2ND EDITION

Financial
MANAGEMENT
PRINCIPLES AND PRACTICE

2ND EDITION

Financial
MANAGEMENT
PRINCIPLES AND PRACTICE

SUDHINDRA BHAT

MBA, MFM, ACS, PGDIR&PM, PGDS&MM, M. Phil, PhD
KSBS Consulting, Bangalore

EXCEL BOOKS

ISBN - 81-7446-508-1

First Edition: New Delhi, 2007
Second Edition: New Delhi, 2008
Reprint: 2009, 2011

EXCEL BOOKS

A-45, Naraina, Phase I,
New Delhi - 110 028

INDIA SALES OFFICES

2/8, Ansari Road, Darya Ganj, New Delhi-110002
106/2, 2nd Floor, Ramnivas, 6th 'C' Cross, Gandhinagar, Bangalore-560009
1st Floor, 19/150, Anand Nagar, Vakola, Santacruz (East), Mumbai-400056
2-2-1167/2H, Near Railway Bridge, Tilaknagar, Nallakunta, Hyderabad-500044
S-3/21-23, Shastri Market, Near "B" Block Circle, Indira Nagar, Lucknow-226016

AFRICA SALES OFFICES

71 Burg Street, Cape Town-8000, South Africa
211 Pietermaritz Street, Pietermaritzburg, South Africa
27/31 Field (Joe Slovo) Street, Durban, 4000, KZN, South Africa
43 Biccard Street, Braamfontein, Johannesburg-2000, South Africa

It is illegal to export this book to Africa without the written permission of the publisher.

Published by Anurag Jain for Excel Books, A-45, Naraina, Phase-I, New Delhi - 110 028
and printed by him at Excel Printers, C-205, Naraina, Phase-I, New Delhi - 110 028

Dedicate to
My students for their inspiration
and
My Parents

Brief Contents

Brief Contents

Detailed Contents

Preface to the Second Edition

Finance in real sense is the cornerstone of the organization. Good financial management is vitally important to the health of the business firm. Finance is an exciting, challenging, ever-changing discipline.

Financial Management – principles and practice, second edition is designed as a reference cum textbook in financial management. It will serve as an introduction to the study of financial management for students and managers. The developments in the capital market and the new avenues available to tackle the traditional financial constraints have placed the present day finance manger in a situation to learn new skills and constantly update knowledge to take financial decisions in a competitive environment. Financial Management - principles and practice is designed as a comprehensive and analytical treatise to fill the gaps. The book seeks to build and develop familiarity with the analytical techniques in financial decision-making.

Changes in the second edition

Seven new chapters titled Funds flow statement, Analysis of financial statement (Ratio), The financial environment: Markets Institutions, Risk & rates of returns, Bonds and their valuation, Stocks & their valuation have been added.

The book is Organized into seven parts and twenty five chapters Part 1: Introduction to FM - Chapter 1: An overview of FM., Chapter 2: Financial statements, Cash Flow, statements, Chapter 3: Funds flow statement, Chapter4: Analyses financial statement (Ratio), Chapter 5: The financial environment: Markets Institutions, Part 2: Fundamental concept in financial Management, Chapter 6: Risk & rates of returns

Chapter 7: Time value of money, Part 3: Financial Assets- Chapter 8: Bonds and their valuation, Chapter 9: Stocks & their valuation, Part 4: Investing in long term assets: Capital Budgeting - Chapter 10: the cost of capital, Chapter 11: the basic capital budgeting, Chapter 12: capital rationing & risk factor in capital budgeting, Part 5: Capital structure & dividend policy - Chapter 13: Capital structure and leverage

Chapter 14: Capital Structure Theory, Chapter 15: Management of profits/ dividend policy, Part 6: Working Capital management - Chapter 16: Working capital management, Chapter 17: Cash management, Chapter 18: Receivable Management

Chapter 19: Inventory Management, Chapter 20: Source of working capital, Part 7: Special topics in financial management - Chapter 21: Financial planning & forecasting

Chapter 22: Leasing & hire purchase financing, Chapter 23: Foreign exchange market

Chapter 24: Security Market, Chapter 25: Mergers & acquisition

Four important advantages of the second edition are

Comprehensive coverage,

Numerous illustrations,

Easy readability and clear explanation as well as extensive use of case studies and projects, which have been included in many chapters for class discussion, EDP and FDP.

Discussion as well as mind stretching questions at the end of each chapter to stimulate financial decision-making.

The Book is structured such a way that it can be used in both, the semester as well as trimester patterns of various PGDM, MBA, PG Courses of all Major Universities and Professional institutions.

The concepts are explained with a number of illustrations and diagrams for clear understanding of the subject matter. It provides complete clarity in a simple style and will help the students, teachers and managers in easy understanding of the financial dimension.

SUDHINDRA BHAT

Preface to the First Edition

The developments in the capital market and the new avenues available to tackle the traditional financial constraints have placed the present day finance manger in a situation to learn the new skills and constant updation of knowledge to take financial decision in a competitive environment. Financial Management; principles and practice designed as comprehensive and analytical treatise to fill the gaps. With the aim of developing the readers/students financial decision making the book has the following special feature

Covers comprehensively the course requirements for MBA, M.Com, CA, CS, ICWA, CFA, PG. COURSES of different university and Autonomous institution .Provides complete clarity in a simple style.397 Solved Problems.159 Unsolved Problems 399 Review questions (theoretical questions) 122 Fill in the blacks with answer. 101 True or falls questions with answer .21 Case Study's for Class discussion .Discussion as well as mind - stretching questions at the end of each chapter to stimulate financial decision making.

The book is divided in to 18 chapters covering the topics like Introduction to financial management, financial planning, time value of money, cost of capital, capital structure with leverage, capital structure theory, capital budgeting, capital rationing and risk factor in capital budgeting, management of profits, dividend policy and theory, working capital management, cash management, receivables management, inventory management, sources of working capital, mergers & acquisition , lease financing, securities markets, foreign exchange market ete.,

In writing this book the author has made use of ideas of erudite scholars who have contributed to the growing body of literature in finance to all such persons the author expresses his obligation and admiration.

The book is primarily targeted at teachers/ students of finance, management, commerce, accounting related professions.

SUDHINDRA BHAT

Acknowledgements

This book could not been produced without the dedicated efforts of many friends and colleagues. I am particularly grateful to Prof. Premraj Jain, Prof. Bhavana, Prof R K Vijasarathy, Prof. Yerriswamy, Dr. S Aithal, Dr. Sathish Kumar, Mr. Srinivas B Pai Chartered Accountant, Dr. Kalyani Rangarajan, Dr. Rangarajan, Dr. Shankaranarayan, Prof. Kiran Reddy, Prof. Narayan Bhatt, Mr. Shivananda, Mr. Raju Pujary, Mrs Susheela Swamy, Ms Suma, K Laxmisha, K GopalKrishna, Pandith Subramany Bhat, Mrs Sharmila SathyaNaraya, Nagraj and Anjali Nagaraj Bhat, Mr. Surayanarana Vitla, Dr. Anuradha, and Dr. Patabiram.

My father Pandith K.Srinivas Bhat and my mother Shakunthala Bhat were always a source of great encouragement and motivation in completing this work. No words can express my sincere thanks to them for their continuous support. Thanks are also due to Mrs Sushma Bhat, who, as usual, provided me with both moral and emotional support during this period.

I would like to thank Prof N.N.Pandey for reviewing the 1st edition and pointing out errors, which have been rectified in this edition. Special thanks are due to many people at Excel Books for their enthusiasm, encouragement and suggestions in making the second edition of this book a reality. I am particularly grateful to Mr. Anurag Jain, Mrs. Vimmi Sethi and Mr. Anish Hazra for all the effort put in by them as a team to make this book a reality. I eagerly look forward to suggestions for improvement in this book.

Acknowledgements

About the Author

Dr. Sudhindra Bhat is Director at SRN Adarsh Department of Management Studies. He is an Investment Consultant and Trainer at KSBS Consulting at Bangalore. He is an MBA, MFM, CFA, ACS, M.Phil., PGDIR&PM, PGS&MM, PhD (Finance). He has rendered his services as consultant, faculty and adjunct faculty at various prestigious companies and B Schools like Bharathi Info tel, AFF, Srinivas B Pai and Co, Alliance Business Academy, MSRIM, AIMS, IFIM, etc. He has presented more then 45 papers in International and National seminars and Conferences. He has published more then 27 articles and research papers in international and national refereed journals and books. He is a recognized evaluator and guide for Rajendra Prasad Institute of Communication and Management, Mumbai, and Bharthiya Vidya Bhavan, Bangalore. He was a visiting Professor of finance at AUT New Zealand and Dallas University, Texas, USA. Along with Financial Management Principles and Practice, he has published four books. He teaches and trains in the area of Corporate Finance, Behavioral Finance, Wealth Management and SAPM.

He has conducted training programmes in the finance area for IFB, Oracle, KMF, MCF, GWASF Quality Costing, Sonal Group of Companies, Aravid Mills, Power Finance Corporation, Airtel, Infosys, Firepro Systems Pvt. Ltd, Yahoo India R&D etc.

PART I

INTRODUCTION TO FINANCIAL MANAGEMENT

An Overview of Financial Management

1

1 Understand the meaning and importance of business finance

2 Give the framework of financial management

3 Explain meaning and objectives of financial management

4 Describe scope of financial management

5 Explain the different methods of financial management

6 Describe the organization of financial function

7 Explain the importance of financial management

FINANCE — A CONCEPT

It would be worthwhile to recall, what Henry Ford had once remarked : "Money is an arm or a leg. You either use it or lose it". This statement, though apparently simple, is quite meaningful. It brings home the significance of money or finance. In the modern money-oriented economy, finance is one of the basic foundations of all kinds of economic activities, it is the master key which provide access to all the sources for being employed in manufacturing and merchandising activities. The Sanskrit saying "arthah sachivah" (....), which means "finance reigns supreme", speaks volumes for the significance of the finance function of an organization. It has rightly been said that, business needs money to make more money. However, it is also true that money begets more money, only when it is properly managed. Hence, efficient management of finances. In conclusion, we can say that "Finance is the backbone of every business"

MEANING OF BUSINESS FINANCE

Business Finance is that business activity which is concerned with the acquisition and conservation of capital funds in meeting financial needs and overall objectives of business enterprises.

MEANING AND DEFINITION OF FINANCIAL MANAGEMENT

According to the *Encyclopedia of Social Sciences*, Corporate finance deals with the financial problems of corporate enterprises. Problems include financial aspects of the promotion of new enterprises and their administration during early development, the accounting problems connected with the distinction between capital and income, the administrative questions created by, growth and expansion, and finally the financial adjustments required for bolstering rehabilitation of a corporation which has come into financial difficulties. Management of all these is financial management. Financial management mainly involves, rising of funds and their effective utilisation with the objective of maximizing shareholders' wealth. To quote, Joseph and Massie, "Financial Management is the operational activity of a business that is responsible for obtaining and effectively utilising the funds necessary for efficient operations".

According to *Van Horne and Wachowicz*, "Financial Management is concerned with the acquisition, financing and management of assets with some overall goal in mind."[1] Financial manager has to forecast expected events in business and note their financial implications. First, anticipating financial needs means estimation of funds required for investment in fixed and current assets or long-term and short-term assets. Second, acquiring financial resources—once the required amount of capital is anticipated, the next task is acquiring financial resources i.e., where and how to obtain the funds to finance the anticipated financial needs and the last one is, allocating funds in business – means allocation of available funds among the best plans of assets, which are able to maximize shareholders' wealth. Thus, the decisions of financial management can be divided into three viz., investment, financing and dividend decision.

Financial Management is broadly concerned with the acquisition and use of funds by a business firm. Its scope may be defined in terms of the following questions.

♦   How large should the firm be and how fast should it grow?

♦   What should be the composition of the firm's assets?

♦   What should be the mix of the firm's financing ?

♦   How should the firm analyze, plan and control its financial affairs?

The entire gamut of management efforts concerned with raising of funds at optimum cost and their effective utilization with a view to maximize the wealth of the shareholders.

Financial Management is concerned with the efficient use of an important economic resource namely, capital funds.

Thus, Financial Management includes – Anticipating Financial Needs, Acquiring Financial Resources and Allocating Funds in Business (i.e., Three A's of financial management)

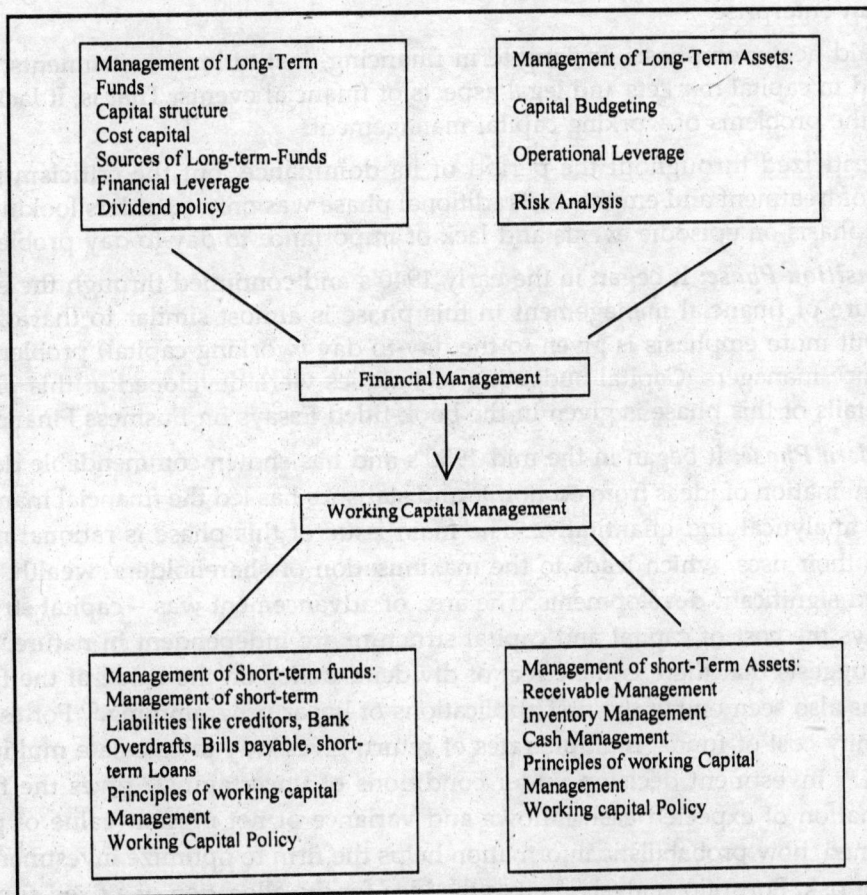

Figure 1.1: Framework of Financial Management

EVOLUTION OF FINANCIAL MANAGEMENT

Financial management has emerged as a distinct field of study only in the early part of this century, as a result of consolidation movement and formation of large enterprises. Its evolution may be divided into three phases (some what arbitrary) – viz.,

1. The Traditional phase,
2. The Transitional phase and
3. The Modern phase[2].

1. *The Traditional Phase:* This phase has lasted for about four decades. Its finest expression was shown in the scholarly work of Arthur S. Dewing, in his book tilted the Financial Policy of Corporation in 1920s."[3] In this phase the focus of financial management was on four selected aspects.

    (i) It treats the entire subject of finance from the outsider's point of view (investment banks, lenders, other) rather than the financial decision maker in the firm.

(ii) It places much importance on corporation finance and too little on the financing problems of non-corporate enterprises.

(iii) The sequence of treatment was on certain episodic events like formation, issuance of capital, major expansion, merger, reorganization and liquidation during the life cycle of an enterprise.

(iv) It laid heavy emphasis on long-term financing, institutions, instruments, procedures used in capital markets and legal aspects of financial events. That is, it lacks emphasis on the problems of working capital management.

It was criticized throughout the period of its dominance, but the criticism is based on matters of treatment and emphasis. Traditional phase was only outsiders looking approach, over emphasis on episodic events and lack of importance to day-to-day problems.

2. *The Transition Phase:* It began in the early 1940's and continued through the early 1950's. The nature of financial management in this phase is almost similar to that of the earlier phase, but more emphasis is given to the day-to-day (working capital) problems faced by the finance managers. Capital budgeting techniques were developed in this phase. Much more details of this phase is given in the book titled Essays on Business Finance.[5]

3. *The Modern Phase:* It began in the mid 1950's and has shown commendable development with combination of ideas from economic and statistics has led the financial management to be more analytical and quantitative. The main issue of this phase is rational matching of funds to their uses, which leads to the maximisation of shareholders' wealth. This phase witnessed significant developments. The area of advancement was – capital structure. The study says the cost of capital and capital structure are independent in nature,[6] Dividend policy, suggests that there is the effect of dividend policy on the value of the firm.[10] This phase has also seen one of the first applications of linear programming.[7] For estimation of opportunity cost of funds, multiple rates of return-gives way to calculate multiple rates of a project.[8] Investment decision under conditions of uncertainty,[9] gives the formula for determination of expected cash inflows and variance of net present value of project and also defined, how probabilistic information helps the firm to optimize investment decisions involving risk. Portfolio analysis[10] gives the idea for the allocation of a fixed sum of money among the available investment securities. Capital Asset Pricing Model (CAPM), suggests that some of the risks in investments can be neutralized by holding a diversified portfolio of securities. Arbitrage Pricing Model (APM),[11] argued that the expected return must be related to risk in such a way, that no single investor could create unlimited wealth through arbitrage. CAPM is still widely used in the real world, but APM is slowly gaining momentum. The Agency theory, [12] emphasizes the role of financial contracts in creating and controlling agency problems. Option Pricing Theory (OPT), [13] applied Martingale pricing principle to the pricing of real estates. The cash management of models (working capital management) by Baumol Model,[14] Miller[15] and Orglers; Baumol models helps to determine optimum cash conversion size; Miller model reorder points and upper control points and Orglers model helps to determine optimal cash management strategy by adoption of linear programming application. Further new means of raising finance with the introduction of new capital market instruments, such as Pads, Fads, PSBs and Caps, etc. Financial engineering that involves the design, development and the implementation of innovative financial instruments, and formulation of creative optional solutions to problems in finance. Even though, the above mentioned developed areas of finance is remarkable, but understanding the international dimension of corporate finance formed a very small part of it, which is not sufficient in this era of globalisation.

IMPORTANCE OF FINANCIAL MANAGEMENT

Financial Management is indeed, the key to successful business operations. Without proper administration and effective utilization of finance, no business enterprise can utilize its potentials for growth and expansion.

Financial management is concerned with the acquisition, financing and management of assets with some overall goals in mind. As mentioned in the contents of modern approach, the discussions on financial management can be divided into three major decisions viz., (1) Investment decision; (ii) Financing decision; and (iii) Dividend decision (see figure 1.2). A firm takes these decisions simultaneously and continuously in the normal course of its business. Firm may not take these decisions in a sequence, but decisions have to be taken with the objective of maximizing shareholders' wealth.

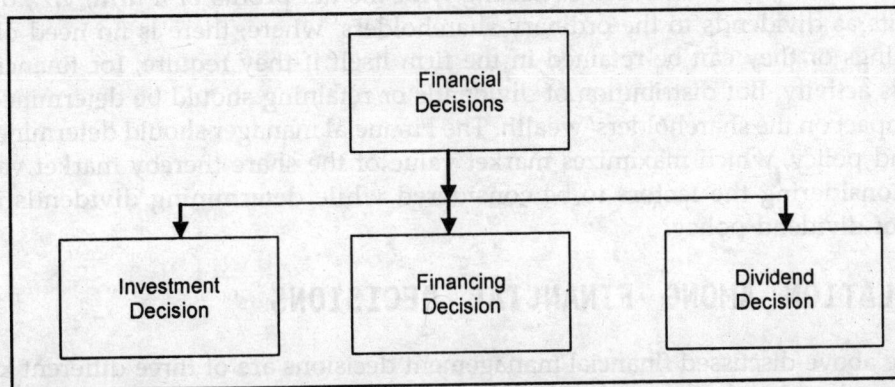

Figure 1.2: Financial Decisions

(a) *Investment Decision:* It is most important than the other two decisions. It begins with a determination of the total amount of assets needed to be held by the firm. In other words, investment decision relates to the selection of assets, that a firm will invest funds. The required assets fall into two groups:

   (i) *Long-term Assets* (Fixed assets: plant & machinery, land and buildings, etc.). Which involve huge investments and yield a return over a period of time in future. Investment in long-term assets is popularly known as "capital budgeting". It may be defined as the firm's decision to invest its current funds most efficiently in fixed assets with an expected flow of benefits over a series of years. It is discussed in detail under the chapter capital budgeting.

   (ii) *Short-term Assets* (Current assets: raw materials, working in process, finished goods, debtors, cash, etc.). That can be converted into cash within a financial year without diminution in value. Investment in current assets is popularly termed as "working capital management". It relates to the management of current assets. It is an important decision of a firm, as short-survival is the prerequisite for long-term success. Firms should not maintain more or less assets. More assets reduce return and there will be no risk, but having less assets is more of a risk as well as more profitable. Hence, the main aspects of working capital management are, the trade-off between risk and return. Management of working capital involves two aspects. First, determination of the amount required for the running of the business and secondly financing these assets. It is discussed in detail in the chapter on Working Capital Management.

(b) *Financing Decision:* After estimation of the amount required and the assets that require purchasing, comes the next financing decision into the picture. Here, the financial manager is concerned with make up of the left hand side of the balance sheet. It is related to the financing mix or capital structure or leverage and he has to determine the proportion of debt and equity. It should be optimum finance mix, which maximizes shareholders' wealth. A proper balance will have to be struck between risk and return. Debt involves fixed cost (interest), which may help in increasing the return on equity alongwith an increase in risk. Rising of funds by issue of equity shares is one permanent source, but the shareholders expect higher rates of earnings. The two aspects of capital structure are : capital structure theories and determination of optimum capital structure. Capital structure theories are out of the scope of this book, but optimal capital structure is discussed in detail under the chapter, Capital Structure.

(c) *Dividend Decision:* This is the third financial decision, which relates to dividend policy. Dividend is a part of profits, that are available for distribution, to equity shareholders. Payment of dividends should be analyzed in relation to the financial decision of a firm. There are two options available in dealing with the net profits of a firm, viz., distribution of profits as dividends to the ordinary shareholders' where, there is no need of retention of earnings or they can be retained in the firm itself if they require, for financing of any business activity. But distribution of dividends or retaining should be determined in terms of its impact on the shareholders' wealth. The Financial manager should determine optimum dividend policy, which maximizes market value of the share thereby market value of the firm. Considering the factors to be considered while determining dividends is another aspect of dividend policy.

INTER-RELATION AMONG FINANCIAL DECISIONS

Although the above-discussed financial management decisions are of three different kinds, they are not independent, but are inter-related as the underlying objective of all the three decisions is (same) maximisation of shareholders' wealth.

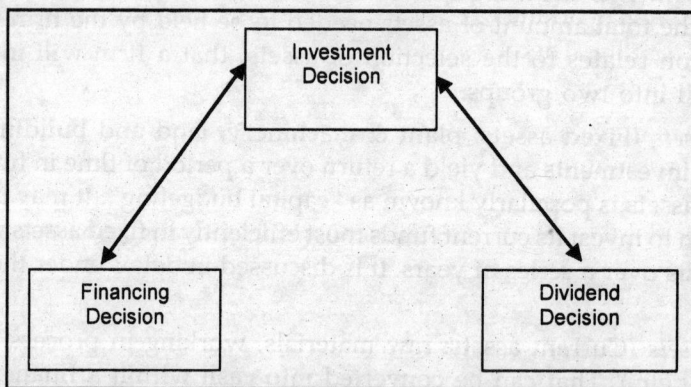

Figure 1.3: Inter-relationship among financial decisions

(a) *Inter-relation between "Investment and Financing Decisions":* While taking the investment decision, the financial manager decides the type of asset or project that should be selected. The selection of a particular asset or project helps to determine the amount of funds required to finance the project or asset. For example, suppose the investment on fixed assets is Rs. 10 crore and investment in current assets or working capital is Rs. 4 crore. So the total fund required to finance the total assets is Rs. 14 crore.

Once the anticipation of funds required is completed then the next decision is financing decision. Financing decision means raising the required funds by various instruments.

There is a inter-relation between investment decision and financing decision, without knowing the amount of funds required and types of funds (short-term and long-term) it is not possible to raise funds. To put it in simple words, investment decision and financing decisions cannot be independent. They are dependent on each other.

(b) *Inter-relation between "Financing Decision and Dividend Decision":* Financing decision influences and is influenced by dividend decision, since retention of profits for financing selected assets or projects, reduces the profit available to ordinary shareholders, thereby reducing dividend payout ratio. For example, in the illustration above, we have decided the amount required to finance a project is Rs. 14 crore. If the financial manager plans to raise only Rs. 7 crore from outside and the remaining by way of retained earnings, and if the dividend decision is 100% payout ratio, then the financial manager has to depend completely on outside sources to raise the required funds. So, dividends decision influences the financing decision. Hence, there is an inter-relation between financing decision and dividend decision.

(c) *Inter-relation between "Dividend Decision and Investment Decision":* Dividend decision and investment decision are inter-related because retention of profits for financing the selected assets depends on the rate of return on proposed investment and the opportunity cost of the retained profits. Profits are retained when return on investment is higher than the opportunity cost of retained profits and vice-versa. Hence, there is inter-relation between investment decision and dividend decision.

The Financial manager has to take an optimal joint decision after evaluating the decisions that will affect the wealth of the shareholders, if there is any negative affect on the wealth it should be rejected and vice versa.

The importance of financial management can be ascertained, after going through the following points :

1. *Successful promotion:* Successful promotion of a business concern depends upon efficient financial management. If the plan adopted, fails to provide adequate capital to meet the requirements of fixed and working capital and particularly the latter, the firm cannot carry on its business successfully. Therefore, sound financial planning is quite essential for the success of a business firm.

2. *Smooth running:* Since finance is required at each stage of the business such as promotion, incorporation, development, expansion and management of day-to-day expenses, proper financial administration becomes necessary for the smooth running of a business enterprise.

3. *Decision making:* Financial management provides scientific analysis of all facts and figures through various financial tools such as ratio analysis, Variance analysis, budgets etc., Such an analysis helps the management to evaluate the profitability of the plan in the given circumstances, so that a proper decision can be taken to minimize the risk.

4. *Solutions to financial problems:* Efficient Financial Management helps the top management by providing solutions to the various financial problems faced by it.

5. *Measure of performance:* Financial Management is considered as a yard stick to measure the performance of the firm.

The importance of Financial Management in an enterprise may very well be realized by the following words. "Financial Management is properly viewed as an integral part of the overall management rather than as a staff specialty concerned with fund raising operation. In addition to raising funds, financial management is directly concerned with production, marketing and other functions within an enterprise, whenever decision are made about the acquisition or distribution of assets".

Thus, financial management has attained a good deal of importance in modern business.

SCOPE AND FUNCTIONS OF FINANCIAL MANAGEMENT

From the below discussion it is evident, that financial management as an academic discipline has undergone notable changes over the years, with regard to its scope and areas of coverage. At the same time, the financial manager's role also has undergone fundamental changes over the years. Study of the changes that have taken place over the years is known as "scope of financial management." In order to have an easy understanding and better exposition to the changes, it is necessary to divide the scope into two approaches.

1. *Traditional Approach:* The traditional approach, which was popular in the early stage, limited the role of financial management to raising and administering of funds needed by the corporate enterprises to meet their financial needs. It deals with the following aspects.

   (i) Arrangement of funds from financial institutions.

   (ii) Arrangement of funds through financial instruments like share, bonds etc.

   (iii) Looking after the legal and accounting relationship between a corporation and its sources of funds.

Thus, the finance manager had a limited role to perform, He was expected to keep accurate financial records, prepare reports on the corporation's status and performance and manage cash in a way that the corporation was in a position to pay its bills on time.

The term "Corporation Finance" was used in place of the present term "Financial Management".

The traditional approach to the scope of the finance function evolved during the 1920s and 1930s, dominated the academic thinking during the 40s and through the early 50s. It has now been discarded as it suffers from serious limitations. Following are the main limitations.

(a) *External approach:* The approach treated the subject of finance only from the view point of suppliers of funds, i.e., outsiders, viz, bankers, investors etc. It followed an outsider – looking- in approach and not the insider-looking-out approach, since it completely ignored the view point of those who had to take internal financing decisions.

(b) *Ignored routine problems:* The subject of financial management was mainly confined to the financial problems arising during the course of incorporation, mergers etc, and the subject did not give any importance to day-to-day financial problems of the business.

(c) *Ignored non-corporate enterprise:* The approach focused mainly on the financial problems of corporate enterprises.

(d) *Ignored working capital financing:* The problems related to financing, short term or working capital were ignored in the approach. The approach focuses mainly on the problems of long term financing.

(e) *No emphasis on allocation of funds:* The approach confined financial management only to procurement of funds. It did not emphasis on allocation of funds.

The conceptual framework of the traditional treatment ignored, what Solomon aptly describes as the central issues of financial management. These are :

(i) Should an enterprise commit capital funds to certain purposes ?

(ii) Do the expected returns meet financial standard of performance?

(iii) How should these standards be set and what is the cost of capital funds to the enterprise?

(iv) How does the cost vary with the mixture of financing methods used ?

In the absence of the coverage of these crucial aspects, the traditional approach implied a very narrow scope for financial management. The modern approach provides a solution to these shortcomings.

2. *Modern Approach:* According to the modern approach, the term financial management provides a conceptual and analytical framework for financial decision-making. That means, the finance function covers both, acquisition of funds as well as their allocation. The new approach views the term financial management in a broader sense. It is viewed as an integral part of the overall management.

The new approach is an analytical way of viewing the financial problems of a firm. The main contents of the modern approach are as follows :

(i)   What is the total volume of funds, an enterprise should commit?

(ii) What specific assets should an enterprise acquire?

(iii) How should the funds required, be financed?

Thus, financial management, in the modern sense of the term, can be divided into four major decisions as functions of finance. They are :

(i)   The investment decision

(ii) The financing decision

(iii) The dividend policy decision

(iv) The funds requirement decision

The functions of financial management may be classified on the basis of Liquidity, Profitability and Management.

1. *Liquidity:* It is ascertained on the basis of three important considerations.

(a) Forecasting cash flows → i.e., matching the inflows against the cash outflows.

(b) Raising funds → i.e., financial manager will have to ascertain the sources fro which funds may be raised and the time when these funds are needed.

(c) Managing the flow of internal funds.

2. *Profitability:* →While ascertaining profitability, the following factors are taken into account.

(a) Cost control

(b) Pricing

(c) Forecasting future profits

(d) Measuring cost of capital

3. *Management:* Asset management has assumed an important role in financial management. It includes : (a) the management of long term funds. (b) The management of short term funds.

Apart from the main functions, mentioned above following subsidiary functions are also performed by the finance management.

THE FUNCTIONAL AREAS OF MODERN FINANCIAL MANAGEMENT

As Modern Financial Management performs several functions, it is a difficult task to identify the functional areas of modern financial management. However, we can refer to the following, as important functional areas of modern management.

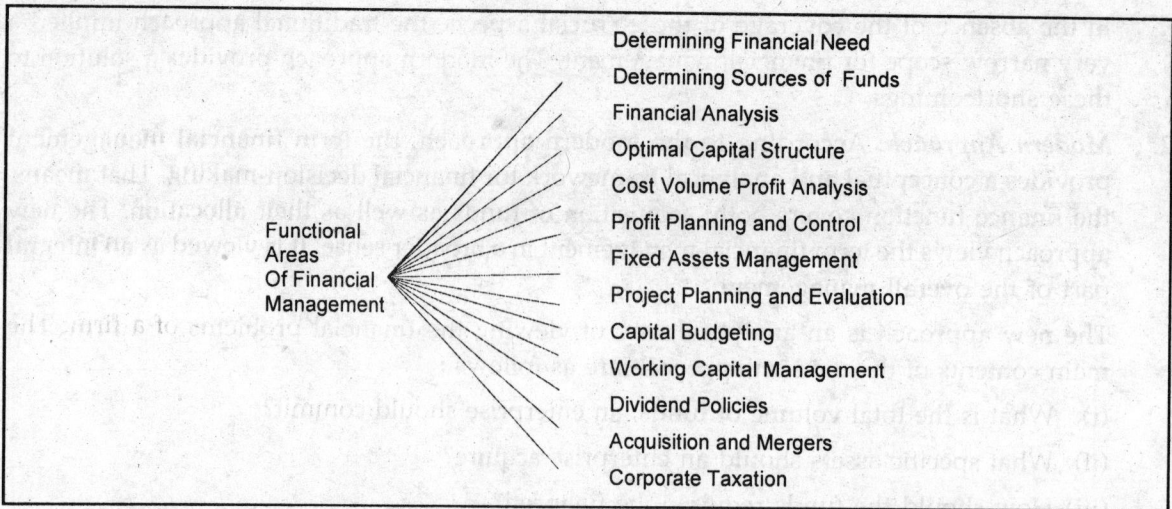

	Determining Financial Need
	Determining Sources of Funds
	Financial Analysis
	Optimal Capital Structure
	Cost Volume Profit Analysis
Functional Areas Of Financial Management	Profit Planning and Control
	Fixed Assets Management
	Project Planning and Evaluation
	Capital Budgeting
	Working Capital Management
	Dividend Policies
	Acquisition and Mergers
	Corporate Taxation

Key Activities of Financial Management

The three activities, broadly speaking, of financial management are : (a) financial analysis ; planning and control (b) management of firm's asset structure and (c) management of the firm's financial structure. Figure 1.4 shows, how these activities are related to the balance sheet of the firm.

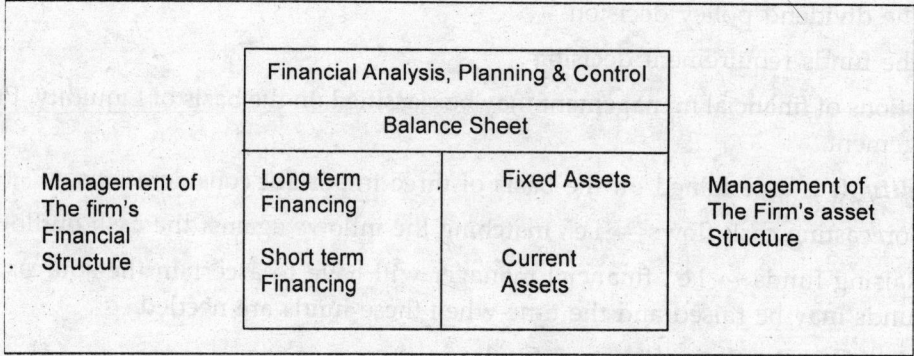

	Financial Analysis, Planning & Control		
	Balance Sheet		
Management of The firm's Financial Structure	Long term Financing	Fixed Assets	Management of The Firm's asset Structure
	Short term Financing	Current Assets	

Figure 1.4 : Key Activities of Financial Management

ORGANIZATION OF THE FINANCE FUNCTIONS

Like any other functional management in a firm, 'finance' is a vital functional organ of the firm. If finance function does not operate well, the whole organizational activity will be ruined. So inefficient financial management paralyses the activity of the firm. That is why, every company will have a separate department to look after the financial aspects of the company.

The finance function can be broadly classified into two parts.

♦ Routine financial matters like, custody of cash and bank accounts, collection or loans, payment of cash etc.

♦ Special financial functions like financial planning and budgeting, profit analysis, investment decisions etc.

These two functions can be looked after by two executives and ultimately by the top management.

Routine matters are looked after by the "Treasurer" and special matters are managed by the "Controller of Finance". The following chart will give an idea about the finance department.

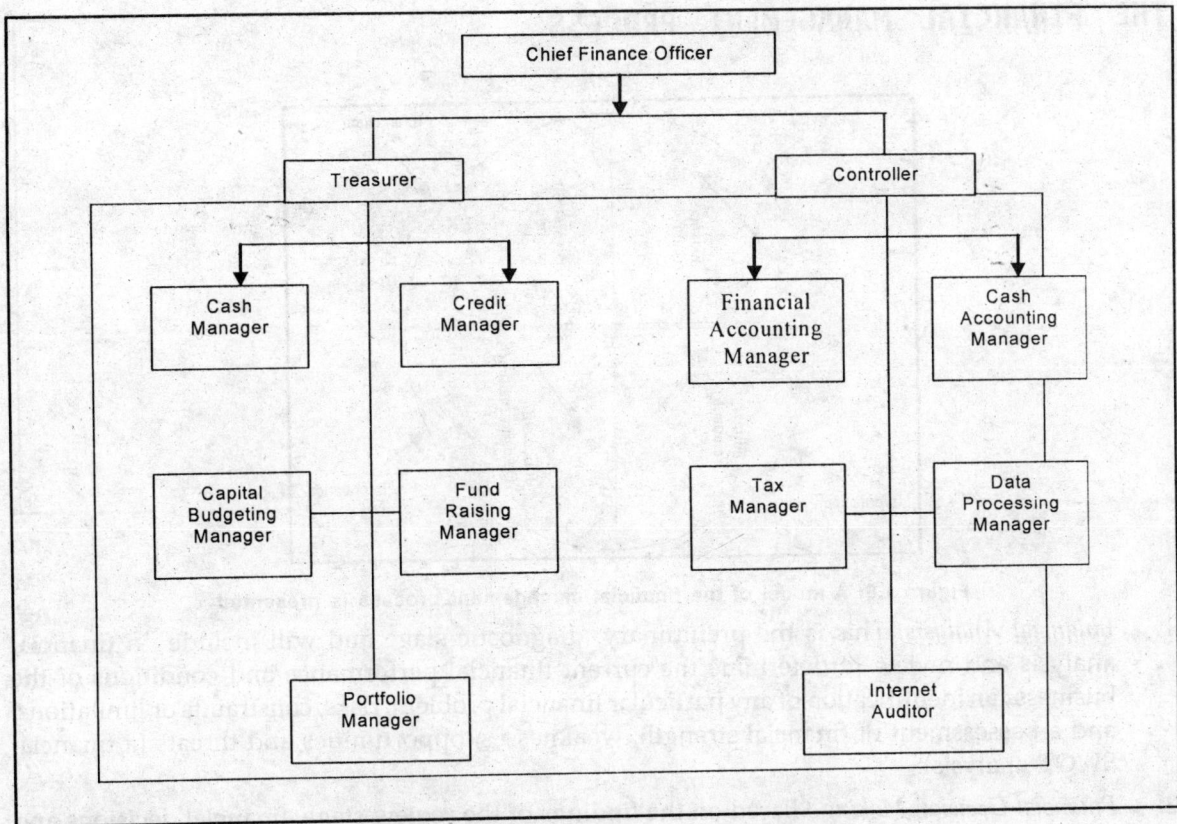

Figure 1.5: Organization of the Finance Function

Treasurer's and Controller's Functions in the Indian Context

The terms treasurer and controller are used by the Financial Executives in American corporations. In USA the functions of financial management or the functions of the financial officer are divided into two, viz., treasurership and controllership functions. However, these terms are not used in India. In India many corporations have given the designation of 'financial controller' or 'controller', who performs the functions of a Chief Accountant or Management Accountant. In majority of Indian corporations, the term General Manager Finance or Chief Finance Manager is given as designation. Government reporting, insurance coverage, other activities related to insurance are the few functions of a treasurer and a controller, which are taken care of, by a company secretary. In India, in many corporations financial managers are appointed to perform the duties of the treasurer and controller both. Financial manager should realise the importance of his/her duties and that, they require extraordinary skills. Hence, he/she should ensure the optimum use of scarce financial resources for maximisation of shareholders wealth.

Table 1.1: Functions of the Treasurer and the Controller

TREASURER	FINANCE CONTROLLER
1. To look after the cash and bank account	1. Accounting
2. Investments	2. Budgeting
3. Tax and Insurance	3. Internal Audit
4. Credit and Collection	4. Finance Planning
5. Investor relations	5. Profit Planning
	6. Investment Decisions
	7. Economic appraisal

THE FINANCIAL MANAGEMENT PROCESS

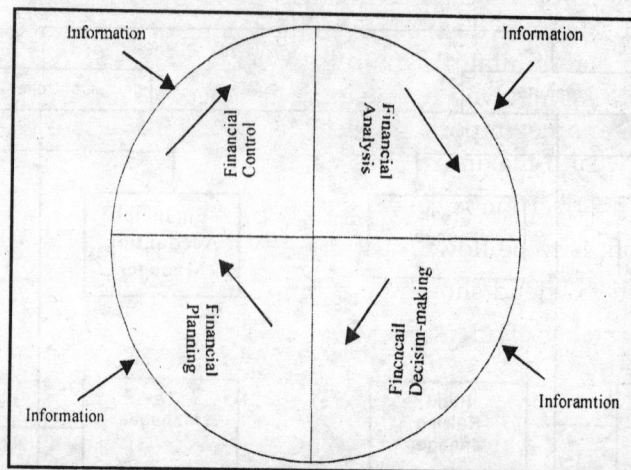

Figure 1.6: A model of the financial management process is presented

1. *Financial Analysis:* This is the preliminary, diagnostic stage and will include : a financial analysis and review to determine the current financial performance and conditions of the business ; an identification of any particular financial problem, risks, constraints or limitations; and an assessment of financial strength, weaknesses, opportunities and threats (a financial SWOT analysis).

2. *Financial Decision Making :* Based on the findings of the review stage, financial decisions and choices are made. These are likely to include strategic investment decisions, such as investing in new production facilities or the acquisition of another company and strategic financing decisions, for example, the decision to raise additional long-term loans.

3. *Financial Planning :* The essence of financial planning is to ensure that, the right amount of funds is available at the right time and at the right cost for the level of risk involved to enable the firm's objectives to be achieved. Budgeting will be a key financial planning tool. The efficiency and effectiveness of the financial planning process will be great, aided by the application of computerized financial modeling.

4. *Financial Control :* The final stage of the process involves the entire organization. This is to ensure that plans are properly implemented, that progress is continually reported to the management, and that, any deviations from plans are clearly identified.

FINANCIAL DECISIONS

The important financial decisions to be taken by the manager are as follows :

1. *Investment Decision :* This is concerned with the allocation of capital. It has to show the funds that can be invested in assets, which would yield benefit in future. This is a decision based on risk and uncertainty. Finance manager has to evaluate the investment in relation to its expected return and risk, to determine whether the investment is feasible or not. Besides, the financial manager is also entrusted with the management of existing assets. The whole exercise is called "Capital Budgeting", this was the first technique developed in financial management. This technique helps to know 'Net Present Value' of the assets. To have a more profitable investment, the companies can think of amalgamations and mergers internally and externally. That is why, we have seen the emergence of multinational companies.

2. *Finance Decision:* This decision is concerned with the mobilization of finance for investment. The finance manager has to take decisions regarding the acquisition of finance. Whether entire capital required, should be raised in the form of equity capital, or the amount should be borrowed capital, has to be decided. Even the timing of acquisition of capital should be well defined. While determining the ratio between debt and equity, the finance manager should ascertain the risk involved in obtaining each type of capital. Thus, determining the best "Finance Mix" is another important task of the finance manager. The best capital structure will always ensure wealth maximization.

3. *Dividend Decision:* This decision is concerned with the divisible profits of the company.

   (i) How much profit is to be flown back of capitalization

   (ii) How much cash dividend should be paid to the shareholders?

   (iii) Maintenance of stable dividend rate over the period, are some of the issues connected with this decision.

   The dividend decision involves the determination of the percentage of profit earned by the enterprise which is to be paid to its shareholders. The dividend payout ratio must be evaluated in the light of the objective of maximizing shareholder's wealth. Thus, the dividend decision has become a vital aspect of financing decision.

4. *Current Assets Management:* The finance manager should also manage the current assets, to have liquidity in the business. Investment of funds in current assets reduce the profitability of the firm. However, at the same time, the finance manager should also look after the current financial needs of the firm to maintain optimum production. While investing funds in current assets, he must see that proper balance (trade off) is maintained between profitability and liquidity.

Every financial decision involves this trade off. At this level the market value of the company's shares would be the maximum.

The inter-relationship between market value, financial decisions, risk-return and trade off is depicted in the chart given below.

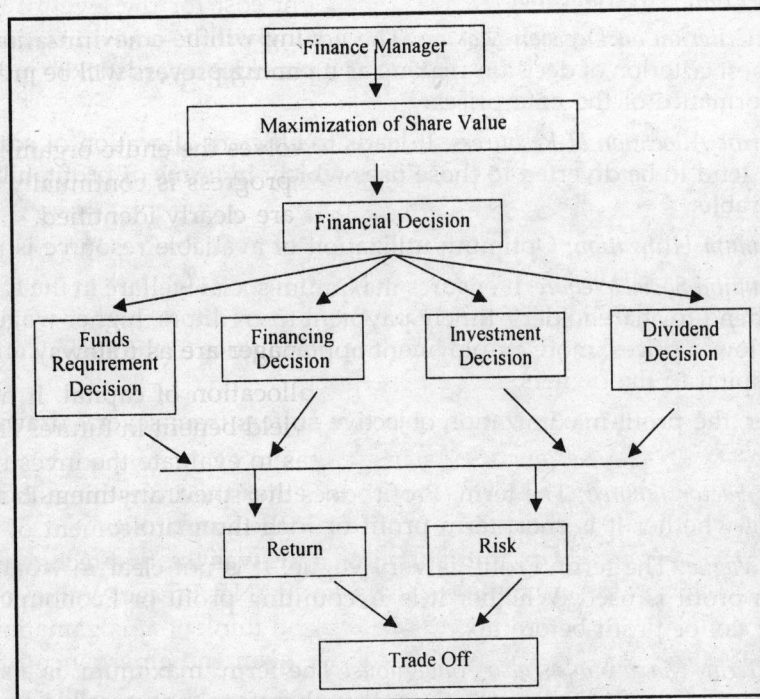

Figure 1.7 : Decision, Return, Risk and Trade off

In conclusion we can say that to maximize the wealth of owners, the finance manager has to be very careful while taking the decisions relating to (i) Investment (ii) Dividend (iii) Financing and (iv) Current Assets.

OBJECTIVE OF FINANCIAL MANAGEMENT

(Profit – Maximization vs Wealth Maximization)

The objectives of financial management can be broadly classified into two categories:

1. *Basic Objectives:* Traditionally, the basic objectives of financial management have been (A) Maintenance of liquid assets and (B) Maximization of profitability of the firm. However, these days, there is a greater emphasis on (C) Shareholders' wealth maximization rather than on profit maximization.

   (A) *Maintenance of Liquid Assets:* Financial management aims at maintenance of adequate liquid assets with the firm to meet its obligations at all times. However, investment in liquid assets has to be adequate – neither too low nor too excessive. The finance manager has to maintain a balance between liquidity and profitability.

   (B) *Maximization of Profit:* "Profit maximization" is a term which denotes the maximum profit to be earned by an organization in a given time period. The profit- maximization goal implies that the investment, financing and dividend policy decision of the enterprise should be oriented to profit maximization.

   The term "Profit" can be used in two senses – first, as the owner-oriented concept and the second, as the operational concept.

   Profit as the owner-oriented concept, refers to the amount of net profit, which goes in the form of dividend to the shareholders. Profit as the operational concept means profitability, which is an indicator of economic efficiency of the enterprise.

   Profitability-maximization implies, that the enterprise should select assets, projects and decisions, that are profitable and reject the non-profitable ones. It is in this sense, that the term profit- maximization is used in financial management.

   Merits of Profit – Maximization

   (i) *Best Criterion on Decision-Making:* The goal of profit – maximization is regarded as the best criterion of decision-making as it provides a yardstick to judge the economic performance of the enterprises.

   (ii) *Efficient Allocation of Resources:* It leads to efficient allocation of scarce resources as they tend to be diverted to those uses which, in terms of profitability, are the most desirable.

   (iii) *Optimum Utilization:* Optimum utilization of available resource is possible.

   (iv) *Maximum Social Welfare:* It ensures maximum social welfare in the form of maximum dividend to shareholders, timely payment to creditors, higher wages, better quality and lower prices, more employment opportunities to the society and maximization of capital to the owners.

   However, the profit-maximization objective suffers from several drawbacks which are as follows.

   (i) *Time Factor Ignored:* The term 'Profit' does not speak anything about the period of profit-whether it is short-term profit or long-term profit.

   (ii) *It is Vague:* The term 'Profit' is very vague. It is not clear in what exact sense the term profit is used. Whether it is Accounting profit or Economic profit or profit after tax or profit before tax.

   (iii) *The Term 'Maximum' is also Ambiguous:* The term 'maximum' is also not clear. The concept of profit is also not clear. It is therefore, not possible to maximize what cannot be known.

(iv) *'It' Ignores Time Value:* The profit maximization objective fails to provide any idea regarding the timing of expected cash earnings. The choice of a more worthy project lies in the study of time value of future inflows of cash earnings. It ignores the fact that the rupee earned to day is more value able than a rupee earned later.

(v) *'It' Ignores the Risk Factor:* According to economists, profit is a reward for risk and uncertainty bearing. It is also a dynamic surplus or profit is a reward for innovation. But when can the organization maximize profits ? Profit – maximization objective does not make this clear.

(C) *Wealth Maximization:* It is now widely and universally accepted that the objective of the enterprise should suitable and operationally feasible. Precise and clear cut and should give weight age to the time value and risk factors. Owing to the various drawbacks of the profit maximization objective, Professor Ezar Solomon rejected it as inappropriate and unsuitable and suggested the adoption of wealth- maximization objective which removes all the drawbacks of the profit maximization objective.

Wealth- maximization is also called value- maximization. The wealth or 'net present worth' of a course of action is the difference between gross present worth and the amount of capital investment required to achieve the benefits. Gross Present-worth represents the present value of expected cash benefits.

In simple words, wealth-maximization means maximizing the present value of a course of action (i.e. NPV = GPC of benefits – Investment). Any financial action which results in positive NPV, creates and adds to the existing wealth of the organization and the course of action which has a negative NPV, reduces the existing wealth and hence be given up. All positive actions can be adopted, as they add to the existing wealth and help in wealth maximization.

Significance of Wealth- Maximization

The company, although it-cares more for the economic welfare of the shareholders, cannot forget the others who directly or indirectly work for the over-all development of the company. Thus, Wealth- Maximization takes care of.

1. Lenders or creditors
2. Workers or Employees
3. Public or Society
4. Management or Employer

2. *Other objectives:* Besides the above basic objectives, the following are the other objectives of financial management.

- Ensuring a fair return to shareholders.
- Building up reserves for growth and expansion.
- Ensuring maximum operational efficiency by efficient and effective utilization of finance.
- Ensuring financial discipline in the management.

METHODS OF FINANCIAL MANAGEMENT

The term "Financial Method" or "Financial Tool" refers to any logical method or technique to be employed for the purpose of accomplishing the following two goals :

(a) Measuring the effectiveness of firm's action and decisions.

(b) Measuring the validity of the decisions regarding accepting or rejecting future projects.

Following are the important financial tools or methods used by the financial manager in performance of his job :

1. *Cost of Capital:* Cost of capital helps the finance manager in deciding, the sources, from which the funds are to be raised. In case of different sources of finance viz, shares, debentures, loans from financial institutions, banks, public deposits etc., the financial management takes into account the cost of capital and opts for the source, which is the cheapest, the cost of capital is also taken into account for determining the optimum capital structure.

2. *Trading on Equity:* Trading on equity is another tool, which helps the finance manager in increasing the return to equity shareholders.

3. *Capital Budgeting appraisal:* Methods such as payback period, average rate of return, internal rate of return, net present value, profitability index etc., help the finance manager in selecting the best among the alternative capital investment proposals.

4. *Ratio Analysis:* This is another method for evaluating different aspects of the firm different ratios serve different purposes.

5. *ABC Analysis:* Cash management models, debtor's turnover ratio etc, help the finance manager in effective management of current assets.

6. *Funds Flow Analysis and Cash Flow Analysis:* These techniques help the finance manager in determining whether the funds have been procured from the best available source and they have been utilized in the best possible way. Projected funds flow analysis and projected cash flow analysis help the finance manager in estimating or arranging, for the future working capital or cash needs.

FINANCIAL MANAGEMENT AND OTHER DISCIPLINES

The study of financial management as a totally independent subject is relatively recent, its roots trace back to the turn or this century. It draws heavily on related disciplines and other fields of study. The most important of these are, Accounting and Economics ; in the latter discipline, macroeconomics and micro-economics are of special significance. Marketing, Production and the study of Quantitative methods also have an impact on the financial management field.

Accounting: Financial Managers play a game of managing a firm's financial and real assets, securing the funding needed to support these assets. Financial managers often turn to the accounting data to assist them in making decisions. Financial managers are primarily concerned with a firm's cash flows, because they often determine the feasibility of certain investment and financing decisions.

FINANCIAL MANAGEMENT VS FINANCIAL ACCOUNTING

Table 1.2: Financial Management vs Financial Accounting

Points of difference	Financial Management	Financial Accounting
Role	Decision-making	Stewardship
Focus	Value creation	Costs
Returns	Cash flows	Profits
Perspective	Future-oriented and Outward-looking	historic and inward looking
Time frame	Long term	Short term

Economics: There are two areas of economics, with which the financial manager must be familiar: micro-economics and macroeconomics. Micro-economics deals with economic decisions of individuals and firms, whereas macroeconomics looks at the economy as a whole.

Marketing, Production and Quantitative Methods

Figure 1.8 depicts the relationship between financial management and its primary important supportive disciplines. Marketing, Production and quantitative methods are indirectly related to the day-to-day decisions, made by financial managers. For example, financial managers should consider the impact of new product development and promotion plans made in the marketing area, because these plans require capital outlay and have an impact on the firm's projected cash flows. Similarly, changes in the production process may necessitate capital expenditures, which the firm's financial managers must evaluate and then finance. And, finally the tools of analysis developed in the quantitative methods area, are frequently helpful in analyzing complex financial management problems.

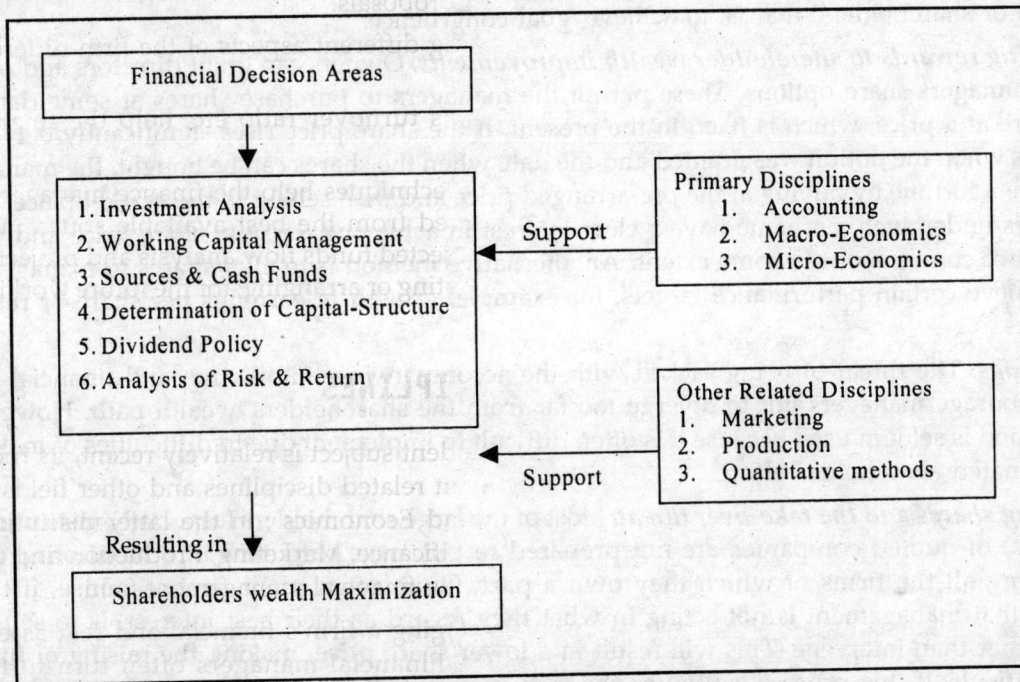

Financial Decision Areas

1. Investment Analysis
2. Working Capital Management
3. Sources & Cash Funds
4. Determination of Capital-Structure
5. Dividend Policy
6. Analysis of Risk & Return

Support

Primary Disciplines
1. Accounting
2. Macro-Economics
3. Micro-Economics

Other Related Disciplines
1. Marketing
2. Production
3. Quantitative methods

Support

Resulting in

Shareholders wealth Maximization

Figure 1.8: Impact of other Disciplines on Financial Management

AGENCY PROBLEM

Conflicts of interest among stockholders, bondholders, and managers.

Agency Theory

The analysis of principal-agent relationships, in which one person, an agent, acts on behalf of another person, a principal.

Agency Costs

The incremental costs of having an agent make decisions for a principal.

The agency problem arises due to the separation of ownership and control of business firms.

◆ In theory, the shareholders, being the owners of the firm, control its activities.

◆ In practice, however, the large modern corporation has a diffuse and fragmented set of shareholders and control often lies in the hands of directors.

It is extremely difficult to marshall thousands of shareholders, each with a small stake in the business, to push for a change. Thus in many firms there exists what is called a separation, or divorce, of ownership and control.

The separation of ownership and control raises worries that the management team may pursue objectives attractive to them, but which are not necessarily beneficial to the shareholders - this is termed 'managerialism.' This conflict is what is known as the principal-agent problem (agency problem). The principals (the shareholders) have to find ways of ensuring that their agents (the managers) act in their interests.

This means incurring costs, 'agency costs', to (a) monitor managers' behaviour, and (b) create incentive schemes and control for managers to pursue shareholders' wealth maximization.

Various methods have been used to try to align the actions of senior management with the interests of shareholders, that is, to achieve 'goal congruence.'

Linking rewards to shareholder wealth improvements: Owners can grant directors and other senior managers share options. These permit the managers to purchase shares at some date in the future at a price, which is fixed in the present. If the share price rises significantly between the dates when the option was granted and the date when the shares can be bought, the manager can make a fortune by buying at the pre-arranged price and then selling in the market place. The managers under such a scheme have a clear interest in achieving a rise in share price and thus congruence comes about to some extent. An alternative method is to allot shares to managers if they achieve certain performance targets, for example, growth in earnings per share or return on shares.

Sackings: The threat of being sacked with the accompanying humiliation and financial loss may encourage managers not to diverge too far from the shareholders' wealth path. However, this method is seldom used because it is often difficult to implement due to difficulties of making a coordinated shareholder effort.

Selling shares and the take-over threat: Most of the large shareholders (especially institutional investors) of quoted companies are not prepared to put large resources into monitoring and controlling all the firms of which they own a part. Quite often, their first response, if they observe that management is not acting in what they regard as their best interest, is to sell the share rather than intervene. This will result in a lower share price, making the raising of funds more difficult. If this process continues the firm may become vulnerable to a merger bid by another group of managers, resulting in a loss of top management posts. Fear of being taken over can establish some sort of backstop position to prevent shareholder wealth considerations being totally ignored.

Corporate governance regulations: There is a considerable range of legislation and other regulatory pressures (e.g. the Companies Act) designed to encourage directors to act in shareholders' interests. Within these regulations for example, the board of directors is not to be dominated by a single individual acting as both the chairman and chief executive. Also, independently minded non-executive directors should have more power to represent shareholder interests; in particular, they should predominate in decisions connected with directors' remuneration and auditing of firm's accounts.

Information flow: The accounting profession, the stock exchange, the regulating agencies and the investing public are continuously conducting a battle to encourage or force firms to release more accurate, timely and detailed information concerning their operations. An improved quality of corporate accounts, annual reports and the availability of other forms of information flowing to investors and analysts such as company briefings and press announcements help to monitor firms, and identify any wealth-destroying actions by wayward managers early.

THE CHANGING SCENARIO OF FINANCIAL MANAGEMENT IN INDIA

In a country like India, the scenario of financial management keeps changing. As the economy is opening up and global participation is increasing very fast, opportunities are practically limitless. Presently, financial management passes through an era of experimentation as a larger part of finance activities are carried out.

Highlights Context

♦ Interest rates are free from regulations.

♦ Rupee is fully convertible in current account.

♦ Optimum debt equity mix is possible.

♦ Merger and Acquisitions

♦ Maintaining share prices are also crucial. In a liberalized scenario, the capital market is an important avenue of funds for business.

♦ Ensuring management control is vital especially in the light of foreign participation.

♦ Foreign portfolio investment

♦ Foreign direct Investment

♦ Growing and volatile capital market.

Efficient financial managers should know how to use the above information to convert them into profit. Profit maximization or wealth maximization is a new challenge for the financial manager.

Profit Maximization: The objective of financial management is the same as the objective of a company, that is, to earn profit. But profit maximization cannot the sole objective of a company.

Wealth Maximization: It is commonly agreed that the objective of a firm is to maximize value or wealth. The value of a firm is represented by the market price of the company's common stocks. The market price of a firm's stock represents the focal judgment of all market participants as to what the value of the particular firm is. It takes in to account present and prospective future earnings per share, the timing and risk of these earnings, the dividend policy of the firm and many other factors that bear upon the market price of the stock. Market price acts as the performance index or report card of the firm's progress. Prices in the share markets are largely affected by many factors like general economic outlook, outlook of a particular company, technical factors and even mass psychology. Normally, this value is a function of two factors as given below

♦ The anticipated rate of earnings per share of the company

♦ The capitalization rate.

The likely rate of earnings per shares (EPS) depends upon the assessment as to how profitably a company is growing to operate in the future. The capitalization rate reflects the liking of the investors for the company.

In a challenging dynamic global environment planning, procurement, allocation and earning the profit and maintaining the same is itself is a challenging task.

SUMMARY

♦ Business finance is the activity concerned with planning, raising, controlling and administering of the funds used in the business.

♦ Business may be sole-proprietary, partnership or corporation/company. *Sole-proprietorship* is a small organisation, which is owned and managed by a single individual. *Partnership* is an association of two or more people joined together, to own and manage and, share its profits and losses. *Corporation* is an association of many persons who contribute money or money's worth to a common stock and employs it in business, and who share profit and loss arising from the business equally.

♦ Financial Management is concerned with the acquisition, financing and management of assets with some overall goal in mind. The main activities of a financial manager are (1) anticipating financial needs, (2) acquiring financial resources, and (3) allocating funds in the business.

♦ The scope of financial management can be studied under two approaches. (1) The traditional approach and (2) The modern approach. In the traditional approach, the role of financial management is limited to fund raising and administering needed, by the corporate enterprises to meet their financial needs. But criticism was stated on this approach in the late 50s because of its various limitations. It ignored day-to-day problems; outsider-looking-in approach; ignored working capital financing and ignored allocation of capital.

♦ The scope of modern approach covers both, procurement of funds as well as their allocation. The main contents of the new approach are: What is the total volume of funds an enterprise should commit? What specific assets should an enterprise acquire ? How should the funds required, be financed ? These three questions are related to the three decisions of financial management : (i) Financing decision, (ii) Investment decision and (iii) Dividend decision.

♦ Investment decision relates to the selection of assets, that a firm will invest fund to procure. The required assets fall into two groups, *long-term assets* (fixed assets), and *short-term assets* (current assets).

♦ Financing decision is related to the financing mix or capital structure or leverage. While taking this decision, the financial manager has to determine the proportion of debt and equity.

♦ Dividend decision relates to dividend policy. Payment of dividends should be analyzed in relation to the financial decision of a firm.

♦ Financial management decisions are of different kinds but they are inter-related because the underlying objective of all the three decisions is (same) the maximisation of shareholders' wealth.

♦ The aim of finance function covers (1) Anticipation of funds needed, (2) to acquire the anticipated funds at low cost, (3) efficient allocation and utilisation of funds, (4) to increase profitability, and (5) maximizing the firm's value.

There are two widely accepted goals of financial management viz., (1) Profit maximization and (2) Wealth maximization. Profit maximisation has been criticized for being vague, and that, it ignores time value of money, and quality of benefits. Shareholders wealth maximization means maximizing net present value (or wealth) of a course of action to its shareholders.

♦ The organisational structure of financial management vary from firm to firm, depending on the factors like the size of the firm, nature of business transactions; type of financing operations; capabilities of financial executives and the philosophy of finance function of the firm. The designation (titles) of financial officers also differs from one organisation to another. The Finance manager exercises his functions through his two subordinates known as (1) Treasurer and (2) Controller. The main concern of the treasurer is towards the financing activities and investment activities, including cash management; relationship management with commercial and investment bankers; credit management; portfolio management; inventory management; insurance/risk management; investors relations; dividend disbursement. The functions of the controller is related to the management and control of assets. The main functions include, cost accounting, financial accounting, internal audit, financial statement preparation; preparation of budgets, taxation, general ledger (payroll) and data processing.

TEST YOUR KNOWLEDGE

1. Fill in the blanks with appropriate word(s):

    (a) Business Finance is wider than the _____.

    (b) _____ Finance deals with the company form of business.

    (c) Modern Financial Management is concerned with proper _____, _____, and _____ of funds effectively.

    (d) 6A's of financial management are _____, _____, _____, _____, _____ and _____.

    (e) Maximization of _____ is the main goal of financial management.

    (f) _____ and _____ maximization are the goals of financial management.

    (g) Profit maximisation ignores _____.

    (h) Equity shareholders' expected return is equal to risk free rate plus _____.

    (i) _____ is a conflict of interest between the agent and the owner.

    (j) Social responsibility means taking decision beyond the _____ activity.

    [**Answers:** (a) Corporate finance, (b) Corporate, (c) anticipation, acquiring and allocation, (d) anticipation, acquiring, allocation, administering, analysis and accounting, (e) Shareholders wealth (f) Profit, Wealth (g) Time value of money, (h) Risk premium (i) Agency conflict (j) Economic.]

2. State whether each of the following statement is true or false:

    (a) Men, Money, Machine, Materials, Methods, Minutes and Management are the 7 M's of management.

    (b) Traditional concept of finance was limited to acquisition of funds.

    (c) Investment decision, financing decision, dividend decision are the decisions of finance.

    (d) There is no relation among finance decisions.

    (e) Profit maximisation is suitable for sole proprietorship concerns.

    (f) A rupee receivable today, is less valuable than a rupee receivable in future.

    (g) Having basic knowledge of economics is necessary for a financial manager.

    (h) The job of a financial manager is confined to raising and effective utilisation of funds.

    (i) There is risk involvement in financial decisions.

    (j) Principles of corporate finance can be applied to all types of organisations.

    [*Answers:* (a) True (b) True (c) True (d) False (e) True (f) False (g) True (h) True (i) True (j) True]

REVIEW QUESTIONS

Short Questions

1. Define financial management.
2. Write a note on the traditional approach of finance.

3. Write a note on profit maximisation approach.
4. What do you understand by shareholders wealth ?
5. What is finance function ?
6. Define social responsibility.
7. What do you mean by agency problem?
8. List out the three limitations of profit maximisation.
9. What is meant by time value of money?
10. How do you compute shareholders wealth ?
11. What is financing decision ? (Finance MDC)
12. What do you mean by dividend decision ?
13. Write a note on investment decision.

Analytical Type

1. Write a note on the evolution of finance function.
2. Contrast the salient features of traditional and modern approaches to financial management.
3. Discuss in detail the scope of financial management.
4. State the objectives of financial management.
5. What do you mean by wealth maximisation and profit maximisation ? Which one do you suggest ? Why ?
6. Briefly explain the functions of financial management.
7. Comment on profit maximisation and wealth maximisation.
8. Explain briefly, the concept of profit maximisation with its limitations.
9. "Investment, financing and dividend decisions are all inter-related". Comment.
10. What is agency conflict? How can they be mitigated ?
11. Discuss in brief, the aims of finance functions.
12. Write a note on the organisation of finance function.
13. What are the major differences between finance and accounting ?
14. Discuss the risk return trade-off in financial decisions.
15. Comment on the emerging role of the finance manager in India.
16. Discuss the general relationship between finance and economics.
17. What do you mean by financial management ? Discuss the approaches to finance function.
18. What do you mean by business finance ? Should the goal of financial decision-making be profit maximisation or wealth maximisation ? Discuss.
19. In what respect is the objective of wealth maximisation superior to profit maximization?
20. "The profit maximization is not an operationally feasible criterion." Do you agree? Illustrate your views.
21. What are the main functions of the modern finance manager? How do they differ from his traditional counterpart ?
22. What are the basic financial decisions ? How do they involve risk return trade-off ?
23. "Finance functions of a business is closely related to its other functions" Discuss.

24. Assuming wealth maximization to be the objective of financial management, show how the financing, investment and dividend decisions of a company can help to attain this objective.

25. Explain what is meant by agency relationships and agency costs. How can the agency costs be mitigated ?

26. "………Finance has changed …….from a field that was concerned primarily with the procurement of funds to one, that includes the management assets, the allocation of capital and valuation of the firm" Elucidate.

REFERENCES

1. Van Horne, J.C and Wachowicz, Jr, J.M., *"Fundamentals of Financial Management,"* New Delhi, Prentice Hall of India Pvt. Ltd., 1996. p. 2.

2. Chandra, P, *"Financial Management-Theory and Practice"*, New Delhi : Tata McGraw Hill Publishing Company Ltd. 2002, p. 3.

3. Arthur, S.D., *"The Financial Policy of Corporations"*, New York: Ronalds 1918.

4. Wilford, J. Eiteman, et al, *"Essays of Business finance"*, Ann Arber, Michigan, Masterco Press Inc.1953.

5. Modigliani, F and Miller, M.H., *"The Cost of Capital, Corporate Finance and the Theory of Investment"*, American Economic Review 48, June 1958, Pp. 261-297.

6. Miller, M.H. and Modigliani. F, *"Dividend Policy Growth and Valuation of Shares,"* Journal of Business 34, October 1961, Pp. 411-433.

7. Charnes, A., Cooper, W.W and Miller, M.H. *"Application of Linear Programming to Financial Budgeting and the Costing of Funds"* Journal of Business, 32 January 1959, Pp. 20-46.

8. Teichroew, D, Rebichek A.A., and Montalbana. M, *"An Analysis of Criteria for Investment and Financing Decisions under Certainty"* Management Science, 12th November 1965, Pp. 151-179.

9. Hillier, F.S, op.cit., Pp. 443-457.

10. Sharpe, W.F, *"A Simplified Model of Portfolio Analysis Management Science"*, January 1963. Lentner. J., *"The Valuation of Risk Assets and the Selection of Risk Investments in Stock Portfolios and Capital Budgets"*, Review of Economics and Statistics, February 1965; Mossin. J., *"Equilibrium in Capital Market"*, Econometrica, October, 1966.

11. Ross, S.A., *"The Arbitrage Theory of Capital Asset Pricing"*, Journal of Economic Theory, December 1976.

12. Jensen, M.C. and Mecking, W.H., *"Theory of the Firm; Managerial Behaviour, Agency Costs and Ownership Structure"*, Journal of Financial Economics, October 1976, pp. 305-360.

13. Black, F., *"A Simple Discounting Rule"*, Financial Management, Summer 1988, pp. 7-11. Sick, G.A., *"A Certainty Equivalent Approach to Capital Budgeting"*, Financial Management, Winter 1986, pp. 23-32.

14. Baumol, W.J., *"The Transaction Demand for Cash: An Inventory Theoretic Approach"*, Quarterly Journal of Economics, LXV, Nov 1952, pp. 545-56.

15. Miller, M.H and Orr, D., *"A Model of the Demand for Money in Firms,"* Journal of Economics, LXX Aug 1966, pp. 413-435.

16. Soloman, E., *"Theory of Financial Management,"* New York: Columbia University, Press 1960, p. 5.

17. Ibid.p.8.

18. Bradely, J.F., *"Administrative Financial Management,"* New York; France & Noble, 1964 p. 104.

19. McAlpine, T.S., *"Profit Planning and Control,"* London: Business Book Ltd., 1969, p. 108.

20. Souvenir published at IV Conference of Asian and Pacific Accounts, New Delhi : 1965, p. 14.

BHATT INDUSTRIES BASIC PLANNING

This case will help the reader, develop an approach to structuring a case solution. It requires a logical approach to solving a general financial problem.

Bhatt Industries has been manufacturing fireworks at a small facility just outside Greensboro, North Carolina. The firm is known for the high level of quality control in its production process and is generally respected by distributors in the states, where fireworks are legalized. Its selling market is fairly well defined ; it has the capacity to produce 800,000 cases annually, with peak consumption in the summer. The firm is fairly confident, that the whole of next year's production can be sold for Rs. 25 a case.

On September 7, the company has Rs. 8,000,000 in cash. The firm has a policy against borrowing, to finance its production, a policy first established by William Bhatt, the owner of the firm. Mr. Bhatt keeps a tight rein on the firm's cash and invests any excess cash in treasury bonds, that pays a 12 per cent return and involve no risk of default.

The firm's production cycle revolves around the seasonal nature of the fireworks business. Production begins right after Labour Day and runs through May. The firms sales occur in February through May ; the firm closes from June 1 to Labour Day, when its employees return to farming. During this time, Mr. Bhatt visits his grandchildren in New York and Pennsylvania. As a result of this scheduling, the firm pays all its expenses during September and in May receives, all its revenues from its distributors within 6 weeks after the 4th of July. The customers send their checks directly to Kenmy National Bank, where the money is deposited in Bhatt's account.

Mr. Bhatt is the only full-time employee of his company and he and his family hold all the common stock. Thus, the company's only costs are directly related to the production of fireworks. The costs are affected by the law of variable proportions, depending on the production level. The first 100,000 cases cost Rs. 16 each; the second 100,000 cases, Rs. 17 each ; the third 100,000 cases, Rs. 18 each and the fourth 100,000 cases, Rs. 19 each ; the fifth 100,000 cases, Rs. 20 each ; the sixth 100,000 cases, Rs 21 each. As an example, the total of 200,000 cases would be Rs. 1,600,000 plus Rs. 1,700,000 or Rs. 3,300,000.

BHATT INDUSTRIES - INCOME STATEMENT (August 31, fiscal year just ended)	
	Rs.
Revenues from operations	50,00,000
Revenues from interest on government bonds	9,20,000
Total revenues	59,20,000
Operating expenses	40,50,000
Earnings before taxes	18,70,000
Taxes	9,48,400
Net income after taxes	9,21,600

Bhatt Industries is a corporation and pays a 30 per cent tax on income, because of the paperwork involved. Mr. Bhatt invests his excess cash on September 6 in one year treasury bonds. He does not invest for shorter periods.

Assignments

1. How does this level affect long-term prospects of wealth maximization ?
2. What should be the level of production to maximize the profit?

Analysis Financial Statement (Ratio)

2

1 Understand the significance of financial statement

2 Explain the nature of financial statements

3 Discuss the objectives of financial statements

4 Understand the limitations of financial statement analysis

5 Know the attributes of financial statements

6 Explain the importance of financial statements

7 Discuss the analysis of financial statements

8 Understand the recent trends in presenting financial statements

9 Know the methods of analysing financial statements

10 Explain the types of financial statement analysis

11 Discuss the according to nature of the analyst and the material used by him

12 Analyse according to modus operandi of analysis

13 Understand the according to the objective of the analysis

14 Know the comparative and common size statements

15 Explain the trend ratios

16 Understand the meaning, significances, classification and problems of ratio analysis

17 Significances of Ratio Analysis

18 Classification of Ratio Analysis

19 Know the capital structure ratios

20 Explain the liquidity ratio

21 Discuss the turnover ratio

22 Understand the profitability ratios

23 Explain the market ratios

24 Know the limitation of ratios

25 Problems on Ratio Analysis

FINANCIAL STATEMENTS ANALYSIS AND INTERPRETATION

Financial statements, as used in corporate business houses, refer to a set of reports and schedules which an accountant prepares at the end of a period of time for a business enterprise. The financial statements are the means with the help of which the accounting system performs its main function of providing summarised information about the financial affairs of the business. These statements comprise Balance Sheet or Position Statement and Profit and Loss Account or Income Statement. Of course to give a full view of the financial affairs of an undertaking, in addition to the above, the business may also prepare a Statement of Retained Earnings and a Cash Flow Statement. In India, every company has to present its financial statements in the form and contents as prescribed under Section 211 of the Companies Act 1956.

The significance of these statements is given below:

(i) *Balance Sheet or Position Statement:* Balance sheet is a statement showing the nature and amount of a company's assets on one side and liabilities and capital on the other. In other words, the balance sheet shows the financial position on a particular date usually at the end of one year period. Balance sheet shows how the money has been made available to the business of the company and how the money is employed in the business.

(ii) *Profit and Loss Account or Income Statement:* Earning profit is the principal objective of all business enterprises and Profit and Loss account or Income Statement is the document which indicates the extent of success achieved by a business in meeting this objective. Profits are of primary importance to the Board of directors in evaluating the management of a company, to shareholders or potential shareholders in making investment decisions and to banks and other creditors in judging the loan repayment capacities and abilities of the company. It is because of this that the profit and loss or income statement is regarded as the primary statement and commands a careful scrutiny by all interested parties. It is prepared for a particular period which is mentioned along with the title of these statements, which includes the name of the business firm also.

(iii) *Statement of Retained Earnings:* This statement is also known as Profit and Loss Appropriation Account and is generally a part of the Profit and Loss Account. This statement shows how the profits of the business for the accounting period have been utilised or appropriated towards reserves and dividend and how much of the same is carried forward to the next period. The term 'retained earnings' means the accumulated excess of earnings over losses and dividends. The balance shown by Profit and Loss Account is to be transferred to the Balance Sheet through this statement after making necessary appropriations.

(iv) *Cash Flow Statement:* This is a statement which summarises for the period, the cash available to finance the activities of an organisation and the uses to which such cash have been put. A statement of cash flow reports cash receipts and payments classified according to the organisation's major activities i.e., operating activities, investing activities and financing activities. This statement reports the net cash inflow or outflow for each activity and for the overall business. The cash flow statement is to be prepared according to the Accounting Standard 3 (Revised) "Cash Flow Statement". The details of this statement have been discussed in a separate study.

NATURE OF FINANCIAL STATEMENTS

Financial statements are prepared for the purpose of presenting a periodical review or report on the progress by the management and deal with the (a) status of the investments in the business and (b) results achieved during the period under review. The data exhibited in these financial statements are the result of the combined effect of (i) recorded facts; (ii) accounting conventions;

(iii) postulates or assumptions made to implement conventional procedures; (iv) personal judgements used in the applications of conventions and postulates and (v) accounting standards and guidance notes. These factors are explained below:

(i)   *Recorded Facts:* The term 'recorded facts' means, facts which have been recorded in the accounting books such as cash in hand, cash at bank, bills receivables, bills payable, debtors, creditors, fixed assets, sales, purchases, wages, capital and so forth. These items are listed on the basis of historical records of the transactions and valued at the price at which such transactions took place. Facts which have not been recorded in the accounting books are not depicted in the financial statements, however, material they might be.

(ii) *Accounting Conventions:* Accounting conventions have reference to certain fundamental accounting principles, the applications of which has been sanctified by long usage. For example, on account of the convention of conservation, provision is made for expected losses but expected profits are ignored.

(iii) *Postulates:* This assumption is referred to as the permanency postulate, and the assets of the business are valued under this assumption at cost less depreciation. In absence of this assumption, the assets may have to be valued at realisable value which may be negligible if the business is not a going concern. Another postulate which accountants make is the monetary postulate. It is the tacit assumption that the value of money, that is its purchasing power, remains constant over different periods. The accountants does not take into consideration the price-level changes while valuing various assets in different periods. Of late, however, accountants in the west have shown growing consciousness for incorporating price-level changes while preparing financial statements. A third postulate is the realisation postulate which takes cognizance of the time lag between production and sales affected. Under this postulate entire revenue is considered to be earned at the moment the sales take place and not at the time when the production took place. This postulate forms the basis for the convention of matching costs with revenues, where under, the costs incurred in the past period are brought forward to be accounted for against the revenues earned at a later period.

(iv) *Personal Judgements:* It may be noted that the application of conventions, assumptions or postulates depends on the personal judgements of the accountant. For example, the choice of selecting methods of depreciation, the mode of amortisation of fictitious assets, the method of valuation of stock, calculation of provision for doubtful debts etc. depend on the personal judgements of the accountant. However, the existence of consistency principle serves as a check on the power of the accountant to use his parsonal judgement. Since the accountant is guided by the past practices, the area of application of his personal judgement is reduced.

OBJECTIVES OF FINANCIAL STATEMENTS

Who is interested in financial statement analysis? According to author, everyone – both internal stake holder and external stake holder. Financial statements are necessary for shareholders and potential shareholders, in addition to management and creditors. The number and types of people interested in financial statements have changed radically in recent times..

The following groups have a direct interest in the financial statements of companies: Suppliers and potential suppliers of funds, i.e., shareholders, debentureholders, employees, customers, suppliers of goods and services on credit, tax authorities, etc. In addition, there are groups which have an indirect interest in these statements: Financial analysts and advisors, stock exchanges, academicians, lawyers, regulatory authorities, trade associations, and labour unions.

The Accounting Principles Board of America mentions the objectives of financial statements as follows:

1. To provide reliable financial information about economic resources and obligations of a business enterprise.

2. To provide reliable information about the net resources (resources less obligations) of an enterprise that results from its activities.

3. To provide financial information that assists in estimating the earning potentials of a business.

4. To provide other needed information about changes in economic resources or obligation.

5. To disclose, to the extent possible, other information related to the financial statements that is relevant to the needs of the users of these statements.

In order to meet the above objectives and to suit the needs of the varied users, the accountant entrusted with the task of compiling and presenting financial statements must follow a set of guidelines to ensure consistency, completeness, and fairness of the statements. These guidelines are called "generally accepted accounting principles". In absence of these 'generally accepted accounting principles' statements prepared may be un-understandable and misleading for the various groups of users. In addition to this, the financial statements prepared must also be authenticated as to their accuracy and fairness so that the confidence of the users is invoked. For this purpose, it is necessary that these statements be reviewed and certified by an independent reviewer, commonly known as auditor.

IMPORTANCE OF FINANCIAL STATEMENTS

The most important objective of financial statements is to present information for the use of different categories of persons as mentioned below:

1. *The Management:* The bigness of modern business and the multiplicity of factors affecting the business operations call for an increasingly scientific and analytical approach in the management of such businesses. This is possible only when up-to-date, accurate and systematic financial records are available to the management team. Financial accounts and statements are of a very great help in understanding the progress, position and prospects of the business vis-a-vis the industry. Financial statements, by helping the management to be acquainted with the causes of the business results, enable them to formulate appropriate policies and courses of action for the future

2. *The Public: Business is a social entity:* Various groups of the society, though not directly connected with business, are interested in the progress, position and prospects of a business enterprise. These groups are financial analysts, lawyers, trade associations, labour unions, financial press, students and teachers, etc. It is only through the published financial statements that these people can analyse, judge and comment upon the business enterprise. It should be noted that these financial statements are available to the public in case of joint stock companies. In case of proprietorships or partnerships, and other form of ownership, no such statements are published or made available to the public.

3. *The Shareholders and the Lenders:* The financial statements serve as a useful guide for the shareholders and probable shareholders, the suppliers, and the lenders and probable lenders of a company. It is through a critical examination of the financial statements that these groups can come to know about the efficiency and effectiveness of the management and position, progress and prospects of the company. For this purpose, it is necessary that the financial statements should contain accurate, complete and systematic facts and figures so that these people can get a full and accurate idea regarding the present position and future of the company. Since published financial statements are the main bases available to such group of people to judge the affairs of the company, it has been found that some managements

have been resorting to 'window dressing' in the presentation of these statements, to project a "better" than "what is" the position of the company.

4.   *The Labour and Trade Unions:* In India, workers are entitled to bonus under the Payment of Bonus Act, depending upon the size of the profit as disclosed by audited Profit and Loss Account. Thus, the Profit and Loss Account becomes greatly important to the workers. In wage negotiations also, the size of profits and the profitability achieved are greatly relevant.

5.   *The Country and Economy:* Economic progress of country is to a great extent, associated with the rise and growth of joint stock companies. The divergence between ownership and management of such companies has provided an opportunity for unscrupulous and fraudulent persons to cheat and defraud the public. Such unscrupulous acts affect the industry and people in the region in which the company operates, to a significant extent. Such fraudulent activities impair the confidence of the general public in joint stock companies as forerunner of economic progress, and thus retard economic growth of the country. The solution lies in raising the level of business and financial morality of the promoters and managements and in imparting knowledge about financial statements to the public so that they can examine and assess the real worth of the company and avoid being cheated by unscrupulous persons. The law endeavours to raise the level of business morality by compelling the companies to draw up financial statements in a clear systematic form and disclose certain minimum information. Such provisions increase the confidence of the public in joint stock companies, thus enabling faster economic progress of the country. This has all the more greater significance in underdeveloped and developing countries. In such countries, capital is not only scarce but also shy. Malpractices on the part of promoters and managements, only help to increase the scarcity and shyness of capital, thus blocking economic progress. Published financial statements provide an opportunity for the critical assessment of the worth of company and thus protect innocent public, increase their confidence, and help faster economic progress.

LIMITATIONS OF FINANCIAL STATEMENTS

The financial statements are based on certain accounting concepts and conventions which can not be said to be foolproof.

The following are the limitations of the financial statements:

1.   Financial statements are essentially interim reports and therefore, cannot be final because the final gain or loss can be computed only at the termination of the business.

2.   Financial statements take into consideration only the financial factors. They fail to bring out the significance of non-financial factors which may have considerable bearing on the operating results and financial conditions of an enterprise. For example, public image of the enterprise, the calibre of its management, efficiency and loyalty of its workers etc.

3.   It is not always possible to discover false figures in financial statements. Unscrupulous managements generally resort to 'window dressing' in the preparation of such statements.

4.   Financial statements only reflect the progress and position of the business at frequent intervals during its life. The decision regarding the period of these statements is a matter of personal judgement and it gives rise to the problem of allocating expenditures over various periods

5.   Financial statements though expressed in exact monetary terms, are not absolutely final and accurate. As the balance sheet is prepared on the basis of a going concern asset valuation represents neither the realisable value nor replacement costs. They depend on the judgement of the management in respect of various accounting policies.

6. Financial statements are prepared primarily for shareholders. Other interested parties have to generally make many adjustments before they use them profitably.

7. Quite often, financial statements do not disclose current worth of the business. Only historical facts are presented and the true current worth is not reflected.

ATTRIBUTES OF FINANCIAL STATEMENTS

Financial Statements prepared for an enterprise should possess the following attributes if they are to serve meaningfully the purpose and objectives for which they are meant:

1. *Relevance:* The financial statements prepared must be relevant for the purpose they are supposed to serve. While irrelevant and confusing disclosures should be avoided, nothing relevant and material should be held back from the public. The accountant so compiles such statements should be clear about relevancy and materiality or otherwise of the various information on the basis of which these statements are prepared.

2. *Accuracy and Freedom from Bias:* Financial Statements should convey a full and correct idea about the progress, position and prospects of an enterprise. For this purpose they must be accurately prepared. Inaccuracy besides invoking legal consequences, may also defeat the objectives for which the statements are meant. It may, however, be noted that absolute accuracy is not always possible, but this does not mean that rash and inaccurate data be deliberately provided, The least one can expect is that those who prepare and present financial statements should not allow their personal prejudices to colour the facts.

3. *Comparability:* Comparability increases the utility of financial statements. Comparison with previous statements helps in assessing the performance and in localising the trends in the progress and position of the business enterprise. Comparisons with other similar concerns or the industry reveals the strength of the enterprise vis-a-vis other firms and industry.

4. *Consistency:* The financial statements for a certain period are affected by the judgment and procedural choices exercised by the accountant. Opinions and procedures other than those employed generally, might cause the statement data to differ materially. Rules of accounting require that having made a selection of procedures, the accountant must strictly follow them in successive periods, unless the situation demands otherwise. Consistency has a direct bearing upon comparability. If inventories are valued on different basis in different periods (LIFO to FIFO to Replacement Cost) the results disclosed, generate doubt and comparison becomes difficult.

5. *Authenticity the financial statements* in order to be accepted as reliable must be reviewed and authenticated by an independent and capable person, generally known as auditor. Statements duly audited and certified by recognised and established auditors are accepted at their face value and are deemed to be more reliable. Unaudited statements give room to doubt and unreliability.

6. *Compliance with Law:* Financial statements must meet the requirements of law, if any, in the matter of form, contents and disclosures, procedures and methods. Non-compliance with legal provisions, besides invoking penalties, impairs the confidence of the public investors. In India, companies are required to present their financial statements according to the provisions of Section 211 of the Companies Act, 1956.

7. *Analytical Presentation:* The financial statements should be prepared in a classified form so that a better and meaningful analysis can be made. Proper classification helps in tracing and understanding in causes of the results as shown in these statements. Detailed and classified information helps to reveal inefficient performance and wasteful activities. Such classification helps in speedier analysis of these documents.

8. *Promptness:* No doubt, that the preparation of financial statement is somewhat complicated, but an undue delay in their preparation would reduce the significance and utility of these statements. They should be prepared as soon as possible, after the end of the period for which they are meant. Undue delay, the time lag between the end of the period and the preparation of these statements, may present difficulty in training the causes of the results as disclosed by the statements. Such delays and the delayed action thereon, may do more harm than good to the enterprise.

9. *Generally Accepted Principles:* Since the financial statements are meant for the use of a wider clientele, they must have general acceptability and understandability. This acceptability and understandability can come only when these statements are prepared in accordance with the "generally accepted accounting principles". This also increases the reliability of these statements and adds to the confidence of the users.

RECENT TRENDS IN PRESENTING FINANCIAL STATEMENTS

In India, every company has to present its financial statements in the form and contents as prescribed under Section 211 of the Companies Act, 1956. Keeping in view the complicacies of statutory forms in the Companies Act, now-a-days it is common practice to add the profit and loss account and balance sheet drawn ir statutory forms, some voluntary supplementary information in a simple manner as would be easily understood by a layman.

This voluntary information may include; the following:

1. *Summarised profit and loss account and balance sheet:* Now-a-days, companies are discarding the preparation of traditional two sided balance sheet and profit and loss account and are following columnar forms of balance sheet and profit and loss account which are simple way of presentation of information.

2. *Provision of important accounting ratios:* Accounting ratios show the interrelationship which exists among various accounting data. Balance sheet is substantiated by the important ratios of the current year and of the last two years.

3. *Disclosure of accounting policies:* Presently, progressive companies disclose accounting policies in their published accounts on the basis of which they have prepared their financial statements. This is done with a view to giving better understanding of the financial statements to the public.

4. *Impact of price level changes:* Since prices go on changing every day financial statements based on historical costs do not reflect the effect of price level changes on the financial position and profitability of the company. In order to accommodate the effect of price level changes in the financial statements now-a-days many companies have started showing this effects on financial statements in a supplementary statement in addition to the conventional statements prepared on historical basis.

5. *Rounding off of figures:* The Sachhar Committee has recommended the companies should be given the option to round off the figures of financial statements to the nearest thousand and/or hundred or ten rupees. This recommendation has been accepted and companies are now-a-days making use of rounding off of figures.

6. *Use of charts, graphs and diagrams:* Many companies incorporate charts, graphs and diagrams in their published accounts. It is known as graphic method of presentation of information. It attracts the attention of the users more quickly and forcibly. Recently, graphs and diagrams have been becoming very popular because they are considered to be the most effective media for disclosing trends and making comparisons over fairly long periods within a short space. The method of presenting information can effectively depict production

costs, fluctuations in output and sales, components of cost of production and income, use of divisible profits as taxes, dividends, other appropriations and retained profits etc.

7. *Use of schedules:* In order to make the balance sheet and profit and loss account as compact as possible, separate schedules for different heads (e.g. share capital, reserves and surplus, secured loans, unsecured loans, current liabilities and provisions, fixed assets, investments, current assets, loans and advances, miscellaneous expenditure, etc.) are prepared and details regarding these heads as prescribed in the Companies Act are given in these schedules. This is done to make the balance sheet and profit and loss account manageable within limited space. These schedules are properly numbered and reference of these is given in the balance sheet and profit and loss account.

8. *Highlights:* Highlights are usually shown at the beginning of the annual report so that the users may come across the important facts of the company immediately as he opens the report. It may usually cover information about sales, production, profit before and after tax, capital projects, working capital, fixed assets, share capital, important landmarks of the year, etc.

9. *Cash flow statements:* The preparation of cash flow statement has become mandatory now-a-days. A statement of cash flow, reports the cash receipts, cash payments and net changes in cash resulting from operating, investing and financing activities of an enterprise during a period in a format that reconciles the beginning and ending cash balances. It reports a net cash inflow or outflow for each activity and for the overall business.

ANALYSIS OF FINANCIAL STATEMENTS

According to Myers, "financial statement analysis is largely a study of relationship among the various financial factors in business as disclosed by a single set of statements and a study of the trend of these factors as shown in a series of statements".

According to author, analysis of financial statements refers to the treatment of information contained in the financial statement in a way so as to afford a full diagnosis of the profitability and financial position of the firm concerned.

The process of analysing financial statements involves the rearranging, comparing and measuring the significance of financial and operating data. Such a step helps to reveal the relative significance and effect of items of the data in relation to the time period and/or between two organisations.

Interpretation, which follows analysis of financial statements, is an attempt to reach to logical conclusion regarding the position and progress of the business on the basis of analysis. Thus, analysis and interpretation of financial statements are regarded as complimentary to each other.

TYPES OF FINANCIAL STATEMENT ANALYSIS

A distinction may be drawn between various types of financial analysis

1. According to Nature of the Analyst and the Material used by him
2. According to Modus Operandi of Analysis
3. According to the Objective of the Analysis

ACCORDING TO NATURE OF THE ANALYST AND THE MATERIAL USED BY HIM

(a) *External Analysis:* It is made by those who do not have access to the detailed records of the company. This group, which has to depend almost entirely on published financial statements, includes investors, credit agencies and governmental agencies regulating a business in nominal way. The position of the external analyst has been improved in recent times owing to the governmental regulations requiring business undertaking to make available detailed information to the public through audited accounts.

(b) *Internal Analysis:* The internal analysis is accomplished by those who have access to the books of accounts and all other information related to business. While conducting this analysis, the analyst is a part of the enterprise he is analysing. Analysis for managerial purposes is an internal type of analysis and is conducted by executives and employees of the enterprise as well as governmental and court agencies which may have regulatory and other jurisdiction over the business.

ACCORDING TO MODUS OPERANDI OF ANALYSIS

(a) *Horizontal Analysis:* When financial statements for a number of years, are reviewed and analysed, the analysis is called 'horizontal analysis'. As it is based on data from year to year rather than on one date or period of time as a whole, this is also known as 'dynamic analysis'. This is very useful for long term trend analysis and planning.

(b) *Vertical Analysis:* It is frequently used for referring to ratios developed for one date or for one accounting period. Vertical analysis is also called 'Static Analysis'. This is not very conducive to proper analysis of the firm's financial position and its interpretation as it does not enable to study data in perspective. This can only be provided by a study conducted over a number of years so that comparisons can be effected. Therefore, vertical analysis is not very useful.

ACCORDING TO THE OBJECTIVE OF THE ANALYSIS

On this basis the analysis can be long-term and short-term analysis:

(a) *Long-term Analysis:* This analysis is made in order to study the long-term financial stability, solvency and liquidity as well as profitability and earning capacity of a business. The objective of making such an analysts is to know whether in the long-term the concern will be able to earn a minimum amount which will be sufficient to maintain a reasonable rate of return on the investment so as to provide the funds required for modernisation, growth and development of the business.

(b) *Short-term Analysis:* This analysis is made to determine the short-term solvency, stability, liquidity and earning capacity of the business. The objective is to know whether in the short-run a business enterprise will have adequate funds readily available to meet its short-term requirements and sufficient borrowing capacity to meet contingencies in the near future.

Objectives of Financial Statement Analysis

Financial statement analysis is very much helpful in assessing the financial position and profitability of a concern. The main objectives of analysing the financial statements are as follows:

1. The comparative study in regard to one firm with another firm or one department with another department is possible by the analysis of financial statements.

2. Analysis of past results in respects of earning and financial position of the enterprise is of great help in forecasting the future results. Hence it helps in preparing budgets.

3. It facilitates the assessments of financial stability of the concern.

4. The analysis would enable the present and the future earning capacity and the profitability of the concern.

5. The operational efficiency of the concern as a whole as well as department wise can be assessed. Hence the management can easily locate the areas of efficiency and inefficiency.

6. The solvency of the firm, both short-term and long-term, can be determined with the help of financial statement analysis which is beneficial to trade creditors and debenture holders.

7. The long-term liquidity position of funds can be assessed by the analysis of financial statements.

Limitations of Financial Statement Analysis

1. Financial statements though expressed in exact monetary terms are not absolutely final and accurate and it depends upon the judgement of the management in respect of various accounting methods. If there is change in accounting methods, the analysis may have no comparable basis and the result will be biased.

2. The reliability of analysis depends on the accuracy of the figures used in the financial statements. The analysis will be vitiated by manipulations in the income statement or balance sheet and accounting procedure adopted by the accountant for recording.

3. The results for indications derived from analysis of financial statements may be differently interpreted by different users.

4. The analysis of financial statement relating to a single year only will have limited use. Hence, the analysis may be extended over a number of years so that results may be compared to arrive a meaningful conclusion.

5. When different firms are adopting different accounting procedures, records, policies and different items under similar headings in the financial statements, the comparison will be more difficult. It will not provide reliable basis to access the performance, efficiency, profitability and financial condition of the firm as compared to industry as a whole.

6. There are different tool of analysis available for the analyst. However, which tool is to be used in a particular situation depends on the skill, training, and expertise of the analyst and the result will vary accordingly.

7. Owing to the fact that financial statements are compiled on the basis of historical costs, while there is a market decline in the value of the monetary unit and resultant rise in prices, the figures in the financial statement loses its functions as an index on current economic realities. Again the financial statements contain both items. So an analysis of financial statements can not be taken as an indicator for future forecasting and planning.

8. Analysis of financial statements is a tool which can be used profitably by an expert analyst but may lead to faulty conclusions if used by unskilled analyst. So the result can not be taken as judgements or conclusions.

9. Financial statements are interim reports and therefore can not be final because the final gain or loss can be computed only at the termination of the business. Financial statement reflects the progress of the position of the business so analysis of these statements will not be a conclusive evidence of the performance of the business.

METHODS OF ANALYSING FINANCIAL STATEMENTS

The analysis of financial statements consists of a study of relationship and trends, to determine whether or not the financial position and results of operations as well as the financial progress of the company are satisfactory or unsatisfactory. The analytical methods or devices, listed below, are used to ascertain or measure the relationships among the financial statements items of a single set of statements and the changes that have taken place in these items as reflected in successive financial statements. The fundamental objective of any analytical method is to simplify or reduce the data under review to more understandable terms.

Analytical methods and devices used in analysing financial statements are as follows:

1. Comparative Statements
2. Common Size Statements
3. Trend Ratios
4. Ratio Analysis
5. Funds Flow Statement
6. Cash Flow Statements.

COMMON-SIZE STATEMENTS

In the comparative financial statements, it is difficult to comprehend the changes over the years in relation to total assets, total liabilities and capital or total net sales. This limitation of comparative statements makes comparison between two or more firms of an industry impossible because there is no common base of comparison for absolute figures. Again, for an interpretation of underlying causes of changes over time period, a vertical analysis is required and this is not possible with comparative statements.

Common size financial statements are those in which figures reported are converted into percentages to some common base. For this, items in the financial statements are presented as percentages or ratios to total of the items and a common base for comparison is provided. Each percentage shows the relation of the individual item to its respective total.

Common-size Income Statement: In a common size income statement, the sales figure is assumed to be equal to 100 and all other figures of costs or expenses are expressed as percentages of sales. A comparative income statement for different periods helps to reveal the efficiency or otherwise of incurring any cost or expense. If it is being prepared for two firms, it shows the relative efficiency of each cost item for the two firms.

Common-size Balance Sheet: In a common size balance sheet, total of assets or liabilities is taken as 100 and all the figures are expressed as percentage of the total. Comparative common size balance sheets for different periods help to highlight the trends in different items. If it is prepared for different firms in an industry, it facilitates to judge the relative soundness and helps in understanding their financial strategy.

Illustration 1: From the following prepare the Common size Income statement and Balance sheet and interpretation the same

ABC and Young XYZ Income Statement Period ending 31st March, 07

	ABC	XYZ
	Amount	Amount
	Rs.	Rs.
Net sales	25,38,000	9,70,000
Cost of goods sold	14,22,000	4,75,000
Gross Profit on Sales	11,16,000	4,95,000
Selling expenses	7,20,000	2,72,000
General and administrative		
Expenses	1,84,000	97,000
Total Operating Expenses	9.04,000	3,69,000
Operating profit	2,12,000	1,26,000
Other income	26,000	10,000
	2,38,000	1,36,000
Other expenses	40.000	29,000
Income before- tax	1,98,000	1,07,000
Income-tax	68,000	28,000
Net Income after tax	1,30,000	79,000

Balance Sheets As on 31 st March, 2007

	ABC	XYZ
	Amount	Amount
	Rs.	Rs.
Assets		
Current Assets:		
Cash	54,000	72,000
Sundry debtors	4,40,000	2.26,000
Trading stock	2,00,000	1,74,000
Prepaid expenses	22,000	21,000
Other current assets	20.000	21,000
Total Current Assets	7,36,000	5,14,000
Fixed Assets (less accumulated depreciation)	12,70,000	5,13,000
Total	20.06,000	10.27.000
Liabilities and Capital:		
Current Liabilities:		
Sundry creditors	84,000	1,34,000
Other current liabilities	1,56,000	62.000
Total Current Liabilities	2,40,000	1,96,000
Mortgage debentures	4,50,000	3JM00
Total Liabilities	6,90,000	5,14,000
Capital and reserves	13,16,000	5,13,000
Total Liabilities and Capital	20,06,000	10,27,000

Solution:

ABC and XYZ Companies Comparative Income Statement Period ending 31st March, 2007

	ABC		XYZ.	
	Amount	%of	Amount	% of
	Rs.	sales	Rs.	sales
Net sales	25,38,000	100.0	9,70,000	100.0
Cost of goods sold	14,22,000	56.0	4,75,000	49.0
Gross Profit on Sales	11,16,000	44.0	4,95,000	51.0
Selling expenses	7,20,000	28.4	2,72,000	28.0
General and administrative				
Expenses	1,84,000	7.2	97,000	10.0
Total Operating Expenses	9.04,000	35.6	3,69,000	38.0
Operating profit	2,12,000	8.4	1,26,000	13.0
Other income	26,000	1.0	10,000	1.0
	2,38,000	9.4	1,36,000	14.0
Other expenses	40.000	1.6	29,000	3.0
Income before- tax	1,98,000	7.8	1,07,000	11.0
Income-tax	68,000	2.7	28,000	2.9
Net Income after tax	1,30,000	5.1	79,000	8.1

Comparative Balance Sheets As on 31 st March, 2007

	ABC.		XYZ.	
	Amount	%of	Amount	%of
	Rs.	Total	Rs.	total
Assets				
Current Assets:				
Cash	54,000	2.7	72,000	7.0
Sundry debtors	4,40,000	22.0	2.26,000	22.0
Trading stock	2,00,000	10.0	1,74,000	17.0
Prepaid expenses	22,000	1.0	21,000	2.0
Other current assets	20.000	1.0	21,000	2.0
Total Current Assets	7,36,000	36.7	5,14,000	50.0
Fixed Assets (less accumulated depreciation)	12,70,000	63.3	5,13,000	50.0
Total	20.06,000	100.0	10.27.000	100.0
Liabilities and Capital:				
Current Liabilities:				
Sundry creditors	84,000	4.2	1,34,000	13.0
Other current liabilities	1,56,000	7.8	62.000	6.0
Total Current Liabilities	2,40,000	12.0	1,96,000	19.0
Mortgage debentures	4,50,000	22.4	3JM00	31.0
Total Liabilities	6,90,000	34.4	5,14,000	50.0
Capital and reserves	13,16,000	65.6	5,13,000	50.0
Total Liabilities and Capital	20,06,000	100.0	10,27,000	100.0

The following conclusions can be drawn from a careful analysis of the above financial statements:

1. ABC company has a better and efficient credit and collection system because its debtors and trading stock amounts to 32% of total assets as compared to 39% in case of XYZ Company.

2. The cash position of XYZ Company (7% of total assets) compares favourably with that of ABC (2.7%).

3. The turnover of ABC is larger (Rs. 25,38,000) than XYZ Company (Rs. 9,70,000), but the cost of goods absorbs a larger i.e. 56% of net sales compared to 49% in case of XYZ Company. This reflects a better pricing mark-up by Young Ones.

4. The selling, administrative and general expenses are 35.6% of net sales in case of ABC while 38% in case of Young Ones. Administration costs in XYZ is higher as compared to Old Guards, reflecting a highly paid or over staffed administrative function.

5. ABC appear to be more traditionally financed with shareholders equity of 65.6% of total liabilities as against 50% in case of Young Ones. This reflects the financial value ability of XYZ.

6. The fixed assets of ABC company is larger (Rs. 12,70,000) than of XYZ Company (Rs. 5,13,000). But, if this is compared with turnover that of the two companies, we find that ABC has a lower asset turnover (50%) than that of XYZ Company (53%). This reflects a better asset utilisation by XYZ Company.

COMPARATIVE STATEMENTS

These financial statements are so designed as to provide time perspective to the various elements of financial position contained therein. These statements give the data for all the periods stated so as to show:

(a) Absolute money values of each item separately for each of the periods stated.

(b) Increase and decrease in absolute data in terms of money values.

(c) Increase and decrease in terms of percentages.

(d) Comparison expressed in ratios.

(e) Percentages of totals.

Such comparative statements are necessary for the study of trends and direction of movement in the financial position and operating results. This calls for a consistency in the practice of preparing these statements, otherwise comparability may be distorted. Comparative statements enable horizontal analysis of figures.

Comparative Profit and Loss Account or Income Statement: Comparative income statement shows the operating results for a number of accounting periods and changes in the data significantly in absolute periods and changes in the dan significantly in absolute money terms as well as in relative percentage. A specimen income statement is given below:

Comparative Balance Sheet: A comparative balance sheet shows the balance of accounts of assets and liabilities on different dates and also the extent of their increases or decreases between these dates throwing light on the trends and direction of changes in the position over the periods.

Illustration 2: The following is the balance Sheet of Bhatt & Sons Ltd. for the year ended 31 march 2006 and 2007. Prepare Comparative Profit and Loss Account or Income Statement and comparative balance sheet interprets the figures:

Bhatt & Sons Ltd.
Comparative Statement of Income
(for year ended 31st March, 2006 and 2007)

(1)	31.3.2006 (2)	313.2007 (3)
	Rs.	Rs.
Net sales	8,50,000	9,52,000
Cost of goods sold	5,25,000	6,00,000
Gross Profit on Sales	3.25.000	3,52,000
Operating Expenses:		
Selling Expenses		
Advertising	15,000	20,000
Delivery expenses	20,000	18,000
Salesmen salaries and		
Commission	1,50,000	1,53,000
Packing and freight expenses	14,000	15,000
Other selling expenses	20,000	23,000
Total Selling Expenses	2,19,000	2,29,000

General and Administrative Expenses

Office salaries	58,000	63,800
Office expenses	2,000	4,000
Stationery and postage	1,000	2,000
Insurance	2,000	1,000
Doubtful debts	3,000	4,000
Total administrative and		
general expenses	66,000	74,800
Total Operating Expenses	2,85,000	3,03,800
Operating Profit	40,000	48,200
Other Incomes		
Interest income	12,000	12,000
Rent income	8,000	16,000
Discount received	12,000	18,000
Total Other Incomes	32,000	46,000
Total of Operating Profit		
and Other Income	72,000	94,200
Other Expenses		
Interest expense	26,000	17,000
Sales discount	8,000	7,000
Total Other Expenses	34,000	24,000
Income before income tax	38,000	70,200
Income tax	19,000	31,000
Income after Income Tax	19,000	39,200

Balance sheet of Bhatt & sons Ltd.

Assets	31.3.2006	31.3.2007
	Rs.	Rs.
Current Assets		
Cash in hand and at bank	1,18,000	10,000
Receivable on customer's		
accounts and bills	2,09,000	1,90,000
Inventory of materials, goods in process and		
finished stock	1,60,000	1,30,000
Prepaid expenses	3,000	3,000
Other current assets	29,000	10,000
Total Current Assets	5,19,000	3,43,000
Fixed Assets		
Land and buildings	2,70,000	1,70,000
Plant and machinery	3,10,000	7,86,000
Furniture and fixtures	9,000	18,000
Other fixed assets	20.000	30,000
Total Fixed Assets	6.09.000	10.04.000
Investments	46,000	59,000
Total Assets	11.74.000	14,06,000

Liabilities and Capital		
Current Liabilities		
Accounts payable (sundry trade creditors and bills payable)	2,55,000	1,17,000
Other short-term liabilities	7,000	10,000
Total Current Liabilities	2,62,000	1,27,000
Debentures	50,000	1,00,000
Long-term loans on mortgage	1,50,000	2.25.000
Total Liabilities	4,62,000	4,52,000
Capital		
Equity share capital	4,00,000	6,00,000
Reserve and surplus	3,12,000	3,54,000
Total Liabilities and Capital	11,74,000	14,06,000

Solution:

Bhatt & Sons Ltd.
Comparative Balance Sheet
(as on 31 st March, 2006 and 2007)

Assets	31.3.2006	31.3.2007	Increase (+) or Decrease (-) in amounts	Increase (+) or Decrease (-) in %age
	Rs.	Rs.	Rs.	
Current Assets				
Cash in hand and at bank	1,18,000	10,000	(-)1,08,000	(-)92
Receivable on customer's accounts and bills	2,09,000	1,90,000	(-) 19,000	(-)9
Inventory of materials, goods in process and finished stock	1,60,000	1,30,000	(-) 30,000	(-)19
Prepaid expenses	3,000	3,000	—	—
Other current assets	29.000	10.000	(-) 19,000	(-)66
Total Current Assets	5,19.000	3.43.000	M1,76,000	M34
Fixed Assets				
Land and buildings	2,70,000	1,70,000	(-)1,00,000	(-)37
Plant and machinery	3,10,000	7,86,000	(+)4,76,000	(+)150
Furniture and fixtures	9,000	18,000	(+) 9,000	(+) 100
Other fixed assets	20.000	30.000	(+) 10,000	(+)50
Total Fixed Assets	6.09.000	10.04.000	(+)3,95,000	(+)65
Investments	46,000	59,000	(+) 13,000	(+)28
Total Assets	11.74.000	14,06,000	M2.32.000	(+)20

Liabilities and Capital				
Current Liabilities				
Accounts payable (sundry trade creditors and bills payable)	2,55,000	1,17,000	(-)1,38,000	(-)54
Other short-term liabilities	7,000	10,000	(+) 3,000	(+)43
Total Current Liabilities	2,62,000	1,27,000	M1.35.000	(-)52
Debentures	50,000	1,00,00C	(+) 50,000	(+) 100
Long-term loans on mortgage	1,50,000	2,25,000	(+) 75.000	(+)50
Total Liabilities	4,62,000	4,52,000	(-) 10,000	(-)2
Capital				
Equity share capital	4,00,000	6,00,000	(+)2,00,000	(+)50
Reserve and surplus	3,12,000	3,54,000	(+) 42,000	(+)13
Total Liabilities and Capital	11,74,000	14,06,000	(+)2.32.000	(+)20

An analysis and interpretation of the above balance sheet reveals:

1. Current assets have decreased by Rs.1,76,000 between 2006 and 2007, while current liabilities have decreased only by Rs. 1,35,000. But this has no adverse affect on current ratio because the percentage decrease in current assets (34%) is much less than the percentage decrease in current liabilities (52%).

2. Fixed assets have increased by Rs. 3,95,000, major increase being a plant and machinery of Rs. 4,76,000, which amounts to the increase in production and profit earning capacities. Increase in fixed assets appears to have been partly financed by an increase in equity capital (Rs. 2,00,000), partly by release of working capital, and partly by increase in debentures and long- term borrowings (Rs. 1,25,000). The increase in reserves and surpluses (Rs. 42,000) may be the result of profits retained, and has gone to account for increase in long-term loans and fixed assets.

3. There has been a drastic fall in cash balance (Rs. 1,08,000). This reflects an adverse cash position.

Bhatt & Sons Ltd.
Comparative Statement of Income
(for year ended 31st March, 2005 and 2006)

(1)	31.3.2005 (2)	313.2006 (3)	Amount of (+) increase or decrease (-) during 2005-06 (4)		Percentage (+) increase or decrease (-) during 2005-06 (5)	
	Rs.	Rs.		Rs.		
Net sales	8,50,000	9,52,000	(+)	1,02,000	(+)	12
Cost of goods sold	5,25,000	6,00,000	(+)	75,000	(+)	14.3
Gross Profit on Sales	3.25.000	3,52,000	(+)	27.000		(±)8,3
Operating Expenses:						
Selling Expenses						
Advertising	15,000	20,000	(+)	5,000	(+)	33.3
Delivery expenses	20,000	18,000	(-)	2,000	(-)	10
Salesmen salaries and						
Commission	1,50,000	1,53,000	(+)	3,000	(+) 2	
Packing and freight expenses	14,000	15,000	(+)	1,000	{+}	7
Other selling expenses	20,000	23,000	(+)	3,000	(+)	15
Total Selling Expenses	2,19,000	2,29,000	(+)	10,000	(+)	4.5

General and Administrative Expenses

Office salaries	58,000	63,800	(+)	5,800	(+)	10
Office expenses	2,000	4,000	(+)	2,000	(+)	100
Stationery and postage	1,000	2,000	(+)	1,000	(+)	100
Insurance	2,000	1,000	(-)	1,000	(-)	100
Doubtful debts	3,000	4,000	(+)	1,000	(+)	33
Total administrative and general expenses	66,000	74,800	(+)	8,800	(+)	13.3
Total Operating Expenses	2,85,000	3,03,800	(+)	18,800	(+)	6.6
Operating Profit	40,000	48,200	(+)	8,200	(+)	20.5
Other Incomes						
Interest income	12,000	12,000	—	——		—
Rent income	8,000	16,000		8,000	(+)	100
Discount received	12,000	18,000	(+)	6,000	(+)	50
Total Other Incomes	32,000	46,000		14,000	(+)	43.7
Total of Operating Profit and Other Income	72,000	94,200	(+)	22,200	(+)	30.8

(1)	(2)	(3)		(4)		(5)
Other Expenses						
Interest expense	26,000	17,000	(-)	9,000	(-)	34.6
Sales discount	8,000	7,000	(-)	1,000	(-)	12.5
Total Other Expenses	34,000	24,000	(-)	10,000	(-)	29.4
Income before income tax	38,000	70,200	(+)	32,200		84.7
Income tax	19,000	31,000	(+)	12,000	(+)	63.1
Income after Income Tax	19,000	39,200	(+)	20,200		106.3

A study of the income statements reveals that there has been an increase of Rs. 1,02,000 in sales, but at the same time cost of goods sold has also increased by Rs. 75,000. In relative terms, sales increased by 12% while cost of goods sold by 14.3%. It means either the addition in sales has been due to lowering of sales price or the increase in cost is due to operational inefficiency. Similarly, increase in advertising has been much more (33%) than the increase in sales (12%). But in absolute terms the amount of increase is only Rs. 5,000. Operating profits have shown an increase of 20.5% over 2006-07 but in absolute terms profits have increased only by Rs. 8,200.

There has been a substantial increase in other incomes both in relative (43.7%) as well as absolute terms (Rs. 14,000). Similarly, there has been substantial decrease in other expenses

(29.4% and Rs. 10,000). These items have gone to increase the total income before tax for the year by Rs. 32,200, thus reflecting that the management has been more concerned for the other incomes than the operating profits.

TREND RATIOS

Trend ratios can be defined as index numbers of the movements of the various financial items in the financial statements for a number of periods. It is a statistical device applied in the analysis of financial statements to reveal the trend of the items with the passage of time. Trend ratios show the nature and rate of movements in various financial factors. They provide a horizontal analysis of comparative statements and reflect the behaviour of various items with the passage of time. Trend ratios can be graphically presented for a better understanding by the management. They are very useful in predicting the behaviour of the various financial factors in future. However, it should be noted that conclusions should not be drawn on the basis of a single trend. Trends of related items should be carefully studied, before any meaningful conclusion is arrived at. Since trends are sometimes significantly affected by externalities, i.e. reasons extraneous to the organisations, the analyst must give due weightage to such extraneous factors like government policies, economic conditions, changes in income and its distribution, etc.

Computation of Trend Percentages: For calculation of the trend of data shown in the financial statements, it is necessary to have statements for a number of years, and then proceed as under:

1. Take one of the statements as the base with reference to which all other statements are to be studied. In selection of the best statement, it should be noted that it belongs to a 'normal' year of business activities. Statement relating to an 'abnormal' year should not be selected as base, otherwise the trend calculated will be meaningless.

2. Every item in the base statement is stated as 100.

3. Trend percentage of each item in other statement is calculated with reference to same item in the base statement by using the following formula:

$$\frac{\text{Absolute Value of item (say cash) in other statements}}{\text{Absolute Value of same item (cash) in base statement}} \times 100$$

Limitations of Trend Ratios: It should be noted that trend ratios are not calculated for all items. They are calculated only for logically connected items enabling meaningful analysis. For example, trend ratios of sales become more revealing when compared with the trend ratios of fixed assets, cost of goods sold and operating expenses. Trend ratios have the following limitations:

(a) If the accounting practices have not been consistently followed year after year, these ratios become incomparable and thus misleading.

(b) Trend ratios do not take into consideration the price level charges. An increasing trend in sales might not be the result of larger sales volume, but may be because of increased sales price due to inflation. In order to avoid this limitation, figures of the current year should be first adjusted for price level changes from the base year and then the trend ratios be calculated.

(c) Trend ratios must be always read with absolute data on which they are based, otherwise the conclusions drawn may be misleading. It may be that a 100% change in trend ratio may represent an absolute change of Rs.1,000 only in one item, while a 20% change in another item may mean an absolute change of Rs. 1,00,000.

(d) The trend ratios have to be interpreted in the light of certain non-financial factors like economic conditions, government policies, management policies etc.

Illustration 3: From the following information extracted from the Balance Sheets of Star Ltd. for four previous financial years, calculate the trend percentages taking 2003-04 as the base year:

	2003-04	2004-05	2005-2006	2006-07
			(Rs. in lakhs)	
Current Assets:				
Cash	200	240	400	220
Bank	260	300	200	240
Debtors	400	600	1,000	1,600
Stock	800	1,200	1,800	2,000
Fixed Assets:				
Building	1,000	1,200	1,200	1,200
Plant and Machinery	2,000	2,400	2,400	2,800
	4,660	5,940	7,000	8,060

Solution:

Trend Percentages

	2003-04	2004-05	2005-06	2006-07	2003-04	2004-05	2005-06	2006-07
	(Rs. in lakhs)				(Trend percentage)			
Current assets:								
Cash	200	240	400	220	100	120.00	200.00	110.00
Bank	260	300	200	240	100	115.38	76.92	92.30
Debtors	400	600	1,000	1,600	100	150.00	250.00	400.00
Stock	800	1,200	1,800	2,000	100	150.00	225.00	250.00
Fixed Assets:								
Building	1,000	1,200	1,200	1,200	100	120.00	120.00	120.00
Plant and Machinery	2,000	2,400	2,400	2,800	100	120.00	120.00	140.00
	4,660	5,940	7,000	8,060	100	127.46	150.21	172.96

INTRODUCTION TO RATO ANALYSIS

According to J. Batty "the term accounting ratio is used to describe significant relationships which exist between figures shown in a balance sheet, in a profit and loss account, in a budgetary control system or in any other part of the accounting organization".

Financial statements contain many information (figures) relating to profit or loss and financial position of the business. If these items in financial statements are considered independently it will be or not be of much use. To make a meaningful reading of financial statements, these items found in financial statements have to be compared with one another. Ratio analysis, as a technique or analysis of financial statement uses this method of comparing the various items found in financial statements.

MEANING

The relationship between two figures expressed mathematically is called a ratio.

It is a numerical relationship between two numbers which are related in some manner.

DEFINITION

"A number expressed in terms of another."

"Ratio is a yardstick used to evaluate the financial condition and performance of a firm, relating to two pieces of financial data to each other."

— *James C. Van Harne*

"The relation of one amount, a to another b, expressed as the ratio of a to b".

— *Kohler*

"Ratio is a fraction whose numerator is the antecedent and denominator the consequent."

"Ratio is the relationship or proportion that one amount bears to another, the first number being the numerator and the later denominator."

— *H.G. Guthmann*

From the above definition we can clearly say that 'ratio' is a relationship between two figures or factors or variables". This relationship helps to analyse and interpret the financial condition and performance when applied to the financial data. The accounting ratios indicate a quantitative relationship which is used for analysis and decision-making.

A ratio is a quotient of two numbers and the relation expressed between two accounting figures is known as 'accounting ratio'. Ratio analysis is a very powerful analytical tool useful for measuring performance of an organization. The ratio analysis concentrates on the inter-relationship among the figures appearing in the aforementioned four financial statements.

ADVANTAGES/IMPORTANCE/SIGNIFICANCE OF RATIO ANALYSIS

Importance of Ratio Analysis

The major benefits arising from ratio analysis are as follows:

1. Ratio analysis is a very powerful analytical tool useful for measuring performance of an organization.

2. Ratio analysis concentrates on the inter-relationship among the figures appearing in the financial statements.

3. Ratios make comparison easy. The said ratio is compared with the standard ratio and this shows the degree of efficiency utilisation of assets, etc.

4. The results of two companies engaged in the same business can be easily compared (inter-firm comparison) with the help of ratio analysis.

5. Short-term liquidity position and long-term solvency position can be easily ascertained with the help of ratio analysis.

6. Ratio analysis helps the management to analyse the past performance of the firm and to make further projections.

7. Ratio analysis allow interested parties to make evaluation of certain aspects of the firm's performance as given below:

8. (i) Its importance lies in analysing the probable casual relationship between two past results.

    (ii) By effectively using the ratios, one can find out the growth or decline of an enterprise with the help of them, future actions can be taken.

9. The ratio analysis helps the management to analyse the past performance of the firm and to make further projections.

10. Ratio analysis allows interested parties like shareholders, investors, creditors, government and analysts to make an evaluation of certain aspects of a firm's performance

11. The appraisal of the ratios will make proper analysis about the strengths and weaknesses of the firm's operations.

Advantages of Ratio Analysis for Shareholders and Prospective Investors

1. Shareholders and prospective investors will analyse ratios for taking investment and disinvestment decisions.

2. The credit rating agencies will analyse the ratios of a firm to give the credit rating to the firm.

3. The government agencies will analyse ratios of a firm for review of its performance.

4. Bankers who provide working capital will analyse ratios for appraising the creditworthiness of the firm.

5. The financial institutions which provide long-term debt will analyse ratios for project appraisal and debt servicing capacity of the firm.

6. The financial analysts will analyse ratios for making comparisons and recommending to the investing public.

LIMITATIONS OF RATIO ANALYSIS

The following limitations must be taken into account.

1. Over use of ratios as controls on managers could be dangerous, in that management might concentrate more on simply improving the ratio than on dealing with the significant issues. For example, the return on capital employed can be improved by reducing assets rather than increasing profits.

2. Ratios provide only guidelines to the management. They are only the means. However, they scratch surfaces and raise questions. This limitation of ratios may force the management to undertake detailed investigation of the situation under question.

3. The standards will differ from industry to industry. Comparison of ratios of firms belonging to different industries is not suggested.

4. Since ratios are calculated from past records, there are no indicators of future.

5. Proper care should be exercised to study only such figures as have a cause and effect relationship, otherwise ratios will only be meaningless or misleading.

6. The reliability and significance attached to ratios depend on the accuracy of data based on which ratios are calculated.

7. Ratios of a company can have meaning only when they are compared against standards. Past performance of the same company cannot be benchmarked when there is change in circumstances.

8. The change in price levels due to inflation will distort the reliability of ratio analysis.

9. The analyst should have through knowledge of methods of window-dressing.

10. Single accounting ratio is not useful, at all, unless it is studied with other accounting ratios. This limitation of ratios necessitates inter-firm and intra-firm comparisons.

11. Ratios are based only on the quantitative information, hence, qualitative information (i.e., character, managerial ability, etc.) puts limit on the ratios.

12. Ratios are subject to arithmetical accuracy of the financial statements. Moreover, financial statements also include estimated data like provision for depreciation, for bad and doubtful debts, etc. Hence, results revealed by ratios are subject to such estimates.

13. Ratios are computed on the basis of financial statements which are historical in nature.

14. Knowledge of ratios alone is meaningless unless it is also ascertained how it is made up.

15. Lack of homogeneity of data, person judgment, lack of consistency etc. are the factors which limit the conclusion to be derived on the basis of accounting ratios.

16. Ratios are calculated form financial statements which are affected by the financial bases and policies adopted on such matters as depreciation and the valuation of stocks.

17. A ratio is a comparison of two figures, a numerator and a denominator. In comparing ratio, it may be difficult to determine whether differences are due to changes in the numerator, or in the denominator or in both.

18. Ratios are inter-connected. They should not be treated in isolation. The effective use of ratios, therefore, depends on being aware of all these limitations and ensuring that, following comparative analysis, they are used as a trigger point for investigation and corrective action rather than being treated as meaningful in themselves.

19. The analysis of ratios clarifies trends and weaknesses in performance as a guide to action, as long as proper comparisons are made and the reasons for adverse trends or deviations from the norm are investigated thoroughly.

20. While making inter firm comparison, the analyst must keep in mind that different firms follow different accounting policies e.g., depreciation allowance, valuation of inventory etc.

Factors affecting the efficacy of Ratios

Ratios by themselves mean nothing. Caution has to be exercised in using ratios. They must always be compared with:

(a) A norm or a target,

(b) Previous ratios in order to assess trends, and

(c) The ratios achieved in other comparable companies (inter-company comparisons).

CLASSIFICATION OF RATIOS

The ratio analysis is made under six broad analysis, according to users categories as follows:

♦ Liquidity ratios

♦ Leverage ratios

♦ Asset management ratios

♦ Profitability ratios

♦ Operating ratios

♦ Market based ratios

Or

1. Calculation according to statement of sources and income statement

2. Classification according to time

3. Classification according to nature or importance in financial analysis

4. Classification according to functions/objectives

5. Classification according to users

The above classifications can be explained as follows:

1. Classification according to statements (source) from which they are calculated.

(i) *Balance Sheet ratios:* Where both numerator and denominator figures are taken from the balance sheet, such as current ratio, quick ratio, proprietary ratio, etc.

(ii) *Profit and loss (revenue) ratios:* Ratios calculated from the figures in the profit and loss account. At times they are also called operating ratios. Some of the profit and loss ratios, gross profit ratio, operating profit ratio, net profit ratio, expenses ratio, etc.

(iii) *Position-cum-revenue ratios:* Where ratios are calculated by taking one figure from balance sheet and another from profit and loss account, they are known as combined or consolidated or complex or position-cum-revenue ratios. For example, return on proprietor's fund, return on capital employed, turnover of debtors and creditors separately, earnings ratio, etc.

2. Classification according to Functions/Objectives

(i) *Financial ratios:* Include solvency and liquidity ratios.

(ii) *Profitability ratios:* For example, Gross profit ratio, net profit ratio, operating ratio, return on capital employed, expense ratios, etc.

(iii) *Turnover or Activity ratios:* For example, Turnover of Stock, Turnover of Debtors, Turnover of Creditors, etc.

(iv) *Market Test ratios:* For example, Earnings Per Share (EPS), Price Earning ratio, Dividend Yield ratio, Equity Dividend Cover, Net Cash inflow, book value per share, etc.

3. *Classification according to Users:*

In view of the requirements of the various uses of ratios, we may classify them into the following four important categories.

(i) Liquidity ratios

(ii) Leverage ratios

(iii) Activity ratios

(iv) Profitability ratios

4. Classification according to time:

    (i) *Structural ratios:* For example, ratios computed from data referring to the same point of time, ratios of a particular month or year. (ii) Trend ratios: i.e., ratios computed between the items referred to different periods of time.

5. Classification according to nature or importance in financial analysis

    (i) Primary ratio, e.g., operating profit to capital employed.

    (ii) Secondary or supporting ratio, e.g., stock velocity, creditors velocity, expenses ratios, etc.

DETAILED ANALYSIS OR DIFFERENT ACCOUNTING RATIO

In the above, we have seen different classification or ratios available on difference basis. From the above, let us understand in detail some of the very important ratios which we use frequently in different situations of decision-making process; they are on the basis or nature or purpose with which a ratio is calculated.

On the basis or the nature or purpose, accounting ratios may be classified into four categories.

1. Liquidity ratios or short-term solving ratios.
2. Capital structure or leverage ratios.
3. Turnover ratios or activity ratios or performance ratios.
4. Profitability ratios.

LIQUIDITY RATIOS

The liquidity ratios measure the liquidity of the firm and its ability to meet its maturing short-term obligations. Liquidity is defined as the ability to realize value in money, the most liquid of assets.

Liquidity refers to the ability to pay in cash, the obligations that are due. Corporate liquidity has two dimensions viz., quantitative and qualitative concepts. The quantitative aspect includes the quantum, structure and utilization of liquid assets and in the qualitative aspect, it is the ability to meet all present and potential demands on cash from any source in a manner that minimizes cost and maximizes the value of the firm. Thus, corporate liquidity is a vital factor in business. Excess liquidity, though a guarantor of solvency would reflect lower profitability, deterioration in managerial efficiency, increased speculation and unjustified expansion, extension of too liberal credit and dividend policies. Too little liquidity then may lead to frustration, business objections, reduced rate of return, missing of profitable business opportunities and weakening of morale. The important ratios in measuring short-term solvency are (1) Current Ratio (2) Quick Ratio (3) Absolute Liquid Ratio, and (4) Defensive-Interval Ratio.

Current Ratio

This ratio measures the solvency of the company in the short-term. Current assets are those assets which can be converted into cash within a year. Current liabilities and provisions are those liabilities that are payable within a year.

$$\frac{\text{Current Assets, Loans and Advances}}{\text{Current Liabilities and Provisions}}$$

A current ratio 2:1 indicates a highly solvent position. A current ratio of 1.33:1 is considered by banks as the minimum acceptable level for providing working capital finance. The constituents of the current assets are as important as the current assets themselves for evaluation of a company's solvency position. A very high current ratio will have adverse impact on the profitability of the organization. A high current ratio may be due to the piling up of inventory, inefficiency in collection of debtors, high balances in cash and bank accounts without proper investment etc.

The composition of current assets are, (i) Cash in hand and at bank (ii) Readily convertible or marketable securities (iii) Stock (iv) Sundry Debtors (v) Bills of exchange i.e. bills receivable, pre-paid expenses.

The current liabilities comprise of bills of exchange, bills payable, sundry creditors, outstanding and occured expenses, income-tax payable, bank over draft etc.

Advantages of Current Ratio

1. This ratio indicates the extent of current assets available to meet the current obligation. It is only from the current assets the immediate obligations (current liabilities) are met with. Therefore, the interest of creditors lie in this ratio.

2. The safe ratio is 2:1. This means, for every current liability of Re.1, there should be current assets of Rs. 2, so that the firm can conveniently meet its current obligations, even if the assets like stock or debtors are not quickly realised.

3. This margin also leaves sufficient amount as working capital to carry out day-to-day transactions.

4. This is useful in assessing the solvency and liquidity position of the company.

Quick Liquid/Acid Test Ratio

Quick ratio is used as a measure of the company's ability to meet its current obligations since bank overdraft is secured by the inventories, the other current assets must be sufficient to meet other current liabilities.

$$\frac{\text{Current Assets, Loans and Advances} - \text{Inventories}}{\text{Current Liabilities and Provisions} - \text{Bank overdraft}}$$

A quick ratio of 1:1 indicates highly solvent position. This ratio serves as a supplement to the current ratio in analyzing liquidity.

Advantages of the Quick Ratio

♦ This ratio is very useful for cross checking the performance in other areas of economic management of an enterprise. Thus, the liquid ratio, cross-checked with inventory throw light on the inventory accumulation. In addition, the liquid ratio can throw light on certain other aspects of inventory management which will be pointed out later.

♦ It is an improved variant of the current ratio in arriving at a liquidity index for an enterprise.

Absolute Liquid/Super Quick Ratio

The ratio of absolute liquid assets to quick liabilities. However, for calculation purposes, it is taken as ratio of absolute liquid assets to current liabilities. Absolute liquid assets include cash in hand, cash at bank and short-term or temporary investments.

$$\frac{\text{Absolute Liquid Assets}}{\text{Current Liabilities}}$$

Absolute Liquid Assets = Cash in Hand + Cash at Bank + Short-term investments

The ideal absolute liquid ratio is taken as 1:2

The stock working capital ratio is defined as (stock + working capital) and is expressed as a per cent ratio, where stock refers to inventory as the rupee value of raw materials, work in-process, finished goods, stores and packing materials. It may be noted that stock is valued at cost price or market price whichever is lower. Stock can mean either the rupee value of the closing stock as on the date of the balance sheet or the average rupee value of the stock i.e.

(Opening stock plus closing stock/2)

Working capital means either gross working capital (current assets) or net working capital (current assets less current liabilities). But generally working capital is assumed to be net working capital.

Stock to working capital ratio is expressed as follows:

(Inventory/Stock)/working capital × 100

Note: Inventory or stock can be taken as either closing stock or average stock (opening + closing/2)

Illustration 4: From the following balance sheet calculate current ratio, liquid ratio and absolute ratio

Balance Sheet

Liability		Rs.	Assets		Rs.
Share Capital		2,00,000	Fixed Assess		1,60,000
Reserves		80,000	CURRENT ASSETS:		
CURRENT LIABILITIES:			Stock	1,20,000	
creditors	80,000		Debtors	60,000	
Bills payable	40,000	1,20,000	Investments	40,000	
			(Short term)		
			Cash	20,000	2,40,000
		4,00,000			4,00,000

Solution:

Current Ratio is = 2,40,000/1,20,000 = = 2:1

Quick ratio = (2,40,000 – 1,20,000)/1,20,000 = 1 or 1:1

Absolute liquid ratio or cash position ratio = Cash on hand and as bank balance/Current liabilities cash position ratio will be = 20,000 / 1,20,000 = 0.167

Stock or inventory to working capital ratio = Stock – 1,20,000 Cap = Current asset – Current liabilities = 2,40,000 – 1,20,000 = 1,20,000

Inventory to working capital ratio = 1,20,000/1,20,000 × 100 = 100%

CAPITAL STRUCTURE RATIOS AND LEVERAGE RATIO

Leverage or capital structure ratios are those ratios which measures the relative interest of lenders and proprietors in a business organisation. These ratios indicate the long-term solvency position of an organisation. These ratios help the management in the proper administration of the capital.

Shareholders Equity Ratio

The ratio is calculated as follows:

$$\frac{\text{Shareholders Equity}}{\text{Total Assets (tangible)}}$$

It is assumed that larger the proportion of the shareholders' equity, the stronger is the financial position of the firm. This ratio will supplement the debt-equity ratio. In this ratio, the relationship is established between the shareholders' funds and the total assets.

Shareholders funds represent equity and preference capital plus reserves and surplus less accumulated losses. A reduction in shareholders' equity signaling the over-dependence on outside sources for long-term financial needs and this carries the risk of higher levels of gearing. This ratio indicates the degree to which unsecured creditors are protected against loss in the event of liquidation.

Long-term Debt to Shareholders Net Worth Ratio

The ratio is calculated as follows:

$$\frac{\text{Long-term Debt}}{\text{Shareholders Net worth}}$$

The ratio compares long-term debt to the net worth of the firm i.e., the capital and free reserves less intangible assets. This ratio is finer than the debt-equity ratio and includes capital that is invested in fictitious assets like deferred expenditure and carried forward losses. This ratio would be of more interest to the contributories of long-term finance to the firm, as the ratio gives a factual idea of the assets available to meet the long-term liabilities.

Capital Gearing Ratio

It is the proportion of fixed interest bearing funds to equity shareholders funds.

$$\frac{\text{Fixed interest bearing funds}}{\text{Equity Shareholder's funds}}$$

The fixed interest bearing funds include debentures, long-term loans and preference share capital. The equity shareholders funds include equity share capital, reserves and surplus.

Capital gearing ratio indicates the degree of vulnerability of earnings available for equity shareholders. This ratio signals the firm which is operating on trading on equity. It also indicates the changes in benefits accruing to equity shareholders by changing the levels of fixed interest bearing funds in the organization.

Advantages of capital gearing ratio

1. Capital gearing ratio measures the company's capitalisation.
2. This ratio is useful to the new investors for making sound investment decisions.
3. Capital gearing ratio shows the claim of owners as against the claim of lenders and preference share holders.

Debt-Equity Ratio

Debt-Equity ratio measures the relative claim of creditor and owners in a business organisation. Debt usually includes all external long term liabilities. In some cases, both short-term and long term liabilities are included in the preview of debt. Equity includes owners or proprietors fund, it comprises of capital, all accumulated reserves and profits. Any accumulated losses should be deducted.

Debt Equity ratio can be expressed as follows:

$$= \frac{\text{Debt}}{\text{Equity}}$$

Debt = All external long term liabilities

Equity = Share capital and all reserves and provisions.

Ideal ratio of the debt-equity ratio is 2:11 i.e., 2 debt for one equity. Any higher ratio is considered as a risky position for the firm as more debt is involved and a lower ratio indicates a sound financial position.

Advantages/uses of Debt-Equity ratio

1. This ratio is a measure of contribution of owners to the business as compared to long-term creditors.

2. It tests the long-term liquidity or solvency of an organisation.

Fixed Assets to Long-Term Funds Ratio

The fixed assets is shown as a proportion to long-term funds as follows:

$$\frac{\text{Fixed Assets}}{\text{Long-term Funds}}$$

This ratio indicates the proportion of long-term funds deployed in fixed assets. Fixed assets represents the gross fixed assets minus depreciation provided on this till the date of calculation. Long-term funds include share capital, reserves and surplus and long-term loans. The higher the ratio indicates the safer the funds available in case of liquidation. It also indicates the proportion of long-term funds that is invested in working capital.

Proprietary Ratio or Net worth Ratio

It express the relationship between shareholders' net worth and total assets.

$$\frac{\text{Shareholders Net Worth}}{\text{Total Assets}}$$

Reserves earmarked specifically for a particular purpose should not be included in calculation of net worth. A high proprietary ratio is indicative of strong financial position of the business.

The higher the ratio, the better it is.

Owners' funds mean the sum of the paid-up equity share capital plus preference share capital plus proprietary reserves (reserves on revenue account like general reserves and profit and loss account credit balance and reserves on capital account i.e. capital reserves). From the sum so arrived at, intangible assets like goodwill and fictitious assets capitalised as 'miscellaneous expenditure' may be deducted.

Or

Net worth = Equity share capital + Preference share capital + Reserves – Fictitious assets

Total assets = Fixed assets + Current assets – fictitious assets

If the ratio equals unity, it implies that all uses of finance are supported by the owner's. In such a case, ownership capital is the exclusive source of finance. Theoretically, the value of this ratio as unity, may be considered to be sound position because it is believed that higher the ratio, sounder the capital structure. And, remember, unity is the highest possible arithmetic value, which this ratio can assume. As the ratio tends to 100% the financial position tends to increasingly improve.

Advantages or uses of Proprietary Ratio: It also shows the relation between own fund and borrowed fund. It shows the amount of proprietors funds invested in the total assets of the firm.

Current assets to net worth ratio

This ratio signifies the relationship between current assets and net worth.

Current assets to net worth ratio can be expressed as follows:

Current assets to net worth ratio = Current Assets/Net worth

Uses of this ratio is, this ratio indicates the current assets financial by owners of the business. And it also shows the relative claim of owners on the fixed assets of the business organisation.

ASSET MANAGEMENT RATIO OR TURNOVER RATIO OR PERFORMANCE RATIO OR ACTIVITY RATIO

Asset management ratios measure how effectively the firm employs its resources. These ratios are also called 'activity or turnover ratios' which involve comparison between the level of sales and investment in various accounts - inventories, debtors, fixed assets, etc. asset management ratios are used to measure the speed with which various accounts are converted into sales or cash. The following asset management ratios are calculated for analysis. These ratios also analyse the use of resources and the utility of each component of total assets. The profitability of the firm can be determined by activity ratios coupled with the degree of leverage.

Inventory Turnover Ratio

A considerable amount of a company's capital may be tied up in the financing of raw materials, work-in-progress and finished goods. It is important to ensure that the level of stocks is kept as low as possible, consistent with the need to fulfill customers' orders in time.

$$\frac{\text{Cost of Goods Sold}}{\text{Average Inventory}} \text{ or } \frac{\text{Sales}}{\text{Average Inventory}}$$

Average Inventory = (opening stock + Closing stock)/2

The higher the stock turnover rate or the lower the stock turnover period the better, although the ratios will vary between companies. For example, the stock turnover rate in a food retailing company must be higher than the rate in a manufacturing concern.

The inventory turnover ratio measures how many times a company's inventory has been sold during the year. If the inventory turnover ratio has decreased from past, it means that either inventory is growing or sales are dropping. In addition to that, if a firm has a turnover that is slower than for its industry, then there may be obsolete goods on hand, or inventory stocks may be high. Low inventory turnover has impact on the liquidity of the business.

Inventory Ratio

The level of inventory in a company may be assessed by the use of the inventory ratio, which measures how much has been tied up in inventory.

$$\frac{Inventory}{Current\ Assets} \times 100$$

Debtors Turnover·Ratio

Debtors turnover, which measures whether the amount or resources tied up in debtors is reasonable and whether the company has been efficient in converting debtors into cash. The formula is:

$$\frac{Credit\ Sales}{Average\ Debtors}$$

The higher the ratio, the better the position

Debtors Collection Period or Debtors Velocity Ratio

Average debtors collection period measures how long it take to collect amounts from

$$\frac{Average\ Debtors}{Credit\ Sales} \times 365\ (in\ days)$$

The actual collection period can be compared with the stated credit terms of the company.

If it is longer than those terms, then this indicates inefficiency in collecting debts.

Use or Advantages of Debtor Turn-over Ratio

1. This ratio helps to monitor credit and collection policies. It can signal the need for corrective action particularly if compared with a norm.
2. This ratio highlights the impact of management policies on the liquidity of the enterprise a well as its profitability. It is a barometer of the general state of health of an enterprise.
3. It is easy to understand, particularly when expressed as debtors collection period.

Illustration 5: Following is the information available of RKV. Ltd.

	Rs.
B/R on 1-1-2006	1,50,000
B/Ron31-12-2006	2,50,000
Opening Debtors (1-1-2006)	2,00,000
Closing Debtors (31-12-2006)	3,00,000
Cash Sales for the year 2006	4,00,000
Total Sales for the year 2005	40,00,000

Calculate Debtors Turnover ratio

Solutions:

To compute the ratio we have to find out certain figures.

		Rs.
1. "Credit Sales : Total Sales		40,00,000
Less: Cash Sales		4,00,000
		36,00,000
2. Average Debtors : Opening Debtors		2,00,000
Opening B/R		1,50,000
		3,50,000
Closing Drs	3,00,000	
Closing B/R	2,50,000	5,50,000

$(3,50,000 + 5,50,000)/2 = 4,50,000$

Debtor's turnover ratio = Credit Sales/Average Debtors

$= 36,00,000/4,50,000 = 8$ times

Bad Debts to Sales Ratio

It measures the proportion of bad debts to sales:

$$\frac{\text{Bad Debts}}{\text{Sales}} \times 100$$

Bad debts to sales ratio indicates the efficiency of the credit control procedures of the company. Its level will depend on the type of business. Mail order companies have to accept a fairly high level of bad debts, while retailing organizations should maintain very low levels of ratio. The actual ratio is compared with the target or norm to decide whether it is acceptable or not.

Creditors Turnover Ratio

The measurement of the credit turnover period shows the average time taken to pay for goods and services purchased by the company. The formula is:

$$\frac{\text{Net Credit Purchase}}{\text{Average Creditors}}$$

Here, purchases refers to net credit purchases and average creditors is given by Opening creditors and Bills payable + Closing creditors and bills payable divided by two.

In general the longer the credit period achieved the better, because delays in payment mean that the operations of the company are being financed interest free by suppliers of materials. But there will be a point beyond which delays in payment will damage relationships with suppliers which, if they are operating in a seller's market, may harm the company. If too long a period is taken to pay creditors, the credit rating of the company may suffer, thereby making it more difficult to obtain supplies in the future.

Creditors Payment Period or Creditors Velocity Ratio

$$\frac{\text{Average Creditors}}{\text{Credit Purchases}} \times 365 \text{ (in days)}$$

Generally Payment period of 50 to 60 days is considered ideal.

Illustration 6: Following information is available relating to RJS company.

B.P on 1-1-05	3,00,000
Creditors on 1-1-0!;	2,50,000
B.P on 31-12-05	3,50,000
Creditors on 31-12-05	3,00,000
Credit purchases for the year	50,00,000

Calculate creditor's turn over ratio and payment period

Average Creditors

Opening creditors & B.P   2,50,000 + 3,00,000 = 5,50,000

Closing creditors & B.P   3,50,000 + 30,00,000 = 6,50,000

Average =   5,50,000 + 6,50,000/2 = 6,00,000

Creditors turnover ratio = Net annual credit purchases/Average Creditors

= 50,00,000/6,00,000 = 8.333 times

Creditor's payment period or Velocity Ratio

Payment Period = 360/Creditors turnover ratio Or

$$= \frac{\text{Average Creditors}}{\text{Credit Purchases}} \times 365 \text{ (in days)}$$

= 360/8.333times = 43 days

Fixed Assets Turnover Ratio

This ratio will be analysed further with ratios for each main category of asset. This is a difficult set of ratios to interpret, as asset values are based on historic cost. An increase in the fixed asset figure may result from the replacement of an asset at an increased price or the purchase of an additional asset intended to increase production capacity.

$$\frac{\text{Sales}}{\text{Fixed Assets}}$$

The ratio of the accumulated depreciation provision to the total of fixed assets at cost might be used as an indicator of the average age of the assets, particularly when depreciation rates are noted in the accounts. The ratio of sales value per square foot of floor space occupied is particularly significant for trading concerns, such as a wholesale warehouse or a departmental store.

Illustration 7:

Balance Sheet of ABC Ltd., as on 31-12-05				
Share capital		20,00,000	Fixed assets	35,00,000
Reserves 6t suplus		5,00,000	Current assets	10,00,000
Long term liabilities		12,00,000		
Current liabilities		8,00,000		
		45,00,000		45,00,000

Net sales Rs. 2,50,00,000

Solution:

Fixed assets turn over ratio = Net Sales/Fixed Assets

$$= 2,50,00,000/35,00,000 = 7.14 \text{ times}$$

Total Assets Turnover Ratio

This ratio indicates the number of times total assets are being turned over in a year.

$$\frac{\text{Sales}}{\text{Total Assets}}$$

The higher the ratio indicates overtrading of total assets, while a low ratio indicates idle capacity.

From the Illustration 6, we can calculate total asset turnover ratio = 2, 50, 00,000 / 45, 00,000 = 5.55 times

Working Capital Turnover Ratio

This ratio is calculated as follows:

$$\frac{\text{Sales}}{\text{Working Capital}}$$

This ratio indicates the extent of working capital turned over in achieving sales of the firm.

Sales to Capital Employed Ratio

This ratio is ascertained by dividing sales with capital employed.

$$\frac{\text{Sales}}{\text{Capital Employed}}$$

This ratio indicates efficiency in utilization of capital employed in generating revenue.

Illustration 8: The following are the Trading and Profit & Loss Account for the year ended 31st March, 2005 and the Balance Sheet as on that date of RKV. Ltd.

Trading and Profit & Loss A/c

Particulars	Rs.		Particulars	Rs.
To Opening stock	9,950		By Sales	85,000
To Purchases	54,525		By Closing Stock	14,900
To Wages	1,425			
To Gross profit	34,000			
	99,900			99,900
To Administrative expenses	15,000		By Gross Profit	34,000
To Selling expenses	2,000		By Interest	300
To Bad debts	1,000		By Profit on sale of shares	600
To Financial expenses	1,500			
To Loss on sale of assets	400			
To Net profit	15,000			
	34,900			34,900

Balance Sheet

Liabilities	Rs.	Assets	Rs.
Share capital	20,000	Land & Buildings	15,000
Reserves	9,000	Plant & Machinery	8,000
Current liabilities	13,000	Stock	14,900
Profit & Loss A/c	6,000	Debtors	7,100
		Cash at bank	3,000
	48,000		48,000

You are required to calculate asset management ratios or turnover ratio.

Solution:

Calculation of Activity or Turnover Ratios

1. **Inventory Turnover Ratio**

$$\frac{\text{Cost of goods sold}}{\text{Average inventory}} = \frac{51,000}{12,425} = 4.10$$

Note:

(i) Cost of goods sold

= Opening stock + Purchases + Wages − Closing stock

= 9,950 + 54,525 + 1,425 − 14,900 = Rs. 51,000

(ii) Average Inventory

= (Opening Stock + Closing Stock)/2

= (9,950 + 14,900)/2 = Rs. 12,425

The company is having low inventory turnover ratio, and the company's working capital might be tied up in financing inventory.

2. *Inventory Ratio*

$$\frac{\text{Inventory}}{\text{Current Assets}} = \frac{14,9000}{25,000} = 0.60$$

Note:

Current Assets

= Stock + Debtors + Cash at bank

= 14,900 + 7,100 + 3,000 = Rs. 25,000

There is a clear indication that 60% of current assets are locked up in the form of inventory. There may be high stock of inventory or piling up of obsolete stocks.

3. *Debtors Turnover Ratio*

$$\frac{\text{Credit sales}}{\text{Average debtors}} = \frac{58,000}{7,100} = 11.97 \text{ times}$$

The high debtors turnover ratio indicates the efficiency of the company in converting debtors into cash quickly.

4. *Creditors Payment Period*

$$\text{In days} = \frac{\text{Average creditors}}{\text{Credit purchases}} \times 365 = \frac{13,000}{54,525} \times 365 = 87 \text{ days}$$

$$\text{In weeks} = \frac{\text{Average creditors}}{\text{Credit purchases}} \times 52 = \frac{13,000}{54,525} \times 52 = 12.4 \text{ weeks}$$

$$\text{In months} = \frac{\text{Average creditors}}{\text{Credit purchases}} \times 12 = \frac{13,000}{54,525} \times 12 = 2.86 \text{ months}$$

The credit payment period may be too long, which would effect the company's creditworthiness in the long run.

5. *Creditors Turnover Ratio*

$$\frac{\text{Credit purchases}}{\text{Average creditors}} = \frac{54,525}{13,000} = 4.19 \text{ times}$$

This ratio represents the substantial amount is payable towards credit purchases. By making early payment of creditors, the company can insist for discount in payments or discount in cash purchases.

6. *Debtors Collection Period*

$$\text{In days} = \frac{\text{Average debtors}}{\text{Credit sales}} \times 365 = \frac{7,100}{85,000} \times 365 = 30.49 \text{ days}$$

$$\text{In weeks} = \frac{\text{Average debtors}}{\text{Credit sales}} \times 52 = \frac{7,100}{85,000} \times 52 = 4.34 \text{ weeks}$$

$$\text{In months} = \frac{\text{Average debtors}}{\text{Credit sales}} \times 12 = \frac{7,100}{85,000} \times 12 = 1 \text{ month}$$

The actual collection period should be compared with the credit terms of the company in analyzing the efficiency of credit control department.

7. **Bad Debts to Sales Ratio**

$$\frac{\text{Bed debts}}{\text{Sales}} \times 100 = \frac{1,000}{85,000} \times 100 = 1.18\%$$

The percentage of bad debts to total sales is negligible. The credit control department is more efficient in collecting the debtors balances.

8. **Fixed Assets Turnover Ratio**

$$\frac{\text{Sales}}{\text{Fixed assets}} = \frac{85,000}{23,000} = 3.70 \text{ times}$$

The ratio appear to be satisfactory and the company is assumed to be using its fixed assets properly in achieving targeted production and turnover.

9. **Total Assets Turnover Ratio**

$$\frac{\text{Sales}}{\text{Total assets}} = \frac{85,000}{48,000} = 1.77 \text{ times}$$

It indicates inefficiency in using the assets for achieving higher sales of the company.

10. **Working Capital Turnover Ratio**

$$\frac{\text{Sales}}{\text{Working Capital}} = \frac{85,000}{12,000} = 7.08 \text{ times}$$

Note:

Working Capital

= Current assets – Current liabilities

= 25,000 – 13,000 = Rs. 12,000

The ratio indicates that working capital is effectively utilized for increase in sales turnover.

11. **Sales to Capital Employed Ratio**

$$\frac{\text{Sales}}{\text{Capital employed}} = \frac{85,000}{35,000} = 2.43 \text{ times}$$

The poor ratio indicates that the capital employed was not properly used in generating sales revenue.

PROFITABILITY RATIOS

This ratios are to help assessing the adequacy of profits earned by the company and also to discover whether profitability in increasing or declining the profitability of the firm is the net result of a large number of policies and decisions. The profitability ratios show the combined effects of liquidity, asset management and debt management on operating results. Profitability ratios are measured with reference to sales, capital employed total assets employed, shareholders funds etc. These ratios are very important from the point of view of different set of people who are interested in the business organization like owners, creditors, employees, suppliers, government organisations etc.

The major profitability rates are as follows:

Gross Profit Margin

The gross profit ratio is also known by the names (i) Gross margin ratio (ii) Trading margin ratio, (iii) Manufacturing margin ratio and (iv) Turnover ratio. This ratio is expressed in per cent. The gross profit margin is calculated as follows:

$$\frac{\text{Sales} - \text{Cost of good sold}}{\text{Sales}} \times 100 \text{ or } \frac{\text{Gross Profit}}{\text{Sales}} \times 100$$

The gross profit represents the excess of sales proceeds during the period under observation over their cost, before taking into account administration, selling and distribution and financing charges. The ratio measures the efficiency of the company's operations and this can also be compared with the previous year's results to ascertain the efficiency.

This ratio shows the gap between revenue and expense at a point after which an enterprise has to meet the expenses related to the non-manufacturing activities, like marketing administration etc. This ratio acts as an index of the mobility of an enterprise to meet (a) marketing expenses (b) administration expenses (c) finance cost (d) taxes (e) appropriations like dividend etc. The following illustration will explain the activity of gross profit ratio.

Illustration 9: RKV Company has Rs. 2,00,000 sales and the cost of sales is Rs. 120000, Calculate gross profit and gross profit ratio.

Solution:

$$\text{G.P} = \text{Sales cost of sales Rs. } 80,000 = \text{Rs. } 2,00,000 - \text{Rs. } 1,20,000$$

$$\text{G.P. Ratio} = 80,000/2,00,000 \times 100 = 40\%$$

Ratio reveals that there is a 40% mark-up on sales and 66.66% mark-up on cost of Sales (40,000/60,000 × 100)

Net Profit Margin

The ratio is calculated as follows:

$$\frac{\text{Net Profit before Interest and Tax}}{\text{Sales}} \times 100$$

The ratio is designed to focus attention on the net profit margin arising from business operations before interest and tax is deducted. The convention is to express profit after tax and interest as a percentage of sales.

This ratio reflects net profit margin on the total sales after deducting all expenses but before deducting interest and taxation. This ratio measures the efficiency of operation of the company. The net profit is arrived at from gross profit after deducting administration, selling and distribution expenses. The non-operating incomes and expenses are ignored in computation of net profit before tax, depreciation and interest in the industry. This measure will depict the correct trend of performance where there are erratic fluctuations in the tax provisions from year to year.

Net Profit Ratio

Net Profit Ratio expresses net profit as a percentage of sales. It can be computed as follows:

$$\text{Net Profit Ratio} = \frac{\text{Net profit}}{\text{Net Sales}} \times 100$$

This ratio indicates the profitability and efficiency of the business. However, the ratio would be more useful if studied with operating ratio. At this stage, it is important to differentiate between (i) Operating profit ratio (ii) Net profit ratio.

Operating profit ratio offers from the net profit ratio in as much as it is calculated after adding non-operating expenses to the net profit and deducting non-operating expenses to the net profit.

Cash Profit Ratio

Cash profit ratio measures the cash generation in the business as a result of the operations expressed in terms of sales.

$$\frac{\text{Cash profit}}{\text{Sales}} \times 100$$

Cash Profit = Net Profit + Depreciation

This ratio is a more reliable indicator of performance where there are sharp volatility in the profit before tax and net profit from year to year owing to difference in depreciation charged. This ratio measures the efficiency of operations in terms of cash generation and is not affected by the method of depreciation charged. It is also useful for inter-firm comparison of performance since different methods of depreciation may be adopted by different companies.

Return on Total Assets

The profitability of the firm is measured by establishing relation of net profit with the total assets of the organisation. This ratio indicates the efficiency of utilization of assets in generating revenue. This ratio is calculated as follows:

$$\frac{\text{Net Profit after Tax}}{\text{Total Assets}} \times 100$$

Return on Shareholders Funds or Return on Net Worth

This ratio expresses the net profit in terms of the equity shareholders funds. This ratio is an important yardstick of performance for equity shareholders since it indicates the return on the funds employed by them. However, this measure is based on the historical net worth and will be high for old plants and low for new plants.

$$\frac{\text{Net Profit after Interest and Tax}}{\text{Net worth}} \times 100$$

Net worth = Equity capital + Reserves and Surplus

This ratio is useful in measuring the rate of return as a percentage of the book value of shareholders equity. The further modification of this ratio is given below:

Return on Equity (ROE)

$$= \frac{\text{Profit after Tax}}{\text{Net Sales}} \times \frac{\text{Net Sales}}{\text{Total Assets}} \times \frac{\text{Total Assets}}{\text{Net Worth}}$$

i.e., ROE = Net profit margin × total assets turnover ratio × total assets to net worth

The ratio indicates: measure of profitability, the efficiency in use of assets in achieving sales, measure of leverage.

Operating Ratio or Operating Cost Ratio

Operating ratio expresses the relationship of cost of goods sold plus operating expenses to net sales. It may be expressed as

$$\text{Operating Ratio} = \frac{\text{Operating Cost}}{\text{Net Sales}} \times 100 \text{ or}$$

$$\text{Operating Ratio} = \frac{\text{Cost of goods sold} + \text{Operating expenses}}{\text{Net Sales}}$$

Operating Expenses

Operating expenses consist of (1) Administrative expenses (2) Financial expenses (3) Selling and distribution expenses. Let us understand this ratio by solving the following illustrations.

Illustration 10: The following information extracted from the KSBS's books of accounts. From the following data, compute the operating ratio.

1. Cost of goods sold   Rs. 1,80,000
2. Operating expenses   Rs. 20,000
3. Net sales   Rs. 2,00,000

$$\text{Operating Ratio} = \frac{\text{Cost of goods sold} + \text{operating expenses}}{\text{Net sales}} \times 100$$

Operating Ratio = 1,50,000 + 20,000/2,00,000 × 100

= 1,70,000/2,00,000 × 100 = 85%

The ratio shows the cost of goods sold plus operating expenses as a percentage of sales. In other words, operating cost of every Rs. 100 worth of net sales amount to Rs. 85.

Uses of Operating Ratio

Operating ratio indicates the operating efficiency of the company. It depicts the cost picture or the debit aspect of the profit margin ratio. Higher the operating ratio, given a level of sales, lower will be the profit margin or the net profit ratio.

Advantages of Operating Ratio

The operating ratio leads itself to the idea of standards and standard costs. Hence, an evaluation of the efficiency of an enterprise can be made with a fair degree of precision. Every enterprise has a typical operating ratio. The idea of hying down norms is, therefore, a feasible proposition.

This ratio is useful as a yardstick to measure the efficiency of the business enterprises, with respect to the inputs associated with the various functional areas of business anagement viz., production (factory cost of sales), marketing, administration and finance.

$$\text{Operating Profit Ratio} = \text{Operating Profit . Net sales} \times 100$$

Expense Ratios

Expense ratios, or otherwise called cost ratios, show the relationship between operating costs and expenses on the one hand and volume of sales on the other. In other words, these ratios express each element of cost and expenses as percentage of sales. It can be expressed as follows:

$$\text{Expense Ratio} = \frac{\text{Expenses}}{\text{Net Sales}} \times 100$$

Expense may be an individual expense or group of expenses. Following are the important expense ratios.

Factory Cost to Sales

This ratio shows factory cost as percentage of Sales

$$= \frac{\text{Factory Cost}}{\text{Sales}} \times 100$$

(a) Administration cost of sales (Administration cost of sales /Sales × 100)

(b) Selling and distribution cost to sales (Selling and distribution cost / Sales × 100)

(c) Bad Debts to sales (Bad debts/Sales × 100)

(d) Cost of goods sold to Net Sales:

This ratio is expressed as follows: = Cost of goods sold / Net Sales × 100

This ratio may also be computed for each element of cost as below:

(i) Material cost of sales (Materials consumed/Sales × 100)

(ii) Labour cost to sales or wages to sales (Labour cost or wages/Sales × 100)

Expense ratios show the portion of net sales revenue which is consumed on account of various operating costs and expenses.

Interest cover

The interest coverage ratio shows how many times interest charges are covered by funds that are available for payment of interest. Interest cover indicates how many times a company can cover its current interest payments out of current profits. It gives an indication of problem in servicing the debt. An interest cover of more than 7 times is regarded as safe and more than 3 times is desirable. An interest cover of 2 times is considered reasonable by financial institutions.

$$\frac{\text{Profit before Interest, Depciation and Tax}}{\text{Interest}}$$

A very high interest cover ratio indicates that the firm is conservative in using debt and a very low interest coverage ratio indicates excessive use of debt.

Dividend cover

This ratio indicates the number of times the dividends are covered by net profit. This highlights the amount retained by a company for financing of future operations.

(a) *Equity Dividend Cover*

$$\frac{\text{Net Profit after Tax} - \text{Preference Dividend}}{\text{Equity Dividend}}$$

(b) *Preference Dividend Cover*

$$\frac{\text{Net Profit after Tax}}{\text{Preference Dividend}}$$

Debt Service Coverage Ratio (DSCR)

Debt Service Coverage Ratio (DSCR) ratio is the key indicator to the lender to assess the extent of ability of the borrower to service the loan in regard to timely payment of interest and repayment of loan instalment. The ratio is calculated as follows:

$$\frac{\text{Profit after Taxes} + \text{Depreciation} + \text{Interest on Loan}}{\text{Interest on Loan} + \text{Loan repayment in a year}}$$

The greater debt service coverage ratio indicates the better debt servicing capacity of the organization. A ratio of 2 is considered satisfactory by the financial institutions. By means of cashflow projection, the borrower should work DSCR for the entire duration of the loan. This will be use full to lender to take correct view of the borrower's repayment capacity. This ratio indicates whether the business is earning sufficient profits to pay not only the interest charges, but also the installments due of the principal amount.

Illustration 11: From the following information calculate the expense ratio and segment ratios viz., administration expense ratio and marketing expense ratio.

	Rs.
Sales	5,50,000
Sales Returns	50,000
Administrative expenses	60,000
Interest on loan	20,000
Marketing expenses	40,000

Solution:

(i) Expense Ratio = Expenses/Net Sales × 100

= 60,000 + 40,000/550,000 × 100 = 18.18%

(ii) Administrative Expense ratio = Administrative expenses / Net sales × 100

$$= 60,000/550,000 × 100 = 10.90\%$$

(iii) Marketing expense ratio = Marketing expenses / Net sales × 100

$$= 40,000/550,000 × 100 = 7.27\%$$

Uses or Advantages of Expense Ratio

The expense ratios indicate the extent to which the credit effects of the revenue are neutralized by the debit impact of the expenses. The expense ratios can, therefore, be said to have an inverse relationship with the profit ratio. These ratios are useful in knowing the following common aspects relating to profit and help the management to know the position of profit i.e., whether the profit is on the increase or on the decrease. (i) Higher the factor cost to sales, lower the gross profit. (ii) Higher the expense ratio, lower the profit and vice-versa. (iii) Higher the non-manufacturing expenses ratio (marketing, administration, finance, etc.) lower the net profit.

1. These ratios are easy to compute and simple to understand. This advantage strongly speaks of these expense ratios as a practical tool of financial analysis.

2. The expense ratios presented in logical form can throw light on the efficiencies of internal operations of a business unit viz., factory and non-manufacturing operations of business.

3. The expense ratios lend themselves to scientific standards and, therefore, provide readymade norms that can be used to compare the actual performance with predetermined performance.

Illustration 12: Following is the summarised income statement and balance sheet of KSBS Ltd. for year ended 31st March, 2007 as under:

Income statement for the year ended 31st March, 2007		(Rs.)
Sales		90,00,000
Less: Cost of good sold		64,00,000
Gross Profit margin		26,00,000
Less: Depreciation	1,50,000	
Selling and administration expenses	2,50,000	4,00,000
Profit before interest and tax		22,00,000

Less: Interest	3,00,000
Profit before tax	19,00,000
Less: Tax @ 40%	7,60,000
Net Profit	11,40,000

Balance Sheet as at 31st March, 2007

Liabilities	Rs.	Assets	Rs.
Share Capital	50,00,000	Fixed assets	63,00,000
Retained earnings	18,00,000	Inventory	9,00,000
Debentures	8,00,000	Debtors	5,00,000
Creditors	2,80,000	Marketable securities	2,10,000
Bills Payable	1,20,000	Cash	90,000
	80,00,000		80,00,000

You are required to calculate: (a) Gross profit margin, (b) Net profit margin, (c) Cash profit ratio, (d) Return on total assets and (e) Return on shareholders net worth.

Solution:

(a) *Gross Profit Margin*

$$\frac{\text{Sales - Cost of goods sold}}{\text{Sales}} \times 100 \text{ or } \frac{\text{Gross profit}}{\text{Sales}} \times 100$$

$$\frac{26,00,000}{90,00,000} \times 100 = 28.88\%$$

(b) *Net Profit Margin*

$$\frac{\text{Net Profit before interest and tax}}{\text{Sales}} \times 100$$

$$= \frac{22,00,000}{90,00,000} \times 100 = 24.44\%$$

(c) *Cash Profit Ratio*

$$\frac{\text{Cash Profit}}{\text{Sales}} \times 100 \text{ or } \frac{\text{Net Profit - Depreciation}}{\text{Sales}} \times 100$$

$$= \frac{22,00,000 + 1,50,000}{90,00,000} \times 100 = 26.11\%$$

(d) *Return on Total Assets*

$$\frac{\text{Net Profit after tax}}{\text{Total Assets}} \times 100 = \frac{11,40,000}{80,00,000} \times 100 = 14.25\%$$

(e) *Return on Shareholders Networth*

$$\frac{\text{Net Profit after tax}}{\text{Shareholders Network}} \times 100 = \frac{11,40,000}{68,00,000} \times 100 = 16.76\%$$

Note: Shareholders net worth

= Share capital + Retained earnings

= Share capital + retained earnings

= 50,00,000 + 18,00,000 = Rs. 68,00,000

Return on Capital Employed (ROCE) or ROI

This ratio is also called Return on Investment (ROI). The strategic aim of a business enterprise is to earn a return on capital. If in any particular case, the return in the long-run in not satisfactory, then the deficiency should be corrected or the activity be abandoned for a more favourable one. The rate of return on investment is determined by dividing net profit or income by the capital employed or investment made to achieve that profit.

ROI consists of two component viz. (a) Profit margin, and (b) Investment Turnover, as shown bellows:

$$\frac{\text{Net Profit}}{\text{Capital Employed}} \quad or \quad \frac{\text{Net Profit}}{\text{Sales}} \times \frac{\text{Sales}}{\text{Capital Employed}}$$

We can seen from the above formula that ROI can be improved by increasing one or both of its component viz. the profit margin and the investment turnover in any of the following ways:

(a) Increasing the profit margin

(b) Increasing the investment turnover, or

(c) Increasing both profit margin and investment turnover.

The obvious generalizations that can be made about the ROI formula are that any action is beneficial provided that it:

(i) Reduces invested capital

(ii) Reduces costs (while holding the other two factors constant) and boosts sales

Advantages or uses of ROI Ratio

Return on investment analysis provides a strong incentive for optimal utilization of the assets of the company. This encourages managers to obtain assets that will provide a satisfactory return on investment and to dispose of assets that are not providing an acceptable return. In selecting amongst alternative long-term investment proposals, ROI provides a suitable measure for assessment of profitability of each proposal. The return on capital employed ratio is helpful in measuring the managerial performance in the following ways:

1. It helps in making comparison of inter-divisional and inter-firm comparison.
2. It helps in measuring the profitability of the firm.
3. It indicates how effectively the operating assets are used in earning return.
4. The actual return on capital employed can be compared with the targeted rate of return.
5. It focus the attention on efficiency of management in managing the investments made into business.
6. It can be used as a sensitive gauge of profit making ability of the firm.
7. Divisional performance measurement can be done easily with ROI.
8. It correlates the return with various assets used in the business.

Capital employed can be calculated as follows

		(Rs.)
Share capital		xxx
Reserves and surplus		xxx
Loans (secured & unsecured)		xxx
		xxx
Less : Capital-in-progress	xxx	
Investment outside the business	xxx	
Preliminary expenses	xxx	
Debit balance of Profit and Loss A/c	xxx	
Capital employed		**xxx**

Return on Proprietors' Funds Ratio

This ratio is calculated as follows:

$$\text{Return on Proprietor's Funds} = \frac{\text{Net Profit (PIT)}}{\text{Share holder's funds}}$$

(P.I.T. – Profit after Interest and Taxes)

Return on proprietors' fund ratio represents the ratio of net profit to proprietors' funds. Here, it is essential to provide an explanation about proprietors' funds.

Proprietors' Funds

This fund consists of share capital (both equity and preference) and reserves and surplus. For the purpose of this ratio, average amount of share holders' funds is taken. It is calculated in the following manner:

Opening balance of share holders funds + Closing balance of share funds / 2

Net Profit:

Net profit for the purposes of this ratio means the profit arrived at after taxation and interest on long-term liabilities.

Illustration 13: The following is the liabilities side of the Balance Sheet of KSBS Ltd.

Liabilities	Rs.	Rs.
Share capital:		
10000 equity shares of Rs. 10 each	2,00,000	
5% 500 Pref. shares of Rs. 50 each	25,000	1,25,000
Reserves and Surplus :		
General Reserve	40,000	
Reserve for Contingencies	15,000	
Capital Reserve	20,000	
Profit and Loss A/C	15,000	95,000

The net profit for the year (after taxation and interest) was Rs. 64.500. Calculate return on proprietors' funds.

Solution:

1. Proprietors Funds= Rs. 2,25,000 + 95,000 = 320,000
2. Net profit after taxation = 64,500

Return on proprietors' funds

$$= 64,500/320,000 \times 100 = 20.15\%$$

This ratio measures the overall efficiency and profitability of an enterprise and reflects the economic productivity of the total resources employed by the business. This ratio is very useful to measure the overall profitability of the concern. It indicates the average return on the share holders' investment in the company. The quality of management is ascertained by making a comparison of the returns on owner's funds over the past few years and the performance of similar units in the same industry. Thus, it facilitates inter-period and inter-firm comparison. It is an index to the operational efficiency of the business as well as an indicator of profitability. This ratio is also called 'Earning Ratio' as it reveals the rate of the earning capacity of the business. The higher the ratio, the greater will be the return for owners and vice-versa.

Return on Equity Capital Ratio

Return on Equity Capital is the ratio of net profit to equity share capital. Return on Equity Capital is calculated as;

$$\text{Return on Equity Capital} = \frac{\text{Net profit} - \text{dividend due to preference share holders}}{\text{Equity Share Capital}} \times 100$$

Notes: (i) Sometimes, earning per equity share may also be calculated. It is calculated as: Net Profit less dividend due to preference shares / Total number of equity shares

Return on Capital Employed Ratio

Return on capital employed is the ratio of adjusted net profit to capital employed. It is expressed in percentage. The return on "Capital Employed" may be based on Gross Capital or Net Capital Employed. Formulation for calculation of return on capital employed is as follows:

$$\text{Return on Capital Employed Ratio} = \frac{\text{Profit}}{\text{Net Capital employed}} \times 100$$

Net capital employed will be calculated as follows:

Net capital employed consists of total assets (i.e. fixed assets, investments and current assets) of the business less is current liabilities (i.e., creditors, bank overdraft etc.) Thus,

Net Capital Employed = Fixed Assets'+ Investments + Current Assets – Current Liabilities

Thus, Net Capital Employed = Fixed Assets + Investments + Working Capital.

In other words, we may also express the Net Capital employed as below:

Net Capital employed = Issued share capital + Capital Reserves + Revenue Reserves +

+ Debentures and Long term loans - Fictitious Assets

Adjusted Net Profit:

Following adjustments should be made, if necessary, with the figure of net profit to arrive at the adjusted net profit for the purpose of computing return on capital employed.

(a) Add any abnormal or non-recurring losses, (b) Add interest on long term liabilities. Moreover, the return on gross capital employed is to be calculated, add interest on short term liabilities also. (c) Add Income-tax paid and provision for income-tax, (d) Deduct additional depreciation based on the replacement cost, (e) Deduct income from investments outside the business, (f) Deduct any abnormal or non-recurring gains.

Uses and advantages of computing Return on Capital Employed

1. Return on capital employed shows overall profitability of business.
2. It shows the overall performance of the business enterprise.
3. It facilitates comparisons of the relative profitability of the various departments and the different types of products.

4. It helps in evaluating and controlling capital expenditure projects.
5. It helps in profit planning.

Illustration 14: Following is the balance sheet of KSBS Ltd. for the period 31-3-2007

Balance sheet for a company

Share capital	60,000	Fixed assets	2,50,000
Reserves & Surplus	50,000	Investments	30,000
P&L a/c	30,000	Current assets	70,000
Long-term liability	1,60,000		
Current liability	50,000		
	3,50,000		3,50,000

Net profit for the year is Rs. 50,000

Solution:

(i) Capital employed

= Fixed assets + Investments + (Current assets – current liability) working capital

= 2,50,000 + 30,000 + (70,000 - 50,000)

= 3,00,000

(ii) Return on capital employed is

N.P./Net capital employed

= 50,000/3,00,000 × 100 = 16.666%

Illustration 15: The following data has been extracted from the annual accounts of the KSBS Company Ltd.

	(Rs.)
Share capital	80,00,000
General reserve	50,00,000
Investment allowance reserve	5,00,000
12% Mortage loan	30,00,000
Sundry creditors	12,00,000
Profit before tax	30,00,000
Provision for taxation	8,00,000
Proposed dividends	10,00,000

From the above details, calculate return on capital employed.

Solution:

	(Rs.)
Share capital	80,00,000
General reserve	50,00,000
Investment allowance reserve	5,00,000
12% Mortage loan	30,00,000
Capital employed	**1,65,00,000**

	(Rs.)
Profit before tax	30,00,000
add: interest on mortage loan (30,000,000 × 12/100)	3,60,000
Total return	**33,60,000**

Return on Capital Employed

$$\frac{\text{Net Profit before interest and tax}}{\text{Capital employed}} \times 100 = \frac{33,60,000}{1,65,00,000} \times 100 = 21.9\%$$

Illustration 16: The Trading and Profit & Loss accounts of SKSS Ltd. for the year ended 31st March, 2007 are given below:

Particulars	Rs.	Particulars	Rs.
To Opening stock	2,50,000	By Sales	24,00,000
To Purchases	10,50,000	By Closing stock	1,50,000
To Wages	4,00,000		
To Factory expenses	2,00,000		
To Gross profit c/d	6,50,000		
	25,50,000		**25,50,000**
To Administration expenses	2,30,000	By Gross Profit b/d	6,50,000
To Selling and distribution expenses	1,00,000	By Miscellaneous income	50,000
To Interest	20,000		
To Net Profit	3,50,000		
	7,00,000		**7,00,000**

You are required to calculate operating ratios.

Solution:

Calculation of Operating Ratios:

(a) **Materials Cost Ratio**

$$\frac{\text{Materials consumed}}{\text{Sales}} \times 100 = \frac{11,50,000}{24,00,000} \times 100 = 47.92\%$$

Note: Materials consumed:

= Opening stock + Purchases − Closing stock

= 2,50,000 + 10,50,000 − 1,50,000 = Rs. 11,50,000

(b) **Labour Cost Ratio**

$$\frac{\text{Labour cost}}{\text{Sales}} \times 100 = \frac{4,00,000}{24,00,000} \times 100 = 16.6\%$$

(c) **Factory Expenses Ratio**

$$\frac{\text{Factory expenses}}{\text{Sales}} \times 100 = \frac{2,00,000}{24,00,000} \times 100 = 8.33\%$$

(d) **Administrative Expenses Ratio**

$$\frac{\text{Administrative Expenses}}{\text{Sales}} \times 100 = \frac{2,30,000}{24,00,000} \times 100 = 9.58\%$$

(e) **Selling and distribution Expenses Ratio**

$$\frac{\text{Selling and distribution expenses}}{\text{Sales}} \times 100 = \frac{1,00,000}{24,00,000} \times 100 = 4.17\%$$

(f) **Operating Ratio**

$$\frac{\text{Cost of goods sold} + \text{Operating expenses}}{\text{Sales}} \times 100$$

$$= \frac{17,50,000 + 3,30,000}{24,00,000} \times 100 = 86.67\%$$

Note:

(i) Cost of Goods Sold

= Opening stock + Purchases – Wages + Factory expenses – Closing stock

= 2,50,000 + 10,50,000 + 4,00,000 – 2,00,000 – 1,50,000

= Rs. 17,50,000

(ii) Operating Expenses

= Administration expenses - Selling and distribution expenses

= 2,30,000 + 1,00,000

= 3,30,000

Net Profit Ratio

= 100% – Operating ratio = 100% – 86.67%

= 13.33%

Illustration 17: From the financial information of Yahoo Ltd. Given below, calculate activity or turnover ratios.

Balance sheet as at 31st March, 2007	(Rs.)
Liabilities:	30,00,000
Equity share capital	10,00,000
10% Preference share capital	14,00,000
Retained earnings	18,00,000
12% Secured Debentures	9,50,000
Sundry creditors	5,00,000
Bills payable	3,50,000
Income tax provision	90,00,000
Assets:	
Fixed assets	62,00,000
Inventory	10,60,000
Sundry debtors	8,50,000
Bills receivable	6,50,000
Cash	2,40,000
	90,00,000

Contd...

Additional information	(Rs.)
Profit before interest and depreciation	25,00,000
Depreciation	8,00,000
Interest	2,16,000

Tax@ 50% Loan Instalment payable during the year Rs. 3,00,000. Equity Dividend declared during the year @ 18% You are required to calculate long-term solvency ratios.

Solution:

PBIDT	25,00,000
Less: Depreciation	8,00,000
PBIT	**17,00,000**
Less: Interest	2,16,000
PBT	**14,84,000**
Less: Income tax @ 40%	5,93,600
PAT	**8,90,400**

(a) **Debt-Equity Ratio**

$$\frac{\text{Long-term Debt}}{\text{Shareholders funds}} = \frac{18,00,000}{30,00,000 + 10,00,000 + 14,00,000} = 0.33\%$$

The company's long-term solvency is more satisfactory. The debt-equity ratio of the company is 0.33:1 and it is well with in the accepted norm of 2:1. Since the proportion of debt to equity is low. The company is said to be low geared and could not reap the benefit of trading on equity.

(b) **Shareholders Equity Ratio**

$$\frac{\text{Shareholders Equity}}{\text{Total assets (tangible)}} = \frac{54,00,000}{90,00,000} = 0.6$$

Since the shareholders equity is larger in proportion of 50% to total assets. Therefore, the financial position of the company is stronger.

(c) **Long-term Debt to Shareholders Net Worth Ratio**

$$\frac{\text{Long-term debt}}{\text{Shareholders Net worth}} = \frac{18,00,000}{30,00,000 + 10,00,000 + 14,00,000} = 0.33$$

Since the long-term debt represents only 33% of the shareholders net worth leaving balance 67% to other current liabilities, it gives an indication of strong short-term as well as long-term solvency of the company.

(d) **Capital Gearing Ratio**

$$\frac{\text{Fixed interest bearing funds}}{\text{Equity shareholders funds}} = \frac{10,00,000 + 18,00,000}{30,00,000 + 14,00,000} = 0.64$$

The fixed interest bearing funds represent 64% of the equity shareholders funds. The financial risk of the company is lower and the earnings available to equity shareholders is less vulnerable.

(e) *Fixed Assets to Long-term Funds Ratio*

$$\frac{\text{Fixed assets}}{\text{Long-term funds}} = \frac{62,00,000}{30,00,000 + 10,00,000 + 14,00,000 - 18,00,000} = 0.86$$

It indicates the long-term solvent position of the company. The high ratio indicates the high proportion of long-term funds deployed in fixed assets.

(f) *Proprietary Ratio*

$$\frac{\text{Shareholders networth}}{\text{Total assets}} = \frac{54,00,000}{90,00,000} = 0.60$$

The high Proprietary ratio indicates the strong financial position of the business.

(g) *Interest Cover*

$$\frac{\text{Profit before interest, depreciation and tax}}{\text{Interest}} = \frac{25,00,000}{2,16,000} = 11.57 \text{ times}$$

An interest cover of 2:1 is ideal. The high ratio of interest in a company indicates the low proportion of debt and the company is following very conservative policy in using the debt component in the capital structure.

(h) *Debt Service Coverage Ratio*

$$\frac{\text{Profit after tax + interest + Depreciation}}{\text{Interest + Periodic loan instalment}}$$

$$= \frac{8,90,400 + 2,16,000 + 8,00,000}{2,16,000 + 3,00,000} = \frac{19,06,400}{5,16,000} = 3.69 \text{ times}$$

The higher debt service coverage ratio of the company indicates the better servicing ability of the company.

(i) *Preference Dividend Cover*

$$\frac{\text{Profit available to preference shareholders}}{\text{Preference dividend}} = \frac{8,90,4000}{1,00,000} = 8.90 \text{ times}$$

The higher preference dividend cover indicates greater assurance to preference shareholders in obtaining their assured return of 10%.

(j) Equity Dividend Cover

$$\frac{\text{Profit after tax - Preference dividend Shareholders}}{\text{Equity Dividend}} \quad \text{or} \quad \frac{\text{Profit available to Equity}}{\text{Equity Dividend}}$$

$$\frac{8,90,400 - 1,00,000}{5,40,000} = \frac{7,90,400}{5,40,000} = 1.46$$

Illustration 18: The following is the Profit and Loss Account and Balance sheet of Daruwala Company.

Trading and P&L A/c

To opening stock	76,250	By sales	5,00,000
" Purchases	3,22,250	" Closing stock	98,500
" Gross profit	2,00,000		
	5,98,500		5,98,500
" Selling & distribution expenses	22,000	By Gross profit	2,00,000
" Administrative Expenses	98,000	" Dividend	9,000
" Loss on sale of assets	2,000	" Profit on sale of shares	3,000
" Net profit	90,000		
	2,12,000		2,12,000

Balance Sheet

Share Capital	2,60,000	Land & building	1,50,000
Reserves	70,000	Plant & Machinery	80,000
P & La/c	20,000	Stock	98,500
Current liabilities	1,30,000'	Debtors	61,500
		Bills receivables	60,000
		Bank	30,000
	4,80,000		4,80,000

Calculate

1. Gross profit ratio
2. Net profit ratio
3. Operating ratio
4. Operating profit ratio
5. Stock turnover ratio

Solution:

1. Gross profit ratio = Gross profit / Sales × 100

    = 2,00,000/ 5,00,000 × 100 = 40%

2. Net profit ratio = Net Profit / Sales × 100

    = 90,000 / 5,00,000 × 100 =18%

3. Operating ratio (operating cost ratio)

$$= \text{Operating cost / Net Sales} \times 100$$

$$= \text{Operating cost} = \text{Cost of goods sold} + \text{operating expenses}$$

$$= \text{Cost of goods sold} = 5,00,000 - 2,00,000 = 3,00,000$$

$$= \text{Operating expenses} = 1,20,000$$

∴ Operating cost $= 4,20,000$

Operating ratio $= 4,20,000 / 5,00,000 \times 100 = 84\%$

4. Operating profit ratio = 100% − operating ratio

$$= 100\% - 84$$

$$= 16\%$$

5. Stock turnover ratio = Cost of goods sold / Average stock

COGS $= 5,00,000 - 2,00,000 = 3,00,000$

Average stock = (Opening stock + closing stock) / 2

$$= (76,250 + 98,500) / 2 = 87,375$$

$$= (3,00,000 / 87,375) = 3.43 \text{ times}$$

MARKET BASED RATIOS

Market-based ratios give management an indication of what investors think of the company's past performance and future prospects. The market based ratios relate the firm's stock price to its earnings and book value per share. If firm's profitability, solvency and turnover ratios are good, then the market based ratios will be high and its share price is also expected to be high. The market based ratios are as follows:

Earnings Per Share (EPS)

The EPS is one of the important measures of economic performance of a corporate entity. The flow of capital to the companies under the present imperfect capital market conditions would be made on the evaluation of EPS.

A higher EPS means better capital productivity. EPS is one of the most important ratios which measure the net profit earned per share. EPS is one of the major factors affecting the dividend policy of the firm and the market prices of the company. A steady growth in EPS year after year indicates a good track of profitability. EPS is computed by dividing the net profit after tax and dividend to preference share holders. This avoids confusion and indicates the profit available to the ordinary shareholders on a "per share basis". This is computed as follows:

$$\text{EPS} = \frac{\text{Net Profit after Tax and Preference Dividend}}{\text{No. of Equity Shares}}$$

Price Earnings Ratio (P/E Ratio)

It measures the number of times the earnings per share discounts the market price of an equity share. The ratio indicates the market price of an equity share to the earnings per share. This is one of the important valuation ratios. Risk involved in the investment and return on investment are the two vital factors which influence the valuation. These two have a combined impact on valuation. The utility of P/E Ratio is that the investor can think of better investment by adopting this ratio. For the management too, this ratio helps in financial forecasting. The share valuation can also be easily assessed. The management can now asses, whether the share is undervalued or overvalued. It is computed as follows: P. E. Ratio = Market Price Share/Earning Per Share or

$$\frac{\text{Current Market Price of Equity Share}}{\text{Earnings per Share}}$$

Benefits of P/E Ratio

1. This ratio indicates how much an investor is prepared to pay per rupee of earnings.
2. P/E ratio reflects high earnings potential and a low ratio reflects the low earnings potential.
3. P/E ratio reflects the market's confidence on company's equity.
4. This ratio helps to ascertain the value of equity share,
5. Price-earning approach to share valuation is simple and more popular.
6. This ratio reflects the market's assessment of the future earnings potential of the company.

Market Price to Book Value Ratio (P/BV ratio)

This ratio measures the relationship between the accounting value of the firm's assets and the market price of its stock. In case of growth firms i.e., firms with high growth of sales and earnings will have this ratio higher than 1, for the reason that the potential future growth in earnings is reflected in the current stock price. The ratio is calculated by dividing the stock price per share by the book value of share.

$$\frac{\text{Market Price per Share}}{\text{Book Value per Share}}$$

Cash Earnings Per Share

Cash earnings per share is a more reliable yardstick for measurement of performance of companies, especially for highly capital intensive industries where provision for depreciation is substantial. This measures the cash earnings per share and is also a relevant factor for determining the price for the company's shares. This method is not as popular as EPS and is used as a supplementary measure of performance only. The cash earnings per share (Cash EPS) is calculated by dividing the net profit before depreciation with number of equity shares.

$$\frac{\text{Net Profit after Tax + Depreciation}}{\text{No. of Equity Shares}}$$

Dividend Payout Ratio

Dividend payout ratio indicates the extent of the net profits distributed to the shareholders as dividend. A high payout signifies a liberal distribution policy and a low payout reflects conservative distribution policy. This ratio is calculated by dividend per share divided by the earnings per share:

$$\frac{\text{Dividend per Share}}{\text{Earnings per Share}}$$

Book Value

The book value is a reflection of the past earnings and the distribution policy of the company. A high book value indicates that a company has huge reserves and is a potential bonus candidate. A low book value signifies a liberal distribution policy of bonus and dividends, or a poor track record of profitability. Book value ratio indicates the net worth per equity share

$$\frac{\text{Equity Capital + Reserves - Profit and Loss A/c Debit balance}}{\text{Total number of Equity Shares}}$$

Dividend Yield

Dividend yield ratio reflects the percentage yield that an investor receives on this investment at the current market price of the shares. This ratio is computed by dividend per share divided by market price multiplied by hundred

$$\text{Divided Yield} = \frac{\text{Dividend per Share}}{\text{Market Price}} \times 100$$

Illustration 19: From the following data, calculate the earnings per share.

1. Net profit before tax Rs. 4 00.000
2. Tax at 40% of net profit
3. 5% preference shares of Rs 100 each Rs 100000.
4. Equity shares Rs. 4,00,000, face value Rs. 10.
5. Market Price per share Rs. 150

   Compute EPS, P/E Ratio

Solution:

Working Notes:

(i) Net Profit after tax/ Net Profit before tax   Rs. 4,00,000

    Less: Tax @ 40%   160,000

     Rs. 2,40,000

(ii) Pref. Dividend

    Pref. Capital 1000 x Rs. 100 = Rs. 1,00,000

    Dividend at 5% = Rs. 5,000

    Earning after Preference dividend = Profit - Dividend = Rs. 240,000 - 5,000 = Rs. 235,000

(iii) Number of shares = 4,00,000/10 = 40 000

    EPS = 235,000/ 40,000 = Rs. 5.875

    P/E Ratio = Market price per share/EPS

    P/E Ratio = 25/5.875 = 4.25 or 4

Illustration 20: The summarized Balance Sheet of Bad Luck Ltd. for the financial year ended 31st March, 2007 are given below:

Liabilities	Rs.	Assets	Rs.
Equity share capital (Rs. 10)	50,00,000	Fixed assets investments	90,00,000
10% Pref. share capital (Rs. 100)	20,00,000	Investments	15,00,000
Reserves and surplus	17,90,000	**Current assets:**	
15% Term loan	40,00,000	Stock	60,00,000
Creditors	19,00,000	Debtors	25,00,000
Accounts payable	6,00,000	Accounts receivable	12,00,000
Provision for taxation	17,60,000	Cash at bank	8,00,000
Provision for dividend	9,50,000		
	1,80,00,000		**1,80,00,000**

You are given the following information for the year 2006-07

	(Rs.)
Provision for tax 40% You are required to calculate: (a) Earnings per share and (b) Cash earnings per share.	
Profit before interest, depreciation and tax (PBIDT)	80,00,000
Less: Depreciation	30,00,000
Profit before interest and tax (PBIT)	**50,00,000**
Less: Interest	6,00,000
Profit before tax	**44,00,000**
Less: Provision for tax (@40%)	17,60,000
Profit after tax	**26,40,000**
Less: Preference dividend	2,00,000
Profit available to Equity shareholders	**24,40,000**

	(Rs.)
Sales	7,50,00,000
PBIDT	80,00,000
Depreciation	30,00,000
Interest	6,00,000
Preference dividend	2,00,000
Equity dividend	7,50,000

Solution:

(a)   Earnings Per Share (EPS)

$$\frac{\text{Net profit available to Equity shareholders}}{\text{Number of Equity shares}}$$

$$= \frac{\text{Rs. } 24,40,000}{5,00,000 \text{ Equity shares}} = \text{Rs. } 4.88$$

(b)   Cash Earnings per Share

$$\frac{\text{Net Profit available to equity shareholders} + \text{Depreciation}}{\text{Number of Equity shares}}$$

$$= \frac{\text{Rs. } 24,40,000 + \text{Rs. } 30,00,000}{5,00,000 \text{ equity shares}} = \text{Rs. } 10,88$$

Illustration 21: The following is the Balance Sheet of ABC Ltd. as on 31-12-06

Liabilities	Rs.	Assets	Rs.
Equity Share capital			
(20,000 shares x Rs 100 each)	20,00,000	Plant & Equipment	12,50,000
Retained earnings	5,00,000	Land & building	5,00,000
Sundry creditors	4,00,000	Sundry debtors	4,50,000
Bill payable	1,50,000	Stock	7,00,000
Other current liabilities	50,000	Bill receivables	1,50,000
		Pre-paid insurance	10,000
		Cash	40,000
	31,00,000		31,00,000

Statement of profit for the year ended 31-12-06

Sales	50,00,000
(-) COGS	38,50,000
Gross profit	11,50,000
(-) Operating expenses	7,50,000
Net profit	4,00,000
(-) Tax at 40%	1,60,000
Net profit after tax	2,40,000

Calculate

1. Current ratio
2. Liquid ratio
3. Stock turnover ratio
4. Debtors turnover ratio
5. Gross profit ratio
6. Net profit ratio
7. EPS

Solution:

1. Current ratio = Current Assets / Current liabilities

Current Assets	
Stock	7,00,000
Sundry Debtors	4,50,000
Bills receivables	1,50,000
Pre-paid insurance	10,000
Cash	40,000
	13,50,000

Current liabilities	
Sundry creditors	4,00,000
Bills payables	1,50,000
Other current liabilities	50,000
	6,00,000

Current ratio = 13,50,000 / 6,00,000 = 2.25

2. Liquid/Quick ratio = Liquid Assets/Current liabilities

Liquid Assets = All current assets – inventory / stock

= 13,50,000 – 7,00,000

= 6,50,000

Liquid Ratio = 6,50,000 / 6,00,000 = 1.08

3. Stock/Inventory turnover ratio = COGS /Avg. inventory

= 38,50,000 / 7,00,000 = 5.5 times

(As average inventory is not available, closing inventory itself is taken as average)

4. Debtors turnover ratio = Net credit sales / Average debtors

= 50,00,000 / (4,50,000 + 1,50,000) 6,00,000 = 8.33 times

Total sales itself is taken as credit sales. Debtors includes sundry debtors and bills receivables.

5. Gross profit ratio = G.P. / Sales × 100

= 11,50,000 / 50,00,000 × 100 = 225

6. Net profit ratio = Net Profit / Sales × 100

= 2,40,000 / 50,00,000 × 100 = 4.8%

7. EPS = Net Profit after tax (available to equity share holders) / Number of equity shares.

= 2,40,000 / 20,000 = Rs. 12

Illustration 22: The following is the balance sheet of a company as on 31-3-06

Liabilities	Rs.	Assets	Rs.
E. Shares	40,00,000	Land & building	40,00,000
Reserves & Surplus	20,00,000	Plant & machinery	40,00,000
Debentures	30,00,000	Investments	30,00,000
Long term loans	50,00,000	Stock	25,00,000
Creditors	8,00,000	Debtors	15,00,000
Other current liabilities	12,00,000	Other current assets	10,00,000
	1,60,00000		1,60,00000

Calculate

1. Current ratio
2. Stock to working capital ratio
3. Debt-Equity ratio
4. Net-worth ratio / proprietor/ ratio
5. Fixed assets to net worth ratio
6. Current assets to net worth ratio
7. Solvency ratio
8. Capital gearing ratio.

Solution:

1. Current ratio = Current Asset / Current Liabilities
    = 50,00,000 / 20,00,000 = 2.5

2. Stock to working capital ratio
    = Stock / Inventory / Working capital × 100
    Working capital = Current Assets − Current Liabilities
    = 50,00,000 − 20,00,000 = 30,00,000
    = 25,00,000 / 30,00,000 × 100 = 83.33%

3. Debt-Equity ratio = Debt / Equity
    Debt = Long term loans 30,00,000 + 50,00,000 = 80,00,000
    Equity = Share capital + Reserves + Surplus
    = 40,00,000 + 20,00,000 = 60,00,000
    = 80,00,000 / 60,00,000 = 1.33

4. Net worth or Proprietary ratio = Net worth (Equity) / Total assets
    (Net worth = Share capital + Reserves & Surplus)
    = 60,00,000 / 1,60,00,000 = 0.375

5. Fixed Assets to net worth ratio = Net fixed assets
    = 80,00,000 / 60,00,000 = 1.33

6.   Current assets to net worth ratio = Current assets / Net worth

$$= 50,00,000 / 60,00,000 = 0.833$$

7.   Solvency ratio   = Total assets / Total liabilities

Total assets   = Total of asset side of balance sheet.

Total liabilities   = Both long-term and current liabilities.

$$= 1,60,00,000 / 1,00,00,000 = 1.6$$

8.   Capital gearing ratio = Fixed dividend bearing loans debentures + fixed dividend bearing preference shares / equity share capital

$$= \text{Debentures } 30,00,000 + \text{long-term loan } 50,00,000 \text{ / equity share capital } 40,00,000$$

$$= 80,00,000 / 40,00,000 = 2$$

Illustration 23: Yahoo Ltd. has the following Profit and Loss Account for the year ended 31st March, 2007 and the Balance Sheet as on that date:

Profit and Loss Account for the year ended 31st March, 2007

Particulars	Rs. Lakhs		Particulars	Rs. Lakhs
Openings stock	1.75		Sales: Credit	12.00
Add: Manufacturing cost	10.75		Cash	3.00
	12.50			
Less: Closing stock	1.50			
Cost of goods sold	11.00			
Gross Profit	4.00			
	15.00			15.00
Administrative expenses	0.35		Gross profit	4.00
Selling expenses	0.25		Other income	0.09
Depreciation	0.50			
Interest	0.47			
Incom-tax	1.26			
Net profit	1.26			
	4.09			4.09

Balance Sheet as on 31st March, 2007

Liabilities	Rs. Lakhs		Assets	Rs. Lakhs
Equity shares of Rs. 10 each	3.50		Plant and machinery	10.00
10% Preference shares	2.00		Less: Depreciation	2.50
Reserves and surplus	2.00		Net plant and machinery	7.50
Long-term loan (12%)	1.00		Goodwill	1.40
Debentures (14%)	2.50		Stock Debtors	1.50
Creditors	0.60		Pre-paid expenses	1.00
Bills Payable	0.20			0.25
Accured expenses	0.20		Marketable securities	0.75
Provision for tax	0.65		Cash	0.25
	12.65			12.65

The market price of the share of Yahoo Ltd. on 31st March, 2007 is Rs. 45

	(Rs. Lakhs)
Reserves at the beginning	1.465
Net profit during the year	1.260
	2.725
Preference dividends	0.200
Equity dividends	0.525
Reserves at the close of year	2.000

Calculate the following ratios – (1) Current ratio (2) Quick ratio (3) Debt-equity ratio (4) Interest coverage (5) Fixed charge coverage (6) Stock turnover (7) Debtors turnover (8) Average collection period (9) Gross profit margin (10) Net profit margin (11) Operating ratio (12) Return on capital employed (ROCE) (13) Earning per share (14) Return on shareholders' equity (15) P/E ratio and (16) Earning yield.

Solution:

1. **Current Ratio**

$$\frac{\text{Current assets}}{\text{Current liabilities}} = \frac{3,75,000}{1.65.000} = 2.27:1$$

2. **Quick Ratio**

$$\frac{\text{Current assets - Inventories}}{\text{Current liabilities - Bank overdraft}} = \frac{2,00,000}{1,65,000} = 1.21:1$$

3. **Debt-Equity Ratio**

$$\frac{\text{Long-term debt}}{\text{Shareholders funds}} = \frac{3,50,000}{7,50,000} = 0.467:1$$

4. **Interest Coverage**

$$\frac{\text{PBIDT}}{\text{Interest}} = \frac{1,26,000 + 47,000 + 1,26,000}{47,000} = 6.36 \text{ times}$$

5. **Fixed Charge Coverage**

$$\frac{\text{PBIDT}}{\text{Interest + Preference dividend}} = \frac{2,99,000}{47,000 + 20,000} = 4.46 \text{ times}$$

6. **Stock Turnover**

$$\frac{\text{Cost of goods sold}}{\text{Average inventory}} = \frac{11,00,000}{(1,75,000 + 1,50,000) / 2} = 6.8 \text{ times}$$

7. **Debtors Turnover**

$$\frac{\text{Credit sales}}{\text{Debtors}} = \frac{12,00,000}{1,00,000} = 12 \text{ times}$$

8. **Average Collection Period**

$$\frac{360 \text{ days}}{\text{Debtors turnover}} = \frac{360}{12} = 30 \text{ days}$$

9.   *G.P Margin*

$$\frac{\text{Sales - Cost of goods sold}}{\text{Sales}} \times 100 = \frac{15,00,000 - 11,00,000}{15,00,000} \times 100 = 26.67\%$$

10.   *N.P. Margin*

$$\frac{\text{PBIT}}{\text{Sales}} \times 100 = \frac{1,26,000 + 1,26,000 + 47,000}{15,00,000} \times 100 = 19.93\%$$

11.   *Operating Ratio*

$$\frac{\text{Operating expenses}}{\text{Sales}} \times 100 = \frac{11,00,000 + 35,000 + 25,000 + 50,000}{15,00,000} \times 100 = 80.67\%$$

12.   *Return on Capital Employed (ROCE)*

	(Rs.)
Equity share capital	3,50,000
Preference share capital	2,00,000
Reserves and surplus	2,00,000
Long-term loan (12%)	1,00,000
Debentures 914%)	2,50,000
Capital employed	11,00,000

$$\frac{\text{Net Profit}}{\text{Capital employed}} \times 100 = \frac{1,26,000}{11,00,000} \times 100 = 11.45\%$$

OR

$$\frac{\text{Net profit before interest and tax}}{\text{Capital employed}} \times 100 = \frac{2,99,000}{11,00,000} \times 100 = 27.18\%$$

13.   *Return on Shareholders' Equity*

$$\frac{\text{Net profit}}{\text{Share holders funds}} \times 100 = \frac{1,26,000}{7,50,000} \times 100 = 16.8\%$$

14.   *EPS*

$$\frac{\text{Net profit - Preference dividend}}{\text{No. of equity shares}} = \frac{1,26,000 - 20,000}{35,000} = \text{Rs.}3.03$$

15.   *Price / Earning Ratio*

$$\frac{\text{Market price}}{\text{EPS}} = \frac{45}{3.03} = 14.85 \text{ times}$$

16.   *Earning Yield*

$$\frac{\text{EPS}}{\text{Market price}} \times 100 = \frac{3.03}{45} \times 100 = 6.73\%$$

Illustration 24: Following is the balance sheet and income statement of Jaynagara Ltd. for the year ended 31st March, 2007 as under: Income Statement for the year ended 31st March, 2007

	(Rs. '000)
Sales	1,600
Less: Cost of Goods sold	1,310
Gross margin	290
Less: Selling and administrative expenses	40
EBIT	250
less: interest expenses	45
Earnings before tax	205
Les: Tax	82
Net profit	123

Balance Sheet as on 31st March, 2007

	(Rs. '000)
Liabilities	
Paid-up capital (40,000 equity shares of Rs. 10 each. Fully paid-up	400
Retained earnings	120
Debentures	700
Creditors	180
Bills payable	20
Other current liabilities	80
	1,500
Assets	
Net fixed assets	800
inventory	400
Debtors	175
Marketable securities	75
Cash	50
	1,500

Price per share: Rs. 15 industry's average ratios are:

Current ratio	2.4	Debt equity ratio	2:01
Quick ratio	1.5	Times interest earned	6
Sales to inventory	8.0 times	Net profit margin	7%
Average collection period	36 days	Price to earnings ratio	15
Debt to assets	40%	Return to total assets	11%

From the above facts and figures, you are required to - (i) Calculate the relevant ratios and interpret them to identify the problems areas. (ii) Based on the ratio analysis, as a Company Secretary, prepare a report for consideration of your Board of Directors, clearly bringing out the reason in respect of identified problem areas and giving suggestions to solve them.

Solution:

	(Rs. '000)
Current	
Inventory	400
Debtors	175
Marketable securities	75
Cash	50
	700
Current Liabilities	
Creditors	180
Bills payable	20
Other Current liabilities	80
	280

1. Current Ratio = $\dfrac{\text{Current assets}}{\text{Current liabilities}} = \dfrac{700}{280} = 2.5$

2. Quick Ratio = $\dfrac{\text{Liquid assets}}{\text{Current liabilities}} = \dfrac{300}{280} = 1.07$

3. Sales to Inventory = $\dfrac{\text{Sales}}{\text{Inventory}} = \dfrac{1600}{400} = 4 \text{ times}$

4. Average collection Period = $\dfrac{\text{Debtors}}{\text{Average daily sales}} = \dfrac{175}{4.4} = 40 \text{ days}$

5. Debts to Assets = $\dfrac{\text{Debts}}{\text{Total assets}} \times 100 = \dfrac{700}{1500} \times 100 = 46.7\%$

6. Debt-Equity Ratio = $\dfrac{\text{Debts}}{\text{Shareholders funds}} = \dfrac{700}{520} = 1.35$

7. Times Interest Earned = $\dfrac{\text{EBIT}}{\text{Interest charges}} = \dfrac{250}{45} = 5.56$

8. Net Profit Margin = $\dfrac{\text{Net Profit}}{\text{Sales}} \times 100 = \dfrac{123}{1600} \times 100 = 7.7\%$

9. Price to Earnings Ratio = $\dfrac{\text{Price per share}}{\text{E.P.S}} = \dfrac{15}{3.075} = 4.88$

10. Return to Total Assets = $\dfrac{\text{Net Profit}}{\text{Total Assets}} \times 100 = \dfrac{123}{1500} \times 100 = 8.2\%$

DU PONT ANALYSIS

The Du Pont Chart is a chart of financial ratios, which analyses the net profit margin in terms of asset turnover. Du Pont analysis is an extension of return on investment (ROI) ratio, which measures the overall profitability and operational efficiency of the firm. The Du Pont company of USA has introduced a system of financial analysis which has received wide acceptance in the financial field. Because of this, this chart is known as Du Pont Analysis.

Advantages/Uses or Plus Point of Du Pont Analysis or Chart

1. The Du Pont analysis is used as a tool in measuring the managerial performance by linking the net profit margin to total assets turnover.

2. The Du Pont chart is useful in segregation and identification of factors that effect the overall performance of the company

3. The Du Pont analysis considers the inter-relationship of accounting information given in financial statements.

4. Comparative analysis can be done with reference to the data of previous period or industry data or competitor's data.

5. Return on investment can be improved by increasing one or both of its components viz., the profit margin and the investment turnover in any of the following ways: (a) Increasing the net profit margin, or (b) Increasing the investment turnover, or (c) Increasing both net profit margin and investment turnover.

6. The Du Pont chart indicates that the return on investment is ascertained as a product of net profit margin ratio and investment turnover ratio.

Du Pont Chart

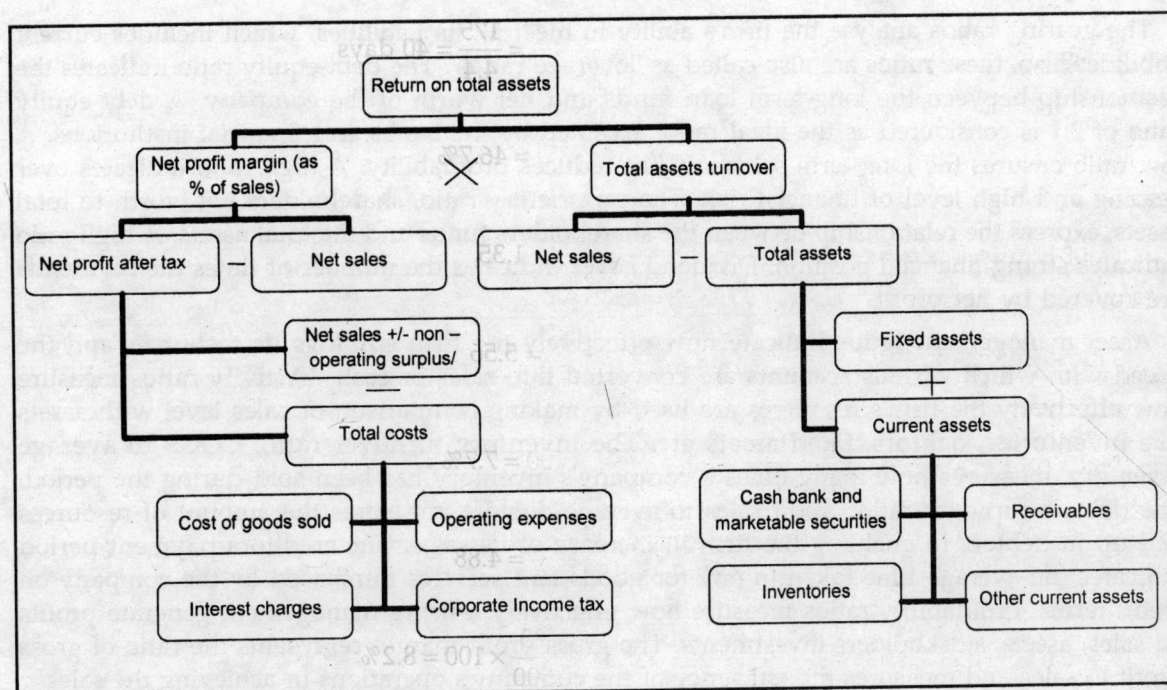

Calculation of Net Profit After Tax

			(Rs.)
Sales			xxx
Less: Cost of goods sold			xxx
Gross profit			xxx
Less: Operating expenses			xxx
Operating profit (EBIT)			xxx
Less: Interest		xxx	
Tax		xxx	xxx
Net profit after tax (PAT)			xxx

Alternatively, total assets can be calculated as follows

	(Rs.)
Shareholders' Equity	xxx
Add: Long-term borrowed funds	xxx
Add: Current liabilities	xxx
Total Assets	**xxx**

SUMMARY

Ratio is a fraction whose numerator is the antecedent and denominator the consequent."Ratio is the relationship or proportion that one amount bears to another, the first number being the numerator and the later one of denominator." Ratio analysis is a powerful analytical tool for measuring performance of an organization. Various ratios are used in analysis of financial health of a business organisation. The liquidity ratios measure the liquidity of the firm and its ability to meet its short-term obligations.

The gearing ratios analyse the firm's ability to meet all its liabilities, which includes current liabilities also, these ratios are also called as 'leverage ratios'. The debt-equity ratio indicates the relationship between the long-term loan funds and net worth of the company. A debt-equity ratio of 2:1 is considered as the ideal ratio, accepted by the banks and financial institutions. A low ratio ensures the long-term solvency, but reduces profitability. A high ratio indicates over gearing and high level of financial risk. The proprietory ratio, shareholders net worth to total assets, express the relationship between the shareholders funds and the total assets. A high ratio indicates strong financial position. Dividend cover indicates the number of times the dividends are covered by net profit.

Asset management ratios indicate how effectively the firm employs its resources and the speed with which various accounts are converted into sales or cash. Activity ratios measure how effectively the firm's resources are used by making comparison of sales level with assets like inventories, debtors, fixed assets etc. The inventory turnover ratio, COGS to average inventory, measures how many times a company's inventory has been sold during the period. The debtors turnover ratio, credit sales to average debtors, measures the amount of resources tied up in debtors in enabling the firm in increase of its sales. The creditors payment period indicates the average time taken to pay for goods and services purchased by the company on credit terms. Profitability ratios measure how effectively a firm's management generate profits on sales, assets, stockholders investments. The gross profit margin represents the ratio of gross profit to sales and measures the efficiency of the company's operations in achieving the sales.

Market-based ratios measure the financial market's evaluation of company's performance and its dividend payment policy. Earnings per share is calculated by dividing the net profit after tax and preference dividend with number of equity shares. EPS is the measure of net profit earned per share. A steady growth in EPS year after year indicates a good track of profitability. Dividend yield indicates the dividend received by shareholder as a percentage of market price of share. Dividend payout ratio indicates the extent of the net profits distributed to the shareholders as dividend. A high payout ratio indicates a liberal dividend distribution policy. Du Pont Analysis is used as a tool in measuring the managerial performance by linking the net profit margin to total assets turnover. Du Pont Analysis is an extension of ROI or ROCE. Du Pont Chart indicates the return on investment, which is ascertained as a product of net profit margin ratio and investment turnover ratio.

Financial statements, as used in corporate business houses, refer to a set of reports and schedules which an accountant prepares at the end of a period of time for a business enterprise. The financial statements are the means with the help of which the accounting system performs its main function of providing summarised information about the financial affairs of the business. These statements comprise Balance Sheet or Position Statement and Profit and Loss Account or Income Statement. Of course to give a full view of the financial affairs of an undertaking, in addition to the above, the business may also prepare a Statement of Retained Earnings and a Cash Flow Statement.

Financial statements are prepared for the purpose of presenting a periodical review or report on the progress by the management and deal with the (a) status of the investments in the business and (b) results achieved during the period under review. The data exhibited in these financial statements are the result of the combined effect of (i) recorded facts; (ii) accounting conventions; (iii) postulates or assumptions made to implement conventional procedures; (iv) personal judgements used in the applications of conventions and postulates and (v) accounting standards and guidance notes.

The number and types of people interested in financial statements have changed radically in recent times. Financial statements are necessary for shareholders and potential shareholders, in addition to management and creditors.

Analysis of financial statements refers to the treatment of information contained in the financial statement in a way so as to afford a full diagnosis of the profitability and financial position of the firm concerned.

The process of analysing financial statements involves the rearranging, comparing and measuring the significance of financial and operating data. Such a step helps to reveal the relative significance and effect of items of the data in relation to the time period and/or between two organisations.

A distinction may be drawn between various types of financial analysis either on the basis of material used for the same or according to the modus operandi or according to the objective of the analysis.

The analysis of financial statements consists of a study of relationship and trends, to determine whether or not the financial position and results of operations as well as the financial progress of the company are satisfactory or unsatisfactory.

Analytical methods and devices used in analysing financial statements are as follows: Comparative Statements, Common Size Statements, Trend Ratios, Ratio Analysis, Cash Flow Statements.

Comparative statements are necessary for the study of trends and direction of movement in the financial position and operating results. This calls for a consistency in the practice of preparing these statements, otherwise comparability may be distorted. Comparative statements enable horizontal analysis of figures.

Common size financial statements are those in which figures reported are converted into percentages to some common base. For this, items in the financial statements are presented as percentages or ratios to total of the items and a common base for comparison is provided. Each percentage shows the relation of the individual item to its respective total.

Trend ratios show the nature and rate of movements in various financial factors. They provide a horizontal analysis of comparative statements and reflect the behaviour of various items with the passage of time. Trend ratios can be graphically presented for a better understanding by the management. They are very useful in predicting the behaviour of the various financial factors in future.

REVIEW QUESTIONS

Section - A (2 marks questions)

1. Define 'Accounting Ratio'.
2. What do you mean by Accounting Ratios?
3. What is Gross Profit Ratio?
4. What is Operating Ratio?
5. What is Expenses Ratio?
6. What is Net Profit Ratio?
7. What do you mean by Combined Ratio?
8. What do you understand by Turnover to Debtors Ratio?
9. What are Solvency Ratios?
10. What is "Return on capital employed"?
11. State the components of liquid ratio.
12. Gross profit of a firm is Rs. 1,60,000, operating expenses are Rs. 50,000. Taxes Rs. 10,000, owner's fund Rs. 2,50,000, calculate return on proprietors fund.
13. Given current ratio 2.5, working capital is Rs. 60,000, calculate the amount of current assets and liabilities.
14. Current ratio 2.5, acid test ratio 1.5, stock Rs. 1,50,000, calculate net working capital.
15. State the utility of operating expenses ratio.
16. What do you mean by current ratio?
17. What do you mean by acid test or liquid ratio?
18. Closing Stock of X Ltd., is Rs. 2,00,000. Total Liquid Assets are Rs. 10,00,000. Liquid Ratio is 2: 1. Find out the working capital.
19. Cost of goods sold is Rs. 1,60,000. Stock turnover is 5 times. Closing stock is Rs. 4,000 more than opening stock. Calculate the opening stock.
20. Total current liabilities are Rs. 80,000. Current ratio 2.5: 1. Acid test ratio 1.5: 1. Total current assets include stock, debtors, and cash only. Cash is 2/3 of debtors. Calculate debtors.
21. What do you mean by Revenue Statement Ratio?
22. How do you calculate "Stock Turnover Ratio"?
23. Total current assets are Rs. 1,20,000, Current Ratio is 2. Fixed assets are 60% of capital, calculate capital and fixed assets.
24. Stock turnover of 5 times. Average stock is Rs. 60,000. Rate of gross profit on sales is 20%, calculate sales and gross profit.
25. State the key steps involved in ratio analysis.

26. Current liabilities of the company are Rs. 3,00,000. Its current ratio is 3:1 and quick ratio 1:1. Calculate value of stock-in-trade.
27. What is Activity Ratio?
28. State the significance of Current Ratio.

Section - B (8 marks questions)

1. "Short-term solvency is the ability to meet all present and potential demands on cash from any source in a manner that minimizes cost and maximizes the value of the firm". Explain.
2. Write short note on 'Liquidity ratios'.
3. Describe the shortcomings of 'Current Ratio' and 'Quick Ratio' as measures of liquidity.
4. Give the meaning of: (answer any one)
   (a) Net profit to total assets ratio
   (b) Return on proprietor's funds
   (c) Learnings per ratio
   (d) Price-earning ratio
   (e) Sales to debtors ratio
   (f) Sales to stock ratio
   (g) Efficiency ratio
   (h) Activity ratio
5. State the importance of ratio analysis.
6. Give an analytical note on combined ratios.
7. Current liability of a company is Rs. 30,000. Its current ratio is 3: 1 and quick ratio is 1: 1. Calculate the value of stock-in-trade.
8. State any four accounting ratios and explain their utility.
9. Analyse the relationship between liquidity, solvency and profitability.
10. "Ratios are mechanical and incomplete" - Analyse.
11. What are Turnover Ratios ? Analyse their utility.
12. Analyse the utility of the following ratios (any two): (1) Current Ratio. (2) Liquid Ratio (3) Debtors' Turnover Ratio (4) Creditors' Turnover Ratio (5) Stock Turnover Ratio (6) Proprietory Ratio.
13. What are the limitations of ratio analysis?
14. State and analyse the significance of current ratio with an imaginary illustration.
15. State and analyse the significance of liquid ratio with an illustration.
16. State and analyse the significance of proprietory ratio with an example.
17. What is window-dressing in current ratio? Analyse this with an illustration.
18. Give an analysis note on revenue statement ratios.
19. Write short notes on 'Acid Test Ratio'.
20. Write short notes on 'Defensive-Interval Ratio'. Illustrate.
21. Define and evaluate of the following ratios : (i) Debt-Equity Ratio (ii) Fixed Assets Ratio, and (iii) Interest Coverage Ratio.
22. "Ratios are the symptoms like blood pressure, pulse or temperature of an individual." Explain. Also name and explain in brief the ratios used to judge the long-term solvency of a concern.

23. Briefly describe the Leverage Ratios.

24. What are the ratios that assess the company's debt capacity?

25. Write short notes on 'Debt Service Coverage Ratio'.

26. "Asset Management Ratios measure how effectively the firm employs its resources in inventories, debtors, fixed assets" Explain.

27. Write short notes on 'Activity/Turnover Ratios'.

28. Distinguish between 'Operating Ratios' and 'turnover ratios'.

29. Briefly explain the 'Profitability Ratios.'

30. Discuss the utility of 'Return on capital used' as a measure of management performance.

31. "Higher profit margins need not necessarily lead to higher rate of return on investments". Elucidate.

Section - C (15 marks questions)

1. "Interpretation of ratios is a highly technical job for a financial analyst". Discuss.

2. "Ratio analysis is only a technique for making judgments and not a substitute for judgments". Examine.

3. "Ratios are indicators - sometimes pointers but not in themselves powerful tools of management". Explain.

4. What are the factors affecting the efficacy of ratios?

5. Discuss the non-financial measures used in evaluation of performance of a company.

6. Give an explanatory note on the various aspects of occuring ratios.

7. Give an explanatory note on balance sheet ratios.

8. What are important profitability ratios? How are they worked out? Explain and illustrate.

9. State the important combined ratios. How are they computed? Explain and illustrate.

10. Describe any five accounting ratios and briefly explain their application.

11. Explain the role of ratio analysis in the interpretation of financial statements. State its limitations.

12. Enumerate and explain which financial ratios will be of interest to the potential investors in a company.

13. Explain in brief the uses of the following groups of ratios and give their formulae: (i) Earnings Per Share (ii) Price Earnings Ratio (iii) Dividend Payout Ratio (iv) Dividend Yield Ratio.

14. Discuss any three ratios computed for investment analysis.

15. What are the major uses of ratio analysis in financial evaluation?

16. "Ratio analysis is an important tool for judgment of the health of any organization". Elaborate.

17. Define and explain Comparative statement.

18. Write a note on Comparative Income statement and Comparative Balance sheet.

19. What are the objectives of financial statements?

20. Discuss the limitations of financial statements and point out how these limitations can be removed through management accounting?

21. How will you interpret and analyse financial statement presented to you?

22. What is the common size balance sheet and income statement? Explain the technique of preparing common size balance sheet.

23. What are the trend ratios? Explain the technique of computing trend ratios.

Funds Flow Statement

3

Objectives

Objectives

*After studying this chapter, you
should be able to:*

1 Meaning of FFS

2 Understand advantages of
funds flow statement

3 Discuss limitations of funds flow
statement

4 Distinguish between funds flow
statement and balance sheet

5 Distinguish between funds flow
statement and income
statement

6 Know preparation of funds flow
statement

7 Explain problems on funds flow
statement

Every company prepares its balance sheet at the end of its accounting year. It is a statement of assets and liabilities of the company, as on a particular date. It reveals the financial position of the company. It does not present a detailed analysis. The balance sheet fails to account for the periodic increase or decrease in the working capital of an enterprise. Hence, another statement has become necessary to show the changes in working capital during a period and explain them. The statement is called funds flow statement.

In a funds flow analysis, the details of financial resources availed and the ways in which such resources are used during a particular accounting period, are given in a statement from called 'Funds Flow Statement'. The sources of funds also include the funds generated from operations internally. The funds flow statement can explain the reasons for liquidity problems of the firm even though it is earning profits. It helps the efficient working capital management and indicates the ability of the firm in servicing its long-term debt obligations. The changes in working capital position can also tracked by observing the surplus/deficit of funds during a particular accounting period. This statement is also called 'Statement of Sources and Application of Funds' and 'Statement of Changes in Financial Position'.

In the words of the author, the meaning of funds flow statement is "a report on the movement of funds or working capital". It explains how working capital is raised and used during an accounting period.

DEFINITION

"A statement of sources and application of funds is a technical device designed to analyze the changes in the financial condition of a business enterprise between two dates" - *Foulke*.

Various names or titles for funds flow statement: Funds flow statement is called by various names such as statement of sources and application of funds, sources and uses of funds, statement of changes in financial position, where got where gone statement, analysis of working capital changes and movement of funds statement.

Meaning of Funds: The term 'funds' has been defined in a number of ways. In a narrow sense, it means cash only. A fund flow statement prepared on cash basis is called a cash flow statement. In a broader sense, the term 'funds' refers to all financial resources. However, the concept of funds as working capital is the most popular and widely accepted. Working capital is the excess of current assets over current liabilities.

Concept of Flow of Funds: The term 'flow' means change and therefore the term 'flow of funds' means 'change of funds' or 'change in working capital'. In other words, 'flow of funds' means any increase or decrease in working capital. If the transaction results in the increase of funds it is called a source of funds; if it results in the decrease of funds it is known as an application of funds. If the transaction does not affect the working capital, there is no flow of funds. The flow of fund occurs only when a transaction involves one current account and another non-current accounts. When a transaction involves non-current accounts only, no flow of funds occurs since working capital is not altered. For example, issue of shares in consideration for machinery. Similarly, if a transaction affects current accounts only, no flow of fund occurs. For instance, collection of cash from debtors or payment of cash to creditors. Thus, to facilitate a flow of fund [change in working capital] the transaction must affect one current account and another non-current account e.g., issue of shares in consideration for stock acquired, cash payment for building etc.

Objectives of Funds Flow Statement

The main objectives of funds flow statement are:

1. To show how the resources have been obtained and used.
2. To indicate the results of current financial management.

3. To throw light upon the most important changes that has taken place during a specific period.

4. To show how the general expansion of the business has been financed.

5. To indicate the relationship between profits form operations, distribution of dividend and raising of new capital or term loans.

6. To have an assessment of the working capital position of the concern.

7. The funds flow statement contain all the details of the financial resources which have become available during an accounting period and the ways in which those resources have been used up.

8. This statement discloses the amounts raised from various sources of finance during a period and then explains how that finance has been used in the business.

9. This statement is valuable in interpretation of the accounts.

10. It is a very useful tool in analysis of financial statements which analyses the changes taking place between two balance sheet dates.

11. The statement analyses the changes between the opening and closing balance sheets for the period. A balance sheet sets out the financial position at a point of time, setting liabilities from which funds have been raised against assets acquired by the use of those funds.

12. A funds flow statement analyses the changes which have taken place in the assets and liabilities during certain period as disclosed by a comparison of the opening and closing balance sheets.

Advantages (uses) and Significance of Funds Flow Statement

The funds flow statement is of primary importance to the financial management. It is an essential tool for financial analysis. It is being widely used by financial institutions, financial managers and analysts. The significance of funds flow statement can be understood from the various uses given below.

1. *Analysis of Financial Operations:* The main purpose of funds flow statement is to analyse the financial operations of the business. The statement explains the causes for changes in the assets and liabilities during a period. It also indicates the effect of these changes on the liquidity of the firm.

2. *Evaluation of the Firm's Financing:* The analysis of sources of funds reveals how the firm has financed its development projects in the past i.e., from internal sources or from external sources. It also reveals the rate of growth of the firm.

3. *Answers to Intricate Questions:* The funds flow statement provides answers to questions such as:

   1. How were the loans repaid?
   2. How much funds were generated from operations?
   3. How were the funds used?
   4. How was the increase the working capital financed?

4. *Allocation of Scare Resources:* A projected funds flow statement is an instrument for allocation of resources. It lays down the plan for efficient use of scarce resources in future. It enables the management to discharge its financial obligations promptly.

5. *Helps in Working Capital Management:* Funds flow statement indicates the adequacy or inadequacy of working capital. The management can take steps for effective use of surplus working capital. In case of inadequacy, arrangement can be made for improving the working capital position.

6. *Acts as a Guide to the Future:* With the aid of projected funds flow statement the management can plan for meeting future financial requirements.

7. *Helps Financial Institutions:* The funds flow statement is also useful to leading institutions like banks, IDBI, ICICI, IFCI and others. It helps them to assess the credit worthiness sand repaying capacity of the borrowing company.

Limitations of Funds Flow Statement

The limitations of funds flow statement are listed below:

1. Funds flow statement is not a substitute for an income statement or balance sheet. It provides only some additional information regarding changes in working capital.

2. Changes in cash are more important and relevant for financial management than the working capital.

3. It is not an original statement. It is only a rearrangement of data given in financial statement.

4. Funds flow statement is essentially historic in nature. A projected funds flow statement, on the basis of it cannot be prepared with much accuracy. It does not estimate the sources and application of funds of the near future.

5. It cannot reveal continuous changes.

Other limitations or drawbacks of FFS are as under

1. New items are not disclosed - The funds flow statement does not disclose any new or original items which affect the financial position of the business. The funds flow statement simply rearranges the data given in conventional financial statements and schedules.

2. Not relevant - a study of changes in cash is more relevant than a study of changes in funds for the purpose of managerial decision-making.

3. Not foolproof - The funds flow statement is prepared from the data provided in the balance sheet and profit and loss account. Hence, the defects in financial statements will be carried over to funds flow statement too.

4. Structural changes are not disclosed - The funds flow statement does not disclose the structural changes in financial relationship in a firm nor it discloses the major policy changes with regard to investment in current assets and short-term financing. Significant additions to inventories financed by short-term creditors are not furnished in the statement as they are offset by each other while computing net changes in working capital.

Distinguish between Funds Flow Statement and Balance Sheet

The distinctions between a funds flow statement and a balance sheet are as follows:

Funds Flow Statement	Balance Sheet
1. It is prepared to know the total sources and their uses in a year.	1. It is prepared to know the financial position.
2. It is dynamic as it reveals the changes in the value of fixed assets and their effect on flow of funds,	2. It shows the assets and liabilities as on a particular date, as such it is a static statement.
3. It is prepared with the help of balance sheets of two consecutive years.	3. It is prepared on the basis of different accounts in the ledger.
4. Its preparation is at the discretion of the management.	4. Its preparation is a statutory obligation and as per the format prescribed under legal provisions.

Contd...

5. In funds flow statement, current assets and current liabilities are used to find out increase or decrease in working capital.	5. In balance sheet, current assets and current liabilities are show itemwise:
6. It is useful for internal financial management.	6. It is useful not only to the management, but also to the shareholders, creditors, outsiders and government agencies etc.

Distinguish between Funds Flow Statement and Income Statement

The funds flow statement and income statement have different functions and their main differences are summarised below:

Funds Flow Statements	Income Statement
1. Its main objective is to ascertain the funds generated from operations. It reveals the sources of funds and their applications.	1. Its main objective is to ascertain the net profit earned or loss incurred by the company out of business operations at the end of particular period.
2. It is prepared based on the financial statements of two consecutive years.	2. It is prepared on the basis of nominal accounts of particular accounting period.
3. Funds flow statement matches the funds raised with funds applied. No distinction is made between capital and revenue items.	3. But the income statement matches cost of goods sold with sales, to ascertain profit or loss. It deals with revenue items only.
4. It takes into account not only the funds available from trading operations but also funds available from other sources like issue of share capital/debentures, sale of fixed assets, etc.	4. It uses only income and expenditure transactions relating to trading operations of a particular period.
5. Income statement is one of the source documents in preparation of funds flow statement.	5. An income statement can be prepared without the help of a funds flow statement.
6. Preparation of funds flow statement is not a statutory obligations and is left to the discretion of management.	6. Preparation of profit and loss account is a statutory obligation and should be prepared in accordance with the legal requirements.
7. It may be prepared much before business operations and act as an instrument of planning and control.	7. It is static in as much as it gives information's on what has happened during the period covered by it.
8. It can be prepared as and when management wants it.	8. It is prepared only at the end of accounting period for the period covered by it.
9. It cannot be easily manipulated by management.	9. The determination of periodic income is necessarily based on number of estimates, judgment and allocations and is subject to manipulations of management.
10. It provides a complete record of transactions involving cash	10. It is prepared on accrual basis of accounting and fails to present the factual history of firm's cash transactions.

Identification of Flow of Funds

A 'flow' of funds takes place only if a current account is involved. To identify a flow, journalise the transaction, identify the two accounts involved as 'current' and 'non-current' and apply the general rule.

♦ Transactions which involve only current accounts do not result in a flow.

♦ Transactions which involve only non-current accounts do not result in a flow.

♦ Transactions which involve one current account and one non-current account result in a flow of funds.

STEPS IN PREPARATION OF FUNDS FLOW STATEMENT

Step 1. Preparation of Changes in Working Capital Position

Step 2. Preparation of Ledger Account (if required)

Step 3. Preparation of Adjusted Profit and Loss Account or Computation of Funds from Operation (FFO)

Step 4. Preparation of Funds Flow Statement

Step 1. Changes in Working Capital Position

This statement follows the Statement of Sources and Application of Funds. The primary purpose of the statement is to explain the net change in working capital, as arrived in the funds flow statement. In this statement, all current assets and current liabilities are individually listed. Against each account, the figure pertaining to that account at the beginning and at the end of the accounting period is shown. The net change in its position is also shown. The changes taking place with respect to each account should add up to equal the net change in working capital, as shown by the funds flow statement.

Increase in Current Assets and Decrease in Current Liabilities: The acquisition of current assets and repayment of current liabilities will result in funds outflow. The funds may be applied to finance an increase in stock, debtors etc. or to reduce trade creditors, bank overdraft, bills payable etc.

Decrease in Current Assets and Increase in Current Liabilities: The reduction in current assets e.g., stock or debtors balance will result in release of funds to be applied elsewhere. Short-term funds raised during the period by any increase in the current liabilities like trade creditors, bank overdraft and tax dues, means that these sources have lent more at the end of the year than at the beginning.

Statement of Changes in Working Capital

Particulars		Beginning of the year	End of the year	Working Capital	
				Increase	Decrease
Current Assets					
Cash in hand		xxx	xxx	Xxx	-
Cash at bank		xxx	xxx	Xxx	-
Bills receivable		xxx	xxx	-	xxx
Sundry debtors		xxx	xxx	-	xxx
Closing stock		xxx	xxx	Xxx	-
Short-term investments		xxx	xxx	Xxx	-
Prepaid expenses		xxx	xxx	Xxx	-
Other current assets		xxx	xxx	-	xxx
	(a)	xxx	xxx		

Contd...

Current liabilities					
Bills payable		xxxx	xxxx	xxxx	-
Sundry creditors		xxxx	xxxx	-	xxxx
Outstanding expenses		xxxx	xxxx	-	xxxx
Bank overdraft		xxxx	xxxx	-	xxxx
Short-term loans taken		xxxx	xxxx	xxxx	-
Proposed dividend		xxxx	xxxx	xxxx	-
Provision for tax		xxxx	xxxx	-	xxxx
Other current liabilities		xxxx	xxxx	xxxx	-
	(b)	xxxx	xxxx		
Working capital	(a) - (b)	xxxx	xxxx	-	-
Net increase or decrease in working capital		xxxx	xxxx	xxxx	xxxx
		xxxx	xxxx	xxxx	xxxx

Basic Rules of Changes in Working Capital

♦ Increase in current asset will increase in working capital.

♦ Decrease in current assets will decrease in working capital.

♦ Increase in current liability will influence to decrease in working capital.

♦ Decrease in current liability will increase the working capital.

Illustration 1: From the following prepare a statement showing changes in working capital during 2007.

Balance Sheet of TV 9 Ltd., as on 31st December

Liabilities	2006	2007	Assets	2006	2007
	Rs.	Rs.		Rs.	Rs.
Share capital	6,00,000	6,00,000	Fixed Assets	10,00,000	11,20,000
Reserves	50,000	1,80,000	Less : Depre-		
			ciation	3,70,000	4,60,000
Profit and Loss					
account	40,000	65,000		6,30,000	6,60,000
Debentures	3,00,000	2,50,000			
Creditors for			Stock	2,40,000	3,70,000

Contd...

goods	1,70,000	1,60,000	Book debts	2,50,000	2,30,000
Provision for			Cash in hand		
Income tax	60,000	80,000	and at Bank	80,000	60,000
			Preliminary		
			expenses	20,000	15,000
	12,20,000	13,35,000		12,20,000	13,35,000

Solution:

Schedule of Changes in Working Capital of TV 9 Ltd.

Particulars	2006	2007	Increase	Decrease
	Rs.	Rs.	Rs.	Rs.
Current assets:				
Stock	2,40,000	3,70,000	1,30,000	
Book debts	2,50,000	2,30,000		20,000
Cash in hand & Bank	80,000	60,000		20,000
	5,70,000	6,60,000		
Less : Current liabilities:				
Creditors for goods	1,70,000	1,60,000	10,000	
Provision for tax	60,000	80,000		20,000
	2,30,000	2,40,000	1,40,000	60,000
Working capital	3,40,000	4,20,000		
	80,000			80,000
	4,20,000	4,20,000	1,40,000	1,40,000

Illustration 2: Prepare a statement showing changes in working capital from the information given below:

Particulars	2006	(Rs.) 2007
Assets:		
Cash	60,000	94,000

Contd...

Debtors	2,40,000	2,30,000
Stock	1,60,000	1,80,000
Land	1,00,000	1,32,000
	5,60,000	**6,36,000**
Capital and Liabilities:		
Share capital	4,00,000	5,00,000
Creditors	1,40,000	90,000
Retained earnings	20,000	46,000
	5,60,000	**6,36,000**

Solution:

Statement showing charges in working capital

Particulars	2006	2007	Increase	Decrease
Current Assets:				
Cash	60,000	94,000	34,000	-
Debtors	2,40,000	2,60,000	-	10,000
Stock	1,60,000	1,80,000	20,000	-
	4,60,000	**5,04,000**	-	-
Current Liabilities				
Creditors	1,40,000	90,000	50,000	-
Working Capital (CA - CL)	3,20,000	4,14,000	-	-
Net increase in working capital	94,000	-	-	94,000
	4,14,000	**4,14,000**	**1,04,000**	**1,04,000**

Step 3: Calculation of Funds from Operation (FFO)

Profit of a period is an important source of funds. The profit and loss account reveals the net profit or loss of a business. The net profit is arrived at after taking into account all items of income and expenditure (both operating and non-operating, both fund items and non fund items). To arrive at funds from operations, adjustments are made in net profit for non-fund and non-operating items. It will be clear from the following.

Calculation of Funds from Operation:

Net profit earned during the year (CY)   ---------------

Add: Non-fund and Non operating items

Which are already debited to P & L a/c,

Depreciation on fixed assets	----------------
Goodwill written off	----------------
Discount on issue of shares, written off	----------------
Preliminary expenses written off	----------------
Patents written off	----------------
Transfer to reserves	----------------
Loss on sale of fixed assets	----------------

Less: Non-fund or Non-operating items

Which are already credited of P & L a/c:

Profit on sale of fixed assets	----------------
Profit on revaluation of assets	----------------
Rent received	----------------
Dividend received	----------------
Refund of income tax	----------------

Funds from Operations	----------------

If the profit and loss a/c shows a net loss, the above procedure will be reversed.

(FFO can also prepared by using T format)

Illustration 3: Calculate funds from operations with the help of the following Profit and Loss Account of XYZ Ltd:

Profit and Loss A/c			
	Rs.		Rs.
To Expenses paid and outstanding	1,50,000	By Gross profit	2,25,000
To Depreciation	35,000	By Gain of sale of land	30,000
To Loss on sale of machine	2,000		
To Discount	100		
To Goodwill	10,000		
To Net profit	57,900		
	2,55,000		2,55,000

Solution:

		Rs.
Net Profit (as given)		57,900
Add: Non-fund or non-operating items which have been debited to P&L A/c		
Depreciation	35,000	

Contd...

Loss on sales of machine	2,000	
Goodwill	10,000	47,000
		1,40,9000
Less: Non-fund non-operating items which have been credited to P&L A/c:		
Gain on sales of land		30,000
Funds From Operations		**74,900**

Illustration 4: Following are the extracts from the balance sheets of a companion two different dates:

Particulars	31-3-2006	(Rs.) 31-3-2007
Profit and Loss A/c	50,000	80,000
Provision for taxation	10,000	15,000
Proposed dividends	5,000	10,000

Additional Information:

1. Tax paid during the year 2006-07 Rs. 2,500
2. Dividends paid for the period 2006-07 Rs. 1,000

On the basis of the above information, calculate 'funds from operations' taking provision for tax and proposed dividend as non-current liabilities.

Provision for Taxation A/c			
	Rs.		Rs.
To Income-tax A/c (tax paid)	2,500	By Balance b/d	10,000
To Balance c/d	15,000	By P& L A/c (current year provision)	7,500
	17,500		17,500

Provision for Dividend A/c			
	Rs.		Rs.
To dividend A/c (dividend paid)	1,000	By Balance b/d	5,000
To Balance c/d	10,000	By P & L A/c (Proposed dividend)	6,000
	11,000		11,000

Adjusted Profit and Loss A/c			
To Provision for taxation A/c	7,500	By Balance b/d	50,000
To Proposed dividend	6,000	By Funds from operations (FFO) (balancing figure)	43,500
To Balance c/d	80,000		
	93,500		93,500

Illustration 5: The following information has been extracted from the balance sheets of Black Shoe Company:

		(Rs.)
Particulars	**31.12.2005**	**31.12.2006**
Machinery	80,000	2,00,000
Accumulated depreciation	30,000	35,000
Profit and loss account	25,000	40,000

The following additional information is also available:

(i)   A machine costing Rs. 20,000 was purchased during the year by issue of equity shares.

(ii)   On January 1, 2006, a machine costing Rs. 15,000 (with an accumulated depreciation of Rs. 5,000) was sold for Rs. 7,000. Find out funds from operation.

Accumulated Depreciation A/c			
	Rs.		Rs.
to Machinery A/c	5,000	By Balance b/d	30,000
To Balance c/d	35,000	By P& L A/c (balancing figure)	10,000
	40,000		40,000

Machinery A/c			
To Balance b/d	80,000	By bank (sales)	7,000
To Share capital A/c	20,000	By Accumulated Depreciation a/c	5,000
To Bank A/c (purchases) (bal.figure)	1,15,000	By P & L A/c (loss on sale)	3,000
		By Balance c/d	2,00,000
	2,15,000		2,15,000

Adjusted Profit and Loss A/c			
To Accumulated depreciation A/c	10,000	By Balance b/d	25,000
To Machinery A/c (loss on sale)	3,000	By Funds from operations (balancing figure)	28,000
To Balance c/d	40,000		
	53,000		53,000

Note:

(a)   Purchase of machinery for Rs. 20,000 by issue of equity shares is neither a source nor an application of funds.

(b) Sale of machinery for Rs. 7,000 is a source of funds.

(c) Purchase of machinery for Rs. 1,15,000 for cash is an application of funds.

(d) Funds from operations of Rs. 28,000 is a source of funds.

Illustration 6: The following are the summarized balance sheets of ABC Ltd., as on 31st December 2005 and 2006.

Balance Sheet

Liabilities	31-December 2005	31-December 2006	Asset	31-December 2005	31-December 2006
	Rs.	Rs		Rs.	Rs.
Capital			Fixed Assets	41,000	40,000
7% Redeemable			Less:		
preference			Depreciation	11,000	15,000
shares	-	10,000		30,000	25,000
Equity shares	40,000	40,000			
	40,000	50,000	Current assets:		
General reserve	2,000	2,000	Debtors	20,000	24,000
Profit & Loss			Stock	30,000	35,000
Account	1,000	1,200	Prepaid expenses	300	500
Debentures	6,000	7,000	Cash	1,200	3,500
Current liabilities					
Creditors	12,000	11,000			
Provision for Tax	3,000	4,200			
Proposed dividend	5,000	5,800			
Bank overdraft	12,500	6,800			
	81,500	88,000		81,500	88,000

You are required to prepare

(i) A statement showing changes in the working capital

Solution:

Schedule of changes in working capital

Particulars	2005	2006	Increase	Decrease
	Rs.	Rs.	Rs.	Rs.
Current Assets:				
Debtors	20,000	24,000	4,000	-

Contd...

Prepaid expenses	300	500	200	-
cash	1,200	3,500	2,300	-
	51,500	63,000		
Less :				
Current Liabilities :				
Creditors	12,000	11,000	1,000	-
Provision for tax	3,000	4,200	-	1,200
Proposed dividend	5,000	5,800	-	800
Bank overdraft	12,500	6,800	5,700	-
	32,500	27,800		
Working capital	19,000	35,200	18,200	2,000
Increase in working				
capital	16,200	-	-	16,200
	35,200	35,200	18,200	18,200

Working

Fixed Assets Account

	Rs.		Rs.
To balance c/d	41,000	By Cash (sale) (?)	1,000
		By balance b/d	40,000
	41,000		41,000

Provision for Depreciation Account

	Rs.		Rs.
		By Balance b/d	11,000
		By Adjusted Profit	
		and loss account	
To balance c/d	15,000	(current year's provision)	4,000
	15,000		15,000

Adjusted Profit & Loss Account

	Rs.		Rs.
To provision for	4,000	By Balance b/d	1,000
depreciation		By Funds from	
To balance c/d	1,200	Operations (?)	4,200
	5,200		5,200

Step 4: Statement Sources and Application or Statement of Funds flow Statement.

The basic rules in preparation of the funds flow statement is as follows:

♦ An increase in an asset over the year is an application of fund.

♦ A decrease in an asset over the year is a source of fund.

♦ A decrease in a liability over the year is an application of fund.

♦ An increase in a liability over the year is a source of fund.

The relationship between sources and application of funds and its impact on working capital is explained in the format of Statement of Sources and Application of Funds given below.

Statement of Sources and Application of Funds of ABC Ltd., for the year ended 31st March,.....

Sources and Application of Funds	(Rs.)
Fund from operations	xxx
Issue of share capital	xxx
Raising of long-term loans	xxx
Receipts from partly paid shares, called up	xxx
Sales of non current (fixed) assets	xxx
Non-trading receipts, such as dividends received	xxx
Sale of investments (long-term)	xxx
Decrease in working capital (as per schedule of charges in working capital	xxx
	xxx
Application or Uses of Funds	
Funds lost in operations	xxx
Redemption of preference share capital	xxx
Redemption of debentures	xxx
Repayment of long-term loans	xxx
Purchase of non-current (fixed) assets	xxx
Purchase of long-term investments	xxx
Non-trading payments	xxx
Payments of dividends'	xxx
Payment of tax'	xxx
Increase in working capital (as per schedule of changes in working capital)	xxx
	xxx

Note: Payment of dividend and tax will appear as an application of funds only when these items are appropriations of profits and not current liabilities.

(Funds flow statement can also prepare by using T format as under)

Sources of Funds	Uses of Application of Funds
1. Issue of shares and debentures	1. Redemption of preference shares and debentures
2. Raising of long term loans	2. Repayment of loans
3. Income from investments	3. Purchase of long term investments
4. Sale of fixed assets	4. Purchase of fixed assets and long term investments
5. Funds form operations	5. Payment of taxes and dividends
6. Decrease in schedule of changes in working capital	6. Drawings (in case of proprietary or partnership business)
	7. Loss of cash by embezzlement
	8. Funds lost in operations.
	9. Increase in schedule of changes in working capital.

Illustration 9: From the following balance sheets of B. Ltd., prepare a sources and uses of funds statement for 2007.

	31 st December	31 st December
	2007	2006
	Rs.	Rs.
Assets:		
Cash	75,000	35,000
Accounts Receivable	90,000	98,000
Merchandise Inventory	1,20,000	87,000
Long-term investments	10,000	15,000
Land	30,000	20,000
	3,25,000	2,55,000
Liabilities:		
Accounts Payable	45,000	50,000
Bills Payable	55,000	20,000
Capital Stock	1,50,000	1,25,000
Retained earnings	75,000	60,000
	3,25,000	2,55,000

Solution:

Schedule of Changes in Working Capital

Particulars	2006	2007	Increase	Decrease
	Rs.	Rs.	Rs.	Rs.
Current Assets:				
Cash	35,000	75,000	40,000	——
Accounts Receivable	98,000	90,000	—	8,000
Merchandise				
Inventory	87,000	1,20,000	33,000	——
	2,20,000	2,85,000		
Less:				
Current Liabilities:				
Accounts				
Payable (creditors)	50,000	45,000	5,000	——
Bills Payable	20,000	55,000	——	35,000
	70,000	1,00,000	78,000	43,000
Working capital	1,50,000	1,85,000		
Increase in working				35,000
capital	35,000			
	1,85,000	1,85,000	78,000	78,000

Statement of Sources and Uses of Funds

Sources	Rs.	Uses	Rs.
Increase in		Purchase of land	10,000
capital stock		Increase in	
(share capital)	25,000	working capital	35,000
Funds from operation			
(increase in retained earnings)	15,000		
Sales of investments	5,000		
	45,000		45,000

Illustration 10: From the following balance sheets of Mr. Ramesh, prepare a funds flow statement.

	30 st June 2006	30 st June 2007
	Rs.	Rs.
Cash	5,000	2,300
Debtors	17,500	19,200
Stock	12,500	11,000
Land	10,000	15,000
Building	25,000	27,500
Machinery	40,000	43,000
	1,10,000	1,18,000
Creditors	18,000	20,500
Bank loan	15,000	19,500
Capital	77,000	78,000
	1,10,000	1,18,000

Drawings of Mr. Ramesh during the year was 20,000. Depreciation charges on machinery was Rs. 4,000.

Solution:

Schedule of Changes in Working Capital

Particulars	30th June	30th June	Increase	Decrease
	2006	2007		
Current Assets:				
Cash	5,000	2,300		2,700
Debtors	17,500	19,200	1,700	
Stock	1,2500	11,000		1,500
	35,000	32,500		
Less: Current Liabilities:				
Creditors	18,000	20,500		2500
Working capital	17,000	12,000	1,700	6,700
Decrease in				
Working capital		5,000	5,000	
	17,000	17,000	6,700	6,700

Funds Flow Statement

Sources	Rs.	Application	Rs.
Bank loan	4,500	Purchase of land	5,000
Funds from		Purchase of building	2,500
operation(3)	25,000	Purchase of	
Decrease in working		machinery (1)	7,000
Capital	5,000	Drawings	20,000
	34,500		34,500

Working

(1) Machinery Account

	Rs.		Rs.
By Balance b/d	40,000	By Adjusted P & L a/c	
		(depreciation)	4,000
To Cash (Purchase)?	7,000	By balance c/d	43,000
	47,000		47,000

Working

(2) Capital Account

	Rs.		Rs.
By Drawings	20,000	By Balance b/d	77,000
To balance c/d	78,000	By Adjusted P&L a/c	
		(net profit)	21,000
	98,000		98,000

(3) Adjusted Profit and Loss Account

	Rs.		Rs.
To machinery	4,000	By Funds from	
To Net Profit (2)	21,000	operation(?)	25,000
	25,000		25,000

Illustration 11: The following are the summarized balance sheets of XYZ Ltd., as on 31st December 2006 and 2007.

Balance Sheet

	31-Dec			31-Dec	
Liabilities	2006	2007	Asset	1988	2007
	Rs.	Rs		Rs.	Rs.
Capital			Fixed Assets	41,000	40,000
7% Redeemable			Less:		

Contd...

preference			Depreciation	11,000	15,000
shares	-	10,000		30,000	25,000
Equity shares	40,000	40,000			
	40,000	50,000	Current assets:		
General reserve	2,000	2,000	Debtors	20,000	24,000
Profit & Loss			Stock	30,000	35,000
Account	1,000	1,200	Prepaid expenses	300	500
Debentures	6,000	7,000	Cash	1,200	3,500
Current liabilities					
Creditors	12,000	11,000			
Provision for Tax	3,000	4,200			
Proposed dividend	5,000	5,800			
Bank overdraft	12,500	6,800			
	81,500	88,000		81,500	88,000

You are required to prepare

(i)   A statement showing changes in the working capital and

(ii) A statement of sources and application of funds

Solution:

Schedule of Changes in Working Capital

Particulars	2006	2007	Increase	Decrease
	Rs.	Rs.	Rs.	Rs.
Current Assets:				
Debtors	20,000	24,000	4,000	-
Stock	30,000	35,000	5,000	-
Prepaid expenses	300	500	200	-
cash	1,200	3,500	2,300	-
	51,500	63,000		
Less:				
Current Liabilities:				
Creditors	12,000	11,000	1,000	-
Provision for tax	3,000	4,200	-	1,200

Contd...

Proposed dividend	5,000	5,800	-	800
Bank overdraft	12,500	6,800	5,700	-
	32,500	27,800		
Working capital	19,000	35,200	18,200	2,000
Increase in working				
capital	16,200	-	-	16,200
	35,200	35,200	18,200	18,200

Statement of Sources and Application of Funds

Sources	Rs.	Application	Rs.
Issue of 7% Redeemable		Increase in	
preference shares	10,000	working capital	16,200
Funds from operation	4,200		
Issue of debentures	1,000		
Sale of fixed assets	1,000		
	16,200		16,200

Working

Fixed Assets Account

	Rs.		Rs.
To balance c/d	41,000	By Cash (sale) (?)	1,000
		By balance b/d	40,000
	41,000		41,000

Provision for Depreciation Account

	Rs.		Rs.
		By Balance b/d	11,000
		By Adjusted Profit	
		and loss account	
To balance c/d	15,000	(current year's Provision)	4,000
	15,000		15,000

Adjusted Profit & Loss Account

	Rs.		Rs.
To provision for	4,000	By Balance b/d	1,000
depreciation		By Funds from	
To balance c/d	1,200	Operations (?)	4,200
	5,200		5,200

Further more problem please refer CD.

SUMMARY

In a funds flow analysis, the details of financial resources availed and the ways in which such resources are used during a particular accounting period, are given in a statement from called 'Funds flow statement'. The sources of funds also include the funds generated from operations internally. The fund flow statement highlights the amounts raised from various sources of finance during a period and then explains how that finance has been used in the business. It analyses the net increase or decrease in working capital into changes in the constituent items i.e., stock, debtors, creditors, cash etc. It is an analysis of funds flow between two balance sheet dates. Along with funds flow statement, another statement is also prepared to analyse the impact of funds flow on working capital position. Such a statement is called 'Statement of changes in working capital position.' The funds flow statement list out the sources from which working capital has been derived during the accounting period and the ways in which working capital has been used up. The funds flow statement indicates the flow of working capital and the statement of changes in working capital position indicates the composition of working capital.

REVIEW QUESTIONS

Section A (2 to 3 Marks Questions)

1. What is Funds Flow Analysis?
2. What are the sources and applications of funds?
3. Draw a Proforma of Fund Flow Statement.
4. How does the Statement of Changes in Working Capital position help in Funds Flow Analysis?
5. Distinguish between 'Funds Flow Statement and Income Statement.'
6. Distinguish between 'Funds Flow Statement and Balance Sheet'.
7. What are the uses of Funds Flow Statement? What are its disadvantages?
8. "Income Statement concentrates on the operating part while Funds Flow Statement throws light on the activities and the direction of operations." Comment.
9. How do you treat provision for taxation while preparing a funds flow statement?
10. State the treatment of profit on sale of investment in a funds flow statement.

Section B (6 Marks questions - answer 30 lines each)

1. State and analyse the basic difference between funds flow and cash flow statements.

2. What is a funds flow statement? Examine its managerial uses.

3. How do you construct a funds flow statement?

4. Analyse some of the transactions that will either increase or decrease the amount of working capital.

5. What is fund from operations ? How do you calculate the same ?

6. Is depreciation a source of fund ? Analyse.

7. How do you treat provision for taxation while preparing a funds flow statement ?

8. State the treatment of profit on sale of investment in a funds flow statement.

Section C (15 Marks Questions)

1. Give an explanatory note on sources and application of funds.

2. "A Funds Flow Statement is a better substitute for an income statement". Elucidate.

3. What is the meaning of the term fund ? How do you treat the following items in the preparation of funds flow statement: (1) Proposed dividend and interim dividend.(2) Provision for taxation. (3) Provision against current assets?

4. From the following balance sheets and information of Little Bad Luck Ltd. for 2006 and 2007 draw out a funds flow statement and statement of changes in working capital for 2007.

Balance Sheets of Everest Ltd.		(Rs.)
Particulars	2006	2007
Liabilities:		
Equity share capital	2,00,000	3,00,000
8% Preference share capital (redeemable)	1,00,000	50,000
General reserve	20,000	30,000
Capital reserve	-	25,000
Profit and loss account	18,000	27,000
Proposed dividend	28,000	39,000
Sundry creditors	25,000	47,000
Bills payable	10,000	6,000
Liabilities for expenses	8,000	6,000
Provision for taxation	28,000	32,000
	4,37,000	5,62,000
Assets:		
Goodwill	50,000	40,000
Land and building	1,00,000	75,000
Plant	90,000	1,91,000
Trade investment	10,000	35,000
Sundry debtors	60,000	90,000
Stock	85,000	78,000
Bills receivable	15,000	18,000
Cash in hand	7,000	6,000
Cash at bank	10,000	22,000
Preliminary Expenses	10,000	7,000
	4,37,000	5,62,000

(a) In 2007, Rs. 18,000 depreciation has been written off from plant account and no depreciation has been charged on land and building.

(b) A piece of land has been sold out and the balance has been revalued. Profits on revaluation and sales being transferred a capital reserve. There is no other entry in Capital Reserve Account.

(c) A plant was sold for Rs. 12,000 (w.d.v. Rs. 15,000).

(d) Rs. 2,100 dividend has been received, but it includes Rs.600 pre-acquisition dividend.

(e) An interim dividend of Rs. 10,000 has been paid in 2005.

5. From the figures given below, prepare a statement showing the application and sources of funds during the year 2006-07.

Particulars	31st March, 2006	31st March, 2007
Assets		
Fixed assets (net)	5,10,000	6,20,000
Investments	30,000	80,000
Current assets	2,40,000	3,75,000
Discount on debentures	10,000	5,000
	7,90,000	10,80,000
Liabilities		
Share capital (equity)	3,00,000	3,50,000
Share capital (preference)	2,00,000	1,00,000
Debentures	1,00,000	2,00,000
Reserves	1,10,000	2,70,000
Provision for doubtful debts	10,000	15,000
Current liabilities	70,000	1,45,000
	7,90,000	10,80,000

You are informed that during the year.

1. A machine costing Rs. 70,000 (book value Rs. 40,000) was disposed of for Rs. 25,000.

2. Preference share redemption was carried out at a premium of 5%.

3. Dividend at 15% was paid on equity shares for the year 2006.

Future:

(a) The provision for depreciation stood at Rs. 1,50,000 on 31-03-2006 and at Rs. 1,90,000 on 31-03-2007.

(b) Stock which was valued at. Rs. 90,000 as on 31-03-2006 was written up to its cost Rs. 1,00,000 for preparing the Profit and Loss account for 2007.

6. The following Balance Sheets of Dummy Products Ltd. for the years 2006 and 2007 are available:

Particulars	2006	2007
Liabilities		
Share capital	6,00,000	7,00,000
General reserve	2,00,000	2,50,000
Capital reserve (Profit on sale of investments)	-	10,000
Profit and loss account	1,00,000	2,00,000
7% debentures	3,00,000	2,00,000

Contd...

Creditors for expenses	10,000	12,000
Creditors for supply of goods	1,60,000	2,50,000
Proposed dividend	30,000	35,000
Provision for taxation	70,000	75,000
	14,70,000	17,32,000
Assets		
Fixed assets	10,00,000	12,00,000
Less: Accumulated depreciation	2,00,000	2,50,000
	8,00,000	9,50,000
Investments (at cost)	1,80,000	1,80,000
Stock (at cost)	2,00,000	2,70,000
Sundry debtors (less provision for Rs. 20,000 and Rs. 25,000 respectively)	2,25,000	2,45,000
Bills receivable	40,000	65,000
Pre-payment of expenses	10,000	12,000
Misc. expenditure	15,000	10,000
	14,70,000	17,32,000

Other Information:

(a) During the year 2007, fixed assets (WDV Rs. 10,000, depreciation written off Rs. 30,000) were sold for Rs. 8,000.

(b) The proposed dividend of the last year was paid in 2007.

(c) During the year 2007, investments costing Rs. 80,000 were sold and later in the year investments of the same cost were purchased.

(d) Debentures were redeemed at a premium of 10% in 2007.

(e) Liability for taxation for 2006 came to Rs. 55,000.

(f) During the year 2007 bad debts written off were Rs. 15,000 against the provision account.

Prepare a fund flow statement.

7. From the following balance sheets of XYZ Co. Ltd. prepare funds flow statement:

					(Rs. '000)
Liabilities	2006	2007	Assets	2006	2007
Equity share capital	600	800	Goodwill	230	180
Preference capital	300	200	Land and buildings	400	340
General reserve	80	140	Plant and machinery	160	400
Profit and loss account	60	96	Debtors	320	400
Proposed dividend	84	10	Stock	154	218
Creditors	110	166	Bills receivable	40	60
Bills payable	40	62	Cash	30	20
Tax provision	80	100	Bank	20	16
	1,354	1,634		1,354	1,634

Additional Information:

(a) Proposed dividend made during 2006 has been paid during 2007.

(b) Depreciation - (i) Rs. 20,000 on plant and machinery, and (ii) Rs. 40,000 on land and buildings.

(c) Interim dividend has been paid Rs. 40,000 in 2007.

(d) Income-tax Rs. 70,000 has been paid during 2007.

Financial Statements, Cash Flow Statements

4

INTRODUCTION

Cash plays an important role in the economic life of a business. A firm receives cash from sales, debtors and other sources like sale of assets, investments etc. It needs cash to make payments to its, suppliers, to incur day-to-day expenses and to pay salaries, wage, rent, interest, dividends etc. Thus, in a firm, there is constant inflow and outflow of cash. What blood is to human body, cash is to business. Therefore, a major responsibility of financial management is to plan cash and maintain adequate cash balance. Cash flow statement is an important tool of cash planning and control. At the same time, it serves as a valuable tool of financial analysis too.

A statement of cash flows reports the inflows (receipts) and outflows (payments) of cash and its equivalents of an organisation during a particular period. It provides important information that compliments the profit and loss account and balance sheet. A statement of cash flow reports cash receipts and payments classified according to the entities' major activities—operating, investing and financing during the period. This statement reports a net cash inflow or net cash outflow for each activity and for the overall business.

It also reports from where cash has come and how it has been spent. It explains the causes for the changes in the cash balance. In substance, the cash flow statement for a business entity is analogous in that it summarises a myriad of specific cash transactions into a few categories. The statement of cash flows reports the cash receipts, cash payments, and net changes in cash resulting from operating, investing and financing activities of an enterprise during a period in a format that reconciles the beginning and ending cash balances.

According to the author, cash flow statement can be defined as: "a statement prepared from the historical data (i.e. income statement and balance sheet) showing sources and uses of cash is called cash flow statement". It reveals the inflow and outflow of cash during the particular period. Cash flow statement can be prepaid for a year, half year, and quarter or for any other duration. The term cash is used to refer bank balance, too.

OBJECTIVES OF CASH FLOW STATEMENT

The objectives of cash flow analysis are:

1. To show the causes of changes in cash balance between two balance sheet dates.
2. To indicate the factors contributing to the reduction of cash balance in spite of increase in profits and vice versa.

Advantages or Significance and uses of Cash Flow Statement

Cash flow statement is of vital significance to the financial management. Its chief advantages are:

1. The cash flow statement explains the reasons for low cash balance in spite of huge profits or large cash balance in spite of low profits.
2. It helps in internal financial management. The cash flow analysis helps in exploring the possibility of repayment of long-term debts, which depends upon the availability of cash.
3. It helps in short-term financial decisions relating to liquidity.
4. It shows the major sources and uses of cash. The management with the aid of projected cash flow statement can know, how much cash will be needed, from which sources it can be obtained, how much can be generated internally, how much could be obtained from outside.
5. It helps the management in planning the repayment of loans, replacement of assets, credit arrangements etc. It is also significant for capital budgeting decisions.

6. It helps in efficient cash management. One of the most important functions of the management is to manage the company's cash resources in such a way that adequate cash is available to meet the liabilities. A projected cash flow statement enables the management to plan and co-ordinate the financial operations of the business efficiently.

7. Cash flow statement supplemental to funds flow statement. Cash flow analysis supplements the analysis provided by funds flow statement, as cash is a part of the working capital.

8. It is better tool of analysis. For payment of liabilities that are likely to be matured in the near future, cash is more important than the working capital. As such, cash flow statement is certainly a better tool of analysis than funds flow statement for short-term analysis.

9. On the basis of past years' cash flow statements, projections can be made for the future. The projected cash flow statement helps in planning for the investment of surplus or meeting the deficit

10. Cash flow statement helps to determine the likely cash flow. Projected cash flow statements help the management to determine the likely inflow or outflow of cash from operations and the amount of cash required to be raised from other sources to meet the future needs of the business.

11. A comparison of actual cash flow statement with the projected cash flow statement helps in understanding the variations and control of cash expenditure.

12. It evaluates management decisions. The statement of cash flows reports the companies' investing and financing activities and thus gives the investors and creditors information about cash flow for evaluating managers' decisions.

Limitations of Cash Flow Statement

The cash flow analysis is criticized for the following reasons:

1. *Influenced by changes in management policies:* The cash balance as disclosed by the cash flow statement may not represent the real liquid position of the business. The cash can be easily influenced by purchases and sales policies, by making certain advance payments or by postponing certain payments.

2. *Misleading inter-firm comparison:* The terms of purchases and sales will differ from firm to firm. Cash inflow does not always mean profit. Therefore, inter-firm comparison of cash flows may also be misleading.

3. *Cannot be equated with income statement:* Cash flow statement cannot be equated with the income statement. An income statement takes into account both cash as well as non-cash items. Hence, net cash flow does not necessarily mean net income of the business.

4. *Misleading comparison over a period of time:* Just because the company's cash flow has increased in the current year, a company may not be better off than the previous year. Thus, the comparison over a period of time can be misleading.

5. *Not a replacement of other statements:* Cash flow statement is only a supplement of funds flow statement and cannot replace the income statement or the funds flow statement as each one has its own function or purpose of preparation.

6. *Misleading inter-industry comparison:* Cash flow statement does not measure the economic efficiency of one company in relation to another. Usually, a company with heavy capital investment will have more cash inflow. Therefore, inter-industry comparison of cash flow statement may be misleading.

DIFFERENCE BETWEEN FUNDS FLOW STATEMENT AND CASH FLOW STATEMENT

The difference between these two statements is given below:

Funds Flow Statement	Cash Flow Statement
1. It is based on accrual accounting system.	1. While preparation of this statement, all transactions effecting the cash and cash equivalents are taken into consideration.
2. It is a broader concept, it takes into account both long-term funds and short-term funds into account in analysis.	2. It only deals with one of the current assets on assets side of balance sheet.
3. A sound fund position does not necessarily mean a sound cash position.	3. A sound cash position is always followed by a sound fund position.
4. It analyses the sources and application of funds of long-term nature and net increase or decrease in long-term funds will be reflected on the working capital of the firm.	4. It considers only the increase or decrease in current assets and current liabilities in calculating the cash flow from operations.
5. It shows the funds generated and applied as regards long-term assets long-term liabilities and capital.	5. It shows the cash flow from operating, financing and investment activities.
6. The changes in current items are adjusted in the statement of changes in working capital.	6. In this statement, cash from operations are calculated after adjusting the increase or decrease in current assets and current liabilities to operating profit before working capital changes.
7. It tallies the funds generated from various sources with various uses to which they are put.	7. It starts with the opening balance of cash and reach to the closing balance of cash by proceeding through sources and uses.
8. It is more useful in long-range planning.	8. It is more useful for identifying and correcting the current liquidity problems of the firm.

AS-3 REVISED CASH FLOW STATEMENTS

♦ Cash flow statement provides information about the cash receipts and payments of an enterprise's for a given period. It provides important information that supplements the profit and loss account and balance sheet.

♦ The statement of cash flows has to be reported by Accounting Standard-3 (revised) issued by the Institute of Chartered Accountants of India in March 1997, which replaces the 'Changes in Financial Position' as per AS-3.

♦ There are certain changes in the preparation of cash flow statement from the previous methods as a result of the introduction of AS-3 (revised).

♦ AS-3 (revised) is mandatory in nature in respect of accounting periods commencing on or after 1-4-2001 for the following.

(i) Enterprises whose equity or debt securities are listed on a recognised stock exchange in India, and enterprises that are in the process of issuing equity or debt securities that will be listed on a recognised stock exchange in India as evidenced by the board of directors' resolution in this regard.

(ii) All other commercial, industrial and business reporting enterprises whose turnover for the accounting period exceeds Rs.50 crores.

CLASSIFICATION OF CASH FLOWS

The cash flow statement during a period is classified into three main categories of cash inflows and cash outflows i.e.

1. Cash flows from operating activities.
2. Cash flows from investing activities, and
3. Cash flows from financing activities.

Cash Flows from Operating Activities

Operating activities are the principal revenue-producing activities of the enterprise and other activities that are not investing and financing activities. Operating activities include cash effects of those transactions and events that enter into the determination of net profit or loss.

A business's normal operations result in both cash receipts and cash payments. Cash receipts result from selling goods and providing services. The cost of goods sold and other operative expenses result in cash disbursements.

Following are examples of cash flows from operating activities:

(a) Cash receipts from the sale of goods and the rendering of services.
(b) Cash receipts from royalties, fees, commissions, and other revenues.
(c) Cash payments to suppliers for goods and services.
(d) Cash payments to and on behalf of employees.
(e) Cash receipts and payments of an insurance enterprise for premiums and claims, annuities and other policy benefits.
(f) Cash payments or refunds of income taxes unless they can be specifically identified with financing and investing activities; and
(g) Cash receipts and payments relating to future contracts, forward contracts, option contracts, and swap contracts when the contracts are held for dealing or trading purposes.

Cash Flows from Financing Activities

Financing activities are activities that result in changes in the size and composition of the owners' capital (including preference share capital in the case of a company) and borrowings of the enterprise. Following are the examples of cash flows arising from financing activities:

(a) Cash proceeds from issuing shares or other similar instruments.
(b) Cash proceeds from issuing debentures, loans notes, bonds and other short-term borrowing.
(c) Cash repayments of amounts borrowed i.e. redemption of debentures, bonds etc.
(d) Cash payments to redeem preference shares.
(e) Payment of dividend.

Cash Flows from Investing Activities

Investing activities are the acquisition and disposal of long-term assets and other investments not included in cash equivalents. In other words, investing activities include transactions and events that involve the purchase and sale of long-term productive assets (e.g. land, building, plant and machinery etc.) not held for resale and other investments.

The following are the examples of cash flows arising from investing activities:

(a) Cash payments to acquire fixed assets (including intangibles). These payments include those relating to capitalised research and development costs and self-constructed fixed assets.

(b) Cash receipts from disposal of fixed assets (including intangibles).

(c) Cash payments to acquire 'shares, warrants, or debt instruments of other enterprises and interests in joint ventures (other than payments for those instruments considered to be cash equivalents and those held for dealing or trading purposes).

(d) Cash receipts from disposal of shares, warrants, or debt instruments of other enterprises and interests in joint ventures (other than receipts from those instruments considered to be cash equivalents and those held for dealing or trading purposes).

(e) Cash advances and loans made to third parties (other than advances and loans made by a financial enterprise); cash receipts from the repayment of advances and loans made to third parties (other than advances and loans of a financial enterprise).

(f) Cash receipts and payments relating to future contracts, forward contracts, option contracts, and swap contracts except when the contracts are held for dealing or trading purposes, or the transactions are classified as financing activities.

Special Items

In addition to the general classification of three types of cash flows, Accounting Standard-3 (revised) provides for the treatment of the cash flows of certain special items as under:

Foreign Currency Cash Flows

Cash flows arising from transactions in a foreign currency should be recorded in an enterprise's reporting currency by applying to the foreign currency amount the exchange rate between the reporting currency and foreign currency at the date of the cash flow. A rate that approximates the actual rate may be used if the result is substantially the same as would arise if the rates at the date of cash flows were used. Unrealised gains and losses arising from changes in foreign exchange rates are not cash flows. However, the effect of exchange rate changes on cash and cash equivalents held or due in foreign currency is reported in the cash flow statement in order to reconcile cash and cash equivalents at the beginning and the end of the period. This amount is presented separately from cash flows from operating, investing and financing activities and includes the differences, if any, had those cash flows been reported at the end of period exchange rates.

Extraordinary Items

Any cash flows relating to extraordinary items should as far as possible be classified into operating, investing or financing activities and those items should be separately disclosed in the cash flow statement. Some of the examples for extraordinary items are bad debts recovered, claims from insurance companies, winning of a lawsuit or lottery etc. The above disclosure is in addition to disclosure mentioned in AS-5, "Net profit or Loss for the Period Prior Period Items and Changes in Accounting Policies."

Interest and Dividends

Cash flows from interest and dividends received and paid should each be disclosed separately. The treatment of interest and dividends, received and paid, depends upon the nature of the enterprise i.e., financial enterprises and other enterprises.

In case of financial enterprises, cash flows arising from interest paid and interest and dividends received, should be classified as cash flows from operating activities.

In case of other enterprises: (a) Cash outflows arising from interest paid on term loans and debentures should be classified as cash outflow from financing activities. (b) Cash outflows arising from interest paid on working capital loan should be classified as cash outflow from operating activities. (c) Interest and dividends received should be classified as cash inflow from investing activities. (d) Dividend paid on equity and preference share capital should be classified as cash outflow from financing activities.

Taxes on Income

Cash flows arising from taxes on income should be separately disclosed. They should be classified as cash flows from operating activities unless they can be specifically identified with financing and investing activities. When tax cash flows are allocated over more than one class of activity, the total amount of taxes paid is disclosed.

Acquisition and Disposals of Subsidiaries and other Business Units

The aggregate cash flows arising from acquisitions and from disposals of subsidiaries or other business units should be presented separately and classified as investing activities.

Non-cash Transactions

Investing and financing transactions that do not require the use of cash or cash equivalents should be excluded from a cash flow statement. Such transactions should be disclosed elsewhere in the financial statements in a way that provides all the relevant information about these investing and financing activities. The exclusion of non-cash transactions from the cash flow statement is consistent with the objective of a cash flow statement, as these do not involve cash flows in the current period. Following are examples of non-cash transactions:

(i) The acquisition of assets by assuming directly related liabilities.

(ii) The acquisition of an enterprise by means of issue of shares.

(iii) Conversion of debt into equity.

PREPARATION OF A CASH FLOW STATEMENT

The following basic information is required for the preparation of a cash flow statement:

(i) *Comparative Balance Sheets:* Balance sheets at the beginning and at the end of the accounting period indicate the amount of changes that have taken place in assets, liabilities and capital.

(ii) *Profit and Loss Account:* The profit and loss account of the current period enables to determine the amount of cash provided by or used in operations during the accounting period after making adjustments for non-cash, current assets and current liabilities.

(iii) *Additional data:* In addition to the above statements, additional data are collected to determine how cash has been provided or used e.g. sale or purchase of assets for cash.

The following procedure may be used for the preparation of a cash flow statement:

(i) Calculation of net increase (decrease) in cash and cash equivalents accounts. The difference between cash and cash equivalents for the period may be computed by comparing these accounts given in the comparative balance sheets. The results will be cash receipts and payments during the period responsible for the increase or decrease in cash and cash equivalent items.

(ii) Calculation of the net cash provided (used) by operating activities. It is accomplished by the analysis of profit and loss account, comparative balance sheet and selected additional information.

(iii) Calculation of the net cash provided (used) by investing and financing activities. All other changes in the balance sheet item must be analysed taking into account the additional information; the effect on cash may be grouped under the investing and financing activities.

(iv) Preparation of a cash flow statement. It may be prepared by classifying all cash inflows and outflows in terms of operating, investing and financing activities. The net cash flow provided by (used) in each of the three activities may be highlighted.

(v) Ensure that the aggregate of net cash flows from operating, investing and financing activities is equal to net increase (decrease) in cash and cash equivalents.

(vi) Report any significant investing/financing transactions that did not involve cash or cash equivalents in a separate schedule to the cash flow statement.

REPORTING OF CASH FLOWS FROM OPERATING ACTIVITIES

The purpose for determining the net cash flow from operating activities is to understand why net profit/loss as reported in the profit and loss account must be converted. The financial statements are generally prepared on accrual basis of accounting, under which the net income will not indicate the net cash provided by or net loss will not indicate the net cash used in operating activities. In order to calculate the net cash flows in operating activities, it is necessary to replace revenues and expenses with actual receipts and payments in cash. This is done by eliminating the non-cash revenues and/non-cash expenses from given earned revenues and incurred expenses. There are two methods of converting net profit into net cash flows from operating activities:

(i) Direct method, and

(ii) Indirect method.

Direct Method

Under the direct method, cash receipts from operating revenues and cash payments for operating expenses are arranged and presented in the cash flow statement. The difference between cash receipts and cash payments is the net cash flow from operating activities. It is in effect, a cash basis profit and loss account. In this case each cash transaction is analysed separately and the total cash receipts and payments for the period are determined. The summarised data for revenue and expenses can be obtained from the financial statements and additional information. We may convert accrual basis of revenue and expenses to equivalent cash receipts and payments. Make sure that a uniform procedure is adopted for converting accrual base items to cash base items.

The following are some examples of usual cash receipts and cash payments resulting from operating activities:

(i) cash sales of goods and services;

(ii) cash collected from debtors (customers);

(iii) cash receipts of interest or dividends;

(iv) cash receipts of royalties, fees, commission and other revenues;

(v) cash payments to suppliers (creditors);

(vi) cash payments for various operating expenses i.e. rent, rates, power etc.

(vii) cash payments for wages and salaries to employees;

(viii) cash payments for income tax etc.

Indirect Method

In this method, the net profit (loss) is used as the base and convert it to net cash provided by (used in) operating activities. The indirect method adjusts net profit for items that affected net profit but did not affect cash. Non-cash and non-operating charges in the profit and loss account are added back to the net profit while non-cash and non-operating credits are deducted to calculate operating profit before working capital changes. It is a partial conversion of accrual basis profit to cash basis profit. Necessary adjustments are made for increase/decrease in current assets and current liabilities to obtain net cash from operating activities.

FORMAT OF CASH FLOW STATEMENT

Cash Flow Statement (Direct Method)

Cash Flow Statement (Direct Method) (Rs.)		
Cash flows from operating activities		
Cash receipts from customers		(xxx)
Cash paid to suppliers and employees		xxx
Cash generated from operations		(xxx)
Income-tax paid		xxx
Cash flow before extraordinary items		xxx
Proceeds from earthquake disaster settlement etc.		xxx
Net cash flow from operating activities	(a)	**xxx**
Cash flows from investing activities		
Purchase of fixed assets		(xxx)
Proceeds from sale of equipment		xxx
Interest received		xxx
Dividend received		xxx
Net cash flow from investing activities		**xxx**
Cash flows from financing activities		
Proceeds from issuance of share capital		xxx
Proceeds from long-term borrowings		xxx
Repayments of long-term borrowings		(xxx)
Interest paid		(xxx)
Dividend paid		(xxx)

Contd...

Net cash flow from financing activities	(b)	xxx
Net increase (decrease) in cash and cash equivalents during the period	(a+b+c)	xxx
Cash and cash equivalents at beginning of period		xxx
Cash and cash equivalents at end of period		xxx

Cash Flow Statement (Indirect Method) (Accounting Standard-3 (revised) (Rs.)		
Cash flow from operating activities		
Net profit before tax and extraordinary items		xxx
Adjustments for:		
-Depreciation		xxx
-Foreign exchange		xxx
-Investments		xxx
-Gain or loss on sale of fixed assets		(xxx)
-Interest/dividend		xxx
Operating profit before working capital changes		xxx
Adjustment for:		
-Trade and other receivables		xxx
-Inventories		(xxx)
-Trade payables		xxx
Cash generated from operations		xxx
-Interest paid		(xxx)
-Direct taxes		(xxx)
Cash before extraordinary Items		xxx
Deferred revenue		xxx
Net cash flow from operating activities	(a)	xxx
Cash flow from investing activities		
Purchase of fixed assets		(xxx)
Sale of fixed assets		xxx
Sale of investments		xxx
Purchase of investments		(xxx)

Contd...

Interest received		xxx
Dividend received		xxx
Loans to subsidiaries		xxx
Net cash flow from investing activities	(b)	**xxx**
Cash flow from financing activities		
Proceeds from issue of share capital		xxx
Proceeds from long-term borrowings		xxx
Repayment to finance/lease liabilities		(xxx)
Dividend paid		(xxx)
Net cash flow from financing activities	(c)	**xxx**
Net increase (decrease) in cash and cash equivalents during the period	**(a+b+c)**	**xxx**
Cash and cash equivalents at the beginning of the year		xxx
Cash and cash equivalents at the end of the year		xxx

Ascertainment of Cash from Operations (CFO)			
Funds from operations (FFO)	**(As learnt in funds flow analysis)**		xxx
Add: Increase in current liabilities	(Excluding back overdraft)	xxx	
Decrease in current assets	(Excluding cash and bank balance)	xxx	xxx
			xxx
Less: Increase in current assets	(Excluding cash and bank balance)	xxx	
Decrease in current liabilities	(Excluding bank overdraft)	xxx	xxx
Cash from operations			xxx

Illustration 1: From the information as contained in the income statement and the balance sheet of SLV Ltd., you are required to prepare a cash flow statement using (i) Direct Method and (ii) Indirect Method.

(A) Income Statement and Reconciliation of Earnings for the year ended 31.3.2007

		Rs.
Net Sales		25,20,000
Less: Cost of sales	19,80,000	
Depreciation	60,000	
Salaries and wages	2,40,000	
Operating expenses	80,000	

Contd...

Provision for taxation	88.000	24.48,000
Net operating profit		72,000
Non-recurring income:		
Profit on sale of equipment		12,000
		84,000
Retained earnings (balance in profit and loss account brought forward)		1,51,800
		2,35,800
Dividend declared and paid during the year		72,000
Profit and loss account balance as on 31.3.2007		1,63,800

(B) Comparative Balance Sheets

	As on	As on
	31.3.2006	31.3.2007
	Rs.	Rs.
Fixed assets		
Land	48,000	96,000
Buildir g and equipments	3,60,000	5,76,000
Current assets		
Cash	60,000	72,000
Debtors	1,68,000	1,86,000
Stock	2,64,000	96,000
Advances	7,800	9,000
	9.07,800	10,35,000
Capital	3,60,000	4,44,000
Surplus in profit and loss A/c	1,51,800	1,63,800
Sundry creditors	2,40,000	2,34,000
Outstanding expenses	24,000	48,000
Income tax payable	12,000	13,200
Accumulated depreciation on building and equipments	1,20,000	1,32,000
	9,07,800	10,35,000

Cost of equipment sold was Rs. 72,000.

Solution:

Direct Method

SLV Limited
Cash Flow Statement for the year ended 31.3.2007

	Rs.	Rs.
Cash flows from operating activities:		
Cash receipts from customers	25,02,000	
Cash paid to suppliers and employees	21,15,200	
Cash generated from operations	3,86,800	
Income tax paid	(86,800)	
Net cash from operating activities		3,00,000
Cash flows from investing activities:		
Purchase of land	(48,000)	
Purchase of building and equipment	(2,88,000)	
Sale of equipment	36,000	
Net cash used in investing activities		(3,00,000)
Cash flows from financing activities:		
Issue of share capital	84,000	
Dividend paid	(72,000)	
Net cash from financing activities		12,000
Net increase in cash and cash equivalents		12,000
Cash and cash equivalents at the beginning		60,000
Cash and cash equivalents at the end		72,000

Working Notes:

(i) Cash receipts from customers:		
Sales revenue		25,20,000
Add: Debtors at the beginning		1,68,000
		26,88,000
Less: Debtors at the end		1,86,000
		25,02,000
(ii) Cash paid to suppliers and employees:		

Contd...

Cost of goods sold		19,80,000
Add: Operating expenses		80,000
Salaries and wages		2,40,000
		23,00,000
Add: Creditors at the beginning	2,40,000	
Stock at the end	96,000	
Advances at the end	9,000	
Outstanding expenses at the beginning	24,000	3,69,000
		26,69,000
Less: Creditors at the end	2,34,000	
Stock at the beginning	2,64,000	
Advances at the beginning	7,800	
Outstanding expenses at the end	48,000	5,53,800
		21,15,200
(Hi) Income tax paid		
Tax payable at the beginning		12,000
Add: Provision for taxation		88,000
		1,00,000
Less: Tax payable at the end		13,200
Tax paid during the year		86,800
(iv) Accumulated depreciation written off on equipments (sold)		
Accumulated depreciation at the beginning		1,20,000
Add: Depreciation for the year		60,000
		1,80,000
Less: Accumulated depreciation at the end		1,32,000
		48,000
(v) Sale price of equipment		
Cost price		72,000
Less: Accumulated depreciation		48,000
		24,000
Add: Profit on sale		12,000
		36,000

Contd...

(vi) Purchase of building and equipments		
Balance at the beginning		3,60,000
Less: Cost of equipment sold		72,000
Balance		2,88,000
Balance at the end		5,76,000
Purchased during the year		2,88,000

Indirect Method

SLV Limited
Cash Flow Statement for the year ended 31.3.2007

	Dr.	Cr.
	Rs.	Rs.
Cash flows from operating activities:		
Net profit before taxation and extra-ordinary item	1,60,000	
Adjustments for:		
Depreciation	60,000	
Operating profit before working capital changes	2,20,000	
Increase in debtors	(18,000)	
Decrease in stock	1,68,000	
Increase in advances	(1,200)	
Decrease in creditors	(6,000)	
Increase in outstanding expenses	24,000	
Cash generated from operation	3,86,800	
Income tax paid	(86,800)	
Net cash from operating activities		3,00,000
Cash flows from investing activities:		
Purchase of land	(48,000)	
Purchase of building and equipments	(2,88,000)	
Sale of equipment	36,000	
Net cash used in investing activities		(3,00,000)
Cash flows from financing activities:		
Issue of share capital	84,000	
Dividend paid	(72,000)	

Contd...

Net cash from financing activities		12,000
Net increase in cash and cash equivalents		12,000
Cash and cash equivalents at the beginning		60,000
Cash and cash equivalents at the end		72,000

Illustration 2: From the following information as contained in the income statement and the balance sheet of RKV Ltd., you are required to prepare a cash flow statement using (i) direct method, and (ii) indirect method:

Income Statement and Reconciliation of Earnings for the year ended 31st March, 2007.

		(Rs.)
Net sales		40,32,000
Less: Cost of sales	31,68,000	
Depreciation	96,000	
Salaries and wages	3,84,000	
Operating expenses	1,28,000	
Provision for taxation	1,40,8000	39,16,800
Net operating profit		**1,15,200**
Non-recurring income:		
Profit on sale of equipment		19,200
Profit for the **year**		**1,34,400**
Retained earnings (balance in Profit & Loss Account b/f)		2,42,880
		3,77,280
Dividend declared and paid during the year		1,15,200
Profit & Loss Account balance as on 31st March, 2007		**2,62,080**

Comparative Balance Sheets (Rs.)		
Particulars	As on 31-3-2006	As on 31-3-2007
Fixed Assets:		
Land	76,800	1,53,600
Building and equipments	5,76,000	9,21,600
Current Assets:		
Cash	96,000	1,15,200
Debtors	2,68,800	2,97,600

Contd...

Stock	4,22,400	1,53,600
Advances	12,480	14,400
	14,52,480	**16,56,000**
Capital	5,76,000	7,10,400
Surplus in Profit & Loss A/c	2,42,880	2,62,080
Sundry creditors	3,84,000	3,74,400
Outstanding expenses	38,400	76,800
Income-tax payable	19,200	21,120
Accumulated depreciation on building and equipments	1,92,000	2,11,200
	14,52,480	**16,56,000**

Cost of equipment sold was Rs. 1,15,200

Solution:

Statement showing cash receipts from customers

	(Rs.)
Sales	40,32,000
Add: Debtors at the beginning	2,68,800
	43,00,800
Less: Debtors at the end	2,97,600
Cash receipts from customers	**40,03,200**

Statement showing cash payments to suppliers and employees

		(Rs.)
Cost of goods sold		31,68,000
Add: Operating expenses		1,28,000
Salaries and wages		3,84,000
		36,80,000
Add: Creditors at the beginning	3,84,000	
Outstanding expenses at the beginning	38,400	
Stocking at the end	1,53,600	
Advances at the end	14,400	5,90,400
		42,70,400
Less: Creditors at the end	3,74,400	

Contd...

Outstanding expenses at the end	76,800	
Stock at the beginning	4,22,400	
Advances at the beginning	12,480	8,86,080
Cash paid to supplies and employees		33,84,320

Income-tax Payable A/c			
	Rs.		Rs.
To Income-tax A/c (tax paid) by figure	1,38,880	By Balance b/d	19,200
To Balance c/d	21,120	By Profit & Loss A/c	1,40,800
	1,60,000		1,60,000

Accumulated Depreciation A/c			
To Buildings and Equipment A/c (Dep. On equipment sold)	76,800	By Balance b/d	1,92,000
To Balance c.d	2,11,200	By Profit and Loss A/c (provision during the year)	96,000
	2,88,000		2,88,000

Building and Equipment A/c			
To Balance b/d	5,76,000	By Accumulated Depreciation A/c (Dep. on equipment sold)	76,800
To Bank A/c (purchase of equip.)	4,60,000	By Bank A/c (sales of equipment)	57,600
To Profit & Loss (A/c) (profit on sale of equipment)	19,200	By Balance c/d	9,21,600
	10,56,000		10,56,000

1. Cash flow Statement of M/s RKV Ltd., for the year ended 31-3-2007 (Direct method) (Rs.)

	(Rs.)
Cash flows from operating activities:	
Cash receipts from customers	40,03,200
Cash paid to suppliers and employees	(33,84,320)
Cash generated from operations	6,18,880
Income-tax paid	(1,38,880)
Net cash inflow from operating activities (a)	4,80,000
Cash flows from investing activities:	
Purchase of land	(76,880)

Contd...

Purchase of building and equipment	(4,60,800)
Sale of equipment	57,600
Net cash outflow in investing activities (b)	(4,80,000)
Cash flows from financing activities:	
Issue of share capital	1,34,400
Dividend paid	(1,15,200)
Net cash inflow form financing activities (c)	**19,200**
Net increase in cash and cash equivalents during the period (a-b+c)	19,200
Cash and cash equivalents at the beginning	96,000
Cash and cash equivalents at the end	**1,15,200**

2.   Cash flow statement of M/s Strong Ltd. for the year ended 31-3-2007 (indirect method) (Rs.)

	(Rs.)
Cash flows from operating activities:	
Net profit before taxation and extraordinary items	2,56,000
Adjustment for:	
Depreciation	96,000
Operating profit before working capital changes	**3,52,000**
Increase in debtors	(28,800)
Decrease in stock	2,68,800
Increase in advances	(1,920)
Decrease in creditors	(9,600)
Increase in outstanding expenses	38,400
Cash generated from operations	**6,18,880**
Income-tax paid	(1,38,880)
Net cash inflow from operating activities (a)	**4,80,000**
Cash flows from investing activities:	
Purchase of land	(76,800)
Purchase of building and equipment	(4,60,800)
Sale of equipment	57,600
Net cash outflow in investing activities (b)	**(4,80,000)**
Cash flows from financing activities:	
Issue of share capital	1,34,400

Contd...

Dividend paid	(1,15,200)
Net cash inflow from financing activities (c)	**19,200**
Net increase in cash and cash equivalents during the period (a-b+c)	19,200
Cash and cash equivalents at the beginning	96,000
Cash and cash equivalents at the end	**1,15,200**

Illustration 3: From the following balance sheets of Sudhir Ltd., for the year ended 31st March, 2006 and 2007, prepare a cash flow statement.

		31.3.2006		31.3.2007
		Rs.		Rs.
Assets				
Property		2,00,000		2,50,000
Plant and machinery	4,00,000		4,50,000	
Less: Depreciation	1.40.000	2,60,000	1.50.000	3,00,000
Loans to subsidiary Co.		—		15,000
Share in subsidiary Co.		20,000		20,000
Stock in trade		1,40,000		1,50,000
Debtors		1,00,000		1,50,000
Bank		35.000		1.57.000
		7.55.000		10.42,000
Liabilities				
Equity Share of Rs.20 each		3,00,000		4,00,000
Share premium		—		10,000
Profit & Loss appropriation A/c		1,00,000		1,00,000
Profit for the year		—		2,00,000
6% Debentures		1,50,000		1,00,000
Profit on redemption of debentures		—		2,000
Sundry creditors		1,40,000		1,10,000
Provision for taxation		50,000		1,00,000
Proposed dividend		15,000		20,000
		7.55.000		10,42,000

Additional information:

During the year, plant costing Rs.50,000 was sold for Rs.10,000. Accumulated depreciation on this plant was Rs.30,000. Loss on sale of plant was charged to profit and loss account. Income tax paid during the year was Rs. 60,000.

Solution:

Sudhir Limited
Cash Flow Statement for the year ended 31.3.2007
Cash Flows from Operating Activities

	Rs.
Net profit before tax and extraordinary items	2,00,000
Adjustments for:	
Depreciation	40,000
Provision for taxation	1,10,000
Proposed dividend	20,000
Loss on sale of machinery	10,000
Operating profit before working capital changes	3,80,000
Adjustments for:	
Increase in debtors	(50,000)
Increase in stock-in-trade	(10,000)
Decrease in creditors	(30,000)
Cash generated from operations	2,90,000
Tax paid	(60,000)
Net cash from operating activities	2.30,000
Cash flows from investing activities	
Purchase of property	(50,000)
Sale of plant	10,000
Purchase of machinery	(1,00,000)
Loans to subsidiaries	(15,000)
Net cash used in investing activities	(1,55,000)
Cash flows from financing activities	
Issue of equity share capital at premium	1,10,000
Redemption of debentures	(48,000)
Dividends paid	115,000)
Net cash from financing activities	47,000
Net increase in cash and cash equivalents	
(Rs.2,30,000 – Rs.1,55,000 + Rs.47,000)	1,22,000
Cash and cash equivalents at the beginning of the year	35,000
Cash and cash equivalents at the end of the year	1,57,000

Working Notes:

Property Account

Dr.			Cr.
	Rs.		Rs.
To Balance b/d	2,00,000	By Balance c/d	2,50,000
To Bank (purchases)			
(balancing figure)	50,000		
	2,50,000		2,50,000

Plant and Machinery Account

	Rs.		Rs.
To Balance b/d	4,00,000	By Bank (plant sold)	10,000
To Bank (purchases)	1,00,000	By Accumulated depreciation	30,000
(balancing figure)		(on plant sold)	
		By Loss on plant sold	10,000
		By Balance c/d	4,50,000
	5,00,000		5,00,000

Accumulated Depreciation Account

	Rs.		Rs.
To Plant and machinery A/c	30,000	By Balance b/d	1,40,000
(on plant sold)		By Dep. for the year	40,000
To Balance c/d	1,50,000	(balancing figure)	
	1,80,000		1,80,000

Loans to Subsidiary Account

	Rs.		Rs.
To Bank (balancing figure)	15,000	By Balance c/d (closing)	15,000
	15,000		15,000

Equity Share Capital Account

	Rs.		Rs.
To Balance c/d	4,00,000	By Balance b/d	3,00,000
		By Bank (balancing figure)	1,00,000
	4,00,000		4,00,000

Share Premium Account

	Rs.		Rs.
To Balance c/d	10,000	By Bank (balancing figure)	10,000
	10,000		10,000

6% Debentures Account

Dr. | | | | Cr.

		Rs.		Rs.
To	Bank (balancing figure)	48,000	By Balance b/d	1,50,000
To	Profit on redemption A/c	2,000		
To	Balance c/d	1.00,000		
		1.50.000		1,50.000

Profit on Redemption Account

		Rs.		Rs.
To	Balance c/d	2,000	By 6% Debentures A/c	2,000
		2,000		**2,000**

Provision for Taxation

		Rs.		Rs.
To	Bank (tax paid)	60,000	By Balance b/d	50,000
To	Balance c/d	1.00,000	By Transfer from P & L A/c	1,10,000
		1,60.000		1,60,000

Proposed Dividend

		Rs.		Rs.
To	Bank (dividends paid)	15,000	By Balance b/d	15,000
To	Balance c/d	20.000	By Transfer from P & L A/c	20,000
		35,000		35,000

Further more problem please refer CD.

SUMMARY

Cash flow statement is an important tool of cash planning and control. At the same time, it serves as a valuable tool of financial analysis too. The cash flow statement provides information about cash receipts and payments of an enterprise for a given period. The Institute of Chartered Accountants of India has issued Accounting Standard-3 (revised) prescribing the formats of cash flow statement and the procedure to be adopted in preparation of it. Now, it is mandatory to annex cash flow statement to the published financial statements. The cash flows are classified into three main categories viz., cash flows from operating activities, cash flows from investing activities and cash flows from financing activities. The purpose for determining the net cash flow from operating activities is to understand why net profit/loss as reported in the profit and loss account must be converted. Under direct method, cash receipts from operating revenues and cash payments for operating expenses are rearranged so as to get cash flow from operating activities. Under indirect method, net profit is taken as a base and is adjusted to arrive at cash flows from operating activities. The main difference between the funds flow analysis and cash flow analysis is that, funds flow statement takes into account the sources and application of funds of long-term nature and the net increase or decrease in long-term funds will be reflected on the working capital position of the firm.

REVIEW QUESTIONS

Section A (2 to 4 marks questions)

1. What is cash flow statement?
2. What are the methods of presentation of a cash flow statement?
3. What is the treatment in presentation of a cash flow statement?
4. In what respects is a cash flow statement is significantly different from a funds flow statement?
5. Distinguish between a cash flow and fund flow statement.

Section B (5 marks or 8 marks questions)

1. (a) What is a cash-flow statement?
   (b) How does it differ from a cash budget and a funds flow statement?
2. Discuss the classification of cash flow statement.
3. Explain the importance of cash-flow analysis.
4. Explain briefly the steps to be followed in preparing a cash-flow statement.
5. Explain how interest and dividend are treated in cash flow statement.
6. What are the uses and significances of a cash flow statement?
7. What are the objectives of cash flow statements?
8. Do cash flow statements have any limitations? If yes, what are the limitations of cash flow statement?
9. What are the objectives of cash flow statements?
10. What are the limitations of cash flow analysis?
11. What are the main categories of cash inflows and cash outflows as per AS-3 (revised)?
12. In the case of a manufacturing company:
    (i) List the items of 'inflows' of cash receipts from operating activities.
    (ii) List the items of 'outflows' of investing activities.
13. Distinguish between 'cash' and 'cash equivalents.'
14. What is the procedure in preparation of a cash flow statement?

15. Distinguish the direct and indirect methods suggested as per 'AS-3 Revised' in the preparation of a cash flow statement.

16. What are the disclosure requirements in reporting cash flows?

17. State the importance and uses of cash flow analysis.

18. Discuss the significance of projected cash flow statement in decision-making.

19. By assuming hypothetical figures prepare a cash flow statement for the period ending 30th June, 2006, for a manufacturing company.

20. From the following information, prepare a cash flow statement for the year ended 31st March, 2006:

   (i) Increase in working capital - Rs.40,000

   (ii) Depreciation provided on fixed assets - Rs.17,500

   (iii) Dividend paid - Rs.35,000

   (iv) Net profit - Rs.1,07,500 before writing off goodwill

   (v) Goodwill written off out of profit - Rs.50,000

   (vi) Machinery purchase - Rs.100,000

   (vii) Further issue of share capital Rs.50,000 for cash.

Section C (15 to 18 marks questions)

1. From the following information you are required to prepare cash flow statement of ABC Ltd., for the year ended 31st March 2006:

(Rs. in '000)

Liabilities	31.3.2005	31.3.2006	Assets	31.3.2005	31.3.2006
	Rs.	Rs.		Rs.	Rs.
Share capital	70,000	74,000	Bank balance	9,000	7,800
Bonds	12,000	6,000	Accounts receivable	14,900	17,700
Accounts payable	10,360	11,840	Inventories	49,200	42,700
Provision for			Land	20,000	30,000
doubtful debts	700	800	Goodwill	10,000	5,000
Reserves and					
Surplus	10,040	10,560			
	1,03,100	1,03,200		1,03,100	1,03,200

Following additional information has also been supplied to you:

   (i) Dividends of Rs.3,500 thousand were paid during the year 2005-06.

2. The balance sheets of RKV Ltd. as at the end of March 2005 and 2006 were given below:

	31.3.2005	31.3.2006
	Rs.	Rs.
Liabilities		
Share capital	1,00,000	1,50,000
Share premium	—	5,000
General reserve	50,000	60,000
Profit & Loss A/c	10,000	17,000
8% Debentures	70,000	50,000
Depreciation reserve:		
Plant	50,000	56,000
Furniture	5,000	6,000
Provision of tax	20,000	30,000
Sundry creditors	86,000	95,000
Reserve for bad debts	2,000	5,000
	3,93.000	4,74,000
Assets		
Freehold land	1,00,000	1,00,000
Plant at cost	1,04,000	1,00,000
Furniture at cost	7,000	9,000
Investment at cost	60,000	80,000
Debtors	32,000	75,000
Stock	60,000	65,000
Cash	30,000	45,000
	3,93,000	4.74.000

A plant purchased for Rs.4,000 (depreciation Rs.2,000) was sold for Rs.800 on 31st December, 2005. On October 2005, an item of furniture was purchased for Rs.2,000. Depreciation on plant was provided at 8% on cost (excluding sold out item) and on furniture at 12.5% on average cost. A dividend of 22.5% on original shares was paid. Prepare a cash flow statement for 2005-06.

3. Following information is available from the books of Olive Company Ltd. (Rs.)

Particulars	2006	2007
Profit made during the year		2,50,000
Income received in advance	500	600
Prepaid expenses	1,600	1,400
Debtors	80,000	95,000
Bills receivable	25,000	20,000
Creditors	45,000	40,000
Bills payable	13,000	15,000
Outstanding expenses	2,500	2,000
Accrued income	1,500	1,200

Prepare cash flow statement from operations.

4. From the following, calculate cash from operations:

Profit & Loss Account for the year ended 31st March, 2007.			
Particulars	Rs '000	Particulars	Rs '000
To Salaries	7,000	By Gross profit	25,000
To Rent	1,000	By Profit on sale of fund	5,000
To Depreciation	2,000	By Income tax refund	3,000
To Loss on sale of plant	1,000		
To Goodwill written off	4,000		
To Proposed dividend	5,000		
To Provision for tax	5,000		
To Net profit	8,000		
	33,000		**33,000**

5. From the following summary cash account of RKV Ltd. prepare a cash flow statement for the year ended 31st March, 2007 in accordance with AS-3 (revised) using the direct method the company does not have any cash equivalents.

Summary Cash Account for the year ended 31-3-2007			
			(Rs. '000)
Balance on 1-4-2006	50	Payment of suppliers	2,000
Issue of equity shares	300	Purchase of fixed assets	200
Receipts from customers	2,800	Overhead expense	200
Sale of fixed assets	100	Wages and salaries	100
		Taxation	250
		Dividend	50
		Repayment of bank loan	300
		Balance on 31-3-2005	150
	3,250		**3,250**

The Financial Environment: Markets Institutions

5

Objectives

After studying this chapter, you should be able to:

1 Introduction - operations of indian stock markets

2 Know the primary market

3 Analyse secondary market

4 Discuss stock exchanges

5 Explain BSE

6 Define NSE

7 Analyse OTCE

8 Understand the integrated stock exchanges

9 Know the merchant banks

10 Analyse the money market

11 Discuss the fund manager

12 Know the universal banking

13 Explain the retail banks

14 Define the private banks

15 Understand CHIPS

16 Analyse the auditing body

17 Discuss the investment banking

18 Describe the investment company

INTRODUCTION - OPERATIONS OF INDIAN STOCK MARKETS

In every economic system, some units that may be individual or institutions are surplus generating, while others are deficit generating. Surplus generating units are called savers while deficit generators are called spenders. In our country, at a spectral level, households are surplus generating while corporates and governments are deficit generating. This is, however, true only at an aggregate/macro level. You would definitely come across individual houses who are deficit generating and corporate bodies who are surplus generating at some point of time. The question that arises here is: What do the surplus generating units do with their surpluses or savings? You can now imagine that they have only two alternatives before them. They can either invest or hold their savings in a liquid form. Liquid cash holdings are required to meet transaction, precautionary or speculative needs. The surplus generating units could invest in different forms. They could invest in physical assets viz. land and building, plant and machine or in precious metal viz. gold and silver, or in financial assets viz. shares and debentures, units of the Unit Trust of India, Treasury bills, commercial paper etc.

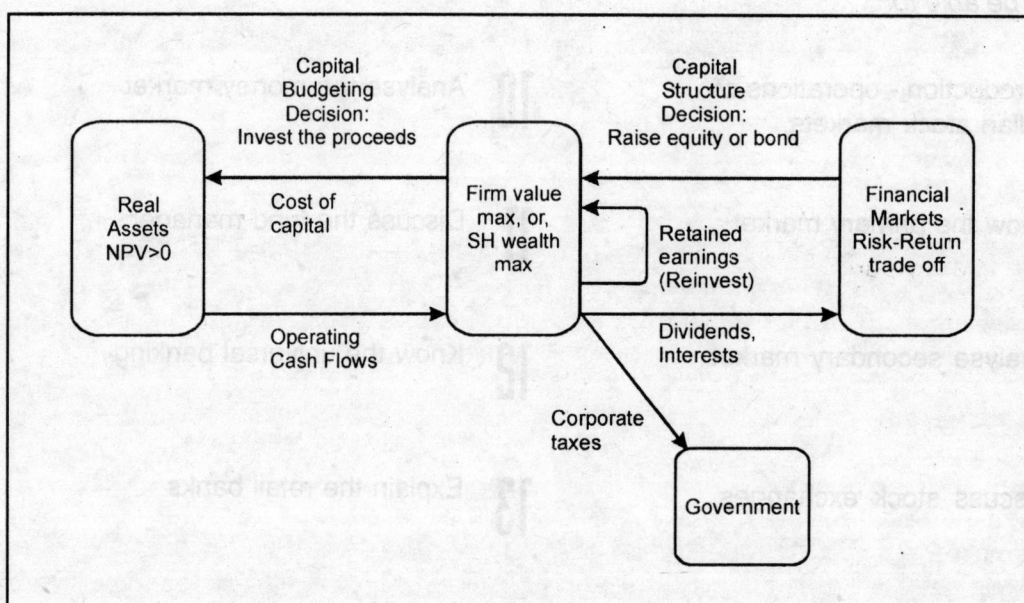

The financial assets are also called financial claims or financial securities or paper assets. These finance securities are issued by deficit generating units in exchange for their savings. It is for this reason that surplus generating units are called investors while deficit generating units are called issuers. These investors and issuers of financial securities constitute two important elements of the securities market. The third critical element of markets is the intermediaries who act as conduits between the investors and issuers. Regulatory bodies, which regulate the functioning of the securities markets, constitute the last but very significant element of securities markets. Thus, there are some important elements of securities markets namely investing issuers, intermediaries and regulators. Now depending upon the nature of the relationship among these elements of securities markets, the markets are classified as primary and secondary. Further, depending upon the main securities markets, the markets are classified as short-term and long-term and depending upon the issuers, they are classified as government securities or industrial securities. Government securities are also called gilt-edged securities. In order to pick up the right kind of securities, an investor or a portfolio manager should be fully conversant with the different segments of securities markets, different types of securities that are traded and different trading arrangement which exists in the market. In this unit, we shall distinguish between primary market and secondary market securities and discuss various traded securities and trading arrangements prevalent in India. Let us begin distinguishing primary and secondary markets.

CLASSIFICATION

Primary market

Secondary market

It can also be classified on the basis of life span of the asset into:

Money market -Less than one year

Capital market proper - More than one year.

Primary or New Issue Market

Primary market is the segment in which new issues are made whereas secondary market is the segment in which outstanding issues are traded. It is for this reason that the primary market is also called new issues market and the secondary market is called the stock market.

In the primary market, new issues may be made in three ways namely, public issue, rights issue and private issue. Public issue involves sale of securities to members of public. Rights issue involves sale of securities of the existing shareholders/debenture holders. Private placement involves selling securities privately to a selected group of investors. In the primary market, equity shares, fully convertible debentures (FCD), are partially convertible investors. In the primary market, equity shares, fully convertible debentures (FCD), partially convertible centres (PCD), and non-convertibles debentures (NCD) are the securities commonly issued by non-government share companies issuing equity shares and bonds.

Secondary Market

Business finance is concerned with the provision of funds for investment in business enterprise; whatever is invested in this way must be provided by an investor, and this means that the investor must forgo consumption and save to provide the funds. Savers and the users of their funds come together in the market for finance, where the normal rules of supply and demand apply, unless there is government interference with interest rates. The price of money is the rate of interest paid for the use. If the demand for investment funds is greater than the funds offered for investment by savers, then the rate of interest will rise until people in the economy are induced to forgo consumption and make their savings available for investment. The new issues of securities are made available in the 'primary market'. The securities that are already outstanding and owned by the investors are usually bought and sold through the 'secondary market', which is popularly known as 'stock market'. In the stock market, the outstanding issues are permitted to trade. In this market, a stock or bond issue has already been sold to the public, and it is traded between current and potential owners. The proceeds from a sale in the stock market do not go to the issuing organisation but to the current owner of the security. Once investors have purchased new issues, they change hands in the stock market. There are two broad segments of the stock markets (i) The organised stock exchanges (if) The Over-the-Counter (OTC) market. The primary middlemen in the stock market are brokers and dealers. The distinction between them is that the broker acts as an agent, whereas the dealer acts as a principal in the transaction. Stock markets are said to reflect the health of the country's economy. On the other hand, major economic indicators determine stock market movements to a large extent. From a thorough analysis of the various economic indicators and its implications on the stock markets, it is known that stock market movements are largely influenced by broad money supply, inflation, credit/ deposit ratio and fiscal deficit, apart from political instability. Besides, fundamental factors like corporate performance, industrial growth etc. always exert a certain amount of influence upon the stock markets. Because the stock market involves the trading of securities initially sold in the primary market, it provides liquidity to the individuals who acquired these securities. The trends in stock market will have impact on the primary market. The secondary market in India comprises of 23 stock exchanges on which about 500 companies are listed. Large volumes of transactions in the secondary markets are put through the BSE and NSE. Presently, the BSE & NSE put together account for 99% of the total turnover as compared to 1% by the other stock exchanges.

Reasons for Transactions on Secondary Market

There are two main reasons why individuals transact in the secondary market:

Information-motivated reasons: Information-motivated investors believe that they have superior information about a particular security than other market participants. This information leads them to believe that the market is not correctly pricing the security. If the information is good, this suggests that the security is currently under-priced, and investors with access to such information will want to buy the security. On the other hand, if the information is bad, the security will be currently overpriced, and such investors will want to sell their holdings of the security.

Liquidity-motivated reasons: Liquidity-motivated investors, on the other hand, transact in the secondary market because they are currently in a position of either excess or insufficient liquidity. Investors with surplus cash holdings (e.g., as a result of an inheritance) will buy securities, whereas investors with insufficient cash (e.g., to purchase a car) will sell securities.

Securities that are traded in the secondary market may be classified as follows:

1.   On the basis of issuer, securities may be classified as

    ❖   Industrial securities
    ❖   Government securities
    ❖   Financial intermediaries securities.

Industrial securities issued by industrial and common undertakings in the private and public sector whereas government, state governments, municipalities and public utilities. Government securities are generally considered risk-free, low-return securities compared to industrial securities. Besides these two classes of issuers, financial intermediaries are emerging as the third important group. The securities issued by financial institutions and banks would fall, in terms of risk-return features, somewhere between the industrial securities and government securities.

On the basis of maturity, securities may be classified into short-term and long-term or money market capital market securities. Treasury bills, commercial bills, commercial paper, certificates of deposit are short-term or money market securities. Equities, preference shares, debentures and bonds are long-term or capital market securities. On the basis of settlement of deals, securities may be classified into forward securities and backward securities. Forward securities are those settlement date for which can be shifted from one settlement date to other by paying badla charges. Cash securities are those for which settlement dates cannot be shifted. For the securities are known by different names viz. specified shares, group A shares or forward section. Cash securities are also known as non-specified shares, group B shares or cash section.

STRUCTURE OF THE SECURITIES MARKET

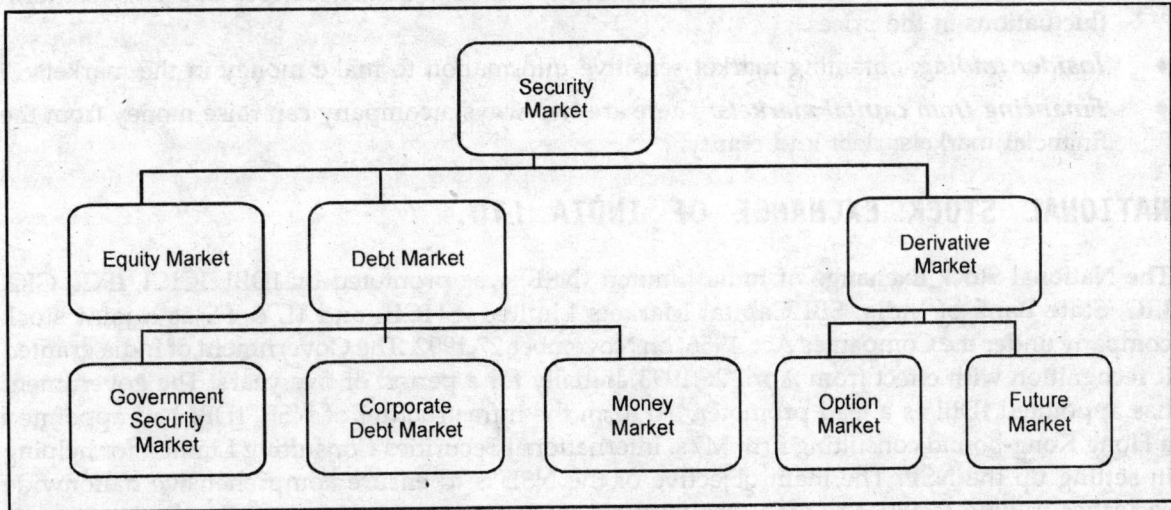

```
                          ┌──────────────┐
                          │   Security   │
                          │   Market     │
                          └──────────────┘
          ┌───────────────────┼───────────────────────┐
   ┌──────────────┐   ┌──────────────┐         ┌──────────────┐
   │ Equity Market│   │  Debt Market │         │  Derivative  │
   │              │   │              │         │   Market     │
   └──────────────┘   └──────────────┘         └──────────────┘
          ┌───────────────┬───────────────┐   ┌───────────┬───────────┐
   ┌──────────────┐┌──────────────┐┌──────────────┐┌──────────┐┌──────────┐
   │  Government  ││  Corporate   ││    Money     ││  Option  ││  Future  │
   │  Security    ││ Debt Market  ││   Market     ││  Market  ││  Market  │
   │  Market      ││              ││              ││          ││          │
   └──────────────┘└──────────────┘└──────────────┘└──────────┘└──────────┘
```

PARTICIPANTS IN THE SECURITIES MARKET

♦   Regulators

CLB, RBI, SEBI,

DEA, DCA

SEC, FRB

Stock Exchanges, Listed Securities, Depositories, Brokers, FIIs, Merchant Bankers or Investment Bankers, Mutual Funds, Custodians, Registrars, Underwriters, Bankers to Issue Debenture Trustees, Venture Capital Funds, Credit Rating Agencies.

DEFINITION OF CAPITAL MARKET

♦   It is a place where people buy and sell financial instruments be it equity or debt.

♦   It is a mechanism to facilitate the exchange of financial assets.

Examples of Capital Market

In India - BSE & NSE are the two capital markets.

Internationally - NYSE, LSE & TSE are the largest capital markets.

PURPOSE OF STOCK MARKET

1.   It helps in capital formation in the country.
2.   It maintains active trading.
3.   It increases the liquidity of assets.
4.   It also helps in price recovery process.

SHORTCOMINGS OF STOCK MARKETS

♦   *Scarcity of floating stocks:* financial institutions, banks and insurance companies own 80% of the equity capital in the private sector.

- ♦ *Speculation:* 85% of the transactions on the NSE and BSE is speculative in nature.
- ♦ *Price rigging:* evident in relatively unknown and low quality scrips. Causes short-term fluctuations in the prices.
- ♦ *Insider trading:* obtaining market-sensitive information to make money in the markets.
- ♦ *Financing from capital markets:* There are two ways a company can raise money from the financial markets: debt and equity.

NATIONAL STOCK EXCHANGE OF INDIA LTD.

The National Stock Exchange of India Limited (NSE) was promoted by IDBI, ICICI, IFCI, GIC, LIC, State Bank of India, SBI Capital Markets Limited, SHCIL and IL & FS as a joint stock company under the Companies Act, 1956, on November 27,1992. The Government of India granted it recognition with effect from April 26,1993, initially for a period of five years. The government has appointed IDBI as a lead promoter. To form the infrastructure of NSE, IDBI had appointed a Hong Kong-bound consulting firm M/s. International Securities Consulting Limited for helping in setting up the NSE. The main objective of the NSE is to ensure comprehensive nationwide securities trading facilities to investors through automated screen-based trading and automatic post-trade clearing and settlement facilities. The NSE will be encouraging corporate trading members with dealer networks, computerised trading and short settlement cycles. It proposes to have two segments, one dealing with wholesale debt instruments and the other dealing with capital market instruments. The Electronic Clearing and Depository System (ECDS) proposed to be set up by the Stock Holding Corporation of India Limited (SHCIL) would provide the requisite clearing and settlement systems.

OVER THE COUNTER EXCHANGE OF INDIA (OTCEI)

Indeed, in the mid-eighties itself, the G.S. Patel Committee on Stock Exchange Reforms and the Abid Ali Committee on Capital Markets had recommended the creation of a second-tier stock market that would ease some of the problems of the present stock exchanges. Over-The-Counter Exchange of India (OTCEI) has promoted by UTI, IDBI, IFCI, LIC, GIC, SBI Capital Market and Canbank Financial Services as a non-profit making company under Section 25 of the Companies Act, 1956. The OTCEI is a recognized stock exchange under Section 4 of the Securities Contracts (Regulation) Act, 1956. Hence companies listed on the OTC Exchange enjoy the same status as companies listed on any other stock exchanges in the country as regards to interest rates on borrowings, etc.

The OTC Exchange of India has picked the model from the NASADQ system (National Association of Security Automated Dealers' Quotations) prevalent in the United States of America. Modifications suited to Indian conditions have been adopted. OTC in America was an offshoot of their government's efforts to regulate the unlisted securities. The Indian version of NASD (National Associations of Securities Dealers) is what is called the OTC Exchange of India. Unlike in the regular exchange, listing on OTCEI is a national listing from day one. Wherever and whenever countries start operating within the country, they can trade in all the scripts of OTCEI. A separate listing in those regular places is not needed at all.

The unique features of OTCEI are as under:

Ringless Trading

OTCEI exchange has eliminated the traditional trading ring with a view to have greater accessibility to the factors. Trading will instead take place through a network of computers (screen-based) of OTC dealers located several places within the same city and even across cities. These computers allow dealers to quote, query and act through a central OTC computer using telecommunication links. Investors can walk into any of centres of members and dealers and see the quote display on the screen, decide to deal and conclude the fraction.

National Network

Unlike other stock exchanges, the OTC Exchange will have a nationwide reach, enabling a widely dispersed ring across the cities, resulting in greater liquidity. Companies, thus, have the unique benefit of nationwide listing trading of their scrips by listing at one exchange, the OTC Exchange.

Totally Computerized

All the activities of the OTC trading will be computerized, making for a more transparent, quick and compliant market.

Exclusive List of Companies

The OTC Exchange will not list and trade in companies listed on any other stock exchange. It will be, therefore, an entirely new set of companies 'sponsored' by members of the OTC Exchange. However, it has recently viewed some 25 companies already listed on other exchanges to list on OTCEI.

Two ways of making a Public Offer

Another unique feature of OTCEI is its 'two ways' of making a public offer. Under 'direct offer', a company can offer its shares directly to the public after getting it sponsored by a sponsor but under 'indirect offer' the company has given its shares first to the sponsor who along with the company can at a later and convenient time, make an offer.

Faster Transfers and Trading Without Shares

OTC trading also provides for transfer of shares of Registrars, up to a certain percentage per folio. This results in faster transfers. The concept of immediate settlement makes it better for the investors. They do not trade with share certificates but with a different tradable document called counter receipt (CR). However, an investor can always exercise his right of having a share certificate by surrendering the CR and again exchanging share certificate for CR when he wants to trade. There will be a custodian who will provide this facility along in a settler who will do the signature verification and CR validation.

Investor Registration

Yet another feature of OTCEI is investor registration, introduced for the first time in India. The investor registration has to be done only once and is valid for trading on any OTC counter in the country in any scrip. The purpose of the investor registration is to facilitate computerized trading. It also provides greater safety of operations the investors.

Trading Mechanism

An investor can buy and sell any listed scrip at any OTC Exchange counter. Similarly, he can sell any listed scrip at by OTC Exchange counter. The investor can also make an application for services like transfer of shares, splitting and consolidation of shares, nomination and revocation of nomination, registering power of attorney, transmission shares and charge of holder's name, et. The parties involved in trading on OTC are investor, counter settler registered custodian, company and bank.

INTER-CONNECTED STOCK EXCHANGE OF INDIA

Inter-connected Stock Exchange of India Limited (ISE) has been promoted by 15 regional stock exchanges to provide trading linkage/connectivity to all the participating exchanges to widen their market. Thus, ISE is a national level exchange providing trading, clearing, settlement, risk management and surveillance support to the inter-connected market system (ICMS). The ISE aims to address the needs of small companies and retail investors with the guiding principle of optimising the infrastructure and harnessing the potential of regional markets to transform these into a liquid and vibrant market through the use of technology and networking. The participating exchanges in ISE have in all about 4,500 traders. In order to leverage its infrastructure and also to expand its nation-wide reach, ISE has also appointed dealers across various cities other than the participating exchange centres. These dealers are administratively supported through strategically located regional offices at Delhi, Calcutta, Chennai and Nagpur. ISE, thus, expects to emerge as a low-cost national level exchange in the country for retail investors and small intermediaries. ISE has also floated a wholly-owned subsidiary namely, ISE Securities and Services Limited (ISS) to take membership of NSE and other premier exchanges, so that traders and dealers of ISE can access other markets in addition to the local market and the ISE. This will provide the investors in smaller cities with a solution for cost-effective and efficient trading in securities.

THE BOMBAY STOCK EXCHANGE

The Indian stock market is one of the oldest in Asia. Its history dates back to nearly two centuries. The earliest records of security dealings in India are meagre and obscure. The East India Company was the dominant institution in those days and business in its loan securities was transacted towards the close of the eighteenth century. By the 1830s, business in corporate stocks and shares in bank and cotton presses took place in Bombay. Though the trading list was broader in 1839, there were only half a dozen brokers recognised by banks and merchants.

In 1860-61, the American Civil War broke out and cotton supply from the United States of America and Europe came to a halt. This resulted in the "share mania" for cotton trading in India. The number of brokers increased to between 200 and 250. However, at the end of the American Civil War, in 1865, a disastrous slump began - for example, a Bank of Bombay share that had touched Rs.2,850 could be sold only at Rs.87. At the same time, brokers found a place in Dalal Street, Bombay, where they could conveniently assemble and transact business. In 1887, they formally established the "Native Share and Stock Brokers' Association." In 1895, the association acquired premises in the same street and it was inaugurated in 1899 as the Bombay Stock Exchange.

The Bombay Stock Exchange is governed by a board, chaired by a non-executive chairman. The executive director is in charge of the administration of the exchange and is supported by elected directors, Securities Exchange Board of India (SEBI) nominees, and public representatives.

MONEY MARKET

A money market is a mechanism that makes it possible for borrowers and lenders to come together. Essentially, it refers to a market for short-term funds. It meets the short-term requirements of the borrowers and provides liquidity of cash to the lenders.

Money market is the market in which short-term funds are borrowed and lent. The money market does not deal in cash or money but in trade bills, promissory notes and government papers, which are drawn for short periods. These short-term bills are known as near money.

Importance of Money Market

♦   Dealing in bills of exchange and commercial papers
♦   Acting as an outlet for the excess short-term funds of commercial banks
♦   Dealing in treasury bills and short-dated government securities
♦   Guiding central banking policies
♦   Making central banking policies effective
♦   Reduction of disparities in interest rates
♦   Influencing the capital market

Features of a Developed Money Market

♦   Existence of a efficient and effective central bank
♦   Well-organized commercial banking system
♦   Existence of specialized sectors
♦   Free flow of funds between the various sub-markets
♦   Adequate facilities for transfer of funds
♦   Uniformity in interest rates
♦   Availability of ample funds
♦   Availability of ample short-term credit instruments
♦   Sensitiveness to internal and external events
♦   Existence of specialized financial institutions

Features and Weaknesses of Indian Money Market

♦   Existence of unorganised money market
♦   Absence of integration
♦   Diversity in money rates of interests
♦   Seasonal stringency of money
♦   Highly volatile call money market
♦   Absence of the bill market
♦   Absence of well-organised banking system
♦   Availability of credit investments

Money market is the market in which short-term funds are borrowed and lent. The money market does not deal in cash or money but in trade bills, promissory notes and government papers, which are drawn for short periods. These short-term bills are known as near money.

Money Market Instruments

Analysing specifically, the money market deals with the transactions of raising and supplying money in a short period not exceeding one year through various instruments. The following are important money market instruments:

♦   Treasury Bills (T-Bills)
♦   Central Government Securities (gilt-edged securities)

♦   State Government and Public Sector Instruments
♦   Municipal Bonds
♦   Commercial Paper
♦   Certificates of Deposit
♦   Bills Rediscounting
♦   Call/Notice Money Market
♦   Repurchase Agreements (Repos)
♦   Inter Bank Participation
♦   Bank Deposits
♦   Term Money
♦   Corporate Debentures and Bonds
♦   Bankers Acceptance
♦   Commercial Bills
♦   Fringe Market

COMPOSITION OF THE INDIAN MONEY MARKET

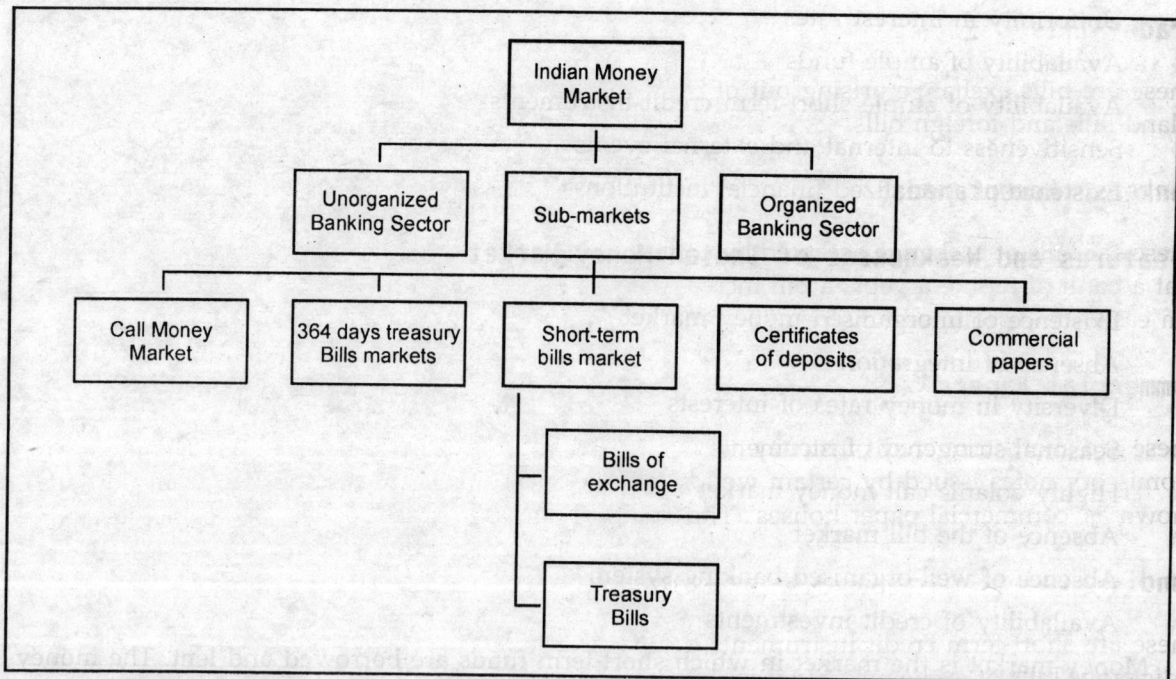

```
                          ┌──────────────────┐
                          │ Indian Money     │
                          │ Market           │
                          └──────────────────┘
            ┌───────────────────┬───────────────────┐
   ┌──────────────┐      ┌──────────────┐     ┌──────────────┐
   │ Unorganized  │      │ Sub-markets  │     │ Organized    │
   │ Banking      │      │              │     │ Banking      │
   │ Sector       │      │              │     │ Sector       │
   └──────────────┘      └──────────────┘     └──────────────┘
   ┌─────────┬──────────────┬──────────────┬──────────────┬──────────────┐
┌─────────┐ ┌────────────┐ ┌────────────┐ ┌────────────┐ ┌────────────┐
│ Call    │ │ 364 days   │ │ Short-term │ │ Certificates│ │ Commercial │
│ Money   │ │ treasury   │ │ bills      │ │ of deposits │ │ papers     │
│ Market  │ │ Bills      │ │ market     │ │            │ │            │
│         │ │ markets    │ │            │ │            │ │            │
└─────────┘ └────────────┘ └────────────┘ └────────────┘ └────────────┘
                          ┌────────────┐
                          │ Bills of   │
                          │ exchange   │
                          └────────────┘
                          ┌────────────┐
                          │ Treasury   │
                          │ Bills      │
                          └────────────┘
```

Treasury Bills (T-Bills)

T-Bills are one of the most important instruments in virtually all the money markets in the world. T-Bills are issued by the government for periods ranging from 14 days to 364 days through regular auctions. They are highly liquid instruments and demand for them is largely from banks, financial institutions and corporations. Fundamentally, T-Bills are short-term instruments issued by RBI on behalf of the Government of India to tide over short-term liquidity shortfalls. T-Bills market is much more liquid than that for dated Government of India securities because of shorter tenure of T-Bills.

There are three categories of T-Bills.

On-Top T-Bills	- These bills can be bought from the RBI at any time at an interest yield of 4.663%. But, with the deregulation of the interest rates, they have lost much of their relevance.
Ad hoc T-Bills	- The RBI creates these bills to replenish the government's cash balances. Thus, they, essentially, are just an accounting measure in RBI's books. They have a maturity period of 91 days, but can be redeemed prior to the final date of maturity, because for them the dealing is only between the government and the RBI.
Auctioned T-Bills	- These bills were first introduced in April, 1992 and are the most active of the three categories. In effect, they are the only one among the three categories that can actually be called an active money market instrument.

Treasury bill is a short-term money market instrument as well as a short-term security by which the government raises finance to meet its short-term requirements. The investment in the Treasury bill is reckoned for the purpose of statutory liquidity reserve (SLR) requirements. The periodicity of the T-Bills is 14 days, 28 days, 91 days, 182 days and 364 days. Periodically, the Reserve Bank of India comes out with auctions of T-Bills, whereas only in the case of 91 days T-Bills, the amount is notified. T-Bills transactions are routed through the Special General Ledger (SGL) Accounts. Being a short-term instrument, it has a good secondary market.

Trade Bills

These are bills exchange arising out of bona fide commercial transactions. They include both inland bills and foreign bills.

Bankers' Acceptances

These are bills of exchange accepted by commercial banks on behalf of their customers. The fact that a bank of repute accepts a bill increases its creditworthiness, which, in turn, means that it can easily be discounted.

Commercial Papers

These are short-term credit instruments dealt with in the Indian money market. They refer to promissory notes issued by certain well-known business houses to the specialized institutions known as 'commercial paper houses'. Their maturity period ranges between 90 to 180 days.

Hundis

These are short-term credit instruments dealt with in the Indian money market. They refer to indigenous bills of exchange drawn in vernacular languages and under various circumstances.

Central Government Securities (Gilt-edged Securities)

The Webster's Dictionary defines gilt-edged as something of "the highest or best quality" and gilt as the thin layer of gold applied in the process of gilding. The government securities/ bonds, the world over, are known as 'gilt-edged securities.' This is due to the near riskless nature of government debt. The maturity pattern of Government of India securities has undergone a sea change over the years. There is a greater emphasis on medium and long-term securities now, as compared to the short-term securities earlier. The ownership of the gilt-edged securities is largely limited to the banking system in India. The return on gilt-edged securities is much lower than virtually all other forms of investment. The Central Government issues securities for terms ranging from 1 year to 10 years either at a fixed rate or through auction. They are relatively less liquid than treasury bills and demand is mainly from banks. The types of Central Government securities that have evolved recently include:

(a) Issue of stock through auction, ushering a new treasury culture enabling development of bidding skills amongst market participants.

(b) Issue of stock with pre-announced coupon rates (e.g. fixed rate bonds).

(c) Issue of stock with variable coupon rates (e.g. floating rate bonds).

(d) Issue of zero coupon bonds (issued at discount).

(e) Issue of capital index bonds (to hedge against inflation).

(f) Issue of stock in conversion of maturing treasury bill/dated securities (converted stocks).

State Government/Public Sector/Municipality Issued Securities

Municipal Bonds: Municipal bonds are bonds raised by municipal bodies or local governments for financing core urban infrastructure facilities like drinking water, sanitary systems, solid waste disposal systems, road, hospitals etc. Generally, municipal bonds are broadly of two types.

General Obligation Bonds (GOBs): GOBs secured by the "full faith and credit" of the local body. In other words, debts repayment is based on the overall credit standing and revenue sources of the municipality. These kinds of issues are more favoured by the corporations who have consistent stream of revenues currently and have sufficient debt-servicing capacity. GOBs are usually issued for shorter maturities.

Revenue Bonds (RBs): RBs, on the other hand, are project specific and can, therefore, be issued by Municipalities or by Special Purpose Vehicles (SPY) created for the purpose of setting up specific projects. Here, the debt is serviced from the income stream generated by the project. The investor profile for the municipal bond market would be a combination of institutional and individual investors.

State Government and Public Sector Instruments: Some of the prominent debt instruments that play an important role in the developed money markets are largely dormant in India. These instruments are state government securities and government-guaranteed bonds. These instruments have practically a negligible presence in the Indian money market. State government securities are issued for a period of five to seven years in order to meet long-term funding needs. The target market for these securities is insurance companies and funds.

Certificate of Deposit

Certificate of Deposits (CDs) was introduced by RBI as a step towards deregulation of interest rates on deposits. Under this scheme, any scheduled commercial banks, co-operative banks excluding land development banks, can issue CDs for a period of not less than three months and up to a period of not more than one year. The financial institutions specifically authorised by the RBI can issue CDs for a period not below one year and not above 3 years duration. CDs can be issued within the period prescribed for any maturity. The various features of CDs are as follows:

♦ CDs can be subscribed by an individual, as well as, by an institution.

♦ CDs are money market instruments in the form of Usance Promissory Notes issued at a discount and are negotiable in character. There is a lock-in-period of 15 days, after which they can be sold.

♦ The minimum size of the deposit is Rs.5 lakhs and thereafter, in multiples of Rs.5 lakhs.

♦ The parties to the transaction determine the rate of interest freely.

♦ The instrument is to be stamped according to the rates prescribed by the Indian Stamp Act.

♦ Premature closure of CDs is not permitted and buy-back of the CDs is prohibited.

♦ The CDs should fall due for payment on a working day. In case the due date falls on a holiday, the payment is to be made on the previous working day.

♦ No advance can be taken against the security of the CDs.

♦ There is no limit for investment in CDs by banks.

♦ Due to the negotiable character of the CD, the same could be sold after the lock-in-period, thus enabling the investing bank to create liquidity. This instrument is useful to the corporates for parking their surplus short-term bonds.

FINANCIAL INSTITUTIONS

Financial Market Participants

♦ Firms are net borrowers, and raise capital (bond or equity) to finance investments in plant and equipment.

♦ Households are net savers, and purchase securities issued by firms.

♦ Government can be borrowers or lenders, depending on tax revenue and government expenditures.

♦ Financial intermediaries

   ❖ Banks take deposits and lend money to borrowers

   ❖ Investment companies pool and manage funds for many investors

   ❖ Investment banks specialize in selling (underwriting) securities to the public

   ❖ Insurance companies, credit unions, mutual funds, pension funds, venture capital firms, etc.

Diagram of the Capital Formation Process

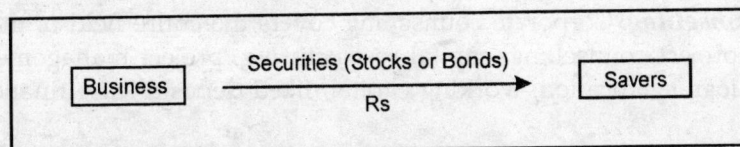

MERCHANT BANKERS/INVESTMENT BANKS

Definition

There is no universal definition for merchant banking. It assumes diverse functions in different countries. Thus, merchant banking may be defined as, "an institution that covers a wide range of activities such as management of customer services, portfolio management, credit syndication, acceptance credit, counselling, insurance etc."

Origin

Merchant banking originated when the London merchants entered into financing foreign trade through acceptance of bills. Later, the merchants assisted the governments of underdeveloped countries in raising long-term funds through flotation of bonds in the London money market.

Over a period, they extended their activities to domestic business of syndication of long-term and short-term finance, underwriting of new issues, acting as registrars and share transfer agents, debenture trustees, portfolio managers, negotiating agents for mergers, takeovers etc. The post-war period witnessed the rapid growth of merchant banking through the innovative instrument like Euro dollar and the growth of various financial centres like Singapore, Hong Kong, Bahrain, Kuwait, Dubai etc.

MERCHANT BANKS AND COMMERCIAL BANKS

There are differences in approach, attitude and areas of operations between commercial banks and merchant banks. The differences between merchant banks and commercial banks are summarised below:

1. Commercial banks basically deal in debt and debt-related finance and their activities are appropriately arrayed around credit proposals, credit appraisal and loan sanctions. On the other hand, the area of activity of merchant bankers is 'equity and equity related finance.' They deal with mainly funds raised through money market and capital market.

2. Commercial banks are asset-oriented and their lending decisions are based on detailed credit analysis of loan proposals and the value of security offered against loans. They generally avoid risks. The merchant bankers are management-oriented. They are willing to accept risks of business.

3. Commercial bankers are merely financiers. The activities of merchant bankers include project counselling, corporate counselling in areas of capital restructuring, amalgamations, mergers, takeovers etc., discounting and rediscounting of short-term paper in money markets, managing, underwriting and supporting public issues in new issue market and acting as brokers and advisers on portfolio management in stock exchanges. Merchant banking activities have impact on growth, stability and liquidity of money markets.

SERVICES OF MERCHANT BANKS

The services of merchant bankers are described in detail in the following section.

(i) **Corporate Counselling:** Corporate counselling covers the entire field of merchant banking activities viz. project counselling, capital restructuring, project management, public issue management, loan syndication, working capital, fixed deposit, lease financing, acceptance credit etc.

(ii) **Project Counselling:** Project reports are prepared to obtain government approval, avail of financial assistance from institutions and plan for the public issue. The financing mix is to be decided keeping in view the rules, regulations and norms prescribed by the government or followed by financial institutions. The projects are appraised, as to the location, technical, commercial and financial viability of the project. Project counselling also includes filling up of application forms with relevant information for obtaining funds from financial institutions.

(iii) **Loan Syndication:** Loan syndication refers to assistance rendered by merchant banks to get mainly term loans for projects. Such loans may be obtained from a single development finance institution or a syndicate or consortium. Merchant bankers help corporate clients to raise syndicated loans from commercial banks.

(iv) **Issue Management:** Management of issue involves marketing of corporate securities viz., equity shares, preference shares and debentures or bonds by offering them to public. Merchant banks act as intermediary whose main job is to transfer capital from those who own it to those who need it.

The issue function may be broadly dividend into pre-issue management and post-issue management. In both the stages, legal requirements have to be complied with and several activities connected with the issue have to be co-ordinated.

The pre-issue management is divided into:

(i) Issue through prospectus, offer for sale and private placement,

(ii) Marketing and underwriting.

(iii) Pricing of Issues.

(v) *Post-issue Management:* The post-issue management consists of collection of application forms and statement of amount received from bankers, screening applications, deciding allotment procedure, mailing of allotment letters, share certificates and refund orders.

(vi) *Underwriting of Public Issue:* Underwriting is a guarantee given by the underwriter that in the event of under-subscription the amount underwritten would be subscribed by him. It is insurance to the company that proposes to make public offer against risk of under subscription. The issues picked by well-known underwriters generally receive a high premium from the public. This enables the issuing company to sell securities quickly.

(vii) *Managers, Consultants or Advisers to the Issue:* The managers to the issue assist in the drafting of prospectus, application forms and completion of formalities under the Companies Act, appointment of Registrar for dealing with share applications and transfer and listing of shares of the company on the stock exchange.

(viii) *Portfolio Management:* Merchant bankers provide portfolio management service to their clients. Today, the investor is very prudent. Every investor is interested in safety, liquidity and profitability of his investment. But investors cannot study and choose the appropriate securities. They need expert guidance. Merchant bankers have a role to play in this regard. They have to conduct regular market and economic surveys to know.

(i) Monetary and fiscal policies of the government.

(ii) Financial statements of various corporate sectors in which the investments have to be made by the investors.

(iii) Secondary market position i.e., how the share market is moving.

(iv) Changing pattern of the industry.

(v) The competition faced by the industry with similar type of industries.

(ix) *Off-shore Finance:* The merchant bankers help their clients in the following areas involving foreign currency.

(i) Long-term foreign currency loans

(ii) Joint venture abroad

(iii) Financing exports and imports and

(iv) Foreign collaboration arrangements.

The bankers render other financial services such as appraisal, negotiations and compliance with procedural and legal aspects.

FUND MANAGER

Fund managers sell the units of funds to investors at the net asset value (NAV) and are also ready to purchase units from the investors at the net asset value. In case of a "no-load" fund, the fund manager sells the units by mail to the investors. Since there are no other intermediaries, this type of fund does not have a sales commission. In terms of a loaded fund, the units are sold through a salesperson. When investors purchase units, a part of the investor's equity is removed as the load at the beginning of the contract. This is called the front-end loading. By adding the commission at the time of sale of units by the investors, exit fees or back-end loading can also be charged. The commission to be paid to the salesperson is added to the net asset value. Apart from this, the fund managers also charge a management fee for the cost of operating the portfolios. These costs include expenses that will be borne by the fund manager such as brokerage fees, transfer costs, book-keeping expenses, and fund managers' salaries.

MUTUAL FUNDS

As defined in the pamphlet of the Association of Mutual Funds in India (AMFI), "A mutual fund is a trust that pools the savings of a number of investors who share common financial goal. Anybody with an investable surplus of as little as a few thousand rupees can invest in mutual funds. These investors buy units of a particular mutual fund scheme that has a defined investment objective and strategy."

According to SEBI Regulations, 1996, "Mutual fund means a fund established in the form of a trust to raise monies through the sale of units to the public or a section of public under one or more schemes for investing in securities, in accordance with Regulations."

Entities in a Mutual Fund Operation

A mutual fund represents a vehicle for collective investment. In India, the following entities are involved in a mutual fund operation.

Sponsor: The sponsor of a mutual fund is like the promoter of a company.

Mutual Fund: The mutual fund is typically constituted as a trust under the Indian Trust Act.

Trustees: Trustees are the internal regulators of the mutual fund entrusted with the job of protecting the interest of unit-holders. Appointed by the sponsor, the trustees are typically a corporate body (a trustee company).

Asset Management Company (AMC): The AMC, referred to also as the Investment Manager, is a separate company appointed by the trustees to run the mutual fund. The AMC is compensated in the form of investment management and advisory fees.

Custodian: The custodian handles the investment back office operation of a mutual fund.

Registrars and Transfer Agents: The registrars and transfer agents handle investor-related services.

MUTUAL FUNDS AND SEBI

The Unit Trust of India was the first mutual fund set up in India in the year 1963. In the early 1990s, the government allowed public sector banks and institutions to set up mutual funds. In the year 1992, the Securities and Exchange Board of India (SEBI) Act was passed. The objectives of SEBI are – to protect the interests of investors in securities and to promote the development of and to regulate the securities market. As far as mutual funds are concerned, SEBI formulates policies and regulates the mutual funds to protect the interests of the investors. SEBI notified regulations for the mutual funds in 1993. Thereafter, mutual funds sponsored by private sector entities were allowed to enter the capital market. The regulations were fully revised in 1996 and have been amended thereafter from time to time. SEBI has also issued guidelines to the mutual funds from time to time to protect the interests of investors. All mutual funds, whether promoted by public sector or private sector entities including those promoted by foreign entities, are governed by the same set of regulations. There is no distinction in regulatory requirements for these mutual funds and all are subject to monitoring and inspections by SEBI.

Open-ended Schemes vs. closed-ended Schemes

The subscription to a closed-ended scheme is kept open only for a limited period whereas an open-ended scheme accepts offers of units on a continuing basis.

A closed-ended scheme does not allow investors to withdraw funds as and when they like, whereas an open-ended schemes permits withdrawal on a continuing basis. A closed-ended scheme has a fixed maturity period whereas an open-ended scheme has no maturity period. Closed-ended schemes are listed on the secondary market, whereas open-ended schemes are ordinarily not listed.

PRIMARY DEALERS

The operations in the government securities market have macro-economic implications like rise in inflation resulting from the growth of money supply in the system. This growth is mainly due to monetisation of ad hoc borrowing of the government to meet the non-plan expenditure and the budget deficit by the RBI. This happens because of the development of the issue on the RBI – the reason being the liquidity of the paper. To ease this burden and reduce the growing resistance from the banks to subscribe to the issue, the RBI has introduced the concept of primary dealers. Primarily, the primary dealers have two major roles to play – that of an underwriter in the primary market and that of a market maker in the secondary market for the government instruments.

Securities Trading Corporation of India Ltd.

The financial sector reforms process has provided an impetus to the government securities market, which is an important segment of financial market. The setting up of the Securities Trading Corporation of India (STCI) has been a measure taken by the RBI to develop an active secondary market in the following government securities.

The main objective of the STCI is to foster the development of an active secondary market in government-dated securities and the bonds issued by the public sector units. With interest now being shown in the government securities by the non-captive investors like corporates, it would be the endeavour of the STCI to facilitate the process of widening the clientele for the government securities market so as to make the market the broad based. The STCI play a role of market-maker in government securities and as such, it would strive to achieve large business turnover, rather than becoming a mere repository of the government securities. In doing so, the STCI would mainly be guided by the commercial considerations.

Discount and Finance House of India

The Discount and Finance House of India (DFHI) was set up by the RBI and it came into existence from April 25, 1988. It is a joint stock company and is jointly owned by the RBI, the public sector banks, and the all-India financial institutions that have contributed its paid-up capital of Rs.150 crores. The main objective of establishing DFHI has been to strengthen the short-term money market and making short-term resources available to the institutions.

BANKING SERVICES

Universal Banking: Universal banks are the one-stop shops, who deal with a wide portfolio of financial products integrating commercial banking, term lending, retail operations investment banking, mutual funds, pension funds, insurance, underwriting of issues securities issuance etc. Universal banks have the ability to offer a full range of financial services. Europe is regarded as the home of universal banking. Universal banks have the potential to leverage on their large capital base, comprehensive portfolio of products and services, technology-enabled distribution and a strong brand image. In India, the development financial institutions (DFIs) are transformed into universal banks following the liberalization of government policies and RBI guidelines. Universal banks derive benefit from economies of scale, direct mobilisation of funds from general public through bank deposits, using such deposit funds for the term lending and retail business. As the universal banks would serve more customers with the same existing network, the customers would be benefited ultimately with the low cost of services.

Correspondent Banking: It is a system of inter-bank relationships in which a bank sells services to other financial institutions. The institution providing the services is the correspondent bank or upstream correspondent. The institution buying the services is the respondent bank or downstream correspondent. Services provided by correspondent bank include cheque collection, data processing, federal funds trading, securities safekeeping or sale of securities, loans to directors and officers, international transactions, investment banking, advice on mergers and acquisitions, loan participation and many others.

Retail Banking: It is a subset of commercial banking. A retail banker provides banking service for individuals. This includes deposit taking, home finance, automobile finance, consumer finance, consumer durable finance, credit card services, retail mutual fund, retail insurance, investment management services etc. provided to individual clients. It is a high volume business, long valued for its ability to gather cheap deposits and generate high margin loans.

Private Banking: In private banking, the banking services, including lending and investment management, are offered only for wealthy individuals. Private banking is primarily a credit-based service and it is less dependent on accepting deposits as in retail banking.

CHIPS: The Clearing House Interbank Payment System (CHIPS) is a computerised fund transfer system for international dollar payments linking major US and foreign banks with offices in New York city. Funds transfer through CHIPS, operated by the New York Clearing House Association, account for 90% of all inter-bank dollar payments relating to international trade. Final settlements occur through adjustments in special account balances at the Federal Reserve Bank of New York. Since 1981, settlement has occurred at the close of each business day when CHIPS members send and receive payments from other the US banks through the Federal Reserve's Federal Wire (Fedwire), the Fed's electronic funds transfer and securities transfer network.

SWIFT: The Society for Worldwide Interbank Financial Telecommunications, a cooperative company that transmits financial messages, payment orders, foreign exchange confirmations and securities deliveries to nearly 7,000 financial institutions on the network, located in 190 countries. SWIFT's global network carried more than 1 billion messages in 1999, with an average daily value of over $ 5 trillion.

INVESTMENT MANAGEMENT COMPANY

The investment management company has to undertake only the management of the scheme; act as a trustee of any scheme; launch any scheme for the purpose of investing in securities but not invest in any schemes floated by it. Every investment management company is responsible for managing the funds or properties of the scheme on behalf of the unit-holders. It has to take all reasonable steps and exercise due diligence to ensure that the scheme is managed in accordance with SEBI regulations, the offer document and the trust deed; and exercise care in managing the assets and funds of the scheme. The company is responsible for the acts of commission and omission by its employees or the persons whose services have been availed by it. The company remains liable to the unit-holders for its acts of commission or omission. The investment management company has to appoint a registrar and share transfer agents;

issue receipts for all the monies received by it; and give a report to SEBI every month, particularly of receipts and payments.

An investment management company appoints a trustee who holds the assets of the scheme for the benefit of unit holders. Only persons registered with SEBI as trustees under SEBI can be appointed as trustees of collective investment scheme. The trustee and the investment management company enter into an agreement for managing the scheme.

The investment management company may launch only schemes that are approved by the trustee. The scheme has to obtain a rating from a credit rating agency. The company has to get the scheme appraised by an appraising agency.

The investment management company has to issue unit certificates to accepted scheme applicants at the most six weeks from the date of closure of the subscription list. A unit certificate issued under the scheme is freely transferable. The investment management company, on production of the instrument of transfer, together with relevant unit certificates, registers the transfer and returns the unit certificate to the transferee within 30 days of the date of such production.

REGULATORY BODIES

There are four regulatory bodies for the Indian capital market. The main capital market regulator is the Securities and Exchange Board of India. The other regulators are the Reserve Bank of India (RBI), Department of Company Affairs (DCA), and Department of Economic Affairs (DEA). These regulators monitor and help in the smooth and uninterrupted flow of activities in the capital market. Though SEBI has been empowered with more powers and is directly linked to the regulation of stock market, it also works with other regulators to govern the capital market are CLB, RBI, SEBI, DEA, DCA, SEC, FRB.

AUDITING BODIES

Good corporate governance recommends that all public companies having a paid-up capital of Rs.5 crores or more have to constitute a committee of the Board of Directors known as the audit committee which will consist of not less than three directors. At least two-thirds of the total number of the members of such a committee should not be managing or whole-time directors. The members have to elect a chairman from amongst themselves.

The Companies (Amendment) Act, 2000, has, among others, provided for the formation and functioning of an audit committee. Similarly, the listing agreement lays down this requirement for listed companies in a stock exchange.

The statutory auditors have to report whether the company has an internal control system commensurate with its size and the nature of its business. However, it was felt that there should be greater interaction and link between the auditors, both statutory and internal, and the top level of the management. Therefore, the necessity arose for an audit committee of the Company's Board of Directors. The statutory and the internal auditor, through the audit committee, are expected to have a greater opportunity to bring forth any problem or difficulty faced by them, particularly deviations, abnormalities, and fraud. The audit committee is also expected to directly interact with the auditors, discuss matters of concern, and take remedial measures wherever required.

CREDIT RATING

Credit rating is a symbolic indication of the current opinion regarding the relative capability of a corporate entity to service its debt obligations in time with reference to the instrument being rated. It enables the investor to differentiate between debt instruments on the basis of their underlying credit quality. To facilitate simple and easy understanding, credit rating is expressed in alphabetical or alphanumerical symbols.

A rating is specific to a debt instrument and is intended to grade different such instruments in terms of credit risk and ability of the company to service the debt obligations as per terms of contract namely - principal as well as interest. A rating is neither a general-purpose evaluation of a corporate entity, nor is an overall assessment of the credit risk likely to be involved in all the debts contracted or to be contracted by such entity. Though credit rating is considered more relevant for gradation of debt securities, it can be applied for other purposes too. The diagram below depicts various types of credit ratings:

Credit Rating

1. Financial instruments rating (a) bond rating (b) equity rating (c) short-term instruments rating

2. Customer rating – sovereign rating – borrower rating

The various purposes for which credit rating is applied are:

1. Long-term/Medium-term debt obligations such as debentures, bonds, preference shares or project finance debts are considered long-term and debts ranging from one to three years like fixed deposits are considered medium-term.

2. Short-term debt obligations – the period involved is one year or less and covers money market instruments such as commercial paper, credit notes, cash certificates etc.

3. Equity grading and assessment, structured obligations, municipal bonds, mutual fund schemes, plantation schemes, real estate projects, infrastructure-related debts, ADR, GDR issues, bank securities etc.

Credit Rating Agencies

Credit Rating and Information Services of India Ltd. (CRISIL)

CRISIL was jointly promoted in 1988, by India's leading financial institutions, ICICI and UTI. Its other shareholders include LIC, SBI, HDFC, GIC, Standard Chartered Bank, Bank of Tokyo, Banque Indo-Suez, Sakura Bank, UCO Bank, Canara Bank, Central Bank of India, IOB, Vysya Bank Ltd. and Bank of Madura Ltd. CRISIL went public in 1992. In 1995, CRISIL entered into a strategic alliance with Standard & Poor's to extend its credit rating services to borrowers from the overseas market. The services offered are broadly classified as rating, information services, infrastructure services and consultancy.

Credit Analysis and Research (CARE)

CARE was promoted in 1992 by IDBI jointly with Canara Bank, UTI, private sector banks and insurance companies. The services offered by CARE include credit rating of debt instruments, credit assessment of companies, advisory services, credit reports and performance ratings.

Investment Information and Credit Rating Agency of India Ltd. (ICRA)

ICRA was promoted by IFCI and 21 other shareholders comprising foreign and nationalised banks and Indian insurance companies. Established in 1991, ICRA is the second rating agency in India. Services offered by ICRA can be broadly classified as analytical services, advisory services and investment services.

- The analytical services comprise rating of debt instruments and credit assessment.
- Advisory services include strategic counselling and general assessment such as restructuring exercise and sector-specific services such as for power, telecom, ports, municipal ratings etc.
- The information or the research desk provides research reports on specific industry, sector and corporate.
- The information services also include equity-related services viz., equity grading and equity assessment.

Duff & Phelps Credit Rating India (OCR)

DCR is a joint venture between Duff and Phelps, USA and Alliance Capital Ltd., Calcutta. This is the youngest of all the credit rating agencies in India. Its expertise is in the rating of structured obligations with international standards. It offers rating of all other short-term, medium-term and long-term debt instruments. In the US, Standard and Poor's (S&P), Moody's Investor Services and Fitch's are some of the important firms engaged in credit rating functions.

TECHNOLOGY PROVIDERS/INTERNET PROVIDERS

In order to smoothen the online trading and terminal updating technology is must. For Internet trading to succeed, it is imperative to have a good business model as well as a comprehensive technology strategy. With net trading in securities and rapid consolidation between multiple stock exchanges, the securities marketplace is fast becoming an international market place.

Bandwidth Optimization

In the Indian context, since the availability of a sufficient bandwidth is limited, the application software optimises the available bandwidth by deploying advanced technologies. Some of the technologies that have already made their mark in the capital market are broadband, narrowband technologies, Electronic Communications Network (ECN), and e-Customer Relationship Management (eCRM). These technologies will influence the way online brokers deal with customers, segment their markets, execute financial transactions, enhance their offerings, develop their businesses, diversify their revenue streams, and differentiate themselves from their competitors.

INVESTMENT COMPANIES

Investment companies are firms that invite individual investors to subscribe to their capital, combine the capital thus collected into a common pool of investable resources and then seek to accomplish the investment objectives of the investors by investing these resources in an appropriate portfolio of securities. Investment companies may have a number of different schemes (or 'funds' as they are sometimes called; we shall use the terms interchangeably) catering to the specific investment objectives of different classes of investors. These investment schemes, offered by investment companies, can be categorized based either on the nature of their capitalization or based on their investment objectives or based on the types of assets held by them.

Portfolio Management Process

Portfolio management in investment companies is a four-stage process comprising the following stages:

Stage 1: Identifying the objectives of, and level of risk acceptable to the target group of investors and setting goals and objectives for the scheme so as to meet the objectives of this target group of investors.

Stage 2: Evaluating individual securities with respect to their risk return characteristics.

Stage 3: Identifying the set of efficient portfolios and selecting optimal (with respect to the expectations of the target group of investors) portfolio out of this set of efficient portfolios.

Stage 4: Reviewing the portfolio on a continuous basis and re-forming it as and when required. We shall, now, elaborate on each of these stages:

Investment Companies in India

By our definition of investment companies (firms which pool the resources of investors and invest them in various financial assets), we can identify quite a large number of investment companies in India. We shall, however, confine our discussion to the activities of the Unit Trust of India (UTI hereafter), Life Insurance Corporation of India (LIC hereafter) and private sector investment companies. Mutual funds of commercial banks will be only touched as they are discussed in detail in Unit 15.

Unit Trust of India (UTI)

The UTI was established in 1964 with the objective of making available the benefits of industrial growth to small savers. The UTI collects investable resources from investors through the sale of securities called 'units.' These funds are then invested by UTI in various financial assets. Holders of 'units' receive dividends from UTI. Since its inception, UTI has offered various schemes to cater to the need of different classes of investors. Most of these schemes are income-oriented thought, of late, UTI also offers growth oriented schemes. It offers both open-ended and closed-ended schemes. Investors can subscribe to the units of open-ended schemes of UTI throughout the year at prices stipulated by UTI. UTI also stands ready to repurchase these units throughout the year at stipulated prices. Subscriptions to the close-ended schemes of UTI, however, are open only during a stipulated period of time and investors in these schemes have to lock their funds in the scheme for the period of the scheme. Some close-ended funds of UTI are traded on the stock markets thus providing liquidity to the investors.

Mutual Funds of Commercial Banks (MFS)

Since 1987, the nationalized commercial banks like Canara Bank, State Bank of India, Indian Bank etc. have been floating mutual fund schemes. Over the years, the merchant banking subsidiaries of these banks have been offering numerous schemes catering to the investment needs of a wide variety of investors. There are both close-ended and open-ended schemes, schemes with re-purchase options and minimum guaranteed returns and without, schemes targeted at small individual investors, large individual investors and corporate investors. In fact, the collective investable resources of these mutual funds put together now rival that of UTI, which till now has been the premier investment institution in India. We shall discuss more about MFs in Unit 5.

Life Insurance Corporation of India (LIC)

The premium collected by the LIC from its insurance policy holders is administered by LIC and invested in the capital markets. LIC has been one of the largest players in the stock market of India. Of late, it has started floating specific investment schemes targeted at different investor groups, which provide both an insurance cover and a share in the returns from the investments made by LIC.

Investment Options for Investment Companies In India

Given the range of financial instruments available in the Indian financial markets and given the regulations and guidelines governing the investment policies of investment companies in India, the possible investment options open to investment companies in India are restricted to the following: shares of public limited companies, company debentures, public sector bonds, government bonds, treasury bills, money market operations and bills discounting. Returns from these investments are of two types: (1) Interest/Dividend Income: this is the money received by the investment company while it holds on to the security (2) Disinvestments Income: This is the proceeds from the sale of those securities which the investment company decides to disinvest from time to time.

Interest/Dividend income is a known sum in the case of fixed-income securities like debentures and bonds, while it is variable and uncertain in the case of shares. The quantum of disinvestments income is always uncertain, especially in the case of shares (the prices of which are very volatile). Of the investment options available to Indian investment companies, interest/dividend returns are least in the case of investments in treasury bills and government bonds. Public sector bonds and debentures offer a higher return. Dividends from equity shares vary widely from company to company. Disinvestments returns (or 'capital appreciation') are normally highest in the case of equity shares. As far as variability/uncertainty of returns (or 'riskiness') is concerned, investments in treasury bills and government bonds are considered the safest and the investments in equity shares care considered the least safe.

SUMMARY

Trading on stock exchanges is done through brokers and dealers. All members can act as brokers and or this purpose they have to maintain security deposits. Brokers act as agents buying and selling or others for which they receive brokerage commission at stipulated rates. Dealers act as principals and sell securities on their own accounts.

The operations in the government securities market have macro-economic implications like rise in inflation resulting from the growth of money supply in the system. This growth is mainly due to monetisation of ad hoc borrowing of the government to meet the non-plan expenditure and the budget deficit by the RBI. This happens because of the development of the issue on the RBI – the reason being the liquidity of the paper.

Universal banks are the one-stop shops, which deal with a wide portfolio of financial products integrating commercial banking, term lending, retail operations, investment banking, mutual funds, pension funds, insurance, underwriting of issues securities issuance etc. Universal banks have the ability to offer full range of financial services. Europe is regarded as the home of universal banking. Universal banks have the potential to leverage on their large capital base, comprehensive portfolio of products and services technology-enabled distribution and a strong brand image.

Merchant banking originated through the entry of London merchants into the financing of foreign trade through acceptance of bills. Later, these merchants assisted the governments of underdeveloped countries in raising long-term funds through flotation of bonds in London money market. Over a period, they extended their activities to domestic business of syndication of long-term and short-term finance, underwriting of new issues, acting as registrars and share transfer agents, debenture trustees, portfolio managers, negotiating agents for mergers, takeovers etc.

Mutual fund means a fund established in the form of a trust to raise monies through the sale of units to the public or a section of public under one or more schemes for investing in securities, in accordance with regulations.

Credit rating is a symbolic indication of the current opinion regarding the relative capability of a corporate entity to service its debt obligations in time with reference to the instrument being rated. It enables the investor to differentiate between debt instruments on the basis of their underlying credit quality. To facilitate simple and easy understanding, credit rating is expressed in alphabetical or alphanumerical symbols.

Investment companies are firms that invite individual investors to subscribe to their capital, combine the capital thus collected into a common pool of investable resources and then seek to accomplish the investment objectives of the investors by investing these resources in an appropriate portfolio of securities. Investment companies may have a number of different schemes (or 'funds' as they are sometimes called; we shall use the terms interchangeably) catering to the specific investment objectives of different classes of investors.

REVIEW QUESTIONS

1. Make a detailed study of merchant bankers.
2. Who is a fund manager? Write a note on fund managers.
3. Explain investment banks in detail.
4. Explain briefly the operations of the Indian stock market.
5. What is the purpose of stock markets in a country like India?
6. Write on primary vs. secondary markets.
7. Explain stock markets in India, their role and functions.
8. Write on membership, organization and management of stock exchanges.
9. What are the principal weaknesses of Indian stock markets?
10. What are the major areas of reform in the functioning of stock exchanges?
11. What do you mean by listing of securities? Explain.
12. Write a note on investment companies.
13. Write on different types of mutual funds.
14. "Mutual funds companies create the market." Do you agree with this statement?
15. Write on different credit rating agencies.
16. What is the role of auditing bodies in the financial market?
17. Explain technology providers in brief.

REFERENCES

1. Clendenin, John C and Christy, George A: *Introduction to Investment*, New York, McGraw Hill, 2005.
2. Coates, Robert C: *Investment Strategy*, McGraw Hill 1978.
3. Cohen, A.W: *Point and Future Stock Market Trading*, Larchmont NY Chacraft, Inc., 2003.
4. Cohen, Jerome, B.: Zinbarg, Edward D., and Zeikel, Arthur, *Investment Analysis and Portfolio Management*, Homewood, Ill.: Richard D. Irwin, 1977.
5. Cottle, C.C., and Whitman, W.T.: *Investment Timing: The Formula Plan Approach*, New York, McGraw Hill, 1953.
6. Criaig, Malcolm: *Investment to survive to 80s: Inside information for businessmen and investments*, Berkshire, Scope Books, 1980.
7. Curley, Anthony J. and Bear, Robert M: *Investment Analysis and Management*, NY, Harper & Row, 1979.
8. D. Ambrosio, Charles A: *Guide to Successful Investing*, Englewood Cliffs, NJ Prentice Hall, 1970.
9. Dicksler, James L. and Samuelson, Paul A.: *Investment Portfolio Decision-making*, London, Lexington Books, 1974.
10. Donaldson, Gordon: *Corporate Debt Capacity*, Boston, Harvard University Press, 1966.
11. Doodhan, Kersi D: *Stock Exchange in a Developing Economy*, University of Bombay, Bombay, 1962.
12. Dougall, Herbert E: *Capital Markets and Institutions*, 2nd ed. Englewood Cliffs, NJ, Prentice Hall, 1970.

PART II

FUNDAMENTAL CONCEPT IN FINANCIAL MANAGEMENT

Risk and Return

6

Objectives

After studying this chapter, you should be able to:

1 Understand return

2 Know risk

3 Analyse security return

4 Discuss systematic risk

5 Explain unsystematic risk

6 Describe the risk in a contemporary mode

7 Understand the using beta in estimate return

8 Know alpha

9 Discuss the measuring historical return and risk

10 Analyse the measuring historical risk

11 Describe the measuring expected return and risk

12 Understand the calculating expected return and risk

INTRODUCTION

Unlike natural science and like medicine, law and economics, investing lies somewhere between an art and a science. Certain aspects of investing lend themselves to a scientific approach. The creation of computer skills has accelerated the use of scientific methods.

However, corporations are managed by people and therefore open to problems associated with their faulty judgments. Moreover, the corporations operate in a highly dynamic and competitive environment, and many operate both nationally and internationally. As a result, the judgment factor still dominates investment decisions.

Whether investing will ever be classified as a science is doubtful, but research, training and experience have developed investing into a discipline. Discipline means a structured, consistent and orderly process without rigidity in either concept or methods.

Financial Analysis

Financial analysis is the informative and predictive function in investing. It provides information about the past and present, and it quantifies expectations for the future. Capital budgeting decisions, corporate financial polices, and informed selections of securities for investment are all products of financial analysis. Analytical resources mobilized for these purposes include economic, capital market, sector and specific security analyses.

Economic Analysis

Economic analysis provides both near-term and longer-term projections for the total economy in terms of the nation's output of goods and services, inflation, profits, monetary and fiscal policy, and productivity. It, thus, provides the foundation for capital market, sector, industry and company estimates of the future.

Capital Market Analysis

Capital market analysis examines the industries and securities of individual companies primarily to develop value and return expectations for securities and thus to distinguish over-priced securities from under-priced ones.

Between capital market analysis and security analysis, incorporating some characteristics of each are sector analysis. Broader than industry and company analysis, sector analysis may be viewed as a bridge between capital market context; sectors consist of major groupings of stocks (i.e. according to economic sector, growth rate, or cyclically in earnings) that either cut across or combine several industries.

Comparative Selection of Securities

Selection among alternative investment opportunities requires appraisal of securities so that their relative attractiveness in terms of return and risk can be judged at any time. This purpose can be accomplished only if consistent analytical procedures are employed and industry and company forecasts are based on an internally consistent set of economic and capital market projections.

If Hindalco is considered for purchase, it must be considered more attractive than Nalco, Indian Aluminium, or other issues with comparable investment characteristics. Thus, isolated analysis and evaluation of an individual security are impractical and inappropriate. One security cannot be effectively appraised apart from other securities, or apart from the general investment climate.

Consistency and comparability are so important that they should be the twin goals of the investment analysis process. Consistency applies to data for an individual company across time, whereas comparability seeks valid data on companies for each time period. Without consistency and comparability, the investor cannot exercise sound judgment in identifying instances of overvaluation and under-valuation.

Investment Decision-making

Investment decision-making can best be viewed as an integrated process to which security analysis makes its unique contribution. Portfolio management requires the consistent application of economic, capital market and sector analysis to the definition of objectives and the measurement of performance. Security analysis serves the investment decision-maker by identifying the fairly priced or under-priced securities that are most likely to produce the desired results.

Investment policies and asset allocation strategies are developed based on the following objectives:

♦   To earn a sufficient "real" rate of return and maintain the purchasing power of its assets adjusted for inflation in perpetuity.

♦   To control portfolio risk and volatility in order to provide as much year-to-year spending stability as possible and still meet.

RISK DEFINED

Risk can be defined as the probability that the expected return from the security will not materialize. Every investment involves uncertainties that make future investment returns risk-prone. Uncertainties could be due to the political, economic and industry factors.

Risk could be systematic in future depending upon its source. Systematic risk is for the market as a whole, while unsystematic risk is specific to an industry or the company individually. The first three risk factors discussed below are systematic in nature and the rest are unsystematic. Political risk could be categorised depending on whether it affects the market as whole, or just a particular industry.

Types of Investment Risk

Systematic versus Non-systematic Risk

Modern investment analysis categorizes the traditional sources of risk causing variability in returns into two general types: those that are pervasive in nature, such as market risk or interest rate risk, and those that are specific to a particular security issue, such as business or financial risk. Therefore, we must consider these two categories of total risk. The following discussion introduces these terms. Dividing total risk into its two components, a general (market) component and a specific (issuer) component, we have systematic risk and non-systematic risk, which are additive:

$$\text{Total risk} = \text{General risk} + \text{Specific risk}$$
$$= \text{Market risk} + \text{Issuer risk}$$
$$= \text{Systematic risk} + \text{Non-systematic risk}$$

Systematic Risk: An investor can construct a diversified portfolio and eliminate part of the total risk, the diversifiable or non-market part. What is left is the non- diversifiable portion or the market risk. Variability in a security's total returns that is directly associated with overall movements in the general market or economy is called systematic (market) risk.

Virtually all securities have some systematic risk, whether bonds or stocks, because systematic risk directly encompasses interest rate, market, and inflation risks. The investor cannot escape this part of the risk because no matter how well he or she diversifies, the risk of the overall market cannot be avoided. If the stock market declines sharply, most stocks will be adversely affected; if it rises strongly, as in the last few months of 1982, most stocks will appreciate in value. These movements occur regardless of what any single investor does. Clearly, market risk is critical to all investors.

Non-systematic Risk: The variability in a security's total returns not related to overall market variability is called the non- systematic (non-market) risk. This risk is unique to a particular security and is associated with such factors as business and financial risk as well as liquidity risk. Although all securities tend to have some non-systematic risk, it is generally connected with common stocks.

Remember the difference: Systematic (market) risk is attributable to broad macro factors affecting all securities. Non-systematic (non-market) risk is attributable to factors unique to a security. Different types of systematic and unsystematic risks are explained as under:

1. *Market Risk:* The variability in a security's returns resulting from fluctuations in the aggregate market is known as market risk. All securities are exposed to market risk including recessions, wars, structural changes in the economy, tax law changes and even changes in consumer preferences. Market risk is sometimes used synonymously with systematic risk.

2. *Interest Rate Risk:* The variability in a security's return resulting from changes in the level of interest rates is referred to as interest rate risk. Such changes generally affect securities inversely; that is, other things being equal, security prices move inversely to interest rates. The reason for this movement is tied up with the valuation of securities. Interest rate risk affects bonds more directly than common stocks and is a major risk that all bondholders face. As interest rates change, bond prices change in the opposite direction.

3. *Purchasing Power Risk:* A factor affecting all securities is purchasing power risk, also known as inflation risk. This is the possibility that the purchasing power of invested dollars will decline. With uncertain inflation, the real (inflation-adjusted) return involves risk even if the nominal return is safe (e.g., a Treasury bond). This risk is related to interest rate risk, since interest rates generally rise as inflation increases, because lenders demand additional inflation premiums to compensate for the loss of purchasing power.

4. *Regulation Risk:* Some investments can be relatively attractive to other investments because of certain regulations or tax laws that give them an advantage of some kind. Municipal bonds, for example, pay interest that is exempt from local, state and federal taxation. As a result of that special tax exemption, municipals can price bonds to yield a lower interest rate since the net after-tax yield may still make them attractive to investors. The risk of a regulatory change that could adversely affect the stature of an investment is a real danger. In 1987, tax law changes dramatically lessened the attractiveness of many existing limited partnerships that relied upon special tax considerations as part of their total return. Prices for many limited partnerships tumbled when investors were left with different securities, in effect, than what they originally bargained for. To make matters worse, there was no extensive secondary market for these illiquid securities and many investors found themselves unable to sell those securities at anything but 'firesale' prices if at all.

5. *Business Risk:* The risk of doing business in a particular industry or environment is called business risk. For example, as one of the largest steel producers, U.S. Steel faces unique problems. Similarly, General Motors faces unique problems as a result of such developments as the global oil situation and Japanese imports.

6. *Reinvestment Risk:* The YTM calculation assumes that the investor reinvests all coupons received from a bond at a rate equal to the computed YTM on that bond, thereby earning

interest on interest over the life of the bond at the computed YTM rate. In effect, this calculation assumes that the reinvestment rate is the yield to maturity.

If the investor spends the coupons, or reinvests them at a rate different from the assumed reinvestment rate of 10%, the realized yield that will actually be earned at the termination of the investment in the bond will differ from the promised YTM. And, in fact, coupons almost always will be reinvested at rates higher or lower than the computed YTM, resulting in a realized yield that differs from the promised yield. This gives rise to reinvestment rate risk. This interest-on-interest concept significantly affects the potential total dollar return. Its exact impact is a function of coupon and time to maturity, with reinvestment becoming more important as either coupon or time to maturity, or both, rise. Specifically:

(a) Holding everything else constant, the longer the maturity of a bond, the greater the reinvestment risks.

(b) Holding everything else constant, the higher the coupon rate, the greater the dependence of the total dollar returns from the bond on the reinvestment of the coupon payments.

Let's look at realized yields under different assumed reinvestment rates for a 10% non-callable 20-year bond purchased at face value. If the reinvestment rate exactly equals the YTM of 10%, the investor would realize a 10% compound return when the bond is held to maturity, with $4,040 of the total dollar return from the bond attributable to interest on interest. At a 12% reinvestment rate, the investor would realize an 11.14% compound return, with almost 75% of the total return coming from interest-on-interest ($5,738/$7,738). With no reinvestment of coupons (spending them as received), the investor would achieve only a 5.57% return. In all cases, the bond is held to maturity.

Clearly, the reinvestment portion of the YTM concept is critical. In fact, for long-term bonds the interest-on-interest component of the total realized yield may account for more than three-fourths of the bond's total dollar return.

7. **Bull-Bear Market Risk:** This risk arises from the variability in the market returns resulting from alternating bull and bear market forces. When security index rises fairly consistently from a low point, called a trough, over a period of time, this upward trend is called a bull market. The bull market ends when the market index reaches a peak and starts a downward trend. The period during which the market declines to the next trough is called a bear market.

8. **Management Risk:** Management, all said and done, is made up of people who are mortal, fallible and capable of making a mistake or a poor decision. Errors made by the management can harm those who invested in their firms. Forecasting errors is difficult work and may not be worth the effort and, as a result, imparts a needlessly sceptical outlook.

An agent-principal relationship exists when the shareholder owners delegate the day-to-day decision-making authority to managers who are hired employees rather than substantial owners. This theory suggests that owners will work harder to maximize the value of the company than employees will. Various researches in the field indicate that investors can reduce their losses to difficult-to-analyse management errors by buying shares in those corporations in which the executives have significant equity investments.

9. **Default Risk:** It is that portion of an investment's total risk that results from changes in the financial integrity of the investment. For example, when a company that issues securities moves either further away from bankruptcy or closer to it, these changes in the firm's financial integrity will be reflected in the market price of its securities. The variability of return that investors experience, as a result of changes in the credit worthiness of a firm in which they invested, is their default risk.

Almost all the losses suffered by investors as a result of default risk are not the result of actual defaults and/or bankruptcies. Investor losses from default risk usually result from security prices falling as the financial integrity of a corporation's weakness - market prices of the troubled firm's securities will already have declined to near zero. However, this is not always the case - 'creative' accounting practices in firms like Enron, WorldCom, Arthur Anderson and Computer Associates may maintain quoted prices of stock even as the company's net worth gets completely eroded. Thus, the bankruptcy losses would be only a small part of the total losses resulting from the process of financial deterioration.

10. *International Risk:* International risk can include both country risk and exchange rate risk.

Exchange Rate Risk: All investors who invest internationally in today's increasingly global investment arena face the prospect of uncertainty in the returns after they convert the foreign gains back to their own currency. Unlike the past, when most US investors ignored international investing alternatives, investors today must recognize and understand exchange rate risk, which can be defined as the variability in returns on securities caused by currency fluctuations. Exchange rate risk is sometimes called currency risk.

For example, a US investor who buys a German stock denominated in marks (German currency), must ultimately convert the returns from this stock back to dollars. If the exchange rate has moved against the investor, losses from these exchange rate movements can partially or totally negate the original return earned. Obviously, US investors who invest only in US stocks on US markets do not face this risk, but in today's global environment where investors increasingly consider alternatives from other countries, this factor has become important. Currency risk affects international mutual funds, global mutual funds, closed-end single country funds, American Depository Receipts, foreign stocks, and foreign bonds.

Country Risk: Country risk, also referred to as political risk, is an important risk for investors today. With more investors investing internationally, both directly and indirectly, the political, and therefore economic stability and viability of a country's economy need to be considered. The United States has the lowest country risk, and other countries can be judged on a relative basis using the United States as a benchmark. Examples of countries that needed careful monitoring in the 1990s because of country risk included the former Soviet Union and Yugoslavia, China, Hong Kong, and South Africa.

Liquidity Risk: Liquidity risk is the risk associated with the particular secondary market in which a security trades. An investment that can be bought or sold quickly and without significant price concession is considered liquid. There is more uncertainty about the time element and the price concession, the greater the liquidity risk. A treasury bill has little or no liquidity risk, whereas a small OTC stock may have substantial liquidity risk.

Liquid Assets Risk: It is that portion of an asset's total variability of return which results from price discounts given or sales concessions paid in order to sell the asset without delay. Perfectly liquid assets are highly marketable and suffer no liquidation costs. Illiquid assets are not readily marketable and suffer no liquidation costs. Either price discounts must be given or sales commissions must be paid, or the seller must incur both the costs, in order to find a new investor for an illiquid asset. The more illiquid the asset is, the larger the price discounts or the commissions that must be paid to dispose of the assets.

Political Risk: It arises from the exploitation of a politically weak group for the benefit of a politically strong group, with the efforts of various groups to improve their relative positions increasing the variability of return from the affected assets. Regardless of whether the changes that cause political risk are sought by political or by economic interests, the resulting variability of return is called political risk, if it is accomplished through legislative, judicial or administrative branches of the government.

Domestic political risk arises from changes in environmental regulations, zoning requirements, fees, licenses, and most frequently, taxes. Taxes could be both direct and indirect. Some types of securities and certain categories of investors enjoy a privileged tax status.

International political risk takes the form of expropriation of non-residents' assets, foreign exchange controls that won't let foreign investors withdraw their funds, disadvantageous tax and tariff treatments, requirements that non-residents investors give partial ownership to local residents, and un-reimbursed destruction of foreign-owned assets by hostile residents of the foreign country.

Industry Risk: An industry may be viewed as group of companies that compete with each other to market a homogeneous product. Industry risk is that portion of an investment's total variability of return caused by events that affect the products and firms that make up an industry. For example, commodity prices going up or down will affect all the commodity producers, though not equally.

The stage of the industry's life cycle, international tariffs and/or quotas on the products produced by an industry, product/industry related taxes (e.g. cigarettes), industry-wide labour union problems, environmental restrictions, raw material availability, and similar factors interact with and affect all the firms in an industry simultaneously. As a result of these common features, the prices of the securities issued by the competing firms tend to rise and fall together.

These risk factors do not make up an exhaustive list, but are merely representative of the major classifications involved. All the uncertainties taken together make up the total risk, or the total variability of return.

MEASUREMENT OF RISK

Volatility

Of all the ways to describe risk, the simplest and possibly most accurate is "the uncertainty of a future outcome." The anticipated return for some future period is known as the expected return. The actual return over some past period is known as the realized return. The simple fact that dominates investing is that the realized return on an asset with any risk attached to it may be different from what was expected. Volatility may be described as the range of movement (or price fluctuation) from the expected level of return. For example, the more a stock goes up and down in price, the more volatile that stock is. Because wide price swings create more uncertainty of an eventual outcome, increased volatility can be equated with increased risk. Being able to measure and determine the past volatility of a security is important in that it provides some insight into the riskiness of that security as an investment.

Standard Deviation

Investors and analysts should be at least somewhat familiar with the study of probability distributions. Since the return an investor will earn from investing is not known, it must be estimated. An investor may expect the TR (total return) on a particular security to be 10% for the coming year, but in truth this is only a "point estimate."

Probability Distributions

To deal with the uncertainty of returns, investors need to think explicitly about a security's distribution of probable TRs. In other words, investors need to keep in mind that, although they may expect a security to return 10%, for example, this is only a one-point estimate of the entire range of possibilities. Given that investors must deal with the uncertain future, a number of possible returns can, and will, occur.

In the case of a treasury bond paying a fixed rate of interest, the interest payment will be made with 100 per cent certainty, barring a financial collapse of the economy. The probability of occurrence is 1.0, because no other outcome is possible. With the possibility of two or more outcomes, which is the norm for common stocks, each possible likely outcome must be considered and a probability of its occurrence assessed. The result of considering these outcomes and their probabilities together is a probability distribution consisting of the specification of the likely returns that may occur and the probabilities associated with these likely returns.

Probabilities represent the likelihood of various outcomes and are typically expressed as a decimal (sometimes fractions are used). The sum of the probabilities of all possible outcomes must be 1.0, because they must completely describe all the (perceived) likely occurrences. How are these probabilities and associated outcomes obtained? In the final analysis, investing for some future period involves uncertainty, and therefore subjective estimates. Although past occurrences (frequencies) may be relied on heavily to estimate the probabilities, the past must be modified for any changes expected in the future. Probability distributions can be either discrete or continuous. With a discrete probability distribution, a probability is assigned to each possible outcome. With a continuous probability distribution, an infinite number of possible outcomes exists. The most familiar continuous distribution is the normal distribution depicted by the well-known bell-shaped curve often used in statistics. It is a two-parameter distribution in that the mean and the variance fully describe it.

To describe the single-most likely outcome from a particular probability distribution, it is necessary to calculate its expected value. The expected value is the average of all possible return outcomes, where each outcome is weighted by its respective probability of occurrence. For investors, this can be described as the expected return.

We have mentioned that it's important for investors to be able to quantify and measure risk. To calculate the total risk associated with the expected return, the variance or standard deviation is used. This is a measure of the spread or dispersion in the probability distribution; that is, a measurement of the dispersion of a random variable around its mean. Without going into further details, just be aware that the larger this dispersion, the larger the variance or standard deviation. Since variance, volatility and risk can, in this context, be used synonymously, remember that the larger the standard deviation, the more uncertain the outcome.

Calculating a standard deviation using probability distributions involves making subjective estimates of the probabilities and the likely returns. However, we cannot avoid such estimates because future returns are uncertain. The prices of securities are based on investors' expectations about the future. The relevant standard deviation in this situation is the *ex ante* standard deviation and not the *ex post* based on realized returns.

Although standard deviations based on realized returns are often used as proxies for *ex ante* standard deviations, investors should be careful to remember that the past cannot always be extrapolated into the future without modifications. *Ex post* standard deviations may be convenient, but they are subject to errors. One important point about the estimation of standard deviation is the distinction between individual securities and portfolios. Standard deviations for well-diversified portfolios are reasonably steady across time, and therefore historical calculations may be fairly reliable in projecting the future. Moving from well-diversified portfolios to individual securities, however, makes historical calculations much less reliable. Fortunately, the number one rule of portfolio management is to diversify and hold a portfolio of securities, and the standard deviations of well-diversified portfolios may be more stable.

Something very important to remember about standard deviation is that it is a measure of the total risk of an asset or a portfolio, including, therefore, both systematic and unsystematic risk.

It captures the total variability in the asset's or portfolio's return, whatever the sources of that variability. In summary, the standard deviation of return measures the total risk of one security or the total risk of a portfolio of securities. The historical standard deviation can be calculated for individual securities or portfolios of securities using total returns for some specified period of time. This *ex post* value is useful in evaluating the total risk for a particular historical period and in estimating the total risk that is expected to prevail over some future period.

The standard deviation, combined with the normal distribution, can provide some useful informations about the dispersion or variation in returns. In a normal distribution, the probability that a particular outcome will be above (or below) a specified value can be determined. With one standard deviation on either side of the arithmetic mean of the distribution, 68.3% of the outcomes will be encompassed; that is, there is a 68.3% probability that the actual outcome will be within one (plus or minus) standard deviation of the arithmetic mean. The probabilities are 95% and 99% that the actual outcome will be within two or three standard deviations, respectively, of the arithmetic mean.

Beta

Beta is a measure of the systematic risk of a security that cannot be avoided through diversification. Beta is a relative measure of risk – the risk of an individual stock relative to the market portfolio of all stocks. If the security's returns move more (less) than the market's returns as the latter changes, the security's returns have more (less) volatility (fluctuations in price) than those of the market. It is important to note that beta measures a security's volatility, or fluctuations in price, relative to a benchmark, the market portfolio of all stocks.

Securities with different slopes have different sensitivities to the returns of the market index. If the slope of this relationship for a particular security is a 45-degree angle, the beta is 1.0. This means that for every one per cent change in the market's return, on average this security's returns change 1%. The market portfolio has a beta of 1.0. A security with a beta of 1.5 indicates that, on average, security returns are 1.5 times as volatile as market returns, both up and down. This would be considered an aggressive security because when the overall market return rises or falls 10%, this security, on average, would rise or fall 15%. Stocks having a beta of less than 1.0 would be considered more conservative investments than the overall market.

Beta is useful for comparing the relative systematic risk of different stocks and, in practice, is used by investors to judge a stock's riskiness. Stocks can be ranked by their betas. Because the variance of the market is constant across all securities for a particular period, ranking stocks by beta is the same as ranking them by their absolute systematic risk. Stocks with high betas are said to be high-risk securities.

RISK AND EXPECTED RETURN

Risk and expected return are the two key determinants of an investment decision. Risk, in simple terms, is associated with the variability of the rates of return from an investment; how much do individual outcomes deviate from the expected value? Statistically, risk is measured by any one of the measures of dispersion such as co-efficient of range, variance, standard deviation etc.

The risk involved in investment depends on various factors such as:

(i) The length of the maturity period - longer maturity periods impart greater risk to investments.

(ii) The credit-worthiness of the issuer of securities - the ability of the borrower to make periodical interest payments and pay back the principal amount will impart safety to the investment and this reduces risk.

(iii) The nature of the instrument or security also determines the risk. Generally, government securities and fixed deposits with banks tend to be riskless or least risky; corporate debt instruments like debentures tend to be riskier than government bonds and ownership instruments like equity shares tend to be the riskiest. The relative ranking of instruments by risk is once again connected to the safety of the investment.

(iv) Equity shares are considered to be the most risky investment on account of the variability of the rates of returns and also because the residual risk of bankruptcy has to be borne by the equity holders.

(v) The liquidity of an investment also determines the risk involved in that investment. Liquidity of an asset refers to its quick saleability without a loss or with a minimum of loss.

(vi) In addition to the aforesaid factors, there are also various others such as the economic, industry and firm specific factors that affect the risk an investment. A detailed analysis of these risk factors will be taken up in the next chapter.

Another major factor determining the investment decision is the rate of return expected by the investor. The rate of return expected by the investor consists of the yield and capital appreciation.

Before we look at the methods of computing the rate of return from an investment, it is necessary to understand the concept of the return on investment. We have noted earlier that an investment is a postponed consumption. Postponement of consumption is synonymous with the concept of 'time preference for money'. Other things remaining the same, individuals prefer current consumption to future consumption. Therefore, in order to induce individuals to postpone current consumption they have to be paid certain compensation, which is the time preference for consumption. The compensation paid should be a positive real rate of return. The real rate of return is generally equal to the rate of return expected by an investor from a risk-free capital asset assuming a world without inflation. However, in real life, inflation is a common feature of a capitalist economy. If the investor is not compensated for the effects of inflation, the real rate of return may turn out to be either zero or negative. Therefore, the investors, generally, add expected inflation rate to the real rate of return to arrive at the nominal rate of return.

For example, assume that the present value of an investment is Rs. 100; the investor expects a real time rate of 3% per annum and the expected inflation rate is 3% per annum. If the investor was to receive only the real time rate, he would get back Rs. 103 at the end of one year. The real rate of return received by the investor would be equal to zero because the time preference rate of 3% per annum is matched by the inflation of 3% per annum. If the actual inflation rate is greater than 3% per annum, the investor would suffer negative returns.

Thus, nominal rate of return on a risk-free asset is equal to the time preference real rate plus expected inflation rate.

If the investment is in capital assets other than government obligations, such assets would be associated with a degree of risk that is idiosyncratic to the investment. For an individual to invest in such assets, an additional compensation, called the risk premium will have to be paid over and above the nominal rate of return.

Determinants of the rate of return

Therefore, three major determinants of the rate of return expected by the investor are:

(i) The time preference risk-free real rate

(ii) The expected rate of inflation

(iii) The risk associated with the investment, which is unique to the investment.

Hence,

Required return = Risk-free real rate + Inflation premium + Risk premium

It was stated earlier that the rate of return from an investment consists of the yield and capital appreciation, if any. The difference between the sale price and the purchase price is the capital appreciation and the interest or dividend divided by the purchase price is the yield. Accordingly

$$\text{Rate of return } (R_t) = \frac{I_t + [P_t - P_{t-1}]}{P_{t-1}} \qquad ...(1.1)$$

Where

R_t = Rate of return per time period 't'

I_t = Income for the period 't'

P_t = Price at the end of time period 't'

P_{t-1} = Initial price, i.e., price at the beginning of the period 't'.

In the above equation 't' can be a day or a week or a month or a year or years and accordingly daily, weekly, monthly or annual rates of return could be computed for most capital assets.

The above equation can be split in to two components. Viz.,

$$\text{Rate of return } (Rt) = \frac{I_t}{P_{t-1}} + \frac{P_t - P_{t-1}}{P_{t-1}} \qquad ...(1.2)$$

Where $\dfrac{I_t}{P_{t-1}}$ is called the current yield,

and $\dfrac{P_t - P_{t-1}}{P_{t-1}}$ is called the capital gain yield.

Or **ROR = current yield + capital gain yield**

Illustration 1: The following information is given for a corporate bond. Price of the bond at the beginning of the year: Rs. 90, Price of the bond at the end of the year: Rs. 95.40, Interest received for the year: Rs. 13.50. Compute the rate of return.

Solution:

The rate of return can be computed as follows:

$$\frac{13.50 + (95.40 - 90)}{90} = 0.21 \text{ or } 21\% \text{ per annum}$$

The return of 21% consists of 15% current yield and 6% capital gain yield.

There is always a direct association between the rates of return and the asset prices. Finance theory stipulates that the price of any asset is equal to the sum of the discounted cash flows, which the capital asset owner would receive. Accordingly, the current price of any capital asset can be expected, symbolically, as

$$P_0 = \sum_{t=1}^{n} \frac{E(I_t)}{(1+r)^t} + \frac{P_n}{(1+r)^n} \qquad ...(1.3)$$

Where

$E(R_t)$ = Expected income to be received in year 't'

P_0 = Current price of the capital asset

P_n = Price of the asset on redemption or on liquidation

R = The rate of return investors expect given the risk inherent in that capital asset.

Thus, 'r' is the rate or return, which the investors require in order to invest in a capital asset that is used to discount the expected future cash flows from that capital asset.

Illustration 2: Mr. Amirican has purchased 100 shares of Rs. 10 each of Kinetic Ltd. in 2005 at Rs. 78 per share. The company has declared a dividend @ 40% for the year 2006-07. The market price of share as on 1-4-2006 was Rs. 104 and on 31-3-2007 was Rs. 128. Calculate the annual return on the investment for the year 2006-07.

Dividend received for 2004 – 05 = Rs. 10 × 40/100 = Rs. 4

Solution:

Calculation of annual rate of return on investment for the year 2006-07

$$R = \frac{d_1 + (P_1 - P_0)}{P_0} = \frac{4 + (128 - 104)}{104} = 0.2692 \text{ or } 26.92\%$$

RISK-RETURN RELATIONSHIP

The most fundamental tenet of finance literature is that there is a trade-off between risk and return. The risk-return relationship requires that the return on a security should be commensurate with its riskiness. If the capital markets are operationally efficient, then all investment assets should provide a rate or return that is consistent with the risks associated with them. The risk and return are directly variable, i.e., an investment with higher risk should produce higher return.

The risk/return trade-off could easily be called the "ability-to-sleep-at-night test." While some people can handle the equivalent of financial skydiving without batting an eye, others are terrified to climb the financial ladder without a secure harness. Deciding what amount of risk you can take while remaining comfortable with your investments is very important.

In the investing world, the dictionary definition of risk is the possibility that an investment's actual return will be different than expected. Technically, this is measured in statistics by standard deviation. Risk means you have the possibility of losing some, or even all, of your original investment.

Low levels of uncertainty (low risk) are associated with low potential returns. High levels of uncertainty (high risk) are associated with high potential returns. The risk/return trade-off is the balance between the desire for the lowest possible risk and the highest possible return. This is demonstrated graphically in the chart below. A higher standard deviation means a higher risk and higher possible return. The figure below represents the relationship between risk and return.

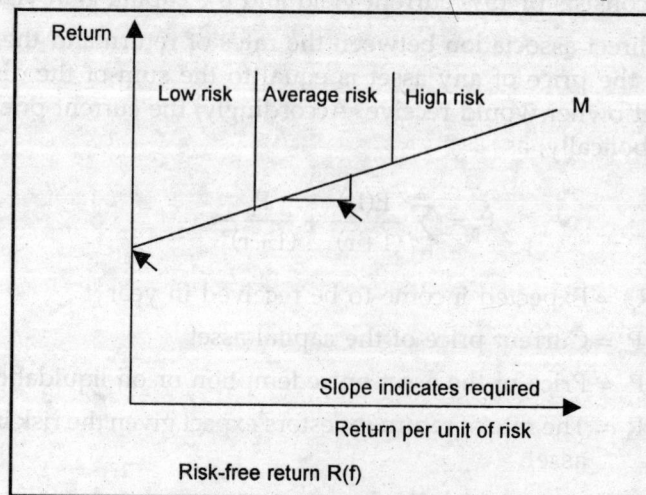

Risk and Return Relationship

The slope of the Market Line indicates the return per unit of risk required by all investors. Highly risk-averse investors would have a steeper line, and vice versa. Yields on apparently similar stocks may differ. Differences in price, and therefore yield, reflect the market's assessment of the issuing company's standing and of the risk elements in the particular stocks. A high yield in relation to the market in general shows an above average risk element.

This is shown in the figure below.

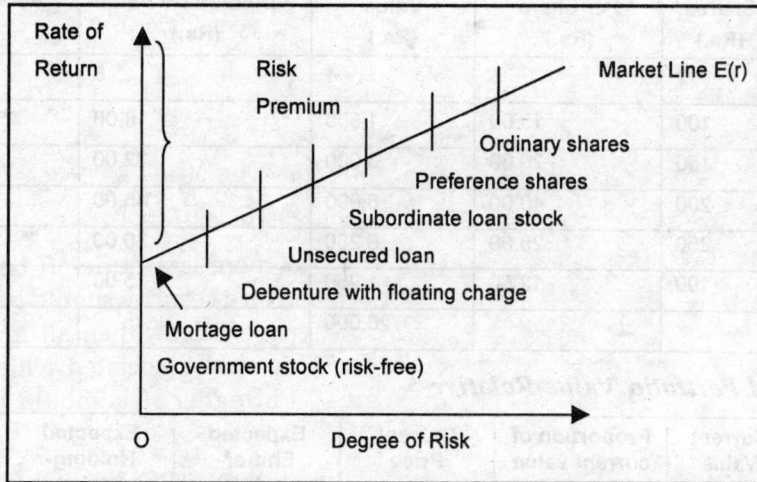

Risk return relationship of different stocks

Given the composite market line prevailing at a point of time, investors would select investments that are consistent with their risk preferences. Some will consider low-risk investments, while others prefer high-risk investments.

A common misconception is that higher risk equals greater return. The risk/return trade-off tells us that the higher risk gives us the possibility of higher returns. But there are no guarantees. Just as risk means higher potential returns, it also means higher potential losses.

On the lower end of the scale, the risk-free rate of return is represented by the return on Treasury Bills of government securities, because their chance of default is next to nil. If the risk-free rate is currently 8 to 10 %, this means, with virtually no risk, we can earn 8 to 10 % per year on our money.

The common question arises: who wants to earn 6% when index funds average 12% per year over the long run? The answer to this is that even the entire market (represented by the index fund) carries risk. The return on index funds is not 12% every year, but rather -5% one year, 25% the next year, and so on. An investor still faces substantially greater risk and volatility to receive an overall return that is higher than a predictable government security. We call this additional return the risk premium, which in this case is 8% (12% - 8%).

Determining what risk level is most appropriate for you isn't an easy question to answer. Risk tolerance differs from person to person. Your decision will depend on your goals, income and personal situation, among other factors.

PORTFOLIO AND SECURITY RETURNS

A portfolio is a collection of securities. Since it is rarely desirable to invest the entire funds of an individual or an institution in a single security, it is essential that every security be viewed in a portfolio context. Thus, it seems logical that the expected return of a portfolio should depend on the expected return of each of the security contained in the portfolio. It also seems logical that the amounts invested in each security should be important. Indeed, this is the case. The example of a portfolio with three securities shown in Table a illustrates this point.

The expected holding period value - relative for the portfolio is clearly shown:

=   1.155

Giving an expected holding period return of 15.50%.

(a) *Security and Portfolio Values*

Security	No. of Shares (Rs.)	Current Price Per Share (Rs.)	Current Value (Rs.)	Expected End-cf-Period Share Value (Rs.)	Expected End-of-Period Share Value (Rs.)
1	2	3	4	5	6
XYZ	100	15.00	1,500	18.00	1,800
ABC	150	20.00	3,000	22.00	3,300
RST	200	40.00	8,000	45.00	9,000
KNF	250	25.00	6,250	30.00	7,500
DET	100	12.50	1,250	15.00	1,500
			20.000		23.100

(b) *Security and Portfolio Value-Relative*

Security	Current Value	Proportion of current value of Properties	Current Price Per Share	Expected End-of-Period Value Per Share	Expected Holding-Period Value-Relative	Contribution to Portfolio Expected Holding-Period Value-Relative
(1)	(2) (Rs.)	3 = (2) Rs. 20,000	(4) (Rs.)	(5) (Rs.)	(6) = (5) / (4)	(7) = (3) X (6)
XUZ	1,500	.0750	15,00	18.00	. 1,200	0.090000
ABC	3,000	.1500	20,00	22.00	1,100	0.165000
RST	8,000	.4000	40,00	45.00	1,125	0.450000
KNF	6,250	.3125	25,00	30.00	1,200	0.375000
DET	1,250	.0625	12,50	15.00	1,200	0.075000
	20,000	1.0000				1.155000

(c) *Security and Portfolio Holding-period Returns*

Security	Proportion of Current Value of Portfolio	Expected Holding Period Return (%)	Contribution to Portfolio Expected Holding Period Return (%)
1	2	3	4
XYZ	.0750	20.00	1.50
ABC	.1500	10.00	1.50
RST	.4000	12.50	5.00
KNF	.3125	20.00	6.25
DET	.0625	20.00	1.25
	1.0000		15.50

Since the portfolio's expected return is a weighted average of the expected returns of its securities, the contribution of each security to the portfolio's expected returns depends on its expected returns and its proportionate share of the initial portfolio's market value. Nothing else is relevant. It follows that an investor who simply wants the greatest possible expected return should hold one security. This should be the one that is considered to have the greatest expected return. Very few investors do this, and very few investment advisers would counsel such an extreme policy. Instead, investors should diversify, meaning that their portfolio should include more than one security. This is because diversification can reduce risk.

Illustration 3: The average market prices and dividend per share of Asian CERC Ltd. for the past 6 years are given below:

Year	Average market price (Rs.)	Dividend per share (Rs.)
2007	68	3.0
2006	61	2.6
2005	50	2.0
2004	53	2.5
2003	45	2.0
2002	38	1.8

Solution:

Calculate the average rate of return of Asian CERC Ltd.'s shares for past 6 years.

Year	Average market price per share (Rs.)	Capital gain (%)	Dividend per share (Rs.)	Dividend yield (%)	Rate of return (%)
2002	38	-	1.8	4.74	-
2003	45	18.42	2.0	4.44	22.86
2004	53	17.78	2.5	4.72	22.50
2005	50	-5.66	2.0	4.00	-1.66
2006	61	22.00	2.6	4.26	26.26
2007	68	11.48	3.0	4.41	15.89

$$R = 1/5 \ (22.86 + 22.50 - 1.66 + 26.26 + 15.89)$$
$$= 1/5(85.85) = 17.17\%$$

RISK

All possible questions which the investor may ask, the most important one is concerned with the probability of actual yield being less than zero, that is, with the probability of loss. This is the essence of risk. A useful measure of risk should somehow take into account both the probability of various possible "bad" outcomes and their associated magnitudes. Instead of measuring the probability of a number of different possible outcomes, the measure of risk should somehow estimate the extent to which the actual outcome is likely to diverge from the expected.

Two measures are used for this purpose: the average (or mean) absolute deviation and the standard deviation.

Illustration 4: The rate of return of equity shares of Wipro Ltd., for past six years are given below:

Year	01	02	03	04	05	06
Rate of return (%)	12	18	-6	20	22	24

Calculate the average rate of return, standard deviation and variance.

Solution:

Calculation of Average rate of Return ($\bar{R}$)

$$\bar{R} = \frac{\Sigma R}{N} = \frac{12 + 18 - 6 + 20 + 22 + 24}{6} = 15\%$$

$$\sigma^2 = \frac{\Sigma(R - \bar{R})^2}{N}$$

Year	Rate of Return (%)	$(R - \bar{R})$	$(R - \bar{R})^2$
2001	12	-3	9
2002	18	3	9
2003	-6	-21	441
2004	20	5	25
2005	22	7	43
2006	24	9	81
		$\Sigma(R - \bar{R})^2$	614

$$\text{Variance } (\sigma^2) = \frac{64}{6} = 102.33$$

$$\sigma = \sqrt{\sigma^2} = \sqrt{\text{Variance}}$$
$$= 10.12\%$$

Illustration 5: Mr. RKV invested in equity shares of Wipro Ltd., its anticipated returns and associated probabilities are given below:

Return %	-15	-10	5	10	15	20	30
Probability	0.05	0.10	0.15	0.25	0.30	0.10	0.05

You are required to calculate the expected rate of return and risk in terms of standard deviation.

Solution:

Calculation of expected return and risk in terms of standard deviation.

Return (R)	Probability (P)	(PXR)	$(R - \bar{R})$	$(R - \bar{R})^2$	$(R - \bar{R})^2 \times P$
-15	0.05	- 0.75	-5.5	30.25	1.5125
-10	0.10	-1.0	-0.5	0.25	0.0250
5	0.15	0.75	-4.5	20.25	3.0375
10	0.25	2.50	0.5	0.25	0.625
15	0.30	4.50	5.5	30.25	9.0750
20	0.10	2.00	10.5	110.25	11.0250
30	0.05	1.50	20.5	420.25	21.0125
	1.00	$\bar{R}$ =9.5%			$\Sigma(R - \bar{R})^2 P$ = 45.75

Expected Return $\bar{R} = \Sigma(PXR) = 9.5\%$

Standard Deviation $= \Sigma(R - \bar{R})^2 P = \sqrt{45.75} = 6.764$

The risk in the above illustration can be measured by taking the range of 45% (i.e. 30%- (-) 15%) and standard deviation of 6.764. The investment carries greater risk in terms of high variation in return.

Illustration 6: The probabilities and associated returns of Modern Foods Ltd., are given below:

Return%	12	15	18	20	24	26	30
Probability	0.05	0.10	0.24	0.26	0.18	0.12	0.05

Calculate the standard deviation.

Solution:

Return (R)	Probability (P)	(P x R)	$(R - \bar{R})^2$	$(R - \bar{R})^2 \times P$
12	0.05	0.60	- 8.56	3.664
15	0.10	1.50	- 5.56	3.091
18	0.24	4.32	- 2.56	1.573
20	0.26	5.20	- 0.56	0.082
24	0.18	4.32	3.44	2.130
26	0.12	3.12	5.44	3.551
30	0.05	1.50	9.44	4.456
	1.00	$\bar{R}$ = 20.56%		$\Sigma (R - \bar{R})^2 \times P = 18.547$

Expected Return $\bar{R} = \Sigma(PXR) = 20.56\%$

Standard Deviation $= \Sigma(R - \bar{R})^2 P = \sqrt{18.547} = 4.31\%$

The expected return is greater at 20.56%, the range of returns is 18% (i.e. 30% - 12%) and the standard deviation is lower at 4.31%. The investment carries lesser risk in terms of low variation in return.

Illustration 7: Mr. Marin provides the following informations, from the same compute his expected return and standard deviation and variance.

Events	1	2	3	4
Probability	.20	.40	.30	.10
Return (%)	–10	25	20	10

Solution:

A. Calculating the Mean Absolute Deviation:

Event	Probability	Return %	P x Return	Deviation	Probability x Deviation	Probability x Absolute Deviation
(1)	(2)	(3)	(4)	(5)	(6)	(7)
A	.20	-10	-2.0	-25.0	-5.0	5.0
B	.40	25	10.0	10.0	4.0	4.0

Contd...

C	.30	20	6.0	.0	1.5	1.5
D	.10	10	-1.0	-5.0	-0.5	0.5
			Expected Return = 5.0		0	Average = 10.0 Absolute Deviation

B.   Calculating the Standard Deviation

Event	Probability	Deviation	Deviation squared	Probability x Deviation
(1)	(2)	(3)	(4) = (3) 2	(5) = (2) x (4)
a	.20	-25.0	625.0	125.0
b	.40	10.0	100.0	40.0
c	.30	5.0	25.5	7.5
d	.10	-5.0	25.5	2.4
			Variation = Weighted average squared deviation = 175.0	
			Standard Deviation = square root of variance = 13.2287	

When an analyst predicts that a security will return 15% next year, he or she is presumably stating something comparable to an expected value. If asked to express the uncertainty about the outcome, he or she might reply that the odds are 2 out of 3 that the actual return will be within 10% of the estimate (i.e., 5% and 25%). The standard deviation is a formal measure of uncertainty, or risk, expressed in this manner, just as the expected value is a formal measure of a "best guess" estimate. Most analysts make such predictions directly, without explicitly assessing probabilities and making the requisite computations.

Illustration 8: The possible returns and associated probabilities of Securities X and Y are given below:

Security X		Security Y	
Probability	Return %	Probability	Return %
0.05	6	0.10	5
0.15	10	0.20	8
0.40	15	0.30	12
0.25	18	0.25	15
0.10	20	0.10	18
0.05	24	0.05	20

Calculate the expected return and standard deviation of securities X and Y.

Solution:

Calculation of expected return and standard deviation of Security X:

Probability (P)	Return % (R)	(P x R)	$(R - \bar{R})$	$(R - \bar{R})^2$ P
0.05	6	0.30	- 9.5	4.5125
0.15	10	1.50	-5.5	4.5375
0.40	15	6.00	-0.5	0.1000

Contd...

0.25	18	4.50	2.5	1.5625
0.10	20	2.00	4.5	2.0250
0.05	24	1.20	8.5	3.6125
1.00		$\bar{R}$ = 15.5		$\sum(R - \bar{R})^2 P$ = 16.35

Expected return of Security X = 15.5%

Standard Deviation of Security X

$$\sigma_y^2 = 16.35$$

$$\sigma_y = \sqrt{16.35} = 4.04\%$$

Calculation of expected return and standard deviation of Security Y

Probability (P)	Return % (R)	(P x R)	(R − R̄)	(R − R̄)² P
0.10	5	0.50	-7.25	5.2563
0.20	8	1.60	-4.25	3.6125
0.30	12	3.60	-0.25	0.0188
0.25	15	3.75	2.75	1.8906
0.10	18	1.80	5.75	3.3063
0.05	20	1.00	7.75	3.0031
		12.25		S17.0876

Expected Return Security Y ($\bar{R}$) = 12.25%

Standard Deviation of Security Y

$$\sigma_y^2 = 17.086$$

$$\sigma_y = \sqrt{17.0876} = 4.134\%$$

Analysis - Security X has higher expected return and lower level of risk as compared to Security Y.

RETURN AND RISK OF PORTFOLIO

Return of Portfolio (Two Assets)

The expected return from a portfolio of two or more securities is equal to the weighted average of the expected returns from the individual securities.

$$\Sigma(R_p) = W_A(R_A) + W_B(R_B)$$

Where,

$\Sigma(R_p)$ = Expected return from a portfolio of two securities

W_A = Proportion of funds invested in Security A

W_B = Proportion of funds invested in Security B

R_A = Expected return of Security A

R_B = Expected return of Security B

$W_A + W_B = 1$

Illustration 9: A Ltd.'s share gives a return of 20% and B Ltd.'s share gives 32% return. Mr. Gotha invested 25% in A Ltd.'s shares and 75% of B Ltd.'s shares. What would be the expected return of the portfolio?

Solution:

Portfolio Return = 0.25(20) + 0.75 (32) = 29%

Illustration 10: Mr. RKV's portfolio consists of six securities. The individual returns of each of the security in the portfolio are given below:

Security	Proportion of investment in the portfolio	Return
Wipro	10%	18%
Latham	25%	12%
SBI	8%	22%
ITC	30%	15%
RNL	12%	6%
DLF	15%	8%

Calculate the weighted average of return of the securities consisting the portfolio.

Solution:

Security	Weight (W)	Return (%) (R)	(W x R)
Wipro	0.10	18	1.80
Latham	0.25	12	3.00
SBI	0.08	22	1.76
ITC	0.30	15	4.50
RNL	0.12	6	0.72
DLF	0.15	8	1.20
			12.98

∴   Portfolio return is 12.98%

Risk of Portfolio (two assets)

The risk of a security is measured in terms of variance or standard deviation of its returns. The portfolio risk is not simply a measure of its weighted average risk. The securities that a portfolio contains are associated with each other. The portfolio risk also considers the covariance between the returns of the investment. Covariance of two securities is a measure of their co-movement; it expresses the degree to which the securities vary together. The standard deviation of a two-share portfolio is calculated by applying formula given below:

$$p = \sqrt{W_A^2 \sigma_A^2 + W_B^2 \sigma_B^2 + 2W_A W_B \rho_{AB} \sigma_A \sigma_B}$$

Where,

σ_p = Standard deviation of portfolio consisting securities A and B

$W_A W_B$ = Proportion of funds invested in Security A and Security B

$\sigma_A \sigma_B$ = Standard deviation of returns of Security A and Security B

ρ_{AB} = Correlation coefficient between returns of Security A and Security B

The correlation coefficient (AB) can be calculated as follows:

$$AB = \frac{Cov_{AB}}{\sigma_A \sigma_B}$$

The covariance of Security A and Security ( ) can be presented as follows:

$$Cov_{AB} = \sigma_A \, \sigma_B \, \rho_{AB}$$

The diversification of unsystematic risk, using a two-security portfolio, depends upon the correlation that exists between the returns of those two securities. The quantification of correlation is done through calculation of correlation coefficient of two securities (ρ_{AB}). The value of correlation ranges between −1 to 1; it can be interpreted as follows:

If $\rho_{AB} = 1$, No unsystematic risk can be diversified.

If $\rho_{AB} = -1$, All unsystematic risks can be diversified.

If $\rho_{AB} = 0$, No correlation exists between the returns of Security A and Security B.

Illustration 11: The returns of Security of Wipro and Security of Infosys for the past six years are given below:

Year	Security of Wipro Return %	Security of Infosys Return %
2003	9	10
2004	5	-6
2005	3	12
2006	12	9
2007	16	15

Calculate the risk and return of portfolio consisting.

Solution:

Calculation of Mean Return and Standard Deviation of Security A:

Year	Return % R	$(R - \bar{R})$	$(R - \bar{R})^2$
2003	8	0	0
2004	5	-4	16
2005	3	-6	36
2006	12	3	9
2007	16	7	49
	45		110

Mean Return ($\bar{R}$) = 45/5 = 9%

Standard Deviation (σ_A) = $\sqrt{110}$ = 10.49%

Calculation Mean Return and Standard Deviation of Security A

Year	Return %	$(R - \bar{R})$	$(R - \bar{R})^2$
2001	10	2	4
2002	-6	14	196
2003	12	4	16
2004	9	1	1
2005	15	7	49
	40		266

Mean Return $(\bar{R})$ = 40/5 = 8%

Standard Deviation (σ_B) = $\sqrt{266}$ = 16.31%

Analysis – Security A has a higher historic level of return and lower risk as compared to Security B. Correlation Coefficient (ρ_{AB}).

$$= \frac{N\Sigma XY - (\Sigma X)(\Sigma Y)}{\sqrt{N\Sigma X^2 - (\Sigma X)^2}\sqrt{N\Sigma Y^2 - \Sigma Y^2}}$$

A's return %		B's return %		
X	X^2	Y	Y^2	XY
9	81	10	100	90
5	25	-6	36	-30
3	9	12	144	36
12	144	9	81	108
16	256	15	225	240
ΣX= 45	ΣX^2 = 515	ΣY = 40	ΣY^2 = 586	ΣXY = 444

$$= \frac{(5 \times 5) - (45)^2 \sqrt{5 \times 586 - (40)^2}}{\sqrt{(5 \times 515) - (45)^2}\sqrt{5 \times 586) - (40)^2}}$$

$$= \frac{2,220 - 1800}{\sqrt{2575 - 2025}\sqrt{2930 - 1600}} = \frac{420}{\sqrt{550}\sqrt{1330}}$$

$$= \frac{420}{23.452 \times 36.469} = \frac{420}{855.271} = 0.491$$

Verification:

Calculation of Covariance of Returns of Securities A and B

Year	Returns %		$(R_A - \bar{R}_A)$	$(R_B - \bar{R}_B)$	$(R_A - \bar{R}_A) \times (R_B - \bar{R}_B)$
	A	B			
2001	9	10	0	2	0
2002	5	-6	-4	-14	56
2003	3	12	-6	4	-24
2004	12	9	3	1	3
2005	16	15	7	7	49
					Cov_{AB} = 84

$$\rho_{AB} = \frac{Cov_{AB}}{\sigma_A \sigma_B} = \frac{84}{10.49 \times 16.31} = 0.491$$

$$Cov_{AB} = \sigma_A \sigma_B \rho_{AB} = 10.49 \times 16.31 \times 0.491 = 84$$

Return of portfolio (R_p)

$$= (0.80 \times 9) + (0.20 \times 8) = 7.2 + 1.6 = 8.8\%$$

Risk of portfolio (σ_p)

$$\sigma_p^2 = (0.80^2 \times 10.49^2) + (0.20^2 \times 16.31^2) + (2 \times 0.80 \times 0.20 \times 10.49 \times 16.31 \times 0.491)$$

$$= (0.64 \times 110.04) + (0.04 \times 266.02) + 26.88$$

$$= 70.43 + 10.64 + 26.88 = 107.95$$

$$\sigma_p = \sqrt{107.95} = 10.39\%$$

Risk and Return of Portfolio (three assets)

Formula for calculating risk of portfolio consisting three securities

$$\sigma_p^2 = W_x^2 \sigma_x^2 + W_y^2 \sigma_y^2 + W_z^2 \sigma_z^2 + 2W_x W_y \rho_{yz} \sigma_y \sigma_z + W_x W_z \rho_{xz} \sigma_x \sigma_z$$

Where,

W_1, W_2, W_3 = Proportion of amount invested in securities X, Y and Z

$\sigma_x, \sigma_y, \sigma_z$ = Standard deviations of securities X, Y and Z

ρ_{xy} = Correlation coefficient between securities X and Y

ρ_{yz} = Correlation coefficient between securities Y and Z

ρ_{xz} = Correlation coefficient between securities X and Z

Illustration 12: A portfolio consists of three securities P, Q and R with the following parameters:

	Security			Correlation coefficient
	P	**Q**	**R**	
Expected return (%)	35	22	20	
Standard deviation (%)	20	26	24	
Correlation coefficient:				
PQ				-0.5
QR				+0.4
PR				+0.6

If the securities are equally weighted, how much is the risk and return of the portfolio of these three securities?

Solution:

Expected Portfolio Return

$$= (25 \times 1/3) + (22 \times 1/3) + (20 \times 1/3) = 22.33\%$$

$$\sigma_p^2 = (30)^2(1/3)^2 + (26)^2 + (24)^2(1/3)^2 + 2(1/3)(-0.5)(30)(26)$$

$$+ 2(1/3)(1/3)(0.4)(26)(24) + 2(1/3)(1/3)(0.6)(30)(24)$$

$$\sigma_p^2 = 100 + 75.11 + 64 - 86.67 + 55.47 + 96 = 303.91$$

$$\sigma_p = \sqrt{303.91} = 17.43\%$$

Optimal Portfolio (Two assets)

The investor can minimise his risk on the portfolio. Risk avoidance and risk minimisation are the important objectives of portfolio management. A portfolio contains different securities; by combining their weighted returns we can obtain the expected return of the portfolio. A risk-averse investor always prefers to minimise the portfolio risk by selecting the optimal portfolio. The minimum risk portfolio with two assets can be ascertained as follows:

$$W_A = \frac{\partial_B^2 - Cov_{AB}}{\partial_A^2 + \partial_B^2 - Cov_{AB}}$$

In continuation to illustration 10 we can calculate the proportion to be invested (W_A) in Security A.

$$= \frac{16.31^2 - 84}{(10.49^2 + 16.31^2) - (2 \times 84)} = \frac{182.02}{208.06} = 0.875$$

Therefore, 87.5% of funds should be invested in Security A and 12.5% should be invested in Security B, which represents the optimal portfolio.

PORTFOLIO DIVERSIFICATION AND RISK

In an efficient capital market, the important principle to consider is that, investors should not hold all their eggs in one basket; investor should hold a well-diversified portfolio. In order to understand portfolio diversification, one must understand correlation. Correlation is a statistical measure that indicates the relationship, if any, between series of numbers representing anything from cash flows to test data. If the two series move together, they are positively correlated; if the series move in opposite directions, they are negatively correlated. The existence of perfectly correlated especially negatively correlated-projects is quite rare. In order to diversify project risk and thereby reduce the firm's overall risk, the projects that are best combined or added to the existing portfolio of projects are those that have a negative (or low positive) correlation with existing projects. By combining negatively correlated projects, the overall variability of returns or risk can be reduced. The figure illustrates the result of diversifying to reduce risk.

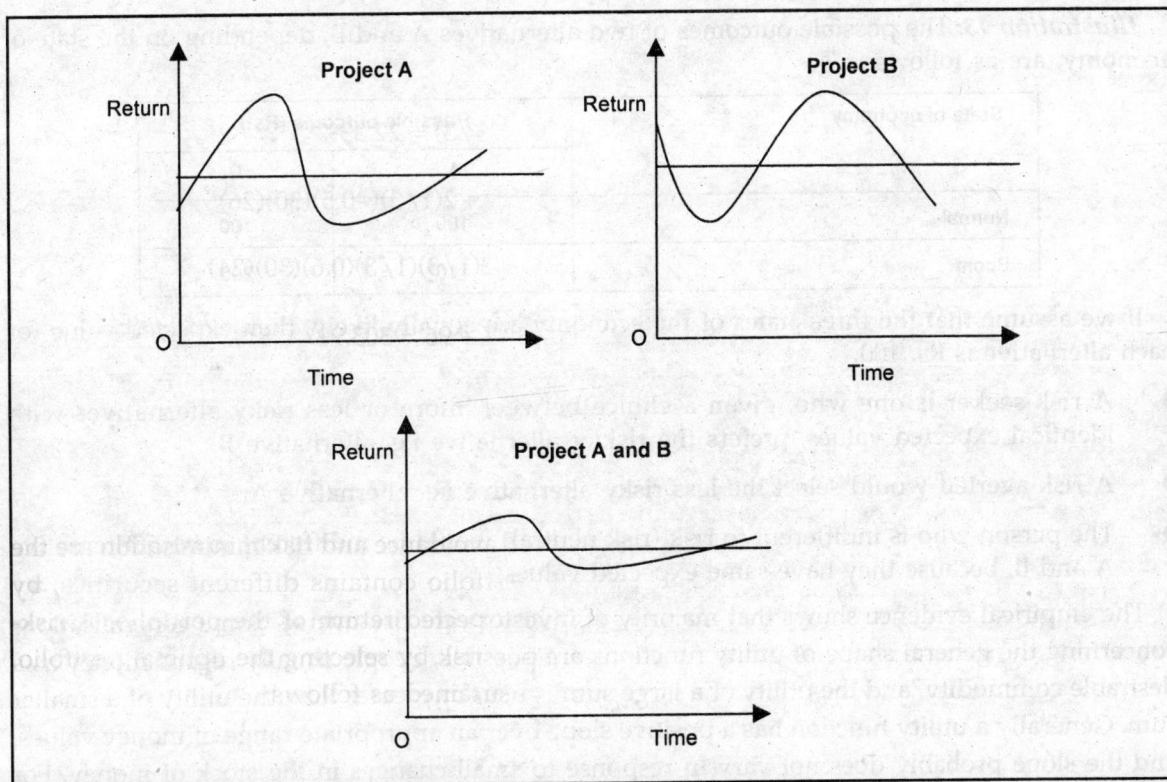

Reduction of Risk through Diversification

It shows that a portfolio is containing the negatively corrected projects A and B, both having the same expected return, E, but less risk (i.e. less variability of return) than either of the projects taken separately. This type of risk is sometimes described as diversifiable or alpha risk. The creation of a portfolio by combining two perfectly correlated projects cannot reduce the portfolio's overall risk below the risk of the least risky project, while the creation of a portfolio combining two projects that are perfectly negatively correlated can reduce the portfolio's total risk to a level below that of either of the component projects, which in certain situations may be zero.

BENEFITS OF DIVERSIFICATION

The gains in risk reduction from portfolio diversification depend inversely upon the extent to which the returns on securities in a portfolio are positively correlated. Ideally, the securities should display negative correlation. This implies that if a pair of securities has a negative correlation of returns, then in circumstances where one of the securities is performing badly, the other is likely to be doing well and vice versa in reverse circumstances. Therefore the average return on holding the two securities is likely to be much 'safer' than investing in one of them alone.

Utility Function and Risk Taking

Common investors will have three possible attitudes to undertake risky course of action (i) an aversion to risk (ii) a desire to take risk, and (iii) an indifference to risk.

The following example will clarify the risk attitude of the individual investors.

Illustration 13: The possible outcomes of two alternatives A and B, depending on the state of economy, are as follows:

State of economy	Possible outcome (Rs.)	
	A	B
Normal	100	100
Boom	110	200

If we assume that the three states of the economy are equally likely, then expected value for each alternative is Rs. 100.

♦ A risk-seeker is one who, given a choice between more or less risky alternatives with identical expected values, prefers the riskier alternative i.e. alternative B.

♦ A risk averted would select the less risky alternative i.e. alternative A.

♦ The person who is indifferent to risk (risk neutral) would be indifferent to both alternative A and B, because they have same expected values.

The empirical evidence shows that majority of investors are risk-averse. Some generalisations concerning the general shape of utility functions are possible. People usually regard money as a desirable commodity, and the utility of a large sum is usually greater than the utility of a smaller sum. Generally a utility function has a positive slope over an appropriate range of money values, and the slope probably does not vary in response to small changes in the stock of money. For small changes in the amount of money going to an individual, the slope is constant and the utility function is linear. If the utility function is linear, the decision-maker maximises expected utility by maximising expected monetary value. However, for large variations in the amount of money, this is likely to be the case. For large losses and large gains, the utility function often approaches upper and lower limits. The slope of the curve will usually increase sharply as the amount of loss increases, because the dis-utility of a large loss is proportionately more than the disutility of a small loss, but the curve will flatten as the loss becomes very large. For a risk-averse decision-maker, the expected utility of a function is less than the utility of the expected monetary value. It is also possible for the decision-maker to be risk preferring, at least over some range of the utility function. In this case, the expected utility of a function is more than the utility of the expected monetary value (EMV).

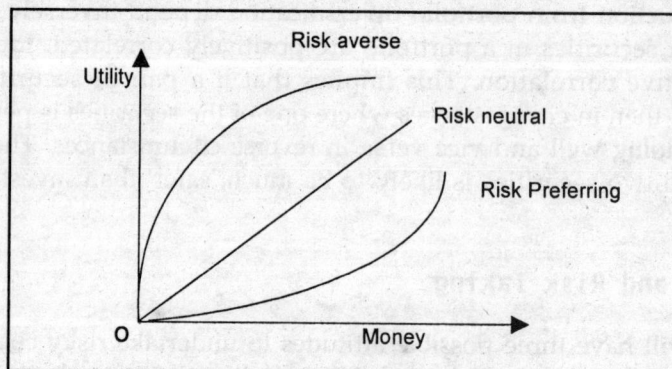

Utility Function and Risk Taking

Illustration 14: Assume the investor in Problem 35 wants to determine how risky his portfolio is and wants you to compute the portfolio variance. If the expected correlations and variance of the stocks are as follows, what is the variance of the portfolio?

Correlations		ABC	BCD	CDE	DEF
	BCD	.50	-	-	-
	CDE	.60	.30	-	-
	DEF	-.30	-.20	-.10	-
Variances:		.04	.16	.02	.10

Solution:

To compute the variance, you need to make a covariance matrix. Using the square roots of the variances and correlations given, the covariance are calculated:

$$Cov(r_{ABC}, R_{BCD}) = .500 \times .200 \times .400 = .040$$
$$Cov(r_{ABC}, R_{CDE}) = .600 \times .200 \times .141 = .070$$
$$Cov(r_{ABC}, R_{DEF}) = -.300 \times .200 \times .316 = -.019$$
$$Cov(r_{BCD}, R_{CDE}) = .300 \times .400 \times .141 = .017$$
$$Cov(r_{BCD}, R_{DEF}) = .200 \times .400 \times .316 = -.025$$
$$Cov(r_{CDE}, R_{DEF}) = .100 \times .141 \times .316 = .004$$

With the given variance and the portfolio weights, the covariance matrix is as follows:

Securities	Weights	ABC .25	BCD .25	CDE .25	DEF .25
ABC	.25	.04	.040	.017	-.019
BCD	.25	.040	.16	.017	-.025
CDE	.25	.017	.017	.02	-.004
DEF	.25	-.019	-.025	-.004	1.0

Multiplying each covariance by the weight at the top of the column and at the left of the row and summing, we get

$$.25 \times .25 \times .04 = .0025$$
$$.25 \times .25 \times .040 = .0025$$
$$.25 \times .25 \times .017 = .0011$$
$$.25 \times .25 \times -.019 = .0012$$
$$.25 \times .25 \times .040 = .0025$$
$$.25 \times .25 \times .160 = .0100$$
$$.25 \times .25 \times .017 = .0011$$
$$.25 \times .25 \times -.025 = .0016$$
$$.25 \times .25 \times .017 = .0011$$
$$.25 \times .25 \times .017 = .0011$$

$$.25 \times .25 \times .020 = .0013$$
$$.25 \times .25 \times -.004 = .0003$$
$$.25 \times .25 \times -.019 = .0012$$
$$.25 \times .25 \times -.025 = -.0016$$
$$.25 \times .25 \times .004 = -.0003$$
$$.25 \times .25 \times .100 = .0063$$

Total portfolio variance = .0223

Illustration 15: Suppose you have Rs. 10,000 to invest and would like to sell Rs. 5,000 in stock XYZ short to invest in ABC. Assuming no correlation between the two securities, compute the expected return and the standard deviation of the portfolio from the following characteristics:

Security	ABC	XYZ
E(R)	.12	.02
σ (R)	.08	.10

Solution:

Expected return:

$$E(R)_p = W_{ABC} \ E(R_{ABC}) + W_{XYZ} \ E(R_{XYZ})$$
$$= \frac{15,000}{10,000} \cdot 2 - \frac{5,000}{10,000} \cdot 2$$
$$= .18 - .01 = .17$$

Standard deviation:

$$[W^2_{ABC} \ \sigma^2 (R_{ABC}) + W^2_{XYZ} \ \sigma^2 (R_{XYZ})]^{1/2} = \sigma_p$$
$$= [(1.5)^2 \times (.08)^2 + (-.5)^2 \times (.10)^2]^{1/2}$$
$$= .130$$

SUMMARY

Corporations are managed by people and therefore open to problems associated with their faulty judgments. Moreover, corporations operate in a highly dynamic and competitive environment, and many operate both nationally and internationally. As a result, the judgment factor still dominates investment decisions. Risk can be defined as the probability that the expected return from the security will not materialize. Every investment involves uncertainties that make future investment returns risk-prone. Uncertainties could be due to the political, economic and industry factors. Risk could be systematic in future, depending upon its source. Systematic risk is for the market as a whole, while unsystematic risk is specific to an industry or the company individually. The first three risk factors discussed below are systematic in nature and the rest are unsystematic. Political risk could be categorised depending upon whether it affects the market as whole or just a particular industry.

Beta is a measure of the systematic risk of a security that cannot be avoided through diversification. Beta is a relative measure of risk - the risk of an individual stock relative to the market portfolio of all stocks. If the security's returns move more (less) than the market's returns as the latter changes, the security's returns have more (less) volatility (fluctuations in price) than those of the market. It is important to note that beta measures a security's volatility, or fluctuations in price, relative to a benchmark, the market portfolio of all stocks.

The risk/return trade-off could easily be called the "ability-to-sleep-at-night test." While some people can handle the equivalent of financial skydiving without batting an eye, others are terrified to climb the financial ladder without a secure harness. Deciding what amount of risk you can take while remaining comfortable with your investments is very important.

The investor can minimise his risk on the portfolio. Risk avoidance and risk minimisation are the important objectives of portfolio management. A portfolio contains different securities; by combining their weighted returns we can obtain the expected return of the portfolio.

REVIEW QUESTIONS

1. Define return.
2. Define risk.
3. What do you mean security return?
4. What are the different types of risk influences on investment?
5. Explain systematic and unsystematic risks.
6. Define Beta. How does it influence the investment decision-making process?
7. Define Alpha.
8. How do you measure historical return and risk?
9. Explain the concepts of expected return and risk.
10. Write about the different steps in calculating expected return and risk.
11. What do you mean by portfolio diversification?

REFERENCES

1. Graham, Benjamin, David, L.; Dodd, Sidney Cottle, et. al.: *Security Analysis: Principles and Techniques,* 4th ed. New York McGraw – Hill Book Co. Inc., 1962.
2. Granger, Clive W and Morgenstem Oskar: *Predictability of Stock Market Prices,* Lexington, Health Lexington, 1970.
3. Granville, Joseph E.: *A Strategy of Daily Timings for Maximum Profit,* Englewood Cliffs, N.J., Prentice-Hall, 1960.
4. Gup, Benton E.: *Basics of Investing,* N.Y. Wiley, 1979.
5. Gupta L.C.: *Rates of Return on Equities: the Indian Experience,* Bombay, Oxford University Press, 1981.
6. Bonus Shares: *A Study of the Dividend and Price Effects of Bonus Shares Issues,* Bombay, Macmillan, 1973.
7. Gupta, S.N.: *Bonds and Guarantees,* Delhi, Commercial Law Publications, 1981.
8. Gupta, Umrao Lal: *Working of Stock Exchange in India,* New Delhi, Thomson Press, 1972.
9. Haavelmlo, T.: *Study in the Theory of Investment,* London, University of Chicago Press, 1960.
10. Hagin, R. and Mader, G.: *What today's investor should know about the new science of investing,* Illinois, Jones – Irwin, 1973.
11. Hardy, C. Colburn: *Investors guide to technical analysis,* N.Y. McGraw-Hill, 1978.
12. Harper, Victor L.: *Handbook of investment products and services,* New York, Institute of Finance, 1975.
13. Hawkins, David F. and Campbell, Walter J.: *Equity Valuation: Models Analysis and Implications,* N.Y. FERF, 1978.
14. Helliwell, J.B. (ed.): *Aggregate Investment: Selected Readings,* Harmondsworth, Penguin Education, 1976. Henin, Claude G. and Ryan, Peter J.: *Options: Theory and Practice,* Lexington, Lexington books, 1977.
15. Henning, Charles, N., William Piggot, and Robert Haney Scott: *Financial Markets and the Economy.* Englewood Cliffs, NJ Prentice – Hall, Inc, 1975.
16. Hester, Donald D. and Tobin, J. (ed): *Risk Aversion and Portfolio Choke,* Cowles – Foundation for Research in Economics, Yale University, monography 19.

17. Hester, Donald D. and Tobin, J. (ed.): *Studies of Portfolio Behaviour,* New York, Wiley, 1967. Haugen, Robert A.: *Modern Investment Theory,* Englewood Cliffs, Prentice Hall, 1990.

18. Hicks, J.R.: *Value and Capital – an enquiry into some fundamental principles of economic theory,* The English Language Book Society and Oxford University Press, 1946.

19. Hirshleifer, J.: *Investment, Interest and Capital,* Englewood Cliffs, N.J. Prentice Hall, 1970. Hirst, F.W.: *The Stock Exchange: A Short Study of Investment and Speculation,* Oxford University Press, 1948.

20. Huang, Stanley S.C.: *Investment Analysis and Management,* Cambridge, Winthrop, 1981.

21. Hull J.C: *Introduction to Futures & Options Markets,* Prentice Hall, Englewood Cliffs, New Jersey, 1995.

22. Jean, William H.: *Analytical Theory of Finance: a study of the investment decisions process,* Jessup, Paul F: *Competing for Stock Market Profits* N.Y. Holt, Rinehart and Winston, 1970.

23. Jessup, Paul F: *Competing for Stock Market Profits,* N.Y., Wiley, 1974. Johnson, Timothy E.: *Investment Principles,* N.J. Prentice Hall, 1978.

24. Jones, Charles P., Donald L. Turtle and Cherrill P. Heaton, *Essentials of Modern Investments,* Ronald Press Company, 1977.

25. Kaufman, George, G.: *Money, the Financial System and the Economy,* 2nd ed.; Chicago, Rand Mc Nally & Co. 1977.

26. Kolb, Rober W.: *Financial Derivatives,* New York Institute of Finance, New York, 1993.

27. Kroos, Herman E., and Blyn, Martin R.: *A history of financial intermediaries,* New York, Random House, 1971.

28. Labys, Walter C., and Granger, Clive W.J.: *Speculation, Hedging and Commodity Price Forecast,* Lexington, Mass, D.C. Health and Company, 1970.

29. Lasry, George: *Valuing Common Stock: The Power of Produce,* N.Y. Amacom, 1979.

30. Latane, Henery, A. Turtle, Donald L.; and Jones, Charles P.: *Security Analysis and Portfolio Management* end (ed.) New York Ronald Press, 1975.

31. Leffler; George L, and Farwell, Loring C.: *The Stock Market,* 3rd ed. New York, Ronald Press, 1963.

32. Lee, Cheng F., Joseph E. Finnerty and Donald H. Wort: *Security Analysis and Portfolio Management,* Foresman and Company, 1990.

33. Lenger, H.V.R.: *Monetary Policy and Economic Growth,* Vora & Co., Bombay, 1962.

34. LEVINE, Sumner N. (ed.) Investment Managers Handbook, Illinois, Dow-Jones Irwin, 1980.

Time Value of Money

7

Objectives

After studying this chapter, you should be able to:

1 Explain the time value of money.

2 Explain the various valuation concepts.

3 Compute the various values based on different valuation concepts.

4 Understand different valuation models concerned with different securities.

INTRODUCTION

It has been explained in the preceding unit that Maximization of the shareholder's wealth is the basic objective of the finance manager of a firm. This requires him to take appropriate decisions on financing, investment and dividends. While taking these decisions, the finance manager must keep the "Time factor" in mind.

For example

(i)   When interest on funds raised, will have to be paid.

(ii) When return on investment will be received.

(iii) Whether it will be received on a consistent basis or otherwise etc.

All this requires that the finance manager knows about the various valuation concepts, viz., Compound Value Concept, Annuity Concept, Present Value Concept etc. All these concepts are basically based upon the fact that, money has time value.

TIME VALUE OF MONEY

"Money has time value" means that the value of money changes over a period of time. The value of a rupee, today is different from what it will be, say, after one year.

Factors contributing to the Time Value of Money

Money has a time value because of the following reasons:

(i)   Individuals generally prefer current consumption to future consumption.

(ii) An investor can profitably employ a rupee received today, to give him a higher value to be received tomorrow or after a certain period of time.

(iii) In an inflationary economy, the money received today, has more purchasing power than money to be received in future.

(iv) 'A bird in hand is worth two in the bush' : This statement implies that, people consider a rupee today, worth more than a rupee in the future, say, after a year. This is because of the uncertainty connected with the future.

Thus, the fundamental principle behind the concept of time value of money is that, a sum of money received today, is worth more than if the same is received after some time. For example, if an individual is given an alternative either to receive Rs. 10,000 now or after six months ; he will prefer Rs. 10,000 now. This may be because, today, he may be in a position to purchase more goods with this money than what he is going to get for the same amount after six months.

Time value of money or time preference of money is one of the central ideas in finance. It becomes important and is of vital consideration in decision making. This will be clear with the following examples.

Example 1 : A project needs an initial investment of Rs. 1,00,000. It is expected to give a return of Rs. 20,000 p.a. at the end of each year, for six years. The project thus involves a cash outflow of Rs. 1,00,000 in the 'zero year' and cash inflows of Rs. 20,000 per year, for six years. In order to decide, whether to accept or reject the project, it is necessary, that the present value of cash inflows received annually for six years is ascertained and compared with the initial investment of Rs. 1,00,000. The firm will accept the project only when the present value of the cash inflows at the desired rate of interest is at least equal to the initial investment of Rs. 1,00,000.

Example 2: A firm has to choose between two projects. One involves an outlay of Rs. 10 crore with a return of 12% from the first year onwards, for ten years. The other requires an investment of Rs. 10 crore with a return of 14% p.a. for 15 years commencing with the beginning of the sixth year of the project. In order to make a choice between these two projects, it is necessary to compare the cash outflows and the cash inflows resulting from the project. In order to make a meaningful comparison, it is necessary that the two variables are strictly comparable. This is possible only when the time element is incorporated in the relevant calculations.

The above examples reflect the need of comparing the cash flows arising at different points of time in decision-making.

VALUATION CONCEPTS OR TECHNIQUES

The Time value of money implies.

(i)   That a person will have to pay in future more, for a rupee received today and

(ii) a person may accept less today, for a rupee to be received in the future.

The above statements relate to two different concepts:

(i)   Compound Value Concept

(ii) Discounting or Present Value Concept

COMPOUND VALUE CONCEPT

In this concept, the interest earned on the initial principal amount becomes a part of the principal at the end of a compounding period.

Illustration 1 : Rs. 1,000 invested at 10% is compounded annually for three years, Calculate the Compounded value after three years.

Solution:

Amount at the end of 1st year will be :   1,100

[1000 x 110/100 = 1,100]

Amount at the end of 2nd year will be :   1,210

[1100 x 110/100 = 1,210]

Amount at the end of 3rd year will be :   1,331

[1210 x 110/100 = 1,331]

This compounding process will continue for an indefinite time period.

Compounding of Interest over 'N' years : The compounding of Interest can be calculated by the following equation.

$A = P (1 + i)^n$

In which,

A = amount at the end of period 'n'.

P = Principal at the beginning of the period.

I = Interest rate.

N = Number of years.

By taking into consideration, the above illustration we get,

$$A = P(1+i)^n$$
$$A = 1000(1 + .10)^3$$
$$A = 1,331$$

Computation by this formula can also become very time consuming if the number of years increase, say 10, 20 or more. In such cases to save upon the computational efforts, **Compound Value table*** can be used. The table gives the compound value of Re. 1, after 'n' years for a wide range of combination of 'I' and 'n'.

For instance, the above illustration gives the compound value of Re. 1 at 10% p.a. at the end of 3 years as 1.331, hence, the compound value of Rs. 1000 will amount to :

$$1000 \times 1.331 = Rs. 1331$$

Multiple Compounding Periods

Interest can be compounded, even more than once a year. For calculating the multiple value above, logic can be extended. For instance, in case of Semi-annual compounding, interest is paid twice a year but at half the annual rate. Similarly in case of quarterly compounding, interest rate effectively is $1/4^{th}$ of the annual rate and there are four quarter years.

Formula:

$$A = P\left[1 + \frac{i}{m}\right]^{m \times n}$$

Where,

A = Amount after a period.

P = Amount in the beginning of the period.

I = Interest rate.

M = Number of times per year compounding is made.

n = Number of years for which compounding is to be done.

Future Value of Series of Cash flows

So far we have considered only the future value of a single payment made at time zero. The transactions in real life are not limited to one. An investor investing money in installments may wish to know the value of his savings after 'n' years.

Illustration 2: Mr. Manoj invests Rs. 500, Rs. 1,000, Rs. 1,500, Rs. 2,000 and Rs. 2,500 at the end of each year. Calculate the compound value at the end of 5 years, compounded annually, when the interest charged is 5% p.a.

Solution:

Statement of the compound value

End of year	Amount deposited	Number of years compounded	Compounded Interest factor from Table A – 1	Future Value (2) X (4)
1	2	3	4	5
1	Rs. 500	4	1.216	Rs.608.00
2	1,000	3	1.158	1158.00
3	1,500	2	1.103	1,654.50
4	2,000	1	1.050	2,100.00
5	2,500	0	1.000	2,500.00

Amount at the end of the 5th Year Rs. 8020.50

It may be noted here, that we are making use of the Compound interest formula for each payment separately. For instance, Rs. 500 put at the end of the first year, compounds for four years, and has a future value of Rs. 608 at 5% interest [Rs.500 $(1 + 0.05)^4$]. Similarly, Rs. 1,000 deposited at n = 2 compounds for 3 years, amounts to Rs. 1,158 [Rs. $1000(1+0.05)^3$] and so on.

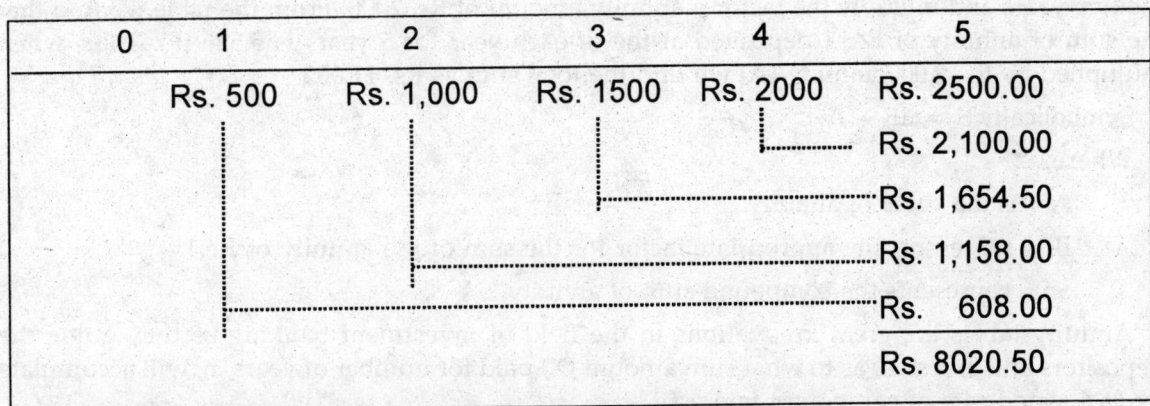

Figure 7.1: Graphic illustration of Compounding Values

Compound sum of an Annuity

An annuity is a stream of equal annual cash flows. Annuities involve calculations based upon the regular periodic contribution or receipt of a fixed sum of money.

Illustration 3: Mr Ramesh deposits Rs. 2,000 at the end of every year for 45 years in his saving account, paying 5% interest compounded annually. Determine the sum of money, he will have at the end of the 5th year.

Solution:

End of Year	Amount Deposited	Number of Years compounded	Compounded Interest factor From Table 3	Future Sum
1	2	3	4	5
1	Rs. 2,000	4	1.216	Rs. 2,432
2	2,000	3	1.158	2,316
3	2,000	2	1.103	2,206
4	2,000	1	1.050	2,100
5	2,000	0	1.000	2,000

Amount at the end of 5th Year Rs. 11,054

Finding the common factor of Rs. 2,000

= Rs. 2,000 (1.216+1.158+1.103+1.050+1.000)

= Rs. 2,000(5.527)

= Rs. 11,054

The above illustration depicts that in order to find the sum of the annuity, the annual amount must be multiplied by the sum of the appropriate compound interest factors. Such calculations are available for a wide range of I and n. They are given in Table A – 2. To find the answer to the annuity question of illustration 3 we are required to look for the 5% column and the row for the five years and multiply the factor y annuity amount of Rs. 2000. From the table we find that the sum of annuity of Re. 1 deposited at the of each year for 5 years is 5.526(IF). Thus, when multiplied by Rs. 2,000 annuity (A) we find the total sum as Rs. 11,052.

Symbolically $S_n = IF \times A$

Where,

A = is the value of annuity.

IF = represents the appropriate factor for the sum of the annuity of Re.1.

Sn = represents the compound sum of annuity.

Annuity tables are great innovations in the field of investment banking as they guide the depositors and investors as to what sum amount (X) paid for number of years, n, will accumulate to, at a stated rate of compound interest.

Illustration 4: Find the compound value of annuity, when three equal yearly payments of Rs. 25,000 are deposited into an account, that yields 7% compound interest.

Solution : The Annuity Table (i.e. Table A – 2) gives the compound value as 3,215, when Re.1 is paid every year for 3 years at 7%. Thus, the compounded value of annuity of Rs. 2,000 is :

$S_n = IF \times A$

$S_n = 3.215 \times 2000$

$S_n = 6,430$

DISCOUNTING OR PRESENT VALUE CONCEPT

The concept of present value is the exact opposite of that of a sum of money or series of payments, while in case of present value concept, we estimate the present worth or a future payment/ instalment or series of payment adjusted for the time value of money.

The basis of present value approach is that, the opportunity cost exist for money lying idle. That is to say, that interest can be earned on the money. This return is termed as 'discounting rate'.

Given a positive rate of interest, the present value of the future Rupee will always be lower. The technique for finding the present value is termed as 'discounting'.

Present value after 'n' Years:

Formula :

$$PV = \frac{A}{(1+i)^n}$$

Where,

PV = principal amount the investor is willing to forego at present

I = Interest rate.

A = amount at the end of the period 'n'.

N = Number of years.

With this formula, we can directly calculate the amount, any depositor would be willing to sacrifice at present, with a time preference rate or discount rate of x%.

Example : If Mr. X, depositor, expects to get Rs. 100 after one year, at the rate of 10%, the amount he will have to forego at present can be calculated as follows :

$$PV = \frac{A}{(1+i)^n}$$

$$PV = \frac{100}{(1+.10)} = Rs.\,90.90$$

Similarly, the present value of an amount of inflow at the end of 'n' years can be computed.

Present Value of a Series of Cash flows

In a business situation, it is very natural that returns received by a firm are spread over a number of years. An investment made now may fetch returns a certain time period. Every businessman will like to know whether it is worthwhile to invest or forego a certain sum now, in anticipating of returns he expects to earn over a number of years. In order to take this decision he needs to equate the total anticipated future returns, to the present sum he is going to sacrifice. The estimate of the present value of future series of returns, the present value of each expected inflow will be calculated.

The present value of series of cash flows can be represented by the following:

$$PV = \frac{C_1}{(1+i)^1} + \frac{C_2}{(1+i)^2} + \frac{C_3}{(1+i)^3} + \frac{C_n}{(1+i)^n}$$

$$PV = \sum_{T=1}^{n} \frac{C_t}{(1+i)^n}$$

Where,

PV = sum of individual present values of each cash flow : C_1, C_2, C_3 ....

C_n = Cash flows after period 1,2,3............n.

I = Discounting rate.

However, a project may involve a series of cash inflows and outflows. The computation of the present value of inflows by the above equation is a tedious problem. Hence , present value Table is used (i.e. Table A – 3).

Illustration 5: Given the time value of money as 10% (i.e. the discounting factor), you are required to find out the present value of future cash inflows that will be received over the next four years.

Year	Cash flows (Rs.)
1	1,000
2	2,000
3	3,000
4	4,000

Solution:

Present Value of Cash flows

1 Year	2 Cash flows	3 Present Value Factor at 10%	4(2x3) Present Value
1	1,000	0.909	909
2	2,000	0.826	1,652
3	3,000	0.751	2.253
4	4,000	0.683	2,732
Present value of series of Cash flows	7,546		

Present value of an Annuity : In the above case there was a mixed stream of cash inflows. An individual or depositor may receive only constant returns over a number of years. This implies that, the cash flows are equal in amount. To find out the present value of annuity either, we can find the present value of each cash flow or use the annuity table. The annuity table gives the present value of an annuity of Re. 1 for interest rate 'r' over number of years 'n'.

Illustration 6: Calculate the present value of annuity of Rs. 500 received annually for four years, when the discounting factor is 10%.

Solution:

Present Value of Annuity of Rs. 500

1 Year	2 Cash flows	3 Present Value Factor at 10%	4(2x3) Present Value
1	500	0.909	454.50
2	500	0.827	413.50
3	500	0.751	375.50
4	500	0.683	341.50
		3,170	
Present value of series of Cash flows Rs. 500	1,585.00		

This basically means to add up the Present Value Factors and multiply with Rs. 500.

i.e. 3,170 × 500 = **Rs. 1,585.**

Formula for calculation of the present value of an annuity can be derived from the formula for calculating the present value of a series of cash flows :

$$PVA_n = \frac{C_1}{(1+i)^1} + \frac{C_2}{(1+i)^2} + \frac{C_3}{(1+i)^3} + \frac{C_n}{(1+i)^n}$$

$$= C\left(\frac{1}{(1+i)^1} + \frac{1}{(1+i)^2} + \frac{1}{(1+i)^3} + \frac{1}{(1+i)^n}\right)$$

$$= C\left(\sum_{t=1}^{n} \frac{Ct}{(1+i)^n}\right)$$

Where,

PVA_n = Present value of an annuity having a duration of 'n' periods.

A = value of single instalment.

I = Rate of interest.

However, as stated earlier, a more practical method of computing the present value would be to multiply the annual instalment with the present value factor.

PVA_n = A × ADF

Where ADF denotes Annuity Discount Factor. The PVA_n in the above example can be calculated as 500 × 3.170 = Rs. 1,585.

The figure of 3,170 has been picked up directly from the Annuity Table for present value (Table A – 4).

Illustration 7: Find out the present value of an annuity of Rs. 5,000 over 3 years when discounted at 5%.

Solution:

$$
\begin{aligned}
PVA_n \quad &= A \times ADF \\
&= 5000 \times 2.773 \\
&= 13,865
\end{aligned}
$$

Present Value of a perpetual Annuity :

A person may like to find out the present value of his investment, in case he is going to get a constant return year after year. An annuity of this kind which goes on for ever is called a 'perpetuity'.

The present value of a perpetual annuity can be ascertained by simply dividing 'A' by interest or discount rate 'I', symbolically represented as A/i.

Illustration 8: Mr. Bharat, principal, wishes to institute a scholarship of Rs. 5,000 for an outstanding student every year. He wants to know the present value of investment which would yield Rs. 5,000 in perpetuity, discounted at 10%.

Solution:

$$P = \frac{A}{1} = \frac{5000}{.10} = 50,000$$

Illustration 9: Mr. Nandan intends to have a return of Rs. 10,000 p.a. for perpetuity, Incase the discount rate is 20%, calculate the present value of this perpetuity.

Solution:

$$P = \frac{A}{i} = \frac{10,000}{.20} = 50,000$$

This means that, Mr. Nandan should invest Rs. 50,000 at 20% to get an annual return of Rs. 10,000 for perpetuity.

VALUATION OF BONDS OR DEBENTURES

Meaning : A bond or debenture is an instrument of long-term debt issued by a borrower.

Technique of Valuation of Bonds or Debentures : The value of bonds or debentures is, generally, determined through the technique known as the Capitalization technique.

The process of determination of the present value of a bond or debenture can be considered under two headings viz.,

1.   When a bond or debenture is redeemable (i.e. definite maturity period).
2.   When a bond or debenture is irredeemable (i.e. as no specified definite maturity period).

Present Value of a Redeemable Bond or Debenture

When a bond or debenture is redeemable, its present value can be determined by estimating its future cash flows, and then, discounting the estimated future cash flows at an appropriate capitalisation rate or discount rate.

The estimated cash flows from the bond or debenture consists of the stream of future interest payments plus the principal repayment.

The appropriate capitalization rate or discount rate to be applied to discount the cash flows from the bond or debenture will depend upon the risk associated with the bond or debenture. If the risk is low, a lower discount rate will be applied. On the other hand, if the risk is high, a higher discount rate would be applied.

The following formula may be used to find out the present value of the bond or debenture (assuming that the bond has a maturity period of 4 years):

$$V = \frac{I_1}{(1+K_d)^1} + \frac{I_2}{(1+K_d)^2} + \frac{I_3}{(1+K_d)^3} + \frac{I_4+M}{(1+K_d)^4}$$

Where,

V	= the present value of the bond or debenture.
I	= annual interest payment.
K_d	= the capitalization rate or the discount rate.
M	= The maturity value of the bond or debenture.

Alternatively, the present value of the bond or debenture can be ascertained through the table called the 'discount rate tables or present value tables'.

Illustration 10: A debenture of Rs. 1,000, issued by a company, matures in 5 years. The rate of interest payable by the company on the debenture is 7% p.a. the appropriate capitalization rate is 5%.

Calculate the present value of the debenture.

Solution:

Through the formula:

$$V = \frac{I_1}{(1+K_d)^1} + \frac{I_2}{(1+K_d)^2} + \frac{I_3}{(1+K_d)^3} + \frac{I_4}{(1+K_d)^4} + \frac{I_5+M}{(1+K_d)^5}$$

$$V = \frac{70}{(1+05)^1} + \frac{70}{(1+05)^2} + \frac{70}{(1+05)^3} + \frac{70}{(1+05)^4} + \frac{100}{(1+05)^5}$$

The present value of interest of Rs. 70 for 5 years (70 × 4.330) = 303.1

The present value of the principal at the end of the 5th year (1000 × 0.784) = 784.0

Present value of the debenture = 1087.1

Note 1: As the interest of Rs. 70 is an annual payment for 5 years, it is an annuity for 5 years. The present value of an annuity of Re. 1 for 5 years, as per the present value tables is Rs. 4.330 (As per Table A – 4).

Note 2: The Principal repayment is a lump sum repayment at the end of the 5th year, so the present value of the principal amount (as per table A – 3) is 0.784 × 1000.

OR

Through Discount Rate Table

1 Year	2 Interest payment & principal Repayment		3 Discount Factor at 5%	4 Present Value (2x3)
1	(1000 x 7/100)	= 70	0.952	66.64
2		= 70	0.907	63.49
3		= 70	0.864	60.48
4		= 70	0.823	57.61
5		= 70	0.784	54.88
	Principal Amount	= 1,000	0.784	784.00
	Present value of the debenture			1087 = 10

Illustration 11: A debenture of Rs. 2,000, issued by a company, matures in 4 years. The rate of interest on the debenture is 8% p.a. The capitalization rate is 6%. Calculate the present value of the debenture.

Solution:

Present Value of the Debenture

1 Year	2 Interest payment & principal Repayment		3 Discount Factor at 6%	4 Present Value (2x3)
1	(2000 x 8/100)	= 160	0.943	150.88
2	(2000 x 8/100)	= 160	0.890	142.40
3	(2000 x 8/100)	= 160	0.840	134.40
4	(2000 x 8/100)	= 160	0.823	131 = 68
	Principal Amount	= 2,000	0.823	1646 = 00
			Present value	= 2205.36

Present Value of a perpetual or Irredeemable Bond or Debenture

When a bond or debenture is irredeemable, its present value can be determined by simply discounting the stream of interest payments for the infinite period by an appropriate capitalization rate or discount rate.

The following formula may be used to determine the present value of the bond or debenture.

$$V = 1/K_d$$

Where,

V - means the present value of the bond or debenture.

I – means annual interest payment.

K_d – means the capitalization rate or the discount rate.

Illustration 12: A perpetual debenture of the face value of Rs. 1,000 is issued by a company. The rate of interest payable by the company is 6% p.a. The appropriate capitalization rate is 5%. Calculate the present value of the debenture.

Solution:

$V = 1/K_d$ Here, I = Annual Interest i.e. $1000 \times 6/100 = 60$

$$K_d = 5\% \text{ or } 0.05$$

Therefore, 60/0.05 = 1,200.

VALUATION OF PREFERENCE SHARES

Meaning : Preference shares are issued by a joint stock company for raising share capital from the public. It may be redeemable preference shares or irredeemable preference shares.

The value of preference shares also is, generally, determined through the capitalization technique.

The process of determination of the present value of preference share is the same as that of bonds or debentures. The process or determination of the present value of a preference share can be considered under two heads viz.

1.   When preference share is redeemable.

2.   When preference share is irredeemable.

1.   *When preference share is redeemable:* Present value of a redeemable preference share can be determined by estimating its future cash flows, and then discounting the estimated future cash flows at an appropriate capitalization rate or discount rate.

The estimated future cash flows from the preference share consists of the stream of future dividend payment plus the par value of the preference share.

The following formula may be used to determine the present value of the preference share (assuming that the preference share has a maturity period of 3 years).

$$V = \frac{D_1}{(1+K_p)^1} + \frac{D_2}{(1+K_p)^2} + \frac{D+M}{(1+K_p)^3}$$

Where,

V = present value of the preference shares

D = Annual dividend payment.

K_p = Capitalization rate or discount rate.

M = Maturity value i,e., the value of the preference share.

Alternatively, the present value of the preference share can be determined though the table called the present value Tables.

Illustration 13: X Ltd. has issued 7% preference shares of Rs. 100 each. The preference shares are redeemable after 5 years. The appropriate capitalization rate is 5%.

Calculate the present value of a preference share

$$V = \frac{D_1}{(1+K_p)^1} + \frac{D_2}{(1+K_p)^2} + \frac{D_3}{(1+K_p)^3} + \frac{D_4}{(1+K_p)^4} + \frac{D_5+M}{(1+K_p)^5}$$

$$V = \frac{7}{(1+05)^1} + \frac{7}{(1+05)^2} + \frac{7}{(1+05)^3} + \frac{7}{(1+05)^4} + \frac{100}{(1+05)^5}$$

That is,

7×4.330	= 30.31	
100×0.784	= 78.40	
Present value	= 108.71	

Note: (i) The present value of an annuity of Re. 1 at the capitalization rate of 5% at the end of the 5th year is 4.330.

(ii) The present value of Re. 1 at the capitalization rate of 5% at the end of the 5th year is 0.784.

1 Year	2 Dividend payment And share Repayment	3 Discount Factor at 6%	4 Present Value
1	$(100 \times 7/100)$ = 7	0.952	6.66
2	$(100 \times 7/100)$ = 7	0.907	6.35
3	$(100 \times 7/100)$ = 7	0.864	6.05
4	$(100 \times 7/100)$ = 7	0.823	5.76
5	$(100 \times 7/100)$ = 7	0.784	5.49
	Share Amount = 100	0.784	78.40
		Present value	=108.71

Present value of perpetual or an irredeemable preference share

The present value of irredeemable preference share can be determined by simply discounting the streams of dividend payment for the infinite period by an appropriate capitalization rate of the discount rate.

Formula:

$$V = \frac{D}{K_p}$$

Where,

V = Present value of the preference share.

D = Annual dividend payment on the preference share.

K_p = Capitalization rate.

Illustration 14: X company issued 8% irredeemable preference shares of Rs. 100 each. The capitalization rate is 6%. Compute the present value of a preference share.

Solution:

$$V = \frac{D}{K_p} = \frac{8}{0.06} = 133.33$$

Here,

D = (8% of 100) = 8

K_p = 0.06

VALUATION OF EQUITY SHARES

The valuation of equity shares is difficult as compared to the valuation of debenture or preference shares. This is because of two reasons.

(a) Equity shares do not carry a fixed dividend or interest rate as is the case with preference shares or debentures. Equity shareholders may or may not get dividends.

(b) Earnings or dividends on equity shares are expected to grow unlike the interest on debentures and preference dividend.

Methods of Valuation : Valuation is basically based upon two approaches :

Dividend Capitalization Approach : This is conceptually a very sound approach. According to this, the value of an equity share is equivalent to the present value of future dividends plus the present value of the price expected to be realized on its re-sale. The approach is based on the following assumptions.

(a) Dividends are paid annually.

(b) The dividend is received after the expiry of one year of purchase equity share.

Two possible valuation models can be used for this purpose.

1. *Single period valuation model :* Here, it is presumed, that the investor expects to hold the equity share for a year only. In such a case, the value of the equity share will be equivalent to, the present value of dividend at the end of the first year plus the present value of the price he expects to receive on selling of share.

$$P_0 = \frac{D_1}{(1+K_e)} + \frac{P_1}{(1+K_e)}$$

Where,

 P_0 = Current price of the equity share

 D_1 = Dividend per share expected at the end of the first year.

 P_1 = Expected market price of the share at the end of the first year.

 K_e = The required rate of capitalization.

Illustration 15: Mr X holds an equity share, giving him an annual dividend of Rs. 20. He expects to sell the share for Rs. 180 at the end of a year. Calculate the value of the share if the required rate of return is 12%.

$$P_0 = \frac{D_1}{(1+K_e)} + \frac{P_1}{(1+K_e)}$$

$$P_0 = \frac{20}{(1+.12)} + \frac{180}{1+.12}$$

$$P_0 = 178.57$$

2. *Multi period Valuation Model:* When the dividend Rate is Constant

Formula

$$P_0 = \frac{D_e}{K_e}$$

Where,

 P_0 = Current value of an equity share.

 D_e = Expected annual dividend per equity share.

 K_e = Capitalization rate.

Illustration 16: ABC Ltd, is currently paying a dividend of Rs. 40 per share. It is expected that, the company will not deviate from this rate in future. The current capitalization rate is 15%. Calculate the present value of an equity share.

Solution:

$$P_0 = \frac{D_e}{K_e} = \frac{40}{.15} = Rs. 267$$

When Growth in Dividends

In the above illustration, we have presumed that, dividend per share remains constant year after year. However, this presumption however, is unrealistic. The earnings and dividends of most companies grow over time at least because of their retention policies.

Illustration 17: A company has a share capital of Rs. 5,00,000. The company has the policy of retaining 60% of its earnings. Calculate the growth rate in dividends if the company earns 10% on its capital employed.

Solution:

1st Year	
Total Earnings (10% of 5,00,000)	50,000
Less : Retained earnings 60% (60% of 50,000)	30,000
Dividend distributed	20,000
2nd Year	
Earnings on capital employed (50,000 + 10% of 30,000)	53,000
Less : Retained earning 60% of 53,000	31,800
Dividend Distributed	21,200

$$\text{Therefore, Growth in Dividends} = \frac{\text{Dividend in 2}^{nd}\text{ Year} - \text{Dividend in 1}^{st}\text{ year}}{\text{Dividend in 1}^{st}\text{ year}} \times 100$$

$$= \frac{21,200 - 20,000}{20,000} \times 100$$

$$= 6\%$$

(a) *Constant growth in dividends* : While valuing equity shares in most of the cases it is presumed that, the dividend grows at a constant rate. This means that, the dividend at the end of the First Year will be :

$$D_1 = D_0 (1+g)$$

Similarly, dividend at the end of the Second Year will be :

$$D_2 = D_0 (1+g)^2 \text{ and so on.}$$

The formula for valuation of the equity shares with a constant growth rate in dividends can now be put as follows :

$$= P_0 = \frac{D_0(1+g)^1}{(1+k_e)^1} + \frac{D_0(1+g)^2}{(1+k_e)^2} + \frac{D_0(1+g)^n}{(1+k_e)^n}$$

$$P_0 = \frac{D_1}{(K_e - g)}$$

Where,

D_1 = Dividend at the end of the year.

P_0 = Current market price of an equity share.

K_e = Capitalization rate.

G = Growth rate in dividend.

Illustration 18: XYA, is expected to pay a dividend at Rs. 40 per share. Dividends are expected to grow perpetually at 10%. Calculate the market value of the share if capitalization rate is 15%.

Solution:

$$P_0 = \frac{D_1}{(K_e - g)}$$

$$= \frac{40}{(.15 - .10)} = \frac{40}{0.05} = \text{Rs. } 800$$

(b) *Variable Growth in Dividends* : In some companies, dividends grow at a super normal rate during the period when, there is a constant increasing demand for the company's products. The dividend starts to grow at a normal rate after the demand for the company's product reaches the normal level.

Illustration 19: A Company is expected to pay a dividend of Rs. 4 per share after a year. Its dividends are then expected to grow at 15% for the next five years and then at the rate of 8% indefinitely. Find out the present value of its share, if the capitalization rate is 12%.

Solution:

I Step

Present value of dividends

Year		Dividends	P.V. Factor @ 12%	Present Value
1		4.00	0.893	3.57
2	4.00 + (15% of 4.00)	4.60	0.797	3.67
3	4.60 + (15% of 4.60)	5.29	0.712	3.77
4	5.29 + (15% of 5.29)	6.08	0.636	3.87
5	6.08 + (15% of 6.08)	7.00	0.567	3.97
6	7.00 + (15% of 7.00)	8.05	0.507	4.08
				22.93

II Step

The dividend for the 7th year is likely to be: [8.05 + 8.05 × 8/100] = 8.695

Apply the formula for valuation of shares under constant growth in dividend, for finding out the present value at the end of the 6th year i.e.

$$P_6 = \frac{D_7}{(K_{e-gn})}$$

Where,

P_6 = Present value of share at the end of the 6th year.

D_7 = Expected Dividend for the 7th year.

gn = Normal growth in dividends.

K_e = Capitalization rate.

On substituting,

$$P_6 = \frac{8.694}{(.12 - .08)} = \text{Rs. } 217.35$$

III Step

Present value of shares = 217.35 × 0.507 = 110.20

IV Step or Final Step

Value of share = Present value of share + Present value of dividend

i.e. = Value of share = 110.20 + 22.93

= 133.13

Earning Capitalization Approach

In the following two cases, the value of an equity share can be determined by capitalizing the expected earnings.

1. When the earnings of the firm are stable.

2. When there is no growth but simply there is only expansion situation.

$$\text{Formula} = P_0 = \frac{E_1}{K_e}$$

Where,

E = Expected earning per share.

K_e = Capitalization rate.

P_0 = Current value of an equity share.

Illustration 20: Calculate the price of an equity share according to dividend capitalization approach and earnings capitalization approach with the help of the following facts.

Earning per share =   Rs. 20

Capitalization rate =   12%

Retained Earning =   Nil

Solution:

Dividend Capitalization Approach

$$P_0 = \frac{D_1}{K_e} = \frac{20}{.12} = Rs.\ 166.67$$

Earnings Capitalization Approach

$$P_0 = \frac{D_1}{K_e} = \frac{20}{.12} = Rs.\ 166.67$$

PRACTICE YOURSELF

Illustration 1: Mr. Bhat has deposited Rs. 1,00,000 in a Savings bank account at 6 per cent simple interest and wishes to keep the same, for a period of 5 years. He requested you to give accumulated interest.

Solution:

$$S_I = P_o(I)(n) = Rs. \ 1,00,000 \times 0.06 \times 5 \ years = Rs. \ 30,000$$

If the investor wants to know his total future value at the end of 'n' years. Future value is the sum of accumulated interest and the principal amount. Symbolically:

$$FV_n = P_o + P_o(I)(n) \ or \ S_I + P_o$$

Illustration 2: Krishna's annual savings is Rs. 1,000, which is invested in a bank saving fund account that, pays a 5 per cent simple interest. Krishna wants to know his total future value or the terminal value at the end of a 8 years time period.

Solution:

$$FV_n = P_o + P_o(I)(n) \ or \ S_I + P_o$$
$$FV_n = Rs. \ 1000 + Rs. \ 1000 \ (0.05)(8) = Rs. \ 14,000$$

COMPOUND INTEREST

Illustration 3: Suppose you have Rs. 10,00,000 today, and you deposit it in a financial institute, which pays you 8 per cent compound interest annually for a period of 5 years. Show how the deposit would grow.

$$Solution: C_{vn} = P_o (1 + I)^8$$
$$FV_5 = 10,00,000(1+0.08)^5 = 10,00,000 \ (1.469)$$
$$FV_5 = Rs. \ 14,69,000$$

Note: See the compound value for one rupee Table for 5 years at 8 per cent rate of interest.

Variable Compounding Periods

Illustration 4 (Semi annual compounding) : How much does a deposit of Rs. 40,000 grow in 10 years at the rate of 6 per cent interest and compounding is done semi-annually. Determine the amount at the end of 10 years.

Solution:

$$CV_{10y} = Rs. \ 40,000 \left(1 + \frac{0.06}{2}\right)^{2 \times 10}$$

$$= Rs. \ 40,000 \ [1.806] = Rs. \ 72,240$$

Note: See the compound value for one rupee Table for year 20 and at 3 per cent interest rate.

Illustration 5 (Quarterly compounding): Suppose a firm deposits Rs. 50 lakhs at the end of each year, for 4 years at the rate of 6 per cent interest and compounding is done on a quarterly basis. What is the compound value at the end of the 4th year.

Solution:

$$FV_4 = Rs. \ 50,000,000 \left(1 + \frac{0.06}{4}\right)^{4 \times 4}$$

$$= Rs. \ 50,00,000 \ [FV1F_{3y....8y}]$$
$$= Rs. \ 50,00,000 \times 1.267 = Rs. \ 63,35,000$$

CALCULATION OF THE COMPOUND GROWTH RATE

Compound growth rate can be calculated with the following formula :

$$g_r = V_0(1 + r)^n = V_n$$

where,

g_r = Growth rate in percentage.

V_0 = Variable for which the growth rate is needed (i.e., sales, revenue, dividend at the end of year '0').

V_n = Variable value (amount) at the end of year 'n'.

$(1 + r)^n$ = Growth rate.

Illustration 6: From the following dividend data of a company, calculate compound rate of growth for period (1998 – 2003).

Year	1998	1999	2000	2001	2002	2003
Dividend per share (Rs.)	21	22	25	26	28	31

Solution:

$$21 (1 + r)^5 = 31$$

$$(1 + r)^5 = 31 / 21 = 1.476$$

Note: See the compound value one rupee Table for 5 years (total years – one year) till you find the closest value to the compound factor, after finding the closest value, see first above it to get the growth rate.

Compounded/Future Value Of Series Of Cash Flows [Annuity]

Illustration 7: Mr. Bhat deposits each year Rs. 5000, Rs. 10000, Rs. 15000, Rs. 20000 and Rs. 25000 in his savings bank account for 5 years at the interest rate of 6 per cent. He wants to know his future value of deposits at the end of 5 years.

Solution:

$$CV_n = 5000(1+0.06)^4+10000(1+0.06)^3+15000(1+0.06)^2+20000(1+0.06)^1+25000(1+0.06)^0$$

$$CV_5 = 5000(1.262)+10000(1.191)+15000(1.124)+20000(1.050)+25000(1.00)$$

$$= 6310 + 11910 + 16860 + 21000 + 25000 = Rs. 81,080/-$$

CV can also be calculated in the following ways.

Year (1)	Amount paid Rs. (2)	No. of years compounded (3)	Compound interest factor (4)	Future value Rs. (5) = (2) x (4)
1	5000	4	1.262	6,310
2	10,000	3	1.191	11,910
3	15,000	2	1.124	16,860
4	20,000	1	1.05	21,000
5	25,000	0	1.00	25,000
TOTAL				81,080

Compound Value of Annuity (Even Cash Flows)

Illustration 8: Mr. Ram deposits Rs. 500 at the end of every year, for 6 years at 6 per cent interest. Determine Ram's money value at end of 6 years.

Solution:

$$FV_n = P_1 (1+I)^{n-1} + P_2 (1+I)^{n-2} + \text{---------}P_{n-1}(1+I)+P^{n-n}$$

$$FV_6 = 500(1+0.06)^5+500(1+0.06)^4+500(1+0.06)^3+500(1+0.06)^2+500(1+0.06)^1 + 500(1+0.06)^0$$

$$= 500(1.338) + 500(1.262) + 500(1.19) + 500(1.124) + 500(1.060) + 500(1.00)$$

$$= 669 + 631 + 595.5 + 562 + 530 + 500 = Rs.\ 3487.5$$

By using table format,

Year	Amount Paid Rs.	No. of years compounded	Compound interest factor	Future value Rs.
1	500	5	1.338	669.00
2	500	4	1.262	631.00
3	500	3	1.191	595.50
4	500	2	1.124	562.00
5	500	1	1.06	530.00
6	500	0	1.00	500.00
TOTAL				**3,487.50**

Short-cut formula

$$CV_n = P\left[\frac{(1+I)^n - 1}{I}\right]$$

Where,

P = Fixed periodic cash flow.

I = Interest rate.

n = Duration of the amount.

$$\frac{(1+I)^n - 1}{1} = (FVIFA_{I.n})$$

$(FVIFA_{I.n})$ = Future value for interest factor annuity at 'I' interest and for 'n' years.

Illustration 9 : Take the above example.

$$CV_6 = 500\left(\frac{(1+0.06)^6 - 1}{0.06}\right)$$

$$= 500\ [6.975] = Rs.\ 3487 = 50$$

Note: See the compound value of annuity table of one rate for 6 years at 6 per cent interest.

Compound Value of Annuity Due

Illustration 10: Suppose you deposit Rs. 2500 at the beginning of every year for 6 years in a saving bank account at 6 per cent compound interest. What is your money value at the end of the 6 years.

Solution:

$$CV_6 = 2500 \left(\frac{(1+0.06)^6 - 1}{0.06} \right) (1 + 0.06)$$

$$= 2500 \, (6.975) \, (1 + 0.06) = Rs. \, 18,483.75$$

Through the Table format

Year	Cash outflow Rs.	No. of times compounded	Compound factor	Compound value (Rs.)
1	2500	6	1.419	3,547.50
2	2500	5	1.338	3,345.00
3	2500	4	1.262	3,155.00
4	2500	3	1.191	2,977.50
5	2500	2	1.124	2,810.00
6	2500	1	1.06	2,650.00
	TOTAL			18,485.00

DOUBLING PERIOD

Doubling period is the time required, to double the amount invested at a given rate of interest. For example, if you deposit Rs. 10,000 at 6 per cent interest, and it takes 12 years to double the amount. (see compound value for one rupee table at 6 per cent till you find the closest value to 2).

Doubling period can be computed by adopting two rules, namely:

1. *Rule of 72 :* To get doubling period 72 is divided by interest rate.

    Doubling period $(D_p) = 72 \div I$

    Where,

    I = Interest rate.

    D_p = Doubling period in years.

    Illustration 11: If you deposit Rs. 500 today at 10 per cent rate of interest, in how many years will this amount double?

Solution:

$$D_p = 72 \div I = 72 \div 10 = 7.2 \text{ years (approx.)}$$

2. *Rule of 69 :* Rule of 72 may not give the exact doubling period, but rule of 69 gives a more accurate doubling period. The formula to calculate the doubling period is:

    $$D_p = 0.35 + 69 / I$$

Illustration 12: Take the above problem as it is and calculate doubling period.

Solution:

$$D_p = 0.35 + 69 / 10 = 7.25 \text{ years.}$$

EFFECTIVE RATE OF INTEREST IN CASE OF DOUBLING PERIOD

Sometimes investors may have doubts as to what is the effective interest rate applicable, if a financial institute pays double amount at the end of a given number of years.

Effective rate of interest can be defined by using the following formula.

(a) *In case of rule of 72*

ERI = 72 per cent Doubling period (D_p)

where,

ERI = Effective rate of interest.

D_p = Doubling period.

Illustration 13: A financial institute has come with an offer to the public, where the institute pays double the amount invested in the institute by the end of 8 years. Mr. A, who is interested to make a deposit, wants to know the affective rate of interest that will be given by the institute. Calculate :

Solution:

ERI = $72 \div D_p$ = $72 \div 8$ years = 9 per cent

(b) *In case of rule of 69*

$$ERI = \frac{69}{D_p} + 0.35$$

Illustration 14: Take the above example:

$$ERI = \frac{69}{8 \text{ years}} + 0.35$$

= 8.98 per cent or 9 per cent

PRESENT VALUE

Illustration 15: An investor wants to find the present value of Rs. 40,000, due 3 years. His interest rate is 10 per cent.

Solution:

$$P_v = FV_3 \left(\frac{1}{1+I}\right)^3$$

$$= \text{Rs. } 40,000 \left(\frac{1}{(1+0.10)}\right)^3$$

$$= \text{Rs. } 40,000 \, [0.751^{\bullet}] \qquad = \text{Rs. } 30,040$$

Note: Present value of one rupee Table at 3 years for the rate of 10 per cent.

Present value of a series of cash flows

Illustration 16: From the following information, calculate the present value at 10 per cent interest rate.

Year	0	1	2	3	4	5
Cash inflow (Rs.)	2,000	3,000	4,000	5,000	4,500	5,500

Solution:

$$P_v = \frac{2000}{(1+0.10)^0} + \frac{3000}{(1+0.10)^1} + \frac{4000}{(1+0.10)^2} + \frac{5000}{(1+0.10)^3} + \frac{4500}{(1+0.10)^4} + \frac{5500}{(1+0.10)^5}$$

$$= 2000 + 2727 + 3304 + 3755 + 3073.5 + 3415.5 = \text{Rs. } 18.275$$

Present value can also be calculated by the following way:

Years	Cash inflow (Rs.)	PV Factor 10 per cent	Present value (Rs.)
0	2000	1.00	2000.0
1	3000	0.909	2727.0
2	4000	0.826	3304.0
3	5000	0.751	3755.0
4	4500	0.683	3073.5
5	5500	0.621	3415.5
Total present value			**18275.0**

(c) *Present value of even cash flows (annuity)*

Present Value of Deferred Annuity

$$PVA_n = \frac{CIF_1}{(1+I)^1} + \frac{CIF_2}{(1+I)^2} + - - - - - - \frac{CIF_n}{(1+I)^{n-1}} + \frac{CIF}{(1+I)^n}$$

or

$$CIF \left(\frac{(1+I)^n - 1}{I(1+I)^n} \right) = CIF \, (PVIFA_{I.n})$$

Where,

PVA = Present value of annuity.

I= Discounting factor or interest rate.

CIF = Cash inflows.

n = Duration of the annuity.

Illustration 17: Mr. Bhat wishes to determine the PV of the annuity consisting of cash flows of Rs. 40,000 per annum for 6 years. The rate of interest he can earn from this investment is 10 per cent.

Solution:

$$= \text{Rs. } 40{,}000 \times \text{PVIFA}_{\text{I.n}}$$
$$= \text{Rs. } 4000 \times 4.355 = \text{Rs. } 17{,}420$$

Note: See present value of annuity table for 6 year at 10 per cent.

Alternate way to find present value

Years	Cash inflow (Rs.)	PV Factor 10 per cent	Present value (Rs.)
1	4000	0.91	364.0
2	4000	0.826	3304.0
3	4000	0.751	3004
4	4000	0.683	2732.0
5	4000	0.621	2484.0
6	4000	0.564	2256.0
PV of Annuity			17420

Alternate way

Years	Cash inflow (Rs.)	PV factor at 10 per cent	PV (Rs.)
1 to 6	4000	4.355	17,420

Present value of Annuity Due

$$\text{PVA}_n = \text{CIF} \, (\text{FVIF}_{\text{I.n}}) \, (1 + I) \text{ or}$$

$$\text{PVA}_n = \text{CIF} \left(\frac{1 - (1+I)^{-n}}{I} \right)(1+I)$$

Illustration 18: Mr. Bhat has to receive Rs. 500 at the beginning of each year, for 4 years. Calculate personal value of annuity due, assuming 10 per cent rate of interest.

Solution:

$$\text{PVA}_4 = \text{Rs. } 500 \, (3.170) \times (1.10) = \text{Rs. } 1743.5$$

Alternatively

Years	Cash inflow (Rs.)	PV Factor at 10 per cent	Present value (Rs.)
1	500	1.00	500.0
2	500	0.909	454.5
3	500	0.826	413.0
4	500	0.751	375.5
PV of Annuity			1743.0

EFFECTIVE VS NOMINAL RATE

The nominal rate of interest or rate of interest per year is equal. Effective and nominal rate are equal only when the compounding is done yearly once, but there will be a difference, that is, effective rate is greater than the nominal rate for shorter compounding periods. Effective rate of interest can be calculated with the following formula.

$$ERI = \left(1 + \frac{I}{m}\right)^m - 1$$

Where,

I = Nominal rate of interest.

m = Frequency of compounding per year.

Illustration 19: Mr. X deposited Rs. 1000 in a bank at 10 per cent of the rate of interest with quarterly compounding. He wants to know the effective rate of interest.

Solution:

$$ERI = \left(1 + \frac{0.10}{4}\right)^4 - 1$$

$$= 1.1038 - 1 = 0.1038 \text{ or } 10.38 \text{ per cent.}$$

SINKING FUND FACTOR

The financial manager may need to estimate the amount of annual payments so as to accumulate a predetermined amount after a future date, to purchase assets or to pay a liability. The following formula is useful to calculate the annual payment.

$$A_p = FVA_n \left(\frac{I}{(1+I)^n - 1}\right)$$

Where,

A_p = Annual payment.

VA_n = Future value after 'n' years.

I = Interest rate.

$$\left(\frac{I}{(1+I)^n - 1}\right) = FVIFA_{I.n}$$

Illustration 20: The finance manager of a company wants to buy an asset costing Rs. 1,00,000 at the end of 10 years. He requests to find out the annual payment required, if his savings earn an interest rate of 12 per cent per annum.

Solution:

$$A_p = 1,00,000 \left(\frac{0.12}{(1+0.12)^{10} - 1}\right)$$

$$= 1,00,000 \ (0.12 \ or \ 2 \ / \ 2.1058) \ = Rs. \ 5698.5$$

$$A_p = 1,00,000 \times \frac{1}{FVIFA_{12\%,10y}}$$

$$= 1,00,000 \times \frac{1}{17.548}$$

$$= Rs. \ 5698.65$$

Present Value of Perpetuity

Perpetuity is an annuity of infinite duration. It may be expressed as :

$$PV_\infty = CIF \times PVIFA_{I,\infty}$$

Where,

PV_∞ = Present value of a perpetuity.

CIF = constant annual cash inflow.

$PVIFA_{I,\infty}$ = PV interest factor for a perpetuity.

$$PV_\infty = CIF \ / \ I$$

Illustration 21: Mr. Bhat an investor, expects a perpetual amount of Rs. 1000 annually from his investment. What is his present value of this perpetuity if the interest rate is 8 per cent?

Solution:

$$PV_\infty = CIF/I \quad = 1000/0.08 = Rs. \ 12,500$$

LOAN AMORTISATION

Loan is an amount raised from outsiders at an interest and repayable at a specified period (lumpsum) or in installments. The repayment of loan is known as amortisation. A financial manager may take a loan and he may interested to know the amount of equal instalment to be paid every year to repay the complete loan amount including interest. Instalment can be calculated with the following formula :

$$L_I = P_A \left(\frac{I(1+I)^n}{(1+I)^n - 1} \right)$$

or

$$L_I = P_A \div PVIFA_{n,I}$$

Where,

L_I = Loan installment.

P_A = Principal amount.

I   = Interest rate.

n   = Loan repayment period.

$PVIFA_{n,I}$ = PV interest factors at loan repayment period at a specified interest rate.

Illustration 22: ABC Company took a loan of Rs. 10,00,000 lakh for an expansion program from IDBI at 7 per cent interest per year. The amount has to be repaid in 6 equal annual installments. Calculate the per instalment amount.

Solution:

$$L_I = 10,00,000 \left(\frac{0.06(1+0.06)^6}{(1+0.06)^6 - 1} \right)$$

or

$$L_I = 10,00,000 \div \text{PVIFA}_{7\%,\ 6y}$$
$$= 10,00,000 \div 4.769 \quad = \text{Rs. } 2,09,687.56$$

Present Value of Growing Annuity

Growing annuity means the cash flow that grows at a constant rate for a specified period of time. In others, the cash flow grows at a component rate.

Steps involved in calculation :

1. Calculate the series of cash flows.
2. Convert the series of cash flows into present values at a given discount factor.
3. Add all the present values, of series of cash flows to get total PV of a growing annuity.

Formula

$$PVG_A = \frac{CIF}{(1+g)} \left(\frac{1 - \dfrac{(1+g)^n}{(1+I)^n}}{(1-g)} \right)$$

Where,

PVG_A = PV of growing annuity.

CIF = Cash inflows.

g= Growth rate.

I = Discount factor.

n= Duration of the annuity.

Illustration 23: XYZ real estate agency has rented one of their apartment for 5 years at an annual rent of Rs. 6,00,000 with the stipulation that, rent will increase by 5 per cent every year. If the agency's required rate at return is 14 per cent. What is the PV of expected (annuity) rent?

Solution:

Step 1 : Calculate on series of annual rent

Year	Amount of rent (Rs.)
1	6,00,000
2.	6,00,000 X (1 + 0.05) = 6,30,000
3.	6,30,000 X (1 + 0.05) = 6,61,500
4.	6,61,500 X (1 + 0.05) = 6,94,575
5.	6,94,575 X (1 + 0.05) = 7,29,303.75

Step 2 : Calculate present values

Years	Cash inflow (Rs.)	Discounting Rate 14 per cent	Present value (Rs.)
1	600,000	0.877	526200.0
2	630,000	0.769	484470.0
3	661,500	0.675	446512.5
4	694,575	0.592	411188.4
5	729,303.75	0.519	378508.6
Total PV of Annuity			**22,46,879.55**

Shorter Discounting Periods

Generally cash flows are discounted once a year, but sometimes cash flows have to be discounted less than one (year) time, like, semi-annually, quarterly, monthly or daily. The general formula used for calculating the PV in the case of shorter discounting period is :

$$PV = CIF_n \left(\frac{1}{1+I/m} \right)^{m \times n}$$

Where,

$$
\begin{aligned}
PV &= \text{Present value.}\\
CIF_n &= \text{Cash inflow after 'n' year.}\\
m &= \text{No. of times per year discounting is done.}\\
I &= \text{Discount rate (annual).}
\end{aligned}
$$

Illustration 24: Mr. A expected to receive Rs.1,00,000 at the end of 4 years. His required rate of return is 12 per cent and he wants to know PV of Rs. 1,00,000 with quarterly discounting.

Solution:

$$PV = 1,00,000 \left(\frac{1}{1+0.12/4} \right)^{4 \times 4}$$

$$= 1,00,000 \times PVIF_{3 \text{per cent } 4y}$$

$$= 1,00,000 \times 0.623 \quad = Rs. 62,300$$

TEST QUESTIONS

Objective Type Questions

1. **Fill in the blanks with appropriate word(s)**

    (a) Simple interest (SI) = P_o (I) (_____).

    (b) _____ is a stream on uniform periodic cash flows.

    (c) _____ an annuity, whose first cash flow occurs at the present time.

    (d) Interest payable or receivable on interest _____.

(e) _____is the process of finding the present value of a future cash flow or a series of future cash flows.

(f) Ignoring time value of money is one of the limitations of _____ Maximisation objective.

(g) A rupee receivable today is more _____than a rupee which is receivable in future.

(h) _____is repayment of loan over a period of time.

(i) _____ opportunity is one of the reasons for time preference of money.

2. **State whether each of the following statement is true or false**

(a) Current consumption is one of the reasons for time preference of money.

(b) Compound value and future value both, are same.

(c) There are two rules available to find out double period.

(d) Effective rate of interest is more than the nominal rate of interest in single period compounding.

(e) Rule 73 is one of the rules of doubling period.

(f) Cost of capital interest rate requires rate of return and discounting rate factor, all are used for calculating of PV of cash flows.

(g) Compound growth rate formula is $V_o (1 + r) = V_n$.

(h) A series of unequal cash flows are called Annuity.

(i) $0.35 + 69/I$ is the formula used to calculate present value of perpetuity.

(j) Cash flows are divided with interest (per cent) rate to calculate future value of perpetuity.

[Answers : (a) True, (b) True, (c) True, (d) False, (e) False, (f) True, (g) False, (h) False, (i) False, (j) False]

REVIEW QUESTIONS

1. What do you understand by "Discounting" ?

2. List out the reasons for time preference of money.

3. How do you calculate the present value?

4. What do you mean by time value of money ?

5. Why does money have time value ?

6. What is compounding interest ?

7. Explain the meaning and importance of valuation concept. How does valuation concept help in decision making ?

8. Explain the procedure to calculate a) The present value of a series of cash flows b) The present value of an annuity.

9. Define Annuity.

10. Give the formula for the compound value of a single amount.

11. Explain the rule of 69. How does it compare with the rule of 72 ?

12. Distinguish between ordinary annuity and annuity due.

13. "A bird in hand is more preferable than two birds in the bush". Explain.

14. "A rational human being has a time preference for money". Give reasons.

15. "Cash flows of different years in absolute terms are incomparable." Discuss.

16. State the relationship between the effective rate of interest and the nominal rate of interest. Explain the mechanics of calculating the present value of cash flows ?

17. "Time value of money is helpful in capital budget." Explain.

18. What happens to the PV of annuity, when the interest rate declines ?

PROBLEMS

1. Mr. X deposited Rs. 1,00,000 in a savings bank account today, at 5 per cent simple interest for a period of 5 years. What is his accumulated interest? [Answer: Rs. 25000]

2. Mr. X invested Rs. 40,000 today, for a period of 5 years. Calculate the future value if his required rate of returns is 10 per cent. [Answer: Rs. 64,440]

3. Suppose you deposit Rs. 1,00,000 with an investment company, which pays 10 per cent interest with semi annual compounding. What is the total deposit amount at the end of 5 years? [Answer: Rs. 162,889]

4. Mr. A deposits at the end of each year Rs. 2000, Rs. 3000, Rs. 4000, Rs. 5000 and Rs. 6000 for the consequent 5 years respectively. He wants to know his series of deposits value at the end of 5 years with 6 per cent rate of compound interest. [Answer: Rs. 21,893]

5. Assume you have been depositing each year for 5 years, the deposit amount of Rs. 100, Rs. 200, Rs. 300, Rs. 400 and Rs. 500 respectively. Calculate your deposits value if you get 7 per cent compound interest and assume you have deposited in the beginning of each year. [Answer: Rs. 1885]

6. If you invest Rs. 500 today, at a compound interest of 9 per cent, what will be its future value after 60 years? [Answer: Rs. 88015]

7. A borrower offers 16 per cent rate of interest with quarterly compounding. Determine the effective rate of income. [Answer: 17 per cent]

8. A finance company has advertised saying that, it will pay a lumpsum of Rs. 44,650 at the end of 5 years to anyone who deposits Rs. 6000 per annum. Mr. A is interested, but he wants to know the implicit rate of interest. [Answer: 20 per cent]

9. What is the present value of Rs. 1,00,000, which is receivable after 60 years. If the investor required rate of interest is 10 per cent. [Answer: Rs. 324.9]

10. From the following information, calculate the present value if the cost of capital is 10 per cent.

Year	0	1	2	3	4	5	6
Cash flow (Rs.)	250	400	700	900	1000	1100	1400

[Answer: Rs. 4023.4]

11. Ramesh deposits Rs. 20,00,000 in a bank account that pays 8 per cent interest. How much can he withdraw annually for a period of 10 years. [Answer: Rs. 298, 063]

12. Mrs. X deposits Rs. 5000 at the end of each year, at 8 per cent per year. What amount will she receive at the end of 6 years ? [Answer: Rs. 36,680]

13. A company has raised a loan of Rs. 50 lakhs from an industrial finance bank at 9 per cent p.a. The amount has to be paid back in 5 equal installments. Calculate the instalment amount. [Answer: Rs. 12,85,347]

14. ABC Company has Rs. 10,00,000, 8 per cent debentures redeemable after 5 years. The company plans to redeem debentures by establishing sinking fund, where company can earn 10 per cent interest p.a. What annual payment must the firm make to ensure, that the needed amount is available on the required date ? [Answer: Rs. 1,63,800]

15. Calculate the present value of Rs. 10,000 received in perpetuity for an infinite period, assuming 12 per cent discount rate. [Answer: Rs. 83, 333]

16. SS purchases a computer system for Rs. 35,000, which is borrowed on a 15 per cent interest. The loan is to be repaid in 12 EMI, payable at the end of each month. Determine the loan instalment amount. [Answer: Rs.3,159]

17. A company purchases a fixed asset for Rs. 4,00,000 by making a down payment of Rs. 1,00,000 and the remaining balance in equal installments of Rs. 1,00,000 for 4 years. What is the rate of interest to the firm. [Answer: Rs. 12 per cent.]

18. For the following cases, calculate the amount money at the end of the deposit period.

Case	Initial Amount	Interest Rate (%)	No. of Years	Compounding period (in months)
1	4000	8	4	3
2	2000	10	5	6
3	1000	11	10	12

[Answer : (1) Rs. 5492 (2) Rs. 3,528 (3) Rs. 2389.40]

19. Find the present value of the following cash flows using a discount rate of 10%.

Year	Cash Flow(Rs.)
1 -3	1,000
4	2,000
5	3,000
6 -14	1,000
15	4,000

[Answer : 10,247. 34]

20. XYS bank pays 12% and the compound interest quarterly. If Rs. 1,000 is deposited initially, how much shall it grow at the end of 5 years.

21. How will you value redeemable preference shares?

22. Explain the two approaches, which are adopted for valuation of equity shares with examples.

23. A debenture of Rs. 1,000 carries a coupon rate of 14%. It is to mature after 5 years. The required rate of return is 13%. Calculate the value of the debenture. [Answer : 1034.40]

24. At present a share of Rs. 1,000, carries a dividend rate of 10%. The current market rate is 15%. The share becomes due for redemption after 10 years. Calculate the value of the equity share. [Answer : 748.90]

25. An equity share of Rs. 10 is expected to earn an annual dividend of Rs. 2 and the share will be sold for Rs. 18 after a year. The required rate of return is 12%. Calculate the value of the equity share. [Answer : 17.86]

PRACTICE YOURSELF

TIME VALUE OF MONEY

Exercise One : Comparing Mortgage Alternatives

The application of the time value of money principles can help you make decisions on loan alternatives. This exercise requires you to compare three mortgage alternatives using various combinations and points. Points on a mortgage refer to a payment that is made upfront to secure the loan. A single point is a payment of one per cent of the amount of the total mortgage loan. If you were borrowing Rs. 200,000 a single point would require an upfront payment of Rs. 2,000.

When you are evaluating alternative mortgages, you may be able to obtain a lower rate by making an upfront payment. This comparison will not include an after-tax comparison. When taxes are considered, the effective costs are affected by interest paid and the amortization of points on the loan. This analysis will require you to compare only before-tax costs.

Zeal.com allows you to compare the effective costs on alternative mortgages. You are considering three alternatives for a Rs. 250,000 mortgage. Assume that the mortgage will start in December, 2006. The mortgage company is offering you a 6% rate on a 30-year mortgage with no points. If you pay 1.25 points, they are willing to offer you the mortgage at 5.875%. If you pay 2 points, they are willing to offer you the mortgage at 5.75%.

1. What are the mortgage payments under the three alternatives?
2. Which alternative has the lowest effective cost?
3. Can you explain how the effective rate is being calculated?

Exercise Two: Comparing Auto Loan Alternatives

You are considering the purchase of a new car. You have negotiated with the salesperson at the dealership and can purchase the vehicle for Rs. 30,000. You have Rs. 8,000 that can be used as a down payment.

Before the going to the dealer, you had made up your mind and set an absolute limit of Rs. 375 as the monthly payment amount that you can make on the car. You are willing to finance over five years but you cannot exceed the payment of Rs. 375 per month. The dealer is offering to finance you at an annual rate of 6.5% for a 5-year loan or at 5.5% financing on a 4-year loan.

1. Can you meet your payment restriction and finance the amount required for the car?
2. What is the maximum amount that you can borrow, to meet your payment restriction if the loan is to be paid off in 5 years?
3. Suppose, you are limited to paying Rs. 375 per month but you want to pay the loan off in 4 years and not 5 years. What is the maximum amount that you can borrow?

WEBSITE REFERENCE

1. http://www.fei.org/

REFERENCES

1. Bierman, H. Jr., "*The Capital Budgeting Decisions*", Mac millan, 1975, p. 69-72.
2. Ibid.

PART III

FINANCIAL ASSETS

Bonds and their Valuation

8

Objectives

After studying this chapter, you should be able to:

1 Understand the types of bond and preference shares

2 Analyse the yield and interest rates

3 Explain the yield to maturity

4 Discuss the bond duration and price volatility

5 Know the pre-emptive rights preference share yields

6 Describe the holding period return

7 Understand the valuation of fixed income securities

THE THREE STEP VALUATION PROCESS

Implicit in all rational buy-sell transactions relating to claims, goods, and services is the question. Is it good or real? The investor surrenders a cost (time or money) in exchange for promised benefits. Both cost and benefits have to face uncertainty since nothing except death and taxes appear certain in this world. The basic valuation process, therefore, is a constant exercise in rationally with cost, benefits, and uncertainty as important variables.

The question of the valuation process following a sequence has been widely examined in the literature and the industry performance, in turn, is linked to performance of the economy and the market in general. The three sequential steps in the valuation process would, therefore, be as follows.

1. Economy analysis
2. Industry analysis
3. Company analysis

Economy Influences

All firms are parts of the overall systems known as the 'general economy' which records ups and downs. It is special to begin the valuation process with projections of the 'macro economy'. What you should grasp is the vast number of influences that affect the 'general economy'. To give only a few examples. Fiscal policy affects spending both directly and through its multiplier effects. Monetary policy affects the supply and cost of funds available to business units. Interest rates and hence required rates of return are influenced by expected inflation. Balance payments position exchange rates and hence required rates of return are influenced by expected inflation. Balance of payments affects the performance of the economy. A well-informed investor will first attempt to project the future course of the economy. Should he anticipate a recession? He should get his cash back and say 'goodbye' to new investments. If this projection indicates conditions of boom, he should select industries most likely to benefit from the expected phase of prosperity.

Industry Influences

All industries are not influenced equally by changes in the economy nor are they are affected by busy cycles at just one single point of time. For example, in an international environment of peace treaties and restrained cold war, profits of defence-related industries would wane as the economy is not likely to benefit from industries. Similarly, a boom or expansion of the economy is not likely to benefit industries subject to foreign competition or product obsolescence. A weak firm in boom industry might prove more rewarding than a leader in a weak or declining industry. Of course, the investor would continuously be through a search process that identifies the best firms in strong industries, and narrow down his area of search for investment out.

THE GENERAL VALUATION FRAMEWORK

Most investors look at price movements in securities markets. They perceive opportunities of capital gains in movements. All would wish that they could successfully predict these and ensure their gains. Few, however, recognize that value determines price and both change randomly. It would be useful for an intelligent investor to be aware of this process. The present section examines this process in detail. We first present a brief outline of the evaluation model and then proceed do discuss the relationship of value with price via investor-market-action and shall also recall active and passive investment strategies and finally figure out the dynamic valuation model.

The Basic Valuation Model

Value of security is a fundamental variable and depends on its promised return, risk, and the discount rate. It may recall your basic understanding of present value concept with the mention of fundamental factors like sum and discount rate. In fact, the basic valuation model is none else than the present value procedure. Given a adjusted a discount rate and the future expected earnings flow of a security in the form of interest, dividend, earnings or cash flow, you can always determine the present value as follows:

$$PV = \frac{CF_1}{1+r} + \frac{CF_2}{(1+r)^2} + \frac{CF_3}{(1+r)^3} + - - - - - - + \frac{CF_n}{(1+r)^n}$$

PV = Present value

CV = Cash, flow, interest, dividend, or earnings per time period upto 'n' number of periods.

R = Risk adjusted discount rate (generally the interest rate)

Expressed in the above manner, the model looks simple. But practical difficulties do make the use or model complicated. For instance, it may be quite in the fitness of this that a single value is generated. Whose does the valuation job (a professional analyst or an intelligent investor), the safest course would be work on margin of error. Thus, the value estimated may be Rs. 100 + Rs. 20 and not just Rs. 100 or Rs. 800 or Rs. 120 will realize that market operations would become tedious with a range of values. Secondly, return risk and value would tend to change over time. Thus security prices may rise or fall with buying and selling pressures respective (assuming supply of securities does not change) and this may affect capital gains and hence returns expect. Consequently, estimates of future income will have to be revised and values reworked. Similarly, the risk complete of the security may change over time. The firm may over borrow (and face operating risk) or engage in a venture (and face operating risk). An increase in risks would raise the discount rate and lower value. It would seem to be a continuous exercise Every new information will affect values and the buying and selling pressed which keep prices in continuous motion would drive them continuously close to new values. The last part of section portrays this dynamic valuation model with ever-changing information inputs.

Value-Price Relationship

You would recall that investments strategies can be 'passive' or 'active'. Following this, investors and investment managers can also be broadly grouped in 'passive' and 'active' categories. You should note that buying and selling pressures dominantly originate with active investors. And they follow certain rules of the game which are:

Rule 1: Buy when value is more than price. This underlines the fact that shares are under priced and it was to be a bargain to buy now and sell when prices move up towards value.

Rule 2: Sell when value is less than price. In a situation like this, shares would be overpriced and it would advantageous to sell them now and avoid less when price later moves down to the level of the value.

Rule 3: Don't trade when value is equal to price. This is a state when the market price is an equilibrium is not expected to change.

An example would make the operation of these rules and the consequential investor action clear. Asses that the share of a hundred-per cent-export-unit (EOV) is currently trading at Rs. 80 against a face value of Rs...? Now the new of the company having lost a value export contract amounting to around 40% its expect total export sales in the coming year is received by most active investors in the market. They revise the estimate of future income downward by 40% and, risk, discount rate and other things remaining unchanged. Review the present value at

Rs. 48 (60% of Rs. 80). Now, this takes you to rule 2 when you value us less than price more appropriately when price is more than value). One would expect a decline in price due to an adverse net affecting the present value. Active investors would price begin selling to avoid probable losses so the selling pressure would be generated and its supply of shares does not change. Such a pressure would reduce price till such time that it nears the new present value viz., Rs. 45. Contrarily, take the case of a company whose share was trading at Rs. 20 (with a par of Rs. 10). Now, the alert and active investors obtain the news of the lifting of a year-long lock-out and signing of three-wage agreement quite beneficial to management much before even media could get hold of it. Other things including risk and discount rate remaining unchanged, analysts revise the estimates of the present value to Rs. 40 (Rs. 10 below the peak of the last year when the company was work normally). You will see the case now falling under rule 1. Investors would expect price to move up towards the next value of Rs. 40 and would immediately start buying at or around the current price of Rs. 20. This will generate buying pressures and the price would increase if supplies of the scrip do not increase at the same time.

VALUATION OF FIXED INCOME SECURITIES

A debenture is a legal document containing an acknowledgement of indebtedness by a company. It contains a promise to pay a stated rate of interest for a defined period and then to repay the principal at a given date of maturity.

In short, a debenture is a formal legal evidence of debt and is termed as the senior securities of a company.

Unlike equity holders, the bond investor does not share in the growth of a company to any appreciable extent. Thus, although serious losses can accrue to bond holders if a company suffers financial reverses, they cannot profit to any significant degree by a spectacular improvement in the company's position. It is a case of heads they lose and tails they cannot win. Therefore, their primary role in an investment portfolio is to provide continuity of income under all reasonably conceivable economic conditions.

BOND FEATURES

Indenture: The indenture is a long, complicated legal instrument containing the restrictions, pledges and promises of the contract. Bond indenture involves three parties. The first party is the debtor corporation that borrows the money, promises to pay interest, and promises to repay the principal borrowed.

Maturities: Maturities vary widely. Bonds are usually grouped by their maturity classes.

Interest Payments: Bond interest is usually paid semi-annually, though annual payments are also popular. The method of payment depends upon whether the bond is a coupon (bearer) or registered bond.

Call Feature: Most modern corporate bonds are callable at the discretion of the issuer. This gives the issuing company the right to recall a bond before it reaches maturity.

Reasons for Issuing Bonds

To Reduce the Cost of Capital: Bonds are the cheapest source of financing.

To Widen the Sources of Funds: By issuing bonds, the corporation can attract funds from individual investors and especially from those investing institutions which are reluctant or not permitted to purchase equity shares.

To Preserve Control: An increase in debt does not diminish the voting power of present owners since bonds ordinarily carry no voting right.

To Gain the Benefit of Leverage: The presence of debt and / or preference shares in the company's financial structure means that it is using financial leverage. When financial leverage is used, changes in earnings before interest and tax (EBIT) translate into the larger changes in earnings per share.

To Effect Tax Saving: Unlike dividends on equity, the interest on bonds is deductible in figuring corporate income for tax purposes. Hence, the EPS increases if the financing is through bonds rather than with preference or equity shares.

Types of Bonds

Convertible and Non-Convertible Bonds: Convertible bonds can be one of the finest holdings for the investor looking for both appreciation of investment and income of bond. A convertible bond is a cross between a bond and a stock. The holder can at his option, convert the bond into a predetermined number of shares of common stock at a predetermined price.

Collateral Trust Bonds: Instead of being secured by a pledge of tangible property, as are mortgage bonds, collateral trust issues are secured by a pledge of intangibles, usually in the form of stocks and bonds of corporation. Collateral trust issues are thus secured by (1) shares, representing ownership in corporation, (2) bonds, representing the indirect pledge of assets, or a combination of both. Usually, the pledged securities are those of other corporations.

Income Bonds: Income bonds are bonds on which the payment of interest is mandatory only to the extent of current earnings. If earnings are sufficient to pay only a portion of the interest, that portion usually is required to be paid, but if the corporation is able to pay the unearned balance out of its cash resources, it is of course free to do so.

Redeemable and Irredeemable Bonds: A redeemable debenture is a bond which has been issued for a certain period, on the expiry of which its holder will be repaid the amount thereof with or without premium. A bond without the aforesaid redemption period is termed as an irredeemable debenture. These may be repaid either in the event of the winding-up of company or the happening of certain specified uncertain or contingent events.

Participating Bonds: Companies with poor credit positions issue participating bonds. They have a guaranteed rate of interest but may also participate in earnings up to an additional specified percentage.

Sinking Fund Bonds: Sinking fund bonds arise when the company decides to retire its bond issue systematically by setting aside a certain amount each year for the purpose. The payment, usually fixed annual rupees amount or percentage instalment, is made to the sinking fund agent who is usually the trustee.

Serial Bonds: Like sinking fund bonds, serial bonds are not special types of bonds but just names given to describe the method of repayment. Thus, any bond can become such by merely specifying it in the indenture.

Mortgage or Secured Bonds: The term mortgage generally refers to alien on real property or buildings. Mortgage bonds may be open-end, close-end, and limited open-end. An open-end mortgage means that a corporation under the mortgage may issue additional bonds. But the open-end mortgage indenture usually provides that the corporation can issue more bonds only if the earnings or additional security obtained by selling the new securities meet certain tests of earnings and asset coverage.

Risk Management in Bonds

A bond ensures a fixed return over a period of time, defined by the bond agreement. In the market-place, the rates of interest are not constant and vary with time. Owing to the changes in interest rate from the date of entering into a debt contract to the date of maturity of the debt contract, the investor faces the risk. Apart from price risk, bond investors also face a reinvestment risk. This risk is inherent since there is an assumption that interest rates are reinvested at the same rate as defined in the bond contract.

Default Risk: Default risk identifies the uncertainty prevalent in the repayment of interest and principal to the bondholders.

Purchasing Power Risk: Debt instrument investors have to look at the real rate of return, or the actual return minus the rate of inflation. Rising inflation has a negative impact on the real rates of return, because inflation reduces the purchasing power of the investment income and principal.

Price Risk: Investors who need their principal prior to maturity have to rely on the available market for the securities.

Liquidity Risk: The exchange listing of debt securities does not guarantee liquidity. The liquidity in the market is mostly influenced by the demand and supply situation for that instrument by the market players.

Reinvestment Risk: The maturity period of bonds is spread over a fixed time duration. Since the par value or repayment value is also fixed, the investor purchasing the debt instrument for such a long duration is holding it for a known fixed rate of interest, irrespective of fluctuations in interest rates in the market.

PLAYERS IN THE DEBT MARKET

Both government and private enterprises that need long-term financial assistance issue fixed interest securities in all countries. Government participants could be the Central Government, state governments, or other regional administrations. When public sector enterprises issue bonds, they are also usually categorised as government bonds since they have characteristics similar to government bonds. The table below shows the value of bonds traded in the Wholesale Debt Market (WDM) segment of the National Stock Exchange in India.

Value of Bonds Traded in WDM Segment of NSE (April 1, 2006)

Sec. Type	Name	Issue Rate (%)	Weighted YTM (%)	Low Price (Rs.)	High Price (Rs.)
BB	SBI08	11.90	5.4911	122.4173	122.5384
DB	LT09	6.0	5.7350	101.0718	101.1142
GF	CG2011	+0.13	5.0109	100.1100	100.1100
GS	CG2008	12.25	4.8029	129.4300	129.4300
IB	IDBI11	12	5.9823	136.7000	136.7000
ID	IDBI05	15.50	8.0238	108.3090	108.3090
PT	NTPC07	8.05	5.4100	107.8226	107.8226
TB	364D (04R05)	-	4.0000	96.7144	96.7144
CP	ICICBK (040804)	-	4.7501	98.4119	98.4119

BB-Bank Bonds, DB-Debentures, GF-Government Floating Rate Instrument, GS-Central Government Security, IB-SLR Bond, ID-Non-SLR Bond, PT-Taxable PSU Bonds, TB-Treasury Bills, CP-Commercial Paper.

Source: The Economic Times, April 1, 2006.

New issues of corporate bonds are similar to the issue of equity instruments. Debt instruments are issued in the primary market of the stock exchange, just like equity instruments. It is usually a public offer for sale at a fixed price. They may also be issued by auction in some markets. In the auction method, no price is fixed. Debt instruments are sold to the highest bidder at the price they submitted at the auction.

The issue of government bonds, on the other hand, is often most crucial since it reflects the monetary policy of the country. The traditional method of issue of government bonds is a sale by tender in which the government offers a specified quantity of debt instruments for sale on a specific day at a minimum price and invites bids. If the offer is undersubscribed, all offers are accepted. In this instance, the government retains the unsold stock and releases it to the market subsequently when conditions are favourable. Such subsequent issues are known as "tap stock". On the other hand, if it is oversubscribed, the highest bids are accepted, but at a common price.

The government may also choose the auction method to issue the instruments in the market. In this method, no minimum price is set. The bonds are sold to the highest bidders at the price they bid. From the point of money supply, sale by auction has the advantage that the issuer can set the volume, knowing that it will be fully subscribed, since the price will adjust to ensure this. The third method is to 'buy' the bond itself and to release it to the market as and when market conditions permit. This is similar to the 'tap stock' issue by the government.

After debt instruments are issued in the stock exchanges, they subsequently come into the secondary market for trading. The secondary market trading systems are either 'quote-driven' or 'order driven', or have a mixed nature. Dealer markets are called quote-driven markets. In dealer markets, the dealer makes a market by holding an inventory of his stocks and announcing (continuously) a price at which he is prepared to buy and sell. Since the quotes are given first, the available price is known beforehand; this is known as a quote-driven market.

In an order-driven market, trade takes place when dealers can match orders to buy and sell. In this case, they are responding to orders and trying to find a price that will match the maximum number of buy and sell orders. The matching process may be continuous or it may take place at specified times. Sometimes, these markets may also work on a call basis rather than on a continuous basis. In case of a call basis, there is a call auction at the beginning of the day where all orders accumulated since the last close of trading are executed, followed by continuous trading throughout the day. Buyers and sellers may specify with their order whether they wish to exercise their order immediately or at the next call. In such cases, auctioneers do not hold their own inventory level since they buy from a seller and simultaneously sell to a buyer.

BOND VALUATION

Debt securities issued by governments, government and quasi-government organizations, and private business firms are fixed income securities. Bonds and debentures are the most common examples.

The intrinsic value of bond or debenture is equal to the present value of its expected cash flows. The coupon interest payments, and the principal repayment are known and the present value is determined by discounting these future payments from the issuer at an appropriate discount rate or market yield. The usual present value calculations are made with the help of the following equation.

$$PV = \sum_{t=1}^{n} \frac{c}{(1+r)t} + \frac{C}{(1+r)n}$$

Where   PV = the present value of the security today (i.e., time period zero)

                      C = coupons or interest payments per time period 't'

TV = the terminal value repayable at maturity; this could be at par, premium, or even at discount (in extraordinary cases)

r = the appropriate discount rate or market yield

n = the number of years to maturity

Illustration 1: Consider Rs. 1,000 bound issued with a maturity of five years at par to yield 10% interest is paid annually and the bond is newly issued.

Solution:

The value of the bond would be as follows.

$$PVA = \frac{Rs.\ 100}{1 + .10} + \frac{Rs.\ 100}{(1 + .10)^2} + \frac{Rs.\ 100}{(1 + .10)^3} + \frac{Rs.\ 100}{(1 + .10)^4} + \frac{Rs.\ 100}{(1 + .10)^5}$$

$$= 100 \times .90.91 + 100 \times .8264 + 100 \times .7513 + 100 \times .6830 + 1100 \times .6209$$

$$= 90.91 + 82.64 + 75.13 + 68.30 + 682.99$$

$$= 999.97 \text{ or Rs. 1000 approximately.}$$

You should recognize that the present value of the bond viz., Rs. 1,000 estimated above is equal to the issue price because the bond was just been sold at par of Rs. 100.

Now, consider another Rs. 1,000 bond B is issued ten years ago at a coupon at 6%. The bond had a maturity period of ten years and as of today, therefore, five more years are left for final repayment at par. The current discount rate is 10% as before. All other characteristics of bond B are identical with bond A.

It is obvious that the present value of bond B will not be Rs. 1,000 because investors will not pay this price and agree to receive Rs. 60 per year as interest for the next five years when bond A with similar characteristics provides annual interest payments of Rs. 100 for the five years. The represent value of bond B will be determined.

$$PVA = \frac{Rs.\ 60}{1 + .10} + \frac{Rs.\ 60}{(1 + .10)^2} + \frac{Rs.\ 60}{(1 + .10)^3} + \frac{Rs.\ 60}{(1 + .10)^4} + \frac{Rs.\ 60}{(1 + .10)^5}$$

$$= 60 \times .90.91 + 60 \times .8264 + 60 \times .7513 + 60 \times .6830 + 1100 \times .6209$$

$$= 54.55 + 48.59 + 45.08 + 40.98 + 657.15$$

$$= Rs.\ 847.35$$

You will observe that the numerator of the PV equation will be given at the time of issuance of the bond or the nature. The maturity period, timing of interest is payments, and maturity value will also be specified. What should to be determined is the denominator of the equation viz., the discount rate. You may notice that the rate is with the same features. In other words, it is an opportunity cost. Thus, the discount rate incorporates the timing of interest rates and reflects the current market yield for the issue.

Should interest payments be semi-annual, the PV equation will have to be modified as follows: divide 'ct' both end and by multiply 'n' by 2. The resultant equation will be.

$$PV = \sum_{t=1}^{2n} \frac{ct/2}{(1 + r/2)^t} + \frac{C}{(1 + r/2)^{2n}}$$

Coming semi-annual payments, present values of bonds A and B the above examples can be solved as under.

$$PV_A = \sum_{t=1}^{10} \frac{Rs.50}{(1.05)^t} + \frac{1000}{(1.05)^{10}}$$

$$= Rs.\ 999.985 \text{ or Rs. 1000 approx.}$$

$$PV_A = \sum_{t=1}^{10} \frac{Rs.30}{(1.05)^t} + \frac{1000}{(1.05)^{10}}$$

$$= 845.551$$

ESTIMATING RETURNS ON FIXED INCOME SECURITIES

Several measures of returns on bonds are available. They are the coupon rate, the current yield and the yield maturity. The coupon rate is specified at the time of issue and is all too obvious. The other two measures can discussed.

Current yield: This is calculated as follows

$$\text{Current yield} = \frac{\text{Stated (coupon) interest per year}}{\text{Current market price}}$$

Illustration 2: 15% Rs. 200 debenture is currently selling for Rs. 220, the annual current yield would be

$$\frac{Rs\ 30}{Rs.\ 220} = 13.64\%$$

You must notice that the 15% debenture is currently selling for Rs. 220 because interest rates subsequently declined and debenture/bond prices move inversely with interest rates. The current yield having declined to 13.64%. The coupon rate of 15% reflects this.

Current yield is a superior measure than coupon rate because it is based on the current market price. However, it does not account for the difference between the purchase price of the bond/debenture and its maturity value.

YIELD-TO-MATURITY (YTM)

This is most widely used measure of return on fixed income securities. It may be defined as (promised) compounded rate of return, the investor will receive from a bond purchased at the current market and held to maturity. Computing YTM involves equating the current market price of bond with the discount value of future interest payments and the terminal principal repayment. Thus, YTM equates the two values, value of the market price and the present value of future payments including the principal repayment.

Illustration 3: Assume that an investor purchased a 15% Rs. 500 fully secured non-convertible debenture at par five year ago. The current market price of the debenture is Rs. 400, which implies increase in market interest rates subsidy to the issue of the security. Five years remain to maturity and the debenture is repaid at par. What is required in this case is a value of YTM that equates Rs. 400 with the sum of present values 75% for 5 years and of Rs. 500 receivable at the end of the fifth year. The yield-to maturity can be estimated as follows.

Solution:

The yield-to maturity can be estimated as follows:

Several values of YTM can be tried till the equating value emerges. Trials can be started with the current with the next trial rate increased if the present value of the preceding trial exceeds the current market and vice versa.

Thus, trying at 15%, the following present value of the right hand side cash flows is estimate.

$$PV_{15\%} = \text{Rs. 75 per annum} \times PVIF_{a.yrs.15\%} + \text{Rs. 500} \times PVIF_{15\%.5yrs}$$

$$= \text{Rs. 75} \times 3.3522 + \text{Rs.500} \times .4972 = \text{Rs. 251.42} + 248.60$$

$$= \text{Rs. 500.08}$$

Since the PV of Rs. 500.08 exceeds Rs. 400, a higher discount rate must be tried.

$$PV_{20\%} = \text{Rs. 75} \times 2.9906 + \text{Rs. 500} \times .8333$$

$$= \text{Rs. 224.295} + \text{Rs. 200.95}$$

$$= \text{Rs. 425.245}$$

Even the second trial has failed to equate the two values. Hence, you can go over to the third trial at, say

$$PV_{24\%} = \text{Rs. 75} \times 2.7454 + \text{Rs. 500} \times .3411$$

$$= \text{Rs. 205.91} + \text{Rs. 170.55}$$

$$= \text{Rs. 376.46}$$

The third trial has lowered the present value to Rs. 376.46 which is less than Rs. 400. Hence, the required must lie between 20% and 24$. The estimate can be obtained by interpolating, thus:

$$YTM = \frac{20\% + 425.245 - 400.00 \times (24\% - 20\%)}{425.245 - 346.46} = \frac{20\% + 25.245 \times 4\%}{48.785}$$

$$20\% + 2.07\% = 22.07\%$$

It may note that YTM calculation is similar to calculating the internal rate of return. Calculators and computers made these calculations and computers made these calculations extremely easy. You may further note that the YTM is just a promised yield and the cannot earn it unless the bond /debenture is held to maturity. And if you have to hold the security till you cannot, at the same time, sell it. Thus, there would be no trading. One significant implication of such of that the investor simply buys and holds and assumes all intermediate cash flows in the form of interest principal repayments be reinvested at YTM. In other words, the YTM concept is a compound interest concept investor earning interest-an-interest at YTM throughout the hold period till maturity. You should understand intermediate cash flows are not reinvested at YTM, the realizes yield actually earned will differ from the rate receipts are reinvested at different rates (interest being receivable semi-annually).

Coupon Interest Income (Rs.) (1)	Assumed Reinvestment (%) (2)	Interest on Interest income (Rs.) (3)	Total return (Rs.) (4)	Realized Return (%) (5)
2000	0	0	2000	5.57
2000	5	1370	3370	7.51
2000	8	2751	4751	8.94
2000	9	3352	5352	9.46
2000	10	4040	6040*	10.00
2000	11	4830	6830	10.56
2000	12	5738	7738	11.14

Notes:

Vol. 1: Coupon interest @ 10% on Rs. 1,000 received for 20 years semi-annually = Rs. 50 × 40 periods = Rs. 2000 Interest on interest at the assumed reinvestment rate for 40%

Vol. 3: Co. 1 + Col. 3 + Co.4

Vol. 4: Sum of an annuity of Rs. 50 for 40 periods at 5% semi-annual reinvestment rate is thus period annuity factor = 120.80 × 50 = Rs.6040*

Vol. 5: Realized return = (Future value per rupee invested)$^{1/N-1}$

$$\text{Future value per rupee invested} = \frac{\text{Total return} + \text{Cost of bond}}{\text{Cost of bond}}$$

The realized return is the compound return on semi-annual basis. For an annual basis, this figure must be doubled. The table above clearly demonstrates the critical nature of the reinvestment rate assumption of YTM. You note that the realized return is equal to the YTM of 10% only when the reinvestment rate is 10%. At a payment rate of zero (i.e., the investor consumes away all intermediate cash flows from the bond), interest-on-interest is zero and the realized return is a low 5.57% in contrast, at a reinvestment rate of 12%, the interest-on-interest is Rs. 5738 (i.e. 5738/7738 = around 75% of total return) and the realized return 11.14%

Investors must make specific assumptions about re-investment rates in order to gain ideas about realisations. Zero coupon bonds eliminate the reinvestment rate risk because investors know at the time of purchase of YTM that will be realized when the bond is held to maturity.

$$\text{Approximate YTM} = \frac{\text{Coupon Interest} + MP_n - MP_t}{[MPn + MP]/2}$$

where MPn is market price at, if maturity and MPt is market price (or cost) at beginning.

Illustration 4: Air Cell pays 12% per annum quarterly interest rates due every March, June, September, and December end. The quoted price in the market is Rs. 86 on January 24, 2003. Determine the accrued interest as on this date.

Solution:

The accrued interest is $(12/4) * (24/97) = 3 * 0.2474 = Rs\ 0.74$

Illustration 5: ABS group 10% per annum half-yearly interest rates are due every March and September end and has a current quoted price of Rs 44 on February 3. What should be the price at which the debentures will be exchanged in the market on this date?

Solution:

The accrued interest amount is $(10/2) * (126/182) = 5 * 0.6923 = Rs\ 3.46$

Exchange price (dirty price) = 44 + 3.46 = Rs 47.46.

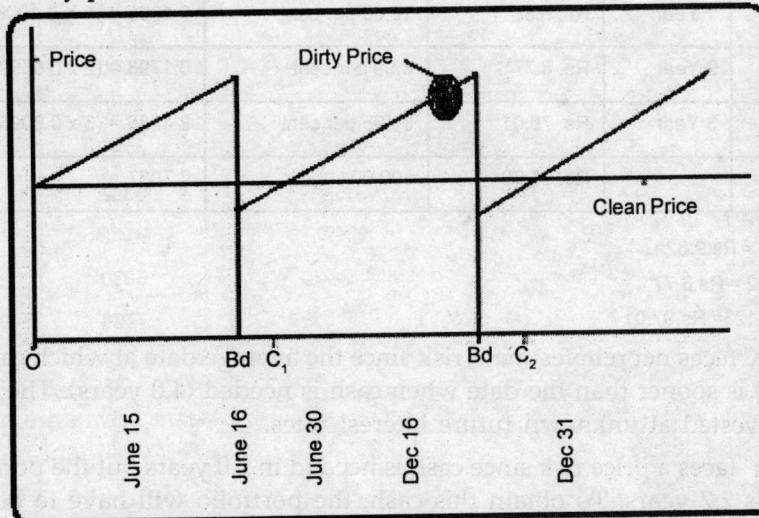

The effect of book-closure dates

Illustration 6: An investor is considering the purchase of the following debenture:

Maturity / 3 years   Coupon / 11%   Par / Rs.100

(a) If the investor requires a YTM of 13% on debentures of equivalent risk and maturity, what does he believe is a fair market price?

(b) If the debenture is selling for a price of Rs.97.59, what is its promised YTM?

(c) If the investor expects the debenture to provide a final payment of Rs.105 in year 3 instead of the promised Rs. 11 (par plus coupon). Using the debenture's market price of Rs.97.59, what is his expected annual return? If the return on three-year risk-free securities is equal to 10.0%, why might this debenture sell at a higher expected return?

(d) Why is the expected return different from the yield to maturity calculated in part (b)?

(e) What is the duration of this debenture?

(f) If an investor 'X' has a horizon date of 4.0 years, why is this debenture risky to investor 'X'?

(g) If an investor 'Y' has a horizon date of 2.0 years, why is this debenture risky to investor 'Y'?

Solution:

(a) Rs. $11/(1 + 0.13)$ + Rs. $11/(1 + /13)^2$ + Rs. $111/(1 + 1.13)^3$ = Rs. 95.28

(b) By trial and error, YTM is found to be 12%:

Rs. $11/(1 + 0.12)$ + Rs. $11/ (1 + /12)^2$ + Rs. $11/(1 + 1.12)^3$ = Rs. 97.59

(c) Again, by trial and error, the expected return is 10.16%:

Rs. $11/1.1016$ + Rs. $11/ (1.1016)^2$ + Rs. $105/(1.1016)^3$ = Rs. 97.59

If the default risk on this debenture is systematic (undiversifiable), a risk premium above the risk-free rate of 10% will be required.

(d) The yield to maturity is the return which is expected only if all promised payments are indeed expected. If this is not the case, YTM will be upwardly biased measure of the true expected return.

(e) Consider the debenture to be a portfolio of three zero-coupon debentures:

Debenture	Duration	Value	Xi	Weighted Duration
1	1 Year	Rs. 9.82*	10.06 per cent	0.1006 = (1 X 0.1006) = 10.06%
2	2 Year	Rs. 8.77**	8.99 per cent	0.1798 = (2 x 0.0899) = 17.98%
3	3 Year	Rs. 79.01***	80.95 per cent	2.4285 = (3 x 0.8095) = 24.29%
		Rs. 97.60	100.00	2.7087

* Rs.11/1.12 = Rs.9.82

** Rs.11/1.12^2 = Rs.8.77

*** Rs. 111/1.12^3= Rs.97.01

(f) Investor 'X' faces net reinvestment risk since the average date at which cash is to be received (2.7 years) is sooner than the date when cash is needed (4.0 years). The portfolio will have to be reinvested at unknown future interest rates.

(g) Investor 'Y' faces a price risk since cash is needed in 2.0 years but the portfolio measures (on average) is 2.7 years. To obtain this cash, the portfolio will have to be sold at unknown future prices.

Illustration 7: RKV recently purchased a bond with a Rs.1,000 face value, a 10% coupon rate, and four years to maturity. The bond makes annual interest payments, the first to be received one year from today. Mr. RKV paid Rs.1,032.40 for the bond.

(i)   What is the bond's yield-to-maturity?

(ii) If the bond can be called two years from now at a price of Rs.1,100, what is its yield-to-call?

Solution:

(i)   A bond YTM is that interest rate that equates the bond's price to the discounted value of its promised cash flows. In this case:

Rs. 1032.40 = Rs. $100/(1 + YTM)$ + Rs.$100/(1 + YTM)^2$ + Rs.$100/(1 + YTM)^3$ + Rs.1.100 $/(1 + YTM)^4$

YTM = 9%

(ii) If the bond can be called in two years for Rs.1,100, its yield-to-call is found by solving for the YTM assuming the receipt of only two coupon payments and a call price of Rs.1,100. That is:

Rs. 1032.40 = Rs. $100/(1 + YTC)^1$ + Rs. $1,200/(1 + YTC)^2$

where   : YTC = Yield-to-call

By solving   : YTC = 125%

Illustration 8: Ravi considering investing in a bond currently selling for Rs.8,785.07. The bond has four years to maturity, a Rs.10,000 face value, and an 8% coupon rate. The next annual interest payment is due one year from today, The approximate discount factor for investments of similar risk is 10%.

(i)   Calculate the intrinsic value of the bond. Based on this calculation, should Ravi purchase the bond?

(ii) Calculate the YTM of the bond. Based on this calculation, should Ravi purchase the bond?

Solution:

(i)   The intrinsic value of a bond is equal to the discounted value of the cash flows. In this particular problem:

V = Rs. $800/(1 + 10)^1$ + Rs. $800/(1 + 10)^2$ + Rs. $800/(1 + 10)^3$ + Rs.$10,800/(1 + 10)^4$

= Rs. 727.27 + Rs. 66116 + Rs. 601.05 + Rs. 7,376.55

= Rs. 9,366.03

Because the bond is actually selling for Rs.8,785.07, the bond is underpriced and Ravi should purchase it.

(ii) The YTM is the interest rate that equates the price of the bond to the discounted value of the bond's cash flows. In this particular problem:

Rs. 8785.07 = Rs. $800/(1 + YTM)1$ + Rs. $800/(1 + YTM)^2$ + Rs. $800/(1 + YTM)^3$

+ Rs. $10,800/(1 + YTM)^4$

YRM = 12%

Because the YTM (12%) is greater than the appropriate discount rate (10%) for this bond, Ravi should purchase it.

Illustration 9: The Reliance Investment Bond 2006 was issued in January 2007 with a maturity of two years. The coupon payment is 6% per annum made every six months (face value Rs 100). If the current market price on January 15, 2007 is Rs 96, what is the yield to maturity?

Solution:

$$96 = (3/(1 + x)^1) + (3/(1 + x)^2) + (3/(1 + x)^3) + (3/(1 + x)^4 + (100/(1 + x)^4);$$

x = 0.04

(r/2) = x

Hence, the annual return from the bond (r) = 0.08(8%).

Illustration 10: RJK has its bonds traded in the Bombay Stock Exchange. The clean price of the instrument as on March 30 is Rs 188.50. An interest of 6% is paid half yearly at the end of March and September. The book closure dates are March 28 and September 27. If the instruments are exchanged as on March 30, what will be the accrued interest? What is the dirty price of the instrument?

Solution:

Accrued interest = (6/2) * [(2 – 3)/184]) = (3 * –0.0054) = –0.0163

Dirty price = clean price + accrued interest = 188.50 – 0.0163 = Rs 188.4837

Besides the concept of YTM, other yield measures are also useful to investors in identifying a possible investment opportunity. They are the running yield, simple yield to maturity, and holding period yield.

Illustration 11: Sen acquired at par a bond for Rs. 1,000 that offered a 15% coupon rate. At the time of purchase, the bond had four years to maturity. Assuming annual interest payments, calculate Sen's actual yield-to-maturity if all the interest payments were reinvested in an investment earning 18% per year. What would Sen's actual yield-to-maturity be if all interest payments were spend immediately upon receipt?

Solution:

Sen receives four Rs.150 coupon payments from the bond. Assuming that they are reinvested at 18%, those coupon payments plus the principal repayment will, after four years, have grown to an accumulated value of:

Ace. value = Rs. $150 \times (1.18)^3$ + Rs. $150 \times (1.18)^2$ + Rs. $150 \times (1.18)^1$ + Rs. $1,150 (1.18)^0$

= Rs. 246.45 + Rs. 208.86 + Rs. 177 + Rs. 1,150

= Rs. 1,782.31

As the bond had a purchase price of Rs.1,000, Sen's actual YTM over the four years is:

Actual yield = $(Rs.1,782.31/Rs.1,000)^{1/4}$ = 15.54%

If the coupon payments were spend immediately upon receipt, men the effective reinvestment rate is 0%. Thus the accumulated value of the cash flow is:

Ace. value = Rs.$150 \times (1.0)^3$ + Rs.$150 \times (1.0)^2$ + Rs.$150 \times (1.0)^1$ + Rs. $1,150 (1.0)^0$

= Rs.1600

Therefore, Sen's actual YTM over the four years is:

Actual yield = $(Rs.1600/Rs.1000)^{1/4}$

= 1.1246828 = 12.47%

Illustration 12: From the price data that follow, compute the holding period returns:

Time	Stock Price (in Rs.)
1	25
2	30
3	24
4	32

Solution:

Time	Stock Price (in Rs.)	Holding-Period Return
1	25	
2	30	(Rs. 30/Rs. 25) - 1 = 20%
3	24	(Rs. 24/Rs. 30) - 1 = - 20%
4	32	(Rs. 32/Rs. 24) - 1 =333%

Illustration 13: Calculate the value and duration for the following bonds:

Bond	Years of Maturity	Annual Interest	Maturity value
Wipro	10	Rs. 80	Rs.1,000
SBI	15	Rs. 65	Rs. 1,000

Solution:

Bond	Wipro Bond	SBI Bond		
Bond value	Rs. 1000	Rs. 872		
Year	Interest (in Rs.)	PV of Interest (in Rs.)	Interest (in Rs.)	PV of Interest (in Rs.)
1	80	74	65	60
2	80	137	65	111
3	80	191	65	155
4	80	235	65	191
5	80	272	65	221
6	80	302	65	246
7	80	327	65	265
8	80	346	65	281
9	80	360	65	293
10	1080	5002	65	301
11			65	307
12			65	310
13			65	311
14			65	310
15			1065	5036
Sum of PV of Interest		Rs. 7,247		Rs. 8,398
Duration		7.25		9.63

Illustration 14: ABC Company has just sold a Rs. 10 crore, 10-year, 12% bond issue. A sinking fund will retire the issue over its life. Sinking fund payments are of equal amount and will be made is semi-annually, and the proceeds will be used to retire bonds as the payments are made. Bonds can be called at par for sinking fund purposes, or the funds paid into the sinking fund can be used to buy bonds in the open market.

(a) How large must each semi-annual sinking fund payment be?

(b) What will happen, under the conditions of the problem thus far, to the company's debt service requirements per year for this issue over time?

(c) Now suppose ABC Ltd. set up its sinking fund so that equal annual amount, payable at the end of each year, are paid into a sinking fund trust held by a bank, with the proceeds being used to buy government bonds that pay 9% interest. The payments, plus accumulated interest, must total Rs. 10 crore at the end of 10 years, and the proceeds will be used to retire the bonds at the time. How large must the annual sinking fund payment be now?

(d) What are the annual cash requirements for covering bond service costs under the trusteeship arrangement described in part c?

(e) What would have to happen to interest rates to cause the company to buy bonds on the open market rather than call them under the original sinking fund plan?

Solution:

(a) Rs. 10,00,00,000/10 = Rs. 1,00,00,000 per year or Rs. 50,00,000 each 6 months. Since the Rs. 50,00,000 will be used to retire bonds immediately, no interest will be earned on it.

(b) The debt service requirements will decline. As the amount of bonds outstanding declines, so will the interest requirements:

Semi-annual Payment Period	Outstanding Bonds on Which Interest is Paid	Interest Payment	Sinking Fund Payment	Total Bond Service
(1)	(2)	(3)	(4)	(3) + (4) = (5)
1	Rs. 10 crore	Rs. 0.6 crore	Rs. 0.5 crore	Rs. 1.10 crore
2	9.5	0.57	0.5	1.07
3	9.0	0.54	0.5	1.04
.	.		.	.
.	.		.	.
.	.		.	.
20	0.5	0.03	0.5 crore	0.53

(a) Interest is calculated as (0.5)(0.12)(Column 2); for example: interest in Period 2 = (0.5)(0.12) (Rs. 9.5 crore) = Rs. 0.57 crore

The company's total cash bond service requirement will be Rs. 2.17 crore per year for the first year. The requirement will decline by 0.12 (Rs. 1,00,00,000) = Rs. 12,00,000 crore per year for the remaining years.

(b) Here we have a 10-year, 9% annuity whose compound value is Rs. 10 crore, and we are seeking the annual payment, PMT.

The solution can be obtained by using this equation:

$$\text{Rs. } 1,00,000,000 = \sum_{t=1}^{10} PMT(1+k)^t$$
$$= PMT(FVIFA_{9\%,\ 10})$$
$$= PMT[(1 + 0.09)^{10} - 1)]/0.09$$
$$= PMT(15.193)$$
$$PMT = \text{Rs. } 65,81,979 = \text{Sinking fund payment.}$$

(c) Annual debt service costs will be Rs. 10,00,00,000 (0.12) + Rs. 65,82,009 = Rs. 18,582.009.

(d) If interest rates rose, causing the bonds' price to fall, the company would use open market purchase. This would reduce its debt service requirements.

Illustration 15: What is the elasticity of a ten-year zero-coupon bond priced to yield 10%?

Solution:

Because it is a zero-coupon bond, its duration is equal to its maturity.

$$e1 = 10(0.10)/(1 + 0.10) = -0.9091$$

This means that for a 1% rise in interest rates (not a rise of one percentage point), the price of the bond should fall by 0.9091%.

RUNNING YIELD

The simple rate of return relating the periodic coupon payments to the clean price of the debt instrument is called the running yield. It is also known as interest yield or current yield. This method is often used to estimate profits of debt instruments held for a short term. For instance, compared to other short term interest rates, if the running yield is higher, then those instruments could be used to fund the debt instrument that has a higher running yield. The borrowing rate, hence, is lower and the investor is able to make a short-term profit by trading in the debt instrument. However, the assumption is that the time to the maturity of the debt instrument is also short.

The formula for the computation of running yield is

$$\text{Yield} = \frac{\text{Coupon}}{\text{Clean price}}$$

Illustration 16: Anil buys a Rs. 100 bond with a coupon interest of 5%. The ex-coupon (clean) price is Rs 97.45. What running yield on the bond?

Solution:

The running yield on the bond will be

$$(5/97.45)^* 100 = 5.13\%$$

The running yield of a 7% coupon bond (face value Rs 100), clean price Rs 104.58, and dirty price Rs. 104.76 will be

$$(7/104.58)^* 100 = 6.69\%$$

Illustration 17: GKB buys a 10% bond at a price of Rs 109.43 with borrowed funds at 9% interest and holds the bond for three months. What is GKB's profit from the transaction, ignoring transaction costs and capital gains/loss?

Solution:

The running yield on the bond is (10/109.43)*100 = 9.14%. The cost of borrowing funds is 9%. Hence, the profit from the transaction would be 0.14%. This, however, is not the exact benefit for GKB since he would also have incurred a capital gain or loss for the three months from the sale of the bond.

SIMPLE YIELD TO MATURITY

Simple yield to maturity takes into account not only the coupon payment but also the capital gains that are realised from holding the debt instrument over a period of time. The formula for computation of simple yield to maturity is

$$YTMs = C/P + (F - P)/(n \times p)$$

where

C = coupon amount

F = face value of the bond

P = clean price

n = number of years to maturity.

Simple yield to maturity, thus, considers the running yield plus the capital gain (the difference between face value and clean price). The assumption is that capital gains accrue evenly throughout the years of the investment.

Simple yield to maturity is useful since investors can compute the return from their bond investments till the date of redemption of these instruments. This method gives only an approximate return from the bond instrument and not the exact return from holding the instrument. This yield measure does not consider the fact that the coupon payments received can be reinvested. Hence the measure understates the yield that actually accrues to the investor.

Illustration 18: A 15-year 12% bond is bought in the market at Rs. 112.45 with five years to maturity. What is the simple yield to maturity?

Solution:

The simple yield to maturity of this instrument is computed as follows:

(12/112.45) + ([100 – 112.45]/[5*112.45]) = 0.1067 – 0.0221 = 0.0846 – 8.46%

Illustration 19: Julie buys a five-year 7% bond at Rs 99.48. What is the simple yield to maturity?

Solution:

The simple yield to maturity of this bond will be

(7/99.48) + ([100 – 99.48]/[5*99.48]) = 0.0704 + 0.0011 = 0.0715 – 7.15%.

Note that if the running yield had been computed, the return would have been merely 7.04%.

Illustration 20: Mr. Rakesh buys a 10-year 8% bond with six months to maturity at Rs 99.89. What is the simple maturity?

Solution:

The simple yield to maturity for Mr. Rakesh will be

(8/99.89) + ([100-99.89]/[0.5 * 99.89]) = 0.0801 + 0.0022 = 0.0823 = 8.23%

HOLDING PERIOD YIELD

The holding period yield further refines the return computations by considering different reinvestment rates and by recognising a holding time period which can be different from the maturity date. The equation for computing the holding period yield is as follows:

$$M_d \times (1 + 1/m\, Y_h)^{mm} = (C/m) \times (1 + 1/mi_1)^{nm-1} + (C/m) \times (1 + 1/mi_2)^{nm-2} + \ldots + (C/m) + P_1$$

where,

Y_h = holding period yield

i_1 and i_2 = rates of interest at which the first coupon, second coupon, and so on can be reinvested

P_1 = the price at which the debt instrument will be sold by the investor.

The above equation can be restated as follows:

$$Y_h = (\{[(C/m) \times (1 + 1/mi_1)]^{nm-1} + \ldots + (C/m) + P_1\}/M_d\} - 1\,) \times m$$

YIELD ON INDEX LINKED BONDS

In certain bond markets, the government and/or corporate enterprises issue bonds that have either or both of their coupon and principal linked to a price index, such as the retail price index, or a consumer index, or a commodity index, or a stock market index. To compute the yield on such index-linked bonds, it is necessary to make forecasts of the relevant index first, which are then used in the yield computation. The linkage of the bond index could vary, that is, in some instances, only coupon rates will be linked to the index while in others only the principal payment will be linked to the index. There are also instances where both principal and coupon payments are linked to the index.

For instance, if a bond linked to a Retail Price Index, (RPI) is issued the coupon payment will be

$$\text{Coupon Payment} = (C/m) \times (RPI_{C-d}/RPI_{base})$$

where,

C = coupon payment

m = times the coupon payment is made

RPI_{base} a base of the index

RPI_{C-d} = index value before the coupon payment time

In case of half-yearly payments, 'd' will be six months plus the delay in publication of index and computation of coupon payment. The computation of principal amount (assuming a principal amount of Rs 100) is principal repayment = $100 \times (RPI_{M-d}/RPI_{base})$

Here, the ratio is the proportion of retail price index value 'd' duration earlier to maturity time 'M' to base index value.

Two types of yield measures are computed for index-linked bonds-nominal yield and real yield. The nominal yield forecasts all future cash flows from the bond. Since future cash flows for the bond are linked to the index, the yield requires a forecast of future index values. In case of price indexes, the forecast is made on the basis of the expected inflation rate.

For example, the forecast of retail price index will be

$$RPI_t = RPI_{base} * (1 + i)^{m/12}$$

where,

RPI_t = the forecasted "retail price index"

RPI base = the current "retail price index"

i = the assumed future annual inflation rate

m = the number of months between base index and forecasted index.

The money/nominal yield is computed using the following equation.

$$M_d = [(C/m) \times (RPI_1/RPI_0)]/(1 + 1/m\, Y_{ri}) + [(C/m) \times (RPI_2/RPI_0)]/(1 + 1/m\, Y_{ri})^2 + \ldots\ldots\ldots\ldots\ldots$$
$$\ldots\ldots\ldots\ldots [(C/m) \times (RPI_n/RPI_0)]/(1 + 1/m\, Y_{ri})^n$$

Where

M_d = market exchange price of the bond

m = number of times coupon payments are made

Y_{ri} = nominal yield

M = maturity payment

n = total number of coupon payments till maturity.

Real yield is related to nominal yield. The computation of real yield is as follows;

$$[1 + (1/m\, Y_{ry})] = [1 + 1/m\, Y_{ri}]/[1 + i]^{1/m}$$

Here Y_{ri} is the nominal yield and 'i' is the forecasted inflation rate and Y_{ry} is the real yield. The equation used for computing the real yield can be restated as follows:

$$M_d = RPI_a/RPI_0 = [(C/m)/(1 + 1/m\, Y_{ry})] + \ldots\ldots.. + [(C/m)+M/(1 + 1/m\, Y_{ry})^n]$$

where,

$$RPI_a = RPI_1(1 + i)^{(1/m)}$$

where,

RPI_1 = index in the first year

i = the inflation rate

m = the number of times interest is compounded

Illustration 21: An index-linked bond (eight years) with a coupon rate of 3% per annum (half-yearly) was issued in April 1996. The base RPI for 1996 was 146.3, while the RPI for 2006 was 183.9. Calculate the actual coupon payment and principal repayment.

Solution:

Coupon payment = (3/2) * (183.9/146.3) = 1.88551

Principal payment = 100 * (183.9/146.3) = 125.70061

The computed nominal yield of a bond is 4.3% per annum (half-yearly interest payment) and the expected inflation rate is 2%. Compute the real yield.

$$Y_{ry}/2 = \{[1 + (.043/2)]/[(1 +.02)^{\wedge(1/2)}]\} - 1$$
$$= \{1.0215/1.0099\} - 1 = 1.01149 - 1 = 0.01149$$
$$Y_{ry} = 0.01149 * 2 = 0.02298 = 2.3\%$$

SUMMARY

The question of the valuation process following a sequence has been widely examined in the literature and the industry performance, in turn, is linked to performance of the economy and the market in general. The three sequential steps in the valuation process would, therefore, be as follows – Economy analysis, Industry analysis, Company analysis.

Most investors look at price movements in securities markets. They perceive opportunities of capital gains in movements. All would wish that they could successfully predict them and ensure their gains. Few, however, organize that value determines price and both change randomly. It would be useful for an intelligent investor to be aware of this process. The present section examines this process in detail. We first presented a brief outline of the evaluation model and then proceeded to discuss the relationship of value with price via investor-market-action shall also recall active and passive investment strategies and finally figure out the dynamic valuation model.

Debt securities issued by governments, government and quasi-government organizations, and private business firms are fixed income securities. Bonds and debentures are the most common examples. The intrinsic value of bond or debenture is equal to the present value of its expected cash flows. The coupon interest payments, and the principal repayment are known and the present value is determined by discounting these future payments from the issuer at an appropriate discount rate or market yield.

REVIEW QUESTIONS

1. What types of investors are interested in debentures in general?
2. Write on the three step valuation process.
3. Explain the general valuation framework.
4. Write on value-price relationship.
5. Write on features of bond and explain them in detail.
6. What are the reasons for issuing bonds?
7. Define a bond. What are the different types of bonds? Explain in detail.
8. What is meant by yield-to-maturity (YTM)?
9. What comprises the appropriate discount rate for a given debenture?
10. Market interest rates and debenture prices are inversely related. Explain why.
11. What are some of the general characteristics found in preference shares?
12. Explain preference shares in detail.

REFERENCES

1. Hirst, F.W.: *The Stock Exchange: A Short Study of Investment and Speculation*, Oxford University Press, 1948.

2. Huang, Stanley S.C.: *Investment Analysis and Management*, Cambridge, Winthrop, 1981.

3. Hull J.C.: *Introduction to Futures & Options Markets*, Prentice–Hall, Englewood Cliffs, New Jersey, 1995.

4. Jean, William H.: *Analytical Theory of Finance: A Study of the Investment Decisions Process* and N.Y. Holt, Rinehart and Winston, 1970.

5. Jessup, Paul F: *Competing for Stock Market Profits* N.Y., Wiley, 1974. Johnson, Timothy E.: Investment Principles, N.J. Prentice–Hall, 1978.

6. Jones, Charles P., Donald L. Turtle and Cherrill P. Heaton, *Essentials of Modern Investments*, Ronald Press Company, 1977.

7. Kaufman, George, G: *Money, the Financial System and the Economy*, 2nd ed.; Chicago, Rand Mc Nally & Co. 1977.

8. Kolb, Robert W.: *Financial Derivatives*, New York Institute of Finance, New York, 1993.

9. Kroos, Herman E., and Blyn, Martin R.: *A History of Financial Intermediaries*, New York, Random House, 1971.

10. Labys, Walter C., and Granger, Clive W.J.: *Speculation, Hedging and Commodity Price Forecast*, Lexington, Mass, D.C Health and Company, 1970.

11. Lasry, George,: *Valuing common stock : The power of produce*, N.Y. Amacom, 1979.

12. Latane, Henry, A. Turtle, Donald L.; and Jones, Charles P.: *Security Analysis and Portfolio Management* 2nd ed. New York Ronald Press, 1975.

13. Leffler; George L, and Farwell, Loring C.: *The Stock Market*, 3rd ed. New York, Ronald Press, 1963.

14. Lee, Cheng F., Joseph E. Finnerty & Donald H. Wort, *Security Analysis and Portfolio Management*, Foresman and Company, 1990.

15. Lenger, H.V.R.: *Monetary Policy and Economic Growth*, Vora & Co., Bombay, 1962.

16. LEVINE, Sumner N.(ed.) Investment Managers Handbook, Illinois, Dow-Jones Irwin, 1980.

17. Levy, Haim and Sarnat, Marshal: *Investment and Portfolio Analysis*, John, Wiley, 1984.

18. *Portfolio and Investment Section Theory and Practice*, Prentice–Hall, 1984.

19. Longstreth, Bevis: *Modern Investment Management and the Prudent Man Ruk (AQ)*, Oxford University Press, 1986.

20. Lister, R.J. (ed.): *Studies in Optimal Financing*, London, Macmillan, 1973.

21. Lorie, James H. and Marry T. Hamilton: *The Stock Market: Theories and Evidence*, Homewood III, Richard D. Envin, Inc, 1973.

22. Lund, Phillips J.: *Investment: The Study of Economic Aggregates*, Edinburgh, Oliver and Boyd. 1971.

23. Maclachlan, DIL: *Guide to Share Investment* N.Y. Longman, 1977.

24. Malkiel, Burton, G.: *A Random Walk Down Wall Street*, New York, W.W. Norton & Co., Inc., 1973.

Stocks and their Valuation

9

Objectives

After studying this chapter, you should be able to:

1 Understand the introduction of equity shares

2 Analyse the equity valuation model

3 Discuss the basic models: zero growth model, constant growth model, variable growth model

4 Understand the valuation models of cyclical stocks

5 Know the models based on price ratio analysis

6 Describe the random valuation model

7 Understand the group rotation model

8 Analyse the considerations in developing and selecting quantitative strategy

9 Describe the preference shares valuation

THE PRESENT VALUE OF EXPECTED STREAM OF BENEFITS FROM EQUITY SHARES

Fundamental analysis is centred on present value, which is computed as the discounted value of future earnings. This poses two problems. One, it is neither specified (as in the case of preference shares) not stated and their timing have both to be estimated in a probabilistic scenario viz., dividends, cash flows, and earnings. The solution to the first problem is offered by past data, which is appropriately modified for future projections. Also, the doing period of investors on the margin (i.e., the major players in the market who influence the pricing in the case of active strategists and 'infinity' in the case of those who follow the 'buy-and-hold strategy' is the base for determining the timing of these benefits. A major modification to past data will be premised on received growth rates of return on equities.

The second problem can also be viewed as a case of three alternatives, not really conflicting with each other. And question is: which cash flows are appropriate in the valuation of equity shares? Now, if you buy equity and place them all in a trust fund for your and your heir's perpetual benefit, what cash flows will be received to fund? The answer is 'dividends' because this is the only cash distribution, which a company makes to that. Even though earnings per share in any year do belong to the shareholders, companies do not distribute them all. There is no doubt that investors who follow the 'buy-and-sell' strategy i.e., active strategists, would sell their whenever price changes are favourable. But since a price is the present value of future dividends investors cash flows from equity shares as a combination of dividends and a future price at which the shares can be this is equivalent to the stream of all dividends to be received on the shares.

Finally, should you regard earnings as important and use them as a measure of future benefits? Obviously, the answer is 'yes'. All dividends are paid out of earnings. Moreover, a popular approach to valuation of equity down as P/E ratio uses earnings as its basis. Hence, earnings are important. Now if all earnings are paid dividends, they will be accounted for as dividends. In the even of a part of earnings being retained, the effect will be to increase future earnings and finally the future dividends too. Present value analysis accounts for earnings reinvested currently and paid later as dividends. This carries a risk of double counting as 'earnings' are used as a measure of future benefits. In fact, the two can be properly defined and in which case the two variables viz., earnings and dividends would produce the same results. You would recognize that more than one present value model is possible in the case of equity shares viz., earnings how (i.e., earnings after tax plus depreciation). However, it is always correct to use dividends as the sum of the present value equation used to estimate the intrinsic value of equity shares. The present value that uses dividends as its variable representing the cash flow stream is known as the dividend valuation. This model is discussed below and is followed by a discussion of the P/E approach to equity shares situation.

ACTIVE EQUITY INVESTMENT STYLES

The primary styles of active equity management are top-down and bottom-up. A manager who uses a top-down equity management style begins with an assessment of the overall economic environment and a forecast of its near-term outlook and makes a general asset allocation decision regarding the relative attractiveness of the various sectors of the financial markets (e.g., equity, bond, real estate, bullion, and cash equivalents).

The top-down manager then analyses the stock market in an attempt to identify economic sectors and industries that stand to gain or lose from the manager's economic forecast. After identifying attractive and unattractive sectors and industries, the top-down manager finally selects a portfolio of individual stocks.

Active Equity Management versus Passive Equity Management

Equity Management	
Active	Passive
Subjective	Objective
Complex rules	Simple rules
Few names	Many names
Appropriate weightings	Precise weightings
Trading	
Active	Passive
Worked transactions	Programme transactions
Few names	Many names
Cash reserves	Fully vested
Monitoring	
Active	Passive
Infrequent	Constant
Approximate	Detailed

SHARE VALUATION

Share valuation is the process of assigning a rupee value to a specific share. An ideal share valuation technique would assign an accurate value to all shares. Share valuation is a complex topic and no single valuation model can truly predict the intrinsic value of a share. Valuation models can provide a basis to compare the relative merits of two different shares.

Equity valuations could be classified into the following categories:

1. Earnings valuation
2. Revenues valuation
3. Cash flow valuation
4. Asset valuation
5. Yield valuation
6. Member valuation

EQUITY VALUATION MODELS

We turn now to some of the actual models of equity valuation. The purpose of these models is to identify whether a stock is mispriced. Under-priced stocks need to be purchased; overpriced stocks should be shorted. As most modern equity valuation models are based upon the present value theory, set forth in detail by John B. Williams in Theory of Investment Value, investment analysts must turn first to the present value estimation to know the intrinsic value of the equities.

Dividend Valuation Model

A difficult problem in using the dividend valuation model is the timing of cash flows from dividends. Since equity shares have no finite term, the investor must forecast all future dividends. This might imply a forecast of intently long stream of dividends. Clearly, this would be almost impossible. And to manage the problem therefore, assumptions are made with regard to the future grown of the dividend of the immediately previous period available at the time the investor wants to determine the intrinsic value of his/her equity shares. The assumptions can be:

(a) Dividends do not grow in future i.e., the constant or zero growth assumption.

(b) Dividends grow at a constant rate in future, i.e., the constant assumption.

(c) Dividends grow at varying rates in future time period i.e., multiple growth assumption.

The dividend valuation model is now discussed with these assumptions.

(a) *The zero-growth case:* The growth rate of dividend D at time 't' will be known by solving for 'g' in the following

$$D_t = D_t - 1(1 + g_t) \qquad\qquad .....(1)$$

Or,

$$D_t = \frac{D_t - 1(1 + g_t)}{D_1 - 1} \qquad\qquad ......(2)$$

You can easily see that when $g_t = 0$, 3 equation 3 will yield $D_t = D_t - 1$ which means all future dividends would equal to be current dividend (i.e., the dividend of the immediately preceding period available as on date).

Now, the present value of dividends for an infinite future period would be

$$V = \frac{D_0}{1 + K} + \frac{D_1}{(1 + K)^2} + \frac{D_2 + \infty}{(1 + K)^3}$$

$$\sum_{t=1}^{\infty} \frac{D_0}{(1 + K)^t}$$

Since, $D_0 = D_1 = D_2 = D_3$, under the zero-grown assumption, the numerator D_1 in equation 5 is replaced D_0

$$v = D\sum_{t=1}^{\infty} \frac{D_0}{(1 + K)^t}$$

You will appreciate that discounting cash flows over a very distant long future period would be meaningless. Mathematics tells us that if $K > 0$ then the value of an infinite series like the one in equation (3.6) is reduced so that the equation (6) results in following:

$$V_0 = \frac{D_0}{K}1 = \frac{D_0}{K_0}$$

And since $D_0 = D_1$, equation 3.7 cam also be written as

$$V = \frac{D_1}{K}$$

You may recall that equation 8 was used for the valuation of preference shares. This is one case for application of the zero-growth assumption.

The calculation underlying the zero-growth model can be illustrated.

Illustration 1: Consider a preference share on which the company expects to pay a cash dividend of RKV Rs.9 per share for an indefinite future period. The required rate return is 10% and the current market price is Rs.80.00. Would you buy the share at its current price?

Solution:

This is a zero-growth case because the dividend per share remains Rs.9 for all future time periods. You find the intrinsic value of the share using equation

V = Rs.9.00/.10 = Rs. 90

The intrinsic value of Rs.90 is more than the market price of Rs.80. You would consider buying the share.

Illustration 2: Assume that the dividend per share is estimated to be Rs.4.00 per year indefinitely and the investor requires a 20% of return.

Solution:

The intrinsic value of the equity share is Rs.4/.20 = Rs. 20. (This model is more appropriate for an analysis of preference share because of the constant dividend assumption).

(b) *Constant growth case:*

When dividends grow in all future periods at a uniform rate 'g'

$$D_t = D_t - 1 (1 + g)^t \qquad \text{.....(9)}$$

Substituting 'D$_0$' in equation 3.5 by the value of D$_1$ in equation 3.9, we get

$$v = \sum_{t=0}^{\infty} \frac{D_0(1+g)^t}{(1+K)^t} \qquad \text{.....(10)}$$

For a constant amount 'D$_0$' can be written out of summation to obtain the following question

$$v = D_0 \sum_{t=0}^{\infty} \frac{D_0(1+g)^t}{(1+K)^t} \qquad \text{......(11)}$$

Constant amount, 'D$_0$'can be written out of summation to obtain the following equation

$$\sum_{t=0}^{\infty} \frac{(1+g)^t}{(1+K)^t} = \frac{1+g}{K-g} \qquad \text{......(12)}$$

Substituting mathematical properties of infinite series, if K > g, then it can be shown that

$$V = \frac{D_0(1+g)}{(K-g)} \qquad \text{......(13)}$$

Equation 13 can be re-written as follows:

$$V = \frac{D_0(1+g)}{(K-g)} = \frac{D1}{K-g} \qquad \text{......(14)}$$

Illustration 3: Dabba Ltd., paid a dividend of Rs.2.00 per share for the year ending March 31, 1991. A constant growth of 10% income has been forecast for an indefinite future period. Investors' required rate of return has been estimated at 15%. You want to buy the share at a market price quoted on July 1, 1991 in the stock market at Rs.60.00. What would be your decision?

Solution:

This is a case of constant-growth-rate situation. Equation 14 can be used to find out the intrinsic value of the equity share as under

$$V = \frac{D_1}{(K-g)} = \frac{Rs.2(1.10)}{.15-.10} = \frac{Rs.2.20}{.05} = Rs.\ 44.00$$

The intrinsic value of Rs.44 is less than the market price of Rs.60.00. Hence, the share is overvalued and you could not buy.

Illustration 4: The company paid its first cash dividend of Rs.2.50 today and dividends are expected to grow at a rate of 30% per year for the next three years. Thereafter, cash dividends will grow at a 10% rate per year. Shareholders expect to earn a 15% return on their investments. Calculate the present value of dividend.

Solution:

Step 1: Calculate the present value of dividends for the first three years.

$$\sum_{t=1}^{n} Do(1 + g_x)^t/(1 + K)^t$$

$$= Rs.\ 8.3473$$

Year	Dividend Do $(1 + g_x)^t$	x Capitalisation Rate x k = 0.15	= Present Value
	Rs. 2.50(1+0.30)^t		
(1)	(2)	(3)	(4) = (2) x (3)
0	Rs.2.500		
1	Rs.3.250	0.870	3.7356
2	4.225	0.756	5.5886
3	5.493	0.658	8.3473

Step 2: Value at the end of 3 years for the remaining life of the company

Dividend in 4th year $D_4 = D_3(1 + g_y)$

$$= Rs.5.493\ (1 + 0.10) = Rs.6.0423$$

Value at the end of the third year

$$V_3 = D_4/(k - g_y)$$
$$V_3 = 6.0423/(0.15 - 0.10)$$
$$= Rs.\ 120.846$$

Step 3: The present value at the end of three years (V3) discounted by the required rate of return k = 0.15

$$(V_3) \times 1/(1 + k)^3$$
$$= Rs.120.846\ (0.658)$$
$$= Rs.79.516668$$

Step 4: The value per share today equals the present value of dividends for the first three years (Step-1) plus the present value of the share price at the end of year 3 (Step-3).

Step 1		Step 2
Vo =Rs.8.343	+	Rs.79.516668
	= Rs.87.8639668	

Step 5: Multiply the number of shares by the price per share to determine the total value of the equity. If there are 10,00,000 ordinary shares the total value of the firm is Rs.8,78,63,967.

(c)   *The multiple-growth case:*

The multiple-growth assumption has to be made in a vast number of practical situations. The infinite future period is viewed as divisible into two or more different growth segments. The investor must forecast the time to which growth would be variable and after which only the growth rate would show a pattern and would be constant. This would mean that present value calculations will have to be spread over two phases viz., one phase would last until time 'T' and other would begin after 'T' in infinity.

The present value of all dividends forecast up to and including time 'T' VT(i) would be

$$V_{T(i)} \sum_{t=1}^{T} \frac{D_t}{(1+K)^t} \qquad \dots \dots 14$$

The second phase present value is denoted by VT(2) and would based on constant-growth divided forecast after time 'T.' The position of the investor at time 'T' after which the second phase commences will be viewed as a point in time, when he is forecasting a stream of dividends for time periods T + 1, T + 2, T + 3 and on which growth occurs at a constant rate. The second phase dividends would be

$$D_{T+1} = D_T (1 + g)$$
$$D_{T+2} = D_{T+1} (1 + g) = D_T(1 + g)^2 \qquad \dots \dots 15$$
$$D_{T+3} = D_{T+2} (1 + g) = D_T(1 + g)^3$$

and so on. The present value of the second phase stream of dividends can, therefore, be estimated using each 14 and at time 'T.'

$$V_T = D_{T+1} \frac{1}{K-g} \qquad \dots \dots 16$$

You may note 'V_T' given by equation 16 is the present value at time 'T' of all future expected dividends. Hence, when this value has to be viewed at time 'zero' it must be discounted to provide the present value at time for the second phase's present value. The latter can also be viewed at time 'zero' as a series of each dividend that grows at a constant rate as already stated. The resulting second phase value VT(2) will be given as following.

$$V_{T(2)} = V_{T+1} \frac{1}{(1-K)^T} \qquad \dots \dots 16$$

$$V_{T(2)} = V_{T+1} \frac{D_{T+1}}{(K-g)(1+K)T}$$

Now, the two present values of phase 1 and 2 can be added to estimate the intrinsic value of an equal that will pass through a multiple growth situation. The following describes the summation of the two phases.

$$V_{T(2)} = V_{T(1)} + V_{T(2)}$$

$$\sum_{t=1}^{T} \frac{D_t}{(1+K)t} + \frac{D_{T+1}}{(K-g)(1+K)^T}$$

Illustration 5: RKV Ltd. paid dividends amounting to Rs.0.75 per share during the last year. The company is to pay Rs.2.00 per share curing the next year. Investors forecast a dividend of Rs.3.00 per share in the year that follows. At this time, the forecast is that dividends will grow at 10% per year into an indefinite future. Would you sell the share if the current price is Rs.54.00? The required rate of return is 15%.

Solution:

This is a case of multiple growth. Growth rates for the first phase must be worked out and the time between the two phases established. It is clear that 'T' = 2 years. Hence, this becomes the time. Partition rates before 'T' are:

$$g_1 = \frac{D_1 - D_g}{D_0} = \frac{Rs.\,2.00 - Rs.\,0.75 = 167\%}{Rs.\,0.75}$$

$$g_2 = \frac{D_2 - D_1}{D_1} = \frac{Rs.\,3.00 - Rs.\,2.00 = 50\%}{Rs.\,0.75}$$

The values $V_{T(1)} + V_{T(2)}$ can be calculated as follows:

$$V_{T(1)} = \frac{Rs.\,2.0}{(1+15)^t} + \frac{Rs.\,3.0}{(1+.15)^2} = Rs.\,4.01$$

$$V_{T(1)} = \frac{Rs.\,3.30}{(.15+.10)^t} + \frac{Rs.\,49.91}{(1+.15)^2}$$

Since $V_0 = V_{T(1)} + V_{T(2)}$ the two values can be summed to find the intrinsic value of a Cromecon equity share time 'zero'. This is given below:

$$V_0 = Rs.\,4.01 + Rs.\,49.91 = Rs.\,53.92$$

At the current price of Rs.54.00, the share is fairly priced and hence you won't trade.

MODELS BASED ON PRICE RATIO ANALYSIS

Price ratios are widely used by financial analysts, more so even than dividend discount models. Of course, all valuation methods try to accomplish the same thing, which is to appraise the economic value of a company's stock

The P/E Approach to Equity Valuation

The first step here consists of estimating future earning per share. Next, the normal price-earnings ratio will be end. Product of these two estimates will give the expected price. For a single year holding period with D1 as respected dividends in the coming year, the expected return of an investor can be found as under.

$$\text{Expected Return} = \frac{D_1(p_1 - P)}{P}$$

Stagnating normal price-earning ratio is central to the P/E approach for valuing equity shares. The procedure has been described in the following paragraphs.

You may go back to equation 5 and introduce the earnings variable in it by expressing.

$$D_t = p_1 - E_1 \tag{....(20)}$$

Where P1 = pay-out ratio, and Et = earnings per share in time 't' so, if you forecast earnings per share and layout ratio you have in fact forecast dividends per share. Now, use equation 20 to restore equation will be replaced by $p_t E_t$ as follows

$$V_0 = \frac{D_1}{1+K} + \frac{D_1}{(1+K)^2} + \frac{D_1}{(1+K)^3} + \cdots\cdots$$

$$= \frac{p_1 E_1}{1+K} + \frac{p_2 E_2}{(1+K)^2} + \frac{p_3 E_3}{(1+K)^3}$$

$$= \sum_{t=1}^{\alpha} \frac{P_1 E_1}{(1+K)^1} \qquad\qquad \cdots\cdots(21)$$

Now, if earnings like dividends also grow at a rate 'ge' in future time periods, that is

$$E_1 = E_{t-1}(1 + g_{et})$$

And which would also imply that

$$E_1 = E_{t-1}(1 + g_{et})$$
$$E_2 = E_1(1 + g_{et}) = E_0(1 + g_{e1})(1 + g_{e2})$$
$$E_3 = E_2(1 + g_{e3}) = E_0(1 + g_{e3})(1 + g_{e3})$$

and so on, where E_0 is the actual level of earnings per share over the past year, E_1 is the expected level of earnings per share for the year after E_1 and E_2 is expected level of earnings per share for the year after E_2

Substituting these equations in equation 21, we get

$$V = \frac{p_1 [E_0(1+g_{e1})]}{1+K} + \frac{p_2 [E_0(1+g_{e1}) + (1+g_{e1})]}{(1+K)^2} + \frac{p_2 [E_0(1+g_{e1}) + (1+g_{e2}) + (1+g_{e3})]}{(1+K)^3} \qquad \cdots(23)$$

Now, you may recall that 'V' is the intrinsic value or the price at which the share would sell if it were priced. Then, V/E0 would be the price-earnings ratio that must prevail if the share were fairly priced. In other words, V/E0 would be the normal price-earnings ratio. To obtain a normal price-earnings ratio from equation 23, divide both sides of the equation by E0 and simplify. The resultant equation would be

$$= \frac{V}{E0} = \frac{p_1 (1+g_{e1})}{1+K} + \frac{p_2 (1+g_{e2}) + (1+g_{e2})}{(1+K)^2} + \frac{p_3 (1+g_{e1}) + (1+g_{e2}) + (1+g_{e3})}{(1+K)^2} + \cdots\cdots \qquad \cdots\cdots(24)$$

You can now interpret equation 25 to show that a share's normal price-earnings ratio will be higher:

$(g_{e1}, g_{e1}, g_{e1}\cdots\cdots)$; the smaller the required rate of return (K).

The above relationships are qualified by the phrase "other things being equal," which means that there is no change in variables. For example, the normal price earnings ratio would increase with an increase in payout ratio but no company can ever achieve this result on concentrating on an increase in the payout ratio. What happens with an increased payout ratio is a corresponding decrease in reinvestment of earnings and consequently, a diminution in the growth rate; increased payout would neutralized by decreased growth and so on. Consequently, intrinsic value and hence the normal price-earnings will not increase.

Second, from equation 24 based on the infinite series of dividends the growth situations, the equations can be derived as follows:

The Constant Growth Situation: $V = \dfrac{p}{E_0} \dfrac{1+g^3}{K-g}$ \qquad\qquad $\cdots\cdots(25)$

$$\text{Zero Growth Situation} \quad \frac{V}{E_0} = \frac{1}{K}$$

REASONS FOR COMPANY TO HAVE NEGATIVE EARNING

There are a number of reasons for a company to have negative earnings. Some of the reasons for negative earnings can be listed as follows:

♦ Cyclical nature of industry
♦ Unforeseeable circumstances
♦ Poor management
♦ Persistent negative earnings
♦ Early growth stage
♦ High leverage cost

Cyclical Nature of Industry

Companies might belong to the cyclical industry. When there is a recession in the economy, the company will post negative earnings. However, once the economic variables change, the companies in these cyclical industries also recover and show a positive growth rate. Normalised Net Income = Average ROE * Current Book Value of Equity

Normalised after-tax Operating Income = Average ROC * Current Book Value of Assets

Unforeseeable Circumstances

The earnings of a company may show a negative result due to a one-time unforeseen event. The extent of downtrend could depend on both external and internal factors relating to the company.

Poor Management

The company might have a team at the top which is responsible for wrong business decisions or the company could have been affected by fraud or mismanagement issues. However, if it is felt that the negative earnings due to this mismanagement has been identified and corrective action by the company is on the agenda of the board, the valuation of such companies has to be done considering the industry earnings record.

Illustration 6: Zee Ltd. is paying dividends on its equity shares at Rs.8 per share and expects to pay the same for an undefined long period in future. The equity share currently sells for Rs.65 and investor's required rate of return is 10. Determine if the Zee share is fairly priced using P/E approach valuation.

Solution:

This is a zero-growth case and the normal price-earnings ratio can be found as under

$$V/E_0 = 1/K = 1/.10 = 10$$

The actual price earnings ratio = P/E = Rs.65/Rs.8 = 81. Since the normal price-earnings ratio of 10 is more than the actual price-earnings ratio of 8.1, the share at Rs.65.0 is under priced.

Illustration 7: Now, assume the Zee paid a dividend of Rs.1.80 per share over the past year and the forecast is that this would grow at 5% per annum forever. The required rate of return is

11% and the current market price is Rs.40 per share. Using P/E approach, determine if the Zee share is fairly priced. E0 may be taken as Rs.2.70.

Solutions:

This is a constant growth case. The normal price earnings ratio (V/E_0) can be

$$\frac{V}{E_0} = P = \frac{(1+g_e)}{K-g}$$

$$= 1.80/2.70 \; \frac{1+.05}{.11-.05}$$

$$= .6667 \; \frac{1.05}{.05} = 11.67$$

$$\frac{P}{E_0} = \frac{Rs.40.0}{Rs.2.70} = 14.81$$

Since $\frac{V}{E_0} = 11.67 < \frac{P}{E_0} = 14.81$, the share is overpriced

Price-Book [P/B] Ratio

A very basic price ratio for a company is its price-book [P/B] ratio, sometimes called the market-book ratio. A price-book ratio is measured as the market value of a company's equity issued divided by its book value of equity. Price-book ratios are appealing because book values represent, in principle, historical costs. The stock price is an indicator of current value, so a price-book ratio simply measures what the equity is worth today relative to what it cost. A ratio bigger than 1.0 indicates that the firm has been successful in creating value for its stockholders. A ratio smaller than 1.0 indicates that the company is actually worth less than it cost.

Price-Sales (P/S) Ratio

A price-sales ratio is calculated as the current price of a company's stock divided by its current annual sales revenue per share. A high P/S ratio would suggest high sales growth, while a low P/S ratio might indicate sluggish sales growth.

CONSIDERATIONS IN DEVELOPING AND SELECTING QUANTITATIVE STRATEGIES

Many models can be used in combination with each other and especially in combination with sound judgement. The quantitative strategy in valuation models may be defined as engineered investment strategies. In developing these strategies, consideration must be given at least to three characteristics. First, the strategy should be based on a sound theory. That is, there should be not only a reason why the strategy worked in the past, but, more importantly, a reason why it should be expected to work in the future. Second, the strategy should be put in quantified terms. Finally, a determination should be made of how the strategy would have performed in the past. This last characteristic is critical and is the reason why investment strategies are back-tested. An equity manager encounters many potential problems in the design, testing and implementation of engineered investment strategies.

These include:

Random Valuation Model

The Random Valuation model begins with the premise that the next three years' growth of earnings, dividends, and price will be similar to those of the past ten years. This is similar to the Trend Valuation equation for estimating the rate of return, r. In Random Valuation, the ten-year growth rate of earnings and dividends is used, along with the ten-year P/E ratio.

Solved Problems to Practice

Illustration 8: Ravi paid Rs.2.75 in dividends on its equity shares last year. Dividends are expected to grow at 12 per cent annual rate for an indefinite number of years.

(a) If Ravi's current market price is Rs.37.50, what is the stock's expected rate of return?

(b) If your required rate of return is 14%, what is the value of the stock for you?

(c) Should you make the investment?

Solution:

(a) Expected Rate of Return = Rs.2.75 (1.12)/(Rs.37.50 + 0.12) = 20.21%

(b) Investor's value = Rs.2.75 (1.12)/(0.14 – 0.12) = Rs.154

(c) The expected rate of return is greater than the required rate of return (20.21% versus 14%). Also, the value of the stock (Rs.154) is larger than the current market price (Rs.37.50). The share is undervalued and should be purchased.

Illustration 9: The market price for Super Iron's equity is Rs.65 per share. The price at the end of one year is expected to be Rs.90, and dividends for next year should be Rs.2.90. What is the expected rate of return?

Solution:

If the expected rate of return is represented by ERR:

Current Price = (Dividend in year 1)/(1 + ERR) + (Price in year 1)/(1 + ERR)

ERR = [(Dividend in year 1 + Price in year 1)/Current Price] – 1

ERR = [(Rs.2.90 + Rs.90)/65] – 1 = 0.30

ERR = 30.0%

Illustration 10: Ravi Petro is expected to pay Rs.3.00 in dividends next year, and the market price is projected to be Rs.75 by the year-end. If the investor's required rate of return is 20%, what is the current value of the stock?

Solution:

V_e = (Dividend in year 1)/(1 + Required rate) + (Price in year 1)/(1 + Required rate)

= Rs.3.00/(1 + 0.20) + Rs.75/(1 + 0.20)

= Rs.2.50 + Rs.62.50

= Rs.65.00

Illustration 11: On Sudha Enterprises' equity shares, the dividend paid was Rs.1.32 per equity share last year and this is expected to grow indefinitely at an annual rate of 7% rate. What is the value of each equity share of Sudha Enterprises if the investor requires an 11% return?

Solution:

$$V_e = \text{(Last year dividend \{1 + Growth Rate\})/(Required rate of return –}$$
$$\text{Growth rate)}$$
$$= \text{Rs.}1.32\ (1.07)/(0.11 – 0.07) = \text{Rs.}35.31$$

Illustration 11: An investor holds an equity share giving him an annual dividend of Rs.30. He expects to sell the share for Rs.300 at the end of a year. Calculate the value of the share if the required rate of return is 10%.

Solution:

The market price of a share in the beginning of the period is equal to the present value of the dividends paid at the end of the period plus the market price of the share at the end of the period. Symbolically:

$$Po = D_1/(1 + i) + P_1\ (1 + i)$$
or $$\qquad Po = (D_1 + P_1)/(1 + i)$$

where

Po = The current price of the share

i   = The required rate of return or the cost of equity

D_1 = Dividend to be received at the end of the period

P_1 = Market price of share at the end of the period

Substituting the values, we get:

$$Po = (\text{Rs.}30 + \text{Rs.}300)/(1 + 0.10)$$
$$= \text{Rs.}330/1.10 = \text{Rs.}300$$

Illustration 12: Ravi equity share currently sells for Rs.23 per share. The company's finance manager anticipates a constant growth rate of 10.5% and an end-of-year dividend of Rs.2.50.

(a)   What is the expected rate of return?

(b)   If the investor requires a 17% return, should he purchase the stock?

Solution:

(a)   Expected rate of return = (Dividend in year 1)/(Market Price) + Growth rate
$$= (\text{Rs.}2.50/\text{Rs.}23.00) + 0.105$$
$$= 21.37\%$$

(b) $$\qquad\qquad Ve = \text{Rs.}2.50/(0.17 – 0.105)$$
$$= \text{Rs.}38.46$$

The value of the stock would be Rs.38.46. Thus, the expected rate of return exceeds the required rate of return, which means that the value of the security is greater than the current market price. Thus the investor should buy the stock.

Illustration 15: Raj's equity shares currently sells for Rs.22.50 per share. The finance manager of Raj anticipates a constant growth rate of 12% and an end-of-year dividend of Rs.2.50.

(a)   What is your expected rate of return if you buy the stock for Rs.25?

(b)   If you require an 18% return, should you purchase the stock?

Solution:

(a)   (Dividend in year 1)/(Market Price) + Growth rate

$$= Rs.2.50/Rs.25 + 0.12$$
$$= 0.22 = 22\%$$

(b) $$V_e = Rs. 2.50/(0.18 - 0.12)$$
$$= Rs.41.67$$

Yes, purchase the equity shares of Raj.

Illustration 17: Firms A, B and C are similar. Firm A is the most progressive and trades at an 18/1 P/E multiple. Firm B is less progressive, is not publicly traded, and has an EPS of Rs.1.20. Firm C is least progressive and trades at a 15/1 P/E ratio. What is the intrinsic value of firm B?

Solution:

$$\text{Average P/E} = 16.5$$
$$\text{Intrinsic value} = 16.5 \times 1.20$$
$$= Rs.19.80$$

Illustration 18: Companies R, S and T are similar. Company R is privately held, and has a book value of Rs.40 per share. Company S has a market price of Rs.15 and a book value of Rs.12. Company T has a market value (MV) of Rs.82 and a book value of Rs.62. What is a possible value for company R?

Solution:

Ratio of book value to market value:

Company R = Rs.40/MV – 0 .78

MV = Rs.51

Company S = Rs.12/Rs. 15 = 0.8

Company T = Rs.62/Rs. 82 = 0.76

Illustration 19: Verma is a conservative investor who demands a 10% interest on his fixed investment but 20% from his equity investments. He has been considering the purchase of an equity that pays Rs.2.50 in dividends this year and whose dividends are expected to grow at 10% per year for the next three years. Earnings this year are Rs.5 per share and are expected to grow at 20% for the next seven years. Stocks growing at this rate generally sell at 40 times earnings. What price does Verma pay for this equity?

Solution:

Using the three year valuation formula:

$$Po = D(1 + g)/(1 + k) + D(1 + g)^2/(1 + k)^2 + D(1 + g)^3/(1 + k)^3$$

where

$$P_3 = (E) (P/E) (1 + g)^3$$
$$P_3 = (Rs.4) (40) (1 + 20\%)^3 = Rs.276.48$$
$$Po = Rs.2.50 (1 + 0.10)/(1 + 0.20) + Rs.2.50 (1 + 0.10)^2/(1 + 0.20)^2 +$$
$$[Rs.2.50 (1 + 0.10)^3 + Rs.276.48]/(1 + 0.20)^3$$

$$\text{Rs.2.50}/(1.20) + \text{Rs.3.035}/(1.44) + (\text{Rs.3.3275} + \text{Rs.276.48})/(1.728)$$
$$= \text{Rs.2.292} + \text{Rs.2.107} + \text{Rs.161.926}$$
$$= \text{Rs.166.32}$$

Illustration 20: KSBS can buy an equity that will pay Rs. 2.00 in dividends annually over the next 3 years. The earnings of the company are expected to grow and the equity is expected to reach a price of Rs.70 per share at the end of three years. This is a conservative investment and Rao expects a yield of 18%. What price should Rao pay for the equity if he wishes to earn 18%?

Solution:

$$\text{Yield (Y)} = [(D + P_3 - Po)/3]/[(P_3 + Po)/2]$$

Solving for

$$Po = [(Y)(P_3 + Po)/2] + [D + (P_3 - Po)/3]$$
$$(3)(Y)(P_3 + Po) = (2)(3)(D) + (2)(P_3 - Po)$$
$$3YP_3 + 3YP0 = 6D + 2P_3 - 2P0$$
$$3YP0 + 2P0 = 6D + 2P_3 - 3YP_3$$
$$Po = (6D + P_3(2 - 3Y)/(3Y + 2)$$

Substituting:

$$Po = [(6 \times \text{Rs.2})\ \text{Rs.78}\ [2 - (3)(0.18)]/[(3)(0.18) + 2]$$
$$= (\text{Rs.12} + \text{Rs.70}\ [2 - 0.54])/(0.54 + 2)$$
$$= (\text{Rs.12} + \text{Rs.102.20})/2.54$$
$$Po = \text{Rs.45}$$

Verification:

$$0.18 = [\text{Rs. 2.00}\ \{(70 - 45)/3\}]/[(70 + 45)/2]$$
$$= (\text{Rs.2} + 8.33)/57.50$$
$$= 18\%$$

Illustration 21: EPS, Rs.5; Market price Rs.60; Growth rate of sales, 6%, and of EPS, 9%; Dividend payout, 70%; Normal capitalisation rate, 12%. Using the capitalisation and dividend growth methods, find out what is the value of the stock?

Solution:

Capitalisation of earnings: Rs.5 (8.33)* = Rs. 41.67

*1/0.12 = 8.33

Capitalisation of dividends: Rs.2 (11.9)* = Rs. 23.80

*833(70) = 119

Capitalisation of earnings and dividends:

8.33 (Rs. 2 + 30% (Rs.5)= Rs.29.16

Capitalisation of growth: Rs.7.06 (8.5 + 2(9)) = Rs. 187

5(10 + 1.5(6)) = Rs.95

Dividend growth model:

Rs.2/(12% – 8.33%*(60%)) 9 Rs.28.57

*5/60 = 8.33%

Illustration 22: On April 1, 2007 the equity share of Gitam stood at Rs.469. The traded options market in the shares quoted in May at Rs.500 puts it at Rs.47. If the share price falls to Rs.450, how much, if any, profit would be investor make? What will the option be worth if the share price moves up to Rs.510?

Solution:

Traded options give the holder the right, but not the obligation, to buy (a call option) or sell (a put option) a quantity of shares at a fixed price on an exercise date in the future. They are usually in contracts of 1,000 shares and for three, six or nine moths.

Holders of a put option in Gitam have the right to sell shares in May at Rs.500. For this right they currently have to pay a premium of Rs.47, or Rs.470 on a contract of 1,000 shares.

If the share price falls below Rs.453 (i.e. Rs.500–Rs.47), the shares become profitable and the holder is in the money. So if they fall to Rs.450, the investor can buy shares at this price, and exercise his put option to sell shares for Rs.500. A profit of Rs.50 per share which, after the initial cost of the option gives a net profit of Rs.3 per share or Rs.3000 per contract.

If the share price moves up to Rs.510 by May, the option becomes worthless, and the investor loses his Rs.47 premium.

Options such as these can be used to either speculate or hedge on share price changes for a relatively low premium.

Illustration 23: A firm's current EPS is Rs.6, its dividend payout is 40%, and its growth rate of EPS is 10%. The normal P/E multiple is 15/1. What is the stock's value using the capitalisation of earnings method? What is its value in three years using the same method?

Solution:

$$P/E \times EPS_{current} = PV$$
$$PV = 15 \times 6 = Rs. \, 90$$
$$EPS_3 = Rs.6 \, (1.10)^3$$
$$= Rs.7.986$$
$$\text{Value in three years} = 15 \times Rs.7.986$$
$$= Rs.119.79$$

Illustration 24: Companies X, Y and Z are in the same industry. Company X has a 5% growth rate, pays @ Rs.2.00 dividend, and sells for Rs.25 per share. Company Y pays a Rs.4 dividend, has an 8% growth rate, and is not publicly traded. Company Z sells for Rs.60, pays a Rs.6 dividend, and has a 2% growth rate. What is the value of the stock of Company Y?

Solution:

$$CR_X = Rs.2/Rs. \, 25 + .05 = 13\%$$
$$CR_Z = Rs.6/Rs. \, 60 + .02 = 12\%$$
$$CR_{Avg} = 12.5\%$$
$$\text{Value of Y} = Rs.4/(12.5\% - 8\%)$$
$$= Rs.89$$

Illustration 25: RKV has invested in Asian Chemicals. The capitalisation rate of the company is 15% and the current dividend is Rs.2.00 per share. Calculate the value of the company's equity share if the company is slowly sinking with an annual decline rate of 5% in the dividend.

Solution:

The value of the firm stock is:

$$V_e = D_1/(k - g)$$
$$= Rs.2 \, (1 - 0.05)/(0.15 - (-0.05))$$
$$= Rs.1.90/0.20$$
$$= Rs.9.50$$

Illustration 26: What would be the value of the equity share of Wipro's of previous problem if the company shows no growth but is able to maintain its dividend.

Solution:

The value of the equity is

$$V_e = D_1/(k - g)$$
$$= (Rs.2.00 \, (1 + 0)/(0.15 - (-0.00))$$
$$= Rs.13.33$$

VALUATION OF PREFERENCE SHARES

Preference shares are a hybrid security. They have some features of bonds and some of equity shares. Theoretically, preference shares are considered a perpetual security but there are convertible, callable, redeemable and other similar features, which enable issuers to terminate them within a finite time horizon. In the case of redeemable preference shares, legal mandates require creation of redemption sinking funds and earmarked investments to ensure funds for repayments.

Preference dividends are specified like bonds. This has to be done because they rank prior to equity share for dividends. However, specification does not imply obligation, failure to comply with which may amount to default. Several preference issues are cumulative where dividends accumulate over time and equity dividends read clearance of preference arrears first.

Preference shares are less risky than equity because their dividends are specified and all arrears must paid before equity holders get dividends. They are, however, more risky than bonds because the latter earn priority in payment and in liquidation. Bonds are secured too and enjoy protection of principal, which is ordinarily not available to preference shares. Investors' required returns on preference shares are more than those on bond, but less than on equity shares. In exceptional circumstances, when preference shares enjoy special tax-shares (like in the US, inter-corporate holdings of preference shares get exemption on 80% of preference dividends) required return on such shares may even be marginally below those on bonds.

Since dividends from preference shares are assumed to be perpetual payments, the intrinsic value of shares will be estimated from the following equation valid for perpetuities in general

$$VP = \frac{C}{(1+K_p)} + \frac{C}{(1+K_p)^2} + \dots\dots$$

Where V_p = the value of a perpetuity today

C = the constant annual payment to be received

Kp = the required rate of return appropriate for the perpetuity

You have only to substitute preference dividend (D) for 'C' and the appropriate required return (K_{ps}) for 'K_p' to obtain the following equation for valuing preference shares.

$$VP = \frac{D}{K_{PS}}$$

You may note that 'D' is a perpetuity and is known and fixed forever. A perpetuity does not involve present value calculations and the equitation provides for computing any of the three variables viz., value of perpetuity (V) preference dividend (D) and the required rate return (K_{ps}) only if the remaining two variables are known. Thus, the value of a preference share can be calculated if the dividend per share and the required rate of return are known. Similarly, the required rate of return (or yield) can be known if the value of the perpetuity and dividend per share are known.

Illustration 27: The valuation process of a preference share. Consider for issuing preference shares of Rs.100 each with a specified dividend of Rs.11.5 per share. Now, if the investor's required rate of return corresponding to the risk-level of firm A is 10%, the value today of the share would be?

Solution:

$$VP = \frac{Rs.11.50 = Rs.115.00}{.10}$$

Should the required return increase (say in the wake of rising interest rates and, in consequence the high opportunity costs) to 12%, value will be:

$$\frac{Rs. 11.50}{.12} = 95.83$$

You may note that the value changes inversely to the required rate of return.

If you are an observer of market prices, you may notice the price of any preference share on any day and calculate its yield on that day using the above formula. Thus, if the current market price of the preference share question is Rs.125.00, the required rate of return or yield can be calculated as under:

$$VP = \frac{D}{K_{PS}} \text{ or, Rs. } 125.00 = \frac{Rs.11.50}{K_{PS}}$$

Or

$$K_{PS} \frac{125.00}{125.00} = 9.2\%$$

Thus, the yield declines after issue of the shares by 'A'. Maybe, interest rates declines or there are other changes to induce the downward shift in the yield.

You can observe price shifts over various spans of time, say weeks, months, and years and examine causes shifts in yields of preference shares.

Relate to 'fundamental approach to 'floatation equity shares.

Illustration 28: What is the value of a preference share where the dividend rate is 18% on a Rs.100 par value? The appropriate discount rate for a stock of this risk level is 15%.

Solution:

$$V_p = (0.18 \times Rs.100)/0.15$$
$$= Rs.18/0.15$$
$$= Rs.120$$

Illustration 29: The preference shares of RKV Group are selling for Rs.47.50 per share and pay a dividend of Rs.2.35 in dividends. What is your expected rate of return if you purchase the security at market price?

Solution:

Expected rate of return = Dividend/Market Price

$$= Rs.2.35/Rs.47.50$$

$$= 4.95\%$$

Illustration 30: You own 250 preference shares of ABC Company, which currently sells for Rs.38.50 per share and pays annual dividends of Rs.6.50 per share.

(a)   What is your expected return?

(b)   If you require a 13% return, given the current price, should you sell or buy more preference shares?

Solution:

(a)   Expected return = Dividend/Market Price

$$= Rs.6.50/Rs.38.50$$

$$= 16.88\%$$

(b)   Given 13 per cent required rate of return, the stock is worth:

$$V_p = \text{Dividend/Required Rate}$$

$$= Rs.6.50/0.13$$

$$= Rs.50.00$$

Because the expected rate of return (16.88%) is greater than the required rate of return (13%) or because the current market price (Rs.38.50) is less than Rs.50.00, the stock is undervalued and it is worth buying.

Illustration 31: Pioneer's preference shares are selling for Rs.44 per share in the market and pay a Rs.4.40 annual dividend.

(a)   What is the expected rate of return on the preference shares?

(b)   If an investor's required rate of return is 12%, what is the value of a preference share for that investor?

(c)   Should the investor acquire the preference shares?

Solution:

(a)   Expected rate of return on preference

$$= Rs.4.40/Rs.44.00$$

$$= 10\%$$

(b) $$V_p = \text{Dividend/Required rate of return}$$

$$= Rs.4.40/0.12$$

$$= Rs.36.67$$

(c)   The investor's required rate of return (12%) is more than the expected rate of return for the investment (10%). Also, the value of the preference share to the investor (Rs.36.67) is less than the existing market price (Rs.44). Therefore, the investor should not acquire the preference shares from the market.

Illustration 32: Consider a share of preferred stock with a par value of Rs.100 that pays an 12% annual dividend, or Rs.12. If the discount rate for this share were 15%, what would the preference share be worth?

Solution:

$$V_p = \text{Rs. } 12/0.15$$
$$= \text{Rs.}80$$

Illustration 33: KSDB pays a Rs.2.76 dividend on each preference share. What is the value of each preference share if the required rate of return of investors is 12%?

Solution:

$$V_p = \text{Rs. } 2.76/0.12$$
$$= \text{Rs.}23$$

SUMMARY

Fundamental analysis is centred on present value, which is computed as the discounted value of future of earnings poses two problems. One, it is neither specified (as in the case of preference shares) not stated and their timing have both to be estimated in a probabilistic scenario viz., dividends, cash flows and earnings. The solution to the first problem is offered by past data which is appropriately modified for future projections. Also, doing period of investors on the margin (i.e., the major players in the market who influence the pricing in the case of active strategists and 'infinity' in the case of those who follow the 'buy-and-hold strategy' is the base for determining the timing of these benefits. A major modification to past data will be premised on received growth rates of return on equities.

The valuation task is relatively straightforward in case of bond and preference shares, because benefits are generally constant and reasonably certain. Equity valuation is different, because the return on equity is uncertain and can change from time to time. It is the size of the return and the degree of fluctuation (i.e. risk), which together determine the value of a share to the investor's equity valuation. The purpose of these models is to identify whether a stock is mispriced. Under-priced stocks need to be purchased; overpriced stocks should be shorted. As most modern equity valuation models are based upon the present value theory, set forth in detail by John B. Williams in *Theory of Investment Value,* investment analysts must turn first to the present value estimation to know the intrinsic value of the equities.

REVIEW QUESTIONS

1. Write a note on the present value of expected stream of benefits from equity shares.
2. Explain passive and active investment styles.
3. What is the difference between active equity management and passive equity management?
4. What do you mean by valuation? Explain different equity evaluation modules in brief.
5. Write a short note with illustrations for the following
    (i)   Dividend Valuation Model:
    (ii) The Zero-Growth Case
    (iii) Constant Growth Case
    (iv) The Multiple-Growth Case

PART IV

INVESTING IN LONG TERM ASSETS: CAPITAL BUDGETING

The Cost of Capital

After studying this chapter, you should be able to

1 Define cost of capital

2 Understand the significance / importance of cost of capital.

3 List out the basic aspects of the concept of cost of capital.

4 Classify the costs.

5 Calculate cost of equity capital, preference share capital

6 Determine marginal preference share and debt or debenture capital.

7 Compute WACC. cost of capital. Discuss the factors that affect cost of capital.

The cost of capital is an important concept in formulating a firm's capital structure. Cost of capital is a central concept in financial management. It is also viewed as one of the corner stones in the theory of financial management. It has received considerable attention from both theorists and practitioners. Two major schools of thought, have emerged having basic difference on the relevance of cost of capital. In one camp, Modigline Miller argued, that a firm's cost of capital is constant and it is independent of the method and level of financing. In another camp (traditionalists) cost of capital is varying and dependent on capital structure. In both the camps, optimal policy is taken as the policy that maximizes the value of a company.

Cost of capital is still largely an academic term and the problem of measuring it in operational terms is a recent phenomena. Prior to this development, the problem was either ignored or by passed. In modern times, it is widely used as basis of investment projects and evaluating the alternative sources of finance.

COST OF CAPITAL — CONCEPT

The term cost of capital is a concept having many different meanings. The three viewpoints, regarding the cost of capital is given below.

♦ *From Investors' View Point:* Investor may define it as "the measurement of the sacrifice made by him in capital formation. For example, Mr. A an investor invested in a company's equity shares, amount Rs. 1,00,000, instead of investing in a bank at the rate of 7 per cent interest. Here he had sacrificed 7 per cent interest for not having invested in the bank.

♦ *Firms Point:* It is the minimum required rate of return needed to justify the use of capital. For example, a firm raised Rs. 50 lakhs through the issues of 10 per cent debentures, for justifying this issue, a minimum rate of return it has to earn is 10 per cent.

♦ *Capital Expenditure Point:* The cost of capital is the minimum required rate of return, the hurdle or target rate or the cut off rate or any discounting rate used to value cash flows.

For example, Firm 'A' is planning to invest in a project, that requires Rs. 20 lakh as initial investment and provides cash flows for a period of 5 years. So for the conversion of future 5 years cash flows into present value, cost of capital is needed.

Cost of capital represents the rate of return that the firm must pay to the fund suppliers, who have provided the capital. In other words, cost of capital is the weighted average cost of various sources of finance used by the firm. The sources are, equity, preference, long-term debt and short-term debt.

MEANING AND DEFINITION OF COST OF CAPITAL

"The rate that must be earned on the net proceeds to provide the cost elements of the burden at the time they are due."

- Hunt, William and Donaldson

"Cost of capital is the minimum required rate of earnings or the cut-off rate of capital expenditures."

- Solomon Ezra

"A cut-off rate for the allocation of capital to investments of projects. It is the rate of return on a project that will leave unchanged the market price of the stock."

- James C. Van Horne

"The rate of return the firm requires, from investment in order to increase the value of the firm in the market place."

- Hampton, John J

Thus, as defined above, we can say, that cost of capital is that minimum rate of return, which a firm must and is expected to earn on its investments so as to maintain the market value of its shares. It is also known as Weighted Average Cost of Capital (WACC), composite cost of capital or combined cost of capital. It is expressed in terms of percentage.

BASIC ASPECTS ON THE CONCEPT OF COST OF CAPITAL

The above definitions indicates, that the following are the three basic aspects of the concept of cost of capital.

(i) *Rates of Return:* Cost of Capital is not a Cost as such, infact it is the rate of return that a firm requires to earn from its investment projects.

(ii) *Minimum Rate of Return:* Cost of Capital of any firm is that minimum rate of return that will at least maintain the market value of the shares.

(iii) *Cost of Capital Comprises three Components*[1]:

    (a) The risk less cost of the particular type of financing (r_j)

    (b) The business risk premium, (b) and

    (c) The financial risk premium (f)

Symbolically cost of capital may be represented as : $K_o = r_j + b + f$

IMPORTANCE/SIGNIFICANCE OF COST OF CAPITAL

The concept of cost of capital is very important and the central concept in financial management decisions. The decisions in which it is useful are as follows:

1. *Designing Optimal Corporate Capital Structure:* This concept is helpful in formulating a sound and economical capital structure for a firm. The debt policy of a firm is significantly influenced by the cost consideration. Capital structure involves determination of proportion of debt and equity in capital structure that provides less cost of capital.

   While designing a firm's capital structure, the financial executives always keep in mind minimisation of the over all cost of capital and to maximise value of the firm. The measurement of specific costs of each source of funds and calculation of weighted average cost of capital help to form a balanced capital structure. By comparing various (sources of finance) specific costs, he/she can choose the best and most economical source of finance and can succeed in designing a sound and viable capital structure.

2. *Investment Evaluation / Capital Budgeting:* Wilson R.M.S., states that the Cost of Capital is a concept, which should be expressed in quantitative terms, if it is to be useful as a cut-off rate for capital expenses. Capital expenditure means investment in long-term projects like investment on new machinery. It is also known as Capital budgeting expenditure. Capital budgeting decisions require a financial standard (cost of capita) for evaluation. The financial standard is Cost of Capital. In the Net Present Value (NPV) method, an investment project is accepted, if the present value of cash inflows are greater than the present value of cash outflow. The present values of cash inflows are calculated by discounting the rate known as Cost of Capital. If a firm adopts Internal Rate of Return (IRR) as the technique for capital budgeting evaluation, investment should be accepted only when cost of capital is less than the calculated IRR. Hence, the concept of cost of capital is very much useful in capital budgeting decisions, particularly if a firm is adopting discounted cash flow methods of project evaluation.

3. *Financial Performance Appraisal:* Cost of capital framework can be used to evaluate the financial performance of top management.[2] Financial performance evaluation involves a comparison of actual profitability of the investment project with the project overall cost of capital of funds raised to finance the project. If the actual profitability is more than the projected cost of capital, then the financial performance may said to be satisfactory and vice versa.

The above discussion clearly shows the role of cost of capital in financial management decisions. Apart from the above areas (decisions), cost of capital is also useful in (distribution of profits), capitalization of profits, making to rights issue and investment in owner assets.

CLASSIFICATION OF COST

Before going to discuss the computation of specific cost of each source of funds and cost of capital, it is wise to know various relevant costs associated with the problem of measurement of cost of capital. The relevance costs are :

1. *Marginal Cost Of Capital*: A marginal cost is the additional cost incurred to obtain additional funds required by a firm. It refers to the change in the total cost of capital resulting from the use of additional funds. The marginal cost of capital is a very important concept in investment decisions (capital budgeting decisions).

2. *Average Cost / Composite / Overall Cost*: It is the average of various specific costs of the different components of equity, preference shares, debentures, retained earnings of capital structure at a given time and this is used as the acceptance criteria for (capital budgeting) investment proposals.

3. *Historic Cost / Book Cost*: The book cost has its origin in the accounting system in which book values, as maintained by the books of accounts, are readily available. They are related to the past. It is in common use for computation of cost of capital. For example, cost of capital may be computed based on the book value of the components of capital structure. Historical costs act as guide for future cost estimation.

4. *Future Cost*: It is the cost of capital that is expected to raise funds to finance a capital budget or investment proposal.

5. *Specific Cost*: It is the cost associated with particular component / source of capital. It is also known as component cost of capital. For example, cost of equity (Ke) or cost of preference share (Kp), or cost of debt (Kd), etc.

6. *Spot Cost*: The costs that are prevailing in the market at a certain time. For example, few years back cost of bank loans (house loans) was around 12 per cent, now it is 6 per cent. 6 per cent is the spot cost.

7. *Opportunity Cost*: The opportunity cost is the benefit that the shareholder foregoes by not putting his/her funds elsewhere because they have been retained by the management. For example, an investor, had invested in a company's equity shares (100 shares, each share at Rs. 10). The company decided to declare dividend of 10 per cent on book value of share, but due to capital requirements it retains its investment on one project that is having return on investment (ROI) of 4 per cent. Elsewhere, the project rate of interest (banks) is at 6 per cent. Here, the opportunity cost to the investor is (6- 4) 2 per cent.

8. *Explicit Cost*: Cost of capital can be either explicit or implicit. Distinction between explicit and implicit is important from the point of view of computation cost of capital. An explicit cost of any source of capital is the discount rate that equates the present value of the cash inflows, that are incremental to the taking of the financing opportunity with present value

of its increments cash outflows. In other words, the discount rate that equates the present value of cash inflows with present value of cash outflows.[3] It is also called as the internal rate of return. For example, a firm raises Rs. 1,00,000 through the sale of 12 per cent perpetual debentures. There will be a cash inflow of Rs. 1,00,000 and a cash outflow of Rs. 12,000 every year for a indefinite period. The rate that equates the PV of cash inflows (Rs. 1,00,000) and PV of cash outflows (Rs. 12,000 per year) would be the explicit cost. Computation of explicit cost is almost similar to the computation of IRR, with one difference.

9. *Implicit Cost:* It is the cost of opportunity, which is given up in order to pursue a particular action. It is also known as implicit cost of capital. The implicit cost of capital of funds raised and invested by the firm may, therefore be defined as "the rate of return associated with the best investment opportunity for the firm and its shareholders that would be foregone, if the projects presently under consideration by the firm were accepted. The cost of retained earnings is an opportunity cost of implicit cost for a shareholder, who is deprived of the opportunity to invest retained earnings elsewhere. Funds raised by any form of financing have implicit capital costs once they are invested.[4] Thus, in a sense, implicit costs may also be viewed as opportunity costs. This implies that a project reflects negative PV, when its cash flows are discounted by the implicit cost of capital.

COMPUTATION OF OVERALL COST OF CAPITAL (WACC)

The term, cost of capital (K_o) means the overall composite cost of capital, defined as the weighed average of the cost of each specific type of fund. It is also known as composite cost or Weighted Average Cost of Capital (WACC). In order to compute the WACC or composite cost of capital a finance manager has to keep in mind the following steps:

1. Determination of the type of funds to be raised and their individual share in the total capitalisation of the firm / company.
2. Computation of cost of each type of funds.
3. Assigning weights to specific costs.
4. Multiplying the cost of each of the sources by the (appropriate) assigned weights.
5. Dividing the total weighted cost by the total weights to get over all cost of capital.

The first aspect has been discussed in capital structure chapter and the sources of finance. The second aspect, discussed below, involves the computation of specific cost of capital.

COMPUTATION OF SPECIFIC COST OF CAPITAL

The financial manager has to compute the specific cost of each type of funds needed in the capitalisation of a company. The company may resort to different financial sources (equity share, preference share, debentures, retained earning public deposits; or it may prefer internal source (retained earnings) or external source (equity, preference and public deposits). Generally, the component cost of a specific source of capital is equal to the investors' required rate of returns. Investors required rate of returns are interest, discount on debt, dividend, capital appreciation, earnings per share on equity shareholders, dividend and share of profit on preference shareholders funds. But investors' required rate of returns should be adjusted for taxes in practice for calculating the cost of a specific source of capital, to the firm.

Compensation of specific source of finance, viz., equity, preference shares, debentures, retained earnings, public deposits is discussed below :

COST OF EQUITY

Firms may obtain equity capital in two ways (a) retention of earnings and (b) issue of additional equity shares to the public. The cost of equity or the returns required by the equity shareholders is the same in both the cases, since in both cases, the shareholders are providing funds to the firm to finance their investment proposals. Retention of earnings involves an opportunity cost. The shareholders could receive the earnings as dividends and invest the same in alternative investments of comparable risk to earn returns. So, irrespective of whether a firm raises equity finance by retaining earnings or issue of additional equity shares, the cost of equity is same. But issue of additional equity shares to the public involves a floatation cost whereas, there is no floatation cost for retained earnings. Hence, issue of additional equity shares to the public for raising equity finance involves a bigger cost when compared to the retained earnings.

In the following cost of equity is computed in both sources point of view (i.e., retained earnings and issue of equity shares to the public).

Cost Of Retained Earnings (K_{re})

Retained earnings is one of the internal sources to raise equity finance. Retained earnings are those part of (amount) earnings that are retained by the form of investing in capital budgeting proposals instead of paying them as dividends to shareholders. Corporate executives and some analysts too normally consider retained earnings as cost free, because there is nothing legally binding the firm to pay dividends to equity shareholders and the company has its own entity different from its stockholders. But it is not so. They involve opportunity cost. The opportunity cost of retained earning is the rate of return the shareholder forgoes by not putting his/her funds elsewhere, because the management has retained the funds. The opportunity cost can be well computed with the following formula.

$$K_{re} = K_e \left(\frac{(1 - T_i)}{(1 - T_b)} \right) \times 100$$

Where,

K_e = Cost of equity capital [D ÷ P or E/P + g].

T_i = Marginal tax rate applicable to the individuals concerned.

T_b = Cost of purchase of new securities / broker.

D = Expected dividend per share.

NP = Net proceeds of equity share / market price.

g = Growth rate in (%).

Illustration 1: A company paid a dividend of Rs. 2 per share, market price per share is Rs. 20, income tax rate is 60 per cent and brokerage is expected to be 2 per cent. Compute the cost of retained earnings.

Solution:

$$K_{re} = \left(\frac{D}{NP} \times \frac{(1 - T_i)}{(1 - T_b)} \right) \times 100$$

$$= \left(\frac{2}{20} \times \frac{(1 - 0.60)}{(1 - 0.02)} \right) \times 100$$

= 0.10 X 0.409 X 100 = 4.1 per cent

Illustration 2: ABC company's cost of equity (K_e) capital is 14 per cent, the average tax rate of individual shareholders is 40 per cent and it is expected that 2 per cent is brokerage cost that shareholders will have to pay while investing their dividends in alternative securities. What is the cost of retained earnings?

Solution

$$K_{re} = \left(K_e \times \frac{(1-T_i)}{(1-T_b)} \right) \times 100$$

$$= 0.14 \times \frac{(1-0.4)}{(1-0.02)} \times 100$$

$$= (0.14 \times 0.613) \times 100 = 8.6 \text{ per cent}$$

Illustration 3: Life Style Garment Manufacturing Company has net earnings of Rs. 20 lakhs and all of its stockholders are in the bracket of 50 per cent. The management estimates that under the present conditions, the stockholder's required rate of returns is 12 per cent. 3 per cent is the expected brokerage to be paid if stockholders want to invest in alternative securities. Compute the cost of retained earnings.

Solution:

$$K_{re} = K_e \left(\frac{(1-T_i)}{(1-T_b)} \right) \times 100$$

$$= \left(0.10 \times \frac{(1-0.50)}{(1-0.03)} \right) \times 100$$

$$= (0.10 \times 0.516) \times 100 = 5.2 \text{ per cent}$$

Illustration 4: BPL company's equity share is currently being sold at Rs. 350.75 and it is currently paying a dividend of Rs. 5.25 per share. The dividend is expected to grow at 15 per cent per annum for one year. Income tax rate is 40 per cent and brokerage is 2 per cent . Calculate cost of retained earnings.

Solution:

$$K_{re} = \left(\frac{D}{NP} + g \times \frac{(1-T_i)}{(1-T_b)} \right) \times 100$$

$$= \left(\frac{5.25}{350.75} + 0.15 \frac{1-0.40}{1-0.02} \right) \times 100$$

$$= [\, 0.165 \times 0.613 \,] \times 100 = 10.2 \text{ per cent}$$

Cost Of Issue Of Equity Shares (K$_e$)

Calculation of cost of equity (K$_e$) capital cost brings forth, a host of problems. It is the most difficult and controversial cost to measure because there is no one common basis for computation. For calculation of cost of debt (K$_d$) interest charge is the base and preference dividend is the base for calculation of cost of preference shares (K$_p$). Interest on debentures/debt and dividend on preference shares is fixed in terms of the stipulations following the issue of such debentures and shares. In contrast, the return on equity shareholders solely depends upon the discretion of the company management. Apart from this, there is no stipulation for payment of dividend to equity shareholders. They are ranked at the bottom as claimants on the assets of the company at the time of liquidation. Though it is quite evident from the above discussion that, equity capital does not carry any cost. However, this is not true, equity capital has some cost.

The cost of equity capital (K_e), may be defined as the minimum rate of returns that a firm must earn on the equity financed portions of an investment project in order to leave unchanged the market price of the shares. The cost of equity is not the out-of-pocket cost of using equity capital as the equity shareholders are not paid dividend at a fixed rate every year.

APPROACHES TO CALCULATE THE COST OF EQUITY (K_E)

There are six approaches available to calculate the cost of equity capital, they are:

(i) Dividends Capitalisation Approach (D/Mp Approach)

According to this approach, the cost of equity capital is calculated on the basis of a required rate of return in terms of the future dividends to be paid on the shares. Accordingly, K_e is defined as the discount rate that equates the present value of all expected future dividends per share, along with the net proceeds of the sale (or the current market price) of a share. It means investor arrives at a market price for a share by capitalizing dividends at a normal rate of return. The cost of equity capital can be measured by the given formula:

$K_e = D / CMP$ or NP

Where,

K_e = cost of equity

D   = Dividends per share

CMP   = Current market price per share

NP   = Net proceed per share

This method assumes that investor give prime importance to dividends and risk in the firm remains unchanged and it does not consider the growth in dividend.

Illustration 5: XYZ Ltd., is currently earning Rs. 1,00,000, its current share market price of Rs. 100 outstanding equity shares is 10,000. The company decides to raise an additional capital of Rs. 2,50,000 through issue of equity shares to the public. It is expected to pay 10 per cent per share as floatation cost. Equity capital is issued at a discount rate of 10 per cent, per share. The company is interested to pay a dividend of Rs. 8 per share. Calculate the cost of equity.

Solution:

$$K_e = \frac{D}{NP} \times 100$$

$$K_e = \frac{Rs.8}{(100 - 10 - 10)} \times 100$$

$$K_e = \frac{Rs.8}{80} \times 100$$

$$= 10 \text{ per cent}$$

Limitations

Dividend Capitalization approach, suffers from the following limitations:

1. It does not consider future earnings
2. It ignores the earnings on retained earnings
3. It ignores the fact that market price raise may be due to retained earnings and not on account of high dividends.
4. It does not take into account the capital gains.

(ii) Earnings Capitalisation Approach (E/MP Approach)

According to this approach, the cost of equity (K_e) is the discount rate that equates the present value of expected future earnings per share with the net proceeds (or current market price) of a share. The advocates of this approach establish a relationship between earnings and market price of the share. They say that, it is more useful than the dividend capitalisation approach, due to two reasons, *one*, the earnings capitalization approach acknowledges that all earnings of the company, after payment of fixed dividend to preference shareholders, legally belong to equity shareholders whether they are paid as dividends or retained for investment, *secondly*, and most importantly, determining the market price of equity shares is based on earnings and not dividends. Computation of retained earnings cost, taken separately leads to double the company's cost of capital. Assumption of earnings capitalization approach is employed under the following conditions:

(a) Constant earnings per share over the future period;

(b) There should be either 100 per cent rotation ratio or 100 per cent dividend pay out ratio and,

(c) The company satisfies the requirements through equity shares and does not employ debt.

Cost of equity can be calculated with the following formula :

$$K_e = \frac{E}{CMP \text{ or } NP}$$

Where,

K_e = Cost of equity

E = Earnings per share

CMP = Current market price per share

NP = Net proceeds per share.

Illustration 6: Well do company Ltd. is currently earning 15 per cent operating profit on its share capital of Rs. 20 lakh (FV of Rs. 200 per share). It is interested to go for expansion for which the company requires an additional share capital of Rs. 10 lakh. Company is raising this amount by the issue of equity shares at 10 per cent premium and the expected floatation cost is 5 per cent. Calculate the cost of equity.

Solution:

$$K_e = \frac{E}{NP} \times 100$$

$$= \frac{Rs.30}{(Rs.200 + 20 - 10)} \times 100$$

$$= \frac{Rs.30}{Rs.210} \times 100$$

$$= 14.3 \text{ per cent}$$

1. *Calculation of EPS*

   Operating Profit = Rs.20,00,000 x 0.15 = Rs.3,00,000

   No.of Equity Shares = 20,00,000 /200 = 10,000 Shares

   EPS = 3,00,000 / 10,000 = **Rs.30**

2. *Net Proceeds (NP)* = Face value + Premium - Floatation cost = 200 +20 - 10 = **Rs.210**

   Illustration 7: A firm is currently earning Rs. 1,00,000 and its share is selling at a market price of Rs. 90. The firm has 10,000 shares outstanding and has no debt. Compute the cost of equity.

Solution:

$$K_e = \frac{E}{MP} \times 100$$

$$= \frac{Rs.10}{90} \times 100 = 11.11$$

Limitations

Earnings Capitalization approach has the following limitations:

1. All earnings are not distributed to the equity shareholders as dividends.
2. Earning per share may not be constant.
3. Share price also does not remain constant.

(iii) Dividend Capitalization plus growth rate approach [(D/MP) + g]

Computation of cost of equity capital based on a fixed dividend rate may not be appropriate, because the future dividend may grow. The growth in dividends may be constant perpetually or may vary over a period of time. It is the best method over dividend capitalisation approach, since it considers the growth in dividends. Generally, investors invest in equity shares on the basis of the expected future dividends rather than on current dividends. They expect increase in future dividends. Growth in dividends will have positive impact on share prices.

Cost of Capital Under Constant Growth Rate Perpetually

The formula for computation of cost of equity under constant growth rate is :

$$K_e = \frac{D}{NP \text{ or } CMP} + g$$

Where,

K_e = Cost of equity capital

D = Dividends per share.

NP = Net proceeds per share.

CMP = Current market price per share.

g = Growth rate (%).

Illustration 8: Equity shares of a paper manufacturing company is currently selling for Rs. 100. It wants to finance its capital expenditure of Rs. 1 lakh either by retaining earnings or selling new shares. If company seeks to sell shares, the issue price will be Rs. 95. The expected dividend next year is Rs. 4.75 and it is expected to grow at 6 per cent perpetually. Calculate cost of equity capital (internal and external).

Solution:

$$K_e = \frac{D}{MP} + g$$

$$K_e = \frac{4.75}{100} + 0.06$$

$$= 0.048 + 0.06$$

$$= 10.8 \text{ per cent}$$

Calculate cost of external equity (Issue of shares)

$$K_e = \frac{4.75}{95} + 0.06$$

$$= 0.050 + 0.06$$

$$= 11 \text{ per cent}$$

Cost of Capital Under Variable Growth Rate

The computation cost of equity after a specific period, is based on the estimation of growth rate in dividends of a company. Expected growth rate will be calculated based upon the past trend in dividend. It may not be unreasonable to project the trend into the future, based on the past trend. The financial manager must estimate the internal growth rate in dividends on the basis of long range plans of the company. Expected growth rate in the internal context requires to be adjusted. Compound growth rate in dividends can be computed with the following formula.

$$gr = Do (1 + r)^n = Dn$$

Where,

gr	=	Growth rate in dividends.
Do	=	First year dividend payment.
$(1 + r)^n$	=	Present value factor for 'nth' year.
Dn	=	Last year dividend payment.

Illustration 9: From the following dividends record of a company, compute the expected growth rate in dividends.

Year	1996	1997	1998	1999	2000	2001	2002	2003
Dividends per share Rs.	21	22	23	24	25	26	27	28

Solution:

$$gr = Do (1 + r)^n = \qquad Dn = 21 (1 + r)^7 = 28$$
$$(1 + r)^7 = 28 \div 21 \qquad (1 + r)^7 = 1.334$$

During seven years the dividends has increased by Rs. 7 giving a compound factor of 1.334. The growth rate is 4 per cent since the sum of Re. 1 would accumulate to Rs. 1.334 in seven year at 4 per cent interest.

Illustration 10: Mr. A an investor, purchases an equity share of a growing company for Rs. 210. He expects the company to pay dividends of Rs. 10.5, Rs. 11.025 and Rs. 11.575 in years 1, 2 and 3 respectively and he expects to sell the shares at a price of Rs. 243.10 at the end of three years.

(a) Determine the growth rate in dividends.

(b) Calculate the current dividend yield.

(c) What is the required rate of return of Mr. A on his equity investment ?

Solution:

(a) Computation of growth rate (gr)

$$gr = Do (1 + r)^n = Dn = Rs.\ 10.5 (1 + r)^2 = Rs.\ 11.575$$

$$(1+r)^2 = \frac{11.575}{10.5}$$

$$(1+r)^2 = 1.103$$

$$gr = 5 \text{ per cent}$$

(b) Calculation of the current dividend yield

3rd year dividend Rs. 11.575

$$\text{Current dividend yield} = \frac{11.575}{100} \times 105 = Rs.\ 12.154$$

Growth in dividend is [12.154 − 11.575] = 0.579

$$\text{Current dividend yield} \quad \frac{0.579}{11.575} \times 100 \quad = 5 \text{ per cent}$$

In simple words, current dividend yield is equal to growth rate in dividends.

(c) Mr. A's required rate of return

$$K_e = \frac{D}{\text{Expected sales price (MP)}} + g$$

$$= \frac{Rs.\ 12.154}{243.10} + 0.05$$

$$= 0.050 + 0.05 = 0.10 \times 100 = 10 \text{ per cent}$$

Illustration 11 (variable growth rates) : A textile company's dividends have been expected to grow in the following manner.

1 – 2 years	15 per cent
3 – 5 years	10 per cent
6 year and beyond	5 per cent

The company currently pays a dividend of Rs. 2 per share, which is currently selling at Rs. 75 per share. What would be the cost of equity capital assuming a fixed dividend pay out ratio ?

Solution:

$$NP = \sum_{t=1}^{n} \frac{D_0(1+gr)^t}{(1+K_e)^t} + \frac{D_{n+1}}{K_e - g^n} \times \frac{1}{(1+K_e)^n}$$

$$75 = \frac{2.3}{(1+K_e)^1} + \frac{2.645}{(1+K_e)^2} + \frac{2.9095}{(1+K_e)^3} + \frac{3.200}{(1+K_e)^4} + \frac{3.52}{(1+K_e)^5} + \frac{3.52(1+0.05)}{(1+K_e)^5} \times \frac{1}{(1+K_e)^5}$$

$$= 2.3(PVIF_{1.K_e}) + 2.645(PVIF_{2.K_e}) + 2.9095(PVIF_{3.K_e}) + 3.2(PVIF_{4.K_e}) + 3.52(PVIF_{5.K_e}) + \frac{3.696(PVIF_{6.K_e})}{K_e - 0.05}$$

By trial and error method using PV tables, we find $K_e = 14$ %

First trial at 14%

$$75 = 2.3(0.877) + 2.645(0.769) + 2.909(0.675) + 3.2(0.592) + 3.52(0.519) + \frac{3.696}{0.14 - 0.05} \times (0.456)$$

$$75 = 2.02 + 2.03 + 1.96 + 1.89 + 1.83 + 18.73$$

$$75 = 28.5$$

Here, 75 is not equal to 28.5, for increasing the 28.5 to 75 we have to try at a lower rate, say 6%

$$75 = 2.3(0.943) + 2.645(0.890) + 2.907(0.840) + 3.2(0.823) + 3.52(0.747) + \frac{3.696}{0.06 - 0.05} \times (0.705)$$

$$= 2.17 + 2.35 + 2.44 + 2.63 + 2.63 + 260.568 = 272.79$$

New PV of cash out flows exceeding cash inflow. So, we will use interpolation formula

$$K_e = 6\% + \left((14\% - 6\%) \frac{272.79 - 75}{272.79 - 28.5} \right)$$

$$= 6\% + 8\% \left(\frac{197.79}{244.29} \right)$$

$$K_e = 6\% + 6.48 = 12.48 \text{ per cent.}$$

(iv) Bond Yield Plus Risk Premium Approach

According to this approach, the rate of return required by the equity shareholder of a company is equal to

$$K_e = \text{yield on long-term bonds} + \text{risk premium}$$

The logic of this approach is very simple, equity investors bear a higher risk than bond investors and hence their required rate of return should include a premium for their higher risk. In other words, bond holders and equity shareholders, both are providing funds to the company, but the company assures a fixed rate of interest to the bond holders and not to the equity shareholders, hence, there is a risk involved due to uncertainty of expected dividends. It makes a sense to base the cost of equity on a readily observable cost of debt. The problem involved in this approach, is the addition of premium, should it be one per cent, two per cent, three per cent or 'n' per cent. There is no theoretical basis for estimating the risk premium. Most analysts look at the operating and financial risks of the business and arrive at a subjectively determined risk premium that normally ranges between 3 per cent to 5 per cent. Cost of equity capital calculated, based on this approach is not a precise one, but it is a ballpark estimation.

Illustration 12: XYZ Company is planning to sell equity shares. Mr. A is planning to invest in XYZ Company by purchasing equity shares. Bond yield of XYZ Company is 12 per cent. Mr. A, an investor requests you to calculate his required rate of return on equity with 3 per cent risk premium.

Solution:

K_e = Bond yield + risk premium = 10% + 3% = 13 per cent

(v) Realised Yield Approach

Computation of the cost of equity based on dividends capitalisation and earnings capitalisation, have serious limitations. It is not possible to estimate future dividends and earnings correctly, both these variables are uncertain. In order to remove the difficulty in the estimation of the rate of return that investors expect on equities, where future dividends, earnings and market price of share are uncertain, Realised Yield Approach is suggested. It takes into consideration that, the actual average rate of returns realised in the past few years, may be applied to compute the cost of equity share capital i.e, the average rate of returns realised by considering dividends received in the past few years along with the gain realised at the time of sale of share.

This is more logical because the investor expects to receive in future at least what he has received in the past. The realised yield approach is based on the following assumptions :

 (a) Firms risk does not change over the period.

 (b) Past realised yield is the base for shareholders expectations.

 (c) There is no opportunity cost to investors.

 (d) Market price of equity share does not change significantly.

Calculation of the cost of equity based on realised yield approach is not realistic, due to unrealistic assumptions.

Illustration 13: An investor purchased equity share of HPH company at Rs. 240 on 01.01.1998 and after holding it for 5 years sold the share in early 2003 at Rs. 300. During this period of 5 years, he received a dividend of Rs. 14 in 1998 and 1999 and Rs. 14.5 from 2000 to 2002. Calculate the cost of equity capital based on realised yield approach with 10 per cent discounting factor.

Solution:

Years	Cash inflows (Rs.)	DF 10%	PV of Cash inflows (Rs.)
1998	14.0	0.909	12.7
1999	14.0	0.826	11.6
2000	14.5	0.751	10.9
2001	14.5	0.683	9.9
2002	14.5	0.621	9.0
2003	300.0	0.621	186.3
			240.4
	(-) Purchase price in 1998		240.0
			0.4

At 10 per cent discount rate, the total PV of cash inflows equals to the PV of cash outflows. Hence, cost of equity capital is 10 per cent.

(vi) Capital Asset Pricing Model Approach (CAPM)

Capital Asset Pricing Model (CAPM) was developed by William F. Sharpe.[5] This is another approach that can be used to calculate cost of equity. From the cost of capital point of view, CAPM explains the relationship between the required rate of return, or the cost of equity capital and the non-diversifiable or relevant risk, of the firm as reflected in its index of non-diversifiable risk that is beta (β). Symbolically,

$$K_e = R_f + (R_{mf} - R_f)\ \beta$$

Where:

K_e = Cost of equity capital.

R_f = Rate of return required on a risk free security (%).

β = Beta coefficient.

R_{mf} = Required rate of return on the market past folio of assets, that can be viewed as the average rate of return on all assets.

Assumptions

CAPM approach is based on the following assumptions:

(A) *Perfect Capital Market:* All investors have the same information about securities:-

♦ There are no restrictions on investments (buying and selling)

♦ Securities are completely divisible

♦ There are no transaction costs

♦ There are no taxes

♦ Competitive market – means no single investor can affect market price significantly

(B) *Investors preferences :* Investors are risk averse:-

♦ Investors have homogenous expectations regarding the expected returns, variances and correlation of returns among all securities.

♦ Investors seek to maximise the expected utility of their portfolios over a single period planning horizon.

Illustration 14: The Capital Ltd., wishes to calculate its cost of equity capital using the Capital Asset Pricing Model (CAPM) approach. Company's analyst found, that its risk free rate of return equals 12 per cent beta equal equals 1.7 and the return on market portfolio equals 14.5 per cent.

Solution:

$$K_e = R_f + (R_{mf} - R_f)\ \beta = 12 + [14.5 - 12]\ 1.7$$
$$= 12 + 4.25 = 16.25 \text{ per cent}$$

COST OF PREFERENCE SHARES

The preference share is issued by companies to raise funds from investors. Preference share has two preferential rights over equity shares, (i) preference in payment of dividend, from distributable profits, (ii) preference in the payment of capital at the time of liquidation of the company.

Computation of cost of preference share capital have some conceptual difficulty. Payment of dividend is not legally binding on the company and even if dividends are paid, they are not a charge on earnings, they are distributed from distributable profits. This may create an idea that preference share capital is cost free, which is not true.

The cost of preference share capital is a function of the dividend expected by the investors. Generally, preference share capital is issued with an intention (a fixed rate) to pay dividends. In case dividends are not paid, it will affect the firm's fund raising capacity. For this reason, dividends on preference share capital should be paid regularly except when the firm does not make profits.

There are different types of preference shares, cumulative and non-cumulative, redeemable and irredeemable, participating and non-participating, and convertible and non-convertible. But computation of cost of preference share will be only for redeemable and irredeemable.

Cost of Irredeemable Preference Share/Perpetual Preference Share

The share that cannot be paid till the liquidation of the company is known as irredeemable preference share. The cost is measured by the following formula:

$$K_p \text{ (without tax)} = \frac{D}{CMP \text{ or } NP}$$

Where,

K_p =   Cost of preference share.

D   =   Dividend per share.

CMP   =   Market price per share.

NP   =   Net proceeds.

Cost of irredeemable preference stock (with dividend tax)

$$K_p \text{ (with tax)} = \frac{D(1 + Dt)}{CMP \text{ or } NP}$$

Where,

Dt = tax on preference dividend

Illustration 15: HHC Ltd., issues 12 per cent perpetual preference shares of face value of Rs. 200 each. Compute cost of preference share (without tax).

Solution:

$$K_p = \frac{D}{NP} \times 100$$

$$K_p = \frac{24}{200} \times 100 = 12 \text{ per cent}$$

Illustration 16: (with dividend tax): A company is planning to issue 14 per cent irredeemable preference share at the face value of Rs. 250 per share, with an estimated flotation cost of 5%. What is the cost of preference share with 10% dividend tax.

Solution:

$$K_p = \frac{D(1+Dt)}{NP} \times 100$$

$$= \frac{35(1+0.10)}{237.5} \times 100 = 16.21 \text{ per cent}$$

Illustration 17: Sai Ram & Co. is planning to issue 14 per cent perpetual preference shares, with face value of Rs. 100 each. Floatation costs are estimated at 4 per cent on sales price. Compute (a) cost of preference shares if they are issued at (i) face / par value, (ii) 10 per cent premium, and (iii) 5 per cent discount, (b) compute cost of preference share in these situation assuming 5 per cent dividend.

Solution:

Without dividend tax	With dividend tax
(i) Issued at face value $$K_p = \frac{14}{(100-4)} = 14.6 \text{ per cent}$$	(i) Issued at face value $$K_p = \frac{14(1+0.05)}{96} = 15.4 \text{ per cent}$$
(ii) Issued at 10% premium $$K_p = \frac{14}{(110-4)} = 13.2 \text{ per cent}$$	(ii) Issued at 10% premium $$K_p = \frac{14(1+0.05)}{106} = 13.9 \text{ per cent}$$
(iii) Issued at 5% discount $$K_p = \frac{14}{(100-5-3.8)} = 15.4 \text{ per cent}$$	(iii) Issued at 5% discount $$K_p = \frac{14(1+0.05)}{91.2} = 16.2 \text{ per cent}$$

Cost of Redeemable Preference Shares

Shares that are issued for a specific maturity period or redeemable after a specific period are known as redeemable preference shares. The explicit cost of redeemable preference shares is the discount rate that equates the net proceeds of the sale of preference shares with the present value of the future dividend and principle repayments. In other words, cost of preference share is the discount rate that equates the present value of cash inflows (sale proceeds) with the present value of cash outflows (dividend + principal repayment). Dividends will be paid at the end of each year, but the principle amount will be repaid either in lump sum at the end of maturity period or in installments (equal or unequal). If the principle amount is paid in installments, then the cash outflow for each year equals to dividend plus part of principal amount. Cost of preference shares, when the principal amount is repaid in one lumpsum amount:

$$NP = \sum_{t=1}^{n} \frac{Dt}{(1+K_p)^t} + \frac{P_n}{(1+K_p)^n}$$

$$NP = \frac{D_1}{(1+K_p)^1} + \frac{D_2}{(1+K_p)^2} + \frac{D_3}{(1+K_p)^3} + \cdots\cdots + \frac{P_n}{(1+K_p)^n}$$

Where,

K_p = Cost of preference share.

NP = Net sales proceeds (after discount, flotation cost).

D = Dividend on preference share.

P_n = Repayment of principal amount at the end of 'n' years.

Illustration 18 (Lump sum repayment): A company issues Rs. 1,00,000, 10 per cent preference shares of Rs. 100 each redeemable after 10 years at face value. Cost of issue is 10 per cent. Calculate the cost of preference share.

Solution:

$$NP = \sum_{t=1}^{n} \frac{Dt}{(1+K_p)^t} + \frac{P_n}{(1+K_p)^n}$$

$$90 = \sum_{t=1}^{10} \frac{10}{(1+K_p)^t} + \frac{Rs.\ 100}{(1+K_p)^{10}}$$

The trial and error method is used here, for the computation of the cost of preference share.

Year	Cash outflow (Rs.)	PV factor		Present Values	
		10%	12%	10%	12%
1 - 10	10	6.145	5.650	61.45	56.5
10	100	0.386	0.322	38.60	32.2
Total PV of Cash outflow				100.05	88.70
(-) PV of Cash inflow				90.00	90.00
				10.05	(-) 1.3

In trials, PV of cash outflow did not equal to the PV of cash inflow (Rs. 100). Hence, cost of preference share is calculated by using interpolation formula.

$$K = LDF(\%) + \left((HDF - LDF) \frac{LDFPV - PV\ of\ CIF}{LDFPV - HDFPV} \right)$$

Where,

LDF = Lower discounting factor in %.

LDFPV = Lower discounting factor present value (Rs.).

HDFPV = Higher discounting factor present value (Rs.).

PV of CIF = Present value of cash inflows.

$$K_p = 10\% + \left((12\% - 10\%)\frac{100.05 - 90}{100.05 - 88.7} \right)$$

$$= 10\% + \left(2 \times \frac{10.05}{11.35} \right)$$

$$= 10\% + 2 \times 0.886 = 10\% + 1.772$$

$$= 11.77 \text{ per cent}$$

Short cut formula :

$$K_p = \frac{D + (f + d + pr - pi)/N_m}{(RV + NP)/2}$$

Where,

D	=	Dividend per share.
f	=	Flotation cost (Rs).
d	=	Discount on issue of preference share (Rs).
pr	=	Premium on redemption of preference shares (Rs).
pi	=	Premium on issue of preference share (Rs).
N_m	=	Term of preference shares.
RV	=	Redeemable value of preference share.
NP	=	Net proceeds realized.

$$K_p = \frac{10 + (10 + 0 + 0 - 0)/10}{(100 + 90)/2}$$

$$= \frac{10 + (1)}{95} = 11.579 \text{ per cent}$$

COST OF DEBENTURES/DEBT/PUBLIC DEPOSITS

Companies may raise debt capital through issue of debentures or loan from financial institutions or deposits from public. All these resources involve a specific rate of interest. The interest paid on these sources of funds is a charge on the profit & loss account of the company. In other words, interest payments made by the firm on debt issue qualify tax deduction in determining net taxable income. Computation of cost of debenture or debt is relatively easy, because the interest rate that is payable on debt is fixed by the agreement between the firm and the creditors. Computation of cost of debenture or debt capital depends on their nature. The debt/debentures can be perpetual or irredeemable and redeemable cost of debt capital is equal to the interest paid on that debt, but from company's point of view it will be less than the interest payable, when the debt is issued at par, since the interest is tax deductible. Hence, computation of debt is always after tax cost.

Cost of Irredeemable Debt/Perpetual debt

Perpetual debt provides permanent funds to the firm, because the funds will remain in the firm till liquidation. Computation of cost of perpetual debt is conceptually relatively easy. Cost of perpetual debt is the rate of return that lender expect (i.e., fixed interest rate). The coupon rate or the market yield on debt can be said to represent an approximation of cost of debt. Bonds / debentures can be issued at (i) par / face value, (ii) discount and (iii) premium. The following formulae are used to compute cost of debentures or debt of bond:

(i) **Pre-tax cost**

$$Kdi = \frac{I}{P \text{ or } NP}$$

(ii) **Post-tax cost**

$$Kdi = \frac{I(1-t)}{P \text{ or } NP}$$

Where,

Kdi	=	Pre-tax cost of debentures.
I	=	Interest
P	=	Principle amount or face value.
P	=	Net sales proceeds.
t	=	Tax rate.

Illustration 19: XYZ Company Ltd., decides to float perpetual 12 per cent, debentures of Rs. 100 each. The tax rate is 50 per cent. Calculate cost of debenture (pre and post tax cost).

Solution:

(i) **Pre-tax cost**

$$Kdi = \frac{Rs. \ 12}{100} = 12 \text{ per cent}$$

(ii) **Post-tax cost**

$$Kd = \frac{12(1-0.5)}{100} = 6 \text{ per cent}$$

Generally, cost of debenture is equal to the interest rate, when debenture is issued at par and without considering tax. Cost will be less than the interest when we calculate cost after considering tax since it is tax deductible. From the cost of capital point of view, debenture cost is always in post tax cost.

Sometimes debentures may be issued at premium or discount. A company, which is having a good track record, will be issued at premium and a company that is new or unknown to the public or has a nominal or poor track record will be issued at discount. Whenever debentures are issued at premium or discount the cost of debenture will be affected, it will decrease or increase respectively.

Illustration 20: Rama & Co. has 15 per cent irredeemable debentures of Rs. 100 each for Rs. 10,00,000. The tax rate is 35 per cent. Determine debenture assuming it is issued at (i) face value / par value (ii) 10 per cent premium and (iii) 10 per cent discount.

Solution:

Issued at	Pre-tax	Post-tax
(i) Face value	$\dfrac{\text{Rs. } 15}{100} = 15$ per cent	$\dfrac{15(1-0.35)}{100} = 9.8$ per cent
(ii) 10% premium	$\dfrac{\text{Rs. } 15}{110} = 13.7$ per cent $(100+10)$	$\dfrac{15(1-0.35)}{110} = 8.9$ per cent
(iii) 10% discount	$\dfrac{\text{Rs. } 15}{90} = 16.67$ per cent $(100-10)$	$\dfrac{15(1-0.35)}{90} = 10.9$ per cent

Cost of Redeemable Debentures/Debt

Redeemable debentures that, are having a maturity period or are repayable after a certain given period of time. In other words, these type of debentures that are under legal obligation to repay the principal amount to its holders either at certain agreed intervals during the duration of loan or as a lumpsum amount at the end of its maturity period. These type of debentures are issued by many companies, when they require capital for fulfilling their temporary needs.

Cost of Redeemable Debentures

$$Kd = \sum_{t=1}^{n} \frac{NI_t}{(1+Kd)^t} + \frac{P_n}{(1+Kd)^n}$$

Where,

Kd = Cost of debentures.

n = Maturity period.

NI = Net interest (after tax adjustment).

P_n = Principal repayment in the year 'n'.

Illustration 21: BE Company issues Rs. 100 par value of debentures carrying 15 per cent interest. The debentures are repayable after 7 years at face value. The cost of issue is 3 per cent and tax rate is 45 per cent. Calculate the cost of debenture.

Solution:

$$(100-3) = \sum_{t=1}^{7} \frac{15(1-0.45)}{(1+Kd)^t} + \frac{100}{(1+Kd)^n}$$

Year	Cash outflow (Rs.)	DF		PV of cash outflows Rs.	
		7%	10%	7%	10%
1 - 7	8.25	5.389	4.868	44.96	40.16
7	100	0.623	0.513	62.30	51.30
	PV of cash out flows			106.76	91.46
(-) PV of Cash inflows				97.00	97.00
				9.76	5.54

Cost of debenture capital lies between 10 per cent and 12 per cent, because net present value Rs. 97 lies between the PV of 10 per cent and 12 per cent. Exact cost can be computed only with interpolation formula:

$$Kd = LDF + \left((HDF - LDF) \frac{LDFPV - NP}{LDFPV - HDFPV} \right)$$

Where,

LDF   = Lower discounting factor.

HDF   = Higher discounting factor.

LDFPV = Lower discounting factor present value.

HDFPV = Higher discounting factor PV.

PVCIF = Present value of cash inflows

NP   = Net proceeds.

$$Kd = 7\% + \left[3 \times \frac{106.76 - 97}{106.76 - 91.46} \right]$$

$$= 7\% + 1.91 = 8.91\%$$

Short cut method

$$K_p = \frac{I(1-t) + (f + d + pr - pi)/N_m}{(RV + NP)/2}$$

Where,

I   = Interest.

t   = Tax rate.

f   = Flotation cost.

d   = Discount.

p_r = Premium on redemption.

p_i = Premium on issue.

RV   = Redeemable value.

NP   = Net proceed.

N_m = Maturity period of debt.

$$K_p = \frac{15(1 - 0.45) + (3 - 0 + 0 - 0)/7}{(100 - 97)/2}$$

$$K_p = \frac{8.68}{98.5} = 8.81\%$$

Illustration 22 (Installment repayment) : Hari Ram & Co. issued 14 per cent debentures aggregate at Rs. 2,00,000. The face value of debenture is Rs. 100. Issue cost is 5 per cent. The company has agreed to repay the debenture in 5 equal installment at par value. Installment starts at the end of the year. The company's tax rate is 35 per cent. Compute cost of debenture.

Solution:

Sales proceeds = face value + flotation cost = Rs. 100 − 5 = Rs. 95

Installment amount = Face value + No. of installments = 100 ÷ 5 = Rs. 20.

Years	Cash outflow (Rs.)	DF Factor		PV of cash Outflows Rs.	
	(NI + Installment)	8%	13%	8%	13%
1	9.1 + 20 = 29.1	0.926	0.885	26.947	25.754
2	7.28 + 20 = 27.28	0.857	0.783	23.379	21.361
3	5.46 + 20 = 25.46	0.794	0.693	20.216	17.644
4	3.64 + 20 = 23.64	0.735	0.613	17.376	14.492
5	1.82 + 20 = 21.82	0.681	0.543	14.860	11.849
PV of cash out flows				102.778	91.230
PV of cash inflows				95.000	95.000
				(+) 7.778	(−)3.770

$$Kd = 8\% + \left((13-8) \times \frac{102.778 - 95}{102.778 - 91.1} \right)$$

$$= 8\% + \left(5 \times \frac{7.778}{11.678} \right)$$

$$= 8\% + 3.33 = 11.33 \text{ per cent}$$

WEIGHTED AVERAGE COST OF CAPITAL (WACC)

A company has to employ a combination of creditors and fund owners. The composite cost of capital lies between the least and most expensive funds. This approach enables the maximisation of profits and the wealth of the equity shareholders by investing the funds in projects earning in excess of the overall cost of capital.

The composite cost of capital implies an average of the costs of each of the source of funds employed by the firm property, weighted by the proportion they hold in the firm's capital structure.

Steps involved in computation of WACC

1. Determination of the type of funds to be raised and their individual share in the total capitalisation of the firm.
2. Computation of cost of specific source of funds.
3. Assignment of weight to specific costs.
4. Multiply the cost of each source by the appropriate assigned weights.
5. Dividing the total weighted cost by the total weights to get overall cost of capital.

Once the company decides the funds that will be raised from different sources, then the computation of specific cost of each component or source is completed after which, the third step in computation of cost of capital is, assignment of weights to specific costs, or specific sources of funds. How to assign weights? Is there any base to assign weights? How many types of weights are there?

Assignment of Weights: The weights to specific funds may be assigned, based on the following:

(i) **Book Values:** Book value weights are based on the values found on the balance sheet. The weight applicable to a given source of fund is simply the book value of the source of fund divided by the book value of the total funds.

  ♦ The merits of book values weights are

  - Calculation of weights is simple.

  - Book values provide a usable base, when firm is not listed or security is not actively traded.

  - Book values are really available from the published records of the firm.

  - Analysis of capital structure in terms of debt – equity ratio is based on book value.[6]

  ♦ *Disadvantages of book value weights*

  - There is no relation between book values and present economic values of the various sources of capital

  - Book value proportions are not consistent with the concept of cost of capital because the latter is defined as the minimum rate of return to maintain the market value of the firm.

(ii) **Capital Structure Weights:** Under this method, weights are assigned to the components of capital structure based on the targeted capital structure. Depending up on the target, capital structures have some difficulties. They are[7] :

  ♦ A company may not have a well defined target capital structure.

  ♦ It may be difficult to precisely estimate the components of capital costs, if the target capital is different from present capital structure.

(iii) **Market Value Weights:** Under this method, assigned weights to a particular component of capital structure is equal to the market value of the component of capital divided by the market value of all components of capital and capital employed by the firm.

  ♦ *Advantages of market value weights*

  - Market values of securities are approximately close to the actual amount to be received from their sale.

  - Costs of the specific resources of funds that constitute the capital structure of the firm, are calculated by keeping in mind the prevailing market prices.

  ♦ *Disadvantages of market value weights*

  - Market values may not be available when a firm is not listed or when the securities of the firm are very thinly traded.

  - Market value may be distorted when securities prices are influenced by manipulation loading.

  - Equity capital gets greater importance.

Most of the financial analysts prefer to use market value weights because it is theoretically consistent and sound.

Illustration 23: A firm has the following capital structure as the latest statement shows:

Source of funds	Rs.	After tax Cost %
Debt	30,00,000	4
Preference shares	10,00,000	8.5
Equity share	20,00,000	11.5
Retained earnings	40,00,000	10
Total	**100,00,000**	

Based on the book values compute the cost of capital.

Solution:

Source of Finance	Weights	Specific Cost (%)	Weighted Cost
Debt	0.30	0.04	0.012
Preference shares	0.10	0.08	0.008
Equity share	0.20	0.11	0.022
Retained earnings	0.40	0.10	0.040
	1.00		0.082

Overall cost of capital (Ko) = Total Weighted Cost x 100

$$= 0.082 \times 100 = 8.2 \text{ per cent}$$

Cost of weight

$$\text{Debt weight} = \frac{\text{Debt capital}}{\text{Total capital}} = \frac{30,00,000}{1,00,00,000} = 0.30$$

Illustration 24: XYZ company supplied the following information and requested you to compute the cost of capital based on book values and market values.

Source of Finance	Book Value (Rs.)	Market Value (Rs.)	After Tax Cost (%)
Equity capital	10,00,000	15,00,000	12
Long term debt	8,00,000	7,50,000	7
Short term debt	2,00,000	2,00,000	4
Total	20,00,000	24,50,000	

Solution:

Computation of cost of capital based on book value

Source of Finance	Book Value (Rs.)	Weights	Specific cost	Weighted cost
(1)	(2)	(3)	(4)	(5) = (3) X (4)
Equity capital	10,00,000	0.50	0.12	0.060
Long term debt	8,00,000	0.40	0.07	0.028
Short term debt	2,00,000	0.10	0.04	0.004
Total	20,00,000	1.00		0.092

Cost of capital = 0.092 x 100 = 9.2 per cent

Cost of capital based on market value weight.

Source of Finance	Book Value (Rs.)	Weights	Specific cost	Weighted cost
(1)	(2)	(3)	(4)	(5) = (3) X (4)
Equity capital	15,00,000	0.613	0.12	0.074
Long term debt	7,50,000	0.307	0.07	0.022
Short term debt	2,00,000	0.080	0.04	0.003
	24,50,000	1.000		0.099

Cost of capital = 100 X 0.099 = 9.9 per cent

Weighted average cost of capital (alternative method)

Source of Finance	Market Value (Rs.)	Cost (%)	Total Cost
(1)	(2)	(3)	(4) = (2) X (3)
Equity capital	15,00,000	0.12	1,80,000
Long term debt	7,50,000	0.07	52,500
Short term debt	2,00,000	0.04	8,000
	24,50,000		2,40,500

$$WACC = \frac{\text{Total Cost}}{\text{Total Capital}}$$

$$= \frac{2,40,500}{24,50,000} \times 100 = 9.9\% \quad \text{approx. 10 per cent}$$

MARGINAL COST OF CAPITAL

Companies may rise additional funds for expansion. Here, a financial manager may be required to calculate the cost of additional funds to be raised. The cost of additional funds is called marginal cost of capital. For example, a firm at present has Rs. 1,00,00,000 capital with WACC of 12 per cent, but it plans to raise Rs. 5,00,000 for expansion, such as additional funds, the cost that is related to this Rs. 5 lakhs is marginal cost of capital.

The weighted average cost of new or incremental, capital is known as the marginal cost of capital. The marginal cost of capital is the weighted average cost of new capital using the marginal weights. The marginal weights represent the proportion of various sources of funds to be employed in raising additional funds. The marginal cost of capital shall be equal to WACC, when a firm employs the existing proportion of capital structure and some cost of component of capital structure. But in practice WACC may not be equal to marginal cost of capital due to change in proportion and cost of various sources of funds used in raising new capital. The marginal cost of capital ignores the long term implications of the new financing plans. Hence, WACC should be preferred, to maximise the shareholders wealth in the long term.

Illustration 25: HLL has provided the following information and requested you to calculate (a) WACC using book-value weights and (b) weighted marginal cost of capital (assuming that specified cost do not change)

Source of Finance	Amount (Rs.)	Weights (%)	After tax cost (%)
Equity capital	14,00,000	0.452	9
Preference capital	8,00,000	0.258	12
Debentures	9,00,000	0.290	16

HLL wishes to raise an additional capital of Rs. 12,00,000 for the expansion of the project. The details are as follows

Equity capital	Rs. 3,00,000
Preference capital	Rs. 3,00,000
Debentures	Rs. 6,00,000

Solution:

Computation of WACC

Source of Finance	Weights	After tax Cost (%)	Weighted Cost
Equity capital	0.452	0.09	0.041
Preference capital	0.258	0.12	0.031
Debentures	0.290	0.16	0.046
			0.118

WACC = 0.118 x 100   = 11.8 per cent

Computation of Weighted Marginal Cost of Capital (WACC)

Source of Finance	Marginal Weights	After tax Cost (%)	Weighted marginal cost
Equity capital	0.50	0.09	0.045
Preference capital	0.25	0.12	0.030
Debentures	0.25	0.16	0.040
			0.115

WACC = 0.115 x 100   = 11.5 per cent

FACTORS AFFECTING WACC

Weighted average cost of capital is affected by a number of factors. They are divided into two categories such as:

(a) Controllable Factors (Internal Factor)

(b) Uncontrollable Factors (External factor)

(a) *Controllable Factors:* Controllable factors are those factors that affect WACC, but the firm can control them. They are is

(i) *Capital Structure Policy*: As we have assured, a firm has a given target capital structure where it assigns weights based on that target capital structure to calculate WACC. However, a firm can change its capital structure or proportions of components of capital that affect its WACC. For example, when a firm decides to use more debt and less equity, which will lead to reduction of WACC. At the same time increasing proportion of debt in capital structure increases the risk of both debt and equity holder, because it increases fixed financial commitment.

(ii) *Dividend Policy*: The required capital may be raised by equity or debt or both. Equity capital can be raised by issue of new equity shares or through retained earnings. Sometimes companies may prefer to raise equity capital by retention of earnings, due to issue of new equity shares, which are expensive (they involve flotation costs). Firms may feel that retained earnings is less costly when compared to issue of new equity. But if it is different it is more costly, since the retained earnings is income that is not paid as dividends hence, investors expect more return and so it affects the cost of capital.

(iii) *Investment Policy*: While estimating the initial cost of capital, generally we use the starting point as the required rate of return on the firm's existing stock and bonds.

Therefore, we implicitly assume that new capital will be invested in assets of the same type and with the same degree of risk. But it is not correct as no firm invest in assets similar to the ones that currently operate, when a firm changes its investment policy. For example, investment in diversified business.

(b) *Uncontrollable Factors :* The factors that are not possible to be controlled by the firm and mostly affects the cost of capital. These factors are known as External factors.

(i) *Tax Rates:* Tax rates are beyond the control of a firm. They have an important effect on the overall cost of the capital. Computation of debt involves consideration of tax. In addition, lowering capital gains tax rate relative to the rate on ordinary income makes stocks more attractive and reduces cost of equity and lower the overall cost of capital.

(ii) *Level of Interest Rates:* Cost of debt is interest rate. If interest rates increases, automatically cost of debt also increases. On the other hand, if interest rates are low then the cost of debt is less. The reduced cost of debt decreases WACC and this will encourage an additional investment.

(iii) *Market Risk Premium:* Market risk premium is determined by the risk in investing proposed stock and the investor's aversion to risk. Market risk is out of control risk, i.e., firms have no control on this factor.

The above are the important factors that affect the cost of capital.

SUMMARY

♦ The cost of capital is viewed as one of the corner stones in the theory of financial management. It has received considerable attention from both, theorists and practitioners. There are two major schools of thought: one Modigline Miller argued that a firms cost of capital is constant and it is independent of the method and level of financing. According to the second group (traditionalists), the cost of capital is varying and dependent on capital structure.

♦ Cost of capital may be viewed in different ways: (i) From investors' view point – the measurement of the sacrifice made by him with regard to capital formation, (ii) Firms view point – it is the minimum required rate of returns needed to justify the use of capital, and (iii) Capital expenditure point -it is the minimum required rate of return used to value cash flows.

♦ Cost of capital is the weight average cost of various sources of finance used by the firm. It comprises the risk less cost of the particular type of financing (r_j), the business risk premium, (b) and the financial risk premium (f). Symbolically $(K_o) = r_j + b + f$.

♦ The cost of capital is useful in designing optimal capital structure, investment evaluation, and financial performance appraisal.

♦ Computation of Cost of capital / of WACC involves five steps: (1) Determination of the type of funds to be raised and their individual share in the total capitalisation of the firm, (2) Computation of the cost of each type of funds, (3) Assigning weights to specific costs, (4) Multiplying the cost of the source by the (appropriate) assigned weights, and (5) Dividing the total weighted cost by the total weights to get over all cost of capital.

♦ The financial manager has to compute the specific cost of each type of funds needed in the capitalisation of a company. Company may resort to different financial sources (equity share, preference share, debentures, retained earning, public deposits.

♦ Firms may obtain equity capital in two ways (a) retention of earnings and (b) issue of additional equity shares to the public. The cost of equity or the returns required by the equity shareholders is the same in both the cases, since the cost of equity is computed in both sources point of view (i.e., retained earnings and issue of equity shares to the public).

♦ Retained earnings are one of the internal sources to raise equity finance. Corporate executives and some analysts too normally consider the retained earnings as cost free, but it is not so. They involve opportunity. The opportunity cost of retained earning is the rate of return the shareholder forgoes by not putting his funds elsewhere.

♦ Cost of equity capital, is the minimum rate of return that a firm must earn on the equity financed portions of an investment project in order to leave unchanged the market price of the shares. There are six approaches available to compute K_e:

(i) Dividends capitalisation approach (D/Mp Approach) – Ke is calculated on the basis of a required rate of returns in terms of the future dividends to be paid on the shares. Symbolically: K_e = D / CMP or D/NP. This approach, suffers from few limitations; it does not consider future earnings, it ignores the earnings on retained earnings, it ignores the fact that market price raise may be due to retained earnings and not on account of high dividends, and it does not take into account the capital gains.

(ii) Earnings capitalisation approach (E/MP Approach)- here the K_e is the discount rate that equates the present value of expected future earnings per share with the net proceeds (or current market price) of a share. Symbolically: K_e = E/ CMP or E/NP. It suffers from few weaknesses; all earnings are not distributed as dividends, EPS may not be constant, and share price also does not remain constant.

(iii) Dividend capitalisation plus growth rate approach $[K_e$ (D/MP) + g] - Computation Ke fixed dividend rate may not be appropriate, because the future dividend may grow.

(iv) Bond yield plus risk premium approach – In this approach Ke is equal to yield on long-term bonds + risk premium.

(v) Realised Yield Approach - In order to remove the difficulty of estimation the rate of return that investors expect on equities where future dividends, earnings and market price of share are uncertain, realised yield approach is suggested. It takes into account the actual average rate of returns realised in the past few years, to K_e.

(vi) Capital Asset Pricing Model Approach (CAPM) – It explains the relationship between the required rate of return, or the cost of equity capital and the non-diversifiable or relevant risk, of the firm as reflected in its index, that is beta (β). Symbolically, $K_e = R_f + (R_{mf} - R_f)$ β. CAPM is based on the assumptions: perfect capital market, and investors' preferences.

♦ Cost of preference share capital (Kp) is a function of the dividend expected by the investors. Kp is having some conceptual difficulty. There are different types of preference shares. But computation of Kp is only done for the redeemable and irredeemable shares.

(a) Cost of Irredeemable Preference Stock (without tax): K_p = D/ CMP or NP.

(b) Cost of irredeemable preference stock (with dividend tax): K_p = D (1 + Dt) / CMP or D/NP.

(c) Cost of redeemable preference shares: Dividends will be paid at the end of every year, but principle amount will be repaid either in lump sum amount at the end of maturity period or in installments (equal or unequal). Kp when the principal amount is repaid in one lumpsum amount-

$$NP = \sum_{t=1}^{n} \frac{NI_t}{(1+Kd)^t} + \frac{P_n}{(1+Kd)^n}$$

♦ Cost of perpetual debenture / debt - Perpetual debt provides permanent funds to the firm. The coupon rate or the market yield on debt can be said to represent an approximation of cost of debt. Bonds / debentures can be issued at (i) par / face value, (ii) discount and premium.

(a) *Cost of Irredeemable debt / debenture:*

   (i)   Pre-tax cost: Kdi = (I/P or NP),

   (ii) post-tax cost: Kd =[I (1-t) / P or NP]

(b) *Cost of redeemable debentures (lump sum):*

♦   Once the company decides the funds that will be raised from different sources and then computation of specific cost of each source is completed, then comes the third step in computation of cost of capital i.e. assignment of weights to specific costs. There are three types of weights; Book value weights, capital structure weights, and market value weights.

♦   The marginal cost of capital is the weighted average cost of new capital using the marginal weights. The marginal weights represent the proportion of various sources of funds to be employed in raising additional funds. Marginal cost of capital shall be equal to WACC, when a firm employs the existing proportion of capital structure and some cost of component of capital structure. But in practice WACC may not be equal to marginal cost of capital due to change in proportion and cost of various sources of funds used in raising the new capital.

♦   The important factors that affect WACC are divided into two: (a) Controllable factors - Controllable factors can be controlled by the firm, they are: capital structure policy, dividend policy, and investment policy. (b) Uncontrollable factors: The factors that are not possible to be controlled by the firm, they are: tax rates, and level of interest rates.

PRACTICE YOURSELF (SOLVED PROBLEMS)

Illustration 1: A company's earnings available to ordinary shareholders is Rs. 5,00,000. It has capital Rs. 50,00,000, face value of Rs. 100 each. The company's share is selling at Rs. 200. Compute cost of equity (Assuming 100% dividend payout ratio).

Solution:

Computation of Dividends per share (DPS)

$$\frac{\text{Earnings available to shareholder (equity)}}{\text{No. of equity shares outstanding}}$$

$$\frac{\text{Rs. }5,00,000}{50,000\,*} = \text{Rs. 10 per share}$$

$$*\,\text{No. of equity shares out standing} = \frac{\text{Equity share capital}}{\text{Face value}}$$

$$= \frac{50,00,000}{100} = 50,000 \text{ shares}$$

(a) *Cost of equity based on face value :*

$$K_e = \frac{D}{Fv} = \frac{\text{Rs. }10}{100} X100 = 10 \text{ per cent}$$

(b) *Cost of equity based on market price :*

$$K_e = \frac{D}{MP} = \frac{\text{Rs. }10}{200} X100 = 5 \text{ per cent}$$

Illustration 2: P & G Company's current earnings per share is Rs. 6 and its share is currently selling at Rs. 25 per share. Compute cost of equity capital.

Solution:

$$K_e = \frac{E}{CMP} = \frac{Rs.\ 6}{25} X 100 = 24 \text{ per cent}$$

Illustration 3: A company has 50,00,000 equity shares outstanding. The market price of the share is Rs. 96, where the book value is Rs. 65. The firm's earnings and dividends per share is Rs. 10 and Rs. 7 respectively. The company wants to issue 10,00,000 shares with a net proceed of Rs. 80 per share. What is the cost of capital of new issue?

Solution:

$$K_e = \frac{D}{NP} = \frac{7}{80} \times 100 = 8.75 \text{ per cent}$$

Illustration 4: MNC Company has paid a dividend of Rs. 6 per share for last 10 years and it is expected to continue so in the future. The company's share was sold for Rs. 50 ten years ago, and its market price is also Rs. 50. What is the cost of equity share ?

Solution:

$$K_e = \frac{6}{50} \times 100 = 12 \text{ per cent}$$

Illustration 5: VS International is thinking of rising funds by the issuance of equity capital. The current market price of the firm's share is Rs. 150. The firm is expected to pay a dividend of Rs. 3.9 next year. At present, the firm can sell its share for Rs. 140 each and it involves a flotation cost of Rs. 10. Calculate cost of new issue.

Solution:

$$K_e = \frac{D}{NP} = \frac{Rs.\ 3.9}{(140 - 10)} \times 100 = \frac{3.9}{130} \times 100 = 3 \text{ per cent}$$

Illustration 6: SSS company is currently earning Rs. 10,00,000 and its share is selling at a market price of Rs. 160. The firm has 2,00,000 shares outstanding and has no debt. The earnings of the firm are expected to remain stable and it has a pay out ratio of 100 per cent. What is K_e ? If firm pay out ratio is assumed to be 70 per cent and that it earns 15 per cent of return on its investment opportunities, then what would be the firms K_e ?

Solution:

$$K_e \left(\text{with 100\% payment} \right) = \frac{D}{CMP} = \frac{5^*}{160} \times 100 = 3.125 \text{ per cent}$$

$$^* \text{Dividend per share} = \frac{10,00,000}{2,00,000} = Rs.\ 5 \text{ per share}$$

$$K_e(\text{with 70\% payout}) = \frac{Rs.\ 3.5}{160} + 0.045 = 6.687 \text{ per cent}$$

growth = br

g = (0.30 x 0.15) = 0.045

where,

b = Retention rate.

r= rate of returns

Illustration 7: Woodlands company's share is currently selling for Rs. 134. Current dividend is Rs. 3.5 per share and is expected to grow at 8 per cent next 4 years and at a rate of 15 per cent every year. Calculate company's cost of equity.

Solution:

Year	Dividend	Year	Dividend
1	3.5 (1.08) = 3.78	3	4.08 (1.08) = 4.41
2	3.78 (1.08) = 4.08	4	4.41 (1.08) = 4.76

$$K_e = \frac{D}{CMP} = \frac{4.76}{134} + 15\% = 18.55\%$$

Illustration 8: ABB is contemplating an issue of new equity shares. The company's equity share is currently selling at Rs. 250 per share. The dividend payment record for past 6 years is as follows :

Year	1	2	3	4	5	6
Dividend per share	22	25	26	27	28	29

The company is expected to spend flotation cash at 3% of the current selling price of the share. The company is requested for

(a) growth rate in dividends

(b) cost of equity assuming growth rate calculated under continuous for ever

(c) cost of new equity

Solution:

(a) Growth rate in dividends: Do $(1 + r)^n$ = Dn

$22 (1 + r)^5 = 29$

$(1 + r)^5 = 29 / 22$ = 1.318

The compound sum of one rupee table suggests that Re. 1 compounds to Rs. 1.318 in 5 years at the compound rate of 6 per cent \ growth rate is 6 per cent.

(b) Cost of equity $= \dfrac{29\ (1.06)}{250} + 0.06 = 18.3$ per cent

(c)   Cost of new equity $= \dfrac{30.74}{242.5} + 0.06 = 18.676$ per cent

Illustration 9: Karvey is planning to sell equity shares. Mr. Ram wishes to invest in Karvy company by purchasing equity shares. The company's bond has been yielding at 13 per cent. You are requested by Mr. Ram to calculate his expected rate of return on equity based on bond yield plus risk premium approach (assuming 3 per cent as risk premium).

Solution:

$$K_e = \text{Bond yield} + \text{risk premium} = 13\% + 3\% = 16 \text{ per cent}$$

Illustration 10: Mr. Krishna, who has purchased equity share of Wipro company at Rs. 100, on 01-01-1997 and after holding it for 6 years, sold the share at the end of 2002 for Rs. 180. During this 6 years period, he had received a dividend of Rs. 15, Rs. 15.50, Rs. 16, Rs. 17, Rs. 17.50, and Rs. 17 for the years 1997, 1998, 1999, 2000, 2001, 2002 years respectively. Calculate cost of equity share based on realised yield approach.

Solution:

Years	Cash inflow (Rs.)	DF		PV of cash inflow (Rs.)	
		10%	24%	10%	24%
1997	15	0.909	0.806	13.635	12.09
1998	15.5	0.826	0.650	12.803	10.075
1999	16	0.751	0.524	12.016	8.384
2000	17	0.683	0.423	11.611	7.191
2001	17.5	0.621	0.341	10.868	5.968
2002	17	0.564	0.275	9.588	4.675
2002	180	0.564	0.275	101.520	49.500
PV of Cash inflow				172.041	97.883
(-) PV of Cash outflow				100.000	100.000
				72.041	(-) 2.117

Cost of equity lies between 10% and 24% since the purchase price Rs. 100 lies between these two present values using interpolation formula K_e

$$K_e = 10\% + \left((24 - 10)\frac{172.41 - 100}{172.41 - 97.883} \right)$$

$$= 10 + \left(14 \frac{72.04}{74.157} \right)$$

$$= 10 + 13.6 = 23.6 \text{ per cent}$$

Illustration 11: Calculate the required rate of return on four equity stocks with the beta values shown against them.

Stock	A	B	C	D
Beta	0.9	1.1	1.6	1.9

The risk free rate is 20 per cent and rate of return on the market portfolio is 32 per cent.

Solution:

Require rate of returns $(K_e) = R_f + (R_{mf} - R_f) \beta$

A	B	C	D
20 + (32-20) 0.9	20 + (32 – 20) 1.1	20 (32 – 20) 1.6	20 + (32 – 20) 1.9
= 30.8 per cent	= 33.2 per cent	= 39.2 per cent	= 42.8 per cent

Illustration 12: Weekly returns of XYZ company for the period of January 2003 to July 20, 2003 containing 223 observations with the weekly returns for the same period on the Economic Times price index they obtained the beta of 1.20. The average market return (based on weekly returns) during the some period is approximately 21.3 per cent. If the risk free rate's assumed to be 10 per cent. How much is XYZ's cost of equity ?

Solution:

$$K_e = 10 + (21.3 - 10) \ 1.18 = 23.33 \text{ per cent}$$

Illustration 13: An investor supplied you the following information and requested you to calculate. Expected rate of returns on market portfolio

Investment in Company		Initial price	Dividends	Year-end market price	Beta risk factor
A	Paper	20	2	55	0.7
	Steel	30	2	65	0.8
	Chemical	40	2	140	0.6
B	GOI Bonds	1000	140	1005	0.99

Risk free returns=10 per cent

Solution:

Calculation of expected return on market portfolio investment

Investment in Security		Returns			Investment
		Dividend	Capital gain	Total	
A	Paper	2	35 (55 - 20)	37	20
	Steel	2	35 (65 - 30)	37	30
	Liquor	2	100 (140 - 40)	102	40
B	GOI Bonds	140	5 (1005 - 1000)	145	1000
		146		321	1090

The expected rate of return on market portfolio $= \dfrac{\text{Total return}}{\text{Total investment}} \times 100$

$$= \dfrac{321}{1090} \times 100 = 29.44 \text{ per cent}$$

Illustration 14: Om Sai Enterprises issued 9 per cent preference share (irredeemable) four years ago. The preference share that has a face value of Rs. 100 is currently selling for Rs. 93. What is the cost of preference share with 8 per cent tax on dividend.

Solution:

$$K_p = \dfrac{D(1+Dt)}{CMP}$$

$$K_p = \dfrac{9(1+0.08)}{93} \times 100 = 10.45 \text{ per cent}$$

Illustration 15: A company issues 12,000, 12 per cent perpetual preference shares of Rs. 100 each. Company is expected to pay 2 per cent as flotation cost. Calculate the cost of preference shares assuming to be issued at (i) face value of par value, (ii) at a discount of 5% and (iii) at a premium of 10%.

Solution:

$$K_p = \dfrac{D}{NP}$$

(i)   Issued at face value

$$K_p = \dfrac{12}{(100-2)} \times 100 = 12.24 \text{ per cent}$$

(ii) Issued at 5% discount

$$K_p = \dfrac{12}{(100-2-5)} = \dfrac{12}{93} \times 100 = 12.90 \text{ per cent}$$

(iii) Issued at a premium of 10%

$$K_p = \dfrac{12}{(100+10-2)} = \dfrac{12}{108} \times 100 = 11.11 \text{ per cent}$$

Illustration 16: A company has 50,000 preference shares of Rs. 100 at par outstanding at 11 per cent dividend. The current market price of the share is Rs. 90. What is its cost ?

Solution:

$$K_p = \dfrac{D}{MP} \times 100$$

$$= \dfrac{11}{90} \times 100 = 12.22 \text{ per cent}$$

Illustration 17: Vani & Co. issues Rs. 100 face value of preference share which carries 11 per cent dividend and is redeemable after 12 years at par value. The net amount realised per share is Rs. 95. What is the cost of preference share ?

Solution:

Year	Cash outflow (Rs.)	PV factor		PV of Cash outflows	
		11%	12%	11%	12%
1 – 12	11	6.492	6.194	71.412	68.134
12	100	0.286	0.257	28.600	25.700
PV of Cash outflows				100.012	93.834

Cost of preference share lies between 11% and 12%. Since the realised value of Rs. 95 lies between these two discount factors. So, by using interpolation formula K_p

$$K_p = 11\% + \left((12-11)\frac{100.012 - 95}{100.012 - 93.834} \right)$$

$$= 11 + \left(1 \times \frac{5.012}{6.178} \right)$$

$$= 11 + 0.811 = 11.81 \text{ per cent}$$

Illustration 18: AMC Engineering Company issues 12 per cent, Rs. 100 face value of preference stock, which is repayable with 10 per cent premium at the end of 5 years. It involves a flotation cost of 5 per cent per share. What is the cost of preference share capital, with 5 per cent dividend tax.

Solution:

$$K_p = \frac{D(1+Dt) + (f+d+pr-pi)/N_m}{(RV+NP)/2}$$

$$K_p = \frac{12(1+0.05) + (5+0+10-0)/5}{(110+95)/2}$$

$$= \frac{12.6+3}{102.5} \times 100 = 15.219 \text{ per cent or } 15.22 \text{ per cent}$$

Illustration 19: A company issues 8 per cent preference of share of Rs. 100 face value at a premium of 10 per cent redeemable after 6 years at par and it involves a brokerage cost of Rs. 10 per share. Calculate cost of preference share.

Solution:

$$K_p = \frac{D + (f+d+pr-pi)/N_m}{(RV+NP)/2}$$

$$K_p = \frac{8 + (10+0+0-10)/2}{(100+95)/2}$$

$$= \frac{8+0}{97.5} \times 100 = 8.205 \text{ per cent}$$

Illustration 20: SSL Company has 12 per cent perpetual debenture of Rs. 1,00,000. The tax rate is 35 per cent. Determine the cost of debenture capital (before as well as after tax), assuming debentures are issued at (i) face value / par value, (ii) 10 per cent discount and (iii) 10 per cent premium.

Solution:

	Issued at	Before tax	After tax
(i)	Face value =	$\dfrac{12,000}{1,00,000} \times 100 = 12\%$	$\dfrac{12,000(1-0.35)}{1,00,000} \times 100$ $\dfrac{7,800}{1,00,000} \times 100 = 7.8\%$
(ii)	Int. 10% discount =	$\dfrac{12,000}{1,00,000 - 10,000} \times 100 = 13.33\%$	$\dfrac{7,800}{90,000} \times 100 = 8.66\%$
(iii)	10% premium =	$\dfrac{12,000}{1,00,000 + 10,000} \times 100 = 10.9\%$	$\dfrac{7,800}{1,10,000} \times 100 = 7.09\%$

Illustration 21: MTR Foods has a series of bonds outstanding which is currently yielding 10% on bondholders. The company is in the 45% tax bracket. Compute after tax cost of bond for MTR foods.

Solution:

$$K_d = I\,(1-T) = 10\,(1-0.45) = 5.5 \text{ per cent}$$

Illustration 22: TTK Ltd., issues 14 per cent debentures par value of Rs. 100. The issue involves a flotation cost of 2 per cent and a 3 per cent discount. The debenture is redeemable at par after 10 years. The company tax rate is 35 per cent. What is the cost of debenture ? Use the shortcut and trial and error method with 5 percent premium on redemption.

Solution:

Cost of debenture :

Short cut method

$$K_d = \frac{I(1-T) + (f + d + pr - pi)/N_m}{(RV + NP)/2}$$

$$K_d = \frac{14(1-0.35) + (2 + 3 + 0 - 0)/10}{(100 + 95)/2}$$

$$= \frac{9.1 + (0.5)}{97.5} \times 100 = 9.85 \text{ per cent}$$

Trial and Error method

Year	Cash outflow (Rs.)	DF		PV of Cash outflows	
		9%	11%	9%	11%
1 - 10	9.1	6.418	5.889	58.400	53.59
10	100	0.386	0.352	38.600	35.20
PV of Cash outflows				97.00	88.79
(-) PV of Cash inflows				95.00	95.00
				2.00	(-) 6.21

Use Interpolation formula : Since the PV of cash out flows did not equate to the PV of net proceeds at 9% and 11% discount factor.

$$K_d = 9 + \left((11-9)\frac{97-95}{97-88.79} \right)$$

$$= 9 + \left(2\frac{2}{8.21} \right)$$

$$= 9 + 0.49 = 9.49 \text{ per cent}$$

Cost of debentures with 5 per cent redemption premium

$$K_d = \frac{14(1-0.35) + (2+5+5-0)/10}{(105+95)/2}$$

$$= \frac{9.1+1.2}{100} = \frac{10.3}{100} \times 100 = 10.3\%$$

Trial and Error method

Year	Cash outflow (Rs.)	DF		PV of Cash outflows	
		9%	11%	9%	11%
1 - 10	9.1	6.418	5.889	58.40	53.59
10	105	0.386	0.352	40.53	36.96
PV of Cash outflows				98.93	90.55
(-) PV of Cash inflows				95.00	95.00
				3.93	(-) 4.45

$$K_d = 9 + \left((11-9)\frac{98.93-95}{98.93-90.55} \right)$$

$$= 9 + \left(2 \frac{3.93}{8.38} \right)$$

$$= 9 + 94 = 9.94 \text{ per cent}$$

Illustration 23: A firm issues 4.8 per cent debentures on the condition that the principles amounting to Rs. 1,44,000 will be repayable in 6 equal yearly installments from the end of the first year. The company is required to pay a tax rate of 60 per cent. Find out the cost of debt.

Solution:

Instalment amount $= \dfrac{1,44,000}{6\,\text{years}} = \text{Rs. } 24,000$

Years	Cash outflow	DF		PV of Cash out flows	
	Interest + Installment	8%	4%	8%	4%
1	6912 + 24000	0.926	0.962	28624.51	29737.34
2	5760 + 24000	0.857	0.925	25504.32	27528.00
3	4608 + 24000	0.794	0.889	22714.75	25432.51
4	3456 + 24000	0.735	0.855	20180.16	23474.88
5	2304 + 24000	0.681	0.822	17913.02	21621.89
6	1152 + 24000	0.630	0.790	15845.76	19870.08
PV of Cash outflow				130782.52	147664.70
(-) PV of Cash inflow				144000.00	144000.00
				(-)13217.48	(-) 3664.70

$$K_d = 4 + \left((8-4)\,\frac{147664.7 - 144000}{147664.7 - 130782.52} \right)$$

$$K_d = 4 + 4 \times \frac{3664.7}{16882.18}$$

$$= 4 + 0.87 = 4.87 \text{ per cent}$$

Illustration 24: A company currently is maintaining 6 per cent rate of growth in dividends. The last year dividend was Rs. 4.5 per share. Equity share holders required rate of return is 15 per cent. What is the equilibrium price per share.

Solution:

$$P = \frac{D}{K_e - g} = \frac{4.5(1+0.06)}{0.15 - 0.06} = \text{Rs. } 53$$

Where,

P = Equilibrium price

D = Last dividend per share.

K_e = Cost of equity or required rate of return.

g = Growth rate in dividends.

Illustration 25: Your company's share is quoted in the market at Rs. 20 currently. The company pays a dividend of Re. 1 per share and investor's market expects a growth rate of 5 per cent per year.

(a) Compute the company cost of equity capital

(b) If the anticipated growth rate is 6% p.a. calculate the indicated market price per share.

Solution:

(a) Cost of equity $(K_e) = \dfrac{D}{MP} + g$

$$= \frac{1}{20} + 0.05 = 10 \text{ per cent}$$

(b) Market price, $P = \dfrac{D}{K_e - g}$

$$P = \frac{1(1+0.06)}{0.10 - 0.06} = \text{Rs. } 26.50$$

Illustration 26: A paper company's raw materials availability have been declining and cost of producing paper decreasing year by year. As a result earnings and dividend of the company are declining at a rate of 5 per cent per year. Company paid Rs. 10 as dividend last year. The company's required rate of return is 15 per cent. What would be the current price of the equity share of the company?

Solution:

$$\text{Market price, MP} = \frac{D}{K_e - g} = \frac{10(1 - 0.05)}{0.15 - 0.05} = \frac{9.5}{0.10} = \text{Rs. } 95$$

Illustration 27: Equity share of Asian Paints Company that engages no external financing is selling for Rs. 100. The total earnings of the company are Rs. 1,00,000 and its outstanding shares are 10,000. The company's dividend payout ratio is 70 per cent and 30 per cent retained to invest in a project which provides 10% rate of returns. Calculate cost of equity.

Solution:

$$K_e = \frac{E(1-b)}{CMP} + b_r$$

where

E	=	Earnings per share.
CMP	=	market price.
b	=	Retention ratio.
r	=	Rate of return on reinvestment.
b_r	=	Growth in earnings

$$\text{EPS} = \frac{\text{Total earnings}}{\text{No. of equity share}} = \frac{\text{Rs. } 1,00,000}{10,000} = \text{Rs. } 10$$

$$b_r = 0.10 \times 0.30 = 0.03$$

$$K_e = \frac{\text{Rs. } 10(1 - 0.3)}{100} + 0.03$$

$$= 0.07 + 0.03 = 0.10 \times 100 = 10 \text{ per cent}$$

Illustration 28: Mico Industries limited has assets of Rs. 3,20,000 that have been financed with Rs. 1,04,000 of debt and Rs. 1,80,000 of equity and a general reserve of Rs. 36,000. The company's initial profits after interests and taxes for the year 31-03-2004 were Rs. 27,000. It pays 8 per cent interest on debt. The company is in the 50 per cent tax bracket. It has 1800 equity shares of Rs. 100 each, selling at a market price of Rs. 120 per share. Calculate WACC.

Solution:

Calculation of specific costs

$$\text{Cost of debt } (K_d) = \frac{I(\text{in Rs.})[1-T]}{\text{Total debt}}$$

or

$$R[1-\text{Tax}]$$
$$= 8 [1-.50]$$
$$= 4\%$$

$$\text{Cost of equity } (K_e) = \frac{D}{MP} \times 100$$

$$= \frac{\text{Rs. } 15}{120} \times 100 = 12.5 \text{ per cent}$$

Calculate Dividend per share	Rs.
Profit after taxes	27,000
(-) Preference dividend	–
Earnings available to equity	27000

$$EPS = \frac{27000}{1800} = \text{Rs. } 15$$

♦ Cost of general reserve is equal to K_e. Because reserve funds belong to equity share holders.

♦ Calculation of WACC:

Source of Finance	Weights	Specific Cost (%)	Weighted Cost
Debt	0.325	0.04	0.013
Equity	0.563	0.125	0.070
General reserve	0.112	0.125	0.014
	1.00		0.097

WACC=0.097×100=9.7 per cent

Illustration 29: Nilgiris company's equity beta is 1.2. The market risk premium is 7 per cent and the risk free rate is 10 per cent. The company has a debt equity rate of 2 : 3. Its pre tax cost of debt is 14 per cent. If the tax rate is 35 per cent, what is the cost of capital ?

Solution:

Cost of equity $(K_e) = R_f + (R_{mf} - R_f) b = 10\% + (7\% - 10\%) 1.2$
$$= 10\% - 3.6 = 6.4 \text{ per cent}$$
Cost of debt $K_d = 14\% (1 - t)$
$$= 14\% (1 - 0.35) = 9.1 \text{ per cent}$$

Source of Finance	Weights	Specific Cost	Weighted Cost
Equity	0.40	0.064	0.0256
Debt	0.60	0.091	0.0546
	1.00		0.0802

WACC = 0.0802 X 100 = 8.02 per cent

Illustration 30: Sam's company manufactures specialty chemicals. Its debt equity ratio is 0.8. Its overall costs of capital is 15 per cent and 30 per cent tax rate.

(i)   If Sam's cost of equity is 20%, what is pre-tax cost of debt.

(ii) If Sam can use debt at an interest rate of 13%, what is cost of equity ?

Solution:

(i)   Debt equity ratio = 0.8, means, for every one rupee equity there is 80 paise debt, i.e., 1 : 0.8

$\therefore$ Debt weight = 0.8/1.8 = 0.44

Equity weight = 1.0/1.8 = 0.56

$WACC = We \times K_e + Wd \times K_d (1 - t)$

$0.15 = 0.56 \times 0.2 + 0.44 \times K_d (1 - t)$

$0.15 = 0.112 + 0.44 \times K_d (1 - 0.30)$

$0.44 \times K_d (1 - 0.30) = 0.15 - 0.112$

$0.44 \times K_d (1 - 0.30) = 0.038$

$K_d (1 - 0.30) = 0.038/0.44 = 0.086$

$K_d = 0.086/0.7 \times 100$

= 12.29 Per cent

(ii) $WACC = 0.56 \times X + 0.44 \times 0.13 (1 - 0.30)$

$0.15 = 0.56 X + 0.44 \times 0.091$

$= 056X + 0.040$

$0.56X + 0.040 = 0.15$

$0.56X = 0.15 - 0.040$

$0.56X = 0.11$

$X = 0.11 / 0.56 = 19.64$ per cent

Illustration 31 : A firm has the following capital structure

Source of Finance	Amount (Rs.)	Specific Cost
• Equity stock (25,000 shares Rs. 50 each)	12,50,000	-
• Preference stock (10,000 shares Rs. 50 each)	5,00,000	8
• Debentures (pre – tax)	13,00,000	12

The firm's equity stock is currently selling at Rs. 70 per share and is expected to get the dividend of Rs. 5. Shareholders anticipate that the equity stock dividend will grow at a rate of 6 per cent per annum in the near future. The company has a tax rate of 60 per cent. Calculate WACC.

Solution:

In the above problem K_e is not available, hence there is a need to calculate K_e.

$$K_e = \frac{D}{CMP} + g = \frac{Rs.5}{70} + 0.06 = 0.07 + 0.06 = 13 \text{ per cent}$$

Post tax cost of debentures

$$K_d = \frac{I(1 - T)}{\text{Debenture capital}} = \frac{1,56,000(1 - 0.6)}{13,00,000} \times 100 = 4.8 \text{ per cent}$$

Calculation of WACC

Source of Finance	Weights	Specific Cost	Weighted Cost
Equity stock	0.41	0.13	0.0533
Preference stock	0.16	0.08	0.0128
Debentures	0.43	0.048	0.0206
	1.00		0.0867

K_o or WACC = 0.0867 X 100 = 8.67 per cent

Illustration 32: A company is considering the most desirable capital structure, the following estimates of the debt and equity capital (after tax) have been made at various levels of debt equity mix.

Debt as a percentage of total capital employed	Cost of debt (%)	Cost of equity (%)
0	6.0	13
10	6.0	13
20	6.0	13.5
30	6.5	14.0
40	7.0	15.0
50	7.5	17.0

Determining the optimal debt – equity mix for the company by calculation of overall cost of capital.

Solution:

Overall cost of capital

Debt (%)	Equity (%)	Cost of Debt (%)	Cost of Equity (%)	Overall cost of capital (%) (Kd)(Wd)+(Ke)(We)100
0	100	6.0	13	(6 x 0) + (13 x 100) = 13.0
10	90	6.0	13	(6 x 10) + (13 x 90) = 12.3
20	80	6.0	13.5	(6 x 20) + (13 x 80) = 12.0
30	70	6.5	14.0	(6.5 x 30) +(14 x 70) = 11.75
40	60	7.0	15.0	(7 x 40) + (15 x 60) = 11.80
50	50	7.5	16.0	(7.5 x 50) + (17 x 50) = 12.25

30 per cent debt and 70 per cent equity gives the optimal debt equity mix or optimal capital structure, since at that proportion of debt equity, the overall cost of capital is minimum.

Illustration 33 : From the following financial statement of BLP you are required to

(a) Calculate the earnings per share.

(b) Calculate the percentage cost of capital to the company for the debenture funds and the equity.

Particulars	Rs. in lakhs
Earnings before interest and tax (EBIT)	210
(-) Interest on debentures	66
Earning before tax	144
(-) Income tax @ 50%	72
Earning after tax	72
Equity share capital (share of Rs. 10 each)	400
Reserves and surplus	200
15% non-convertable debentures (of Rs. 100 each)	440
	1040

The market price per equity share is Rs. 12 and per debenture is 94.

Solution:

(a) $\text{Earning per share (EPS)} = \dfrac{\text{Profit after tax}}{\text{No. of equity share}}$

$$= \dfrac{72,00,000}{40,00,000} = \text{Rs. } 1.8$$

(b) (i) Cost of equity (K_e) (Earnings approach) $= \dfrac{E}{CMP} = \dfrac{\text{Rs. } 1.8}{12} \times 100 = 15$ per cent

(ii) Cost of debenture (K_d) (book value) $= \dfrac{\text{Interest}}{\text{Debenture capital}} = \dfrac{66,00,000 \,(1-0.35)}{4,40,00,000} = \text{Rs. } 9.75$ per cent

(iii) Cost of debenture (K_d) (based on market values) $= \dfrac{15\,(1-0.35)}{94} \times 100 = 10.37$ per cent

Illustration 34 : From the following information of Excel Ltd., determine the WACC using (a) book value weights and (b) market value weights. How are they different ? Can you think of a situation, where the WACC would be the same using either of the weights ?

Source of finance	Book Value (Rs.)	Market Value (Rs.)	Costs (%)
Equity capital	3,00,000	6,00,000	15
Retained earnings	1,00,000		13
Preference capital	50,000	60,000	8
Debt capital	2,00,000	1,90,000	6
	6,50,000	8,50,000	

Solution:

(a) *WACC based on book value weights*

Source of finance	Book Value Weights	Cost	Total weighted Cost
Equity capital	0.461	0.15	0.069
Retained earnings	0.154	0.13	0.020
Preference capital	0.077	0.08	0.006
Debt capital	0.308	0.06	0.018
	1.000		0.113

K_o or WACC = 0.113 X 100 = 11.3 per cent

(b) *WACC based on market value weights*

Source of finance	Market Value (Rs.)	Weights	Costs	Total Weights (%)
Equity capital	4,50,000*	0.53	0.15	0.080
Retained earnings	1,50,000*	0.18	0.13	0.023
Preference capital	60,000	0.07	0.08	0.006
Debt capital	1,90,000	0.22	0.06	0.013
	8,50,000	1.00		0.122

WACC = 0.122 x 100 = **12.2 per cent**

* *Note 1* : According to Gitman[12] retained earnings are treated as equity capital for purpose of calculation of cost of specific source of funds, the market value of equity shares may be taken to represent the combined market value of equity shares and retained earnings. The total market value of equity shares and retained earnings is apportioned respectively on the basis of their book values, i.e., 3 : 1

◆ The difference in MV weights COC and BV weights of COC WACC calculated based on market value weights is considerably larger than the book value weights WACC, since, the sources of long-term funds have higher specific costs (in terms of rupees).

◆ The WACC would be the same with both the book value weights and market value weights, when there is no difference between the book value and market value of source of finance used in raising the capital.

Illustration 35: Zee Ltd., is foreseeing a growth rate of 13 per cent p.a in the next two years. The growth rate is likely to fall to 10 per cent for the third year and the fourth year, after that, the growth rate is expected to stabilize at 7 per cent per annum. If the last dividend was Rs. 2 per share and cost of equity capital is 15 per cent, find out the intrinsic value per share of Zee Ltd., as of date.

Solution:

Intrinsic value is the sum of

(a) PV of dividend payments during 1 – 4 year and

(b) PV of expected market price at the end of the fourth year based on a constant growth of 7 %.

(a) *Present value of dividends during 1 – 4 year*

Years	Dividend	DF 15%	PV of cash inflow (Rs.)
1	2.26	0.870	1.966
2	2.55	0.756	1.928
3	2.81	0.658	1.849
4	3.09	0.572	1.767
			7.51

(b) Market price at the end of year $4\left(P_4\right) = \dfrac{D_5}{K_e - g}$

$$= \frac{3.09(1+0.07)}{0.15-0.07} = \text{Rs. } 41.33$$

Present value of Rs. 41.33 = 41.33 x 0.572 = Rs. 23.64

∴ Intrinsic value of share = Rs. 7.51 + Rs. 23.64 = Rs. 31.15

Illustration 36: The following information is available for your perusal.

The Company's present BV capital structure is as follows:

	Rs.
Debentures (Rs. 100 per debenture	7,00,000
Preference shares (Rs. 100 per share)	3,00,000
Equity shares (Rs. 10 each)	10,00,000
	20,00,000

All these securities are traded in the capital market and their recent prices are :

Debentures Rs. 110 per debenture

Preference stock Rs. 120 per share

Equity share Rs. 22 per share

Anticipated external financing opportunities are :

(a) Rs. 100, redeemable debenture at face value after 8 years, 13 per cent interest rate, 4 per cent flotation cost.

(b) 14 per cent redeemable preference shares (5 years), it involve a flotation cost of 5 per cent and the sales price Rs. 100.

(c) Equity share : Rs. 2 per share brokerage, Rs. 22 sales price.

In addition, the dividend expected as the equity share at the end of the year is Rs. 2 per share. The anticipated growth rate in dividends is 6 per cent and the firm has the practice of paying all its earnings in the form of dividends. The corporate tax rate is 35 per cent .

Solution:

Calculation of specific cost

(a) $K_d = \dfrac{I(1-t)+(f \div N_m)}{(RV+NP)/2} = \dfrac{\text{Rs. } 13(1-0.35)+(4 \div 8)}{(100+96)/2} = 9.13 \text{ per cent}$

(b) $K_p = \dfrac{D + (f \div N_m)}{(RV + NP)/2} = \dfrac{14 + (5 \div 5)}{(100 + 95)/2} = 15.38$ per cent

(c) $K_e = \dfrac{D}{NP} + g = \dfrac{2}{22 - 2} + 0.06 = 16$ per cent

Source of finance	WACC based on Book value weights		Weighted
	Book value (Rs.)	Cost	Costs
Debentures	7,00,000	0.0913	63,910
Preference shares	3,00,000	0.1538	46,140
Equity shares	10,00,000	0.16	1,60,000
	20,00,000		2,70,050

$K_0 = \dfrac{2,70,050}{20,00,000} \times 100 = 13.50$ per cent

Source of finance	WACC based on Market value weights		Weighted
	Book value (Rs.)	Cost	Costs
Debentures (17,000 x Rs.110)	7,70,000	0.0913	70,301
Preference shares (3,000 x Rs.120)	3,60,000	0.1538	55,368
Equity shares (1,00,000 x Rs.22)	22,00,000	0.16	3,52,000
	33,30,000		4,77,669

K_0 or WACC $= \dfrac{4,77,669}{33,30,000} \times 100 = 14.34$ per cent

Illustration 37: A company has the following capital structure on 31-12-2003

	Rs.
Equity shares (20,000 shares)	10,00,000
10% preference shares	2,50,000
14% debentures	7,50,000
	20,00,000

The company's share is currently selling at Rs. 20. Next year's expected dividend is Rs. 2 per share, that will grow at 6 per cent forever. The company is in the tax bracket of 50 per cent. You are required to calculate :

(a)   WACC based on the existing capital structure

(b)   New WACC if the company raises an additional Rs. 5,00,000 debt by issuing 15 per cent debenture. This will increase the existing dividend by Re. 1 but leave growth rate unchanged, and the price of share will fall to Rs. 15.

Solution:

(a) Calculation of WACC based on existing capital structure

Source of finance	Weights	After Tax Cost	Total weighted cost
Equity shares	0.50	0.16[Note 1]	0.08
10% Preference shares	0.125	0.10	0.0125
14% debentures	0.375	0.07	0.0263
	1.00		0.1188

∴ WACC = 0.1188 × 100 = 11.88 per cent

Note:

1. Cost of equity share (K_e) = Rs. 2 / 20 + 0.06 = 16 per cent
2. K_e = Rs. 3 / 15 + 0.06 = 26 per cent
3. K_d = 15 (1 – 0.5) = 7.5 per cent

(b) WACC based on new capital structure

Source of finance	Weights	After Tax Cost	Total weighted cost
Equity shares	0.40	0.26[Note 2]	0.104
10% Preference shares	0.10	0.10	0.010
14% debentures	0.30	0.07	0.021
15% debentures	0.20	0.075[Note 3]	0.015
	1.00		0.150

∴ WACC = 0.150 x 100 = 15 per cent

Illustration 38: A company issues 5,000, 12% debentures of Rs. 100 each at a discount of 5%. The commission payable to underwriters and brokers is Rs. 25,000. The debentures are redeemable after 5 year. Compute the after tax cost of debt assuming a tax rate of 50 %.

Solution:

$$K_d = \frac{I(1-t)+(f+d+Pr-Pi)/N}{(RV+SC)/2} = \frac{60,000(1-0.5)+(25,000+25,000+0-0)/5}{(5,00,000+4,50,000)/2} = 8.42 \text{ per cent}$$

Illustration 39: An electric equipment manufacturing company wishes to determine the weighted average cost of capital budgeting projects. You have been supplied with the following information:

Balance Sheet

Capital and Liabilities	Amount (Rs.)	Assets	Amount (Rs.)
Equity share capital	12,00,000	Fixed Assets	25,00,000
Preference Share Capital	4,50,000	Current Assets	15,00,000
Debentures	9,00,000		
Retained Earnings	4,50,000		
Current Liabilities	10,00,000		
	40,00,000		40,00,000

Anticipated external financing information:

1. 20 years, 14% debentures of Rs.2,500 face value redeemable at 5 % premium sold at par 2 % flotation costs,

2. 15% preference shares: sales price Rs. 100 per share 2% flotation cost

3. Equity share: sales price Rs. 115 per share. Flotation cost Rs. 5 per share

The corporate tax rate is 55 % and expected growth in equity dividend is 8 % per year. The expected dividend at the end of the future financial year is Rs. 11 per share. Assume that the company is satisfied with its present capital structure and intends to maintain it.

Solution: Calculation of WACC

Source of Finance	Amount (Rs.)	Specific Cost (%)	Cost of Source of Finance (Rs.)
Equity Capital 12,000x115	13,80,000	18	2,48,400
Preference Capital	4,50,000	15.13	68,085
Debentures	9,00,000	6.55	58,950
Retained Earnings	4,50,000	18	81,000
Total Capital	31,80,000		4,56,435

$$\text{WACC} = \frac{\text{Total Cost (Rs.)}}{\text{Total Capital}} \times 100 = \frac{4,56,435}{31,80,000} \times 100 = 14.35\%$$

Assumptions

♦ Cost of equity capital calculated on market price base

♦ WACC computed on market value base

Working Notes:

1. **Cost of Debt**

$$K_d = \frac{I(1-t)+(f+d+Pr-Pi)/N}{(RV+SC)/2} = \frac{350(1-0.55)+(50+0+125-0)/20}{(2,625+2,450)/2} = 6.55 \text{ per cent}$$

2. Cost of Preference shares:

$$K_p = \frac{d}{NS} = \frac{15}{(100-2)} \times 100 = 15.3 \text{ per cent}$$

3. Cost of Equity:

$$K_e = \frac{d}{(MP-f)} + g = \frac{11}{(115-5)} + 0.08 = 18 \text{ per cent}$$

Illustration 40: A Ltd. Company with net operating earnings of Rs. 6,00,000 wants you to evaluate possible capital structures, shown below. Which capital structure will you select? Why?

Capital Structure	Debt in Capital Structure (Rs.)	Cost of Debt (%)	Cost of Equity (%)
1	6,00,000	10	12
2	8,00,000	10	13
3	10,00,000	11	15

Solution:

Evaluation and selection of capital structure plans is based on cost of capital. WACC is the only structure available, where there is total capital, debt capital, and equity capital but in the above problem debt in capital structure is given, and proportion of debt in not given. Here, we need to assume total capital structure. Total capital is Rs. 10,00,000 now we determine proportions of debt and equity in capital structure.

Capital Structure Plan	Capital (Rs.)		Weights (%)		Specific Cost		WACC (%)
	Debt	Equity	Debt	Equity	Debt	Equity	
1	6,00,000	4,00,000	0.60	0.40	0.10	0.12	10.8
2	8,00,000	2,00,000	0.80	0.20	0.10	0.13	10.6
3	10,00,000	------	0.00	0.100	0.11	0.15	15.0

WACC = [Wd x Kd + We x ke] 100

Capital Structure Plan 1 = [0.60 x 0.10 + 0.40 x 0.12] 100 = 10.8 per cent

Capital Structure Plan 2 = [0.80 x 0.10 + 0.20 x 0.13]100 = 10.6 per cent

Capital Structure Plan 3 = [0.0 x 0.11 + 1.00 x 0.15]100 = 15 per cent

Decision: Capital Structure Plan 2 is selected, since WACC is minimum at that structure.

Illustration 41: PES has the following capital structure, which is considered to be optimal. The components of capital proportions are: Equity – 60%, Debt –25%, Preference stock – 15%. PES's expected net income this year is 30%, and its tax rate is 40%. In the future the dividends are expected to grow at a constant rate of 9%. Last year Rs.3.6 was paid as dividend. The company's share is selling at (currently) Rs.54 per share. PES can obtain new capital in the following ways:

1. Preferred – New preferred stock with a dividend of Rs.11 and it can be sold at Rs. 95 per share.

2. Debt - at 12%

   (a) Determine specific cost of components of capital structure

   (b) Calculate WACC.

Solution:

(a) *Computation of specific cost of capital*

$$\text{Equity cost}(K_e) = \frac{D_0 + (1+g)}{P_0} + g = \frac{3.6(1+0.09)}{54} + 0.09 = 16.27 \text{ per cent}$$

Cost of Debt (Kd) = I (1-T) = 12% (1-0.4) = 7.2 per cent

Cost of Preferred Stock (Kp) = D / NS = 11 / 95 = 11.58 per cent

(b) *Computation of WACC:*

[We X Ke + Wd X Kd + Wp X Kp] 100

[0.60 X 0.1627 + 0.25 X 0.072 + 0.15 X 0.1158] 100 = 13.30 per cent

TEST QUESTIONS

Objective Type Questions

1. Fill in the blanks with appropriate word(s)

    (a) Cost of capital is the _____ required rate of return expected by investors.

    (b) Cost of capital, is the measurement sacrifice made by _____ with regard to capital formation.

    (c) According to _____ cost of capital is the minimum required rate of earnings or the cut off rate of capital expenditure.

    (d) Cost of Capital $(K_o) = r_f +$ ____ +f.

    (e) The explicit cost is the _____, which equates the present value of cash inflows with present value of cash outflows.

    (f) An average of the cost of each source of funds employed by the firm for capital formation is known as _____.

    (g) Cost of capital is not useful in capital budgeting if a firm is depended on ___ methods.

    (h) _____ is the additional cost incurred to obtain additional funds required by a firm.

    (i) Bond yield plus _____ is one of the approaches available to calculate cost of equity capital.

    (j) _____ is the cost associated with particular component at capital structure.

    [Answers: (a) Minimum, (b) Investor, (c) Soloman Izra, (d) 'b' business risk premium, (e) discount rate, (f) Overall cost of capital, (g) Traditional approach, (h) Marginal cost, (i) Risk premium, (j) Specific cost.]

2. State whether each of the following statement is true or false

    (a) Cost of capital comprises three components.

    (b) Cost of capital with minimum required rate of return needs to be justified.

    (c) There is no cost for internally generated funds.

    (d) According to traditional approach, cost of capital is affected by debt equity MPC.

    (e) Cost of capital is useful in capital budgeting, in evaluation based on discounted cash flow techniques only.

    (f) CAPM approach is one of the approaches used in computation of cost of equity capital.

    (g) In Bond yield plus risk premium approach of cost of equity, risk premium ranges between 2% to 6%.

    (h) Opportunity costs are technically referred to as implicit cost.

    (i) Existence of perfect capital market is one of the assumptions of CAPM.

    (j) Incremental value is the sum of present value of dividend payments during the holding period and present value of expected market price at the end of the specified period.

    [Answers: (a) True, (b) True, (c) False, (d) True, (e) True, (f) True, (g) True, (h) True, (i) True, (j) True]

REVIEW QUESTIONS

1. What is cost of capital ?
2. Explicit vs Implicit Cost.
3. Define marginal cost of capital.
4. How to compute growth rate ?
5. What do you mean by CAPM ?
6. What do you understand by bond yield plus risk premium approach ?
7. How is cost of perpetual debt computed ?
8. What is retained earnings ?
9. How is the cost of retained earnings computed ?
10. List out any two approaches to calculate cost of equity.
11. Define cost of capital. Explain the significance of cost of capital.
12. What is the relevance of cost of capital in capital budgeting decisions?
13. Write a note on CAPM approach for calculation of cost of equity.
14. State any four methods of computing cost of equity.
15. Distinguish between WACC and MCC.
16. "Marginal cost of capital nothing but the average cost of capital", explain.
17. The basic formula to calculate the cost of equity is D/P + g. Explain its rationale.
18. How is cost of debt calculated ?
19. How is cost of preference share calculated ?
20. Discuss the following bases for determining the weights in cost of capital calculation, book values, target capital structure and market values.
21. How should you handle the flotation costs in the determination of cost of capital ?
22. What are the steps involved in calculating a firm's WACC?
23. What is cost of equity ? Write a detailed note on the approaches available for computation of cost of equity.
24. Define cost of capital. Discuss in detail the steps involved in computation of WACC.
25. "Evaluating capital budgeting proposals without cost of capital is not possible". Discuss.
26. Critically evaluate the different approaches to the calculation of cost of equity capital.
27. Explain the problems faced in determining the WACC ? How is it relevant to capital budgeting decisions ?
28. WACC (K_o) may be determined using book value and market value weights. Compare the pros and cons of using market value weights rather than book value weights in calculating K_o.
29. What are the components of capital ? Discuss in detail about the individual components of capital.

CASE STUDY FOR CLASS DISCUSSION - I

NIKE, INC.-COST OF CAPITAL

On July, Kimi-ford, a portfolio manager at North Point Group, a mutual-fund-management firm, pored over analysts' write-ups of Nike, Inc., the athletic-shoe manufacturer. Nike's share price had declined significantly from the start of the year. Ford was considering buying some shares for the fund she managed, the North Point Large-Cap Fund, which invested mostly in fortune 500 companies, with an emphasis on value investing. Its top holdings included Exxon Mobile. General Motors, McDonald's, 3M, and other large-cap. It had performed extremely well. In 2000, the fund earned a return of 20.7 per cent even as the S&P 500 fell 10.1 per cent. The fund's year-to-date returns at the end of June 2001 stood at 6.4 versus the S &P – 7.3 per cent.

Only a week ago, on June 28,2001, Nike held an analyst' meeting to disclose its fiscal-year 2001 results. The meeting, however had another purpose : Nike management wanted to communicate a strategy for revitalizing the company. Since 1997 Nike's revenues had plateaued at around $9 billion, while net income had fallen from almost $ 800 million to $580 million (see Exhibit 1). Nike's markets in the U.S. had fallen from 48 per cent in 1997 to 42 per cent in 2000. In addition, recent supply-chain issues and the adverse effect of a strong dollar had negatively affected revenue.

At the meeting, the management revealed plans to address both-line growth and operating performance. To boost revenue, the company would develop more athletic-shoe products in the mid-priced segment – a segment that had been overlooked in the recent years. Nike also planned to push its apparel line, which, under the recent leadership of industry veteran Mindy Grossman had performed extremely well. On the cost side, Nike would exert more effort on expense control, finally, the company's executives reiterated their long-term revenue growth targets of 8-10 per cent and earnings-growth targets of above 1 percent.

The Analysts reactions were mixed. Some thought, the financial targets too aggressive ; other saw significant growth opportunities in apparel and in Nike's international businesses.

Ford read all the analysts reports that she could find about the June 28 meeting, but the reports gave her no clear guidance : a Lehman Brothers report recommended a "Strong Buy", while UBS analysts expressed misgiving about the company and recommended a "Hold". Ford decided instead to develop her own discounted-cash-flow forecast to come to a clearer conclusion.

Her forecast showed that, at discount rate of 12 per cent, Nike was overvalued at its current share price of $42.09 (see Exhibit 2). She had, however, done a quick sensitivity analysis that revealed Nike was valued at discount rates below 11.2 per cent. As she was about to go into a meeting, she asked her new assistant, Joanna Cohen, to estimate Nike's cost of capital.

Cohen immediately gathered all the data she though she might need (Exhibits 1,2,3 and 4) began to work on her analysis. At the end of the day, she submitted her cost-of-capital estimate and a memo (Exhibit 5) explaining her assumption to Ford.

Exhibit 1: Consolidated Income Statements Year ended May 31							
(in millions excepts per share data)	2000	2001	2002	2003	2004	2005	2006
Revenues	4,760.8	6,470.6	9,816.5	9,553.1	8,776.9	8,995.1	9,488.8
Cost of goods sold	2,865.3	3,906.7	5,503.0	6,065.5	5,493.5	5,403.8	7,784.9
Gross profit	1,895.6	2,563.9	3,683.5	3,487.6	3,283.4	3,591.3	3,703.9
Selling and administrative	1,209.8	1,588.6	2,303.7	2,623.8	2,426.6	2,606.4	2,689.7
Operating Income	685.8	975.3	1,379.8	863.8	856.8	984.9	1,014.2
Interst expense	24.2	39.5	52.3	60.0	44.1	45.0	58.7
Other expense net	11.7	36.7	32.3	20.9	21.5	23.2	34.1
Restructuring charge,net	---	---	---	129.9	45.1	2.5	---
Income before Income taxes	649.9	899.1	1,295.20	653.0	746.1	919.2	921.4
Income taxes	250.2	345.9	499.4	253.4	294.7	340.1	331.7
Net Income	399.7	553.2	795.8	399.6	451.4	579.4	589.7
Diluted earning per Annum Shares	1.4	1.9	2.7	1.4	1.6	2.1	2.2
Average shares outstanding (diluted)	294.0	293.6	297.0	296.0	287.5	279.8	273.3
Growth(%)							
Revenue		35.9	42.0	4.0	8.1	2.5	5.5
Operating income		42.2	41.5	37.4	0.8	15.0	3.0
Net income		38.4	43.9	49.8	13.0	28.3	1.8
Margins (%)							
Gross margin		39.6	40.1	36.5	37.4	39.9	39.0
Operating margin		15.1	15.0	9.0	9.8	10.9	10.7
Net margin		8.5	8.7	4.2	3.1	6.4	6.2
Effective tax rate (%)		38.5	38.6	38.8	39.5	37.0	36.0

Exhibit 2: Discounted - Cash - flow Analysis										
	2007	2008	2009	2010	2011	2012	2013	2014	2015	2016
Assumption										
Revenue growth (%)	7.0	6.5	6.5	6.5	6.0	6.0	6.0	6.0	6.0	6.0
COGS/Sales (%)	60.0	60.0	59.5	59.5	59.0	59.0	58.5	58.5	58.0	58.0
S & A / Sales (%)	28.0	27.5	27.0	26.5	26.0	25.5	25.0	25.0	25.0	25.0
Tax rate (%)	38.0	38.0	38.0	38.0	38.0	38.0	38.0	38.0	38.0	38.0
Current Assets / sales (%)	38.0	38.0	38.0	38.0	38.0	38.0	38.0	38.0	38.0	38.0
Current liabilities/ sales (%)	11.5	11.5	11.5	11.5	11.5	11.5	11.5	11.5	11.5	11.5
Yearly depreciations Equals capex.										
Cost of Capital (%)	12.0									
Terminal growth rate (%)	3.0									
Discounted cash flow										
Opeating income	1,218.4	1,351.6	1554.6	1717.0	1950.0	2135.9	2410.2	2554.8	2790.1	2957.5
Taxes	463.0	513.6	590.8	652.5	741.0	811.7	915.9	970.8	1060.2	1123.9
NOPAT	755.4	838.0	963.9	1064.5	1209.0	1324.3	1494.3	1584.0	1729.9	1833.7
Capex.net of dereciation	---	---	---	---	---	---	---	---	---	---
Change in NWC	8.8	-174.9	186.3	198.4	195.0	206.7	219.1	232.3	246.2	261.0
Free cash flow	764.1	663.1	776.6	866.2	1014.0	1176.6	1275.2	1351.7	1483.7	1572.7
Terminal value										17998.7
Total flows	764.1	663.1	776.6	866.2	1014.0	1176.6	1275.2	1351.7	1483.7	19571.5
Present value of flows	682.3	528.6	553.5	550.5	575.4	566.2	576.8	545.9	535.0	6301.5
Enterprise value	11415.7									
Less : current outstanding dept.	1296.6									
Equity value	10119.1									
Current shares outstanding	271.5									
Equity value per share	$37.27		Current share price	$42.09						

Exhibit 3: Sensitivity of equity value of discount rate	
Discount rate	**Equity value**
8.00%	$75.80
8.50	67.85
9.00	61.25
9.50	55.68
10.00	50.92
10.50	46.81
11.00	43.22
11.17	42.09
11.50	40.07
12.00	37.27

Exhibit 4: Consolidated Balance Sheets (in millions)
May 31

	2005	2006
Assets		
Current assets		
Cash and equivalents	$254.3	$304.0
Accounts receivable	1,569.4	1,621.4
Inventories	1,446.0	1,424.0
Deferred income taxes	111.5	113.3
Prepaid expenses	215.2	162.5
Total Current assets	3,596.4	3,625.3
Property, plant and equipment, net	1,583.4	1,618.8
Identifiable, intangible assets and goodwill, net	410.9	397.3
Deferred income taxes and other assets	266.2	178.2
Total assets	$5,856.9	$5,819.6
Liabilities and shareholder's equity		
Current liabilities		
Current portion of long-term debt	$50.1	$5.4
Notes payable	924.2	855.3
Accounts payable	543.8	432
Accrued liabilities	621.9	472.1
Income taxes payable	-----	21.9
Total current liabilities	2,140.0	1,786.7
Long-term debt	470.3	435.9
Deferred income taxes and other liabilities	110.3	102.2
Redeemable preferred stock	0.3	0.3
Share holder equity		
Common stock, par	2.8	2.8
Capital in excess of stated value	369.0	459.4
Unearned stock comper	11.7	9.9
Accumulated other comprehensive income	111.1	152.1
Retained earnings	2887.0	3194.3
Total share holder equity	3136.0	3494.5
Total liabilities and shareholder's equity	$5,856.9	$5,819.6

Exhibit 5: Dr. Bhatt's Analysis

SUBJECT : Nike's Cost of Capital

Based on the following assumptions, my estimate of Nike's cost of capital is 8.4 percent :

Single or Multiple Costs of Capital

The first question I considered was whether to use single or multiple costs of capital given that Nike has multiple business segments. Aside from footwear, which makes up 62 per cent of revenue. Nike also sells apparel (30 per cent of revenue) that complement its footwear products. In addition, Nike sells sport balls, time-pieces, eyewear, skates, bats and other equipment designed for sports activities. Equipment products account for 3.6 per cent of revenue. Finally, Nike also sells some non- Nike branded products such as Cole-Haan dress and casual footwear, and ice stakes, skate blades, hockey sticks, hockey jerseys and other products under the Bauer trademark, non-Nike brands account for 4.5 per cent of the revenue.

I asked myself, whether Nike's different business segments shad enough risks from each other to warrant different costs of capital. Were their profiles really different? I concluded that it was only the Cole-Haan line that was somewhat different : the rest were all sports-related businesses. However, since Cole-Haan makes up only a tiny fraction of the revenues, I did not think it necessary to compute a separate cost of capital. As for the apparel and footwear lines, they are sold through the same marketing and distribution channels and are often marketed in "collections" of similar design. I believe, they face the same risk factors, as such, I decided to compute only one cost of capital of the whole company.

Methodology for Calculating the Cost of Capital; WACC

Since Nike is funded with both debt and equity, I used the Weighted Average Cost of Capital (WACC) method. Based on the latest available balance sheet, debt as a proportion of total capital makes up 27.0 per cent and equity accounts for 73.0 per cent:

Capital sources	Book Values	
Debt		
Current portion of long-term debt	$ 5.4	
Notes payable	855.3	
Long-term debt	435.9	
	$ 1.291.2	→ 27.0% of total capital
	$ 3.494.5	→ 72.0% of total capital

Cost of Debt

My estimate of Nike's cost of debt is 4.3 per cent. I arrived at this estimate by taking total interest expense for the year 2001 and dividing it by the company's average debt balance. The rare is lower than Treasury yields but that is because Nike raised a portion of its funding needs through Japanese yen notes, which carry rates between 2.0 per cent to 4.3 per cent.

After adjusting for tax, the cost of debt comes to 2.7 per cent. I used a tax rate of 38 per cent, which I obtained by adding state taxes of 3 per cent to the U.S. statutory tax rate. Historically, Nike's state taxes have ranged from 2.5 per cent to 3.5 per cent.

Cost of Equity

I estimated the cost of equity, using the Capital Asset Pricing Model (CAPM). Other methods such as the Dividend Discount Model (DDM) and the Earnings capitalization Ratio can be used to estimate the cost of equity. However, in my opinion, the CAPM is the superior method.

My estimate of Nike's cost of equity is 10.5 per cent I used the current yield on 20-year Treasury bonds as my risk-free rate, and the compound average premium of the market over Treasury bonds (5.9 per cent) as my risk premium. For beta, I took the average of Nike's beta from 1996 to the present.

Putting it all Together

After inputting all my assumptions into the WACC formula, my estimate of Nike's cost of capital is 8.4 per cent.

$$WACC = K_d (1 - t) \quad *D/(D + E) \quad + K_c * E/(D + E)$$
$$= 2.7\% \quad * 27.0\% \quad + 20.5\% * 73.0\%$$
$$= 8.4\%$$

COMPANY BACKGROUND : COCA – COLA

In 2000, the Coca-Cola Company's (ticker symbol : KO) annual sales were $20.5 billion, and its marker value reached $110.1 billion. The company was the largest manufacturer, distributor, and marketer of soft-drink concentrates and syrups in the world and also marketed and distributed a variety of noncarbonated – beverage products, which included Minute Maid orange juice, Fruitopia, Dasam bottled water, and Nestea, among others.

From 1993 to 1998, the Coca-Cola Company had consistently garnered the first or second spot in-fortune's annual ranking of the top wealth creators. One of the main reasons for this, was the company's strategy of spinning off its bottling operations in order to avoid consolidation on its balance sheet. This move, implemented in 1985, contributed to a dramatic rise in returns on equity from 23 per cent to as much as 57 per cent over the last two decades (see Exhibit 2).

Recently however, the company had run into difficulties. The Asian financial crisis, South America's difficulties, and Russia's devaluation of the rouble all hurt KO. But business mistakes by Doug Ivester, CEO from 1997 aggravated the situation.

An example of one such mistake occurred in November 1999, when Ivester instituted a 7.7 percent hike on syrup, a rate that was double that of usual increases. The Coca-Cola Company's bottlers were infuriated, and felt that Ivester was gouging them in order to increase KO's profits. In response, the bottlers raised prices for the first time in years in order to improve profitability, resulting in a decrease in volume (see Exhibit 3). During Ivester's approximately two-year term, net income fell by 41 per cent. The company's board of directors eased Ivester out in December 2000.

Douglas Daft, head of Coca-Cola's middle and Far East and Africa groups, was Chosen to succeed Ivester. Upon taking over, he immediately instituted major organizational changes such as cutting staff and reducing bureaucratic involvement. But perhaps the most important change was his acknowledgement that KO needed to be a dominant player in the noncarbonated-beverages market. In contrast to Ivester, who had insisted on pushing the company's core self-drink brands – Coca-Cola, Fanta, Sprite, and Diet Coke. Daft and his executives worked hard to come up with new noncarbonated products.

Some analysts were optimistic that the change in management would return the Coca-Cola Company lost its glory. Perhaps through improved relations with bottlers and acquisitions of noncarbonated beverages, KO would return to the pre -1998 profit margins. Other analysts were less enthusiastic. One thing was certain, however,: with PepsiCo's invigorated management, KO would need to get back on its feet as quickly as it could.

Company Background : Pepsico, Inc.

In 2000, PepsiCo, Inc., was a $20-billion company involved in snack-food, soft-drink and noncarbonated-beverage businesses. The company sold and distributed salt and sweet snacks under the Frito-Lay trademark, and manufactured concentrates of Pepsi, Mountain Dew, and other brands for sale to franchised bottlers. The company also produced and distributed juices and other noncarbonated beverage. Snack foods accounted for roughly two-thirds of PepsiCo's sales and operating income, while beverages accounted for the remainder.

PepsiCo, as a focused snack-and- beverage company in 2000 was due mostly to the efforts of Roger Enrico, CEO from 1996 to 2000. During his tenure, Enrico instituted a massive overhaul of PepsiCO. In 1997, he sold off the fast-food chains KFC, Taco Bell, and Pizza Hut, ridding PepsiCo of a business that had long been a drag on returns. In 1999. he spun-off Pepsi's capital-intensive bottling operations into an independent public company. By spinning off the bottling operations, PepsiCo was left with just the higher-margin business of selling concentrate to bottlers. At the same time, independent PepsiCo bottlers were be able to raise capital on their own, freeing up cash flow within the parent company form other uses. Enrico also took aggressive steps to make PepsiCo a "total beverage company". He brokered the acquisitions of Tropicana, the market leader in orange juice, and Quaker Oats, whose Gartorade brand dominated the energy-drink market.

During Enrico's term PepsiCo's return on equity almost doubled, from 17 per cent in 1996 to 30 per cent in 2000. (See Exhibit 2 for historical returns and Exhibit 1 for a historical EVA analysis). On Wall Street, analysts were upbeat about PepsiCo's prospects.

Industry Overview and Competitive Events

In 2000, the beverage industry was undergoing a rapid transformation in the noncarbonated-drinks segment, although still representing only a small fraction of the beverage maket, it had grown by 62 per cent in volume over the last five years, while soft-drink volume growth had been sluggish. According to the beverage Digest, the share of the carbonated soft-drink industry fell from 71.3 per cent in 1990 to 60.5 per cent in 2000.

In Soft-drink volume, PepsiCo still lagged behind Coke, although it seemed to have caught up somewhat in recent years (see (Exhibit 3). In the fall of 1999, for instance, PepsiCo, for the first time in its history, occupied two of the top three places in U.S. soft-drink brands, as its Mountain Dew dislodged Diet Coke from third place".

Recent developments in both the companies signaled an aggressive new round of competition. Given below is a summary of recent competitive moves made by both companies in several beverage categories.

Soft Drinks

Over the last five years, Pepsi had launched aggressive and exciting campaigns (e.g. Generation Next." "Joy of Pepsi") that helped boost volumes and visibility. In addition, Pepsi launched the "Power of One campaign – a strategy that entailed moving Pepsi drinks next to Frito-Lay chips on store shelves to entice shoppers to pick up a Pepsi when they bought chips. This strategy also helped boost bottle, Frito Lay's and Pepsi's volumes. In response to the success of the Pepsi campaigns, Coca-cola resorted to a number of tactics such as veering away from its traditional feel-good ads and launching trendier ones in the summer of 2000. Unfortunately, the new ads were highly unpopular and elicited negative reaction from customers and bottlers. Coca-cola pulled the ads and replaced them with the "Life Tastes Good" series, which marked a return to Coke's traditional "Feel-good" themes while being trendy at the same time.

Noncarbonated beverage

Coke and PepsiCo raced to position themselves in this important and fast-growing market segment :

Orange Juice : 1998, PepsiCo acquired Tropicana, the clear market leader in orange juice. Tropicana held more than 40 per cent of the total chilled-orange-juice market and 70 per cent of the not-form-concentrate orange-juice segment in the United States. Coke's Minute Mate had less than 20 per cent of the chilled-orange-juice market.

Bottled water : PepsiCo test-marketed Aquafina as early as 1994, while Coke did not enter the bottled-water market until 1999, with its Dasani brand. Aquafina was the number-one bottled-water brand in the U.S. market in 2000.

Sports drinks : Pending the Federal Trade commission's approval of the Pepsi Co-Quaker Oats deal, PepsiCo would own Gatorade, which held 83 per cent of the U.S. sports drink market coca-Cola's Powerade was a distant second at 11 per cent.

Special drinks : PepsiCo, in alliance with Starbucks, introduced the highly popular Starbucks Frappucino in 1996. It took Coca-Cola until 2000 to announce that it was going to test-market a frozen coffee beverage. In October 2000, PepsiCo beat Coca-Cola in acquiring south Beach Beverage Company, maker of the SoBe brand teas and fruit juices.

Financial Comparison

Analyst expected that the coming months would be among the most exciting in the Coke-Pepsi saga. It would be interesting to see how the revived "cola wars" would play out. In the meantime, a look at some performance measures might provide clues as to what the future holds.

♦ Ratio analysis. Exhibits 4 and 5 present a variety of analytical ratios computed from the financial statements of each firm.

♦ Economic Profit Analysis. Also known as Economic Value Added, EVA can be used to estimate the value created or destroyed by comparing a firm's cash operating profits or "net operating Profits After Tax" (NOPAT) against a capital charge :

EVA = NOPAT – (weighed Average Cost of Capital X Invested Capital

Alternatively, the formula could be written as:

EVA = (Return on Invested Capital – WACC) x Invested Capital

Return on Invested Capital (ROIC), as the name suggests, could be calculated by dividing NOPAT by Invested Capital. The second formula highlights the idea that a "spread" earned beyond a company's cost of capital results in value creation.

Conclusion

Coke and Pepsi had created one of the strongest rivalries in business history. Carolyn Keene wanted to term a clean view regarding of the two companies future performance. She obtained pro forma projections for the two firms form reports prepare by analysts at Credit Suisse first Boston. (see Exhibits 6 and 7), and gathered information about current capital-market conditions (Exhibit 8), and gathered information about current capital-market conditions (Exhibit 8). She also took out her guidelines for estimating the components of EVA (Exhibit 9). It would be nice to finish her analysis going off for Christmas break.

EXHIBIT 1

Historical EVATM Estimation and Return Comparisons for Coca-cola Company and Pepsi Co. Inc.,

The Coca-Cola company ($MM)							
	1994	1995	1996	1997	1998	1999	2000
NOPAT	2,547	2,783	2,583	3,381	3,178	1,605	2,349
Invested Capital	7,769	8,466	9,649	13,825	15,896	15,644	15,864
Return on invested capital	32.8%	32.9%	26.8%	24.5%	20.0%	16.6%	14.8%
WACC	12.2%	11.4%	13.4%	12.9%	11.1%	6.9%	8.4%
ROIC-WACC Spread	20.6%	21.4%	13.4%	11.6%	8.9%	6.8%	6.4%
EVA	1.602	1,814	1.601	1.601	1,422	1,063	1,016

EXHIBIT-2 PEPSICO, Inc., ($MM)							
	1994	1995	1996	1997	1998	1999	2000
NOPAT	2,122	2,204	1,899	1,922	2,522	1,794	2,292
Invested Capital	22,507	27,009	26,823	16,392	19,439	12,849	13,146
Return on invested capital	9.4%	8.2%	7.1%	11.7%	13.0%	14.0%	17.4%
WACC	11.5%	11.0%	10.5%	11.6%	10.8%	9.9%	8.3%
ROIC-WACC Spread	-2.1%	-2.8%	-3.4%	0.1%	2.2%	4.1%	9.1%
EVA	(464)	(760)	(916)	24	428	522	1,201

Source : Casewriter estimates

Exhibit 3: U.S. soft-Drink Market Shares and volume, Coca-cola and Pepsi Co.,											
	1990	1991	1992	1993	1994	1995	1996	1997	1998	1990	2000
Coca-cola											
Gallonage (in million)	4,915.5	5,038.4	5,108.9	5,310.0	5,580.0	5,915.4	6,223.9	6,473.0	6,767.4	6,730.5	6,737.2
Growth	4.0%	2.5%	1.4%	3.9%	5.1%	6.0%	5.2%	4.0%	4.5%	0.5%	0.1%
Market share	41.0%	41.3%	41.3%	41.7%	42.0%	42.9%	43.8%	44.1%	44.6%	44.1%	44.0%
Market share gain/(loss)	0.6%	0.3%	0.0%	0.4%	0.3%	0.9%	0.9%	0.3%	0.5%	-0.5%	-0.1%
Pepsi Co											
Gallonage (in million)	3,970.5	4,010.2	3,827.6	3,899.0	4,070.6	4,201.8	4,370.2	4,500.2	4,704.1	4,732.3	4,736.1
Growth	3.0%	1.0%	-4.6%	1.9%	4.4%	3.2%	4.0%	3.0%	4.5%	0.6%	0.1%
Market share	33.1%	32.9%	30.9%	30.6%	30.7%	30.6%	30.8%	30.7%	31.0%	531.0%	30.9%
Market share gain/(loss)	0.1%	-0.2%	-2.0%	-0.3	0.1%	-0.1%	0.2	-0.1%	0.3%	0.0%	-0.1%
Soft Drink Industry							5				
Gallonage (in million)	11.996.1	12.200.4	12,473.2	12,72.7	13,275.0	13,752.9	14,199.5	14,655.8	15,160.6	15,251.6	15,328.0
Growth	2.6%	2.2%	2.2%	2.0%	4.3%	3.6%	3.2%	3.3%	3.4%	0.6%	0.5%

Exhibit 4: Analytical financial Ratios for the Coca-Cola company							
	1994	1995	1996	1997	1998	1999	2000
Activity Analysis							
Average days outstanding	31.24	32.61	32.83	31.73	32.06	31.92	31.71
Working capital turnover	(16.33)	(11.27)	(10.62)	(8.90)	(6.14)	(5.49)	(6.52)
Fixed assets turnover	3.59	3.60	3.87	4.33	4.36	3.79	3.32
Total assets turnover	1.08	1.12	1.15	1.12	1.05	0.92	0.93
Liquidity Analysis							
Current ratio	0.64	0.59	0.80	0.75	0.87	0.90	0.87
Cash ratio	0.25	0.18	0.22	0.21	0.18	0.18	0.20
Cash from operations ratio	0.54	0.45	0.47	0.47	0.35	0.39	0.38
Long-term Debt and Solvency Analysis							
Debt equity ratio	0.67	0.75	0.73	0.61	0.65	0.65	0.61
Times interest earned	18.63	14.80	13.69	19.38	17.93	11.82	8.26
Fixed charge coverage ratio	10.02	9.87	7.18	8.99	8.70	6.03	5.77
Capital expenditure ratio	3.83	3.55	3.50	3.69	3.98	3.63	4.89
Cash from operations-debt ratio	0.96	0.82	0.77	0.78	0.55	0.62	0.63
Profitability analysis							
Operating margin	22.9%	22.3%	21.1%	26.5%	24.4%	20.1%	18.0%
Net profit margin	15.8%	16.6%	18.8%	21.8%	18.8%	12.3%	10.6%
ROA	16.8%	17.7%	19.1%	21.1%	22.9%	17.3%	11.5%
ROE	44.3%	48.1%	51.7%	48.0%	46.1%	37.1%	25.8%
Financial leverage effect*	70.1%	68.9%	74.2%	89.2%	82.6%	71.1%	61.0%
Growth							
Sales	15.9%	11.4%	2.9%	1.7%	-0.3%	5.3%	-3.3%
Book assets	15.4%	8.4%	7.4%	4.5%	13.4%	12.9%	-3.6%
Net income before unusual gain/loss	16.7%	16.9%	16.9%	18.2%	-14.4%	-31.2%	-10.4%
Adjusted NOPAT	19.5%	8.6%	-2.8%	27.7%	-0.7%	-19.8%	-7.3%
Net income	17.4%	16.9%	16.9%	18.2%	-14.4%	-31.2%	-10.4%
Operating income	19.5%	8.6%	-2.8%	27.7%	-0.7%	-19.8%	-7.3%

*Net income/operating income

Source: Case-writer estimates

Exhibit 5 : Analytical financial Ratios for PepsiCo., Inc.							
	1994	1995	1996	1997	1998	1999	2000
Activity Analysis							
Average days outstanding	25.33	26.89	28.39	40.71	37.59	37.25	31.28
Working capital turnover	(34.07)	513.67	200.28	20.98	(28.69)	(12.86)	38.78
Fixed assets turnover	1.64	1.72	1.82	1.42	1.57	1.55	2.05
Total assets turnover	1.17	1.20	1.27	0.94	1.05	1.01	1.14
Liquidity Analysis							
Current ratio	0.96	1.06	1.00	1.47	0.55	1.10	1.17
Cash ratio	0.28	0.29	0.15	0.68	0.05	0.28	0.34
Cash from operations ratio	0.71	0.72	0.82	0.80	0.41	0.80	0.99
Long-term Debt and Solvency Analysis							
Debt equity ratio	1.39	1.73	1.97	0.71	1.24	0.44	0.33
Times interest earned	4.96	4.38	4.24	5.57	6.54	7.76	14.59
Fixed charge coverage ratio	3.03	2.72	2.48	3.41	3.09	3.73	4.36
Capital expenditure ratio	1.65	1.78	1.83	2.27	2.29	2.71	3.67
Cash from operations-debt ratio	0.39	0.30	0.32	0.69	0.40	0.99	1.62
Profitability analysis							
Operating margin	11.3%	9.9%	8.0%	12.7%	11.6%	13.8%	15.8%
Net profit margin	6.2%	5.3%	3.6%	10.2%	8.9%	10.1%	10.7%
ROA	7.2%	6.4%	4.6%	9.6%	9.3%	10.2%	12.2%
ROE	24.1%	24.7%	23.0%	16.9%	32.1%	30.0%	29.0%
Financial leverage effect*	54.6%	54.7%	53.8%	45.1%	80.5%	77.1%	72.7%
Growth							
Sales	13.3%	6.7%	4.6%	-33.9%	6.8%	-8.9%	-0.3%
Book assets	4.6%	2.6%	-3.6%	-18.0%	12.7%	-22.5%	-4.5%
Net income before unusual gain/loss	12.3%	-10.0%	-28.5%	29.8%	33.7%	2.9%	-6.5%
Adjusted NOPAT	10.1%	-6.7%	-14.8%	4.6%	-2.9%	9.1%	-14.4%
Net income	10.3%	-8.3%	-28.5%	86.4%	-7.0%	2.9%	-6.5%
Operating income	10.1%	-6.7%	-14.8%	4.6%	-2.9%	9.1%	-14.4%

* Net income/operating income
Source: Case-writer estimates

Exhibit 6: Income-Statement and Balance-Sheet forecast for the Coca-cola company							
Income statement	2001E	2002E	2003E	Balance sheet	2001E	2002E	2003E
Net operating revenue	20,223	21,223	22,508	Cash & equivalents	2,238	2,406	2,432
Cost of goods sold	6,092	6m285	6,617	A/R, Net	1,838	1,930	2,046
Gross profit	14,131	14,949	15,891	Inventories	1,015	1,048	1,103
				Prepaid expenses & other	1,834	1,868	1,964
				Total current assets	6,925	7,252	7,545
Selling expense	7,508	7,569	7,985				
General & admin.	1,224	1,248	1,273				
	8,732	8,817	9,258	Investment in bottles	5,962	6,189	6,449
				Marketable securities	2,364	2,364	2,364
Operating income	5,399	6,132	6,633	PP&E	7,334	0,084	8,834
				Less : Acc. depreciation	(2,935)	(3,476)	(4,073)
Interest income	295	244	254	Net PP&E	4,399	4,608	4,761
Interest expense	(310)	(280)	(264)	Goodwill & other	1,783	1,488	1,193
Equity income	197	227	261	Total assets	21,434	21,901	22,311
Other income/							
Deductions), net	24	(10	(10)	A/P & accrued liabilities	3,796	3,868	4,066
				Loans and notes payable	3,600	3,500	3,400
Pretax Taxes	5,605	6,313	6,874	Current portion of long-term debt.	154	153	2
				Accrued income taxes	643	724	788
Income Taxes	1,682	1,894	2,062	Total current liabilities	8,193	8,245	8,256
Net Income	3,923	4,419	4,812				
				Long-term debt	681	528	526
Supplemental information:				Other	991	991	9991
Depreciation	489	542	597	Deferred income taxes	302	239	3,196
Amortization	295	295	295	Total liabilities	10,167	10,003	9,943
Cash taxes	1,738	1,957	2,131				
Capital expenditures	700	750	750	Common stock	870	870	870
				Additional paid-in capital	3,196	3,196	3,196
Accumulated goodwill amortization at the end of		Retained earnings	23,466	26,097	29,067		
2000 was expected to be $192 million.....			Accumulated other				
				Comprehensive losses	(2,722)	(2,722)	(2,722)
The reader should assume net income reflects the		Treasury stock	(13,543)	(15,543)	(18,043)		
Deduction of depreciation and amortization.			Total equity	11,267	11.898	12,368	
				Total liabilities and equity	21,434	21,901	22,311

Exhibit 7: Income-Statement and Balance-Sheet forecast for Pepsi Co. Inc..,							
Income Statement	2001E	2002E	2003E	Balance sheet	2001E	2002E	2003E
Revenue	10,553	11,307	12,116	Cash	1,775	3,677	2,457
Frito-Lay	14,498	15,373	16,273	Investment	466	466	466
Quacker Foods	2,042	2,109	2,179	Cash and equivalents	2,241	4,143	2,923
	27,093	28,789	30,568				
				A/R,Net	2,292	2,435	2,585
Operating profit				Inventories	1,284	1,364	1,449
Beverages	1,667	1,818	1,976	Prepaid Exp. & Other	886	942	1,000
Frito-Lay	2,675	2,855	3,239	Total current assets	4,462	4,741	5,034
Quaker foods	408	426	446				
Synergies	-	60	90	PP&E	7,449	8,021	8,493
Corporate expense	(365)	(374)	(382)	Intangibles	4,556	4,556	4,556
	4,385	4,885	5,369	Investment in unconsol, affiliated	3,095	3,235	3,414
Net Interest expense	148	92	37	Other Total assets	952	1,019	1,090
Equity income	157	186	239		22,757	25,716	25,511
Pretax income	4,394	4,979	5,571	Short-term borrowings	202	-	-
Provision for taxes	1,406	1,593	1,783	Current portion of long-term debt.	281	444	64
				Accts payable & other current liabs	5,017	5,2484	5,573
Net Income	2,988	3,386	3,788	Total current liabilities	5,500	5,728	5,637
				Long-term debt	2,106	1,825	1,381
Supplemental information:				Other liabilities	2,444	4,541	4,859
Depreciation	900	950	1,000	Deferred income taxes	1,625	1,974	2,252
Amortization	236	295	295	Total liabilities	13,475	14,068	14,129
Cash taxes	1,142	1,245	1,504				
Capital expenditures	1,860	1,583	1,528	Preferred stock			
				Common stock & add'	690	690	690
	Accumulated goodwill amortization at the end of 2000 was expected to be $751 million.....		Retained earnings	18,420	20,786	23,520	
			Accumulated other				
				Comprehensive losses	(1,394)	1,394)	(1,394)
The reader should assume net income reflects the deduction of depreciation and amortization.		Treasury stock	(8,434)	(8,434)	(11,434)		
			Total equity	9,282	11,648	11,382	
				Total liabilities and equity	22,757	25,716	25,511

Source (except for accumulated goodwill amortization) : "Third Quarter Review of 10Q : flat Revenue and Varied Operating Performance". By Andrew Conway, Chirs O'donnell, and Corey Horsch, Credit Suisse first Bostan Equity Research, November 19,2001.

Exhibit 8: Capita-Market Information on December 4, 2000					

The Coca-Cola Company

Publicity Trade Debt.

Coupon	5.75% paid semi-annually		
Maturity	4/30/2009		
Current price	91.54		
Rating	A1		

Historic Betas

1994	0.88
1995	0.83
1996	1.19
1997	1.11
1998	0.97
1999	0.71
2000	0.44
Average	0.88

Dividend History and forecasts

Payment Dates	31-mar	30-June	30-Sep	31-Dec	Total
1996	-	0.125	0.125	0.25	0.50
1997	-	0.14	0.14	0.28	0.56
1998	-	0.15	0.15	0.30	0.60
1999	-	0.16	0.16	0.32	0.64
2000	-	0.17	0.17	0.34E	0.68

E – Estimate

Value Line Forecast of Dividend Growth from 1997-99 to 2003-05	7.50%
Value Lines EPS Estimate for FY 2001	$1.75
Coke Share price on December 4 2000	$ 62.75
Outstanding shares (in millions)	
Basic	2,477
Diluted	2,487

The Pepsi co,Inc.

Publicity Trade Debt.

Coupon	5.75% paid semi-annually				
Maturity	1/15/2008				
Current price	93.26				
Rating	A2				

Historic Betas

1994	1.05	1995	1996	1997	1998	1999
2000	1.07	2001	2002	2003	2004	2005
2006	0.93	2007	2008	2009	2010	2011
2012	0.96	2013	2014	2015	2016	2017
2018	1.03	2019	2020	2021	2022	2023
2024	0.73	2025	2026	2027	2028	2029
2030	0.42	2031	2032	2033	2034	2035
Average	0.88					

Dividend History and Forecasts

Payment Dates	31-Mar	30-June	30-Sep	31-Dec	Total
1996	0.20	0.115	0.115	-	0.43
1997	0.13	0.125	0.125	-	0.48
1998	0.25	0.13	0.13	-	0.51
1999	0.26	0.135	0.135	-	0.53
2000	0.27	0.14	0.14	-	0.55

E – Estimate

Value Line forecast of Dividend Growth from 1997-99 to 2003-05		7.50%	
Value Lines EPS Estimate for FY 2001		$1.63	
PepsiCo., Share price on December 4, 2000		$ 43.81	
Outstanding shares (in millions)			
Basic		1,446	
Diluted		1,475	

Exhibit 9: Some Guidelines for Estimating Components of Eva

NOPAT- "Net Operating Profit After Taxes" (NOPAT) is calculated with the aim of arriving at the actual cash generated by the concern. Adjustments might include adding goodwill amortization and other non-cash expenses. Taxes must similarly be adjusted to reflect only actual cash taxes. Depreciation is not added to NOPAT despite being a non-cash expense, because of the assumption that depreciation represents the true economic cost (i.e. it is the amount that must be reinvested to maintain operations at the existing level). For consistency, invested capital is measured net of depreciation.

Invested Capital- Invested capital means, simply, the amount of capital invested in the business. It may be calculated either from the asset side or from the liabilities + equity side of the balance sheet. The latter is the simpler method.

Invested capital includes debt, equity, and other near-capital items that represent economic value employed on behalf of the firm, such as the present value of operating leases, write-offs and cumulative losses, and accumulated goodwill amortization. The rationale for including losses and write-offs in continuing capital is that, these represent unproductive assets, or failed investment.

Were they excluded from the capital equation, the sum would only count successful efforts and not accurately reflect the performance of the firm Accumulated goodwill amortization likewise needs to be included in invested capital because it represent a true investment. Excess cash not needed for operations, such as marketable securities, may be deducted from the invested capital base.

Cost of capital The capital charge applied against NOPAT should be based on a blend of the costs of all the types of capital the firm employs, or the weighted-average cost of capital.

$$WACC = \{K_d(1 - 1) *D/(D+E) + K_c*/(D+3)\}$$

Where, K_d = Cost of debt.

T = Effective marginal tax rate.

K_c = Cost of equity.

D = total debt.

E = Total equity.

The cost of debt (used for both debt and leases) is the annual rate consistent with each firm's bond rating. The cost of equity may be estimated in a variety of ways – a usual practice is, to use the capital-asset-pricing model.

$$K_4 = R_f + b (R_m - R_f)$$

Where, R_f =   Risk-free rate, typically the yield on 10-years U.S. Treasury bonds.

β =   Beta, a measure of the volatility of a company's stock price with respect to market movements.

R_m-R_f =   Mark-risk premium. The additional return, investors require over the risk-free rate to compensate them for investing in companies.

REFERENCES

1.   Khan M.Y., and Jain P.K, op. cit., p.43.

2.   Bhattacharya S.K, *"A Cost-of-Capital Frame Work for Management Control"*, Economic and Political Weekly, Vol. 35, 29 August 1970.

3.   Porterfield, ITS, *"Investment Decisions and Capital Gains Costs"*, Prentice Hall, 1965, p. 45.

4.   Porter field, ITC, Op.cit, p.61

5.   William F.S, *"Capital Asset Prices – A Theory of Market Equilibrium under Conditions of Risk"*, Journal of Finance, September 1964.

6.   Brigham E.F, and Houston J.F, *"Fundamentals of Financial Management"*, Singapore: Harcourt Asia Pvt. Ltd., 2001, p. 472.

7.   Gitman L.J., *"Principles of Managerial Finance"*, New York, Harper & Row, 1997, p. 353.

Capital Budgeting

11

INTRODUCTION

Capital project planning is the process by which companies allocate funds to various investment projects designed to ensure profitability and growth.

Evaluation of such projects involve estimating their future benefits to the company and comparing these with their costs.

In a competitive economy, the economic viability and prosperity of a company depends upon the effectiveness and adequacy of capital expenditure evaluation and fixed assets management.

MEANING AND DEFINITION

Capital budgeting refers to planning the deployment of available capital for the purpose of maximizing the long-term profitability of the firm. It is the firm's decision to invest its current funds most efficiently in long-term activities in anticipation of flow of future benefits over a series of years.

In other words, Capital budget may be defined as the firm's decision to invest its current funds most efficiently in the long-term assets in anticipation of an expected flow of benefits over a series of years. [10] Therefore, it involves a current outlay or series of outlay of cash resources in return for an anticipated flow of future benefits. Capital budgeting is the process to identify, analysis and select investment projects, whose returns (cash flows) are expected to extend beyond one year. [11] Firm's investment decisions would generally include expansion, acquisition, modernization, replacement of fixed assets or long-term assets. From the above definition, we may identify the basic features of capital budgeting viz., potentially large anticipated benefits, relatively a high degree risk, and a relatively long-time period between the initial outlay and anticipated return.

Capital budgeting involves

- The search for new and more profitable investment proposals
- The making of an economic analysis to determine the profit potential of each investment proposal.

In simple, capital budgeting refers to the total process of generating, evaluating, selecting and following upon capital expenditure alternatives.

Capital budgeting may be defined as the firm's formal process for the acquisition and investment of capital. It involves the firm's decision to invest its current funds for addition, disposition, modification and replacement of fixed assets.

FEATURES OF CAPITAL BUDGETING DECISIONS

Capital budgeting decisions have the following features:
a) It involves exchange of current funds for future benefits.
b) They benefit future periods.
c) They have the effect of increasing the capacity, efficiency, span of life regarding future benefits.
d) Funds are invested in long-term activities.

Some of the examples of capital budgeting decision are :
a) Introduction of a new product.
b) Expansion of business by investing in plant and machinery.

c)   Replacing and modernizing a process.

d)   Mechanization of process.

e)   Choice between alternative machines.

SIGNIFICANCE

Capital budgeting decisions are significant due to the following reasons:

Growth: The fixed assets are earning assets, since they have decisive influence on the rate of return and direction of firm's growth. A wrong decision can affect the other projects, which are already running under profits. In other words unwanted or unprofitable investments will result in heavy operating costs.

More Risky: Investment in long-term assets increases average profit but it may lead to fluctuations in its earnings, then firm will become more risky. Hence, investment decision decides the future of the business concern.

Huge investments: Long-term assets involve more initial cash outflows, which makes it imperative for the firm to plan its investment programmes very carefully and make an advance arrangement of funds either from internal sources or external sources or from both the sources.

Irreversibility: Long-term asset investment decisions are not easily reversible and that too, with much financial loss to the firm; due to difficulties in finding out market for such capital items once they have been used. Hence, firm will incur more loss in that type of capital assets.

Effect on other Projects: Whenever long-term asset investment is a part of the expansion programme, its cashflow effects the projects under consideration, if it is not economically independent. The effect may be increased in profits or decrease in profits. So, while taking investment in long-term assets, the decision maker has to check the impact of this project on other projects, if the effect is in terms of increase in profits then he / she has to accept the project and vice versa.

Difficult Decision: Capital budgeting decision is very difficult due to (a) decision involves future years cash inflows, (b) uncertainty of future and more risk.

Other reasons regarding the significance of capital budgeting are:

1.   The decision-maker loses some of his flexibility, for the results continue over an extended period of time. He has to make a commitment for the future.

2.   Asset expansion is related to future sales.

3.   The availability of capital assets has to be phased properly.

4.   Asset expansion typically involves the allocation of substantial amounts of funds.

5.   Many firms fail, because they involve the allocation of substantial amount of funds.

6.   Decision relating to capital investment is among the most difficult and, at the same time, most critical that a management has to make. These decisions require an assessment of the future events which are uncertain.

7.   The most important reason for capital budgeting decisions is that, they have long-term implications for a firm. The effects of a capital budgeting decision extends into the future and have to be put up with, for a longer period than the consequences of current operating expenditures.

8.   Capital budgeting is an important function of the management because it is one of the critical determinants of success or failure of the company, advised or excessive capital spending may create excessive capacity and increase in operating costs limits the viability of company funds and reduce its profit earning capacity.

OBSTACLES FOR CAPITAL BUDGETING

Capital budgeting decisions are very important, but they pose difficulties, which shoot from three principle sources:

Measurement Problem: Evaluation of project requires identifying and measuring its costs and benefits, which is difficult since they involve tedious calculations and lengthy process. Majority of replacement or expansion programmes have impact on some other activities of the company (introduction of new product may result in the decrease in sales of the other existing product) or have some intangible consequences (improving morale of the workers).

Uncertainty: Selection or rejection of a capital expenditure project depends on expected costs and benefits in the future. Future is uncertain, if anybody tries to predict the future, it will be childish or foolish. Hence, it is impossible to predict the future cash inflows.

Temporal Spread: The costs and benefits, which are expected, are associated with a particular capital expenditure project spread out over a long period of time, which is 10-20 years for industrial projects and 20-50 years for infrastructure projects. The temporal spread creates some problems in estimating discount rates for conversation of future cash inflows in present values and establishing equivalences.

CAPITAL BUDGETING PROCESS

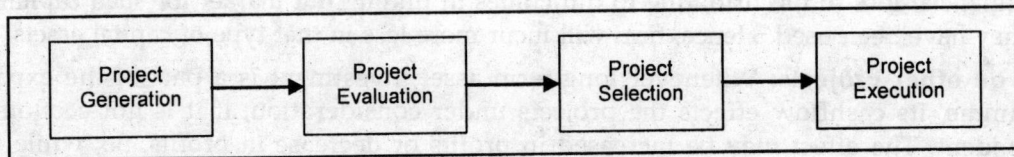

Figure 11.1 : Exhibits Capital Budgeting process

While steps are essential to any capital budgeting process, but individual situations of capital budgeting may demand other steps relevant to the situation to make the process an effective one:

1. **Project Generation:** Investment proposals of various types may originate at different levels within a firm. The investment proposals may fall into one of the following categories.
   i) Proposals to add new product to the product line.
   ii) Proposal to expand capacity in existing product lines.
   iii) Proposals to reduce the costs of the output of the existing at any level; from top management level to the level of the workers. The proposals may originate systematically or haphazardly.

2. **Project Evaluation :** Project Evaluation involves two steps :
   i) Estimation of benefits and costs. The benefits and costs must be measures in terms of cash flows.
   ii) Selection of an appropriate criterion to judge the desirability of the project.

3. **Project Selection :** Since capital budgeting decisions are of considerable significance, the final approval of the project may generally rest on the top management. However, projects are screened at multiple levels.

4. **Project Execution :** The funds are appropriated for capital expenditure after the final selection of investment proposals. The formal planning for the appropriation of funds is called the capital budget. The project execution committee or the management must ensure that the funds are spent in accordance with appropriations made in the capital budget.

According to Finance managers, the Capital Budgeting Process is classified as under:

1. Planning/Idea Generation
2. Evaluation/Analysis
3. Selection
4. Financing
5. Execution/Implementation
6. Review

PROCESS/STEPS OF CAPITAL BUDGETING

The process of Capital budgeting may be divided into six broad phases/steps, viz., planning or idea generation, evaluation/analysis, selection, financing, execution/implementation and review. Figure 8.1 depicts the relationship among phases of capital budgeting.

1. **Planning / Idea Generation:** The search for promising project ideas is the first step in capital budgeting process. In other words the planning phase of a firm's capital budgeting process is concerned with articulation of its broad investment strategy and the generation and preliminary search of project proposals. Identifying a new worthwhile project is a complex problem. It involves a careful study from many different angles. Ideas can be generated from the sources like, performance analysis of existing industries, examination of input and output of various industries, review of import and export data, study plans outlays and government guidelines, looking at the suggestions of financial institutions and developmental agencies, study of local materials and resources, analysis of economic and social trends, study of new technological developments, draw clues from the consumption abroad, explore the possibility of reviving sick units, identity unfulfilled psychological needs, attending trade fairs, stimulate creativity for generating new product ideas among the employees.

2. **Evaluation / Analysis:** In the preliminary screening, when a project proposal suggests that the project is prima facie worthwhile, then it is required to go for evaluation/analysis. Analysis has to consider aspects like, marketing, technical, financial, economic and ecological analysis. This phase focuses on gathering data, preparing, summarizing relevant information about various alternative projects available, which are being considered for inclusion in the capital budgeting process. Costs and benefits are determined based on the information gathered about other alternative projects.

3. **Selection:** Selection or rejection follows the analysis phase. If the project is worthwhile, after using a wide range of evaluation techniques, which are divided into traditional/non-discounted and modern/discounted. Selection and rejection of a project depends on the technique used to evaluate and its rule of acceptance. The acceptance rules are different for each and every method. Apart from the use of techniques of evaluation, there are few techniques available for measurement (range, standard deviation, coefficient of variation) and incorporation of risk (risk adjusted discount rate, certainty equivalent, probability distribution approach and decision tree approach) in capital budgeting.

4. **Financing of the Project:** After the selection of the project, the next step is financing. Generally the amount required is known after the selection of the project. Under this phase financing arrangements have to be made. There are two broad sources available such as equity (shareholders' funds – paid up share capital, share premium, and retained earnings) and debt (loan funds – term loans, debentures, and working capital advances). While deciding the capital structure, the decision maker has to keep in mind some factors, which influence capital structure. The factors are Flexibility, Risk, Income, Control, and Tax benefits (referred to by the acronym FRICT). Capital should consist of debt and equity.

5. **Execution / Implementation:** Planning of paper work and implementation is physically different in implementing the selected project. Implementation of an industrial project involves the stages, project and engineering designs, negotiations and contracting, construction, training, and plant commissioning. Translating an investment proposal from paper work to concrete work is complex, time consuming and a risky task. Adequate formulation of project, use of the principle of responsibility accounting and use of network techniques (PERT and CPM), are very much helpful for the implementation of a project at reasonable cost.

6. **Review of the Project:** Once the project is converted from paper work to concrete work, then, there is need to review the project. Performance review should be done periodically, under this performance review, actual performance is compared with the predetermined or projected performance.

PRINCIPLES OF CAPITAL BUDGETING

Capital expenditure decisions should be taken on the basis of the following factors :

1. Creative search for profitable opportunities : profitable investment opportunities should be sought to supplement existing proposals.

2. Long-range capital planning : It indicates sectoral demand for funds to stimulate alternative proposals before the aggregate demand for funds is finalized.

3. Short-range capital planning : It indicates sectoral demand for funds to stimulate alternative proposals before the aggregate demand for funds is finalized.

4. Measurement of project work : here, the project is ranked with the other projects.

5. Screening and selection : The project is examined on the basis of selection criteria, such as the supply cost of capital, expected returns alternative investment opportunities, etc.,

6. Retirement and disposal : The expiry of the life cycle of a project is marked at this stage.

7. Forms and procedures : These involve the preparation of reports necessary for any capital expenditure programme.

RANKING OF CAPITAL BUDGETING PROPOSALS OR CLASSIFICATION OF INVESTMENT PROPOSALS

A firm should select its own projects after considering the advantages and disadvantages of each one of them. For this purpose, it should rank the proposals. Proposals are ranked on the basis of the following considerations.

1. Mutually Exclusive Investment Proposals

This kind of Proposal connote those proposals which represent alternative methods of doing the same job. In case one proposal is accepted, the need to accept the other is ruled out. For Example, there are 5 pieces of equipment available in the market to carry out a job. If the management chooses one piece of the equipment, others will not be required because they are mutually exclusive projects.

2. Contingent Investment Proposals

There are certain projects utility which is contingent upon the acceptance of others. For example, management of an enterprise may be contemplating to construct, employee's quarters and a co-operative shops. If it decides not to build quarters, the need for the shop does not arise. If the management decides to construct quarters but not shops, the employees will have no shop to make purchases. These are contingent projects.

3. Independent investment proposals

It includes all such investment proposals as are being considered by the management for performing different tasks with in the organization. Investments in machinery, automobiles, buildings, parking lot, recreation centre and so on are the examples of the independent investment proposals. Acceptance of each of these projects is done on its own merit without depending on other projects.

4. Replacement

The investments, which are contemplated for replacing, old and antiquated equipment so that the job could be performed more efficiently, are termed as replacements.

CAPITAL BUDGETING APPRAISAL METHODS

In view of the significance of capital budgeting decisions, it is absolutely necessary that the method adopted for appraisal of capital investment proposal is a sound one. Any appraisal method should provide for the following:

i.   A basis of distinguishing between acceptable and non-acceptable projects.

ii. Ranking of projects in order of their desirability.

iii. Choosing among several alternatives.

iv. A criterion which is applicable to any conceivable project.

v.   Recognizing the fact, that bigger benefits are preferable to smaller ones and early benefits are preferable to later ones.

There are many methods for evaluating and ranking the capital investment proposals. In all these methods, the basic method is to compare the investments in the projects regarding the benefits derived.

TECHNIQUES OF PROJECT EVALUATION

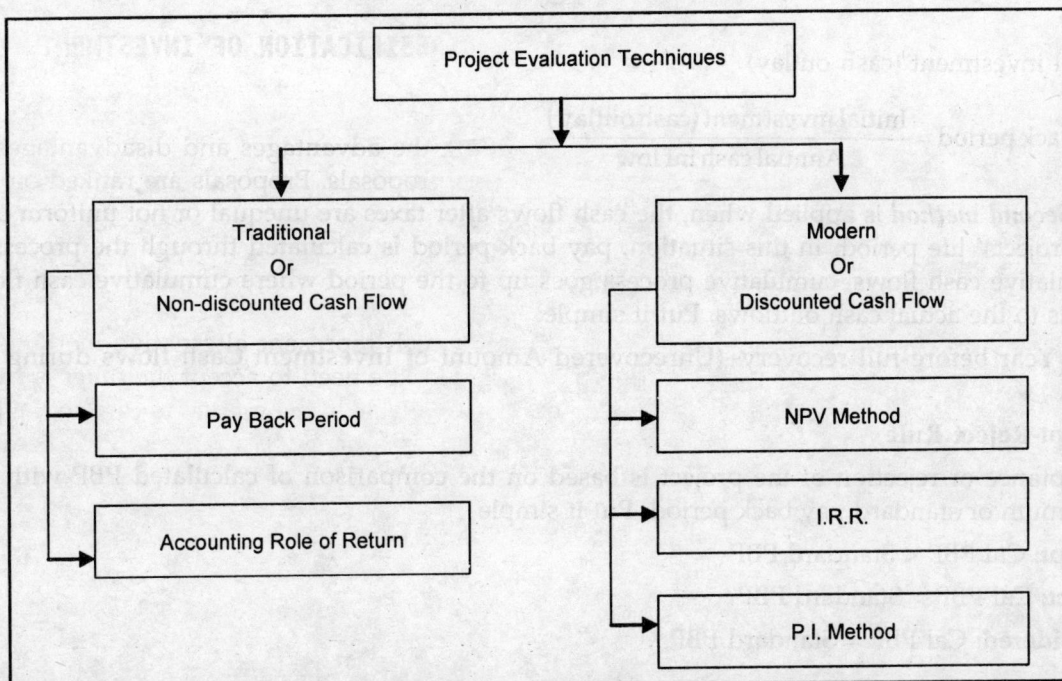

1. Traditional Methods :
    a. Payback period method
    b. Accounting rate of return method
2. Discounted cash flow methods :
    a. The net present value of method
    b. Internal rate of return
    c. Profitability index or benefit-cost-ratio

It should be kept in mind that different firms may use different methods. Which method is appropriate to a specific project of the firm, depends upon the relevant circumstances of the proposed project under evaluation.

INVESTMENT EVALUATION CRITERIA

(I) TRADITIONAL TECHNIQUES OR NON-DISCOUNTED CASH FLOW TECHNIQUES

The traditional techniques are further subdivided into two, such as

    (A) Pay back period, and

    (B) Accounting Rate of Return or Average Rate of Return (ARR).

(A) Pay Back Period: Pay back period is one of the most popular and widely recognized technique of evaluating investment proposals. Pay back period may be defined as that period required, to recover the original cash outflow invested in a project. In other words it is the minimum required number of years to recover the original cash outlay invested in a project. The cash flow after taxes is used to compute pay back period.

Pay back period can be calculated in two ways, (i) Using formula (ii) Using Cumulative cash flow method. The first method can be applied when the cash flows stream of each year is equal / annuity in all the years' or projects life, i.e., uniform cash flows for all the years. In this situation the following formula is used to calculate pay back period.

Pay Back Period = Original Investment ÷ Constant Annual Cash Flows After Taxes

or

Initial investment (cash outlay)

$$\text{Payback period} = \frac{\text{Initial investment}\left(\text{cash outlay}\right)}{\text{Annual cash inflow}}$$

The Second method is applied when, the cash flows after taxes are unequal or not uniform over the projects' life period. In this situation, pay back period is calculated through the process of cumulative cash flows, cumulative process goes up to the period where cumulative cash flows equals to the actual cash outflows. Put it simple:

PBP=Year before full recovery+(Unrecovered Amount of Investment‚Cash flows during the year)

Accept-Reject Rule

Acceptance or rejection of the project is based on the comparison of calculated PBP with the maximum or standard pay back period. Put it simple

Accept: Cal PBP < Standard PBP

Reject: Cal PBP > Standard PBP

Considered: Cal PBP = Standard PBP

Advantages Pay Back Period

The *Merits* of pay back period are,

- It is very simple and easy to understand.
- Cost involvement in calculating pay back period is very less as compared to sophisticated methods.

Limitations of Pay Back Period

Pay back period method suffers from certain Limitations such as:

- It ignores cash flows after pay back period.
- It is not an appropriate method of measuring the profitability of an investment, as it does not consider all cash inflows yielded by the investment.
- It does not take into consideration time value of money.
- There is no rationale basis for setting a minimum pay back period.
- It is not consistent with the objective of maximizing shareholders' wealth. Share value does not depend on pay back periods of investment projects.

For calculating payback period we need cash flows after taxes (CFAT)

Calculation of Cash flows after taxes (CFAT):

Particulars	Rs.
Sales revenue	xxx
Less: Variable cost	xxx
Contribution	xxx
Less: Fixed cost	xxx
Earning Before Depreciation and Taxes (EBDT)	xxx
Less: Depreciation	xxx
Earning Before Taxes (EBT)	xxx
Less: Taxes	xxx
Earnings After Tax (EAT)	xxx
Add: Depreciation	xxx
Cash Flows After Tax (CFAT) or Earnings After Taxes but Before Depreciation (EATBD)	xxx

Illustration 1 : A project requires an initial investment of Rs. 1,20,000 and yields annual cash inflow of Rs. 12,000 for 12 years. Find the payback period

Solution:

1,20,000/12,000 = 10 years.

In case of unequal annual cash inflows, cumulative cash inflows will be calculated and by interpolation, the exact payback period can be found out.

Illustration 2 : The project requires an initial investment of Rs. 20,000 and the annual cash inflows for 5 years is Rs. 6,000, Rs. 8,000, Rs. 5,000, Rs. 4,000 and Rs. 4,000 respectively. Find the payback period.

Solution:

Year	Cash inflow	Cumulative Cash Inflow
1	Rs. 6,000	Rs. 6000
2	Rs. 8,000	Rs. 14,000
3	Rs. 5,000	Rs. 19,000
4	Rs. 4,000	Rs. 23,000
5	Rs. 4,000	Rs. 27,000

The above table shows that in 3 years, Rs. 19,000 has been recovered, Rs. 1000 is left out of initial investment. In the fourth year, the cash inflow is Rs. 4000. It means the payback period is between three and four years, ascertained as follows :

$$Pay - back\ period = 3 years + \frac{1000}{4000} = 3.25\ years$$

Accept or Reject Criterion

The decision to accept or reject a proposal depends upon how the computed pay-back figures compares with a standard. For example, if the pay-back standard were 7 years, the project with the 5 years pay-back period would be accepted. Therefore, the decision rule is accepted if the computed pay-back period is less than the standard ; other wise it is rejected.

Illustration 3: A company is considering expanding its production. It can go either for an automatic machine costing Rs. 2,24,000 with an estimated life of 5 years or an ordinary machine costing Rs.60,000 having an estimated life of 8 years. The annual sales and costs are estimated as follows:

	Automatic Machine (Rs.)	Ordinary Machine (Rs.)
Sales	1, 50,000	1, 50,000
Costs:		
Materials	50,000	50,000
Labour	12,000	60,000
Variable overheads	24,000	20,000

Calculate the payback period and advice the management.

Solution:

Calculation of PBP needs cash flows after tax. Hence, now calculate CFAT

Calculation of Cash inflows after taxes CFAT

Calculation of Cash inflows after taxes CFAT

Particulars	Automatic Machine (Rs.)	Ordinary Machine (Rs.)
Sales	1, 50,000	1, 50,000
Less costs:		
Material +Labour +V. overheads	86,000	1, 30,000
EBDT	64,000	20,000
Less: Depreciation (WNi)	44,800	7,500
EBT	19,200	12,500
Less: Taxes at 50 per cent	9,600	6,250
EAT	9,600	6,250
Add: depreciation	44,800	7,500
Cash inflow (CFAT)	54,400	13,750

Payback period = Initial Investment ÷ Constant Annual Cash Inflows

PBP of Automatic Machine = 2, 24,000 ÷ 54,400= **4.11 Years**

PBP of Ordinary Machine = 60,000 ÷ 13,750= **4.36 Years**

Advice: The payback period in case of automatic machine is shorter. Hence automatic machine is preferable.

Working Note: Depreciation = (Original Investment – Scrap Value) ÷ Life Period

Automatic Machine: (2, 24,000 – 0) / 5 = Rs. 44,800

Old Machine: (60,000 – 0) / 8= Rs. 7,500

Assumption : Tax rate assumed as 50 per cent

Illustration 4 : A project costs Rs.20 lakh and yields annually a profit of Rs.3, 00,000 after depreciation at 12½ per cent but before tax at 50 per cent. Calculate payback period and suggest whether it should be accepted or rejected based on 6 year standard pay back period.

Solution

Calculation of Cash Flows After Tax

Particulars	Amount (Rs.)
Profit After Depreciation Before Taxes	3, 00,000
Less: Taxes at 50 %	1, 50,000
EAT	1, 50,000
Add: Depreciation (Note) Cash inflow	2, 50,000
(CFAT)	4, 00,000

Payback period = Initial Investment ÷ Constant Annual Cash Inflows

Payback period = Rs.20,00,000 ÷ Rs.4,00,000 = 5 years

Decision: Project should be accepted since calculated PBP is less than the standard PBP

Working Note: Depreciation = Cost of Project X Depreciation Rate

$$= 20, 00,000 \times 0.125 = Rs.2, 50,000$$

Illustration 5: (when cash inflows are uneven)

XYZ Ltd. is considering two projects. Each requires an investment of Rs.10, 000. The firm's cost of capital is 10 per cent. The net cash inflows from investments in two projects X and Y are as follows:

Year	1	2	3	4	5
X (Rs.)	5,000	4,000	3,000	1,000	--
Y (Rs.)	1,000	2,000	3,000	4,000	5,000

The company has fixed three years payback period as the cut-off point. State which project should be accepted.

Solution

Calculation of pay back period

Year	Project X		Project Y	
	CFAT (Rs.)	Cumulative CFAT (Rs.)	CFAT (Rs.)	Cumulative CFAT (Rs.)
1	5,000	5,000	1,000	1,000
2	4,000	9,000	2,000	3,000
3	3,000	1,000/3,000* =0.33	3,000	6,000
4	1,000		4,000	10,000
5	......		5,000	15,000
6	......		6,000	21,000

Recoverable Amount ÷ Concerned year cash flows

PBP of Project X is **2.33 years**   PBP of Project Y is   **4 years**

Since the cut-off point is 3 years, project X should be accepted i.e. 2.33 years is less than 3 years.

Merits

1. It is an important guide to investment policy.
2. It lays great emphasis on liquidity.
3. The rate which capital is recouped has a positive significance.
4. The method enables a firm to choose an investment which yields a quick return on cash funds.
5. It is easy to understand, calculate and communicate to others.
6. Other than its simplicity, the main advantage claimed for the payback method is, that it is a built-in safeguard against risk.
7. It enables a firm to determine the period required to recover the original investment with some percentage return and thus, arriving at the degree of risk associated with the investment.

Demerits:

1. It does not measure the profitability of a project.
2. The time value of money is ignored.
3. It does not value projects of different economic lives.
4. It is only a rule-of-thumb method. It is often difficult to judge objectively whether one proposed project is superior to another and, if so, by how much.
5. No allowance is made for taxation nor is any capital allowance made.

(B) ACCOUNTING RATE OF RETURN / AVERAGE RATE OF RETURN (ARR): Accounting rate of return method uses accounting information as revealed by financial statements, to measure the profitability of the investment proposals. It is also known as the *return on investment (ROI)*. Some times it is known as average rate of return (ARR). Average annual earnings after depreciation and taxes are used to calculate ARR. It is measured in terms of percentage. **ARR can be calculated in two ways.**

(i) Whenever it is clearly mentioned as *accounting rate of return*

If accounting rate of return is given in the problem, return on original investment method should be used to calculate accounting rate of return.

$$\text{Accounting Rate of Return (ARR)} = \frac{\text{Average annual EAT or PAT}}{\text{Original investment (OI)}^*} \times 100$$

* OI = Original investment + Additional NWC + Installation Charges + Transportation Charge

(ii) Whenever it is clearly mentioned as *average rate of return*

If Average rate of return is given in the Illustration, return on average investment method should be used to calculate average rate of return.

$$\text{Average Rate of Return} = \frac{\text{Average annual EAT}}{\text{Average investment (AI)}^*} \times 100$$

* AI = (Original investment − scrap)1/2 + Additional NWC + Scrap value

(iii) If ARR is given in the problem, any one of the above method can be used to calculate ARR (preferably return on average investment method).

Accept-Reject Rule

Acceptance or rejection of the project is based on the comparison of calculated ARR with the predetermined rate or cut of rate.

Accept: Cal ARR > Predetermined ARR or Cut-off rate

Reject: Cal ARR < Predetermined ARR or Cut-off rate

Considered: Cal ARR = Predetermined ARR or Cut-off rate

Advantages of ARR Method

The ARR method has some *merits*.

- The most significant merit of ARR is that, it is very simple to understand and easy to calculate.
- Information can easily be drawn from accounting records.
- It takes into account all profits of the projects' life period.
- Cost involvement in calculating pay back period is very less in comparison to the sophisticated methods, since it saves analysts' time.

Limitations of ARR Method

ARR method suffers form serious demerits.

- It uses accounting profits instead of actual cash flows after taxes, in evaluating the projects. Accounting profits are inappropriate for evaluating and accepting projects, since they are computed based on arbitrary assumptions and choices and also include non-cash items.
- It ignores the concept of time value of money.
- It does not allow profits to be reinvested.
- It does not differentiate between the size of the investment required for each project.

- It does not take into consideration any benefits, which can accrue to the firm from the sale of equipment, in abundance which is replaced by the new investment.
- It feels that, 10 per cent rate of return for 10 years is more beneficial than eight per cent rate of return for 25 years.
- It is incompatible with the objective of wealth maximization to the equity shareholders.
- It uses arbitrary cut-off as yardstick or standard for acceptance or rejection rule.

Illustration 6 :

The working result of two machines are given below

	Machine X Rs.	Machine Y Rs.
Cost	45,000	45,000
Sales per year	1,00,000	80,000
Total Cost Per Year (excluding depreciation	36,000	30,000
Expected Life	2 years	3 years

Which of the two should be preferred?

Solution

Computation of average income

	Machine X Rs.	Machine Y Rs.
Sales per year	1,00,000	80,000
Less : cost per year	36,000	30,000
	64,000	50,000
Less : Depreciation	22,500	15,000
Net profit	41,500	35,000
Average Income	41,500	35,000
Average Investment	22,500	22,500

$$ARR = \frac{Average\ Income}{Average\ investment} \times 100$$

For 'X' $\frac{41,500}{22,500} \times 100 = 184\%$

For 'Y' $= \frac{35,000}{22,500} \times 100 = 156\%$

Machine X has higher ARR. Hence, Machine X should be preferred.

Illustration 7 : A limited firm has under consideration the following two projects. Their details are as follows:

	Project X Rs.	Project Y Rs.
Investment in machinery	10,00,000	15,00,000
Working capital	5,00,000	5,00,000
Life of machinery (Years)	4	6
Scrap value of machinery (%)	10	10
Tax rate (%)	50	50

Income before depreciation and tax at the end of

Year	1	2	3	4	5	6
X (Rs.)	8,00,000	8,00,000	8,00,000	8,00,000	--	----
Y (Rs.)	15,00,000	9,00,000	15,00,000	8,00,000	6,00,000	3,00,000

You are required to calculate the average rate of return and suggest which project is to be preferred.

Solution:

Calculation of ARR: (Average annual income after taxes ÷ Average investment) × 100

Project X = (2,87,500 /10,50,000)×100 = **27.38 per cent**

Project Y = (3,54,167/ 13,25,000) ×100 = **26. 73 per cent**

ARR of Project X is higher than that of Project Y. Hence Project X is preferred.

Working Notes:

1. Calculation of Average Annual Income After Depreciation and Taxes:

	Project X Rs.	Project Y Rs.
Average EBDT	8,00,000	9,33,333
Less: Depreciation	2,25,000	2,25,000
Average EBT	5,75,000	7,08,333
Less: Taxes at 50 %	2,87,500	3,54,166
Average EAT	2,87,500	3,54,167

2. Calculation of Average Investment

(Original investment - scrap value)1/2 + Additional Working Capital + Scrap value

Project X: (10,00,000-1,00,000) 1/2 +5,00,000+1,00,000 = **Rs.10,50,000**

Project Y: (15,00,000-1,50,000) 1/2 +5,00,000+1,50,000 = **Rs.13,25,000**

3. Depreciation: (Original Investment – Scrap Value) ÷ Life Period

Project X: (10,00,000-1,00,000)/4 = Rs. 2,25,000

Project Y: (15,00,000-1,50,000)/6 = Rs. 2,25,000

4. Average EBDT = 32,00,000/4 = 8,00,000   56,00,000 /,6 =,9,33,333

Illustration 8: A project costs Rs. 5,00,000 and has a scrap value of Rs. 1,00,000. Its stream of income before depreciation and taxes during first year through five years is Rs. 1,00,000, Rs. 1,20,000, Rs. 1,40,0000, Rs. 1,60,000 and Rs. 2,00,000. Assume a 50 per cent tax rate and depreciation on straight-line basis. Calculate the accounting rate for the project. Also state whether you recommend the project for investment when the management expects a rate of return of 10 per cent.

Solution

ARR: (Average EAT ÷ Original investment) x 100

ARR = (Rs.32,000 / 5,00,000) ×100 = 6.4 per cent

As accounting rate of return for Project is less than the 10 per cent set by the management, hence the project can be rejected.

Working notes: i) Calculation of Average EAT

	Rs.
Average EBDT (Note iii)	1,44,000
Less: Depreciation (Note ii)	80,000
Average EBT	64,000
Less: taxes at 50 per cent	32,000
Average EAT	32,000

ii) **Depreciation** = (5,00,000 – 1,00,000) / 5 = Rs. 80,000

iii) **Average EBDT** = Total profits / No. of years = 7,20,000 / 5 = Rs.1,44,000

Illustration 9 : Determine the accounting rate of return from the following data of two machines A and B.

	Machine A Rs.	Machine B Rs.
Original cost	56,125	56,125
Additional investment in networking capital	5,000	6,000
Estimated life in years	5	5
Estimated salvage value	3,000	3,000
Average income-tax rate (%)	55	55

Annual estimated income after depreciation and taxes (EAT)

Year	1	2	3	4	5
Machine A (Rs.)	3,375	5,375	7,375	9,375	11,375
Machine B (Rs.)	11,375	9,375	7,375	5,375	3,375

Depreciation has been charged on straight line basis.

Solution

Accounting Rate of Return: (Average EAT ÷ Original investment) x 100

Machine A: Average annual income after tax = 36,875 / 5 = 7,375

Original investment = 56,125 + 5000 = 61,125

Accounting rate of return = (7,375 ÷ 61,125)100 = 12.06 per cent

Machine B: Average annual income after tax = 36,875 / 5 = 7,375

Original investment = 56,125 + 6,000 = 62,125

Accounting rate of return = (7,375 ÷62,125) 100 = 11.87 per cent

Note:

i)   If accounting rate of return is given in the illustration, return on original investment method should be used to calculate accounting rate of return.

Original investment = original investment + additional net working capital

ii)   If Average rate of return is given in the illustration, return on average investment method should be used to calculate average rate of return.

(Average annual income after taxes ÷ Average investment) x 100

(Original investment - scrap value) 1/2 + Additional Working Capital + Scrap value

iii)   If ARR is given in the problem, any one of the above methods can be used to calculate ARR (preferably return on average investment method).

(2) MODERN TECHNIQUES OR DISCOUNTED CASH FLOW (DCF) TECHNIQUES

Modern / discounted cash flow techniques take into consideration almost all the deficiencies of the traditional methods and consider all benefits and cost occurring during the projects' entire life period. Modern techniques can be again subdivided into three, viz., (A) Net Present Value (NPV) (B) Internal Rate of Return (IRR) or trail and error (C) Profitability Index (PI) or Discounted Benefit Cost Ratio (DBCR).

(A) Net Present Value Method (NPV)

The net present value method is one of the discounted cash flow methods. It is also known as discounted benefit cost ratio method. NPV can be defined as preset value of benefits minus preset value of costs. It is the process of calculating present values of cash inflows using cost of capital as an appropriate rate of discount and subtract present value of cash outflows from the present value of cash inflows and find the net present value, which may be positive or negative. Positive net present value occurs when the present value of cash inflow is higher than the present value of cash outflows and vice versa.

Steps involved in computation of NPV are,

(i) Forecasting of cash inflows of the investment project based on realistic assumptions.

(ii) Computation of cost of capital, which is used as discounting factor for conversion of future cash inflows into present values.

(iii) Calculation of cash flows using cost of capital as discounting rate / factor.

(iv) Finding out NPV by subtracting present value of cash outflows from present value of cash inflows.

Accept-Reject Rule

Acceptance or reject rule of the project is decided based on the NPV.

Accept: NPV> Zero   **Reject:** NPV< Zero   **Consider:** NPV= Zero

Advantages of NPV Method: The *Merits* of NPV are,

- It takes into account the time value of money.

- It uses all cash inflows occurring over the entire life period of the project including scrap value of the old project.

- It is particularly useful for the selection of mutually exclusive projects.

- It takes into consideration the changing discount rate.

- It is consistent with the objective of maximization of shareholders' wealth.

Limitations of NPV Method: NPV is the most acceptable method in comparison with traditional methods. Nevertheless, it has certain *Limitations* also.

- It is difficult to understand when compared with PBP and ARR.

- Calculation of required rate or discounting factor or cost of capital is difficult, which involves a lengthy and time consuming process and presents illustrations. At the same time calculation cost of capital is based on different methods.

- In case of projects involving different cash outlays, NPV method may not give dependable results.

- It does not give satisfactory results when comparing two projects with different life periods. Generally a project, having a shorter economic life would be preferable, other things being equal.

Illustration 10: A choice is to be made between the two competing proposals which require an equal investment of Rs. 50000 and are expected to generate net cash flows as under :

Years	Project A Rs.	Project B Rs.
1	25000	10000
2	15000	12000
3	10000	18000
4	Nil	25000
5	12000	8000
6	6000	4000

Cost of capital of the company is 10%. The following are the present value factor at 10% p.a.

Year	:	1	2	3	4	5	6
P.V. Factor At 10%	:	0.909	0.826	0.751	0.683	0.621	0.564

Which proposal should be selected using NPV method? Suggest the best project.

Solution:

Comparative Statement of NPV

Year	PV Factor @10%	Project A		Project B	
		Cash Inflow	Present Value	Cash Inflow	Present Value
1	0.909	25000	22725	10000	9090
2	0.826	15000	12390	12000	9912
3	0.751	10000	7510	18000	13518
4	0.683	Nil	Nil	25000	17075
5	0.621	12000	7452	8000	4968
6	0.564	6000	3384	4000	2256
	Total present Value :		53461		56819
	Less : Initial Investment :		50000		5000
	NPV :		Rs. 3461		Rs. 6819

Since project B has the highest NPV, Project B should be selected.

Illustration 11 : The Gama Co., Ltd., is considering the purchase of a new machine. Two alternative machines (X and Y have been suggested, each having an initial cost of Rs. 400000 and requiring Rs. 20000 as additional working capital at the end of the 1st year. Earnings after taxation are expected to be as follows :

Year	Cash inflows	
	Machine X Rs.	Machine Y Rs.
1	40000	120000
2	120000	160000
3	160000	200000
4	240000	120000
5	160000	80000

The company has a target of return on capital of 10% and on this, you are required to compare the profitability of the machines and state which alternative you consider financially preferable.

Note : The present value of Re. 1 due in 'n' number of years :

Year	:	1	2	3	4	5
P.V. At 10%	:	0.91	0.83	0.75	0.68	0.62

Solution

Statement showing the profitability of the two machines

Year	PV Factor @10%	Machine X Cash Inflow	Machine X Present Value	Machine Y Cash Inflow	Machine Y Present Value
1	0.91	40000	36400	120000	109200
2	0.83	120000	99600	160000	132800
3	0.75	160000	120000	200000	150000
4	0.68	240000	163200	120000	81600
5	0.62	160000	99,200	80000	49600
Total present value of cash inflows :			518400		523200
Total present value of cash outflows :					
(Rs. 400000 + 20000 x 0.91) :			418200		418200
Net Present value :			100200		105000

Recommendation : Machine Y is preferable to machine X

Accept or Reject criterion

In case, NPV is positive, the project should be accepted. If the NPV is negative, the project should be rejected.

It can be summarized as under:

1. NPV> Zero → Accept
2. NPV< Zero → Reject
3. NPV = Zero → Consider

Illustration 12: Calculate the NPV for a project, which requires an initial investment of Rs.20,000 and which, involves a net cash inflow of Rs.6, 000 each year for 6 years. Cost of funds is at 8 per cent.

Solution

Years	Net Cash inflow (Rs.)	Discount Factor 8 %	Present Value (Rs.)
1 to 6	6,000	4.623*	27,738
Present Value of Cash inflows			27,738
Less: Present Value of cash outflows			20,000
Net Present Value			7,738

Note: See TABLE A-4 The Present Value of Annuity One Rupee for PV of one rupee at 8 per cent discounting factor, because the cash inflow occurs evenly for a period of 6 years.

Illustration 13: Which amount is worth more at 10 per cent: Rs.1,000 in hand today or Rs.2,000 due after 8 years.

Solution:

A rupee received today is more valuable than a rupee received tomorrow. Based on the time value of money, Rs. 1,000 in hand today is worth more than the sum due after 8 years.

Computation of Present Value

Cash Flows (Rs.)	Discounting Factor 10 %	Present Value (in Rs.)
1,000	1.00	1,000
2,000	0.467*	934

Rs. 1,000 today is more valuable than Rs. 2,000 due after 8 years because the value of Rs.2,000 after 8 years is only Rs.934.

*Note: See TABLE A-3 The Present Value of One Rupee for PV of one rupee at 10 per cent discounting factor, because the cash inflow occurs only in one point of time.

Illustration 14: A new machine costs Rs. 20,000, requires no increased investment in working capital and is expected to yield Rs.6, 000 profit per year for 10 years, at which time its scrap value will be negligible. Assume straight-line depreciation and a 30 per cent tax rate.

If management requires at least a 10 per cent return on any new investment, would this investment qualify? At a rate of return what is the present value per rupee of investments.

Solution:

Calculation of CFAT

	Rs.
EBDT	**6,000**
Less: Depreciation	2,000 (20,000÷10)
EBT	**4,000**
Less: Taxes 30 %	1,200
EAT	**2,800**
Add: Depreciation	2,000
CFAT	**4,800**

Computation of NPV

Year	Cash Flows (in Rs.)	D F 10%	PV's (in Rs.)
1 to 10	4,800	6.145*	29,496
Present Value of cash inflows			29,496
Less: Cash outflows			20,000
Net Present Value (NPV)			**9,496**

Since the NPV is greater than zero, this investment quality to be accepted.

*Note: See TABLE A-4 The Present Value of Annuity One Rupee for PV of one rupee at 10 per cent discounting factor, because the cash inflows occurs evenly for a period of 10 years.

PV per rupee of investment = Total present value cash inflows ÷ Total investment

= Rs. 29,496 ÷ 20,000 = Rs. 1.47

Illustration 15:

No project is acceptable unless the yield is 10 per cent. Cash inflows of a certain project along with cash outflows are given below:

Year	0	1	2	3	4	5
Cash outflow (Rs.)	1,50,000	30,000	-----	-----	-----	-----
Cash outflow (Rs.)	-----	20,000	30,000	60,000	80,000	30,000

The salvage value at the end of 5th year is Rs.40,000. Calculate the NPV.

Solution:

Calculation of NPV

Year	Cash Flows (in Rs.)	D F 10%	PV's (in Rs.)
1	20,000	0.909*	18,180
2	30,000	0.826	24,780
3	60,000	0.751	45,060
4	80,000	0.683	54,640
5	30,000	0.621	18,630
5	Scrap Value 40,000	0.621	24,840
Present Value of cash inflows			1,86,130
Less: Cash outflows•			1,77,270
Net Present Value (NPV)			8,860

• **Working Note: Calculation of PV of cash outflows**

Year	Cash Outflow	DF 10%	PV Rs.
0	1,50,000	1	1,50,000
1	30,000	0.909	27,270
Total PV of Cash outflows			**1,77,270**

*Note: See TABLE A-3 The Present Value of One Rupee for PV of one rupee at 10 per cent discounting factor, because the cash inflow occurs unevenly for a period of 5 years.

(B) Internal Rate Of Return (IRR)

This method advocated by Joel Dean, takes into account the magnitude and timing of cash flows.

IRR is that rate at which the sum of Discounted Cash Inflow (DCF) equals the sum of discounted cash outflow. It is the rate at which the net present value of the investment is zero. It is called Internal Rate of Return because it depends mainly on the outlay and proceeds associated with the project and not on any rate determined outside the investment. This method is also known by following names :

- Marginal efficiency of capital
- Rate of return over cost
- Time adjusted rate of return
- Yield on investment

Internal rate of return may be defined as that discounting factor at which the present value of cash inflows equals to the present value of cash outflows. It takes into account the magnitude and timing of cash flows.[12] In case of NPV method, the discount rate is the required rate of return and that is predetermined, usually by cost of capital, which determines based on external point of view, where as IRR is based on facts, which is internal to the proposal. It is the best available concept. We shall see that although frequently a used concept in finance, yet at times quite a misleading measure of investment worth. [13]

Computation of IRR is based on the cash flows after taxes. IRR is mathematically represented as 'r'. It can be found by trial and error method. In this method the evaluator selects any discount rate to compute present value of cash inflows. Generally the cost of capital is taken as first trial. If calculated present value of the cash inflows is higher than the present value cash outflows then evaluator has to try at higher rate. On the other hand if the present value of cash inflows is lower than the present value of cash outflows then evaluator has to try lower discounting factor. This process will be repeated till the present value of cash inflows equals to the present value of cash outflows. Generally, IRR may lie between two discounting factors; in that case analyst has to use interpolation formula for calculation of IRR. The formulae is as follows:

$$IRR = LDF\% + \left[\Delta DF \frac{LDPV - OI}{LDPV - HDPV} \right]$$

Where, LDF = Discount factor of low trial

ΔDF = Difference between low discounting factor and High discounting factor

LDPV= PV of cash inflows at low discounting factor trial

HDPV = PV of cash inflows at high discounting factor trial

OI = Original investment

Or

$$IRR = A + \frac{C - 0}{C - D} \times (B - A)$$

Where,

A = Discounted factor of low trial

B = Discounted factor of high trial

C = Present value of cash inflow in the low trial

D = Present value of cash inflow in the high trial

O = Original or initial outlay

Accept-Reject Rule

Acceptance or reject rule of the project decides based upon the calculated IRR and Cost of capital (Ko).

Accepted: IRR > Cost of capital (Ko)

Reject: IRR < Cost of capital (Ko)

Consider IRR = Cost of capital (Ko)

MERITS OF IRR

1. IRR attempts to find the maximum rate of interest at which funds invested in the project could be repaid out of the cash inflows arising from that project.

2. It considers the time value of money.

3. It considers cash flows thought out the life of the project.

4. It is not in conflict with the concept of maximizing the welfare of the equity shareholders.

5. It is calculated by the method of trial and error, usually it gives more psychological satisfaction to the user.

6. It is consistent with the objective of shareholders; wealth maximization.

DEMERITS OF IRR

1. Calculation of IRR is quite tedious and it is difficult to understand.

2. Both NPV and IRR assume that the cash inflows can be reinvested at the discounting rate in the new project. However, reinvestment of funds at the cut-off rate is more appropriate than at the IRR. Hence, NPV method is more reliable than IRR to ranking two or more projects.

3. It implies that profits can be reinvested at internal rate of return, which is not logical.

4. It produces multiple rate of returns which can be confusing.

5. It does not help in the evaluation of mutually exclusive projects, since a project with highest IRR would be selected. However, in practice, it may not turn out to be the one, that is the most profitable and consistent with the objective of shareholders i.e. wealth maximization.

6. It may not give fruitful results in case of unequal projects life, unequal cash outflows, and difference in the timing of cash flows.

7. It may give results inconsistent with NPV method. This is especially true in case of mutually exclusive projects, i.e, projects where acceptance of one would result in the rejection of the other. Such conflict of results arises due to the following.

   i.   Differences in cash outlays
   ii. Unequal lives of projects
   iii. Different pattern of cash flows.

COMPARE AND CONTRAST 'NPV' WITH 'IRR'

NPV and IRR are the discounted cash flow methods available for evaluation of capital budgeting projects. These are similar in certain respects. In certain situations, they would give same (accept or reject) decision. But they differ in the sense, that the results regarding the choice of assets are under certain circumstances mutually contradictory. The comparison of these methods is therefore, involves a discussion of (a) Similarities between the methods, and (b) Differences.

NPV with IRR: Similarities

- The two methods use cash inflows after tax (CFAT).

- Both the methods take into consideration the time value of money.

- They consider CFAT throughout the projects life period.

- Both methods give consistent results in terms of acceptance or rejection of investment proposals in certain situations. That is, if a project is viable it will be indicated by both the methods. If a project is not qualified, both methods will indicate that it should be rejected.

- The situations in which the two methods will give a concurrent accept or reject decision will be in respect of conventional and independent projects.

- According to NPV the decision rule is that a project will be accepted if NPV is greater than zero, the IRR would support projects where IRR is greater than the cost of capita (Ko).

NPV with IRR: Differences

- In case of mutually exclusive projects, if NPV method accepts the project while IRR rejects.
- If there is a size disparity the NPV and the IRR will give different rankings.
- When there is an incremental approach, the NPV method is superior to the IRR, because the former supports projects, which are compatible with the goal of shareholders wealth maximization while the latter does not.
- When there is time disparity the NPV would give results superior to the IRR method.
- In Projects with unequal lives, NPV and IRR would give conflicting ranking to mutually exclusive projects.

Comparison of NPV and IRR Methods:

NPV Method	IRR Method
1. Interest rate is a known factor	1. Interest rate is an unknown factor
2. It involves computation of the amount that can be invested in a given project so that the anticipated earnings will be sufficient to repay this amount with market rate of interest.	2. It attempts to find out the maximum rate of interest at which funds are invested in the project. Earnings from the project in the form of cash flow will help us to get back the funds already invested.
3.It assumes that the cash inflows can be reinvested at the discounting rate in the new projects.	3. It also assumes that the cash inflows can be reinvested at the discounting rate in the new projects.
4. Reinvestment is assumed to be at the cut-off rate.	4. Reinvestment in funds is assumed to be at the IRR.

The Present value method always provides for correct ranking of mutually exclusive investment projects, whereas, IRR method sometimes, does not. In the latter method, the implied reinvestment rate will differ depending upon the cash flow for each investment proposal under consideration. For proposal with a high internal rate of return, a high reinvestment rate is assumed, for proposals with a low rate of return, a low reinvestment rate is assumed. The IRR calculated, may rarely represents the relevant rate as assumed and the relevant rate for reinvestment of intermediate cash flows.

(C) Profitability Index (PI) / Discounted Benefit Cost Ratio (DBCR)

This is another discounted cash flow method of evaluating investment proposals. It is also known as discounted benefit cost ratio method. It is similar to NPV method. It is the ratio of the present value of cash inflows, at the required rate of return, to the initial cash outflow of the investment proposal. PI method measures the present value of future cash per rupee, where as NPV is based on the difference between present value of cash inflows and present value of cash outflows. NPV method is not reliable to evaluate projects requiring unequal initial investments. PI method provides solution to this problem. PI is the ratio, which is derived by dividing present value of cash inflows by present value of cash outflows.

PI is the ratio of present value of future cash benefits at the required rate of return at the initial cash outflow of the investment.

$$PI = \frac{PV \text{ of cash inflows}}{Initial \text{ cash outlay}}$$

Like IRR and NPV methods, profitability index is a conceptually sound method of appraising investment projects. It provides ready comparisons between investment proposals of different magnitudes.

Accept-Reject Rule

Accept: PI > 1   **Reject:** PI < 1   **Considered:** PI = 1

Characteristics of Sound Investment Criterion

The characteristics should be possessed by a sound investment criterion.

(i)   It should consider all cash flows to determine the true profitability,

(ii) It should provide for an objective and unambiguous way of separating good projects from bad projects,

(iii) It should help ranking of projects according to their true profitability,

(iv) It should recognize the fact that bigger cash flows are preferable to smaller ones and early cash flows are preferable to later ones,

(v)   It should help to choose among mutually exclusive projects that particular project which maximizes the shareholders' wealth,

(vi) It should be a criteria, which is applicable to any conceivable investment project independent of others.

Merits of PI

The PI Method satisfies almost all the requirements of a sound investment criterion. The characteristic, as we recollect are:

● It gives due consideration to time value of money.

● It considers all cash flows to determine PI.

● It help to rank projects according to their PI.

● It recognizes the fact that bigger cash flows are better than smaller ones and early cash flows are preferable to later ones.

● It can also be used to choose mutually exclusive projects by calculating the incremental benefit cost ratio.

● It is consistent with the objectives maximization of shareholders' wealth.

Illustration 16

The initial cash outlay of a project is Rs. 50000 and it generates cash inflows of Rs. 10000, Rs. 20000, Rs. 30000 and Rs. 10000. Assume 10% rate of discount. Find Pl.

Solution:

Computation of PI

Year 1	Cash inflow 2	Present Value Factor @ 10%	Present Value of Cash inflow
1	10000	0.909	9090
2	20000	0.826	16520
3	30000	0.751	22530
4	10000	0.683	6830
		Total	**54970**

$$PI = \frac{PV\ of\ cash\ inflows}{Initial\ cash\ outlay}$$

$$= 54970/50000 = 1.0994$$

Accept or reject criterion

Accept the project if its profitability index is greater than one. Such a project will have the positive net present value. Projects can be ranked on the basis of PI. Highest rank will be assigned to the project with highest PI, while the lowest rank will be given to the project having lowest PI.

Illustration 17: A project requires an investment of Rs.10,000 and the expected cash flows are:

1st year Rs.12,000; and 2nd year Rs.4,000

The cost of capital is 10 per cent and the PV factors at 10 per cent are 1st year-0.909, 2nd year-0.826. Compute the profitability index.

Solution:

Profitability index   = Total PV of cash inflows ÷ Initial investment

= (Rs.12,000 X 0.909 + Rs.4,000 X 0.826) ÷ 10,000

= 14,212 ÷ 10,000 =1.42

It indicates that for every one rupee investment, there is (1.42-1) 0.42 paise profit.

Illustration 18

The initial cash outlay of a project is Rs.1,00,000 and it generates cash inflows of Rs.40,000, Rs.30,000, Rs.50,000 and Rs.20,000. Assume a 10 per cent rate of discount. Calculate Profitability index.

Solution

Calculation of Profitability Index

Year	CFAT (Rs.)	DF 10%	Present Values (Rs.)
1	40,000	0.909	36,360
2	30,000	0.826	24,780
3	50,000	0.751	37,550
4	20,000	0.683	13,660
PV of Cash inflows			1,12,350

Profitability Index = PV of cash inflows ÷ Initial investment= 1,12,350 ÷1,00,000 = **1.12**

TAXATION AND CAPITAL BUDGETING

Inflation and capital budgeting

Inflation - its expectations and its effects

When a manager evaluates a project, or when a shareholder evaluates his/her investments, he/she can only guess what the rate of inflation will be. These guesses will probably be wrong, at least to some extent, as it is extremely difficult to forecast the rate of inflation accurately. The only way in which uncertainty about inflation can be allowed for in project evaluation is by risk and uncertainty analysis. Inflation may be general, that is, affecting prices of all kinds, or specific to particular prices. Generalised inflation has the following effects:

(a) Inflation will mean higher costs and higher selling prices. It is difficult to predict the effect of higher selling prices on demand. A company that raises its prices by 30%, because the general rate of inflation is 30%, might suffer a serious fall in demand.

(b) Inflation, as it affects financing needs, is also going to affect gearing, and so the cost of capital.

(c) Since fixed assets and stocks will increase in money value, the same quantities of assets must be financed by increasing amounts of capital. If the future rate of inflation can be predicted with some degree of accuracy, the management can work out how much extra finance the company will need and take steps to obtain the same, e.g. by increasing retention of earnings, or borrowing.

However, if the future rate of inflation cannot be predicted with a certain amount of accuracy, then management should estimate what it is likely to be and accordingly make plans to obtain the extra finance. Provisions should also be made to obtain access to 'contingency funds' should the rate of inflation exceed expectations, e.g. a higher bank overdraft facility might be arranged, should the need arise.

Many different proposals have been made for accounting for inflation. Two systems known as "Current purchasing power" (CPP) and "Current cost accounting" (CCA) have been suggested.

CPP is a system of accounting that makes adjustments to income and capital values to allow for the general rate of price inflation.

CCA is a system that takes account of specific price inflation (i.e. changes in the prices of specific assets or groups of assets), but not of general price inflation. It involves adjusting accounts to reflect the current values of assets owned and used.

At present, there is very little measure of agreement as to the best approach to the problem of 'accounting for inflation'. Accountancy bodies are still debating both these approaches.

Illustration 65: On Inflation Delta Corporation is considering two capital expenditure proposals. Both proposals are for similar products and both are expected to operate for four years. Only one proposal can be accepted.

The following information is available:

Profit/(loss)		
	Proposal A	**Proposal B**
	$ or Rs	$ or Rs
Initial investment	46,000	46,000
Year 1	6,500	4,500
Year 2	3,500	2,500
Year 3	13,500	4,500
Year 4	Loss 1,500	Profit 14,500
Estimated scrap value at the end of Year 4	4,000	4,000

Depreciation is charged on a straight-line basis. Problem:

(a) Calculate the following for both proposals: i) the payback period to one decimal place ii) the average rate of return on initial investment, to one decimal place.

Allowing for inflation

So far, the effect of inflation has not been considered on the appraisal of capital investment proposals. Inflation is particularly important in developing countries, as the rate of inflation tends to be rather high. As inflation rate increases, so will the minimum return required by an investor. For example, one might be happy with a return of 10% with zero inflation, but if inflation was 20%, one would expect a much greater return.

Illustration 66: Keymer Farm is considering investing in a project with the following cash flows:

TIME	ACTUAL CASH FLOWS
	Z$
0	(100,000)
1	90,000
2	80,000
3	70,000

Keymer Farm requires a minimum return of 40% under the present conditions. Inflation is currently running at 30% a year, and this is expected to continue indefinitely. Should Keymer Farm go ahead with the project?

Solutions:

Let us take a look at Keymer Farm's required rate of return. If it invested $10,000 for one year on 1 January, then on 31 December it would require a minimum return of $4,000. With the initial investment of $10,000, the total value of the investment by 31 December must increase to $14,000. During the year, the purchasing value of the dollar would fall due to inflation. We can restate the amount received on 31 December in terms of the purchasing power of the dollar at 1 January as follows:

Amount received on 31 December in terms of the value of the dollar on 1 January:

$$= \frac{\$14,000}{(1.30)^1}$$

$$= \$10,769$$

In terms of the value of the dollar or rupee at 1 January, Keymer Farm would make a profit of $769, which represents a rate of return of 7.69% in "today's money" terms. This is known as the real rate of return. The required rate of 40% is a money rate of return (sometimes known as a nominal rate of return). The money rate measures the return in terms of the dollar, which is falling in value. The real rate measures the return in constant price level terms. The two rates of return and the inflation rate are linked by the equation:

(1 + money rate) = (1 + real rate) x (1 + inflation rate)

where all the rates are expressed as proportions. In the above case ,

(1 + 0.40) = (1 + 0.0769) x (1 + 0.3)

= 1.40

So, which rate is used in discounting? As a rule of thumb: a) If the cash flows are expressed in terms of actual dollars that will be received or paid in the future, the money rate for discounting should be used.

(b)   If the cash flows are expressed in terms of the value of the rupee or dollar at time 0 (i.e. in constant price level terms), the real rate of discounting should be used.

In the above questions (in Keymer Farm's case), the cash flows are expressed in terms of the actual dollars that will be received or paid at the relevant dates. Therefore, we should discount them using the money rate of return.

TIME	CASH FLOW	DISCOUNT FACTOR	PV
	$	40%	$
0	(150,000)	1.000	(100,000)
1	90,000	0.714	64,260
2	80,000	0.510	40,800
3	70,000	0.364	25,480
			30,540

The project has a positive net present value of Rs or $30,540, so Keymer Farm should go ahead with the project. The future cash flows can be re-expressed in terms of the value of the dollar or rupee at time 0 as follows, given inflation at 30% a year:

TIME	ACTUAL CASH FLOW	CASH FLOW AT TIME 0 PRICE LEVEL	
	$ / Rs	$ / Rs.	
0	(100,000)	(100,000)	
1	90,000	$90,000 \times \dfrac{1}{1.30^1} =$	69,231
2	80,000	$80,000 \times \dfrac{1}{1.30^2} =$	47,337
3	70,000	$70,000 \times \dfrac{1}{1.30^3} =$	31,862

The cash flows expressed in terms of the value of the dollar at time 0 can now be discounted using the real value of 7.69%.

TIME	CASH FLOW	DISCOUNT FACTOR	PV
	$/Rs	7.69%	$/Rs
0	(100,000)	1.000	(100,000)
1	69,231	$\dfrac{1}{(1.0769)^1}$	64,246
2	47,337	$\dfrac{1}{(1.0769)^2}$	40,804
3	31,862	$\dfrac{1}{(1.0769)^3}$	25,490
			30,540

The NPV is the same as before.

MULTINATIONAL COMPANIES AND CAPITAL BUDGETING

Multinational companies are constantly acquiring and disposing of assets globally in the normal course of business. Shareholder wealth is created when the MNC makes an investment that will return more (in present value terms) than what it costs. Among the most important decisions that MNC managers face is the choice of capital projects globally. These investments will determine the firm's competitive position in the marketplace, its overall profitability, and, ultimately, its long-run survival.

Multinational capital budgeting, like domestic capital budgeting, focuses on the cash flows of prospective long-term investment projects. It is used both in traditional foreign direct investment analysis, such as the construction of a chain of retail stores in another country, as well as cross-border mergers and acquisitions activity. Capital budgeting for a foreign project uses the same net present value (NPV) discounted cash flow model used in domestic capital budgeting. However, multinational capital budgeting is considerably more complex due to a number of additional factors that need to be considered.

Factors influencing multinational companies' capital budgeting are as follows

1. *Parent versus project cash flows:* Parent (that is, home-country) cash flows must be distinguished from project (that is, host-country) cash flows. While parent cash flows reflect all cash flow consequences for the consolidated entity, project cash flows look only at the single country where the project is located. For example, cash flows generated by an investment in Spain may be partly or wholly taken away from one in Italy, with the end

result that the net present value of the investment is positive from the Spanish affiliate's point of view, but contributes little to the firm's world-wide cash flows.

2. *Financing versus operating cash flows:* In multinational investment projects, the type of financing package is often critical in making otherwise unattractive projects attractive to the parent company. Thus, cash may flow back to the parent because the project is structured to generate such flows via royalties, licensing fees, dividends, and so on. Unlike in domestic capital budgeting, operating cash flows cannot be kept separate from financing decisions.

3. *Foreign currency fluctuations:* Another added complexity in multinational capital budgeting is the significant effect that fluctuating exchange rates can have on the prospective cash flows generated by the investment. From the parent's perspective, future cash flows abroad have value only in terms of the exchange rate at the date of repatriation. In conducting the analysis, it is necessary to forecast future exchange rates and to conduct sensitivity analysis of the project's viability under various exchange rates scenarios.

4. *Long-term inflation rates:* Differing rates of national inflation and their potential effect on competitiveness must be considered. Inflation will have the following effects on the value of the project: a) it will impact the local operating cash flows both in terms of the prices of inputs and outputs and also in terms of the sales volume depending on the price elasticity of the product, b) it will impact the parent's cash flow by affecting the foreign exchange rates, c) it will affect the real cost of financing choices between foreign and domestic sources of capital.

5. *Subsidised financing:* In situations where a host government provides subsidised project financing at below-market rates, the value of that subsidy must be explicitly considered in the capital budgeting analysis. If a company uses the subsidised rates in the analysis, there is an implicit assumption that the subsidy will exist through the life of the project. Another approach might be to incorporate the subsidised interest rates into the analysis by including the present value of the subsidy rather than adjusting the cost of capital.

6. *Political risk:* This is another factor that can significantly impact the viability and profitability of foreign projects. Whether it be through democratic elections or as a result of sudden developments such as political upheavals or military coups, changes in a country's government can affect the attitude in that country towards foreign investors and investments. This can affect the future cash flows of a project in that country in a variety of ways. Political developments may also affect the life and the terminal value of foreign investments.

7. *Terminal values:* While terminal values of long-term projects are difficult to estimate even in the domestic context, they become far more difficult in the multinational context due to the added complexity from some of the factors discussed above. An added dimension is that potential acquirers may have widely divergent perspectives on the value to them of

acquiring the terminal assets. This is particularly relevant if the assets are located in a country that is economically segmented due to a host of restrictions on cross-border flow of physical or financial assets.

In conducting multinational capital budgeting analyses from a parent's perspective, the additional risk arising from projects located abroad can be handled in at least two ways. One possibility is to add a foreign risk premium to the discount rate that would be used for a domestic project.

This higher rate is intended to capture the additional uncertainties arising from exchange risk, political risk, inflation, and such factors. The second possibility is to adjust the cash flows for the foreign projects to reflect the additional risk. The discount rate stays the same as for domestic projects. Thus, the additional complexities resulting from doing business abroad must be incorporated in the analysis through adjustments to either the discount rate or the projected cash flows. Rather than make these adjustments arbitrarily, firms can use wide-ranging publicly available data, historical analysis, and professional advice to make reasonable decisions.

Incorporating Country Risk in Capital Budgeting

Adjustment of the discount rate

- The higher the perceived risk, the higher the discount rate that should be applied to the project's cash flows.

  Adjustment of the estimated cash flows

- By estimating how each form of risk could affect the cash flows, the MNC can determine the probability distribution of the net present value of the project

SUMMARY

- Modern financial manager's function is efficient allocation of capital among available investment opportunities. The investment opportunity may be long-term investment or fixed assets; short–term or current assets.

- One of the important problems confronting the top management of a firm is to determine whether the firm should invest funds in fixed assets. Fixed assets may be tangible as well as intangible. While the former represent assets like land and buildings, plant and machinery and, furniture and fixtures, the latter group consists of copyrights, patents and goodwill.

- Capital budgeting is the firm's decision to invest its current funds most efficiently in the long-term assets in anticipation of an expected flow of benefits over a series of years.

- Capital budgeting decisions are important since growth of the firm depends on fixed assets, it is a more risky decision as huge investments are involved, an irreversible decision, it has effect on other projects too, a and difficult decision (became the decision is based on future years cash inflows, and involves uncertainty of future and hence more risk).

- Capital budgeting decisions are very important, but they pose difficulties, which shoot form three principle sources: measurement problem, uncertainty, and temporal spread.

- The capital budgeting process may be more or less depended on the type of the project. So firm normally classify the projects into different categories. It may differ from one firm to another firm, but the most important classification of projects are: new projects, expansion projects, diversification projects, replacement and modernization projects, research and development projects, interior decoration, recreational facilities, executive aircrafts, landscaped gardens etc.

- The process of Capital budgeting may be divided into six broad phases / steps. They are: (1) planning or idea generation, (2) evaluation / analysis, (3) selection, (4) financing, (5) execution / implementation, and (6) performance review.

- The methods of evaluation capital investment play a vital role, since the selection of profitable project will help to maximize value of the firm through the maximization of profits. Project evaluation involves market analysis, financial analysis, technical analysis, economic analysis, and ecological analysis. In financial analysis after estimation of the cash flows and required rate of return on the project, the next step is evaluation of various investment alternatives and selection of the most profitable project.

- A wide range of criteria has been suggested to judge the worthwhileness of investment projects. They are divided into two broad categories, viz., (I) Traditional techniques or non-discounted techniques and (II) Modern techniques or discounted cash flow techniques. The traditional techniques are further subdivided into two, such as (a) Pay back period, and (b) Accounting rate of return or average rate of return (ARR). The discounted cash flow techniques are again subdivided into three, such as (A) Net present value (NPV) technique, (B) Internal rate of return (IRR) or trial and error technique, and (C) Profitability index (PI) of benefit cost ratio (BCR).

- Pay back period is that period required to recover the original cash outflow invested in a project. It can be calculated in two ways, First, using formula and the second, cumulative cash flow method. The first method can be applied only when the cash flows stream is uniform for all the years. Symbolically Pay Back Period = Original Investment ÷ Constant Annual Cash Flows After Taxes. The Second method is applied when the cash flows stream is unequal. In this situation, pay back period is calculated through the process of cumulative cash flows, cumulative process goes up to the period where, cumulative cash flows equal to the actual cash outflows. Acceptance or rejection of the project are decided based on the comparison of calculated PBP with the standard pay back period. If a Cal PBP < Standard PBP then, the project is accepted and vice versa. A project is considered when the Cal PBP = Standard PBP.

- The main merits of PBP are: cost involvement in calculating pay back period is very less. But it suffers from serious shortcomings it ignores cash flows after pay back period, it does not consider all cash inflows yielded by the investment, it does not take into consideration time value of money, there is no rationale basis for setting a minimum pay back period, and it is not consistent with the objective of maximizing shareholders 'wealth.

- Accounting Rate of Return (ARR) method uses accounting information as revealed by financial statements, to measure the profitability of the investment proposals. It is also known as the return on investment (ROI). Some times it is known as average rate of return (ARR). Average annual earnings after taxes are used to calculate ARR. It is measured in terms of percentage. ARR is calculated in two ways. One, whenever it is clearly mentioned as accounting rate of return. Average annual EAT is divided by original investment (original investment + additional net working capital) and multiplied by 100 to get accounting rate of return. Second, whenever it is clearly mentioned as average rate of return. Average annual EAT is divided by average investment [1/2 (Original investment – scrap) +additional NWC + scrap value and multiplied by 100 to get average rate of return. Acceptance or reject of the project decides are based on the predetermined rate or cutoff rate. A project is accepted when the Cal. ARR > Cut off rate and vice versa. A project is considered when the Cal ARR = Cut off rate.

- ARR is very simple to calculate, information can easily be drawn from accounting records, it takes into account all profits of the projects life period, cost involvement in calculating pay back period is very less. However, it suffers from some disadvantages: it uses accounting profits, instead of actual cash flows after taxes, it ignores the concept of time value of money, it does not allow the fact that the profits can be reinvested, it does not differentiate between the size of the investment required for each project, it is incompatible with the objective of wealth maximization.

- Discounted cash flow techniques take into consideration almost all the deficiencies of the traditional methods. Net present value (NPV) is the present value benefits minus present value of costs. Symbolically:

$$NPV = \frac{n \cdot NIFt}{t = 1(1+k_0)^t} - II$$

NPV may be positive or negative. The decision rule of NPV: accept the project when NPV>0, and vice versa. Project is considered when NPV = 0.

- NPV is the most acceptable method with comparison to traditional methods due to it: if considers time value of money; uses entire life period cash inflows, is useful for the selection of mutually exclusive projects, takes into consideration the changing discount rate, and is consistent with the objective of maximization. But it suffers from some limitations: it is difficult to calculate, calculation of required rate is difficult, in case of projects involving different cash outlays, NPV method may not give dependable results, and it does not give satisfactory results when the comparison involves two projects with different life periods.

- Internal rate of return (IRR) is that discounting factor at which the present value of cash inflows equals to the present value of cash outflows. Symbolically:

$$IRR = \frac{n \, CIFt}{t = 1(1+k_0)^t} + \frac{CIFn + SVn}{(1+k_0)^n} - II$$

Computation of IRR is based on the cash flows after taxes. In this method, the evaluator selects any discount rate to compute present value of cash inflows. Generally cost of capital is taken as first trial. If calculated present value of the cash inflows is higher than the present value cash outflows then evaluator has to try at higher rate and vice versa. This process will be repeated till the present value of cash inflows equals to the present value of cash outflows. Generally, IRR may lies between two discounting factors; in that case analyst has to use interpolation formula for calculation of IRR. The formulae-

$$IRR = LDF\% + \left[\Delta DF \frac{LDPV - OI}{LDPV - HDPV} \right]$$

Project should be accepted if the IRR > K_o and vice versa. When IRR = K_o the project should be considered.

- IRR is a theoretically sound for evaluating capital expenditure projects. It has the advantages offered by the NPV method. But theoretical soundness is not withstanding due to some serious limitations: it is difficult to calculate, it assumes that profits can be reinvested at internal rate of return, which is not logical, it produces multiple rate of returns that can be confusing, it does not help in the evaluation of mutually exclusive projects, it may not give fruitful results in case of unequal projects life, unequal cash outflows, and difference in the timing of cash flows.

- NPV and IRR are similar in certain respects and also differ in certain respects. (a) Similarities between methods: the two methods use cash inflows after tax, considers the time value of money, considers CFAT throughout projects life period, gives consistent results in terms of acceptance or rejection of investment proposals in certain situations. That is if a project is viable it will be indicated by both the methods, concurrent accept or reject decision will be in respect of conventional and independent projects, decision rule is almost same (return base). (b) NPV with IRR- differences occur; in case of mutually exclusive projects if NPV method accepts the project while IRR rejects, if there is a size disparity the NPV and IRR will give different rankings, when there is an incremental approach, the NPV method is superior to the IRR, when there is time disparity the NPV would give results superior to the IRR method, In projects with unequal lives, NPV and IRR would give conflicting ranking to mutually exclusive projects.

- PI method measures the resent value of future cash per rupee. Present value of cash inflows is divided by present value of cash outflows to get PI. Using the PI method, a project will qualify for acceptance if PI > 1, and vice versa. It is considered when PI = 1.

PRACTICE YOURSELF SOLVED PROBLEMS

1. What is the present value of Rs.10,000 at the end of second year at a discount rate of 10 per cent?

Solution:

PV of Rs.10,000 at the end of second year = 10,000 × 0.826 = **Rs.8,260**

2. What is the present value of Rs.40,000 due, three years hence at a discount rate of 10 per cent?

Solution:

PV of Rs.40,000 at the end of three years = 40,000 × 0.751 = Rs.30,040

3. What is the present value of Rs. 30,000 due, three years hence at a discount of 10 per cent?

Solution:

Formula for calculation of discount factor $= [1 \div 1 + r]^n$

Discount Factor at 10 per cent $= [1 \div 1+0.10]^3 = 0.751$

Present Value of Rs.30, 000 = Rs.30, 000 × 0.751 = Rs. 22,530

4. Which amount is worth more at 12 per cent Rs.10, 000 in hand today or Rs.15, 000 due after 5 years.

Solution:

A rupee received today is more valuable than a rupee received tomorrow. Based on the time value of money, Rs. 10,000 in hand today is worth more than the Rs.15,000 due after 5 years.

Computation of Present Value

Cash Flows (in Rs)	DF12 %	Present Value (in Rs.)
10,000	1.00	10,000
15,000	0.567	8,505

Rs. 10,000 today is more valuable than Rs. 15,000 due after 5 years because the value of Rs.15, 000 after 5 years is only **Rs.8,505**.

5. After conducting a survey that cost Rs.2,00,000, X Ltd., decided to undertake a project for placing a new product on the market. The company's cut-off rate is 12 per cent. It was estimated that the project would cost Rs.40,00,000 in plant and machinery in addition to working capital of Rs.10,00,000. The scrap value of plant and machinery at the end of 5 years was estimated at Rs.5,00,000. After providing for depreciation on straight-line basis, profits after tax were estimated as follows:

Year	1	2	3	4	5
PAT (Rs.)	3,00,000	8,00,000	13,00,000	5,00,000	4,00,000

Ascertain the net present value of the projects with 12% cost of capital.

Solution:

Working Note 1 Calculation of Cash outflows

	Rs.
Cost of Equipment	40,00,000
Add: Survey Cost	2,00,000
Additional Working Capital	10,00,000
	52,00,000

Calculation of NPV

Year	PAT (Rs.)	CFAT (Rs.)	DF 12%	Present Values (Rs.)
1	3,00,000	10,40,000	0.893	9,28,720
2	8,00,000	15,40,000	0.797	12,27,380
3	13,00,000	20,40,000	0.712	14,52,480
4	5,00,000	12,40,000	0.636	7,88,640
5	4,00,000	11,40,000	0.567	6,46,380
		PV of cash inflows		50,43,600
	Add: PV of working capital 10,00,000 × 0.567			5,67,000
	Add: PV of Scrap value 5,00,000 × 0.567			2,83,500
	Total PV of Cash inflows			**58,94,100**
	Less: PV of cash outflows			52,00,000
	NPV			6,94,000

Working Notes 2- Depreciation: Original cost + Survey cost – Scrap value ÷ Life of machinery

$$= (40,00,000 + 2,00,000 - 5,00,000)/5 \quad = \textbf{Rs. 7,40,000}$$

Depreciation should be added to PAT of every year to get CFAT

6. A firm has two investment opportunities, each costing Rs.1,00,000 and each having an expected profit as shown below:

Year	1	2	3	4
Project X (Rs.)	50,000	40,000	30,000	10,000
Project Y (Rs.)	20,000	40,000	50,000	60,000

After giving due consideration to the risk criteria in each project, the management has decided that project A should be evaluated at a 10 per cent cost of capital and project B, a risky project with a 15 per cent cost of capital.

Compare the NPV and suggest the course of action for the management if

a) Both the projects are independent.

b) Both are mutually exclusive.

Solution:

Calculation of NPV

Year	CFAT (Rs.)		DF %		PVs (Rs.)	
	Project A	Project B	10	15	Project A	Project B
1	50,000	20,000	0.909	0.780	45,450	17,400
2	40,000	40,000	0.826	0.756	33,040	30,240
3	30,000	50,000	0.751	0.657	22,530	32,850
4	10,000	60,000	0.683	0.572	6,830	34,320
Present Value of cash inflows					1,07,850	1,14,810
Less: Cash outflows					1,00,000	1,00,000
Net Present Values (NPV)					7,850	14,810

a) If both the projects are independent, accept both the projects, as NPV of both projects are positive.

b) If both the projects are mutually exclusive, accept project B as its NPV is higher than that of Project A.

7. Bhatt petrochemicals Ltd., which has a 50 per cent tax rate and a 10 per cent after tax cost of capital, is evaluating a project, which will cost Rs.1,00,000 and will require an increase in the level of inventories and receivables of Rs.50,000 over its effective life.

The project will generate additional sales of Rs.1,00,000 and will require cash expenses of Rs.30,000 each year of its 5-year lifespan. It will depreciate on straight-line basis. What is its NPV?

Solution:

Calculation of cash inflows

Particulars	Amount (Rs.)
Sales	1,00,000
Less: Cash expenses	30,000
EBDT	70,000
Less: Depreciation	20,000
EBT	50,000
Less: Taxes at 50 per cent	25,000
EAT	25,000
Add: Depreciation	20,000
CFAT	45,000

Calculation of PVs (Rs.)

PV of Cash inflows 45,000 × 3.790	1,70,550
Add: PV of working capital 50,000 × 0.621	31,050
Total PV of cash inflows	2,01,600
Less: PV of cash outflows (1,00,000 + 50,000)	1,50,000
NPV	51,600

8. A project costs an initial investment of Rs.40,000 and is expected to generate annual cash inflows of Rs.16,000 for 4 years. Calculate IRR.

Solution:

Fake pay back period = Initial investment ÷ Avg. Annual cash inflow = 40,000 ÷ 16,000 = 2.5

Referring to the PV of an annuity of one rupee table, we find that the fake pay back period of 2.5 lies in between 21 per cent (2.540) and 22 per cent (2.494) in the line of 4 years.

Calculation of PV of cash inflows

PV of cash inflows at 21 per cent = 16,000 × 2.540 = 40,640

PV of cash inflows at 22 per cent = 16,000 × 2.494 = 39,904

Calculation of IRR

$$IRR = LDF\% + \left[\Delta DF \frac{LDPV - OI}{LDPV - HDPV}\right]$$

$$IRR = 21 + \left[1 \frac{40,640 - 40,000}{40,640 - 39,904}\right]$$

$$IRR = 21 + \left[1 \frac{640}{736}\right] = 21 + 0.87 = 21.87 \text{ per cent}$$

9. There are two alternative machines. You are asked to compute the profitability of the investment on the basis of payback profitability.

	Machine X Rs.	Machine Y Rs.
Purchase price	25,000	42,000
Estimated life (years)	8	10
Net earnings (after tax but before Depreciation p.a.)	5,000	6,000

Solution:

Calculation of payback profitability

PBP =   Initial investment ÷ Constant Annual cash inflows

Machine X =Rs.25,000 ÷ 5,000 = 5 Years;   Machine Y =Rs.42,000 ÷ 6,000 = 7 Years

Post payback period = (Life of machine – payback period)

Payback profitability:

Machine X =(5,000×3)=**Rs.15,000**   ;   **Machine Y** = (6,000×3) = **Rs. 18,000**

10. X Ltd., is considering the purchase of a new machine, which will carry out some operations at present performed by labourer. Two alternative models A and B are available for the purpose. From the following information, prepare a profitability statement for submission to the management and calculate PBP.

	Machine A Rs.	Machine B Rs.
Estimated life (Years)	5	6
Cost of Machine (Rs.)	80,000	1, 50,000
Estimated additional cost (Rs.)		
Indirect material (p.a)	2,000	3,000
Maintenance (p.m)	500	750
Supervision (per quarter)	3,000	4,500
Estimated savings in scrap (p.a.)	8,000	12,000
Estimated savings in direct wages		
a. Workers not required	10	15
b. Wages per worker p.a.	7,200	7,200

Depreciation is calculated under straight-line method. Taxation may be taken at 50 per cent of net profit (net savings).

Solution:

(PROFITABILITY STATEMENT)

Particulars	Machine A (Rs.)	Machine B (Rs.)
Estimated savings p.a.		
Scrap	8,000	12,000
Direct Wages: A - 10x7,200 ; B – 15 x 7,200	72,000	1,08,000
Total savings	**80,000**	**1, 20,000**

contd...

Additional costs			
Indirect material		2,000	3,000
Maintenance: A – 500 × 12 ; B – 750 × 12		6,000	9,000
Supervision: A – 3,000 × 4 ; B – 4500 × 4		12,000	18,000
Total cost		**20,000**	**30,000**
Net savings (EBDT)	(Savings – cost)	**60,000**	**90,000**
Less: Depreciation		16,000	25,000
EBT		**44,000**	**65,000**
Less: Taxes at 50 per cent		22,000	32,500
EAT		**22,000**	**32,500**
Add: Depreciation		16,000	25,000
Annual cash inflow (CFAT)		**38,000**	**57,500**

PBP = Initial investment ÷ Constant annual cash inflows

Machine A =Rs.80,000 ÷ 38,000 = **2.1 Years**

Machine B =Rs.1,50,000 ÷ 57,500 = **2.61 Years**

Depreciation: Machine A=Rs.80,000÷5=**Rs. 16,000; Machine B**=Rs.1,50,000÷6=**Rs. 25,000**

11. The following two projects A and B require an investment of Rs. 2, 00,000 each. The income after taxes for these projects is as follows:

Year	Project A (in Rs.)	Project B (in Rs.)
1	80,000	20,000
2	80,000	40,000
3	40,000	40,000
4	20,000	40,000
5	-------	60,000
6	-----	60,000

Using the following criteria, determine which of the project is preferable:

(i) 8 years pay back; (ii) Average Rate of Return

(iii) Present value approach if the company's cost of capital is 10 per cent

Solution:

Note 1: Depreciation = Initial cost – Salvage value ÷ Life period

Project A: (Rs.2,00,000 – 0) ÷ 4 = **Rs.50,000; Project B:** (Rs.2,00,000 – 0) ÷ 6 = **Rs.33,333**

Calculation of Cash inflows

Year	Project A			Project B		
	EAT (Rs.)	Cash inflow (Rs.)	Cumulative CFAT (Rs.)	EAT (Rs.)	Cash inflow (Rs.)	Cumulative CFAT (Rs.)
1	80,000	1,30,000	1,30,000	20,000	53,333	53,333
2	80,000	1,30,000	2,60,000	40,000	73,333	1,26,666
3	40,000	90,000	3,50,000	40,000	73,333	1,99,999
4	20,000	70,000	4,20,000	40,000	73,333	2,73,332
5	-------	--------	--------	60,000	93,333	3,66,665
6	-------	--------	--------	60,000	93,333	4,59,998

i) **Initial investment** = 2, 00,000

PBP: Project A: 1+ (70,000÷1,30,000) = 1.54 Years;   **Project B** = 3 years

Decision: Based on 8 years pay back both the projects should be selected. Project A should be selected since the PBP is less than the 8 years pay back period which is to be considered as standard pay back period and also because its pay back period is less than Project B.

ii) **Computation of Average Rate of Return = (**Annual Avg. IAT ÷ Average investment) 100

   Annual Average Income (AAI)= Total EAT ÷ No. of years

   Project A: 2,20,000 ÷ 4 = Rs.55,000;

   Average Investment = 2,00,000 ÷ 2 = Rs.1,00,000

   Average rate of return = (55,000 / 1,00,000)100 = **55** per cent

Project B: AAI = 2,60,000 ÷ 6 = Rs. 43.333

   Average investment = 2,00,000 ÷ 2 = Rs. 1,00,000

   Average rate of return = (43,333/1,00,000)100 = **43.33** per cent

Decision: Project A should be selected since its ARR is greater than the Project B.

iii) **Computation of Net Present Value (NPV)**

Year	CFAT (in Rs.)		DF 10 %	PV's (in Rs.)	
	Project A	Project B		Project A	Project B
1	1,30,000	53,333	0.909	1,18,170	48,480
2	1,30,000	73,333	0.826	1,07,380	60,573
3	90,000	73,333	0.751	67,590	55,073
4	70,000	73,333	0.683	47,810	50,086
5	--------	93,333	0.621	--------	57,960
6	--------.	93,333	0.564	------	52,640
	Present Value of cash inflows			**3,40,950**	**3,24,812**
	Less: Cash outflows			2,00,000	2,00,000
	Net Present Values (**NPV**)			**1,40,950**	**1,24,812**

Decision: Based on NPV both the Projects A and B are eligible to be accepted. However, Project A is preferable since its NPV is more than that of Project B.

12. A company is considering an investment proposal to install a new machine. The project will cost Rs. 50,000 and will have life and no salvage value. Tax rate is 50 per cent, the company follows straight-line method of depreciation. The net income before depreciation and tax is as follows:

Year	1	2	3	4	5
NIBDT (Rs.)	10,000	11,000	14,000	15,000	25,000

Evaluate the project using:

(a) PBP (b) ARR (c) NPV at 10 per cent and (d) PI at 10 per cent

Solution:

CALCULATION OF CFAT (RS.)

Year	EBDT (Rs.)	EBT (Rs.) (EBDT-Dep.)	EAT (Rs.) (EBT-Tax)	CFAT (Rs.) (EAT+Dep.)	Cumulative CFAT (Rs.)
1	10,000	-	-	10,000	10,000
2	11,000	1,000	500	10,500	20,500
3	14,000	4,000	2,000	12,000	32,500
4	15,000	5,000	2,500	12,500	45,000
5	25,000	15,000	7,500	17,500	62,500

Note: **Depreciation** = (Original cost – Salvage value) ÷ Life period

= (Rs. 50,000 – 0) ÷5 = Rs. 10,000

(a) Calculation of Pay back period:

Pay Back Period = 4+ (5,000 / 17,500) = **4.29 years**

(b) Computation of ARR: (Annual Average Income After Tax ÷ Average Investment) 100

Annual Average Income = 12,500÷5 = **Rs. 2,500**

Average Investment = 50,000÷2 = **Rs.25,000**

ARR = (2,500÷25,000)100 = **10 per cent**

(c) Computation of Net Present Value (NPV)

Year	CFAT (Rs.)	DF 10 %	PVs (Rs.)
1	10,000	0.909	9,090
2	10,500	0.826	8,673
3	12,000	0.751	9,012
4	12,500	0.683	8,538
5	17,500	0.621	10,868
Present Value of cash inflows			**46,181**
Less: Cash outflows			50,000
Net Present Value (-)			**3,819**

(d) Computation of Profitability Index (PI): PV of cash inflows ÷ Initial investment

= Rs. 46,181 ÷ 50,000 = **0.92 paise**

PI indicates that for every one rupee of investment the project will generate only 0.92 paise, in other words the project will incur a loss of 0.08 paise for every one rupee of investment.

13. ABC limited has under consideration two mutually exclusive proposals for the purchase of new equipment.

Particulars	Machine X	Machine Y
Net cash outlay	1,00,000	75,000
Salvage value	Nil	Nil
Life (Years)	5	5
PBDT (Rs.)	Rs.	Rs.
1	25,000	18,000
2	30,000	20,000
3	35,000	22,000
4	25,000	20,000
5	20,000	16,000

Assuming the tax rate to be 50 per cent, suggest to the management, the best alternative using.

(a) Pay back period, (b) ARR, and (c) NPV at 10 per cent

Solution:

Computation of CFAT for Machine A

Year	EBDT (Rs.)	EBT (Rs.)	EAT (Rs.)	CFAT (Rs.)	Cumul. CFAT (Rs)
1	25,000	5,000	2,500	22,500	22,500
2	30,000	10,000	5,000	25,000	47,500
3	35,000	15,000	7,500	27,500	75,000
4	25,000	5,000	2,500	22,500	97,500
5	20,000	Nil	Nil	20,000	1,17,500

Computation of CFAT for Machine B

Year	EBDT (Rs.)	EBT (Rs.)	EAT (Rs.)	CFAT (Rs.)	Cumul. CFAT (Rs)
1	18,000	3,000	1,500	16,500	16,500
2	20,000	5,000	2,500	17,500	34,000
3	22,000	7,000	3,500	18,500	52,500
4	20,000	5,000	2,500	17,500	70,000
5	16,000	1,000	500	15,500	85,500

Note 1:Depreciation

Machine A: Initial cost – Salvage value ÷ Life period = (Rs.1,00,000 – 0) ÷ 5 = **Rs.20,000**

Machine B: Initial cost – Salvage value ÷ Life period = (Rs.75,000 – 0) ÷ 5 = **Rs.15,000**

Depreciation should be deducted from EBDT, and added back to EAT.

a) Computation of pay back period (PBP)

Machine A: 4+ (2,500 /20,000) = **4.125 years**

Machine B: 4+(5,000/ 15,500) = **4.323 years**

Decision: Based on PBP Machine A should be selected since its PBP is less than the Machine B, even though the initial investment is greater than the other Machine.

b) Computation of ARR: Annual Average Income after taxes ÷ Average Investment

Annual Average Income (AAI):

Machine A: AAI = 17,500 ÷ 5 = **Rs.3,500;**   Avg. Investment = 1,00,000 ÷ 2 = **Rs.50,000**

ARR = (3,500 ÷ Rs.50,000)100 = **7 per cent**

Machine B: AAI = 10,500÷5 = **Rs.2,100;** Avg. Investment = 75,000 ÷ 2 = **Rs. 37,500**

ARR = (2,100 ÷ Rs.37,500) 100 = **5.6 per cent**

Decision: Machine A should be selected since its ARR is greater than the Machine B.

c) Computation of Net Present Value (NPV)

Year	CFAT (Rs.)		DF 10 %	PVs (Rs.)	
	Machine A	Machine B		Machine A	Machine B
1	22,500	16,500	0.909	20,452.50	14,998.50
2	25,000	17,500	0.826	20,650.00	14,455.00
3	27,500	18,500	0.751	20,652.50	13,893.50
4	22,500	17,500	0.683	15,367.50	11,952.50
5	20,000	15,500	0.621	12,420.00	9,625.50
Present Value of cash inflows				89,542.50	64,925.00
Less: Cash outflows				1,00,000	75,000
Net Present Values (NPV)				**(-) 10,457.50**	**(-) 10,075**

Decision: Based on the NPV, both the Machine A and B should be rejected, since their NPV's are negative.

14. Zoom and Camp, a joint stock company is considering purchase of equipment. There are three alternatives available with an investment of Rs.40 lakhs as purchase consideration. The estimated life and the net cash inflow for three years is are as under:

Particulars	Machines		
	A	B	C
Estimated Life	3 years	3 years	3 years
Cash inflow (Rs. in lakhs)			
1 year	27	06	12
2 year	18	21	08
3 year	55	33	30

Which machine should be selected on the basis of pay back period? Compute the NPV for each of the machines at 15 per cent cost of capital.

Solution:

Computation of pay back period (Rs. In lakhs.)

Year	Machine A		Machine B		Machine C	
	Cash inflow	Cumul. CFAT	Cash inflow	Cumul. CFAT	Cash inflow	Cumul. CFAT
1	27	27	6	6	12	12
2	18	45	21	27	8	20
3	55	100	33	60	30	50

PBP: Machine A: 1 + (13 / 18) = **1.72 years** ; Machine B: 2 + (13 / 33) = **2.39 years**
Machine C: 2 + (20 / 30) = **2.67 ears**

Decision: Based on PBP Machine A should be selected, because its PBP is less than the other machines.

Computation of NPV

Year	Cash flows (Rs. in lakhs)			DF 15 %	PV's (Rs. in lakhs)		
	Machine A	Machine B	Machine C		Machine A	Machine B	Machine C
1	27	06	12	0.870	23.490	5.220	10.440
2	18	21	08	0.756	13.608	15.876	6.048
3	55	33	30	0.658	36.190	21.714	19.740
			PV of Cash inflows		73.288	42.810	36.228
	Less: Cash outflows				40.000	40.000	40.000
Net Present Values (**NPV**)					33.288	2.810	(-)3.772

Decision: Based on the NPV, Machine A and Machine B should be selected, since both these machines have positive NPV, but profitability point of view only Machine A should be selected, as it is generating more profit.

15. Raj Company is considering the purchase of one of the following machines whose relevant data is as follows:

Particulars	Machine - X	Machine -Y
Estimated Life (Years)	3	3
Capital cost	Rs. 90,000	Rs. 90,000
Earnings after Tax	Rs.	Rs.
1	40,000	20,000
2	50,000	70,000
3	40,000	50,000

The company follows the straight-line method of depreciation; the estimated salvage value of both the machines is zero. Assume 10 per cent cost of capital.

Show the most profitable investment based on:

(a) Pay Back Period,

(b) Accounting Rate of Return,

(c) NPV and

(d) Profitability Index.

Solution:

Calculation of NCF's

Year	Machine –X			Machine -Y		
	EAT (Rs.)	NCF (Rs.)	Cum. CFAT(Rs.)	EAT (Rs.)	NCF (Rs.)	Cum. CFAT (Rs.)
1	40,000	70,000	70,000	20,000	50,000	50,000
2	50,000	80,000	1,50,000	70,000	1,00,000	1,50,000
3	40,000	70,000	2,20,000	50,000	80,000	2,30,000

(a) PBP:

Machine X=1+(20,000 / 80,000) = **1.25 years; Machine Y**=1+(40,000/1,00,000)=**1.4 years**

Decision: Machine X's pay back period is 1.25 years which is less than the Machine Y. Hence, Machine X can be selected.

(b) Account Rate of Return: Annual Average Income after taxes÷Original Investment

Annual Average Income:

Machine X = 1,30,000 ÷ 3 = **Rs.43,333**

Machine Y = 1,40,000 ÷ 3 = **Rs.46,667**

Average Investment: Machine X=90,000 ÷ 2= Rs.45,000; **Machine** Y= 90,000 ÷ 2= Rs.45,000

(c) ARR: Machine X = (Rs.43, 333 ÷ Rs.45, 000) 100 = **96.30 per cent**

Machine Y = (Rs.46, 667 ÷ Rs.45, 000) 100 = **103.70 per cent**

Decision: Based on ARR, Machine Y should be selected, since its ARR is greater than the Machine X.

Net Present Value

Year	Cash Flows (in Rs.)		DF 10 %	Total Present Values (in Rs.)	
	Machine X	Machine Y		Machine X	Machine Y
1	70,000	50,000	0.909	63,630	45,450
2	80,000	1,00,000	0.826	66,080	82,600
3	70,000	80,000	0.751	52,570	60,080
Present Value of Cash Flows				1,82,280	1,88,130
Less: Cash out flows				90,000	90,000
Net present values				92,280	98,130

Decision: According to the NPV, both the machines are selected, but the NPV of Machine Y is greater than that of Machine X, Hence Machine Y is selected.

(d) Profitability Index: PV Cash inflows ÷ Initial investment

$$\text{Machine X} = 1,82,280 ÷ 90,000 = \textbf{2.025}$$

$$\text{Machine Y} = 1,88,130 ÷ 90,000 = \textbf{2.090}$$

Decision: Based on PI, both machines should be selected since their PI is greater than one. But from the point of view of net profits generated, Machine Y should be selected since it is going to generate 2.090 paise (which is greater than the Machine X net PI) for every one rupee of investment.

16. Green field Ltd., Bombay, has to make a choice between three possible investments– Project A, B and C. The immediate capital outlays for each being Rs. 1,10,000. Each will continue for 5 years and it has been decided that a discount rate of 12 per cent is acceptable for all the proposals. The cash flows for the three projects are as follows:

Year	Projects	(in Rs.)	
	A	B	C
1	10,000	20,000	30,000
2	20,000	30,000	40,000
3	30,000	50,000	35,000
4	40,000	30,000	25,000
5	50,000	20,000	20,000

Which project would you recommend and why? Use the following evaluating techniques:

(1) NPV Method (2) PI Method

Solution

(1) **Calculation of NPV**

Year	Cash Flows (in Rs.)			DF 12 %	Present Values (in Rs.)		
	Project A	Project B	Project C		Project A	Project B	Project C
1	10,000	20,000	30,000	0.8929	8,929	17,858	26,787
2	20,000	30,000	40,000	0.7972	15,944	23,916	31,888
3	30,000	50,000	35,000	0.7118	21,354	35,590	24,913
4	40,000	30,000	25,000	0.6355	25,420	19,065	15,888
5	50,000	20,000	20,000	0.5674	28,370	11,348	11,348
Present Value of cash inflows					1,00,017	1,07,777	1,10,824
Less: Cash outflows					1,10,000	1,10,000	1,10,000
Net Present Values (NPV)					(-) 9,983	(-) 2,223	824

Recommendation: Project C should be selected since its NPV is positive.

(2) **Computation of Profitability Index (PI):** PV of cash inflows ÷ Cash outflows

Project A = 1,00,017 ÷ 1,10,000 = **0.9092 Paise**

Project B = 1,07,777 ÷ 1,10,000 = **0.980 Paise**

Project C = 1,10,824 ÷ 1,10,000 = **1.007 Paise**

Recommendation: Based on PI also Project C should be selected since its PI is greater than one.

17. A company is considering, purchase of machinery which costs Rs.8, 00,000 and which has an estimated life of 10 years. This machine will generate additional sales of Rs.4, 00,000 per year while increased costs and maintenance will be Rs.1, 00,000 per year. The cost of the machine is depreciated on a straight line and has no salvage value at the end of its 10 year life. The company has a cost of capital of 12 per cent and a corporate tax rate of 40 per cent.

You are required to calculate (a) annual cash flow (b) the NPV (c) the payback period (d) internal rate of return should the company purchase the new machine.

Solution:

a) Calculation of Annual Cash Inflow

	Rs.
Sales	4,00,000
Less: Cost and maintenance	1,00,000
EBDT	**3,00,000**
Less: Depreciation	80,000 (8,00,000÷10)
EBT	**2,20,000**
Less: Taxes	88,000
EAT	**1,32,000**
Add: Depreciation	80,000
Annual cash inflow	**2,12,000**

b) The NPV

PV of an annuity of Re.1 at the end of 10th year = 5.651

Total PV of cash inflows = 2,12,000 × 5.651	11,98,012
Less: PV of cash out flows	8,00,000
Net Present Value	3,98,012

c) The Pay Back Period

PBP = Original investment ÷ Annual cash inflow = 8,00,000 ÷ 2,12,000 = **3.77 years**

d) IRR

Fake payback period = 3.77

Referring to PV of an annuity of Re.1 table, the fake payback period of 3.77 lies in between 23 per cent (3.799) and 24 per cent (3.682) in the line of years.

PV of cash inflows at 23 per cent = 2,12,000 × 3.799 = 8,05,388

PV of cash inflows at 24 per cent = 2,12,000 × 3.682 = 7,80,584

Calculation of IRR

$$IRR = LDF\% + \left[\Delta DF \frac{LDPV - OI}{LDPV - HDPV}\right]$$

$$IRR = 23\% \left[(24-23)\frac{8,05,388 - 8,00,000}{8,05,388 - 7,80,584}\right]$$

$$IRR = 23 + \left[1\frac{5,388}{24,804}\right] = 23 + 0.22 = 23.22 \text{ per cent}$$

18. Karnataka Ltd., plans to undertake a project for placing a new product in the market. The company's cut-off rate is 12 per cent. It was estimated that the project would cost Rs.40,00,000 in plant and machinery in addition to working capital of Rs.10,00,000, which will be recovered in full when the project's 5 years life is over. The scrap value of plant and machinery at the end of 5 years was estimated at Rs.5,00,000. After providing for depreciation on straight line basis, profit after tax were estimated as follows:

Year	1	2	3	4	5
PAT (Rs.)	3,00,000	8,00,000	13,00,000	5,00,000	4,00,000

Evaluate the project under:

(a) Payback period method, (b) Average rate of return method, and (c) Net present value method

Solution

Depreciation = (40,00,000 – 5,00,000) ÷ 5 = **Rs. 7,00,000**

Depreciation Rs. 7,00,000 should be added to all the years EAT to get CFAT

Calculation of Cash Inflows (Rs.)

Year	EAT (Rs.)	Depreciation Rs.	CFAT (Rs.)	Cum. CFAT (Rs.)
1	3,00,000	7,00,000	10,00,000	10,00,000
2	8,00,000	7,00,000	15,00,000	25,00,000
3	13,00,000	7,00,000	20,00,000	15,00,000÷20,00,000
4	5,00,000	7,00,000	12,00,000	= 0.75
5	4,00,000	7,00,000	11,00,000	

a) Pay back period: 2 + 0.75 = **2.75 years**

b) Avg. Rate of Return: (Average annual EAT / Average investment) 100

Average annual EAT = 33,00,000 ÷ 5 = 6,60,000

Avg. Investment = (Original investment – scrap value)1/2 + Net working capital + Scrap value

= (40,00,000 – 5,00,000)1/2 + 10,00,000 + 5,00,000 = **Rs.32,50,000**

Average rate of return = (6,60,000 / 32,50,000) × 100 = **20.31 per cent**

c) NPV (Rs.)

Year	Cash inflow (Rs.)	DF 12%	PVs (Rs.)
1	10,00,000	0.893	8,93,000
2	15,00,000	0.797	11,95,500
3	20,00,000	0.712	14,24,000
4	12,00,000	0.636	7,63,200
5	11,00,000	0.567	6,23,700
PV of Cash inflows			48,99,400
Add: PV of working capital (10,00,000 x 0.567)			5,67,000
PV of scrap value (5,00,000 x 0.567)			2,83,500
PV of cash inflows			57,49,900
Less: PV of Cash outflows			50,00,00
NPV			7,49,900

19. A Limited Company is considering the purchase of a new machine, which will replace some manual operations. There are two alternatives 'X 'and 'Y'. From the following information prepare a profitability statement and work out the payback period for each.

	Model X	Model Y
	Rs.	Rs.
Cost of the machine	1,50,000	2,50,000
Estimated life	5 years	5 years
Cost of indirect materials	6,000	8,000
Estimated savings in scrap	10,000	15,000
Additional cost of maintenance	19,000	27,000
Estimated savings in direct wages:		
Employees not required	15	20
Wages per employee p.a.	6,000	6,000

Tax rate is 50 per cent. Suggest which machine is preferred.

Solution:

Profitability Statement

Particulars	Model X (Rs.)	Model Y (Rs.)
Estimated savings p.a.		
Scrap	10,000	15,000
Direct Wages: A – 15 × 6,000 ; B – 20 × 6,000	90,000	1,20,000
Total savings	**1,00,000**	**1,35,000**
Additional costs		
Cost of Indirect material	6,000	8,000
Maintenance	19,000	27,000
Total cost	**25,000**	**35,000**
Net savings (EBDT) (Savings – cost)	75,000	1,00,000
Less: Depreciation	28,000	47,000
EBT	**47,000**	**53,000**
Less: Taxes at 50 per cent	23,500	26,500
EAT	**23,500**	**26,500**
Add: Depreciation	28,000	47,000
Annual cash inflow (CFAT)	**51,500**	**73,500**

PBP = Initial investment ÷ Constant Annual cash inflows

Model X=Rs.1,50,000 ÷51,500=**2.91 years**;   **Model Y** =Rs.2,50,000÷73,500 = **3.40 years**

As the payback period for Model 'X' is less than that of Model 'Y', hence, Model 'X' is recommended.

20. An enterprise has to decide on either of the following proposals. Assuming a required rate of return of 10 per cent p.a., evaluate the investment proposals as under:

(a) Average rate of return method (ARR), (b) Payback method, and (c) Profitability index.

	Proposal A	Proposal B
Cost of investment	Rs.20,000	28,000
Life (Years)	4	5
Scrap value	NIL	NIL
Inflows after depreciation and tax	Rs.	Rs.

Year	1990	1991	1992	1993	1994
Proposal A	500	2,000	3,500	2,500	---
Proposal B	---	3,400	3,400	3,400	3,400

Each project will require an additional working capital of Rs.2,000, which will be received back in full after the expiry of each project life. Depreciation is provided under straight line method.

Solution:

Calculation of Cash Inflows

Year	Proposal A		Proposal B	
	EAT	CFAT	EAT	CFAT
1990	500	5,500	----	5,600
1991	2,000	7,000	3,400	9,000
1992	3,500	8,500	3,400	9,000
1993	2,500	7,500	3,400	9,000
1994	---	----	3,400	9,000

(a) Pay back period

Year	Proposal A		Proposal B	
	Cash inflow	Cumulative CFAT	Cash inflow	Cumulative CFAT
1990	5,500	5,500	5,600	5,600
1991	7,000	12,500	9,000	14,600
1992	8,500	7,500÷8,500	9,000	23,600
1993	7,500	=0.88	9,000	4,400÷9,000
1994	----		9,000	=0.49

PBP: Proposal A = **2.88 years**; Proposal B = **3.49 years**

(b) Average rate of return method: (Average annual EAT ÷ Average investment)100

Proposal A: Average annual EAT = 8,500 ÷ 4 = **Rs.2,125**

Average investment = (20,000-0)1/2 +2,000+0 = **Rs. 12000**

ARR = (2,125 / 12,000)100 = **17.71 per cent**

Proposal B: Average annual EAT = 13,600÷5 = **Rs.2,720**

Average investment = (28,000-0)1/2 +2,000+0 = **Rs. 16000**

ARR = (2,270 / 16,000)100 = **17 per cent**

(c) Profitability Index

Year	CFAT (Rs.)		DF 10%	PVs (Rs.)	
	Proposal A	Proposal B		Proposal A	Proposal B
1990	5,500	5,600	0.909	5,000	5,090
1991	7,000	9,000	0.826	5,782	7,434
1992	8,500	9,000	0.751	6,384	6,759
1993	7,500	9,000	0.683	5,123	6,147
1994	----	9,000	0.621	-----	5,589
PV of cash inflow				22,289	31,019
Add: PV of Working Capital				1,366	1,242
PV of total cash inflows				23,655	32,261

Profitability Index = Total PV of cash inflows ÷ Initial investment

Proposal A = 23,655 ÷22,000 = **1.075**;   **Proposal B** = 32,761 ÷ 30,000 = **1.092**

21. A company has to select one of the following two projects. Cash flow is

Year	0	1	2	3	4
Project X	11,000	6,000	2,000	1,000	5,000
Project Y	10,000	1,000	1,000	2,000	10,000

Calculate: (a) Pay back period, (b) ARR, (c) NPV at 10 per cent (d) PI at 15 per cent (e) IRR Suggest the best alternative on the above basis.

Solution: a) Pay back period

Year	Project X		Project Y	
	CFAT (Rs.)	Cum. CFAT (Rs.)	CFAT (Rs.)	Cum. CFAT (Rs.)
1	6,000	6,000	1,000	1,000
2	2,000	8,000	1,000	2,000
3	1,000	9,000	2,000	4,000
4	5,000	2,000÷5,000= 0.4	10,000	6,000÷10,000=0.6
PBP	3.4 Years		3.6 Years	

b) ARR (Average Rate of Return)

Calculation of EAT

Year	CFAT (Rs.)		EAT = CFAT – Dep (Rs.)	
	Project X	Project Y	Project X	Project Y
1	6,000	1,000	3,250	-1,500
2	2,000	1,000	-750	-1,500
3	1,000	2,000	-1,750	-500
4	5,000	10,000	2,250	7,500

ARR = (Average Annual IAT ÷ Average investment) 100

Project X: ARR = (750 /5,500)100 = **13.64** per cent

Project Y: ARR = (1,000 / 5,000)100 = **20** per cent

c) NPV at 10 per cent discount rate

Year	CFAT (Rs.)		DF	Present Values (Rs.)	
	Project X	Project Y	10%	Project X	Project Y
1	6,000	1,000	0.909	5,454	909
2	2,000	1,000	0.826	1,652	826
3	1,000	2,000	0.751	751	1,502
4	5,000	10,000	0.683	3,415	6,830
PV of Cash inflows				11,272	10,067
Less: PV of Cash outflows				11,000	10,000
NPV				272	067

d) Profitability Index at 15 per cent

Year	CFAT (Rs.)		DF	Present Values (Rs.)	
	Project X	Project Y	15%	Project X	Project Y
1	6,000	1,000	0.870	5,220	870
2	2,000	1,000	0.756	1,512	756
3	1,000	2,000	0.658	658	1,316
4	5,000	10,000	0.572	2,860	5,720
PV of Cash inflows				10,250	8,662

Profitability Index: Project X: 10,250÷11,000 = **0.93; Project Y:** 8,662÷10,000 = **0.87**

e) Internal Rate of Return

Year	CFAT (Rs.)		DF	Present Values (Rs.)	
	Project X	Project Y	12%	Project X	Project Y
1	6,000	1,000	0.893	5,358	893
2	2,000	1,000	0.797	1,594	797
3	1,000	2,000	0.712	712	1,424
4	5,000	10,000	0.636	3,180	6,360
PV of Cash inflows				10,844	9,474

Project X: Calculation of fake pay back period

Fake PBP =(11,000 ÷ 3,500) = **3.143**

Referring to PV of an annuity of Re.1, the fake pay back period of 3.143 lies in between 10 per cent (3.169) and 12 per cent (3.038) in the line of 4 years.

PV of cash inflows at 10 per cent = 11,272

PV of cash inflows at 12 per cent = 10,844

$$IRR = IDF\% + \left[\Delta DF \frac{LDPV - OI}{LDPV - HDPV} \right]$$

$$IRR = 10 + \left[2 \frac{11,272 - 11,000}{11,272 - 10,844} \right]$$

$$IRR = 10 + \left[2 \frac{272}{428} \right] = 10 + 1.27 = 11.27 \text{ per cent}$$

Project Y: Factor = 10,000 / 3,500 = 2.857

Referring to PV of an annuity of Re.1, the factor of 2.857 lies in between 10 per cent (3.169) and 15 per cent (2.856) in the line of 4 years.

PV of cash inflows at 10 per cent = 10,067

PV of cash inflows at 15 per cent =   8,662

$$IRR = LDF\% + \left[\Delta DF \frac{LDPV - OI}{LDPV - HDPV} \right]$$

$$IRR = 10 + \left[5 \frac{10,067 - 10,000}{10,067 - 8,662} \right]$$

$$IRR = 10 + \left[5 \frac{67}{1,405} \right] = 10 + 0.24 = 10.24 \text{ per cent}$$

Evaluation of the projects based on the ranking method

Techniques	Project X	Project Y
PBP	1	2
ARR	2	1
NPV	1	2
PI	1	2
IRR	1	2

According to the ranking method, Project X can be selected as it has got the highest ranking than that of Project Y.

22. A company has an investment opportunity costing Rs.4,00,000 with the following expected net cash inflows:

Year	1	2	3	4	5	6	7	8	9	10
CIFs	70,000	70,000	70,000	70,000	70,000	80,000	1,00,000	1,50,000	1,00,000	40,000

Determine the following:

(a) Pay back period, (b) Profitability Index at 10per cent discount rate and (c) IRR

Solution:

a) Calculation of payback period

Year	Cash inflow (Rs.)	Cumulative CFS (Rs.)
1	70,000	70,000
2	70,000	1,40,000
3	70,000	2,10,000
4	70,000	2,80,000
5	70,000	3,50,000
6	80,000	50,000 ÷ 80,000 =0.625
7	1,00,000	
8	1,50,000	
9	1,00,000	
10	40,000	

PBP = 5 + (50,000 / 80,000) = 5 + 0.625 = **5.625 years**

b) Calculation of Profitability Index:

Year	Cash inflow (Rs.)	DF 10%	PVs (Rs.)
1	70,000	0.909	63,630
2	70,000	0.826	57,820
3	70,000	0.751	52,570
4	70,000	0.683	47,810
5	70,000	0.621	43,470
6	80,000	0.564	45,120
7	1,00,000	0.513	51,300
8	1,50,000	0.467	70,050
9	1,00,000	0.424	42,400
10	40,000	0.386	15,440
Total PV of Cash inflows			4,89,610

Profitability Index = 4,89,610 / 4, 00,000 = **1.22**

c) Calculation of Internal Rate of Return

Year	Cash inflow (Rs.)	DF 15%	PVs (Rs.)
1	70,000	0.870	60,900
2	70,000	0.756	52,920
3	70,000	0.658	46,060
4	70,000	0.572	40,040
5	70,000	0.479	34,790
6	80,000	0.432	34,560
7	1,00,000	0.376	37,600
8	1,50,000	0.327	49,050
9	1,00,000	0.284	28,400
10	40,000	0.247	9,880
Total PV of Cash inflows			3,94,200

$$IRR = LDF\% + \left[\Delta DF \frac{LDPV - OI}{LDPV - HDPV} \right]$$

$$IRR = 10 + \left[5\frac{4,89,610 - 4,00,000}{4,89,610 - 3,94,200} \right]$$

$$IRR = 10 + \left[5\frac{89,610}{95,410} \right] = 10 + 4.696 = 14.7 \text{ per cent}$$

23. Modern Co. Ltd., is considering the purchase of a machine. There are two machines A and B each costing Rs.50,000. While comparing the profitability of these machines a discount rate of 10 per cent is to be used. Earnings after taxation are expected to be as follows:

Year	1	2	3	4	5
Machine A	15,000	20,000	25,000	15,000	10,000
Machine B	5,000	15,000	20,000	30,000	20,000

Depreciation is provided at 10 per cent on original cost.

Evaluate the project using: (a) ARR method,   (b) Net Present Value method, and (c) Profitability Index

Solution:

a) ARR: (Average Annual EAT ÷ Average investment)100

Machine A: Average Annual EAT = 85,000/5 = **Rs.17,000**

Average investment = 50,000/2 = **Rs.25,000**

ARR = (17,000/25,000) × 100 = **68 per cent**

Machine B: Average annual EAT = 90,000/5 = **Rs.18,000**

Average investment = 50,000/2 = **Rs.25,000**

ARR = (18,000/25,000) × 100 = **72 per cent**

b) Calculation of CFAT and Net Present Value

Year	EAT (Rs.)		CFAT (Rs.)		DF 10%	PVs (Rs.)	
	Machine A	Machine B	Machine A	Machine B		Machine A	Machine B
1	15,000	5,000	20,000	10,000	0.909	18,180	9,090
2	20,000	15,000	25,000	20,000	0.826	20,650	16,520
3	25,000	20,000	30,000	25,000	0.751	22,530	18,775
4	15,000	30,000	20,000	35,000	0.683	13,660	23,905
5	10,000	20,000	15,000	25,000	0.621	9,315	15,525
PV of cash inflow						84,335	83,815
Less: PV of Cash outflows						50,000	50,000
NPV						34,335	33,815

c) Profitability Index: PV of cash inflows ÷ cash outflows

Machine A: 84,335 / 50,000 = 1.69;   **Machine B** = 83,815 / 50,000 = 1.68

24.   A company has to choose one of the following two mutually exclusive projects. Both the projects have to be depreciated on straight line basis. The tax rate is 50 per cent.

Year	X (Rs.)	Y (Rs.)
0	30,000	30,000
1	8,400	8,400
2	9,600	9,000
3	14,000	8,000
4	16,000	10,000
5	4,000	20,000

Use payback period as the criterion for project selection.

Solution:

Calculation of payback period

Year	Project X (Rs.)		Project Y (Rs.)	
	CFAT	Cumulative CFAT	CFAT	Cumulative CFAT
1	8,400	8,400	8,400	8,400
2	9,600	18,000	9,000	17,400
3	14,000	32,000	8,000	25,400
4	16,000	48,000	10,000	35,400
5	4,000	52,000	20,000	55,400

PBP: Project X =2+(12,000/14,000) =2.86 Years; Project Y =3+(4,600/10,000)=3.46 Years Project X should be preferred as the payback period of Project X is less than that of Project Y.

25.   A project costs Rs. 2, 50,000 and yields an annual profit of Rs.40, 000 after depreciation at 12 per cent p.a. but before tax at 50 per cent. Calculate the payback period.

Solution:

Calculation of payback period needs CFAT, but in the above problem only EBT is given, hence there is a need to calculate CFAT:

EBT	40,000
Less: Tax 50 %	20,000
EAT	20,000
Add: Depreciation (at 12per cent on 2, 50,000)	30,000
Annual cash inflow	50,000

Pay Back Period = **Rs.2,50,000 ÷ Rs.50,000 = 5 years**

26. Determine the average rate of return from the following data of two machines A and B.

	Machine A	Machine B
	Rs.	Rs.
Original cost	56,125	56,125
Additional investment in net working capital	5,000	6,000
Estimated life in years	5	5
Estimated salvage value	3,000	3,000
Average income-tax rate (%)	55	55

Annual estimated income after depreciation and taxes

Year	1	2	3	4	5
Machine A	3,375	5,375	7,375	9,375	11,375
Machine B	11,375	9,375	7,375	5,375	3,375

Depreciation has been charged on straight line basis.

Solution:

Average rate of return = (Average annual EAT ÷ Average investment) 100

Machine A: Average annual income after tax = 36,875 / 5 = Rs. 7,375

Average investment = (56,125 – 3,000) 1/2+ 5,000 + 3,000 = Rs. 34,562

Average rate of return = (7,375 / 34, 562) × 100 = 21.34 per cent

Machine B: Average annual income after tax = 36,875 / 5 = Rs. 7,375

Average investment = (56,125 – 3,000) 1/2+ 6,000 + 3,000 = Rs. 35,562

Average rate of return = (7,375 / 35,562) 100 = 20.74 per cent

27. A limited company has, under consideration the following two projects. Their details are as under:

	Project X	Project Y
	Rs.	Rs.
Investment in machinery	10,00,000	15,00,000
Working capital	5,00,000	5,00,000
Life of machinery (Years)	4	6
Scrap value of machinery (%)	10	10
Tax rate (%)	50	50

Income before depreciation and tax at the end of

Year	1	2	3	4	5	6
Project X	8,00,000	8,00,000	8,00,000	8,00,000	----	----
Project Y	15,00,000	9,00,000	15,00,000	8,00,000	6,00,000	3,00,000

Calculate the Accounting rate of return and suggest which project is to be preferred.

Solution:

Average rate of return = (Average annual EAT ÷ Original investment) 100

Project X: Average annual EAT = 2,87,500

Original investment = 10,00,000 + 5,00,000 = 15,00,000

Accounting rate of return = (2,87,500 / 15,00,000) ×100 = 19.17 per cent

Project Y: **Average annual EAT = 3,54,167**

Original investment = 15,00,000 + 5,00,000 = 20,00,000

Accounting rate of return = (3,54,167 / 20,00,000) ×100 = 17.71 per cent

28. ABC Ltd. is proposing to take up a project, which will need an investment of Rs. 40,000. The net income before depreciation and tax is estimated as follows:

Year	1	2	3	4	5
IBDT (Rs.)	10,000	12,000	14,000	16,000	20,000

Depreciation is to be charged according to the straight-line method. Tax rate is 50 per cent. Calculate the Accounting rate of return.

Solution:

Accounting rate of return = (Average annual EAT ÷ Original investment) x100

Average EBDT	14,400
Less: Depreciation	8,000
Average EBT	6,400
Less: Tax 50 %	3,200
Average EAT	3,200

Accounting rate of return = (3,200 / 40,000) ´100 = 8 per cent

29. The directors of Alpha Limited are contemplating the purchase of a new machine to replace a machine, which has been in operation in the factory for the last five years. Ignoring interest but considering tax at 50per cent of net earnings, suggest which of the two alternatives should be preferred. The following are the details:

	Old machine	New machine
Purchase price	Rs.40, 000	60,000
Estimated life of machine (Years)	10	10
Machine running hours p.a.	2,000	2,000
Units per hour	24	36
Wages per running hour	Rs.3	Rs.5.25
Power	Rs. 2,000	Rs. 4,000
Consumable stores p.a.	Rs.6,000	7,5000
All other charges p.a.	Rs.8,000	9,000
Material cost per unit	Re.0.50	Re.0.50
Selling price per unit	Rs.1.25	1.25

You may assume that the above information regarding sales and cost of sales will hold good throughout the economic life of each of the machines.

Solution:

Profitability Statement

Particulars	Old Machine (Rs.)	New Machine (Rs)
Production p.a. Old: (2,000x24), New: (2,000x36)	48,000	72,000
Sales: Old: (48,000x1.25), New: (72,000x1.25)	**60,000**	**90,000**
Cost of Sales pa		
Wages: Old: (2,000x3), New: (2,000x5.25)	6,000	10,500
Power	2,000	4,500
Consum ble stores	6,000	7,500
All other charges	8,000	9,000
Materials cost: Old: (48,000x0.5), New: (72,000x0.5)	24,000	36,000
	46,000	67,500
EBDT: (Sales – Cost of Sales	14,000	22,500
Less: Depreciation	4,000	6,000
EBT	**10,000**	**16,500**
Less: Tax 50%	5,000	8,250
EAT	**5,000**	**8,250**

Incremental profit = RS.3,250 (8,250-5,000);   Incremental investment = 20,000

ARR Old Machine: (5,000 / 40,000) 100 = **12.5 per cent**

ARR New Machine : (8,250 / 60,000) 100 = **13.7 5per cent**

Avg. Rate of Return: (5,000 / 20,000) 100 = **25 per cent**

ARR New Machine: (8,250 / 30,000) 100 = **27.5 per cent**

Incremental ARR: (Incremental EAT ÷ Incremental investment)´100

= (Rs.3,200 ÷40,000) 100 = 8 per cent

Thus, replacement of the old machine (ignoring interest) is profitable.

Working note:

1. Incremental investment in new machine: **Rs.**

   Investment in new machine   60,000

   Less: Sale value of old machine

   (cost – depreciation for 5 years)   20,000

   [40,000- (4,000/5)]   40,000

2. Depreciation: Old machine = (40,000 ÷10) = **Rs. 4,000**; New: **60,000 ÷10= Rs.6000**

30. Delhi Works manufactures a part of the air cooler, which it sells. The quantity required is 7,000 units per year. The direct cost of manufacturing this part is Rs.4 per unit. It has received a proposal from a Tumkur firm offering to meet the entire needs at Rs.5 per unit.

If works discontinues making this part, it can expand its existing facilities for manufacturing a new product for sale, which would involve the following:

Investment in new machine (life 40,000 hours) Rs.40, 000

Material cost   Rs.3 per unit.

Direct labour Rs.2 per unit

Indirect expenses (other than depreciation) for 8,000 hours Rs.12, 000

Estimated volume of sales 8,000 units at Rs.9 per unit. State whether the proposal of Tumkur firm should be accepted or not if (i) the current cut-off rate is 25 per cent.

(ii) the current cut-off rate is 30 per cent.

Solution:

Profitability Statement

Particulars		Amount (Rs.)
Sales (8,000 × 9)		72,000
Less: Cost of production		
Material (8,000 × 3):	24,000	
Direct labour (8,000×2):	16,000	
Indirect expenses:	12,000	52,000
EBDT (Sales – Cost)		20,000
Less: Depreciation		
8,000 (40,000 ÷ 40,000)		8,000
EBT		12,000
Less: Extra cost of part A payable (If Bought from Tumkur firm instead of manufacturing (5-4) 7,000		7,000
Net Earnings		5,000

Average investment in the new project 20,000 (40,000 ÷2)

i) Rate of return at 25 per cent cut-off rate = 20,000×0.25 = **Rs. 5,000**

ii) Rate of return at 30 per cent cut-off rate = 20,000×0.30 = **Rs. 6,000**

The proposal may be accepted at cut-off rate of 25 per cent. However, it is not acceptable at cut- off rate of 30 per cent.

31. A Company is considering an investment proposal of Rs. 50,000 to install new milling controls. The facility has a life expectancy of 5 years and his salvage value. The company's tax rate is 55% and no investment tax credit is allowed. The firm uses straight – line depreciation. The estimated Cash Flow Before Tax (CFBT) from the proposed investment proposal is as follows

Year	:	1	2	3	4	5
CFBT(Rs.)	:	10000	11000	14000	15000	25000

Compute the following :

(a) Payback period

(b) Average rate of return

(c) Internal rate of return

(d) Net present value at 10% discount rate

(e) Profitability index at 10% discount rate.

Solution:

First We Should Determine CFAT

Year 1	CFBT 2	Depreciation 3	Net Profits (4(2-3))	Taxes 5	Net Profit 6(4-5)	CFAT 7(6+3)
1	10000	10000	Nil	Nil	Nil	10000
2	11000	10000	1000	550	450	10450
3	14000	10000	4000	2200	1800	11800
4	15000	10000	5000	2750	2250	12250
5	25000	10000	15000	8250	6750	16750
					11250	61250

Depreciation = Cost of machine – salvage value/life years of machine

= 50000 – Nil/5

= Rs. 10000

(a) Calculation of payback period :

Year	CFAT	Cumulative CFAT
1	10000	10000
2	10450	20450
3	11800	32250
4	12250	44500
5	16750	61250

4th year CFAT is 44500. To recover the investment Rs. 50000, the remaining amount needed is (50000-44500) = 5500

Therefore, payback period is = 4 + 5500/16750

i.e., 4.328 years.

(b) Computation of average rate of return :

ARR = (Average income investment) x 100

Average income = 11250/5 = 2250

Average investment = 50000/2 = 25000

= (2250/25000) x 100

= 9%

(c) Computation of IRR

First Step : Calculation of Fake payback period :

Fake payback period : (Original Investment/average cash flow)

= (50000/12250)

= 4.0816

Next, look at table II, close to the take payback period of 4.0816 against 5 years. The relevant factor is 4.22 against 6%.

Statement showing present value at 6%

Year	CFAT	P V Factor @ 6%	Present Value
1	10000	0.943	9430
2	10450	0.890	9300
3	11800	0.840	9912
4	12250	0.823	10082
5	16750	0.747	12512
			51236
		Less : Original Investment	50000
			1236

Since PV is more than Rs. 50000, let us try with 8%

Statement showing present value at 8%

Year	CFAT	P V Factor @ 8%	Present Value
1	10000	0.926	9260
2	10450	0.857	8956
3	11800	0.794	9369
4	12250	0.763	9347
5	16750	0.681	11407
			48339
		Less : Original Investment	50000
			(–)1661

By interpolation IRR will be

$$IRR = A + \frac{C-0}{C-D} \times (B-A)$$

= 6 + (51,236 − 50000/51236 − 48,339) x (8 − 6)

= 6 + (1236/2897) × 2

= 6 + 0.85

= 6.85

(d) Computation of NPV at 10% discount rate :

Statement showing present value at 10%

Year	CFAT	P V Factor @ 6%	Present Value
1	10000	0.909	9090
2	10450	0.826	8632
3	11800	0.751	8862
4	12250	0.683	8367
5	16750	0.621	10401
		PV Of CFAT	45352
		Less : Original Investment	50000
		NPV	-4648

$$PI = \frac{PV \, of \, cash \, inflows}{Initial \, cash \, Outlay}$$

$$= \quad 45352/50000$$

$$= \quad 0.907$$

TEST YOUR KNOWLEDGE

(1) **Fill in the blanks with appropriate word(s)**

   (a) Fixed assets represent _____and _____elements.

   (b) _____ is the firm's decision to invest its current funds most efficiently in the long-term assets in anticipation of an expected flow of benefits over a series of years.

   (c) Capital budgeting decisions are _____ without _____

   (d) Capital budgeting evaluation techniques are divided into _____broad categories.

   (e) Traditional techniques of capital budgeting evaluation is also known as _____.

   (f) Pay back period and Accounting rate of return methods are _____.

   (g) Modern techniques are also known as _____.

   (h) Discounted cash flow techniques are subdivided into _____.

   (i) Net present value (NPV), _____, and profitability index are three discounted cash flow techniques.

   (j) Profitability index technique is also known as _____.

   (k) Original investment is divided by _____ to get pay back period.

   (l) Internal Rate of Return (IRR) is also called _____method.

   (m) The discount rate at which present value of cash inflows equals to the present value of cash outflows is called _____.

   (n) The intermediate cash flows reinvested at the discount rate is the assumption of ____.

   (o) Profitability index is equal to one the project should be _____

[**Answers:** (a) Non-liquid, long-term; (b) Capital budgeting; (c) Irreversible, loss; (d) Two, (e) Non-discounted; (f) Traditional; (g) Discounted cash flow techniques; (h) Three; (i) Internal Rate of Return (IRR); (j) Benefit cost ratio, (k) Constant annual cash in flows; (l) Trail and error; (m) Internal Rate of Return (IRR); (n) Net present value; (o) Considered]

(2) **State whether each of the following statement is true or false**

   (a) Capital budgeting is a short-term decision.

   (b) CFAT is the base for computation of pay back period.

   (c) When cash flows after taxes are unequal then cumulative cash flow method is used to compute pay back period.

   (d) Intermediate cash flows are reinvested at the rate of IRR is the assumption of IRR.

   (e) Additional working capital required is not added to the cost of the project when evaluation is based on DCF techniques.

   (f) Additional, scrap value and cost of project are the components of average investment.

   (g) NPV and IRR both, are DCF methods.

   (h) If there is a size disparity the NPV and IRR will give different rankings.

[**Answers: (a)** False; **(b)** True; **(c)** True; **(d)** True; **(e)** False; **(f)** True; **(g)** True; **(h)** True]

REVIEW QUESTIONS

1. Define capital budgeting.
2. What do you understand by capital budgeting?
3. What is Cut-Off rate ?
4. Bring out the difference between The NPV and IRR method.
5. State the difference between mutually exclusive and independent proposals.
6. Explain the circumstances under which the payback period is useful.
7. List the stages of capital budgeting process.
8. What do you mean by discounting of cash flows?
9. State the techniques of capital budgeting.
10. What do you mean by mutually exclusive project?
11. Explain the nature and concept of capital budgeting.
12. Discuss the process of capital budgeting.
13. Discuss the significance of capital budgeting.
14. Why is pay back period so popular?
15. How do you calculate the Accounting rate of return? What are its limitations?
16. Compare and contrast NPV with IRR.
17. Discuss the traditional techniques of capital budgeting evaluation.
18. What is NPV? Discuss the steps involved in computation of NPV.
19. How do you calculate cash flows after tax (CFAT)?
20. What is BCR? What are its merits?
21. How should working capital and sunk costs be treated in evaluating capital budgeting decision?
22. What do you mean by pay back period?
23. What is the accept or reject criterion under PBP technique?
24. List three limitations of pay back period.
25. Name the discounting cash flow methods.
26. What is NPV?
27. What is the accept or reject criterion under NPV technique?
28. What is Profitability Index?
29. What is IRR?
30. What is the accept or reject criterion under IRR technique?
31. What are limitations of capital budgeting?
32. What is capital rationing?
33. What is capital budgeting? The process and techniques of capital budgeting.
34. Briefly discuss the techniques of capital budgeting with their merits and limitations.
35. What is capital budgeting? Discuss its nature, importance and deficiencies of capital budgeting.

PRACTICE YOURSELF

1. A project requires an investment of Rs.100,000. It is expected t yield an annual cash flow after taxes of Rs. 20,000 for 10 years. Calculate payback period.**[Answer:** 5 years]

2. ABC company is planning to buy an equipment, that had two alternatives A and B. Each equipment requires an initial investment of Rs 30,000. From the following additional information you are required to calculate payback period and suggest which equipment should be preferred ? why ?

Years		1	2	3	4	5
CFAT	A(Rs.)	10,500	8,000	6,000	7,500	12,000
	B(Rs.)	3,000	6,000	8,000	12,000	80,000

[Answer: A: 3.73 years, B: 4.12 years, Project A is preferred since its PBP is less than other]

3. An equipment costs Rs. 10,00,000 and it is expected to yield a profit after depreciation but before loss is Rs. 150,000. Depreciation rate is 10 per cent on straight-line method, and company's tax rate is 50 per cent, calculate the pay back period. **[Answer:**4 years]

4. A project expected cash flows are as follows:

Year	0	1	2	3	4	5
CFAT (Rs.)	50,000	10,000	15,000	20,000	25,000	20,000

Calculate pay back period **[Answer:**4 years]

5. A project costs Rs.30, 00,000 and yields annually Rs.4, 50,000 after depreciation at 15 per cent but before tax at 40 per cent. Calculate payback period.

(Answer: CFAT Rs. 7,20,000, Pay Back Period = 4.17 years)

6. From the following information calculate pay back period and Accounting Rate of Return

Projects	Original Investment	CFAT(Rs)	Economic life
A	25,000	3,000	10
B	3,000	1,000	5
C	12,000	2,000	8
D	20,000	4,000	10
E	40,000	8,000	2

[Answer: PBP: A-8.33 years, B – 3years, C- 6years, D - 5 years, and E - 5 years,

ARR: A–12 per cent, B - 33.33 per cent, C – 16.7 per cent, D – 20 per cent; and E – 20 per cent]

7. A company is planning to consider any one of the three alternatives A,B and C. Calculate ARR.

Alternatives	CFAT(Rs)		
	0	1	2
A	5,000	0	6,610
B	5,000	1,080	3,080
C	5,000	5,750	0

[Answer: A – 132.2 per cent; b – 41.6 per cent, and C – 115 per cent]

8. From the following cash flow (CFAT) stream of X and Y, calculate (a) PBP (b) ARR (c) NPV, and (d) PI.

Years	0	1	2	3	4	5	6	7	8	9	10
X (Rs. in Lakhs)	4	0.80	0.80	0.80	0.80	0.80	0.80	0.80	0.80	0.80	0.80
Y (Rs. in Lakhs)	6	0.80	0.80	0.80	0.80	0.80	0.60	0.70	0.30	0.30	0.40

Assume 10 per cent discounting rate.

[**Answer:** (a) PBP: X – 5 years and Y – 9.25 years; (b) ARR : X – 10 per cent and Y – 5 per cent (c) NPV : X – Rs, 91,600 and Y – Rs. 84,800; and (d) PI : X – 1.229, and Y – 0.692]

9. VS International co, Ltd, is evaluating a project that costs Rs 2,00,000 and it require an all additional net working capital of Rs. 1,00,000. It is expected to generate a net cash flow of Rs. 1,05,000 for 5 years. What is the NPV and IRR of the project assuming 50 per cent tax rate and 10 per cent cash of capital. [**Answer:** NPV: Rs, 160.155, IRR: 29.86 per cent]

10. XYZ company is considering the following projects P and Q.

Year	0	1	2	3
P	25,000	5,000	5,000	25,640
Q	28,000	12,672	12,672	12,602

Calculate NPV and IRR of both projects. [**Answer:** NPV:P–Rs.1700, Q–Rs.2436, IRR:P–15 per cent, Q–17 per cent]

11. XYX., Ltd, company is considering the purchase of machines. Two machines P and Q each costing Rs. 50,000 are available. EAT are a follows.

Year	1	2	3	4	5
Machine P	15,000	20,000	25,000	15,000	10,000
Machine Q	5,000	15,000	20,000	30,000	2,000

Evaluate the two alternatives according to NPV Method. Assuming cost of capital 10 per cent. Which Machine should be selected why?

[**Answer:** NPV : Machine P: 53,309, Machine Q: 52,783. Machine P is preferable since its NPV is greater than the other]

12. Philips India Ltd is considering the following proposals. Assuming a required rate of return of 10 per cent pa. evaluate the investment proposals order.

(a) PBP (b) Average Rate of Return (ARR), (c) PI

	Project A	**Project B**
Cost of Project	Rs. 24,000	Rs. 35,000
Life	4 years	5 years
Scrap value	Rs. 2000	Rs. 4000

In flows after depreciation and tax

Year	1996	1997	1998	1999	2000
Project A	1,000	2,500	4,000	3,000	-
Project B	-	4,200	4,200	4,200	4,200

Each project will require an additional working capital of Rs.2000, which will be received back in full after expire of the project life. Depreciation is provided under straight line method.

Answer:

Method	Project A	Project B
(a) PBP	3 years	3.36 years
(b) ARR (%)	17.5	15.63
(c) PI (Rs)	1.06	1.126

13. Three projects have been suggested to BPL Company, The CFAT is as follows:

Years		0	1	2	3	4
	X	10,000	2,800	3,000	4,000	4,000
Projects	Y	18,000	6,500	6,500	6,500	6,500
	Z	30,000	6,000	10,000	12,000	16,000

Assuming 12 per cent cost of capital, rank the projects based on PI method.

Answer:

Project	PI	Rank
Project X	1.0281	3
Project Y	1.9068	1
Project Z	1.068	2

14. A company is considering the purchase of a new machine, which will carry out some operations at present being performed by hands. The two machines A and B are under consideration regarding which one should be selected. Details about two machines are.

	Machine A Rs.	Machine B Rs.
Estimated life (Years)	10	12
Cost of Machine (Rs.)	12,00,000	18,00,000
Estimated additional cost (Rs.)		
Indirect material (p.a.)	30,000	40,000
Maintenance (p.a.)	40,000	60,000
Supervision (p.a.)	60,000	80,000
Estimated savings in scrap (p.a.)	1,00,000	1,20,000
Estimated savings in direct wages		
a. workers not required	100	130
b. wages per worker p.a.	9,000	9,000

Using the method of pay back period, suggest which machine should be purchased assuming that tax rate is 40 per cent.

[Answers: CFAT: Machine A - 5,70,000;   Machine B - 7,26,000; **PBP:** Machine A – 2.11 Years; Machine B – 2.48 Years)

Decision: As the payback period for Machine A is less than that of Machine B. Hence, Machine A is profitable.

15. KMF wants to replace the manual operations by a new machine. There are two alternative models, A and B of the new machine.

Using payback period, suggest the most profitable investment.

	Machine A	Machine B
	Rs.	Rs.
Cost of Machine	9,000	18,000
Estimated life of the Machine	4 years	5 years
Estimated savings in scrap	500	800
Estimated savings in direct wages	6,000	8,000
Additional cost of the maintenance	800	1,000
Additional cost of supervision	1,200	1,800

Ignore taxation.

[Answers: Net Savings or CFAT: Machine A – Rs. 4,500; Machine B – Rs.6,000;

PBP: Machine A – 2 Years; Machine B – 3Years]

Decision: As the payback period for Machine A is less than that of Machine B. Hence, Machine A is profitable.

16. Ramnath Washing Machines Ltd., is considering the purchase of a new machine, which would carry out some operations at present performed by manual labour. A and B are alternative models. The following information is available. Using payback period, identify the most profitable investment.

	Machine A	Machine B
	Rs.	Rs.
Cost of Machine	15,000	25,000
Estimated life of the Machine	5 years	6 years
Estimated cost of indirect material p.a.	600	800
Estimated savings in scrap	1,000	1,500
Estimated savings in direct wages		
a. workers not required	15	20
b. wages per worker p.a.	600	600
Additional cost of the maintenance p.a.	700	1,100
Additional cost of supervision p.a.	1,200	1,600

Assume a tax rate of 50 per cent.

[Answers: CFAT: Machine A – Rs. 5,250; Machine B – Rs.7,083;

PBP: Machine A – 2.86 Years; Machine B – 3.53Years]

Decision: As the payback period for Machine X is less than that of Machine Y. Hence, Machine X is recommended.

17. The working results of two machines are as follows:

	Machine I	Machine II
	Rs.	Rs.
Cost	45,000	45,000

Sales per year	1,00,000	80,000
Cost per year	36,000	30,000
Expected life	2 years	3 years

Which of the two should be preferred?

(Answer: EAT: Machine I-Rs. 20,750; Machine II- Rs. 17,500

Avg. Rate of Return: Machine I-92.22 per cent; Machine II- 77.78 per cent)

Machine I has higher average rate of return as compared to Machine II. Hence, Machine I is better.

18. M/s. Bharath Industrial Limited purchased a machine five years ago. A proposal is under consideration to replace it by a new machine. The life of the machine is estimated to be 10 years. The existing (old) machine can be sold at its written down value. As cost accountant of the company you are required to submit your recommendations based on the following information:

	Existing (Old) machine	New machine
Initial cost	Rs.25, 000	Rs.50, 000
Machine hours per annum	2,000	2,000
Wages per running hour	1.25	1.25
Power per hour	0.50	2.00
Indirect material p.a.	3,000	3,000
Other expenses p.a.	12,000	12,000
Cost of materials per unit	1	1
No. of units produced per hour	12	12
Selling price per unit	2	2

Interest to be paid at 10per cent on fresh capital invested.

(Answer: Total profit: Existing Machine – Rs. 3,000, New Machine – Rs. 750; Total Profit Before Interest: Rs.750 + Rs.3,750 = Rs.4,500; Incremental profit = 4,500 – 3000 = 1,500; Incremental investment = 37,500; Accounting rate of return - 4 per cent; Average rate of return - 8 per cent

Decision: This is not even sufficient to pay interest at 10 per cent on additional investment required. Thus, it will be advised to continue with the existing machine.

19. A company has just purchased patent rights to a new milling process for Rs. 60000. The patents are to run for a period of 3 years, after which they are to be renewed. The future earning after taxes (EAT) are given below :

Year	:	1	2	3
EAT	:	10000	10000	10000

Compute the following :

a) Payback period

b) ARR

c) IRR

d) NPV at 15% rate of discount

CASE STUDY FOR CLASS DISCUSSION - I

RNS MOTORS LTD

RNS Adwani, an ITI diploma holder had been working with M/s. RNS and workshop for the last ten years. He had joined as a technician. He was recognized as the best mechanic of Supreme Garage. A good number of clients preferred to get their cars repaired by RNS Adwani . In three years time, he was promoted as a supervisor. RNS Adwani then joined distance education programme of IGNOU and completed his graduation. He studied accounts and would assist the owner Mr. Gupta in maintaining the accounts. Mr. Gupta liked him very much and two years back, RNS Adwani was promoted as the manager of RNS and Workshop.

Gupta had set up this business about 18 years back when he had retired from the Indian Army due to a leg injury. Due to good customer relations and quality service, RNS and workshop had earned a very good reputation and was known as the best motor garage in the district. A large number of clients form the neighbouring district would bring in their vehicles to Supreme Garage. The workshop was known for engine overhauling. It had an electrical section for auto electrical and an agency for Exide batteries. RNS specialized in denting and painting and maintained good relations with insurance companies. It maintained its own tow truck and did good business during accidents and break-downs. It presently employed ten full time mechanics, one supervisor besides RNS Adwani and Gupta who were manager and the owner respectively. During the rush season the workers worked overtime and additional casual labour was also employed to meet the delivery schedules.

Since past one year, Mrs. Gupta was not keeping well. Six months ago, she had a minor heart attack. Mrs and Mr. Gupta decided to shift to USA and join their daughter, who was a heart specialist at Los Angles, USA. Gupta had no one to succeed him, he decided to sell the business. He wanted the buyer to run the business on similar lines and maintain its reputation.

He called RNS Adwani and made him an offer to sell his business. The initial offer was for Rs. 57.50 lakh. He also proposed to assist RNS in financing the purchase.

Gupta provided him with the information on past earnings with projections for five years. He also provided him with the Balance Sheet and Profit and Loss Accounts of RNS Motors as on 31st March 2000. He informed RNS that based upon the business flow, he had valued the goodwill as Rs. 15 lakh.

RNS was excited about the offer. He knew that the business was very profitable and its profits had been increasing over the years. It had never been at loss. He consulted a friend who was a banker and also a Chartered Accountant. He advised him differently. He knew there was a scope of negotiation over the price of the business. Now RNS now needs assistance.

Sales and Profit of Previous Years

Net sales	81,95,000	90,34,000
PBT	7,37,500	7,56,600
PAT	5,25,000	6,23,200

Summary of Projected sales and earnings

Year	2001	2002	2003	2004	2005
Net Sales	11,00,000	120,00,000	125,00,000	130,00,000	135,00,000
PBT	8,65,000	9,50,000	10,50,000	12,00,000	12,50,000
PAT	7,00,000	7,80,000	8,60,000	9,30,000	9,75,000

QUESTIONS

1. Evaluate the value of RNS Motors using discounted cash flow and multiple earning method (Assume 20% required rate of return).

2. How do you think the banker will value this business? Discuss the method and calculate the value.

3. If you were the banker, will you finance?

4. How would you evaluate the good will of RNS Motors.

5. As a consultant would you advice Mr. RNS Adwani to buy RNS Motors or not. Explain with reasons.

RNS MOTORS
Balance sheet (As on 31.03.2000)

Liabilities	Rs.
Capital	16,00,000
Retained profits	18,10,880
Building loan	26,99,200
Term loan	12,16,000
Current liabilities	8,14,400
Total liabilities	81,40,480
Assets	
Gross block	66 56,000
Depreciation	14,22,720
Net blocks (at the end)	52,33,280
Current assets	
Stocks	6,65,600
Receivables	13,31,200
Cash in hand	9,10,400
Total current assets	29,07,200
Total assets	81,40,440

Depreciation Schedule

Asset	Gross Block	Depreciation	Net Block
Land Building	38,40,000	6,16,000	32,24,000
Plant Eqpt.	26,24,000	7,34,720	18,89,280
Other Assets	1,92,000	72,000	1,20,000
Total	66,56,000	14,22,726	55,33,280

RNS MOTORS
Profit & Loss Account (for the year ending 31.03.2000)

	Rs.
Net Sales	99,64,800
Direct Wages	30,78,400
Contract Materials	18,83,200
Supplies	2,36,800
Mix Costs	4,24,000
Cost of Sales	56,22,400
Gross Profit from Operation	43,42,400
Operating Expenses	26,35,200
Total Depreciation for the Year	3,76,272
Net Income before Interest and Taxes	13,30,928
Interest	4,97,440
Profit Before tax	8,33,488
Income tax	1,58,240
Net Profit after tax	6,75,248

CASE FOR CLASS DISCUSSION 2

MAVIS MACHINE SHOP

The case is set in an metalworking shop in West Virginia, one of whose products is drill bits for oil exploration. The time is 1980, in the midst of an oil drilling boom resulting from the oil crises of 1974 and 1979.

Early in 1980, Tom Mavis, President of Mavis Machine shop was considering a project to modernize his plant facilities. The company operated out of a large converted warehouse in Salem, West Virginia. It produced machinery or assorted machined metal parts for the oil and gas drilling and production industry in the surrounding area. One of Mavis major customer was Buckeye Drilling, Inc., which purchased specialized drill bits and replacement parts for its operations. Mavis had negotiated an annual contract with Buckeye to supply its drill bit requirements and related spare parts in each of the past 8 years. In 1978 and 1979 the requirements had been about 8,400 bits per year. All Buckeye's rigs were busy. Mavis knew, there were 30 rigs operating in the state and that it had resin up from 17 in 1972. Wells drilled was up even more, from 679 in 1972 to 1,474 last year.

The arrangement of the machine shop included four large manual lathes currently devoted to the Buckeye business. Each lathe was operated by a skilled worker, and each bit required mechanical keep. Mavis was considering replacing these manual lathes with an automatic machine, capable of performing all four machinery operations necessary for a drill bit. This machine would produce drill bits at the same rate as the four existing lathes, and would only require one operator. Instead of skill in metalworking, the job would now involve more skill in computerized automation.

The four existing manual lathes were 3 years old and had cost a total of $590,000. Together they produced 8,400 drill bits on a two-shift, 5-day/week basis. The useful life of these lathes, calculated on a two-shift/day, 5 day/week basis, was estimated to be 15 years. The salvage value at the end of their useful life was estimated to be $5,000 each. Depreciation of $114,000 had been accumulated on the four lathes. Cash for the purchase of these lathes had been partially supplied by a 10-year, unsecured, 10% bank loan, of which $180,000 was still outstanding. The best estimate of the current selling price of the four lathes in their present condition was $240,000, after dismantling and removal costs. The loss from the sale would be deductible for tax purposes, resulting in a tax savings of 46% of the loss.

The automatic machine being considered needed only one skilled operator to feed in raw castings, observe functioning, and make necessary adjustments. It would have an output of 8,400 drill its annually on a two-shift, 5-day basis. As it would be specially built by a machine tool manufacturer, there was no catalogue price. The cost was estimated to be $680,000, delivered and installed, the useful life would be 15 years. Using a 12-year life (the remaining life of the current lathes). The estimated salvage value would be 10% of the cost.

The automatic lathe was first introduced in 1975 at a cost of $ 750,000. It was expected that as the manufacturing techniques became more generally familiar, the price would continue to drop over the next few years. This price decline was in stark contrast to the inflation in oil services products and supplies which was 18% in both, 1978 and 1979.

A study prepared by the cost accountant to help decide, what action to take, showed the following information. The direct labour rate for lathe operations was $10 per hour including fringe benefits. Pay rates for operators would not change as a result of machining changes. The new machine would use less floor space, which would save $15,000 annually on the allocated charges for square footage of space used, although the layout of the plant was such that the left space unoccupied would be difficult to utilize and no other use was planned. Miscellaneous cash expenses for supplies, maintenance, and power would be $20,000 less per year, if the automatic machine were used. The purchase price was subject to 10% investment tax credit that did not reduce the depreciable cost.

Assignment

1. Summarize the net cash flows for the proposed project.
2. For the project, calculate the internal rate of return, the accounting rate of return, the payback period, the net present value and the profitability index.
3. What qualitative factors should be considered in evaluating this project?
4. What decision would you recommend?

EXHIBIT I

Mavis Machine Shop

Selected Financial Information

Condensed Income Statement, 1979

Neat Sales	:	85,364,213
Cost of Goods Sold	:	3,494,941
Selling, General & Administrative	:	643,706
Profit before Taxes	:	81,225,566
Income Taxes	:	602,851
Net Income	:	8622,715

Condensed Balance Sheet, 12/31/79

Cash	8532.122	Current liabilities	8930.327
Accounts Receivable	622.107	long-Term Notes Outstanding (at 10%)	500.000
Inventory	1,858.120	Common Stock	1,000,000
Property Assets	4,390.701	Retained Earnings	5,011,723
	87,442,050		87,442,050

REFERENCES

1. Finny, H.A. and Miller, H.E., "*Principles of Accounting*", New Delhi: Prentice-Hall of India, 1968, P. 163.
2. Gitman, L. J., "*Principles of Management Finance*", New York: Harper & Row Publishers, 1982, P. 381.
3. Chowdhary, S.B., "*Analysis of Company Financial Statements*", Bombay: Asia Publishing House, 1964, P. 31.
4. Paton & Paton., "*Corporation Accounts and Statements*", New York: Macmillan Company, 1964, P. 362.

5. Kulshrestha, N.K., *"Analysis of Financial Statements of Indian Paper Industry"*, Aligarh: Navman Publishing House, 1972, P. 133.

6. Anthony, R. N. and Reece, J.S., *"Management Accounting – Text and Cases"*, Illinois: Richard D. Irwin, 1975, P. 98.

7. Homer, J.M., Poul, E.F. and Donald, F.I., *"Using Accounting Information"*, New York: Harcourt Brace, 1975, P. 399.

8. Kulshrestha, N.K., Op. cit., p. 133.

9. Kulshrestha, N.K., Op. cit., p. 134.

10. Pandey, I.M., *"Financial Management"*, New Delhi: Vikas Publishing House, 2002, p.407.

11. Van Horne, J.C. and Wachowicz Jr, J.M., *"Fundamentals of Financial Management"*, New Delhi: Prentice-Hall of India Private Ltd, 1996, p. 314.

12. The use of IRR for appraising capital investment was emphasized in the formal terms, for the first time by Joel Dean in his article titled, *"Capital Budgeting"*, Colombia University Press, 1951.

13. Breadly, R.and Mayers., *"Principles of Corporate Finance"*, Tata McGraw-Hill Publishing Company Ltd., 1991, p.8.

Capital Rationing and Risk Factor in Capital Budgeting

*After studying this chapter, you
should be able to:*

1 Explain the Meaning of Capital
Rationing.

2 Discuss the objective and the
effects of Capital Rationing.

3 Explain the steps involved in
Capital Rationing.

4 Understand Risk Analysis in
Capital Budgeting.

5 Understand the Techniques
used for in Corporation of Risk
Factor in Capital Budgeting
decision.

INTRODUCTION

Theoretically speaking, a concern should accept all profitable capital projects which add to the wealth of the owners and increase the market value per share. The profitability of a capital project can be determined under any of the discounted cash flow techniques, such as the net present value method, profitability index method or internal rate of return method. The acceptable criteria under these methods are :

(i)   In the case of net present value method, the net present value of the project must be more than zero.

(ii) In the case of profitability index method, the profitability index must be more than 1.

(iii) In the case of internal rate of return method, the internal rate of return should be more than the cost of capital.

No doubt, if a concern has more funds it can accept and implement all profitable projects.

However, in real situation, a concern may not have enough funds to undertake all profitable projects. Further, there may be restrictions imposed by the management on the amount of funds that could be used for financing capital projects during a specified period. In such a situation, there arises the need for rationing of capital. That is, in such a situation, all the profitable investment proposals or projects cannot be taken up. Only some of the profitable proposals or projects have to be taken up and the other profitable proposals have to be given up. So, capital rationing arises in a situation where a concern has more profitable investment proposals than it can finance.

MEANING OF CAPITAL RATIONING

Capital rationing means the allocation of the limited funds available for financing the capital projects to only some of the profitable projects in such a manner that the long-term returns are maximized. In other words, it means the selection of only some of the profitable investment proposals or projects out of the several profitable investment proposals available. In short, it means the selection of only some of the profitable investment proposals and the rejection of the other profitable investment proposals due to limited availability of funds or other considerations, say, the desire of the management to keep the growth of the firm within limit, the preference of the management to safety and control as compared to profit.

OBJECTIVE OF CAPITAL RATIONING

The main objective of capital rationing is, to ensure the selection of only those profitable investment proposals that will provide the maximum long-term returns. In short, the objective of capital rationing is to maximise the value of the firm.

EFFECT OF CAPITAL RATIONING

The effects of capital rationing are:

(i)   When there is capital rationing, a firm will not be able to undertake all the profitable investment proposals. It has to accept only some of the profitable investment proposals and reject the other profitable investment proposals.

(ii) When there is capital rationing, it will be possible for the firm to maximize the wealth of the owners and to maximize the market value per share.

STEPS INVOLVED IN CAPITAL RATIONING

Capital rationing involves two important steps. They are :

a) **Ranking of the different investment proposals:** First, the different investment proposals or capital projects available, should be ranked on the basis of their profitability (i.e., on the basis of their net present value or profitability index or the internal rate of return), in the descending order.

b) **Selection of some of the profitable investment proposals:** Then, on the basis of their profitability in the descending order, the selection of that combination of profitable investment proposals, which would provide the highest profitability, should be made subject to the budget constraint for the period.

Illustration 1 : A firm has the following investment opportunities :

Proposal	Initial outlay Rs.	Profitability index
1	3,00,000	1.20
2	1,50,000	1.15
3	2,50,000	1.10
4	2,00,000	1.05

The available fund amount is Rs. 4,00,000.

Which proposals the firm should accept ?

Solution:

First Step- Ranking of the proposals in the descending order of their Profitability Index.

Proposal	Profitability index	Rank
1	1.20	I
2	1.15	II
3	1.10	III
4	1.05	IV

Second Step- Selection of the proposals: Here, the profitability index of all the proposals is above unity, i.e., above one. As such, all the proposals are profitable or acceptable. However, as the funds available are limited, there should be capital rationing and only the most profitable combination of the proposals should be accepted.

For determining the most profitable combination of proposals, first, we should determine the net present value of the various acceptable proposals. The net present value of each of the various acceptable proposals can be computed with the help of the following formula :

Net present value of a proposal = Initial capital cost of a project X Profitability index of the proposal - 1

Accordingly, the net present value of each of the various investment proposals is:

Proposal	Net Present value of the Proposal
1	3,00,000 x 1.20 – 1 i.e. = Rs. 60,000
2	1,50,000 (1.15 – 1) i.e. = Rs. 22,500
3	2,50,000 (1.10 – 1) i.e. = Rs. 25,000
4	2,00,000 (1.05 –1) i.e. = 10,000

After the ascertainment of the net present value of each of the various profitable proposals, the selection of the combination which will yield the highest total net present value has to be made. Such a combination of proposals can be :

Various possible combination of proposals:

i) Proposal involving a capital outlay of Rs. 3,00,000 and yielding a net present value of Rs. 60,000.

ii)   Proposals 2 and 3 involving capital outlay of Rs (1,50,000 + 2,50,000) 4,00,000 and yielding total net present value of Rs (22,500+10,000) 32,500.

iii) Proposals 2 and 4 involving capital outlay of Rs. (1,50,000 + 2,00,000) 350,000 and yielding a net present capital outlay of Rs. (22,500 + 10,000) 32,500.

Of the three possible combinations, the net present value of the first combination is the highest. So, this combination has to be selected.

Note: It is assumed that the uninvested capital of Rs. (4,00,000 - 3,00,000) 1,00,000 has a net present value of zero.

Illustration 2 : A firm has Rs. 5,00,000 available for investment. The firm's cost of capital 10%. The investment opportunities available are as follows :

Proposal	Cost of the Project	Internal Rate of Return	Net present value
	Rs.		Rs.
1	1,50,000	5%	-14,000
2	2,00,000	11%	3,000
3	1,80,000	12%	18,000
4	1,90,000	20%	1,20,000
5	1,00,000	18%	70,000
6	1,50,000	9%	12,000

Solution:

First Step: Ranking of the proposals in the descending order of Internal Rate of Return

Proposal	Internal Rate of Return Taking 10% as Cut-off Rate	Rank
1	5%	-
2	11%	IV
3	12%	III
4	20%	I
5	18%	II
6	9%	-

Note : the internal rate of return of proposals 2,3,4 and 5 is above the cut-off rate or firm's cost of capital of 10%, and the internal rate of return of proposals 1 and 6 is less than the cut-off rate of 10%. So, proposals 2,3,4 and 5 are profitable or acceptable and proposals 1 and 6 are not acceptable (i.e., to be rejected).

Second Step : Selection of the proposals: Here, though proposals 2,3,4 and 5 are acceptable or profitable, all these proposals cannot be selected because of the limited availability of funds and credit rationing. Under credit rationing, only that combination of acceptable proposals, which will yield the highest total net present value has to be selected. Accordingly, here, only the combination of proposals 4,5, and 3 involving a capital expenditure of Rs. (1,90,000 + 1,00,000 + 1,80,000) 4,70,000 and yielding a total net present value of Rs. (1,20,000 + 70,000 + 18,000) 2,08,000 should be selected.

Note: It is assumed that the uninvested capital of Rs. (5,00,000- 4,70,000) 30,000 has zero net present value.

Illustration 3: A firm having Rs. 15,00,000 to invest wishes to select from the following project those that maximize the present value of cash inflows :

Project	Initial cost Investment	B/C Ratio
	Rs.	
1	6,00,000	1.20
2	2,00,000	1.40
3	3,00,000	1.10
4	8,00,000	1.30
5	5,00,000	1.50
6	4,00,000	1.20
7	9,00,000	1.30
8	7,00,000	1.45

i) Calculate the present value of cash flow of each project.

ii) Using a trial and error approach, select the group of projects that maximize the firm's present value of cash inflows. The firm earns zero return on any uninvested portion of the budget.

Solution :

First step : Ranking of the proposals in the descending order of their profitability.

Proposal or Project	B/C Ratio or Profitability Index of the Proposal	Rank
1	1.20	V
2	1.40	III
3	1.10	VI
4	1.30	IV
5	1.50	I
6	1.20	V
7	1.30	IV
8	1.45	II

Note: Here, the B/C ratio or the profitability index of all the projects is above unity, i.e., above 1. That means, all the projects are profitable or acceptable.

Second Step: Selection of the proposals: Here, no doubt, all the projects are acceptable. But the funds available for capital investment are limited. So, there should be capital rationing. Under capital rationing, only the most profitable group or combinations or proposals should be selected.

For selecting the most profitable group of proposals, first, we should ascertain the net present value of each of the various proposals. The net present value of each of the various proposals can be ascertained as follows :

Initial cost of the project x (profitability of index-1). Accordingly the net present value of the various proposals is as follows :

Proposal	Net Present Value of the Proposal
1	6,00,000 X (1.20 – 1) = Rs. 1,20,000
2	2,00,000 X (1.40 – 1 = Rs. 80,000
3	3,00,000 X 1.10 – 1) = Rs. 30,000
4	8,00,000 X (1.30–1) = Rs. 2,40,000
5	5,00,000 X (1.50–1) = Rs. 2,50,000
6	4,00,000 X (1.20–1) =Rs. 80,000
7	9,00,000 X (1.30–1) = Rs. 2,70,000
8	7,00,000 X (1.45–1) = Rs. 3,15,000

After ascertaining the net present value of the various proposals, the selection of the most profitable combination or group of proposals has to be made. Such a combination of proposals, in this case, are 5, 8 and 2 involving the capital expenditure of Rs. (5,00,000 + 7,00,000 + 2,00,000) 14,00,000 and yielding the highest total net present value of Rs. (2,50,000 + 3,15,000 + 80,000) 6,45,000.

Note: It is assumed that the uninvested capital of Rs. (15,00,000 - 14,00,000) 1,00,000 has zero net present value.

RISK ANALYSIS IN CAPITAL BUDGETING

Need for Risk Analysis in Capital Budgeting : If a capital budgeting decision is made on the assumption that the capital project or investment proposal does not involve any risk (i.e., there is certainly regarding the future estimate of cash inflows from capital project during its estimated life), then, there is no question of risk analysis is capital budgeting.

However, in real saturation, the assumption that the investment proposal does not involve any risk does not hold good. In real situation, owing to a number of reasons, such as technical, economic, political, cyclical fluctuation, financial, foreign exchange, taxation etc., the actual return from an investment proposal will be usually different from the estimated returns. In other words, there is uncertainly regarding the future estimation of cash inflows from capital project. In short, there is risk in capital budgeting or investment decision. (Of course, the risk from one investment proposal to another. Some proposals will be less risky and some may be more risky).

As risk is involved in every investment proposal, in real situation, it is necessary to take into account the risk factor, while taking the capital budgeting decision.

Meaning of Risk Investment Proposal: Risk in an investment refers to the variability that is likely to future between the estimated returns and the actual returns from the proposal. The greater is the variability between the two returns, the more is the risk involved in the project, and vice versa.

Incorporation of the Risk in Investment Proposal: As stated earlier, risk is involved in very capital budgeting decision. As risk is involved in every capital budgeting proposal, the management of a firm must take the risk factor into account, while determining the returns or cash inflows and the profitability of a project for the purpose of capital budgeting.

It, may be noted that the incorporation of the risk factor in capital budgeting decisions is a difficult task.

Techniques used for Incorporation of Risk Factor in Capital Budgeting Decisions

There are a number of techniques used for the incorporation of the risk factor in capital budgeting decisions. The most popular techniques are :

A) Ordinary techniques or general techniques, such as (a) risk adjusted discount rate and (b) certainly equivalent coefficient.

B) Quantitative techniques such as (a) sensitivity analysis, (b) probability assignment, (c) standard deviation, (d) coefficient of variation and (e) decision tree.

Now, let us consider the various techniques used for the incorporation of the risk factor in capital budgeting decisions.

A) GENERAL TECHNIQUES

Risk Adjusted Discount Rate Method

Meaning and features of Risk Adjusted Discount Rate Method : Under the risk adjusted discount rate method, the future cash flow from capital projects are discounted at the risk adjusted discount rate and decision regarding the selection of a project is made on the basis of the net present value of the project computed at the risk adjusted discount rate.

The risk adjusted discount rate is based on the assumption that investors expect a higher rate of return on more risky projects and a lower rate of return on less risky projects, and so, a higher discount rate is used for discounting the cash flows of more risky project and a lower discount rate is used for discounting the cash flows of less risky project.

The risk adjusted discount rate comprises two rates, viz.,

(i) risk-free rate, normal rate, usual discount rate or unity rate that takes care of time element and

(ii) risk premium rate, surplus rate or extra rate that takes care of the risk factor. So, the risk adjusted discount rate is the usual or normal discount rate for the time factor plus the extra or additional discount rate for the risk factor.

Risk-free rate is the rate at which the future cash flows of a project which is not subject to risk are discounted. In short, it is the normal or usual discount rate at which the future cash flows of a risk less project are discounted.

Risk premium rate is the extra or additional discount rate at which the future cash flows of a risky project are discounted. The risk-premium rate or the extra discount rate for the risk factor varies with the degree of risk involved in the capital projects. So, for a less risky investment proposal, the extra discount rate will be lower and for a more risky investment proposal, the extra discount rate for the risk factor will be more.

Let us consider the risk-adjusted discount rate with an example. Suppose there are two investment proposals, X and Y. Proposal X is less risky, and Proposal Y is more risky. The normal discount rate for the time factor is 5%. The extra discount rate for the risk factor is 5% for proposal X and 10% for proposal Y. In this case, the risk-adjusted discount rate for proposal X will be 10% (i.e., the normal discount rate of 5% plus the extra discount rate for the risk factor 5% and the risk-adjusted discount rate for proposal Y will be 15% (i.e., the normal discount rate of 5% plus the extra discount rate for the risk factor 10%).

Merits of Risk-Adjusted Discount Rate Method

a) It is easy to understand and simple to calculated.

b) The risk-premium rate included in the risk adjusted rate takes care of the risk element in the future cash flows of the project.

c) It takes into account the risk averse attitude of investors.

Demerits of Risk-Adjusted Discount Rate Method

a) The risk-premium rates, determined under this method, are arbitrary. So, this method may not give objective results.

b) It is the future cash flows which are subject to risk and not the discount rate. So, the future cash flows must be adjusted and not the discount rate. But, under this method, it is the discount rate that is adjusted and not risk, and not the future cash flows. Thus, this method adjusts the wrong element.

c) Under the method, the risk is compounded over time, since the risk premium is added to the discount rate. Which means, this method presumes that the risk necessarily increases with the passage of time. But this may not happen in all situations or cases.

d) This method presumes that investors are averse to risk (i.e., investors avoid facing risk). This may not be true in all cases. There are many investors who would like to take risks and are prepared to pay premium for taking risk.

Illustration 4: From the following data, state which project is preferable :

	A(Rs.)	B (Rs.)
Year 1	6,000	8,000
Year 2	5,000	6,000
Year 3	4,000	5,000
Initial cost of the project	12,000	12,000

Riskless discount rate is 5%. Project A is less risky as compared to project B and so, the management considers risk premium rates at 5% and 10% respectively as appropriate for discounting the cash inflows.

Note: The discount factors at 10% and 15% are :

Year	10%	15%
1	0.909	0.876
2	0.826	0.756
3	0.751	0.650

Solution:

First Step: Calculation of Risk-Adjusted Discount Rate

For Project A

Riskless discount rate	5%
Add Risk-premium rate	5%
Risk adjusted discount rate	10%

For project B

Riskless discount rate	5%
Add Risk premium rate	10%
Risk-adjusted discount rate	15%

Second Step : Calculation of discounted cash inflows (i.e., present value and net present value of the projects):

Year	Project A	Project B
	Discounted Cash Inflows at 10%	**Discounted Cash Outflows at 15%**
	Rs.	Rs.
1	(6,000 X .909) 5,454	(8,000 X .876) 7,008
2	(5,000 X .826) 4,130	(6,000 X .756) 4,536
3	(4,000 X .751) 3,004	(5,000 X .658) 3,250
	12,588	14,794
Less : Initial outlay	12,000	12,000
Net present value	588	2,794

Comment : The net present value of Project B is higher than that of Project A. So, Project B is preferable.

Certainty Equivalent Coefficient method:

Introduction: Certainty equivalent co-efficient method is a method which makes adjustment against risk in the estimates of future cash inflows for a risky capital investment project.

Features of certainty equivalent coefficient method: Under this method, adjustment against risk is made in the estimates of future cash inflows of a risky capital project by adjusting (i.e, reducing) to a conservative level the estimated cash flows of a capital investment proposal by applying a correction factor termed as certainty equivalent coefficient.

The certainty equivalent coefficient is the ratio of riskless cash flow to risky cashflow. Riskless cash flow means the cash flow which the management expects, when there is no risk in investment proposal. Risky cash flow means the cash flow which the management expects when there is risk in investment proposal.

The certainty equivalent coefficient can be calculated with the help of the following formula:

$$\text{Certainty equivalent coefficient} = \frac{\text{Riskless cash flow}}{\text{Risky cash flow}}$$

Suppose the risky cash flow is Rs. 20,000 and the riskless cash flow is Rs. 14,000.

$$\text{The certainty equivalent co-efficient is} : \frac{14,000}{20,000} = 0.7$$

Steps involved in certainty equivalent coefficient method: The various steps involved in the certainty equivalent coefficient method are :

1. First, the certainty equivalent coefficient has to be calculated for each year of a project.

2. Secondly, the risk-adjusted cash flow of a project for each year has to be calculated. The risk-adjusted cash flow of a year can be calculated as follows : Estimated cash flow for the year X Certainty equivalent coefficient.

   Suppose the estimated cash flow of a project for a year is Rs. 20,000 and the certainty equivalent coefficient for the cash flow of that year is 7, the risk adjusted cash flow for the year will be : 20,000 × .7 = Rs. 14,000.

3. Thirdly, we have to find out the present value of the capital project. The present value of the capital project can be found by adopting the following procedure. First, the risk-adjusted

cash flow for each year should be multiplied by the present value factor applicable to that year to get the present value of the risk-adjusted cash flow of each year.

4. Fourthly, we have to ascertain the net present value of the project. The net present value of the project will be :

	Rs.
Present value of the project	_____
Less Initial investment on the project	_____
Net present value of the project	_____

5. After the net present value of a project is computed, decision is taken as to the selection of the project. The selection of a project is, usually, made on the following lines :

i) Generally, a project becomes acceptable, if it has a positive (i.e., +) net present value.

ii) If there are two or more mutually exclusive projects, generally, the project whose net present value is higher (if there are only two projects) or highest (if there are three or more projects) is selected.

Merit of this method: This method is an improvement over the previous method, as it provides for adjustment against risk.

Demerit: Even this method is not strictly objective, as an element of subjectivity is bound to arise while converting risky cash flows into riskless cash flows.

Illustration 5: Two mutually exclusive investment proposals, X and Y are under consideration before the management of a company. The initial outlay of each project is Rs. 30,000. Both the projects are estimated to have a useful economic life-span of 5 years.

The estimates of cash inflows and their certainty equivalent coefficient are as follows :

Year	Project		Project	
	Estimated Cash Flows	Certainly Equivalent Coefficient (C.E.C.)	Estimated Cash Flow	Certainly Equivalent Coefficient (C.E.C.)
	Rs.		Rs.	
1	25,000	.7	30,000	.6
2	30,000	.5	35,000	.5
3	20,000	.4	25,000	.4
4	15,000	.3	12,000	.2
5	10,000	.2	10,000	.1

The cost of capital for the company is 15%.

Compare the net present value of the two projects and suggest which project should be accepted by the management.

Note: The present value factor at 15% is :

Year	Present Value Factor at 15%
1	.870
2	.756
3	.658
4	.572
5	.497

Solution:

First Step - Computation of the net present value of the projects :

		Project X				
Years	Estimated cash Flows	Certain Equivalent Coefficient (C.E.C.)	Risk Adjusted Cash Flows	Present Value Factor at 15%	Present Value	
	Rs		Rs			Rs
1	25,000	0.7	(25000x.7)17,500	0.870	(17,500x.870)	15,225
2	30,000	0.5	(30,000x.5)15,000	0.756	15,000x.756)	11,340
3	20,000	0.4	(20,000x.4)8,000	0.658	(8,000x.658)	5,264
4	15,000	0.3	(15,000x.3)4,500	0.572	(4,500x.572)	2,574
5	10,000	0.2	(10,000x.2)2,000	0.497	(2,000x.497)	994
		Gross present value				35,397
		Less initial capital outlay				30,000
		Net present value				5,397

		Project X				
Years	Estimated cash Flows	Certainly Equivalent Coefficient (C.E.C.)	Risk Adjusted Cash Flows	Present Value Factor at 15%	Present Value	
	Rs.		Rs.			Rs.
1	30,000	0.6	(30,000x.6)18,000	0.870	(18,000x.870)	15,660
2	35,000	0.5	(35,000x.5)17,500	0.756	15,000x.756)	13,230
3	25,000	0.4	(25,000x.4)10,000	0.658	(10000x.658)	6,580
4	12,000	0.2	(12,000x.2)2,400	0.572	(2,400x.572)	1,373
5	10,000	0.1	(10,000x.2)1,000	0.497	(1,000x.497)	497
		Present value of the project				37,340
		Less initial capital outlay				30,000
		Net present value of the project				7,340

Second Step - Decision - making as to selection of the project : Here, both the projects have positive net present value. So, both are acceptable.

However, the net present value of Project Y is more than that of Project X. That means, project Y is preferable.

B)   QUANTITATIVE TECHNIQUES

Sensitivity Analysis

Introduction: While making capital investment decision, if we consider only one figure of estimated cash inflows, there are chances of estimation errors creeping into the capital investment decision. So, to avoid this, the sensitivity analysis has been introduced. The sensitivity analysis tries to check the estimation errors creeping into the capital investment decision by providing more than one estimate of cash inflows of a project.

Meaning of Sensitivity Analysis: Sensitivity analysis is a way of analyzing the changes in the net present value or the internal rate of return of a project to a given change in one of the variables of capital investment proposal like the estimated cash inflows of the project, the rate of return or the estimated economic life of the project. It indicates how sensitive is a projects" net present value to a change in any particular variable of investment proposal.

Under the sensitivity analysis, usually, estimation of the cash inflows of a project is made under three assumptions or situations, viz, (i) pessimistic, (ii) most likely and (iii) optimistic outcomes associated with the project. After estimating the cash inflows and determining the net present value of the project under the three different situations, conclusion is drawn about the riskiness of the project. Under this analysis, it is usually concluded that the larger is the difference between the pessimistic and optimistic cash inflows and the resultant net present value, the more is the risk of the project and vice versa.

Steps involved in the Technique of Sensitivity Analysis : The technique of sensitivity analysis involves three steps. They are :

a) Identification of all the variables which have influence on the project's net present value or internal rate of return

b) Determination of the mathematical relationship between the various variables which affect the project's net present value or internal rate of return.

c) Analysis of the impact of the change in each of the variables on the project's net present value or internal rate of return.

Advantages of the Techniques of Sensitivity Analysis: The technique of sensitivity analysis has certain advantages. They are :

a) It is a popular method of assessing the risk associated with a project.

b) It shows how sensitive a project is to a change in any variable influencing the investment proposal.

c) It is helpful to locate and assess the impact of risk on a project's profitability.

Disadvantages of the Technique of Sensitivity Analysis : The technique of sensitivity analysis is not free from drawbacks. It suffers from the following drawbacks.

i) Unless the combined effect of changes in a set of inter-related variables is examined, the technique of sensitivity analysis will be useless. Single variable sensitivity testing may lead to wrong conclusion.

ii) Examination of the combined effect of changes in a set of variables is a very complex process.

Illustration 6: A company has under consideration, two mutually exclusive projects X and Y for increasing its plant's capacity. Each project requires net investment of Rs. 10,000. Each project has an economic life of 10 years.

The company's cost of capital is 10%. The management of the company has made the following pessimistic, most likely and optimistic estimates of the annual cash inflows associated with each project.

Estimated annual cash inflows	Projected A	Projected B
	Rs.	Rs.
Pessimistic	2,000	1,000
Most likely	2,500	2,500
Optimistic	3,000	5,000

a) Determine the net present value of each project.

b) Which project do you consider should be selected by the management.

Note: The present value factor of an annuity of Re. 1/- at 10% for 10 years is Rs. 6.145.

Solution:

First Step: Computation of the net present value of the Projects :

		Project A		
Situation	Cash Inflows of the Project	Discount Factor at 10%	Present Value of the Project	Net Present value of the Project
	Rs.		Rs.	
Pessimistic	2,000	6.145	12,290	(12,290 – 10,000) 2,290
Most likely	. 2,500	6.145	15,363	(15,363–10,000) 5,363
Optimistic	3,000	6.145	18,435	(18.'35–10,000) 8,435

		Project B		
Situation	Cash Inflows of the Project	Discount Factor at 10%	Present Value of the Project	Net Present value of the Project
	Rs.		Rs.	
Pessimistic	1,000	6.145	6,145	(6,145 – 10,000) –3,855
Mcst likely	2,500	6.145	15,363	(13,363–10,000) 3,363
Optimistic	5,000	6.145	30,725	(30.725–10,000) 20,725

Second Step: Decision- making regarding the selection of the project : The difference between the pessimistic net present value and optimistic net present value of Project A is Rs. (8,435 – 2,290) 6,145 and of project B is Rs. (20,725 + 3,855) 24,580. The difference between the pessimistic net present value and the optimistic net present value of Project B is more than that of Project A. Hence, Project B is more risky than Project A. So, Project A may be selected.

Probability Assignment Method

Introduction: Sensitivity analysis method suffers from a limitation. It, no doubt, provides cash inflow estimates under three different assumptions or situations, viz., pessimistic, most likely and optimistic. But it does not indicate the chances of occurrence of each of these three estimates. That is, it does not indicate how far these three cash flow estimates would come true. A better capital budgeting decision may be made only if one can assign approximate probabilities to these three cash inflow estimates. The cash inflows as adjusted by probabilities will give a more precise estimates of the likely cash inflows as compared to the cash inflows which are not adjusted by probabilities. This realization has contributed to the introduction of probability assignment in capital budgeting decisions.

Features of probability Assignment Approach : Under the probability assignment approach, probabilities are assigned to the various cash inflow estimates and the expected monetary values for the various cash inflow estimates are ascertained. On the basis of the sum total expected monetary values of the various cash flow estimates of each project, decision-making as to the selection of a project is made. Generally, a project whose expected monetary value is greater or greatest is selected.

Meaning of Probability: Probability means the degree of likelihood of occurrence of even in future. When an event is said to have '1' probability, it means that it is bound to occur. If an event is said to have '0' (zero) probability, It means that the event is not going to occur.

The probability of an event is determined on the basis of repeated observation of the event under identical situations over a period of time.

Probability may be objective or subjective: An objective probability is based on a larger number of observations under independent and identical conditions repeated over a period of time. Objective probability is of little utility in a capital budgeting decision. As no two independent investment situations can be identical.

A subjective probability is not based on a large number of observations under independent and identical conditions repeated over a period of time. It is based on the personal judgment of the person concerned. For this reason, a subjective probability is also known as personalized probability. In capital budgeting decisions, probabilities are of subjective type.

Steps involved in Probability Assignment Approach : The various steps involved in the probability assignment approach are :

1. First, probabilities are assigned to a series of cash inflow estimates (i.e., cash inflow estimates for different events) for each year.

2. Second, the expected monetary value of each figure of the cash inflow estimate is computed. The expected monetary value of each figure of the cash inflow estimate can be calculated as follows :

   Each figure of cash flow estimate x probability assignment to each figure of cash flow estimate.

3. Third, the total monetary value of the project is computed by adding the monetary values of the various figures of cash inflow estimates.

4. Lastly, decision- making as to the selection of the project is made. Generally, the project whose total expected monetary value is higher or highest is preferred.

Illustration 7 : A company has two capital investment proposals, A and B under consideration. Both the projects require investment of Rs. 6,000.

The following are the details of possible events, cash inflows and probability assignments:

Possible events or Series of Probable Cash inflows	Project A		Project B	
	Cash inflows	Probability Assignments	Cash inflows	Probability Assignments
	Rs.		Rs.	
A	5,000	0.20	10,000	0.15
B	6,000	0.30	8,000	0.25
C	8,000	0.40	8,000	0.30
D	8,000	0.20	6,000	0.25
E	10,000	0.10	5,000	0.20

You are required to give your opinion regarding the selection of the project.

Solution:

First Step: Computation of expected monetary value of the project :

Possible events or Series of Probable Cash inflows	Project A			
	Cash inflows	Probability Assignments	Expected Monetary Value	
	Rs.			Rs.
A	5,000	0.20	(5,000X.20)	1,000
B	6,000	0.30	(6,000X.30)	1,800
C	8,000	0.40	(8,000X.40)	3,200
D	8,000	0.20	(8,000X.20)	1,600
E	10,000	0.10	(10,000X.10)	1,000
Total expected monetary value				8,600

Possible events or Series of Probable Cash inflows	Project B			
	Cash inflows	Probability Assignments	Expected Monetary Value	
	Rs.			Rs.
A	10,000	0.15	(10,000X.15)	1,500
B	8,000	0.25	(8,000X.25)	2,000
C	8,000	0.30	(8,000X.30)	2,400
D	6,000	0.25	(6,000 X .25)	1,500
E	5,000	0.20	(5,000 X .20)	1,000
Total expected monetary value				8,400

Second Step: Decision - making as to the selection of the project : The expected monetary value of Project A is more than project B. So, Project A is preferable.

Standard Deviation Approach

Introduction : Probability assignment approach is, no doubt, a good technique of risk analysis in capital budgeting. But it does not give precise results about the extend of variability of cash inflows. So, to overcome this drawback of probability assignment method, standard deviation method or approach has been introduced.

Standard deviation method is a statistical technique of risk measurement in capital budgeting. It is regarded as an improvement over the probability assignment method.

Meaning and Features of Standard Deviation Approach: Standard deviation is the square root of the squared deviations calculated from the mean. This measure (i.e., standard deviation) is used to compare the variability of probable cash inflows of different projects from their respective mean or expected values.

This technique indicates that a project having a larger standard deviation will be more risky as compared to a project having smaller standard deviation.

Steps involved in the calculation of standard deviation: A number of steps are involved in the calculation of standard deviation. They are :

1. First, we have to compute the mean value (i.e., the arithmetic average) of the projected cash inflows.

2. Second, we have to square up the deviations between the mean value and the projected cash inflows.

3. Third, we have to square up the deviations so arrived at. This gives squared deviations.

4. Fourth, we have to multiply the squared deviations by the assigned probabilities. This gives weighted squared deviations.

5. Fifth, we have to total up the weighted squared deviations.

6. Lastly, we have to find out the square root of the total weighted squared deviations. The resulting figure is the standard deviation.

7. The formula for calculating standard deviation is : $\sqrt{\Sigma pdcf^2}$

    Where,

    'S' means standard deviation

    'p' means probability assigned.

    'dcf' means deviation from the mean (i.e., the expected monetary value).

Advantage of Standard Deviation approach: The main advantage of standard deviation approach is that it gives a precise measure of risk associated with a project. It indicates that a project having higher standard deviation is more risky as compared to a project having a lower standard deviation.

Drawback of Standard Deviation Approach: No doubt, standard deviation approach is an improvement over the probability assignment approach. But it suffers from a drawback. That is, it is only an absolute measure of dispersion or variation and not a relative measure of variation. As a result, when the values of mean expected monetary value show wide variations in the case of two or more projects, the results shown by the standard deviation method may not be precise.

Illustration 8: A company has two Projects A and B, under consideration. Both the projects involve an equal initial investment of Rs. 6,000.

The following particulars are available :

Possible Events	Project A		Project B	
	Cash Inflows	Probability Assigned	Cash Inflows	Probability Assigned
	Rs.		Rs.	
A	5,000	0.2	12,000	0.20
B	7,000	0.15	10,000	0.20
C	9,000	0.3	9,000	0.40
D	9,000	0.2	8,000	0.15
E	10,000	0.1	6,000	0.10

Find out which project is more risky by adopting standard deviation approach

Solution:

Computation of Standard Deviation

Project A					
Possible Events	Cash Inflow	Deviation from the Arithmetic Mean of Rs 8,000	Deviations Squared up	Probability Assigned	Product of Squared Deviations and Probability (Squarred deviations x probability assigned)
A	5,000	(8,000–5,000)=3,000	3,000X3,000=90,00,000	0.20	(90,00,000X.20) 18,00,000
B	7,000	(8,000–7,000)=1,000	1,000X1,000=10,00,000	0.15	(10,00,000X.15) 1,50,000
C	9,000	(9,000–8,000)=1,000	1,000X1,000=10,00,000	0.30	(10,00,000X.30) 3,00,000
D	9,000	(9,000–8,000)=1,000	1,000X1,000=10,00,000	0.20	(10,00,000X.20) 2,00,000
E	10,000	(10,000–8,000)=2,000	2,000X2,000=40,00,000	0.10	(40,00,000X.10) 4,00,000
					28,50,000

Standard Deviation: Square root of 28,50,000, i.e., $\sqrt{28,50,000}$ = 1688.19

Note: In this case, the arithmetic mean of cash inflows is calculated as follows :

Total cash inflows of five events	Rs.
A	5,000
B	7,000
C	9,000
D	9,000
E	10,000
Total	40,000

Arithmetic mean or

Average: 40,000/5 = Rs. 8,000.

Project B					
Possible Events	Cash Inflow	Deviation from the Arithmetic Mean of Rs. 9,000	Deviations Squared up	Probability Assigned	Product of Squared Deviations and Probability (squared deviations x probability assigned)
A	12,000	(12,000–9,000) = 3,000	3,000X3,000=90,00,000	0.20	(90,00,000X.20) 18,00,000
B	10,000	(10,000–9,000) = 1,000	1,000X1,000=10,00,000	0.20	(10,00,000X.20) 2,00,000
C	9,000	(9,000–9,000) = 0	0	0.40	0
D	8,000	(8,000–9,000) = 1,000	1,000X1,000=10,00,000	0.15	(10,00,000X.15) 1,50,000
E	6,000	(6,000–9,000) = 3,000	3,000X3,000=90,00,000	0.10	(90,00,000X.10) 9,00,000
					30,50,000

Standard Deviation

Square Deviation

Square root of 30,50,000, i.e., $\sqrt{30,50,000}$ = 1,746.42

Note: In this case, the arithmetic mean of cash inflows is cash as follows :

Total cash inflows of five events

	Rs.
A	12,000
B	10,000
C	9,000
D	8,000
E	6,000
Total	45,000

Arithmetic mean or average : 45,000/5 = Rs. 9,000

Comment: The standard deviation of Project B is more than that of Project A. That means the variability of cash flow is more in the case of Project B than in the case of Project A. So, Project B is more risky.

Coefficient of Variation Approach

Introduction: Standard Deviation is an absolute measure. It is not suitable for comparison, particularly when investment proposals involve different capital outlay or different monetary values of probable cash inflows. In such cases, a relative measure of dispersion should be employed for comparison. For comparison in such cases, coefficient of variation approach is the best measure. This realization is responsible for the emergence of coefficient of variation approach in capital risk analysis.

Coefficient of variation approach is a relative measure of dispersion. It is considered superior to standard deviation approach in capital risk evaluation associated with investment proposals.

Features of Coefficient Variation Approach: There may be cases where the standard deviations of two investment projects are the same, but the expected monetary values of probable cash flows of the two projects differ. Again, there may be cases where the expected monetary values of probable cash flows of two projects are the same, but the standard deviations of the projects may be different. In such cases or situations, the coefficient of variation of each of the investment projects is computed to get a more precise relative measure of risk.

Coefficient of variation is found by dividing the standard deviation by the mean. (i.e., the arithmetic mean of the estimated cash inflows).

The formula for the calculation of coefficient of variation is :

$$\text{Coefficient of variation} = \frac{\text{Standard Deviation}}{\text{Mean (i.e., the arithmetic mean of the estimate cash inflows)}}$$

Advantages of Coefficient of Variation Approach: The Coefficient of variation is a relative measure. It is quite useful for comparison where the projects involve different cash outlays or different monetary values of cash inflows.

The coefficient of variation suggests that, the more is the coefficient of variation of a project, the greater is the risk associated with that project.

Illustration 9: Taking the illustration given under standard deviation approach, calculate the coefficient of variation and suggest which project is more risky.

Solution:

The coefficient of deviation (i.e., variation) of the projects is :

Project A

$$\frac{\text{Standard Deviation of the Project i.e. } 1688.19}{\text{Arithmetic mean of the estimated cash inflows of the project, i.e, Rs. 8,000}} = 0.21$$

Project B

$$\frac{\text{Standard Deviation of the Project i.e. } 1746.42}{\text{Arithmetic mean of the estimated cash inflows of the project, i.e. Rs. 9,000}} = 0.19$$

Comment:

The coefficient of deviation of Project B is more than that of project A. That means, Project B is more risky.

In this context, It may be noted that with higher risk, the profitability of the project is also higher. As such, the selection of a project depends upon the capacity of the investor to bear risk. If the investor is not averse to risk, he may prefer project B and in case he is averse to risk he may prefer Project A.

Decision Tree Analysis

Introduction: Investment decisions are, generally, sequential in nature. That is, they involve a sequence of decisions over time. An investment decision taken at one point of time results in a series of decision alternatives at some other time in future, depending upon the nature and extent of outcomes and events. As a result investment decisions become complex.

The complex investment decisions can be handled through the technique of decision tree analysis. The technique of decision tree analysis can be employed effectively to analyse and evaluate sequential investment decisions. It is an important technique for taking risky capital investment proposals.

Meaning of Decision Tree Analysis: A present decision depends upon the future events, and the alternatives of a whole sequence of decisions in future are affected by the present decision and the future events. That means, there is inter-relationship between the decision made at the present moment and the future probable decision alternatives emerging out of the sequential outcomes of the original decision. The relationship between a present decision and possible future events, future decisions and their consequences can be displayed graphically or pictorially. The graphic display of the relationship between a present decision and the possible future events, future decisions and their consequences is shown in a format resembling the branches of a tree. Such an analysis is called decision tree analysis, and the graph is called decision tree. So, decision tree analysis is a graphic or pictorial representation in tree form, which presents the relationship between a present decision and possible future events, future decisions and their consequences.

This is clear from the definition of decision tree as given by Prof. Hampton. In the words of Prof. Hampton, "Decision tree is a graphic display of relationship between a present decision and possible future events, future decisions and their sequences. The sequences of events is mapped out over time in a format resembling branches of a tree".

Steps involved in the Decision Tree Process:

A number of steps are involved in the decision tree process. The major steps are :

1. *Defining the investment opportunity or proposal:* First, the investment opportunity or proposal must be clearly defined or determined.

    The investment proposal may be to enter a new market, to introduce a new product line, etc. The investment proposal may be sponsored by any department say, the marketing department or the production department or any other department.

2. *Identification of alternatives:* Every investment proposal will have at least two alternatives, ie. acceptance or rejection of the proposal. But most investment proposals have more than two alternatives. For instance, when a firm is considering the purchase of a new plant for the manufacture of a new product, it may have four alternatives, viz., i) not to purchase the plant, (ii) to purchase a small plant, (iii) to purchase a medium-sized plant and (iv) to purchase a large plant.

    As every investment proposal has two or more alternatives, once a proposal has been defined, the various decision alternatives have to be identified and analysed thoroughly.

3. *Delineation of the decision tree:* After the identification of the various decision alternatives, the delineation of the decision tree must be taken up. Delineation of the decision tree involves the layout of the decision points. Decision branches, chance events and other data. The decision points represent various offshoots requiring varying amount of cash outlays. The decision branches represents the various alternatives which are available. The decision points, decision branches, chance events and other data are required to be determined, as they are to be laid down in the decision tree graph.

4. *Forecasting cash flows and probability assignment:* Once the decision tree has been delineated, the next step is to make a forecast of probable cash flows which are likely to emerge from each decision branch (i.e., decision alternative). Probabilities should also be assigned to each cash flow.

5. *Computation of the expected monetary values:* On the basis of the forecasted probable cash flows and the probabilities assigned to them, the expected monetary value (i.e., expected present values) have to be computed. As the final decision rests on the total expected monetary values, the computed monetary values have to be totalled.

6. *Evaluating or analyzing the results and choosing the best alternative:* After computing the expected monetary values, the results of the various alternatives have to be evaluated or analysed and on the basis of the profitability, the best (i.e. the most profitable alternative) has to be chosen.

Advantages of the Technique of Decision Tree Analysis :

The technique of decision tree analysis has certain advantages. They are:

a) This technique facilitates investment decisions in a scientific way.

b) This technique gives an overall view of all the possibilities associated with a project, helps the management to take decisions keeping the entire picture in mind.

c) As this technique links the probable outcomes of a decision one after another in an inter-related manner along with probabilities assigned to each sequential outcome, it is very useful in tackling investment situations requiring decisions to be taken in a sequence.

Disadvantages of the Technique of Decision Tree Analysis

The technique of decision tree analysis is not free from drawbacks. It suffers from the following drawbacks:

a) A prime decision may have a number of sequential decision points and each one of such decision points may have numerous decision branches or decision alternatives.

b) The decision tree analysis becomes very complex, when a project has a life of more than 2 years. For instance, when a project has a life of 3 years, with three possible outcomes, the number of decision branches or paths may be as many as 27. In such situation, it becomes almost impossible to understand and derive proper conclusion from the decision tree analysis. So, it is necessary that out of the numerous decision alternatives of choices, only a few have to be selected through the process of elimination. In other words, there should be pruning or decision alternatives. "Decision trees are like grape vines, they are production only if vigorously pruned". (Myers) otherwise, the decision tree will become unwieldy, resulting in confusion.

Illustration 10: M.Ltd. is considering the purchase of a new plant, requiring a cash outlay of Rs. 20,000. The plant is expected to have a useful life of 2 years without any scrap value.

The cash flows and their associated probabilities for the two years are as follows

1ˢᵗ Year

	Cash flow	Probability
(i)	Rs. 10,000	0.2
(ii)	Rs. 15,000	0.4
(iii)	Rs. 18,000	0.4

2ⁿᵈ year

If cash flows in 1st year is:

	Rs.10,000		Rs.15000		Rs.18,000	
	Cash Flow	Probability	Cash Flow	Probability	Cash Flows	Probability
i)	Rs. 8,000	0.3	Rs. 12,000	0.4	Rs. 15,000	0.3
ii)	Rs. 12,000	0.4	Rs. 15,000	0.4	Rs. 20,000	0.5
iii)	Rs. 15,000	0.3	Rs. 20,000	0.2	Rs. 25,000	0.2

Presuming that 10% is the cost of capital, plot the above data in the form of a decision tree and suggest whether the project should be accepted or not.

Note

Discount factor   10%

1ˢᵗ Year   .909

2ⁿᵈ Year   .826

Solution

First Step: Computation of Net Present Value

Alternatives	Cash Inflow First Year	Second Year	Present Values at 10% First Year Cash Inflow x 0.909	Second Year Cash Inflow x 0.826	Total Present Value of Two Years	Total Present Value – cost of the Project = NPV
	Rs.	Rs.	Rs.	Rs.	Rs.	Rs.
(a) (i)	10,000	8,000	9,090	6,608	15,698	-4,302
(ii)	10,000	12,000	9,090	9,912	19,002	-998
(iii)	10,000	15,000	9,090	12,390	21,480	1,480
(b) (i)	15,000	12,000	13,635	9,912	23,547	3,547
(ii)	15,000	15,000	13,635	12,390	26,025	6,025
(iii)	15,000	20,000	13,635	16,520	30,155	10,155
(c) (i)	18,000	15,000	16,362	12,390	28,752	8,752
(ii)	18,000	20,000	16,362	16,520	32,882	12,882
(iii)	18,000	25,000	16,362	20,650	37,012	17,012

Second Step: Construction of Decision Tree

Year	First Year		Second Year		Net present value of the project (as calculated earlier)	Joining Probability (Probability of first Year & probability of second year	Expected net Present Value (Net present value x joint Probability)
	Probability	Cash Inflows	Probability	Cash Inflows			
		Rs.		Rs.	Rs.	Rs.	
			0.3	8,000	– 4302	0.06	-258
	0.2	10,000	0.4	12,000	– 998	0.08	-80
Cash Outlay			0.3	15,000	1,480	0.06	89
	0.4	15,000	0.4	12,000	3,547	0.16	568
Rs. 20,000			0.4	15,000	6,025	0.16	964
	0.4	18,000	0.2	20,000	10,155	0.08	812
			0.3	15,000	8,752	0.12	1,050
			0.5	20,000	12,882	0.20	2,576
			0.2	25,000	17,012	0.08	1,361
						1.00	7,082

Decision-making: The above decision tree analysis indicates that the project gives a positive expected net present value of Rs. 7,082 at 10% discount factor. That means the Project may be accepted.

EXERCISES

1. How do you compare the risk factor of two capital projects with the help of standard deviation?
2. Explain the technique of "Certainty Equivalent Coefficient".
3. What is "Decision Tree Analysis"?
4. What is capital rationing? How would capital projects be ranked under capital rationing?

PART V

CAPITAL STRUCTURE AND DIVIDEND POLICY

Capital Structure and Leverage

13

Every organisation requires funds to run and maintain its business. The required funds may be raised from short-term sources or long-term sources or a combination both the sources of funds, so as to equip itself with an appropriate combination of fixed assets and current assets. Current assets to a considerable extent, are financed with the help of short-term sources. Normally, firms are expected to follow a prudent financial policy, as revealed in the maintenance of net current assets. This net positive current asset must be financed by long-term sources. Hence, long-term sources of funds are required to finance for both (a) long-term assets (fixed assets) and (b) networking capital (positive current assets).

The long-term financial strength as well as profitability of a firm is influenced by its financial structure. The term 'Financial Structure' refers to the left hand side of the balance sheet as represented by "total liabilities" consisting of current liabilities, long-term debt, preference share and equity share capital. The financial structure, therefore, includes both short-term and long-term sources of funds.

A firm can easily estimate the required funds by a detailed study of the investment decision. In other words, anticipation of the required funds may be estimated by analyzing the investment decision. Once anticipation of required funds is completed then the next step is financial for the manager to make decisions related to the finance or the selected investment decisions. Generally capital is raised from two prime sources (a) equity and (b) debt. What should be the proportion of equity and debt in the capital structure of a company?

MEANING OF CAPITAL STRUCTURE

Capital structure is that part of financial structure, which represents long-term sources. The term capital structure is generally defined to include only long-term debt and total stockholder investment.[1] The term capital structure refers to the mix of long-term sources of funds, such as equity shares capital, reserves and surpluses, debenture, long-term debt from outside sources and preference share capital. To quote Bogen, "Capital structure may consists of a single class of stock, or it may be complicated by several issues of bonds and preferred stock, the characteristics of which may vary considerably". [2] In other words, capital structure refers to the composition of capitalisation, i.e., to the proportion between debt and equity that make up capitalisation. [3] Capital structure indicated by the following equation. [4]

Capital Structure = Long-term Debt + Preferred Stock + Net worth

or

Capital Structure = Total Assets - Current Liabilities

Thus, the capital structure of a firm consists of the shareholder ' funds and debt. The inherent financial stability of an enterprise and risk of insolvency to which it is exposed, are primarily dependent on the source of its funds as well as the type of assets it holds and relative magnitude of such asset categories.[5]

OPTIMUM CAPITAL STRUCTURE

In taking a financing decision, the financial manager's job is to come out with an optimum capital structure. Optimum capital structure is that capital structure at that level of debt - equity proportion, where the market value per share is maximum and the cost of capital is minimum. The same to quote, Ezra, "optimum leverage is that mix of debt and equity which will maximise the market value of the company and minimise the company's overall cost of capital." [6] The study of capital structure involves a discussion of the nature of the industry and specific circumstances of the business enterprise in question, besides the general theory of finance. It is difficult to define an ideal capital structure. A company's capital structure is a function of the nature of its business and how risky the particular business is, and therefore, a matter of business judgment. [7] As observed by Van Horne, "In the optimum capital structure, the marginal real cost of each available method of financing is the same". [8] As Guthmann and Dougall rightly remark, from a strictly financial point of view, the optimum capital structure is achieved by balancing the financing, so as to achieve the lowest average cost of long-term funds. This in turn produces that maximum market value for the total securities issued against a given amount of corporate income. [9] The optimum capital structure keeps balance between share capital and debt capital. The primary reason for the employment of debt by an enterprise can be stated as upto a certain point, debt is from the point of view of the ownership, a less expensive source of funds than equity capital. [10] Hence, optimum capital structure keeps a balance between debt capital and equity capital.

FEATURES OF AN APPROPRIATE CAPITAL STRUCTURE

Construction of optimum capital structure is very important for a firm, since its value depending on the capital structure. Hence, the financial manager or the concerned person should develop an appropriate capital structure, which is helpful to maximise shareholder wealth. This can be done only when all those factors., which are relevant to the company's capital structure decision, are properly analysed and balanced. Capital structure should be planned, keeping in view the interest of ordinary shareholder because they are the ultimate owners of a business enterprise and have the right to select the directors. However, the interest of the other groups, such as, employees, customers, creditors, society and government should also receive reasonable consideration. There is no tailor-made capital structure for all business enterprises. There are certain common characteristics that categorise industries. The study of capital structure involves a study of the debt-equity mix with the object of lowering the overall cost of capital and with a view to maximizing the market value of the firm's securities.

An appropriate capital structure should have the following features[11]:

(a) *Profitability/Return:* As we have seen in the above discussion the appropriate capital structure is one, which is most advantageous. With the constraints, maximum use of leverage at a minimum cost should be made. In other words, it should generate maximum returns to the owners without adding additional cost.

(b) *Solvency/Risk:* The use of more or excessive debt threatens the solvency of the firm. Debt should be used till the point where, debt does not add significant risk, otherwise use of debt should be avoided.

(c) *Flexibility:* Flexible capital structure means it should allow the existing capital structure to change according to the changing conditions without increasing cost. It should also be possible for the firm to provide funds whenever needed to finance its possible activities. The Firm should also repay the funds if not required.

(d) *Conservation/Capacity:* Capital should be conservative in the sense that the debt capacity of a firm should not be exceeded. In other words, the capital structure should be determined within the debt capacity of the firm and not beyond the firm's capacity. The debt capacity of a firm depends on its ability to generate future cash inflows. It should have enough cash to pay its fixed charges and principal sum.

(e) *Control:* Use of more equity may lead to loose my control of the company. The competitors from (closely held firms) are particularly concerned about the dilution of control. Hence, construction of capital structure should not involve the risk of loss of control over the firm.

The above stated are the general features of an appropriate capital structure. There may be particular features for a firm, which may be additional. Further, the weight given to each of these features will differ from firm to firm.

COMPUTATION OF OPTIMAL CAPITAL STRUCTURE

As we already know that optimum capital structure is that capital structure at debt equity proportion where the market value per share and value of the firm is maximum or the overall cost of capital is minimum. But here, since, calculation of market value of share or value of the firm is beyond the scope of this book. Hence, capital structure is calculated based on overall cost of capital.

Illustration 1: In considering the most desirable capital structure of a company. Financial manager has estimated the following.

Debt as a % of total Capital Employed	Cost of Equity (%)	Cost of Debt (%)
0	10.0	6.0
10	10.0	6.0
20	10.5	6.0
30	11.0	6.5
40	12.0	7.0

You are required to determine the optimal debt - equity mix or optimal capital structure by the calculation of overall cost of capital.

Solution

Calculation of overall cost of capital

Equity Weight (W_e)	Debt Weight (W_d)	Cost of Equity (K_c)	Cost of Debt (K_d)	Overall cost of Capital (Ko = %) $K_o = [K_c (W_e) + K_d (W_d)] \times 100$
1.00	0.00	0.100	0.06	$[(0.10 \times 1.0) + (0.06 \times 0.0)] \times 100 = 10$
0.90	**0.10**	0.100	0.06	$[(0.10 \times 0.90) + (0.06 \times 0.10)] \times 100 = $ **9.6**
0.80	0.20	0.105	0.06	$[(0.105 \times 0.80) + (0.06 \times 0.20)] \times 100 = 9.68$
0.70	0.30	0.110	0.065	$[(0.11 \times 0.70) + (0.065 \times 0.30)] \times 100 = 9.65$
0.60	0.40	0.120	0.07	$[(0.12 \times 0.60) + (0.07 \times 0.40)] \times 100 = 10$

Here optimal capital structure is one, with 90 per cent equity and 10 per cent debt since K is less (9.6).

DETERMINANTS OF CAPITAL STRUCTURE

Capital structure may be determined at the time of promotion of the firm or during the latter stages. But determining optimal capital structure at the time of promotion is very important and it should be designed very carefully. Management of any firm should set a target capital structure and the subsequent financing decisions should be made with a view to achieve the target capital structure. Construction of capital structure, is difficult, since it involves a complex trade off among several factors or considerations. Keeping the objective of wealth maximisation in mind, capital structure has to be determined. The following factors affect optimal capital structure.

1. *Tax benefit of Debt:* Debt is the cheapest source of long-term finance, when compared with other source equity, because the interest on debt finance is a tax-deductible expense. Hence, debt can be accepted as a tax-sheltered source of finance, which helps in shareholder ' wealth maximisation.

2. *Flexibility:* Flexibility is one of the most important and serious factors, which is considered in determining capital structure. Flexibility is the firm's ability to adopt its capital structure to the needs of changing conditions. Changing conditions may be, need of more funds for investments or having substantial funds that are already raised. Whenever there is a need to have more funds to finance profitable investments, the firm should be able to rise without delay and less cost. On the other hand, whenever there are surplus funds, the firm should be able to repay them. The above two conditions are fulfilled only when there is a flexible capital structure. In other words, the financial plan of a firm should be able to change according to their operating strategy and needs. The flexibility of capital structure depends on the flexibility in fixed charges, the covenants and debt capacity of the firm.

3. *Control:* The equity shareholder have voting right to elect the directors of the company. Raising funds by way of issue of new equity shares to the public may lead to loss of control. If the management wants to have total control on the firm then, it may require to raise funds through non-voting right instrument that is debt source of finance. But the firm needs to pay interest compulsory on debt finance. Debt finance is preferred only when the firm's debt service capacity is good. Otherwise the creditors may seize the assets of the firm to satisfy their claims (interest). In this situation management would lose all control. It might be better to sacrifice a measure of control by some additional equity finance rather than run the risk of loosing all control to creditors by employing too much debt. (12) Widely held companies can raise funds by way of issue of equity shares, since the shares are widely scattered and majority of shareholder are interested in the return. At the same time if they are not satisfied with the firm, they will switch over to some other firm, where they expect higher return.

4. *Industry Leverage Ratios:* The Industry standards provide benchmark. Firm can use industry leverage ratio as standard for construction of capital structure. Because industry standard may be appropriate to the firm. It does not mean that all firms in the industry are having optimum capital structure. Put it simple, they may be using more leverage or less leverage, but it suggests that whether the firm is out of line or not, if it is it should know the reasons why and be satisfied with the reasons.

5. *Seasonal Variations:* Use of more or less financial leverage depends on the seasonal variations of the business. Low degree of financial leverage (less debt) is preferable when a firm's business is seasonal in nature. Example, Businesses such as production and sale of umbrellas, fans, air coolers., industries requires less debt capital in their capital structure. Use of more debt may make the firm unable to pay interest obligations in lean years, which would lead to financial distress. On the other hand, industries involved in business, where there is no seasonality, like consumer non-durable products (food items, soaps, etc) or with items in habitual use (cigarette) or all those products, which have an inelastic demand are not likely to be subject to wide fluctuations in sales can use more debt in their capital structure, since they are able to earn regular profit.

6. *Degree of Competition:* Competition in the industry also determines the capital structure. When, there is no or less competition then, the firms can use less equity or more debt in their capital structure, since they can sell more products at higher prices. Example, public utility corporations like gas, electricity, etc. On the other hand, competitive firms have to use more equity in their capital structure, because of competition; they may not be able to sell more units and cannot earn more profits. Example., garment industry, home appliances industry.

7. *Industry Life Cycle:* The Industry life cycle consists of introduction stage; growth stage; maturity stage and declining stage. The industry in infancy should use less debt capital or more equity capital in capital structure, since the profit earning capacity is less due to less sales where as when a firm is in its growing stage (fast) and having more profits, it can go for more debt or less equity that helps to maximise shareholder wealth.

8. *Agency Costs:* Agency costs arises when there is a conflict of interest among owners, debenture holders and the management. Conflict may arise due to the transferring of wealth to debt holders in their favour. The agency problem is handled through monitoring and restrictive covenants, which involve costs that are called agency costs. The financing strategy of a firm should seek to minimise the agency costs, by way of employing an external agent who specialises in low-cost monitoring. Management should use debt finance to the extent that it maximises the wealth of shareholders, not beyond that.

9. *Company Characteristics:* Characteristics like size and credit standing among other companies (within or outside industry). Small firm's ability to raise funds from outside is limited when compared to large firms. Small firms have to depend on owners' funds for financing activities. In other words, investors perceive that investment in small firms is more risky than the large firms. On the other hand, large firms are forced to make use of different sources of funds, because no single source is sufficient to their needs.

When it comes to the credit rating characteristics a firm enjoying high credit rating may get funds easily from the capital market, as compared to other firms, which are having low credit rating. Because investors and creditors prefer to invest and grant loans to high credit rating firms, since the risk is less.

10. *Timing of Public Issue:* Timing of public offer is also one of the most important factors considered while planning the capital structure. Public offering should be made at a time when, that state of the economy as well as capital market is ideal to provide the funds. For example during 2003 to 2004 period, many firms like Vijaya Bank, IOB, Union Bank, TCS, IOC, NTPC come up with IPO due to ideal capital market and the economy. Prices as well as yields on securities depend on the money policy pursued by the government. Scarcity of debt money and equity funds leads to high interest rates and low price earnings (P/E) ratios. Therefore, company has to decide whether to finance infancy stage with equity funds and latter stages (except declining) with debt funds or vice versa.

11. *Requirements of Investors:* Before going to issue a particular instrument to the public or investors to raise funds, there is a need to know the investors requirements. Investors may be institutional investors. (LIC, GIC, UTI) as well as individual investors. Some investors are ready to take risk (bold investors.), who prefer capital gains and control and hence, equity shares are suitable to them. On the other hand, investors. (cautious), who are interested in the safety of their investment and stable returns, prefer to invest in debentures, since satisfying their needs and preference share are more suitable to the investors. (less cautious), who prefers stable returns and share in profits.

12. *Period of Finance:* Period of finance also plays a crucial role in determining the capital structure. A firm can issue redeemable debentures or preference shares, when the finance is required for a limited period. For example, for 5 years, firm can issue 5 years redeemable debentures or preference shares. But equity share capital is the best source when the firm needs finance for unlimited period (unknown).

13. *Purpose of Finance:* Debt source of finance is suitable when a firm is planning to invest in productive (avenues) purpose. For example, investment on machinery, where as, if the firm is planning to raise funds for non-productive purpose, it can raise funds from equity source for example social responsibility or general development on a permanent basis.

14. **Legal Requirements:** There are some guidelines on shares and debentures issued by the government that are very important for the construction of the capital structure. For example, the controller of capital issues, now SEBI grants to consent for capital issue when, (a) debt equity ratio does not exceed 2 : 1 (higher ratio may be allowed for capital intensive projects), (b) the ratio of preference capital to equity capital does not exceed 1 : 3 and (c) promoters hold at least 2.5 per cent of the equity capital.

PATTERNS/FORMS OF CAPITAL STRUCTURE

While making or farming the capital structure, a firm may use equity share capital or preference share capital or debt capital (debentures or loans) or a combination of them all. However, the use of any one of the above sources does not help to come up with an optimum capital structure. Optimum capital structure is possible only when there is a mix of all the above sources (debt and equity). The following are the forms of capital structure.

(i)   Complete equity share capital;

(ii)   Different proportions of equity and preference share capital;

(iii)   Different proportions of equity and debenture (debt) capital and

(iv)   Different proportions of equity, preference and debenture (debt) capital.

APPROACHES TO DETERMINE APPROPRIATE CAPITAL STRUCTURE:

The following are the approaches to determine a firm's capital structure[13]

(a) EBIT - EPS Approach (b) Valuation Approach and (c) Cash flow Approach

(a)   **EBIT - EPS Approach:** This approach is helpful to analyse the impact of debt on earnings per share.

(b)   **Valuation Approach:** This approach determines the impact of debt use on the shareholder value.

(c)   **Cash Flow Approach:** This approach analyses the firm's debt service capacity.

Apart from the above ROI - ROE analysis, ration analysis is also used. But here in this book, we will discuss the first (EBIT - EPS) approach only.

(a)   **EBIT - EPS (Approach) Analysis:** Leverage effects on shareholder ' return and risk, has been discussed in detail in the next part of this Chapter, under leverages. But here we shall try to understand how sensitive are earnings per share (EPS) to the changes in earnings before interest and tax (EBIT) under different financial plans / capital structures / alternatives. It is known as EBIT - EPS analysis. Use of fixed cost sources of finance in capital structure of a firm is known as financial leverages / trading on equity. In other words, use of less cost source of finance to maximise earnings per share (EPS), but the benefits are more when a firm uses debt as a source of finance, due to cheap and interest is tax deductible source. Use of debt can be used to maximise shareholder wealth only when a firm has a high level of operating profit (EBIT). EBIT - EPS analyses is one way to study the relation between earnings per share (EPS) and various possible levels of operating profit (EBIT), under various financial plans.

Illustration 2: XYZ Co. Ltd. has a share capital of Rs. 1,00,000 face value of Rs. 10 each. It requires Rs. 50,000 to finance expansion programme and is considering three alternative financial plans.

(i)   Issue of 5000 ordinary shares of Rs. 10 each

(ii)   Issue of 500 preference shares of Rs. 100 each at 10 per cent and

(iii)   Issue of 10 per cent debentures of Rs. 50,000

The company's operating profit (EBIT) after additional investment is Rs. 40,000 per annum. Tax rate is 50 per cent. Show the effect of use of debt in financial plan.

Solution

Calculation EPS

Particulars.	I (Equity) Rs.	II (Preference) Rs.	III Debt - Equity Rs.
EBIT	40,000	40,000	40,000
Less : Interest	---	---	5,000
EBT / or PBT	40,000	40,000	35,000
Less : Tax at 50%	20,000	20,000	17,500
PAT or EAT	20,000	20,000	17,500
Less: Preference dividend	---	5,000	---
Earnings available to share holders.	20,000	15,000	17,500
No. of shares outstanding	15,000	10,000	10,000
EPS = $\dfrac{\text{Earnings available to shareholder}}{\text{No. of equity shares}}$	1.333	1.5	1.75

Illustration 3: VS International Ltd., has a capital structure (all equity) comprising of Rs. 5,00,000 each share of Rs. 10. The firm wants to raise an additional Rs. 2,50,000 for expansion project. The firm has the following four alternative financial plans I, II, III and IV. If The firm is able to earn an operating profit at Rs. 80,000 after additional investment and 50 per cent tax rate. Calculate EPS for all four alternatives and select the preferable financial plan. Financial plans

I.   Raise the entire amount in the form of equity capital.

II. Raise 50 per cent as equity capital and 50 per cent as 10 per cent debt capital.

III. Raise the entire amount as 12 per cent debentures.

IV. Raise 50 per cent equity capital and 50 per cent preference share capital at 10 per cent.

Solution

Calculation of EPS

Particulars.	I Rs.	II Rs.	III Rs.	IV Rs.
EBIT	80,000	80,000	80,000	80,000
Less: Interest	---	12,500	30,000	---
EBT	80,000	67,500	50,000	80,000
Less: Tax at 50%	40,000	33,750	25,000	40,000
EAT	40,000	33,750	25,000	40,000
Less: Preference dividend	---	---		12500
Earnings available to share holders.	40,000	33,750	25000	27500
No. of shares (equity) outstanding	75,000	62,500	50,000	62,500
EPS	0.53	0.54	0.50	0.44

As EPS is maximum as per plan-II, this is most-preferable financial plan.

INDIFFERENCE POINT

The break-even EBIT level of indifference point, is when the EPS is same for two alternative capital structures. It may be defined as the level of EBIT beyond which the benefits of financial leverage begin to operate with respect to earnings per share (EPS). In other words, if the expected level of EBIT is less than the indifference point, it is advantageous with the use of equity capital to maximise EPS.

Indifference point between two capital structures can be obtained by using the following formula:

$$\frac{(x - I_1)(1-t) - PD(1+Dt)}{ES_1} = \frac{(x - I_2)(1-t) - PD(1+Dt)}{ES_2}$$

Where

    X = EBIT   I1I2 = Interest under alternatives 1 and 2

    t = Tax rate   PD = Preference dividend

    Dt = Preference dividend tax

    ES_1, ES_2 = No. of equity share outstanding under alternative 1 and 2

Illustration 4: WDC Ltd., has a total capitalisation of Rs. 10 lakh consisting entirely of equity capital (Rs. 10 each share). It is planning to raise an additional funds of Rs. 5 lakh for implementing capital budgeting project. There are two alternatives available to the company.

a)   Entire equity share capital by issue of shares.

b)   Entire amount by debt at 10 per cent interest.

The company is in the tax brackets of 50 per cent. Calculate indifference point.

Solution:

Indifference point formula

$$\frac{(x - I)(1 - 0.5)}{ES_1} = \frac{(x - 1)(1 - 0.5)}{ES_2}$$

$$\frac{x(1 - 0.5)}{(1,00,000 + 50000)} = \frac{(x - 50,000)(1 - 0.5)}{1,00,000}$$

$$\frac{0.5x}{1,50,000} = \frac{0.5x - 25000}{1,00,000}$$

$$50,000x = 75,000x - 3,75,00,00,000$$

$$3,75,00,00,000 = 75,000x - 50,000x$$

$$= 25,000x$$

$$x = 3,75,00,00,000/25,000$$

$$x = Rs. 150,000$$

Calculation of EPS

Particulars.		Financial Plan			
		Alternative 'A'		Alternative 'B'	
		Rs.		Rs.	
EBIT		1,50,000		1,50,000	
Less : Interest		---		50,000	
EBT / or PBT		1,50,000		1,00,000	
Less : Tax at 50%		75,000		50,000	
EAT		75,000		50,000	
Less : Preference dividend		---		---	
Earnings available to share holders.		75,000		50,000	
No. of shares (existing + new)		(1,00,000 + 50,000)		(1,00,000 + 0)	
EPS =	Earnings available to share holders.	75,000	= 0.5	50,000	= 0.5
	No. of equity shares	1,50,000		1,00,000	

LEVERAGES

As we have seen in the above discussion, that a firm can raise its required finance either equity or debt or both the sources. While constructing capital structure, a firm can use fixed cost bearing securities for maximisation of shareholder ' wealth. Leverage has been defined as, the action of a lever and mathematical advantage gained by it. In other words, leverage allows accomplishing certain things that are otherwise not possible. The concept is valid in business also. From the financial management point of view, the term leverage is commonly used to describe the firm's ability to use fixed cost assets or sources of funds to magnify the returns to its owners. According to James Home, leverage is, "the employment of an asset or sources of funds for which the firm has to pay a fixed cost or fixed return." Here fixed cost (operating cost) or fixed returns (financial cost) remains constant irrespective of the level of output.

TYPES OF LEVERAGES

There are two types of leverages, such as

i)   Operating leverage

ii) Financial leverage

Now let us discuss about types of leverages.

(i)   *Operating Leverage:* operating leverage is present any time, a firm has operating costs regardless of the level of production. These fixed costs do not vary with sales. They must be paid regardless of the amount of revenue available. Hence, operating leverage may be defined as the firm's ability to use operating costs to magnify the effects of changes in sales on its earnings before interest and taxes. Operating leverage is associated with investment (assets acquisition) activities.[14] Hence, operating leverage results from the present fixed operating expenses with in firm's income stream. The operating costs are categorised into three: One - fixed costs, which do not vary with the level of production, they must be paid regardless of the amount of revenue available. Example, depreciation plant and machinery, buildings, insurance, etc,. Second - variable costs that varies directly with the level of production. Example, raw materials, direct labour costs, etc. Third - Semi-variable costs, which partly vary and is partly fixed.

The degree of operating leverage may be defined as the change in the percentage of operating income (EBIT), for the change in percentage of sales revenue. The degree of operating leverage at any level of output is arrived at by dividing the percentage change in EBIT with percentage change in sales.[15]

That is

$$\text{Degree of Operating Leverage} = \frac{\text{Percentage change in EBIT}}{\text{Percentage change in sales}}$$

or

$$\text{DOL} = \frac{\text{Contribution}}{\text{Operating Profit(EBIT)}}$$

Operating leverage may be favourable or unfavourable. High degree of operating leverage indicates high degree of risk. It is good, when revenues are rising and bad when they are falling. Operating risk (business risk) is the risk of the firm not being able to cover its fixed operating costs. The larger the magnitude, the larger is the volume of sales required to cover all fixed costs.

Before solving the problems, there is a need to know the calculation of earnings available to equity shareholder from the sales revenue. The following table clearly gives a picture about the calculation of earnings available to ordinary shareholder.

Particulars	Amount (Rs.
Sales Revenue (units sold x selling price pu)	X X X X
Less : Variable cost	X X X
[Units produced x cost per unit]	
Contribution	X X X X
Less: Fixed cost	X X X
Earnings Before Interest & Taxes (EBIT)	X X X X
Less: Interest	X X X
Earnings Before Tax (EBT)	X X X X
Less: Tax	X X X
Earnings After Taxes (EAT)	X X X X
Less: Preference Dividend	X X X
Earnings available to Equity shareholder (EAES)	X X X X

Illustration 5: XYZ Ltd., produced and sold 1,00,000 units of a product at the rate of Rs.100. For production of 1,00,000 units, it has spend a variable cost of Rs. 6,00,000 at the rate of Rs. 6 per unit and a fixed cost of Rs. 2,50,000. The firm has paid interest Rs. 50,000 at the rate of 5 per cent and Rs. 1,00,000 debt. Calculate operating leverage.

Solution:

$$DOL = \frac{\text{Contribution}}{\text{EBIT or Operating profit (EBIT)}}$$

Particulars.	Amount Rs.
Sales Revenue (1,00,000 x Rs. 100)	10,00,000
Less: Variable cost (1,00,000 x Rs. 6)	6,00,000
Contribution	4,00,000
Less: Fixed cost	2,50,000
EBIT	1,50,000

$$\text{Operating leverage} = \frac{4,00,000}{1,50,000} = 2.66$$

Illustration 6: From the following particulars of ABC Ltd., calculate operating leverage.

Particulars.	Previous Year 2003	Current Year 2004
Sales revenue	10,00,000	12,50,000
Variable cost	6,00,000	7,50,000
Fixed cost	2,50,000	2,50,000

Solution:

Calculation of EBIT on a percentage change

Particulars.	2002	2004	% change
Sales Revenue	10,00,000	12,50,000	25
Less : Variable cost	6,00,000	7,50,000	25
CONTRIBUTION	4,00,000	5,00,000	25
Less : Fixed cost	2,50,000	2,50,000	
EBIT	1,50,000	2,50,000	66.67

$$\text{Percentage change} = \frac{\text{Increase in revenue/profit/amount}}{\text{Base or previous year revene/profit}}$$

$$\text{Degree of operating leverage (DOL)} = \frac{\text{Percentage change in EBIT}}{\text{Percentage change in sales}}$$

$$\text{DOL} = \frac{66.67}{25} = 2.667$$

Operating leverage 2.667 indicates that when, there is 25 per cent change in sales, the change in EBIT is 2.667 times.

Application of Operating Leverage

- It is helpful to know how operating profit (EBIT) would change with a given change in units produced.
- It will be helpful in measuring business risk.

(ii) *Financial Leverage:* A firm may need long-term funds for long-term activities like expansion, diversification, modernization etc. , the financial managers job is to compose funds. The required funds may be raised by two sources: equity and debt. Use of various sources to compose capital is known as financial structure. The use of fixed charges, sources of funds such as debt and preference share capital along with the equity share capital in capital structure is described as financial leverage. According to Lawrence, financial leverage is the ability of the firm to use fixed financial charges to magnify the effects of changes in EBIT on the firm's earnings per share. (16) In other words, financial leverage may be defined as the payment of fixed rate of interest for the use of fixed interest bearing securities, to magnify the rate of return as equity shares. It is also known as "trading as equity". Hence, financial leverage results from the presence of fixed financial charges in the income statement. Financial leverage associates with financing activities. (17) The fixed charges do not vary with firm's EBIT. They must be paid regardless of the amount of EBIT available to the firm. It indicates the effect on EBIT created by the use of fixed charge securities in the capital structure of a firm. Financial leverage is computed by the following formula:

$$\text{Financial (Leverage)} = \frac{\text{EBIT or operating profit}}{\text{EBT or taxable income}}$$

or

$$\text{Degree of financial leverage (DFL)} = \frac{\text{Percentage change in EPS}}{\text{Percentage change in EBIT}}$$

A Financial leverage may be positive or negative. Favourable leverage occurs when the firm earns more on the assets purchased with the funds, than the fixed cost of their use and vice versa. High degree of financial leverage leads to high financial risk. The financial risk refers to the risk of the firm not being able to cover its fixed financial costs. Hence, the financial manager should take into consideration, the level of EBIT and fixed charges while preparing the firm's financial plan.

Illustration 7: A firm has sales of 1,00,000 units at Rs. 10 pu. Variable cost of the produced products is 60 per cent of the total sales revenue. Fixed cost is Rs. 2,00,000. The firm has used a debt of Rs. 5,00,000 at 20 per cent interest. Calculate the operating leverage and financial leverage.

Solution:

Calculation of EBT

Particulars.	Amount Rs.
Sales Revenue (1,00,000 units x Rs. 10 P.u)	10,00,000
Less: Variable cost (10,00,000 x 0.60)	6,00,000
Contribution	4,00,000
Less: Fixed cost	2,00,000
EBIT	2,00,000
Less: Interest (5,00,000 x 20 /100)	1,00,000
Earning before tax (EBT)	1,00,000

Operating leverage = contribution of EBIT = 4,00,000 ÷ 2,00,000 = 2

Financial leverage = 2,00,000 ÷1,00,000 = 2

Illustration 8: From the following particulars of PQR Company, calculate operating and financial leverages. The company's current sales revenue is Rs. 15,00,000 lakh and sales are expected to increase by 25 per cent. Rs. 9,00,000 incurred on variable expenses for generating Rs.15 lakh sales revenue. The fixed cost is Rs. 2,50,000. The company has Rs. 20 lakh equity shares capital and Rs. 20 lakh, 10 per cent debt capital. Calculate operating leverage and financial leverage. Rs. 10 equity and 50 per cent tax rate.

Solution:

Calculation of EPS

Particulars.	Current position	Expected change	Percentage of change
Sales Revenue	15,00,000	18,75,000	25
Less: Variable cost	9,00,000	11,25,000[(1)]	
Contribution	6,00,000	7,50,000	
Less: Fixed cost	2,50,000	2,50,000	
EBIT	3,50,000	5,00,000	42.86
Less: Interest	2,00,000	2,00,000	
EBT	1,50,000	3,00,000	
Less: Tax 50%	75,000	1,50,000	
EAT	75,000	1,50,000	
Less: Preference dividend	---	---	
Earnings available to shareholder	75,000	1,50,000	
EPS	0.375	0.75	100%

Working Notes

1) *Variable cost in percentage of Sales:*

$$VC\% = \frac{\text{Total variable cost}}{\text{Sales}} \times 100 = \frac{9,00,000}{15,00,000} \times 100 = 60 \text{ per cent}$$

Increase in variable cost = 3,75,000 x 60/100 = 2,25,000

Total variable cost = 9,00,000 + 2,25,000 = Rs. 11,25,000

2) *Percentage change in EBIT:*

$$\frac{\text{Increase or decrease in EBIT}}{\text{Base EBIT}} \times 100 = \frac{1,50,000}{3,50,000} \times 100 = 42.86 \text{ percent}$$

3) *Interest on Debt:*

$$20,00,000 \times \frac{20}{100} = \text{Rs. } 4,00,000$$

4) *EPS*

$$EPS = \frac{\text{Earnings available to shareholders}}{\text{No. of ordinary shares}}$$

Current position = 75000 ÷ 2,00,000 = 0.375

Expected change = 1,50,000 ÷ 2,00,000 = 0.75

- Operating leverage $= \dfrac{\text{Contribution}}{\text{EBIT}}$ or $\dfrac{\%\text{ change in EBIT}}{\%\text{ change in Sales}}$

$$= \frac{6,00,000}{3,50,000} \text{ or } \frac{42.86}{25} = 1.714$$

- Financial leverage $= \dfrac{\text{EBIT}}{\text{EBT}}$ or $\dfrac{\%\text{ change in EPS}}{\%\text{ change in Sales}}$

$$= \frac{3,50,000}{1,50,000} \text{ or } \frac{100}{42.86} = 2.333$$

Application of Financial Leverage:

♦ It is helpful to know, how EPS would change with a change in operating profit (EBIT).

♦ It will be helpful for measuring the financial risk.

Combined Leverage: The operating leverage has its effects on operating risk and is measured by the percentage change in EBIT due to the percentage change in sales. The financing leverage has its effects on financial risk and is measured by the percentage change in EPS due to the per centage change in EBIT. Since, both these leverages are closely related with the ascertainment of the firm's ability to cover fixed charges (fixed operating costs in the case of operating leverage and fixed financial costs in the case of financial leverage), the sum of both, gives us the total leverage or combined leverage and the risk associated with combined leverage is known as total risk. The degree of combined leverage may be defined as the percentage change in EPS due to the percentage change in sales. Thus the combined leverage is:

$$\frac{\%\,Change\,in\,EBIT}{\%\,Change\,in\,Sales}\times\frac{\%\,Change\,in\,EPS}{\%\,Change\,in\,EBIT}=\frac{\%\,Change\,in\,EPS}{\%\,Change\,in\,Sales}$$

$$\frac{Contribution}{EBIT}\times\frac{EBIT}{EBT}=\frac{Contribution}{EBT}$$

Illustration 9: VST Corporation has sales of Rs. 40 lakh, variable cost 70 per cent of the sales and fixed cost is Rs.8,00,000. The firm has raised Rs.20 lakh funds by issue of debentures at the rate of 10 per cent. Compute operating, financial and combined leverages.

Solution:

Calculation of EBT or PBT

Particulars.	Amount Rs.
Sales Revenue	40,00,000
Less: Variable cost (40,00,000 x 0.70)	28,00,000
Contribution	12,00,000
Less: Fixed cost	8,00,000
EBIT	4,00,000
Less: Interest (20,00,000 x 0.10)	2,00,000
EBT	2,00,000

Operating leverage = Contribution ÷ EBIT = 12,00,000 ÷ 4,00,000 = 3

Financial leverage = EBIT ÷ EBT = 4,00,000 ÷ 2,00,000 = 2

Combined leverage = OL x FL = 3 x 2 = 6

The combined leverage can work in both directions. It is favourable if sales increase and unfavourable when sales decrease. This is because the change in sales results in more than proportion returns in the form of EPS. Financial leverage and operating leverage are something like an double-edged sword. They have tremendous acceleration or deceleration effects on EBIT and EPS. A right combination of these leverages is a blessing for the corporate growth, while an improper combination may prove a curse. Operating leverage also acts as a check on financial leverage.

The following table shows various combination of operating and financial leverage and the effect of combination.

Operating leverage	Financial leverage	Combined effect
High	High	This combination is very a dangerous policy, which should be avoided.
Low	Low	This combination is a very cautious policy and is not assuming risk.
High	Low	This combination has adverse effect of operating leverage, that is taken care of by having low financial leverage.
Low	High	This combination is an ideal situation. The company can follow aggressive debt policy.

SUMMARY

♦ Organisation requires funds to run and maintain the business. The required funds may be raised from short-term sources or long-term sources or a combination of both the sources of funds, so as to equip itself with an appropriate combination of fixed assets and current assets. Generally, capital is raised from two prime sources (a) equity and (b) debt. What should be the proportion of equity and debt in the capital structure of a company?

♦ Capital structure refers to the mix of long-term sources of funds, such as equity shares capital, reserves and surpluses, debenture, long-term debt from outside sources, and preference share capital.

♦ Capital structure is indicated by the equation: Capital structure = long-term debt + preferred stock + net worth or Capital structure = total assets - current liabilities.

♦ In a financing decisions the financial manager's job is to come out with an optimum capital structure, which maximizes market value per share by minimizing cost of capita. An appropriate capital structure should take into consideration profitability, solvency, flexibility of capital structure, firm's debt capacity, and control.

♦ The construction of capital structure is difficult, since it involves a complex trade off among several factors The important factors that affect optimal capital structure: (1) tax benefit of Debt, (2) flexibility, (3) control, (4) industry leverage ratios, (5) seasonal variations, (6) degree of competition, (7) industry life cycle, (8) agency costs, (9) company characteristics, (10) timing of public issue, (11) requirements of investors., (12) period of Finance, (13) purpose of finance, and (14) legal requirements.

♦ While construction of a firm's capital structure, the firm may use equity share capital, preference share capital and debt capital (debentures or loans) or combination of them. Optimum capital structure is possible only when there is a mix of debt and equity. The forms of capital structure are: (i) complete equity share capital, (ii) different proportions of equity and preference share capital, (iii) different proportions of equity and debenture (debt) capital, and (iv) different proportions of equity, preference and debenture (debt) capital.

♦ Appropriate capital structure can be determined by adopting: EBIT-EPS approach, valuation Approach and cash flow approach.

♦ Indifference point is that EBIT level at which, the EPS is same for two alternative capital structures. Indifference point between two capital structures, symbolically:

$$\frac{(x - I_1)\,(1\text{-}t)\text{-}PD\,(1 + Dt)}{ES_1} = \frac{(x\text{-}I_2)\,(1\text{-}t)\,\text{-}PD\,(1 + Dt)}{ES_2}$$

♦ Leverage has been defined as, the action of a lever and mathematical advantage gained by it. From the financial management point of view, the term leverage is commonly used to describe the firm's ability to use fixed cost assets or sources of funds to magnify the returns to its owners.

♦ There are two types of leverages: (i) operating leverage and (ii) financial leverage.

♦ Operating leverage (OL) refers as the firm's ability to use operating costs to magnify the effects of changes in sales on its earnings before interest and taxes. The degree of operating leverage (DOL) may be defined as the change in the percentage of operating income (EBIT), for the change in percentage of sales revenue. Symbolically: Percentage change in EBIT ÷ Percentage change in sales (or) contribution ÷ Operating profit (EBIT). OL may be favourable or unfavourable. High DOL indicates high degree of risk. It is good when revenues are rising and bad when they are falling. OL is helpful in knowing, how the operating profit (EBIT) would change with a given change in units produced, and in measuring business risk.

♦ Financial leverage (FL) is the ability of the firm to use fixed financial charges to magnify the effects of changes in EBIT on the firm's earnings per share. It is also known as "trading as equity". Symbolically (DFL): Percentage change in EPS ÷ Percentage change in EBIT (or) EBIT ÷ EBT pertaining profit (EBIT). FL may be positive or negative favourable leverage occurs when the firm earns more on the assets purchased with the funds, than the fixed cost of their use and vice versa. High DFL leads to high financial risk. Financial leverage is helpful to know how EPS would change with a change in operating profit (EBIT), and for measuring financial risk.

♦ Both the leverages are closely related with the ascertainment of the firm's ability to cover fixed charges (fixed operating costs in the case of OL and fixed financial costs in the case of FL), the sum of them all gives us the total leverage or combined leverage and the risk associated with combined leverage is known as total risk. The degree of combined leverage is the percentage change in EPS due to the percentage change in sales. Symbolically:

$$\frac{\% \text{ Change in EBIT}}{\% \text{ Change in Sales}} \times \frac{\% \text{ Change in EPS}}{\% \text{ Change in EBIT}} = \frac{\% \text{ Change in EPS}}{\% \text{ Change in Sales}}$$

$$\frac{\text{Contribution}}{\text{EBIT}} \times \frac{\text{EBIT}}{\text{EBT}} = \frac{\text{Contribution}}{\text{EBT}}$$

The combined leverage can work in both directions. It is favourable if sales increase and unfavourable when sales decrease. A right (low operating and high financial leverage) combination of operating and financial leverages is a blessing for corporate growth, while an improper combination may prove as a curse.

SOLVED PROBLEMS

Illustration 1: From the following information determine optimal capital structure by the calculation of cost of capital.

Particulars.	Plan 1	Plan 2	Plan 3	Plan 4	Plan 5	Plan 6	Plan 7
Debt as a percentage of total capital	0	0.1	0.2	0.3	0.4	0.5	0.6
Debt cost (Kd %)	6	6	6	6.5	7	7.5	8.5
Equity cost (Ke %)	14	14	14.5	15	16	18	19

Solution: Calculation of Cost of capital

Financial Plan	Capital Structure		Specific Cost		WACC (%)
	Debt	Equity	Debt	Equity	
1	0.0	1.0	0.06	0.14	[0.0 x 0.06 + 1.0 x 0.14] 100 = 14
2	0.1	0.9	0.06	0.14	[0.1 x 0.06 + 0.9 x 0.14] 100 = 13.2
3	0.2	0.8	0.06	0.145	[0.2 x 0.06 + 0.8 x 0.145] 100 = 12.8
4	0.3	0.7	0.065	0.15	[0.3 x 0.065 + 0.7 x 0.15] 100 = 12.45
5	0.4	0.6	0.07	0.16	[0.4 x 0.07 + 0.6 x 0.16] 100 = 12.40
6	0.5	0.5	0.075	0.18	[0.5 x 0.075 + 0.5 x 0.18] 100 = 12.75
7	0.6	0.4	0.085	0.19	[0.6 x 0.085 + 0.4 x 0.19] 100 = 12.7

From the above calculation, we can observe that WACC has decreased from 15 per cent to 12.4 per cent and thereafter increased, which was due to the use of heavy debt. Hence, optimal capital structure is where, the WACC is minimum, 12.4 per cent at 40 per cent debt and 60 per cent equity. In other words, fifth financial plan is optimum capital structure.

Illustration 2: If debt is cheaper than equity, why do companies not finance their assets with 80 per cent or 90 per cent debt ratio?

The capital structure is the mixture of the various types of long-term sources of funds namely, equity share including retained earnings, preference shares debentures and long-term loans from financial institution. It is also known as financial structure.

Companies can use any source of finance for their assets requirements. The required capital can be raised through any one of the following financial plans.

(a) Fully equity share capital plan,

(b) Fully debt capital plan,

(c) Fully preference share capital plan,

(d) Combination of (a) and (b) in different proportions,

(e) A combination of (a), (b) and (c) in different proportions, and

(f) A combination of (a) and (c) in different proportions and so on.

Of all the sources of long-term finance, debt is the cheapest source no doubt, because the interest paid on debt is allowed for tax purpose. The company can save tax due to the interest, but company cannot use debt beyond certain limit, up to certain limit use of debt reduces overall cost of capital; beyond the limit it will increase. This can be illustrated with the following example.

Finance source and their cost	Plan 1	Plan 2	Plan 3	Plan 4	Plan 5	Plan 6	Plan 7
Debt as a percentage of total capital	0	10	20	30	40	50	60
Debt cost (Kd %)	7	7	7	7.5	8	8.5	9.5
Cost of Equity (Ke %)	15	15	15.5	16	17	19	20

You are required to find out optimal debt-equity mix of the company.

Solution: Calculation of debt-equity mix for financial plans

Financial Plan	Capital Structure		Specific Cost (%)		Weighted Average Cost of Capital (in %)
	Debt	Equity	Debt	Equity	
1	0.0	100.0	7	15	[0.0 x 0.07 + (.1) x 0.15] 100 = 15
2	10	90	7	15	[0.1 x 0.07 + (.9) x 0.15] 100 = 14.2
3	20	80	7	15.5	[0.2 x 0.07 + (.8) x 0.155] 100 = 13.8
4	30	70	7.5	16	[0.3 x 0.075 + (.7) x 0.16] 100 = 13.45
5	40	60-	8	17	[0.4 x 0.08 + (.6) x 0.17] 100 = 13.40
6	50	50	8.5	19	[0.5 x 0.085 + (.5) x 0.19] 100 = 13.75
7	60	40	9.5	20	[0.6 x 0.095 + (.4) x 0.20] 100 = 13.7

From above table we can observe that the WACC has decreased from 15 per cent 13.4 per cent and thereafter increased due to the use of debt. Company's optimum debt-ration is 40 per cent (i.e., out of total funds required for financing of assets, company can use 40 per cent of debt funds and 60 per cent of equity funds). So, companies cannot finance their assets with 80 per cent or 90 per cent, since the WACC is increasing after 40 per cent.

Illustration 3: Calculate operating leverage. Interest Rs. 5,0000; sales Rs. 50,000; Variable cost Rs. 25,000; Fixed cost Rs. 15,000.

Solution: Computation of EBIT or Operating Profit

Particulars.	Amount Rs.
Sales	50,000
Less: Variable cost	25,000
Contribution	25,000
Less: Fixed cost	15,000
EBIT or Operating Profit	10,000

Operating leverage = Contribution ÷ EBIT or Operating profit = Rs. 25,000 ÷ Rs.10,000 = 2.5

Illustration 4: Given the operating income Rs. 2,00,000 and taxable income Rs. 1,25,000, calculate the financial leverage.

Solution

Financial leverage = Operating income ÷ Earnings before tax

= Rs. 2,00,000 ÷ Rs. 1,25,000 = 1.6

Illustration 5: Given: Financial leverage is 2, Fixed interest charges Rs. 1,00,000. Find out the operating profit.

Solution

Financial leverage = Operating profit ÷ (operating profit - interest)

= X ÷ (X - Rs. 1,00,000) = 2

X = Rs. 2,00,000

Illustration 6: AMC Company Ltd., provided the following information and requested you to calculate (a) operating leverage with 4000 and 6000 quantity of sales, (b) operating BEP (Q)

Selling price Rs. 300, variable cost Rs. 200, Fixed cost Rs. 2,40,000

Solution: Calculation of EBIT

Particulars.	4000 units	6000 units
Sales revenue	12,00,000	18,00,000
Less: Variable cost	8,00,000	12,00,000
Contribution	4,00,000	6,00,000
Less: Fixed cost	2,40,000	2,40,000
EBIT or Operating Profit	1,60,000	3,60,000

(a) Operating leverage (OL) = Contribution ÷ EBIT

OL (4000 units) = 2.5; OL (6000 units) = 1.66

(b) Operating BEP (Q) = Fixed cost ÷ Contribution per unit

= 2,40,000 ÷ (300 - 200) = 2400 units

Illustration 7: BOL Ltd., currently selling 800 units per annum at the rate of Rs. 2000 per unit. For manufacture of one unit the company has to spend Rs. 1200 variable cost per unit and a fixed cost of Rs. 2,00,000. What is the operating leverage at present level of activity ? Also calculate the operating leverage if the company sells 1200 units per annum.

Solution: Calculation of EBIT

Particulars.	800 units Activity level	1200 units activity level
Sales at Rs. 2000 p.u.	16,00,000	24,00,000
Less: Variable cost	9,60,000	14,40,000
Contribution	6,40,000	9,60,000
Less: Fixed cost	2,00,000	2,00,000
EBIT or Operating Profit	2,40,000	7,60,000
Operating leverage = Contribution ÷EBIT	2.66	1.263

Illustration 8: From the following information, calculate operating leverage, financial leverage and combined leverage.

Sales 50,000 units at Rs. 4 per unit; Variable cost Rs. 2 per unit;

Fixed cost Rs. 75,000;   10% debentures of Rs. 2,00,000

Solution : Calculation of EBIT

Particulars.	Amount Rs.
Sales revenue (50,000 x 4)	2,00,000
Less: Variable cost (50,000 x 2)	1,00,000
Contribution	1,00,000
Less: Fixed cost	75,000
EBIT	25,000
Less: Interest	20,000
EBT	5,000

Operating leverage = Contribution ÷ EBIT = 1,00,000 ÷ 25,000 = 4

Financial leverage = EBIT ÷ EBT   = 25,000 ÷ 5,000 = 5

Combined leverage = OL x FL or = (C ÷ EBIT) (EBIT ÷ EBT)

$$= 4 \times 5 = 20 \text{ or} = (1,00,000 ÷ 25,000) (25,000 ÷ 5,000) = 20$$

Illustration 9: X Ltd. has a total capitalisation of Rs. 10 lakh consisting entirely of equity share capital of Rs. 50 each. It wishes to raise another 5 lakh for expansion through one of its two possible financial plans.

a)   All equity shares of Rs. 50 each;

b)   All debentures carrying 9 per cent interest.

c)   Present leverage of EBIT is Rs. 1,40,000 and tax 50 per cent. Calculate EBIT level at which EPS would remain same, irrespective of raising funds through equity or debentures.

Solution:

$$\frac{X(1-t)}{ES_1} = \frac{(X-I)(1-t)}{ES_2}$$

$$\frac{X(1-0.5)}{30,000} = \frac{(X-45,000)(1-0.5)}{20,000}$$

$$\frac{0.5X}{30,000} = \frac{0.5X - 22,500}{20,000}$$

$$10,000X = 15,000X - 67,50,00,000$$
$$67,50,00,000 = 15,000X - 10,000X$$
$$67,50,00,000 = 5,000x$$
$$X = 67,50,00,000 / 5,000 = 1,35,000 /-$$

Proof

Particulars.	Plan A	Plan B
EBIT	1,35,000	1,35,000
Less: Interest	---	45,000
EBT	1,35,000	90,000
Less: Tax 50 %	67,500	45,000
EAT	67,500	45,000
Less: Preference dividend	---	---
Earnings available to share holders.	67,500	45,000
EPS	67,500 ÷ 30,000 Rs. 2.25	45,000 ÷ 20,000 Rs. 2.25

Illustration 10: KPMG Ltd., has currently an ordinary share capital of Rs. 25 lakh, consisting of 25,000 shares of Rs. 100 each. The management is planning to raise another Rs. 20 lakh to finance a major programme of expansion through one of the four possible financial plans.

i) Entirely through ordinary shares.

ii) Rs.10 lakh through ordinary shares and Rs. 10 lakh through long-term borrowings at 8 per cent interest p.a.

iii) Rs.5 lakh through ordinary shares and Rs. 15 lakh through long-term borrowing at 9 per cent interest p.a.

iv) Rs. 10 lakh through ordinary shares and Rs. 10 lakh through preference shares with 5 per cent dividend.

The company's expected EBIT will be Rs. 8 lakh. Assuming a corporate tax rate of 46 per cent. Determine the EPS in each alternative and comment which alternative is best and why ?

Solution: Calculation of EPS

Particulars.	Financial Plan I	II	III	IV
EBIT	8,00,000	8,00,000	8,00,000	8,00,000
Less: Interest	---	80,000	1,35,000	---
EBT	8,00,000	7,20,000	6,65,000	8,00,000
Less: Tax 46 %	3,68,000	3,31,200	3,05,900	3,68,000
EAT	4,32,000	3,88,800	3,59,100	4,32,000
Less: Preference dividend	---	---	---	50,000
Earnings available to equity	4,32,000	3,88,800	3,59,100	3,82,000
EPS = Equity earnings Equity shares	9.6	11.108	11.97	10.91

Notes: Calculation of No. of Equity Shares

Plan 1: Existing + new shares = 25,000 + 20,000 = 45,000

Plan 2: 25,000 + 10,000 = 35,000

Plan 3: 25,000 + 5,000 = 30,000

Plan 4: 25,000 + 10,000 = 35,000

The above calculation indicates that financial plan (iii) is the best since EPS under this plan is highest, when compared to other financial plans.

Illustration 11: A firm has sales of Rs. 10,00,000, variable cost Rs. 7,00,000 and fixed cost Rs. 2,00,000 and debt of Rs. 5,00,000 at 10 per cent rate of interest. What are the operating and financial leverages.

Solution: Calculation of EBT

Particulars.	Amount Rs.
Sales	10,00,000
Less: Variable cost	7,00,000
Contribution	3,00,000
Less: Fixed cost	2,00,000
EBIT	1,00,000
Less: Interest (5,00,000 x 10 / 100)	50,000
EBT	50,000

Operating leverage = Contribution ÷ EBIT = 3,00,000 ÷ 1,00,000 = 3

Financial leverage = EBIT ÷ EBT = 1,00,000 ÷ 50,000 = 2

Illustration 12: Penta Four Ltd., has currently adopted an all equity structure, consisting of 15,000 equity shares of Rs. 100 each. The management is planning to raise another Rs. 25 lakh to finance a major expansion programme and is considering three alternative methods of financing.

i)   To issue 25,000 equity shares of Rs. 100 each.

ii)   To issue 25,000, 8% debentures of Rs. 100 each.

iii) To issue 25,000, 8% preference shares of Rs. 100 each.

The company's expected EBIT will be Rs. 8 lakh. Assuming a corporate tax rate of 46 per cent. Determine the EPS in each financial plan and determine the best one and why ?

Solution: Calculation of EPS

Particulars.	Financial Plan		
	I	II	III
EBIT	8,00,000	8,00,000	8,00,000
Less: Interest	---	2,00,000	---
EBT	8,00,000	6,00,000	8,00,000
Less: Tax 46 %	3,68,000	2,76,000	3,68,000
EAT	4,32,000	3,24,000	4,32,000
Less: Preference dividend	---	---	2,00,000
Earnings available to equity	4,32,000	3,24,000	2,32,000
EPS = Equity earnings Equity shares	4,32,000	3,24,000	2,32,000
	(25000 + 15000) Rs. 10.8	15,000 Rs. 21.6	15,000 Rs. 15.47

Plan (ii) is the best financial plan since EPS under this is the highest.

Illustration 13: Bangalore traders with total capitalisation of Rs. 10 lakh consisting of entirely equity capital has before it, two choices to meet the additional capital needs of Rs. 15 lakh. You are required to calculate the indifference point in each of the following cases assuming 35 per cent tax rate and the face value of equity shares.

i)   Equity capital of Rs. 15 lakh or Rs. 7.5 lakh 10 per cent debentures and Rs. 7.5 lakh equity capital.

ii) Equity capital of Rs. 15 lakh or Rs. 7.5 lakh equity capital and Rs. 7.5 lakh 15 per cent preference shares.

Solution: Computation of indifference point:

Case - ie. : $(X - I)(1 - t) \div N_{1a} = (X - I)(1 - t) - PD \div N_{1b}$

Where,

X = EBIT or Point of indifference.   I = Interest on debentures.

t = Corporate tax rate.   PD = Preference dividend.

N_{1a} = No. of equity shares in case (i), with fully equity.

N_{1b} = No. of equity shares in case (i), with 50% equity and 50% debentures.

Case - i: $X(1 - t) \div N_{1a} = (X - I)(1 - t) \div N_{1b}$

$X(1 - 0.35) \div 25,000 = (X - 75,000)(1 - 0.35) \div 17,500$

$X(0.65) \div 25,000 = (X - 75,000)(0.65) \div 17,500$

$0.65 X \div 25,000 = (0.65 X - 18,750) \div 17,500$

$11,375 X = 16,250 X - 1,21,87,50,000$

$11,375 X - 16,250 X = - 1,21,87,50,000$

$- 4,875 X = - 1,21,87,50,000$

$X = - 1,21,87,50,000 \div - 4,875$

$X = $ Rs. 2,50,000

Proof

Particulars.	Case – ia (Rs.)	Case – ib (Rs.)
EBIT	2,50,000	2,50,000
Less: Interest on debentures	---	75,000
EBT	2,50,000	1,75,000
Less: Tax 35%	87,500	61,250
EAT	1,62,500	1,13,750

Computation of Earnings Per Share (EPS)

Case - ia: Rs.1,62,500 ÷ 25,000 = Rs. 6.50

Case - ib: Rs.1,13,750 ÷ 17,500 = Rs. 6.50

Point of indifference is proved since its EPS is same under both plans ia and ib.

Note : Face value of share is Rs. 100

No. of shares (N_{1a})

= Existing equity capital Rs. 10,00,000 ÷ Rs. 100 = 10,000 shares.

= Proposed equity capital Rs. 15,00,000 ÷ Rs. 100 = 15,000 shares.

Total shares = 25,000 shares

No. of shares (N_{1b})

= Existing equity capital Rs. 10,00,000 ÷ Rs. 100 = 10,000 shares.

= Proposed equity capital Rs. 7,50,000 ÷ Rs. 100 = 7,500 shares.

Total shares = 17,500 shares

Case - ibis: $(X - I)(1 - t) ÷ N2a = (X - I)(1 - t) - PD ÷ N_{2b}$

Where,

X = EBIT or Point of indifference.   I = Interest on debentures.

t = Corporate tax rate.   PD = Preference dividend.

N_{2a} = No. of equity shares in case (i), with fully equity.

N_{2b} = No. of equity shares in case (i), with 50% equity and 50% preference capital.

Case - ibis:

$$X(1 - t) ÷ N_{2a} = (X - I)(1 - t) - PD ÷ N_{2b}$$
$$X(1 - 0.35) ÷ 25,000 = X(1 - 0.35) - 1,12,500 ÷ 17,500$$
$$X(0.65) ÷ 25,000 = X(0.65) - 1,12,500 ÷ 17,500$$
$$0.65\ X ÷ 25,000 = (0.65\ X - 1,12,500) ÷ 17,500$$
$$11,375\ X = 16,250\ X - 2,81,25,00,000$$
$$11,375\ X - 16,250\ X = -2,81,25,00,000$$
$$-4,875\ X = -2,81,25,00,000$$
$$X = -2,81,25,00,000 ÷ -4,875$$
$$X = Rs.\ 5,76,923$$

Proof

Particulars.	Case – iia (Rs.)	Case – iib (Rs.)
EBIT	5,76,923	5,76,923
Less: Interest on debentures	-----	-----
EBT	5,76,923	5,76,923
Less: Tax 35%	2,01,923	2,01,923
EAT	3,75,000	3,75,000
Less: Preference dividend at 15%	-----	1,12,500
Earnings available to equity shareholder	3,75,000	2,62,500

Computation of Earnings Per Share (EPS)

Case - iia : Rs.3,75,500 ÷ 25,000 = Rs. 15

Case - iib : Rs.2,62,500 ÷ 17,500 = Rs. 15

Point of indifference is proved since its EPS is same under both plans ia and ib.

Note : Face value of share is Rs. 100

No. of shares (N_{2a})

= Existing equity capital Rs. 10,00,000 ÷ Rs. 100 = 10,000 shares.

= Proposed equity capital Rs. 15,00,000 ÷ Rs. 100 = 15,000 shares.

Total shares = 25,000 shares

No. of shares (N_{2b})

= Existing equity capital Rs. 10,00,000 ÷ Rs. 100 = 10,000 shares.

= Proposed equity capital Rs. 7,50,000 ÷ Rs. 100 = 7,500 shares.

Total shares   = 17,500 shares

Illustration 14: A newly established company wishes to determine an appropriate capital structure. It can issue 12 per cent debentures and 10 per cent preference capital and the existing tax rate is 35 per cent. The company requires Rs. 50 lakh.

The possible capital is

Plan	Debenture capital (%)	Preference capital (%)	Equity capital (%)
1	00	00	100
2	30	00	70
3	30	20	50
4	50	00	50
5	50	20	30

If EBIT is 12 per cent calculate EPS.

Solution: Calculation of EBIT

In the above problem if the company earns 15 per cent EBIT on required capital (investment), then the EBIT is:

Required amount = 50,00,000 x 12% = Rs. 6,00,000

Particulars.	Financial Plans				
	1 (in Rs.)	2 (in Rs.)	3 (in Rs.)	4 (in Rs.)	5 (in Rs.)
EBIT	6,00,000	6,00,000	6,00,000	6,00,000	6,00,000
Less: Interest on debentures at 12%	------	1,80,000	1,80,000	3,00,000	3,00,000
EBT	6,00,000	4,20,000	4,20,000	3,00,000	3,00,000
Less: Tax 35 %	2,10,000	1,47,000	1,47,000	1,05,000	1,05,000
EAT	3,90,000	2,73,000	2,73,000	1,95,000	1,95,000
Less: Dividend on Preference capital	------	------	1,00,000	------	1,00,000
Earnings available to equity shares	3,90,000	2,73,000	1,73,000	1,95,000	95,000

Computation of Earnings Per Share (EPS):

EPS = Earnings available to equity shares ÷ No. of shares outstanding

Plan 1 : Rs. 3,90,000 ÷ 50,000 = Rs. 7.80

Plan 2 : Rs. 2,73,000 ÷ 35,000 = Rs. 7.80

Plan 3 : Rs. 1,73,000 ÷ 25,000 = Rs. 6.92

Plan 4 : Rs.   1,95,000 ÷ 25,000 = Rs. 7.80

Plan 5 : Rs.   95,000 ÷ 15,000 = Rs. 6.33

Note: Assumption face value of share is Rs. 100.

From the above illustration we can observe that financial leverage does not increase earnings per share always. Use of debt upto 30 per cent, increased EPS and when the proportion increased to 50 per cent, EPS has come down. Hence, financial leverage does not increase EPS.

Illustration 15: A manufacturing company has the following capital structure:

	Rs.
40,000 equity shares of Rs. 50 each	20,00,000
Retained earnings	10,00,000
10% debentures	10,00,000
12% preference shares	10,00,000
Long term debts at 11 per cent	5,00,000
Rs.	55,00,000

The present EBIT is Rs. 10,00,000. The company is contemplating an expansion programme requiring an additional investment of Rs. 10,00,000.

It is hoped, that the company will be able to maintain the same rate of earnings. To raise the additional capital the company has the following alternatives:

i) To issue debentures at 11per cent

ii) To issue preference shares at 13 per cent

iii) To raise the entire additional capital through equity shares.

Examine these alternatives and suggest which alternative is best for the company. Assure tax rate to be at 35 per cent.

Solution: Calculation of EPS

Particulars.	Alternatives		
	i	ii	iii
EBIT	10,00,000	10,00,000	10,00,000
Less: Interest	1,10,000	---	---
EBT	8,90,000	10,00,000	10,00,000
Less: Tax 35%	3,11,500	3,50,000	3,50,000
EAT	5,78,500	6,50,000	6,50,000
Less: Preference dividend	---	1,30,000	---
Earnings available to equity	5,78,500	5,20,000	6,50,000
EPS = Equity earnings Equity shares	5,78,500	5,20,000	6,50,000
	40,000 Rs. 14.46	40,000 Rs. 13	(40,000 + 20,000) Rs. 10.83

Plan (i) is the best financial plan since EPS under this is highest.

Calculation of existing number of shares = Total equity share capital / face value of each share = Rs. 20,00,000 / Rs. 50 = 40,000 Shares

Calculation of the number of shares to be issued to public to raise Rs. 10 lakh

= Amount to be raised / face value of each share

= Rs. 10,00,000 / Rs. 50 = 20,000 Shares

Note: assumed the shares will be issued at Rs.50 per share

Illustration 16: A firm has sales of Rs. 5 lakh, variable cost Rs. 3.5 lakh and fixed cost Rs. 1,00,000 and debt of Rs. 2.5 lakh at 10 per cent. Calculate the operating, financial and combined leverage.

Solution: Calculation of EBT

Particulars.	Amount Rs.
Sales	5,00,000
Less: Variable cost	3,50,000
Contribution	1,50,000
Less: Fixed cost	1,00,000
EBIT	50,000
Less: Interest (2,50,000 x 10 / 100)	25,000
EBT	25,000

Operating leverage = Contribution ÷ EBIT = 1,50,000 ÷ 50,000 = 3

Financial leverage = EBIT ÷ EBT = 50,000 ÷ 25,000 = 2

$$\text{Combined leverage} = \frac{\text{Contribution}}{\text{EBIT}} = \frac{\text{EBIT}}{\text{EBT}}$$

or

= Operating leverage X financial Leverage

$$= \frac{1,50,000}{50,000} \times \frac{50,000}{25,000} = 6$$

Illustration 17: The following is the balance sheet of Venson Ltd., as on 31-03-01.

Liabilities	Amount Rs.	Assets	Amount Rs.
Equity capital	1,80,000	Fixed assets	4,50,000
(Rs. 10 per share)		Current assets	1,50,000
10% Debentures	2,40,000		
Retained earnings	60,000		
Current liability	1,20,000		
	6,00,000		6,00,000

The company's total assets turnover ratio is 2.5 times. The fixed operating costs are Rs. 2 lakh. Variable operating cost ratio is 40 per cent. Income tax rate is 50 per cent.

(i) Calculate the leverages and

(ii) Determine the likely level of EBIT if EPS is Rs. 6

Solution:

i) *Computation of Sales (in Rs.)*

Asset turn over = Sales 'X' ÷ Total assets = 2.5

Sales 'X' = Total Assets X 2.5 = 6,00,000 X 2.5 = Rs.15,00,000

Computation of Net Profit

Particulars.	Amount Rs.
Sales	15,00,000
Less: Variable cost (15,00,000 x 0.40)	6,00,000
Contribution	9,00,000
Less: Fixed cost	2,00,000
EBIT	7,00,000
Less: Interest (10% on debentures)	24,000
EBT	6,76,000
Less: Tax 50%	3,38,000
Net profit	3,38,000

Operating leverage = Contribution ÷ EBIT = 9,00,000 ÷ 7,00,000 = 1.285

Financial leverage = EBIT ÷ EBT = 7,00,000 ÷ 6,76,000 = 1.035

Combined leverage = Contribution ÷ EBT = 9,00,000 ÷ 6,76,000 = 1.33

ii) *Likely level of EBIT if EPS is Rs. 6*

$$EPS = \frac{\text{Earnings available to ordinary shareholders (net profit)}}{\text{No. of ordinary shares outstanding}}$$

$$Rs. 6 = \frac{'X'}{18,000}$$

Net profit = Rs. 6x 18,000 = Rs. 1,08,000

Net profit is after payment of tax at 50 per cent

Hence EBT = 1,08,000 × 2 = Rs. 2,16,000

EBIT = EBT + Interest = 2,16,000 + 24,000 = Rs. 2,40,000

Illustration 18: Bhatt Co Ltd., balance sheet is as follows.

Liabilities	Amount	Assets	Amount
Equity capital (each Rs. 10)	60,000	Fixed assets	1,50,000
10% Long-term debt	80,000	Current assets	50,000
Retained earnings	20,000		
Current liability	40,000		

The company's total assets turnover is 3. Its fixed operating costs are Rs. 1,00,000 and its variable cost ratio is 40%, income tax rate is 50%.

Calculate (1) Operating leverage, (2) Financial leverage, (3) Combined leverage

Solution: Computation of sales (in Rs.)

Assets turnover = Sales 'X' ÷ Total assets (current + net assets) = 3

Sales 'X' = Total assets x 3 = 2,00,000 x 3 = Rs. 6,00,000

Particulars.	Amount Rs.
Sales	6,00,000
Less: Variable cost (6,00,000 x 0.40 ÷ 100)	2,40,000
Contribution	3,60,000
Less: Fixed cost	1,00,000
EBIT	2,60,000
Less: Interest (10% on debentures)	8,000
EBT	2,52,000
Less: Tax 50%	1,26,000
Net profit	1,26,000

Operating leverage = Contribution ÷ EBIT or Operating profit = 3,60,000 ÷ 2,60,000 = 1.38

Financial leverage = EBIT or Operating profit ÷ EBT = 2,60,000 ÷ 2,52,000 = 1.0317

Combined leverage = Operating leverage X Financial leverage = 1.3846 X 1.0317 = 1.428

Illustration 19: Reliance Ltd., has a share capital of Rs. 2 lakh divided into shares of Rs. 10 each. It has a major expansion programme requiring an additional investment of Rs. 1,00,000. The management is considering the following alternatives.

i)   Issue of 10%, debentures of Rs. 1,00,000

ii) Issue of 10,000, 15% preference shares of Rs. 10 each,

iii) Issue of 10,000 equity shares Rs. 10 each

The company's present EBIT is Rs. 60,000 p.a. Calculate the EPS for the above three alternative financial plans presuming.

(a) EBIT continues to be the same, and

(b) EBIT increases by Rs. 20,000. Tax rate is 50%.

Solution:

a) *Calculation of EPS with EBIT Rs. 60,000*

Particulars.		Financial Plan		
		I	II	III
EBIT (60,000 + 20,000)		60,000	60,000	60,000
Less: Interest		10,000	------	------
EBT		50,000	60,000	60,000
Less: Tax 50%		25,000	30,000	30,000
EAT		25,000	30,000	30,000
Less: Preference dividend		------	15,000	------
Earnings available to ordinary shareholder		25,000	15,000	30,000
EPS =	Earnings available to shareholder	25,000	15,000	30,000
	No. of ordinary shares outstanding	20,000	20,000	30,000
		Rs. 1.25	Rs. 0.75	Rs. 1

b) *Calculation of EPS when EBIT increased by Rs. 20,000*

Particulars.	Financial Plan		
	I	II	III
EBIT (60,000 + 20,000)	80,000	80,000	80,000
Less: Interest	10,000	------	------
EBT	70,000	80,000	80,000
Less: Tax 50%	35,000	40,000	40,000
EAT	35,000	40,000	40,000
Less: Preference dividend	------	15,000	------
Earnings available to ordinary shareholder	35,000	25,000	40,000
EPS	35,000	25,000	40,000
	20,000	20,000	30,000
	= Rs. 1.75	= Rs. 1.25	= Rs. 1.33

Illustration 20: A newly established company wishes to determine an appropriate capital structure. It can issue 12 per cent debentures and 10 per cent preference capital and the existing tax rate is 35 per cent. The company requires Rs. 50 lakh. The possible capital is:

Plan	Debenture capital (%)	Preference capital (%)	Equity capital (%)
1	00	00	100
2	30	00	70
3	30	20	50
4	50	00	50
5	50	20	30

If EBIT is 12 per cent, calculate EPS.

Solution: Calculation of EBIT

In the above problem, if the company earns 15 per cent EBIT on required capital (investment), then the EBIT is: Required amount = 50,00,000 X 12% = Rs. 6,00,000

Particulars.	Financial Plans				
	1 (in Rs.)	2 (in Rs.)	3 (in Rs.)	4 (in Rs.)	5 (in Rs.)
EBIT	6,00,000	6,00,000	6,00,000	6,00,000	6,00,000
Less: Interest on debentures at 12%	------	1,80,000	1,80,000	3,00,000	3,00,000
EBT	6,00,000	4,20,000	4,20,000	3,00,000	3,00,000
Less: Tax 35 %	2,10,000	1,47,000	1,47,000	1,05,000	1,05,000
EAT	3,90,000	2,73,000	2,73,000	1,95,000	1,95,000
Less: Dividend on Preference capital	------	------	1,00,000	------	1,00,000
Earnings available to equity shares	3,90,000	2,73,000	1,73,000	1,95,000	95,000

Computation of Earnings Per Share (EPS):

EPS = Earnings available to equity shares ÷ No. of shares outstanding

Plan 1 : Rs. 3,90,000 ÷ 50,000 = Rs. 7.80

Plan 2 : Rs. 2,73,000 ÷ 35,000 = Rs. 7.80

Plan 3 : Rs. 1,73,000 ÷ 25,000 = Rs. 6.92

Plan 4 : Rs. 1,95,000 ÷ 25,000 = Rs. 3.80

Plan 5 : Rs. 95,000 ÷ 15,000 = Rs. 6.33

Note: Assumption face value of share is Rs. 100.

Illustration 21: The capital structure of XL Ltd., consists of the following securities.

10% Debentures	Rs. 5,00,000
12% Preference shares	Rs. 1,00,000
Equity shares of Rs. 100	Rs. 4,00,000

Operating profit (EBIT) of Rs. 1,60,000 and the company is in 50 per cent tax bracket

i) Determine the company's EPS

ii) Determine the percentage change in EPS associated with 30% increase and 30% decrease in EBIT

iii) Determine the degree of financial leverage.

Solution: Computation of earnings available to equity shareholder

Particulars.	Case II 30% decrease (Rs.)	Base EBIT (Rs.)	Case I 30% increase (Rs.)
EBIT	1,12,000	1,60,000	2,08,000
Less: Interest on debentures	50,000	50,000	50,000
EBT	62,000	1,10,000	1,58,000
Less: Tax 50%	31,000	55,000	79,000
EAT	31,000	55,000	79,000
Less: Preference dividend at 12%	12,000	12,000	12,000
Earnings available to equity shareholder	19,000	43,000	67,000

i) *Earnings per share (EPS)*

Earnings available to equity shareholder ' ÷ No. of shares outstanding

Case I = Rs. 67,000 ÷ 4,000 = Rs. 16.75

Base = Rs. 43,000 ÷ 4,000 = Rs. 10.75

Case II = Rs. 19,000 ÷ 4,000 = Rs. 4.75

ii) *Change in EPS*

30 per cent increase = (6 ÷ 10.75) 100 = 55.8 per cent

30 per cent decrease = (-6 ÷ 10.75) 100 = -55.8 per cent

iii) *Degree of financial leverage = DOFL - EBIT ÷ EBT:*

Case I = Rs. 2,08,000 ÷ Rs. 1,58,000 = Rs. 1.316

Base = Rs. 1,60,000 ÷ Rs. 1,10,000 = Rs.1.455

Case II = Rs. 1,12,000 ÷ Rs. 62,000 = Rs. 1.806

Illustration 22: Determine the earnings per share (EPS) of a company, which the opening profit (EBIT) of Rs. 1,60,000. Its capital structure consists of the following securities :

10%	Debentures	Rs. 5,00,000
12%	Preference shares	Rs. 1,00,000
	Equity shares of Rs. 100	Rs. 4,00,000

The company is in the 55% tax bracket

i) Determine the company's EPS

ii) Determine the percentage change in EPS associated with 30% increase and 30% decrease in EBIT

iii) Determine the degree of financial leverage.

Solution:

Computation of earnings available to equity shareholder

Particulars	Case II 30% decrease (Rs.)	Base EBIT (Rs.)	Case I 30% increase (Rs.)
EBIT	1,12,000	1,60,000	2,08,000
Less: Interest on debentures	50,000	50,000	50,000
EBT	62,000	1,10,000	1,58,000
Less: Tax 55%	34,100	60,500	86,900
EAT	27,900	49,500	71,100
Less: Preference dividend at 12%	12,000	12,000	12,000
Earnings available to equity shareholder	15,900	37,500	59,100

i) *Earnings per share (EPS)*

Earnings available to equity shareholder ' ÷ No. of shares outstanding

Case I = Rs. 59,100 ÷ 4,000 = Rs. 14.78

Base = Rs. 37,500 ÷ 4,000 = Rs. 9.38

Case II = Rs. 15,900 ÷ 4,000 = Rs. 3.98

ii) *Change in EPS*

30 per cent increase = (5.40 ÷ 9.38) 100 = 57.6 per cent

30 per cent decrease = (-5.4 ÷ 9.38) 100 = -57.6 per cent

iii) *Degree of financial leverage = DOFL - EBIT ÷ EBT*

Case I = Rs. 2,08,000 ÷ Rs. 1,58,000 = Rs. 1.32

Base = Rs. 1,60,000 ÷ Rs. 1,10,000 = Rs.1.46

Case II = Rs. 1,12,000 ÷ Rs. 62,000 = Rs. 1.806

Illustration 23: The capital structure of Bhatt Software Ltd., Bangalore, consists of an equity share capital of Rs. 10,00,000 (shares of Rs. 100 each) and Rs. 10,00,000 of debentures. Sales increased by 20% from 1,00,000 units to 1,20,000 units, the selling price is Rs. 10 per unit, variable cost amount to Rs. 6 per unit and fixed expenses amount to Rs. 2,00,000. The IT rate is assumed to be 50 per cent.

a) You are required to calculate the following:

i) The percentage increase in EPS.

ii) The degree of financial leverage at 1,00,000 and 1,20,000 units.

iii) The degree of operating leverage at 1,00,000 and 1,20,000 units.

b) Comment on the behaviour of operating and financial leverage in relation to increase in production from 1,00,000 to 1,20,000 units.

Solution: Computation of earnings available to equity shareholder

Particulars	Base (in Rs.)	Increase (in Rs.)
Sales (in units)	1,00,000	1,20,000
Sales revenue (Rs. 10 per unit)	10,00,000	12,00,000
Less: Variable cost (Rs. 6 per unit)	6,00,000	7,20,000
Contribution	4,00,000	4,80,000
Less: Fixed cost	2,00,000	2,00,000
EBIT	2,00,000	2,80,000
Less: Interest on debentures	1,00,000	1,00,000
EBT	1,00,000	1,80,000
Less: Tax 50%	50,000	90,000
EAT	50,000	90,000
Less: Preference dividend at 12%	--------	--------
Earnings available to equity shareholder '	50,000	90,000

i)   *Percentage increase in (EPS)*

EPS = Earnings available to equity shareholder ' + No. of shares outstanding

Base = Rs. 50,000 ÷ 10,000 = Rs. 5

Increase (20%) = Rs. 90,000 ÷ 10,000 = Rs. 9

Percentage increase in (EPS) = [(9 - 5) ÷ 5] 100 = 80 per cent

ii) *Operating leverage = Contribution   EBIT*

Base = Rs. 4,00,000 ÷ 2,00,000 = 2

Increase (20%) = Rs. 4,80,000 ÷ 2,80,000 = 1.71

iii) *Degree of financial leverage = EBIT   EBT*

Base = Rs. 2,00,000 ÷ 1,00,000 = 2

Increase (20%) = Rs. 2,80,000 ÷ 1,80,000 = 1.6

Comment: An account of increase in sales from 1,00,000 to 1,20,000 units at the rate of 20 per cent, EPS increased by 80 per cent. While operating leverage comes down from 2 to 1.71 and financial leverage also declined from 2 to 1.6. Therefore, there is a significant decrease in both the business risk and financial risk of the company. An account of reduction in both leverages. This is generally the result when there is increase in sales without any increase in fixed operating or financial risk.

Illustration 24: A new project under consideration by your company requires a capital investment of Rs. 150 lakh. Interest on term loans is 12 per cent and tax rate is 50 per cent. If the debt-equity ratio insisted by the financing agencies is 2:1, calculate the point of indifference for the project.

Solution:

With reference to project under consideration the debt-equity ratio insisted upon by the financing agencies is 2 : 1.

There are two alternatives available to the company.

a)   Raising the entire amount by issue of equity shares

b)   Raising Rs. 100 lakh by way of debt and Rs. 50 lakh by way of issue of equity shares, thus maintaining a debt-equity ratio 2:1.

Computation of indifference point

$$(X - I)(1 - t) \div N_1 = (X - I)(1 - t) - PD \div N_2$$

Where,

X = EBIT or Point of indifference.   I = Interest on debentures.

t = Corporate tax rate.   PD = Preference dividend.

N_1 = No. of equity shares in alternative (a) N_2 = No. of equity shares in alternative (b)

$(X - 0)(1 - 0.50) \div 15,000 = (X - 12,00,000)(1 - 0.50) - 0 \div 5,000$

0.5 X ÷ 15,000 = (0.5X - 6,00,000) ÷ 5,000

2,500 X = 7,500 X - 9,00,00,00,000

2,500 X - 7,500 X = - 9,00,00,00,000

-5,000 X = - 9,00,00,00,000

X = - 9,00,00,00,000 ÷ - 5,000 = Rs. 18,00,000

Note: It has been assumed that face value of each equity share is Rs. 1000.

Proof

Particulars	Alternative - A (Rs.)	Alternative – B (Rs.)
EBIT	18,00,000	18,00,000
Less: Interest on debentures	-----	12,00,000
EBT	18,00,000	6,00,000
Less: Tax 50%	9,00,000	3,00,000
EAT	9,00,000	3,00,000

EPS = Rs. 9,00,000 ÷ 15,000 = Rs. 60   Rs. 3,00,000 ÷ 5,000 = Rs. 60

Note: No. of shares (N_1) = Rs. 1,50,00,000 ÷ 1,000 = 15,000 shares

No. of shares (N_2) = Rs. 50,00,000 ÷ 1,000 = 5,000 shares

Since both alternative A and B have same EPS, hence, the point of indifference is proved.

Illustration 25: A project under consideration by your company requires a capital investment of Rs. 120 lakh. Interest on term loans is 10 per cent and tax rate is 50 per cent. Calculate the point of indifference for the project, if the debt-equity ratio insisted by the financing agencies is 2:1.

Solution:

With reference to the project under consideration the debt-equity ratio insisted upon by the financing agencies is 2 : 1.

There are two alternatives available to the company.

a) Raising the entire amount by issue of equity shares.

b) Raising Rs. 80 lakh by way of debt and Rs. 40 lakh by way of issue of equity shares, thus maintaining a debt-equity ration 2 : 1.

Computation of Indifference Point

$(X - I) (1 - t) ÷ N^1 = (X - I) (1 - t) - PD ÷ N^2$

Where,

X = EBIT or Point of indifference.   I = Interest on debentures.

t = Corporate tax rate.   PD = Preference dividend.

N^1 = No. of equity shares in alternative (a). N^2 = No. of equity shares in alternative (b).

X (1 - 0.50) ÷ 1,20,000 = (X - 8,00,000) (1 - 0.50) ÷ 40,000

0.5X ÷ 1,20,000 = (0.5X - 4,00,000) ÷ 40,000

1,20,000X (0.5X - 4,00,000) = 40,000 (0.50X)

60,000X - 48, 00,00,00,000 = 20,000X

60,000X - 20,000X = 48,00,00,00,000

40,000X = 48,00,00,00,000

X = 48,00,00,00,000 ÷ 40,000 = Rs. 12,00,000

Proof

Particulars.	Alternative - A (Rs.)	Alternative - B (Rs.)
EBIT	12,00,000	12,00,000
Less: Interest on debentures	-----	8,00,000
EBT	12,00,000	4,00,000
Less: Tax 50%	6,00,000	2,00,000
EAT	6,00,000	2,00,000

Note: It has been assumed that face value of each equity shar is Rs. 100.

Calculation of EPS:

Alternative - a = Rs. 6,00,000 ÷ 1,20,000 = Rs. 5

Alternative - b = Rs. 2,00,000 ÷ 40,000 = Rs. 5

Note: No. of shares (N_1) = Rs. 1,20,00,000 ÷ 100 = 1,20,000 shares

No. of shares (N_2) = Rs. 40,00,000 ÷ 100 = 40,000 shares

Since both alternative A and B have same EPS, hence the point of indifference is proved.

Illustration 26: A project under consideration by your company requires a capital investment of Rs. 6,00,000. Interest on term loans is 10% pa and tax rate is 50%. Calculate the point of indifference for the project if the debt-equity ratio insisted by the financial institutions is 2:1.

Solution:

With reference to project under consideration the debt-equity ration insisted upon by the financing agencies is 2 : 1.

There are two alternatives available to the company.

a) Raising the entire amount by issue of equity shares

b) Raising Rs. 4,00,000 lakh by way of long-term loans, Rs. 2,00,000 lakh by way of issue of equity shares, thus maintaining a debt-equity ration 2 : 1.

Interest obligation: In case (i) there will be no interest, but in case (ii) there will be Rs. 40,000 on loans raised from financial institutions.

Computation of Indifference Point

$$X (1 - t) \div N_1 = (X - I) (1 - t) \div N_2$$

Where,

X = EBIT or Point of indifference.   I = Interest on debentures.

t = Corporate tax rate.   PD = Preference dividend.

N^1 = No. of equity shares in alternative (a) N^2 = No. of equity shares in alternative

(b) X (1 - 0.50) ÷ 6,000 = (X - 40,000) (1 - 0.50) ÷ 2,000

0.5X ÷ 6,000 = (0.5X - 20,000) ÷ 2,000

1,000X = 3,000X - 12,00,00,000

1,000X - 3,000 X = - 12,00,00,000

-2,000 X = - 12,00,00,000

X = - 12,00,00,000 ÷ - 2,000 = Rs. 60,000

Proof

Particulars	Alternative - a (Rs.)	Alternative - b (Rs.)
EBIT	60,000	60,000
Less: Interest on debentures	-----	40,000
EBT	60,000	20,000
Less: Tax 50%	30,000	10,000
EAT	30,000	10,000

Note: It has been assumed that face value of each equity share is Rs. 100.

Calculation of EPS:

Alternative - a = Rs. 30,000 ÷ 6,000 = **Rs. 5**

Alternative - b = Rs. 10,000 ÷ 2,000 = Rs. 5

Note: No. of shares (N^1) = Rs. 6,00,000 ÷ 100 = 6,000 shares

No. of shares (N^2) = Rs. 2,00,000 ÷ 100 = 2,000 shares

Since both alternative a and b have same EPS, hence the point of indifference is proved.

Illustration 27: The installed capacity of a factory is 700 units. The actual capacity is 500 units. Selling price per unit is Rs. 10 and variable cost is Rs. 6 per unit. Calculate the operating leverage in each of the following situations.

  (i)   When fixed cost are Rs. 500;

  (ii) When fixed cost are Rs. 1,100; (iii) When fixed cost are Rs. 1,500.

Solution: Computation of EBIT

Particulars.	Situations		
	I (Rs.)	II (Rs.)	III (Rs.)
Sales revenue (500 u x Rs. 10 p.u)	5,000	5,000	5,000
Less: Variable cost (500 u x Rs. 6 p.u)	3,000	3,000	3,000
Contribution	2,000	2,000	2,000
Less: Fixed cost	500	1,100	1,500
EBIT	1,500	900	500

Operating leverage = Contribution ÷ EBIT

I = 2,000 ÷ 1,500 = 1.33;   II = 2,000 ÷ 900 = 2.22;   III = 2,000 ÷ 500 = 4

Illustration 28: The financial data of Madhu Industries for the year ended 31-12-98 is as follows:

  Variable expenses as a percentage of sales 75 per cent

  Interest expenses Rs. 300;   Degree of operating leverage = 6

  Degree of financial leverage = 3   Income tax rate = 50 per cent

  Prepare an income statement.

Solution:

Income statement

Particulars	Amount Rs.
Sales (Note 1)	9,600
Less: Variable cost (Note 2)	7,200
Contribution	2,400
Less: Fixed cost (Sales – VC – EBIT)	2,000
EBIT	400
Less: Interest	300
EBT	100
Less: Tax 50%	50
EAT	50

Working notes:

(1)   Degree of financial leverage (DFL) = 3

$$DFL = \frac{EBIT}{EBIT - 1}$$

$$4 = \frac{EBIT}{EBIT - 300}$$

$$EBIT = 400$$

Degree of Operating Leverage (DOL) $= \dfrac{\text{Sales-Variable cost}}{\text{EBIT}}$

$$6 = \frac{\text{Sales} - 0.75 \text{ sales}}{\text{EBIT}}$$

$$6 = \frac{\text{Sales} - 0.75 \text{ sales}}{400} \quad \text{or} \quad 0.25 \text{ Sales} = 2400$$

$$\text{or} \quad \text{Sales} = \frac{2400}{0.25} = \text{Rs. } 9600$$

or   Sales = DOL x EBIT x DFL = 6 x 400 x 4 = Rs. 9,600

(2)   Variable cost = 75% of sales

$$\therefore \ 9600 \times 0.75 = \text{Rs. } 7,200$$

Illustration 29: Loss Industries Ltd., gives the following information for the year ended 31-12-01.

Variable expenses as a percentage of sales = 66 2/3 %

Interest expenses = Rs. 200; Degree of operating leverage = 5

Degree of financial leverage = 3 Income tax rate = 50%

Prepare an income statement.

Solution:

Income statement

Particulars	Amount Rs.
Sales (Note 1)	4,500
Less: Variable cost (Note 2)	3,000
Contribution	1,500
Less: Fixed cost (Sales – VC – EBIT)	1,200
EBIT	300
Less: Interest	200
EBT	100
Less: Tax 50%	50
EAT	50

Working notes:

Degree of financial leverage (DFL) = 3

$$DFL = \frac{EBIT}{EBIT - 1}$$

$$3 = \frac{EBIT}{EBIT - 200}$$

$$EBIT = \text{Rs.} 300$$

Degree of Operating Leverage (DOL) $= \dfrac{\text{Sales-variable cost}}{\text{EBIT}}$

$$5 = \frac{\text{Sales} - 0.6667 \text{ sales}}{\text{EBIT}}$$

$$5 = \frac{\text{Sales} - 0.6667 \text{ sales}}{300} \quad \text{or } 0.333 \text{ Sales} = 1500$$

$$\text{or Sales} = 4500$$

Sales = DOL x EBIT x DFL = 5 x 300 x 3 = Rs. 4,500

(3)   Variable cost = 75% of sales

$$\therefore\ 4,500 \times 0.6667\ = Rs.\ 3,000$$

Illustration 30: From the following data ascertain the degree of operating leverage, which company has greater amount of business risk?

Solution:

Calculation of EBIT

Particulars	Naveen Ltd., (Rs.)	Praveen Ltd., (Rs.)
Sales	80,00,000	1,00,00,000
Less: Variable cost	40,00,000	30,00,000
Contribution	40,00,000	70,00,000
Less: Fixed cost	24,00,000	35,00,000
EBIT	16,00,000	35,00,000

Solution:

Operating leverage = Naveen Ltd., has greater amount of risk.	Contribution	40,00,000	70,00,000
	EBIT	16,00,000 = 2.5	35,00,000 = 2

Illustration 31: From the following information, prepare income statement and comment on the financial position and structure of P, Q and R companies.

Financial data	P	Q	R
Interest expenses	300	400	1000
Income tax rate (%)	50	50	50
Degree of operating leverage	6	7	3
Degree of financial leverage	4	5	3
Variable expenses as a percentage of sales	65	75	70

Solution: **Income statement of P, Q, R companies**

Particulars	P Amount Rs.	Q Amount Rs.	R Amount Rs.
Sales (Note 1)	9,600	17,500	27,000
Less: Variable cost (Note 2)	6,240	13,125	18,900
CONTRIBUTION	3,360	4,375	8,100
Less: Fixed cost (Sales – VC – EBIT)	2,960	3,875	5,000
EBIT	400	500	3,000
Less: Interest	300	400	1,000
EBT	100	100	2,000
Less: Tax at 50%	50	50	1,000
EAT	50	50	1,000

Working Notes

1. **Sales Revenue**

$$DFL = \frac{EBIT}{EBIT-I}$$

$$P: 4 = \frac{EBIT}{EBIT-300} \quad EBIT = Rs.400$$

$$Sales = DOL \times EBIT \times DFL = 6 \times 400 \times 4 = Rs.9,600$$

$$Q: 5 = \frac{EBIT}{EBIT-400} \quad \therefore EBIT = Rs.500$$

$$Sales = 7 \times 500 \times 5 = Rs. 17.500$$

$$R: 3 = \frac{EBIT}{EBIT-1000} \quad \therefore EBIT = Rs. 3000$$

$$Sales = 3 \times 3000 \times 3 = Rs.27,000$$

2. **Variable cost:** P = 65% of sales: 9,600 x 0.65 = Rs. 6,240

   Q = 75% of sales: 17,500 x 0.75 = Rs. 13,215

   R = 70% of sales: 27,000 x 0.70 = Rs. 18,900

'R' company's financial position is better as compared to other companies since its financial leverage is minimum. And from the point of combined leverage also, company 'R' is better positioned due to minimum combined leverage (3 x 3 = 9). Indicating that the total risk (business + financial) is minimum. Based on interest coverage ratio also, company 'R' is in a better position (interest coverage ratio : P - 1.33; Q - 1.25 and R - 3 times).

Illustration 32: BPM Ltd., is a large scale paper mill, and is planning to finance expansion of its production capacity and developed the following four financial plans, 1, 2, 3 and 4. The expected rate of returns before interest and tax is 40 per cent. The corporate tax rate is 35 per cent which alternative would you choose based up on ROR on equity capital.

Source of capital	Financial Plans			(Rs. in 000)
	1	2	3	4
Equity share capital	7,500	3,000	1,500	2,250
10% debentures	------	3,000	2,250	1,500
Long-term loan form FI's at 12%	------	1,500	3,750	------
Preference share capital at 12%	------	------	------	3,750

Solution: Calculation of ROR on equity capital (%)

Particulars	Financial Plans			
	1 (in Rs.)	2 (in Rs.)	3 (in Rs.)	4 (in Rs.)
EBIT (75,00,000 x 0.4)	30,00,000	30,00,000	30,00,000	30,00,000
Less: Interest on debentures				
• On debentures @ 10%	------	3,00,000	2,25,000	1,50,000
• On long-term loan @ 12%	------	1,80,000	4,50,000	------
EBT	30,00,000	25,20,000	23,25,000	28,50,000
Less: Tax 35 %	10,50,000	8,82,000	8,13,750	9,97,500
EAT	19,50,000	16,38,000	15,11,250	18,52,500
Less: Preference Dividend	------	------	------	4,50,000
Earnings available to equity shares	19,50,000	16,38,000	15,11,250	14,02,500
Rate of return on equity (%) Equity earnings ÷ equity share capital	26	54.6	100.75	62.33

Illustration 33: From the following cost information of a firm, find out the percentage change in sales and EBIT or operating profits when:

(a) without fixed cost; and

(b) with fixed cost

Sales Rs. 3 lakh in previous year and Rs. 375,000 in current year

Variable Cost = 60% of sales; and Fixed cost Rs., 30,000

Solution: Operating Profit

(a) Without fixed cost

Particular	Previous year	Present year	Change %
Sales Revenue	3,00,000	3,75,000	25
Variable cost	1,80,000	2,25,000	25
EBIT or operating profit	**1,20,000**	**1,50,000**	25

(b) With Fixed cost Rs. 30,000

Particular	Previous year	Present year	Change %
Sales Revenue	3,00,000	3,75,000	25
(-) Variable cost	1,80,000	2,25,000	25
Contribution	**1,20,000**	**1,50,000**	25
(-) Fixed cost	30,000	30,000	------
EBIT or Operating Profit	**90,000**	**1,20,000**	33.33

In case (a) where, there is no fixed cost the percentage change in sales and percentage change in EBIT is few since, there is no leverage.

In case (b) with fixed costs the percentages change in profits is more than percentage change in sales by 8.33 per cent due to percentage of financial leverage.

Illustration 34: A company needs Rs. 10,00,000 for developing a new product. It would yield an annual operating profit of (EBIT) Rs. 2,40,000, share price is Rs. 50. The company has the objective of maximizing the earnings per share (EPS). Company is in the tax rate of 50 per cent.

Funds can be raised at the following interest rates:

Upto Rs. 1,00,000 at 8 per cent

Over Rs. 1,00,000 to Rs. 5,00,000 at 12 per cent

Over Rs. 5,00,000 at 15 per cent

The company has developed three financing plans that are given below:

a) Raise Rs. 1,00,000 debt, with expected operating profit (EBIT) Rs. 3,40,000

b) Raise Rs. 3,00,000 debt, with expected operating profit (EBIT) Rs. 4,40,000

c) Raise Rs. 6,00,000 debt, with expected operating profit (EBIT) Rs. 5,90,000

Calculate EPS for all the above financing plans and give the best plan based on higher EPS.

Solutions: Calculation of EPS

Particulars	Plan A	Plan B	Plan C
Operating profit (EBIT)	3,40,000	4,40,000	5,90,000
Less: Interest [working note (1)]	8,000	32,000	71,000
EBT	3,32,000	4,08,000	5,19,000
Less: Tax 50%	1,66,000	2,04,000	2,59,500
EAT	1,66,000	2,04,000	2,59,500
Less: Preference shared dividend	-	-	-
Net profit	166000	2,04,000	259500
EPS= Net profit / No of equity share note (2) working	1,66,000 = Rs. 9.22 / 18,000	2,04,000=Rs.14.57 / 14,000	2,59,500=Rs.32.44 / 8,000

Best plan is 'C' since EPS is the highest.

Working Notes

1. **Calculation of Interest**

   Plan (A) : Amount raised Rs. 1,00,000 by debt finance

   Interest upto Rs. 1,00,000 is 8%

   Therefore Interest = 1,00,000 x (8/100) = Rs. 8000

   Plan (B) : Amount raised Rs. 300,000. But interest rate varies

   upto Rs. 1,00,000 is 8% = Rs.   8000

   Rest Rs. 200000 at 12%   = Rs. 24000 = Rs. 32,000

   Plan (C) : Amount raised Rs. 600,000

   upto Rs. 1,00,000 is 8% = Rs.   8000

   Rs. 400,000 at 12%   = Rs. 48000

   Rs. 1,00,000 at 15%   = Rs. 15000 = Rs. 71000

2. **Calculation of No. of Shares**

   Plan (A) : Required amount of Rs. 10,00,000

   Amount raised Rs. 1,00,000 by debt

   Remaining Rs.900,000 : [10,00,000 - 1,00,000]

Share price Rs. 50

No of shares = Amount raised by shares÷Share price = 9,00,000 ÷ 50 = 18,000 shares

Plan (B): Amount raised by debt Rs. 3,00,000

Amount raised by share capital Rs. 7,00,000

Share price Rs. 50

No of shares = Amount raised by shares÷Share price = 7,00,000 ÷ 50 = 14,000 shares

Plan (C): Amount raised by debt Rs. 6,00,000

Amount raised by share capital Rs.4,00,000

Share price Rs. 50

No of shares = Amount raised by shares÷Share price = 6,00,000 ÷ 50 = 8000 shares

Illustration 35: A company needs Rs. 12 lakh for the installations of new factors which would yield an annual EBIT of Rs. 2.4 lakh. The company has the objective of maximizing the EPS. It is considering the possibility of issuing equity share of Rs. 10 each, plus raising adjust of Rs. 2 lakh, Rs. 6 lakh, or Rs.10 lakh. The current market price of share is Rs. 40 which is expected to drop to Rs. 25 per share if the market borrowings were to exceed Rs. 7,50000. Cost of borrowings is as follows :

Upto Rs. 2,50,000 at 10% p.a

Between Rs. 2,50,001 to Rs. 650000 at 14% p.a

Between Rs.6,50,001 to Rs. 10,00,000 at 16% p.a

Assume tax rate of 50 per cent, calculate EPS and Share which would be worth an objective of management.

Solution: Calculation of EPS

Particulars	Debt Plans		
	1. Amount Rs. 2,00,000	2. Amount Rs. 6,00,000	3. Amount Rs. 10,00,000
EBIT	2,40,000	2,40,000	2,40,000
Less: Interest [WN (1)]	20,000	74000	1,37,000
EBT	2,20,000	1,66,000	10,3,000
Less: Tax 50%	1,10,000	83,000	51,500
EAT	1,10,000	83,000	51,500
Less: Preference shared divided	-	-	-
Net profit	1,10,000	83,000	51,500
EPS= Net profit / No of equity share note(2) working	$\frac{1,10,000}{1,00,000}$ = Rs.1.1	$\frac{83,000}{60,000}$ = Rs.1.38	$\frac{51,500}{20,000}$ = Rs.2.575

Raising Rs. 6,00,000 through debt is helpful to maximize EPS, where EOS is Rs. 41.38. [Assuming issue of equity at Rs. 10 each]. At this level of debt there will be no change in market price (Rs. 40) of share, where as the market price come down, when debt amount goes beyond Rs. 7.5 lakh, hence raising Rs. 10 lakh by debt is not preferable.

Working notes

1. **Interest of Calculation:**

   When debt raised is Rs. 2,00,000

   Interest = 2,00,000 X (10/100) = Rs. 20,000

   Debt Rs., 6,00,000

Upto Rs. 2,50,000 at 10%   = Rs. 25,000

[above Rs. 2,50,000] Rs. 3,50,000 at 14% = Rs. 49,000 = Rs.74000

Debt Rs. 10,00,100

Upto Rs. 2,50,000 at 10 %= Rs. 25,000

Rs. 4,00,000 at 14%   = Rs. 56,000

Rs. 3,50,000   at 16%   = Rs. 56,000 = Rs.1,37,000

2. **No. of Shares:**

When debt raised is Rs. 2,00,000

Remaining amount needed = Rs. 10,00,000

No. of shares = 10,00,000 ÷ 10 = 1,00,000

When debt raised is Rs. 6,00,000

No. of shares = 6,00,000 ÷ 10 = 60,000 shares

When debt raised is Rs. 10,00,000

No. of shares = 2,00,000 ÷ 10 = 20,000 shares

Illustration 36: (OCTOBER 2003 MBA BU):

From the following data, calculate debt-equity mix.

Debt as a % of total Capital Employed	Cost of Debt (%)	Cost of Equity (%)
0	7.0	15.0
10	7.0	15.0
20	7.0	15.5
30	7.5	16.0
40	8.0	17.0
50	8.5	19.0
60	9.5	20.0

Solution:

Evaluation and selection of capital structure plans is based on cost of capital.

Capital (Rs.)		Specific Cost(%)		WACC (%) $K_o = [W_e \times K_e + W_d \times K_d] \, 100$
Debt	Equity	Debt	Equity	
0	100	0.07	0.15	[(0x0.07)+(1.0x0.15)] 100 = 15
10	90	0.07	0.15	[(0.1x0.07)+(0.9x0.15)] 100 = 14.2
20	80	0.07	0.155	[(0.2x0.07)+(0.8x0.155)] 100 = 13.8
30	70	0.075	0.16	[(0.3x0.075)+(0.7x0.16)] 100 = 13.45
40	60	0.08	0.17	[(0.4x0.08)+(0.6x0.17)] 100 = **13.40**
50	50	0.085	0.19	[(0.5x0.085)+(0.5x0.19)] 100 = 13.75
60	40	0.095	0.20	[(0.6x0.095)+(0.4x0.20)] 100 = 13.7

Decision: Optimum debt -equity mix is Capital Structure, 40% debt and 60% equity.

Illustration 37: In considering the most desirable capital structure for an export company, the following estimates of cost of debt and equity (after tax) is seen at various levels of debt equity mix.

Debt as a % of total Capital Employed	Cost of Debt (%)	Cost of Equity (%)
0	7.0	15.0
10	7.0	15.0
20	7.0	15.5
30	7.5	16.0
40	8.0	17.0
50	8.5	19.0
60	9.5	20.0
70	10	22

You are required to compute the optimum debt equity mix for the company.

Solution

Evaluation and selection of capital structure plans is based on cost of capital.

Capital (Rs.)		Specific Cost(%)		WACC (%) $Ko = [We \times Ke + Wd \times Kd] \, 100$
Debt	**Equity**	**Debt**	**Equity**	
0	100	0.07	0.15	[(0x0.07)+(1.0x0.15)] 100 = 15
10	90	0.07	0.15	[(0.1x0.07)+(0.9x0.15)] 100 = 14.2
20	80	0.07	0.155	[(0.2x0.07)+(0.8x0.155)] 100 = 13.8
30	70	0.075	0.16	[(0.3x0.075) + (0.7x0.16)] 100 = 13.45
40	**60**	0.08	0.17	[(0.4x0.08) +(0.6x0.17)] 100 = **13.40**
50	50	0.085	0.19	[(0.5x0.085) + (0.5x0.19)] 100 = 13.75
60	40	0.095	0.20	[(0.6x0.095)+(0.4x0.20)] 100 = 13.7
70	30	0.10	0.22	[(0.7x0.1)+(0.3x0.22)] 100 = 13.6

Decision: Optimum debt -equity mix is Capital Structure 40% debt and 60% equity.

Illustration 38: Calculate the degree of operating leverage, degree of financial leverage, and the degree of combined leverage for the following firms and interpret the results:

Particulars	P	Q	R
Output (Units)	3,00,000	75,000	5,00,000
Fixed Cost (Rs.)	3,50,000	7,00,000	75,000
Variable Cost per unit (Rs.)	1.00	7.5	0.1
Interest Expenses (Rs.)	25,000	40,000	----
Selling Price per unit (Rs.)	3.00	25.00	0.50

Solution: Calculation Earnings After Taxes

Particulars	P (Rs.)	Q (Rs.)	R (Rs.)
Sales Revenue (output X Selling Price)	9,00,000	18,75,000	2,50,000
Less: Variable Cost (output X Selling Price)	3,00,000	5,62,500	50,000
Contribution	6,00,000	13,12,500	2,00,000
Less: Fixed Cost	3,50,000	7,00,000	75,000
EBIT	2,50,000	6,12,500	1,25,000
Less: Interest Expenses	25,000	40,000	----
Earnings Before Taxes	2,25,000	5,72,500	1,25,000

Calculation Leverages

Particulars	P	Q	R
Operating Leverage: Contribution / EBIT	6,00,000/2,50,000 =2.4	13,12,500/6,12,500 =2.14	2,00,000/1,25,000 =1.6
Financial Leverage: EBIT / EBT	2,50,000/2,25,000 =1.11	6,12,500/5,72,500 =1.07	1,25,000/1,25,000 =1.0
Combined Leverage: Contribution / EBT	6,00,000/2,25,000 =2.67	13,12,500/5,72,500 2.29	2,00,000/1,25,000 =1.6

Illustration 39: Sales Rs. 1,00,000 units at Rs. 2 per unit, variable cost Re.0.70 per unit, fixed cost Rs.1, 00,000, interest charges Rs. 3,668. Compute degree of operating leverage, financial leverage, and combined leverage.

Solution

Computation of leverages

Operating leverage = Contribution / EBIT = 1,30,000 / 30,000 = 4.33

Financial leverage = EBIT / EBT = 30,000 / 26,332 = 1.14

Combined leverage = Contribution / EBT = 1,30,000 / 26,332 = 4.94

Illustration 40 : Jawahar Company has the following income statement for the year 2000:

Particulars.	Amount (Rs.)
Sales	5,00,00,000
Less: Variable operating costs	1,00,00,000
Fixed operating costs	2,00,00,000
Earnings Before Interest and Taxes (EBIT)	2,00,00,000
Interest	50,00,000
Earnings Before Taxes (EBT)	1,50,00,000
Less: Tax 40 %	60,00,000
Earnings After Taxes (EAT)	90,00,000
Less: Preference Dividend	10,00,000
Earnings Available to equity shareholder	80,00,000

Number of equity shares issued - 4,00,000

Compute: 1. Degree of operating leverage, financial leverage, and combined leverage

2. If sales increases to Rs. 5,50,00,000, what is your forecast for EPS?

Solution:

1. *Computation of leverages*

   Operating leverage = Contribution / EBIT

   = (5,00,00,000-1,00,00,000) / 2,00,00,000 = **2**

   Financial leverage = EBIT / EBT

   = 2,00,00,000 / 1,50,00,000 = **1.33**

   Combined leverage = Contribution / EBT

   = (5,00,00,000-1,00,00,000) / 1,50,00,000 = **2.67**

2. *Forecast of EPS if sales is Rs. 5,50,00,000*

Particulars.	Amount (Rs.)
Sales	5,50,00,000
Less: Variable operating costs	1,10,00,000
Contribution	4,40,00,000
Fixed operating costs	2,00,00,000
Earnings Before Interest and Taxes (EBIT)	2,40,00,000
Interest	50,00,000
Earnings Before Taxes (EBT)	1,90,00,000
Less: Tax 40 %	76,00,000
Earnings After Taxes (EAT)	1,14,00,000
Less: Preference Dividend	10,00,000
Earnings Available to equity shareholder	1,04,00,000

$$\text{Forecasted EPS} = \frac{\text{Earnings Available to equity shareholder}}{\text{No. of Equity Shares outstanding}}$$

$$= \frac{1,04,00,000}{4,00,000} = \text{Rs. 26}$$

TEST YOUR KNOWLEDGE

Conceptual Type

1. Define capital structure.
2. What is optimum capital structure?
3. List out the features of optimal capital structure.
4. What is point of indifference?
5. Define operating leverage.
6. What do you mean by financial leverage?
7. What is trading on equity?
8. What is financial structure?

9. Distinguish between capital structure and financial structure.
10. What do you mean by Agency cost?
11. List the approaches available to determine appropriate capital structure.
12. What are the different forms of capital structure?
13. What do you mean by flexibility in capital structure
14. What is EBIT - EPS analysis
15. How do you compute EBIT?
16. How do you compute net profit from sales?
17. What do you mean by optimum capital structure? Discuss its features.
18. What is leverage? Discuss the types of leverages.
19. What is operating leverage? How does it help to maximize, revenue of a firm?
20. What is trading an equity? How does it maximize the equity earnings?
21. Distinguish between operating and financial leverage.
22. write a note on EBIT-EPS analysis.
23. Define capital structure? Discuss the important factors that should be considered while determining capital structure.
24. What basic principles will you advocate in the matter of deciding on a proper constitution of capital structure for a firm?

PRACTICE YOURSELF PROBLEMS

1. A firm has Rs. 40,00,000 lakh sales, variable cost is 70 per cent of sales, and fixed cost is Rs. 8 lakh and debt of Rs. 20 lakh at 10 per cent. Calculate operating financial and combined leverages. [**Answer:** OL - 3, FL - 2 ; CL - 6]

2. A firm has sales of Rs. 5 lakh, variable cost Rs. 3.5 lakh and fixed cost Rs. 1 lakh, and debt of Rs. 2.5 lakh at 10 per cent. [Answer: OL - 3, FL - 2]

3. From the following information calculate EPS

Particulars	Venkat Ltd (Rs. In lakh)	Sai Ltd (Rs. In lakh)
Equity (shares of Rs. 10 each)	200	100
Debentures at 12 %	-	100
Assets	100	200

Calculate EPS assume (i) 20 per cent before tax rate of return of assets, (ii) 10 per cent before tax return on assets, company is in 50 per cent tax bracket.

[*Answer:* (i) Venkat - Re. 1, Sai ltd Rs. 05, (ii) Venkat Rs. 1.4, Sai ltd Rs. 0.4]

4. ABC companies capital structure is of Rs. 5 lakh, [Rs. 100 each share] and 10 per cent debt capital equity of Rs. 2,00,000. The sales are increased by 20 per cent from 50,000 to 60,000 units. Rs. 10 is the selling price per unit, and Rs. 6 is variable cost per unit and fixed expenses amount to Rs. 1,00,000. Tax rate is 10 per cent calculate.

(a) Percentage increase in EPS
(b) The degree of operating leverage at 5,0000 units and 60,000 units
(c) The degree of financial leverage at 50,000 units and 60,000 units

[*Answer:* (a) 50%, (b) 1.25 and 1.17, (c) 2 and 1.71]

5. From the following data, calculate operating leverage.

Year	EBIT Rs.	Sales in units
1998	60,000	3,00,000
1999	70000	3,60,000

   [*Answer:* 0.834]

6. WD Coy Ltd's capital structure consists of an ordinary share capital of Rs. 10,00,000 (shares of Rs. 10 face value) and Rs. 10,00,000 or 20 per cent. Debentures sales increased by 25 per cent from 2,00,000 to 2,50,000 units, Rs. 10 is the selling price per unit, Rs. 6 is the variable cost per unit, and Rs. 2,50,000 are fixed expenses. The companies tax rate is 50 per cent. You are required to calculate the following:

   (a) The percentage increase in EPS

   (b) The degree of operating leverage at 2,00,000 and 2,50,000 units,

   (c) The degree of financial leverage at 2,00,000 and 2,50,000 units

   [*Answer:* (a) 57 per cent (b) sales at 2,00,000 units 1.45, and sales at 2,50,000 units 1.33 times, (c) Sales at 2,00,000 - 1.57 times and sales at 2,50,000 - 1.36 times]

7. Calculate operating and financial leverage under situations A and B financial plans I and II respectively, the following is the date available:

   Installed capacity - 2000 units   Actual production - and sales 80 per cent

   Selling price per unit - Rs. 40   Variable cost per unit - Rs. 30

   Fixed expenses : Situation - A, Rs. 1000; Situation - B, Rs. 3000

   Capital Structure:

Particulars	Financial Plan	
	I	II
Equity share capital	Rs. 10,000	Rs. 14,000
Debt (20%)	Rs. 10,000	Rs. 4,000

   [*Answer:* Situation A: OL : Plan I and II = 1.01; FL: Plan I - 1.02 and Plan II - 1.015 Situation B: OL: Plan I and Plan II=1.019; FL: Plan I - 1.01 and Plan II - 1.0]

8. It is proposed to start a business and so required a capital of Rs. 10 lakh and an assured return of 15 per cent on investments. Calculate EPS if

   (a) Total capital required, by way of Rs. 100 equity

   (b) If 50 per cent of equity capital and 50 per cent, 10 per cent debentures.

   [*Answer:* (a) Rs. 7.5 (b) Rs. 10]

9. The following data is available for X Ltd:

   Selling price Rs. 120 pu;   Variable cost Rs. 70 pu;   Total fixed cost Rs. 200,000

   (a) What is the operating leverage when, X Ltd produces and sells 6000 units,

   (b) What is the percentage change that will occurring in the operating profit (EBIT) of X Ltd, if output increases by 5 per cent [Answer: (a) OL = 3 (b) 15%]

10. Calculate operating and financial leverages under situations A, B and C and Financial plan 1,2, and 3 respectively from the following functions of XYZ Co. Also find out the combination of operating and financial leverage that gives the highest value and least value:

    Installed capacity = 12,000 units; Actual production & sales = 800 units

Selling price = Rs. 15 p.u; Variable cost = Rs. 10 p.u

Fixed Cost = Situation A, Rs. 1000; Situation B, Rs. 2000; Situation C, Rs. 3000

REFERENCES

1. Solomon, Egra, "The Theory of Financial Management", University Press, 1963, p.42

2. Gestonberg, O.W, "Financial Organization and Management of Business", Eaglewood Cliff, New Jersey: Prentice Hall Inc., 1959, p.168

3. Van Horne, J.C, "Financial Management and Policy", New Delhi: Prentice Hall of India Pvt. Ltd, 1975, p.249

4. Guthmann, H.G, and Dougall, H.E, "Corporate Financial Policy, " New Jersey: Prentice Hall 1962, p.234

5. Leopold, A,B, Op.cit, p.434

6. Johnson, R.L, "Financial Decision Making", Good Year, 1973

7. Johnson, R.W, "Financial Management", Allyn and Bacon, Boston, 1971, p.227

8. Walker, E.W., "Essentials of Financial Management", New Delhi : Prentice Hall of India Pvt. Ltd 1978, p.81

9. Bogen, J.I, "Financial Hand Book", New York ; The Ronald Press, 1957, p.893

10. Philips, F.C, "The Economics of Regulation - Theory and Practice", Home Wood, Illinois: Richard D.Irwin Inc, 1970, p.167

11. Weston, F.J and Brigham, F.F, "Managerial Finance", New York: Rinehart and Winston Inc., 1972, p.254

12. Leo Pold, A.B, "Financial Statement Analysis - Theory, Application and Interpretations", Home Wood, Illinois: Richard D. Irwin Inc, 1974, p.428

13. Van Horne, J.C and Wachowicz, J.M "Fundamentals of Financial Management", New Delhi: Practice Hall of India Pvt. Ltd, 1996, p.434

14. Joy, O.M, "Introduction to Financial Management", Illinois, Richard D. Irwin, Inc, 1977, p.226

15. Solomon, E and Pringle, J.J, Op.cit, p.65

16. Gitman, L.J, "Principles of Managerial Finance", New York: Harper & Row Publisher Inc, 1976, p.84

17. Joy, O.M, Op.cit, p.226

RAJART AND ASSOCIATES CASE : FINANCIAL ALTERNATIVES

This case provides the opportunity to match financing alternatives with the needs of different companies. It allows the reader to demonstrate a familiarity with different types of securities.

George Thomas was finishing some weekend reports on a Friday afternoon in the downtown office of Wishart and Associates, an investment-banking firm. Meenda, a partner in the firm, had not been in the New York office since Monday. He was on a trip through Pennsylvania, visiting five potential clients, who were considering the flotation of securities with the assistance of Wishart and Associates. Meenda had called the office on Wednesday and told George's secretary that he would cable his recommendations on Friday afternoon. George was waiting for the cable.

George knew that Meenda would be recommending different types of securities for each of the five clients to meet their individual needs. He also knew Meenda wanted him to call each of the clients to consider the recommendations over the weekend. George was prepared to make these calls as soon as the cable arrived. At 4:00 p.m. a secretary handed George the following telegram.

George Thomas, Wishart and Associates STOP Taking advantage of offer to go skiing in Poconos STOP Recommendations as follows : (1) common stock, (2) preferred stock, (3) debt with warrants, (4) convertible bonds, (5) callable debentures STOP. See you Wednesday STOP Meenda.

As George picked up the phone to make the first call, he suddenly realized that the potential clients were not matched with the investment alternatives. In Meenda's office, George found folders on each of the five firms seeking financing. In the front of each folder were some handwritten notes that Meenda had made on Monday before he left. George read each of the notes in turn.

APT, Inc, needs $8 million now and $4 million in four years. Packaging firm with high growth rate in tri-state area. Common stock trades over the counter. Stock is depressed but should rise in year to 18 months. Willing to accept any type of security. Good management. Expects moderate growth. New machinery should increase profits substantially. Recently retired $7 million in debt. Has virtually no debt remaining except short-term obligations.

SANDFORD ENTERPRISES

Needs $16 million. Crusty management. Stock price depressed but expected to improve. Excellent growth and profits forecast in the next two year. Low debt-equity ratio, as the firm has record of retiring debt prior to maturity. Retains bulk of earnings and pays low dividends. Management not interested in surrendering voting control to outsiders. Money to be used to finance machinery for plumbing supplies.

SHARMA BROTHERS., INC.

Needs $20 million to expand cabinet and woodworking business. Started as family business but now has 1200 employees, $50 million in sales, and is traded over the counter. Seeks additional shareholder but not willing to stock at discount. Cannot raise more than $12 million with straight debt. Fair management. Good growth prospects. Very good earnings. Should spark investor's interest. Banks could be willing to lend money for long-term needs.

SACHEETEE ENERGY SYSTEMS

The firm is well respected by liberal investing community near Boston area. Sound growth company. Stock selling for $16 per share. Management would like to sell common stock at $21 or more willing to use debt to raise $ 28 million, but this is second choice. Financing gimmicks and chance to turn quick profit on investment would appeal to those likely to invest in this company.

RANBAXY INDUSTRY

Needs $25 million. Manufactures boat canvas covers and needs funds to expand operations. Needs long-term money. Closely held ownership reluctant surrender control. Cannot issue debt without permission of bondholders and First National Bank of Philadelphia. Relatively low debt-equity ratio. Relatively high profits. Good prospects for growth. Strong management with minor weaknesses in sales and promotion areas.

As George was looking over the folders, Meenda's secretary entered the office. George said, "Did Meenda leave any other material here on Monday except for these notes?".

She responded, "No, that's it, but I think those notes should be useful. Meenda called early this morning and said that he verified the facts in the folders. He also said that he learned nothing new on the trip and he sort of indicated that, he had wasted his week, except of course, that he was invited to go skiing at the company lodge up there".

George pondered over the situation. He could always wait until next week, when he could be sure that he had the right recommendations and some of the considerations that outlined each client's needs and situation. If he could determine which firm matched each recommendation, he could still call the firms by 6:00 P.M. and meet the original deadline. George decided to return to his office and match each firm with the appropriate financing.

REQUIRED

1. Which type of financing is appropriate to each firm?

2. What types of securities must be issued by a firm which is on the growing stage in order to meet the financial requirements?

CASE FOR CLASS DISCUSSION 2

SUSHMA ENTERPRISES

Sushma Enterprises was set up in 1950 as a public limited company to manufacture goods used for decoration in drawing rooms. The company is situated in Calicut and it distributes its products throughout the western region of the country. The company expects to earn just over Rs. 30,00,000 and expects sales of Rs. 33,00,000 next year. Variable costs will stay at approximately the same percentage of sales and fixed costs will not increase next year.

Recently the management is seized with investigating the possibility of diversifying the production activities to manufacture small metallic fountains for residential purposes and marble statues to be placed in public gardens. Both products would be compatible with Sushma's existing product line and neither would require any increase in net working capital.

Mr. Arvind, the Production Manager, has been entrusted with the task of analyzing the new product proposals. He estimates that the company would require an investment of Rs. 9,00,000 for the fountains and Rs. 11,00,000 for the statues. In either case, it would take less than 80 days to install the equipment, so production could begin by January 1st.

Mr. Prakash the Sales Manger, estimates that the company could sell fountains, worth Rs. 6,00,000 and Rs. 9,00,000 atues annually. The company's cost accountant predicts variable cost of two-thirds of sales for the fountains and 64 per cent for the ues. Fixed ost is estimated to be around Rs. 90,000 and Rs. 1,90,000 respectively.

The management requested Mr. Sahu, the Finance manager, to find out sources of funds that could be obtained for financing the additional requirements and the terms and conditions of financing. Mr Sahu after investigating the capital market of the country, submitted to the management that, the company could borrow upto Rs. 25,00,000 by floating 25 year bonds at 6 per cent for either or both the projects. The company could also raise funds by issuing preferred stock with 8 per cent dividend upto Rs. 11,00,000. He informed the management that the common stock financing would not be currently available.

Performa Income Statement and Balance Sheet of Sushma Enterprises are shown in Exhibits 1 and 2 below.

Exhibit 1: Performa Income Statement For December 31, 2001	
Sales	30,00,000
Variable Cost	18,56,000
Marginal Contribution	11,44,000
Fixed Costs	5,60,000
Earnings before interest and tax (EBIT)	5,84,000
Interest	80,000
Earning before tax (EBT)	5,04,000
Taxes	2,62,000
Net Income after tax	2,42,000

Exhibit 2: Performa Balance Sheet For December 2001			
Liabilities	**Rs.**	**Assets**	**Rs.**
Current Liabilities	3,00,000	Cash	1,40,000
Long-term debt 10%	8,00,000	Accounts Receivable	3,00,000
Common stock (Rs. 2%)	4,00,000	Inventory	2,40,000
Retained earnings	15,80,000	Fixed Assets	24,00,000
Total	30,80,000	Total	30,80,000

Normal profit margin is 20 per cent and normal asset turnover is 1.2/1

Assignments

1. What will be the effect on EPS of the company in each financing alternative and how the acceptance of each project will affect the leverage.

2. Without the new projects, what would the firms operating, fixed shares, and combined leverage be, the next year? Does it have a favourable financial leverage?

CLASS DISCUSSION CASE 3

RKV CASE : LEVERAGE

This case provides the reader with the opportunity to apply different concepts of leverage to the planning process of the firm.

RKV is an important manufacturer of swimming pools. The firm is located in a semi-urban area. The firm's primary markets are hardware and discount stores located in five Northeastern states. Lucid products reach its market mostly by truck.

Most of RKV's financial planning is done by George Lee, GM of finance. Lee has recently prepared financial statements estimating next year's operating results. He believes that, the firm will earn just over $800,000 in the current year on sales of $8 million and is forecasting sales of $13 million next year. It is likely, that variable costs will remain at approximately the same percentage of sales next year as this year. Fixed costs will probably rise to 12 per cent next year.

Company A has an EBIT of $2.6 million, no debt, $8 in equity (300,000 shares), $18 million. Company B has the same level of sales, an EBIT of $2.85 million, $3.3 and sales of debt at 11 per cent, and $8 in equity (300,000 shares). The tax rate is 35 per cent.

RKV has been investigating the addition of a number of new product lines to be sold through its existing distribution channels. Two items have been of particular interest. The first would involve the production and sale of chaise lounges for use around swimming pools. The product would be aimed at commercial users, such as hotels, but could be sold through hardware and discount stores as a residential product. The second new item would be a patio umbrella. The umbrella would be a large, 12-rib, multicolored canvas with fringe and would be aimed at the residential market. Both products would fit in with RKV's existing product line and neither would require any increase in networking capital.

In his analysis regarding the new product proposals, George Lee recognized that, the firm would have to build new facilities to produce each product. The lounges would require an investment of $3.8 million which would include the purchase and installation of manufacturing and packaging machinery. The umbrellas, although a relatively simple concept, would require an investment of $6 million for efficient production. For both products, it would take 80 days to install the equipment. This means that production could begin by January 1st.

Len haton, the firm's vice-president of sales, has prepared sales estimates for the two products. He forecasts $4 million in sales for the lounges and $ 4.3 million in sales for the umbrellas on annual basis. The report from the cost accounting department estimates variable costs of two-third of the sales value for the lounge unit and 61 per cent for the umbrellas. Fixed costs would be $400,000 and $ 650,000, respectively.

To finance the new projects, Lee has been working with Lucid's investment bankers. At a recent meeting, Lee was told that the firm could raise money from two sources under the current market conditions. First, it could borrow on an 11 year note at 12 per cent for either or both the projects in an amount not exceeding $ 8.5 million. Second, the investment bankers felt confident that they could underwrite a preferred stock issue with a 12 per cent dividend upto a dollar amount of $6 million. The issue would have to be cumulative with respect to dividends. Common stock financing would not be a possibility at present.

RKV

Balance Sheet

(Projected through December 31 this year)

Cash	$ 425,000
Accounts receivables	750,000
Inventory	500,000
Fixed Assets	7,650,000
	$ 9,325,000
Current liabilities	$ 600,000
Long-term debt (10%)	3,800,000
Common stock ($3 par)	1,500,000
Retained earnings	3,425,000
	$ 9,325,000

Assignment

What would be the effect of acceptance of each project on leverages? Would it give a favourable financial leverage to RKV?

RKV

Income Statement

(Projected through December 31 this year)

EBIT	1,926,520
EBT	1,536,520
Fixed Costs	1,043,480
Interest	390,000
Marginal contribution	2,970,000
Net Income	1,027,303
Sales	$ 8,000,000
Taxes	509,217
Variable Costs	5,030,000

Capital Structure Theory

Objectives

After studying this chapter, you should be able to:

1 Understand the relevance and irrelevance theories of capital structure.

2 Understand the relationship between capital structure and the value of the firm.

3 Understand the practical considerations in determining the firm's capital structure.

INTRODUCTION

The Capital structure decision is yet another important area under financial management. Capital structure refers to the mix of proportions of a firm's permanent long-term financing represented by debt, preference capital and equity cDetailed Contentsapital.

While taking any financial decisions, the firm must ensure the maximization of wealth of shareholders. So even the Capital structure decision must be taken in the light of wealth maximization objective. That particular mix of debt and equity which maximizes the value of the firm, is known as optimum capital structure.

ASSUMPTION OF CAPITAL STRUCTURE THEORIES

1) There are only two sources of funds i.e. debt and equity.

2) The total assets of the company are given and do not change.

3) The total financing remains constant. The firm can change the degree of leverage, either by selling the shares and retiring debt or by issuing debt and redeeming equity.

4) Operating profits (EBIT) are not expected to grow.

5) All the investors are assumed to have the same expectation about the future profits.

6) Business risk is constant over time and assumed to be independent of its capital structure and financial risk.

7) Corporate tax does not exit.

8) The company has infinite life.

9) Dividend payout ratio = 100%.

DEFINITIONS AND SYMBOLS USED

S= Total market value of equity shares.

B= Total market value of debt

I= Total interest payments.

V=Total market value of the firm

NI= Net income available to equity shareholders.

V=B+S

Cost of debt (K_d) = 1/ B

Value of debt (B) = 1/ K_e

Cost of equity capital (K_e) = D1/P + g

Because of assumption no-4 growth rate =O. So, K_e= D/P and since payout ratio = 100% D= earnings or dividends.

Therefore, K_d= E/P

Multiplying both, numerator and denominator by the number of shares, we get :

$$K_e = \frac{E*N}{P*N} \qquad \frac{EBIT-1}{S} \, or \, NI$$

$$K_e = \frac{\text{Net income available to the shareholder}}{\text{Total market value of equity shares.}}$$

Overall costs of Capital (K_o)

$K_o = W_1 K_d + W_2 K_e$ (W_1 & W_2 are weights.)

$$B/V(K_d) + S/V(K_e) \text{ or } \frac{B}{B+S}(K_d) + \frac{S(K_e)}{B+S}$$

OR

$$K_o = \frac{1+NI}{V} = \frac{EBIT}{V}$$

SO $\qquad V = \frac{EBIT}{K_o}$

CAPITAL STRUCTURE DECISIONS

The two principal sources of finance for a company are equity and debt. What should be the proportion of equity and debt in the capital structure of the firm? One of the key issues in the capital structure decision is the relationship between the capital structure and the value of the firm. There are several views on how this decision affects the value of the firm.

CAPITAL STRUCTURE THEORIES

Basic assumptions

There are only two kinds of funds used by a firm i.e. debt and equity.

Taxes are not considered.

The payout ratio is 100% .

The firm's total financing remains constant.

Business risk is constant over time.

The firm has perpetual life.

THEORY OF CAPITAL STRUCTURE

The long-term source of finance, which a company may use for investments, may be broadly classified into 2 types. They are **debt capital** and **equity capital.** The financial manager must determine the proportion of debt and equity and financial leverage. Understanding the relationship between financial leverage and cost of capital is extremely important for taking capital structure decisions. Theoretically the value of a firm can be maximized when the cost of capital in minimized. That capital structure, where the cost of capital is minimum, is known as optimum capital structure. Existence of optimum capital structure is not accepted by all. There exist extreme views. The first viewpoint strongly supports the argument that, the financing or debt equity mix has a major impact on the shareholders wealth. The second, however, is of the opinion that, capital structure is irrelevant.

There are 4 major theories explaining the relationship between capital structure, cost of capital and valuation of the firm. They are:

1) Net income approach (NI)
2) Net operating income approach (NOI)
3) Traditional approach
4) Modigliani-Miller approach

NET INCOME APPROACH (NI)

According to this approach, the cost of debt and the cost of equity do not change with a change in the leverage ratio. As a result, the average cost of capital declines as the leverage ratio increases. This is because when the leverage ratio increases, the cost of debt, which is lower than the cost of equity, gets a higher weightage in the calculation of the cost of capital.

This approach has been suggested by David Durand. According to this approach, capital structure decision is relevant to the valuation of the firm. According to the theory it is possible to change the cost of capital by changing the debt equity mix. In other words, a change in the capital structure causes a change in the overall of capital as well as the value of the firm.

The formula to calculate the average cost of capital is as follows:

$K_o = K_d (B/ (B+S)) + K_e (S/(B+S))$

Where,

K_o is the average cost of capital

K_d is the cost of debt

B is the market value of debt

S is the market value of equity

K_e is the cost of equity

The NI approach is based on the following assumptions:

- The use of debt does not change the risk of investors and therefore, cost of debt (K_d) and cost of equity (Ke) remains the same irrespective of the degree of leverage.
- Cost of debt is less than the cost of equity.
- The corporate income tax does not exist.

According to the theory, cost of debt is assumed to be less than the cost of equity. Therefore, when the financial leverage is increased (proportion of debt in the total capital), the overall cost of capital will decline and the value of the firm will increase. The implications of the 3 assumptions of NI approach is that, as the degree of leverage increases, the proportion of a cheaper source of funds (debt) in the capital structure increases. As a result, the weighted average cost of capital tends to decline leading to an increase in the total level of the firm. Thus, even if the cost of debt and cost of equity remains same regardless of leverage, increased use of low cost debt will result in the decline of overall cost of capital and thereby, maximize the value of the firm. So the overall cost of capital will be minimum when the proportion of debt in the capital structure is maximum. Hence, optimum structure exists when the firm employs 100% debt or maximum debt in the capital structure.

The NI approach may be compared to a dishonest trader who wants to sell 10 litres of milk @ Rs. 15 per litre. He can add water and pure milk to prepare the 10 litres of milk. If the cost of 1 litre of water is Re. 1, and cost of 1 litre of pure milk is Rs.10, he can maximise his profit or minimize his cost per litre of milk by adding more and more of low cost water. For example : if he purchases only pure milk, his cost will be Rs. 10*10= Rs. 100. If he adds 5 litres of water to 5 litres of milk, the cost of 10 litres would be 1*5+10*5=(Rs. 5.5/litre). Here, pure milk is compared to equity , which is a costly source, and water is compared to debt, which is a cheaper source.

Illustration 1: A Company's expected net operating income (EBIT) is Rs. 1,00,000. The company has issued Rs. 5,00,000, 10% debentures at Rs. 100 each. The cost of equity is 12.5%. Assuming no taxes, find out the overall cost of capital and the value of the firm according to NI approach.

Solution:

S= Value of equity shares (NI/K_e) (Rs.)	4,00,000
Net operating income (Rs.)	1,00,000
Less: Interest, on debentures (Rs.)	50,000
Earning available to ESH (NI) (Rs.)	50,000
Cost of equity (K_e)	12.5%

Value of debt (B) (Rs.)	5,00,000
Total Value of the firm (S+B=V) (Rs.)	9,00,000
Overall cost of capital (EBIT/V)	11.1%

Alternatively, $K_o = K_d$ (W1) + K_e (W2)

$$\frac{5,00,000(0.10)}{9,00,000} + \frac{4,00,000(0.125)}{9,00,000} = 11.1\%$$

Assuming the market price per share to be Rs. 100, there will be 4000 shares of Rs. 100 each. Find out the effect of increase in leverage on the cost of capital (Ko) and value of the firm.

Assume that the above company increases the debt from Rs. 5,00,000 to Rs. 6,00,000 and the cost of the debt and equity remains at the same level. We can calculate the overall cost of capital, value of the firm and the market value of equity shares as shown below.

EBIT	1,00,000
Less: Int on debt	60,000
Earnings available to ESH (NI)	40,000
K_e	0.125
Value of equity shares (NI/K_e) =S	3,20,000
Value of debt (B)	6,00,000
Value of the firm (S+B=V)	9,20,000

$$K_o = \frac{EBIT}{V} = \frac{1,00,000}{9,20,000} = 10.86\%$$

Alternatively K_o can be calculated as below:

$$K_o = Kd(W1) + K_e(W2)$$

$$\frac{6,00,000(0.10)}{9,20,000} + \frac{3,20,000(0.125)}{9,20,000} = 10.87\%$$

Market value of equity shares

Before increasing the debt, there were 4000 ES of Rs. 100 each . Then the firm increased the debt by Rs. 1,00,000 and used the proceeds to retire equity shares. So the company redeemed 1000 shares of Rs. 100 each. So the number of shares outstanding is 4000 – 1000=3000. Therefore, value of 1 equity share is:

$$Rs. \frac{3,20,000}{3000} = Rs.106.67$$

So, the market value of equity shares has increased to Rs. 106.67.

To sum up, according to the NI approach, as the debt content is increased in the capital structure, K_o falls, value of the firm increases and the market value of the equity shares also increases.

We can graph the relationship between K_o, K_e and K_d with the degree of leverage as shown below.

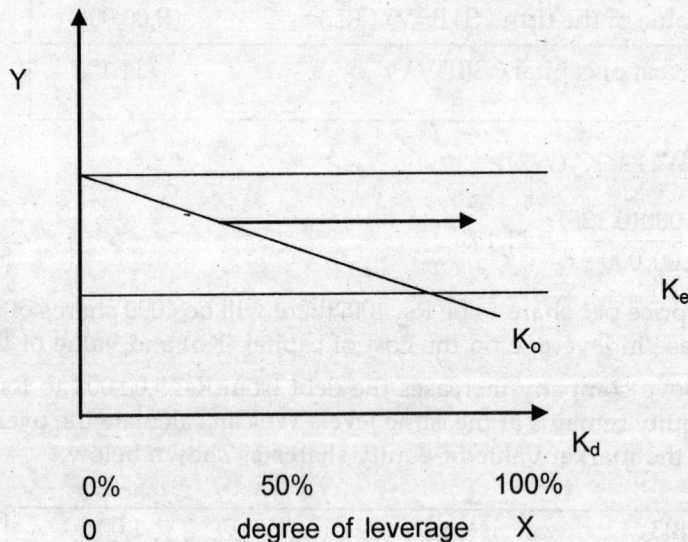

The degree of leverage is plotted along the X-axis, while the cost of Capital in per cent is plotted on Y-axis. As the cost of debt and cost of equity is constant with leverage, we find that both the curves are horizontal to X-axis. As the degree of leverage increases (% of debt in the total capital increase) overall cost of capital continuously falls. K_o is minimum when, there is 100% debt. So optimum capital structure exists at 100% debt and 0% equity capital. But in practice, 100% debt may not be possible. There should be some equity capital in the capital structure of any company.

NOI APPROACH

This theory is also given by David Durand. This is just the opposite to NI approach. According to NOI approach, the capital structure decision is irrelevant and there is nothing like optimum capital structure. All the capital structures are optimum.

According to this theory, the market value of the firm is not affected by the capital structure changes. The market value of the firm is found by capitalizing (dividing) the net operating income by the overall cost of capital, which is constant. The market value of the firm is obtained by using the following formula.

$$V = \frac{NOI}{K_o} = (V = B + S)$$

The overall cost of capital depends on the business risks of the firm, which is assumed to be constant. NOI depends on the investments made by the company and not on the capital structure decisions. So, if NOI and K_o are constant, the value of the firm must remain same regardless of leverage.

Assumptions

The market capitalizes the value of the firm as a whole. Thus, the split between debt and equity is not important. The value of the firm is obtained by capitalizing NOI by the K_o, which depends on the business risks. If business risks is constant, K_o is also constant.

The use of debt increases the risks of shareholders, So, K_e increases with the leverage and eats completely the advantage of low cost debt.

a) Cost of debt remains same regardless of leverage.

b) Corporate income tax does not exist.

The critical assumptions of this approach are that K_o remains same regardless of the degree of leverage. The market capitalizes the value of the firm as a whole and the split between debt and equity is unimportant. The benefits from the increase in the use of cost debt is completely offset (neutralised) by the increases in the cost of equity. So even if the leverage is increased, overall cost of capital remains at the same level. When the company increases the leverage, the firm becomes more risky and equity shareholders penalize the firm by demanding higher and higher rate of returns. So, K_e is the function of the debt equity ratio. Since overall cost of capital structure remains static according to the theory.

Illustration 2: A company's expected annual net operating income (EBIT) is Rs. 1,00,000. The company has 5,00,000, 10% debentures. The overall cost of capital is 12.5%. Calculate the value of the firm and cost of equity according to NOI approach.

Solution:

Net operating income (EBIT) (Rs.)	1,00,000
Overall cost of capital (K_o)	0.125
Total value of the firm (V=EBIT/K_o) (Rs.)	8,00,000
Market value of the debt (B) (Rs)	5,00,000
Total market value of the equity (S=V-B) (Rs)	3,00,000

$$\text{Cost of equity} = \frac{NI}{S} = \frac{\text{earning available to ESH}}{\text{market value of equity shares}}$$

$$K_e = \frac{EBIT - I}{V - B} = \frac{1,00,000 - 50,000}{8,00,000 - 5,00,000} = 16,66\%$$

Market value of equity shares : Assuming the market price of shares to be Rs. 100, there are 3000 shares of Rs. 100 each.

If the company increases the debt from Rs.5,00,000 to Rs. 6,00,000 the Ke and the value of the firm are as below :

Net operating income (EBIT) (RS)	1,00,000
Overall cost of capital (Ko)	0.125
Total value of the firm (V=EBIT/Ko)(Rs.)	8,00,000
Market value of debt (B) (Rs.)	6,00,000
Market value of the equity (S) (Rs)	2,00,000

$$\text{Cost of equity} = \frac{NI}{S} = \frac{40,000}{2,00,000} = 20\%$$

Market value of the equity shares

The firm has increased the debt by Rs.1,00,000 and used the proceeds to reduce equity capital. The number of shares has reduced from 3000 to 2000. Therefore, the price per share can be calculated as below.

$$\text{Price per share} = \frac{\text{total market value of the shares}}{\text{number of shares}}$$

$$= \frac{2,00,000}{2000} = Rs. 100.$$

So, there is no change in the price per share, total value of the firm and overall cost of the capital when the leverage is changed.

NOI approach can be graphically shown as below:

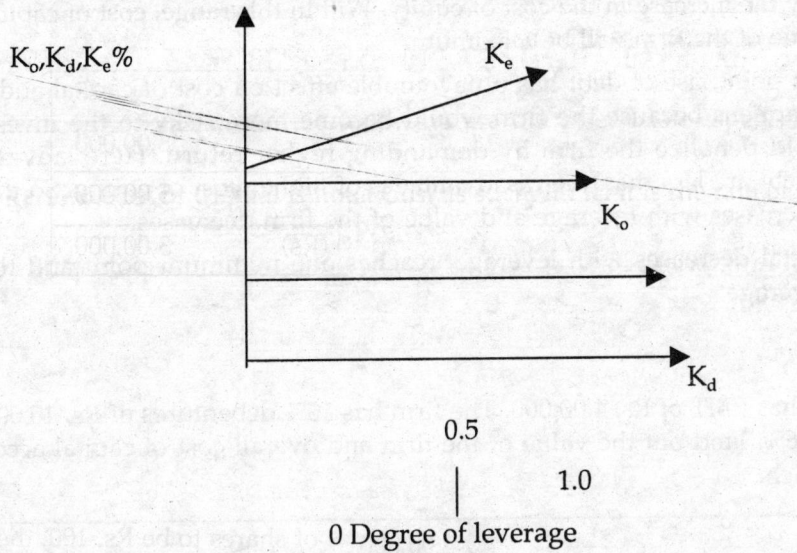

From the above graph, it is clear that, as the degree of leverage is increased, K_o and K_d remains at the same level. But cost of equity increases with leverage and exactly neutralises the benefits of low cost debt. So overall cost of Capital remains at the same level.

TRADITIONAL OR INTERMEDIATE APPROACH OR WACC APPROACH

This approach is midway between the NI and the NOI approach. The main propositions of this approach are:

The cost of debt remains almost constant upto a certain degree of leverage but rises thereafter, at an increasing rate. The cost of equity remains more or less constant or rises gradually up to a certain degree of leverage and rises sharply thereafter. The cost of capital due to, the behaviour of the cost of debt and cost of equity, decreases upto a certain point and remains more or less constant for moderate increases in leverage, thereafter, rises beyond that level at an increasing rate.

In other words NI approach and NOI approach represents two polar cases. The traditional or the intermediate approach is a midway between these two approaches, because it partly takes the features of both the approaches.

According to the theory, the value of the firm can be increased or cost of capital can be reduced by a judicious mix of debt and equity capital. This approach states that, cost of capital is a function of leverage. So cost of capital decreases upto a certain degree of leverages then it remains at the same level for certain degrees of leverage and thereafter it rises sharply with the leverage. So optimum capital structure exists when the cost of capital is minimum or value of the firm is maximum.

The manner in which cost of capital reacts to the changes in the capital structure can be divided into 3 stages.

1. In the first stage, cost of equity remains constant or rises slightly with the debt. But when it increases, it does not increase fast enough to offset the advantage of low cost debt. Cost of debt also remains same or rises slightly with the leverage. As the cost of debt is less than cost of equity, increased use of debt reduces the cost capital during the 1st stage.

2. Once the firm has reached the certain degree of leverage, increased use of debt does not result in the fall in the overall cost of capital. This is due to the fact that, benefits of low cost debt are offset by the increase in the cost of equity. Within this range, cost of capital will be minimum or value of the firm will be maximum.

3. Beyond a certain point, use of debt has unfavourable effect on cost of capital and value of the firm. This happens because the firm would become more risky to the investors and hence they would penalize the firm by demanding higher return. Here, advantages of using low cost debt are less than the disadvantages of higher cost of equity. So the overall cost of capital increases with leverage and value of the firm decreases.

Thus, the cost of capital decreases with leverage, reaches one minimum point and thereafter, increases with the leverage.

Illustration 2

Assume that the firm has EBIT of Rs. 4,00,000. The firm has 10% debentures of Rs. 10,00,000 and the cost of equity is 16%. Find out the value of the firm and overall cost of capital according to the traditional approach.

EBIT (Rs.)	4,00,000
Less : Interest (Rs.)	1,00,000
Earnings available to ESH (Rs.)	3,00,000
Cost of equity	0.16
Market value of the equity shares (Rs.) NI/Ke = 3,00,000/0.16	18,75,000
Market Value of the debt (B)	10,00,000
Total Value of the firm (S+B)	28,75,000

Overall cost of capital $(K_o) = \dfrac{EBIT}{V} = \dfrac{4,00,000}{28,75,000} = 13.9\%$

Now, let us assume that the firm increases the debt to another Rs. 5,00,000. So cost of debt increases to 11% and cost of equity rises to 17%. Calculate the overall cost of capital and the value of the firm.

EBIT (Rs.)	4,00,00,00
Less: Interest (Rs.)	1,65,000
Earnings available to ESH (Rs.)	2,35,000
Cost of equity	0.17
Value of equity shares (S = NI / K_e) (Rs.)	13,82,352
Value of debt (Rs.)	15,00,000
Value of the firm (V)(Rs.)	28,82,352

Overall cost of capital $K_o = \dfrac{EBIT}{V} = \dfrac{4,00,000}{28,82,353} = 13.8\%$

If the debt is further increased to Rs. 5,00,000 the cost of debt increases to 12.5% and the cost of equity is increased to 20%. Find out the overall cost of capital and value of the firm.

EBIT	4,00,000
Less: Interest (Rs.)	2,50,000
Earning available to ESH (Rs.)	1,50,000
Cost of equity	0.20
Value of equity shares (S=NI/K_e)	7,50,000
Value of debt (B) (Rs.)	20,00,00
Value of the firm (V=S+B) (Rs.)	27,50,000

Over all cost of capital $K_o = \dfrac{EBIT}{V} = \dfrac{4,00,000}{27,50,353} = 14.5\%$

MODIGLIANI MILLER APPROACH (MM)

MM theory relating to the relationship between cost of capital and valuation is similar to the NOI approach. According to this approach, the value of the firm is independent of its capital structure. However, there is a basic difference between the two. The NOI approach is purely a definitional term, defining the concept without behavioural justification. MM approach provides analytically sound, logically consistent, behavioral justification in favour of the theory and considers any other theories of Capital structure as incorrect.

Assumption

- Capital markets are perfect. This means,
- Investors are free to buy and sell securities.
- Inventors can borrow and lend money on the same terms on which a firm can borrow and lend.
- There are no transaction costs.
- They behave rationally.
- Firms can be classified into homogenous risk categories. All the firms within the same class will have the same degree of business risks.
- All the investors have the same expectations from a firm's NOI with which to evaluate the value of the firm.
- Dividends Payout ratio is 100% and there are no retained earnings.
- There are no corporate income taxes. This assumption is removed later.

THERE ARE 3 BASIC PROPOSITIONS OF MM APPROACH

The overall cost of capital (K_O) and the value of the firm (V) are independent of leverage. The K_o and V are constant for all the degree of leverage. The total value of the firm is obtained by capitalizing the EBIT at a discount rate appropriate for its risks class.

1. Cost of equity (K_e) is equal to the capitalization rate of a pure equity stream plus a premium for financial risk. The financial risks increases with the leverage and therefore, K_e increases in a manner to offset exactly the benefit from the use of low cost debt.

$K_e = K_o + (K_o - K_d) B/S$.

2.   The cut-off rate for investment purposes is completely independent of the way in which an investment is financed. This is true because cost of capital remains same regardless of the degree of leverage. So both, investment decision and financing decision are independent.

PROOF OF MM ARGUMENT

The value of a firm depends on its profitability and risks. It is in variant with respect to relative changes in the firm's capitalization. Similarly, according to the theory, cost of capital and market value of the firm must be same regardless of the degree of leverage.

The operational justification for the MM hypothesis is the " Arbitrage Argument". The term arbitrage refers to the act of buying a security in the market, where the price is less and simultaneously selling it in another market where the price is more, to take advantage of the difference in price prevailing in two different markets. Arbitrage process helps to bring equilibrium in the market. Because of arbitrage, a security cannot be sold at different prices in different markets. MM approach illustrates the arbitrage process with reference to valuation in terms of two firms, which are exactly similar in all aspects with respect to leverage, so that one of them has debt in the capital structure while other does not. Such homogenous firm's are, according to MM, perfect substitutes. If the market value of the two firms which are exactly same in all the respects, except with the leverage, which is not equal, investors of the overvalued firm would sell their shares, borrow additional funds on their personal account and invest in the undervalued firm, in order to obtain the investors for arbitrage is termed as home-made or personal leverage. So investor undertaking arbitrage would be better off. This behaviour of arbitrage will have investors of overvalued firm. Arbitrage would be counting till the market prices of two identical firms become identical.

Illustration 3

The operation of arbitrage process is illustrated below.

Assume that there are two firms L and U which are identical in all the respects except that, the firm L has 10% Rs. 5,00,000 debentures. The EBIT of both the firms are Rs. 80,000. The cost of equity of the firm L is higher at 16% and firm U is lower at 12.5%. The total market values of the firm are computed as below.

	FIRM L	FIRM U
EBIT	80,000	80,000
Less:Interest	50,000	-
Earnings available to ESH (NI)	**30,000**	**80,000**
Cost of equity (K_e)	0.16	0.125
Market value of equity shares (S=NI/K_e)	**1,87,500**	**6,40,000**
Market value of debt	5,00,000	------
Total value of the firm	**6,87,500**	**6,40,000**

$$K_O = \frac{EBIT}{V} = \qquad\qquad 11.63\% \qquad 12.5\%$$

Thus, the total value of the firm which employed debt is more than the value of the other firm. According to MM, this previous arbitrage would start and continue till the equilibrium is restored.

WORKING OF THE ARBITRAGE PROCESS

Suppose there is an investor X, who holds 10% of the outstanding shares in the firm L. This means his holding amounts to Rs. 18,750 and his shares in the earning which belongs to equity shareholders is Rs. 3000 (10% of Rs. 30,000). Mr. X will sell his holding in the firm L and invest money in the firm U. The firm U has no debt in the capital structure and hence, the financial risk to Mr. X would be less in the firm U than firm L . In order to have the same degree of financial risk as of the firm U, Mr. X will borrow additional funds equal to his proportionate shares in substituted personal leverage in place of corporate leverage.

The position of Mr.X is summarized as below.

Firm L

Investment amount	(10% holding)	18,750
Dividend income	(10% 0f 30000)	3,000
Return on funds	$\dfrac{3000}{18,750} = 16\%$	

Firm U

Investment amount (18,750+50,000)   =   68,750

(50,000 borrowed at 10%)

$$\text{Total income} \dfrac{68,750}{6,40,000} \times 80,000 = 8,593.75$$

Less: Interest on loan	5,000
Return on investment	3,593.75

$$\text{ROI} = \dfrac{3,593.75}{18,750} = 19.16\%$$

So Mr. X gets a higher income after shifting his investment to company U (Rs 3,000 and 3,593.75) His ROI increases from 16% to 19%. The other investors will also wish to make profit out of arbitrage. This increases the demand for securities of the firm U and will lead to increase in its price. At the same time, the price of the security of the firm L will decline due to the selling pressure. This will continue till the prices of the securities of the firms become identical.

Taxes: If the corporate taxes are taken into consideration. MM argues that the value of the firm will increase and cost of capital will decrease with leverage. Interest paid on the debt is tax deductible and therefore, effective cost of debt is less than the coupon rate of interest. Therefore, levered firm would have a greater market value than the unlevered firm (cost capital of levered firm would be lower).

Symbolically:

VL=   VU+BT

VL = Value of levered firm

V_u=   Value of unlevered firm

B=   Amount of debt

T =   Tax rate

DESIGNING CAPITAL STRUCTURE

Capital structure refers to the mix of long term sources of funds. Theoretically the financial manager must plan an optimum capital structure for his company. But it is very difficult to design an optimum capital structure for a company. There are a host of factors, both quantitative and qualitative, including subjective judgement of financial managers, which determines the capital structure of a firm. These factors are highly complex and cannot fit entirely into theoretical frameworks.

FEATURES OF AN APPROPRIATE CAPITAL STRUCTURE

The financial manager should develop an appropriate capital structure which is most advantageous to the company. This can be done only when all the factors, which are relevant to the company's capital structure decision are properly analysed and balanced. Capital structure so arrived, may not be optimum but most reasonable. So some people call it as appropriate or sound capital structure. A capital structure is considered as appropriate if it possesses the following features:

Profitability: A capital structure is most profitable when the overall cost of capital is minimum and gives higher EPS.

Solvency: Excess use of debt threatens the solvency and liquidity of the company. While designing the capital structure, the financial manager must try to reduce cost of capital and also limit the financial risk to the acceptable level.

Flexibility: The capital structure should be such that, it can be easily adjusted to meet the changing conditions. It should also maintain the ability of the firm to borrow for future growth and development.

Control: Capital structure should be so designed that, it involves minimum risk of loss of control of the company. This is highly relevant because many of the Indian promoters do not have a majority stake.

Conservatism: According to this principle, the debt content should not exceed the limit, which the company can bear. The company should be extremely careful while borrowing because, things and circumstances suddenly change against the interest of the company.

GUIDELINES FOR CAPITAL STRUCTURE DECISIONS

The capital structure decision involves taking into consideration several factors including income, risk, flexibility, control, timing etc. The following guidelines could help managers in taking capital structure decisions: -

Exploiting the tax advantage of debt

Interest on debt is a tax-deductible expense and hence reduces the tax burden. The advantage of a tax shelter motivates the company to raise more loans from the market. The market value of the firm would increase with the decreased tax burden.

Ensuring flexibility

Utilising the maximum loan capacity to reduce tax expenses is not always the right decision for a company. The company should have the flexibility to borrow when the situation changes, due to changes in government policies, disruption in supplies, labour unrest etc. Unused debt capacity at such a time could enhance this flexibility.

Limiting risk exposure to reasonable limits

The managers need to ensure that, the total risk exposure of a company is within controllable limits. Business risk is based on the proportion of fixed costs and variability in demand, price and input prices. Financial risks, which indicate the financial leverage of the company, arise from the debt portion of its capital structure. A company cannot keep both the risks at a very high level.

Retaining control

If more equity is issued to the public, control will get diluted for the promoters, whereas with debt issue it will be retained with the company.

Integrating financial policies and corporate strategies

Financial policy makers are from the capital market whereas corporate policy makers are from the product market. To integrate these two policies the chief executive of a company should:

- Thoroughly check the factors underlying the financial policy
- Ensure that the financial policy will support corporate strategy
- Increase the involvement of operating managers in determining financial policy
- Restrict financial policy from becoming the corporate goal

Issuing at the proper time

Although it is difficult to predict the proper timing for raising capital in the market, the following thumb rules may be helpful in improving a company's performance in terms of timing into the market:

- Take the best possible opportunity available at present in the market rather than waiting for a more advantageous time in the future. It may or may not materialise.
- Follow the trend in the financial market
- Wait till the market captures the full potential of the company and reflects it in the share price

Complying with the norms of lenders and credit rating agencies

Debt can be obtained easily if backed by tangible assets as security and accompanied by good credit rating. Companies can take advantage of the same.

Issuing innovative securities

Subject to the guidelines issued by the SEBI from time to time, a company can issue different kinds of financial instruments for raising resources from the market. However, these should be attractive and easily understandable by investors.

FACTORS DETERMINING THE CAPITAL STRUCTURE

Deciding about the capital structure of a company is all about achieving the correct proportion between debt and equity. Equity represents owner's capital. It looks like a free source but it is not so. Perhaps it is the costliest source of funds. Debt is a totally different cup of tea. It carries contractual pay interest at a predetermined rate. In the event of financial crisis, it may even force the company to liquidate.

not so. Perhaps it is the costliest source of funds. Debt is a totally different cup of tea. It carries contractual pay interest at a predetermined rate. In the event of financial crisis, it may even force the company to liquidate.

The capital structure of a company is determined initially when the company carries a fixed rate of return. If the internal rate is more than the cost of capital the excess return goes to the shareholders. So shareholders are able to earn on their capital and also eligible to enjoy excess return earned on the fixed income securities issued by the company. This phenomenon is known as trading on equity.

Example: A company issued 1000 shares of Rs.10 each and 10% of 5000 debentures of Rs. 10 each. It earns Rs. 30,000 as operating profit (50% on investment of Rs 60,000), calculate return on equity.

Operating Profit (Rs.)	30,000
Less: Interest (Rs.)	5,000
Profit available	25,000
Share capital	10,000
Return on equity	= 250%

So even if the company earns only 50% return on investment, the shareholders are able to enjoy 250% return on their capital. This is due to the fact that interest on debt is just 10% and the company earns on their money 50% return. After paying 10% to debentures holders the balance 40% is transferred to equity shareholders (Rs 20,000). So equity shareholders are getting Rs.25,000 (50% on their capital (5000)+ 40% debentures capital (20,000) as return on their capital.

Retaining control: The capital structure of a company is also affected by the extent to which the existing management of the company desires to maintain control over the affairs of the company. If the company issues debt capital or preference capital, there is no risk of dilutions of control. The company can also buy back the shares to increase the control of the promoters over the company.

Nature of the enterprise: Business firms with stable earnings or monopoly firms supplying basic necessaries can have more or debt capital because they have the capacity to service the debt. The firms without the above advantages should rely more on equity.

Purposes of financing: If the purpose is productive, the firm may use the debt capital otherwise it is better to rely more on equity capital.

Period of finance: If the finance is required for a very long time, equity shares should be issued because it is a permanent source. If the funds are required only for a short period, short term debt may be raised.

Requirement of investors: The company requiring large amount of capital must issue different kinds of securities to suit the requirements of different investors.

Example: Regular income bonds, deep discount bonds, partly convertible bonds, equity shares, preference shares etc.

Size of the company: Small companies, and companies with low credit ratings must rely more on equity capital market as it is very easy to issue equity capital. On the other hand, large companies with good credit ratings can raise debt capital easily.

Market sentiments: This is another factor influencing the capital structure decision. When

Cash flow ability : The issue of debt depends on the future cash flow ability of the company.

Floating costs: Floatation costs are incurred when the funds are raised externally. So retained earnings do not involve floatation costs. Floatation costs for the issue of share is more than that of debentures and bonds. Further the floatation costs are much less when the company issues securities on private placement basis instead of public issue.

THE TRADE-OFF THEORY: COST OF FINANCIAL DISTRESS AND AGENCY COSTS

As the dedt equity ratio (ie leverage) increases, there is a trade-off between the interest tax shield and bankruptcy, causing an optimum capital structure, D/E*

The Trade-Off Theory of Capital Structure is a theory in the realm of Financial Economics about the corporate finance choices of corporations. Its purpose is to explain the fact that firms or corporations usually are financed partly with debt and partly with equity. It states that there is an advantage to financing with debt, the tax benefit of debt and there is a cost of financing with debt, the costs of financial distress including bankruptcy costs of debt and non-bankruptcy costs (e.g. staff leaving, suppliers demanding disadvantageous payment terms, bondholder/stockholder infighting, etc). The marginal benefit of further increases in debt declines as debt increases, while the marginal cost increases, so that a firm that is optimizing its overall value will focus on this trade-off when choosing how much debt and equity to use for financing. Although the empirical success of the alternative theories is often dismal, the relevance of this theory has often been questioned. For example, Miller's (1977) metaphor speaks of the balance between those two as equivalent to the balance between horse and rabbit content in a stew of one horse and one rabbit. Other critics have suggested it is the mechanical change in asset prices that makes up for most of the variation in capital structure.

Recognize that costs of financial distress and agency costs are real.

Trade-Off Model

Financial distress costs (includes bankruptcy)

1. Direct costs

   Lawyer's fees, court costs, administrative expenses, assets disappear or become obsolete

2. Indirect costs

   Managers make short-run decisions; customers and suppliers may impose costs

Agency costs

More debt is likely to be experienced. Distress stockholders (thus management) want risk, while bondholders do not.

Use covenants to align interests costs: monitoring to ensure they are followed; also may hamper business. In essence, lost efficiency and monitoring costs reduce advantage of debt, given agency costs and financial distress.

VL = VU + TD – (PV of expected costs of financial distress) – (PV of agency costs)

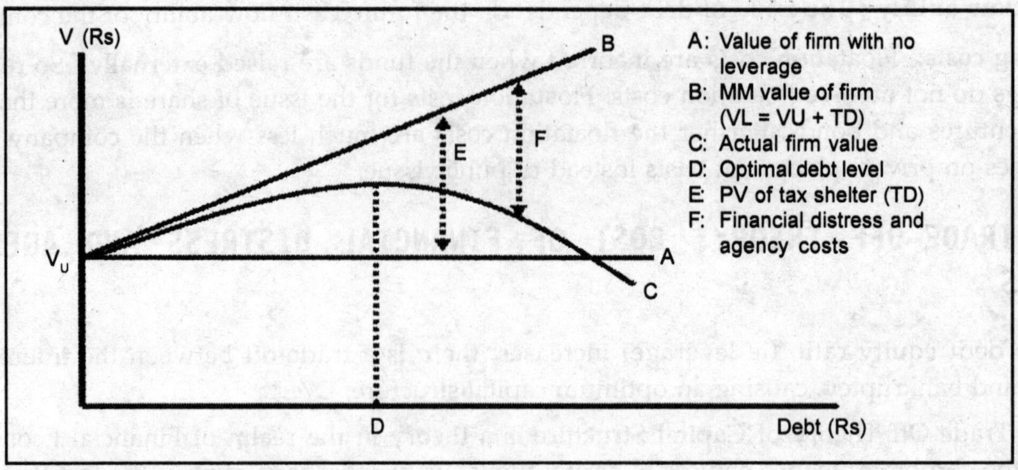
V (Rs)
B
E
F
V_U
A
C
D
Debt (Rs)
A: Value of firm with no leverage
B: MM value of firm (VL = VU + TD)
C: Actual firm value
D: Optimal debt level
E: PV of tax shelter (TD)
F: Financial distress and agency costs

CONSEQUENCES OF FINANCIAL DISTRESS

Bankruptcy Costs

Specific bankruptcy costs include legal and administrative costs along with the sale of assets at 'distress' prices to meet creditor claims. Lenders build into their required interest rate the expected costs of bankruptcy, which reduces the market value of equity by a corresponding amount.

Indirect Costs

- Investing in risky projects
- Reluctance to undertake profitable projects
- Premature liquidation
- Short-term orientation

Debt Policy and Shareholders Conflicts

Shareholder-manager conflicts

Managers have a tendency to consume some of the firm's resources in the form of various perquisites.

Managers have a tendency to become unduly risk-averse and shirk their responsibilities as they have no equity interest, or when their equity interest falls. They may be passing up profitable opportunities.

Shareholder-bondholder conflicts

Shareholder value is created either by increasing the value of the firm or by reducing the value of its bonds. Increasing the risk of the firm or issuing substantial new debt are ways to redistribute wealth from bondholders to shareholders. Shareholders do not like excessive debt.

FINANCIAL DISTRESS

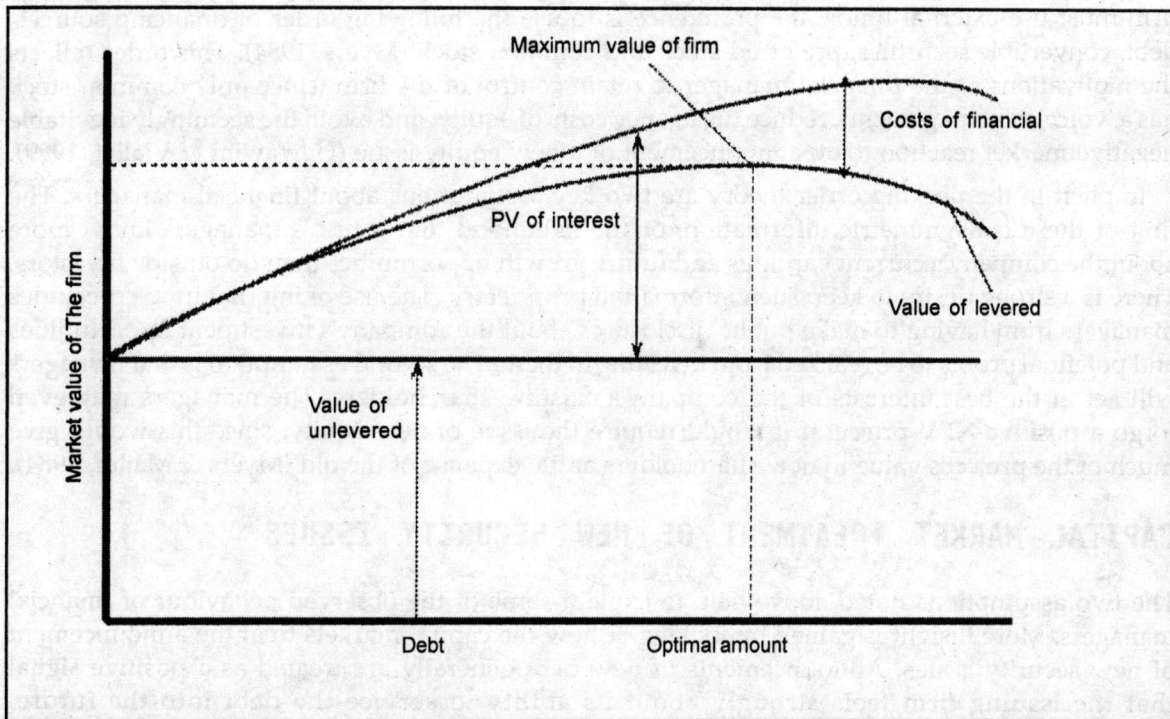

OPTIMUM CAPITAL STRUCTURE: TRADE-OFF THEORY

The optimum capital structure is a function of:

♦ Agency costs associated with debt

♦ The costs of financial distress

♦ Interest tax shield

The value of a levered firm is:

Value of unlevered firm

+ PV of tax shield

- PV of financial distress

Pecking Order Theory Overview

In the theory of firm's capital structure and financing decisions, the Pecking Order Theory or Pecking Order Model was developed by Stewart C. Myers in 1984. It states that companies prioritize their sources of financing (from internal financing to equity) according to the law of least effort, or of least resistance, preferring to raise equity as a financing means "of last resort.". Hence, internal funds are used first, and when that is depleted, debt is issued, and when it is not sensible to issue any more debt, equity is issued. This theory maintains that businesses adhere to a hierarchy of financing sources and prefer internal financing when available, and debt is preferred over equity if external financing is required. —

Pecking order theory of capital structure states that firms have a preferred hierarchy for financing decisions. The highest preference is to use internal financing (retained earnings and the effects of depreciation) before resorting to any form of external funds. Internal funds incur no flotation costs and require no additional disclosure of proprietary financial information that could lead to more severe market discipline and a possible loss of competitive advantage. If a firm must use external funds, the preference is to use the following order of financing sources: debt, convertible securities, preferred stock and common stock (Myers, 1984). This order reflects the motivations of the financial manager to retain control of the firm (since only common stock has a 'voice' in management), reduce the agency costs of equity, and avoid the seemingly inevitable negative market reaction to an announcement of a new equity issue (Hawawini & Viallet, 1999).

Implicit in the pecking order theory are two key assumptions about financial managers. The first of these is asymmetric information, or the likelihood that a firm's managers know more about the company's current earnings and future growth opportunities than do outside investors. There is a strong desire to keep such information proprietary. The use of internal funds precludes managers from having to make public disclosures about the company's investment opportunities and potential profits to be realized from investing in them. The second assumption is that managers will act in the best interests of the company's existing shareholders. The managers may even forgo a positive-NPV project if it would require the issue of new equity, since this would give much of the project's value to new shareholders at the expense of the old (Myers & Majluf, 1984).

CAPITAL MARKET TREATMENT OF NEW SECURITY ISSUES

The two assumptions noted above help to explain some of the observed behaviour of financial managers. More insight is gained by looking at how the capital markets treat the announcement of new security issues. Announcements of new debt generally are treated as a positive signal that the issuing firm feels strongly about its ability to service the debt into the future. Announcements of new common stock are generally treated as a negative signal that the firm's managers feel the company's stock is overvalued (i.e. earnings are likely to decline in the future) and they wish to take advantage of a market opportunity. So it is easy to see why financial managers use new common stock as a last resort in capital structure decisions. The mere announcement of a new stock issue will cause the price of the firm's stock to fall as the market participants try to sort out the implications of the firm choosing to issue a new equity issue.

HOW PECKING ORDER IS SUPERIOR TO THE TRADE-OFF MODEL

While the trade-off model implies a static approach to financing decisions based upon a target capital structure, the pecking order theory allows for the dynamics of the firm to dictate an optimal capital structure for a given firm at any particular point in time (Copeland & Weston, 1988). A firm's capital structure is a function of its internal cash flows and the amount of positive-NPV investment opportunities available. A firm that has been very profitable in an industry with relatively slow growth (i.e. few investment opportunities) will have no incentive to issue debt and will likely have a low debt-to-equity ratio. A less profitable firm in the same industry will likely have a high debt-to-equity ratio. The more profitable a firm, the more financial slack it can build up.

Financial slack is defined as a firm's highly liquid assets (cash and marketable securities) plus any unused debt capacity (Moyer, McGuigan, and Kretlow, 2001). Firms with sufficient financial slack will be able to fund most, if not all, of their investment opportunities internally and will not have to issue debt or equity securities. Not having to issue new securities allows the firm to avoid both the flotation costs associated with external funding and the monitoring and market discipline that occurs when accessing capital markets.

Prudent financial managers will attempt to maintain financial flexibility while ensuring the long-term survivability of their firms. When profitable firms retain their earnings as equity and build up cash reserves, they create the financial slack that allows financial flexibility and, ultimately long-term survival.

The pecking order theory explains these observed and reported managerial actions, while the trade-off model cannot. It also explains stock market reactions to leverage-increasing and leverage-decreasing events, which the trade-off model cannot.

Limitations of Pecking Order Theory

The pecking order theory, however, does not explain the influence of taxes, financial distress, security issuance costs, agency costs, or the set of investment opportunities available to a firm upon that firm's actual capital structure. It also ignores the problems that can arise when a firm's managers accumulate so much financial slack that they become immune to market discipline. In such a case, it would be possible for a firm's management to preclude ever being penalized via a low security price and, if augmented with non-financial takeover defences, immune to being removed in a hostile acquisition. For these reasons, the pecking order theory is offered as a complement to, rather than a substitution for, the traditional trade-off model.

Conclusions and implications: While the traditional trade-off model is useful for explaining corporate debt levels, the pecking order theory is superior for explaining capital structure changes. By including a discussion of pecking order theory in the capital structure unit, students will be exposed to a broad base of both theory and practice that will enable them to better understand how important financing decisions are made. In addition to the traditional discussion of the impact of taxes, financial distress, and agency costs upon capital structure decisions, students will gain insight to how management motivations and market perceptions also impact these decisions. Students will readily appreciate the concern managers have regarding the reporting requirements required to access capital markets. They will also be able to explain why observed practice does not seem to always follow theory.

Furthermore, the addition of the pecking order theory into the basic debate about capital structure provides one more opportunity for critical thinking to occur. For example, the instructor can show how the debt ratios of leading companies, in particular industries, differ from the so-called industry averages to which most companies are usually compared during a cross-sectional financial analysis. Thus, a given ratio (such as a debt ratio only half the industry average) might be argued as a 'good' thing (since the firm has a large supply of financial slack and financial flexibility) rather than as a point of concern (the firm has opportunity costs due to not making efficient use of debt). Students will have to critically evaluate that particular condition to judge which conclusion is correct.

To summarize, by studying the pecking order theory in conjunction with trade-off theory, students will have a more all-round exposure to optimal capital structure. We also briefly look at the important differences between the two theories.

Comparison of Trade-off and Pecking Order Theory Traits

	TRADE-OFF THEORY		PECKING ORDER THEORY
1.	Conforms with value-maximizing construct	1.	Considers managerial motivations
2.	Assumes a relatively static capital structure	2.	Allows for a dynamic capital structure
3.	Considers the influence of taxes, transaction costs and financial distress	3.	Considers the influence of financial slack and availability of positive-NPV projects
4.	Ignores the impact of capital market 'signals'	4.	Acknowledges capital market 'signals'
5.	Ignores concerns regarding proprietary data	5.	Acknowledges proprietary data concerns
6.	Cannot explain many real-world practices	6.	Explains many real-world practices

SUMMARY

Capital structures refers to the mix of different sources of long terms funds such as debt, preference capital and equity capital in the total capitalization of a company. There are difference of opinion on the relationship between capital structure, cost of capital and valuation.

According to the NI approach overall cost of capital continuously decreases as and when the debt content is increased in the capital structure. So optimum capital structure exists when the firm borrows maximum.

NOI is just opposite to NI approach and argues that capital structure is irrelevant. According to the theory, Ko depends on business risk, which is assumed to be constant. So, K_o does not change when leverage is changed.

The MM approach to capital structure is akin to that of NOI approach and argues that capital structure is irrelevant.

According to the traditional approach, Ko decreases with the leverage in the beginning, then reaches the minimum point and rises thereafter. So optimum capital structure exists according to the theory. Thus traditional theory strikes a balances between NI and NOI approach.

Thus, by going through the various theories, we can conclude that there is no unanimity regarding the relationship between leverage and the cost of capital.

TRY YOURSELF

1. What is the relationship between leverage and cost of capital according to NI and NOI approach?
2. What are the main propositions of MM approach?
3. There is nothing like optimum capital structure for a firm. Critically evaluate the statement.
4. Write briefly a note on the arbitrage process.
5. Briefly explain the traditional approach of capital structure.
6. What do you mean by appropriate capital structure? What are the features ?
7. Explain the factors that determine the capital structure for a firm.

Management of Profits/ Dividend Policy

15

Objectives

After studying this chapter, you should be able to :

1 Explain the meaning of dividend policy of management of profits.

2 Discuss the different types of dividend policies, advantages and dangers of stable dividend policy.

3 Understand the factors that influence a firm's dividend policy.

4 Explain the forms of dividend payment.

5 Understand what is stock dividend? Reasons for issue, advantages to shareholders and company, disadvantages to shareholders and the company.

6 Give the meaning of stock split.

7 Compare bonus share and stock split.

8 Give the reasons for stock split.

INTRODUCTION

Finance is the life-blood of business, without which a firm cannot promote, maintain and expand and achieve its predetermined objective. Whether it is big, medium or small it needs finance. Profit is the primary motivating force for any economic activity, a business enterprise essentially being an economic organization, it has to maximise the welfare of its stakeholders. To this end, the business undertaking has to earn profit from its operations. Profit is the excess of revenue over expenses on conducting operations. In fact, profits are useful intermediate beacon towards which a firm's capital should be directed.[1] In this connection McAlpine rightly remarked that profit cannot be ignored since it is both, a measure of the success of business and the means of its survival and growth.[2] To quote Bradly, "if an enterprise fails to make profit, capital invested is eroded and if this situations, prolongs the enterprise ultimately ceases to exist.[3] A well organised profit planning programme will help towards maintaining a level of profit, which will ensure the concentration of the business and fulfillment of other responsibilities. Certainly, profit growth coupled with high level of profit and the ability to maintain reasonable profit will help towards.[4]

(i)   Ensuring that shareholders receive an adequate dividend;

(ii) Preserving the assets worth of the business;

(iii) Generating a sufficient cash flow out of profits to provide capital for expansion; and

(iv) Providing funds for research, and development of new and improved products to replace the existing products before they decline.

MANAGEMENT OF PROFITS

From the point of view of dividend decision it is better to call management of profits as management of earnings. Earnings mean net earnings available to equity shareholders from where a firm actually declares dividends or retain profits for financing of investment opportunities.

Net earnings = Operating Profit - (Interest + Tax + Preference Dividend)

MEANING OF MANAGEMENT OF EARNINGS

Management of earnings means, how the earnings of a firm are determined and how they are utilised or appropriated or allocated or distributed. In other words, how the business firm apportions their earnings is between dividends and retentions for financing of investment opportunities. Retention of earnings's also known as plough back of profits. Management of earnings is an important finance activity of a business undertaking. Since proper management of earnings helps to maximise shareholder's wealth. Particularly in Joint Stock companies where owners are different from the management team, who are selected / appointed by owners. Usually management team or Board of Directors (BOD's) do not distribute the total net earnings to the shareholders as dividends. They may retain a part of it for financing of investment opportunities or expansion programmes by keeping future growth of the firm in mind. Management of earnings policy must maximise value of the firm, thereby maximise benefits to its owners. On the other hand improper retained earnings and absence of financial control measures are the indicators of inefficient management of earnings that may not help to maximise value of the firm, but they may lead to the liquidation of the company.

DIVIDEND POLICY

As we have seen in the above, management of earnings means allocation of earnings among dividends and plough of profits. The term 'dividend' refers to that portion of company's net earnings that is paid out to the equity shareholders (not for preference shareholders, since they are entitled to have a fixed rate of dividend). Dividend policy of a firm decides the portion of earnings is to be paid as dividends to ordinary shareholders and the portion that is ploughed back in the firm for investment purpose. The total net earnings of equity may be paid as dividends (100% dividend payout ratio), which may consequently result in slower growth and lower market price or a part of net earnings may be paid as dividends, higher capital gains and higher market price. When a company uses a part of its net earnings for dividend payments then, the remaining earnings are retained. Thus, there is an inverse relationship between retained earnings and payment of cash dividend—the larger the cash dividends and lesser the retention, smaller the cash dividends and larger retentions. Hence, the alternative use of net earnings or net profit dividends and retained earnings are competitive and conflicting.

Dividend decision affects the value of the firm. The cash available for the payment of dividends is affected by the firm's investment decision, and financing decision. A decision, which is related to investment leads to less cash available for payment of dividends. Thus, there is a relation between investment decision and financing decision. Distribution of net earnings between dividends and retention would obviously affect owners' wealth. Now the company is in dilemma which alternative is consistent to maximise shareholders wealth. The firm has to pay dividends to shareholders if dividends lead to the maximisation of wealth for them, otherwise the company should retain them for financing profitable investment opportunities.

TYPES OF DIVIDEND POLICIES

Dividend decision of a firm is taken after taking into consideration, its operating and financial condition. When there are variations in these conditions the firm may require to adopt the one that is suitable for the present conditions. What are the different types of dividend policies available to the financial manager? The types of dividend policies are as follows :

Stable Dividend Policy: The term "stability" refers to the consistency or lack of variability in the stream of dividend payments. In more precise terms, stable dividend means payment of a certain minimum amount of dividend regularly. There are three distinct forms of stability, they are:

(a) *Constant Dividend Per Share:* A company that follows this policy will pay a fixed amount per share as dividend. For example Rs. 2 as a dividend on the face value of share of Rs. 10 each. The level of earnings would not affect this policy or the dividend payments. This type of dividend policy is more suitable for the company whose earnings are stable over a number of years. Stability of dividend does not mean stagnation in dividend payout. In fact, the prime feature of this policy is to study positive change.

(b) *Constant Payout Ratio:* The ratio of dividend to earnings is known as payout ratio. In other words, dividend per share is divided by earnings per share to get dividend payout ratio. It is also known as constant percentage of net earnings. In this policy a fixed percentage of earnings are paid as dividends each year. Here the ratio is fixed or constant, but dividend per share varies according to the fluctuations in the earnings.

For example, it a company follows a 30 per cent payout ratio it means for every one rupee of net earnings, Re. 0.30 ,paid as dividends. Assume if a company earned Rs. 10 last year and Rs. 15 in the current year. Then the dividend amount for last year is Rs. 3 (10 x 30/100) and Rs. 4.5 (15 x 30/100) for the current year. The relationship between EPS and DPS is shown in figure 15.1.

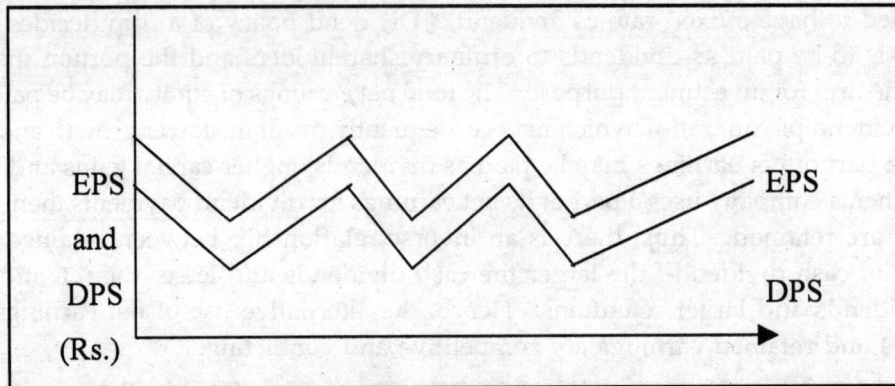

Figure 15.1

This policy is suitable for a company that is not confident getting stable earnings.

(c) *Stable Rupee Dividend Plus Extra Dividend:* Under this policy the management fixes the minimum dividend per share to reduce the possibility of net paying dividend. An extra dividend is paid in the years of prosperity. This type of policy is more suitable to the company having minimum earnings and over the minimum, the earnings may fluctuate.

Advantages of Stable Dividend Policy

A stable dividend policy is advantageous for both the company and the shareholders because:

1) *Building Confidence Among Investors:* Payment of stable dividends may help the company in creating and building confidence among shareholders with regard to regularity. A company that follows stable dividend policy will not change the amount of dividends, even though there are any variations in its earnings. Thus, when the earnings of a firm go down, the company does not cut the amount of dividend. But to its presents investors,a very bright future, and thus, gains confidence of the shareholders.

2) *Investors Desire for Current Income:* A company may have many investor categories, of them a few groups of investors depend on dividend income to meet their portion of living expenses. Investor group may include old and retired persons etc., who require the current income. Their living expenses are fairly stable from the period to period increase over time. Therefore, sharp changes in dividend income may create a need to sell shares to get funds in order to meet current expenses and vice versa. Sale of securities involves inconvenience and it involves transaction costs. Stable dividend policy avoids sale of securities, which automatically avoids inconvenience and transaction cost, hence, such investors may prefer stable dividends.

3) *Information about Firms Profitability:* There is another reason for adopting a stable dividend policy that is, investors are thought to use dividends and the fluctuation in dividends as a source of information about the company's profitability. A growth in dividends indicates improved earnings prospects, a downward trend in dividends implies less earnings and stable dividends means unchanged prospects. In other words, the dividend decision of a

firm resolves uncertainty in the minds of investors. Variation in dividend policy cannot resolve uncertainty in the investor minds. Hence, companies may tries to change dividend policy in response to a certain long-term changes in future prospects.

4) *Institutional Investors Requirements:* Companies shares are not only purchased by individuals but also institutional investors like LIC companies, GIC's, MF's, educational institutes and social institutes. Normally, companies are very much interested to have these institutional investors in the list of their investors. Generally, this type of institutional investors have large size of their ingestible funds, these funds will be invested in the shares of those companies that have the record of paying stable dividends. So, to attract institutional investors a firm may prefer to adopt a regular or stable dividend policy.

5) *Raising Additional Finances:* This is another advantage to the company that is following a stable dividend policy, in raising external finance. Shares of this type of company appear as investment rather than a speculation. Investors, who invest in this type of company's shares hold them for a long period of time and their loyalty and goodwill towards the firm increase by adoption of stable dividend policy. If the company wants to raise additional funds by issuing shares to the public, they would be more receptive to that offer. For example recently in beginning of the year 2004, the public issue of ONGC, ICICI, IPTCL, GAIL are over subscribed. Thus, rising of additional funds required by the firm becomes very easy, even with high premium.

6) *Stability in Market Price of Shares:* Other things remains unchanged, the market price of shares varies with the stability in dividend rates. The share price of a firm having stable dividend policy may not have wide fluctuation on even if the earnings of the firms less than the past year. Thus, this is good for investors and the company.

7) *Easy Availability of Debt Funds:* If the company feels raising additional funds by issue of equity shares, leads to loss of control over the firm, it can easily raise funds from debt source. Because, the firm has been paying dividends regularly with stability, it becomes an assurance to the debenture holders, financial institutions and public (to invest in public deposits).

Limitations of Stable Dividend Policy

In spite of the above discussed advantages the stable dividend policy suffers from certain limitations. They are :

(a) *Difficult to Change:* Once a stable dividend policy is established, it cannot be changed without affecting investors' attitude and financial position of the company, in the minds of investor.

(b) *Adverse Effect on Market Price of Share:* As we have discussed in the advantages, about the investors desire for current income to meet their living expenses, the investors who prefer or depend on stable dividends, may feel bad, when the firm cuts dividend, consequently they may sell some of their shares to fulfill the gap between expected dividend and the actual dividend received (negative dividend. This leads to the reduction in the share price. Hence, directors have to maintain stability in dividends, in lean years.

(c) *Long-Run Effect on Company:* When a firm maintains stable dividend policy in lean years over a period of time with borrowed funds it may lead to death in the long-run.

FACTORS INFLUENCING DIVIDEND POLICY

Maximisation of owners' wealth is the objective of the financial managers job. Whatever decision he/she takes, whether it is investment decision, financing decision or dividend decision, he/she has to maximise value of the firm. There is a positive relation between dividend policy of a firm and value of the firm, that is payment of dividend affects the value (increases) of the firm. Dividend policy means, the formation of a policy by the company regarding the payment of dividend from profits to ordinary shareholders year to year. It determines the ratio between dividend and retained earnings. Then, what type of dividend policy do firms adopt ? Whether it is 20 per cent, or 40 per cent or 80 per cent or any other percentage of earnings available to shareholders? The two important dimensions of dividend policy are, what should be the dividend payout ratio ? How stable should the dividends be over time ? The policy relating to dividend payout ratio and earnings retention varies not only from industry to industry but also among companies within a given industry and within a company from time to time. These variations are because of factors influencing/affecting dividend policy. But financial executives have to make a balanced judgement between the financial needs of the company and desires of the shareholders. In other words, financial executive have to determine optimum dividend policy that should strike the balance between current dividends and future growth which maximises the price of the firm's shares.[5] The dividend payout ratio of a firm should be determined with reference to two objectives - *one* maximisation of shareholders' wealth and *second* providing sufficient funds to finance growth. The determinants of dividend policy will vary from firm to firm. The following are the various factors that have a bearing on the dividend policy.

1) *Nature of Business:* The nature of business has an important bearing on the dividend policy. The industrial units that are having stability of earnings may formulate (adopt) stable or a more consistent dividend policy than other, that are having unstable earnings, because they can predict easily their earnings. Firms that are involved in necessities suffer less from stable incomes than the firms that are involved in luxury goods. The industries / firms that are having stable earnings can adopt stable or high dividend policy, while the other firms that are having instable earnings should follow a variable or low dividend policy.

2) *Age of Company:* The age of company has more impact on distribution of profits as dividends. A newly started and growing company may require much of its earnings for financing expansion programs or growth requirements and it may follow rigid dividend policy, where in, most of the earnings are retained while an old company with good track record and good name in the public can formulate a clear cut and more consistent dividend policy. This type of companies may even pay 100 per cent dividend payout ratio and the required amount for growth can be raised from the public.

3) *Liquidity Position of Company:* Generally dividends are paid in the form of cash, hence, it entails, cash. Although, a firm may have sufficient profits to declare dividends, but it may not have sufficient cash to pay dividends. Thus, availability of cash and sound financial position of the firm is an important factor in taking dividend decision. The liquidity of a company depends very much on the investment and financial decisions of a firm, while in turn determining the rate of expansion and the manner of financing. If cash position of a firm is weak, stock dividend will be better and if cash position is good it can go for payment of dividend by cash.

4) *Equity Shareholders Preference for Current Income:* Legally, the Board of Directors has discretion to decide the distribution of the earnings of a firm. The shareholders who are legal owners of the firm appoint the (BOD's). Hence, directors have to take into consideration owners' preferences, while deciding dividend payment. Shareholders' preference for current dividends or capital gains, that is, depend on their economic status and the effect of tax

differential on dividends and capital gains. When shareholders' have more preference in current dividend than capital gains, the firm may be required to follow liberal dividend policy, on the other hand if shareholders have preferred capital gains (it may be due to tax or economically sound) than the current dividend, then the firm may be required to retain more earnings.

5) *Requirements of Institutional Investors:* Institutional investors like LICs, GICs and Mutual funds (UTI), have investment policy, which says that these type of institutes have to invest only in companies that have a continuous dividend payment record with stability. These purchase large blocks of shares for relatively, to hold a long period of time. Hence, they represent a significant force in the financial markets, and their demand for company's securities may increase the share price and there by owners' wealth. To attract institutional investors firms may require to follow stable dividend policy. Apart from theoretical postulates for the desirability of stable dividends, there are also many empirical studies, classic among them being that of Lintner[5], to support the viewpoint that companies pursue a stable dividend policy. Most firms are in favour of stable dividend per share but they are very careful not to raise dividends per share a level that can safely be sustained in, the future. This cautious creep up of dividends per share results in, stable dividend per share pattern during fluctuating earnings per share periods, and a rising step function pattern of dividends per share during increasing earning per share periods.[6]

6) *Legal Rules:* Legal rules restrictions are significant as they provide framework within which dividend policy is formulated. In other words, dividend policy of a firm has to be evolved within the legal framework and rules and regulations. The legal rules have to do with capital impairment rule, net profits and insolvency rule.

    Capital Impairment Rule: First these provisions require that, the dividend can be paid from earnings either from current years earnings or from past years earnings and be reflected in the earned surplus. If firm pays dividend out of capital, that adversely affects the security of its lenders. The purpose of this rule is to protect creditors (preference shareholders and creditors of the firm) by providing sufficient equity base because they have originally relied on that base. Therefore, the financial manager should keep in mind the legal rules while declaring dividends.

    Net Profits: This rule is essentially a result of the earlier rule. A firm can pay cash dividends within the limits of current profits plus accumulate balance of retained earnings. According to Sec. 205 of the companies Act, 1956, dividends shall be declared or paid only from current profits or past profits after recovery of depreciation'. But Central Govt. is empowered to all (only in public interest) any company to pay dividends for any financial year out of profits of the company without providing depreciation. A firm can take profits of past years if the current year's profits are not sufficient to maintain stable dividend policy. If there are any losses that are to be carried forward, they should be set apart from current years earnings before declaration of dividends. So financial manager has to strong within the boundaries, at the same time has to consider many financial variables and constraints in deciding the amount that is to be paid as dividends.

    Insolvency Rule: A firm is said to be insolvent in two cases. *One*, in a legal sense, the recorded value of liabilities exceeding the recorded value of assets, or *second*, as in a technical sense, as the firm's inability to pay its creditors as obligations came due. If the firm is insolvent in either sense, it is prohibited the payment of dividends. The rationale of this rule is to protect the creditors.

7) *Contractual Requirements:* Generally lenders may put conditions in a bond indenture or loan agreement often includes a restriction of the payment of dividend. This is done to protect their interests when the firm is experiencing low liquidity or profitability. The restrictions may be in three forms. *Firstly*, firms may be prohibited from paying dividends

in excess to a certain percentage say 10 per cent. *Secondly*, a ceiling in terms of net profits that may be used for dividend payment may be laid down. Say only 50 per cent of net profits or a given absolute amount of net profits can be paid as dividends. *Finally*, dividends may be restricted by insisting upon a minimum of earnings to be retained. Reinvestment reduces debt equity ratio, which enhances the margin of pillow for the lenders. Therefore, keeping in mind all the restrictions of lenders dividend declaration should be done.

8) *Financial Needs of the Company:* This is one of the key factors, which influence the dividend policy of a firm. Financial needs means funds required for foreseeable future investment. The required funds may be determined with the help of long-term financial forecasts. A firm that has sufficient profitable investment opportunity, should follow low dividend payout ratio. On the other hand, a firm that has no profitable investment opportunities or few investment opportunities adopts high dividend payout ratio policy (that low retention) because owners' can reinvest dividends elsewhere at higher rate of return then the firm can do, and nominal retention of profit is required to replace the modernize firm's assets.

9) *Access to the Capital Market (External Sources):* Access to the capital market means the firms ability to raise funds from the capital market. A company, which has easy access to the capital market provides that flexibility in deciding dividend policy. Easy access is possible only to the companies that are well established and hence here a profit track record. Generally dividend policy and investment decisions are interrelated, but in this situation they are independent. The management may tempt to declare a high rate of dividend that attract investors and maintain existing shareholders.

On the other hand, a firm that has difficulty in accessing capital market to raise required funds, will not be able to pay more dividends. It has to depend on internal funds, so management should follow a conservative dividend policy by maintaining a low rate of dividend and plough back a sizeable portion of profits to face any contingency. Likewise, the lending financial institutions advance loans in stiffer terms, it may be desirable to rely on internal sources of financing and accordingly conservative dividend policy should be pursued.

10) *Control Objective:* Control over the company is also an important factor, which influences dividend policy. When a firm distributes more earning as dividends in the form of cash it reduces its cash position. As a result, the firm will have to issue shares to the public to raise funds required to finance investment opportunities that leads to loss of control, since, the existing shareholders will have to share control with new owners. Financing investment projects by way of internal source avoids, loss of control. Hence, if the shareholders and management of the firms are reluctant to dilution of control, thus the firm should retain more earnings for investment programmes, by following conservative dividend policy.

11) *Inflation:* Inflation is the state of economy in which the prices of products or goods have been increasing. Inflation is a factor that influences dividend policy indirectly. Indian accounting system is based on historical costs. The funds accumulated from depreciation may not be sufficient to replace the absolute asset or equipment, since depreciation is provided based on historical costs. Consequently, to replace assets and equipment, firm has to depend upon retained earnings, this leads to the payment of low dividend, during inflation period.

12) *Dividend Policy of Competitors:* Keeping one eye on competitors' dividend policy is very important. If the firm wants to retain the existing shareholders or it want to maintain share price in the market, and if it is planning to raise funds from public for expansion programs, it has to pay dividends at par with its competitors. Hence, it is one of the factors that influence dividend policy of a firm.

13) *Past Dividend Rates of the Company:* This is the factor that influences the dividend policy of an existing company (that has already paid dividends). Owners' and prospective investors prefer stability in dividends. Stability of dividends means the payment of dividend regularly, at a constant dividend per share (it may be a fixed percentage on book value or a fixed percentage on earnings available to equity share holders). Generally firms' tries to maintain stability in dividends that is based on past dividend rates of the company. Hence, directors will have to keep in mind the past dividend rates.

14) *Others:* Apart from the above discussed, there are some other factors, which influence dividend policy of a firm, such as Trade Cycles, Corporate taxation policy, attitude of investors group and repayment of loan.

FORMS OF DIVIDENDS

Dividend is the portion of earnings available to equity shareholders that equally (per share bias) is distributed among the shareholders. General practice is to pay dividends in cash, this form may take place when the cash is available or during liquidity of the company. Sometimes firms may declare dividends in the form of Scrip, bond, stock and property dividends. The following discussion deals with the different forms of dividends.

1) *Cash Dividend:* Generally many companies pay dividends in the form of cash. But payment of dividend in the form of cash requires enough cash in the bank or in hands. In other words, there should not be any shortage of cash for payment of dividends. Sufficient cash is available only when a company prepares cash budget to estimate the required amount for the period for which the budget is prepared. If the company finds any shortage of cash, it should make arrangements to borrow funds. But it may be difficult to prepare a cash budget with the expected amount needed for payment of dividends.

2) *Scrip Dividend:* In this form of dividends, the equity shareholders are issued transferable promissory notes for a shorter maturity period that may or may not be interest bearing. It is a simple payment of dividends in the form of promissory notes. Payment of dividend in this form takes place only when the firm is suffering from shortage of cash or weak liquidity position. Payment of dividends in the form of cash is justifiable only when the company has earned profits and it will take some time to convert current assets into cash.

3) *Bond Dividend:* Both scrip dividend and bond dividend are same, but they differ in terms of maturity. Bond dividends caries longer maturity whereas, scrip dividend carries shorter maturity. The effect of both forms of dividends on the company is the same. Bond dividend bears interest.

4) *Property Dividend:* The name itself suggests that payment of dividend takes place in the form of property. In other words, payment of dividends in the form of assets. This form of dividends takes place only when a firm has assets that are no longer necessary in the operation of business and shareholders are ready to accept dividend in the form of assets. This form of dividend payment is not popular in India.

5) *Stock Dividend (Bonus Shares):* Stock dividend is the payment of additional shares of common stocks to the ordinary shareholders. In other words, distribution of bonus shares to the stockholders instead of cash dividend. It is known as stock dividend in USA to the existing shareholder. Bonus shares are shares issued to the existing shareholders as a result of capitalisation of resources. The declaration of bonus shares will increase the paid up share capital and reduces retention of earnings. But there would not be any change in net worth. Issue of bonus shares increases the number of outstanding shares. Distribution of bonus shares is done proportionately. Payment of dividend in the form of bonus share does not affect the wealth of owners', since earnings per share and market price per share

will fall proportionately. When there is no wealth maximisation why do firms pay dividend in the form of bonus shares ?

REASONS OR OBJECTIVES FOR ISSUING THE STOCK DIVIDEND

Payment of dividend through issue of bonus share is a financial gimmick, since it will not affect the owners' wealth. Payment of dividend through issue of bonus share by a firm takes place due to following reasons or objectives.[7]

♦   Issue of bonus share tends to bring the market price per share within a more popular range.

♦   It promotes more active trading, since the issue increases the number of outstanding shares.

♦   It reduces the nominal rate of dividend, which may attract the impression of profiteering.

♦   It increases the paid up share capital and the company may achieve more respectable size in the eyes of the investors.

♦   Shareholders regard a bonus issue as a firm indication that the prospects of the firm as brightened and they can reasonably look for an increase in total dividends.

♦   It improves prospects of raising additional funds. In recent (2004) Infosys has issued 3 bonus shares for every one-bonus share to the existing shareholders.

Advantage of Issue of Bonus Share

As we have read in the above discussion, that issue of bonus shares do not affect the wealth of shareholders. But in practices, it carries some advantages for both, to the company and to the shareholders.

a)   *Advantages to the Company:* The following are some of the advantages enjoyed by the issuing company.

   •   *Conversion of Cash / Maintenance of Liquidity Portion:* Issue of bonus share/stock will not reduce the cash position of firm. In other words, payment of dividend by way of stocks does not affect the cash position of the company. Through this form of dividends firms will be able to retain earnings and at the same time it can satisfy shareholders. So it can maintain liquidity position.

   •   *Only way to pay Dividends under Financial Difficulty and Contractual Restrictions:* Some times companies when, there are no profits, will issue bonus shares just to justify the shareholders. Payment of dividend in the form of bonus shares at the difficult times does not convey the company's position to the shareholders and the investing community. This form of dividend payment is also necessary when there are restrictions from the loan granters to pay dividends in the form of cash. Hence, under the financial difficulty or contractual constraints from creditors to cash dividend, issue of stock dividend is needed to retain the confidence of the shareholders in the firm.

   •   *Attractive Share Price:* Generally higher share price is attractive to investors, but it is not for small investors. Issue of bonus shares reduces market price of share and attracts small investors. Therefore, many companies follow issue dividends in the form of bonus shares.

   •   *Enhances Prestige:* Though the payment of dividend by way of issue of stock, the company increases its borrowing capacity. The company, which pays stock dividend will increase credit standing in the market and it also increases the borrowing capacity of the company in the eyes of lending institutions.

- *Widening the Share for Market:* A company that is interested in widening ownership shares, may pay dividend by way of issue of stock. Because of increased prestige of the firm, there will be a good demand for the share of the company.

- *Availability of Funds for Expansion Programme*: Through the retention of profits, expansion programmes can be financed. As the retention takes place through the issue of stock dividend it becomes a permanent part of the capital structure of a company. Hence, it helps for expansion programmes.

b) *Advantages to Owners' or Ordinary Shareholders:* The following are some of the advantages enjoyed by the owners.[8]

- *Tax Savings:* Receipt of cash dividend involves payment of tax according to ordinary tax rates. By receipt of dividends in the form of stock dividend, there is no payment of tax.

- *Indication of Future Benefits:* As we have seen in the above features, issue of bonus shares is an indication of profiteering. With payment of stock dividend the existing owner receives more shares. If the company maintains the present rate of dividend, the shareholders receive more income since their number of shares are increased.

- *Psychological Value:* Receipt of bonus shares may have a favourable psychological impact on the investors.

Disadvantages of Stock Dividend/Bonus Share

Apart from the above advantages, payment of dividend by way of stock dividends will have the following disadvantages.

a) *Disadvantages for the Company*

- Payment of dividend in the form of stock dividend is costly when compared to cash form of dividends. Stock dividend invokes administrative costs, like printing certificates, and posting them to lakhs of shareholders.

- The most important demerit of issue of stock dividend is adjusting earnings per share (EPS) and price earnings ratio (PE Ratio). Investment analysts do not adjust the EPS share for small issue of bonus shares, as a recent PE Ratio would decrease since the measured growth in earning per share will be less than the true growth based on adjusted EPS.

- It may prevent new investors from becoming the shareholders of the firm.

- It may lead to misuse of management power, since there is no dilution of control.

b) *Disadvantages for Shareholders*

- Disappointment of shareholders, who prefer dividend in the form of cash.

- Shareholders wealth remains unaffected—bonus shares represent simply a division of corporate pie into a large number of pieces.[9]

- Stack dividend or bonus shares issue lowers the market value of existing shares too.

- Less security to investors, done to reduction in reserves

STOCK DIVIDEND (BONUS SHARE) AND STOCK SPLITS (SHARES)

Stock dividend or bonus shares are issued by firm to existing shareholders by conversion of reserves into capitalisation. Stock splits is an increase in the number of shares outstanding by reducing the face value of the stock. For example, shares of Rs. 10 may split into two shares of Rs. 5 each.

Comparison between Bonus Issue (Stock dividend) and Stock Split

a) *Par Value of Share:* Is unchanged in issue of bonus share, whereas it is reduced in stock split.

b) *Capitalisation of Reserves:* Capitalisation (part of reserves) take place in issue of bonus shares, whereas there is no capitalisation in stock split.

c) *Shareholders' Proportion:* There is no change in the shareholders' proportion, it remains unchanged in both cases (bonus issue as well as stock split).

d) *Book Value, Earnings and Market Price Per Share:* In both cases book value, earnings and market price per share decline.

e) *Market Price Per Share:* The market price per share is brought within a popular trading range, where as in stock split it is brought within a more popular trading range.

Reasons for Stock Split

The following are the reasons for splitting of a firm's ordinary (equity) shares.[10]

1) *To Make Share Trading Attractive:* The prime reason of stock split is to reduce the market price to the share, to attract small investors. In other words, firm provides broader and stable market for its stock. With stock split, the shares are placed in a more popular trading range that helps in providing marketability and liquidity to the firm's shares.

2) *Indication of Higher Profits in the Future:* Share split sends wrong signals to the investors that the firm is expecting higher profits in near future. Blue chip or high growth firm's share price (market price) goes up very fast, that puts the firm's shares out of the popular trading range. To put shares in a popular range firms split shares periodically.

3) *To give Higher Dividends to Shareholders:* Share split is the only way through which a company can increase or reduce the cash dividend per share proportionately. However, the total dividends of a shareholder increases after a share split.

Reverse Split

It is quite opposite to the share split, where a company reduces the number of outstanding shares to increase the market price per share. For example, a company has 8 lakhs outstanding shares (equity) of Rs. 10 each. If company declares a reserve split, two for four. Now the company will have 4 lakh shares of Rs. 40 per share.

DIVIDEND POLICY AND SHARE VALUE

There are conflicting opinions as far as the impact of dividend decision on the value of the firm. According to one school of thought, dividends are relevant to the valuation of the firm. Others opine that dividends does not affect the value of the firm and market price per share of the company.

RELEVANT THEORY

If the choice of the dividend policy affects the value of a firm, it is considered as relevant. In that case a change in the dividend payout ratio will be followed by a change in the market value of the firm. If the dividend is relevant there must be an optimum payout ratio. If the dividend is irrelevant, there must be an optimum payout ratio. Optimum payout ratio is that which gives highest market value per share.

WALTER'S MODEL (RELEVANT)

Prof. James E Walter argues that the choice of dividend payout ratio almost always affects the value of the firm Prof. Walter has very scholarly studied the significance of the relationship between internal rate of return (R) and cost of capital (K) in determining optimum dividend policy which maximizes the wealth of shareholders.

Walters models is based on the following assumptions

1) The firm finances its entire investments by means of retained earning only.

2) Internal rate or return (R) and cost of capital (K) of the firm remains constant.

3) The firms earning are either distributed as dividend or reinvested internally.

4) Beginning earnings and dividends of the firm will never change.

5) The firm has a very long or infinite life.

$$P = \frac{D + r/k(E-D)}{K}$$

P= Market price per share.

D= Dividend per share

E= Earning per share

R= Interest rate per capital

K= Cost of capital.

According to the theory, the optimum dividend policy depends on the relationship between the firm's internal rate of return and cost of capital. If R>K , the firms should retain the entire earnings.

Walter's view on optimum dividend payout ratio can be summarized as below :

a) *Growth Firms:* **(R>K):** The firms having R>K may be referred to as growth opportunities. These firms naturally can earn a return which is more than what shareholders could earn on their own. So optimum payout ratio for growth firm is 0%.

b) *Normal Firms* **(R = K):** If R is equal to K the firm is known as normal firm. These firms earn a rate of return which is equal to that of shareholders in this case dividend policy will not have any influence on the price per share. So there is nothing like optimum payout ratio for a normal firm. All the payout ratios are optimum.

c) *Declining Firms* **(R<K):** If the company earns a return which is less than, what the shareholders can earn on their investments, it is known as declining firm. Here it should not make any sense to retain the earnings. So entire earnings optimum payout ratio for a declining firms is 100%.

So according to walter the optimum payout ratio is either 0% (when R>K) or 100% (when R<K).

CRITICISMS

Walter's model based on certain assumptions, which are true for walter but not true in the real world. The following are the limitations of the Walter's model.

1) Walter assumes that there is no external financing. When R>K , the firm must issue additional security and finance its profitable investments, if the company uses only retained earnings, all the profitable investments cannot be undertaken. So the investment decision of the firm will be sub-optimum.

2) Constant R, Internal rate of return cannot remain same. It actually diminishes as and when we make more and more investments.

3) Constant K, Cost of capital of a company cannot remain same. Risk of the company definitely changes with additional investments of retained earnings.

Illustration 1: Given the following information about Sunrise Industries Ltd. Show the effect of the dividend policy on the market price per share, using Walter's model.

EPS= Rs.8

Cost of capital (K) = 12%

Assumed rate of return

a) 15%

b) 10%

c) 12%

Solution:

To show the effect of different dividend policies on the shareholders of the firm for 15% and 12%, let us consider 0%, 25%, 50%, 75% and 100% payout ratios.

I when R>K (15>12)

At 0% payout ratio (dividend=0)

$$P = \frac{D + R/K(E-D)}{K}$$

$$= \frac{0 + 0.15/0.12(8-0)}{0.12}$$

= Rs. 83.33

At 25% payout ratio.

$$P = \frac{2 + 0.15/0.12(8-2)}{0.12}$$

= Rs. 79.16

At 50% payout ratio

$$P = \frac{4 + 0.15/0.12(8-4)}{0.12}$$

= Rs. 75.

At 75% payout ratio

$$P = \frac{6 + 0.15/0.12(8-6)}{0.12}$$

= Rs. 70.83

At 100% payout ratio

$$P = \frac{8 + 0.15/0.12(8-8)}{0.12}$$

= 66.67

Therefore, when R>K, price share will be maximum at 0% payout ratio. Price per share decreases as and when payout ratio is increased.

II when R<K (10%<12%)

At 0% payout ratio

$$P = \frac{0 + 0.10/0.12(8-0)}{0.12}$$

= Rs. 55.55

At 25% payout ratio

$$P = \frac{2 + 0.10/0.12(8-2)}{0.12}$$

= Rs. 58.33

At 50% payout ratio

$$P = \frac{4 + 0.10/0.12(8-4)}{0.12}$$

= Rs. 61.11

At 75% payout ratio

$$P = \frac{6 + 0.10/0.12(8-6)}{0.12}$$

= Rs. 63.88

At 100% payout ratio

$$P = \frac{8 + 0.10/0.12(8-8)}{0.12}$$

= Rs. 66.66

Therefore, when R<K, price per will be maximum at 100% payout ratio. Price per share increases as and when the payout ratio is increased.

III when R=K (12%=12%)

At 0% payout ratio

$$P = \frac{0 + 0.12/0.12(8-0)}{0.12}$$

= Rs. 66.66

At 25% payout ratio

$$P = \frac{2 + 0.12/0.12(8-2)}{0.12}$$

= Rs. 66.66

At 50% payout ratio

$$P = \frac{4 + 0.12/0.12(8-4)}{0.12}$$

= Rs. 66.66

At 75% payout ratio

$$P = \frac{6 + 0.12/0.12(8-6)}{0.12}$$

= Rs. 66.66

At 100% payout ratio

$$P = \frac{8 + 0.12/0.12(8-8)}{0.12}$$

= Rs. 66.66

Therefore, when R=K, price per share remains the same at all payout ratios. So, there is no one-payout ratio, which is optimum.

GORDON'S MODEL

Another theory, which contents that dividends are relevant, is the Gordon's model. This model which opines that dividend policy of a firm affects its value is based on the following

Assumptions.

a) The firm is an all equity firm (no debt).

b) There is no outside financing and all investments are financed exclusively by retained earnings.

c) Internal rate of return (R) of the firm remains constant.

d) Cost of capital (K) of the firm also remains same regardless of the changes in the risk complexion of the firm.

e) The firm derives its earnings in perpetuity.

f) The retention ratio (b) once decided upon is constant. Thus, the growth rate (g) is also constant ($g = b_r$).

g) K>g .

h) A corporate tax does not exist.

Gordon used the following formula to find out price per share

$$P = \frac{E_1(1-b)}{K - b_r}$$

P = price per share
K = cost of capital
E_1 = earnings per share
b = retention ratio
(1-b) = payout ratio

g = b_r growth rate. (r = internal rate of return)

According to Gordon, when R>K, the price per share increases as the dividend payout ratio decreases.

When R<K the price per share increases as the dividend payout ratio increases.

When R=K the prices per share remains unchanged in response to the change in the payout ratio.

Thus, Gordon's view on the optimum dividend payout ratio can be summarized as below:

1. The optimum payout ratio for a growth firm (R.K) is zero.

2. There is no optimum ratio for a normal firm (R = K).

3. Optimum payout ratio for a declining firm R<K is 100%.

Thus, the Gordon's Model's conclusions about dividend policy are similar to that of Walter. This similarity is due to the similarities of assumptions of both the models.

Bird in hand Argument

(Dividends and uncertainty)

Gordon revised this basic model later to consider risk and uncertainty. Gordon's model, like Walter's model, contends that dividend policy is relevant. According to Walter, dividend policy will not affect the price of the share when R=K. But Gordon goes one step ahead and argues that dividend policy affects the value of shares even when R=K. The crux of Gordon's argument is based on the following 2 assumptions.

(a) Investors are risk averse and

(b) They put a premium on a *certain* return and discount (penalise) uncertain return.

The investors are rational. Accordingly they want to avoid risk. The term risk refers to the possibility of not getting the return on investment. The payment of dividends now completely removes any chance of risk. But if the firm retains the earnings the investors can expect to get a dividend in the future. But the future dividend is uncertain both with respect to the amount as well as the timing. The rational investors, therefore, prefer current dividend to future dividend. Retained earnings are considered as risky by the investors. In case earnings are retained, the price per share would be adversely affected. This behaviour of investor is described as "**Bird in Hand Argument**". A bird in hand is worth two in bush. What is available today is more important than what may be available in the future. So the rational investors are willing to pay a higher price for shares on which more current dividends are paid. Therefore, the discount rate (K) increases with retention rate. This is shown below.

Thus Gordon concludes that dividend policy affects the values of the shares even in a situation where R=K

Illustration 2: If K= 11% and earnings per share is Rs.15. Calculate the price per share of Sushma Ltd. For r = 12%, 11% and 10% for the following levels of D/P ratios.

	D/P ratios	Retention ratio
1.	10%	90%
2.	30%	70%
3.	50%	50%

Solution:

I   If R>K (12% > 11%)

$$P = \frac{E_1(1-b)}{K - b_r}$$

1. D/P ratio of 10%. Retention ratio = 90%

$$P = \frac{15(1-0.9)}{0.11 - 0.9 \times 0.12}$$

= Rs. 750

2. D/P ratio of 30%. Retention ratio = 70%

$$P = \frac{15(1-0.7)}{0.11 - 0.7 \times 0.12}$$

= Rs. 173.08

3. D/P ratio of 50%. Retention ratio = 50%

$$P = \frac{15(1-0.5)}{0.11 - 0.5 \times 0.12}$$

= Rs. 125

II   **If R=K (11% = 11%)**

   a)   D/P ratio of 10%. Retention ratio = 90%

$$P = \frac{15(1-0.9)}{0.11-0.9\times0.11}$$

$$= \text{Rs. } 136.36$$

   b)   D/P ratio of 30%. Retention ratio = 70%

$$P = \frac{15(1-0.7)}{0.11-0.7\times0.11}$$

$$= \text{Rs. } 136.36$$

   c)   D/P ratio of 50%. Retention ratio = 50%

$$P = \frac{15(1-0.5)}{0.11-0.5\times0.11}$$

$$= \text{Rs. } 136.36$$

III   **If R<K (10% < 11%)**

   1.   D/P ratio of 10%. Retention ratio is 90%

$$P = \frac{15(1-0.9)}{0.11-0.9\times0.10}$$

$$= \text{Rs. } 75$$

   2.   D/P ratio of 30%. Retention ratio is 70%

$$P = \frac{15(1-0.7)}{0.11-0.7\times0.10}$$

$$= \text{Rs. } 112.50$$

   3.   D/P ratio 50%. Retention ratio = 50%

$$P = \frac{15(1-0.5)}{0.11-0.5\times0.10}$$

$$= \text{Rs. } 125$$

From the above it is clear that, when R>K, the price per share increases and the payout ratio decreases, if R=K price per share remains same at all payout ratios. When R<K, the price per share increases with the increases in the payout ratio.

MODIGLIANI-MILLER MODEL

Irrelevance theory

According to MM, the dividend policy of a firm is irrelevant, as it does not affect the wealth of shareholders. The model which is based on certain assumptions, sidelined the importance of the dividend policy and its effect thereof on the share price of the firm. According to the theory, the value of a firm depends solely on its earnings power resulting from the investment policy and not influenced by the manner in which its earnings are split between dividends and retained earnings.

Assumption

1.   *Capital markets are perfect:* Investors are rational as information is freely available, transaction cost are nil, securities are divisible and no investor can influence the market price of the share.

2.   *There are no taxes:* No difference between tax rates on divisible and capital gains.

3.   *The firm has a fixed investment policy:* Which will not change. So if the retained earnings are reinvested, there will not be any change in the risk of the firm. So K remains same.

4. *Floatation costs does not exist:*

The substance of MM arguments may be stated as below:

If the company retains the earnings instead of giving it out as dividends, the share holders enjoy capital appreciation, which is equal to the earnings, retained.

If the company distributes the earnings by the way of dividends instead of retention, the shareholders enjoy the dividend, which is equal to the amount by which his capital would have been appreciated had the company chosen to retain the earnings.

Hence, the division of earnings between dividends and retained earnings is irrelevant from the point of view of shareholders.

Criticisms

MM theory of division irrelevance is based on some assumptions. When these assumptions hold good, the conclusions derived by them are logically consistent and intuitively appealing. But the assumption will not hold water in the real world. So MM theory lacks practical relevance. The following are some of the limitations.

1. *Tax differentials:* MM's assumption that taxes does not exist is far from reality. Dividends are not taxed where as tax is levied on capital gains. So the shareholders may prefer dividend to capital gains.

2. *Floatation cost:* MM argue that payment of dividend and raising external funds are equivalent. This is not true in practice due to the presence of flotation costs. So a rupee of dividend cannot be replaced by a rupee by external funds. So it is advantageous to retain the earnings.

3. *Transaction costs:* In the absence of transition cost a rupee of capital value can be converted into a rupee of current income and vice versa. This implies that if the dividends are not paid, the shareholders desiring current income can sell a part of their holdings without incurring transaction cost. Because of the presence of the transaction cost, investors may prefer current dividend than retained earnings.

4. *Diversification:* If the company retains the earnings, investors cannot diversify their portfolios. As the investors are willing to pay a higher value to the company which pays more current dividend.

5. *Uncertainty:* MM argues that the prices of the 2 firms which are exactly identical in all the respect except with the dividend policy cannot be different. But this is not true due to "bird in hand argument".

6. *Informational content of dividend:* (financial signaling) - According to this argument dividends contain some information vital to the investors. The payment of dividends conveys the information from the managers to the shareholders about the prospects and profitability of the company. When the company changes its dividend policy, investor will assume that it is in response to the expected changes in the firms' profitability which will last long. An increase in the payout ratio implies a permanent increase in the firms expected earnings and vice versa. So dividend policy becomes relevant because of informational value.

MM accept the informational content of a dividend but still argue that dividends are irrelevant and that dividends are merely proxy for the expected future earnings, which really determines values. Or in other words dividend reflects the profitability of the company. They cannot by themselves determine the market value of the shares.

Illustration 4: The following is the information relating to the acquiring company (A) and the Target Company (T)

	A	T
Earnings after Tax (EAT) (Rs).	50,00,000	10,00,000
Number of shares	5,00,000	2,00,000
Earnings per shares (Rs)	10	5
P/E Ratio	15	10
Market price per share (Rs)	150	50

Based on the evaluation of T, A has agreed to offer Rs. 65 per shares to T. This is 30% premium over the premerger market price of Rs. 50. If the offer price is Rs. 65, exchange ratio is determined as below.

$$ER = \frac{\text{Offer price}}{\text{Share price of the acquires}}$$

$$= \frac{65}{150} = 0.4333 \text{ shares}$$

So A will issue 0.4333 shares for every one share of the target company. The total number of shares to be issued is exchanged ratio x number of shares of T Company.

$0.4333 \times 2,00,000 = 86666$ shares

Earnings per shares of the surviving company after the merges is calculated as below.

$$\frac{\text{Combined earnings}}{\text{Total Number of shares}}$$

$$= \frac{\text{Rs. } 60,00,000}{5,00,000 + 86666}$$

In the above case the EPS of A has increased from Rs. 10 to Rs. 10.22

Assuming that the offer price of Rs. 65 is rejected by the target company. So A company will offer Rs. 90 per shares to the target company. Now the exchange ratio would be:

$$ER = \frac{90}{150} = 0.60 \text{ shares}$$

So 0.6 shares of A must be issued for every shares of T company.

Total number of shares to be issued is $0.6 \times 2,00,000 = 120,000$ shares.

Now EPS of the surviving company after the merger would be:

$$EPS = \frac{60,00,000}{5,00,000 + 1,20,000} = \text{Rs. } 9.67$$

So when the offer prices is Rs. 90 per shares, the EPS of the A company falls to Rs. 9.67 from Rs. 10.

CRITERIA FOR DELUSION IN EPS

The dividend policy of a company determines what proportion of earnings is distributed to the shareholders by way of dividends, and what proportion is ploughed back for reinvestment purposes. Since the main objective of financial management is to maximise the market value of equity shares, one key area of study is the relationship between the dividend policy and market price of equity shares.

There are four models available to show the above relationship, these are briefly described as follows:

DIVIDEND POLICY-STABILITY

Stability of dividends depends on the payout policy followed by the companies.

STABLE DIVIDEND PAYOUT RATIO

According to this policy, the percentage of earnings paid out as dividends remains constant irrespective of the level of earnings. Thus, as earnings of a company fluctuates, dividends paid by it also fluctuates accordingly. The following figure shows the behaviour of dividends in case this policy is adopted:

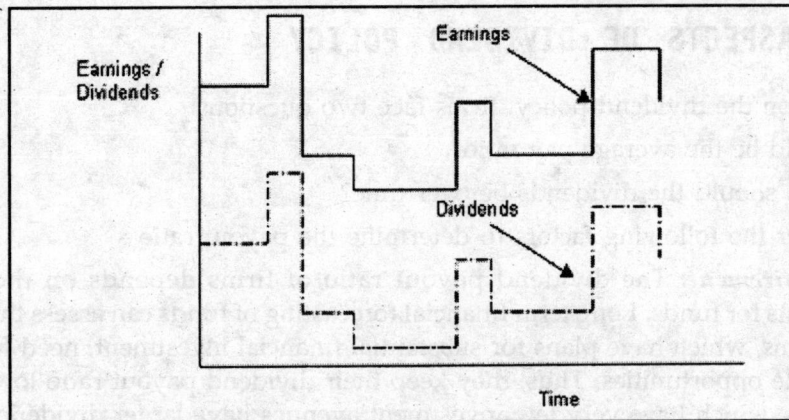

STABLE DIVIDENDS/STEADILY CHANGING DIVIDENDS

According to this policy, dividends in rupee terms mostly remain constant irrespective of the level of earnings. Most of the times, it is gradually increased over a period. The following figure shows the profile of dividend payout according to this policy. Most of the business firms uses this policy.

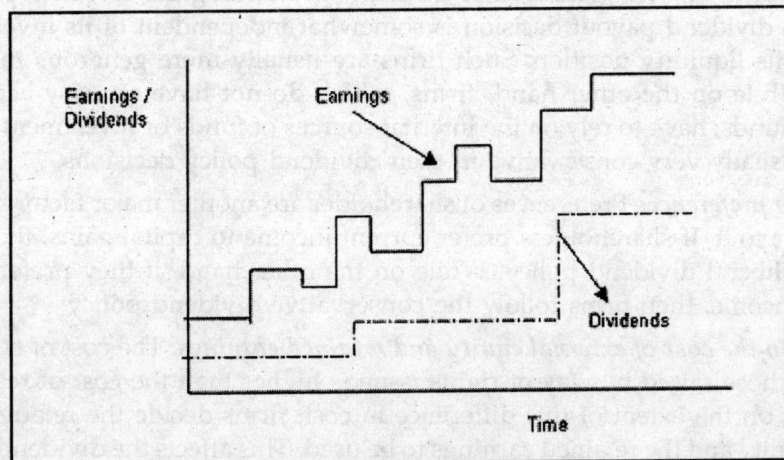

RATIONALE FOR STABILITY OF DIVIDEND

Most of the firms follow stable dividends or gradually increasing dividends due to following reasons:

♦ Many investors consider dividends as a part of regular income to meet their expenses. Hence, they prefer a predictable pattern of dividends rather than a fluctuating pattern. A fall in the dividend income may lead to sale of some shares, on the other hand when the dividend income increases, an investor may invest some of the proceeds as reinvestment in shares. Both the cases involve transaction cost and inconvenience for investor. Hence they, prefer regular dividends.

♦ The dividend policy of firms convey a lot to the investors. Increasing dividends mean better prospects of the company. On the contrary, decreasing dividends suggest bad earnings expectations. In addition, stable dividends are signs of stable earnings of the company. On the other hand, varying dividends lead to uncertainty in the mind of shareholders.

♦ Certain investors mainly institutional, consider the stability of dividends as an important criteria before they decide on the investment in that particular firm.

PRACTICAL ASPECTS OF DIVIDEND POLICY

While deciding on the dividend policy, firms face two questions:

1. What should be the average pay ratio?
2. How stable should the dividends be over time?

Firms consider the following factors to determine the payout ratio :

1. *Funds requirement:* The dividend payout ratio of firms depends on the firm's future requirements for funds. Long term financial forecasting of funds can assess this requirement. Usually firms, which have plans for substantial financial investment, need funds to exploit the available opportunities. Thus, they keep their dividend payout ratio low. On the other hand, firms, which have very few investment avenues have larger dividend pay out ratio.

2. *Liquidity:* It is another factor which influences the dividend payout ratio as dividends involve cash payment. Firms, which desire to pay dividends may not do so, because of insufficient liquidity. This usually happens in the case of profitable and expanding firms, which have very low liquidity because of substantial investments.

3. *Availability of external sources of financing:* Firms which have easy access to external sources of funds enjoy a great deal of flexibility in deciding the dividend payout ratio. For such firms, dividend payout decision is somewhat independent of its investment decision as well as its liquidity position. Such firms are usually more generous in their dividend policies. While on the other hand, firms, which do not have an easy access to external sources of funds, have to rely on the internal sources of funds or investment purposes. Such firms are usually very conservative in their dividend policy decisions.

4. *Shareholder preference:* Preferences of shareholder are another major factor, which influence dividend payout. If shareholders prefer current income to capital gains, then the firm may follow the liberal dividend policy. While on the other hand, if they prefer capital gain to dividend income, then firms follow the conservative dividend policy.

5. *Difference in the cost of external equity and retained earnings:* The cost of equity in all cases except for those raised by way of rights issue is higher than the cost of retained earnings. Depending on the extent of this difference in cost, firms decide the relative proportion of external equity and the retained earnings to be used. This affects the dividend policy decision of the company.

6. *Control:* Raising money from external resources may lead to dilution of control, in case money is raised by issuing public equity. Internal financing on the other hand does not lead to any dilution of control. Hence, if management and shareholders are averse to dilution of control, then firms prefer to rely more on retained earnings. Thus, such companies may adopt, the conservative dividend policy.

7. *Taxes:* In India dividend income for the individuals is free, however capital gains are taxable. Thus, in that case shareholders who are in high tax bracket may prefer dividend income rather than capital gains. However, if tax on dividends is viewed from point of view of corporates, they have to pay dividend tax. Thus, this may influence the companies' dividend policy.

EMPLOYEE STOCK OPTION PLAN (ESOP)

ESOP (Employee stock option plan) is a stock option conferring an employee the right to purchase the share of the company at a set price, after a set period of time.

ADVANTAGES OF ESOPS

ESOPs provide advantages like aligning the interest of the managers with those of the owners. It is a non-cash compensation tool to compete for the best human resources.

The main advantage is the accounting advantage that gives an opportunity to the corporate to pay, without a reduction in book profits.

US GAAP(Generally Accepted Accounting Principles) laid by FASB (Financial Accounting Standard Board), is the standard setting body of the US. India also follows this standard for new instruments like ESOP.

VARIATIONS IN OPTION VALUE USING BLACK AND SCHOLES MODEL

There are five variables that could change the option value:

1. Fall in the share price at the time of announcement of ESOP.
2. Increase of the exercise price.
3. Use of lower interest rate.
4. Use of lower standard deviation.
5. Use of shorter vesting period.

COSTS

Companies may sell shares to their employees under ESOP in any of three ways:-

♦ Sell from treasury stocks
♦ Sell after issuance of new shares
♦ Buyback shares and sell.

All these options either bear opportunity cost or borrowing cost. Any method will dilute control for the owners. In some cases, a corporate may resort to borrowing for buyback and get into a debt trap that is not beneficial.

SEBI GUIDELINES

A guideline issued by the SEBI for stock options requires companies to show expenses in either of the following ways.

♦ Show in the form of option discount (difference between issue price and exercise price).
♦ Or, the fair value of the option measured by the Black and Scholes model.

The accounting value as measured above should be accounted as employee compensation and has to be amortised on a straight-line basis over the vesting period.

An individual should evaluate the choice of a stock option with respect to personal as well as external factors.

FACTORS TO CONSIDER WHILE ADOPTING ESOPS

Personal Factors

♦ Financial situation

♦ Tax bracket

♦ Net worth

♦ Objectives

♦ Acceptable level of risk

♦ Need for cash

EXTERNAL FACTORS

♦ Opportunity of investing in other instruments and their return in comparison to risk.

♦ Prospects for an increase in value of the company's stock.

IMPORTANCE OF UNDERSTANDING ESOPS

As an employee of a company whose stock is publicly traded, you may earn benefits. However, choices are available with respect to:

♦ The timing of your stock option exercises (say, you have 3 months exercise period for ESOP. You have to decide the time to exercise the option to the utmost profit)

♦ Whether to hold or sell acquired shares (they affect your overall financial security.)

Therefore, it is critical that you understand the potential effects of these decisions before taking actions.

TO MAXIMISE THE BENEFITS OF ESOPS

To maximise the potential benefit, you need to consider numerous factors:

♦ Quantify the decision after factoring

♦ Specific tax bracket

♦ Anticipated values of company stock options

♦ Targeted rate of return on other assets

♦ Coordinate these decisions with respect to your overall financial needs and long-term goals

♦ Facilitate wealth management, as company stock options will form a significant portion of your net worth

Each corporate compensation award programme is unique. Likewise every individual has concerns specific to his/her financial situation. It is important to review your stock option awards in the context of your overall financial picture.

EARNED VALUE ANALYSIS (EVA)

EVA is simply net operating profits after tax, minus a charge for the use of capital employed in the business. The capital charge is the minimum rate of return necessary to compensate shareholders, and lenders for the risk of their investments in a company. Research shows that changes in EVA has a closer correlation to changes in shareholder value, when compared to other metrics like Earnings Per Share (EPS), Earnings Growth, Return on Equity (ROE), and Return on Assets (ROA).

TO IMPROVE EVA

♦ Invest in projects that earn more than the cost of capital will help in achieving growth to improve EVA

♦ Increase profits without using additional capital will help in increasing EVA through productivity improvement.

♦ Divesting non-strategic assets that do not generate operating profits greater than the cost of capital.

STEPS INCREASE EVA

By focusing on EVA, employees throughout an organisation have to make strategic and operating decisions that would increase EVA and in turn, the shareholder's value.

Example

Consider a company XYZ Ltd. The significant actions the company has taken in the last 2-3 years include the following:

♦ Sale of its Metal Services company

♦ Acquisition of the Kerr brand of home canning products

♦ Improved operating efficiencies at Plastic Packaging

Operating profits in the Metal services unit had been well below the cost of capital. Long-term prospects in this industry did not show signs of a turnaround. On the other hand, the acquisition and integration of the brand of home canning products provided an opportunity to increase EVA significantly. Improved operating efficiency, combined with reduction in capital employed in Plastic packaging operation in the last two years has contributed to XYZ's recent EVA improvement.

EVA-RELATED INCENTIVE COMPENSATION

To assure that the management's interest is in line with that of XYZ's shareholders, the management's incentive compensation is tied to EVA. XYZ's incentive compensation plan is based on a specific formula. Annual EVA targets are established for each operation based upon the previous year's actual performance. This target setting approach rewards managers for continuous EVA improvement. It is also consistent with XYZ's long-term value creation strategy.

THE IMPORTANCE OF EVA AND ITS INDIAN IMPLICATION

This concept has been picking up in India. Some companies have already made EVA a part of their annual reports-- Infosys Technologies, Hindustan Lever Limited and Dr. Reddy laboratories, to name a few. The reasons for EVA being adopted by only a few companies in India are: -

♦ There is more than one set of shareholders for Indian companies and the company cannot satisfy one set without displeasing other.

♦ Lack of transparency and consistency in reporting.

Calculation of EVA

For calculation of EVA the following elements are needed as inputs: -

Beta (β)

Market Return (R_m)

Risk free rate of return (R_f)

Cost of equity (K_e)

Cost of Debt (K_d)

Weighted Average Cost of Capital (WACC)

Total borrowings

Weightage of debt in total capital employed (W_d)

Weightage of networth in total capital employed (W_e)

Capital employed = debt + networth (equity + reserve and surplus)

Operating profit before interest and tax (OPBIT)

Illustration 5:

Say,

ß = 0.90

R_m = 19 % = 0.19

R_f = 11 % = 0.11

Using CAPM we can get cost of equity (K_e) = ($R_f + b(R_m - R_f)$)

K_e = 0.11+0. 9 (0.19 - 0.11) = 0.18

K_e = 18 % = 0.18

K_d = 3 % = 0.03

W_d = 11 % =0. 11

W_e = 89% = 0.89

Now WACC = $K_e * W_e + K_d * W_d$

= 0.18 * 0.89 + 0.03 * 0.11

= 16 % = 0.16

Capital employed = 2165 crores

Tax = 225 crore.

Now, calculation of EVA

Sales = 1000 crores

Less:

Manufacturing cost = 200 crores

Operating cost = 100 crores

Depreciation = 4 crores

Total = 304 crores

OPBIT = 696 crores

Less:

Tax = 225

= 471 crores

WACC (2165 Cr. * .16)= 346 crores

EVA =125 crores

SHARES BUYBACK

The buying back of outstanding shares (repurchase) by a company in order to reduce the number of shares on the market. Companies will buyback shares either to increase the value of shares still available (reducing supply), or to eliminate any threats by shareholders, who may be looking for a controlling stake.

A buyback is a method for company to invest in itself since it can't own itself. Thus, buybacks reduce the number of shares outstanding on the market, which increases the proportion of shares the company owns. Buybacks can be carried out in two ways:

1. Shareholders may be presented with a tender offer whereby they have the option to submit (or tender) a portion or all of their shares within a certain timeframe and at a premium to the current market price. This premium compensates investors for tendering their shares rather than holding on to them.

2. Companies buy back shares on the open market over an extended period of time.

SUMMARY

♦   Profit is the primary motivating force for any economic activity, business enterprise, essentially being an economic organisation has to maximize the welfare of its stakeholders. To this end, the business undertaking has to earn profit from its operations. Profit is the excess of revenues from operations over expenses on conducting such operations over expenses on conducting such operations.

♦   Profit growth coupled with high level of profit and the ability to maintain reasonable profit will help towards ensuring that shareholders receive an adequate dividend; preserving the assets worth of the business; generating a sufficient cash flow out of profits to provide capital for expansion; and providing funds for the research and development of new and improved products to replace existing products before they go into decline.

♦   From the point of view of dividend decision it is better to call management profit as management of earnings. Earnings mean net earnings available to equity shareholders from where a firm actually declare dividends or retain profits for financing of investment opportunities.

Net earnings = operating profit – (Interest + tax + preference dividend)

♦   Management of earnings means how the earnings of a firm are be determined and how they are utilized or appropriated or allocated or distributed. Management of earnings policy must maximise value of the firm, there by maximise benefits to its owners.

♦   The term 'dividend' refers to that portion of company's net earnings that is paid out to the equity shareholders (not for preference shareholders, since they are entitled to have a fixed rate of dividend).

♦   Dividend policy of a firm decides the portion of earnings to be paid as dividends to ordinary shareholders and what portion is ploughed back in the firm for investment purpose. The alternative use of net earnings or net profit dividends and retained earnings are competitive and conflicting, since it affects the value of the firm.

♦ There are different types of dividend policies: stable dividend policy, here "stability" refers to the consistency or lack of variability in the stream of dividend payments. In more precise terms, stable dividend means payment of a certain minimum amount of dividend regularly. There are three distinct forms of stability, they are (a) Constant dividend per share, (b) Constant payout ratio, and (c) Stable rupee dividend plus extra dividend.

♦ As there is a positive relation between dividend policy of a firm and the value of that firm. The dividend payout ratio of a firm should be determined with reference to two objectives - *one* maximisation of shareholders' wealth and *second* providing sufficient funds to finance growth. There is a need to consider the factors that affect the dividend policy. They are: (1) Nature of earnings, (2) Age of company, (3) Liquidity position of the company, (4) Equity shareholders preference for current income, (5) Requirements of institutional investors, (6) Legal rules, (7) Capital impairment rule, (8)Contractual requirements, (9) Financial needs of the company, (10) Access to the capital market (external sources), (11) Control objective, (12) Inflation, (13) Dividend policy of competitors, (14) Past dividend rates of the company, and (15) others that includes - Trade cycles, corporate taxation policy, attitude of investors group and repayment of loan.

♦ Once determination of dividend policy is over then there a need to decide the form of dividends. General practice is to pay dividends in cash. Some times firms may declare dividends in the form of (a) cash - dividend paid in the form of cash, (b) Scrip - payment of dividends in the form of promissory notes, (c) bond - payment of dividends in the form of long-term bonds, (d) stock (bonus) - payment of additional shares of common stock the ordinary share holders and (e) property - payment of dividends in the form of assets.

♦ Payment of dividend through issue of bonus share is a financial gimmick, since it will not affect the owners' wealth. The reasons for payment of dividend in the form of stock are to: bring the market price per share within a more popular range, promotes more active trading, reduce the nominal rate of dividend, increase paid up share capital, indicate the prospects of the firm, improve prospects of raising additional funds.

♦ Stock dividend is advantages for company and the owners. Advantages enjoyed by the issuing company are: Maintenance of liquidity portion, manage financial difficulties, attractive share price, enhances prestige, widening the share for market, availability of funds for expansion programme. Stock dividend is also beneficial to owners by tax savings, indication of future benefits, psychological value.

♦ Apart from the advantages stock dividend has the following disadvantages. Costly, reduces EPS and price earnings ratio, prevents new investor from becoming the shareholders of the firm, misuse of management power, since there is no dilution of control it is disadvantageous to the company. Disappointment of shareholders, shareholders wealth remains unaffected, lowers the market value of existing shares, less security to investors, done to reduction in reserves are the few disadvantages to owners.

♦ The company law governs the amount of dividend that can be distributed. The important provisions of company law pertaining to dividends are: companies can pay only cash dividends, dividends can be paid out of the profits earned during the financial year after providing for depreciation and after transferring to reserves such as percentage of profits as prescribed by law. Due to inadequacy or absence of profits in any year, dividend may be paid out of the accumulated profits of previous years and dividends cannot be declared for the past years for which accounts been closed.

♦ The procedural aspects of dividend decision are: (1) Board resolution, (2) Shareholders approval, (3) Record date (The dividend is payable to shareholders whose names appear in the Register of Members as on the record date), (4) Dividend payment - once the dividend declaration has been made dividend warrants must be posted within 30 days. Within 7 days, after the expiry of 30 days, unpaid dividends must be transferred to a special account opened with a scheduled bank.

Stock split is done to make share trading attractive, indication of higher profits in the future, give higher dividends to shareholders. From economic point of view stock split and stock dividend are similar to each other, but there are some differences from accounting point of view. They differ in par value of share, capitalisation of reserves, shareholders' proportion, book value, earnings and market price per share

TEST YOUR KNOWLEDGE

Objective Type Questions

1) **Fill in the blanks with appropriate word(s)**

   a) Dividend refers to that portion of companies _____ that are paid out to the equity shareholders.

   b) Distribution of profits between dividends and retained earnings affects the _____ of the firm.

   c) Dividend policy of a firm affects both _____ and owners' wealth.

   d) Investors' desire for current income is one of the advantages of _____ policy.

   e) Making share trading attractive is one of the reasons of _____.

   f) Dividend warrants must be posted within _____ days.

   g) _____ is the payment of additional shares of common stock to ordinary shareholders.

   h) _____ promises to pay the shareholders at a future date.

   i) Usual forms of paying dividend is_____.

   j) The issue of bonus shares amounts to a corresponding increase in the _____ of a firm.

   [**Answers:** (a) Net earnings, (b) value, (c) Long-term finance, (d) Stable dividend, (e) Stock split, (f) 30, (g) Stock dividend, (h) Scrip dividend, (i) Cash, (j) Paid up capital.]

2) **State whether each of the following statement is true of false**

   a) Dividend decision involves legal as well as financial considerations.

   b) Capital impairment rule says that dividends can be paid from capital.

   c) Sec 205 of the Companies Act says that dividends can be declared only from current years profits or from past reserves after providing depreciation.

   d) Payment of dividend is prohibited when the firm is insolvent.

   e) Stock dividend affects the liquidity position of the firm.

   f) There is no relation between financing decisions and dividend decision.

   g) Management of earnings has nothing to do with retention of profits.

   h) Ploughing back of profits is the same as self-financing.

   i) Bonus issue amounts to reduction in the amount of accumulated profits and reserves.

   j) Reduction in the number of outstanding shares is known as reverse split.

   [**Answers:** (a) True, (b) False, (c) True, (d) True, (e) False, (f) False, (g) False, (h) True, (i) True (j) True.]

TRY YOURSELF

Conceptual Type

1) What is dividend ?
2) What is property dividend ?
3) What is stock dividend ?
4) What is bonus share ?
5) List any five objectives of issuing stock dividend.
6) What is stock split ?
7) What is reverse split ?
8) Compare between bonus share and stock split.
9) List out the reasons for stock split.
10) What is free reserve ?
11) How do you compute net earnings ?
12) What is dividend policy ?
13) Name different types of dividend policies.
14) What is scrip dividend ?
15) What do you understand by Bond dividend ?
16) What is stable dividend policy ? Discuss the different forms of stable dividend policy.
17) List the advantages and disadvantages of stock dividend.
18) 'Payment of dividend involves legal considerations' - Discuss.
19) 'Stock dividends are unfair to those stockholders who desire cash income', comment.
20) What is stock split ? Why is it used ? How is it different from a bonus share ?
21) 'Bonus shares represents simply a division of corporate pie into a large number of pieces', explain.
22) What is stock dividend ? Discuss the advantages of stock dividend to the company.
23) Discuss the dividend procedural aspects.
24) Briefly discuss the different types of dividend policies.
25) What is stock dividend ? Discuss in detail the advantages and dangers of stock dividend.
26) Explain the factors that influence the dividend policy of a company.
27) Briefly discuss the legal and procedural aspects of dividends according to company's law.
28) Write short notes on :
    (a) Stock split,
    (b) Stock dividend,
    (c) Stable dividend policy
    (d) Property dividend.
29) Distinguish between Scrip dividend and Bond dividend.

CASE FOR CLASS DISCUSSION 1- FUTURE EARNINGS PER SHARE

RAMESH PRODUCTS CASE

This case allows the reader to apply the concept of future EPS in evaluating a course of action in terms of its effect on the market value of the firm's common stock.

Ramesh Products (RKP) is a medium-sized producer of chemicals and vinyl coating used in a variety of industrial processes. The company's main facilities are located in an industrial park in East Baltimost, a central site by a rail line that is linking the firm with its major customers on the east coast.

Last year the firm recorded over $200 million in sales, showed a net income of $53 million and concluded a very successful year. For the coming year, the firm expects a 15 per cent improvement in sales and operating income figures.

The firm's management committee, consisting of the president and the vice-presidents of production, marketing, and finance, will be meeting with in a week to discuss a major new activity for the next year. Products has been invited to bid on a long-term contract to produce a line of plastics for a large chemical company in Wilmington, Delaware. It appears that the firm can easily get the $50 million contract which should yield an additional $14 million in operating income. These figures are for next year only, and the firm estimates even higher sales and profits in the future.

Chowdhary vice -president of finance, has been studying the financial data related to the new line of plastics. The production manager knows of a small plastic company located about three miles from RKP's facilities. The plastics company has all the equipment needed to produce the new line of plastics; the company is for sale for $104 million. This price represents largely the value of the assets, since the company has lost its only large contracts. Chowdhary Prasad has discussed the purchase of this plastics company with a local real estate agent and has confirmed that it is available for $100 million.

Chowdhary Prasad figures that RKP has sufficient working capital to add the new plastics line but does not have the cash to buy the 100 million of machinery and equipment needed to begin the production. Discussion with a representative of a large Baltimore bank reveals that RKP can borrow $39 million through a 12 per cent mortgage on its main facilities. A mortgage company has indicated that it would help finance the plastic machinery with a $51 million, 13.6 per cent mortgage. Chowdhary Prasad is considering these choices but knows that RKP has traditionally kept its debt-asset ratio below 41 per cent He does not want to borrow if the additional debt causes the ratio to exceed 41 per cent.

Chowdhary Prasad discussed equity financing with RKP's investment banker on a recent trip to New Jersy City. He learned that the firm could probably issue upto $150 million in 15 per cent preferred stock or class A common stock. If the common stock were offered, it could net $20 per share to RKP. Chowdhary Prasad called new Jersy and confirmed that these options were still open to the firm.

In making decision on new investments, Chowdhary Prasad believes in the validity of the future-earnings per share technique. He knows that RKP has traditionally traded at a 6/1 price-earning multiple and he expects that this will hold. Thus, if a new project increases future earnings per share, it will increase the value of the firm for its shareholders.

Assignment

According to the future earning share approach and after detailed analysis what do you feel about the plastic project. Is it worth while to accept.

REFERENCES

1. Bradley, J.F, *Administrative Financial Management*, New York : Frances & Noble 1964, p. 104.
2. McAlpine T.S, *Profit planning and Control*, London : Business Book Ltd., 1969, p. 108.
3. Souvenir Published at IV Conference of Asian and Pacific Accounts, New Delhi : 1965, p. 143.
4. Townsend C, *Financial Management*, Hand book, Essex : Grower Press Ltd., 1972, p. 13.
5. Lintner K, "Distribution of Income of Corporations among Dividends, Retained Earnings and Taxes", *American Economic Review*, May 1956, pp. 97 - 113.
6. Joy O.M, *Introduction to Financial Management*, Homewood : Richard D. Irwin, 1977, p. 274.
7. Chandra P, *Financial Management Theory and Practice*, New Delhi : Tata McGraw Hill Publishing Company, 2002, p. 503.
8. Eismann P.C and Mosel E.A, "Stock Dividends : Managements - Views", *Financial Analysis Journal*, July - August, 1978, pp. 77 - 80.
9. Poterfield James T.S, "Dividend, Dilution and Delusion, *Harvard Business Revies*, Nov - Dec 1959 pp. 156 - 161 (reproduced in Pandy I.M, op. cit. p. 786).
10. Hansman W.H, et. al, "Stock Split, Price changes and Trading Profit : A Synthesis, *Journal of Business*, 44 January, 1971, pp. 69 - 77.

PART VI

WORKING CAPITAL MANAGEMENT

Working Capital Management

16

Working capital management is significant in financial management due to the fact that it plays a vital role in keeping the wheel of the business running. Every business requires capital, without which it cannot be promoted. Investment decision is concerned with investment in current assets and fixed assets. There are two assets required to be financed by fixed capital and working capital. In other words, the required capital can be divided into two categories, such as fixed capital and working capital. *Fixed capital* required for establishment of a business, where as working capital required to utilize fixed assets. Fixed assets cannot be utilized without current assets. It is just like a blood in the human body, without which there is no body.

Working capital plays a key role in a business enterprise just as the role of heart in human body. It acts as grease to run the wheels of fixed assets. Its effective provision can ensure the success of a business while its inefficient management can lead not only to loss but also to the ultimate downfall of what otherwise might be considered as a promising concern. In other words, efficiency of a business enterprise depends largely on its ability to manage its working capital. Working capital management, therefore, is one of the important facets of a firm's overall financial management.[1]

MEANING AND DEFINITION OF WORKING CAPITAL

Working capital refers to short-term funds to meet operating expenses. To quote Ramamoorthy, "It refers to the funds, which a company must possess to finance its day-to-day operations". [2] It is concerned with the management of the firm's current assets and current liabilities. It relates to the with the problems that arise in attempting to manage the current assets, current liabilities and their inter-relationship that exists between them.[3] If a firm cannot maintain a satisfactory level of working capital, it is likely to become insolvent and may even be forced into bankruptcy.

CONCEPTS OF WORKING CAPITAL

The concept of working capital has been a matter of great controversy ,among the financial wizards and they view it differently. There is no universally accepted definition of working capital. Broadly, there are two concepts of working capital commonly found in the existing literature of finance such as:

- Gross Working Capital (Quantitative Concept) and
- Net Working Capital (Qualitative Concept).

Both these concepts of working capital have operational significance. The two concepts are not to be regarded as mutually exclusive. Each has its relevance in specific situations from the management point of view.

Each concept of working capital has its own significance – the 'gross concept' emphasising the 'use' and the 'net concept' the 'source' – an integration of both these concepts is necessary in order to understand working capital management in the context of risk, return and uncertainty.

Gross Working Capital Concept

According to this concept, the total current assets are termed as the gross working capital or circulating capital. Total current assets include; cash, marketable securities, accounts receivables, inventory, prepaid expense, advance payment of tax; etc. This concept also called as 'quantitative or broader approach'. To quote Weston and Brigham, "Gross Working Capital refers to firm's investments in short term assets such as cash, short term securities, accounts receivables and inventories".[4] The concept helps in making optimum investment in current assets and their financing. According to Walker, "Use of this concept is helpful in providing for the current amount of working capital at the right time so that the firm is able to realise the greatest return on investment".[5] The supporters of this concept like Mead,[6] Field[7], and Baker and Malott (8), argue that the management is very much concerned with the total current assets as they constitute the total funds available for operating process.

Significance

Gross Working Capital Concept focuses attention on the two aspects of current assets management, they are:

(i) *Optimum Investment in Current Assets*: Investment in current assets must be just adequate to the needs of the firm. In other words, current assets investment should not be inadequate or excessive. Inadequate working capital can disturb production and can also threaten the solvency of the firm, if it fails to meet its current obligations. On the other hand, excessive investment in current assets should be avoided, since it impairs the firm's profitability.

(ii) *Financing of Current Assets*: Need for working capital arise due to the increasing level of business activity. Therefore, there is a need to provide/arrange it quickly. Similarly, some times surplus funds may arise, thus they should be invested in short-term securities. They should not be kept as idle.

Net Working Capital Concept

As per this concept, the excess of current assets over current liabilities represents net working capital. Similar view is expressed by Guthmann and Dougall[9], Gerstenberg[10], Goel[11], Park and Gladson[12], Kennedy and McMullen[13], and Myer[14] in their distinguished works. 'Accounts Hand Book' has also fully supported this view. [15] The famous economists like, Sailer[16], Lincoln[17], and Stevens[18], fully supported this concept and viewed that the net working capital helps creditors and investors to judge the financial soundness of a firm.

Net Working Capital Concept represents the amount of the current assets, which would remain after all the current liabilities were paid. It may be either positive or negative. It will be positive, if current assets exceed the current liabilities and negative, if the current liabilities are in excess of current assets. Another alternative definition is that net working capital refers to that portion of firm's current assets, which financed with long-term funds[19].

Net Working Capital Concept indicates or measures the liquidity and also suggests the extent to which working capital needs may be financed by the permanent source of funds. To quote Roy Chowdary, "Net Working Capital indicates the liquidity of the business whilst gross working capital denotes the quantum of working capital with which business has to operate". [20]

Significance

Net Working Capital Concept focuses attention on the two aspects of current assets management, they are: i) Maintaining liquidity position, and ii) To decide upon the extent of long-term capital in financing current assets.

i) *Maintaining Liquidity Position*: For maintaining liquidity position there is a need to maintain current assets sufficiently in excess of current liabilities. In other words, excess current assets helps in meeting its financial obligation within the operating cycle of the firm. Generally for every one rupee of current asset there will be one rupee of current liability. As discussed above, negative and excess working capital both are bad to the firm.

ii) *To decide upon the Extent of Long-term Capital in Financing Current Assets*: Net Working Capital (NWC) means the portion of current assets that should be financed by long–term funds. This concept helps to decide the extent of long-term funds required in finance current assets. For example, if there are Rs. 1,00,000 current assets and Rs. 75,000 current liabilities, the extent of current assets should be decided by the NWC base. The NWC is the difference between current assets and current liabilities. In the above example NWC is Rs. 25,000. This is the amount that is supposed to be financed by long–term funds. Hence, NWC helps management to decide the extent to which current assets should be financed with equity capital and borrowed funds.

KINDS OF WORKING CAPITAL

The categorization of working capital can be made either based on its concept or the need to maintain current assets either permanently and/or temporarily. As per conceptual view, it may be classified into *gross working capital* or *net working capital*, which were already explained in detail

Gerstenberg has conveniently classified the working capital into *regular* or *permanent* working capital and *temporary* or *variable working* capital. The variable working capital is again bifurcated into seasonal and special working capital. [21] See Figure – 16.1

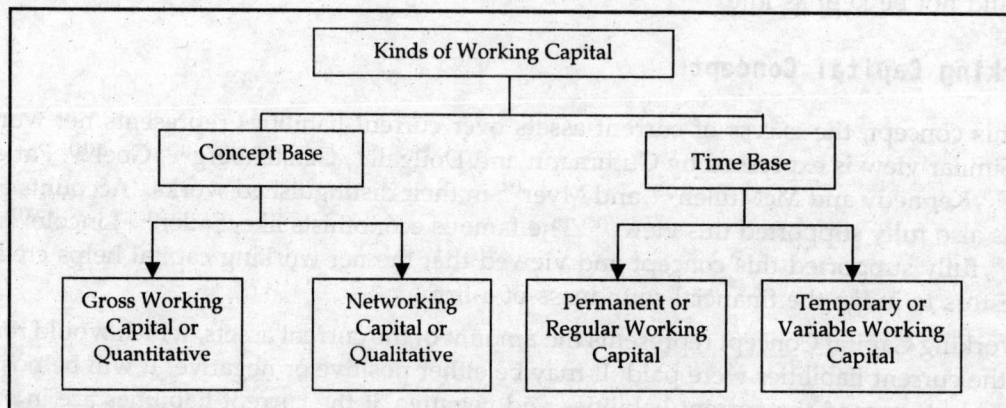

Figure 16.1

Permanent Working Capital

Permanent working capital is the minimum investment kept in the form of inventory of raw materials, work-in-process, finished goods, stores & spares, and book debts to facilitate uninterrupted operation in a firm. Though this investment is stable in short run, it certainly varies in long run depending upon the expansion programmes undertaken by a firm. It may increase or decrease over a period of time. The minimum level of current assets maintained in a firm is usually known as permanent or regular working capital.

Temporary Working Capital

A firm is required to maintain an additional current assets temporarily over and above permanent working capital to satisfy cyclical demands. Any additional working capital apart from permanent working capital required to support the changing production and sales activities is referred to as temporary or variable working capital. In other words, an amount over and above the permanent level of working capital is temporary, fluctuating or variable working capital. [22] At times, additional working capital is required to meet the unforeseen events like floods, strikes, fire, and price hike tendencies and contingencies.

DISTINCTION BETWEEN PERMANENT AND TEMPORARY WORKING CAPITAL

The difference between permanent and temporary working capital can be shown in the following Figure 16.2 and 16.3.

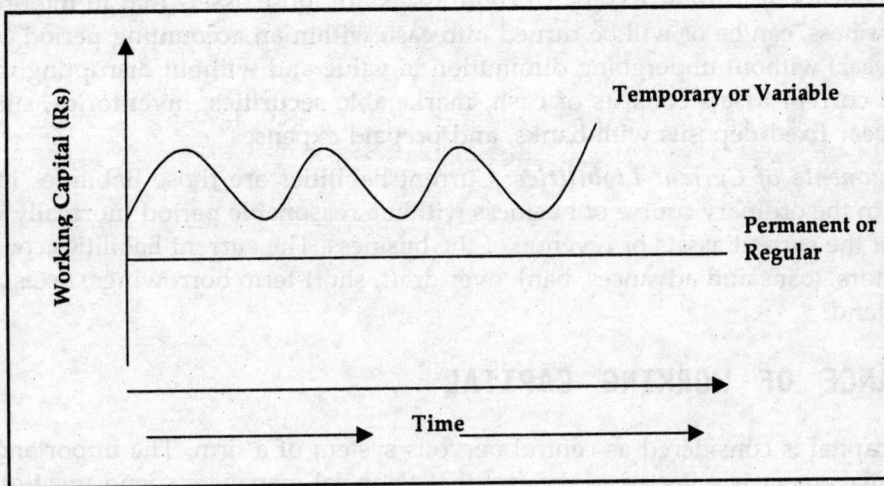

Figure 16.2

The above figure depicts the permanent or regular working capital that is stable over a period, where as temporary or variable working capital is oscillating, or showing ups and down – some times working capital requirement has increased or decreased. The above figure 16.2 will hold good to those firms, where there is no development and have seasonal or cyclic fluctuations.

But for the growing firms figure 16.3 will be suitable as follows:

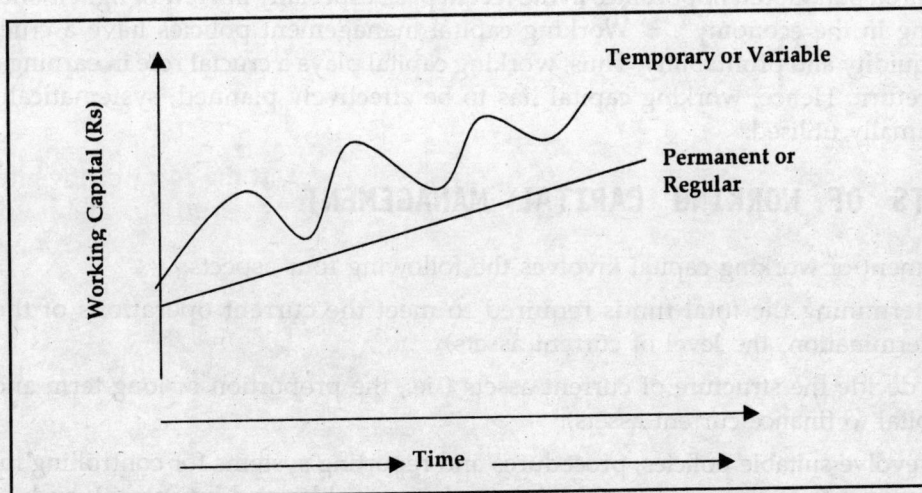

Figure 16.3

Over a long period, permanent working capital also changes with the additional funds, required for expression programs.

COMPONENTS OF WORKING CAPITAL

Efficient management of working capital involves effective control over the current assets and current liabilities, which are the main components of working capital.

(a) *Components of Current Assets:* Current assets are those assets that in the ordinary course of business, can be or will be turned into cash within an accounting period (not exceeding one year) without undergoing diminution in value and without disrupting the operations. Total current assets consists of cash, marketable securities, inventories, sundry debtors, one year fixed deposits with banks, and prepaid expenses.

(b) *Components of Current Liabilities:* Current liabilities are those liabilities intended to be paid in the ordinary course of business within a reasonable period (normally within a year) out of the current assets or revenue of the business. The current liabilities consist of sundry creditors, loans and advances, bank over-draft, short-term borrowings, taxes and proposed dividend.

IMPORTANCE OF WORKING CAPITAL

Working capital is considered as central nervous system of a firm. The importance of working capital management is reflected in the fact that financial managers spend most of their time in managing current assets and current liabilities. Adequate working capital needs to be maintained in order to discharge day-to-day liabilities and protect the business from adverse effects in times of calamities and emergencies. It aims at protecting the purchasing power of assets and maximise the return on investment. [23] In other words, the goal of working capital management is to minimize the cost of working capital while maximizing a firm's profits. [24] Management is required to be vigilant in maintaining appropriate levels in the various working capital accounts. [25] The working capital management is concerned with determination of relevant levels of current assets and their efficient use as well as the choice of the financing mix. "The efficiency of firm to earn profits depends largely on its ability to manage working capital. Working capital management has acquired paramount importance in the recent past, especially in view of tight money conditions prevailing in the economy". [26] Working capital management policies have a crucial effect on firm's liquidity and profitability. Thus, working capital plays a crucial role in earning a reasonable rate of return. Hence, working capital has to be effectively planned, systematically controlled and optimally utilised.

ASPECTS OF WORKING CAPITAL MANAGEMENT

Management of working capital involves the following four aspects:

(i) Determining the total funds required to meet the current operations of the firm (i.e., determination the level of current assets).

(ii) To decide the structure of current assets (ie., the proportion of long-term and short-term capital to finance current assets).

(iii) To evolve suitable policies, procedures and reporting systems for controlling the individual components of current assets (Mainly cash, receivables and inventory); and

(iv) To determine the various sources of working capital.

For determining the sources of working capital (short term and long term) capital the net concept becomes useful. However, for determining the level and composition of working capital it is the gross concept, which becomes more meaningful.

OBJECTIVES OF WORKING CAPITAL MANAGEMENT

The objectives of working capital management could be stated as,

i) To ensure optimum investment in current assets.

ii) To strike a balance between the twin objectives of liquidity and profitability in the use of funds.

iii) To ensure adequate flow of funds for current operations.

iv) To speed up the flow of funds or to minimize the stagnation of funds.

OPERATING CYCLE AND CASH CYCLE

Maximization of shareholders' wealth of a firm is possible only when there are sufficient returns from their operations. But profits can be earned will naturally depend, among other things, upon the magnitude of the sales. In other words, successful sales activity is necessary for earning profits. Sales do not convert into cash immediately. There is invisible time lag between the sale of goods and receipt of cash. There is, therefore, a need for working capital. In other words, sufficient working capital is necessary to sustain sales activity. The operating cycle concept penetrates to the heart of working capital management in a more dynamic form. The time that elapses to convert raw materials into cash is known as operating cycle. In other words the time that elapses between the purchase of raw materials and the collection of cash for sale is referred to as the operating cycle. [27] To quote Joy, The continuing flow from cash to suppliers, to inventory, to accounts receivables and back into cash is what is called the operating cycle. [28] The operating cycle involves the following procedure:

a) Conversion of cash into raw materials.

b) Conversion of raw materials into work-in-process.

c) Conversion of work-in-process into finished goods.

d) Conversion of finished goods into sales [debtors and cash].

If firm sells good on cash basis with (d) operating cycle then returns to the operating cycle (a). But if, firm sells goods on credit basis then there will be another cycle that is,

e) Conversion of debtors into cash.

The following figure 16.4 shows the operating cycle.

Figure 16.4

Stock of raw material is held in order to ensure smooth production. Similarly, stocks of finished goods have to be carried to meet the demand from the consumers on the continuous basis. Goods are sold on credit for competitive reasons. Thus, adequate amount of funds has to be invested in current assets for a smooth and uninterrupted production and sales process.

The operating cycle will be different in different types of business units:

- *Operating Cycle of Manufacturing Firm:* The above stated cycle will be suitable to a manufactures firm.

- *Operating Cycle of a Non-manufacturing Firm:* Non-manufacturing firms are wholesale sellers and retailers, which do not have manufacturing process. They will have the direct conversion of cash into finished goods and then into cash. In other words, they will purchase finished goods from manufacturing firm and sell them either on cash or credit. If they sell goods on credit, the following figure 16.5 gives their operating cycle.

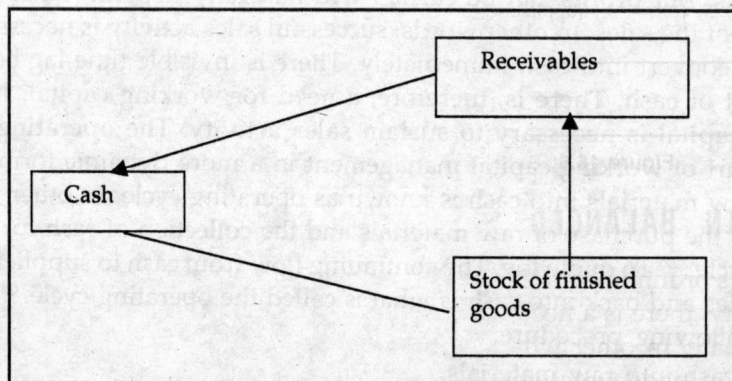

Figure 16.5

CASH CONVERSION CYCLE

The amount of time a firm's resources are tied up calculate by subtracting the average payment period from the operating cycle. [29] In other words the time period between the dates from when pays it suppliers to the date till it receives the cash from its customers.

Calculation of Cash Conversion Cycle (CCC) [See *Figure 16*.6].

CCC = OC – APP

where: OC = Operating Cycle   APP = Accounts Payable Period OC = AAI + ARP.

AAI = Average Age of Inventory   ARP = Average Collection Period.

From the financial statements, it can be determined as the constituents of Cash Conversion Cycle i.e., AAI, ACP, APP:

$$AAI = \frac{Average\ Inventory}{Cost\ of\ Goods\ sold\ /\ 365}$$

$$ARP = \frac{Average\ Accounts\ Receivables}{Annual\ Sales\ /\ 365}$$

$$APP = \frac{Averagae\ Accounts\ Payables}{Cost\ of\ Goods\ Sold\ /\ 365}$$

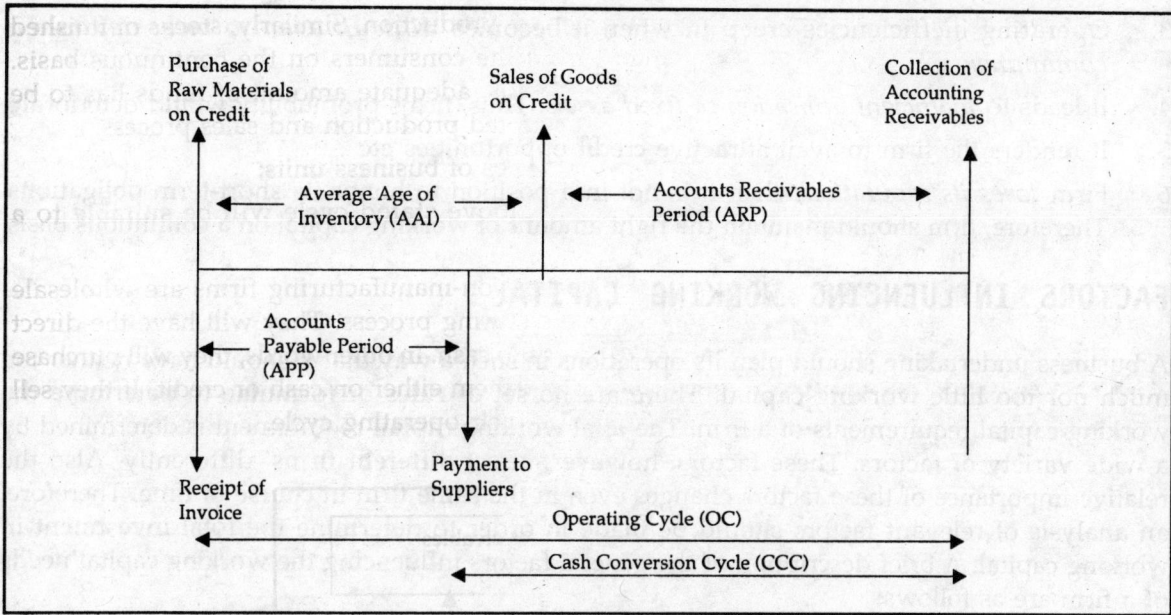

Figure 16.6: Depicts Operating and Cash Cycle

NEED TO MAINTAIN BALANCED WORKING CAPITAL

For maximization profits or minimization of working capital cost or to maintain balance between liquidity and profitability, there is a need to maintain a balance in working capital. It should not be excessive or inadequate. In other words, it should manage adequate working capital to run its business. Excessive or inadequate working capital both are dangerous from firm's point of view. Excessive working capital means idle funds that can earn no profit but involve costs, and inadequate working capital disturbs production and impairs the firm's profitability.

THE DANGERS OF EXCESSIVE WORKING CAPITAL

The dangerous excessive working capital are as follows: [30]

1. It results in *unnecessary accumulation of inventories*, which leads to mishandling of inventories, waste, theft and losses in increase.

2. It is *indication of defective credit policy and slack in collection period*. These lead to higher bad debt losses that reduce profits.

3. It makes management complacent which *degenerates in to managerial inefficiency*.

4. Accumulation inventories tend to make *speculative profits grow*. This type of speculation makes the firm to follow liberal dividend policy and difficult to cope with in future is unable to make speculative profits.

DANGERS OF INADEQUATE WORKING CAPITAL

The following are the dangers of inadequate working capital: [31]

1. It *stagnates growth*. It becomes difficult for the firm to undertake profitable or the firm to undertake profitable of the firm to understand profitable projects for non-availability of working capital.

2. It becomes *difficult to implement operating plans* and achieve the firm's target profit.

3. Operating inefficiencies creep in when it becomes *difficult even to meet day-to-day commitments*.

4. It leads to *inefficient utilisation of fixed assets*. Thus, firms profitability would deteriorate.

5. It renders the firm to avail attractive credit opportunities etc.

6. Firm *loses its reputation* when it is not in a position to honor its short-term obligations. Therefore, firm should maintain the right amount of working capital on a continuous basis.

FACTORS INFLUENCING WORKING CAPITAL

A business undertaking should plan its operations in such a way that it should have neither too much nor too little working capital. There are no set of rules or formulae to determine the working capital requirements of a firm. The total working capital requirement is determined by a wide variety of factors. These factors, however, affect different firms' differently. Also the relative importance of these factors changes even in the same firm in course of time. Therefore, an analysis of relevant factors should be made in order to determine the total investment in working capital. A brief description of the general factors influencing the working capital needs of a firm are as follows:

1. *Nature of Business:* The amount of working capital is basically related to the nature of business. The proportion of current assets needed in some lines of business activity varies from other lines. For instance, trading and finance firms have a very small investment in fixed assets, but they require more working capital. In contrast, public utility concerns rendering public services require huge investment in fixed assets. The requirement of current assets in such concerns is usually less due to cash nature of business and selling service. In trading concerns, the amount of working capital required is less than the manufacturing concern, since there is no production of goods and services involved, but in service industry like banks the amount of working capital required is very high. The relative importance of current assets to total assets will indicate the required intensity of planning and control efforts in working capital management area. [32]

2. *Size of Business:* It may be argued that a firm's size, measured in terms of assets or sales, affects need for working capital. Size may be measured in terms of a scale of operation. A firm having with large-scale operations will need more working capital required then a small firm having small-scale operations. A small firm may use extra current assets as a cushion against cash flow interruptions. [33]

   Bigger firms have many sources of funds, thereby it will require less amount of working capital as compared to the smaller ones.

3. *Production Cycle Process*: This is another factor, which has bearing on the quantum of working capital, is the production cycle. The term production or manufacturing cycle refers to the time involved in the manufacturing of goods. It covers the time span between the procurement of raw materials and the completion of the manufacturing process leading to the production of finished goods. Longer the production cycle, the higher will be the working capital requirement and vice versa. Manufacturing firms have large production cycle, so they require high working capital, but in the case of short production cycle firms require less working capital. Working capital requirements can be reduced with the help of certain policy steps, like terms of credit for raw materials and the suppliers. Unless the sequences of production process leading to conversion into finished goods are kept under close observation to achieve better production and productivity, more and more working capital funds will be tied up. In this context, it should be noted that production planning and control are vital.

4. *Production Policy*: Production policy means whether, it is continuous or seasonal demand for products. What kind of production policy should be followed in above cases? There are two options to such companies, either they confine their production only to periods when goods are purchased or they follow a steady production policy throughout the year and produce goods at a level to meet peak demand. Suppose in the case where, production and sales goes simultaneously, the amount of working capital required is less (example is FMCG goods business), but the sales will be only seasonal and production will take place throughout the year thus continuously the amount of working capital required is very high. (Umbrella business).

5. *Credit Policy or Terms of Purchase and Sales*: The credit policy relating to sales and purchases also affects the working capital. If a company purchases raw materials in cash and sells goods on credit, it will require larger amount of working capital. On the contrary, a concern having credit facilities for the purchase of raw materials and allowing no credit to its customers, will require lesser amount of working capital.

6. *Business Cycle*: The amount of working capital requirements of a firm varies with every movement of business cycle. The variations in business conditions may be in two directions[34] (a) *Upward phase* – when boom conditions prevail, in this case more working capital is required to cover the lag between the increased sales and receipt of cash as well as to finance purchase of additional material. (b) *Downswing phase* – in this case, the need for working capital will be very less, since there is no growth in sales.

7. *Growth and Expansion*: As company grows, it is logical to expect that a larger amount of working capital in required. It is very difficult to determine the relationship between the growth in the volume of business of a company and increase in its working capital required. Other things being equal, growth industries require more working capital than those the static. The critical fact, however is that the need for increased working capital funds does not follow the growth in business activities but proceeds it. Advance planning of working capital is therefore, a continuing necessity for a growing concern, or else, the company may have substantial earnings but little cash.

8. *Scarce Availability of Raw Materials*: The availability of certain raw materials on a continuous basis without interruption would sometimes affect the working capital requirement. There may be some materials, which cannot be procured easily either because of either their sources are few or they are irregular. Therefore, the firm might be compelled to purchase more than required to manage smooth production. In this case, the amount of working capital required is large. In other case, the availability of raw materials are easy and there is no fluctuations thus the amount of working capital required is less.

9. *Profit Level*: Firms may differ in their capacity to generate profit from business. Some firms enjoy a dominant position, due to quality product or good marketing management or monopoly power in the market and earn a high profit margin. Other firms may earn low profits. The net profit is a source of working capital to the extent that it has been earned in cash. A high net profit margin contributes towards the working capital pool. A firm with high profit level requires less working capital and vice versa.

10. *Level of Taxes*: The net profit is calculated after deduction of tax. The amount of taxes to be paid is determined by the tax authorities. So the management has no discretion in this respect. Hence, companies very often pay taxes in advance on the basis of the profit of the previous year. Therefore, tax is an important aspect of working capital planning. If tax liability increases, it leads to an increase in the requirement of working capital and vice versa. So tax planning can, therefore, be said to be an integral part of working capital planning.

11. *Dividend Policy*: Dividend has a bearing on working capital, since it is appropriation profits. The payment of dividend reduces cash resources and thereby, affects working capital to that extent. Conversely, if the firm does not pay dividends but retains profits, the working capital increases. In other words, declaration of dividends leads to more working capital requirement and vice versa.

12. *Depreciation Policy*: It is also exerts an influence on the quantum of working capital required. Depreciation charge is out of pocket cost. The affect of depreciation policy on working capital is indirect. More depreciation provisions reduce the amount of required working capital and vice versa.

13. *Price Level Changes*: Increasing prices necessitate the use of more funds for managing an existing level of activity. In the same level of current assets, higher cash outlays are required. The effect of raising prices is that a higher the amount of working capital is required. However, in the case of companies, which can raise their prices proportionately, there is no serious problem regarding working capital required. Moreover, the price rise does not have a uniform effect on all commodities. The effects of raising price levels will be different for different firms depending upon their pricing policies, nature of the product etc.

14. *Operating Efficiency*: The operating efficiency of the firm relates to the optimum utilisation of resources at minimum costs. Efficiency of operations accelerates the pace of cash cycle and involves the working capital turnover. In this case the amount of working capital needed is less since it releases pressure by improving profitability and improving the internal generation of funds.

15. *Availability of Credit*: The need for working capital in a firm will be less, if it avails liberal credit facilities. Similarly, the availability of credit from banks also influences the working capital needs of the firm. A firm enjoying bank credit facilities can secure funds to finance its working capital requirement very easily, whenever it requires. It can therefore, perform its business activities with less working capital than a firm without such credit facility.

16. *Other Factors*: In addition to the above factors, there are a number of other factors, which affect the requirement of working capital. Some of them are: close co-ordination between production and distribution policies, an absence of specialization in the distribution of products, the means of transportation and communication, the hazards and contingencies inherented in a particular type of business, credit policy of RBI and so on.

The amount of working capital is also influenced by the inventory policies, depreciation policies, management attitude and wages and government policies.

DETERMINATION OF REQUIRED WORKING CAPITAL

Working capital is equal to the current assets minus current liabilities. In other words, working capital consisting two components, such as current assets and current liabilities. Hence, for estimation of working capital, there is a need to follow the following *Four*-step procedure :

1. Estimation of cash cost of the various current assets required by the firm.

2. Estimation of spontaneous current liabilities of the firm.

3. Compute net working capital by subtracting the estimate current liabilities (step 2) from current assets (step 1).

4. Add some percentage (given in the problem) of net working capital if there is any contingency or safety working capital required, to get the required working capital.

Statement of Working Capital Needed

Particulars		Amount (in Rs.)	Amount (in Rs.)
A. Estimation of Current Assets:			
i) Raw materials		XXX	
ii) Work-in-process			
Raw materials (full cost)	XX		
Direct labour (to the extent of completed stage)	XX		
Overheads (to the extent of completed stage)	XX	XXX	
iii) Finished goods inventory		XXX	
iv) Debtors		XXX	
v). Cash balance required		XXX	
Total Current Assets			XXX
B. Estimation of Current Assets:			
i) Creditors		XXX	
ii) Expenses			
Overheads	XX	XXX	
Labour	XX		
Total Current Liabilities			XXX
C. Working Capital (A-B)			XXX
Add: Contingency (Percentage on working capital)			XXX
D. Working Capital Required			XXXX

Estimation of Working Capital (Formulae)

Working capital required is calculated based on the assumption that the production or sales is carried on evenly throughout the year and all costs accrue similarly. Exclusion of depreciation is necessary from sales price since it is out of profit costs [it does not involve cash outflow. In other words, computation of working capital required is based on the cash cost only.

Symbols used in the formulas:

BP	= Budgeted production (in units)
RMC	= Raw Materials cost per unit
ARM HP	= Avg. Raw Materials Holding Period
EWIP	= Estimated work-in-process cost per unit
ATSWIP	= Avg. Time Span of work-in-process inventory
CGP	= Cost of Goods Produced (excluding depreciation) per unit
FGHP	= Finished Goods Holding Period
BCS	= Budgeted Credit Sales in units
CS	= Cost of Sales (excluding depreciation) per unit
ADCP	= Avg. Debt Collection Period
CPAS	= Credit Period Allowed by Suppliers
DWC	= Direct Wages Cost per unit
LPW	= Lag in Payment of Wages
OHC	= Overhead Cost per unit of production
LPOH	= Lag in Payment of Overheads

Estimation of components of current assets and current liabilities:

1. **Estimation of Current Assets:**

   a) *Investment in Raw Materials Inventory:* BP (in units) × RMC per unit × ARM HP (months/ days) ÷ 12 months / 365 days.

   b) *Investment in Work-in-process Inventory:* Work-in-process cost (permit) is proportionate share of the cost of direct materials and conversion costs. Conversion costs include labor and manufacturing overheads costs excluding depreciation, since it is out of pocket cost. Generally, raw materials cost is fully considered, if there is no information about the raw materials requirement. With regards to the share of labor and overhead cost, it is based on the work completion stage. For example if the work is completed to the extent of 50 per cent then only 50 per cent labour cost and overhead cost is taken into consideration for estimation of work-in-process cost. If there is no information about the completion stage then the option is left out to the estimation of working capital (it is better to consider that work completion stage is 50 per cent).

   BP (in units) × EWIP per unit × ATSWIP (months/ days) ÷ 12 months / 365 days

   c) *Investment in Finished Goods Inventory:* BP (in units) x CGS per unit × FGHP (months/ days) ÷ 12 months / 365 days

   d) *Investment in Debtors:* BCS (in units) × CS per unit × ADCP (months/ days) ÷ 12 months / 365 days

   e) *Cash and Bank Balance:* Maintenance of minimum working capital includes a minimum cash balance, but it is very difficult to calculate minimum cash balance required. Generally determination of minimum cash balance would be based on the motives for holding cash of business firm, attitude of management towards risk, accessibility of the firm to the sources of finance, when needed and past experience etc. Generally in examinations the minimum cash balance will be provided

2. **Estimation of Current Liabilities**

   a) *Trade Debtors:* BP (in units) × RMC per unit production × CPAS (months/ days) ÷ 12 months / 365 days.

   b) Direct Wages: BP (in units) × DWC per unit × LPW (months/ days) ÷ 12 months / 365 days.

   c) Overheads: BP (in units) × OHC per unit of production × LPOH (months/ days) ÷ 12 months / 365 days.

Illustration 1: From the following information of VSGR Company Ltd., estimate the working capital needed to finance a level of activity of 1,10,000 units of production after adding a 10 per cent safety contingency.

	Amount (per unit)
Raw materials	78
Direct labour	29
Overheads (excluding depreciation)	58
Total cost	**165**
Profit	24
Selling price	**189**

Additional information:

Average raw materials in stock: One month

Average materials-in-process (50 per cent completion stage): Half a month

Average finished goods in stock: One month

Credit allowed by suppliers: One month

Credit allowed to customers: two months

Time lag in payment of wages: One and half weeks

Overhead expenses: one month

One fourth of the sales is on cash basis. Cash balance is expected to be Rs. 2,15,000. You may assume that production is carried on evenly throughout the year and wages and overhead expenses accrue similarly.

Solution:

Estimation of working capital needed

Particulars	Amount (Rs)	Amount (Rs)
A. Estimation of Current Assets:		
i) Raw materials inventory: One month: (1,10,000 x 78 x 4/52)	6,60,000	
ii) Work-in-process inventory: Half a month		
Raw materials (1,10,000 x 78 x 2/52) = 3,30,000		
Direct labour (1,10,000 x 14.5 x 2/52) = 61,346.15		
Overheads (1,10,000 x 29 x 2/52) = 1,22,692.31	5,14,038.46	
iii) Finished goods inventory: One month: (1,10,000x165x4/52)	13,96,153.85	
iv) Debtors: Two months: (82,500 x 165 x 8/52)	20,94,230.77	
v). Cash balance required	2,15,000	
Total Current Assets	48,79,423.08	
B. Estimation of Current Liabilities:		
i) Creditors: One month: (1,10,000 x 78 x 4/52)	6,60,000	
ii) Expenses:		
Overheads (1,10,000 x 58 x 4/52) = 4,90,769.23		
Labour (1,10,000 x 29 x 3/104) = 92,019.23	582,788.46	
Total Current Liabilities		12,42,788.46
C. Working Capital(A-B)		36,36634.62
Add: 10% Contingency		3,63,663.46
D. Working Capital Required		40,00,298.08

SOURCES OF WORKING CAPITAL (FINANCING OF CURRENT ASSETS)

Once the estimation or determination of the current assets is over then the next step in working capital management is financing of the current assets. There are three financing policies vis-a-vis' to financing current assets. Adoption of the specific policy is left out to the firm. The three financing policies are:

1. *Short-term Financing*: Generally current assets should be financed by only short-term financial sources. Short-term finance is obtained for a period of less than one year. The sources of short-term finance are loans from banks, public deposits, commercial papers,

factoring of receivables, bills discounting, retention of profits etc. , a firm, which required short-term finance, can go for any one of these sources. In other words, a firm that required short term finance can raise through any one of the sources.

2. *Long-term Financing*: Net current assets or permanent current assets or working capital are supposed to be financed by long-term sources of finance. Long-term finance is raised for a period of more them five years. Long-term finance sources include, ordinary share capital, preference share capital, debentures, long-term loans from bankers, and surpluses (includes retained earnings). A firm that needs to finance net current assets can go for any of these sources, but it depends on company's attitude towards risk or control over the company, companies earnings, capacity and period of loan reserved.

3. *Spontaneous Financing*: It refers to the automatic sources of short-term funds arising in the normal course of a business. The source includes trade credit (suppliers') and outstanding expenses. Spontaneous sources of finance is available at no cost. A firm that wishes to maximize owner's wealth, it must and should utilize these sources to the fullest extent. The real choice of financing current assets, is between short–term and long-term sources. In other words, some extent of current assets can be financed with the use of spontaneous source, and the requiring current assets should be financed with the combination of long-term and short-term sources of finance.

APPROACHES FOR FINANCING CURRENT ASSETS

As we have seen in above discussion there are three types of sources for financing the working capital, such as short-term financing, long-term financing and spontaneous financing. But financing of working capital, there are only two sources available, short-term and long-term sources. What should be the proportion on of working capital to be financed by short term and long term sources? They are three approaches available for a company which are Matching, Conservative and Aggressive approach. Adoption of a particular technique depends on the company's attitude towards risk and return. The following figure 16.7 depicts the three approaches available to finance working capital.

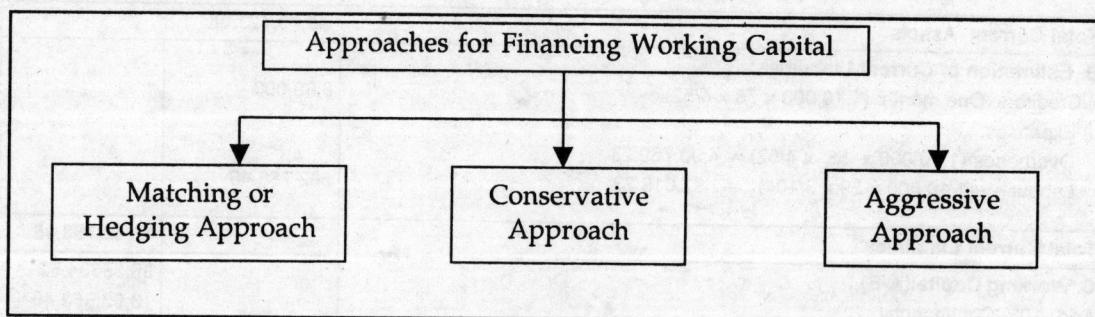

Approaches for Financing Working Capital		
Matching or Hedging Approach	Conservative Approach	Aggressive Approach

Figure 16.7

1. *Matching or Hedging Approach*: Matching approach is that approach in which, the expected life of an asset is matched with the source of finance period with which an asset is financed. For example, an asset, which is having an expected life of 15 years, should be financed only through 15 years loan, or 15 years debentures, or 15 years redeemable preference shares. In other words, the life of an asset should match with the maturity of source of funds. Hence, it is known as matching approach. The term hedging is used in the sense of a risk reducing investment strategy involving transactions of a simultaneous but opposing nature that counter balance the effect of each other with reference to finance mix, the term hedging can be said to refer to the process of matching maturing of debt with the matching of financial needs. [35] Fixed assets and permanent current assets should be financed by long

term funds and temporary current assets should be financed by short term funds. The same can be shown in the following figure 16.8. [36]

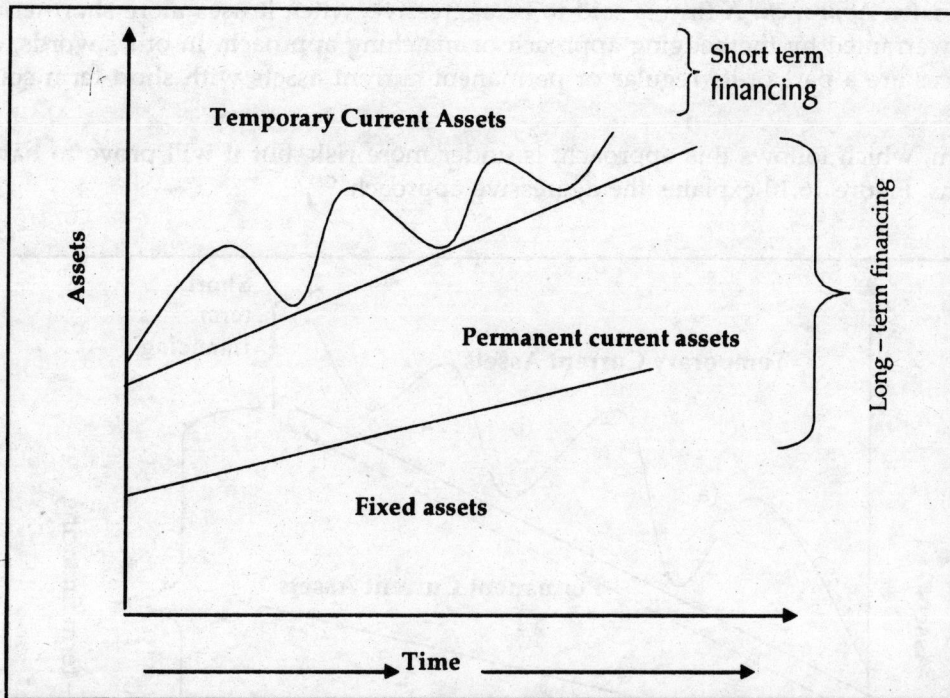

Figure 16.8

The above figure says that there is a need to match the period of source of finance and the assets life, which is financed by funds. But it may not be possible to match, because of uncertainty of assets expected life. As the level of assets increases, the amount of finance also increases in both assets.

2. *Conservative Approach*: According to this approach, a firm depends more on long-term funds for financing needs. In this plan, the firm finances its regular or permanent current assets and a part of temporary or variable current assets with long term source of funds. In the year, when the firm has no need of funds for temporary current assets, the idle funds (long-term) can be invested in the marketable securities so that the firm conserves liquidity. Figure 16.9 shows the conservative policy. [37]

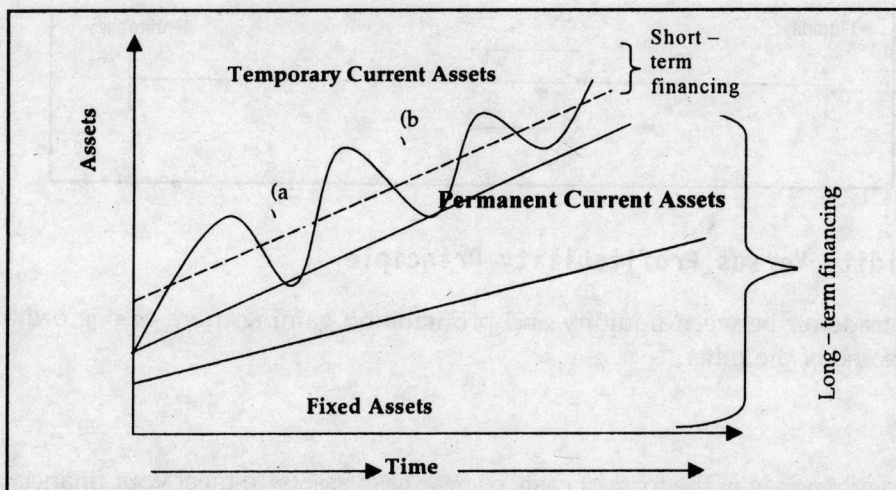

Figure 16.9

A firm, that follows this policy/approach will be under less risk since, it relies an long term finance but the returns are also less.

3. *Aggressive Approach*: A firm is said to be aggressive, when it uses more short-term funds than warranted by the hedging approach or matching approach. In other words, a firm's finances are a part of its regular or permanent current assets with short-term sources of funds.

A firm, which follows this approach, is under more risk, but it will prove to have more returns. Figure 16.10 explains the aggressive approach. [38]

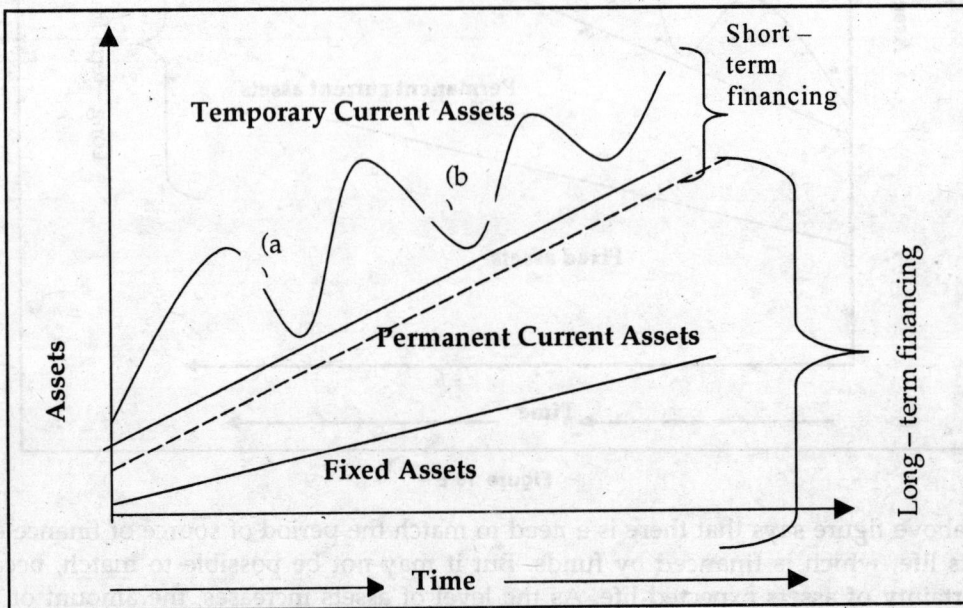

Figure 16.10

TRADE-OFF BETWEEN PROFITABILITY, RISK AND LIQUIDITY

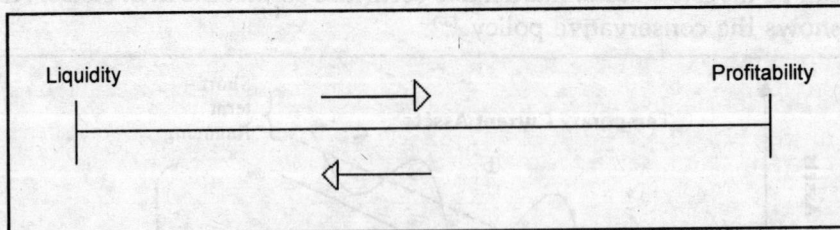

The Liquidity Versus Profitability Principle

There is a trade-off between liquidity and profitability; gaining more of one ordinarily means giving up some of the other.

Liquidity

Having enough money in the form of cash, or near-cash assets, to meet your financial obligations. Alternatively, the ease with which assets can be converted into cash.

Profitability

A measure of the amount by which a company's revenues exceed its relevant expenses.

'Liquidity' as being on one end of a straight line and 'Profitability' on the other end of the line. If you are on the line and move towards one, you automatically move away from the other. In other words, there is the trade-off between liquidity and profitability.

This is easy to illustrate with a simple example. The items on the asset side of a company's balance sheet are listed in order of liquidity, i.e., the ease with which they can be converted into cash. In order, the most important of these assets are:

♦ Cash
♦ Marketable Securities
♦ Accounts Receivable
♦ Inventory
♦ Fixed Assets

Notice that as we go from the top of the list to the bottom, the liquidity decreases. However, as we go from top to bottom, the profitability increases. In other words, the most profitable investment for company is normally in its fixed assets; the least profitable investment is cash.

Bankruptcy Risk

Is it possible for a company to go bankrupt if it has a lot of cash but is not profitable? Sure it is! It may take a while, but if it remains unprofitable, it will eventually go bankrupt. Its available cash will be used to finance the losses, but when the cash runs out, the assets of the company will have to shrink because there will be insufficient funds to replace them as they wear out. The company will become smaller and smaller and will eventually fail.

Is it possible for a company to go bankrupt if it is very, very profitable but is not very liquid (i.e., does not have much cash)? Certainly! For example, if a company expands so rapidly that it is constantly building new buildings and buying new equipment, it may very well get behind on its payments to the contractors and vendors due to the lack of cash. In other words, the company is spending money much faster than it is making it, even though it is making a lot. Eventually, the creditors (i.e., contractors and vendors) will demand their money and, if the company does not have enough cash to pay up, the creditors will take the company to court. A judge may very well decide that the creditors are entitled to their money and will start selling off the assets of the company in order to raise cash to pay them. (Half-finished construction projects don't bring in much cash at a sheriff's auction.) At that point, the owners of the company have lost control and may very well be forced into bankruptcy.

So, you can see that it's dangerous to be on either extreme of the line: (1) highly liquid but not very profitable, and (2) highly profitable but not very liquid. There's a broad middle ground between the two extremes where the company wants to reside.

Managing Current Assets and Liabilities

♦ The greater the firm's investment in current assets,
   ❖ the greater its liquidity, the lower the illiquidity risk
♦ However, current assets (cash, marketable securities) earn very low or no income,
   ❖ trade-off between low income and low illiquidity risk

Working-Capital Management and the Risk-Return Trade-off

♦ Working Capital = the firm's total investment in current assets or assets which it
   ❖ expects to be converted into cash within a year or less.

♦ Risk-Return Trade-off in managing working capital is
   ❖ trade-off between the firm's liquidity and its profitability

Large investment in current assets (cash, inventories)

♦ reduces the chance of production stoppages, lost sales, and inability to pay bills on time
♦ no corresponding increase in profits
♦ return on investments drops (asset increases, profit is the same)

Larger the firm's reliance on short-term debt or current liabilities in financing its asset investments,
♦ the greater the risk of illiquidity
♦ but short-term is less costly and more flexible than long-term

Working Capital

The firm's total investment in current assets or assets that it expects to be converted into cash within a years or less.

Net Working Capital

The difference between the firm's current assets and its current liabilities. Frequently when the term working capital is used, it is actually intended to mean net working capital.

The Risk-Return Trade-Off in Managing a Firm's Net Working Capital

	Firm Profitability	Firm Liquidity
Investing in additional marketable securities and inventories	Lower	Higher
Increasing the use of short-versus long-term sources of financing	Higher	Lower

SUMMARY

● Working capital management is concerned with the problems that arise in attempting to manage the current assets, current liabilities and their inter-relationship that exists between them.

● Working capital management goal is maintain a satisfactory level of working capital.

● There are two concepts of working capital: Gross Working Capital (Quantitative Concept) and Net Working Capital (Qualitative Concept). Gross Working Capital, refers to the total current assets. Net Working Capital refers to the excess of current assets over current liabilities or it is that portion of firm's current assets, which financed with long-term funds.

● *Gross Working Capital Concept* focuses attention on the two aspects of current assets management, they are: Optimum investment in current assets, and financing of current assets.

● Net working capital concept focuses attention on the two aspects of current assets management, they are: Maintaining liquidity position, and to decide upon the extent of long-term capital in financing current assets.

● Working capital has conveniently classified the working capital into two: regular or permanent and temporary or variable working capital. Permanent working capital refers to the minimum level of current assets maintained in a firm. Temporary working capital refers to additional current assets temporarily over and above permanent working capital to satisfy cyclical demands.

- The main components of working capital: Current assets (cash, marketable securities, inventories, sundry debtors, one year fixed deposits with banks, prepaid expenses) and current liabilities (sundry creditors, loans and advances, bank over-draft, short-term borrowings, taxes and proposed dividend).

- The importance of working capital management is reflected in the fact that financial managers spend most of their time in managing current assets and current liabilities. The working capital management is concerned with determination of relevant levels of current assets and their efficient use as well as the choice of the financing mix.

- Management of working capital involves the following four aspects, viz, determination the level of current assets, decide the proportion of long-term and short –term capital to finance current assets, to evolve suitable policies, procedures and reporting systems for controlling the individual components of current assets, and to determine the various sources of working capital.

- The objectives of working capital management could be stated as, to ensure optimum investment in current assets, to strike a balance between the twin objectives of liquidity and profitability in the use of funds, to ensure adequate flow of funds for current operations, and to speed up the flow of funds or to minimize the stagnation of funds.

- The operating cycle concept penetrates to the heart of working capital management in a more dynamic form. The time that elapses to convert raw materials into cash is known as operating cycle. Operating Cycle (OC) = AAI + ARP, Cash Conversion Cycle (CCC) is the time length between the payment for suppliers of raw materials and the collection of cash for sales, CCC = OC – APP.

- There is a need to maintain a balance working capital for maximization profits or minimization of working capital cost or to maintain balance between liquidity and profitability.

- The dangerous excessive working capital are: unnecessary accumulation of inventories, indication of defective credit policy and stack collection period, degeneration in to managerial inefficiency, and speculative profits grow.

- The dangers of inadequate working capital are: stagnates growth, difficult to implement operating plans, difficult even to meet day-to-day commitments, inefficient utilisation of fixed assets, unable to avail attractive credit opportunities, firm loses its reputation.

- Working capital requirement is determined by a wide variety of factors, they are: Nature of Business, Size of Business, Production Cycle Process, Production Policy, Credit Policy or Terms of Purchase and Sales, Business Cycle, Growth and Expansion, Scarce Availability of Raw Materials, Profit Level, Level of Taxes, Dividend Policy, Depreciation Policy, Price Level Changes, Operating Efficiency, Availability of Credit, close co-ordination between production and distribution policies, an absence of specialization in the distribution of products, the means of transportation and communication, the hazards and contingencies inherent in a particular type of business, credit policy of RBI and so on.

- Working capital is equal to the current assets minus current liabilities. Determination/ estimation of working capital, involve four steps: (1) Estimation of cash cost of the various current assets required by the firm, (2) Estimation of spontaneous current liabilities of the firm, (3) Compute net working capital by subtracting the estimate current liabilities (step 2) from current assets (step 1), and (4) Add some percentage (given in the problem) of net working capital, if there is any contingency or safety working capital required, to get the required working capital. (costs and profits are calculated excluding depreciation)

- There are three financing policies vis – a-vis', to finance current assets: (1) Short-term financing, generally current assets should be financed by only short-term financial sources.

The sources of short-term finance are loans from banks, public deposits, commercial papers, factoring of receivables, bills discounting, retention of profits etc., a firm, which required short-term finance can go for any one of these sources. (2) Long-term financing, net current assets or permanent current assets or working capital are supposed to be financed by long-term sources of finance. Long-term finance sources include, ordinary share capital, preference share capital, debentures, long-term loans from bankers, and surpluses (includes retained earnings). (3) Spontaneous financing, it refers to the automatic sources of short-term funds arising in the normal course of a business. The source includes trade credit (suppliers') and outstanding expenses.

- They are three approaches available for a company, that are matching, conservative and aggressive approach. (1) Matching or Hedging Approach, is that approach in which, the expected life of an assets is matched with the source of finance period with which the asset is financed. (2) Conservative Approach, according to this approach a firm depends more on long-term funds for financing needs. In this plan, the firm finances its regular or permanent current assets and a part of temporary or variable current assets with long term source of funds. In the year, when the firm has no need for temporary current assets, the idle funds (long-term) can be invested in the marketable securities so that the firm conserves liquidity. (3) Aggressive Approach, a firm is said to be aggressive, when it uses more short-term funds then warranted by the hedging approach or matching approach.

PRACTICE PROBLEMS

Illustration 1:

X and Y who want to buy a business seek your advice about the average working capital requirements in the first year's trading. The following estimates are available and you are asked to add 5% to allow for contingencies.

		Rs.
a)	**Average amount locked with Stocks :**	
	Stock of finished goods and WIP	10,000
	Stock of stores, materials etc	8,000
b)	**Average Credit given :**	
	Local sales 3 week's credit	90,000
	Outside the states – 5 week's credit	3,20,000
c)	**Time available for payment:**	
	For purchases – 5 weeks	1,10,000
	For wages – 3 weeks	2,90,000

Calculate the average amount of working capital required. Give details of your working.

Solution

Current Assets :		
Inventories :		
Stock of finished goods & WIP	10,000	
Stock of stores, materials etc	8,000	18,000
Accounts Receivable :		

Contd...

Local sales 90,000 x 3/52 =	5,192	
Outside the state 3,20,000 x 5/52 =	30,769	35,961
Total Current Assets		53,961
Less : Current Liabilities		
Accounts, payable 1,10,000 x 5/52 =	10,577	
Outstanding wages 2,90,000 x 3/52 =	16,731	27,308
		26,653
Add 5% for contingencies (26,653 x 5%)		1,333
Working capital required		27,986

By Determining the cash costs of Current Assets and Current Liabilities : It has been stated that the working capital is the differences between current assets and current liabilities. In order to estimate the requirements of working capital one has to forecast the amount of current assets and the current liabilities. However, in case of certain current assets, the cash costs involved are much less than the value of the current assets. This is true that the cost of finished goods add to work-in-progress which may include the amount of depreciation. Many experts, therefore, calculate the working capital requirements by taking into account only the cash cost blocked in sundry debtors, stock in work-in-progress and finished goods.

According to this approach, the debtors are computed not as a percentage sales but as a percentage of cash costs. Similarly, the finished goods and work-in-progress are valued according to cash cost.

The steps involved in estimating the different items of current assets and Current liabilities are as follows:

Estimation of Current Assets :

Raw Materials Inventory : The investment in raw-material inventory can be estimated on the basis of equation given below:

$$\frac{\text{Budgeting Production (in units)} \times \text{Cost of raw material(s) per unit} \times \text{Average inventory holding period (months/days)}}{\text{12 months / 365 days}}$$

Work-in-process Inventory : The relevant cost determine WIP investments are the proportionate share of cost of raw-materials and conversion costs (labour cost and manufacturing overheads excluding depreciation). Here, it is to be noted that administrative overheads are ignored for valuation of WIP and depreciation is excluded as it does not involve any cash expenditure.

Symbolically

$$\frac{\text{Budgeting Production (in units)} \times \text{Estimated WIP Cost per unit} \times \text{Average time span of WIP inventory (months/days)}}{\text{12 months / 365 days}}$$

Finished Goods Inventory : The working capital required to finance the finished goods inventory is given by factors summed up in equations given below:

| Budgeting Production (in units) | ✕ | Manufacturing cost per unit (excluding depreciation) | ✕ | Finished Goods holding periods (months/days) |

12 months / 365 days

Debtors : The working capital tied in debtors should be estimated in relation to total cost price (excluding depreciation). Symbolically,

| Budgeted Credit Sales (in units) | ✕ | Manufacturing cost Per unit (excluding depreciation) | ✕ | Average debt collection period (months/days) |

12 months / 365 days

Estimation of Current Liabilities :

The important liabilities, in this context are, trade-creditors, wages and overheads :

Trade Creditors

| Budgeted yearly production (in units) | ✕ | Raw material requirement per unit | ✕ | credit period allowed by creditors (months/days) |

12 months / 365 days

Direct Wages :

| Budgeted yearly production (in units) | ✕ | Direct labour cost per unit | ✕ | Average time-lag in payment of wages (months/days) |

12 months / 365 days

Overheads (Other than deprecation and amortization)

| Budgeted yearly production (in units) | ✕ | Overhead cost per unit | ✕ | Average time-in payment of oHs (months/days) |

12 months / 365 days

The amount of overheads may be separately calculated for different types of overheads. In the case of selling overheads, the relevant item would be sales volume instead of production volume,

The computation of working capital is summarized in the following format:

Format

Determination of working capital for the Budget Year

	Amount
	(Rs.)
A. Estimation of Current Assets :	
(i) Minimum desired cash and bank balance	x x x
(ii) Inventories:	
Raw-material	x x x
Work-in-progress	x x x
Finished goods	x x x
(iii) Debtors	x x x
Total Current Assets (A)	x x x x
B. Estimation of Current Liabilities	
(i) Creditors	x x x
(ii) Wages	x x x
(iii) Overheads	x x x
Total Current Assets (B)	x x x x
C. Net working Capital (A-B)	x x x x
Add : Margin for Contingency	x x x
D. Average Working Capital i.e.	
[(A-B) + Contingencies]	x x x x

Illustration : 2

X & Y company is desirous to purchase a business and has consulted you. You are asked to advise them regarding the average amount of working capital, which will be required in the first year's working.

You are given the following estimates and are instructed to add 10% to your computed figure to allow for contingencies.

		Amount for the year
		(Rs.)
(i) Average amount backed up for stocks		
Stocks of finished goods		5,000
Stocks of stores, materials etc.		8,000
(ii) Average credit given :		
Island sales 6 weeks' credit		3,12,000
Export sales 1½ week's credit		78,000
(iii) Average time lag in payment of wages and other		
Outgoings :		
Wages	1½ Weeks	2,60,000
Stock, materials etc.	1½ months	48,000

Contd...

Rent Royalties, etc.	6 months	10,000
Clerical staff	1½ months	62,400
Manager	1½ months	4,800
Miscellaneous expenses	1½ months	48,000

(iv) Payment in advance :

Sundry expenses (paid quarterly in advance)   8,000

Undrawn profits on the overage throughout the year 11,000

Set up your calculations for the average amount of working capital required.

Solution

Statement showing working capital for X & Y Company

	Amount (Rs.)
A. Current Assets	
(i) Stock of finished goods	5,000
(ii) Stock of stores, materials etc.	8,000
(iii) Debtors	
Credit sales	36,000
Debtors turnover	
$\left[\dfrac{Rs.\,3,12,000 \times 6\ weeks}{52\ Weeks}\right]$	
Export Sales for 1½ Weeks	
$\left[\dfrac{Rs.\,78,000 \times 1\frac{1}{2}\ weeks}{52\ Weeks}\right]$	2,250
(iv) Advance payment of sundry expenses:	
$\left[\dfrac{Rs.\,8,000 \times 3\,months}{12\,months}\right]$	2,000
Total investment in Current Assets (A)	53,250
B. Current Liabilities	
(i) Wages $\left[\dfrac{Rs.\,2,60,000 \times 1\frac{1}{2}\ weeks}{52\,weeks}\right]$	7,500
(ii) Stocks, materials etc. $\left[\dfrac{Rs.\,48,000 \times 1\frac{1}{2}\,months}{12\,months}\right]$	6,000

Contd...

(iii) Rent, Royalties, etc $\left[\dfrac{\text{Rs.}10,000 \times 6 \text{ months}}{12 \text{ months}}\right]$		5,000
(iv) Clerical Staff $\left[\dfrac{\text{Rs.}62,400 \times \frac{1}{2} \text{ months}}{12 \text{ months}}\right]$		2,600
(v) Manager $\left[\dfrac{\text{Rs.}48,000 \times \frac{1}{2} \text{ months}}{12 \text{ months}}\right]$		200
(vi) Miscellaneous expenses $\left[\dfrac{\text{Rs.}48,000 \times 1\frac{1}{2} \text{ months}}{12 \text{ months}}\right]$		6,000
Total estimated of Current Liabilities (B)		27,3000
C. Net working capital (A-B) (53,250-27,300)		25,950
Add : 10% contingency allowance (10% of 25,950)		2,595
D. Average working capital		28,545

Notes:

(i) For calculations, a time period of 52 weeks/12 months has been assigned in a year.

(ii) Undrawn profit has been ignored in the working capital computation for the following reasons:

 (a) For the purpose of determining working capital provided by net profit, it is necessary to adjust the net profit for income – taxes and dividends.

 (b) Profit need not always be a source of finance working capital. It may be used for other purposes like purchases of fixed assets, repayment of long-term loans etc.

(iii) Actual working capital requirement would be more than what is estimated here as in the problem cash component of current assets is not given.

Illustration 3

XYZ Company sells goods on a gross profit of 25% depreciation is taken into account as a part of cost production. The following are the annual figures given to you:

Sale (Two month's Credit)	18,00,000
Materials consumed (One month's credit)	4,50,000
Wages paid (One month lag in payment)	3,60,000
Cash manufacturing expenses (One month lag in payment)	4,80,000
Administration expenses (One month lag in payment)	1,20,000
Sales promotion expenses (Paid quarterly in advance)	60,000
Income tax payable in four installments of which one lies in the (next year)	1,50,000

The company keeps one month's stock of both raw-materials and finished goods. It also keeps Rs. 1,00,000 in cash. You are required to estimate the working capital requirements of the company on cash cost basis assuming 10% safety margin.

Solution

Statements showing working capital requirements on cash cost basis:

	Amount (Rs.)
A. Current Assets	
Debtors (cash cost of goods sold) $\left[\dfrac{14,70,000 \times 2\,\text{months}}{12\,\text{months}}\right]$	2,45,000
Prepared sales expenses $\left[\dfrac{\text{Rs.}60,000 \times 3\,\text{month}}{12\,\text{months}}\right]$	15,000
Inventories	
Raw – materials $\left[\dfrac{\text{Rs.}4,50,000 \times 1\,\text{month}}{12\,\text{months}}\right]$	37,500
Finished goods $\left[\dfrac{\text{Rs.}12,90,000 \times 1\,\text{month}}{12\,\text{months}}\right]$	10,7,500
Cash in hand (given)	1,00,000
Total current Assets (A)	5,05,000
B. Current Liabilities	
Sundry Creditors $\left[\dfrac{\text{Rs.}4,50,000 \times 1\,\text{month}}{12\,\text{months}}\right]$	37,500
Outstanding manufacturing expenses $\left[\dfrac{\text{Rs.}4,80,000 \times 1\,\text{month}}{12\,\text{months}}\right]$	40,000
Outstanding administration expenses $\left[\dfrac{\text{Rs.}1,20,000 \times 1\,\text{instalment}}{12\,\text{months}}\right]$	10,000
Provision for taxation $\left[\dfrac{\text{Rs.}1,50,000 \times 1\,\text{month}}{4\,\text{installments}}\right]$	37,500
Wages paid $\left[\dfrac{\text{Rs.}3,60,000 \times 1\,\text{month}}{12\,\text{months}}\right]$	30,000
Total Current Liabilities (B)	1,55,000
C. Net working capital (A-B) (5,05,000 – 1,55,000)	3,50,000
Add : 10% contingency allowance (10% of 3,50,000)	35,000
D. Average working capital	3,85,000

Working Notes

1.	Calculation of manufacturing expenses :		
	Sales		18,00,000
	Less : Gross profit 25% on sales		4,50,000
	Total cost manufacture		13,50,000
	Less : Cost of materials	4,50,000	
	Cost wages	3,60,000	
	Manufacturing Expenses	8,10,000	
			5,40,000
2.	Depreciation :		
	Manufacturing Expenses		5,40,000
	Less : Cash manufacturing expenses		4,80,000
			60,000
3.	Calculation of Total cash cost :		
	Total cost of manufacture		13,50,000
	Less: Depreciation		60,000
			12,90,000
	Administration expenses	1,20,000	
	Sales expenses	60,000	
			1,80,000
	Total Cost		14,70,000

Illustration 4: Cost sheet of XYZ company provides the following particulars :

Amount per unit

	(Rs)
Raw –materials	80
Direct labour	30
Overhead	60
Total cost	170
Profit	30
Selling price	200

The following further particulars are available :

Raw materials in stock, on average one month: Materials are in process, on an average of half a month ; Finished Goods in Stock, on an average of one month.

Credit allowed by suppliers in one month : credit allowed to debtors is two months ; average time-lag in payment of wages is 1½ weeks and is one month in overhead expenses; one fourth of the output is sold against cash ; cash in hand and at bank is expected to be Rs. 3,65,000. You are required to prepare a statement showing the working capital needed to finance a level of activity of 1,04,000 units of production.

You may assume that production is carried on evenly throughout the year, and wages and overheads accrue similarly (WIP at 50% completion stage).

Solution

Statement showing working capital requirements

		Amount (Rs.)
A. Current Assets		
(i) Stock of materials for 1 month [i.e. 4 weeks]		
$\left[\dfrac{1,04,000\,\text{units} \times \text{Rs}.80 \times 4\,\text{weeks}}{52\,\text{Weeks}}\right]$		6,40,000
(ii) Work in progress for 2 weeks		
a) Material	$\left[\dfrac{1,04,000 \times 80 \times 2\,\text{weeks}}{52\,\text{weeks}}\right] \times 50\%$ completion	1,60,000
b) Labour	$\left[\dfrac{1,04,000\,\text{units} \times \text{Rs}.30 \times 2\,\text{Weeks}}{52\,\text{weeks}}\right] \times 50\%$ completion	60,000
c) Overheads	$\left[\dfrac{1,04,000\,\text{units} \times \text{Rs}.60 \times 2\,\text{weeks}}{52\,\text{weeks}}\right] \times 50\%$ completion	1,20,000
(iii) Finished goods for 1 month (ie. 4 weeks)		
a) Material	$\left[\dfrac{1,04,000 \times 80 \times 4\,\text{weeks}}{52\,\text{weeks}}\right]$	6,40,000
b) Labour	$\left[\dfrac{1,04,000 \times 30 \times 4\,\text{weeks}}{52\,\text{weeks}}\right]$	2,40,000
c) Over heads	$\left[\dfrac{1,04,000 \times 60 \times 4\,\text{weeks}}{52\,\text{weeks}}\right]$	4,80,000
(iv) Debtors for 2 months (i.e. 8 weeks)		
$\left[\dfrac{78000\,\text{units} \times \text{Rs}.170 \times 8\,\text{weeks}}{52\,\text{weeks}}\right]$		20,40,000
(v) Cash in hand and at Bank (Given)		3,65,000
Total investments in Current Assets (A)		**47,45,000**

Contd...

B. Current Liabilities

(i)   Creditors for one month

      1 month's purchase of Raw – Materials i.e.

$$\left[\frac{1,04,000 \times Rs.80 \times 4\,weeks}{52\,weeks}\right] \qquad = 6,40,000$$

(ii) Average time-lag in payment of expenses :

      a) Overheads (a month) $\left[\dfrac{1,04,000 \times 60 \times 4\,weeks}{52\,weeks}\right]$ = 4,80,000

      b) Labour (1½ weeks) $\left[\dfrac{1,04,000 \times 30 \times 1\frac{1}{2}\,weeks}{52\,weeks}\right]$ = 90,000

Total estimate of current Liabilities (B)	12,10,000
C. Net Working Capital (A - B) (47,45,000 – 12,10,000)	35,35,000
Contingencies allowance	NIL
D. Average working capital required	35,35,000

Notes: 26,000 units have been sold for cash

[1,04,000 x ¼= 26,000] and credit sales for remaining units i.e.

1,04,000 is 78,000 only.

2.   Profits are to be adjusted for income. Tax and dividend payments. For these reasons, profits have been ignored.

3.   All overheads are assumed to be variable. Presence of depreciation element in overheads will lower the working capital requirement.

Illustration 5: Shubha Pvt. Ltd. makes on an average of 20% on sales. In working out the profit margin., depreciation is added to the cost of production

The company maintains one month's stock for raw-materials and also for finished product. In order to maintain a minimum degree of solvency and liquidity. The company does not allow the cash balance to drop below Rs. 1,50,000. The management desires of carry a 20% margin in managing working capital.

Other yearly estimates of the Company are as follows :

	Rs.
Sales of 2 month's credit	30,00,000
Materials to be consumed (suppliers extend one month credit)	7,00,000
Wages (time lag-one month)	6,00,000
Manufacturing expenses payable at the end of the year	
(These are paid one month in arrears)	60,000
Total administration expenses for the year	

(These are paid one month in arrears)   2,60,000

Advertising and promotional expenses

(Payable quarterly in advance)   1,00,000

The company pays income-tax in 4 equal installments, and one installment is paid in the next year. The total income-tax liability of the year amounts to Rs. 3,20,000. Prepare forecast for working capital requirements on Cash Cost Basis.

Solution

Statement showing working capital requirements on Cash Cost Basis

		Amount Rs.
A.	**Current Assets**	
	Debtors (cash cost of goods sold) $\left[\dfrac{23,80,000 \times 2\,\text{months}}{12\,\text{months}}\right]$	= 3,96,667
	Prepaid sales expenses $\left[\dfrac{1,00,000 \times 3\,\text{months}}{12\,\text{months}}\right]$	= 25,000
	Raw materials $\left[\dfrac{7,00,000 \times 1\,\text{month}}{12\,\text{months}}\right]$	= 58,333
	Finished product $\left[\dfrac{20,20,000 \times 1\,\text{month}}{12\,\text{months}}\right]$	1,68,333
	Cash in hand (given)	1,50,000
	Total current Assets (A)	7,98,333
B.	**Current Liabilities**	
	Creditors $\left[\dfrac{7,00,000 \times 1\,\text{month}}{12\,\text{months}}\right]$	= 58,333
	Manufacturing expenses	60,000
	Administrative expenses $\left[\dfrac{2,60,000 \times 1\,\text{month}}{12\,\text{months}}\right]$	= 21,667
	Provision for Taxation $\left[\dfrac{3,20,000}{4}\right]$	= 80,000
	Wages outstanding $\left[\dfrac{6,00,000 \times 1}{12}\right]$	= 50,000
	Total Current Liabilities (B)	2,70,000

Contd...

C. Net Working Capital (A-B)		5,28,333
Add 20% for contingency allowance		
[5,28,333 + 20% of 5,28,333]		= 1,05,667
D. Average working Capital		6,34,000

Working Notes :

(1) **Calculation of Manufacturing expenses**

Sales		30,00,000
Less G. profit 20% on sales		6,00,000
Total cost of manufacture		24,00,000
Less: Cost of material	7,00,000	
Wages	6,00,000	13,00,000
Manufacturing expenses		11,00,000

(2) **Calculation of Depreciation**

Manufacturing expenses		11,00,000
Less Cash manufacturing exp.		7,20,000
		3,80,000

$$\begin{bmatrix} 60,000 \text{ for one month} \\ \text{for12 months 7,20,000} \\ 60,000 \times 12 = 7,20,000 \end{bmatrix}$$

(3) **Calculation of Total cash Cost**

Total cost of Manufacture		24,00,000
Less Depreciation		3,80,000
		20,20,000
Add Administration expenses		2,60,000
Add Sales expenses		1,00,000
Total Cash Cost		23,80,000

Illustration 6: CP Paper Mills Ltd. provided the following information and requested to you to calculate Cash Conversion Cycle (CCC).

Sales – Rs. 3069.14 lakhs

Cost of goods sold – Rs. 2686.24 lakhs

Inventory: Opening – Rs.615.61 lakhs

Closing – Rs. 482.79 lakhs

Receivables: Opening – Rs.926.30 lakhs

Closing – Rs. 986.58 lakhs

Payables: Opening – Rs.832.06 lakhs

Closing – Rs. 901.79 lakhs

Solution:

CCC = Operating cycle (OC) – Accounts Payables Period (APP)

OC = Inventory Conversion Period (ICP) + Accounts Receivables Period (ARP)

ICP = Average Inventory / (Cost of goods sold / 365)

= Rs. 549.2 / (2686.24 / 365) = **74.62 days**

ARP = Average Accounts Receivables / (Sales / 365)

$$= Rs. 956.44 / (3069.14 / 365) = \textbf{113.74 days}$$

OC $= ICP + ARP = 74.62 + 113.74 = \textbf{188.36 days}$

APP   = Average Payables / Cost of goods sold / 365)

$$= Rs. 866.925 / (2686.24 / 365) = \textbf{117.795 days}$$

CCC $= 188.36 - 117.795 = \textbf{70.565 days}$

Illustration 7: Determine the working required to finance a level of activity of 1,80,000 units of output for a year. The cost structure is as under

	Cost per unit (Rs.)
Raw Materials	20
Direct Labour	5
Overheads (including depreciation of Rs. 5)	15
Total cost	**40**
Profit	10
Selling Price	**50**

Additional information

- Minimum desired cash balance is Rs.20,000
- Raw materials are held in stock, on an average, for 2 months
- Work-in-progress (assume 50% completion stage) will approximate to half-a-month production.
- Finished goods remain in warehouse, on an average for a month.
- Suppliers of materials extend a months credit and debtors are provided 2 months credit. The cash sales are 25% of total sales.
- There is a time lag in payment of wages of a month and half-a-month in the case of overheads.

SOLUTION

Estimation of Working Capital Required

Particulars	Amount (Rs.)	Amount (Rs.)
A. CURRENT ASSETS		
Raw materials: (1,80,000 x 20 x 2/12)	6,00,000	
Work-in-process: [(1,80,000 x 27.5 x 0.5/12]	2,06,250	
Finished goods: (1,80,000 x 35 x 1/12)	5,25,000	
Debtors (75% of total units produced):		
(1,35,000 x 35 x 2/12)	7,87,500	
Cash	20,000	
Current Assets		21,38,750
B.CURRENT LIABILITIES		
Suppliers: (1,80,000 x 20 x 1/12)	3,00,000	
Wages: (1,80,000 x 5 x 1/12)	75,000	
Overheads: (1,80,000 x 10 x 0.5/12)	75,000	
Current Liabilities		4,50,000
C.WORKING CAPITAL (A-B)		16,88,750

Illustration 8: A proforma cost sheet of R & Co. Ltd., provides the following information. You are required to estimate the working capital needed to finance a level of activity of 52,000 units of production.

	Amount (per unit)
Raw materials	40
Direct labour	15
Overheads (excluding depreciation)	30
Total cost	**85**
Profit	30
Selling price	**115**

Additional information

Average raw materials in stock: one month; average materials-in-process (50 per cent completion stage): half a month; average finished goods in stock: one month.

Credit allowed by suppliers: one month; credit allowed to customers: two months; time lag in payment of wages: one and half weeks; time lag in payment of overhead expenses: one month; half of the sales is on cash basis. Cash balance is expected to be Rs. 12, 500. You may assume that production is carried on evenly throughout the year, and wages and overhead expenses accrue similarly.

Solution

Estimation of Working Capital Needed

Particulars	Amount (Rs)	Amount (Rs)
A. Estimation of Current Assets:		
i) Raw materials inventory: one month: (52,000 x 40 x 4/52)	1,60,000	
ii) Work-in-process inventory: Half a month		
Raw materials (52,000 x 40 x 2/52) = 80,000		
Direct labour (52,000 x 7.5 x 2/52) = 15,000		
Overheads (52,000 x 15 x 2/52) = 30,000	1,25,000	
iii) Finished goods inventory: one month: (52,000 x 85 x 4/52)	3,40,000	
iv) Debtors: two months: (26,000 x 85 x 8/52)	3,40,000	
v) Cash balance required	12,500	
Total current assets	9,77,500	
B. Estimation of Current Assets:		
i) Creditors: one month: (52,000 x 40 x 4/52)	1,60,000	
ii) Expenses:		
Labour (52,000 x 15 x 3/104) = 22,500		
Overheads (52,000 x 30 x 4/52) = 1,20,000	1,42,500	
Total current liabilities		3,02,500
C. Working capital (A-B)		6,75,000
Add: Contingency		-----------
D. Working capital required		6,75,000

Illustration 9: While preparing a project report on behalf of a client, you have collected the following information. Estimate working capital required (for the level of activity 1,50,000 units)

for the firm after adding 10% contingency. You may assume that production is carried on evenly throughout the year and wages and overhead expenses accrued similarly.

	Amount (per unit)
Raw materials	38.5
Direct labour	11.8
Overheads (including depreciation Rs.5)	32.0
Total cost	**823**
Profit	17.7
Selling price	**100**

Additional Information

Average raw materials in stock: four weeks; average materials-in-process (50 per cent completion stage): half a month; average finished goods in stock: four weeks; credit allowed by suppliers: one month; credit allowed to debtors: eight weeks; lag in payment of wages: two weeks. Cash at bank is expected to be Rs.1,00,000. All sales are credit sales.

Solution

Estimation of working capital needed

Particulars	Amount (in Rs.)	Amount (in Rs.)
A. Estimation of Current Assets:		
i) Raw materials inventory: four weeks		
(1,50,000 x 38.5 x 4/52)	4,44,230.77	
ii) Work-in-process inventory: half a month		
Raw materials (1,50,000 x 38.5 x 2/52) = 222115.38		
Direct labour (1,50,000 x 5.9 x 2/52) = 34038.46		
Overheads (1,50,000 x 13.5x 2/52) = 77884.62	3,34,038.46	
iii) Finished goods inventory: one month		
(1,50,000 x 82.3 x 4/52)	9,49,615.38	
iv) Debtors: two months		
(1,50,000 x 82.3 x 8/52)	18,99,230.8	
v) Cash balance required	1,00,000	
Total current assets		**37,27,115.41**
B. Estimation of Current Assets:		
i) Creditors: one month	4,44,230 = 77	
(1,50,000 x 38.5 x 4/52)		
ii) Expenses:		
Wages (1,50,000 x 11.8 x 2/52)	68,076.92	
Total current liabilities		**5,12,307.69**
C. Working capital(A-B)		**32,14,807.72**
Add: 10% contingency		**3,21,480.28**
D. Working capital required		**35,36,288.00**

Computation of overheads per unit:
Overhead cost per unit Rs. 32 less depreciation Rs. 5 = Rs. 27

TEST KNOWLEDGE

1. Fill in the blanks with appropriate word(s)

   (a) Total of all current assets_____.

   (b) The excess of current assets over current liabilities_____.

   (c) Permanent working capital is the _____ of current assets needed to conduct a business during the normal season of the business.

   (d) The time elapses between the receipt of raw materials and collection of cash from debtors_____.

   (e) Gross operating cycle equal to inventory conversion period plus_____.

   (f) The time elapses between the receipt of raw materials and payment to suppliers_____.

   (g) Net operating cycle equal to gross operating cycle less_____.

   (h) When current assets are less than current liabilities then the resulting figure is_____.

   (i) Components of working capital are_____.

   (j) The automatic sources of short-term funds arising in the normal course of business is known as _____.

   (k) A firm's financial plan that matches the expected life of assets with the expected life of funds raised to finance that assets is referred as _____.

   (l) A firm when depends on more long-term funds for financing needs _____.

   (m) _____ is, use of more short-term funds than warranted by the matching plan.

   [**Answers:** (a) Gross working capital; (b) Net working capital; (c) Minimum amount; (d) Gross operating cycle; (e) Debtors collection period; (f) Cash cycle; (g) payables differed period; (h) Negative working capital; (i) Current assets and current liabilities; (j) Spontaneous; (k) Matching; (l) Conservative, and (m) Aggressive]

2. State whether each of the following statement is true of false

   (a) Working capital is the part of current assets that are supposed to be financed by long-term sources of finance.

   (b) Net working capital is the excess of current assets over current liabilities.

   (c) Negative working capital is the excess of current assets over current liabilities.

   (d) Trade credit is the source of working capital.

   (e) Operating cycle and cash cycle both are one and the same.

   (f) Depreciation is source of working capital.

   (g) In boom period working capital requirement is less.

   (h) Manufacturing companies require less amount of working capital.

   (i) Utilization of fixed assets depends on the availability of working capital.

   (j) Net operating cycle is equal to the gross operating cycle plus payables differed period.

   [**Answers:**(a) True; (b) True; (c) False; (d) True; (e) False; (f) True; (g) False; (h) False; (i) True; and (j) True]

REVIEW QUESTIONS

1. What is working capital?
2. What do you mean by gross working capital?
3. What do you understand by net working capital?
4. Distinguish between permanent working capital and variable working capital.
5. Give the meaning of permanent working capital.
6. What do you mean by variable working capital?
7. What is negative working capital?
8. What is working capital management?
9. List out the components of current assets.
10. List out the components of current liabilities.
11. List out the components of working capital.
12. Distinguish between permanent working capital and variable working capital.
13. What is gross operating cycle or operating cycle?
14. What are various stages of operating cycle?
15. What is cash cycle or net operating cycle?
16. Mention the sources of short-term working capital.
17. List out the approaches of finance mix. What is need for working capital management?
18. Write a note on gross working capital and net working capital.
19. Give a note on different types of working capital.
20. Distinguish between gross operating cycle and net operating cycle.
21. Distinguish between fixed assets and current assets.
22. Discuss the significance of gross working capital and net working capital.
23. Outline the dangers of inadequate working capital.
24. Narrate the dangers of excess working capital.
25. "Working capital must be adequate but at the same time not excessive". Comment.
26. Give a note regarding the factors determining working capital needs of a business firm.
27. Discuss briefly the sources of financing working capital needs.
28. Give a brief note on approaches of finance mix.
29. Write a brief note on operating cycle.
30. Discuss the steps involved in estimation of working capital needed by a firm.
31. What do you mean by matching approach?
32. What do you understand by conservative approach?
33. Give the meaning of aggressive approach.
34. What is working capital? Is there any significant difference in the concepts of gross working capital and net working capital? Discuss in detail.
35. Distinguish between permanent working capital and variable working capital. Explain the significance of distinguish in financing working capital needs of a firm.
36. What is working capital management? What is the need to maintain optimum working capital? Discuss the consequences of inadequate and excess working capital.

37. What is working capital? Discuss the factors that can be considered while estimating working capital requirement of a business firm.

38. Briefly discuss the sources of financing working capital in detail.

39. What is hedging approach of current assets financing? Discuss the basic premise of the hedging approach to finance funds requirements. What are the effects of this approach on the profitability and risk?

40. "Working capital deals with the decisions regarding the appropriate mix and level of current assets and current liabilities". Elucidate that statement.

DO IT YOURSELF PROBLEMS

1. From the following information RRR Company Ltd., for the next year, you are required to estimate the working capital needed to finance a level of activity of 2,08,000 units of production after adding a five per cent safety contingency.

	Amount (per unit)
Raw materials	160
Direct labour	60
Overheads (including depreciation of Rs.10)	130
Total cost	350
Profit	50
Selling price	400

Additional information

Average raw materials in stock: one month

Average materials-in-process (50 per cent completion stage): half a month

Average finished goods in stock: one month

Credit allowed by suppliers: one month

Credit allowed to customers: two months

Time lag in payment of wages: one and half weeks

All sales are credit sales. Cash balance is expected to be Rs. 75,000. You may assume that production is carried on evenly throughout the year and wages and overhead expenses accrued similarly. [**Answer:** 1) Total current assets: Rs.1, 05,40,000; Total liabilities Rs.14, 60,000; Working capital Rs. 90,80,000; Estimated working capital Rs.95, 34,000]

2. From the following information estimate working capital required for the level of activity 78,000 units. You may assume that production is carried on evenly throughout the year and wages and overhead expenses accrue similarly and a time period of four weeks is equivalent to a month.

	Amount (per unit)
Raw materials	45
Direct labour	20
Overheads	37.5
Total cost	102.5
Profit	22.5
Selling price	125

Additional information

Raw materials in stock: two weeks; Materials-in-process: one week; Finished goods in stock: two weeks; Credit allowed by suppliers: half month; Credit allowed to customers: four weeks; Overheads: two weeks; Cash at bank is expected to be Rs.30, 000. 80% of sales are credit sales.
[Answer: 2) Rs.34, 86,250]

3. You are requested by A.P. Paper Mills Limited to estimate working capital required for the level of activity of 6,24,000 units of production. Add 5 per cent for safety. It provides the following information. You may assume that production is carried on evenly throughout the year and wages and overhead expenses accrued similarly and a time period of four weeks is equivalent to a month.

	Amount (per unit)
Raw materials	90
Direct labour	40
Overheads	80
Total cost	210
Profit	60
Selling price	270

Additional information

Raw materials in stock: one month; Materials-in-process: half month; Finished goods in stock: four weeks; Credit allowed by suppliers: one month; Credit allowed to customers: eight weeks; lag in payment of wages: one and half week; Overheads: one weeks; 20 per cent of sales are cash sales and cash at bank is expected to be Rs.60, 000.

[Answer: 3) Total current assets Rs. 3,41,28,000; Total current liabilities Rs. 88,80,000; Working capital Rs. 2, 52,48,000; Estimated working capital Rs. 2,77,72,800]

4. DP Mills Limited has the following information as for the year 2003.

Sales – Rs 3782.79 lakhs   Cost of Goods sold – Rs 3444.47 lakhs

Opening inventory – Rs 856.25 lakhs closing inventory Rs 1037.73 lakhs

Accounts Receivables: Opening – Rs 852 lakhs, Closing – Rs 636.88 lakhs

Accounts Payables: Opening : Rs 832.96 lakhs Closing : 84689 lakhs

Calculate (a) OC and (b) CCC

[Answer: 4) (a) OC = 172.17 days; and (b) CCC = 83.17 days]

CASE FOR CLASS DISCUSSION - I

CREATIVE PROMOTION COMPANY

Mr. Bhatt is a young man of bright ideas. Although he is employed as an engineer in one of the large engineering concerns in Lahore (Pakistan), he spends all his spare time developing new products in his private laboratory at home. Currently, he has commercially provided a domestic appliance called Lavex, which would be a great convenience kitchen to help housewives. He is not interest in manufacturing and selling his new products; his only interest in developing new products is to make money by way of selling patent rights to some established concerns. However, he releases that till he succeeds in selling the patent rights at the price he expects, he has to manufacture and sell the new products on ad hoc basis so as to demonstrate the commercial superiority of his products and thereby, to induce the parties to buy the patents from him. With this objective, he is currently thinking of manufacturing and selling 'Lavex'. He will not give up his full-time job; he will supervise and guide 'Lavex' production and sales during his spare time.

Bhatt has already spent Rs. 30,000 in developing the product. He proposes to buy the component from other parties and keep the production activity to a minimum. The minimum equipment required would cost Rs. 11,000. He would need to rent a small place for Rs. 1,200 per month for production. He proposes to use his residence as office for sales activity.

Bhatt proposes to introduce the product in Chennai city only. His sales projections are as follows :

January	60
February	40
March	110
April	140
May	220
June	180

He is not interested in pushing sales beyond 220 units per month as he cannot cope with the production. He has budgeted Rs. 20,000 for sales promotion, which will be spent mostly for demonstration in leading department stores in the city. The promotion budget is scheduled as follows :

	Rs
January	7,000
February	7,000
March	3,000
April	3,000

This selling price per units will be Rs. 280 and the dealers will be given 15 percent trade discount. He calculates that about 50 unit will be needed for "demonstration and display" in the leading sores at his cost. Although the sales to dealers will be made on one month's credit, he knows that the actual collections will be realized in about 4 weeks time. He rules out cash sales.

Assembling is one of the activity in the production process. Components and materials, which will be purchased from outside parties strictly on 30 days credit will cost Rs. 160 per unit. Wages per month will be Rs. 6000. The production capacity per month will be 220 units. Wages will be paid weekly. Overhead expenses are estimated at Rs. 2800 per month. Materials and components need to be ordered at least one month in advance. There will be inventory of finished goods or goods in process as the production will be strictly against firm orders. Bhatt proposes to employ a full-time production, sales supervisor for Rs. 880 per month.

Mr Bhatt wants to know how much finance will be needed for his first six months of operation and when, so that he may plan accordingly.

Assignments

1. Discuss the nature of the financial problem involved.
2. Prepare the monthly cash budget for the first six months period of the proposed venture.
3. How can the above-mentioned problem be sorted out?

CASE 2

MYSORE LAMPS LIMITED

Mysore Lamps Limited is a company specializing in the production of fluorescent lamps. The company has been maintaining the quality of its products and due to the efforts of its marketing manager, the company has been able to capture a sizeable share of the product market in the recent past. The company is planning to expand in the same product line. Mr. Mysore, the Managing Director of the company, is confronted with the problem of increasing working capital due to the expansion plans of the company.

Mysore Lamps Limited was set up in 1991 with an authorized capital of Rs. 110 crore and faced heavy competition in the initial years of commencement of business. During 2006, the company could make a dent in the fluorescent lamps market and its position as on December 31, 2006, was as shown in **Exhibit 1**.

Exhibit I
Balance Sheet

(Rs. In lakh)

Liabilities	Rs.	Assets	Rs.
Capital	1500	Fixed assets	1000
Reserves	762	Current assets	1862
Long-term loan	400	Raw materials	200
Current liabilities	200	Work-in-progress	287
Finished goods	450	Accounts receivables	675
Bank overdraft	962	Cash	250
Total	4274	Total	4274

During the year 2006, the company was able to sell 50 lakh pieces of fluorescent lamps a Rs. 60 with a profit margin of 10 per cent. The raw material comprised about 50 per cent of the selling price ; while wages and overheads accounted for 12 and 18 per cent, respectively.

As a policy, the company keeps raw material stock for two months of its requirements. In order to make prompt supply to customers on orders received, finished goods stock for two months requirements is maintained, and sales credit of 3 months is given to customers. Due to the standing of the company in the market, the company is able to enjoy 2 months from its suppliers. The production process is of 30 days duration.

Mr. Mysore is seriously considering the proposal for expansion by installing an automatic plant costing Rs. 30 crores. The expansion will bring in an additional capacity of 100 lakh units per annum. Mr. Mysore is not worried about the financing of this plant as the same would be done for the retained earnings supplemented by finances from Mr. Mysore's personal sources. He expects that the company would be able to increase its sale from 50 lakh pieces after the expansion scheme.

Assignments

1. As a manager, what steps would you take to effectively manage the working capital in an inflationary situation?

2. What additional informations are required while evaluating the additional working capital requirement and expansion plans?

3. What steps must be taken to manage the working capital effectively under inflationary situation? What would be the effect of expansion plan on working capital requirement?

REFERENCES

1.   Gitman, L.J., *Principles of Managerial Finance,* New York: Harper and Row Publishers, 1976, p.148.

2.   Ramamoorthy, V.E., *Working Capital Management,* Madras: Institute of Financial Management and Research, 1978, p.5.

3.   Smith, K.V., *Management of Working Capital,* New York: West Publishing Company, 1975, p.5.

4.   Weston, J.F., and Brigham, E.F., *Managerial Finance,* Illinois: The Dryden Press, 1975, p.123.

5.   Walker, E.W., *Essentials of Financial Management,* New Delhi: Prentice-Hall of India Pvt. Ltd., 1974, pp.59-60.

6.   Mead, E.S., *Corporation Finance,* New York: Appleton-Century Co., 1933, p.303.

7.   Field, K., *Corporation Finance,* New York: The Ronald Press Co., 1938, p.173.

8.   Baker, J.C. and Mallet, D.W., *Introduction to Corporate Finance,* New York: McGraw Hill Book Company, 1936, p.92.

9.   Guthmann, H.G. and Dougall, H. E., *Corporate Financial Policy,* New York: Prentice-Hall, 1955, p.387.

10.   Gerstenberg, C.W., *Financial Organisation and Management,* New York: Prentice-Hall, 1959, p.282.

11.   Goel, V.L., *The Management of Working Capital,* The Australian Accountant, Melbourne, Vol. XXIX, No. 6, June 1959, p.319.

12.   Park, C. and Gladson, J.W., *Working Capital,* New York: Macmillan Company, 1963, p.2.

13. Kennedy, R. D. and McMullen, S. Y., *Financial Statement-Form, Analysis and Interpretation,* Illinois: Richard D. Irwin, 1968, p.61.

14. Myer, J. N., *Financial Statement Analysis,* New York: Prentice-Hall of India Pvt. Ltd., 1974, pp.99.

15. Wixon, Rufus (ed.), *Accountants Handbook*, New York: The Ronald Press Company, 1957, p.254.

16. Sailers, E.A., *Handbook of Corporate Management and Procedure*, New York: McGraw-Hill, 1927, p.728.

17. Lincoln, E. E., *Applied Business Finance,* New York: McGraw-Hill, 1929, p.312.

18. Stevens, W.M., *Financial Organisation and Administration*, New York: McGraw-Hill, 1934, p.84.

19. Gitman, L.J., *Op.cit.,* p.150.

20. Roy Chowdary, A. B., *Working Capital Management: A Work Book on Corporate Liquidity,* Calcutta: Management Technologists of 6 Southern Avenue, 1987, p.10.

21. Gerstenberg, C.W., *Op. cit.,* 1960, p.288

22. Joy, O.M., *Introduction to Financial Management,* Homewood Illinois: Richard D. Irwin, 1977, P.407.

23. Zenoff, D. B. and Zack Zwick, *International Financial Management*, New Jersey: Prentice Hall Inc., 1969, p.228.

24. Nargaard, C.T., *Management Accounting,* New Jercy: Prentice Hall Inc., 1985, p.668.

25. Donaldson, E.F., *Corporate Finance*, New York: Ronald Press Co., 1957, p. 479.

26. Agarwal, H.L., *Working Capital Policy – Developing an Analytical Model*, The Management Accountant, Vol.19, No.2, February 1987, p.68.

27. Chandra, P., *Op.cit.,* (2002), p.598.

28. Joy, O.M., *Op.cit.,* p.406.

29. Gitman, L.J., *Op.Cit.,* 2004.p.601

30. Ramamoorthy, V.E., *Op.cit.,*(1976), , p.11.

31. *Ibid.,* p.11.

32. *Ibid.,* 1978, p.60.

33. Hampton, J. J., *Financial Decision Making-Concepts, Problems and Cases*, New Delhi: Prentice-Hall of India Ltd., 1983, p.219.

34. Ramamoorthy, V.E., *Op.cit.,*(1976), p.54.

35. Gitman, L.J., *Op.cit.,* (1997), p.157.

36. Weston, J.F., and Brigham, E.F., *Op.cit., (1975), P.510*

37. *Ibid.,* p.511.

38. Ibid

Cash Management

17

Cash is one of the components of current assets. It is a medium of exchange for purpose of goods and services and for discharging liabilities. Cash management is one of the key areas of working capital management as cash is both beginning and the end of working capital cycle-cash, inventories, receivables and cash. It is the most liquid asset and the basic input required to keep the business running on a continuous basis. To quote Gitman, "liquid assets provide a pool of funds to cover unexpected outlays, thereby reducing the risk of a liquidity crisis'.[1] It is like blood stream in the human body, gives vitality and strength to the firm. Adequate availability of cash is essential to meet the business needs. Since, it is necessary in daily business operations and is productive, the cash owned by an enterprise at any time should be carefully regulated. [2]

Efficient management of the inflow and outflow of cash plays a crucial role in the overall performance of a firm. Shortage of cash will disrupt the firm's manufacturing process while excess cash will remain idle without any contribution towards profit. Cash is not an end itself, but is a means to achieve the end. To quote Brigham, "Cash is a non-earning asset, so excessive cash balance simply lowers the total assets turnover, thereby reducing both the rate of return on net worth and the value of the stock."[3] The steady and healthy circulation of cash throughout the entire business operation is the business solvency.[4] Like any other asset of a company, cash is a tool for profit. Thereby, the emphasis is laid on the a right amount of cash at the right time, at the right place and at the right cost.[5]

Therefore, effective management of cash involves an effort to minimise investment in cash without impairing to liquidity of the firm. It implies a proper balancing between the two conflicting objectives of the liquidity and profitability.

NATURE OF CASH

Cash is the medium of exchange for purchase of goods and services, and for discharging liabilities. In cash management the term cash has been used in two senses.

a) *Narrow Sense:* Under this cash covers currency and generally accepted equivalents of cash, viz., cheques, demand drafts and banks demand deposits.

b) *Broad Sense:* Here, cash includes not only the above stated but also cash assets. There are bank's time deposits and marketable securities. The marketable security can easily sold and converted into cash. Here, cash management is in broader sense.

MOTIVES FOR HOLDING CASH

Cash is the most crucial component of the working capital of a firm, as every transaction results either in an inflow or outflow of cash. Cash has no earning power, then why does a firm need cash? John Maynard Keynes[6] puts forth that there are three possible motives for holding cash.

♦ *The Transaction Motive:* This motive arises due to the necessity of having cash for various disbursements like purchase of raw materials, payment of business expenses, payment of tax, payment of dividend and so on. The need to hold cash would not arise, if there is perfect synchronization between the cash receipts and the cash payments. Hence, the firm must have an adequate cash balance particularly when payments are in excess of receipts to meet its obligations. The requirement of cash to meet routine cash needs is known as the transaction motive and such motive refers to the holding of cash to meet anticipated obligations whose timing is not perfectly synchronized with each receipts. The transaction motive, thus, refers to the holding of cash to meet anticipated obligations whose timing is not perfectly synchronized with cash receipts.

♦ *The Precautionary Motive:* Apart from the non-synchronization of anticipated cash flows in the ordinary course of business, firm may require cash for the payment of unexpected disbursements. The unexpected cash needs at short-notice may be the result of floods, strikes and failure of important customers, bills may be presented for settlement earlier than expected, slow down in collection of accounts receivables, sharp increase in cost of raw materials. It provides a cushion or buffer to withstand some unexpected emergency. The precautionary balance may be held in near-money assets like marketable securities. The amount set aside for precautionary motive is not expected to earn anything. As matter of abundant caution, many companies had learnt the art of 'cultivating the rich uncle', by establishing and maintaining good lasting link with progressive banking institutions. Ready borrowing power is the best antidote to emergency cash drains and facilities release available cash resources for remunerative applications.

♦ *The Speculative Motive:* It refers to the desire of a firm to take advantage of opportunities, which present themselves at unexpected moments and that are typically outside the normal course of business. In simple words, it is a motive of holding cash relates for investing in profitable opportunities as and when they arise. In other words, this motive comes from a desire of holding cash to gain in speculative transactions such as, purchase of raw materials at reduced price on payment of immediate cash, dealing in commodities in bulk purchasing and selling when rates are considered favourable. Hence firms, which have such speculative dealings, may carry additional liquidity.

OBJECTIVES OF CASH MANAGEMENT

One of the prime responsibilities of the financial manager is that managing cash to make balance between profitability and liquidity. In other words, he/she has to maintain optimum cash balance. Optimum cash means it should not be excess or inadequate. Maintenance of excess cash reserve to meet the challenges, the excess cash will remain idle, and idle cash earn nothing, but involves cost. So it will reduce profit. On the other hand, having inadequate cash balance will affect the liquidity of the firm. Hence, there is need to maintain balance between profitability and liquidity. In other words, there should not be excess cash or inadequate cash.

From the above, we can trace the following as the objectives of cash management:

1) To meet cash payment needs, and

2) To maintain minimum cash balance.

1) *To Meet Cash Payments:* The prime objective of cash management is to meet various cash payments needed to pay in business operations. The payments are like payment to supplier of raw materials, payment of wages and salaries, payment of electricity bills, telephone bills and so on. Firm should maintain cash balances to meet the payments, otherwise it will not be able to run business. To quote Bollen, "Cash is an oil to lubricate the ever-turning wheels of business: without it, the process grinds to a stop". Hence, one of the cash management objective is to meet the payments with the maintenance of sufficient cash.

2) *To Maintain Minimum Cash Balance (Reserve):* This is second important objective of cash management. It means the firm should not maintain excess cash balances. Excess cash balance may ensure prompt payment, but if the excess balance will remain idle, as cash is a non-earning asset and the firm will have to forego profits. On the other hand, maintenance of low level of cash balance, may not help to pay the obligations. Hence, the aim of cash management is to maintain optimum cash balance.

ASPECTS OF CASH MANAGEMENT

The aspects or problems of cash management can be examined under three heads, such as:

a) Cash inflows and outflows,

b) Cash flow within the firm, and

c) Cash balances held at the point of time.

Cash inflows (receipts) and outflows (payments) may not match, they may be excess or less over cash outflows. Surplus cash arise when the cash inflows are excess over cash outflows and deficit will arise when the cash inflows are less than the cash outflows. The balance known as synchronisation firm should develop appropriate strategies for resolving the uncertainty involved in cash flow prediction and in balance between cash receipts and payments. Firm has to come up with some cash management strategies regarding the following four facets of cash management.[7]

♦ *Cash Planning:* Cash planning is required to estimate the cash surplus or deficit for each planning period. Estimation of cash surplus or deficit can be arrived by preparation of cash budget.

♦ *Cash Flows Management:* Cash flows means cash inflows and cash outflows. The cash flows should be properly managed that the cash inflows should be accelerated (collected as early as possible) and cash outflows should be decelerated (cash payments should be delayed without affecting firm name).

♦ *Determination of Optimum Cash Balance:* Optimum cash balance is that balance at which the cost of excess cash and danger of cash deficiency will match. In other words, it is the cash balance at that the total cost (total cost equals to transaction cost and opportunity cost) is minimum. Firm has to determine optimum cash balance.

♦ *Investment of Surplus Cash:* Whenever there is surplus cash it should be properly invested in marketable securities, to earn profits. Firms should not invest in long-term securities, they cannot be converted into cash within a short period.

FACTORS DETERMINING CASH NEEDS

From the above, we can say that a firm has to decide the cash balance based on their needs, which is determined after taking into consideration of the following factors.[8]

1) *Synchronisation of Cash Flows:* Synchronisation of cash flows arises only when there is no balance between the expected cash inflows and cash outflows. There is no need to manage cash balance, if there is perfect match between cash inflows and cash outflows. Otherwise, there is a need to manage cash balance for managing synchronisation. This synchronisation is forecasted through the preparation of cash budget for a period of 12 months or the planning period. A well-prepared cash budget will definitely point out the months or periods when the firm will have surplus or deficit cash.

2) *Short Costs:* This is another factor to be considered while determining the cash needs. Short costs are those costs that arise with a short fall of cash for the firm requirements. Shortage of cash can be found through preparation of cash budget. Cash shortage is not cost free, it involves cost whether it is expected or unexpected shortage. The expenses incurred as a result of shortfall are called short costs.[9] They include the following :

❖ *Cost of Transaction:* Whenever there is a shortage of cash it should be financed. Financing may be done through the borrowings from banks or sale of marketable securities (if the firm have). If the firm is planning to finance the deficit cash by sale of marketable securities, then the firm is expected to spend some expenses for brokerage.

❖ *Cost of Borrowing:* If the firm does not have marketable securities with it, then it prefers borrowing as a source of financing, shortage of cash. It involves costs like interest on loan, commitment charges and other expenses relating to the loan.

❖ *Cost of Deterioration of the Credit Rating:* Generally credit rating is given by credit rating agencies (CRISIL, ICRA and CARE). Low credit rating firms may have to go for bank loans with high interest charges, since they cannot raise the required amount from the public. Low credit rating may also leads to the stoppage of supplies, demands for cash payment refusal to sell, loss of image and attendant decline in sales and profits.

❖ *Cost of Loss of Cash Discount:* Sufficient cash helps to get cash discount benefits, but shortage of cash cannot help to obtain cash discounts.

❖ *Cost of Penalty Rates:* Whenever there is shortage of cash firm may not be able to honor currently returned obligations, which in turn demand penalty.

3) *Surplus Cash Balance Costs:* It is self-explanatory. It means that the cost associated with excess or surplus cash balance. Cash is not an earning asset. Surplus cash funds are idle, an impact of idle cash is that the firm losses opportunities to invest those funds and thereby lose interest, which would otherwise have been earned.

4) *Management Costs:* Management costs are those costs involved with setting up and operating cash management staff. These cost are generally fixed over a period, and are mainly include staff, salary, storage, handling cost of security and so on.

CASH PLANNING OR CASH BUDGET

Cash planning and control of cash is the central point of finance functions. Maintenance of adequate cash is one of the prime responsibilities of financial manager. It is possible only through preparation of cash planning.

Cash control is also included in cash planning. Since planning and control are the twins of management. Cash planning is a technique to plan and control the use of cash. A projected cash flow statement prepared based on expected cash receipts and payments, is the anticipation of the financial condition of the firm. Cash planning may be prepared on daily, weekly, monthly or quarterly basis. The period for which the cash planning is prepared depends on the size of the firms and managements philosophy. Large firms, prepare daily and weekly forecasts. Medium size firms prepare weekly and monthly forecasts. Small firms may not prepare cash forecasts due to non-availability of data and less scale of operations. But in a short period they may service but over a long period they have to prepare cash planning for the success of the firm.

Cash Forecasting and Budgeting

Cash forecast is used as a method to predict future cash flow because it deals with the estimation of cash flows (i.e., cash in flows and cash outflows) at different stages and offers the management an advance notice to take appropriate and timely action.[10]

Cash budget is an important tool for the flow of cash in any firm over a future period of time. In other words, it is a statement showing the estimated cash inflows and cash outflows over a planning period. It pinpoints the surplus or deficit cash of a firm as it moves from one period to another period. The surplus of deficit data helps the financial manager to determine the future cash needs of the firm, plan for the financing of those needs and exercise control over the cash and liquidity of the firm. Cash budget is also known as short-term cash forecasting.

Purpose of Cash Budget

Cash budget has proved to be of great help and benefit in the following areas:
♦   Estimating cash requirements
♦   Planning short-term finance planning
♦   Scheduling payments, in respect of acquiring capital goods
♦   Planning and phasing the purchase of raw materials
♦   Evolving and implementing credit policies
♦   Checking and verifying the accuracy of long-term cash forecasting.

Preparation of Cash Budget or Elements of Cash Budget

The above benefit areas clear that the main aim of preparing cash budget is to predict the cash flows over a given period of time and to determine whether at any point of time there is likely to be surplus or deficit of cash. Preparation of cash budget involves the following steps:

Step 1: Selection of period of time (planning horizon). Planning horizon is that period for which cash budget is prepared. There are no fixed rules for cash budget preparation. Planning horizon of a cash budget may differ from firm to firm, depending upon the size of the firm. Cash budget period should not be too short or too long. If it is too short many important events may come out in the planning period and cannot be accounted for the preparation of cash budget, which becomes expensive. On the other hand, if it is too long the estimates will be inaccurate. Then how to determine planning horizon? It is determined on the basis of situation and the necessity of a particular case. A firm whose business is affected by seasonal variations may prepare monthly cash budgets . If the cash flow fluctuates, daily or weekly cash budgets should be prepared. Longer period cash budgets may be prepared when the cash flows are stable in nature.

Step 2: Selection of factor that has bearing on cash flows. The factors that generate cash flows are divided into two broad categories. (a) Operating, and (b) Financial.

♦   *Operating Cash Flows:* Operating cash inflows are cash sales, collection of accounts receivables and disposal of fixed assets and the operating cash outflows are bills payables, purchase of raw materials, wages, factory expenses, administrative expenses, maintenance expenses and purchase of fixed assets.

♦   *Financial Cash Flows:* Loans and borrowings, sale of securities, dividend received, refund of tax, rent received, interest received and issue of new shares and debentures cash outflows are redemption of loan, repurchase of shares, income tax payments, interest paid and dividend paid.

Illustration 1: From the following information prepare cash budget for VSI Co. Ltd.:

Particulars	Jan	Feb	March	April
Opening cash balance	20,000			
Collection from customer	1,30,000	1,60,000	1,65,000	2,30,000
Payments :				
Raw materials purchase	25,000	45,000	40,000	63,200
Salary and wages	1,00,000	1,05,000	1,00,000	1,14,200
Other expenses	15,000	10,000	15,000	12,000
Income tax	6,000	----	----	----
Machinery	----	----	20,000	----

The firm wants to maintain a minimum cash balance of Rs. 25,000 for each month. Creditors are allowed one-month credit. There is no lag in payment of salary, other expenses.

Solution

Cash budget for the period Jan to April (Rs.)

Particulars	Jan	Feb	March	April
Opening cash balance	20,000	29,000	49,000	34,000
Cash collection from customer	1,30,000	1,60,000	1,65,000	2,30,000
(A) Total receipts	1,50,000	1,89,000	2,14,000	2,64,000
Payments :				
Raw materials	----	25,000	45,000	40,000
Salary	1,00,000	1,05,000	1,00,000	1,14,200
Other expenses	15,000	10,000	15,000	12,000
Income tax	6,000	----	----	----
Machinery	----	----	20,000	----
(B) Total payments	1,21,000	1,40,000	1,80,000	1,66,200
Closing Balance (A – B)	29,000	49,000	34,000	97,800

Illustration 2: Prepare cash budget for the 3 months ending on 30-06-2004 from the following information.

(a)   *(Amount in Rs.)*

Month	Sales	Materials	Wages	Overheads
Feb	14,000	9,600	3,000	1,700
March	15,000	9,000	3,000	1,900
April	16,000	9,200	3,200	2,000
May	17,000	10,000	3,600	2,200
June	18,000	10,400	4,000	2,300

(b) *Credit terms are:*

Sales / Debtors - 10 per cent, sales are on cash, 50 per cent of the credit, sales are collected next month and the balance in the following month.

 ❖ Creditors (suppliers) - 2 months

 ❖ Wages - ¼ month; overheads - ½ month

(c) Cash and Bank balance as on 1st April 2004 is expected to be Rs. 6,000.

(d) *Other information:* Machinery will be installed in Feb.'04 at a cost of Rs. 96,000. The monthly installment of Rs. 2,000 is payable from April onward.

Dividend at 5 per cent on preference share capital of Rs. 2,00,000 will be payable on 1st June.

Advance to be received for sale of vehicles Rs. 9,000 in June.

Dividends from investments amounting to Rs. 1,000 are expected to be received in June.

Income tax (advance) to be paid in June is 2,000 (ICWA - Inter)

Solution

Particulars	April	May	June
(A) Opening balance	6,000	3,950	3,000
Receipts: Sales Note (1)	14,650	15,650	16,650
Dividend	----	----	1,000
Advance	----	----	9,000
(B) Total receipts	14,650	15,650	26,650
Payments:			
Creditors	9,600	9,000	9,200
Wages Note (2)	3,150	3,500	3,900
Overheads Note (3)	1,950	2,100	2,250
Installment (on machinery)	2,000	2,000	2,000
Dividend	----		10,000
Tax	----	----	2,000
(C) Total payments	16,700	16,600	29,350
(D) Surplus / Deficit (B – C)	(2,050)	(950)	(2,700)
(E) Balance cash (A – B)	3,950	3,000	300

Working Note:

(1) Cash collection from Sales

Particulars	April	May	June
Feb (14,000 – 10% of 14,000) 50%	6,300	----	----
March (15,000 – 10% of 15,000) 50%	6,750	6,750	----
April (10% of 16,000)	1,600	----	----
(16,000 – 10% of 16,000) 50%	----	7,200	7,200
May (10% of 17,000)	----	1,700	----
(17,000 – 10% of 17,000) 50%	----	----	7,650
June (10% of 18,000)	----	----	1,800
	14,650	15,650	16,650

(2) 75 per cent of the April + 25 per cent of the previous month

(3) 50 per cent of the month + 50 per cent of the previous month

MANAGING CASH FLOWS

After estimation of cash flows, then the next financial manager's job is to ensure that there should not be more deviation between the projected cash flows and the actual cash flows, for that efficient cash management is must. That financial manager will have the control on collection of receipts and cash disbursements. As the objectives of cash management is to accelerate cash receipts as much as possible and decelerate or delay cash payments as much as possible. In other words, the various collection and disbursement methods can be employed to improve cash management efficiently constitutes two sides of the same coin.[11] Both collections and disbursements exercise a joint impact on the overall efficiency of cash management. The idea is that speed collection of accounts receivables so that the firm can use money sooner, otherwise, it has to borrow money, wherein costs are involved. Conversely, firm wants to pay accounts payables late without affecting credit standing with suppliers, so that firm can make use of the money it already has. Hence, for efficient cash management firm has (A) to collect accounts receivables as early as possible, and (B) it has to delay the accounts payables without affecting credit standing.

(A) Accelerating Cash Collections

Accelerating speedy cash collection can conserve cash and reduce its requirements for cash balances of a firm. Cash inflow process can be accelerated through systematic planning. The following are the methods of accelerating cash collections:

1) **Prompt Payment of Customers:** In speed collection, the first hurdle could be the firm itself. It may take a long time to process the invoice. Prompt payment by customers will be possible by prompt billing. The seller has to inform to customers about the amount of payment and period of payment in advance. Automation of billing and enclosure of self-addressed enveloped, will be helpful for speed payment of cash. The other way of prompting customers to pay earlier is to offer cash discount. Cash discount helps customer to save money and they would readily avail discounts.

2) **Early Conversion of Payments into Cash:** After using cheques by customer in favour of the firm collections can be quickened. Conversion of cheques into cash is the second hurdle. There is a time lag between the time a cheque is prepared by customer and the time the funds are credited to firm's account. It is also known as cash cycle. Cash cycle is the time required to convert the raw materials into cash. There are three steps involved in the cash cycle, viz., (i) Mailing time—The time taken by the post offices in transferring the cheques from the customer to the firm. The time lag is referred to as "postal float". (ii) Lethargy - time taken in processing the cheques within the company and sending them to bank for deposit and (iii) Bank Float - Collection within the bank or the time taken by the bank in collecting the payment from the customer's bank. The postal float, lethargy and bank float-collectively known as "deposit float". To quote Rama Moorthy, deposit float as the sum of cheques written by the customer that are not yet usable by the firm.[12] In India deposit float can assume sizeable opportunities as cheques normally take a longer time to get realised than in most countries.[13] Accelerated collection of cash is possible when a firm reduces the transit, lethargy and bank float.

How can the deposit float be reduced ?

It is possible through the options of decentralised collection policy. There are two important methods available to use in a decentralised collection network, they are concentration banking and Lock-Box system.

3) **Concentration Banking or Decentralised Collections:** A firm operating its business spread over a vast area and its branches located at different places would do well to decentralise its collections. The decentralised collection procedure in US is called as "concentration banking." Concentration banking is a system of operating through a number of collection centers, instead of a single collection centre centralised at the company's head office premises. Under this system, a firm will have a large number of bank accounts in the operated areas, but all the areas may not have collection centres. Opening it collection centre depends on the volume of business. In this system, the customers' are instructed to send their payments to the collection centre covering the area under which they come and these are deposited in the local account of the concerned collection centre. On realisation of the proceeds of the cheques, these may be remitted for credit to the Head Office Account, by way of telegraphic transfer, daily or weekly, as per the quantum of collections and the local requirements of funds for expenses. Hence, concentration banking reduces float, which saves time and reduces in the operating cash needs. This system should be adopted only when the savings are higher than the cost.

4) *Lock-Box System:* This is another technique of accelerating collection of cash. It is more popular in USA and European countries. Under this arrangement, a firm rents a post office box and authorises its bank to pick up remittances in the box. The boxes will be placed at different centres on the basis of number of consumers. Customers are billed with instructions to mail remittances to the box. The local authorised bank of the firm, at the respective places pick up the mail several times a day and the same deposits into the firm's account. After the collection of cheques the bank, send a deposit slip along with the list of payments and other required encloses.

Advantages of Lock-box system are:

(a) The bank handles the remittances prior to deposit at a lower cost;

(b) The process of collection through the banking system begins sooner the receipt of cheque and saves time.

(c) Lock-box system involves cost, since the services provided by the bank are chargeable or requires to maintain a minimum cash balance that involves an opportunity cost. A financial manager has to compare the benefits derived from use of lock-box system and when benefits are higher than the cost involved then it should be adopted.

(B) Slowing Down Cash Payments

Operating cash requirement can be reduced by accelerating cash collections and slowing down cash payments. Increased availability of cash depends on the combination of speed collections and slow payments. Following methods can be used to showing down the payments.

♦ *Paying on Last Date:* A prudent businessman would always prefer to make the payment only on the last day, when it is due and never earlier. But early payments entitles a firm to cash discounts. If there is no discount offer on early payments of accounts payables has no advantage, but delayed beyond trade credit period affects the firms credit standing that makes difficult to get trade credit in future. Hence, a firm would be well advised to pay payments only on the last dates.

♦ *Centralised Payments:* Under this system, all payments are made from one central place that is Head Office. The benefits of centralised payment system are :

It increases the transit time. In other words, payment from a centralised place takes more time to send the cheques to customers.

Reduction in operating cash requirement since the firm has centralised bank account, a relatively smaller total cash balance will be needed.

Controlled schedules and payments made exactly on the last day.

Paying the Float: Float is the amount of money tied up in cheques that have been written, but have yet to be collected. In simple words, float refers to the difference between the balance in firms cash book (bank column) and balance in passbook of the bank. There is a time lag between issue of cheque by the company and its presentation to the bank by the customer's bank for collection of money, where cash is required later when the cheque is presented for collection. So, firm can issue cheque without having sufficient cash in its bank account at the time of its issue to its customers, because by the time of presentation of the Cheque for encashment, firm can arrange funds. Use of float in this way referred to as cheque kiting. Cheque kiting[14] can be done in two ways—(a) paying from a distant bank and (b) cheque encashment analysis.

a) *Paying From a Distant Bank:* As discussed in centralised payments.

b) *Cheque Encashment Analysis:* On the basis of firm's past experience (if firm has been paying from a few years onward), it can find out the lag in the issue of cheques and their encashment. If more time lag is there then the firm will pay with delay and vice versa. It will help the firm to save cash.

COMPUTATION OF OPTIMUM CASH BALANCE

A firm has to maintain sufficient liquidity by managing minimum cash balance. Firm needed cash to pay suppliers of raw materials, pay salaries and other expenses as well as paying interest, tax and dividends. Sufficient liquidity means the availability of cash to pay the firm obligations in time. Generally, the minimum cash balance is equal to the cash needed for transaction plus safety cash that can be maintained based on firm's past experience. Maintenance of cash balance provides sufficient liquidity but involve opportunity cost (loss of interest), whereas less cash balance maintenance weakens liquidity and involves profitability. A firm has to maintain optimum cash balance. Optimal cash balance is that cash balance where the firm's opportunity cost equals to transaction cost and the total cost are minimum. Then how to determine optimum cash balance ?

Optimum cash balance can be determined by a number of mathematical models. But here the most important two models are discussed. They are:

Baumol Model (Inventory Model)

Miller—Orr Model (Statistical Model)

Baumol Model

This model was developed by Baumol.[15] This model is suitable only when the cost flows are predictable (under certainty). It considers optimum cash balance similar to the economic order quantity, since it is based on EOQ Concept and also in both the cases there is trade off between cost of borrowing (sale of securities cost) and opportunity the cost. The point where the total cost is minimum. Figure 8.1 shows Baumol model.

Assumptions: Baumol model is based on the following:

The firm knows its cash needs with certainty.

The cash payments (disbursement) of the firm occur uniformly over a period of time and is known with certainty.

The opportunity cost of holding cash is known and it remains stable over time.

The transaction cost is known and remains stable.

Elements of Total Cost

The total cost associated with management of cash under this model involves two elements (a) Conversion cost (transaction cost) and (b) Opportunity cost (interest cost).

a) *Conversion Cost (Transaction cost):* Conversion costs are those costs that are associated with sale of marketable security and raise whenever firm converts marketable security into cash. Conversion Cost (C) = C [F/M]

Where: C = Cost per conversion; F = Expected cash need for future period

M = Amount of marketable securities sold in each sale.

b) *Opportunity Cost:* Is the (cost benefit) foregone by holding idle cash. In other words, opportunity cost is the interest forgone on an average cash balance. Symbolically,

Opportunity cost (O) = I (M ÷ 2)

Where, I = Interest rate that could have been earned

M ÷ 2 = Average can balance [(Opening cash + Closing cash) / 2]

Total cost = Conversion cost + Opportunity cost

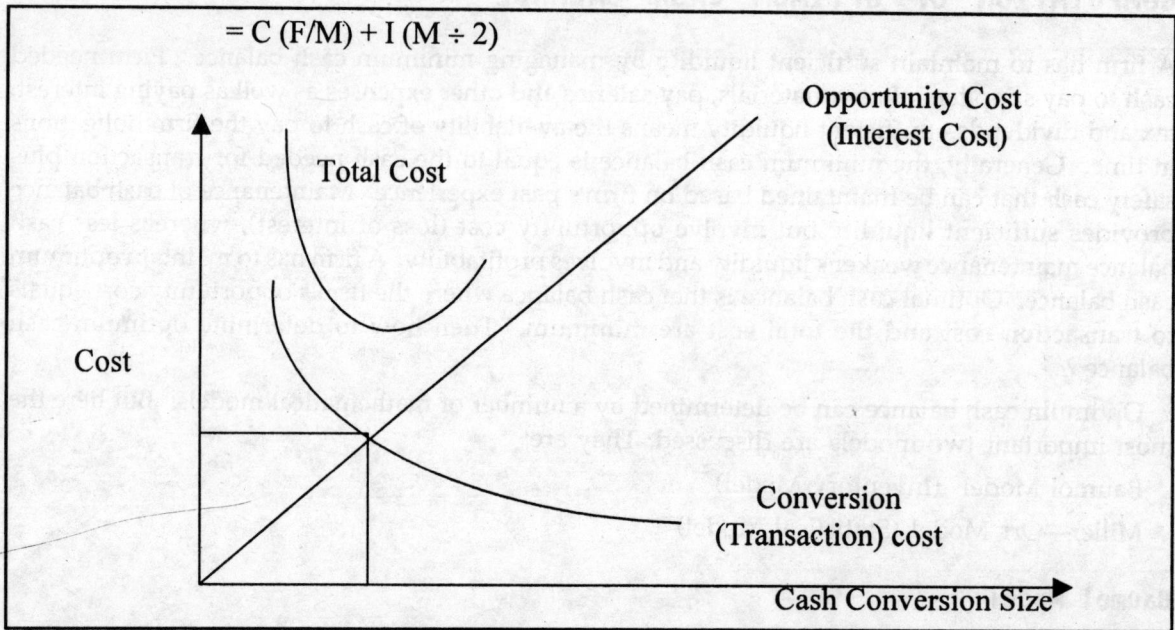

Economical (optimal) Conversion lot size :

$$ECL = \sqrt{\frac{2CF}{O}}$$

Where,

ECL = Economic Conversion Lot;   F = Expected cash needed for future period

C = Cost per conversion;   O = Opportunity cost

Illustration 3: VS International Coy Ltd., estimated cash needs of Rs. 20 lakhs for a year. Cost of transaction of marketable securities is Rs. 2000 per lot. The company has marketable securities in lot sizes of Rs. 1,00,000, Rs. 2,00,000, Rs. 4,00,000, Rs. 5,00,000 and Rs. 10,00,000. Determine economic conversion lot size if 20% is the opportunity cost.

Solution

$$ECL = \sqrt{\frac{2 \times 2000 \times 20,00,000}{0.20}} = Rs.2,00,000$$

Miller and Orr Model

The Miller and Orr model[16] is in fact an attempt to make Baumol model more elastic with regards to the pattern of periodic changes in cash balances. Baumol's model is based on the assumption that uniform and certain level of cash balances. But in practice firms do not use uniform cash balances nor are they able to predict daily cash inflows and outflows. The Miller

Orr Model overcomes the limitations of Baumol model. It's augmented on the Baumol Model and came out of a statistical model. That is useful for the firms with uncertain cash flows. The Miller and Orr model provides two control limits—the upper control limit and the lower control limit along with a return point. The following figure 8.2 shows the two control limits and return point.

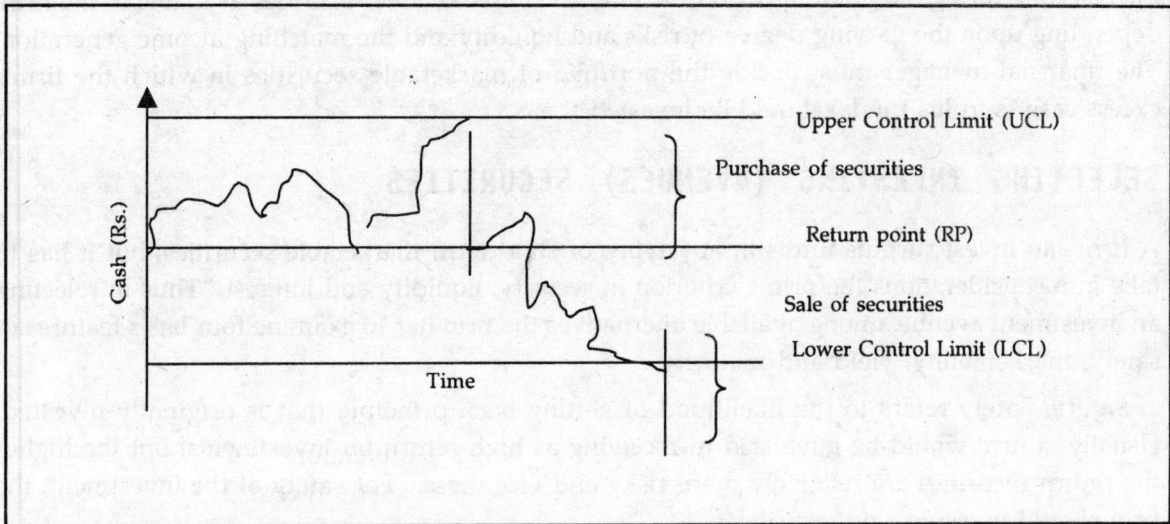

According to this model, cash balance fluctuates between LCL and UCL. Whenever, cash balance touches UCL then the firm purchases sufficient (UCL - RP) marketable securities to take bank cash balance to return point. On the other hand when the firm touches the lower control limit, it will sell the marketable securities to the extent of (RP - LCL), take back cash balance to return point.

The cash balance at the lower control limit (LCL) is set by the firm as per requirement of maintaining minimum cash balance. The cash balances at upper control limit (UCL) and record points will be determined on the basis of the transaction cost (C), the interest rate (O) and standard deviation (σ) of net cash flows.

The following formula is used to determine the spread between UCL and LCL (called Z) as per MO model

$$Z(RP) = \sqrt[3]{\frac{3C\sigma^2}{4O}} + LCL \text{ or } \left(\frac{3}{4} \times \frac{C\sigma^2}{O}\right)^{1/3} + LCL$$

Where: Z = Control limit of cash balance (or) return point

C = Transaction cost   σ = Variance of net cash flow   LCL = Lower control limit

O = Opportunity cost or interest rate earned on marketable security

INVESTMENT OF SURPLUS FUNDS

Components may have surplus (excess cash) funds in several occasions that are required after sometime. Therefore, it would be an efficient decision, if the excess cash invested in some investment avenues that may be safe and liquid, and which may even earn some reasonable interest too, during the holding period. A number of marketable securities available to the firm, depending upon the varying degree of risks and liquidity and the matching income generation. The financial manager must decide the portfolio of marketable securities in which the firm's excess cash (surplus funds) should be invested.

SELECTING INVESTING (AVENUES) SECURITIES

A firm can invest surplus funds in any types of short-term marketable securities, but it has to take into considerations the prime criterion in security, liquidity and interest. Thus in selecting an investment avenue among available alternatives the firm has to examine four basis features of safety, marketability, yield and maturity.

Safety: Safety refers to the likelihood of getting back principle that is originally invested. Usually, a firm would be interested in receiving as high return on investments, but the higher the return securities are relatively more risky and vice versa. For safety of the investment, the firm should invest in safe securities.

Marketability: Marketability of securities refers to the owner's ability to convert the securities into cash on short notice. The two important aspects of marketability are price and time. If the security can be sold within short period without loss, it is highly liquid asset. Firm has to invest its surplus finds only in marketable securities.

Yield: The yield or return, on a security is related to the interest and appreciation of principle amount invested on a security. Some securities do not pay interest, since they are sold at discount. (Treasury bills). If the firm prefers return it may require to bare risk.

Maturity: Maturity refers to the time over which interest and principle amount are to paid. Almost all the short-term securities are having different maturity periods. Financial manager has to decide in which securities surplus cash should be invested.

MONEY MARKET INSTRUMENTS OR MARKETABLE SECURITIES

Money market refers to the market for short-term securities. It has no physical market place and it consists of a loose agglomeration of banks and dealers linked together by telex, telephones and computers.[17] A huge volume of securities is regularly traded on the market and the competition is energetic. The following are most prominent short-term securities available for investment of surplus cash.

(a) *Units of Unit 1964 Scheme:* This scheme is one of the units of Unit Trust of India (UTI), it is known as the Unit Scheme 1964 (in short US 64). It is the most popular mutual fund scheme in India, which comprises the following features : (i) it is an open ended scheme - as it can be purchased and sold back to the UTI itself on the continuous basis, (ii) the units have face value of Rs. 10 for sale and the purchase of units are not determined on the basis of the Net Asset Value (NAV) of the units, as should be the case for a truly open-ended scheme. It is

instead, they are determined administratively by the UTI taking into account the element of accrued interest, from time to time, usually at monthly intervals.   Thus the units of the US 64 scheme offer a convenient and attractive investment avenue for short-term funds for the following reasons: (i) Existence of active secondary market, (ii) Units appreciates over time in a fairly predictable manner as the UTI makes a gradual upward revision in its selling and repurchase price from July to June, each year.

(b) *Ready Forward (RPs or repos):* In the ready forward deal, a commercial bank or some other organisation may enter into an arrangement with a company, intending to park its surplus funds for a short period, under which the bank may sell some securities to one company and repurchases the same securities at prices (i.e., both buying and selling prices) determined as mutually agreed. Hence, it is termed as 'ready forward'. Ready forwards, are however, permitted only in a limited number of specified securities. Ready forward does not provide any income to the company in the form interest, but the company's income is the difference between the buying and selling prices. The income earned on the ready forward is taxable as usual. The rate of return on a ready forward deal is closely related to the market conditions prevailing in the money market, which is generally tight during the busy season, also at the time of the annual closing.

(c) *Treasury Bills:* Treasury bills are the obligations of the government for a short-term period of less than one year, ranging from 91 days to its multiple like 182 days and 364 days. They are sold at a discount rate and redeemed at the face value and the difference between the rates constitutes to the income. In other words, they are not issued at any interest rate. The yield on treasury bills is low, when compared to other gainful short-term investment avenues. But it has several attractive features, like First, they are issued in a bearer form, which makes them easily transferable mere by delivery of the documents, without any endorsement. Second, the secondary market for bills make them highly liquid, and also allows to purchase of bills with very short maturities. Third, they are risk free since they are having financial backing of the government.

(d) *Commercial Papers (CPs):* Commercial paper is short-term, unsecured promissory note issued by large companies. It was introduced in 1990 with a view to enabling the highly rated corporate borrowers to diversify the sources of their short-term borrowings, as also provide an additional instrument to the investors, to park their surplus funds for a short period.[18] Eligibility, any firm which planning to issue of commercial papers is has to fulfill the guidelines given by RBI, such as (i) the tangible net worth of the issuing company should not be less than Rs. 4 crore, as per latest balance sheet. (ii) the company should have been sanctioned a working capital limit by the bank(s) or all India Financial Institutions (IFIs) (iii) the company should have been classified as a Standard Asset by the financing bank(s) financial institutions, and (iv) a minimum credit rating of P-2 of CRISIL (Credit Rating Information Services of India Limited), or such equivalent rating by any other agency approved by RBI (like ICRA - Investment Information and Credit Rating Agency of India Limited, CARE - Credit Analysis and Research Limited).

Mode of Issue: Commercial papers can be directly (companies with high credit rating) issued or through dealers. These are generally sold at a discount (in bearer form) to the face value, as determined by the buyer, but some times they can be issued carrying interest and made payable to the order of the investor. Commercial paper should not be under written or co-accepted. They can be issued with a maturity of minimum period of 15 days (reduced from 30 days) to a maximum period of up to one year. They are issued in the denomination of Rs. 5 lakh or multiples thereof. Any single investor has to invest a minimum amount of Rs. 5 lakh. The main attraction of CPs is interest rate that is typically higher than that offered by the treasury bills or certificates of deposits. The only disadvantage is that it does not have an active secondary market.

(e) *Certificate of Deposit (CDs):* Certificate of deposit represents the receipts of funds deposited with a bank specified period, like the bank term deposits, but the only difference is CDs are negotiable. CDs may be issued in registered form or bearer form. The later form is more popular since, it can be transacted more easily in the secondary market. Not like treasury bills (issued at discount) CDs are issued at an explicit rate of interest. On maturity, the investor gets the principle amount along with interest accumulated.

Certificate of deposits are popular form of short-term investment of surplus funds for companies due to the following reasons: (i) these can be issued by banks in the required denominations and maturities period suits to the needs of investors, (ii) CDs are fairly liquid, (iii) They are virtually risk-free and (iv) CDs generally offer higher rate of interest then the treasury bills and even bank term deposits.

(f) *Banker's Acceptance:* Banker's acceptances are time drafts drawn on a bank by a firm (the drawer or exporter) in order to obtain payment for goods that he/she has shipped to a customer which maintains an account with that specific bank. In other words, it is a short-term promissory trade note for which a bank (by having 'accepted' them) promises to pay the holder the face amount at maturity. The draft guarantees payment by the accepting bank at a specific point of time. Hence, the acceptance becomes a marketable security. The document is not issued in specialised denominations, since one party uses acceptances to finance the acquisition of good. The size of bank acceptances is determined by the cost of goods being purchased. They serve a wide range of maturities and are sold on a discount basis, payable to the bearer. There is no secondary market for acceptances of large banks. Due to their greater financial risk and lesser liquidity, acceptances provide investors a yield advantage over treasury bills of same maturity. Acceptances of major banks are safe investment.

(g) *Inter-Corporate Deposits (ICDs):* This is a popular short-term investment avenue for companies in India. As the name itself suggests, an inter-corporate deposit is that deposit made by one corporate body (company) with another corporate company. The deposits are usually made for a maximum of six months.

There are three types inter-corporate deposits:

(i) *Call Deposits:* These types of deposits are expected to be paid on call, which is whenever its repayment is demanded. Generally, these deposits are called back giving a day's notice. But in actual practice the lender has to for at least three days.

(ii) *Three-month Deposits:* These are more popular among the corporate bodies for parking the surplus funds correspondingly for tiding over the short-term financial crunch faced by some others.

(iii) *Six-month Deposits:* Generally, inter-corporate deposits do not extend beyond six months period. This type of deposits is usually made with 'A' category companies only.

Inter-corporate deposits are in the nature of unsecured deposits. Hence, due care has to be taken to asses and ascertain the credit worthiness and willingness of the company concerned, with whom it is intended to be made. In addition, it must make sure that it adheres the following requirements, as stipulated by sections 370 and 372 of the Company's Act, 1956 which states a company cannot lend more than 10 per cent of its net worth without prior approval of the central government and a special resolution permitting such excess lending.

(h) *Badla Financing:* A company providing badla financing is essentially lending money to a stock market operator who wishes to carry forward his/her transaction from one settlement period to another. Generally, such finance is provided through a broker and that too against the security of the shares already brought by the stock market operator. Badla has single greatest advantage that it offers very attractive rate of interest. But it is coupled with gain there are several risks like the stock market broker may not honor his commitment, or the broker may become a defaulter. Soothe following precautionary and safety measures should borne in mind while providing badla financing: (i) provide finance only for reputed and financially strong stockbroker, (ii) select intrinsically sound shares, (iii) ask or keep adequate margin, if share is highly volatile, and (iv) secure possession of share certificates.

(i) *Bills Discounting:* Generally bill arises out of trade transaction. Bill is drawn by the seller (drawer) on the buyer (drawee) for the value of goods delivered to him. During the pendency of the bill, if the seller needs finds he/she may get it discounted. On the maturity, the bill is presented to the drawee for payment. A bill of exchange is a self-liquidating instrument. Discounting is superior to the inter-corporate deposits. While participating in bill discounting a company should ensure that the bill is trade bill and not accommodation bill, try to go for bills backed by letters of credit rather than open bills as the former are more secure.

SUMMARY

Cash is one of the components of current assets and it is a medium of exchange for purpose of goods and services and for discharging liabilities.

Cash management is one of the key areas of working capital management as cash is both beginning and the end of working capital cycle-cash, inventories, receivables and cash. It is the most liquid asset and the basic input required to keep the business running on a continuous basis.

Efficient management of cash involves an effort to minimise investment in cash without impairing to liquidity of the firm. It implies a proper balancing between the two conflicting objectives of the liquidity and profitability.

In cash management, the term 'cash' has used in two senses: Narrow sense and Broad sense. In narrow sense, cash covers currency and generally accepted equivalents of cash, viz., cheques, demand drafts and banks demand deposits. Broad Sense, cash includes not only the above stated but also near cash assets. There are bank's time deposits and marketable securities. The marketable security can easily sold and converted into cash. Here cash management is in broader sense.

John Maynard Keynes, put forth that there are three possible motives for holding cash:

(1) The Transaction Motive,

(2) Precautionary motive, and

(3) Speculative motive.

Objectives of cash management are to meet cash payment needs; and to maintain minimum cash balance.

Aspects of cash management can be examined under three heads: cash inflows and outflows, cash flow within the firm and cash balances held at the point of time.

Facets of cash management strategies:

(1) Cash Planning,

(2) Cash Flows Management,

(3) Determination of Optimum Cash Balance, and

(4) Investment of Surplus.

The required cash balance is estimated after taking into consideration of the factors: (1) Synchronisation of Cash Flows, (2) Short Costs, (3) Surplus Cash Balance Costs, and (4) Management Costs.

Cash planning is a technique to plan and control the use of cash. A projected cash flow statement prepared based on expected cash receipts and payments, anticipation the financial condition of the firm. Cash planning may be prepared on daily, weekly, monthly or quarterly basis.

Cash budget is a statement showing the estimated cash inflows and cash outflows over a planning period. It pinpoints the surplus or deficit cash of a firm as it moves from one period to another period. Cash budget is prepared for the purpose of estimating cash requirements; Planning short-term finance planning; Scheduling payments, in respect of acquiring capital goods; Planning and phasing the purchase of raw materials; Evolving and implementing credit policies; Checking and verifying the accuracy of long-term cash forecasting. Preparation of cash budget involves two steps: (1) Selection of period of time (planning horizon). Planning horizon is that period for which cash budget is prepared. (2) Selection of factor that has bearing on cash flows.

There are two types of cash forecasts: (1) Short-term cash forecast and (2) Long-term cash forecast. Short-term cash forecast is that forecast, which covers less than one year's period. The most commonly used methods of short-term cash forecasting are: The receipt and disbursements method; and the adjusted income method. Long-term forecast may be prepared for a period of more than one year. Long-term forecasts may be done for a period of 2 to 5 years and it provides a broader picture of the firm's cash position (excess or inadequate). In simple words, it highlights the firm's ingestible surplus and financing needs in future. This type of forecast is useful for planning capital investments and long-term financing.

For efficient cash management firm has (A) to collect accounts receivables as early as possible, and (B) it has to delay the accounts payables without affecting credit standing. Accelerating cash collections can conserve cash and reduce its requirements for cash balances of a firm. Cash inflow process can be accelerated through systematic planning that includes the methods of accelerating cash collections (Prompt Payment of Customers, Early Conversion of Payments into Cash, Concentration Banking, and Lock-Box System). Slowing Down Cash Payments, involves, Paying on Last Date, Centralised Payments.

A firm has to maintain optimal cash balance is that cash balance where the firm's opportunity cost equals to transaction cost and the total cost are minimum. They are: (1) Baumol Model (Inventory Model)—This model is suitable only when the cost flows are predictable (under certainty). It considers optimum cash balance similar to the economic order quantity, since it is based on EOQ concept, and determines the cash conversion size. and (2) Miller—Orr Model (Statistical Model), is in fact an attempt to make Baumol model more elastic as regards to the pattern of periodic changes in cash balances.

A firm can invest surplus funds in any types of short-term marketable securities, but it has to take into considerations the prime criterion in security, liquidity and interest. Thus in selecting an investment avenue among available alternatives the firm has to examine four basis features, of a security safety, marketability, yield and maturity.

Money market refers to the market for short-term securities. The most prominent short-term securities available for investment of surplus cash are: Units of Unit 1964 Scheme, Ready Forward (RPs or repos), Treasury Bills, Commercial Papers (CPs), Certificate of Deposit (CDs), Banker's Acceptance, Inter-Corporate Deposits (ICDs), Badla Financing, and Bills Discounting.

TRY YOURSELF - SOLVED PROBLEMS

1. The annual cash requirement of a company is Rs. 20 lakhs, firm has short-term marketable securities is lot size of Rs. 50,000; Rs. 1,00,000; Rs. 1,50,000; Rs. 2,00,000; Rs. 2,50,000; Rs. 5,00,000 and Rs. 5,50,000. The cost of conversion of marketable securities is Rs. 4,000 per lot. The company's opportunity cost is 6 per cent. Determine the economic lot size.

Solution

$$ECL = \sqrt{\frac{2CF}{O}}$$

Where: C = Cost of conversion of security (per conversion)

F = Expected cash needs for future period

O = Opportunity cost of the firm

$$ECL = \sqrt{\frac{2 \times 4000 \times 20,00,000}{0.06}} = Rs.5,16,398$$

2. A firm has a stable demand for a monthly net cash outflow at Rs. 1,80,000. Every month cash is procured by selling marketable securities. The cost of per conversion is Rs. 100. The firm earn 12 per cent interest on invested securities. You are required to determine economic conversion lot size. The firm has securities in the lot sizes of Rs. 30,000; Rs. 60,000; Rs. 90,000 and Rs. 1,20,000.

Solution

$$ECL = \sqrt{\frac{2CF}{0}}$$

$$ECL = \sqrt{\frac{2 \times 100 \times 1,80,000}{(0.12 \div 12)}} = Rs.60,000$$

3. A financial manager of VSI Co. Ltd., estimates that the firm needs an estimated net cash flow of Rs. 5,00,000 for the next month. The cost of raising funds in the market is 18 per cent and that of transaction involve a cost of Rs. 500 per transaction. The firm is planning to sell its 8 per cent marketable securities. You are required to determine the optimal amount of securities to be converted into cash.

Solution

$$ECL = \sqrt{\frac{2CF}{0}}$$

$$ECL = \sqrt{\frac{2 \times 500 \times 5,00,000}{0.08}} = Rs.79,057$$

Opportunity cost is the difference between the cost of raising funds and the interest on marketable securities is 8 per cent. The effective opportunity cost (interest) per month is

$$\frac{18-8}{Rs.100 \times 12 \text{ months}} = 0.08$$

4. Krishna Co. requires Rs. 15 lakhs to meet its transactions needs during next 6 months planning period. It holds short-term marketable securities of an equal amount at 20 per cent. Rs. 1500 is required to convert the securities into cash. The firm has marketable securities in the lot size of Rs. 75,000, Rs. 1,50,000, Rs. 3,00,000, Rs. 3,75,000 and Rs. 7,50,000. Determine economic lot size by using Baumol Model.

Solution:

$$ECL = \sqrt{\frac{2CF}{O}}$$

$$ECL = \sqrt{\frac{2 \times 1500 \times 15,00,000}{(0.20 \div 2)}} = Rs.2,12,132$$

5. XYZ requires Rs. 1.5 million in cash for meeting its transactions needs over the next 3 months. It has marketable securities in lot sizes of Rs. 1lakhs, Rs. 2 lakhs, Rs. 3 lakhs, 4 lakhs and Rs. 5 lakhs. The firm can earn 15 per cent annual interest on its short-term marketable securities. Rs. 500 (per transaction) is the concession. You are required to prepare a table indicating the economic lot size using numerical analysis.

Solution:

Computation of the economic cash conversion size

A.	Cash needed (Rs. in million)	1.5	1.5	1.5	1.5	1.5
B.	Lot size (Rs. in lakhs)	1.0	2.0	3.0	4.0	5.0
C.	No. of lots (A ÷B)	15	7.5	5	3.75	3
D.	Conversion cost [per transaction Rs.]	500	500	500	500	500
E.	Conversion cost (Rs. 000) (C x D)	7,500	3,750	2,500	1,875	1,500
F.	Avg cash balance (Rs.)	0.5	1.0	1.5	2.0	2.5
G.	Interest cost (F x 0.375)	1,875	3,750	5,625	7,500	9,375
H.	Total Cost (E + G)	9,375	7500	8,125	9,375	10,875

Economic cash conversion size is Rs. 2,00,000, at that lot size the total cost is minimum (Rs. 7500).

6. The annual cash need on Dream Well Co. Ltd., is Rs. 40 lakhs. The firm has short-term marketable securities into sizes of Rs. 2 lakhs, Rs. 4 lakhs, Rs. 8 lakhs, Rs. 10 lakhs and Rs. 20 lakhs. All securities are at 5 per cent yield rate. Cost of conversion of these securities is Rs. 1000 per conversion. Determine Economic cash conversion size, using Baumol model and numerical analysis.

Solution:

Baumol Model

$$ECL = \sqrt{\frac{2 \times 1000 \times 40,00,000}{0.05}} = Rs.4,00,000$$

Computation of economic cash conversion lot size based on numerical analysis.

A.	Cash needed (Rs. in million)	40	40	40	40	40
B.	Lot size (Rs. in lakhs)	2	4.0	8	10	20
C.	No. of lots (A ÷B)	20	10	5	4	2
D.	Conversion cost (PC) (Rs. 000)	1000	1000	1000	1.00	1000
E.	Conversion cost (Rs. 000) (C x D)	0.20	0.10	0.5	0.04	0.02
F.	Avg. cost size (Rs. lakhs)	1.0	2.0	4.0	5.0	10.0
G.	Interest cost (F x 0.05)	0.05	0.10	0.2	0.25	0.5
H.	Total Cost (E + G)	0.25	0.20	0.70	0.29	0.7

The economic cash conversion size is Rs. 4,00,000 since at this lot the total cost is minimum (Rs. 20,000)

7. A firm requires to be insured that an average cash balance of Rs. 16,000 is maintained. The firm has 10 per cent marketable securities and the average cost per transaction is Rs. 100. The standard deviation of a change in daily cash balance is Rs. 1,60,000. You are required to use the Miller and Orr model for determining the upper control limit and returns point.

Solution:

$$Z \text{ or } = \sqrt[3]{\frac{3C\sigma^2}{4.0}} + LCL$$

(RP)

$$UCL = 3Z - 2LL$$

Where: Z = Return point,   C = conversion cost   σ = Change in daily cash balance

LCL = lower control limit,   UCL = upper control limit,   O = interest cost

$$RP = \sqrt[3]{\frac{3(100)(1,60,000)^2}{4 \times 0.00027}} + 16,000 = Rs.207,365.96$$

Interest per day = [0.10 ÷ 365 = 0.00027]

UCL = 3 x RP − 2 x 16000

= 3 x 207,365.96 − 2 x 16000 = Rs 5,90,097.88

8. EAJ Co. has a policy of maintaining a minimum cash balance on Rs. 10,00,000. The standard deviation of firm's daily cash flows is Rs. 4,00,000. The firm has 16 per cent short-term marketable securities, which may require Rs. 300 as sales expenditure or purchasing expenditure (transaction cost). Compute the company's upper control limit and return point using Miller and Orr model.

Solution :

$$RP \text{ or } Z = \sqrt[3]{\frac{3(300)(4,00,000)^2}{4[0.16 \div 365]}} + 10,00,000 = Rs.14,34,670.8$$

UCL = 3 RP − 2 LCL

= 43,04,012.4 − 20,00,000 = Rs. 23,04012

9. A company has experienced a stochastic demand for its product with the result that cash balance fluctuates randomly. The SD of change in the daily net cash flows is Rs. 10,000. The company is interested to security into cash and vice versa as automatic as possible by setting upper control limit and return point. The firm's rate of return on security is 7 per cent. Rs. 200 is the transaction cost. The firm wants to maintain a minimum cash balance of Rs. 1000. Assuming 365 days in a year determine UCL and RP.

Solution

$$RP \text{ or } Z = \sqrt[3]{\frac{3(100)(10,000)^2}{4(0.07/365)}} + 1000 = Rs.30,652.07$$

VCL = 3 RP − 2 x 1000

= (3 x 30,652.07) − (2 x 1000) = Rs 89,956.21

10. From the following particulars, prepare a monthly cash budget for the quarter ended 31st March 2004. (Rs. in Lakhs)

Month	Sales	Purchases	Wages	Expenses
Nov '03	5.00	1.00	2.00	0.40
Dec '03	6.00	2.00	2.00	0.40
Jan '04	4.00	3.00	2.20	0.50
Feb '04	5.00	2.00	2.20	0.50
March '04	6.00	1.00	2.40	0.50

Additional information:

10 per cent sales and purchases are on cash

Credit to debtors: one month on an average, 50% of debtor will make payment on the due date while the rest will make payment one month thereafter.

Credit from creditors : 2 months

Wages to be paid twice in a month on the 1st and 16th, respectively.

Expenses are generally paid within the month.

Plant costing Rs. 1.00 lakh will be installed in February on payment of 25% of the cost in additions to the installation cost of Rs. 5,000, balance to be paid in three equal installments from the following month.

Opening cash balance is 2,00,000.

Solution:

Cash budget for three months from January to March 2004 (Rs. in Lakhs)

Particulars	Jan	Feb	March
(A) *Receipts :*			
Opening cash balance	2.00	3.55	3.55
Cash sales (10% of sales)	0.40	0.50	0.60
Collection during the 1st month (50% of the credit sales)	2.70	1.80	2.25
Collection during the 2nd month (50% of credit sales)	2.25	2.70	1.80
Total receipts	*7.35*	*8.55*	*8.20*
(B) *Payments :*			
Payments to Creditors (10% cash)	0.30	0.20	0.10
Payment at end of credit period	0.90	1.80	2.70
Wages (50% last month's and 50% current month's)	2.10	2.20	2.30
Expenses	0.50	0.50	0.50
Plant (25% of the cost plus installation charge)	---	0.30	---
First installment	---	---	0.25
Total payments	*3.80*	*5.00*	*5.85*
Closing Balance (A) - (B)	*3.55*	*3.55*	*2.35*

11. Venkat Industries (New company) requested to prepare a cash budget for the period of 6 months from January to June 2004. They have provided the following information.

(Rs. in lakhs)

Particulars	Jan	Feb	March	April	May	June
Sales	80.00	100.00	120.00	120.00	120.00	120.00
Purchases	2.00	3.00	4.00	4.00	4.00	2.00
Wages	12.00	14.00	16.00	16.00	16.00	12.00
Manufacturing expenses	26.00	27.00	28.00	28.00	28.00	26.00
Administration expenses	4.00	4.00	4.00	4.00	4.00	4.00
Distribution expenses	4.00	6.00	8.00	8.00	8.00	4.00

Additional financial cash flows:

Receipt of interest Rs. 2 lakhs each in the months of Jan and May.

Receipt of dividend Rs. 3 lakhs each in the months of March and June.

Sale of securities in the month of June for Rs. 3 crore.

Payment of interest during January for Rs. 50,000.

Payment of loan in the month of June for Rs. 1,50,00,000.

Interim dividend payment of Rs. 10,00,000 in the month of April.

Installment of machine in the month of June for Rs. 42 lakhs.

You may assume: 10 per cent of each month's sales for cash; customers are allowed a credit period of one month; creditors are allowing a credit of two months; wages are paid on the 1st of the next month.

Solution: Cash budget for 6 months from January to June 2004

(Rs. in Lakhs)

Particulars	Jan	Feb	March	April	May	June
(A)Receipts: Opening cash balance	---	(24.50)	8.5	57.5	108.5	170.5
Cash sales (10% of sales)	8.00	10.00	12.00	12.00	12.00	12.00
Collections from customer	0.00	72.00	90.00	108.00	108.00	108.00
Interest received	2.00	---	---	---	2.00	---
Dividend received	---	---	3.00	---	---	3.00
Sale of securities	---	---	---	---	---	300.00
Total receipts	10.00	57.5	113.5	177.5	230.5	593.5
(B)Payments :						
Purchases	0.00	0.00	2.00	3.00	4.00	4.00
Wages	0.00	12.00	14.00	16.00	16.00	16.00
Manufacturing expenses	26.00	27.00	28.00	28.00	28.00	26.00
Administration expenses	4.00	4.00	4.00	4.00	4.00	4.00
Distribution expenses	4.00	6.00	8.00	8.00	8.00	4.00
Interest paid	0.50	---	---	---	---	---
Loan paid	0.00	---	---	---	---	150.00
Interim dividend	---	---	---	10.00	---	---
Installment payment of machine	---	---	---	---	---	42.00
Total payments	34.50	49.00	56.00	69.00	60.00	246.00
Closing Balance (A) - (B) (Deficit) - surplus	(24.50)	8.5	57.5	108.5	170.5	347.5

12. God Luck Coy provides the following information and requested you to prepare a cash budget for 6 months starting from July to December 2004.

(Rs. in Lakhs)

Particulars	May	June	July	Aug	Sept	Oct	Nov	Dec	Jan
Sales (net of cash discounts)	15.00	15.00	25.00	35.00	45.00	25.00	25.00	15.00	15.00
Materials	8.00	15.00	22.00	29.00	15.00	15.00	8.00	8.00	---
Rent	---	---	0.50	0.50	0.50	0.50	0.50	0.50	---
Salaries	---	---	1.50	2.00	2.50	1.50	1.50	1.00	---
Miscellaneous expenses	---	---	0.20	0.30	0.40	0.20	0.20	0.10	---
Taxes	---	---	---	---	---	5.00	---	5.00	---
Building construction	---	---	---	---	---	15.00	---	---	---

Credit terms—customers are allowed 40 days, if they pay within 20 days cash discount will be given. 20 per cent sales are paid in the same months of sales. 70 per cent of the sales paid during the second and the 10 per cent of sales are paid in third month.

Materials amount to 70% of sales and are bought in the month before the company expects to sell the finished goods. Suppliers are allowed one-month credit.

The company wants to maintain a minimum cash balance of Rs. 6,00,000 in all the months. It is assumed that the firm will have a beginning balance of Rs. 5 lakhs on July 1. Determine the company's requirements of cash for the period from July to December.

Solution: Cash budget

(Rs. in Lakhs)

Particulars	July	Aug	Sept	Oct	Nov	Dec
(A) *Receipts :*						
Sales collections						
During the month of sales (20%)	5.00	7.00	9.00	5.00	5.00	3.00
During the second month (70%)	10.50	17.50	24.50	31.50	17.50	17.50
During the third month (10%)	1.50	1.50	2.50	3.50	4.50	2.50
Total receipts	*17.00*	*26.00*	*36.00*	*40.00*	*27.00*	*23.00*
(B) *Payments :*						
Materials (1 month lag)	15.00	22.00	29.00	15.00	15.00	8.00
Rent	0.50	0.50	0.50	0.50	0.50	0.50
Salaries	1.50	2.00	2.50	1.50	1.50	1.00
Misc. expenses	0.20	0.30	0.40	0.20	0.20	0.10
Taxes	---	---	---	5.00	---	5.00
Building construction	---	---	---	15.00	---	---
Total payments	*17.20*	*24.80*	*32.40*	*37.20*	*17.20*	*14.60*
Net cash – Receipts (A) – (B)	(0.20)	1.20	3.60	2.80	9.80	8.40
Opening cash	5.00	6.00	6.00	6.00	6.00	6.00
(-) Minimum cash balance	(6.0)	(6.0)	(6.0)	(6.0)	(6.0)	(6.0)
Borrowing (cumulative)	1.20	---	---	---	---	---
Surplus (cumulative)	---	1.20	4.80	7.60	17.40	25.80

Cash at the beginning plus net receipts / less payments, equals to the cash at the end.

13. From the following balance sheet, salary expenses and sales forecast prepare a cash budget for the 6 months January to July.

Balance sheet

Liabilities	Amount Rs.	Assets		Amount Rs.
Capital	1,00,000	Fixed assets	3,00,000	
Reserves	9,00,000	(-) Depreciation	50,000	2,50,000
		Inventory		4,90,000
		Debtors		1,00,000
		Bank		1,60,000
	10,00,000			**10,00,000**

Month	Salary	Sales forecast
Jan	30,000	2,00,000
Feb	50,000	4,00,000
March	70,000	5,00,000
April	90,000	6,00,000
May	1,10,000	9,00,000
June	60,000	5,00,000
July	1,00,000	1,00,000

Additional Information:

Sales are on a 30-days basis, but payments are not received until the following month.

All purchases are on cash basis.

Sales & distribution expenses are expected to be 10 per cent on each month sales.

Depreciation charges are one per cent per month.

The firm's purchases are enough to cover 120 per cent of the following months sales. The firm has a policy of maintaining 10 per cent gross profit margin on sales.

Interest received Rs. 50,000 in the month of April.

A minimum cash balance of Rs. 1,00,000 is required to be maintained.

New plant purchased for Rs. 50,000 and the cost is to be paid in to equal installments in the months of April and May.

Solution: Cash budget

Particulars	Jan	Feb	March	April	May	June
(A) Receipts :						
Cash collections	1,00,000	2,00,000	4,00,000	5,00,000	6,00,000	9,00,000
Interest	---	---	---	50,000	---	---
Total Receipts	**1,00,000**	**2,00,000**	**4,00,000**	**5,50,000**	**6,00,000**	**9,00,000**
(B) Payments :						
Purchases	4,80,000	6,00,000	7,20,000	10,80,000	6,00,000	1,20,000
Salary	30,000	50,000	70,000	90,000	1,10,000	60,000
Plant	---	---	---	25,000	25,000	---
Selling expenses	20,000	40,000	50,000	60,000	90,000	50,000
Total payments	**5,30,000**	**6,90,000**	**8,40,000**	**12,55,000**	**8,25,000**	**2,30,000**
Net cash receipts (A) - (B)	(4,30,000)	(4,90,000)	(4,40,000)	(7,05,000)	(2,25,000)	6,70,000
Cash at the beginning of month	1,00,000	1,00,000	1,00,000	1,00,000	1,00,000	1,00,000
Minimum cash	(1,00,000)	(1,00,000)	(1,00,000)	(1,00,000)	(1,00,000)	(1,00,000)
Borrowing (cumulative)	4,30,000	9,20,000	13,60,000	20,65,000	22,90,000	16,20,000

14. As a financial consultant, prepare a cash budget for a firm whom you have to advise on the amount of overdraft they will require during the months of August and September. Details are given below:

1. 50 per cent of credit sales are realized in the month following the sales, and the remaining sales in the second month following, creditors are paid in the month following the purchase.

2. Cash in Bank on August 1 is Rs. 50,000.

Month	Sales	Purchases	Wages
June	3,60,000	2,24,000	24,000
July	2,84,000	2,88,000	28,000
August	2,16,000	4,86,000	22,000
September	3,48,000	4,92,000	20,000

Solution: Cash budget on August 1

Particulars	August (Rs.)	September (Rs.)
Opening cash in Bank	50,000	62,000
(A) Receipts		
Month following	1,42,000	1,08,000
After two months	1,80,000	1,42,000
(A) Total Receipts [incl .op. balance]	3,72,000	3,12,000
(B) Payments		
Purchases	2,88,000	4,86,000
Wages (assumed, no time)	22,000	20,000
(B) Total Payments	3,10,000	5,06,000
Balance (A) – (B)	62,000	(–)1,94,000

Comment: In August, there is no Cash Deficit (CD), but in the month September there is a need to arrange an CD of Rs. 1,94,000.

TEST YOUR KNOWLEDGE

Objective Type Questions

1. **Fill in the blanks with appropriate word(s)**
   a) Cash is one of the components of _____.
   b) Cash is the most_____asset.
   c) The two types of cash forecasting are _____ and _____.
   d) Surplus cash is_____.
   e) _____ and _____ are short-term cash forecasting methods.
   f) ___is the time taken by the bank in collecting the payment from the customer's bank.
   g) _____the time taken in processing the cheques within the company and sending them to bank for deposit.
   h) The _____, _____, and _____are collectively known as deposit float.
   i) The decentralised collection procedure in US is called as _____.

j) _____ system is a method of accelerating cash outflows.

k) Total cost under Baumol Model equals to _____ plus _____.

l) _____ is also known as short-term cash forecasting.

[*Answer:* (a) Current assets, (b) Liquid, (c) Short-term and Long-term, (d) Unproductive, (e) The receipt disbursement, adjusted income, (f) Bank float, (g) Lethargy, (h) Postal float, Lethargy and bank float, (i) Concentration banking, (j) Lock box, (k) Conversion and opportunity, and (l) Cash budget]

2. **State whether each of the following statement is true of false**

a) There is no time gap between cash inflows and outflows.

b) The time taken by post offices in transferring the cheques from the customer to the firm is referred to as postal float.

c) There are four motives for holding cash.

d) Conversion cost is the cost of converting securities into cash.

e) Cash management is a trade off between the liquidity and profitability.

f) Baumol model cash is based on statistical technique.

g) A cash budget is an account of the expected cash receipts and cash payments.

h) UCL is equal to 3 Z minus 2 LCL.

i) Safety, marketability, yield and maturity are the factors that should be considered while selecting investing securities.

j) Commercial paper is short-term, unsecured promissory notes issued by large companies.

k) CRISIL, ICRA and CARE are the three credit rating agencies.

l) CDs are the one of the surplus cash investing avenues.

[*Answers:* (a) False, (b) True, (c) False, (d) True, (e) True, (f) False, (g) True, (h) True, (i) True, (j) True, (k) True, and (l) True]

DO IT YOURSELF

1) What is the nature of cash ?

2) What is cash management ?

3) List out the motives for holding cash.

4) Name the objectives of cash management.

5) List out the aspects of cash management.

6) How do you determine (Baumol) economic conversion lot size?

7) List out the factors considered while selecting investment avenues.

8) Give the meaning of repos.

9) What is commercial paper (CP) ?

10) What is certificate of deposits (CD) ?

11) What is cash planning ?

12) What do you mean by short costs ?

13) What is cash budget ?

14) List out the objectives of preparing cash budget.

15) What is float ?

16) What do you understand by lethargy ?

17) What is deposit float ?

18) Write a few lines on concentration bank.

19) What do you mean by lock box system ?

20) What do you understand by Cheque encashment analysis?

21) What is cash management ? Discuss the objectives.

22) Briefly discuss the aspects of cash management.

23) Explain the factors that determine the cash needs of a firm.

24) What is cash budget ? Explain the 'purposed preparing cash budget.'

25) Briefly discuss the elements of cash budget.

26) Explain and contrast deposit float and payment float.

27) What is lock box system ? How does it help to reduce the cash balances ?

28) Discuss the receipts and payments method of cash forecasting.

29) Discuss the options available to a firm for investing surplus cash.

30) What represents the optimal cash balance for a firm ?

31) What do you understand by Badla financing ?

32) Explain various motives for holding cash.

33) Write a brief not on Baumol cash management model.

34) Discuss the important features of the Miller and Orr model.

35) What are the major sources of cash receipts and cash payments ?

36) Efficient cash management will aim at maximizing the cash inflows and slowing cash outflows". Discuss.

37) "Cash budgeting or short-term cash forecasting (budgeting) is the principal tool of cash management." Discuss.

38) Discuss in detail the factors that determine the cash needs of a firm. Give examples to necessary factors.

39) Discuss the types of cash forecasting methods.

40) How do you determining optimum level of cash balances? How does uncertainty of cash balance affects this problem?

41) "Management of cash flows plays a very important role in cash management". Discuss.

42) Briefly discuss the various avenues or opportunities available to the companies to park their surplus funds for a short-term.

43) Write short notes on :
    a) US 64 scheme
    b) ICD's
    c) CD's
    d) Discounting of (time) bills, and
    e) Purchase of demand drafts.

44) Write short notes on :
    a) Ready Forward,
    b) Commercial Papers (CPs)

c) Badla Financing, and

d) Treasury Bills (TBs)

DO IT YOURSELF PROBLEMS

1. ABC Ltd., estimates its total cash requirement as Rs. 5 crore in the next year. Rs. 300 is the conversion cost of securities in cash on which the firm was earning 15 per cent interest per annum. Determining the optimum cash balance. [Answer: Rs. 4,47,213.59]

2. Best of Luck Co. Ltd., firm estimated its total cash requirements of Rs. 2,00,000 for next six months. The firm has to spend Rs. 200 as conversion cost, if it wants to convert its securities into cash. The firm has 10 per cent securities. What is the economic conversion size of cash. Assume the firm has securities in the lot sizes of Rs. 20,000, Rs. 40,000, Rs. 60,000, Rs. 80,000 and Rs. 1,00,000. [Answer:Rs.40,000]

3. Rama & Co., has a policy of maintaining a cash balance (minimum) of Rs. 1,00,000. The standard deviation of the changes in daily cash flowing is Rs. 20,000. Rs. 75 is the transaction cost. The company has 10 per cent short-term marketable security in different lot sizes. You are required to determining the ULC and Z or RP as per Miller Orr model (assuming 360 year). [Answer: RP or Z : Rs. 168, 689 ; UCL : Rs. 3,06,068]

4. Venkat & Co., expects its cash flow to behave in a random manner, as it was assumed by Miller Orr model. Venkat & Co. requested you to set an UCL and RP, with the following information. The management of firm would like to maintain a minimum cash balance of Rs. 70,000. The standard deviation its daily cash balances in Rs. 7,000. Firm earns a 12 per cent yield on its short-term marketable securities. Conversion of securities into cash is net cost free it involves Rs. 120 (Assume 366 days a year). [Answer: RP or Z : Rs. 93,784 ; UCL : Rs. 1,41,351]

5. Softeck Ltd., commences business on 1st April 2003 and deposits Rs. 1,00,000 in the SBI. The sum deposited would not be sufficient to finance its operations over a period of four months. As a company secretary, prepare a cash budget from 1st April 2003 to 31st July 2003, to ascertain company's bankers. Additional data :

Furniture purchases – Rs. 10,000 prepared to be made in April 2003.

Sales are made to one distributor only on 30 days terms 2 per cent discount and cheques are received on the first date of the following due date.

Budgeted figures:

Particulars	April	May	June	July
Materials purchases	50,000	40,000	30,000	40,000
Cash expenses	4,000	5,000	4,000	4,000
Salaries	40,000	50,000	40,000	40,000
Sales	60,000	70,000	80,000	80,000

All purchases are made on net 30 days terms and cheques are posted to creditors on the last day of the month due.

Answer

Net cash receipts	April	May	June	July
	(Rs. 54,000)	(Rs. 46,200)	(Rs. 15,400)	(Rs. 4,400)
Overdraft	Nil	Rs. 200	Rs. 15,400	Nil

Prepare cash budget for the 3 months ended 30th Sept 1998 based on the following information.

- Cash at bank on 1st July 1998   - Rs. 25,000
- Monthly salaries and wages (estimated)   - Rs. 10,000
- Interest payable in August 1998   - Rs. 5,000

Estimated	June	July	August	September
Credit sales (actual)	1,20,000	1,40,000	1,52,000	1,21,000
Credit sales	1,00,000	80,000	1,40,000	1,20,000
Material purchases	1,60,000	1,70,000	2,40,000	1,80,000
Other expenses	18,000	20,000	22,000	21,000

Credit sales are collected 50 per cent in the month of sale and 50 per cent in the following month. Collections from credit sales are subject to 10 per cent discount, if received in the month of sale and to 50 per cent if received in the month following. 10 per cent of the purchases are in cash and balance is paid in next month.

Answer

Particulars	July	Aug	Sept
Total collections	90,000	1,10,000	1,30,000
Net collections	83,500	1,01,000	1,20,500
Payments to creditors	1,61,000	1,77,000	2,34,000
Total cash receipts	2,48,500	3,10,500	3,38,000
Total payments	1,91,000	2,14,000	2,65,000
Closing balance	57,500	96,500	73,000

6. Well Do Coy, has a policy to maintain a cash balance of Rs. 20,000 at the end of each quarter. Cash can be borrowed or repaid in multiplies of Rs. 500 at an interest rate of 10 per cent. Management does not want to borrow cash more than what is required and wants to repay as early as possible. In any event, loans cannot be extended beyond four quarters. Interest is computed and paid when the principal is repaid. Assume the borrowing take place at the beginning and repayments are made at the end of the quarters.

Budget expenses:

	1st Qtr.	2nd Qtr.	3rd Qtr.	4th Qtr.
Opening cash balance	10,000	---	---	2,21,000
Collections	1,25,000	1,50,000	1,00,000	54,200
Raw materials	20,000	35,000	35,000	54,200
Other expenses	25,000	20,000	20,000	17,000
Wages	90,000	95,000	95,000	1,09,200
Income tax	5,000	---	---	---
Machinery	---	---	---	20,000

Prepare cash budget.

[Answers: closing balances: 1st Qtr – Rs 15000, 2nd Qtr – 15000, 3rd Qtr – 15,325 and 4th Qtr – 23825]

CASE FOR CLASS DISCUSSION FOR BETTER UNDERSTANDING - I
BHATT ENTERPRISES CASE : CASH FORECASTING AND INVESTING

Sushma is the Treasurer of Bhatt Enterprises, a poorly organized collection of financial services companies. The composition of Bhatt's activities can best be seen in a statement of forecasted cash flow by each major business line, namely :

	Annual Cash Flow
Insurance policies	$ 85,000,000
Insurance underwriting	55,000,000
Assets based lending	200,000,000
Consumer paper	155,000,000
Auto dealer paper	80,000,000
	$ 575,000,000

Sushma has inherited a concentration banking system, as shown in Figure 11.1. After examining its features, he felt satisfied that it meets the needs of Bhatt

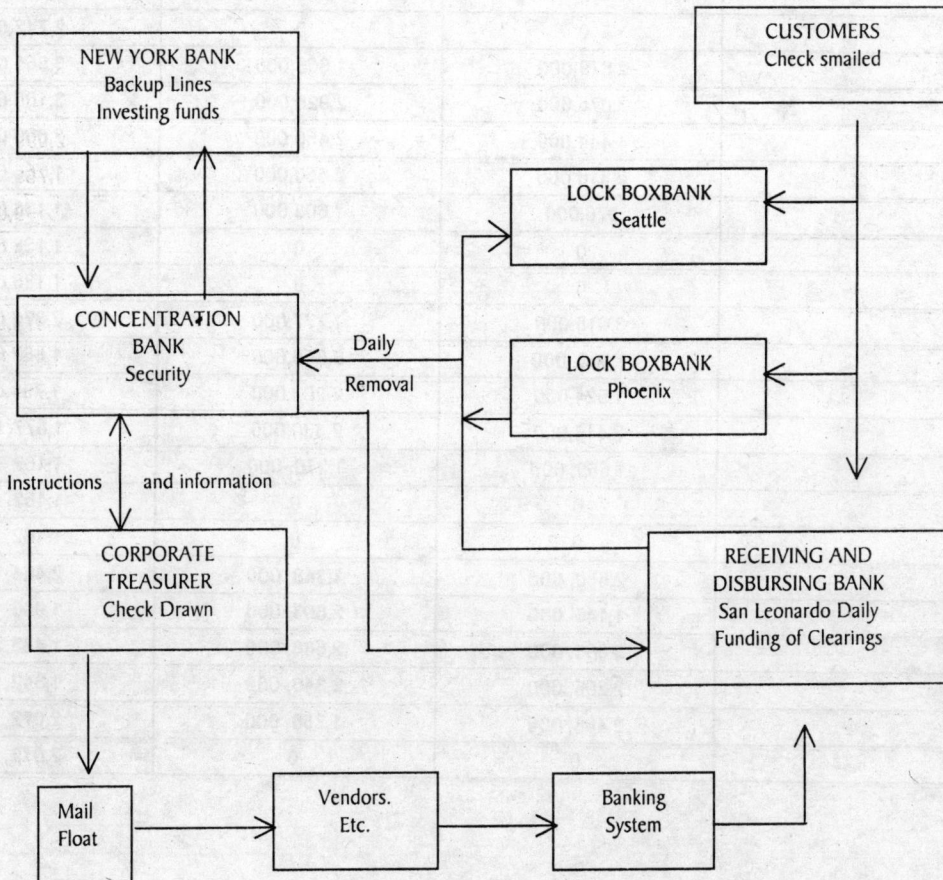

FIGURE 17.1: Bhatt Enterprises Concentration Banking System

Enterprises. The hometown bank in San Franciso. California is not a member of any clearinghouse; all cheques are processed through a correspondent relationship with security. The lockboxes in Phoenix and Seattle are efficiently managed by security and thus, average only one day float. This is the same as for funds deposited directly as security. Excess funds are wired daily to New Jersey for same day investment.

On September 8, Sushma is preparing his monthly report on funds invested during August. Table 11.1 B shows the deposits each day during the month. It also shows the book disbursements: that is, checks written but not clearing each day. This information comes directly from the ledger accounts of Bhatt Enterprises.

Table 17.1: Daily Deposits and Cheques Drawn, Bhatt Enterprises

For the Month of August Starting Balance	Daily Deposit	Cheques Drawn	Books Balance
			3,20,000
1	2,150,000	1,740,000	7,30,000
2	1,340,000	1,765,000	3,05,000
3	0	0	3,05,000
4	0	0	3,05,000
5	2,330,000	1,292,000	1,343,000
6	1,475,000	1,628,000	1,191,000
7	2,567,000	1,555,000	1,202,000
8	2,300,000	1,432,000	3,070,000
9	1,278,000	1,606,000	2,742,000
10	0	0	2,742,000
11	0	0	2,742,000
12	2,879,000	1,666,000	3,955,000
13	2,075,000	2,925,000	3,105,000
14	1,444,000	2,450,000	2,099,000
15	2,316,000	2,650,000	1,765,000
16	978,000	1,605,000	1,138,000
17	0	0	1,138,000
18	0	0	1,138,000
19	3,015,000	1,777,000	2,376,000
20	1,866,000	2,355,000	1,887,000
21	1,924,000	2,202,000	1,791,000
22	2,416,000	2,330,000	1,877,000
23	1,555,000	1,270,000	1,162,000
24	0	0	1,162,000
25	0	0	1,162,000
26	2,650,000	1,348,000	2,464,000
27	1,145,000	2,603,000	1,006,000
28	3,065,000	2,588,000	1,483,000
29	2,205,000	2,346,000	1,342,000
30	2,488,000	1,758,000	2,072,000
31	0	0	2,072,000

Table 17.2: New Goods Funds Credited Daily, Bhatt Enterprises.

For the Month of August Starting Balance	New Goods Funds	Cheques Cleared	Books Balance
			700.000
1	1,832,000	1,460,600	1,069,400
2	2,055,000	1,832,250	1,292,150
3	0	0	1,292,150
4	0	0	1,292,150
5	8,69,480	1,352,650	808,980
6	2,123,400	2,303,750	628,630
7	1,467,300	2,292,950	(197,020)
8	2,454,400	1,524,900	723,480
9	2,300,120	1,142,700	1,880,900
10	0	0	1,880,900
11	0	0	1,880,900
12	3,40,600	1,645,160	576,350
13	2,790,680	1,511,950	1,855,080
14	2,040,240	1,492,900	2,402,420
15	1,481,680	1,043,900	2,840,200
16	2,070,120	3,072,850	1,837,470
17	0	0	1,837,470
18	0	0	1,837,470
19	1,174,834	2,758,750	253,554
20	3,366,940	2,555,000	1,065,494
21	1,860,300	2,349,250	576,544
22	1,903,860	1,043,250	1,437,154
23	2,400,000	3,100,740	736,414
24	0	0	736,414
25	0	0	736,414
26	1,699,680	2,237,750	198,344
27	2,986,200	2,128,500	1,056,044
28	1,195,500	2,309,000	(57,456)
29	2,882,200	1,475,500	1,349,244
30	2,246,300	506,800	3,088,744
31	0	0	3,088,744
Total	44,917,294	41,385,850	

Separately, Table 17.2 shows the new good funds credits to Bhatt account each day in August. It also shows the cheques that cleared, as reported by the bank.

Assignment

1. Draw the monthly report giving the real picture about:
    (a) Total Cheques Written
    (b) Average Cash Balance

2. For how many days, the firm have negative cash balance and also mention the day of week, which has highest level of deposit and highest level of cheques written

BAJAJ ELECTRONICS CASE : CASH FORECASTING

This case tests the reader's ability to develop a basic cash forecast for a firm and prepare a recommendation for backup financing over a period of 12 months.

A leading producer of telecommunications components and a major contender in shorter antennas is Bajaj Electronics Company. Bajaj's business has grown tremendously in recent years despite increased competition. The primary reasons for increased growth are technological advancement that have expanded production capacity, an aggressive marketing effort, and a reputation for quality products and excellent service.

Loofer the financial analyst for the company, has been assigned the task of preparing a quarterly cash forecast for the next fiscal year. After checking with marketing, he was given a monthly breakdown of actual sales for last month and the current month and a forecast for the next 12 months. These are given in Table 17.3 and reflect the somewhat seasonal nature of the firm's marketing activities.

Table 17.3: Actual and Forecast Sales from Marketing

Month	Actual Credit Sales	Forecast Sales
November	$ 4,338,000	
December	5,204,000	
January		$ 4,600,000
February		4,500,000
March		4,500,000
April		52,00, 000
May		5, 000, 000
June		4,700, 000
July		6, 000, 000
August		6,000,000
September		5,800,000
October		4,500,000
November		4,600,000
December		4,600,000

From the accounting department, Loofer obtained information on the historical mix of sales and collection information. During the first half of the year, credit sales generally mad up about 80 per cent of all sales. In the second half, this dropped to 75 per cent. With respect to the credit sales, collection patterns varied seasonally. This information is contained in Table 17.4. Once again, the collection pattern is also seasonal Note, however, that the collections do not total to 100 per cent of credit sales. This is the case because the firm allows a margin for bad debts and unexpected collection costs.

The firm follows a unique and highly controlled system for its trade payables. Each month during the first half of the year, the accounts payable section pays suppliers cash equal to 50 per cent of the monthly sales. During the second half of the year, this rises to 55 per cent. Over a full year, this pattern of payment seems to be adequate to pay all bills. At times, suppliers are pressing for more payments and some maneuvering is needed. Still, this policy assists the firm's cash management during the busy third quarter and will be followed next year.

Cash operating expenses are paid as they occur. During the first and fourth quarters, they are estimated at 50 per cent of sales. During the second and third quarters, they rise to 55 per cent of sales.

Loofer knows that the firm includes the impact of interest and taxes in its operating cash flow forecasts. The levels of such debt, along with the forecasted average interest rate for each month, are given in Table 17.5. Interest will be calculated to reflect changes in debt levels.

The firm pays estimated tax payments monthly at a 35 per cent rate. It uses a cost of goods sold estimate at 50 per cent of sales, not including depreciation. Loofer assumes that monthly depreciation for the next year will be $ 185,000.

Table 17.4: Collection Pattern of Receivables

| Months | Collected in Same Month | Percent of Credit Sales | |
		Collected One Month Later	Collected Two Months Later
November	0.20		
December	0.60	0.15	
January	0.20	0.60	0.15
February	0.30	0.60	0.50
March	0.25	0.60	0.10
April	0.25	0.60	0.10
May	0.15	0.60	0.20
June	0.20	0.60	0.15
July	0.10	0.60	0.25
August	0.20	0.60	0.15
September	0.15	0.60	0.20
October	0.20	0.60	0.15
November	0.15	0.60	
December	0.10		

Table 17.5: Debt Forecast, Last Day of Each Month, and Average Monthly Interest Rates

Months	Interest-Bearing Debt (,000s)	Interest Rate
December	1600	
January	1800	0.120
February	1500	0.100
March	1600	0.110
April	1500	0.100
May	1600	0.110
June	1500	0.100
July	1500	0.090
August	1400	0.080
September	1300	0.090
October	1400	0.080
November	1200	0.095
December	1600	0.095

The final information for the forecast involves establishing a safety level. The firm requires cash or equivalents equal to 20 per cent of the monthly cash operating expenses. The firm began the year with $6,10,000 in the form of cash and equivalents.

Question

Prepare a statement showing cash forecast for the next 12 months, and in case where firm needs additional cash, draw the recommendation with the tune of credit that must be arranged from bank.

REFERENCES

1. Gitman, L.J., *"Principles of Managerial Finance"*, London : Harper & Row Publishers, 1976, p. 168.

2. Accountants Handbook, New York : A Ronald Press Publications; John Wiley & Sons, 1970 Section 10, p. 9.

3. Brigham, E.F., *"Fundamentals of Financial Management"*, Illinois : The Dryden Press, 1978. p. 168.

4. Howard, B.B and Uptan .M, *"Introduction to Business Finance"*, New York : McGraw Hill Book Co., Inc., 1953, p. 188.

5. Gitman, L.J., op. cit., p. 170.

6. Keynes, J.M., *"The General Theory of Employment, Interest on Money"*, New York : Harcourt Brace Jovanovich, Inc., 1956, pp. 170-174.

7. Pandey, I.M., *"Financial Management"*, New Delhi : Vikas Publishing House, 2002, p. 912.

8. Khan, M.Y and Jain, P.K., *"Basic Financial Management"*, New Delhi : Tata McGraw Hill Publishing Co. Ltd.

9. Bottan S.E., op. cit., p. 390 (Reproduced in Khan M.Y and Jain P.K, *"Basic Financial Management"*, New Delhi : Tata McGraw Hill Publishing Co. Pvt., Ltd., 2000, p. 7.4).

10. Hartely, W.C.F and Meltzer, Y.L., *"Cash Management, Planning, Forecasting and Control"*, New Jersey : Prentice - Hall Inc., 1967, p. 58.

11. Orgler, Y.E, *"Cash Management : Method and Models"*, California : Wordsworth Publishing Company, 1970, p. 392.

12. Joy, O.M, *"Introduction to Financial Management"*, Irwin Homewood Ill, 1977, p. 431.

13. Ramamoorthy V.E, *"Working Capital Management"*, Madras: Institute of Financial Management and Research, 1978, p. 136.

14. Gitman L.J, Op.cit, p. 180 (reproduced in Khan M Y and Jain P.K, op. cit., p. 7.17).

15. Baumol, W.J, *"The Transaction Demand for Cash : An Inventory Theoretical Approach"*, Journal of Economics (Quarterly), LXV, No. 66, Nov. 1952, pp. 545 - 556).

16. Miller M.H and Orr D, *"A Model of the Demand for Money in Firms"*, Quarterly Journal of Economics, LXY (Nŏ. 80), August 1966, pp. 413 - 435.

17. Brealey, R.A and Myers, S.C, *"Principles of Corporate Finance"*, New Delhi : Tata McGraw Hill International, 2002, p. 893.

18. Mathur, S.B, *"Working Capital Management and Control - Principles & Practice"*, New Delhi: New Age International Pvt. Ltd., 2002, p. 70.

Receivables Management

Objectives

After studying this chapter, you should be able to:

1 Say what are accounts receivables and their characteristics.

2 Define accounts receivables management.

3 Explain, objectives, benefits, and costs of receivables management

4 Discuss the modes of payment if credit.

5 Define credit policy. Types of credit policies with their advantages and disadvantages.

6 Explain the credit policy variables.

7 Discuss the aspects of receivables management.

8 Explain the steps involved in credit evaluation.

Accounts Receivables occupy an important position in the structure of current assets of a firm. They are the outcome of rapid growth of credit sales granted by the firms to their customers. Credit sales are reflected in the value of Sundry Debtors [SD's In India]. It is also known as Trade Debtors (TD's), Accounts Receivables (AR's), Bills Receivables (BR's) on the asset side of balance sheet.[1] Trade credit is most prominent force of modern business. It is considered as a marketing tool acting as a bridge between production and customers. Firm grants credit to protect its sales from the competitors and attract the potential customers. It is not possible to increase sales without credit facility, increase in sales also increases profits. But investment on accounts receivables involve certain costs and risks. Therefore, a great deal of attention is normally paid to the effective and efficient management of accounts receivables.

MEANING OF ACCOUNTS RECEIVABLES

The term receivable is defined as "debt owed to the firm by customers arising from sale of goods or services in the ordinary course of business".[2] When the firm sells its products services on credit, and it does not receive cash for it immediately, but would be collected in near future. Till collection they form as a current assets.

CHARACTERISTICS OF RECEIVABLES

The accounts receivables arising out of credit sales have the following characteristics'.[3]

1. *Risk Involvement:* Receivables involve risk, since payment takes Bajaj in future, and future is uncertain so they should carefully analyzed.

2. *Based on Economic Value:* Accounts receivables are based on economic value. The economic value in goods or services passes to the buyer currently in return the seller expects an equivalent value from the buyer latter.

3. *Implies Futurity:* Buyer will make cash payment of the goods or services received by him/her in a future period. [i.e generally after credit period]

MEANING OF ACCOUNTS RECEIVABLES MANAGEMENT

Accounts Receivable Management means making decisions relating to the investment in these current assets as an integral part of operating process, the objective being maximization of return on investment in receivables. In other words, accounts receivables management involves maintenance of receivables of optimum level, the degree of credit sales to be made, and the debtors collection. In simple words, the key function of credit management is to optimize the sales at the minimum possible cost of credit. According to Joseph, "The purpose of any commercial enterprise is the earning of profit. Credit in itself is utilized to increase sales, but sales must return a profit".[4] The offer of goods on credit should not only optimise sales but also lead to maximization of overall return on investment. Management of receivable, therefore, should be based on sound credit policies and practices.

OBJECTIVES OF ACCOUNTS RECEIVABLES MANAGEMENT

The following are the main objectives of accounts receivables management:

1. *Maximizing the Value of the Firm:* The basic objective of debtors' management is to maximise the value of the firm by achieving a trade off between liquidity (risk) and return. The main purpose of receivables management is to minimise the risk of bad debts and not maximisation of order. Efficient management of receivables expands sales by retaining old customers and attracting new customers.

2. ***Optimum Investment in Sundry Debtors:*** Credit sales expand, but they involve block of funds, that have an opportunity cost, which can be reduced by optimum investment in receivables. Providing liberal credit increases sales consequently profits will increase, but increasing investment in receivables results in increased costs.

3. ***Control and Dr. Bhatt the Cost of Trade Credit:*** When there are no credit sales, there will not be any trade credit cost. But credit sale increases profits. It is possible only when the firm is able to keep the costs at minimum. The costs are discussed below.

COSTS OF ACCOUNTS RECEIVABLES MANAGEMENT

Management of accounts receivables is not cost free. The following are the main costs associate with accounts receivables management:

a. ***Opportunity Cost / Capital Cost:*** Providing goods or services on credit involves block of firm's funds. In other words, the increased level of accounts receivables is an investment in current assets. These blocked funds or investment in receivables need to be financed, by shareholders funds or from short-term borrowings. They involve some cost. If receivables are financed by shareholder funds, there involves opportunity cost to shareholders. If they are financed by borrowed funds, it involves payments of interest, which is also a cost.

b. ***Collection Cost:*** Collection of receivable is one of the tasks of receivables management. Collection costs are those costs that are increased in collecting the debts from the customers to whom the credit sales have been granted. The collection costs may include, staff, records, stationary, postage they are related to maintenance credit department, and exposes details involved in collecting information about prospective customers, from specialized agencies, for evaluation of prospective customer before going to grant credit.

c. ***Bad Debts:*** Some times customer may not be able to honour the dues to the firm because of the inability to pay. Such costs are referred as bad debts, and they have to be written off, because they cannot be collected. These cost can be reduced to some extent, if the firm properly evaluates customer before granting credit, but complete avoidance is not possible.

BENEFITS OF ACCOUNTS RECEIVABLES MANAGEMENT

Accounts receivables management involves, not only costs but also benefits. The benefits are:

a) ***Increased Sales :*** Providing goods or services on credit expands sales, by retaining old customers and attraction of prospective customers.

b) ***Market Share Increase:*** When the firm's able to retain old customer and attract new customer automatically market share will be increased to the extent of new sales.

c) ***Increase in Profits :*** Increased sales, leads to increase in profits, because, it need to produce more products with a given fixed cost and sales of products with a given sales network, in both cost per unit comes down and the profit will be increased.

MODES OF PAYMENT

After evaluation and selection of individual customers or accounts, the firm may decide to provide credit facility, it may be unlimited or limited. The economic value of goods or services that have provided under credit, will be paid in future. If the firm is financially sound it may extend liberal credit to the buyer and vice versa. Investment in receivable will be financed by three people-buyer, seller and financed intermediary. Buyer pays a part of goods or services purchased, seller puts his/her own amount a part and the remaining by financial institute all these financing will be done in the trade cycle. The economic value of goods or services sold on credit, will be paid by adoption of different modes.

(a) *Cash Mode:* Whenever a firm sells goods or services on cash terms, the value of goods or services will be received either cash in advance (before the goods are shifted) or on delivery (after the goods are delivered). Receipt of advance is necessary whenever the goods are manufactured on a special order. It is for financing productions and to avoid the non-acceptability goods ordered by the order or buyer. Immediate cash payment will take Bajaj only when the seller has high bargaining power due to monopoly power or the customer is risky customer.

(b) *Open Account:* Majority of the credit sales takes Bajaj on an open account mode. Open account means, after the sale and purchase agreement between seller and buyers, the seller first shifts goods and he sends the invoice (bill), which consists of credit terms, credit period allowed, cash discount for early payment, and the period of cash discount offer, quantity of goods with their total value and so on. The invoice is generally acknowledged by the buyer.

Credit Period: It is the period allowed by seller to customer to pay economic value of goods.

Cash Discount: It is the discount [some percentage] allowed to buyer for an early payment. For example, a seller has given "2/15, not 45". It means that discount of 2 per cent is allowed, if the payment is made on or before 15th days, other wise full payment is due by the 45th day.

(c) *Bill of Exchange:* A bill of exchange represents an unconditional order issued by the seller asking the buyer to pay the amount maintained on it as per demand at a certain future date. This type of demand is made only when the seller does not have strong evidence of the buyer's obligation. Hence, there is a need of secured arrangement in the form of a bills of exchange. In other words, if the seller wants a clear commitment from the buyer, before he/she delivers the goods, seller can arrange a commercial draft.[5] Generally, the bill accompanied by documents (shipping or some other transport documents) that are delivered to the drawee when he/she pays or accepts the bill. When the buyer accept a bill than it becomes a trade acceptance, which may be hold till the maturity or get it discounted. The advantages of bills of exchange are (i) it represents negotiable instrument. (ii) It serves as a written evidence of a definite obligation. (iii) It helps in reducing cost of finance to some extent, since it can be discounted.

(d) *Letter of Credit:* Letter of credit is a formal document issued by a bank on behalf of customer, stating the conditions under which the bank will honor the commitments of its customer (buyer). Payment through the letter of credit arises whenever trade takes Bajaj at international level, but now days it has been used in domestic trade also. In other words, whenever trade takes Bajaj in the absence of Bajaj-to-Bajaj unknown people, issue of letter of credit [L/C] arises.

Functions of the letter of credit are, (i) it eliminates risk, since letter of credit issued by good standing bank. (ii) It reduces uncertainty, as the seller knows the conditions that should be fulfilled to receive payments. (iii) It provides safety to the buyer, who wants to ensure that payment is made only in conformity with the conditions of the letter of credit.

(e) *Consignment:* In consignment business, consignor (seller) sends goods to consignee (agent of the seller). In this case goods sent are just shipped but not sold to the consignee since the consignor retains the title of the goods till they sold by the consignee to a third party. In this consignment only sales proceeds are remitted to the consignor by the consignee.

FACTORS INFLUENCING THE SIZE OF INVESTMENT IN RECEIVABLES

The level of investment in receivables is affected by the following factors:

(a) **Volume of Credit Sales:** Size of credit sale is the prime factor that affects the level of investment in receivables. Investment in receivable increase when the firm sells major portion of goods on credit base and vice versa. In other words an increase in credit sales, increase the level of receivables and vice versa.

(b) **Credit Policy of the Firm:** There are two types of credit policies such as lenient and stringent credit policy. A firm that is following lenient credit policy tends to sell on credit to customers very liberally, which will increase the size of receivables. On the other hand, a firm that following stringent credit policy will have low size of receivables because the firm is very selective in providing of stringent credit. A firm that is providing string one credit, may be able to collect debts promptly this will keep the level of receivables under control.

(c) **Trade Terms:** It is the most important factor (variable) in determining the level of investment in receivables. The important credit terms are credit period and cash discount. If credit period is more when compared to other companies/industry, then the investment in receivables will be more. Cash discount reduces the investment in receivables because it encourages early payments.

(d) **Seasonality of Business:** A firm doing seasonal business has to provide credit sales in the other seasons. When the firm provides credit automatically the level of investment in receivables will increase with the comparison of the level of receivables in the season; because in season firm will sell goods on cash basis only. For example, refrigerators, air-cooling products will be sold on credit in the winter season, and on cash in summer season.

(e) **Collection Policy:** Collection policy is needed because all customer do not pay the firm's bill in time. A firm's liberal collection policy will not be able to reduce investment in receivables, but in future sales may be increased. On the other hand, a firm that follow stringent collection policy will definitely reduce receivables, but it may reduce future sales. Therefore, the collection policy should aim at accelerating collections from slow payers and reducing bad debt base.

(f) **Bill Discounting and Endorsement:** Bill discounting and endorsing bill to the third party, which the firm has to pay, will reduce the size of investment in receivables. If the bills are dishonored on the due date, again the investment in receivable will increase because discounted bills or endorsed bills have to be paid by the firm.

CREDIT POLICY

A firm's credit policy regarding its credit standards, credit period, cash discounts, and collection procedures. The credit policy may be lenient or stringent (tight).

Lenient Credit Policy

It is that policy where the seller sells goods on very liberal credit terms and standards. In other words, goods are sold to the customers whose creditworthiness is not up to the standards or whose financial position is doubtful.

Advantages of Liberal Credit Policy

- **Increase in Sales:** Lenient credit policy expands sales because of the liberal credit terms and favorable incentives granted to customers.

- **Higher Profits:** Increase in sales leads to increase in profits, because higher level of production and sales reduces permit cost.

Disadvantages of Lenient credit policy

Apart from the advantages it has some disadvantages:

- *Bad Debt Loss:* A firm that follows lenient credit policy may suffer from bad debt losses that arise due to the non-payment credit sales.

- *Liquidity Problem:* Lenient credit policy not only increases bad debt losses but also creates liquidity problem, because when the firm is not able to receive the payment at a due date, it may became difficult to pay currently maturing obligations.

STRINGENT CREDIT POLICY

Stringent credit policy seller sells goods on credit on a highly selective basis only i.e., the customers who have proven creditworthiness and financially sound.

Advantages of Stringent Credit Policy

- *Less Bad Losses:* A firm that adopts stringent credit policy will have minimum bad debt losses, because it had granted credit only the customers who are creditworthy.

- *Sound Liquidity Position:* The firm that follows stringent credit policy will have sound liquidity position, due to the receipt of all payments from customers on due date, the firm can easily pay the currently maturing obligations.

Disadvantages of Stringent Credit Policy

- *Less Sales:* Stringent credit policy restricts sales, because it is not extending credit to average creditworthiness customers.

- *Less Profits:* Less sales automatically reduces profits, because firm may not be able to produce goods economically, and it may not be able to use resources efficiently that leads increase in production cost per unit.

In fact, firms follow credit policy that lies between lenient and stringent credit policy. In other words, they follow optimum credit policy. Optimum credit policy involves a balance between costs and benefits. The major considerations in costs are liquidity and opportunity costs. The optimum credit policy occurs at point where there is a trade off between liquidity and profitability. Therefore, the management has to strike a balance between easy credit to promote sales and profit and tight credit to improve liquidity. The important variables of credit policy should be identified before establishing an optimum credit policy.

CREDIT POLICY VARIABLES

As we have seen in the credit policy that majority of firms follow a credit policy that lies between stringent and lenient, that is optimum credit policy. Optimum credit policy is one, which maximizes firm's operating profit. For establishing optimum credit policy, the financial manager must consider the important decision variables, which have bearing on the level of receivables. In other words, the credit policy variables have bearing on level of sales, bad debt loss, discounts taken by customers, and the collection expenses. The major credit policy variable include the following:

(a) Credit Standards, (b) Credit Terms, and (c) Collection Policy and Procedures.

(a) *Credit Standards:* Firm has to select some customers for extension of credit. For this firm has to evaluate the customer. In evaluation of customers what standards should be applied? Credit standards refer to the minimum criteria for the extension of credit to a customer. Credit ratings, credit references, average payment periods, and certain financial ratios provide a quantitative basis for establishing and enforcing credit standards. The firm's decision, to accept or reject a customer, and to extend credit depends on credit standards. Firms may have more number of standards in this respect, but at one point it may decide not to extend credit to any customer, even though his/her credit rating is strong. On the other point, firm may decide to provide goods on credit to all customers irrespective of their credit creditworthiness. Practical ones lies between these two points.

Adoption of liberal credit standards increases sales by attracting more customers, but these credit standards increase bad debt loss, loss of opportunity cost and higher collection costs. On the other hand, rigid credit standards, opposite effects. They reduce sales, bad debt loss, save opportunity cost due less investment in receivables. When ever firms plans to go for new standards (generally liberalization of standards) they have to determine the changes in net profit after taking into consideration all the benefits and costs of the change of policy. If the change in net profit is positive, it is better to go for new standards and vice versa.

Calculation of Change in Net Profit

Particulars	Amount (Rs.)
Increase in Sales	X X X X
Less: Variable Cost	X X X
Contribution	X X X
Less: Bad debt loss on new sales	XX
Earnings Before Tax (EBT)	XXX
Less: Tax	XX
Earnings After Tax (EAT)	XXX
Less: Opportunity cost	XX
Change in Net Profit	XXX

(1) Calculation of Bad Debt Loss on New Sales

Increase in Sales × Ratio of bed debt loss on sales

Or

Bad Debt Loss with proposed credit period	XXXX
Less: Bad Debt Loss with proposed credit period	XXXX
Bad Debt Loss on New Sales	XXXX

(2) Opportunity Cost = Increase in Investment × Cost of Capital

Increase in Investment = (Increase in Sales ÷365) x Average Collection Period x Ratio of Variable Cost to Sales

Or

= Cost of Sales ÷ Receivables Turnover

Or

= Total Variable Cost of Annual Sales ÷ Receivables Turnover

Receivable Turnover = 365 ÷ Average Collection Period

Average Collection Period

= (Trade Debtors x No. of Working Days) ÷Net Credit Sales

Illustration 1:

Dream Well Company's present annual sales are Rs. 5,00,000, cost of capital is 15 % and the company is in the 40% tax bracket. Company categorized its customers into four categories, viz.,

C1, C2, C3 and C4 (C1 customer have the highest credit standing and those in C4 have lowest credit standing). At present, Company has provided unlimited credit to categories C1 and C2, where as limited credit facility to Category C3 and no credit to Category C4, since their credit standing (rating) is very low. Due to the present credit standards the company foregoing sales to the extent of Rs. 50,000 to the customers in category C3 and Rs. 40,000 to the C4 category customers. To attract for the foregoing sales to the C3 and C4 category customers, company is considering to relax, credit standards, thus C3 customers would be provided unlimited credit facility and C4 category would be provided limited credit facility. As a result of relaxation in credit standards the sales are expected to increase by Rs.75,000 and it involves 12 per cent bad debt loss on increased sales. The estimated contribution margin ratio is 25 per cent and average collection period if 50 days.

Determine the change in net profit and suggest whether the company consider the relaxation of credit standards or not.

Solution:

Calculation of Change in Net Profit

Particulars	Amount (Rs.)
Increased Sales	75,000
Less: Variable Cost (Rs.75,000 × 0.75)	56,250
Contribution	**18,750**
Less: Bad debt loss on new sales (Rs.75,000 × 0.12)	9,000
Earnings Before Tax (EBT)	**9,750**
Less: Tax at 40 %	3,900
Earnings After Tax (EAT)	**5,850**
Less: Opportunity cost (See Note)	1,156
Increase in Net Profit	**4,694**

Note: Calculation of Opportunity Cost: Increase in Investment × Cost of Capital

Increase in Sales =Avg. Collection Period × Ratio of Variable Cost to Sales × Cost of Capital

$(75,000 \div 365) 50 \times 0.75 \times 0.15 = Rs.1,156$

Suggestion: The firm can relax its credit standards since the change in net profit is positive.

Illustration 2:

Good Luck Ltd's present sales are Rs. 5,00,000 annual. Company categorized its customers into four categories, viz., A1, A2, A3 and A4 (A1 customer have the highest credit rating and those in A4 have lowest credit rating). At present, Company has provided unlimited credit to categories A1 and A2, where as limited credit facility to Category A3 and no credit to Category A4, since their credit rating is very low. Presently the Company's bad debt loss percentage is 10%. Due to the present credit standards, the company is foregoing sales to the extent of Rs. 50,000 to the customers in category A3 and Rs. 40,000 to the A4 category customers. To attract the foregoing sales to the A3 and A4 category customers, company is considering to relax credit standards, under that category A3 customers would be provided unlimited credit facility and customers in A4 category would be provided limited credit facility. As a result of relaxation in credit standards the sales are expected to increase by Rs.75,000 and it involves a bad debt loss ratio of 20%. Variable cost to sales ratio is 80% and average collection period if 50 days. It required rate of return is 20% and the company's tax rate is in the 35%. Assume 360 days year.

You are required to suggest whether the company consider the relaxation of credit standards or not.

Solution:

Calculation of Change in Net Profit

Particulars	Amount (Rs.)
Increased Sales	75,000
Less: Variable Cost (Rs.75,000 × 0.80)	60,000
Contribution	**15,000**
Less: Bad debt loss on new sales (Note –1)	65,000
Earnings Before Tax (EBT)	– 50,000
Less: Tax at 35 %	-------
Earnings After Tax (EAT)	– 50,000
Less: Opportunity cost (Note –2)	1,667
Increase in Net Profit	**– 51,667**

Note:

1. **Calculation of Bad debt loss:**   Rs.

   Bad debt loss with new policy (5,75,000 × 0.20)   1,15,000

   Less: Bad debt loss with present policy (5,00,000 × 0.10)   50,000

                  Increase in Bad debt loss   65,000

2. **Calculation of Opportunity Cost:** Increase in Investment × Cost of Capital

   Increase in Sales = Avg. Collection Period x Ratio of Variable Cost to Sales x Cost of Capital

                  (75,000 ÷ 360) 50 × 0.80 × 0.20 = Rs.1666.667 or Rs. 1667.

Suggestion: The proposed policy is not feasible, since the change in net profit is negative (i.e.net loss).

(b) *Credit Terms:* The second decision criteria in receivables management are the credit terms. Credit terms means the stipulations under which goods or services are sold on credit. Once the credit terms have been established and the credit worthiness of the customers has been assessed, then the financial managers has to decide the terms and conditions on which the credit will be granted. The credit terms specify the lengthy of time over which credit is extended to a customer and the discount, if any, given for early payment. Credit terms have three components such as: (i) credit period, and (ii) cash discount, and (iii) cash discount period.

(i) *Credit Period:* The period of time, for which credit is allowed to a customer to economic value of purchases. It is generally expressed in terms of a net data [i.e., if a firm's credit [1]terms are "net 60"], it is understandable that payment will be made within 60 days from the date to credit sales. Generally the credit period is decided with the consideration of industry norms and depending on the firm's ability to manage receivables.

A decision regarding lengthening of credit period increases sales by inducing existing customers to purchase more and attracting new customers. But it also increases investment in receivables and lowers the quality of trade credit.[6] In other words, it increases investment in receivables and bad debt loss. On the other hand, shortening of the credit period (existing) will lead to lower sales, decrease investment in debtors, and reduce the bad debt loss. A firm should finalize the decision relating to credit period [either lengthening or shortening credit period] only after cost, benefit analysis. If the change in net profit is positive, it is better to go for credit period and vice versa.

Calculation of Change in Net Profit

Particulars	Amount (Rs.)
Increase in Sales	X X X X
Less: Variable Cost	X X X
Contribution	X X X
Less: Bad debt loss on new sales	XX
Earnings Before Tax (EBT)	XXX
Less: Tax	XX
Earnings After Tax (EAT)	XXX
Less: Opportunity cost	XX
Change in Net Profit	XXX

Opportunity Cost = Increase in Investment × Cost of Capital

Increase in Investment is the sum of average investment with present credit period plus incremental investment with new proposed credit period. In other words, average investment with proposed credit period less average investment with present credit period.

Increase in Investment = (DOS x NACP) + (DVCIS x ACP_n)

Or

(Daily Old Sales x Net Avg. Collection Period) + (Daily Variable Cost of Incremental Sales x New Avg. Collection Period)

Where: DOS = Daily old sales = Old Sales ÷365

NACP= Net average collection period = New ACP – Old ACP

DVCIS= Daily variable cost of incremental sales = (Incremental Sales x Variable Cost Per Unit)÷ 365

ACP_n = New average collection period

Illustration 3:

Long Lost Pvt. Ltd, currently provides 20 days of credit to its customers. Its current sales level is Rs. 4,00,000. The company's cost of capital is 12% and the tax rate is 40%. The ratio of variable cost to sales is 75%. Long Lost is considering extending its credit period by 40 days, such an extension is expected to increase sales by Rs. 1,00,000, and also increases the bad debt portion on new sales would be 5%. Determine the change in net profit and suggest whether the company should consider the relaxation of credit period or not.

Solution:

Calculation of Change in Net Profit

Particulars	Amount (Rs.)
Increased Sales	1,00,000
Less: Variable Cost (Rs.1,00,000 × 0.75)	75,000
Contribution	**25,000**
Less: Bad debt loss on new sales (Rs.1,00,000 × 0.05)	5,000
Earnings Before Tax (EBT)	**20,000**
Less: Tax at 40 %	8,000
Earnings After Tax (EAT)	**12,000**
Less: Opportunity cost (See Note)	6,740
Increase in Net Profit	**5,260**

Note:

Opportunity Cost = Increase in Investment × Cost of Capital

Increase in Investment = (DOS × NACP) + (DVCIS × ACP_n)

= (1095.89 × 40) + (205.48 × 60)= Rs.56,164.3

DOS = Rs. 4,00,000 ÷365 = Rs.1,095.89

NACP = 60 − 20 = 40 Days

DVCIS = (Rs.1,00,000 × 0.75) ÷ 365 = Rs.205.48

Opportunity Cost = Rs.56,164.3 × 0.12 = Rs.6,739.7

Suggestion: Extension of credit period is feasible, since the change in net profit is positive.

(ii) *Cash Discount:* The second part of credit terms is cash discount. Cash discount represents a percent reduction in sales or purchase price allowed for early payment of invoices. It is an incentive for credit customers to pay invoices in a timely fashion. In other words, it encourages the customers to pay credit obligations within a specified period of time, which will be less than the normal credit period. It is generally stated, as a percentage of sales. Cash discount terms specify, the repayment terms required of all credit customers, which involve rate of cash discount. For example, '2/20 net 60', which means creditor (sells) grants 2 per cent discount, if debtor (buyer) pays his/her accounts with 20 days after beginning of the credit period. Financial managers before going to offer cash discount, he/she is suppose to estimate the change in net profit, it is positive, then he can go for providing cash discount and vice versa.

Calculation of Change in Net Profit

Particulars	Amount (Rs.)
Increase in Sales	X X X X
Less: Variable Cost	X X X
Contribution	X X X
Less: Increase in discount cot ($\triangle CDC$)	X X
Earnings Before Tax (EBT)	XXX
Less: Tax	XX
Earnings After Tax (EAT)	XXX
Add: Savings on Investment (K$\triangle$I)	XX
Change in Net Profit	XXX

Note:

1. Calculation of Increase in Cash Discount Cost ($\triangle CDC$) = NCDC − OCDC

   Where: NCDC = New cash discount cost

   OCDC = Old cash discount cost

   NCDC = Total Sales × New Cash Discount × New Percentage of Availing Cash Discount

   OCDC = Old Sales × Old Cash Discount × Old Percentage of Availing Cash Discount

2. Opportunity Cost = Increase in Investment × Cost of Capital

   Increase in Investment = (DOS × NACP) − (DVCIS × ACP_n)

   DOS = Old Sales ÷365

   NACP = Old ACP − New ACP

   DVCIS = (Incremental Sales × Variable Cost Per Unit) ÷ 365

Illustration 4:

2/10, net 30 is the present credit term of Well Do Company Ltd,. Its present level of sales are Rs.6,00,000, with an average collection period of 30 days. The contribution margin ratio is 15%. The proportion of sales on which currently customers take discount is 1%. The Company's cost of capital is 10%. Now the Company is considering to increase the discount term to 4/10, net 30, which is expected to push up sales to Rs. 6,50,000 and reduces the average collection period by 10 days. Such relaxation increases the proportion of discount sales to 2%. Determine the change in net profit with the assumption of 40% tax rate.

Solution:

Calculation of Change in Net Profit

Particulars	Amount (Rs.)
Increased Sales	50,000
Less: Variable Cost (Rs.50,000 × 0.85)	42,500
Contribution	7,500
Less: Increase in discount cots ($\triangle$CDC (Note 1)	400
Earnings Before Tax (EBT)	7,100
Less: Tax at 40 %	2,840
Earnings After Tax (EAT)	4,260
Add: Savings on Investment (K$\triangle$I) (Note –2)	1,411
Increase in Net Profit	5,671

Note:

1. Increase in Cash Discount Cost ($\triangle$CDC) = NCDC –OCDC = Rs.520–Rs.120 =Rs.400

   Where: NCDC = New cash discount cost

   OCDC = Old cash discount cost

   NCDC = Total Sales x New Cash Discount x New Percentage of Availing Cash Discount

   NCDC = Rs. 6,50,000 x 0.04 x 0.02 = Rs. 520

   OCDC = Old Sales x Old Cash Discount x Old Percentage of Availing Cash Discount

   OCDC = Rs. 6,00,000 x 0.02 x 0.01= Rs.120

2. Opportunity Cost = Increase in Investment x Cost of Capital

   Increase in Investment = (DOS x NACP) – (DVCIS x ACP_n)

   = (1,643.84 x 10) – (116.44 x 20)

   = Rs.1,6438.4 – Rs.2,328.8 = Rs.14,109.6

   DOS = Old Sales ÷365 = 6,00,000 ÷ 365 =Rs.1,643.84

   NACP = Old ACP – New ACP = 30 – 20 = 10 Days

   DVCIS = (Incremental Sales x Variable Cost Per Unit) ÷ 365

   = (50,000 x 0.85) ÷ 365 = Rs. 116.44

   Opportunity Cost = Rs.14,109.6 x 0.10 = Rs. 1,410.96

(iii) *Cash Discount Period:* It refers to the duration in which the discount can be availed from collection of receivable and is influenced by the cash discount period. Extension of cash discount period may prompt some more customer to avail discount and more payments, which will release additional funds. But extension of cash discount period will result in late collection of funds, because the customer who are able to pay will have less cash discount thus now they may delay their payments. It will increase collection period of the firm. Hence, financial manager has to match the effect on collection period with the increased cost associated with additional customers availing the discount.

(c) *Collection Policy:* This is the third aspect in receivables management. The collection of a firm is the procedures passed to collect amount receivables, when they become due. It is needed because all customers do not pay the bill receivables in time collection procedures includes monitoring the state of receivables, dispatch of letters to customers whose due date is approaching, electronic and telephonic advice to customers around the due date, threat of legal action to overdue customers, and legal action against overdue accounts.

Customers may be divided into two categories. Such as slow payer and non-payers. Hence, there is a need for accelerating collections from slow payers and reduce bad debt losses. Collection policies may be divided into two categories. (i) strict / rigorous, and (ii) lenient/lax collection policy. Adoption of strict collection policy tends to decrease sales, reduces average collection period, bad debt percentage, and increases the collection expenses. On the other hand, lenient collection policy will increase sales average collection period, bad debt losses, and reduce collection expenses. Financial manager has to see the benefits and costs from adopting one credit policy, if the change in net profit is positive, he/she has to go with new credit policy and vice versa.

Calculation of Change in Net Profit

Particulars	Amount (Rs.)
Increased Sales	X X X X
Less: Variable Cost (Rs.50,000 x 0.85)	X X X
Contribution	**X X X**
Less: Increase in bad debt cost (Note 1)	XX
Earnings Before Tax (EBT)	**XXX**
Less: Tax at 40 %	XX
Earnings After Tax (EAT)	**XXX**
Less: Opportunity cost (K∆I) (Note –2)	XX
Increase in Net Profit	**XXX**

Note:

1. **Calculation of Bad Debt Loss on New Sales**

   Bad Debt Loss with proposed credit period   XXXX

   Less: Bad Debt Loss with proposed credit period   XXXX

   Bad Debt Loss on New Sales   **XXXX**

   Increase in Investment = (DOS x NACP) + (DVCIS x ACP_n)

   Or

   (Daily Old Sales x Net Avg. Collection Period) + (Daily Variable Cost of Incremental Sales x New Avg. Collection Period)

   Where: DOS = Daily old sales = Old Sales ÷365

   NACP= Net average collection period = New ACP – Old ACP

   DVCIS= Daily variable cost of incremental sales = (Incremental Sales x Variable Cost Per Unit) ÷ 365

   ACP_n = New average collection period

Illustration 5:

Honey Well Company is contemplating to liberalize its collection effort. Its present sales are Rs. 10 lakhs, its average collection period is 30 days, its expected variable cost to sales ratio is 85 per cent and its bad debt ratio is 5 per cent. The Company's cost of capital is 10 per cent and tax rate is 40 per cent. The proposed liberalisation in collection effort increases sales to Rs. 12 lakhs, increases average collection period by 15 days, and increases the bad debt ratio to 7 per cent. Determine the change in net profit.

Solution:

Calculation of Change in Net Profit

Particulars	Amount (Rs.)
Increased Sales	2,00,000
Less: Variable Cost (Rs.2,00,000 × 0.85)	1,70,000
Contribution	**30,000**
Less: Increase in bad debt cost (Note 1)	3,4000
Earnings Before Tax (EBT)	**– 4,000**
Less: Tax at 40 %	-----
Earnings After Tax (EAT)	-----
Less: Opportunity cost (KΔI) (Note –2)	3,465
Increase in Net Profit	**– 7465**

Note:

1. Calculation of Bad debt loss: Rs.

   Bad debt loss with new policy (Rs.12,00,000 x 0.070)   84,000

   Less: Bad debt loss with present policy (Rs.10,00,000 x 0.05)   50,000

   Increase in Bad debt loss   34,000

2. Calculation of Opportunity Cost = Increase in Investment x Cost of Capital

   Increase in Investment = (DOS x NACP) + (DVCIS x ACP_n)

   = (2,739.73 x 5) + (465.75 x 45) = 13,698.65 + 20,958.75= Rs.34,657.4

   DOS = Rs.10,00,000 ÷365 = Rs.2,739.73

   NACP = 45 – 30 = 15 Days

   DVCIS = (Rs.2,00,000 x 0.85) ÷ 365 = Rs.465.75

   Opportunity Cost = Rs.34,657.4 × 0.1 = Rs.3,465.74

CREDIT EVALUATION OF INDIVIDUAL ACCOUNTS

Receivables management requires a lot of decision making exercises, setting credit standards, identifying credit terms (credit period and cash discount), collection policy, evaluation of individual accounts. Evaluation of individual accounts is the prime activity, which affects firm's profitability. In this, firm should develop procedures for evaluating credit applicants and consider the possibilities of bad debt or slow payment. Mere determination of appropriate credit policy will not serve the purpose of minimizing investment in receivables and reducing bad debt losses, without credit evaluation of individual accounts and identification of their credit worthiness. In other words, the firm has to evaluate the customers before extension of credit. The credit evaluation procedure involves three related steps(7): (i) obtaining credit information, (ii) analyzing the information, and (iii) making the credit decision.

(i) ***Obtaining Credit Information:*** Credit should be granted to those customers who have ability to make payment on time. To ensure this, a firm should evaluate an individual's accounts properly, for which it require information. Hence, there is a need to obtain information. Collection of credit information involves some cost. Some accounts, small accounts, the cost of collecting information may outweigh the potential profitability of the account. In addition, the cost, the firm must consider the time factor in collecting information. The decision to grant credit to a customer cannot be delayed unnecessarily due to long time involved in collecting information. Hence, while collecting information there is a need to consider cost and time. Depending on these two factors, the credit analyst may use one or more of the following sources of information. The information may be divided into two sources, such as (a) internal source and (b) external source. The following secondary sources are available for the collection of credit information.

(a) ***Internal Sources:*** Internal source is that source that is available with in an organization and it provides information free of cost. This type of source is useful only while evaluating existing customers. A particular customer may have enjoyed credit facility in the past. Now for extension of credit period or cash discount firm may ask the internal receivable department to provide this past record, based on which firm may make decision.

(b) ***External Sources:*** External sources of information are very important when a firm is planning to evaluate a new customer. Secondary source of information is available based on the development of institutional agencies facilities and industry practices. India, has little progress in the matter of developing the sources of credit information in the name of secrecy and confidentiality. But in advanced countries, there are number of independent information agencies, banks, fellow business undertakings and associates, competitors, suppliers etc. Based on the availability, the following are the secondary sources information that can be used to obtain information:

Financial Statements or Annual Reports: Financial statements are the profit & loss account and balance sheet that give the prospective customer's financial condition in terms of financial viability, liquidity, profitability and debt capacity. They are dumb figures, proper analysis provides vivid stories of the prospective customer, which is very much helpful in determining the credit standing position of the prospective customer. There are difficulties in obtaining financial statements of partnership firms or individuals and small private firms.

Bank References: This is another secondary source to credit information. Bank references means collection of information about prospective customer from the bank where the customer is maintaining account. Here the firm is required to write a letter to the bank requesting for a credit report on the prospective customer, the bank may, at its sole discretion, decide to send a report and oblige the firm (seller). Information collected from bank may not be useful, because banker's written report may not provide much of the desired clue, or even a small clue, due to the use of certain self-terminologies, which may have different bases and connotations. These may vary from bank to bank. Some times, they give information favourable to its customers, it cannot be relied upon in granting credit. Firm may require more information from other sources, which may be supplemented. In advanced countries like USA, many banks have separate credit departments that provide detailed information required by the firm that can be believed and can take base for credit granting.

Trade References: Trade reference is the source of information from firm's with whom the prospective customer has dealings. Firms magnify the applicant to give the names of references. This is useful and cost free source. If the firm feels that the information given by the applicant in application is misleading then the firm may need to go to trade references, where all the relevant information may be obtained. Firm should examine honesty and seriousness of the references and may insist on furnishing the references of reputed people.

Credit Rating Agencies: This is the suitable source of information, when the customer insists to give products on credit immediately. Then financial managers cannot spend much time in collection of financial statements. At that time reports of credit rating agencies can be collected and can relieve upon them. In India, there are three important credit rating agencies, such as CRISIL, ICRA, and CARE. But in developed counties like USA, Credit Bureau Reports are an important source of information.

(ii) *Analysis of Information/Credit Analysis:* After having collected the required information about applicant from different sources, the information should be analyzed to determine the credit worthiness of the prospective customers. There are no tailored made procedures to analyze the credit information that are suitable to one. The analysis should cover two aspects. (a) Quantitative, and (b) Qualitative.

(a) *Quantitative:* This type of assessment is very much useful, which is done on the basis of financial statements, and firm's past records. Preparation of aging schedule is the prime one. Aging schedule is statement showing age-wise distribution of receivables (Bills). It gives a clear picture about the past payment patterns of the applicant. Next the firm can go for ratio analysis, where it can study, liquidity, profitability and debt capacity of the perspective customer. Calculated ratios must be compared with industry ratios (standards).

(b) *Qualitative:* Evaluation of prospective customer from the quantitative analysis point, some times it should be fortified by qualitative analysis for interpretation of credit worthiness. Qualitative analysis would cover the aspects relating to quality of management, management, philosophy, management vision etc. The stated external sources may form the basis for conclusion to be drawn.

The above mentioned are the two, methods of evaluation. But in traditional credit analysis takes 6C's into consideration.

1. *Character:* It is the prime C' in as much as it means the moral integrity and noble intentions and willingness in the part of the prospective buyers to honor the obligation of making the full payments on the due date because, there may be cases, where the buyer may be able to pay but may not have the good intention to do so.

2. *Capacity:* It means the ability of prospective customers to pay. In other words, customers capacity as the financial capability to make the payment on the due date. It may be ascertained from the net cash position, after assessing the cash inflows and cash out flows.

3. *Capital:* It refers to the capital base and capital structure of the company. If the applicant is a person then capital refers the personal assets value of financial reserve value of the customer. In any case, the value should be more than the goods are going to be sold on credit. It may be required when the customer has difficulties in meeting obligations out of the current generation of surplus, it may offered to make the payment out of its resources and surplus, till its present financed position improves.

4. *Collateral:* It means offering assets as a pledge against providing credit. It acts as a cushion, when the above three C's are not sufficient to take decision. The assets generally may be security deposits of bank sureties, these are movable.

5. *Conditions:* The term 'condition' here refers to the economic conditions and climate providing at the material time, which may have favourable or unfavourable impact on the financial position and prospects of the prospective customer.

6. *Case History [past expense] (8):* If the credit extension decision to a existing customer than these is a need to go back to old needs and check customs record. The past date may be reliable for decision-making.

(iii) *Making Credit Decision:* The prime objective of evaluation of prospective customer credit worthiness is to asset whether he/she is worthy of granting the credit or not. Actual credit worthiness is compared with the predetermined standards, if the actual are up to the standards or above to the standards, goods would be provided on credit, and vice versa. Credit decision is difficult to make when the credit worthiness is marginal. Decision can be taken only, after comparing the benefits of credit extension with likely bad debt losses. In case, where customers credit worthiness is less than the standards, firm may not reject the customer, but it may give some alternative facilities. Customer may be asked to pay after delivery of goods, or invoices may be sent through bank and it may release after collecting dues on basis of a third party guarantee. This will help to the firm to retain the present or old customs and continuation delays may help in receiving their requests (credit facilities) at a future date.

MONITORING ACCOUNTS RECEIVABLES

Just evaluation of individual accounts does not help in efficient accounts receivables management without continuous monitoring and control of receivables. In other words success of collection effort depends on mp\monitoring and controlling receivables. Then how to monitor and control receivables? There are traditional techniques available for monitoring accounts receivables. They are (a) Receivables turnover, (b) Average Collection period, (c) Aging Schedule and (d) Collection matrix.

(a) *Receivables Turnover:* Receivables turnover provides relationship between credit sales and debtors (receivables) of a firm. It indicates how quickly receivables or debtors are converted into cash. Ramamurthy observes "collection of debtors is the concluding stage for process of sales transaction".[9] The liquidity of receivables is therefore, is measured through the receivables (debtors) turnover rate.

Debtors or Receivables Turnover Rate = Credit Sales ÷ Average Debtors or receivables

Debtors turnover rate is expressed in terms of times. Analyst may not be able to access credit sales information, average debtors and bills receivables.

To avoid of non-availability of the above information and to evaluate receivables turnover there is another method available for analyst.

Debtors or Receivables Turnover Rate = Total Net Sales ÷ Average Debtors (including receivables)

(b) *Average Collection Period (ACP):* Turnover rate converted into average collection period is a significant measure of the collection activities of debtors.[10] Average collection period is a measure of how long it takes from the time sales is made to the time to cash is collected from the customers.

ACP = 365 ÷ Debtors or Receivables turnover.

Illustration 6:

A company's credit sales are Rs. 20 lakhs in a year. The opening debts are Rs.2 lakhs and closing debtors are Rs.2,10,000. Determine Debtors turnover and ACP.

Solution:

Debtors Turnover Ratio = Rs. 20,00,000 ÷ (Rs.2,00,000+Rs.2,10,000)/ 2 = 9.75 times

ACP = 365 ÷ 9.75 = 37.43 Days

(c) *Aging Schedule:* As we have seen in the above average collection period measures quality of receivables in an aggregate manner, which is the limitation of ACP. This can be overcome by preparing aging schedule. Aging schedule is a statement that shows age wise grouping of debtors. In other words, it breaks down debtors according to the length of time for which they have been outstanding. A hypothetical aging schedule is as follows:

Age Group (in days)	Amount Outstanding (Rs.)	Percentage of Debtors to total Debtors
Less than 30	40,00,000	40
31 – 45	20,00,000	20
46 – 60	30,00,000	30
Above 60	10,00,000	10
Total	1,00,00,000	100

Aging schedule is helpful for identifying slow paying debtors, with which firm may have to encounter a stringent collection policy. The actual aging schedule of the firm is compared with industry standard aging schedule or with bench mark aging schedule for deciding whether the debtors are in control or not.

(d) *Collection Matrix:* Traditional methods (debtors turnover rate, average collection period) of receivables management are very popular, but they have limitations, that they are on aggregate data and fail to relate the outstanding accounts receivables of a period with credit sales of the same period. The problem of aggregating data can be eliminated by preparing and analyzing collection matrix. Collection matrix is a method (statement) showing percentage of receivables collected during the month of sales and subsequent months. It helps in studying the efficiency of collections whether they are improving or deteriorating. Following table shows hypothetical collection matrix.

Percentage of Receivables collected During the	April	May	June	July	August
Sales (Rs. Lakhs)	350	340	320	300	250
Month of Sales	10	12	14	11	08
First Month following	30	38	40	30	34
Second Month following	25	24	22	20	21
Third Month following	20	26	22	19	18
Fourth Month following	15	10	02	15	20
Fifth Month following	-	-	-	05	09

From the above table, it may be read for April sales are Rs. 350 lakhs. The pattern of collections are 10 per cent in the same month (April), 30 per cent of sales in May, 25 per cent of sales in June, 20 per cent of sales in July and the remaining 15 per cent in the August.

SUMMARY

- Accounts Receivables occupy an important position in the structure of current assets of a firm. They are the outcome of rapid growth of credit sales granted by the firms to their customers. Credit sales are reflected in the value of Sundry Debtors [SD's in India].

- The term receivable is defined as debt owed to the firm by customers arising from sale of goods or services in the ordinary course of business. The accounts receivables arising out of credit sales has the characteristics Risk Involvement, Based on Economic Value, and Implies Futurity.

- Accounts Receivable management involves maintenance of receivables of optimum level, the degree of credit sales to be made, and the debtors collection.

- The objectives of accounts receivables management are: Maximising the value of the Firm, Optimum Investment in Sundry Debtors, Control and Dr. Bhatt the Cost of Trade Credit.

- The management of accounts receivables is not cost free. It involves cost and its association with accounts receivables results in: Opportunity Cost / Capital Cost, Collection Cost, and Bad Debts.

- The economic value of goods or services sold on credit, will be paid by adoption of different modes—(1) Cash Mode, (2) Open Account, (3) Letter of Credit and (4) Consignment.

- The level of investment in receivables is affected by the factors: Volume of Credit Sales, Credit Policy of the Firm, Trade Terms, Seasonality of Business, Collection Policy, Bill Discounting and Endorsement.

- Receivables management involves the decisions areas: credit standards, credit period, cash discounts, and collection procedures.

- Liberal credit policy is that policy where the seller sells goods on very liberal credit terms and standards, which increase in sales, higher profits. But it involves bad debt loss, and liquidity problem.

- Stringent credit policy seller sells goods on credit on a highly selective basis only, which reduces bad losses, sound liquidity position. These benefits are accompanied by less sales less profits.

- Firms should follow optimum credit policy that lies between lenient and stringent credit policy. Optimum credit policy involves a balance between costs and benefits. The optimum credit policy occurs at point where there is a trade off between liquidity and profitability.

- The major controllable variables of credit policy are: (a) Credit Standards, (b) Credit Terms, and (c) Collection Policy and Procedures.

- Credit Standards refer to the minimum criteria for the extension of credit to a customer. The firm's decision, to accept or reject a customer to extend credit depends on credit standards. Practical ones lies between these two points, liberal credit standards and rigid credit standards.

- Credit Terms: The second decision criterion in receivables management is the credit terms. Credit terms means the stipulations under which goods or services are sold on credit. Credit terms have three components such as: (i) credit period, and (ii) cash discount, and (iii) cash discount period.

- The collection policy of a firm is the procedures passed to collect amount receivables, when they become due. Collection policies may be divided into two categories. First strict / rigorous, and Second lenient/lax collection policy.

- The credit evaluation (individual's accounts) procedure involves three related steps: viz., (i) obtaining credit information, (ii) analyzing the information, and (iii) making the credit decision. (i) Credit Information can be obtained from one or more of the following sources of information. The information may be divided into two sources, such as (a) internal source and (b) external source. Internal Sources is that source that is available with in the organization and it provides information at free cost. External Sources of information (information agencies, banks, fellow business undertakings and associates, competitors, suppliers etc). (ii) Analysis of Information, there are no tailored made procedure to analyze the credit information. But the analysis should cover two aspects. (a) Quantitative, and (b) Qualitative. Quantitative analysis involves preparation of aging schedule, ratio analysis. Qualitative analysis would cover the aspects relating to quality of management, management, philosophy, management vision etc.

- Traditional credit analysis takes 5C's into consideration, they are Character, Capacity, Capital, Collateral, Conditions, and Case History [past expense].

- The success of collection effort depends on mp\monitoring and controlling receivables. Then how to monitor and control receivables? There are traditional techniques available for monitoring accounts receivables. They are (a) Receivables turnover, (b) Average Collection period, (c) Aging Schedule and (d) Collection matrix.

DO IT YOURSELF

1. Calculate the interest cost (on annual percentage basis) associated with the following credit terms for the sellers and to the buyers.

(a) 2/10 net, 50, (b) 2/15 net, 45, (c) 2/5 net, 25, and (d) 3/20 net, 80.

Solution:

Calculation of interest cost from sellers point of view

(a) $(0.02 \times 365) / (50 - 10) = 0.1825$ or 18.25%

(b) $(0.02 \times 365) / (45 - 15) = 0.2433$ or 24.33%

(c) $(0.02 \times 365) / (25 - 5) = 0.365$ or 36.5%

(d) $(0.03 \times 365) / (80 - 20) = 0.1825$ or 18.25%

Calculation of interest cost from Buyers point of view

(a) $(0.02 \times 365 \times 100) / (50 - 10)(100 - 2) = 0.1862$ or 18.62%

(b) $(0.02 \times 365 \times 100) / (45 - 15)(100 - 2) = 0.2483$ or 24.83%

(c) $(0.02 \times 365 \times 100) / (25 - 5)(100 - 2) = 0.3724$ or 37.24%

(d) $(0.03 \times 365 \times 100) / (80 - 20)(100 - 3) = 0.1881$ or 18.81%

2. Hare Ram & Co, produces 1,00,000 units and sells at Rs.80 per unit. 70 per cent of sales are credit sales. Average receivables amount is Rs.2,00,000. Determine average collection period (ACP).

Solution:

$$ACP = \frac{\text{Average receivables} \times 360}{\text{Credit Sales}}$$

$$= \frac{Rs.2,00,000 \times 360}{(1,00,000 \times 0.7 \times Rs.80)} = 12.86 \text{ days or } 13 \text{ days}$$

3. Dream Well Company's credit sales for the year 2004 are Rs. 1,50,000. The company was started 2004 year with opening balance of receivables Rs.15,000 and 2004 year business is closed with Rs.11,000 receivables. Calculate receivables turnover and ACP.

Solution:

Debtors Turnover Ratio = Rs. 1,50,000 ÷ (Rs.15,000+Rs.11,000)/ 2 = 11.538 times

ACP = 365 ÷ 11.538 = 31.63 Days

4. The present annual sales of Info Way Company are Rs. 30 lakhs. The company classifies its customers into three categories, viz., 1, 2, and 3. At present, it provides unlimited credit to category 1, limited credit to customers in category 2 and no credit to category 3 customers. Due to the present credit policy, the company foregoing sales extent Rs. 5 lakhs to the customers in category 2 and Rs. 8 lakhs to the 3 category customers. Now the company is considering the adoption of more liberal credit, in which the customers in category 2 would be provided unlimited credit facility and customers in 3 categories would be provided limited credit facility. Such relaxation would increase the sales by Rs. 9 lakhs on which bad debt losses would be 5 per cent. The variable cost to sales ratio is 70 per cent, the average collection period is 50 days, and cost of capital is 15 per cent, and tax rate is 40%.

Determine the change in net profit and suggest whether the proposed change is desirable? Give specific reasons.

Solution:

Calculation of Change in Net Profit

Particulars	Amount (Rs.)
Increased Sales	9,00,000
Less: Variable Cost (Rs.9,00,000 x 0.7)	6,30,000
Contribution	**2,70,000**
Less: Bad debt loss on new sales	
(Rs.9,00,000 x 0.05)	45,000
Earnings Before Tax (EBT)	**2,25,000**
Less: Tax at 40 %	90,000
Earnings After Tax (EAT)	**1,35,000**
Less: Opportunity cost (See Note)	12,945
Increase in Net Profit	**1,22,055**

Note:

Calculation of Opportunity Cost = KΔI

$$\text{Cost of capital} \frac{\text{Increase in sales}}{365} \times \text{Average Collection Period} \times \text{Ratio of Variable Cost to Sales}$$

$$0.15 \frac{9,00,000}{365} \times 50 \times 0.7 = \text{Rs. } 12,945$$

Suggestion: The proposed change is desirable since the change in net profit is positive.

5. Gokul Plastics currently provides 20 days of credit to its customers. Gokul's present sales are Rs. 9 lakhs. The contribution margin ratio is 25 per cent. Gokul is considering extending its credit period by 10 days, such an extension of credit increases sales to Rs. 10 lakhs. At the same time it involves 5 per cent bad debt loss on new sales. Calculate the change in net profit with the assumption of 40 per cent and cost of capital is 12 per cent credit and also

suggest that should Gokul implement the proposed extension of credit period? Give reason. And also increase the bad debt portion on new sales is 5%. Determine the change in net profit and suggest whether the company consider the relaxation of credit standards or not.

Solution:

Calculation of Change in Net Profit

Particulars	Amount (Rs.)
Increased Sales	1,00,000
Less: Variable Cost (Rs.1,00,000 x 0.75)	75,000
Contribution	**25,000**
Less: Bad debt loss on new sales (Rs.1,00,000 x 0.05)	5,000
Earnings Before Tax (EBT)	**20,000**
Less: Tax at 40 %	8,000
Earnings After Tax (EAT)	**12,000**
Less: Opportunity cost (See Note)	3,699
Increase in Net Profit	**8,301**

Note:

Opportunity Cost = Increase in Investment x Cost of Capital

Increase in Investment = (DOS x NACP) + (DVCIS x ACP_n)

= (2,465.75 x 10) + (205.48 x 30) = (24,657.5) + (6,164.38)= Rs.30,821.88

DOS = Rs. 9,00,000 ÷365 = Rs.2,465.75

NACP = 30 – 20 = 10 Days

DVCIS = (Rs.1,00,000 x 0.75) ÷ 365 = Rs.205.48

Opportunity Cost = Rs.30,821.88 x 0.12 = Rs.3,698.63

Suggestion: Gokul should implement proposed extension of credit period due to the change in net profit is positive.

6. 1/15, net 30 is the present credit term of DD Company. Its sales level is Rs.10 lakhs, with an average collection period of 30 days, its contribution margin ratio is 20 per cent and the cost of capital is 12 per cent. The proportion of sales on which currently customers take discount is 0.5 per cent. The company is contemplating with the idea of increasing the discount term to 2/15, net 30. Such extensions of discount push up sales by Rs. 1 lakh, and reduce the average collection period by 5 days and increase the proportion of discount sales by 0.3. What will be the effect of relaxing the discount policy on its net profit, with an assumption of 45 per cent tax and 365 days to a year.

Solution:

Calculation of Change in Net Profit

Particulars	Amount (Rs.)
Increased Sales	1,00,000
Less: Variable Cost (Rs.1,00,000 x 0.80)	80,000
Contribution	**20,000**
Less: Increase in discount cost (Note 1)	1,260
Earnings Before Tax (EBT)	**18,740**
Less: Tax at 45 %	8,433
Earnings After Tax (EAT)	**10,307**
Add: Savings on Investment (K△I) (Note –2)	986
Increase in Net Profit	**9,321**

Note:

1. Increase in Cash Discount Cost (ΔCDC)=NCDC–OCDC = Rs.1,760–Rs.500 =Rs.1,260

   Where: NCDC = New cash discount cost

   OCDC = Old cash discount cost

   NCDC = Total Sales x New Cash Discount x New Percentage of Availing Cash Discount

   NCDC = Rs. 11,00,000x 0.02 x 0.08 = Rs. 1,760

   OCDC = Old Sales x Old Cash Discount x Old Percentage of Availing Cash Discount

   OCDC = Rs. 10,00,000 x 0.01 x 0.05= Rs.500

2. Opportunity Cost = Increase in Investment x Cost of Capital

   Increase in Investment = (DOS x NACP) – (DVCIS x ACP_n)

   = (2,739.73 x 5) – (219.18 x 25)

   = Rs.13,698.65 – Rs.5,479.5 = Rs.8,219.15

   DOS = Old Sales ÷365 = 10,00,000 ÷ 365 =Rs.2,739.73

   NACP = Old ACP – New ACP = 30 – 25 = 5 Days

   DVCIS = (Incremental Sales x Variable Cost Per Unit) ÷ 365

   = (1,00,000 x 0.8) ÷ 365 = Rs. 219.18

   Opportunity Cost = Rs.8,219.15 × 0.12 = Rs. 986.30

3. XXX Company Ltd., is considering relaxing its collection efforts. Its present sale level is Rs. 20 lakhs, its average collection period is 40 days, its expected variable cost to sales ratio is 0.75 per cent, its cost of capital is 10 per cent, and bad debt ratio is 3 per cent. XXX's tax rate is 45 per cent. Relaxation in collection efforts is expected to increase sales to Rs.22 lakhs, increase average collection period to 50 days, and ratio of bad debts by 2 per cent. What will be the changes in net profit?

Solution:

Calculation of Change in Net Profit

Particulars	Amount (Rs.)
Increased Sales	2,00,000
Less: Variable Cost (Rs.2,00,000 x 0.75)	1,50,000
Contribution	50,000
Less: Increase in bad debt cost (Note 1)	50,000
Earnings Before Tax (EBT)	-------
Less: Tax at 45 %	-----
Earnings After Tax (EAT)	-----
Less: Opportunity cost (KΔI) (Note –2)	7,534
Increase in Net Profit	– 7534

Note:

1. **Calculation of Bad debt loss:** Rs.

   Bad debt loss with new policy (Rs.22,00,000 x 0.05)   1,10,000

   Less: Bad debt loss with present policy (Rs.20,00,000 x 0.03)   60,000

   Increase in Bad debt loss   **50,000**

Calculation of Opportunity Cost = Increase in Investment x Cost of Capital

Increase in Investment = (DOS x NACP) + (DVCIS x ACP_n)

= (5,479.45 x 10) + (410.96 x 50) = 54,794.5 + 20,548= Rs.75,342.5

DOS = Rs.20,00,000 ÷365 = Rs.5,479.45

NACP = 50 − 40 = 10 Days

DVCIS = (Rs.2,00,000 x 0.75) ÷ 365 = Rs.410.96

Opportunity Cost = Rs.75,342.5 x 0.1 = Rs.7,534.25

TEST QUESTIONS

Objective Type Questions

1. **Fill in the blanks with appropriate word(s)**

    (a) In India accounts receivables are known as _____.

    (b) Debt owed to the firm by customers arising from sale of goods or services in the ordinary course of business is known as _____.

    (c) _____ involvement is one of the characteristic features of receivables.

    (d) ____ is a formal document issued by a bank on behalf of its customers, stating the conditions under which the bank will honor the commitments of the customer (Buyer).

    (e) Credit terms have three components _____, _____ and _____.

    (f) _____ represents a percentage of reduction in sales or purchase price allowed for early payment of invoices.

    (g) "2/10, net 60" – 2 denotes _____

    (h) Credit evaluation procedure involves three steps viz., _____, _____ and _____.

    (i) CRISIL, ICRA, and CARE are the three prominent _____ agencies.

    (j) Character, Capacity, Capital, Collateral, Conditions, and _____ are the 6'c' of credit.

[**Answers:** (a) Sundry debtors; (b) Bills receivables; (c) Risk; (d) Letter of credit; (e) Credit period; Cash discount and Cash discount period; (f) Cash discount; (g) Discount; (h) Obtaining credit information, analyzing the information and making the credit decision, (i) Credit rating (j) Case history].

2. **State whether each of the following statement is true of false**

    (a) Receivables constitute to a significant potential current assets.

    (b) Credit period is one of the terms of credit.

    (c) Letter of credit is one of the modes of payment.

    (d) "Net 60", means payment will be made within 60 days form the date of credit sale.

    (e) Optimum credit policy occurs where there is a trade of between liquidity and profitability.

    (f) Bad debt loss is are the losses of receivables management.

    (g) In "2/10, net 30", 10 denotes credit period.

    (h) Credit standards, Credit period, Cash discount and Collection are the variables of credit policy.

    (i) Monitoring the state of receivables does not include receivables collection procedure

    (j) Cost is one of the 6 'C' s of credit.

[**Answers:** (a) True, (b) True, (c) True, (d) True, (e) True, (f) True, (g) False, (h) True, (i) False, (j) False]

TEST YOUR KNOWLEDGE

1. What do you mean by Receivables ?
2. What do you understand by "2/15, net 45"?
3. What do you mean by "net 60"?
4. List out the steps involved in credit evaluation.
5. Name three credit rating agencies.
6. Name the characteristics of Receivables?
7. What is Receivables Management?
8. List out the objectives of receivables management.
9. Name various costs of accounts receivables management.
10. Give three benefits of receivables management.
11. What is open account mode of payment?
12. What do you mean of L/C ?
13. List out the variables of credit policy.
14. Give the 6 'c' s of credit.
15. What is receivables management? Discuss the benefits of it.
16. Explain the objectives of receivables management.
17. Discuss the various costs of receivables management.
18. Discuss the major modes of payment.
19. Discuss the issues involved in receivables management.
20. What is credit policy? Discuss the different types of credit policy.
21. Describe the 6 'c' s of credit.
22. Discuss the consequences of liberal versus stiff credit standards.
23. What are the effects of liberating cash discount policy.
24. Discuss the sources of credit information.
25. What is receivables management? Discuss in detail the objective benefits and cost of receivables management.
26. Briefly discuss the factors that influence the size of investment in receivables.
27. What is credit policy? Discuss the types of credit policy's with their advantages and disadvantages.
28. What is the role of credit policy variables in the credit policy of a firm? Discuss.
29. "The credit policy of a firm is criticized because the bad debt losses have increased". Discuss under what situations this criticism may not be justified.
30. What is credit evaluation? Discuss the steps involved in it.
31. What do you mean by aging schedule?

DO IT YOURSELF PROBLEMS

1. What is the interest cost (on annual percent basis) associated with the following credit terms from seller as well as buyers point of view.

    (a) 1/20 net, 60, (b) 2/10 net, 30, (c) 3/5 net, 25, and (d) 3/15 net, 75.

Answers:

Calculation of interest cost from Sellers' point of view:

(a) 9.125%, (b) 36.5%, (c) 54.75%, and (d) 18.25%

Calculation of interest cost from Buyer's point of view

(a) 9.311%, (b) 24.83%, (c) 37.24%, and (d) 18.81%

2. STC Corporation is considering extending its credit period from 35 to 50 days the corporation's expected sales to increase from Rs. 15 lakhs to Rs. 20 lakhs and the average collection period increases from 30 to 45 days. The bad debt loss ratio and collection costs ratio are expected to remain at 5 % and 8%, respectively. The corporation's contribution margin ratio is 20%. Calculate increase in net profit with the assumption of 40% tax rate and 15% cost of capital.

Answer:

Contribution – Rs.1, 00,000, Bad debt loss on new sales – Rs.65,000, Opportunity cost Rs. 17,465, net profit Rs. 3,535.

3. Green Land Company Ltd., is considering to tighten up its credit standards by reducing credit period from 40 days to 20 days. Such tight credit policy would be to reduce sales from Rs. 15 lakhs to Rs.13 lakhs and bad-debt loss ratio also reduces from 3% to 1%. The company's variable cost ratio to sales is 70%, tax rate is 40 % and required rate of return is 10%. Determine change in net profit.

Answer:

Contribution – Rs.60,000, Bad debt loss – Rs.32,000, Savings on investment Rs. 9,315, net loss Rs. 18,685.

4. Good Life Corporation is considering relaxing its collection effort. The following is the information.

The present sales are Rs. 20 lakhs, its contribution margin ratio is 0.70, its cost of funds is 12% and its bad debt ratio is 2%.

The proposed relaxation in collection effort is expected to increases sales to Rs. 28 lakhs, increases average collection period to 30 days, and increase the bad debt ratio to 4%. Determine the change in net profit with 40% tax rate.

Answer:

Contribution – Rs.2,40,000, increase in bad debt cost – Rs.62,000, Opportunity cost Rs. 12,099.

5. Ram & Co's present sales are Rs.25 lakhs. Its credit terms are 1/20, net 50, average collection period is 30 days, variable cost to sales ratio is 60% and cost of capital is 20%. The proportion of sales on which currently customers take discount is 2%. The Company is contemplating to relax its discount terms to 2/20 net, 50. Such relaxation is expected to increase sales to Rs. 30 lakhs, and reduce average collection period by 20 days, and increase the proportion of discount sales to 4%. Determine the change in net profit with the assumption of 40% tax rate.

Answer:

Contribution – Rs.2,00,000, increase in discount cost – Rs.19,000, savings on investment Rs. 27,945, net profit Rs. 1,36,545.

6. Calculate the interest cost (on annual percentage basis) associated with the following credit terms for the sellers and to the buyers.

(a) 1/10 net, 40, (b) 2/15 net, 50 (c) 3/20 net, 60, and (d) 7/10 net, 80.

Answer:

Calculation of interest cost form sellers point of view

(a) 12.17% (b) 20.87% (c) 27.38% (d) 20.86%

Calculation of interest cost form Buyers point of view

(a) 12.29% (b) 21.28% (c) 28.22% (d) 21.17%

7. VST Co. produces plastic home appliances and it has annual credit sales of Rs. 20 lakhs, the average accounts receivables amount to Rs.4,00,000. Compute ACP assuming 365 day year.

Answer:

73 days.

CASE FOR CLASS DISCUSSION - I

YAHOO. PRODUCTS LIMITED

Yahoo.. Products Limited manufactures a special variety of industrial which are used by other manufacturing units to produce shoes and chappals. The market for the company's product comprises a few large public limited companies and a number of small units run as proprietary or partnership concerns. The sales had in the past proved to be seasonal, with peak sales being recorded in the period January to July (year).

One year back, the company had expanded its production capacity form 4,000 to 9,000 MT per annum. However, the actual production in the financial year Just ended was restricted to 6,000 MT, mainly on account of lack of orders. The cost statement for the year indicated the following :

	Rs/MT
Raw Materials (V)	2,500
Direct Labour and Supervision (F)	800
Indirect Materials, Fuel, etc. (F)	500
Depreciation, Insurance, etc. (F)	2,700
Factory Cost of Production	6,500
Administration, Selling and Interest Charges (F)	500
Selling Price per MT	7,000
(exclusive of all discounts, allowance for freight, etc.)	------

Dr. Bhatt the Director was not satisfied by the under utilization of installed capacity and its effect on the profitability of the company. He called his senior managers to discuss the situation and means of improving the profitability of the concern. The Sales Manager, on whom the pressure was tried to described the limitation of sales to be the stringent credit policy pursued by the company. He argued that under the strict norms for grant of credit followed by the company, only the larger public limited companies among the customers were on the approved credit list of the company and the smaller customers were put on the cash and carry list. This, he maintained, led to an overdependence on the larger customers and an almost complete neglection of a section of the market consisting of the small manufacturers, who were cultivated by the competition by offering them attractive discounts. In fact, the smaller manufacturers came to his company, only if, the market was starved of the product. The Sales Manager pleaded for a more liberal credit policy which would also help increase the sales volume. He ruled out the possibility of procuring additional volume of business from the big customers who had already evolved a scheme sharing out their business among the different suppliers. Any attempt to obtain more business by offering discounts to the bigger firms, the sales manager argued, will only lead to a retaliatory action by competitors and ultimately escalate into a price war which will only prove disastrous for the company. On the other hand, granting credit to the smaller customer will bring the company's policy in line with competitors and will actually stimulate growth in the consuming industry with beneficial effects to the company.

Dr. Bhatt obviously undecided about the wisdom of extending credit to the smaller customers to boost sales volume, called for a detailed note from both the Sales Manager and the Credit Manager. He, However, pointed out that any such change of credit policy, even if approved, would bring in results only in long run while there was an immediate need to boost sales. The Sales Manager, at this point, conveyed to Dr. Bhatt, an offer he had just received from the Shoe Manager. An offer he had just received from the Shoe Plast Limited, one of the larger public limited company. The controller referred to the substantial investment in receivables that this transaction would entail and reckoning interest at 18 percent per annum which was the rate the company was paying to its bankers; he argued that this transaction would involve an interest burden of Rs. 1,64,250 whereas the profits from the transaction would only be Rs. 90,000. As such the offer was wholly unattractive. Shoe Plast Limited would pay for these additional supplies to be effected in the next three months, in the seventh month from date. It was, however, unwilling to pay an interest on the extended credit term. The Sales Manager pointed out that Shoe Plast Limited ranked high in the ratings by the Credit Department and therefore, there should be no hesitation in accepting this offer for additional business.

The customer company wads carrying out an expansion scheme at that time using partly its current resources to finance the same and was, therefore, finding itself in a difficult liquid situation. It, however, expected this to be only temporary and anticipated that the position would improve considerably after six months. Shoe Plast Limited had made an offer to take 100 MT additional each month in the next three months over and above the regular off-take, if Plastic Products Limited agreed to give special credit terms. The Credit Manager, intervening at this stage, pointed to the high rate of mortality among the smaller firms. He read out a long list of the smaller firms in the industry which had closed their creditors in the last few years. He points out with pride the excellent record of the company in the matter of credit management and to the fact that the company has had no incidence of bad debts in the last smaller manufacturers. He further argued that the company would be taking grave risk if it chose to adopt such a policy, as it would lead to bad debts. About 6 per cent each year, which he was quick to point out, was about the profit margin company appears to have from its products.

QUESTIONS

1. What consideration he should take into account, while revising the credit policy of a company?
2. Advice Dr. Bhatt how he should deal with the circumstances?
3. Define factoring. Briefly discuss the services provided by a factor.
4. What are the various types of factoring?
5. Distinguish between factoring and bill financing.
6. Briefly discuss the appraisal technique followed by a factor.
7. What are the benefits, limitations and constraints of factoring in India?
8. Write a short note on international factoring.

CLASS DISCUSSION CASE 2 - CREDIT LIMIT DECISION: BAJAJ ELECTRONICS COMPANY

This case has been framed in order to test the skills in evaluating a credit request and reaching a correct decision.

Perluence International is large manufacturer of petroleum and rubber-based products used in a variety of commercial applications in the fields of transportation, electronics, and heavy manufacturing. In the northwestern united States, many of the Perluence products are marketed by a wholly-owned subsidiary, Bajaj Electronics Company. Operating from a headquarters and warehouse facility in San Antonio, Strand Electronics has 950 employees and handles a volume of $85 million in sales annually. About $6 million of the sales represents items manufactured by Perluence.

Gupta is the credit manager at Bajaj electronics. He supervises five employees who handle credit application and collections on 4,600 accounts. The accounts range in size form $120 to $85,000. The firm sells on varied terms, with 2/10, net 30 mostly. Sales fluctuate seasonally and the average collection period tends to run 40 days. Bad-debt losses are less than 0.6 per cent of sales.

Gupta is evaluating a credit application from Booth Plastics, Inc., a wholesale supply dealer serving the oil industry. The company was founded in 1977 by Neck A. Booth and has grown steadily since that time. Bajaj Electronics is not selling any products to Booth Plastics and had no previous contact with Neck Booth.

Bajaj Electronics purchased goods from Perluence International under the same terms and conditions as Perluence used when it sold to independent customers. Although Bajaj Electronics generally followed Perluence in setting its prices, the subsidiary operated independently and could adjust price levels to meet its own marketing strategies. The Perluence's cot-accounting department estimated a 24 per cent markup as the average for items sold to Pucca Electronics. Bajaj Electronics, in turn, resold the items to yield a 17 per cent markup. It appeared that these percentages would hold on any sales to Booth Plastics.

Bajaj Electronics incurred out-of pocket expenses that were not considered in calculating the 17 per cent markup on its items. For example, the contact with Booth Plastics had been made by James, the salesman who handled the Glaveston area. James would receive a 3 per cent commission on all sales made Booth Plastics, a commission that would be paid whether or not the receivable was collected. James would, of course, be willing to assist in collecting any accounts that he had sold. In addition to the sales commission, the company would incur variable costs as a result of handling the merchandise for the new account. As a general guideline, warehousing and other administrative variable costs would run 3 per cent sales.

Gupta Holmstead approached all credit decisions in basically the same manner. First of all, he considered the potential profit from the account. James had estimated first-year sales to Booth Plastics of $65,000. Assuming that Neck Booth took the, 3 per cent discount. Bajaj Electronics would realize a 17 per cent markup on these sales since the average markup was calculated on the basis of the customer taking the discount. If Neck Booth did not take the discount, the markup would be slightly higher, as would the cost of financing the receivable for the additional period of time. In addition to the potential profit from the account, Gupta was concerned about his company's exposure. He knew that weak customers could become bad debts at any time and therefore, required a vigorous collection effort whenever their accounts were overdue. His department probably spent three times as much money and effort managing a marginal account as compared to a strong account. He also figured that overdue and uncollected funds had to be financed by Bajaj Electronics at a rate of 18 per cent. All in all, slow -paying or marginal accounts were very costly to Bajaj Electronics.

With these considerations in mind, Gupta began to review the credit application for Booth Plastics.

Assignment

How would you judge the potential profit of Bajaj Electronics on the first year of sales to Booth Plastics and give your suggestion regarding Credit limit. Should it be approved or not, what should be the amount of credit limit that electronics give to Booth Plastics.

CASE STUDY FOR CLASS DISCUSSION 3 - CREDIT DECISION
AGARWAL CASE

On August 30, 2006, Agarwal Cast Company Inc., applied for a $200,000 loan from the main office of the National bank of New York. The application was forwarded to the bank's commercial loan department.

Gupta, the President and Principal Stockholder of Agarwal cast, applied for the loan in person. He told the loan officer that he had been in business since February 1976, but that he had considerable prior experience in flooring and carpets since he had worked as an individual contractor for the past 20 year. Most of this time, he had worked in Frankfert and Michigan. He finally decided to "work for himself" and he formed the company with Berry Hook, a former co-worker. This information seemed to be consistent with the Dun and Bradstreet report obtained by the bank.

According to Gupta, the purpose of the loan was to assist him in carrying his receivables until they could be collected. He explained that the flooring business required him to spend considerable cash to purchase materials but his customers would not pay until the job was done. Since he was relatively new in the business, he did not feel that he could compete if he had to require a sizeable deposit or payment in advance. Instead, he could quote for higher profits, if he were willing to wait until completion of the job for payment. To show that his operation was sound, he included a list of customers and projects with his loan application. He also included a list of current receivables.

Gupta told the loan officer that he had monitored his firm's financial status closely and that he had financial reports prepared every six months. He said that the would send a copy to the bank. In addition, he was willing to file a personal financial statement with the bank.

Assignment

Prepare your recommendation on Agarwal Cast Company

REFERENCES

1. Hampton, J. J., *"Financial Decision Making-Concepts, Problems and Cases"*, New Delhi: Prentice-Hall of India Ltd., 1983, p.248.

2. Joy, O.M, *"Introduction to Financial Management"*, Illinois: Irwin Homewood, 1977, P.456.

3. Ramamoorthy, V.E., *"Management of Working Capital"*, Chennai: Institute for Financial Management and Research, 1978, p.210.

4. Joseph, L., *"Business Finance HandBook"*, New York: Prentice Hall, 1953, p. 243.

5. Mayers, S.C., and Brealey, R.A., *"Principles of Corporate Finance"*, New Delhi: Tata McGraw-Hill Publishing Company Limited, 2003, p.910.

6. Seiden, M.H., *"The Quality of Trade Credit,"* New York: National Bureau of Economic Research, 1964, p.39.

7. Van Horne, J.C. and Machowicz, Jr, J.M., *"Fundamentals of Financial Management"*, New Delhi: Prentice-Hall of India, 1996, p254.

8. Satish, B.M, *"Working Capital Management and Control, Principles & Practice"*, New Delhi: New Age International (p) Limited, 2002, p.121.

9. Ramamoorthy, V.E., Op.cit., 1978, p.210.

10. Lewis, E.P., *"Monitoring Accounts Receivables"*, Management Accountant, Sept. 1973, pp.18-21.

11. Lawrance, D.S. and Charles, W.H., *"Introduction to Financial Management"*, New York: McGraw Hill Book Company, 1977, p.417.

Inventory Management

19

After studying this chapter, you should be able to:

1 Define inventory management.

2 List out components of inventory.

3 Explain the motives for holding inventory.

4 Identify the areas, objectives and need for balanced investment in inventory.

5 Highlight costs, risks and benefits of holding inventory.

6 Explain the techniques of inventory management.

Inventory management occupies the most significant position in the structure of working capital. Management of inventory may be defined as the sum of total of those activities necessary for the acquisition, storage, disposal or use of materials.[1] It is one of the important component of current assets. Inventory management is an important area of working capital management, which plays a crucial role in economic operation of the firm. Maintenance of large size of inventories by a firm required a considerable amount of funds to be invested on them. Efficient and effective inventory management is necessary in order to avoid unnecessary investment and inadequate investment.

A considerable amount of funds is required to be committed in inventories. It is absolutely imperative to manage inventories efficiently and effectively in order to optimize investment in them. Prudent inventory management is one of the challenging tasks of the financial manager. Efficient management of inventory reduces the cost of production and consequently increases the profitability of the enterprise by minimising the different types of costs associated with holding inventory.[2] An undertaking, neglecting the management of inventories, will be jeopardising its long term profitability and may fail ultimately. It is possible for a firm to reduce its level of inventories to a considerable degree, i.e., 10 to 20 per cent of current assets without adverse effects on production and sales by using simple inventory planning and control techniques.[3] If business planning can be perfect, a firm may succeed even in attaining the "Zero inventory"[4] norm which as the Japanese management seems to suggest, is not too unrealistic a goal. The reduction in inventories carries a favourable impact on the company's profitability. The efficiency of inventory management in any firm depends on the inventory management practices adopted by it.

MEANING AND DEFINITION OF INVENTORY

The term "Inventory" is originated from the French word "Inventaire" and the Latin "Inventariom", which implies a list of things found. The term inventory has been defined by the American Institute of Accountants[5] as the aggregate of those items of tangible personal property which (a) are held for sale in the ordinary course of business, (b) are in the process of production for such sales, or (c) are to be currently consumed in the production of goods or services to be available for sale. The term inventory refers to the stockpile of the products a firm is offering for sales and the components that make up the product.[6] Inventories are the stocks of the product of a company, manufacturing for sale and the components that make up the product. The various forms in which inventories exist in a manufacturing company are: (i) raw materials, (ii) work-in process, (iii) finished goods, and (iv) stores & spares. However, in commercial parlance, inventory usually includes stores, raw materials, work-in-process and finished goods.[7] The term inventory includes materials – raw materials in process, finished packaging, spares and others stocked in order to meet an unexpected demand or distribution in the future.[8]

COMPONENTS OF INVENTORY

From the above definitions, we can draw the components of inventory. The various forms in which inventories exist in a manufacturing firm are, raw materials, work-in process, finished goods, and stores & spares. The following figure-1 gives the components:

(i) *Raw Materials:* Raw materials are those inputs that are converted into finished goods through a manufacturing or conversion process. These form a major input for manufacturing a product. In other words, they are very much needed for uninterrupted production.

(ii) *Work-in-Process:* Work-in-process is a stage of stocks between raw materials and finished goods. Work-in-process inventories are semi-finished products. They represent products that need to under go some other process to become finished goods.

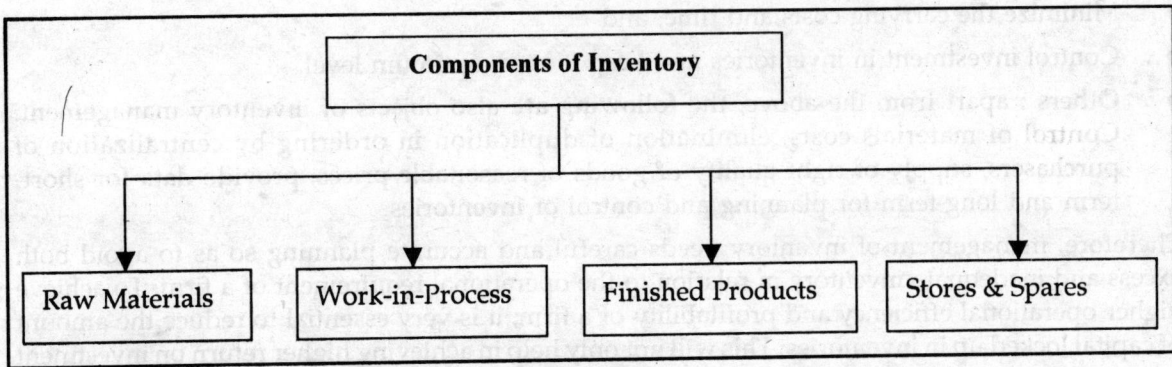

```
┌─────────────────────────────────────────────────────────┐
│                ┌──────────────────────────┐              │
│                │  Components of Inventory  │              │
│                └──────────────────────────┘              │
│         │            │              │             │       │
│         ▼            ▼              ▼             ▼       │
│  ┌────────────┐ ┌──────────────┐ ┌─────────────┐ ┌──────────────┐ │
│  │Raw Materials│ │Work-in-Process│ │Finished Products│ │Stores & Spares│ │
│  └────────────┘ └──────────────┘ └─────────────┘ └──────────────┘ │
└─────────────────────────────────────────────────────────┘
```

Figure 19.1

(iii) *Finished Products:* Finished products are those products, which are completely manufactured and ready for sale. The stock of finished goods provides a buffer between production and market.

(iv) *Stores & Spares:* Stores & spares inventory (include office and plant cleaning materials like soap, brooms, oil, fuel, light, bulbs etc.) are purchased and stored for the purpose of maintenance of machinery.

INVENTORY MANAGEMENT MOTIVES

Managing inventories involves lack of funds and inventory holding costs. Maintenance of inventory is expensive, then why should firms hold inventories? There are three general motives for holding inventories[9]:

(i) *The Transaction Motive:* Transaction motive includes production of goods and sale of goods. Transaction motive facilitates uninterrupted production and delivery of order at a given time (right time).

(ii) *The Precautionary Motive:* This motive necessitates the holding of inventories for unexpected changes in demand and supply factors.

(iii) *The Speculative Motive:* This compels to hold some inventories to take the advantage of changes in prices and getting quantity discounts.

INVENTORY MANAGEMENT - OBJECTIVES

The objectives of inventory management may be viewed in two ways and they are *operational* and *financial*. The *operational* objective is to maintain sufficient inventory, to meet demand for product by efficiently organizing the firm's production and sales operations, and *financial* view is to minimise inefficient inventory and reduce inventory-carrying costs.

These two conflicting objectives of inventory management can also be expressed in terms of *costs* and *benefits* associated with inventory. The firm should maintain investments in inventory which implies that maintaining an inventory involves cost, such that smaller the inventory the lower the carrying cost and vice versa. But inventory facilitates (benefits) the smooth functioning of the production. An effective inventory management should[10]:

- Ensure a continuous supply of raw materials and supplies to facilitate uninterrupted production.

- Maintain sufficient stocks of raw materials in periods of short supply and anticipate price changes.

- Maintain sufficient finished goods inventory for smooth sales operation, and efficient customer service.

- Minimize the carrying costs and time, and
- Control investment in inventories and keep it at an optimum level.
- Others : apart from the above, the following are also objects of inventory management. Control of materials costs, elimination of duplication in ordering by centralization of purchasers, supply of right quality of goods of reasonable prices, provide data for short-term and long-term for planning and control of inventories.

Therefore, management of inventory needs careful and accurate planning so as to avoid both excess and inadequate inventory in relation to the operational requirement of a firm. To achieve higher operational efficiency and profitability of a firm, it is very essential to reduce the amount of capital locked up in inventories. This will not only help in achieving higher return on investment by minimizing tied-up working capital, but will also improve the liquidity position of the enterprise.[11]

NEED FOR BALANCED INVESTMENT IN INVENTORY

Management of optimum level of inventory investment is the prime objective of inventory management. Inadequate or excess investment in inventories is not healthy by for any firm. In other words a firm should avoid inadequate (under) investment or excess (over) investment in inventory. The investment in inventories should be sufficient. The optimum level of investment in inventories lies between excess investment and inadequate investment.

(A) Dangers of Excessive (over) Investment in Inventory

The following are the dangers of excessive investment in inventory.

- The excessive level of inventories consumes funds of the company, they cannot be used for any purpose since they have locked in inventory, and they involve an opportunity costs.
- The excessive investment in inventory increases carrying cost, that include cost of storage, capital cost (interest on capital in inventories, insurance, handling, recording, inspection, obsolescence cost, and taxes. These cost will reduce the firm's profits).
- Carrying excessive inventory over a long-period leads to the loss of liquidity. It may not be possible to sell the inventories in time without loss.
- Another danger of carrying excessive inventory is the physical deterioration of inventories while in storage. In case of certain goods or raw materials deterioration occurs with the passage of time or it may be due to mishandling and improper storage facilities.
- Excess purchases or storage leads to theft, waste and mishandling of inventories.

(B) Dangers of Inadequate Investment in Inventories

Under investment in inventory is also not healthy one. It has some negative points, they are:

- Inadequate raw materials and work-in-progress inventories will disturb production.
- When the firm is not able to produce goods without interruption, that leads the inadequate storage of finished goods. If finished goods are not sufficient to meet customer demand, the customers may shift to the competitors, which will lead to loss of customers permanently.

COSTS OF HOLDING INVENTORIES

Minimizing cost is one of the operating objectives of inventory management. The costs (excluding merchandise cost), there are three costs involved in the management of inventories.[12]

(i) ***Ordering Costs:*** Ordering costs are those costs that are associated with the acquisition of raw materials. In other words, the costs that are spend from placing an order to raw materials to the receipt of raw materials. They include the following:

    (a) Cost of requisitioning the items (raw materials)

    (b) Cost of preparation of purchase order (i.e., drafting typing, dispatch, postage etc.).

    (c) Cost of sending reminders to get the dispatch of the items expedited.

    (d) Cost of transportation of goods (items).

    (e) Cost of receiving and verifying the goods.

    (f) Cost of in unloading of the (items) of goods.

    (g) Storage and stocking charges.

However, incase of items manufactured in house the ordering costs would comprise the following costs:

    (a) Requisitioning cost,

    (b) Set-up cost,

    (c) Cost of receiving and verifying the items,

    (d) Cost of placing and arranging/stacking of the items in the store etc.,

Ordering costs are fixed as per order placed, irrespective of the amount of the order but ordering costs increases in proportion to the number of orders placed. If the firm maintains small inventory levels, then the number of orders will increase, there by ordering cost will increase and vice versa.

(ii) ***Inventory Carrying Costs:*** Inventory carrying costs are those costs, which are associated in carrying or maintaining inventory. The following are the carrying costs of inventory :

    (a) Capital cost [interest on capital locked in the inventories]

    (b) Storage cost [insurance, maintenance on building, utilities serving costs]

    (c) Insurance [on inventory - against fire and theft insurance]

    (d) Obsolescence cost and deterioration

    (e) Taxes

Carrying costs usually constitute to around 25 per cent of the value of inventories held.

(iii) ***Shortage:*** *Costs [Costs of stock out]:* Shortage costs are those costs that arise due to stock out, either shortage of raw materials or finished goods.

    (a) Shortage of inventories of raw materials affect the firm in one or more of the following ways:

       • The firm may have to pay some higher prices, connected with immediate (cash) procurements.

       • The firm may have to compulsorily resort to some different production schedules, which may not be as efficient and economical.

    (b) Stock of finished goods - may result in the dissatisfaction of the customers and the resultant lead, to loss of rules,

Thus, with a view to keep inventory costs of minimum level, we may have to arrive at the optional level of inventory cost, its total order's cost plus carrying costs are minimum.

In other words, we have to determine Economic Order Quantity (EOQ), at that level in which the total inventory [ordering plus carrying less] cost is minimum.

RISKS OF HOLDING INVENTORY

Holding of inventories involves above said cost, they also exposes the firm to take some risks. Risk in inventory management refers to the chance that inventories cannot be turned over into cash through normal sales without loss. Risks associated with inventory management are as follows:

(i) *Price Decline:* Price decline is the result of more supply and less demand. In other words, it may be the result due to introduction of competitive product. Generally, prices are not controllable in the short-run by the individual firm. Controlling inventory is the only way that a firm can counter act with these risks. On the demand side, a decrease in the general market demand when supply remains the same way also cause prices to decrease. This is also a long – run management problem, because, decrease in demand may be due to change in consumer buying habits, tastes and incomes.

(ii) *Product Deterioration:* Holding of finished goods for a long period or storage under improper conditions of light, heat, humidity and pressure lead to product deterioration. For example: Cadbury's chocolate. Recently, there were some live worms in the chocolate, it was due to improper storage. Deterioration usually prevents selling the product through normal channels.

(iii) *Product Obsolescence:* Product may become obsolete due to improved products, changes in customer tastes, particularly in high style merchandise, changes in requirements etc. This risk may prove very costly for the firms whose resources are limited and tied up in slow moving inventories. Obsolescence cost risk is least controllable except by reduction in inventory investment.

Thus, inventories are risk assets to manage in an effective way by minimizing risks.

BENEFITS OF HOLDING INVENTORY

Optimum level of inventory is that level where the total costs of inventory is less. The major benefits of inventory are the basic function of inventory. Proper management of inventory will result in the following benefits to a firm:

- Inventory management ensures an adequate supply of materials and stores, minimizes stock outs and shortages and avoids costly interruptions in operations
- It keeps down investment in inventories; inventory carrying costs, and obsolescence losses to the minimum.
- It facilitates purchasing economies through the measurement of requirements on the basis of recorded experience.
- It eliminates duplication in ordering stocks by centralizing the source from which purchase requisitions emanate.
- It permits better utilisation of available stocks by facilitating inter-department transfers within a firm.
- It provides a check against the loss of materials through carelessness or pilferage.
- Perpetual inventory values provide a consistent and reliable basis for preparing financial statements a better utilisation.[13]

TOOLS AND TECHNIQUES OF INVENTORY MANAGEMENT/CONTROL

Financial manager should aim at determination of optimum inventory level based on costs and benefits to maximize shareholders' wealth. In other words, determination and maintenance of optimum inventory level, helps to maximize owner's wealth. Inventory management problems can be handled by sophisticated/refined mathematical techniques. The major problem areas are (a) classification problem to determine the type of control required, (b) the order quantity problem, (c) the order point problem, and (d) determination of safety stocks. (14) But these are more suitable parts of production and operations management, and out of the scope of this book. In other words, they are out of the area of financial manager. Financial manager needs to be familiar with these techniques because inventory management involves financial costs. Use of a particular technique depends on the convenience of the company. Whatever the techniques may used by the firm the ultimate objective of inventory control programme is to provide maximum customer service at a minimum cost. In the following, some of the inventory control techniques are discussed:

(1) ABC Analysis

This is the one of the widely used technique to identify various items of inventory for the purpose of inventory control. In other words, it is very effective and useful tool for classifying, monitoring and control of inventories. The firm should not keep same degree of control on all the items of inventory. It is based on Pareto's Law. It is also known as *Selective Inventory Control*. The firm should put maximum control on those items whose value is the highest, with the comparison of the other two items. The technique concentrates on important items and is also known as Control by Importance and Exception [CIE].[15] Usually a firm has to maintain several types of inventories, for proper control of they, firm should have to classify inventories in the instance of their relative value. Hence it is also known as *Proportional Value Analysis (PVA)*. The higher value items are classified 'A items' and would be under tight control. At the other end of the classification, we find category 'C items', on this type of inventory, we cannot afford expenses of rigid controls, frequent ordering and expending, because of the low value or low amounts in this area. Thus with the 'C items', we may maintain somewhat higher safety stocks, order more months of supply, expect lower levels of customer service, or all the three. 'B items' fall in between 'A item' and 'C item' and require reasonable attention of management.

According to this technique the task of inventory management is proper classification of all inventory items in to three categories namely A, B and C category. The ideal categorization of inventory items is show in Table 19.1.[16]

Table 19.1

Category	No. of Items(%)	Item value (%)
A	15	70
B	30	20
C	55	10
Total	100	100

The above table indicates that only 15 per cent of the items may account for 70 percent of the value [A category items], on which greater attention is required, where as 55 per cent of items may account for 10 per cent of the table value of inventory (C category items), will be paid a reasonless attention. The remaining 30 per cent of inventory account for 20 per cent of total value of inventory (B category items) will be paid a reasonable attention as this, category value lies between the two other categories. The above data can be shown by the following Figure 19.2.

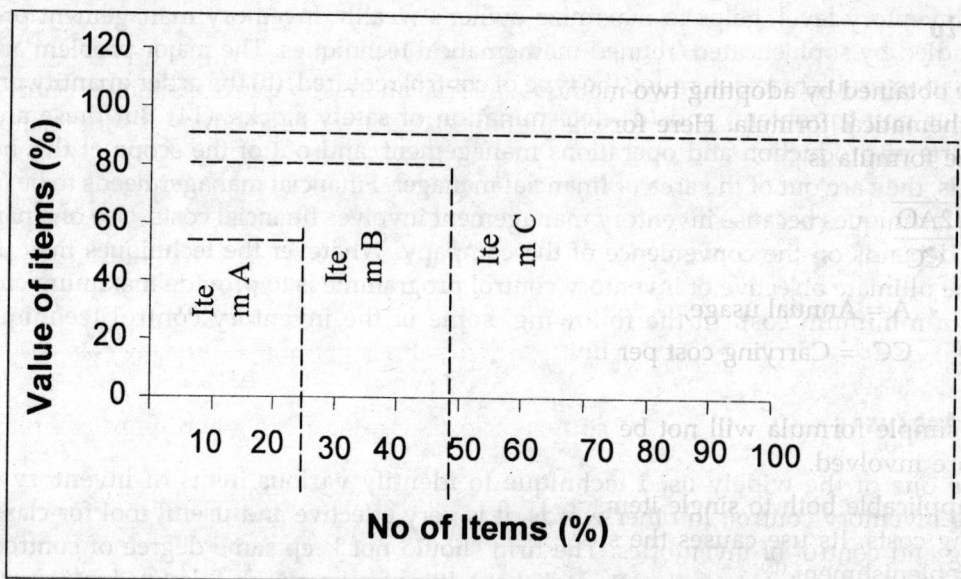

Figure 19.2

In the above figure number of items (%) are shown on 'X' axis and value of items (%) are represented on 'Y' axis. Greater attention will be paid on category 'A' item, because of greater benefit. The control of 'C' items may be released due to less benefits (some times control cost may exceed benefit of control) and reasonable attention should be paid to category 'B' items.

(2) Economic Order Quantity (EOQ)

Once categorization of inventory items is completed, then the next question is how much inventory should be bought in one order on each replenishment? Should quantity to be purchased be large or small? Buying inventory items in large quantities has its own virtues, but it increases carrying costs. Then what is the solution for the determination of an order where the total inventory costs are minimum? To this problem the answer is Economic Order Quantity (EOQ).

Meaning of EOQ

Economic order quantity refers to that level of inventory at which the total cost of inventory is minimum. The total inventory cost comprising ordering and carrying costs. Shortage costs are excluded in adding total cost of inventory due to the difficulty in computation of shortage cost. EOQ also known as Economic Lot Size (ELS).

Assumptions of EOQ Model

The following assumptions are implied in the calculation of EOQ:[17]

- Demand for the product is constant and uniform throughout the period.
- Lead time (time from ordering to receipt) is constant.
- Price per unit of product is constant.
- Inventory holding cost is based on average inventory.
- Ordering costs are constant.
- All demands for the product will be satisfied (no back orders are allowed).

EOQ Formula

EOQ can be obtained by adopting two methods (a) Trial and Error approach and (b) Short cut or Simple mathematical formula. Here for calculation of EOQ we have adopted simple short cut method. The formula is

$$EOQ = \sqrt{\frac{2AO}{CC}}$$

Where: A = Annual usage,   O = Ordering cost per order
         CC = Carrying cost per unit   CC = Price per unit x Carrying cost per unit in percentage

The above simple formula will not be sufficient to determine EOQ when more complex cost equations are involved.

EOQ is applicable both to single items and to any group of stock items with similar holding and ordering costs. Its use causes the sum of the two costs to be lower than under any other system of replenishment.[18]

Limitations of EOQ

Apart from the above application it has its own limitations that are mainly due to the restrictive nature of the assumptions on which it is based.

- *Constant Usage:* This may not be possible to predict, if usage varies unpredictably, as it often does, no formula will work well. [19]
- *Faulty Basic Information:* Ordering and carrying costs is the base for EOQ calculation. It assumes that ordering cost is constant per order is fixed, but actually varies from commodity to commodity. Carrying cost also can vary with the company's opportunity cost of capital.[20]
- *Costly Calculations:* In many cases, the cost estimation, cost of possession and acquisition and calculating EOQ exceeds the savings made by buying that quantity.[21]

(3) Order Point Problem

After determination of EOQ, then at what level should the order be placed? If the inventory level is too high, it will be unnecessary blocks the capital, and if the level is too low, it will disturb the production by frequent stock out and also involves high ordering cost. Hence, an efficient management of inventory needs to maintain optimum inventory level, where there is no stock out and the costs are minimum. The different stock levels are (a) Minimum level, (b) Reorder level, (c) Maximum level, (d) Average stock level, and (e) Dangers level.

(a). Minimum Level : Minimum stock is that level that must be maintained always production will be disturbed, if it is less than the minimum level. How to fix minimum level? While determination of minimum stock level, lead time, consumption rate, the material nature must be considered

- Lead-time is the time taken to receive the delivery after placing orders with the supplier. In other words, the number of days required to receive the inventory from the date of placing order. Lead time also called as procurement time of inventory.
- The average quantity of raw materials consumed daily. The consumption rate is calculated based on the past experience and production plan.

- Requirement of materials for normal or regular production or special order production. If the material is required for special order production, then the minimum stock level need not maintain.

Formula for calculation Minimum Stock Level

Minimum stock level = Re-order level – [Normal Usage x Average delivery time]

(a) *Reordering Level:* Reorder level is that level of inventory at in weeks, which an order should be placed for replenishing the current stock of inventory. Generally, the reorder level lies between minimum stock level and maximum stock level.

Re-order point = Lead time (in days) x Average Daily usage

The above formula is based on the assumption that (a) Consistent daily usage, and (b) Fixed lead-time.

(b) *Safety Stock:* Prediction of average daily usage and lead-time is difficult. Raw materials may vary from day-to-day or from week-to-week, it is in the case of lead-time also. Lead-time may be delayed, if the usage increases then the company faces problem of stock out. To avoid stock out firm may require to maintain safety stock. Formula (under uncertainty of usage and lead time).

Re-order point = Lead time (in days) × Average usage + Safety stock

(c) *Maximum Level:* Maximum level of stock, is that level of stock beyond which a firm should not maintain the stock. If the firm stocks inventory beyond the maximum stock level it is called as overstocking. Excess inventory (overstock) involves heavy cost of inventory, because it blocks firms funds in investment inventory, excess carrying cost, wastage, obsolescence, and theft cost. Hence, firm should not stock above the maximum stock level. Safety stock is that minimum additional inventory to serve as a safety margin or better or buffer or cushion to meet an unanticipated and increase in usage resulting from an unusually high demand and or an uncontrollable late receipt of incoming inventory.

Maximum Stock Level = Reorder Level + Reorder Quantity - (Minimum Usage x Minimum Delivery Time)

(d) *Average Stock Level:*

Average Stock Level = Minimum level + [Reorder Quantity ÷ 2]

(e) *Danger Stock Level:* Danger level is that level of materials beyond which materials should not fall in any situation. When it falls in danger level it will disturb production. Hence, the firm should not allow the stock level to go to danger level, if at all falls in that level then immediately stock should be arranged even if it costly.

Danger Level = Average Usage x Minimum Deliver Time [for emergency purchase]

(4) Two-Bin Technique

It is the oldest techniques of inventory control. Generally, it is used to control 'C' category inventories. According to this technique, stock of each item is separated into two piles, bins or groups. First bin contains stock, just enough to last from the date a new order is placed until it is received for inventory. The second bin contains stock, which is enough to meet current demand over the period of replenishment. First stock is issued from first bin whenever the first bin is completed, then an order for replenishment is placed, and the stock in the second is utilized until the ordered material is received.

(5) VED Classification

According to this classification, inventories are grouped based on the effect of production and inventories are grouped into three, they are Vital, Essential and Desirable inventories. It is specially used for classification of spare parts. If a part is vital, in production, then it is classified as 'V', if it is essential, then it is assigned 'E' and if it is not so essential, desirable that is given 'D'. 'V' category item are stocked high and category 'D' items are maintained at minimum level.

(6) HML Classification

Here the materials are classified based on the unit value and not on the annual usage value. The inventory is classified into three categories such as High, Medium, and Low, as it is adopted in selective inventory control (ABC) technique. The inventory items should be listed in the descending order of unit value and it is up to the management to fix limits for three categories. This classification is useful for keeping control over consumption at departmental levels, for deciding the frequency of physical verification, and for controlling purchases.

(7) SDE Classification

This SDE classification is made based on the availability of materials. It is very much useful in the case of scarcity of supply of inventories. Here 'S' refers to 'scarce' inventory item, generally imported and those, which are in short supply category referred to as 'D' – 'difficult' inventory item that are available indigenously but are difficult to procure. 'E' refers to items, which are easy to acquire and are available in the local markets.

(8) FSN Classification

Under this technique inventory is classified based on movement of inventories from stores. FSN stands for fast moving (F), slow moving (S), and non-moving (N). This technique particularly involved in inventory useful for avoiding obsolescence. For determination whether a particular inventory is fast moving or not the date of receipt or the last date of the issue, whichever is later, is taken, which have lapsed since the last transaction. The items are usually grouped in periods of 12 months. Active moving items need to be reviewed regularly and surplus items, which have to be examined further. Non-moving items may be examined further and their disposal can be considered.

(9) Order Cycling System

In this system, periodic reviews are made of each item of inventory and orders are placed to restore stock to a prescribed supply level. What is the frequency of review? Frequency of review depends upon the criticality of the inventory item. At each review date the required number of items are ordered to bring the inventory to the predetermined supply level.

Approaches to Inventory Systems : There are two general approaches to inventory system, such as (a) Fixed Order Quantity System ('Q' system) and (b) Fixed Order Periodic System ('P' system). Under fixed order quantity system, a fixed quantity of materials is ordered whenever the stock level researches to the re-order level. It is nothing but EOQ. Where in Fixed order periodic system, stock position of each item of material is reviewed periodically. The frequency of reviews varies from company to company and also depending on the importance of materials.

(10) Just in Time (JIT)

Popularly known in its acronym JIT. JIT may be applied for either raw materials purchase or producing finished goods. From raw materials purchases it means that no inventories are held at any stage of production and the exact requirement is bought in each and every successive stage of production of the right time. In other words, maintenance of a minimum level of raw materials, where by the inventory carrying cost could be minimized, and the risk of loss due to stock-out position could be well avoided. From production of goods view, JIT means goods are produced only when the orders are received, there by no storage of finished goods, can avoid costs of carrying finished goods. JIT is also known as "Zero Inventory Production System" (ZIPS), Zero Inventories (ZIN), Materials as Needed (MAN), or Neck of Time (NOT).

SUMMARY

- Inventory management occupies the most significant position in the structure of working capital. Management of inventory may be defined as the sum of total of those activities necessary for the acquisition, storage, disposal or use of materials.

- Efficient management of inventory reduces the cost of production and consequently increases the profitability of the enterprise by minimising the different types of costs associated with holding inventory.

- The components of inventory are: (1) raw materials, (2) work-in process, (3) finished goods, and (4) stores and spares.

- There are three general motives for holding inventories are: (1) The Transaction Motive, (2) The Precautionary Motive, and (3) The Speculative Motive.

- The two conflicting objectives of inventory management are: (1) maintain investments in inventory and (2) to facilitate (benefits) the smooth functioning of the production, which in turn meet the demand.

- An effective inventory management should: Ensure a continuous supply of raw materials and supplies to facilitate uninterrupted production; maintain sufficient finished goods inventory for smooth sales operation, and efficient customer service; minimize the carrying costs and time; and control investment in inventories and keep it at an optimum level.

- The areas of inventory management covers: determining the size of inventory to be carried, establishing timing schedules, procedures and lot sizes for new orders, ascertaining minimum safety levels, co-coordinating sales, arranging the receipt, disbursement and procurement of materials, developing the forms of recording these transactions, assigning responsibilities for carrying out the inventory control functions, and providing the reports necessary for supervising this overall activity.

- Management of optimum level of inventory investment is the prime objective of inventory management. Inadequate or excess investment in inventories is not healthy by for any firm. The optimum level if investment in inventories lies between excess investment and inadequate investment.

- The dangers of excessive investment in inventory are: unnecessary tie-up of funds, excessive carrying costs, impairing liquidity, physical deterioration of inventories, and chance of theft, waste and mishandling of inventories.

- Under investment in inventory is also not healthy one. It has some negative points, they are: stoppage of production, and loss of customers.

- Minimizing cost is one of the operating objectives of inventory management. The costs (excluding merchandise cost), there are three costs involved in the management of inventories. They are: (1) Ordering Costs, and (ii) Inventory Carrying Costs.

- Risk in inventory management refers to the chance that inventories cannot be turned over into cash through normal sales without loss. Risks associated with inventory management are: (1) Price Decline, (2) Product Deterioration, and (3) Product Obsolescence.

- Proper management of inventory will result in the benefits to a firm: ensures an adequate supply of materials and stores, minimizes stock outs and shortages, and avoids costly interruptions in operations, keeps down investment in inventories; inventory carrying costs, and obsolescence losses to the minimum, facilitates purchasing economies, eliminates duplication in ordering stocks, permits better utilisation of available stocks, provides a check against the loss of materials through careless or pilferage. Perpetual inventory value provides a consistent and reliable basis for preparing financial statements a better utilisation.

- Inventory management problems can be handled by sophisticated/refined mathematical techniques. The major problem areas are (a) classification problem to determine the type of control required, (b) the order quantity problem,(c) the order point problem, and (d) determination of safety stocks.

- The most widely used inventory control technique is ABC Analysis [classification problem]. According to this technique, the task of inventory management is proper classification of all inventory items in to three categories namely A, B and C category. 'A' item, because greater benefit. The control of 'C' items may be released due to less benefits (some times control cost may exceed benefit of control) and reasonable attention should be paid on category 'B' items.

- Economic Order Quantity (EOQ) [Order Quantity Problem] refers to that level of inventory at which the total cost of inventory is minimum. The total inventory cost comprising ordering and carrying costs. EOQ also known as Economic Lot Size (ELS). EOQ can be obtained by adopting two methods (a) Trial and Error approach and (b) Short cut or Simple mathematical formula. Here, for calculation of EOQ we have adopted simple short cut method. The formula is:

$$EOQ = \sqrt{\frac{2AO}{CC}}$$

- Order Point Problem relates to the determination of the different stock levels are (a) Minimum level, (b) Reorder level, (c) Maximum level, (d) Average stock level, and (e) Dangers level. (a) Minimum Level is that level that must be maintained always production will be disturbed if it is less than the minimum level. Symbolically,

Minimum stock level = Re-order level – [Normal Usage x Average delivery time]

(b) Reordering Level is that level of inventory in weeks, which an order should be placed for replenishing the current stock of inventory. Generally the reorder level lies between minimum stock level and maximum stock level. Symbolically,

Re-order point = Lead time (in days) x Average Daily usage

Safety stock is that minimum additional inventory to serve as a safety margin or better or buffer or cushion to meet an unanticipated and increase in usage resulting from an unusually high demand and or an uncontrollable late receipt of incoming inventory. To avoid stock out, firm may require to maintain safety stock. Formula (under uncertainty of usage and lead time).

Re-order point = Lead time(in days) x Average usage + Safety stock

(c) Maximum Level of stock, is that level of stock beyond which a firm should not maintain the stock. Symbolically,

Maximum Stock Level = Re-order Level + Re-order Quantity – (Minimum Usage x Minimum Delivery Time)

(d) Average Stock Level Average Stock Level = Minimum level + [Reorder Quantity ÷ 2]

(e) Danger Stock Level is that level of materials beyond which materials should not fall in any situation. Symbolically,

Danger Level = Average Usage x Minimum Deliver Time [for emergency purchase]

- Strategies that help to succeed in inventory management are: (1) Rationality, complete understanding is the most prominent prerequisite for the success of any monitoring and control system of inventory by all affected parties. (2) Flexibility is the strategy that is required for successful monitoring and control of inventory management system. (3) Punctuality, right action in right time is of essence in inventory management.

PRACTICE YOURSELF SOLVED PROBLEMS

1. From the following information of VST Company, compute re-order level, minimum level, maximum level, and average stock level. The company uses two components X and Y for manufacturing a product.

   Normal usage – 100 units per week; Minimum usage – 50 units per week

   Maximum usage – 150 per week

   Re-order period – Component X: 4 to 10 weeks; Component Y: 2 to 8 weeks

   Re-order quantity – Component X: 600 units; Component Y: 900 units

Solution:

Re-order Level = Maximum usage x Maximum delivery time

    Component X = 150 units x 10 weeks = 1,500 units

    Component Y = 150 units x 8 weeks = 1,200 units

Minimum Level = Re-order level – (Normal usage x Average delivery time)

    Component X = 1,500 units – (100 units x 7 weeks) = 800 units

    Component Y = 1,200 units – (100 units x 5 weeks) = 700 units

Maximum Level = Re-order level + re-order quantity – (minimum usage x minimum delivery time)

    Component X   = 1,500 units + 600 units – (50 units x 4 weeks) = 1,900 units

    Component Y   = 1,200 units + 900 units – (50 units x 2 weeks) = 2,000 units

Average Stock Level = Minimum level + (re-order quantity ÷ 2)

    Component X   = 800 units + (600 units ÷ 2) = 1,100 units

    Component Y   = 700 units + (900 units ÷ 2) = 1,150 units

2. Determine re-order level, minimum level, maximum level, and average stock level.

   Normal usage – 100 units per week; Lead-time – 4 to 6 weeks

   Minimum usage – 50 units per week; Maximum usage – 150 per week

   Re-order quantity – 600 units

Solution:

Reorder Level = Maximum usage x Maximum delivery time

    = 150 units x 6 weeks = 900 units

Minimum Level = Re-order level – (Normal Usage x Average delivery time)

    = 900 units – (100 units x 5 weeks) = 400 units

Maximum Level = Re-order level + reorder quantity – (minimum usage x minimum delivery time)

$\qquad$ = 900 units + 600 units – (50 units x 4 weeks) = 1,300 units

Average Stock Level = Minimum level + (re-order quantity ÷ 2)

$\qquad$ = 400 units + (600 units ÷ 2) = 700 units

3. Calculate maximum, minimum and re-order levels of stock from the following information.

Maximum Consumption – 2,000 units/week; Minimum Consumption – 1,500 units/week

Maximum lead-time – 5 weeks; Minimum lead-time – 3 weeks

Reorder quantity – 1,000 units

Solution:

Reorder Level = [Maximum usage x Maximum delivery time]

$\qquad$ = 2,000 units x 5 weeks = 10,000 units

Minimum Level = Re-order level – [Normal usage x Average delivery time in weeks]

$\qquad$ = 1,0000 units – [1,750 units x 4 weeks] = 3,000 units

Maximum Level = Re-order level + Re-order quantity – [Minimum usage x Minimum delivery time]

$\qquad$ = 10,000 units + 1,000 units – [1,500 units x 3 weeks] = 6,500 units.

4. A company purchases a component of a product at the rate of Rs. 50 per piece. The annual consumption of that component is 25,000 pieces. If the ordering cost is Rs.230 per order and carrying cost is 20 per cent per annum, what would be the EOQ?

Solution

Annual usage – 25,000 units; Cost of placing and receiving one order – Rs. 230;

Cost of materials – Rs. 50 per unit; Annual carrying cost of one unit – 20 per cent of inventory value

$$EOQ = \sqrt{2AO \div CC}$$

$$EOQ = \sqrt{(2 \times 25,000 \times 230) \div (50 \times 20/100)} = 1,072 \text{ units.}$$

5. XYZ Company buys 75,000 glass bottles per year. Price of each bottle is Re.0.90. Cost of purchase is Rs. 100 per order; Cost of holding one bottle per year is Re. 0.20. Bank interest is 15 per cent including a charge for taxes and insurance. Find out EOQ quantity.

Solution:

Annual usage – 75,000 units; Cost of placing and receiving one order – Rs. 100

Cost of bottle – Re. 0.90 per bottle; Annual carrying cost of one bottle – Re.0.20 per bottle

$$EOQ = \sqrt{2AO \div CC}$$

$$EOQ = \sqrt{(2 \times 75,000 \times 100) \div 0.335^*} = 6,691.50 \text{ units.}$$

* Inventory carrying cost = Re. 0.20 + [Re.0.90 x 0.15] = Re.0.335

6. A company uses annually 25,000 units of raw materials, which costs Rs. 1.75 per unit. Cost of placing an order is Rs. 30 and carrying cost is 8 per cent per year. Find out EOQ.

Solution:

Annual usage – 25,000 units; Cost of placing and receiving one order – Rs. 30;

Cost of bottle – Rs. 1.75 per unit.

Annual carrying cost of one unit – (Rs.1.75 x 0.08 per cent) = Re. 0.14

$$EOQ = \sqrt{2AO \div CC}$$

$$EOQ = \sqrt{(2 \times 25,000 \times 30) \div 0.14} = 3,273 \text{ units.}$$

7. The demand for a certain item is random. It has been estimated that the monthly demand of the item has a normal distribution with a mean of 780 and a standard deviation of 140 units. The unit price of the item is Rs. 25. Ordering cost is Rs. 28 and the inventory carrying cost is estimated to be 35 per cent per year. Determine EOQ.

Solution:

Mean of monthly demand = 780 units; Annual demand–780 x 12 months = 9,360 units

Ordering cost – Rs. 28 per order; Cost per item   – Rs. 25 per unit

Inventory carrying cost of one unit – (Rs.25 x 0.35 per cent) = Rs. 8.75

$$EOQ = \sqrt{2AO \div CC}$$

$$EOQ = \sqrt{(2 \times 9,360 \times 28) \div 8.75} = 244.75 \text{ or } 245 \text{ units.}$$

8. AIM Company Ltd. uses quarterly 50,000 units of raw materials. Cost of raw materials is Rs. 100 per unit, cost of placing an order is Rs. 100 and carrying cost is 9 per cent per year. Calculate EOQ.

Solution:

Annual usage – (50,000 x 4 Quarters) = 2,00,000 units

Cost of raw materials – Rs. 100 per unit; ordering cost – Rs. 100 per order

Carrying cost of one unit – (Rs.100 x 0.09 per cent) = Rs. 9

$$EOQ = \sqrt{2AO \div CC}$$

$$EOQ = \sqrt{(2 \times 2,00,000 \times 100) \div 9^*} = 2,108 \text{ units.}$$

* Annual demand = 50,000 x 4 quarts = 2,00,000 units

* Inventory carrying cost = Rs. 100 x 0.09 = Rs 9.

9. Best of Luck Company Ltd., uses annually 80,300 units of raw materials at a price of Rs. 8 per unit. Its estimated carrying cost is 14 per cent and its ordering cost is Rs. 20 per order. What will be the economical number of units to order and how often will an order needs to be placed?

Solution:

Annual usage – 80, 300 units; Cost of raw materials – Rs. 8 per unit

Ordering cost – Rs. 20 per order; Carrying cost of one unit – (Rs.8 × 0.14 per cent) = Rs. 1.12

$$EOQ = \sqrt{2AO \div CC}$$

$$EOQ = \sqrt{(2 \times 80,300 \times 20) \div 1.12} = 1,693 \text{ units}$$

Ordering period: Time after which an order to be placed is determined by the following formula:

Ordering period = [EOQ ÷ Consumption per day]

Consumption per day = Annual Consumption ÷ 365 = 80,300 ÷ 365 = 220 units

Ordering period = [1,693 ÷ 220] = 7.695 days or approximately 8 days

10. Hindustan Engineering Factory consumes 75,000 units of a component per year. The ordering, receiving and handling costs are Rs. 6 per order while transportation cost is Rs.24 per order. Depreciation and obsolescence cost Re. 0.008 per unit per year; interest cost Re. 0.12 per unit per year; storage cost Rs. 2,000 per year for 75,000 units. Calculate EOQ.

Solution:

Annual usage – 75,000 units; Cost of raw materials – Rs. 8 per unit

Ordering cost = (Ordering cost + Transportation cost) = (Rs. 6 + Rs. 24) = Rs. 30

Carrying cost of one unit:

Interest cost	0.120
Deterioration and obsolescence cost	0.008
Storage cost (2,000 ÷ 75,000)	0.026
Total carrying cost	0.154

$$EOQ = \sqrt{(2 \times 75,000 \times 30) \div 0.154} = 5,406 \text{ units}$$

11. A wholesale fruit dealer sells 16,000 boxes of dry fruits during the year. The cost of placing an order is Rs. 500 and each box of dry fruit costs Rs. 2,000. The cost of carrying inventory is 20 per cent. Find out economic order quantity.

Solution

$$EOQ = \sqrt{(2 \times 16,000 \times 500) \div (2,000 \times 0.20)} = 200 \text{ units}$$

12. The following information relating to inventory in WTS Ltd. is made available to you. The company wants to introduce the scheme of ordering only the economic order quantity.

Annual demand : 480 units;   Price per unit   : Rs.4

Carrying cost   : 40 paise per unit;   Cost per order   : Rs. 5 per unit

Determine the economic order quantity. Also determine the number of orders per year and frequency of purchases.

Solution:

(i) $EOQ = \sqrt{(2 \times 480 \times 5) \div 0.40}$ = 109.54   or 110 units

(ii)   No. of orders per year = Demand per year ÷ EOQ size = 480 ÷ 110 = **4.36 orders**

(iii) Frequency of purchase = No. of months in a year ÷ No. of orders per year

$$= 12 \div 4 = \textbf{3 months}$$

13. The following relating to inventory costs have been established for XYZ Ltd.,
    - Orders must be placed for the year in multiples of 1,000 units.
    - Requirements for the year are 3,00,000 units.
    - The purchase price per unit is Rs. 3.00.
    - Carrying cost is 25 per cent of the purchase price of goods.
    - Cost per order placed is Rs. 20.

    Find EOQ.

Solution:

$$EOQ = \sqrt{2AO/CC}$$

$$= \sqrt{(2 \times 3,00,000 \times 20)/(3 \times 0.25)} = 4,000 \text{ units}$$

TEST YOUR KNOWLEDGE

1. **Fill in the blanks with appropriate word(s)**
   (a) Inventory is one of components of _____ assets.
   (b) The term inventory is originated from the _____ "Inventoried", and the Latin _____.
   (c) Raw materials, work-in-process, finished goods and stores and spares are the components of _____ .
   (d) _____ motive necessitates the holiday of inventories for unexpected changes in demand and supply factors.
   (e) The time required to process and execute an order is called _____ time.
   (f) _____ costs are those costs that are associated with the acquisition of raw materials.
   (g) ___refers to the level of inventory at which the total inventory cost is minimum.
   (h) _____ also known as ZIPS.
   (i) _____ is that level of inventory at which an order should be placed for replenishing the current stock of inventory.
   (j) Minimum stock level plus half of the re-order quantity is equal to _____.

[**Answers:** (a) Current; (b) French, Inventariom; (c) Inventory; (d) Precautionary, (e) Lead; (f) Ordering; (g) EOQ; (h) JIT; (i) Re-order, level; (j) Average stock level].

2. **State whether each of the following statement is true of false:**
   (a) Holding of inventories to take the advantages of changes in prices and getting quantity discounts are known as speculative motive.
   (b) Inventory carrying costs are those costs that are associated with the carrying of goods from supplies to the firm.
   (c) Price decline, product deterioration, and product obsolescence are the risks of holding inventory.
   (d) Classification of inventor, order quantity, and order point are the three problems of inventory management.

(e)   ABC Analysis is also known at PAV.

(f)   In EOQ Formula $\sqrt{2AO \div CC}$, 'A' stands for Annual usage.

(g)   VED classification is applied to spare parts.

(h)   Just in time system was developed in Japan by Taichi Okno.

(i)   Capital cost is one of the components of inventory carrying cost.

(j)   Cost of carrying goods from supplies to firm factory premises is included in ordering cost.

[**Answers:** (a) True; (b) False; (c) True; (d) True; (e) False; (f) True; (g) True; (h) True; (i) True; and (j) True].

3.   **Answer the Following Question**

1.   What is EOQ ?

2.   What is inventory management?

3.   Name the three main components of inventory.

4.   Name various motives for holding inventories.

5.   List out the risks associated with holding inventory.

6.   Give three problems of inventory management.

7.   What is ordering cost ?

8.   What is inventory-carrying cost. ?

9.   State any two objectives of inventory management.

10.   Define VED analysis.

11.   What do you understand by ABC analysis. ?

12.   How do you compute EOQ?

13.   State the assumption of EOQ.

14.   What do you understand by shortage costs?

15.   What is Lead Time.?

16.   What do you understand by JIT system.?

17.   Write note on FSN system of inventory control.

18.   What do you understand by HML system of inventory control.

19.   What is inventory management? Discuss in detail the objectives of inventory management.

20.   Write a brief note on ABC analysis.

21.   "There are two dangerous situations that management should usually avoid in controlling inventories". Explain.

22.   What is safety stock?

23.   What is order cycling system?

DO IT YOURSELF PROBLEMS

1.   The Management of Shesha Sai Textiles has predicted sales of 1,00,000 units of a product in the next 12 months. The product cost is Rs.18 per unit. Its estimated carrying cost is 25 per cent of inventory value and ordering cost is Rs.10 per order. What is the EOQ ?

[**Answer: 730.29 units**]

2. Bharath Engineering Factory consumes 3,00,000 units of a component per year. The ordering, receiving and handling costs are Rs. 60 per order and the firm is estimating its carrying cost at 20 per cent. Component cost per unit is Rs. 20. Calculate EOQ.

[Answer: 2,683.28 units]

3. Finance Department of RRR Cement Company gathered the following information. You are required to compute EOQ, number of orders in a year, the time gap between the two orders and the total cost of ordering and carrying. Monthly usage 150 units, ordering cost Rs 20, cost of purchase of the component Rs 5 and carrying cost are 16 per cent.

[Answer: EOQ–300 units; Orders – 6; Time Gap between orders – 1 month; Total ordering cost – 120]

4. A manufacturing company has an expected usage of 1,00,000 units of certain product during the next year. The cost of an order is Rs. 40 and carrying cost is Re. 0.5 per unit for one year. Lead-time on an order is five days and company will keep a reserve supply of two days' usage. You are required to calculate (a) EOQ and (b) the Re-order point (assuming 250-day year).

[Answer: EOQ – 4,000; Re-order point – 3,600 units]

5. A company received an order for 15,000 units at the rate of 1,000 units per order. The production cost per unit is Rs. 24 per unit – Rs. 10 for raw materials and Rs. 14 as overhead cost. It costs Rs. 1,500 to set up for one run of 1,000 units and inventory-carrying cost is 20 per cent of the production cost. Since the customer may buy at least 15,000 this year, the company would like to avoid making five different production runs. Determine most economic production run.

[Answer: 3,062 units]

6. From the following information of ABC Co, Ltd., calculate minimum, maximum and re-order stock levels.

Minimum consumption – 300 units per day

Maximum consumption – 400 units per day

Normal consumption – 320 units per day

Re-order period – 10-20 days

Re-order quantity – 1,500 units

Normal re-order period – 14 days.

[Answers: Re-order level – 8000 units; Mini.level – 3200 units; Maxi.level – 3500 units]

REFERENCES

1. Richard, J. W. and Eagle, Robert. H., *"Modern Inventory Management"*, New York: John Wiley & Sons, 1965, p.2.

2. Nageswara Rao and Omji Gupta, *"Management of Inventory Position"*, The Management Accountant, June. 1986, p.355.

3. Howard, L. R., *"Working Capital: Its Management and Control"*, London: Macdonald and Evans Ltd., 1971, p.92-93.

4. Ibid., p.179.

5. Committee on Accounting Procedure, *"Restatement and Review of Accounting Research"* Bulletin, No.42, New York: American Institute of Accountants, June 1953, p.27.

6. Bolten, S.E., *"Managerial Finance"*, Houghton Mifflin Co., Boston, 1976, p.426.

7. Om Prakash, *"Ratio Analysis for Management in New Perspective (Management Ratios)"*, Bombay: Himalaya Publishing House, 1987, p.179.

8. Richard J.T, *"Materials Management and Inventory Systems"*, North Holland Publication Co.p.4.

9. Starr, M.K. and Miller, D.W., *"Inventory Control: Theory and Practice"*, New Jersey: Prentice - Hall, 1962, p.17.

10. Pandey, I.M., *"Financial Management"*, New Delhi: Vikas Publishing House Private Limited, 1985, p.887.

11. Public Enterprises Survey 1979-80, Vol. I, Annual Report on the Working of Industrial and Commercial Undertakings of the Central Government, p.175.

12. Satish, B.M, *"Working capital management and control - Principles & practice"*, New Delhi; New Age International(P) Ltd, 2002, pp.157-158.

13. Chadda, R.S., *"Inventory Management in India"*, Allied publishers, p.1.

14. Solomon, E. and Pringle, J.J., *"Introduction to Financial Management"*, Goodyear Publishing Co., Santa Monica, Calif., 1977, p.211.

15. Richmond, H.J., *"Effective Inventory Management - Fact or Fiction?"*, Financial Executive, March, 1969, pp.74-78.

16. Synder, A, *"Principles of Inventory Management"*, Financial Executive, April, 1964, pp 13-21.

17. Richard, B.Chase, et.al, *"Materials Management and Inventory systems"*, North Holland Publication Co. p.337.

18. Greene, J.H., *"Production and Inventory Control Handbook"*, New Delhi: McGraw-Hill, p.16.3.

19. Dean, S.A., *"Materials Management and Purchasing"*, Taraporevala & Sons, p.326.

20. Ibid, p.326.

21. Ibid, p.327.

Sources of Working Capital

20

Objectives

After studying this chapter, you should be able to:

1 Say the two major sources to working capital finance.

2 List out the sources of short term working capital.

3 Explain the benefits and cost of trade credit.

4 Narrate the features of commercial paper.

5 Discuss the different modes of bank finance for working capital.

6 Explain the different modes of security required by banks for operating credit.

7 Discuss different types of letter of credit .

8 Say what is factoring ? Its features.

9 Discuss the sources of long-term sources of working capital finance.

Once, estimation of working capital required is completed, then the next step is financing of working capital. Statement of working capital gives clear picture about the components, (raw materials, work-in-process, finished goods and receivables) and required investment in these components of working capital. Generally investment in these components varies a great deal during the course of the year. Financing of current assets is the responsibility of finance manager who may require spending lot of time for raising finance.

As we have seen earlier discussion, there are two types of working capital (a) permanent or fixed and (b) temporary or variable working capital. In simple words, working capital should be financed by suitable and optimal mix of short-term source of funds and long-term source of funds.

FINANCING OF TEMPORARY OR VARIABLE OR SHORT-TERM WORKING CAPITAL

Sources of short-term funds have to be used (exclusively) for meeting the working capital requirements only and not far financing fixed assets and for meeting the margin money for working capital loans.

The various sources of short-term financing are as follows :

1) *Trade Credit:* Trade credit refers to the credit extended by the supplier of goods or services to his/her customer in the normal course of business. Trade credit occupies very important position in short-term financing due to the competition. Almost all the traders and manufacturers are required to extend credit facility (a portion), without which there is no possibility of staying back in the business. Trade credit is a spontaneous source of finance that arises in the normal business transactions of the firm without specific negotiations (automatic source of finance). In order to get this source of finance, the buyer should have acceptable and dependable credit worthiness and reputation in the market. Trade credit generally extended in the format open account or bills of exchange. Open account is the form of trade credit, where supplier sends goods to the buyer for the payment to be received in future as per terms of the sales invoice. As such trade credit constitute a very important source of finance, it represents 25 per cent to 50 per cent of the total short-term sources for financing working capital requirements.

Getting trade credit may be easy to the well-established or well-reputed firm, but for a new or the firm with financial problems will generally face problem in getting trade credit. Generally suppliers look for earning record, liquidity position and payment record which is extending credit. Building confidence in suppliers is possible only when the buyer discussing his/ her financial condition future plans and payment record. Trade credit involves some benefits and costs.

Advantages of Trade Credit: The main advantages are:

❖ Easy availability when compared to other sources of finance (except financially weak companies).

❖ Flexibility is another benefit, as the credit increases with the growth of the firm's sales.

❖ Informality as we have already seen that it is an automatic finance.

The above discussion on trade credit reveals two things. One, cost of trade credit is very high beyond the cash discount period, company should not have cash discount for prompt payment and *Second*, if the company is not able to avail cash discount it should pay only at the end of last day of credit period, even if it can delay by one or two days, it does not affect the credit standing.

2) **Accruals:** Accrued expenses are those expenses which the company owes to the other persons or organisations, but not yet due and not yet paid the amount. In other words, accruals represent a liability that a firm has to pay for the services or goods, which it has already received. It is spontaneous and interest-free sources of financing. Salaries, wages, interest and taxes are the major constituents of accruals. Salaries and wages are usually paid on monthly and weekly basis respectively. The amounts of salaries and wages have owed but not yet paid and shown them as accrued salaries and wages on the balance sheet at the end of financial year. Longer the time lag in payment of these expenses, the greater is the amount of funds provided by the employees. Similarly, interest and tax are other accruals, as source of short-term finance. Tax will be paid on earnings. Income tax is paid to the government on quarterly basis and some other taxes may be payable half-yearly or annually. Amount of taxes due as on the date of the balance sheet but not paid till then and they are showed as accrued taxes on the balance sheet. Like taxes, interest is paid periodically in the year but the funds are used continuously by a firm. All other such items of expenses can be used as a source of short-term finance but shown on the balance sheet.

The amount of accrual varies with the level of activities of a firm. When the level of activity expands, accruals increase, they automatically act as a source of finance. Accruals are treated as "cost free" source or finance, since it does not involve any payment of interest. But in actual terms, it may not be true, since payment of salaries and wages is determined by provisions of law and industry practice. Similarly, tax payment governed by laws and delay in payment of tax leads to pay penalty. Hence, a firm must be noted that use of accruals as a source of working capital or it may not be possible to delay in payment of these items of expenses.

3) **Deferred Income:** Deferred incomes are incomes received in advance by the firm for supply of goods or services in future period. These income receipts increase the firm's liquidity and constitute an important source of short-term source finance. These payments are not showed as revenue till the supply of goods or services, but showed in the balance sheet as income received in advance. Advance payment can be demanded by only firms having monopoly power, great demand for its products and services and if the firm is manufacturing a special product on a special order.

4) **Commercial Papers (CPs):** Commercial paper represents a short-term unsecured promissory note issued by firms that have a fairly high credit (standing) rating. It was first introduced in USA and it was an important money market instruments. In India, Reserve Bank of India introduced CP on the recommendations of the Vaghul Working Group on money market. CP is a source of short-term finance to only large firms with sound financial position.

Features of CP

❖ The maturity period of CP ranges from 15 to 365 day (but in India it ranges between 91 to 180 days).

❖ It is sold at a discount from its face value and redeemed at its face value.

❖ Return on CP is the difference between par value and redeemable value.

❖ It may be sold directly to investors or indirectly (through) dealers.

❖ There is no developed secondary market for CP.

"Eligibility" Criteria for issuing CP:

CP is unsecured promissory note, the issue of CP is being regulated by the Reserve Bank of India. RBI has laid down the following conditions to determine the eligibility of a company that wishes to raise funds through the issue of CPs.

❖ The Tangible Net Worth (TNW) of the company, as per latest audited balance sheet should not be less than Rs. 4 crore.

❖ The company should have been sanctioned as a fund based limit for bank(s) finance and / or the All India Financial Institutions.

❖ Company can issue CPs amounting to 75% of the permitted bank (working capital limit) credit.

❖ Company's CPs receives a minimum rating of (P2 from CRISIL, A-2 form ICRA, etc).

❖ The minimum size of each CP is Rs. 5 lakhs or multiples thereof.

❖ The size of any single issue should not be less than Rs. 1 crore.

❖ The CP is in the form of usance promissory note negotiable by endorsement and delivery.

Advantages of CP

❖ It is an alternative source of finance and proves to be helpful during the period of tight bank credit.

❖ It is a cheaper source of short-term finance when compared to the bank credit.

Disadvantages of CP

❖ It is available only for large and financially sound companies.

❖ It cannot be redeemed before the maturity date.

5) **Public Deposits:** Public deposits or term deposits are in the nature of unsecured deposits, have been solicited by the firms (both large and small) from general public primarily for the purpose of financing their working capital requirements.

Regulations

Fixed deposits accepted by companies are governed by the Companies (Acceptance of Deposits) Amendment Rules 1978. The main features of this regulation are :

♦ A firm cannot issue public deposits for more than 25 per cent of its share capital and free reserves.

♦ The public deposits can be issued for a period ranging from a minimum 6 months to maximum 3 years. Public deposits for a period of three months, however, can as well be issued, but only for an amount up to 10% of the company's share capital and free reserves. Maximum period of 5 years is allowed for non-banking financial corporation (NBFC's).

♦ The company that had raised funds by way of issue of public deposits is required to set aside, a deposit and / or investment, by the 30th April each year an amount equal to 10 per cent of the maturity deposits by the 31st March of the next year. The amount, so set aside can be used only for repairing the amount of deposits.

♦ Finally, a company's and accepting the public deposits is required to disclose some true, fair, vital and relevant facts in regards to its financial position and performance.

Advantages: Advantages of public deposit can be studied from two different views.

a) Company point of view

❖ Simple procedure involved in issuing public deposits.

❖ No restrictive covenants are involved.

❖ No security is offered against public deposits.

❖ Cheaper (post-tax cost is fairly reasonable).

b) Investors point of view

❖ Higher interest rates when compared to other investment avenues.

❖ Short maturity period.

Disadvantages : These also can be studied from two different points :

a) Company point of view

- ❖ Limited amount of funds can be raised.
- ❖ Funds available only for a short period.

b) Investor point of view

- ❖ Risk since there is no security against PD.
- ❖ Income received (interest) is taxable.

6) *Inter-Corporate Deposits (ICDS)*

A deposit made by one firm with another firm is known as inter-corporate deposits (ICDs). Generally, these deposits are usually made for a period up to six months. Such deposits may be of three types :

♦ *Call Deposits:* Deposits are expected to be payable on call. In other words, whenever its repayment is demanded on just one days notice. But, in actual practice, the lender has to wait for at least 2 or 3 days to get back the amount. Inter corporate deposits generally have 12 per cent interest per annum.

♦ *Three Months Deposits:* These deposits are more popular among companies for investing the surplus funds. The borrower takes this type of deposits for tiding over a short-term cash inadequacy. The interest rate on these types of deposits is around 14 per cent per annum.

♦ *Six-Months Deposits:* Generally, the inter-corporate deposits are made for a maximum period of six months. These types of deposits are usually given to 'A' category borrowers only and they carry an interest rate of around 16% per annum.

Features of ICDs

♦ There are no *legal regulations, which* makes an ICD transaction very convenient.

♦ Inter-corporate deposits are given and taken in *secrecy.*

♦ Inter-corporate deposits are given based on borrowers financial sound, but in practice lender lends money based on personal contacts.

7) *Commercial Banks:* Commercial banks are the major source of working capital finance to industries and commerce. Granting loan to business is one of their primary functions. Getting bank loan is not an easy task since the lending bank office may ask number of questions about the prospective borrower's financial position and its plans for the future. At the same time bank will want to monitor of the borrower's business progress. But there is a good side to this, that is borrower's share price tends to rise, because investor know that convince banks is very difficult.

Forms of Bank Finance: Banks provide different types of tailored made loans that are suitable for specific needs of a firm. The different types of forms of loans are:

(1) Loans, (2) Overdrafts, (3) Cash credits, (4) Purchase or discounting of bills and (5) Letter of Credit.

(1) *Loans:* Loan in an advance is lumpsum given to borrower against some security. Loan amount is paid to the applicant in the form of cash or by credit to his/her account. In practice the loan amount is paid to the customer by crediting his/her account. Interest will be charged on the entire loan amount from the date the loan is sanctioned. Borrower can repay the loan either in lumpsum or in installments depending on conditions. If the loan is

repayable in installment basis interest will be calculated on quarterly and on reduced balances. Generally, working capital loans will be granted for one-year period.

(2) *Overdrafts:* Overdraft facility is an agreement between the borrower and the banker, where the borrower is allowed to withdraw funds in excess of the balance in his/her current accounts up to a certain limit during a specified period. It is flexible from the borrower's point of view because the borrower can withdraw and repay the cash whenever he/she wants within the given stipulations. Interest is charged on daily over drawn balances and not on the overdraft limit given by the bank. But bank charges some minimum charges.

(3) *Cash Credit:* It is the most popular source of working capital finance in India. A cash credit facility is an arrangement where a bank permits a borrower to withdraw money up to a sanctioned credit limit against tangible security or guarantees. Borrower does not require to withdraw the total sanctioned credit at a time, rather, he can withdraw according to his/her requirements and he can also repay the surplus cash in his cash credit account. Interest is chargeable on actually used amount and there is no commitment charge. Cash credit is a flexible source of working capital from borrower's point of view.

(4) *Purchasing or Discounting of Bills:* Bills receivable arises out of sales transaction, where the seller of goods draws the bill on the purchaser. The bill may be documentary or clean bill. Once the bill is accepted by the purchaser, then the drawer (seller) of the bill can go to bank for discount or sale. The credit worthiness of the drawer (seller) is satisfactory, then bank purchases or discounts the bill and reduces funds by way of crediting to customers account. The credited amount will be less than the bill amount. At the end of maturity period of the bill, bank presents the bill to drawee (acceptor) for payment. If the bill is discounted and dishonored by the drawee, then the customer (seller) is liable to pay the bill amount and any other expenses incurred to bank.

(5) *Letter of Credit [L/C]:* There are two non-fund based sources of working capital, viz., letter of credit (L/Cs) and Bank Guarantees (B/Gs). These are also known as quasi-credit facilities, due to non-payment of amount immediately. A Letter of Credit (L/C) is a written document issued by the Buyer's Banker (BB) at the request of the buyer's, in favour of the seller, where by the Buyers Banker gives an undertaking to the seller, that the bank pay the obligations of its customer up to a specified amount, if the customer fails to pay the value of goods purchased. It helps to bank's customer to obtain credit from the seller (supplier), which is possible by assurance of the payment. Thereby, it allows the supplier to extend credit, since the risk of non-payment is transferred to the BB. Letter of credit facility is available from bank only for the companies that are financially sound and Bank charges the customer for providing this facility.

Security Required in Bank finance

No doubt bank finance is most important source of working capital finances. But getting bank finance without giving adequate security is impossible. In how many modes the borrower can give security? The following are the modes of security required by a bank:

a) *Hypothecation:* Under this arrangement, the loan applicant is provided money against the security of movable property, usually inventories. The owner / loan applicant does not transfer the possession of the property to the bank. Hypothecation is in the nature of floating charge. It is merely a charge against property for the amount of debt. This type of security is accepted for granting credit, only to the first class customers with highest integrity. In other words, they do not grant credit to new customer and low class customers with hypothecation. If the borrower fails to honour the dues to the bank, the banker may realise his due by sale of the goods hypothecated.

b) **Pledge:** Under this arrangement, the loan applicant / borrower is required to transfer the physical possession of the goods / property to the bank as security. As per section 172 of the Indian Contract Act, pledge is a bailment of goods, as a security, for payment of a debt, or performance of a promise, against some advances. Transfer of possession of goods is a precondition for pledge. Once the goods are shifted to the lender or bank, he is expected to take reasonable care of goods pledged with him. The lender has a right of lien and can retain the possession of goods pledged unless the debt (including interest and expenses) is cleared. If the borrower defaults in paying his dues, the bank has the right to sell goods and recover the dues. But this should be done only after giving due notice to the borrower.

c) **Mortgage:** Apart from the hypothecation and pledge some times banks ask for mortgage as collateral security. Mortgage is the transfer of legal or equitable interest in a specific immovable property for the payment of a debt. In this arrangement, the possession of property remain with the owner / loan applicant, but the full legal title is transferred to the bank. If the borrower fails to pay dues, the bank can get decree from the court to sell the immovable property is given as security and it can recover its dues.

FACTORING

Introduction

Cash lubricates the wheels of trade, business and industry. Cash flow is necessary to meet commitments - statutory or otherwise. But, unfortunately for the sellers of goods and services, credit sale is the order of the day, worldwide. The most vulnerable segments are the small and medium sector enterprises. Delayed realization of the sales receivables elongates their working capital cycles. Poor bookkeeping and collection mechanisms along with inadequate and delayed institutional credit hasten their untimely sickness. In this backdrop, factoring has evolved as an innovative portfolio of complementary financial services. It is an alternative way of providing post-sales working capital finance to trade and industry, which they traditionally get from commercial banks. In this unit, we will discuss the features, types and appraisal techniques of factoring. We will also briefly analyse its promises, problems and prospects.

Concept and Features

Factoring is a financial service covering the financing and collection of book debts and receivables arising from credit sale of goods and services, both in the domestic as well as international market. It aims at exonerating the supplier from the burden of complicated administrative and financial tasks involved in receivables management.

From the above definition, we can derive that the main functions of a Factor comprise:

(i) **Maintenance of sales ledgers and collection of receivables:** The Factor takes up the responsibility of sales ledger administration. It includes (a) Bookkeeping (b) Invoice raising (c) Follow-up and monitoring (d) Collection of receivables (e) liaisoning with clients and customers by informing them periodically about collection and outstanding (f) maintaining a management information system (MIS). The service charges paid by the client to the Factor is more than off-set by the host of administrative expenses saved on account of debt administration by the Factor.

(ii) **Credit Control:** A Factor, as a professional, has the wherewithal for credit intelligence on customers. His staff is trained in the assessment of creditworthiness and have access to extensive information on the financial standing and credit rating of individual customers. This enables him to advise his clients accordingly.

(iii) *Credit Protection:* In "without recourse factoring", the Factor assumes credit risk. Based on the credit information of customers, the Factor approves 'credit limits' on individual debtors. Thus, he provides credit insurance facility against possible losses arising from insolvency/bankruptcy - financial failure of the debtors. However, under 'recourse factoring', the client bears the credit risks.

(iv) *Financing of Receivables:* Factor advances funds to the client to the extent of about 80% of the outstanding debts ahead of maturity. This credit input helps the client to expand his business.

(v) *Advisory Services:* With his pool of expertise, the Factor also offers consultancy services to the clients in areas of production, finance and marketing. For example, the Factors' personnel with extensive manufacturing experience can provide guidance on workload analysis, machinery replacement programmes and other technical aspects of clients' business.

Mechanics

By now you have understood that there are three players in a domestic factoring service viz. the Factor (who provides the services), the Client (the seller of goods/services for whom the Factor provides facilities) and the Customer (who purchases goods/services). Presently, in India, a factor can entertain with-recourse factoring services. The system of a domestic factoring is as follows:

(i) On receiving order from the buyer (Customer), the seller (the Client) approaches the Factor for establishing factoring relationship. The seller furnishes information about his business, his banker and credit facilities availed, turnover-size, names and addresses of regular customers, their bankers; average outstanding invoices, the last few years' financial statements, range of factoring service required etc.

(ii) Based on the information supplied by client and additional information collected from other sources, the Factor decides the coverage of factoring services to be provided.

(iii) Factor checks the credit credentials and approves the buyers. For each approved buyer, a credit limit and the period up to which credit can be given are fixed. Factor fixes limits to the client aggregating individual limits to buyers.

(iv) Client sells the goods/services to the buyers.

(v) Client notifies in the invoice, a direction to the customer to pay the invoice value to the Factor.

(vi) Client assigns the debt in favour of the Factor. The invoice is sent to the Factor along with receipted delivery challan. The invoice is accounted for in the buyer's account in the sales ledger maintained by the Factor.

(vii) The Factor provides credit to the client to the entitled extent say 80% of invoice value, retaining a margin of 20%.

(viii) The Factor sends the notice of assignment/copy of invoice to the buyer.

(ix) The Factor periodically sends details of collections and outstanding dues to the client and customer.

(x) On the expiry of the agreed credit period, the buyer makes the payment of the invoice to the Factor. Then the Factor pays to the seller the margin money retained after recovery of interest and other charges.

(xi) If the customer does not pay, the Factor takes recourse to the client under recourse factoring.

The above process can be depicted as follows:

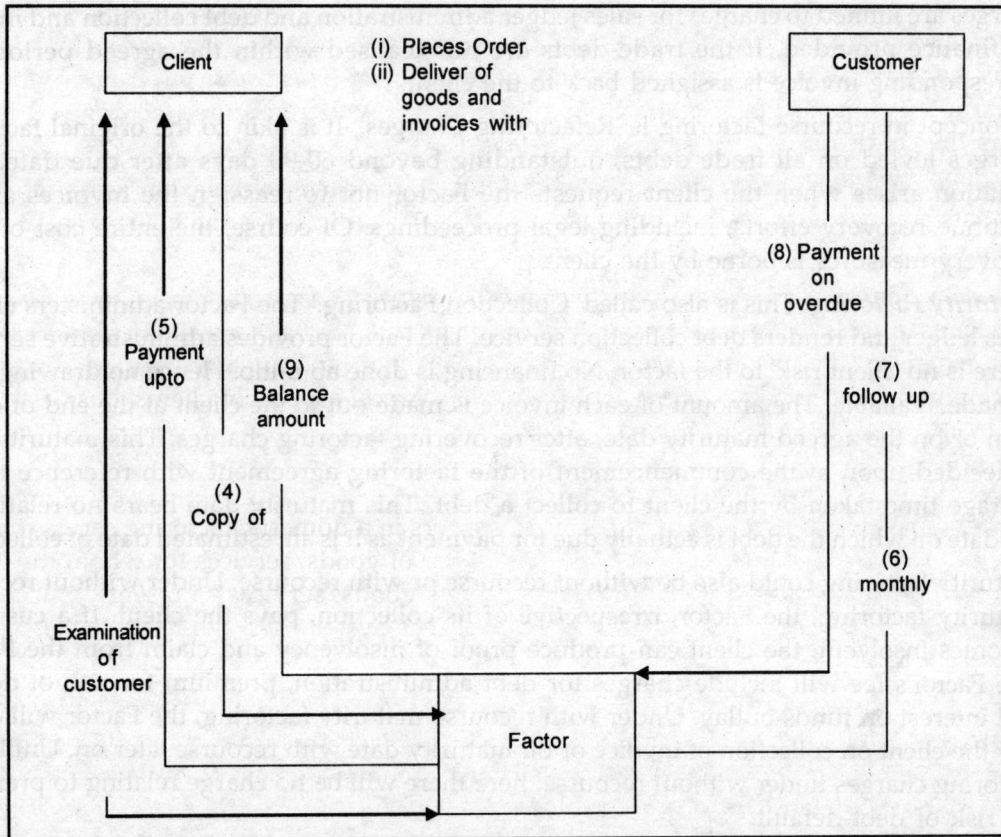

```
  ┌──────────┐     (i) Places Order              ┌──────────┐
  │  Client  │     (ii) Deliver of               │ Customer │
  └──────────┘          goods and                └──────────┘
                        invoices with

                                                 (8) Payment
                                                     on
                                                     overdue

     (5)
   Payment
    upto        (9)                               (7)
              Balance                          follow up
               amount

     (4)
   Copy of
                                                 (6)
                                              monthly
  Examination
      of
   customer
                           ┌──────────┐
                           │  Factor  │
                           └──────────┘
```

TYPES

Depending on the arrangement between the Factor and the Client, factoring can be of six different types:

(i) *Full Factoring:* This is also called "without recourse factoring" or "old-line factoring." This classical form of factoring is most comprehensive and includes services such as maintenance of sales ledger, collection of receivables, credit control, credit protection and financing of receivables. Here the Factor approves the customers for credit risks based on his credit worthiness. Factor assumes the debt risk (within the approved limit). The client is totally absolved of his responsibilities as the invoice representing the receivables/trade debts are assigned to the factor on a 'without recourse' basis up to a specified limit only. Client is free to exceed limit at his risk. But this 'non-recourse' aspect is only towards financial inability of the debtors. Because, if payment is withheld for reasons of dispute regarding quality, quantity, counter-claim etc., recourse will be available to the Factor against the client.

Corresponding to the types of services provided, the Factor's charges include the following:

(a) Charge for rendering sales ledger administration and debt collection

(b) Premium for taking risk of debt-default

(c) Interest on funds provided to client from date of drawing to maturity date of the invoice.

(ii) *Recourse Factoring:* Under this factoring, all the facilities of full factoring except that of credit protection are available to the client. Thus the factor assumes no credit risks. Hence, it may not approve customers or fix credit limits. It acts merely as a collection agent of the supplier besides providing finance and maintaining sales ledger. Accordingly, Factor's charges are limited to charges for sales ledger administration and debt collection and interest on finance provided. If the trade-debts are not realised within the agreed period, the corresponding invoice is assigned back to the client.

A concept in recourse factoring is 'Refactoring Charges.' It is akin to the original factoring charges levied on all trade debts, outstanding beyond 60-90 days after due date. This situation arises when the client requests the Factor not to reassign the invoices and to continue recovery efforts, including legal proceedings. Of course, the entire cost of such recovery measures is borne by the client.

(iii) *Maturity Factoring:* This is also called 'Collection Factoring.' The Factor administers clients' sales ledger and renders debt collection service. The Factor provides administrative services. There is no 'client risk' to the factor. No financing is done ab initio. Hence no drawing limit is made available. The amount of each invoice is made out to the client at the end of credit term or on the agreed maturity date, after recovering factoring charges. This maturity date is decided upon at the commencement of the factoring agreement with reference to the average time taken by the client to collect a debt. This maturity date bears no relation to the date on which the debt is actually due for payment as it is an 'estimated date of collection.'

Maturity factoring could also be without recourse or with recourse. Under without recourse maturity factoring, the Factor, irrespective of its collection, pays the client. If a customer becomes insolvent, the client can produce proof of insolvency and claim from the Factor. The Factor's fee will include charges for debt administration, premium for risk of default and interest on funds outlay. Under with recourse maturity factoring, the Factor will either pay the client on collection of invoice or on maturity date with recourse later on. Unlike the factoring charges under without recourse, here there will be no charge relating to premium for risk of debt-default.

(iv) *Credit Factoring:* It is also known as 'Invoice Discounting.' Under this arrangement, the Factor purchases all or selected invoices of its clients at a discount. The Factor neither maintains the sales ledger nor undertakes debt collection. It only provides finance. The client obtains liquidity by taking advance without having to commit itself to regular factoring services. The debtor (customer) is not aware that the seller (client) has availed factoring facility because there is no notice of assignment to him. Thus this is a type of undisclosed factoring or confidential factoring.

Thus the special features of such an undisclosed factoring are as follows:

❖ Debts are assigned to Factor but client maintains sales ledger. Customers are not notified of Factor's involvement.

❖ Of course, the Factor gets a copy of the invoice, which it accounts for and provides the client with either debt-default cover or finance or both, as desired.

❖ Debt collection is organised by the client who makes over payment of each invoice to the Factor, if advance has been received against such invoices.

❖ Factor maintains the age-wise analysis of debts of the client.

❖ Factor's charges vary with the range of service provided to client.

(v) *Bulk Factoring:* It is a kind of Invoice Discounting. Under this factoring, the Factor provides finance to the client only after notification to the debtors (customers) to make payment to the Factor.

The client himself undertakes sales ledger administration, credit control and collection of receivables. This arrangement runs on with-recourse basis.

(vi) *Agency Factoring:* Under this arrangement, the Factor provides prepayment facility and protection against bad debts. But the client carries out sales ledger administration, collection of receivables and credit control. Thus, it amounts to bulk factoring with additional facility of insurance against credit risk. Moreover, unlike bulk factoring, agency factoring operates on a without recourse basis.

Comparative Position: The above types of factoring show the range of factoring services offered and availed. These types are only illustrative and not exhaustive. There could be any variation of services. A comparative picture is given below.

Types of factoring	Types of Services				
	Sales Ledger Administration & Collection of Book Debts	Credit Control	Credit Protection or Risk Absorption	Finance	Advisory Services
Full factoring (without recourse)	✓	✓	✓	✓	✓
Recourse factoring	✓	✓	X	✓	✓
Maturity factoring	✓	✓	✓	X	✓
Credit factoring	X	X	X	✓ (without notification)	✓
Bulk factoring	X	X	X	✓ (without notification)	✓
Agency factoring	X	X	✓ (sometimes)	✓	✓

✓ P indicates availability and X indicates non-availability of facility

Comparison With Bill Finance

Both Bill Financing and Factoring provide finance by discounting receivables. But they differ in some aspects. Let us discuss their dissimilarities.

	Area	Bill Finance	Factoring
1.	Approach	Specific and limited to providing finance	Total service approach which, inter alia, includes sales ledge administration, collection of receivables, credit control, credit protection, finance and advisory services
2.	Mode of Lending	Advance is given against Bills of Exchange	Outright purchase of trade debt
3.	Registration of charges relating to company advances	Registration is compulsory except with case of documents against payment	There is no need of registration as the Factor is the owner of the debt
4.	Principles of Transaction	Bill by bill basis evaluation	Total (bulk financing) and is available against unpaid and trade generated invoices
5.	Existence of arrangement	Known to the drawee of the bill in all cases	It is unknown to the debtor (customer) only in cases of undisclosed or credit or invoice factoring

Contd...

6.	Treatment in Balance Sheet	On balance sheet item reflected in both sides of balance sheet of the client	In cases of without recourse factoring/full factoring, factoring finance is an off-balance sheet item
7.	Security	Generally additional security is provided	Purchase of debt is the consideration
8.	Misuse	Misuse of bill facility occurs. For example, prevalence of accommodation bill is one type of misuse	Factoring provides built-in checks to prevent and detect misuse

FACTORING IN INDIA

The Working Group on Money Market (1986), under the Chairmanship of N Vaghul, recommended the introduction of factoring services in India to solve the financial problems of small-scale enterprises, arising out of delayed realisation of their receivables. The Sukhamoy Chakravarti Committee also, inter alia, had highlighted the inadequacy of institutional credit against high percentage of Open Account Sales of the small and medium scale enterprises. In 1988, the Reserve Bank of India, set up a Study Group under the Chairmanship of C S Kalyansundaram to examine the scope and need of factoring in India.

Kalyansundaram Committee

The Committee submitted its report in November 1989. The main recommendations/observations of the Committee are as follows:

♦ Factoring service has relevance in India.

♦ Factoring can play a complementary role to the existing bill financing system.

♦ With considerable expertise in bill financing and with large network of branches, the commercial banks have a distinct advantage in setting up factoring services subsidiaries. Four or five such subsidiaries could be floated by banks.

♦ There should be linkage between banks and factors to avoid double financing against some current asset.

♦ SSI units need factoring, especially finance and credit protection services of factors.

♦ Factors need to have fund raising windows like rediscounting, lines of concessional credit from banks etc.

♦ Export factoring should be started concurrently with the domestic factoring.

♦ Comprehensive legal framework should be developed to encourage factoring. Factored invoices should be treated on par with other negotiable instruments for initiating legal proceedings.

Accepting the Kalyansundaram Committee's report, the RBI amended the Banking Regulation Act 1949 in July 1990. It directed that domestic factoring could be undertaken by banks through specialized subsidiaries.

Initially, the RBI suggested setting up four factoring subsidiaries on a zonal basis. In line were the four banks ready to provide factoring services, which were the State Bank of India in Western Region, Canara Bank in the Southern Region, Punjab National Bank in the Northern Region and Allahabad Bank in the Eastern Region. The honour of initiating factoring in India goes to the State Bank of India when it set up on February 26, 1991, in collaboration with the Small Industries Development Bank of India (SIDBI), Union Bank of India, State Bank of Saurashtra and State Bank of Indore, a new subsidiary called SBI Factors and Commercial Services Pvt. Ltd. (SBI

Factors) to serve industrial and commercial units in western region. In the South, Canbank Factors Ltd. was established by Canara Bank with SIDBI and Andhra Bank as co-promoters.

On representation by the SBI, the zonal restrictions were removed by the RBI in 1993, paving the way for these factoring companies to operate in centres outside their allotted zones. To provide further impetus to factoring, the RBI directed in February 1994 that banks could undertake factoring activity departmentally. The RBI also recommended certain other guidelines as follows:

♦ Since factoring services require special skills and adequate infrastructure, it should be undertaken only by certain select branches of banks.

♦ It is like loans and advances and should be assigned 100% risk weight for Capital Adequacy Purpose.

♦ The guidelines on Income Recognition, Asset Classification, Provisioning and Exposure Norms as applicable to banks will also apply for factor financing.

♦ A bank's exposure through factor financing should not exceed 10% of its total advances.

♦ The Factor financing should not result in double-financing client's receivables.

♦ Banks and Factors should exchange information on the client. Factors/Departments doing factoring services should intimate the bank extending working capital facility about the factoring limit of the client. Banks should issue letter of disclaimer to the Factor on book debts factored to facilitate assignment of debt. The Factor, in turn, should route the proceeds through the banks.

♦ For the purpose of propagation of bill culture, it may be restricted to receivable finance availed from banks and factor finance may be excluded from the ambit of Credit Monitoring Arrangement.

However, departmental factoring is yet to take off.

APPRAISAL TECHNIQUE

Appraisal of factoring proposal is more complicated than normal bank lending. It is because in the latter only the client's (seller's) risk is appraised whereas in the former the debtor's (buyer's) risk also needs to be assessed. It is necessary to assess debtor-risk to approve debtor-wise limits. The edifice of sound factoring decision comprises the following:

♦ Financial, operational and managerial competence of the client along with his ability to assign valid debts.

♦ Collectability of debts i.e. strength of the customers.

♦ Continued profitability of the client's business.

Moreover, unlike normal bank lending, the limits for factoring are fixed on the basis of turnover figures of the client and not on the basis of current assets and liabilities position. Once a client's factoring limit is sanctioned, it is generally renewed when the sales position of his unit improves. Hence, factoring is also known as sales finance. Let us discuss the basic issues involved in the appraisal of a factoring.

Appraisal of Risk

The basic objective of assessment of both client's and debtor's risk is to evaluate the strength and weakness of the parties.

Client's Risk: The major business policy relating to client's risk are as follows

(a) *Organisation of the client:* A Factor may accept only partnership firm and companies with sound financial position.

(b) *Client's line of business:* A Factor may stipulate the lines of business, say manufacturing, trading etc. as eligible for factoring as the factor may not be in a position to assess risk in all activates.

(c) *Client's standing:* A minimum period of standing in the line of business may be stipulated.

(d) *Minimum Turnover:* This is fixed to discourage unviable business proportion.

(e) *Credit Period:* Factoring being receivable financing, a credit period of about three months may be fixed so that the factor is not saddled with obsolete debt.

(f) *Quantum of client's limit:* The Factor may fix minimum limit, to discourage uneconomical proposals. Similarly, maximum limit is fixed to limit exposure and risk.

(g) *Client's margin:* This is stipulated to ensure the client's stake in the business. Depending upon the Factor's perception, 10% to 20% margin may be fixed. Even nil margins may be allowed in some transaction.

(h) *Credit opinion on client:* The factor seeks opinion from client's banker to form his assessment.

(i) *Survey:* The factor also studies the managerial competence, financial compatibility, credit control mechanism, condition of sale, existence of any onerous conditions relating to title and assignment, credit management practices, efficiency of management, general functional aspects etc. to form a bankable opinion on the client.

(j) *Rating of client:* A Factor generally rates his clients against major parameters like financial soundness, operational issues, customer base, potential, value of the account to the Factor's business etc.

(k) *Factorability:* A Factor may decide the client's business as non-factorable on the following counts to limit his risk exposure.

❖ High concentration on a few debtors

❖ Large number of small products of various types for sale to general public

❖ 'Big' list of debtors for small-value

❖ Having high percentage of bad debts or disputed cases

❖ With business of fluctuating fortunes

❖ Having 'made to order' specialised/capital goods

❖ Having high Debt Turn Around (DTA)

❖ Having customers of client who refuse to accept letters of assignment of the Factor

❖ Sale on approval basis or consignment basis

❖ Sale of goods/services to allied concerns or group companies

l. *Analysis of Financial Statements:* The factor analyses the financial data of the client based on the last two years' audited balance sheets and Profit & Loss a/c, current year's projection and next two years' estimation. The following major ratios are calculated for a trend and comparative analysis.

❖ Current Ratio: $\dfrac{\text{Current Assets}}{\text{Current Liabilities}}$ (Ideal Ratio 1.33: 1)

❖ Liquid Ratio: $\dfrac{\text{Current Assets} - \text{Stock}}{\text{Current Liabilities}}$ (Ideal Minimum Ratio 1:1)

❖ Debt Equity Ratio: $\dfrac{\text{Long Term Debt}}{\text{Tangible Networth}}$

(Ideally not more than 2 : 1 for SSI units and 1.5 : 1 for other units)

❖ Borrowing Ratio: $\dfrac{\text{Total Borrowings}}{\text{Tangible Net worth}}$ (Factor may limit it to 3 times)

❖ Debt Service Coverage Ratio: $\dfrac{\text{Profit After Tax + Depreciation + Interest}}{\text{Principal Instalments + Interest}}$

(A minimum DSCR of 1.5 may be stipulated)

❖ Debtors' Turnover Ratio: $\dfrac{\text{Sundry Debtors}}{\text{Annual Credit Sales}} \times 360$

❖ Profit (Gross/Operating/Net) Ratio: $\dfrac{\text{Profit(Gross/Operating/Net)}}{\text{Net Sales}} \times 100$

The various profit ratios and debtor's turnover ratio should be compared with industry averages to draw a comparative picture.

(m) *Other aspects:* The following aspects are also considered.

❖ Clients should co-operate to realise payment

❖ Letter of disclaimer from client's banker is obtained

❖ Assignment note should be pre-printed in client's invoices

❖ Personal guarantee of the parties or third party guarantee should be available, if required.

Debtor's Risk: In a with-recourse factoring, the debtor's risk is limited and it is absolute in a without recourse one. However, the debtor's risk can also be assessed in line with client's risk as discussed above.

EVALUATION OF FACTORING PROPOSAL

While evaluating a factoring proposal, it is kept in mind that factoring is a high risk and unsecured business. Hence, it calls for high degree of professional skill and diligence. The assessment and fixation of limit may vary from client to client depending upon various factors and prevailing guidelines.

(a) In cases where the clients do not enjoy any working capital finance from bank, the Factor may adopt the following:

Projected Annual Factorable Turnover _____   T

Accepted Debt Turn Around Period (in months) _____   P

Retention Margin (%)' _____   M

(i) Debts Purchased Limit: $\dfrac{T \times P}{12}$

(ii) Prepayment Limit: $\dfrac{TP}{12} \times \dfrac{(1-M)}{100}$

(b) In case where the clients enjoy working capital finance from bank, the following procedures may be followed.

The prepayment limit may be calculated as above. Thereafter, the permissible limit may be arrived as under.

1. If the client's working capital requirement is less than Rs.2 crores, permissible finance from all sources (banking system) will be 20% of the projected and accepted sales turnover. Of

course, the client has to bring 5% of such sales turnover as net working capital (i.e. current assets minus current liabilities).

2. If the client's working capital requirement is more than Rs.2 crores, the Factor generally goes with the assessment, made by the working capital financing bank(s) and carves out repayment.

3. In respect of non-industrial (say trading) sector, the eligible prepayment limit may be calculated as in (a) above or three times the tangible net worth of the client, whichever is lower.

Within the sanctioned limit calculated as above, the drawing limit is arrived as under:

Gross Value of the approved invoices ....

Less Margin Stipulated ....

....

Drawing Limit ....

Less service charges and the outstanding funds in use ....

....

Available fund for withdrawal ....

ADMINISTRATION OF FACTORING

The steps in administration of factoring at operational level are as follows:

(i) Application (ii) Credit Appraisal (iii) Decision (iv) Documentation (v) Disbursement (vi) Recovery of charges (vii) Accounting & Collection (viii) Monitoring and follow-up (ix) Reporting.

Documentation: Once a factor decides to finance a client, based upon the credit appraisal, documentation is done keeping the legal issues in mind. The legal issues relating to factoring fall within the ambit of statutes like Indian Contract Act, Indian Sale of Goods Act, Transfer of Property Act etc., as no specific law for factoring exists. The rights of a Factor, being the assignee of the debts, are governed by the Transfer of Property Act. His charge of assignment on the client's debt, is the 'actionable claim' as per Section 3 of this Act which reads as under:

"Actionable Claim means a claim to any debt, other than a debt secured by mortgage of immovable property or by hypothecation or pledge of immovable property, or to any beneficial interest in movable property not in the possession, either actual or constructive, of the claimant, which the Civil Courts recognize as affording grounds for relief, whether such debt or beneficial interest be existent, accruing, conditional or contingent."

An illustrative list of documents obtained for a with-recourse factoring facility is as follows:

(i) Factor's sanction letter duly acknowledged by the client.

(ii) Letter of disclaimer from client's lending banker

(iii) Factoring Agreement

(iv) Prepayment Facility Agreement

(v) Duly notarised Power of Attorney

(vi) Personal/Corporate guarantee letter

(i) Client's Constitution-specific documents such as Partnership Deed for Partnership firm, Articles of Association & Memorandum of Association ? In case of limited companies etc.

Documents need to be stamped as per Indian Stamp Act, 1899 and the Stamp Acts of respective states, wherever applicable.

Disbursement: Pre-payments against invoices factored are made by the Factor by cheques through the client's account with the bank that has extended working capital finance, offering the latter automatic control.

Charges: The Factor's charges may include (i) service charge (ii) discount charge and (iii) other charges.

(i) *Service charge:* This is levied towards provision of various services such as sales ledger administration, credit control including processing, operational overhead cost, providing protection against bad debt etc. Service charges are normally based on certain projected sales figures submitted by client and accepted by the Factor, which are reviewed periodically. Service charge is generally calculated as a percentage of invoice value and collected at the time of acceptance of invoice for factoring. It is recovered to the debit of prepayment account of the client. The basic principle of service is that it should be sufficient to cover the factor's establishment cost, possible bad debt and contribute a portion towards profit. A minimum service charge per invoice may be stipulated. Factors generally charge 0.25% to 1% of invoice value as service charge.

(ii) *Discount charge:* It is charged towards providing instant credit to client. It is arrived at depending upon Factor's cost of fund, anticipated return on Capital, competition from others, level of growth of business etc.

(iii) *Other charges:* These may include processing charge, reassignment charge etc. Processing charge may be calculated as a percentage of total pre-payment limit sanctioned, subject to a minimum stipulation. This is collected in advance whenever fresh limit/renewal/enhancement is accorded.

When factored bills are reassigned in favour of the client, a reassignment charge is levied. It indicates that the bills of the client drawn on the customer are not paid even after a reasonable time. Such transactions are not to be encouraged. So the reassignment charge is intended to act as a disincentive for client to refrain from drawing bills whose readability is remote. In this case too, a minimum charge may be prescribed.

It is worthwhile to note that the Kalyansundaram Committee was of the opinion that Factor charges, apart from discount charges, in the range of 2% to 2.5% of the debts factored, towards service charges etc.

Accounting and Collection Procedures vary from Factor to Factor but the basic accounting standards are followed. When factoring is undertaken as a subsidiary, the subsidiary is treated as a Non-Banking Financial Company (NBFC). So all the regulatory guidelines of the RBI relating to Capital Adequacy, Income Recognition, Asset Classification, Provisioning, and Exposure Limits etc. as applicable to NBFCs are followed.

Monitoring and Follow-up: In the post-sanction stage, the Factor monitors the receivables to ensure payment on due dates. In the documentation stage, we have seen that the letter of disclaimer is obtained from the financing bank as a precondition for availing factoring facility. The following precautions are also observed.

1. All invoices should be drawn in round sum to facilitate easy computerised operation.

2. All invoices should be accompanied by Receipted Copy of Delivery Challan/Inspection Note/Customers' acknowledgement of receipt or Lorry Receipt/Railway Receipt/Postal Courier Receipt/Airway Bill etc.

3. Where goods are excisable, the invoice should be sent along with prescribed gate pass.

4. Invoice should contain assignment notice printed on the face of it.

5. Factor's charge is stated by way of assignment.

Reminders are sent to debtors and clients for overdue and sticky debts.

Reporting: Development of computer-based programmes to follow up the debts is a prerequisite for the success of a Factor. The Factor must have a well-developed Management Information System (MIS). Through such computerized data base, it should be able to generate information not only to facilitate decision-making by the management, but also to report to the client and debtor periodically about the collection and outstanding. The reports to clients may include:

♦ Daily report on transactions entered and funds-in-use

♦ Statement of charges as and when recovered

♦ Monthly statements on debts purchased, prepayment a/c, age-wise analysis of outstanding debts, sticky debt report etc.

The report to debtors may include monthly statement of invoices purchased, realized and outstanding. This will act as reminders and enable the debtor to plan and pay promptly.

Benefits, Limitations And Constraints

There are certain intrinsic benefits accruing under factoring which have increased its popularity.

Benefits

1. *Improvement in liquidity:* Factoring provides additional source of funding the receivables which eliminates the uncertainty in realizing receivables. The immediate availability of cash reduces the operating cycle and increases the turnover. This improves client's performance greatly.

2. *Technical advantage:* Apart from the financial aspects, the technical advantage of the factoring is that the client receives guidance on credit decisions, examination of creditworthiness of the customers, selection of accounts receivables; feedback data on regional developments, turnover of the client; information regarding product design/mix, prices, market conditions, general economic prospect etc.

3. *Savings in cost and time:* Factoring has a cost and time saving effect on the operation of the client as it relieves him of the responsibility of maintaining a credit department, book-keeping, servicing the receivables, demand and collection of the same etc. All these activities are taken over by the Factor at about 2% higher than bank charges. This additional cost is more than compensated by the reduction in expenditure effected in sales administration and debt collection. The client can concentrate more on planning, production and sales.

4. *Improves profitability:* Factoring improves profitability of the client by avoiding the risk of bad debts. It ensures perfect debt turnaround, which is very rare in business.

5. *Better purchase/sale terms:* With the availability of advance against receivables, the client can make cash purchase of his inputs. He can negotiate better prices for such inputs. The client can offer finer terms to his customers. His customers may avail credit facility. So he need not offer trade discount for early payment. Thus, factoring facilitates flow of inputs one side and the market prospect improves on the other.

6. *Flexibility:* Factoring provides flexibility to the client as he can draw continuously against receivables - overdraw during peak periods, receive interest on undrawn balances etc.

7. *Improves leverage:* With the release of funds under operating assets, the client can invest more in fixed assets. This increases his degree of operating leverage. Factoring is beneficial especially for those companies facing liquidity problems due to expansion, diversification, necessity of offering longer credit, rising input prices etc. It is most suitable for small-scale enterprises.

8. ***Encourages bill culture:*** Factoring helps in systemising trade credit. Though the RBI has been trying to encourage the bill market in India, it has not been very popular. Factoring encourages clients and customers to transact their business through invoicing.

9. ***A useful alternative method of finance:*** Factoring is useful to the client in ascertaining the payment performance of the customers. This helps in cash management for the clients. It also helps in ascertaining the percentage share of each customer in the client's total turnover. Factoring is also useful in ascertaining the location-wise concentration of debts and the labour cost of business.

10. ***Operationally easy:*** The client need not register his debt under Section 125 of the Companies Act, 1956. Thus it is operationally easy - compared to traditional borrowing from banks.

Limitations

(i) ***May not be attractive:*** Companies with established credit procedures and continuing contracts with their bankers, may not find factoring so attractive to switch over from the traditional method of assigning the receivables to selling the receivables.

(ii) ***Restricted coverage:*** Sound corporate bodies operating in a sellers' market, where credit for payment of receivables is ruled out, will not need factoring. On the other hand, in a buyers' market, where sellers have to offer long credit, it may be difficult for factors to enforce financial discipline. Thus the coverage of factoring may be restricted.

(iii) ***Sign of financial weakness:*** Resorting to factoring is, sometimes, viewed as a sign of weakness of the client indicating at his liquidity problems. For this reason, some companies prefer undisclosed factoring.

(iv) ***Too costly:*** Companies may find factoring too costly when compared to other methods of receivable financing. Though it is theoretically said that cost of factoring compares well with the cost of bad debts, collection and credit costs, interest charged on finance availed etc., factoring cost may prove burdensome because the Factor purchases only good debts and client may have to maintain bad debts. The position of client in a with-recourse factoring is also similar.

(v) ***Constraints:*** To encourage factoring in India, it is necessary to remove the constraints. The Kalyansundaram Committee also raised some of these issues.

INTERNATIONAL FACTORING

Factoring operations can be broadly classified into two categories i.e., domestic factoring and international factoring. When both the seller and buyer are in the same country, it is called domestic factoring, which we have already discussed. International factoring is also called cross-border factoring or export factoring. Such factoring involves exporters, importers and their Factors located in different countries. Unlike forfeiting, export factoring deals with short-term export receivables. It is intended to boost exports under open account sales terms.

Export factoring is preferred to LC-based export because the latter is costly and involves examination of export documents applying 'Doctrine of Strict Compliance'. All these make such transactions less flexible. Moreover, LC is transaction-oriented and not ideal for repetitive transactions where fast delivery schedules are insisted. Export factoring is best suited to a regular pattern of trading amongst buyers and sellers of goods/services. 'Open Account Sales' terms facilitate faster and regular despatch of goods/services necessitating lesser dependence on working capital financing and lines of credit. The principal types of international factoring are:

1. Two Factor System

2. Single Factoring System

3.   Direct Export Factoring, and

4.   Direct Import Factoring

Two Factor System: This system involves four parties viz., exporter, exporter's Factor in exporting country, importer and importer's Factor in importing country. The exporter's Factor provides prepayment but the importer's Factor undertakes bookkeeping and collection of debt. The latter also undertakes to pay to his counterpart as per prior agreement, if the importer does not pay within the agreed credit period.

Single Factoring System: Under this system, as per the special agreement between the exporter's and importer's Factors, the importer's Factor provides credit protection in case of debt-default by importer. But prepayment, bookkeeping and collection responsibilities primarily vest with the exporter's factor. In case of difficulties in realization of debt, the importer's Factor is required to ensure recovery including initiation of legal proceedings. The cost of such recovery efforts is borne by exporter's Factor. If the debt still remains outstanding, the importer's Factor reimburses the exporter's Factor as per the agreement. Here the factoring charges are lower than that of the Two Factor System.

Direct Export Factoring: Under this system, the importer's Factor is not involved. The exporter's Factor provides all elements of factoring service. It is less expensive. But it calls for a high degree of professional skill and knowledge about the systems, procedures, cultures and languages of different countries, on the part of export factor.

Direct Import Factoring: Under this system, the exporter's Factor is not involved. Under a factoring agreement between exporter and the importer's Factor, the invoices representing the shipped goods are assigned to the latter. The importer's factor undertakes sales ledger administration, collection of debts, providing bad debt protection up to an agreed level and consultancy. It is cheaper, but lack of proximity between the exporter and importer's Factor is the disadvantage.

To assist international factoring, Factors Chain International (FCI) has developed Edifactoring i.e. a special communication system to be used by its member Factors. EDI stands for Electronic Data Interchange between computers and speeds up business communication effectively. Sellers and debtors exchange their communication (Purchase Order, Invoice, Payment and remittance etc.) by standard EDIFACT message. EDIFACT is a full communication language, officially adopted by United Nations Organisations, facilitating paperless trading as in the case of use of SWIFT (Society for Worldwide Interbank Financial Transaction) message in banks. The members of FCI can beneficially sublet the system for direct client EDIFACToring for domestic and/or international factoring to capitalize in communications efficiency.

FINANCING OF PERMANENT OR LONG TERM WORKING CAPITAL

Permanent working capital or fixed working capital is that working capital required to maintain the minimum sales. As we have read that networking capital means a part of current assets that should be financed by long-term sources of finance. The following are the sources of long-term working capital or long-term sources of finance.

INTERNAL FINANCING SOURCES

As we have classified source of finance as internal and external, which is based on the generation of finance source. A new company can raise the required long-term funds from external sources, but an undertaking, which is well established, can generate funds not only from external sources but also from internal sources. Internal source of finance is available only for firms that are existing and well established.

The internal sources of finance are:

A. Retained earnings/ploughing back of profits, and

B. Depreciation charges.

The following discussion gives clear view about the internal sources of finance.

A. Retained Earnings/Ploughing Back of Profits

Retained earnings is an important source of internal financing of well-established companies. Retained earnings are the portion of earnings available to equity shareholders, which are ploughed back in the company. In other words, a part of earnings available to equity shareholders that are retained for future investment. Accumulation of profits by a firm for financing developmental programmes. Hence, the process of accumulating company profits regularly and their utilisation in the business is known as retained earnings or ploughing back of profits or internal financing or self-investment. Retained earnings are part of equity, since they are part of equity, which are sacrificed by equity shareholders. In this source of finance companies, generally retained or ploughed back about 20 per cent to 70 per cent of earnings available to equity shareholders for the purpose of financing of the growth of the company. This becomes a main source of long-term finance, when the management capitalizes profits. It is known as capitalization of profits or issue of bonus shares.

Retained earnings may be used for expansion programmes of company, replacement of obsolete assets, modernisation of plant and equipment, redemption of preference shares or debentures, loans etc.

FACTORS INFLUENCING RETAINED EARNINGS

As we have read that use of internal funds as a source of finance is only for well-established companies. Retained earnings are influenced by a number of factors:

1) *Earnings Capacity of a Company:* Ploughing back of profits arise only when the company have sufficient (profits) earnings. Larger the earnings, larger the ploughing back of profits. It can be supported by Psychological Law of Consumption given by Keynes who is a famous economist.

2) *Types of Dividend Policy:* Ploughing back of profits depends on the dividend policy of a firm. In other words, a retained earning depends on the dividend policy adopted by the top management (BOD's) with regards to distribution of earnings. A company, which intended to retain more earnings, needs to follow conservative dividend policy. The retained earnings policy is also affected by the expectation of shareholders. When there is more percentage of shareholders who are in high income tax bracket, expects to retain profits. On the other hand, where the shareholders who are depend on regular income, expects more dividends, i.e., less retained earnings.

3) *Taxation Policy of the Government:* Earnings available to shareholders are the profit after taxes minus preference shareholders dividend. When there is high tax rate less profit after tax and less retained earnings and vice versa.

4) *Profitable Investment Opportunities:* A firm that has more profitable investment opportunities feels to retain profits for financing of that investment and vice versa.

5) *Other Factors:* Apart from the above-discussed factors, the following will also affect retained earnings.

   ❖ Top management attitude and philosophy

   ❖ Custom of the industry

❖   Economic and social environment of the country (Prevailing)

❖   Industry life cycle, etc.

Advantages/Merits of Retained Earnings

The advantages of retained earnings may be studied under three view points:

(a)   Advantages/Merits to Company

❖   Firm can raise funds easily, since there are no obligations involved with shareholders.

❖   It is less costly, when compared to other sources of long-term finance (equity shares, preference shares, and debentures), since it does not involve flotation cost.

❖   It increases credit worthiness of the company because retained earnings increases owners' equity.

❖   No dilution of control, when a company depends on retained earnings.

❖   It helps to maintain stable dividend policy in the year of less or no profits, the company can use to retain earnings to pay uniform dividend.

❖   It helps in improving efficiency, by the use of retained earnings to replace the depletion and obsolescence assets.

❖   It enables to redeem long-term liabilities such as debentures, long-term loans, preference shares, which involve a fixed cost.

❖   It acts as a cushion to absorb hazards refers to the down in the trade cycle (depression, recession, declining).

(b)   Advantages/Merits to Shareholders/Owners

❖   *It increases in the value of shares* in the long-run of stable dividend policy, improvement of efficiency, credit worthiness etc..

❖   *Increase in the collateral value of shares,* since the value of share price increased and it is accepted by the lenders as collateral security.

❖   *It enhances (earnings) dividends,* when the retained earnings are invested in profitable investment avenues.

❖   *It reduces income tax burden,* which is needed to be paid if dividends are declared.

(c)   Advantages/Merits to the Society/Nation

❖   *It increases the rate of capital formation,* which indirectly helps to promote economic development of the nation.

❖   *It stimulates industrialization,* by internal financing.

❖   *It provides employment,* by establishment of more industries (profitable investment avenues).

❖   *It helps to increase productivity,* since retained earnings used for modernization, replacement of old machineries and formulation of new companies, which help to utilize the scarcely available resources optimally.

❖   *It improves standard of living* by providing employment, efficient use of scarce resources, increase in productivity, producing good quality products at reasonable prices.

Disadvantages/Demerits of Retained Earnings

The following are the important disadvantages of retained earnings:

◆   *Limited funds available* by way of retained earnings.

- Continuous retention of profits may *lead to over capitalization.*

- *Creation of monopolies*, since retained earnings in bigger organisations helps to grow bigger which may lead to the monopoly.

- *Loss to shareholders*, when a firm pays less dividends or no dividends due to retained earnings, shareholders may sell their shares for meeting their expenditure.

- *The management may misuse the retained earnings*, which is not helpful to maximize shareholders wealth.

- *The cost of retained earnings is high*, retained earnings are the dividends foregone by ordinary shareholders, which involve an opportunity cost.

- Retained earnings leads to evasion of super profit tax, which is the revenue loss to the Government.

B. Depreciation Charges

Depreciation is the distribution cost or the basic value of tangible capital assets, over the estimated useful life of the asset in a systematic and rational manner. In other words, depreciation is the allocation of capital expenditure to various periods over which the capital expenditure is expected to benefit the company. For example, a machinery costing Rs. 1,00,000, has 5 years life period with no scrap value. If the machine is depreciated based on straight line method of depreciation, the depreciation charge for a year is Rs. 20,000 (Rs. 1,00,000 / 5), which is shown in profit & loss account debt side and it reduces profit by Rs. 20,000. But it is only book entry and not cash outflow. It is out of pocket cost. There is a lot of debate among academicians and business executives regarding the treatment of depreciation as source of finance. What ever may be the arguments either for or against, but one thing is clear that it is a out of pocket cost or non-cash item of expense. Hence, it is considered as a internal source of finance.

EXTERNAL FINANCING SOURCES

A. Share Capital

Meaning of Share

A share is a small unit of capital of a company. In other words, share capital of a company (planned to raise) divided into number of equal parts that known is share. Section 2 (46) of the Companies Act, 1956, defines share as, "a share in the share capital of a company and includes stock, except when a distinction between stock and share is expressed or implied". It is a legal definition of share. Stock and share have different meanings. According to Section 94 (i)(c) of the Companies Act, 1956 stock means, a share, which is fully paid up. Lord Justic James Lindley gives a good definition, as "A share is that proportionate part of capital to which a member is entitled."[1] For example, XYZ company has share capital of Rs. 1,00,000, of Rs. 10 each. Then the capital is divided into 10,000 shares (i.e., Rs.1,00,000 / Rs.10). Shareholder is a person who buys one or more shares in the company.

Kinds of Shares

In our country Companies used to raise funds (before Companies Act, 1956) by issue of three types of shares, i.e., preference shares, equity (ordinary) shares, and deferred shares. But the Companies Act has limited the type of shares into two - preference shares, and equity (ordinary) shares.

EQUITY SHARES

Equity means 'equal'. Equity share is a share that gives equal right to holders. Equity shareholders have to share the reward and risk associated with ownership of company. For example, ABC Company has 10,000 equity shareholders and it has earned Rs. 10,000 profit last year and assume it may earn a loss of Rs. 10,000 in the next year. Here, the shareholder will get Re. 1 as profit from last year and Re. 1 loss in the coming year's loss. It is also called as ordinary share capital. Equity shareholders are the owners of the company, who have control over the working of the company. They are paid dividend at the rate recommended by Board of Directors (BoDs). The dividend rate depends on the profits, more profits more dividends and vice versa. If there are no profits, no dividends will be payable. But some companies pays dividends even if the company has no profits to maintain dividends stability. The amount required to pay dividends will be transferred from general reserve account. The equity shareholders take more risk when compared to preference shareholders.

Features of Equity Stock

The following are the features of equity stock:

♦ *Permanent Capital:* An equity source is the main long-term or permanent source of finance. They can be redeemed or refunded only at the time of liquidation that too from the residue left after meeting all the obligations. In other words, there is no agreement between equity shareholders and the company with regard to refund of capital. Shareholders cannot sell shares to company, but he / she can sell shares in the stock market to others, if he/she wants to get back his / her money. Hence, it is permanent source of finance for company.

♦ *Residual Claim to Income:* Equity shareholders have a residual claim to the income of a company. Residual claim means the income leftover after paying all outsider claims. The residual income is also known as earnings available to equity shareholders, which is equal to profit after tax minus preference dividend. But the total residual income may or may not be paid as dividends, since the BoDs have the right to decide the portion of earnings available to shareholders that will be paid as dividends. Payment of dividend depends on retention or plough back of profits. For example, if the earnings available to equity shareholders are Rs. 1,00,000, and the BoDs decide to retain 50 per cent of them, then the remaining 50 per cent (i.e., Rs.50,000) is paid as dividends. There is no legal obligation to pay dividends even if residual income is available.

♦ *Residual Claim to Assets:* Equity shareholders have a residual claim on firm's assets. In an event of liquidation of a firm, the assets are used first to settle the claims of outside creditors and preference shareholders, if anything left that is equity shareholders residue. In other words, equity shareholders have last priority on assets, hence, their capital become cushion to absorb losses on liquidation.

♦ *Voting right/ Right to Control:* Equity shareholders as real owners of the company they have voting right, in appointing Directors and Auditors of the company, participate and vote in annual general meeting, which helps to control the company. BoDs have the control power of company, because the major decisions are take by BoDs. But in actual practice majority of individual shareholders never bother to utilize the voting right, since they are scattered and they are unorganized. So the control over the company is ineffective.

♦ *Pre-emptive Right:* Equity shareholders have pre-emptive right, which means they have legal right to buy new issues, before offering to the public. Section 81 of the Companies Act 1956, puts company under legal compulsion to offer new shares to the existing shareholders before offering to the public. The number of additional shares offered depends on the number of shares owned in relation to the total shares outstanding and on the issue new shares. For example, Mr. B owns four shares of a company having 200 shares of equity outstanding. Mr. B is entitled the pre-emptive right to buy 2 per cent [(4/200) 100 = 2 per cent] additional shares to be offered by the company. Pre-emptive right is the option given to the shareholders to buy a specified number of shares at a given price. The shareholder can exercise or sell in the market or leave the option partially or fully.

♦ *Limited Liability:* This is the prime feature of equity share. Although, equity shareholders are the owners of the company, their liability is limited to the extent of the investment in the share.

Advantages/Merits of Equity Shares

The advantages of equity shares can be discussed from the point of view of company and investors.

(a) Advantages/Merits to Company

* ❖ It is permanent long-term source of finance.
* ❖ There is no repayment liability.
* ❖ It does not create any obligation to pay dividend.
* ❖ This capital can be issued without creating any charge over assets of the company.
* ❖ Issue of equity share capital increases the credit worthiness of the company.

(b) Advantages / Merits to Investors

* ❖ Equity share provides more income (residual income).
* ❖ Equity shares gives right to participate in the control and management of the company.
* ❖ Capital appreciation (if share price increased when compared to purchase price).

Disadvantages/Demerits of Equity Shares

The advantages of equity shares can be discussed from the point of view of company and investors.

(a) Disadvantages/Demerits to Company

* ❖ High cost source of fund.
* ❖ Involves high flotation costs.
* ❖ Issue of additional shares dilutes control.
* ❖ No tax advantage (dividends are not tax deductible).
* ❖ It make capital structure rigid.

(b) Disadvantages/Demerits to Investors

* ❖ No guarantee, and regularity in receipt of dividend.
* ❖ No guarantee in receipt of principle amount of investment.
* ❖ Loss of capital due to fluctuations in share prices.

TYPES OF EQUITY SHARES

Sweet Equity Shares: The Companies (Amendment) Act of 1999, has inserted a new Section 79A that allows issue of Sweet Equity shares. Sweet equity share defined as, "equity shares issued at a discount or for consideration other than cash for providing know-how or making available rights in the nature of intellectual property rights or value additions by whatever name called". Issue of sweet equity by listed company should be according to SEBI guidelines. The issue should be authorized by a special resolution passed by the company in the general meeting, which specifies the number of shares, price, and consideration, if any. However, non-listed company can issue sweet equity in accordance with prescribed guidelines.

Par-value Shares: Unlike bonds, which always have a par value, equity stock may be sold with par value or without par value. Par value means the nominal value of a share in the Memorandum of Association (MOA) established for legal purpose. The par value decided by promoters of first - directors of company such may be issued at par, at premium, or at a discount price to the public.

No-par Value Shares: These types of shares are without par value. In this arrangement, MOA specifies the number of shares and not the price. They will be issued to the public at a stated price decided by the BoD's. Payment of dividend on this type of shares is so many rupees per share, i.e., Rs. 5 per share or Rs. 6 per share.

In India, Company Law does not allow Indian companies to issue no-par value of share. But in America and Canada, no-par value shares are more popular.

PREFERENCE SHARE CAPITAL

Preference share capital gives certain privileges to its holders on the equity shareholders. Preference shareholders have privileges in two ways:

a) A preferential privilege in payment of a fixed dividend. The fixed dividend may be in the form of fixed rate or fixed amount per share; and

b) Preferential right as to repayment of capital in case of liquidation / winding up of the company.

Preference share capital is a hybrid form of long-term finance, since it has the features of equity and debentures. *Preference share resembles equity in the following ways:*

a) Preference dividends are payable only after tax profits (PAT).

b) Payment of preference dividend depends on the discretion of BoD's, (it is not an obligatory payment).

c) Preference dividend is not a tax deductable payment.

d) Irredeemable preference shares are long-term in nature (they have no maturity date).

Preference share capital is similar to debenture capital in the following ways:

a) It carries a fixed rate of dividend.

b) It has prior claim on assets like debenture capital,

c) It normally does not have voting rights.

d) It is redeemable in nature (if it is redeemable preference share).

e) It does not have right to share residual profits/ assets.

Features of Preference Shares

The features of preference share/ capital are as follows:

♦ *Claim on Assets:* Companies does not create any charge on assets while issue of preference shares, still preference shareholders have prior claim on assets of the company in the event of liquidation. It means before payment of ordinary shareholders, the preference shareholders are paid.

♦ *Claim on Income:* Not only the prior claim on assets at the time of liquidation, they also have prior claim on income or profits. Preference dividend must be paid in full before payment of any dividend on the equity share capital. As preference share capital lies between debenture capital and equity share capital with regards to claim on assets and income of the company. Hence, it is called as "senior security".

♦ **Accumulation of Dividend:** Most of the preference shares dividend is cumulative. It means that all the unpaid / arrears dividends are carried forward for the next year and paid with the current years dividend before payment of any dividend to equity shareholders. For example, company A issues 10 per cent preference shares of Rs. 100 each, in the beginning of the financial year. The company needs to pay Rs. 10 as dividend but due to loss it was not able to pay, in this case the Rs. 10 is carried to the next year. If there are any profits in next year the company has to pay last years dividend and the current year's dividend. Thereby the total dividend is Rs.20.

♦ **Redeemable:** Preference share capital has limited maturity period (if issued as redeemable) after that the share capital has to be refunded. It provides flexibility in capital structure, which is beneficial to the company.

♦ **Fixed Rate of Dividend:** Issue of preference shares are at a fixed rate of dividend. The rate is at par value basis. It helps the management to avoid the provision of equal participation in earnings. The fixed dividend rate may be lower when compared to ordinary shareholders dividend. Hence, it helps the company to maximize equity shareholders wealth. But there is no legal obligation and failure to pay will not force bankruptcy.

♦ **Convertible:** Convertible preference shares capital has the feature of conversion of preference shareholders investment into fully or partly paid equity shares at a pre-determined ratio within a given / specified period. In India, we have a preference share that has convertibility and cumulative features but so far no company has issued.

♦ **Participation in Surplus Profits:** Sometimes preference share capital is in the nature of participation in surplus profits. Here, surplus profits means the amount of profits left out after payment of a fixed / stable rate of dividend to equity shareholders. Same case preference shareholders participate in surplus assets in the event of liquidation. Share of surplus assets arises only when the company goes to liquidation by court order (when assets value is greater than the liabilities value) to protect public interest.

♦ **Voting Rights:** Generally preference shareholders do not have voting rights, so they can not control working of company, but Section 97 of the Companies Act, 1956, entitled to vote on a resolution that directly affects the rights to be attached to their preference shares.

Advantages/Merits of Preference Shares

The advantages of preference shares can be studied under two heads, they are companies and investors.

(a) Advantages/Merits to Company

- There is no legal obligation to pay preference dividend.
- There is no share in control of the company through participation in voting.
- They provide flexibility in capital structure by issue of redeemable preference shares.
- It enhances credit worthiness, because preference share capital is generally treated as a part of net worth.
- Preference shares provide long-term capital for the company.
- Mortgageable assets are conserved, due to the issue of preference share capital without pledging assets.

(b) Advantages/Merits to Investors

- Stable rate of preference dividend.

- Prior claim on assets.
- Less risk when compared to equity shareholders.

Disadvantages/Demerits of Preference Shares

The disadvantages of preference shares can be studied under two heads, they are companies and investors.

(a)   Disadvantages/Demerits to Company

- Tax disadvantage, because preference dividend is not a tax deductible, which makes preference share capital as costly source of finance.
- Adverse effect on creditworthiness, if the company avoids payment of dividend.
- Permanent burden of payment of dividends, if the preference shares are cumulative in nature.

(b)   Disadvantages/Demerits to Investors

- Limited return, as preference shareholders do not have voting rights, their return depends on managerial decision, which is arbitrary, and shareholders cannot force management to pay more dividends.
- The rate of preference dividend is generally less than the rate of dividend on equity shares.
- The market prices of preference shares fluctuate more when compared to debentures

CLASSIFICATION OF PREFERENCE SHARES

Preference shares are may be of several types:

1.   *Cumulative Preference Shares:* Cumulative preference shares are those shares on, which the amount of dividend payable goes on accumulating until it is fully paid. If the full dividend or partial dividend can not be paid in any year (due to less profits), the same can be paid out of future profits. Even if the company is not able to pay the last year's dividend in the next year, the same is cumulated for the future period till the full payment. Preference shares are generally cumulative unless otherwise expressly stated in the Articles of Association or if there are terms of the issue of those shares.

2.   *Non-Cumulative Preference Shares:* Non-cumulative preference shares are those shares on which the unpaid dividend does not cumulate to the next year's dividend. It means in any year, the company fails to earn profit to pay fixed dividend for that year, the preference shareholders cannot ask (or cumulate) from the next years' profit. Thus it is the right to claim unpaid dividends will lapse.

3.   *Redeemable Preference Shares:* Redeemable preference shares are those shares, which can be redeemed or repaid to the holders after a lapse of the stipulated period, which is stated while issue of such a share. A company limited by a share may redeem, if articles permit.

4.   *Irredeemable Preference Shares or Perpetual Shares:* Perpetual preference shares that are not repayable and redeemable only at the time of liquation. These shares are also called perennial shares.

5.   *Participatory Preference Shares:* These are the shares that enjoy the right to participate in surplus profit that are left out after payment of a fixed rate of dividend to equity shareholders. This is the additional return apart from getting a fixed rate of preference dividend. Not only share in surplus profits, they may also participate in surplus assets of the firm at the time of liquidation. Generally, preference shares are deemed to be non-

participatory, if there is no clear provision in Articles of Association or in the terms stated while issue of shares.

6. *Non-participatory Preference Shares:* The preference shares that have no claim in the surplus profit or assets of the firm are deemed to be non-participatory preference shares.

7. *Convertible Preference Shares:* Here convertible means into equity not into cash. The preference shares, which are having the right to convert their holdings into equity shares with a specific period, are known as convertible preference shares. Generally, preference shares are non-convertible in nature unless otherwise stated in Articles of Association or in the terms of issue of the shares.

8. *Non-convertible Preference Shares:* The preference shares that do not enjoy the option of converting their holdings into equity are known as non-convertible preference shares.

The above discussed are some of the types of preference shares.

CREDITORSHIP SECURITIES

Creditorship securities are those securities, which are issued to creditors for raising finance. The securities are debentures/bonds. The amount of raised by issue of debentures/bonds is known as debt capital. Debenture and bond capital is one of the cheapest sources of long-term finance. A debenture and bond is an acknowledgement given by the firm for having received a sum of amount as debt. Here, there is no need to understand the two terms debenture and bond. Debenture and bond, both are issued by a corporate concern to raise long-term capital, but there is a difference between them. The term bond refers a security that has secured by tangible fixed assets of a corporate, and debentures are not secured, (i.e., they are secured by credit worthiness of a corporate and not by assets). In US, the debt securities are called as bonds. In India and UK, the securities are called as debentures, and they are treated as synonym. According to the Companies Act 1956, the term debenture includes, "debenture stock, bonds and other securities of a corporate concern, whether contributing a charge on the assets of a corporate or not". Hence, in the following discussion, the two terms debenture and bond have been used interchangeably.

DEBENTURES/BONDS

Debenture/bonds are an important source of long-term finance. Raising of funds by issue of debentures/bonds is allowed to public limited Companies, if Memorandum of Association is (MoA) permitted.

Meaning of Debenture

The term 'Debenture' is derived from the Latin word 'debere', which means 'to be a debtor'. Companies Act of 1956 defines 'debenture' as including debenture stock, bonds and other security of a company, whether constituting a charge on the assets of the company or not. It is not clear or does not explain fully what is debenture. According to Naidu and Datta, "a debenture is an instrument issued by the company under its common seal acknowledging a debt and setting forth the terms under which they are issued and are to be paid". A person who buys debentures is debenture holder and creditor of the company. Debenture can be priced as the same manner as share. In other words, they can be issued at face (par) value, at premium or at a discount.

Features of Debentures

The features of debentures / bonds are as follows:

◆ *Fixed Rate of Interest:* In general the debentures are issued at a fixed rate of interest, but they may also issued at a floating rate of interest or a zero interest. The fixed rate debentures are more popular in India. The rate of interest is on face value of the debenture that will be paid out annually or semi-annually. The interest payable on debentures is tax deducible. Company is free to determine the interest rate, which may be fixed or floated.

◆ *Maturity:* The debenture capital is a cheapest source of long-term finance, but it should be repaid after a specific period. In other words, debentures are issued for a specific period (i.e., 10 years or 5 years debentures). The period in which the debentures are issued or the period after which the debenture capital is repaid is known as maturity period. The maturity period may vary between 1 year to 20 years. In India, non-convertible debentures are redeemed after 7-10 years.

◆ *Redemption:* Debentures can be repaid either in installment wise or lump sum. If it is repaid in one lump sum amount, it can be done by creation of debenture redemption reserve. It is compulsory for all debentures whose maturity period exceeds 18 months. Company should create dividend redemption reserve (DRR) equivalent to at least 50 per cent of the amount of issue before commencement of repayment.

◆ *Call and Put Option:* Debentures may have 'call' option, which gives the right to 'buy' to issuing company at a certain price before the maturity period. The buy back (call) price may be more than the face value of debenture generally 5 per cent, which is known as premium on redemption. Sometimes, debentures may also put an option, which gives a right to the debenture holder to seek redemption at specified times and at predecided prices.

◆ *Debenture Indenture:* A debenture indenture is a legal document, which specifies the rights of both the issuing company and the debenture holder. The debenture indenture includes descriptions of the amount and timing of the interest and principle amount payments (installments or lump sum), various standard and restrictive provisions, and frequently sinking fund requirements and security interest provisions. The indenture gives the responsibility to the trustee to protect the interest of debenture holders by fulfilling the above stated descriptions.

◆ *Security Interest:* Debenture may be either secured or insecured. In India most of the debenture are secured debentures. A secured debenture is a debenture which is secured by a charge on the company's immovable assets and a floating charge on other assets. An unsecured debenture is one which is without any charge on firm assets, these are known as naked debenture.

◆ *Convertibility:* Companies can also issue convertible debentures. It is the debenture that is convertible into equity shares at the option of the debenture holder. The conversion ratio and the period during which conversion can be affected are specified at the time of issue of debentures.

◆ *Credit Ratings:* Before issue of debentures to the public, the issuing company need to get the debentures rated by anyone of the credit rating agencies. The four credit rating agencies are:

Credit Rating Information Services Of India Limited (CRISIL), Investment Information and Credit Rating Agency of India Limited (ICRA), Credit Analysis and Research Limited (CARL), FITCH India and Duff & Phelps Credit Rating India Pvt. Ltd (DCRI).

◆ *Claim on Income and Assets:* Debenture interest is tax deductible. In other words, debenture interest is paid from earnings before interest and taxes (EBIT) or operating profit. The interest is payable before payment of tax, preference dividend and equity dividend. So, debenture holders have priority of claim on income. At the same time they also have priority of claim on company assets at the time of winding up. Failure of interest force to bankruptcy.

Types of Debentures

The following are the different types of debentures:

1. From the redemption point of view, the debentures are sub divided into two:

   a) *Redeemable Debenture:* Redeemable debentures are those debentures, which are to be repaid by the company at the end of specified period or within the specified period at the option of the company by giving a notice to debenture holders with the intention to redeem debentures either lump sum or installments.

   b) *Irredeemable Debenture:* Irredeemable debentures that are not redeemable during the existence (life) of the company. They are repayable either if the company fails to pay interest on them or at the time of liquidation of the company. These types of debentures are also known as perpetual debentures.

2. From the conversion point of view, the debentures are sub divided into two:

   a) *Convertible Debenture:* Convertible debentures are those debentures that are convertible into equity shares at the option of the debenture holders after stating period at a predetermined price. The debenture capital may be Fully Convertible Debentures (FCDs) or Partially Convertible Debentures (PCDs). This type of debentures is attractive, even though they carry a low rate of interest when compared to non-convertible debentures.

   b) *Non-Convertible Debenture:* As the name itself suggests that the debenture does not carry the option of conversion into equity.

3. From the security point of view, the debentures are sub divided into two:

   a) *Secured or Mortgaged Debenture:* Secured or Mortgaged debentures are those debentures that are issued with a charge on the immovable assets of the company. The charge may be fixed or floating or on particular assets. In case of failure in payment of interest or principle amount, debenture holders can sell the assets in order to satisfy their claims.

   b) *Necked or Simple or Unsecured Debenture:* Necked debentures does not carry any charge on company's assets as regards to the payment of interest and repayment of principle amount. But being creditors of the company, they have general charge on the assets of the company.

4. From the transfer or registration point of view, the debentures are sub divided into two:

   a) *Registered Debenture:* Registered debentures are those debentures that are registered with the issuing company. Names, addresses and other particulars of holders are recorded in debenture register, which is kept by the issuing company. Transfer of this type of debentures needs a regular transfer deed, at the time of transfer of such debentures. The interest is paid only to the person on whose name the debenture is registered.

   b) *Bearer Debenture:* Bearer debentures are those debentures that are payable to the bearer and transferable by delivery only. Bearer debentures are negotiable instruments and the company keeps no records for them. The interest is paid to the bearer of debenture.

5. Other types of Debentures

   a) *Zero Interest (Coupon) Debentures (ZID):* Zero interest (coupon) debentures are of the innovative debt instruments. This type of debenture does not carry any interest (coupon) rate. Generally, they are issued at a discount from their maturity / redeemable value.

The return for the holders of this type of debenture is the difference between purchase (issue) price and maturity (redeemable) value. For example, Mr. A has purchased a debenture at Rs. 50, having a maturity period of 10 years, and debenture redeemable value is Rs. 200. hence, the return to holder is Rs. 150 (Rs200-Rs.50).

b) **Deep Discount Debenture/Bond (DDB):** Deep discount bond is the same as zero coupon bond but deep discount bond is issued at a deep discount from its redeemable (maturity) value. In India, DDBs are being issued by the public financial institutions. They are Industrial Development Bank of India (IDBI), Small Industries Development Bank of India (SIDBI), etc. For example in the year 1992 IDBI sold deep discount bonds at deep discount price of Rs. 2,700, with maturity value of Rs.1 lakh and its maturity period is 25 years. It was the first institution to issue DDB. DDBs enable the issuing company to consume cash during maturity period. In other words, the issuing company need not serve the debt by paying interest. It reduces the risk of reinvestment of interest, which is receivable at the end of every year. However, DDBs exposed to high risk since the entail a balloon payment at the end of maturity period.

c) **Floating Rate Bonds (FRBs):** Floating rate bonds are those bonds in which the rate of interest is not fixed. The interest rate is floating and its linked interest rate on Treasury Bills (TBs), Bank Rate (BR), which are considered as benchmark. In India, State Bank of India (SBI) was the one of earliest financial institution to successfully sell floating rate bonds. Later, IDBI also issued this type of debentures. Floating rate bonds provide protection against inflation risk to investors or bondholders.

d) **Secured Premium Notes (SPNs):** SPN is a type secured debenture redeemable at a premium over the face or purchase price. It is like zero interest debenture, since there will be no interest payment in the lock-in-period. SPN holders have the option to sell back the debenture / note to the issuing firm at face value after the given lock-in-period. SPNs are tradable instruments. For example, Tata Iron & Steel Company (TISCO) issued this type of notes in 1992, face value of Rs. 300. No interest would accrue during the first year after allotment. During 4-7 years the principle amount will be repaid in installments of Rs.75, in addition Rs. 75 in each year as interest and redemption on premium. The buyer was given an option to sell back SPNs at the Rs. 300.

e) **Guaranteed Debentures:** These are the one type of debentures on which the payment of interest and principle amount is guaranteed by third party at the time of their issue. The third parties are financial institutions, government, etc.

f) **Callable Bonds:** Callable bonds are those bonds that can be called in and purchased at a price. Companies generally call back bonds only when the interest rates fall in the market less than the bond's interest rate. Companies redeem high interest bonds and raise funds by issue of low interest bonds. IDBI was the first bank to issue bonds with call features in 1992.

Advantages/Merits of Debentures/Bonds

The advantages of debentures / bonds may be studied under two heads:

(a) Advantages/Merits to Company

- Debenture capital is one of the *cheapest sources* of long-term finance, since interest payment on debentures is a *tax-deductible expenditure and low flotation cost.*

- *Issue of debenture does not dilute control*, since they do not entitled voting right.

- *Debentures enable the company to take advantage of trading on equity*, which results shareholders wealth maximization.

- *Debenture capital provides flexibility in capital structure*, if they are issued as redeemable or if not also, since they have call option.

- *Debenture holders does not participate in the surplus profits* of the company since, payments to them are limited to interest and principle amount.

- *Debenture capital provides protection against inflation* since, the interest rate is fixed.

(b) Advantages/Merits to Debenture holders

- *Debentures provide a fixed, regular and stable source of income.*

- *Debenture holders' investment is safe and secured* since, debentures with a charge on company is assets.

- Debentures are issued for a *definite maturity period.*

- *Debentures holders' interests* (payment of interest and principle amount) *are protected* by the debenture indenture.

Disadvantages/Demerits of Debentures or Bonds

The following are the important disadvantages of debentures:

(a) Disadvantages/Demerits to Company

- Raising debenture capital is *risky one*, since it involves payment of fixed interest charges and repayment of principle amount, which are legal obligations of the issuing company failure to (pay) honour, it may lead to bankruptcy.

- Raising debenture capital increases financial leverage (risk perception on investors), which raise the cost of equity (according to Capital Assets Pricing Model (CAPM) of the company.

- Raising debenture capital involves restrictions, like limit the borrowing, limit dividend payment etc.

- Debenture (irredeemable) capital is costly one, when the rate of inflation decreases. Since the interest rate comes down in the market.

- This is not stable source of long-term finance for a firm with variable earnings.

(b) Disadvantages/Demerits to Debenture holders'

- Debentures do not carry any voting rights, which give no controlling power on the working of the company.

- Debenture holders' does not have claim on surplus profits since they are not the owners of the company.

- Receipt of debentures is fully taxable under the head income from other sources.

- Debenture holders' loose interest charges, if the inflation increases.

- Debenture prices are vulnerable with changes interest rates.

DISTINGUISH BETWEEN EQUITY SHARES AND DEBENTURES

Point of Distinction	Equity Shares	Debentures
Nature of Security	Ownership security	Creditorship security
Form of Return	Dividend	Interest
Rate of Return	Not fixed (no guarantee)	Fixed rate
Refund of principle amount	May be refunded at the time of liquidation.	Refunded at the end of maturity period.
Voting Rights	Have voting rights.	No voting right.
Charge of Return	Dividend is a charge against profit & loss apparition account.	Interest is a charge on profit& loss account.
Exemption of return from tax	Not exempted from tax (dividend is paid after payment of tax).	Exempted from tax (interest is paid before payment of tax).
Claim on assets and income	Equity holder does not have claim on assets and income.	Debenture holders have claim on assets and income.

1) **Issue of Shares:** There are two types of shares (a) ordinary or equity shares and (b) preference shares.

    The following discussion covers the equity shares and preference shares.

    a) **Equity Shares:** The ordinary or equity shareholders of the company are considered to be the owners of the company. Issue of equity shares is the most important source for raising long-term capital, since they will be repaid only after closing down the company. In other words, ordinary shares do not have a maturity date. Further, they do not entitled any fixed rate of dividend. Generally, it is decided by the company's Board of Directors. Dividend payment is subject to the earnings available to equity shareholders. Hence, company should raise the maximum funds by the issue of shares, without losing control over the company.

    b) **Preference Share:** It represents a hybrid source of financing. Since it is a pure combination of the main features of both equity and debentures. It is similar to equity share in the following ways (i) preference dividend is payable only out of earnings after taxes, (ii) payment of dividend is not compulsory, and (iii) preference dividend is not a tax-deductible payment.

    On the other hand, it resembles debenture in the following ways. (i) fixed dividend rate, (ii) they do not have voting right, (iii) preference shareholders have claims on income and (iv) assets prior to equity shareholders. There are different types of preference shares cumulative and non-cumulative, callable and non-callable, convertible and non-convertible, participating and non-participating, redeemable and non-redeemable. This source is helpful only when the firm is planning to raise finance for a long period and not for permanently. Firm can raise finance through issue of preference shares that are redeemable after a given (needed) period.

2) **Debentures:** Debenture is an instrument given by the company under company seal acknowledging the receipt of debt to its holder. It is a long-term promissory note for raising loan capital. Debenture holders are the creditors of company. Company has a legal obligation to pay the amount of interest at a specified rate and on the specified time. Interest is a charge against profit & loss account that save tax. Generally, debentures are given floating charge on the assets of the company. There are different types of debentures - secured and unsecured, redeemable and irredeemable, convertible and non-convertible. The debenture as a source of finance has advantage to the company like trading on equity, retention of control and tax benefits.

3) **Public Deposits:** Public deposits or term deposits are in the nature of unsecured deposits accepted by business firms directly from public. It is very popular for medium term finance,

when there is no availability of finance from banks. Public deposits as a source of finance have a benefit like simple and convenient tax benefit, trading on equity, no security etc.. NBFCs cannot borrow by issue of public deposits more than 25 per cent of its paid up capital and free reserve.

4)   *Loan from Financial Institutions:* Financial institutions such as Commercial Banks, Life Insurance Corporation of India (LICI), General Insurance Corporation (GIC), Unit Trust of India (UTI), State Financial Corporations (SFC's), Industrial Development Bank of India (IDBI), etc., provide short-term medium term and long-term loans. It is most suitable for financing medium-term demand of working capital. There will be a fixed rate of interest charge that is changed to profit and loss account and can get tax benefit. Functions of FIS have discussed in detail under by this term sources of finance.

BANKING NORMS FOR FINANCING WORKING CAPITAL

RBI Directives for Lending Working Capitals by Banks

The concept of maximum permissible bank finance (MPBF) was introduced in November 1975 as part of implementation of the recommendations of the study group to frame guidelines for follow-up of bank credit (Tandon Working Group). Over the years, various improvements had been brought about in the loan delivery system. Consistent with the policy of liberalisation, greater operational freedom has been provided to banks in dispensation of credit. The Reserve Bank of India accordingly has withdrawn (w.e.f. 15th April, 1997) the prescription in regard to assessment of working capital needs based on the concept of MPBF enunciated by Tandon Working Group. Banks, according to their perception of the borrower, may henceforth determine working capital credit and the credit needs.

Working Capital Assessment

Except the State Bank of India (SBI) which is the largest commercial bank in the country, no other bank has come out with any guideline after dissolution of the Tandon Committee guidelines (known as Maximum Permissible Bank Finance - MPBF). Most banks are virtually following the same MPBF with or without slight modification. Brother banks are keenly watching SBI guidelines for slowly adopting the same in one form or other. The methods that are being followed by SBI are given in detail below:

(a)   Projected Balance Sheet Method;

(b)   Cash Budget Method;

(c)   Turnover Method;

(d)   Other Assessment Methods

A Projected Balance Sheet Method (PBS Method)

The PBS method of assessment is applicable to all borrowers who are engaged in manufacturing, services and trading activities, including merchant exports and who require fund-based WC (Working Capital) finance of Rs.25 lakhs and above. In the case of SBI borrowers who require WC finance of Rs.25 lakhs to Rs.200 lakhs, their requirement is first assessed under PBS method. The limit so assessed is sanctioned if it exceeds 20% of the projected turnover.

1.   Presently, a borrower's total business operations, financial position, management capabilities etc. are analysed in detail to assess the WC finance required and to evaluate the overall risk of the exposure.

2.   It is decided that while in the PBS method, the analysis as above will continue to be carried out, some of the present assessment procedures will be rationalized and simplified to facilitate complete flexibility in decision-making. In particular, there will not be a prescription like the minimum level of liquidity or maximum level of a current asset under PBS method, because over the years, such prescriptions have brought in certain rigidities in the assessment process.

Under the PBS method, assessment of WC requirement will be carried out in a flexible manner in respect of each borrower with proper examination of all parameters relevant to the borrower and their acceptability. The assessment procedures, which have been modified for this purpose, are as follows:

A (1) Collection of Financial Data

In the present system of working capital assessment, the required financial data are obtained from the borrower in the following forms:

Form I: Particulars of existing/proposed limits from the banking system;

Form II: Operating statement;

Form III: Analysis of balance sheet;

Form IV: Comparative statement of CA/CL;

Form V: Computation of MPBF for working capital;

Form VI: Funds flow statement

The Form V, which is used for computation of MPBF is not required for assessment under the PBS method. In Form I, information relating to working capital and term-loan borrowings (existing and proposed) is obtained now. Henceforth additional information regarding borrowings from NBFCs, borrowings from term-lending institutions for WC purposes, ICDs (Inter Corporate Deposits) taken, lease finance availed will also be collected in Form I.

A (2) Classification of CA/CL (form III)

The classification is substantially the same as the analysis now done in MPBF but subject to the changes detailed below:

(i)   **Bills negotiated under L/Cs:** As mentioned herein later, the facility for purchase of demand and usance bills drawn under LCs will be computed outside the main assessment of WC finance. Therefore, receivables in the form of sale bills (inland/export) drawn under LCs need not henceforth be included in CA in Form III. Correspondingly, bank borrowings in the form of LC bill purchase limits will not be included in the projected bank finance under CL.

(ii) **Cash margin for LCs and Guarantees:** Margins deposited for LCs and guarantees relating to working capital will be included in the CA.

(iii) **Investments:** Fixed deposits with banks and trustee securities (including units of UTI) are now classified as investments under CA. In addition, from now on temporary investments of a borrower in SBIMF (SBI Mutual Fund) and money market instruments like MMMF, CP, CD etc., which are for the purpose of parking short-term surplus, will also be classified as current assets. All other investments like ICDs, investments in shares and debentures (including investments in subsidiaries and associates) will be classified as non-current assets.

(iv) **ICDs taken:** This will be part of current liabilities (short-term borrowings from others). It should also be shown separately under 'additional information'.

A (3) Verification of Levels of Inventory/Receivables/Sundry Creditors

Under the PBS method, the projected levels of inventory, receivables and creditors for purchases will be examined in the same manner as hitherto done (based on terms of past levels and inter-firm comparison) except that the levels earlier prescribed as norms will not in any manner be treated as ceiling levels to be imposed on strict terms; these will henceforth serve only as historic reference levels.

A (4) Evaluation of Liquidity

The CR (Current Ratio) of 1.33 will be considered as a benchmark level of liquidity instead of the minimum acceptable level. In cases where the CR is projected at a level lower than the benchmark or a slippage in the CR is proposed, it alone will not be a reason for rejection of the loan proposal or for sanction of the loan at a lower level. In each such case, the reasons for low CR or slippage should be carefully examined and in deserving cases, the CR as projected may be accepted under MPBF1.33, which was rigidly followed, unless it would be waived by RBI guidelines.

An illustrative list of the various aspects of liquidity management (under PBS method) in a borrower's business is given below:

(i)   Whether cheques drawn on the cash credit/current accounts were referred due to insufficiency of drawing power/funds; if so, how frequently and for what reasons this happened.

(ii) Frequency and nature of irregularities in the accounts and how these were set right,

(iii) Payment record in respect of inward bills (like LSCs).

(iv) Resort to outside borrowings (to be seen from Fund Flow (FF) Reports and Balance Sheet).

(v)   Adverse changes in the terms of purchases (reduction in credit period, denial of credit etc.).

In the cases where projected CR is found acceptable, WC finance as requested may be sanctioned. In specific cases where warranted, such sanction can be with a condition that the borrower should bring in additional long-term funds to a specified extent by a given future date. Where it is felt that the projected CR is not acceptable but the borrower deserves assistance subject to certain conditions, suitable written commitment should be obtained from the borrower.

A (5) Validation of Bank Finance Sought

Working capital finance will not be computed using any rigid formula. The projected bank borrowing that reflects the finance sought by the borrower, will be validated with reference to the operating cycle of the borrower, projected level of operations, nature of projected build up of CA/CL profitability, liquidity etc. Where these parameters are acceptable, the projected bank borrowing will stand validated for sanction. This amount will be termed as 'Assessed Bank Finance' (ABF).

1.   As mentioned earlier, the assessment exercise should be carried out with due focus on the specific nature and needs of each borrower. As it happens now, under PBS method too, in certain cases it may become necessary to revise the business/financial plan of the borrower, if in the opinion of the bank these require changes. For example, planned levels of CA or CL are not realistic; a higher level of NWC is necessary, etc. In these cases, the operating officials should discuss in detail these aspects with the borrower to facilitate revision of the business plan and financial projections.

2. The following information relating to WC assessment and ABF (Assessed Bank Finance) will be presented under the head 'Working Capital Assessment and Assessed Bank Finance' (in lieu of WC assessment and MPBF calculation).

	Previous Year	Current Year	Next Year
Total CA			
Other CL			
Working Capital Gap			
Net Work Capital (Actual/Projected)			
Assessed Bank Finance (ABF)			
NWC to TCA (%)			
Bank Finance to TCA (%)			
S. Creditors to TCA (%)			
Other CL to TCA (%)			
Inventories to Net Sales (days)			
Receivables to Gross Sales (days)			
S. Creditors to Purchases (days)			

A (6) Ready Reckoner of Changes in the Guidelines on Assessment & Supervision of WC Finance-(MPBF vs PBF)

Assessment of WC	Existing guidelines	Revised guidelines
(a) WC assessment Method	MPBF method as prescribed by the RBI	Projected Balance Sheet (PBS) method
(b) Bank finance assessed is named as	Maximum Permissible Bank Finance (MPBF)	Assessed Bank Finance (ABF)
(c) Formats on which financial data are collected	CMA Forms I to VI prescribed by the RBI	CMA formats I to IV & VI (with additional information in Form I)
(d) Classification of CA/CL	As below	As below
(i) Bills negotiated under LCs	CA under receivables	Not taken as CA
(ii) Bank finance for bills drawn under LCs	CL under short-term borrowings from banks	As a contingent liability under the 'Additional information'
(iii) Cash margin for LCs/ Guarantees (relating to WC)	Non-Current Asset (NCA)	CA
(iv) Investments	Trustee securities & government securities are CAs	Investments in SBIMF, CP, CD are also taken as CAs

Contd...

sheets. The requirements of this break-up of assets and liabilities differs slightly from that mandated by the Company Law Board (CLB). The analysis of balance sheet in CMA data is said to give a more detailed and accurate picture of the affairs of a corporate. Corporates are required by all banks to analyse their balance sheet in this specific format called CMA data format and submit it to the banks. While most qualified accountants working with the firms are aware of the method of classification in this format, professional help is also available in the form of chartered accountants and financial analysts for this analysis.

Tandon Committee: A study group set up by the Reserve Bank of India (RBI) in 1974, to examine the then prevailing system of working capital financing by banks and to make suitable recommendations on the same.

The contribution of the committee, headed by Prakash Tandon, that stands out relates to:

♦   The framing of norms for inventory and receivables for 15 major industries.

♦   Determining the amount of permissible bank finance.

The committee suggested norms, i.e., ceilings for inventory and receivables, which could be considered for bank finance. The 15 industries included cotton and synthetic textiles, paper, cement, pharmaceuticals and engineering. Thus, for instance, the norms proposed for the pharmaceutical industry were:

Raw materials: 2.75 months' consumption

Stocks in process: □ month's cost of production

Finished goods: 2 months' cost of sales

Receivables: 1.25 months' sales

For determining the maximum permissible bank finance (MPBF), the methods suggested were:

Method I: 0.75 (CA - CL)

Method II: 0.75 CA - CL

Method III: 0.75 (CA - CCA) - CL

Here CA stands for current assets, corresponding to the suggested norms or past levels if lower, CL represents current liabilities, excluding bank lending and CCA stands for the 'Core Current Assets', i.e., permanent current assets. Method I and, following the Core Committee recommendations, Method II have been used by banks in assessing working capital needs of businesses, for the last several years. In October 1993, the RBI infused operational autonomy by permitting banks to determine appropriate levels of inventory and receivables, based on production, processing cycle, etc. These lending norms were made applicable to all borrowers enjoying an aggregate (fund-based) working capital limit of Rs.1 crore and above from the banking system. However, the requirement of the current ratio at 1.33 was retained.

SUMMARY

♦   Estimation of working capital required is completed, then the next step is financing of working capital. Statement of working capital gives clear picture about the components, (raw materials, work-in-process, finished goods and receivables) and required investment in these components of working capital. Financing of current assets is the responsibility of finance manager who may require spending lot of time for raising finance.

♦   Working capital should be financed by suitable and optimal mix of short-term source of funds and long-term source of funds.

♦   Sources of short-term financing funds are: trade credit, accruals, differed incomes, commercial papers (CPs), public deposits (PDs), inter corporate deposits (ICDs), and commercial banks.

♦ Trade credit refers to the credit extended by the supplier of goods or services to his customer in the normal course of business. Trade credit is a spontaneous source of finance that it arises in the normal business transactions of the firm without specific negotiations (automatic source of finance).

♦ Accrued expenses are those expenses which the company owes to the other persons or organisations, but not yet due to pay the amount.

♦ Deferred Incomes are income received in advance by the firm for supply of goods or services in future period.

♦ Commercial Papers (CPs) represents a short-term unsecured promissory notes issued by firm's that have a fairly high credit (standing) rating. CP is an alternative source of finance and proves to be helpful during the period of tight bank credit, it is a cheaper source of short-term finance when compared to the bank credit. But CP is available only for large and financially sound companies, and it cannot be redeemed before the maturity date.

♦ Public Deposits or term deposits are in the nature of unsecured deposits, have been solicited by the firms (both large and small) from general public primarily for the purpose of financing their working capital requirements. But fixed deposits accepted by companies are governed by the Companies (Acceptance of Deposits) Amendment Rules of 1978. Benefits of public deposits are simple procedures involved in issuing public deposits, no restrictive covenants are involved, no security is offered against public deposits, and its cheaper (post-tax cost is fairly reasonable). But it has some disadvantages they are: limited amount of funds can be raised, and funds available only for a short period.

♦ Inter-Corporate Deposits (ICDS): A deposit made by one firm with another firm is known as Inter-Corporate Deposits (ICDs). Generally, these deposits are usually made for a period up to six months. Such deposits may be of three types: call deposits, (its repayment is demanded on just one days notice), three months deposits, and six-months deposits. These types of deposits are usually given to 'A' category borrowers only and they carry an interest rate of around 16% per annum.

♦ Commercial banks are the major source of working capital finance to industries and commerce. The loaning of funds to business is one of their primary functions. Forms of Bank Finance are: Loans, (2) Overdrafts, (3) Cash credits, (4) Purchase or discounting of bills and (5) Letter of Credit.

♦ Bank finance is available on providing adequate security. The modes of security required by a bank are (a) hypothecation, (b) pledge, and (c) mortgage.

♦ Factoring service may be offered to the client in two ways: (a) with recourse to the drawer(s) and (b) without recourse to the drawer(s). Advantages relating to the facility factors which ensure certain pattern of cash in flows from credit sales, and elimination of debt collection department, if it continuously goes in for factoring. Apart from the services observed by factor, the arrangement suffers from some limitations they are: services would be provided on selective accounts basis and not for all accounts (debts). The cost of factoring is higher and compared to other sources of short-term working capital finance. Factoring of debt may be perceived as an indication of financial weakness, and reduces future sales due to strict collection policy of factor.

♦ Net working capital should be financed by long-term sources of finance. The sources of long-term working capital are: retained earnings, issue of shares (ordinary or equity shares and preference shares), debentures, public deposits, loan from financial institutions, life insurance corporation of India (LICI), General Insurance Corporation (GIC), Unit Trust of India (UTI), State Financial Corporations (SFC's), Industrial Development Bank of India (IDBI), etc.

TEST QUESTIONS

Objective Type Questions

1. **Fill in the blanks with appropriate word(s)**

   a) _____ and _____ working capital the two types of working capital.

   b) Trade credit is a _____ source of short-term finance.

   c) ____ income is income received in advance by the firm for supply of goods in future.

   d) CPs are sold at _____ and redeemed at _____.

   e) A firm cannot issue public deposits for more than ____ of its share capital and free reserves.

   f) _____ interest rate ceiling on public deposits.

   g) There are no commitment charge for _____.

   h) _____ letter of credit is one that can be withdrawn by the issuing banker any time after it is issued.

   i) _____ means borrower is provided money against the security of movable property.

   j) _____ is a financial institution, which render services relating to the management of and financing of sundry debtors that arises from credit sale.

   [*Answers:* (a) Permanent, variable; (b) Spontaneous; (c) Differed (d) Discount, face value; (e) 25 %; (f) 15 %; (g) Cash credit account; (h) Revocable; (i) Hypothecation ; (j) Factor].

2. **State whether each of the following statement is true of false**

   (a) Minimum size of CP is Rs. 6 lakhs.

   (b) Pubic deposits are governed by the companies (Acceptance of deposits) Amendment Rules 1978.

   (c) There are three types of inter-corporate deposits.

   (d) In India, the factoring services are providing by four financial institutions

   (e) Factor charges a commission ranging between 1% and 2%.

   [*Answers:* (a) False; (b) True; (c) True; (d) True; (e) True].

REVIEW QUESTIONS

Section-A

1. Name the sources of short-term working capital.

   1) What is factoring ?

   2) What is CP ?

   3) What do you mean by L/C ?

   4) Distinguish between pledge and hypothecation.

   5) How do you compute cost of trade credits ?

   6) List out the important forms of working capital advance given by banks.

7) Distinguish between ordinary share and preference share.

8) How do you compute yield of CP's?

9) What do you mean by mortgage?

Analytical Type

1) "Is Trade Credit is source of working capital finance". Discuss.

2) "Accruals are a free source of finance", comment.

3) Write a brief note on CP as a source of finance.

4) What is public deposit ? Discuss its advantages and disadvantages.

5) Discuss the types of ICD's.

6) Write a brief note on L/C.

7) Discuss the different modes of security required by a bank for granting credit.

8) What is factoring ? List out its features.

9) Briefly discuss the sources of short-term working capital.

10) Discuss in detail the sources of long-term working capital.

11) What are the sources of working capital finance? Discuss.

12) Write short note on (a) CP's, (b) L/C, (c) Trade Credit and (d) Accruals.

PART VII

SPECIAL TOPICS IN FINANCIAL MANAGEMENT

Financial Plan Forecasting

Objectives

After studying this chapter, you should be able to

1 Explain the meaning of Financial Planning.

2 Explain the steps involved in Financial Planning.

3 Explain the principles of a Sound Financial Plan.

4 Understand over capitalisation and under capitalisation.

Financial Planning and Forecasting

Objectives

After studying this chapter, you should be able to

1 Explain the meaning of Financial Planning.

2 Explain the steps involved in Financial Planning.

3 Explain the principles of a Sound Financial Plan.

4 Understand over capitalisation and under capitalisation.

INTRODUCTION

At the time of the formation of a company, the promoters or the persons responsible for the management of the company must estimate the total amount of funds, finance or capital the company requires. Determine the sources from which the funds have to be raised and decide about the proper time at which, the funds have to be obtained through proper financial planning.

MEANING OF FINANCIAL PLANNING

Financial Planning is deciding in advance, the course or line of action for the future with respect to the financial management of a concern, It includes :

(i)   Estimating the amount of funds to be raised.

(ii) Determining the forms and the proportionate amount of the securities to be issued for raising the capital and;

(iii) Laying down the policies as to the administration of the financial plan.

DEFINITION OF FINANCIAL PLAN

Financial plan may be defined as the plan, which properly estimates the amount of funds required, proportion of debt-equity, and the policies for administration of financial plan.

Financial plan is a statement estimating the amount of capital required, determination of finance mix and formulation of policies for effective administration of the financial plan. Financial plan states:

(a)   The amount of capital required to be raised.

(b)   The proportion of debt in total capital and its form.

(c)   Policies bearing on the administration of capital.

Opinion of Coben and Robbins, that financial plan should:

(a)   Determine the *financial resources required* to meet the company's operating programme;

(b)   Forecast the extend to which, these requirements will be met by *Internal generation* of funds and to what extent, they will be met from external sources;

(c)   Develop the best plans to obtain the required external plans;

(d)   Establish and maintain a system of financial controls, governing the allocation and use of funds.

(e)   Formulate programmes to provide the most effective *profit-volume-cost relationship*;

(f)   Analyse the financial *results* of operations;

(g)   Report the facts to the top management and make recommendations on the future operations of the firm.

From the above, we can conclude that financial plan is an advance programming of all the plans of financial management and integration and co-ordination of all these plans with other functions of a company.

The meaning of financial planning may be well understood with the help of the following definitions :

"The financial plan of a corporation has two-fold aspects: it refers not only to the capital structure of the corporation, but also to the financial policies, which the corporation has adopted or intends to adopt"

- **J.H. Bourneville.**

"Financial planning pertains only to the function of finance and includes the determination of the firm's financial objectives, formulating and promulgating financial policies and developing financial procedures"

– Walker and Boughn.

The above definitions highlights the main aspects of financial planning, they are :

(a)   Determining the financial objectives;

(b)   Formulation of financial policies;

(c)   Development of financial procedures.

NEED FOR FINANCIAL PLANNING

Many technically sound and economically viable industrial projects have failed simply because of poor financial planning. Thus, it is an essential tool for any business undertaking.

Financial Planning is needed, not only in the case of enterprises proposed to be setup, but is equally needed for on-going enterprises as well.

The need for financial planning arises from the following reasons :

Good financial planning :

(a)   Would ensure liquidity throughout the year.

(b)   Would bring to light, the surplus of funds available for expansion.

(c)   Would contribute to the rational utilisation of the available resources, to get the maximum benefit.

(d)   Would make things easy for the management team to function smoothly.

STEPS IN FINANCIAL PLANNING

1.   *Estimating the Capital Requirements:* It is the first step in financial planning. Requirement of the concern will be estimated on the basis of the following factors :

   (a)   The cost of fixed assets like land, buildings, plant and machinery, furnitures and fittings, needed to be acquired.

   (b)   The cost of intangible assets like patents, goodwill etc., to be acquired.

   (c)   The amount required to be invested in current assets like stock of raw materials, stores, stock of finished goods, sundry debtors, cash etc.

   (d)   The cost of promotion and the cost of financing i.e., the amount of expenses to be incurred on the promotion of the concern like registration fee, stamp duty, legal charges etc., and the amount of expenses to be incurred on the printing of prospectus, share application forms, etc.

2.   *Determination of the Form and the Proportionate Amount of Securities to be issued:* The second step in Financial Planning is the determination of the forms and the proportion of the various securities to be issued by the concern, for raising capital.

3.   *Other Steps*

   •   Projection of Financial Statements

   •   Determination of Funds Needed

   •   Forecast the Availability of Funds

   •   Establish and Maintain Systems of Control

   •   Develop Procedures

   •   Establishment of Performance-Based Management Compensation System

The financial planning process can be broken down into six major steps[3]:

(1) *Projection of Financial Statements:* Financial statements are profit & loss account, and balance sheet. Projection of financial statement is very much needed, since it helps to analyse the effects of the operating plan on projected profits and various financial plans. The same projects can also ensure the proper monitor of the implemented financial plan. Success of a firm depends on the ability to identify the deviations from the financial plan.

(2) *Determination of Funds Needed:* Anticipation of funds needed to invest on fixed assets (Plant & Machinery and equipment) as well as current asset (inventories and receivables) for R & D programmes and for major promotional campaigns.

(3) *Forecast the Availability of Funds:* The required funds may be generated from two sources, internal and external sources. This step involves estimation of funds to be generated internally, which automatically identifies the amount of funds to be raised from outside.

(4) *Establish and Maintain System of Control:* Planning and control are the twins of management. Control system is necessary to see the proper and effective utilisation of funds within the firm. It helps the basic financial plan to be carried out properly.

(5) *Develop Procedures:* Developing procedures ensure consistency of actions. Procedures should be developed for adjusting the basic plan, if the economic forecasts upon which, the plan was based, do not materialise. For example, if the economy turns out to be stronger than was forecasted, then the procedures will help. This step is really a "feedback loop" which triggers modifications in the financial plan.

(6) *Establishment Performance-Based Management Compensation System:* It is very much needed, to reward the managers for doing what the stockholders want them to do i.e., maximization of share prices.

The Financial planning process begins with long-term (strategic) financial plans, which in turn guide the formulation of short-term, (operating plans) and budgets. Generally, the short-term plans and budgets implement the firm's long-term strategic objectives. Whereas a detailed discussion of long-term (strategic) financial plans is out of the scope of this book but a few preliminary comments on long-term financial plan are in order. Preparation of short-term (operating) financial plan is discussed in the chapter of Cash Management.

LONG-TERM (STRATEGIC) FINANCIAL PLANS

Long-term financial plans lay out a company's planned financial actions and the anticipated impact of those actions over a time period, ranging from 2 to 10 years. Generally, companies that are subject to a high degree of operating uncertainty, relatively short production cycles, or both, tend to use shorter planning horizons. These strategic plans are part of an integrated strategy that are carried out along with the other functions of the organisation. Long-term financial plans consider the proposed outlays of fixed assets, R & D, product development actions, capital structure and sources of financing. Termination of products, projects, repayment of debts are also included in the long-term financial plans. These plans tend to be supported by a series of annual budgets and profit plans.

SHORT-TERM (OPERATING) FINANCIAL PLANS

These plans generally cover a period of 1 to 2 years. These plans include the sales forecast and various forms of operating and financing data. The result of short-term financial plans are operating budgets, cash budget and proforma financial statements.

Generally, short-term financial planning process begins with the sales forecast, which helps to develop production plans. In turn, it is in the production plans, that the firm can estimate direct labour requirements, factory overhead out lays and operating expenses. Then the next step is to prepare proforma income statement and then the cash budget can be prepared, which in turn helps to prepare proforma balance sheet.

FACTORS AFFECTING FINANCIAL PLAN

Planning is the prime function of management, so as to financial planning. As we have seen that the main aims of the preparation of the financial plan are: procurement of needed funds at minimum cost and establishment of effective coordination between costs and risks. A sound financial plan is the one which takes into account the short term and the long-term financial needs of a firm and the mix of various securities or means for raising the required funds. The following are the most important points that must be considered n the formulation of a financial plan.

(1) *Nature of the Industry:* Taking into consideration, the nature of the industry is very important in financial planning. Here, nature of industry refers, whether the industry is capital intensive or labour intensive. The nature of industry helps to decide the (amount) quantum of capital and the sources of procurement. Generally labour intensive industries require less amount of capital in comparison to the capital-intensive industry. For example, banks are labour intensive and paper, cement, textile industries are capital-intensive industries that require more capital when compared to the banking industry. Apart from the above stated nature, there is a need to consider the stability and regularity of earnings. Raising funds from capital market is very easy for an industry, which has stability and regularity in its earnings when compared to the other industries, where the earnings are not stable.

(2) *Status of the Company within the Industry:* Status of the company is one, which is considered by the investors while investing in equities or debentures. Hence, a financial manager needs to assess his / her company's status in terms of size, age and goodwill, area operation and the promoters' and management's goodwill, because these affect financial planning. A company, which is having good will in the market or public may be able to raise funds easily (by issue of equity or debentures or public deposits) when compared to other firms that are new. New firms may prefer to raise funds from financial institutes, since they cannot sell equity or debentures or public deposits to the public.

(3) *Evaluation of Alternative Sources of Finance:* Procurement of the needed funds at minimum cost is possible only when there is debt and equity combination. For determination of optimum debt-equity or finance mix, financial manager needs to evaluate various sources of finance in the light of cost, availability, contractual conditions (debt case), limitations etc., before going to formulate the financial planning.

(4) *Attitude of Management Towards Control:* Management's attitude towards control is another factor that should be considered while formulating a financial plan. Any firm or management that is interested to retain the control, would not like to raise funds by issue of equity shares to the public, if at all they issue, they would purchase a majority of the issue to hold control. Additional funds that may be required for modernization or expansion may be raised by debt source of funds if its capital structure permits, otherwise by retentions of profits is always preferred.

(5) *Magnitude of External Capital Requirements:* A financial manager needs to formulate financial plan after taking into account short-term and long-term financial needs of the firm. To put it in a simple way, financial manager needs to consider the working capital and the fixed capital requirements, while formulating a financial plan. Funds for long-term financial requirements should be raised by means of long-term sources, equity, irredeemable preference shares, debentures, but the preferable source is internal that helps ploughing back of profits, reserve and surpluses etc. On the other hand short-term finances may be

obtained from external sources of finance, like redeemable preference shares or debentures or short-term loans from financial institutions.

(6) *Capital Structure:* The construction of capital structure as a part of financial structure should be determined with a combination of debt and equity, but at the same time, the financial manager should try to minimize fixed charge. This is possible only when the firm is able to raise long-term finances by means of equity source.

(7) *Flexibility:* Flexibility is the main principle of a financial plan. It should be flexible enough to adjust according to the needs of the changing conditions. It should allow the flexibility to raise and to repay whenever the need be, without difficulty and delay, which is possible only by determination of capital structure. A firm should arrange its capital structure in such a manner that it can substitute one form of financing by another. Flexibility is possible only when the firm uses redeemable preference shares and redeemable debentures or convertible debentures. These help to reduce the capital whenever the firm needs and the convertible debentures help in increase capital when firm feel the need to have funds for long-term requirements.

(8) *Government Policy:* Government policies, financial controls and other statutory provisions should also be taken into consideration while formulating a firm's financial plan. For example, in India, a firm is needed to obtain the approval of the controller of capital issues, for raising funds by issue of shares and debentures to the public, but the approval will be given only when the mix of securities is an ideal one. Besides Securities Exchange Board of India (SEBI) is also needs to be considered.

LIMITATIONS OF FINANCIAL PLANNING

The above-discussed factors must be taken into consideration while formulating an optimum financial plan of a firm, but it is subject to certain limitations. The following are some of the limitations of financial planning.

(1) *Difficult in Accurate Forecasting:* Financial plans are formulated by taking into account the expected circumstances in the future. But future is uncertain and nothing can be said about it exactly, if the expectancy about future circumstances were wrong, then the financial plan would not be effective. Hence, the reliability of financial planning is uncertain. But this limitation may be overcome by periodical review of the financial plan.

(2) *Absence of Co-Ordination:* Financial function may be the most vital of all other functions, but efficiency of the finance function depends on the co-ordination of other departments with functions related to finance. Determination of financial needs depends on personnel requirements, production policy, marketing possibilities and the research & development policies. Formulation of optimum financial plan may be possible only when there is proper coordination among all functions. But generally, there is a lack of co-ordination among the functions of a firm.

(3) *Rigidity of Financial Plans:* Generally, financial plans are rigid in nature. Rigidity means that the financial plan may not allow changes, if at all it (allows) has flexibility in nature, managers may not like to change. It may not be ready, even to make the changes that are necessary for the smooth running of the firm. There are a good number of reasons that may make financial plan rigid. For example, commitment of investment on large projects, assets might have been purchased, arrangement for raw materials are also made but managers are not psychologically prepared.

(4) *Rapid Technological Changes in Industry and Customer Preferences:* Rapid technological changes in the industry like, automated machinery, improved or new manufacturing process, new marketing mechanism and consumer preferences demand changes in financial plan.

Because, the adoption of a new technology or purchase of new machinery needs funds. Technological changes are unexpected; hence, it is very difficult to adjust a financial plan for the adoption of the fast changing technological environment. But adoption changes in technology, or changing of the manufacturing process or consumer preferences is a must in the globalised economy. So, it is a limitation of the financial plan.

PRINCIPLES GOVERNING A SOUND FINANCIAL PLAN

The various consideration or principles that should be kept in mind by a concern, while formulating its financial plan are :

1. *Simplicity:* The financial plan should contain a simple financial structure that can be implemented and managed easily.

2. *Long-term view:* The financial plan should be formulated, keeping in view the long-term requirements and not just the immediate or short-term requirement of the concern.

3. *Flexibility:* The financial plan should be such, that it can be revised or changed according to the changing needs of the business with the minimum possible delay.

4. *Foresight:* The financial plan must be visualized with much foresight. A financial plan visualized without foresight may fail to meet the present as well as the future requirement of funds and bring disaster to the concern.

5. *Optimum use:* A business should neither starve for funds nor should have unnecessary idle funds. That means, the financial plan should provide for the optimum use of funds. While framing the financial plan, the financial planners should keep in view, the maximization of wealth and at the same time there must be proper balance between long-term funds and short-term funds.

6. *Contingencies:* The financial plan should make adequate provision of funds for meeting the contingencies likely to arise in the future.

7. *Liquidity:* There should be adequate liquidity in the financial plan. Adequate liquidity in the financial plan will act as a shock absorber in the event of business operations deviating from the normal course.

8. *Economy:* The Financial Plan should ensure, that the cost of raising the funds is the minimum. This is possible by having a proper debt-equity mix in the capital structure.

9. *Investor's Temperament:* Investors, who are bold and venturesome, prefer equity shares. Investors, who are not very bold, have a liking for preference shares. Investors, who are cautious, go for debentures. As such, the financial plan should keep in mind the temperament of preferences of investors. That is, the financial plan should be formulated in consonance with the preferences of the investors.

ESTIMATION OF THE FINANCIAL REQUIREMENTS OF A FIRM

Forecasting or estimation of the financial or capital requirements is the most important financial decision or financial function of an enterprise. The amount of capital estimated by a concern should neither be more nor less than the amount which can be profitably employed. So, a concern should estimate or assess its capital or financial requirements properly.

The financial or capital requirements of a business enterprise can be broadly classified into two categories. They are :

1. Fixed capital requirements or fixed capital.
2. Working capital requirements or working capital.

Meaning of Fixed Capital: Fixed Capital refers to the capital or finance required for meeting the permanent or long-term needs of the business.

Estimation of Fixed Capital Requirements: The estimation of the fixed capital requirements of a business organization is made after preparing a list of fixed assets needed to be acquired by the business and the promotion and setting up costs to be incurred by the concern.

OBJECTIVES OF THE FINANCIAL PLAN

A Financial plan has the following prime objectives:

(i)   *Ensure the availability of sufficient funds* to invest in feasible projects, thereby achieving company goals.

(ii) *Balances of risk and costs* while raising the required funds there is a need to balance risk and costs to protect the investor.

(iii) *Simplicity:* Simplicity in this context means that, the firm should issue few securities, since the issue of a variety of securities is complicated.

(iv) *Flexibility:* Flexibility means that, the plan should be flexible enough, to adjust according to the changing conditions.

(v)   *Liquidity:* Liquidity means, the ability of an enterprise to honour the currently maturing obligations. Hence, financial plan should be able to provide funds not only when it is running under profits, but also in the periods of depression or abnormal business situation/ phase.

(vi) *Optimum Use:* The Financial plan should ensure sufficient funds only for genuine needs. Plan should not allow the firm to suffer shortage of cash or should have excess of funds than needed, which will be a waste. Put in simple terms, the funds should be raised according to the needs and should be utilized properly.

(vii) *Economy:* The main objective of the financial manager is to raise funds at least cost, the same is the case with financial planning. The plan should help the firm to raise funds at minimum cost. It should not impose disproportionate burden on the firm, which means the plan should ensure optimum debt-equity mix.

CAPITALISATION

At the very outset, it must be noted, that the concept of capitalization is used only in the case of joint stock companies and not in the case of other forms of business undertaking like sole trading concerns and partnership firms. Again, in financial management, the term 'Capitalisation' is concerned only with the quantitative aspects and not with the qualitative aspects of business finance.

In financial management the term 'capitalisation' is used in two different senses, viz. (1) in a broad sense and (2) in a narrow sense. In a broad sense, the term 'capitalisation' is considered synonymous with financial planning. So, the term is taken to refer to the determination of the amount of capital to be raised, the securities through which the capital is to be raised and the relative proportions of the various types of securities to be issued, and also the administration of the capital .

In a narrow sense, the term 'capitalisation' is taken to mean the determination of only the quantity of finance required by a company.

Components of Capitalisation

The components of capitalisation are :

(a) Par value of share capital i.e., paid-up value of both equity and preference share capital.

(b) Reserves and surplus i.e., all types of reserves, capital reserves as well as revenue reserves and surplus.

(c) Long-term borrowed funds i.e., debentures issued and other long-term borrowings.

Capitalisation vs Capital: The term 'capitalisation' confines itself to only long term sources of finance. But the term 'capital' includes all the sources of finance i.e., long-term, as well as short-term.

The concept of capitalization is used only in the case of companies. But the concept of capital is used in the case of all forms of business undertakings.

Capitalisation vs Share Capital: The terms 'capitalisation' includes not only share capital but also reserves and surplus and long-term borrowings. But, the term 'share capital' includes only the share **capital (i.e., equity as well as preference share capital).**

Estimation of Capitalisation: There are two approaches, basis or theories for the determination of the amount of capitalization of a company. They are :

1. Cost approach or cost theory of capitalisation

2. Earnings approach or earning theory of capitalisation.

Cost Approach or Cost Theory of Capitalisation: Under the Cost Approach or Cost Theory of Capitalisation, the capitalization of a company is based on the cost of acquisition of fixed assets, the establishment of the company and the amount of regular working capital requirement. So, under this method, the amount of capitalisation or the value of a company is arrived at, by adding up the following items.

(a) Costs of acquisition of fixed assets, such as land, buildings, plant and machinery, furniture and fixtures etc.

(b) Cost of establishing the company, comprising the preliminary expenses, underwriting commission, expenses on the issue of shares etc.

(c) The amount of regular working capital requirements.

For instance, if the acquisition of fixed assets would cost Rs. 5,00,000 the cost of establishing the company would amount to Rs. 50,000 and the regular working capital requirements of the company would amount to Rs. 1,00,000, then the amount of capitalization of the company would be taken as Rs. (5,00,000+50,000+1,00,000) = 6,50,000.

The Cost approach, no doubt provides a basis for the determination of the capitalisation of the new company. But it is not a good basis for the determination of capitalization for the following reasons.

(a) The capitalization or the value of a company is based more on its earning capacity (i.e., on its productive or earning capital) rather on the total value of the assets held by it.

(b) The earnings of a company may decline, when some of its assets remain idle and some assets become obsolete. But this will not be revealed, if capitalization is made on the basis of the cost of the assets.

(c) The cost approach is not the right basis for the capitalization of a company having irregular earnings.

Earnings Approach or Earnings Theory of Capitalisation

Under the earnings approach or earnings theory of capitalization, the capitalization or the value of a company is determined on the basis of its earnings. According to this approach, the capitalization or value of a company is equal to the value of its earnings. For instance, if the average annual earnings or profit of a company is Rs. 50,000 and the capitalization rate (i.e., the fair rate of return of the average rate of return in the industry) is 10% on the capital employed, then, the capitalization of the company will be :

$$\text{Average amount of profit of the company} \times \frac{100}{\text{Fair rate of return}}$$

$$\text{i.e. } 50,000 \times \frac{100}{10} = \text{Rs. } 5,00,000$$

The earnings approach provides a good basis for determining the capitalization of an existing company. However, this approach may not be quite suitable for determining the capitalization of a new company. This is because, estimation of the future average annual profits of a new company is not only difficult, but also highly risky, as the future is dependent on a number of considerations.

To sum up, the cost approach of capitalization is quite suited to a new company while the earnings approach of capitalization is quite satisfactory for an existing company.

OVER-CAPITALISATION

Meaning of Over – Capitalisation: A company is said to be over- capitalized, when its actual earnings or profits are not sufficient to pay dividend at proper rate to the shareholders. In short, when the actual capitalization of a company (i.e., the capitalization of a company arrived at, by adding up the par value or paid-up value of share capital, reserves and surplus, debentures and other long-term borrowings) is more than the proper capitalization (i.e. the capitalization determined on the basis of either the cost approach or the earnings approach).

The company is said to be over- capitalized. For instance, if the fair rate of return or the average rate of return in the industry is 10% on the investment or capital employed, the company earns a profit of Rs 75,000 and it has raised funds through the issue of shares and debentures and other long-term borrowings to the extent of Rs. 9,00,000, then the company is said to be over-capitalised. The company is over-capitalised, because the earning of the company is just.

$$\frac{75,000}{9,00,000} \times 100 \text{ i.e. } 8\frac{1}{3}\%, \text{ Which is less than the fair rate return in the industry.}$$

Viz., 10%

Symptoms of Over–Capitalisation

There are certain symptoms of over-Capitalisation. They are:

1. The actual capitalization of the company exceeds the Capitalisation warranted by its activity level and requirements.

2. The earnings or profits of the company are lower than the general expected return in the industry (i.e., the fair rate of return in the industry). In short, there is a fall in the earning capacity of the company.

3. There is a fall in the rate of dividend declared by the company over a long period. (It may be noted that fall in the dividend rate of a company in some of the years does not make the company over- capitalised. It is only when, there is fall in the rate of dividend of the company over a long period, that the company can be said to be over- capitalised).

4. There is a fall in the market value or market price of the shares of the company.

Over-Capitalisation vs. Excess Capital: Over-Capitalisation arises, when the existing capital of a company is not effectively or properly utilized, as indicated by the fall in the earning of the company. On the other hand, excess capital arises, when the company has raised capital in excess of its requirements.

It may be interesting to note that, sometimes, a company may be over-capitalised, but it may suffer from shortage of capital.

Causes of Over – Capitalisation: Over- Capitalisation is caused by a number of factors or causes. The important causes of over- capitalization are :

1. If a company is promoted by acquiring assets at inflated prices (i.e., at prices higher than their real values or worth), there arises over- capitalization as the booked values of the assets are higher than their real worth.

2. Acquisition of unproductive intangible assets like goodwill, patents etc., on a large scale, higher costs render a large portion of the capital of the company unproductive and will lead to over- capitalization.

3. Heavy preliminary and promotional expenses incurred by a company, will render a greater portion of the capital of the company unproductive and will contribute to over-capitalisation.

4. If a company is promoted during the boom period, it will have to pay higher prices for the acquisition of assets. The value of the assets may fall, when the recession sets in. The result is over-capitalisation.

5. When a company raises more capital through the issue of shares and debentures than what it can profitably use, a part of the capital of the company remains unutilised or under-utilised. This results in over-capitalisation.

6. If a company borrows large sums of money at a rate of interest higher than its rate of earning, there results a fall in the earnings of the company as well as over-capitalisation.

7. When a company does not make adequate provision for depreciation or postpones essential repairs to plant and machinery and equipments, the efficiency of plant and machinery and equipments is reduced. Consequently, the earnings of the company decline and this results in over-capitalisation.

8. If a company follows liberal dividends policy, the earnings of the company are dissipated in the form of dividends and adequate reserves are not created. In such a case, after a few years, the book values of the assets of the company tend to be higher than, their real values. Which means, there is over-capitalisation.

9. When there is excessive taxation by the Government, very little fund is left with the company. The meager funds left with the company may not be sufficient even to carry out essential repairs and renewals. As a result, the efficiency of the assets will decline. The decline in the efficiency of the assets will result in a fall in the earnings capacity of the company and over-capitalisation.

Consequences or Effects of Over-Capitalisation: Over-Capitalisation is disadvantageous to the company, the shareholders, the consumers and the society. The disadvantage or the adverse effects of over-capitalisation on the company are:

1. Over-capitalisation results in a fall in the earnings or profits of the company.

2. The fall in the earnings of the company will lead to reduction in the rate of dividend that could be declared by the company. The reduction in the rate of dividend of the company will lead to fall in the market values or market prices of the shares of the company. The fall in the market prices of the company's shares will lead to loss of confidence of the investors in the company.

3. The loss of confidence of the investors in the company will lower the credit-worthiness of the company and will make it very difficult for the company to raise new capital for expansion and modernization.

4. When there is over-capitalisation, the company may resort to window-dressing of accounts (i.e., manipulation of accounts) to show, higher profits and to declare, dividends. Declaration of dividends out of the fictitious profits, shown by the window-dressing of accounts, will result in payment of dividend, out of capital. Declaration of dividends out of capital will be detrimental to the company.

5. An over-capitalised company may be forced to adopt the scheme of re-organisation or if reconstruction has not helped the over-capitalised company to improve its situation, the over-capitalised company has to go into liquidation.

6. When the earnings of the company fall owing to over-capitalisation, the company may try to increase its earnings by raising the prices of its products. When the prices of the products are raised, the company may not be able to face the competition from the rival firms.

Adverse Effects of Over-Capitalisation on the Shareholders: The adverse effects of Over-Capitalisation on the shareholders are :

1. Over-capitalisation results in a fall in the rate of dividends to the shareholders.

2. Over-capitalisation will result in a fall in the market values or market prices of the shares held by the shareholders.

3. On account of the fall in the market values of the shares, resulting from over-capitalisation, the holdings of the shareholders (i.e. the shares held by the shareholders) will have lesser value as securities for raising loans.

4. The shareholders of an over-capitalised company may find it difficult to dispose of their shares. Even if they are able to dispose of their shares, they have to sell those shares at a loss.

5. The fall in the market values of the shares of a company, caused by over-capitalisation, will encourage speculation in such shares. Speculation in the shares of an over-capitalised company is not in the interests of the shareholders.

6. If a company facing Over-Capitalisation resorts to re-organisation of capital as a remedy, the shareholders will be the worst affected, as they have to agree to forego a major part of their share capital for writing –off the past losses of the company.

Adverse Effects of Over-Capitalisation on the Consumers: The adverse effects of over-capitalisation on the consumers are :

1. An over-capitalised company is forced to raise the prices of its products so as to increase its earnings. The rise in the prices of the products will be detrimental to the consumers.

2. An over-capitalised company may not be able to keep up the quality of its products. The fall in the quality of the products will be harmful to the consumers.

3. An over-capitalised company is unable to face competition and survive in the market. The result is, its liquidation. The consumers will be affected adversely by the stoppage of the production by the liquidated company.

Adverse Effects of Over-Capitalisation on the Society: The adverse effects of over-capitalisation on the society are :

1. An over-capitalised company may find it difficult to pay the wages of the workers on time. This will affect the morale of the workers and will lead to strained industrial relations.

2. If an over-capitalised company resorts to wage cuts to reduce its costs and to improve its earnings, there will be resentment amongst the workers. As a result, the industrial relations will be strained.

3. An over-capitalised company with a large amount of debenture issue may, on account of its lower earning-capacity, find it difficult to pay the fixed interest on its debentures. This will affect the interests of the debenture holders adversely.

4. An over-capitalised company may, on accounts of its lower earning capacity, find it difficult to repay the creditors and the debenture holders.

5. Over-Capitalisation will lead to misapplication and wastage of the resources of the society.

6. Over-capitalisation will lead to a fall in the market values of the shares of a company. The fall in the market values of the shares of an over-capitalised company may encourage speculation in the shares and affect the climate of investment adversely (i.e., will be detrimental to the interest of the society).

7. An over-capitalised company is unable to face competition and survive in the market. The result is its liquidation. The liquidation or closure of the over-capitalised company will affect the interests of the creditors and the labourers adversely.

Remedies or Corrective Steps for Over-Capitalisation

The real remedy for over-capitalisation lies in the scheme of re-organization or reconstruction of the over-capitalised company. The scheme of re-organisation or reconstruction helps the over-capitalised company to write off the past losses, to bring down the assets to their real values by providing the necessary depreciation and to undertake repairs and renewals and additions to its plant and machinery, to improve the earnings capacity of the assets and thereby the earnings or profits of the company.

The scheme of re-organization or reconstruction can take the following forms:

(a) The shareholders may be asked to forego a part of their share capital. The share capital of the shareholders can be reduced in any of the following two ways :

   (i) The par value or the paid-up of the shares may be reduced. For instance, if the share capital of the over-capitalised company consists of 10,000 shares of Rs. 100 each, fully paid, it (i.e, the share capital) can be reduced to 10,000 shares of Rs. 50 each, fully paid.

   (ii) The number of shares may be reduced. For instance, if the share capital of an over-capitalised company consists of 10,000 shares of Rs. 100 each, fully paid it (i.e., the share capital) can be reduced to 5,000 shares of Rs. 100 each, fully paid.

(b) Even the debenture holders and the creditors may be induced to forego a reasonable amount of their claims against the over-capitalised company.

(c) High dividend bearing preference shares may be replaced by low dividend bearing preference shares. This will help the over-capitalised company to have more profits available for dividend to equity shareholders or to have more retained earnings.

(d) High interest bearing debentures may be replaced by low interest bearing debentures, if necessary, by offering some inducement to the debenture holders i.e., by offering some premium on the redemption of the old debentures.

(e) Sub-division of the shares of the over-capitalised company may be thought of. This step will increase the marketability of the company's shares and thereby, will increase the market value of the shares of the company.

(f) If funds are available, redemption of some debentures and repayment of some debts may be thought of.

Besides the various schemes of re-organisation or reconstruction enumerated above, efforts should be made by the over-capitalised company to reduce its cost of operation and to improve its earnings or profits.

UNDER-CAPITALISATION

Meaning of Under-Capitalisation: Under-Capitalisation is just the reverse of over-capitalisation. Under-Capitalisation refers to a situation, where the actual capitalization of a company is much less than its proper capitalization (i.e., the capitalization warranted by its earnings). For instance, if the general rate of return or fair rate of return on the investment or capital employed in the industry is 10%, the average annual earnings or profits of a company are Rs. 60,000 and the actual capitalization of the company is Rs. 5,00,000, the company is said to be under-capitalised. The company is under-capitalised, because its actual capitalisation viz., Rs.5,00,000 is much less than its proper or fair capitalization viz.,

$$\text{Rs.}\left(\text{Average annual profits of the company} \times \frac{100}{\text{Fair rate of return}}\right) = 5{,}00{,}000 \text{ i.e. } 60{,}000 \times \frac{100}{10} = 6{,}00{,}000$$

In other words, a company is said to be under-capitalised, when its actual rate of earnings is much higher than the general rate or fair rate of earnings in the industry. For instance, if a company is earning a return of 20% on investment or capital employed, as compared to 12% earned by similar companies engaged in the same industry (i.e., the general or fair rate of return of the industry), the company is said to be under-capitalised.

Symptoms of Under-Capitalisation: The various symptoms of Under-Capitalisation are:

1. The actual capitalization of the company is much less than its fair or proper capitalization (i.e., capitalization warranted by its earnings).

2. The actual rate of earnings of the company is much higher than the general rate or fair of earnings in the industry.

3. The dividend rate of the company will be much higher than, that of similar companies in the industry over a long time.

4. The market value or market price of the shares of the company will be much higher than the market values of the shares of similar companies in the industry.

Under-Capitalisation vs Inadequate Capital

Under-Capitalisation refers to a situation, where the existing capital of a company is very effectively used and as a result, its actual capitalisation is much less than its proper or fair capitalization warranted by its earnings. On the other hand, inadequate capital refers to a situation, where a company does not have sufficient funds at its disposal to carry out its activities.

Causes of Under-Capitalisation

The following are the causes of Under-Capitalisation.

1. Under-estimation of the initial earnings of a company is one of the causes of Under-Capitalisation.

2. If a company is set up during the period of recession, its assets would be acquired at low prices. In such a case, the company becomes Under-Capitalised after the recession is over.

3. Maintenance of high standards of efficiency in the working of a company will contribute to higher earnings and Under-Capitalisation.

4. Creation of adequate reserves for depreciation and renewals, conservative dividend policy followed and large-scale ploughing back of profits result in the availability of large funds for expansion and modernization. This will contribute to higher earnings and Under-Capitalisation.

Consequences or Effects of Under-Capitalisation

Under-Capitalisation has certain consequences or effects. They are:

1. Under-Capitalisation may encourage competition from new companies in the sense, that the high profits earned by an Under-Capitalised company may encourage new companies to enter the field. As a result, the profits of the company may decline.

2. Under-Capitalisation may encourage the management to manipulate the share prices.

3. Higher profits, arising from Under-Capitalisation may lead to more government control and higher taxation.

4. Higher profits, gained due to Under-Capitalisation, may give an opportunity to the workers to demand higher wages and better welfare facilities.

5. The higher profits earned by an Under-Capitalised company may make the consumers develop the feeling that they are being exploited by the company.

Remedies for Under-Capitalisation

The situation of Under-Capitalisation can be set right through a number of corrective steps or remedies. They are :

1. Issue of bonus shares, by capitalizing accumulated earnings, is the most effective remedy for Under-Capitalisation, (i.e., issue of bonus shares reduces the average rate of earning as well as the rate of dividend of the company).

2. Raising the par value of the company's shares is an important remedy for Under-Capitalisation. The par value of the company's assets and giving the shareholders new shares of higher denomination, out of the profits arising from the upward revision of the company's assets, in place of the existing shares.

3. Splitting of the shares of the company is another remedy for Under-Capitalisation. The splitting of the shares of the company results in an increase in the number of shares and a fall in the rate of earning per share. (It may be noted that the splitting of the shares of the company will not lower the average earning rate of the company. It will only lower the rate of earning per share).

Over-Capitalisation Vs. Under-Capitalisation

Both, Over-Capitalisation and Under-Capitalisation are not based on the working results of a company just for a year or two. They represent chronic conditions of the business.

Both, Over-Capitalisation and Under-Capitalisation are post-mortem diagnosis of the disease. That is, they can be observed only when a company has worked for some years. Both are deviations from the ideal pattern of capitalization.

Both, Over-Capitalisation and Under-Capitalisation are detrimental to the society. Over-Capitalisation involves a strain on the financial resources of the company, an evil, for the shareholders and a big danger for the consumers and moreover, it endangers the economic prosperity of the country. Similarly, Under-Capitalisation may accentuate unhealthy competition from business rivals and sow seeds of dissension, cause discontentment among the employees and thus, may lead to exploitation of consumers.

Though both, Over-Capitalisation and Under-Capitalisation are bad, Over-Capitalisation is considered more dangerous than Under-Capitalisation for the following reasons :

1. Over-Capitalisation is a more common phenomenon, whereas Under-Capitalisation is a rare phenomenon.

2. Under-Capitalisation is not an economic problem, but a problem of adjusting the capital structure.

3. Under-Capitalisation is indicative of effective utilization of resources, sound financial position and good management.

4. Over-Capitalisation has more serious effect on the company, the shareholders, the consumers and the society than Under-Capitalisation.

5. Under-Capitalisation can be remedied more easily than Over-Capitalisation.

6. The remedial process of Over-Capitalisation is more painful and has to be carried out at a higher cost to the shareholders than Under-Capitalisation.

It is true that, of the two situations, Over-Capitalisation is more dangerous than Under-Capitalisation or Under-Capitalisation is a lesser evil than Over-Capitalisation. But both the situations should be avoided.

Few years ago, a corporation could run its business without planning for different aspects in technological advancement, that were not directly related to its products, or services. But those times are gone forever. Now, this period of liberalisation, privatisation and globalisation (LPG), business environment, with even expanding opportunities and changing market conditions, strategic planning (long-range) has greater importance for the growth as well as for its survival. To quote Oscar Hauptmann (Harvard Professor) today's business firms are *"Aiming at a moving target"*[1], by long-range planning. The cost of keeping up with change is quite high no matter what procedure is followed and careful environmental scanning and long-range planning is becoming more critical every day.

The (long-range) strategic plan of a corporation consists, its corporate purpose, corporate scope; corporate objectives; and corporate strategies.[2] The *corporate purpose* defines the mission of the company. Put it simple, Coca-Cola company has expressed its purpose as "we exist to create value for our shareholders/owners". The *corporate scope* describes a company's line of business and geographic area of operations. For example, Coca-Cola's mission statement indicates that the company limits its productions to soft drinks, but on a global geographic scale. Nucer Corporation, a firm listed in the New York Stock Exchange, has described its scope as "we are a manufacturing company producing primarily steel products". The corporate purpose and scope states the general philosophy of the business but it does not provide its manager with operational objectives. The *corporate objectives* spell out the specific goals set by the company, which guide the management. The objectives may be in the qualitative or quantitative form. Examples of qualitative objective is the maintenance of distribution system as the worlds' most effective and pervasive method to satisfy customers. On the other hand quantitative objectives can be fixed in terms of quantity. For example, accomplish 60 per cent market share, 30 per cent return on equity (ROE), Rs. 50 crore economic value added (EVA). The *corporate strategies* are the instruments for achieving corporate objective. Put it simple, corporate strategies are broad policies rather than detailed plans. For example, one airline may have a strategy of offering no-frills service between a limited numbers of cities, while another's strategy may be to offer "safe rooms in the sky". Strategies should be both, achievable and compatible with the company's purpose, scope and objectives.

(i) All the functional managers should formulate a strategic plan. Financial manager has to formulate financial plan. Planning is one of the principles of management, so financial management planning means, deciding in advance, what is to be done. The finance function is primarily concerned with the economic procurement and efficient use of funds, which is possible only with the help of a well-prepared financial plan. Financial plan is a systematic approach to attain economic procurement and utilisation of funds. Preparations for this financial plan is the responsibility of the promoter or the consultant (if promoter doesn't have knowledge to prepare the plan) and after promotion, it is the financial manager's responsibility.

TEST QUESTIONS

Objective Type Questions

(1) **Fill in the blanks with appropriate word(s)**

(i) The Financial plan is a statement estimating the amount of capital required, estimation _____ mix and formulation of financial policies for the effective administration of the financial plan.

(ii) Financial planning begins with _____financial plans that in turn, guide the formulation of operating plans and budgets.

(iii) Flexibility is the main _____ and _____of sound a financial plan.

(iv) There are _____types of financial plans.

(v) Planning and controlling are the _____of management.

[Answers: (i) Finance (ii) Long-term or Strategic (iii) Objective, Principle (iv) Two (v)Twins]

(2) **State whether each of the following statement is true or false**

(i) Financial planning depends upon future estimations.

(ii) Planning and finance functions make financial planning.

(iii) Long-term and short-term are the two types of financial plans.

(iv) Cash budget is a long-term financial plan.

(v) Excess capital is good for a sound financial plan.

[Answers: (i) False, (ii) True, (iii) True, (iv) False, (v) False]

REVIEW QUESTIONS

SECTION – A Conceptual Type

(1) What is financial planning ?

(2) List out the elements of a corporate financial plan.

(3) List out the objectives of a financial plan.

(4) Name any four principles of a financial plan.

(5) What do you mean by flexibility of financial plan ?

(6) Give the meaning of economy principle of financial plan.

(7) What do you mean by strategic financial plan ?

(8) What is operating financial plan ?

(9) What are the limitations of financial planning ?

SECTION – B Analytical Type

(1) State the steps involved in financial planning.

(2) What are the principles governing a financial plan?

(3) Explain the theories of Capitalisation.

(4) What are the effects of Under-Capitalisation ?

(5) What are the causes of Over-Capitalisation ?

(6) What is financial planning ? Discuss the principles of sound financial plan.

(7) What are the benefits of financial planning.

(8) Briefly explain the objectives of financial planning.

(9) What are the factors that determine financial plan. Discuss.

(10) What are the limitations of financial planning.

REFERENCES

1. Burton, G and Thakur, M, *"Management Today – Principles and Practice"*, New Delhi: Tata McGraw Hill Publishing Company Ltd., 1995, p. 131.

2. Brigham E.F and Houston J.F., *"Fundamentals of Financial Management"*, Singapore: Harcourt Publishers International Company, 2001, p. 136.

3. Ibid, p. 139

Leasing and Hire Purchase Financing

22

After studying this chapter, you
should be able to:

1 Understand the concept of leasing
and the importance of lease financing

2 Know the various types of leasing,
documentation and legal aspects
involved in leasing and to understand
the fixation of lease rentals;

3 Gain a thorough knowledge in
evaluating a lease and the accounting
involved in leasing; and

4 Gain an overview of leasing industry
in India.

MEANING AND CONCEPT OF LEASING

Leasing has become a timely and flexible source of term financing for industries, especially when not everyone could have access to all types of projects and classes of assets.

The practice of leasing is an age-old one. The leasing of lands and buildings were common. Leasing of equipments, plants and machineries are comparatively of recent development in India. Business communities facing tight money conditions have developed leasing as a method of funding. The use of leasing as a financing device runs as far back as the 1940s, though it emerged in India in an organized manner only in the early seventies.

The credit for inventing lease financing in its present form goes to the USA. There, it developed from the sale and lease back techniques utilized by the large departmental stores and supermarkets. Even before 1940s the idea was prevalent in chain grocery stores and in 1936 itself this type of financial leasing was used by Safeway Stores Inc. However, till the 1960s, leasing was looked at with suspicion as it was mostly identified with lack of commercial means to obtain financing. Only in 1963, did leasing begin to gain importance when permission was granted by the controller of currency of the US to the banks to engage in leasing of moveable properties? This afforded respectability to leasing as a financing method.

In the UK, hire purchase led the way to lease financing. It is believed that lease financing took shape in 1960, in the UK and by 1970 it had expanded threefold. However, after the US, Japan is the second largest leasing nation, and France is the fourth largest shareholder in the leasing market. In India, leasing entered in 1973 with the advent of the first leasing company of India banks entered leasing after the Banking Laws Amendment Act, 1984.

DEFINITION

Simply put, a lease provides a person the right to use and to have control over the asset of another person without receiving the title to it and on payment of a specific consideration for such right for a specific period. The person who lets the asset to be used by another is called the lessor and the person who utilizes it without the title is called the lessee.

Lease is defined by the international accounting standard as an agreement whereby the lessor conveys to the lessee in return for rent the right to use an agreed period of time.

According to Jack Broyles, lease is the method of acquiring the right to use equipment of real property for consideration.

Principally there are two types of leasing arrangements. They are –

1. Financial lease
2. Operating lease

In a financial lease, the rental payments paid by the lessee to the lessor will in total exceed the purchase price of the asset. The rentals are so structured to facilitate the recovery of the purchase price of the assets over the economic life of the asset, whereas, the operating leases are generally for shorter term of two or three years. While the responsibility of maintaining the asset lies with the lessee in case of a financial lease, in case of an operating lease the same rests upon the lessor. But in operating leases, the lessor does not recover his full investment during the lease period itself. However, he retains the benefit of resale value of the asset being leased out.

T.M. Clark, I defines 'leasing', a financial lease as a contract involving payment over an obligatory period of specified sums sufficient in total to amortize the capital outlay of the lessor and give some profit', and defines the operating lease as 'type of lease – where the asset is not wholly amortised during the noncancellable period, if any, of the lease and where the lessor does not reply for his profit on the rentals in the noncancellable period'.

According to the guidance note of the Institution of Chartered Accountant's (ICAI) on accounting for leasees, a financial lease is explained as follows.

"A lease is classified as a financial lease if it secures for the lessor the recovery of his capital outlay plus a return on the funds invested during the lease term."

"A lease is an operating lease", according to the said guidance note of ICAI, "if it does not secure for the lessor the recovery of his capital outlay plus a return on the funds invested during the lease term."

The Transfer of Property Act, 1882 defines a lease as, "the transfer of a right to enjoy an immovable property, made for a certain time, express or implied, or in perpetuity, in consideration of a price paid or promised, or of money, a share of corps, service or any other thing of value, to be rendered periodically or on specified occasions to the transferor by the transferee, who accepts the transfer on such terms." The transferor is called the lessor, the transferee is called the lessee, the price is called premium and the money, share, service or other thing to be so tendered is called the rent. This definition is confined to real estate leasing.

WHY LEASING?

Acquisition of new plants and equipments are often required by business organizations. While it is necessary to see the profitability in investing on new equipment, one must equally be aware of the necessity to conserve cash resources to maintain liquidity. Under such circumstances, leasing arrangements may come in handy for various reasons.

Frees Working Capital

A liquidity crisis is often the cause of business failures. Hence burdening of a company's cash resources in capital investments have to be considered carefully. Conservation of cash resources by avoiding outright purchases will be helpful. Often, loan facilities are burdensome as they require security and affect the cash flows. By adopting lease financing, the capital assets and cash resources of a company can be kept for productive use.

Financing the Cost of the Equipment to the full Extent

Leasing provides 100% financing of the cost of capital goods. Since the lessor owns the leased assets there is no necessity for security. So, the demand for deposits and advance payments is very less. Heavy down payments are not required.

♦ *Flexibility:* Flexibility in lease financing makes it easier to the lessees while planning their finance. Ricard F. Vancil (*Harvard Business Review,* Nov. – Dec 1961) states that "there is no overriding characteristics of lease financing which is sufficiently important to make all leasing plans either better or worse than alternative methods of raising money to purchase equipment. If leasing does have one significant attribute, however, it is its flexibility to adopt the terms of the contract to the needs of borrower."

♦ *Increase in credit capacity:* A lease is not a borrowing and so restrictive loan arrangements and capital budgeting constraints are avoided. It increases the borrowing capacity of the lessee, which will be helpful for future borrowing. There is no accounting necessity to record a lease obligation in the balance sheet of the lessee and it is not depicted as a debt in the balance sheet and thus helps to maintain the lessee's debt-equity ratio lower.

♦ *Tax efficiency:* Lease rentals are fully tax-deductible. While the cost of a fully-owned asset is written off by depreciation, which is often very low, by the fully tax-deductible rentals, the cost of the assets is written of in the books very rapidly.

♦ **Avoiding obsolescence risks:** The purchase of an equipment has the inherent risk that it will become obsolete before its service life is completed; it results in the sale or salvaging of the equipment at a considerable loss. By a lease arrangement, this risk of obsolescence is shifted from the lessee to the lessor instead of bearing the risk by being the owner of the equipment.

♦ **Release from bad investments:** Every organization purchases assets under the assumption that they will be profitable. Sometimes a business may be found to be not profitable and the owner of the assets will want to get rid of the assets purchased for the business. But there is the risk of unsaleableness resulting in serious losses. But in case of a lease, the lessee will be able to return the asset to the lessor if the asset is found to be unprofitable or not satisfactory.

As far as the lessor is concerned leasing as an additional financials product. It tends to increase profitability by tax benefits and reduces the risk. The requirement of security and complex and elaborate documentation are found to be unnecessary.

However, it should not be deemed that there are no disadvantages or unfavourable aspects in lease financing. But the advantages outweigh them.

CONCEPTS

Leasing

Definition

Leasing is a contractual transaction in which the owner of an asset (called lessor) gives the same to another party (called lessee) the right to use it for a specified period of time (called lease period) in consideration of certain payments (called lease rentals). The International Accounting Standard No.17 (IAS - No.17) defines Leasing as "an agreement whereby the Lessor conveys, to the lessee in return for rent, the right to use an asset for an agreed period of time."

Features

(i) **The Parties:** There are mainly two parties – lessor and lessee. In a type of lease called 'Leveraged Lease', there is a third party, the financier, who provides the whole or part of the finance needed for acquiring the asset. A lessor may be a leasing company, a manufacturer, a banker or a subsidiary or an associate. A lessee may be a company, a co-operative society, a firm, an individual, the government or its agencies.

(ii) **The Asset:** The subject of lease transactions is a tangible asset, which can be anything ranging from a plant to an aircraft, land, building or an industry etc.

(iii) **The Agreement:** Written lease agreement is not a legal necessity. It is desirable to execute a written lease agreement when the period is large and considerations complex. Such written agreements attract stamp duty according to the rates prescribed in respective statutes.

(iv) **The Period:** The term of a lease is the period for which the lease agreement will be in operation. When the lease period expires the asset reverts back to the lessor.

(v) **The Rent:** The lease rentals are the regular fixed payments made by the lessee over a period of time at the beginning or at the end of say a month, a quarter, a half-year or year. The same may be based on the cost of lessor's investment, depreciation in the asset other service charges if any. Although generally fixed, the amount and timing of lease rentals can be tailored to the lessee's cash flows. In up-fronted leases, more rentals are charged in the initial years and less in the later years of the contract. The opposite happens in back-ended leases. Sometimes, the lease contract is divided into two parts – primary lease and secondary lease – for the purpose of lease rentals. Primary lease provides for the recovery of the cost of the asset and profit through lease rentals during a period of about five years. It may be followed by a perpetual secondary lease on nominal lease rentals. Various other combinations are also possible.

(vi) *The use:* In a lease transaction, the lessee (user) acquires only the usage or custody of the asset and is not the owner thereof. Legal ownership vests with the lessor. As the legal owner, it is the lessor not the lessee, who is entitled to claim depreciation of leased asset. Although, the lessor is the legal owner of a leased asset, the lessee bears the risk and enjoys the return. Leasing separates ownership and use as two economic activities and facilitates asset use without ownership.

Modus Operandi

Lease financing normally goes through the following stages:

♦ The lessee selects the asset. This involves specification of the asset item, supplier, price, terms of warranties, delivery period, installation and service etc. The lessor normally does not involve himself at this stage.

♦ The lessee approaches the lessor (s) and submits the formal application.

♦ Terms of lessee are negotiated and finalised with the lessor offering the best.

♦ The lessor and lessee sign the lease agreement giving details such as length of the lease period, the distribution of rentals, mechanism of collection of rentals, etc. The lessee assigns purchase rights to the lessor.

♦ The lessor purchases the asset from the manufacturer/dealer.

♦ The asset is delivered to the lessee who issues a certificate to the lessor for having inspected the asset and conforming to the specifications.

♦ The assignable guarantees and service terms are passed on to the lessee. The lessee insures the equipment and endorses the insurance policy in favour of the lessor.

♦ During the lease period, the lessee pays the rental regularly as agreed upon and enjoys the use of the asset.

♦ At the end of the lease period, the asset is transferred back to the lessor. However, in long-term lease contracts, the lessee may be given an option to buy or renew the lease.

HIRE PURCHASE

Definition

As per Sec 2(c) of The Hire Purchase Act, 1972, "a hire purchase is an agreement under which goods are let on hire and under which the hirer has an option to purchase them."

Features

(i) *Cancellability:* A hire-purchase transaction comprises two elements – hire and purchase – in line with bailment and sale respectively. Initially, the bailment takes place when the owner (hire-purchase financier) delivers possession of the goods to the hirer (for deferred sale). On payment of all the instalments and other dues specified in the agreement, the hirer has the option of purchasing the goods but is under no obligation to do so. The hirer can return the goods before the payment of the last instalment. Thus, hire purchase is usually a cancellable contract. This feature of hire purchase distinguishes it from a conditional sale or credit sale.

(ii) *Termination of Hire Purchase Agreement:* A hire purchaser can terminate the agreement, after giving the owner at least 14 days notice in writing. He has to redeliver the goods to the owner and pay any instalment of the hire, which might have been due before the termination. In order to protect the hire purchaser from requiring paying an unreasonable amount, which may be named by the hire vendor in the hire purchase agreement in case of termination, the following provisions have been made under Section 9 of the Hire Purchase Act.

Where the sum total of the amounts paid and the amount due in respect of the hire purchase price immediately before the termination, a) exceeds one-half of the hire purchase price, the hirer shall not be liable to pay the sum so named; b) where it does not exceed one-half of the hire purchase price, the hirer shall be liable to pay the difference between the said sum total and the said one-half, or the sum named in the agreement, whichever is less.

1. *Ownership:* The goods are regarded as the property of the financier/seller until the final instalment is paid. If the hirer decides to purchase the goods on his paying the last instalment, the legal ownership (title) passes on to him. If the hirer defaults the payment of the instalment, the financier/seller is entitled to exercise his right to repossess the without prior notice to the hirer.

2. *Period:* Because of the cancellability/risk of deterioration, hire periods are usually short compared to the useful life of the asset. The hire period is between the point of inception of the transaction/contract and the point at which ownership is transferred.

3. *Instalments:* There is usually a down payment and the purchase price is spread over a period. The periodic payments are called instalments.

4. *Add-on-Rate:* In hire purchase transactions, normally, the rates are quoted at flat rate for the entire period and added to the principal. The total amount so arrived at is divided into equal periodical instalments. Thus, in hire purchase, it is customary to state the financing charges, not as a percentage of the outstanding balances, but as percentage of the principal amount of finance (i.e. cost of asset less down payment). This percentage is called add-on rate of interest. So the add-on rate is not a true rate as the actual outstanding goes on declining with periodical repayments.

5. *Parties:* The hire purchase agreement is usually a tripartite agreement – the three parties being the hiree (hire vendor) the hirer (hire purchaser) and the dealer or it may take place with any two of these three parties.

6. *Arbitration:* Generally, a hire purchase agreement provides an arbitration clause for settling disputes under the agreement, subject to the provisions of the Indian Arbitration Act.

7. *Assignment:* In the absence of any stipulation to the contrary in the agreement, either the financier/owner or the hirer may transfer to a third party his rights by assignment. However, contractual liabilities can be assigned by act of the parties, only by a process called novation i.e. replacement, of one hire-purchase agreement by another. But both rights and obligations may pass on to a third party by operation of law. This involuntary assignment occurs only in case of death or bankruptcy of the parties.

8. *Other charges:* Some financiers also collect in advance service charges of say 1/2 % to 3 % of amount financed. Additional Finance Charges (AFC) are also levied on delayed payment of instalments. The financiers also recover incidental charges like bank commission, insurance premium/tax/penalty, if any, legal charges, etc..

Modus Operandi

The hirer will select the asset required by him. He either directly contacts the hire purchase company for finance or through the dealer. Normally a triangular relationship is established between the dealer, hirer and the financier, particularly if the asset is a consumer durable. In case of industrial finance, the dealer may not be present between the financier and the financee.

Initially, the financier and dealer may enter into a master agreement detailing conditions upon which the former agrees to consider hire-purchase proposals mobilized by the later. Both parties are mutually benefited. The dealer acts as the marketing agent for the financer's hire purchase business. The dealer, in turn, receives sales support because of the credit facility from financier.

Once the customer (hirer) selects the asset he wishes to acquire on hire purchase, the dealer helps him fill up the hire-purchase agreement.

♦ The hirer is usually required to deposit the initial payment with the dealer, which is adjusted towards the cost of the asset payable to the dealer by the finance company.

♦ Then the dealer sends the hire-purchase documents to the finance company requesting to purchase the identified asset for the hirer.

♦ If the finance company agrees to accept the deal, its designated official signs the hire-purchase agreement and a copy of it is sent to the hirer with instructions as to the manner of instalment payment. Simultaneously, the dealer is notified by the financier of its acceptance of the deal and is requested to deliver the asset to the hirer.

♦ On being so notified, the dealer delivers the asset to the hirer against his due acknowledgement.

♦ The hirer pays the hire instalments regularly throughout the hire period.

♦ On completion of the hire period with due payments, the finance company issues a completion certificate to the dealer. Thereupon the hirer becomes the owner of the asset.

TYPES OF LEASE

Leasing is a unique type of commercial contract. Lease financing is often termed as equipment leasing and it is broadly classified into:

John J. Hampton classifies leases into three basic types; they are:

(a) *Operating Lease:* In operating lease, the lease is usually for a shorter term and is generally cancellable. As the asset is leasable repeatedly to several persons, the operating lease is usually said to be a non-payout lease.

(b) *Service Lease:* It is an equipment leasing under which the lessor provides financing as well as servicing of the assets during the lease period. The lessor will covenant with the lessee to provide maintenance and servicing of the leased asset during the existence of the lease.

(c) *Financial Lease:* Financial lease is a long-term lease usually coinciding with the economic life of the asset and is non-cancellable. It operates as a long-term debt financing and is usually full-payout as in contrast to operating lease, it is usually a single lease repaying the cost of the asset. They play a major role in financing of building of buildings and equipments to industries.

According to the Financial Accounting Standards Board Statement No. 13, if at the inception, a lease meets one or more of the following criteria, the lease shall be classified as a capital or financial lease by the lessee.

(i) The lessor transfers title to the lessee at the end of the lease period,

(ii) The lease contains an option to purchase the asset at a bargain price

(iii) The lease period is equal to or greater than 75% of the estimated economic life of the asset.

(iv) At the beginning of the lease, the present value of the minimum lease payments/ rentals equals or exceeds 90% of the fair value of the leased property to the lessor (less any investment or tax credit realized by the lessor).

Any lease that does not satisfy any one of the above four conditions, is an operating lease or a true lease or non-financial lease or open-ended lease or service lease.

Let us compare financial and operating lease.

Financial Lease	Operating Lease
1. The leased asset is use-specific. Usually the lessor buys the asset identified by the lessee and leases out to him.	1. The leased asset is of common-use activity. The lessor already owns the asset and leases it out to several users successively.
2. The risks and rewards incidental to ownership are passed on to the lessee. The lessor only remains the legal owner of the asset.	2. The lessee is given the use of the asset for certain period. Ownership and benefits and risks associated with it remain with the lessor.
3. Therefore, the lessee bears the risk of obsolescence. He is responsible for maintenance, insurance, taxes, etc.	3. Therefore, the lessor bears the risk of obsolescence. He is responsible for maintenance, insurance, tax, etc.
4. It is an intermediate to long-term lease essentially covering the expected useful life of the asset.	4. It is a short-term lease, the lease period being significantly less than the useful life of the asset.
5. During the primary lease period, usually the initial 3 or 5 or 8 years, the lease cannot be cancelled.	5. The lease is usually cancellable at short notice.
6. The lessors' capital outlay is fully amortized during the primary lease period. During a single lease, the lessor recovers through the lease rentals his investment on the leased asset along with interest and profit. Hence, it is called full-pay-out lease.	6. The lessors' capital outlay is not fully amortized during the period of a single lease. The lease rentals recovered during a lease-period are not sufficient to cover fully the cost of leased asset along with an acceptable return thereon. Hence, it is called a non-payout lease.
7. A financial lease is basically a debt equivalent i.e. it is a form of borrowing in disguise. Since, it is a financing decision, the lessee has to decide whether to lease or borrow and buy the asset.	7. An operating lease is basically a rental agreement. Since it is an investment decision, the lessee has to decide whether to lease or buy the asset.
8. The lessor takes the role of a financier. Usually, the lessor is a financial institution and cannot render specialized service connection with the asset.	8. The lessor is specialized in handling and operating the particular asset and usually provides in specialized services.
9. This type of lease is generally suitable for equipment that is tailor-made and does not have ready resale or release market, e.g. heavy machines, etc	9. This type of lease is suitable for equipment that has longer economic life and ready resale or re-lease market i.e., automobiles, computers and office equipments.

In addition to these two major forms of leases, certain other types of lease are also in vogue.

OTHER TYPES

They are further categorized according to need and are described here under.

Full Payout and Non-payout Lease

A full payout lease is defined as one from which the lessor can reasonably expect to expect to realize a return of its full investment in the leased property plus estimated cost of financing the property over the term of the lease from the following resources viz.

♦ Rentals

♦ Estimated tax benefits

♦ The estimated residual value of the property at the expiration of the initial term of the lease.

In full payout leases, the lessor is able to recover his entire capital investment in the assets, out of the rentals payable during the first lease itself along with an assured residual yield on the funds.

In contrast to the full payout leases, there are non-payout or part-payout leases. In these types of leases the assets are leased out repeatedly and so any particular lease will not be a fully paying out one.

Generally, financial leases are fully paying out leases and operating leases are non-payout leases.

Sale and Leaseback

Under this type of transaction, the owner of an asset sells it to a leasing company while it still has useful life, gets the payment for the asset and gets the asset back for lease. The asset is sold at its current market value. By this sale, the funds that are tied up with the asset are released and at the same time the selling person retains the use of the equipment. While there will be cash inflow providing working capital, the cash outflow will be in the form of rentals. In case the market value of the asset being sold exceeds the depreciation written down value, there may be capital gains tax.

(i) *Conveyance Type Lease:* This is a lease of very long tenure. The intention is to convey the title on property. In immovable properties, lease as a mode of conveyance is widely prevalent. Leasing of land for 99 years or even 999 years is a typical example.

(ii) *Sale and Leaseback:* Under this arrangement, a firm sells an asset to a leasing company, which in turn leases the asset back to the firm. The asset is generally sold at market price. The firm receives the sale price in cash. Through this transaction, the firm unlocks its investment in the existing asset by its sale, improves its liquidity, but still retains the right to possess and use the asset during the basic lease period.

This arrangement is beneficial to both the lessor and lessee. The lessor gets periodic lease rentals and gets the benefit of tax credits due to depreciation. The lessor, as the legal owner of the asset, is also entitled to any residual value the asset might have at the end of the lease period. Besides, retaining the use of the asset the lessee gets immediate cash, which improves his cash flow position. It also improves ratio of return on investment and increases the borrowing power of the unit. Where the asset has been fully depreciated, the seller (lessee) is also in a position to improve the bottom line. For this purpose the block concept of depreciation under Income Tax Act has come very handy to these sellers (lessees). The RBI has, however, not permitted banks to finance sale and leaseback transaction.

The sale and leaseback arrangement can be an operating lease or financial lease, depending upon the intentions of the parties in the agreement. It is widely prevalent in the retail market in Western countries. Companies facing short-term liquidity problem also favour it.

(iii) *Sales-aid Lease:* If a leasing firm enters into a tie-up with a manufacturer for marketing the latter's product through his own leasing operation, it is a sale-aid lease. The lessor in consideration of the aid in sales may get either credit or commission. Thus he augments his earning from both the lessees and the manufacturer.

(iv) *Big-Ticket Lease:* Lease of the assets of bigger value running into several crores is called a big-ticket lease. Leasing aircraft, satellite, etc., are typical examples. Converse to this is small-ticket lease where the leased asset is of small value.

(v) *Leveraged Leases:* These are often referred to as big ticket leases as the value of the leased asset is very high, making it difficult for the lessor to finance the purchase by himself. In such cases, the lessor provides a part of the capital and the balance of the requirement is borrowed from or provided by institutional investors or other persons. This person is known as the debt funds. In reality, all the investors would be equity participants. The persons financing the purchase secure their funds by charge or lien over the assets and by getting the lease rentals and other benefits assigned in their favour.

As there are a number of persons interested in a leveraged lease, frequently complex legal and tax aspects are involved. It may not be possible to manage the rights and obligation of the debt and investors by any single person. Hence there is a type of trust arrangement for the management. There will be owner trustees and indenture trustees.

The owner trustee holds title to the leased asset and it normally required only when there are more equity participants. The owner trustee will act as the lessor on behalf of the equity participants and will receive and distribute any surplus that may remain after debt service.

The indenture trustee performs a larger role of receiving the funds required for the purchase of the asset, from the lenders and equity-holders. They pay the price of the asset to the equipment supplier or manufacturer and hold the charge over the leased asset. The indenture trustee will receive the rentals and other sums due from the lessee and will distribute them first towards debt service and the surplus to the equity participants through the owner trustee.

In case of complex lease arrangements an additional party, called the packagers, may also be involved. The packager may be a merchant or even an independent leasing company and also may act as a trustee. For a fee, the package may arrange and or lease transaction on behalf of either party.

Leveraged lease is employed when financing of an asset requires large capital outlay. By investing a proportion of the cost, the equity participants acquire the title to leased asset and investment tax credits with government subsidies are made available along with the deprecation charges associated with the assets. These advantages benefit the lessee by reduced rentals.

Such a lease is called a leveraged lease. Thus, there are three parties to such a transaction – the lessor (the equity participant), the financier (the debt participant) and the lessee. However, the lease is not affected by whether it is leveraged lease or non-leveraged lease. In fact, most leases are leveraged.

(vi) *International leasing:* This type of leasing covers three distinct types of activities:

    (a) Cross-border leasing

    (b) Overseas subsidiaries

    (c) Import leasing,

Cross Border Lease

A cross-border lease is one in which a lessor in one country leases out his asset to a lessee in another country. It is usually a leveraged lease. It differs from international leasing in which giant leasing companies operate and do leasing business through their branches in different countries. Exchange restrictions and the differing fiscal and legal systems have hampered the development of cross-border leasing but they are likely to be the principal growth areas in the future.

Cross border lease may be structured as 'double dip' or 'triple dip'. When it is structured as a double dip there will be benefits of tax positions either in the lessor's country or the lessee's country or in both countries. Depreciation may be claimed on the same asset twice.

Triple dip is an extension of the idea of capitalizing upon the differences in jurisdictions. In this, three nations may be involved and in each of which the transfer may be in the form of hire purchase, true lease or capital lease.

Japan dominates in these types of leases. There is 'Samurai lease' which is aimed at reducing the huge surplus in balance of payments by acquiring large value items like aircrafts. In 'Shogun lease', Japanese leasing companies are allowed to enter into transactions concerning assets located outside Japan to non-residents. They are yen-dominated and are based on international interest rate differential. Japanese leasing companies are also marketing a third type of cross border lease called the "Musashi lease" in which leasing is in foreign currencies.

The biggest hindrance to cross-border leasing is foreign exchange regulations.

Other types of leases are tax-based or tax-oriented leases, specialized service leases, lease receivables discounting, net leases and purchase option leases.

DOCUMENTATION OF LEASE AGREEMENT

Though an agreement to lease a moveable asset is an ordinary one without the necessity of being reduced into writing, generally they are written down, as there will be a long-term relationship. The lease agreement is treated as an ordinary agreement under the Indian Stamp Act and registration of an equipment lease agreement is optional. No prescribed format is available at present and clauses are incorporated according to the need of the parties. Inter alia, the agreement will mention about the period, lease rentals, exemptions, repairs and alternations, default, insurance, delivery and surrender of the equipment and arbitration, beside the rights and liabilities of the lessee and lessor.

Legal Aspects

No specific or particular law deals with leases. The lease contract is mainly subject to the provisions of the Indian Contract Act, but numerous legislations and regulations are also applicable at one point or another. The general issues involved are the right to repossession, subletting and the potential tortious liability of the lessor. In international leasing transactions, there will be more legal factors involving different jurisdictions and interpretations. 'Unidroit' has made an attempt to contract uniform law, to regulate cross border lease. The 'Unidroit' International Institute for the unification of private law is based at Rome and was involved in the project of drafting an uniform law governing international equipment leasing since 1974. On May 26, 1988, the Unidroit conversation on international financial leasing was adopted at Ottawa, Canada. The aim of the conversation was to remove the legal impediments to the international financial leasing of equipment, while maintaining a fair balance of interests between the different parties to the transaction.

TYPES OF HIRE PURCHASE

Based on whether the underlying assets are consumer goods or producer goods, hire purchase, as a type of instalment credit, are of two varieties:

(i)   Consumer instalment credit and

(ii) Industrial and commercial credit.

Consumer Instalment Credit

Consumer instalment credit is a method of financing the consumers for acquisition of consumer durables. Such instalment credit is generally extended in one of the following forms:

Personal Loan: Here loan, either secured or unsecured, is granted by financier directly to the consumer.

(a)   *Hire Purchase or Conditional Sale:* Under a hire purchase agreement, the consumer has the option to buy the financed goods by paying a token consideration. Under a conditional sale agreement, property automatically passes to the consumer after the last instalment is paid. Retail hire-purchase finance may take any of the following forms:

   (i)   *Direct Collection:* The dealer sells the goods to the finance company that in turn lets them on hire purchase to the consumer. Thus, the instalments are collected by the finance company directly without recourse to the dealer.

   (ii) *Agency Collection:* This is a type of direct collection but the dealer acts, by agreement, as an agent of the financier to collect the instalments.

   (iii) *Block Discounting:* Here, the dealer enters into a hire purchase agreement directly with his customers. Later on, he discounts these agreements in blocks, with the financier, making the latter entitled to receive rentals from the hirers. But again the dealer is made agent to collect the instalments and ensure periodical payments as per the discounted agreement.

(b)   *Credit Sale:* Here, the title passes on to the customer from the beginning. The agreement may be either directly between customer and financier or between customer and dealer (later on discounted with the financier).

(c)   *Rental:* Sometimes, the financier enters into rental (leasing) agreement directly with a customer. ·

DIFFERENCE BETWEEN LEASE AND HIRE PURCHASE

	Lease		Hire Purchase
1.	Financing company is called the lessor and the user of the leased asset is called the lessee.	1.	Financing company is called the hiree (hire vendor) or owner and the user of the asset is called hirer.
2.	During the entire period of operation of the contract, the ownership of the asset remains with the lessor. The lessee has only the right to the exclusive use of the asset. After completion of the contract the possession of the asset is passed to the lessor and the same can be leased out to some other lessee at the option of the lessor.	2.	During the period of operation of the contract, the ownership of the asset, for all practical purposes vests with the hirer. After completion of the contract period and subject to payment of total amount of instalments, the ownership legally passes on to the hirer.
3.	Since the ownership of the asset is legally vested with the lessor, the same appears as fixed asset in his balance sheet.	3.	As the hiree transfers all the risks and rewards of ownership the asset appears either as stock in trade or as receivables in the balance sheet of the hirer (user). The amount shown in the balance sheet is the total of instalments paid by him less the interest component.

Contd...

4. Depreciation can also be claimed by the lessor for computation of his taxable income.	4. Depreciation can also be claimed by the hirer for computation of his taxable income.
5. Lease rentals are 100% tax deductible.	5. Hire purchase instalments are partly treated as capital repayment and the balance as interest expenses – the latter amount is only tax deductible.
6. Usually, a lease contract is non-cancellable.	6. Usually a hire purchase agreement is cancellable.
7. The period of a lease can range from very short period (even few hours) to very long period (say 999 years).	7. Normally, a hire-purchase agreement is a medium term contract.

ADVANTAGES AND DISADVANTAGES

Advantages of Leasing

1. *Convenience:* If an asset is needed for a short period, leasing makes sense. Buying an asset and arranging to resell after use is time-consuming, inconvenient and costly.

2. *Flexibility:* A leasing plan can always be tailor-made to suit the requirements and cash flows of the lessee and the financing structure of the lessor.

3. *Faster and cheaper:* Leasing companies are more accommodating than banks and financial institutions. Hence, acquisition of asset through lease contract is faster and cheaper than any other mode of asset financing.

4. *Non-restrictive:* Financial institutions, while lending, stipulate restrictions on the borrower as regards management, debt-equity norm, payment of dividend, repayments, etc. Such restrictive covenants are absent in leasing.

5. *Better use of funds:* Leasing permits 100% finance. Compared to borrowing and buying, there may not be margin contribution for the acquisition of the asset. To that extent, leasing permits alternative productive use of margin money funds.

6. *'Off Balance Sheet' finance increases borrowing capacity:* The leased asset and leasing obligation do not figure in the balance sheet of the lessee. Acquiring assets through leasing does not alter his debt/equity ratio. Thus, leasing helps the lessee to borrow more.

7. *Protects lessee against obsolescence:* Through operating lease arrangements, the lessee can shift the risk of obsolescence to the lessor in respect of assets, which become obsolete at a faster rate.

8. *Specialised services and maintenance:* Leasing high specialisation assets is advantageous to a lessor who is equipped to service and maintain such assets. It is equally cheaper for the lessee to acquire such assets on full-service lease basis.

9. *Tax Benefits:* Leasing is advantageous to lessee because the entire lease rent (principal plus interest) is deductible as business expenses in computing his taxable profits. Hence tax-paying companies prefer to acquire assets on lease. Companies that are not paying tax at present would be benefited by taking machinery on a lease basis, since such lease rentals constitute their business loss, which can be carried forward and set-off against the business profits of future years. Companies that are incurring losses or making low profits, cannot take full advantage of depreciation tax shields on purchase of assets. It makes business sense for them to allow the lessor own the asset, take full advantage of tax benefits and expect that the lessor passes on at least some part of the benefits in the form of reduced lease rentals. A manufacturer-lessor enjoys sales tax benefits since the rental income is

spread over years compared to one time sale attracting higher sales tax. Thus both lessor and lessee stand to benefit financially.

10. *MRTP Act/FERA:* Acquisition of assets though lease saves a lessee from application of Monopolies and Restrictive Trade Practices Act and Foreign Exchange Regulation Act.

Disadvantages of Leasing

1. *Disguised Debt-financing:* Leasing is only another method (disguised one) of debt-financing. Though it is an off-balance sheet item, its implication is known to a financial analyst/creditor.

2. *Sale Tax Burden:* After the 46th Constitutional amendment many states levy sales tax on leasing. So there is double taxation – once when the lessor purchases the asset and again when it is leased on. Moreover, a lessor who is not a manufacturer, is not eligible for lower sales tax though issue of 'C' or form 15. This naturally makes the cost of capital more expensive resulting in charging higher lease rentals.

3. *Psychological Dissatisfaction:* Leasing does not provide the lessee the pride of ownership. Many people would not be satisfied merely by the right to use provided under a lease. They psychologically crave for 'ownership'.

4. *Higher Cost:* In many cases, leasing may be costlier than straightaway borrowing, because the lessor is only a financial intermediary. He borrows from the market at prevailing or even higher rate and adds to it his profit, too.

5. *Loss of Subsidy/Attraction:* Leased assets are not entitled to capital subsidy eligible for projects in backward areas. Generally, lease rental structure do not provide for moratorium period as is available in respect of borrowing from banks/financial institutions. Thus, leasing is considered unattractive for projects with long gestation period. Moreover, in case of financial lease the lessee cannot avail of after-sale warranties from the supplier even though he spends heavily in repairs/maintenance.

Advantages and Disadvantages of Hire Purchase

Advantages of Hire Purchase

1. *Tax benefits:* The hirer (hire purchaser) can charge depreciation in his books on the cash or the initial value of the asset (the amount for which the hired asset would have been sold for cash on the date of agreement). For tax purposes, such depreciation has to be charged according to diminishing balance method. The interest or hire purchase charges are spread evenly over the terms of the agreement and are allowed as a separate deduction out of the profits of the relevant year.

2. *Premature termination:* The hirer can terminate the contract by outright purchase or return of the asset during the continuance of the agreement. In that event, the tax deduction would seize from the date of such termination.

3. *Salvage value:* Unlike in a lease agreement the hirer on payment of all instalments of the asset become its owner and therefore enjoys the salvage value.

Disadvantages of Hire Purchase

Reduced Taxable Deduction: In leasing the entire lease rental is tax deductible. But in hire purchase only the interest component or finance charges included in the hire purchase instalments is deductible as an expense for tax purpose.

LEASE EVALUATION

A leasing transaction has to be beneficial to both the lessee and lessor. Each party evaluates the transaction from his points of view and arrives at the cost-benefit analysis. Let us understand their viewpoints and techniques used to evaluate a lease transaction.

Lessee's View

There are many models to evaluate a lease from lessee's angle. Some treat leasing as a finance decision and compare the advantages of buying and leasing according to discounted cash flow technique, using either Net Present Value (NPV) or Internal Rate of Return (IRR) method. Some treat leasing as an investment decision while some others treat leasing as financial-cum-investment decision.

After establishing the economic viability of acquiring an asset, a lessee has to weigh the various options to finance such acquisition. The cost of alternative sources of finance – through cash accrual, hire-purchase, leasing, public deposits, share capital, debentures, term loans, deferred credit, etc. – has to be kept is mind. Broadly the decision variables boil down to 'buy' or lease'.

Buy or Lease

The following features of 'buying' and 'leasing' are noted for comparing both the options.

Features	Buying	Leasing
Initial cost/Deposit	Incurred (cash outflows)	Not incurred
Depreciation charges	Available (cash inflows)	Not available
Residual value	Available (cash inflows)	Not available
Management fees and lease rentals.	Not payable.	Payable (cash outflows).

Once the lessee accepts leasing as a financing proposition, for the sake of comparison, we limit ourselves to after-tax cash flows. Let us evaluate separately under NPV and IRR method.

NPV Method

Under this method, the present value of cash flows associated with the buying and leasing alternatives are independently ascertained and compared. The alternative that shows higher NPV is preferred. But the basic question is to decide the rate at which the cash flows will be discounted to arrive at the Net Present Values. However, we can evaluate a 'Buy or Lease' preposition by assuming certain discount rate as worked out in the following cases.

Illustration 1: A firm wishes to acquire a machine costing Rs.12000/-. It has two options. It can acquire the machine by borrowing Rs.10000/- and meeting the balance as margin from own sources. The loan is repayable in 5 year-end instalments at an interest rate of 15% p.a. Alternatively, it can lease-in the asset at yearly rental of Rs.3200/- payable at year-end. The firm can claim 25% depreciation on WDV method. It also has an effective tax rate of 50% and expects a discounting rate of 18%. Let us assume that at the end of 5th year, the machine is sold for Rs.4000 and the excess realization, if any over the written down value is subject to tax. Which option is advisable for the firm?

Solution:

Since there is no cash inflow, the net post-tax discounted cash flow under lease' option is Rs.5003.47 which is lesser than the net post-tax discounted cash outflow of Rs.5191.91 under 'Borrow and Buy' option. Hence, leasing should be advisable for the firm in the above example.

IRR Method

Under this method, a lessee's evaluation will proceed as follows:

(i) IRR under the 'buying' alternative is computed.

(ii) IRR under the 'leasing' alternative is computed. IRR computation is made based upon the post-tax net cash outflows.

(iii) A choice between buying and leasing is taken by comparing the IRR under the two alternatives. The alternative having a higher IRR is preferred.

In the IRR analysis, the lessee's evaluation is based on cash flows associated with various options. But the effect of other variables like lease management fee, sales tax on lease rental, lessee's tax position, issues relating to flexibility of lease agreement in the event of contingencies, alternative sources and cost of capital, lessee's capital structure, urgency of finance, etc., will influence the decision to 'buy or lease.'

Lessor's Perspective

While evaluating a lease, a lessor faces a problem of whether to accept a lease plan or not, or which plan among the various alternatives to accept, or how to quote lease rates. In answering these questions, lessors commonly adopt the technique of Internal Rate of Return (IRR). This simple analytical technique of capital budgeting is used since a lessor's expected cash inflows and outflows are known with near certainty. IRR is the rate which discounts these cash flows to zero. If this IRR is higher than the weighted after-tax average cost of capital (of the lessor), the lease plan is accepted.

Cash Inflows

The lessors' inflows from a financial lease are:

(i) Initial/security deposit, (ii) Lease rentals, (iii) Management fees, (iv) Tax benefit on account of depreciation, etc. (v) Salvage/residual value at the termination of agreement.

Cash Outflows

The following outflows are most perceptible in a lease deal.

(i) Purchase cost of the asset, (ii) Financing cost, (iii) Administrative charges, (iv) Tax outflows, including sales tax.

Cost of Capital

A lease deal entails initial outflow in year O on the acquisition of the asset. The lessor receives cost-free initial deposit from the lessee, wherever available. Apart from this the balance outflow has a cost.

Lease Rentals

While pricing, the lessor has to consider the following:

(i)   The rates should be competitive;

(ii) The rates should be adequate to earn a reasonable (risk adjusted) rate of return on investment.

The lessor calculates as follows the present value of cash inflows arising from his ownership of the asset.

$$\sum_{t=1}^{n} \frac{Dt(T)}{(1+K)^t} + \frac{(SV)_n}{(1+K)^n}$$

D = Depreciation charge for year 't' which varies from 1 to n

T = Lessor's tax-rate

K = Lessors' post-tax required rate of return

n = Duration of the primary lease period

SVn = Net Salvage/residual value after the primary lease period.

The net recovery through lease rentals should be equal to cost of leased asset (net of initial deposit) minus the present value of ownership benefits.

The Post-Tax Lease Rental (PTLR) can be worked out as:

$$PTLR = \frac{\text{Net recovery of lease rentals}}{PVIFA}$$

Where K = required post-tax rate of return duration of the primary lease period Present Value Interest Factor for Annuity.

n = duration of the primary lease period

PVIFA = Present Value Interest Factor for Annuity

The actual return of the lessor will also depend upon the timing of rental payments. So the cash inflows by way of lease rentals may be discounted at appropriate post-tax rate of return. The present value of all these lease rentals should be equal to the net recovery through lease rentals

Post tax lease rentals is adjusted for the tax factor to get the lease rentals (LR) as follows:

$$LR = \frac{PTLR}{1 - \text{tax rate}}$$

Illustration 2: KSBS Ltd. is planning to install a captive generator set at its plant. Its finance manager is asked to evaluate the alternatives either to purchase or acquire generator on lease basis.

Buying	**Initial cost Rs.5,00,000**	**Residual Value Rs.1,60,000**
Leasing for 5 years	Annual lease rentals Rs.1,50,000	Residual value Rs.90,000 returned to Lessee in 5 years time

Depreciation @ 20% p.a on written down value. Corporate tax rate 40%. After tax cost of debt is 14%. The time gap between the claiming of the tax allowance and receiving the benefit is one year. Evaluate the lease or buy decision based on the above information.

Solution:

Alternative (1): Buying

Year	Cost or W.D.V	Depreciation @ 20%	Corporate Tax @ 40%
1	5,00,000	1,00,000	40,000
2	4,00,000	80,000	32,000
3	3,20,000	64,000	25,600
4	2,56,000	51,200	20,480
5	2,04,800	-	-
Less: Residual Value	1,60,000	-	-
	44,800	44,800	17,920

Calculation of Net Present Value

Year	Cost Rs.	Tax relief Rs.	Net cash flow Rs.	P.V. Factor @ 14%	P.V. Rs.
0	(5,00,000)	-	(5,00,000)	-	(5,00,000)
1	-	-	-	0.8772	-
2	-	40,000	40,000	0.7695	30,780
3	-	32,000	32,000	0.6750	21,600
4	-	25,600	25,600	0.5921	15,158
5	(1,60,000)	20,480	1,80,480	0.5194	93,741
6	-	17,920	17,920	0.4556	8,164
				NPV =	(3,30,557)

Alternative 2: Leasing

Year	Lease rentals Rs.	Tax Relief	Net cash flow Rs.	P.V. Factor @ 14%	P.V. Rs.
0	(1,50,000)	-	(1,50,000)	-	(1,50,000)
1	(1,50,000)	-	(1,50,000)	0.8772	(1,31,500)
2	(1,50,000)	60,000	(90,000)	0.7695	(69,750)
3	(1,50,000)	60,000	(90,000)	0.6750	(53,289)
4	(1,50,000)	60,000	(90,000)	0.5921	77910
5	90,000	60,000	(1,50,000)	0.5194	10,934
6	(Share residual value) Tax on residual value	60,000 36,000	24,000	0.4556	
				NPV =	(3,76,030)

Analysis: From the above analysis, by applying the discounted cash flow technique, we can observe that the net present value of cash outflow is higher in case of leasing decision i.e., Rs.3,76,030 as compared to buying decision it is only Rs.3,30,557. The company may go for purchase of the generator instead of acquiring on lease basis.

Illustration 3: Mysore Limited is faced with a decision to purchase or acquire on lease a mini car. The cost of the mini car is Rs.1, 26,965. It has a life of 5 years. The mini car can be obtained on lease by paying equal lease rentals annually. The leasing company desires a return of 10% on the gross value of the asset. Mysore Limited can also obtain 100% finance from its regular banking channel. The rate of interest will be 15% p.a. and the loan will be paid in five annual equal instalments, inclusive of interest. The effective tax rate of the company is 40%. For the purpose of taxation it is to be assumed that the asset will be written off over a period of 5 years on a straight-line basis.

(a)   Advise Mysore Limited about the method of acquiring the car.

(b)   What should be the annual lease rental to be charged by the leasing company to match the loan option?

For your exercise, use the following discount factors:

Discount rate	Year 1	Year 2	Year 3	Year 4	Year 5
10%	0.91	0.83	0.75	0.68	0.62
15%	0.87	0.76	0.66	0.57	0.49
9%	0.92	0.84	0.77	0.71	0.65

Solution:

(a)   Annual loan repayment $= \dfrac{\text{Loan amount}}{\text{Annuity factor of 15\%}} = \dfrac{\text{Rs.1,26,965}}{3.86} = \text{Rs.32,892}$

Note: Annuity factor is based on the assumption that loan instalment is repaid at the beginning of the year to be at par with lease rentals. Such annuity factor at 15% works out to be 3.86.

Computation of Interest in Debt Payments

Year	0	1	2	3	4
Opening balance of principal	1,26,965	94,073	75,292	53,694	28,856
Interest @ 15%	Nil	14,111	11,294	8,054	4,036
Total	1,26,965	1,08,184	86,586	61,748	32,892
Repayment of instalment	32,892	32,892	32,892	32,892	32,892
Closing balance	94,073	75,292	53,694	28,556	Nil

Difference between the instalment amount and opening balance of 4th year

Schedule of Cash Outflows in Debt Financing

End of year	Loan re-payment	Interest @ 15%	Depreciation	Tax shield	Net cash outflows (1)-(4)	PV factpr @ 9%	P.V. of cash outflows
0	32,892	-	-	-	32,892	1.00	32,892
1	32,892	14,111	25,393	15,802	17,090	0.92	15,723
2	32,892	11,294	25,393	14,675	18,217	0.84	15,302
3	32,892	8,054	25,393	13,379	19,513	0.77	15,025
4	32,892	4.036	25,393	11,772	21,120	0.71	14,995
5	32,892	-	25,393	10,157	(10,157)	0.65	(6,602)

Total present value of cash outflows: Rs.87,335

(a) Annual lease rentals = $\dfrac{\text{Cost of assets}}{\text{Annuity factor of 10\%}} = \dfrac{\text{Rs.1,26,965}}{4.17} = \text{Rs. 30,447}$

Schedule of Cash Outflows – Leasing Alternative

End of the year	Lease payment	Tax shield	After tax cash outflows	PV factors at 9%	Present value of cash out flows
0	30,447	-	30,447	1.00	30,447
1-4	30,447	12,179	18,268	3.24	59,188
5	-	12,179	(12,179)	0.65	(7,916)

Total present value of cash outflows = 81,719

Decision: The present value of cash outflow under lease financing is Rs.81,719 while that of debt financing (i.e., owning the asset) is Rs.87,335. Thus leasing has an advantage over ownership in this case.

(b) Let the Annual Rental be 'x'

Therefore the after tax cost of lease rentals will be 0.60x

Present value will be 0.60 × X4.17 = 2,502x

Equating 2,502x = Rs. 87,335

The value of x is obtained at Rs.34,906

Therefore, the lease rentals should be Rs.34,906 to match the loan option

Illustration 4: Zonal garment factory needs an equipment for use. It has the option of outright purchase or leasing the equipment. The data are given below. Recommend the best option that the factory should choose.

Option I

Purchase outright for a cost of Rs.80 lakhs. It is to be entirely financed by a term loan @ 18% p.a. interest and outstanding payable on a yearly basis. The term loan is to be repaid in eight equal instalments of Rs.10 lakhs each, beginning from second year-end. The economic life of the equipment is assessed to be ten years. The equipment will be depreciated @ 10% p.a. on a straight-line basis, with insignificant salvage value at the end of the economic life.

The estimated maintenance expenses would be as detailed below:

Year	1	2	3	4	5	6	7	8	9	10
MC	4.00	4.40	4.88	5.47	6.18	7.05	8.11	9.41	11.01	13.00

(*) MC - Maintenance cost in Rs. lakhs

Option 2

The equipment may be leased for a ten-year period. The lessor will do the maintenance of the equipment. The lessee has to pay Rs.18 lakhs annual rental at the beginning of each year over the lease period.

Note: Assume that the lessee is in a tax bracket of 50% and average cost of capital of the lessee firm as 14% p.a.

Present value factors for discounting at 14% p.a. given below may be used for ready reference:

1	2	3	4	5	6	7	8	9	10
.877	.769	.675	.592	.519	.465	.400	.351	.308	.270

Solution:

Option I: Purchase

Year	Loan repaid	Amount balance	Interest on balance	Mainte-nance Cost	Interest + Maintenance + Depreciation	Tax saved 50%	Outflow Interest + Maintenance	Total outflow
1	.				26.40	13.20	5.20	5.20
2	10				26.80	13.40	5.40	15.40
3	10			4.88	25.48	12.74	4.74	14.74
4	10			5.47	24.27	12.13	4.14	14.14
5	10			6.18	23.18	11.59	3.59	13.59
6	10			7.05	22.25	22.25	11.13	13.13
7	10			8.11	21.51	10.76	2.76	12.76
8	10			9.41	21.01	10.50	2.50	12.50
9	10			11.01	20.81	10.41	2.41	12.41
10	-	-		13.00	21.00	10.50	2.50	2.50

Calculation of Present Value

Year	Total cash outflow	DCF @ 14%	Present value
1	5.20	0..877	4.56
2	15.40	0.769	11.84
3	14.74	0.675	9.95
4	14.14	0.592	8.37
5	13.59	0.519	7.05

Contd...

6	13.13	0.465	6.11
7	12.76	0.400	5.10
8	12.50	0.351	4.39
9	12.41	0.308	3.82
10	2.50	0.270	0.67

Total present value of cash outflows =61.86

Option II: Lease

Year	Lease rent	Lease rent after tax shield	DCF @ 14%	Present value
1	18	9	1.000	9.00
2	18	9	0..877	7.89
3	18	9	0.769	6.92
4	18	9	0.675	6.07
5	18	9•	0.592	5.33
6	18	9	0.519	4.67
7	18	9	0.465	4.19
8	18	9	0.400	3.60
9	18	9	0.351	3.16
10	18	9	0.308	2.77

Total present value of cash outflows = 53.60

Analysis: The present value of net cash flows is lowest for lease option. Hence it is suggested to take equipment on lease basis.

Illustration 5: RKV Ltd. is considering the possibility of purchasing a multipurpose machine which cost Rs.10 lakhs. The machine has an expected life of 5 years. The machine generates Rs.6 lakhs per year before depreciation and tax and the management wishes to dispose the machine at the end of 5 years, which will fetch Rs.1 lakh. The depreciation allowable for the machine is 25% on written down value and the company's tax rate is 50%. The company approached a NBFC for a five-year lease for financing the asset, which quoted a rate of Rs.28 per thousand per month. The company wants you to evaluate the proposal with purchase option. The cost of capital of the company is 12% and for lease option it wants you to consider a discount rate of 16%.

	0	1	2	3	4	5
PV@ 12%	1,000	0.893	.797	0.712	0.636	0.567
PV@ 16%	1,000	0.862	0.743	0.641	0.552	0.476

Solution:

Evaluation of Purchase Option

Particulars	0	1	2	3	4	6
Initial outlay	(10)	-	-	-	-	-
Operating Profit		6.00	6.00	6.00	6.00	6.00
Less: Depreciation		2.50	1.88	1.40	1.06	0.79
Profit before tax		3.50	4.12	4.60	4.94	5.21
Less Tax @ 50%		1.75	2.06	2.30	2.47	2.60
Profit after		1.75	2.06	2.30	2.47	2.61
Add: Depreciation		2.50	1.88	1.40	1.06	0.79
Salvage value of machine		-	-	-	-	1.00
Net cash inflow		4.25	3.94	3.70	3.53	4.40
Present value factor @ 12%	1.00	0.893	0.797	0.712	0.636	0.567
Present values	(10)	3.80	3.14	2.63	2.25	2.49

Net present value of the purchase option is Rs.4,31,000

Evaluation of Lease Option

Particulars	1	2	3	4	5
Operating profit	6.00	6.00	6.00	6.00	6.00
Less: Lease rent	3.36	3.36	3.36	3.36	3.36
Profit before tax	2.64	2.64	2.64	2.64	2.64
Tax @ 50%	1.32	1.32	1.32	1.32	1.32
Profit after tax	1.32	1.32	1.32	1.32	1.32
Discount factor @ 16%	0.862	0.743	.641	0.552	0.476
Present values	1.14	0.98	0.85	0.73	0.63

The net present value of the lease option is Rs.4,33,000

Analysis: From the analysis of the above we can observe that NPV of lease option is more than that of purchase option. Hence lease of machine is recommended.

Illustration 6: DLF Ltd. is engaged in the business of leasing and hire purchase. The company also functions as a merchant banker equity researcher, corporate financier, portfolio manager, etc. The company provides fund based as well as non-fund based financial solutions to both wholesale and retail segments.

DLF Ltd. has been approached by A Ltd., Mumbai, for financial help. A Ltd. manufacturers process system for food processing, pharmaceuticals, engineering, dairy and chemical industries. A wide range of centrifugal separators, plate, spray drudgers, custom fabricated equipment for exotic metals, refrigeration compressors, are also manufactured by the company. One of the major strengths of the company is project management.

A Ltd. has a well-equipped R&D centre. It has pilot plant facilities and a modern laboratory for chemical, metallurgical and mechanical analyser. The company has also set up a technology centre with advanced testing facilities. Recently, the manager of the technology centre has requisitioned for the acquisition of computerised sophisticated equipment for conducting important tests.

The equipment is likely to have the useful life of three years. The cost of the equipment is Rs.10 crore. The scrap value of the equipment at the end of its useful life will be zero for the company. The finance manager of A Ltd. has suggested that the company should take a loan for three years from a commercial bank. Repayment of the loan would be made at the end of each year in three equal instalments. The repayments would comprise of the (i) principal, and (it) interest at 10% p.a. (on the outstanding amount in the beginning of the year). A Ltd. uses a cost of capital of 15% to evaluate the investments of this type. The equipment will be depreciated @ 33.3% p.a. (WDV).

P. Securities Ltd. has agreed to give the equipment to the company on a three-year lease. The annual rental for the lease, payable in the beginning of each year, would be Rs.4 crore. P. Securities Ltd. discounts its cash flows @ 14%. The equipment is depreciable at 33.3% p.a. (straight line method). The lessee may exercise its option to purchase the equipment for Rs.4 crore at the termination of the lease.

A Ltd. would bear all maintenance, insurance and other charges in both the alternatives. Both the companies pay tax @ 35%.

You are a practicing Company Secretary. You are approached by the Managing Director of A Ltd. to help the company in evaluating the proposal.

Prepare a report for the Managing Director of A Ltd. showing the effect of the lease alternative on the wealth of its shareholders. Support your answer with appropriate calculations.

Note: Present value of Re.1 is:

Year	6%	7%	10%	14%	15%
1	0.943	0.935	0.909	0.877	0.870
2	0.890	0.873	0.826	0.769	0.756
3	0.840	0.816	0.751	0.675	0.658
4	0.792	0.763	0.683	0.592	0.572

Present value of an annuity of Re.1 is:

Year	6%	7%	10%	14%	15%
1	0.943	0.935	0.909	0.877	0.870
2	1.833	1.808	1.736	1.647	1.626
3	2.673	2.624	2.487	2.322	2.283
4	3.465	3.387	3.170	2.914	2.855

Solution:

Alternative: Purchase of equipment by financing it through bank loan

Cost of equipment = Rs.10,00,000

Useful life = 3 years

Loan period = 3 years (payment in three equal instalments)

Interest rate = 10% p.a

Scrap value after 3 years = NIL

$$\text{Annual repayment amount} = \frac{\text{Rs.10,00,00,000}}{\text{Annuity factor of 10\% of 3 years}}$$

$$= \frac{\text{Rs.10,00,00,000}}{2,487} = \text{Rs.4.021 crore}$$

Calculation of Principal and Interest Amount payments

Year	Principle amount	Instalment at the end of the year	Interest @ 10%	Repayment of principal	Balance amount
1	10.00	4.021	1.000	3.021	6.979
2	6.979	4.021	0.698	3.323	3.656
3	3.656	4.021	0.365	3.656	

Calculation Depreciation on WDV basis

Year	Principle	Depreciation @ 33-1/3% p.a	Balance
1	10.00	3.333	6.667
2	6.667	2.222	4.445
3	4.445	1.482	2.693

Calculation of Present Value of Net Cash Outflows

Year	Loan Instalment	Principal repayment	Interest @ 10% (Rs.)	Depreciation @ 33-1/3% p.a (WDV)	Tax shield @ 35%	Net cash outflow	PV factor @ 15%	PV of Nt cash outflows
1	4.021	3.021	1.000	3.333	1.517	2.504	0.870	2.178
2	4.021	3.323	0.698	2.222	1.022	2.999	0.756	2.267
3	4.021	.3.656	0.365	1.482	0.646	3.375	0.658	2.221
					Total P.V. of net cash outflows			=6.666

Alternative II: Lease the Equipment

Year	Lease rent	Tax savings @ 35%	Net cash outflow	PV factor @ 15%	PV of net cash outflows
0	4.00		4.0	1.000	4.000
1	4.00	1.40	2.60	0.870	2.262
2	4.00	1.40	2.60	0.756	1.966
3		1.40	(1.40)	0.658	(0.921)
		Total P.V of net cash outflows			= 7,307

Suggestion: The present value of net cash outflows is lowest, if the equipment is purchased by taking a loan from the bank. Hence it is suggested to consider Alternative I.

Illustration 7: KSBD Ltd. is thinking of installing a computer. Decide whether the computer is to be purchased outright (through 15% borrowing) or to be acquired on lease rental basis. The rate of income tax may be taken at 40%. The other data available are as under:

Purchase of Computer

Purchase price	Rs.20,00,000
Annual Maintenance (to be paid in advance)	Rs.50,000 per year
Expected economic useful life	6 years
Depreciation (for tax purposes)	straight-line method
Salvage value	Rs.2,00,000

Leasing of Computer

Lease charges to be paid in advance	Rs.4,50,000
Maintenance expenses to be borne by lessor	

Payment of loan: 6 year end equal instalments of Rs.5,28,474

Note: Present value of Re.1 for six years.

Year	P.V. @ 6%	P.V. @ 9%	P.V. @ 15%
1	0.9434	0.9174	0.8696
2	0.8900	0.8417	0.7561
3	0.8396	0.7722	0.6575
4	0.7921	0.7084	0.5718
5	0.7473	0.6499	0.4972
6	0.7050	0.5963	0.4323

Solution:

Calculation of interest on loan

Year end	Loan at the beginning of the year	Loan instalment	Interest on loan	Principle repayment	Principal outstanding at the year end
1	20,00,000	5,28,474	3,00,000	2,28,474	17,71,526
2	17,71,526	5,28,474	2,65,729	2,62,745	15,08,781
3	15,08,781	5,28,474	2,26,317	3,02,157	12,06,624
4	12,06,624	5,28,474	1,80,994	3,47,480	8,59,144
5	8,59,144	5,28,474	1,28,872	3,99,602	4,59,542
6	4,59,542	5,28,474	68,932	4,59,542	

$$\text{Annual depreciation} = \frac{20,00,000 - 2,00,000}{6} = \text{Rs.3,00,000 p.a}$$

Calculation of Present Value of Cash Outflows if computer is purchased outright

Year end	Principal repayment	Interest after tax saving	Tax saving on depreciation	Net cash outflow	Discount factor @ 9%	Present values
(1)	(2)	(3)	(4)	(2)+ (3)- (4)		
1	2,28,474	1,80,000	1,20,000	2,88,474	0.9174	2,44,646

Contd...

2	2,62,745	4,59,437	1,20,000	3,02,182	0.8417	2,54,347
3	3,02,157	1,35,790	1,20,000	3,17,947	0.7722	2,45,519
4	3,47,480	1,08,596	1,20,000	3,36,076	0.7084	2,38,076
5	3,99,602	77,323	1,20,000	3,56,925	0.6499	2,31,966
6	4,59,542	41,359	1,20,000	3,80,901	0.5963	2,27,131
						14,61,685
Less: P.V. of salvage value (Rs.2,00,000 x 0.5963)						1,19,260
P.V. of cash outflow						13,42,425

Calculation of P.V. of cash outflows if computer is taken on Lease basis

Year end	Lease rent (after tax savings)	P.V. Factor @ 9%	Present value
0	4,00,000	1.000	4,00,000
1-5	2,40,000	3.8896	9,33,504
6	(1,60,000)	0.5963	(95,403)
P.V. of cash outflow			12,38,096

Assumption: Tax advantage is accrued at the end of the year.

Analysis: The present value of cash outflow is the lowest if computer is taken on lease basis. Hence it is suggested to acquire computer on lease basis.

RISK FACTOR

Apart from considering the cash inflows arising from leasing out the assets, the lessor also makes an assessment of the risk involved in the transaction. A lease is similar to a term loan in the form of an asset. Hence, while appraising a lessee, a lessor will apply the sound principles of lending as a banker does. Depending upon his risk perception on the lessee, the lessor may demand higher rentals, increased initial/security deposit, personal guarantees, shorter lease term, additional collateral security, etc.

Illustration 8: Let us take an illustration to evaluate a lease plan from lessors' perspective using IRR technique.

A firm wishes to let on lease a machine costing Rs.1 lakh financed 75% through debt and the balance through equity. Pre-tax explicit cost of debt is 18% and that of equity is 15% per annum.

The firm has an effective tax rate of 45% and can claim 25% on WDV method. The residual value of the machine is Rs.15,000 at the end of 5th year. The lessor has to spend Rs.2000/- per year towards maintenance of machine and administration. The lessee agrees to pay annual year-end rent of Rs.35,000 for 5 years; security deposit of Rs.1000/- and one-time management fee of Rs.1000/- at the beginning of the lease. Is the above plan beneficial to the lessor?

Solution:

The lessor's cash flow profile:

(i)   Cash outflow at year 0

			Rs.
Cost of Machine			100000.00
Less: Security Deposit		1000.00	
Management Fee		1000.00	2000.00
Net Cash Outflow			98000.00

(ii)   Annual Net Cash Inflow

(a) Inflow	I	II	III	IV	V
Lease Rentals	35000	35000	35000	35000	35000
Residual Value of Machine	-	-	-	-	15000
	35000	35000	35000	35000	50000
(b) Outflow					
Maintenance /Admn. cost	2000	2000	2000	2000	2000
Tax (see working below)	3600	6413	8522	10104	11290
C. Net Cash Inflow (A-B)	29400	26587	24478	22896	36710
Working:	**Computation of Annual Tax**				
(a) Income Lease Rentals	35000	35000	35000	35000	35000
(b) Expenditure					
Maintenance & Admn	2000	2000	2000	2000	2000
Depreciation	25000	18750	14063	10547	7910
	27000	20750	16063	12547	9910
(c) Taxable Income (a-b)	8000	14250	18937	22453	25090
(d) Tax @ 45%	3600	6413	8522	10104	11290
Post Tax Profit	4400	7837	10415	12349	13800

(iii)   Computation of Internal Rate of Return (IRR)

Year	Cash Outflow	Cash Inflow	Discount Factor at 12%	Present Value	Discount Factor at 14%	Present Value
0	98000					
1	-	29400	0.8928	26248	0.8771	25787

Contd...

2	-	26587	0.7971	21192	0.7694	20456
3	-	24478	0.7117	17421	0.6749	16520
4	-	22896	0.6355	14550	0.5920	13554
5	-	36710	0.5674	20829	0.5193	19063
				100240		95380
NPV				+2240		-2620

$$IRR = 12 + (2240/2240 + 2620) \times 2 = 12 + 0.92 = 12.92\%$$

(iv) Weighted Average Cost of Capital

$$Ko = Kd\,(1 - t)\, \frac{D}{D + S} + Ke\, \frac{S}{D + S}$$

$$= (18(1 - 45/100) \times 75000/100000) + (15 \times 25000/100000)$$

$$= 7.425 + 3.75 = 11.175\%$$

Since, the tax-adjusted weighted average cost of capital works out to 11.175%, which is less than the IRR of 12.92%. The lessor can take up this beneficial lease plan.

Sources of Leasing Benefits

A lease deal could prove beneficial to both the lessor and lessee because of their capital structure and tax brackets. It makes business sense to let the lessor own the assets, take full advantage of tax benefits and expect that the lessor passes on at lease some part of the benefits in the form of reduced lease rentals. Both the lessor and lessee may stand to gain at the government's expense by maximising the utilisation of their tax shields. The society also stands to gain by ensuring provision of faster and less cumbersome credit facilities to productive ventures. Thus it results in a win-win situation.

ACCOUNTING ASPECTS

The assets acquired on lease do not appear in the balance sheet of the lessee. In order to give a true and fair view of the financial statements, the lessee should be required to disclose the amount of leased assets and financial obligations as a footnote to the balance sheet. Total lease rentals, however, appear as chargeable expenses in the Profit & Loss Account.

The lessors show in their balance sheets, leased assets at cost less depreciation as fixed assets. Lease rentals earned are taken as income in the Profit & Loss Account.

The lending banker should ensure that the asset is depreciated within the primary lease period. Even in respect of the companies, which depreciate the leased assets over the primary lease period different depreciation methods, are followed. These methods include:

(a) Equal depreciation over the primary lease period
(b) Depreciation based on lease rentals ratio
(c) Sum of year digit method
(d) ICAI method and its variations

It can be seen that the same leasing transaction reflects difference operational results based on the depreciation policy adopted by the lessor. It makes inter-firm comparison difficult.

The Institute of Chartered Accountants of India (ICAI) has published guidance note for lease accounting in line with International Accounting Standard – IAS 17.

The accounting of finance lease as recommended by ICAI guidelines are as follows:

(a) Calculate the IRR built in the lease rental structure

(b) Apply the IRR on the principal sum that is outstanding at the beginning of the period. This would be the net income earned during the period.

(c) Net-off from the lease rental receipt the amount received as in (b) above. This would be the principal component built into the lease rental.

(d) Depreciate the asset as required under company law. If the depreciation as per company law is less than the principal recovery calculated as per (c) above then debit the difference to the Profit & Loss Account as a "Lease Equalisation Account" debit. On the other hand, if the depreciation as per company law is more than the principal recovery calculated as per (c) above, then credit the difference to the P & L A/c as a "Lease Equalisation Account" credit.

(e) Corresponding to the "Lease Equalisation Account" credit/debit there would be a "Lease Terminal Adjustment" debit/credit shown under the head "current Asset/Liability" in the balance sheet.

The essence of the ICAI guidelines is to bring leases at par with loans and hire purchase finance. This is because the net income recognized as per the guidelines for leases would be lease rentals minus the principal recovery, which in effect is the interest component, built into the lease transaction. Thus, ICAI's guidelines should be followed.

It may be noted that ICAI's guidelines are different from IAS-17 as follows:

(i) ICAI's guidelines aim to show the leased asset as a fixed asset in the balance sheet of a lessor. IAS-17 shows the discounted value of the future lease rentals as an asset. ICAI's logic is to emphasize ownership status and claim depreciation allowance under Section 32 of Income Tax Act.

(ii) Amortization of the principal sum is directly charged to asset under IAS-17 whereas as per ICAI's guidelines it is shown as two items i.e. statutory depreciation and lease equalization credit/debit.

The requirement of charging the principal recovery as statutory depreciation and lease equalization charge has arisen because our Companies Act, 1956 does not look at a leasing transaction in the right perspective. This calls for suitable changes in company law. Thereafter ICAI's guidelines can be amended in line with IAS-17.

ACCOUNTING FOR HIRE-PURCHASE

The guidance note of ICAI as discussed above expressedly excludes hire-purchase transaction from its applicability, unlike International Accounting Standards-17 (where hire-purchase contracts have been defined as included in leasing contracts). In the absence of any accounting standards, the accounting practices of hire purchase companies are neither uniform nor appropriate. The prevailing practice of apportioning finance charges equally/between hire-vender and hirer is not according to international standards. Following IAS-17, a hire purchase transaction should be accounted for like a secured loan. The asset under hire purchase should appear in the hirer's books. The finance charges should be distributed in the books of both the hire-vendor and hirer so as to bear a constant ratio with the amount of investment outstanding. The sum of digits method or the actuarial method can be used to distribute the finance charges, in a manner accepted by International Accounting Standard.

Legal Aspects

Leasing, which is as much a financing transaction as a pure lending or hire purchase, acquires a special status only on the basis of its documentation. There is no separate statute for equipment leasing in India. The obligations of lessor and lessee are akin to those of the bailor and bailee (other than those expressedly specified in the lease contract) as defined by the provisions of Indian Contract Act.

The Hire Purchase Act 1972, which was withdrawn in 1973, has not been brought into force as yet since the Act contains certain lacunae. So hire purchase transactions continue to be governed by the Indian Contract Act, Sale of Goods Act, etc. and also by the various decisions of the Supreme Court of India.

INCOME TAX

Lease

As seen earlier, the principal income tax provisions relating to leasing are as follows:

(i) The lessee can claim full lease rentals as (which comprises a component of recovery of capital and a component for finance charges) as tax deductible expenses;

(ii) The full lease rentals received by the lessor are taxable under the head "Profits and Gains of Business or Profession" and

(iii) The lessor can claim depreciation on the investment made in leased assets after obtaining a certificate from lessee clearly indicating that the leased asset has been installed and put into use. An analysis of the above shows that lease transactions become viable only when the lessee is not able to avail of the tax benefit immediately as he does not have taxable profit and the lessor should have taxable income from other sources so that the depreciation benefit may be set-off against such income. Thus, the tax liability of the lessor gets deferred to future period. Discounting the future cash outflows on account of taxes to the present value, the lessor is able to pass on some concessions to the lessee by way of reduced lease rentals. If the objective of tax shelters is to promote capital formation, lease finance like diversification and expansion achieves it.

Hire Purchase

The hirer is entitled to avail asset based tax benefits like depreciation etc. He is also entitled to claim a deduction in respect of finance charges levied under the hire purchase agreement, the amount of this allowance being evenly spread over the term of the agreement.

SALES TAX

In leasing/hire purchase, the incidence of sales tax is attracted at multiple points (when asset is purchased/sold or right to use the asset is transferred). Also, sales tax is charged on the entire lease rentals, which includes finance charges. This has to be kept in mind while taking a lease or buy decision. Of course, some states have exempted such second or subsequent taxation. But, the Central Sales Tax has not been suitably amended. Again, there are implications on account of inter-state transactions. All these need rationalisation.

MOTOR VEHICLES ACT

As a major portion of hire purchase transactions in India involves motor vehicles, the provisions of the Motor Vehicles Act 1939 have great relevance.

The Act, inter alia, provides the following to safeguard the interest of the financers:

(i) Noting of hire purchase endorsements in the vehicle Registration Certificate,

(ii) Though the hirer is the 'Owner' as per Section 2 (19) of the Act, the financer is effectively a joint owner and his signature is required in the application for Registration.

(iii) Cancellation of endorsement in favour of a financer can be effected only on the basis of hire purchase termination form issued by financer along with No Objection Letter.

(iv) Issue of a fresh registration certificate in the name of the hire purchase company, in the event of repossession of vehicle upon default committed by the hirer.

Leasing and hire purchase as innovative methods of financing assets have been popular only in the recent past. Leasing is an arrangement under which a lessee acquires the right to use an asset, without owning it, in return for a series of periodic lease rentals to the lessor (owner). In the absence of explicit specification, even after payment of lease rentals throughout, the ownership of assets will rest with lessor only. On the contrary, in case of hire purchase, ownership in assets gets automatically transferred to the hirer, if all instalments are paid.

Hire purchase is thus, bailment for deferred sale where the hirer (bailee) has the option to purchase or return the goods before the payment of last instalment. Financial lease and operating lease are two most important categories of lease. Financial leases are long term, non-cancellable leases where the lessee enjoys the returns and bears the risk of obsolescence too. In contrast, operating leases are short-term cancellable leases where the risk of obsolescence is borne by the lessor. Instalment credit for both consumer durables and industrial assets are major forms of hire purchase.

The choice between leasing and buying depends upon the relative financial desirability arising out of net cash flow after taking into account tax advantages. Convenience and flexibility are two other major advantages of leasing. Leasing could be beneficial to both lessor and lessee if the tax benefits by lessor are shared with lessee by way of lower lease rentals. Tax planning is also a major source of advantage in hire purchase. The decision to buy or lease is analysed by mainly using the Net Present Value method and the Internal Rate of Return method.

REVIEW QUESTIONS

1. Define leasing. How does it differ from hire purchase?

2. Differentiate between financial lease and operating lease.

3. Write short notes on i) Sale and leaseback ii) Leveraged lease and iii) Cross-border lease.

4. Explain the meaning and concept of leasing.

5. Why leasing?

6. What does freeing working capital mean?

7. Write a brief note on types of lease, documentation and legal aspects of leasing

8. What is operating lease?

9. What is services lease?

10. Write a note on financial lease.

11. What are the advantages and disadvantages of leasing?

12. Briefly discuss the various aspects of appraisal considered by a banker while financing to a leasing and hire purchase company.

13. A company can acquire equipment either by outright buying or through leasing. The following information is available:

    (i) Cost of equipment is Rs.1,00,100/-

    (ii) To buy outright it can invest Rs.10,100/-from its own source and arrange the balance as a term loan carrying interest @ 16% p.a. The loan is repayable in 5 equal yearly instalments.

(iii) To lease in the asset, it has to pay annual year-end, lease rentals of Rs.36.000/-for 5 years apart from paying a token initial deposit of Rs.100/- and a one-time management fee of Rs.500/- at the beginning of the lease.

(iv) The company can claim depreciation @ 25% on WDV method. It also has an effective tax rate of 45% and expects a discounting rate of 18%.

(v) At the end of the 5th year, the salvage value of the equipment is twice its book value.

Which of the options – buy or lease – is beneficial to the company?

14. With the above information will it be beneficial to a lessor if he faces the following additional situation?

(i) He can finance the equipment by raising debt and equity in proportion of 3:1.

(ii) Its cost of debt is 20% and that of equity is 18%.

(iii) Its effective tax rate is 45% and it can avail depreciation @ 25% on WDV method.

Foreign Exchange Market 23

Objectives

After studying this chapter, you should be able to:

1 Know what is international Financial system?

2 Understand the Role of an International Financial manager.

3 Know economic framework of international financial management.

4 Know about Globalization and International Financial System.

5 Understand the Goals of Global Financial System.

6 Understand the financial system architecture and challenges.

7 Understand the unique elements of International Financial Systems.

8 Understand global benefits from International Financial Systems.

9 Know about International Monetary Systems.

10 Understand bretton woods agreement.

11 Understand International monetary fund.

12 Understand International bank for reconstruction and development (IBRD).

13 Know about foreign exchange transactions

14 Know about foreign exchange risks.

15 Know about types of exchange risks.

16 Understand the techniques of hedging foreign exchange risk.

17 Know about foreign exchange bonds and instruments.

INTRODUCTION TO INTERNATIONAL FINANCIAL MARKET

The international financial system is central to the functioning of the global economy. It provides a framework that facilitates the exchange of goods, services and capital, and that sustains sound economic growth.

An information system comprised of one or more applications that is used for any of the following: collecting, processing, maintaining, transmitting, and reporting data about financial events.

The Global Financial System refers to those financial institutions and regulations that act on the international level, as opposed to those that act on a national or regional level. The main players are the global institutions, such as IMF and World Bank, national agencies and government departments, e.g. central banks and finance ministries, and private institutions acting on the global scale e.g. banks and hedge funds.

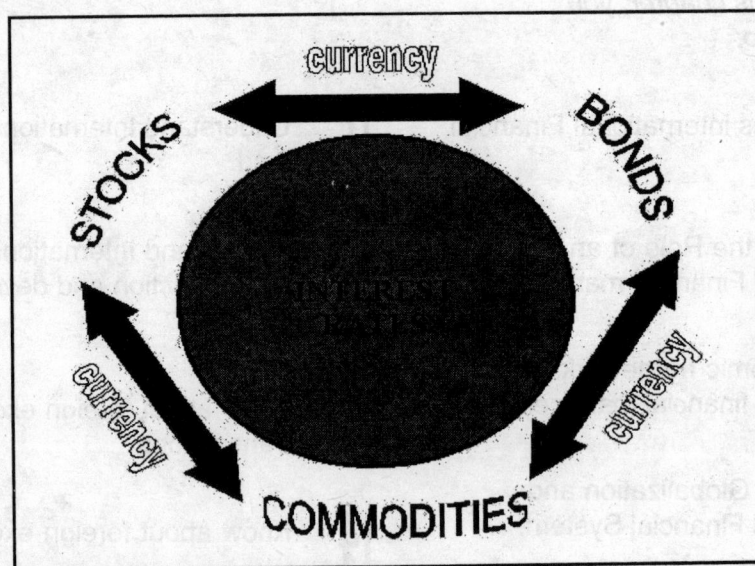

FINANCIAL INSTITUTION

A financial institution acts as an agent that provides financial services for its clients. Financial institutions generally fall under financial supervision from a government authority.

"Financial supervision is government supervision of financial institutions by regulators. The objective is to uphold existing regulations for the financial sector and ultimately to maintain stability of financial markets."

Financial markets play a central role in promoting economic well being by bringing buyers and sellers together. Market prices, which result from this interaction, promote economic efficiency by providing signals to both producers and consumers about the size of the demand and supply of the traded commodity.

ROLE OF AN INTERNATIONAL FINANCIAL MANAGER

a. *Fore casting the financial environment* – prices, inflation rates, interest rate and exchange rate.

b. *Management of asset* – from cash management to international capital budgeting, at home and abroad, in domestic and foreign currencies.

c. *Management of liabilities* – borrowing relationships and decisions, in domestic and foreign currencies and markets, short term and long term.

d. *Exchange risk management* – measuring the effect of exchange rate changes on balance sheets, income and cash flows, managing these risks.

e. *Performance evaluation and control* – accounting for outsiders, the tax authorities, and for management, and doing so across countries and currencies without distortion.

GLOBALIZATION AND INTERNATIONAL FINANCIAL SYSTEM

Two ingredients strongly influence historic trends in international finance: integration and technical change. These basic forces have shaped the evolution of international finance for centuries. Global integration of money and capital markets is the essence of international finance; through such channels purchasing power over real resources today is transferred from areas of the world where expected rates of return are lower to areas of the world where expected rates of return are higher. (At least that is the theory.) This process, in turn, is facilitated in important respects by technical changes that have helped to speed not only the flow of funds but also the flow of information about investment opportunities.

Concerning the structure of international financial flows, many start from the position that the international financial system facilitates the reallocation of savings from locations with lower expected rates of return to higher expected rates of return.

SOME OF THE MAIN AIMS OF THE GLOBAL FINANCIAL SYSTEM ARE AS FOLLOWS

- Transparency
- The goal is to make timely, reliable data, plus information about economic and financial policies, practices, and decision-making, readily available to financial markets and the public.
- Developing and Assessing Internationally Accepted Standards.
- Adherence to international standards and codes of good practices help ensure that economies function properly at the national level, which is a key prerequisite for a well-functioning international system.
- Financial Sector Strengthening.
- Banks and other financial institutions need to improve internal practices, including risk assessment and management, and the official sector needs to upgrade supervision and regulation of the financial sector to keep pace with the modern global economy.
- Involving the Private Sector.
- Better involvement of the private sector in crisis prevention and resolution can limit moral hazard, strengthen market discipline by fostering better risk assessment, and improve the prospects for both debtors and creditors.
- Modifying IMF Financial Facilities and Other Systemic Issues.

FINANCIAL SYSTEM ARCHITECTURE

Interactions in domestic financial systems are governed by a set of norms, rules and regulations - 'financial system architecture' - that has largely arisen out of concerns for the unfettered operations of markets and their participants.

While the International Monetary Fund (IMF) has a central role in actual international financial crisis management, two new international groupings - the Financial Stability Forum and the

Group of Twenty - have broadened the debate and allowed for increased international co-operation on the reform effort.

1. Financial Stability Forum

A landmark development was the creation of the Financial Stability Forum (FSF) in early 1999 to promote international financial stability through enhanced information exchange and co-operation in financial supervision and surveillance. It brings together senior representatives from international financial institutions, international groupings of regulators and supervisors, committees of central bank experts and national authorities responsible for financial stability.

2. The Group of Twenty

The Group of Twenty (G20) was formed in December 1999 to broaden the dialogue on major economic and financial policy issues among systemically significant economies at different stages of development and to promote co-operation so as to achieve stable and sustainable world economic growth. As well as the Annual Ministerial meeting, which the Treasurer and the RBA Governor attend, Deputies' meeting of central bank and finance officials are held twice yearly.

3. IMF

IMF is working in three major directions:

- The gradual increase in the quality and candor of economic information that governments and other institutions are making available to the public.
- The growing implementation of codes of good practices that are essential to a well-functioning economy, and
- The creation of Contingent Credit Lines (CCL), an IMF facility that enables the funds for the first time to be given preemptively to help prevent a crisis.

CHALLENGES TO FINANCIAL SYSTEM ARCHITECTURE

1. Transparency

In its surveillance of members' economies, the Fund continues to actively encourage members to release Public Information Notices (PINs), which describe the IMF Executive Board's assessment of a country's economy and policies. Over 80 percent of countries now release PINs. Under a pilot project for the voluntary release of the staff reports that are the foundation of the surveillance process, almost one-third of member countries have published the reports.

In the use of IMF financial resources, the Fund encourages members to release details of the policies the member will follow to restore economic stability under its IMF-supported program, and about 90 percent of members now release this information. The Fund also releases the key points of Executive Board discussions on those programs.

2. Developing and Assessing Internationally Accepted Standards

In consultation with others, the IMF has developed standards or codes of good practices in its main areas of responsibility: the Special Data Dissemination Standard; the Code of Good Practices on Fiscal Transparency; the Code of Good Practices on Transparency in Monetary and Financial Policies; and Guidelines concerning Financial Sector Soundness.

Other standard-setting bodies are working on developing, strengthening, and disseminating international standards in the areas of accounting and auditing, bankruptcy, corporate governance, securities market regulation, and social policy.

To help foster countries' implementation of these "rules of the road," the IMF has prepared experimental country case studies known as ROSCs (Reports on the Observance of Standards and Codes) that assess a country's progress in observing internationally recognized standard and codes.

3. Financial Sector Strengthening

Banks and other financial institutions need to improve internal practices, including risk assessment and management, and the official sector needs to upgrade supervision and regulation of the financial sector to keep pace with the modern global economy.

The IMF and the World Bank have intensified and enhanced their assessment of countries' financial system through joint Financial Sector Assessment Programs (FSAPs), which serves to identify potential vulnerabilities in countries' financial system. A pilot program of FSAPs for 12 countries is almost complete.

4. Involving the Private Sector

The Fund is encouraging members during periods of relative calm to put in place mechanisms that could help facilitate the orderly resolution of crisis, including collective action clauses in contracts and contingent lines of credit.

When crises inevitably occur, it is important to maintain the involvement of private creditors. In some cases, it may be possible to rely on the catalytic impact of lending by the Fund or other official sources to persuade creditors to maintain exposure. In others, it will be necessary to use mechanisms such as debt restructuring to ensure that countries' programs of economic adjustment are fully financed without excessive reliance on capital from official sources.

Modifying IMF Financial Facilities and Other Systemic Issues.

The IMF created a new instrument for crisis prevention in 1999, Contingent Credit Lines (CCL). The CCL is a precautionary line of defense readily available to member countries with strong economic policies designed to prevent future balance of payment problems that might arise from international financial contagion. The IMF has undertaken a fundamental review of all of its non-concessional financing facilities to ensure that they meet member needs in a changing world economy.

The design of the CCL draws on the other major components of the reform efforts, creating further incentives for countries to adopt strong policies, be transparent, accordingly to internationally accept standards, and have a sound financial system.

UNIQUE ELEMENTS OF INTERNATIONAL FINANCIAL SYSTEMS

First unique element is that some parties must be transacting in currencies that are foreign to them. That is the decision to finance or invest in abroad shows that the financial contracts are denominated in the foreign currency. As a consequence, the market for the exchange of currencies, the forex market, is a basic and unique element of the international financial system.

Second unique element is that participants are financing or investing outside their national boundaries. They finance or invest in foreign countries.

GLOBAL BENEFITS FROM INTERNATIONAL FINANCIAL SYSTEMS

A complete, efficient, and stable foreign exchange market supports and encourages trade between nations; the economics gains from production specialization are shared by all. A related benefit is the foreign direct investment that is encouraged by the availability of foreign financing.

The markets rely on the activities of banks securities dealers, brokers, and underwriters who are increasingly international; they have tended to specialize in international markets as the demand for these services has grown.

Increased financial opportunities also increase the supply and demand for loanable funds.

PARTICIPANTS IN INTERNATIONAL FINANCIAL SYSTEMS

The markets are the channels through which funds flow from one market participant to another. There are three types of market participants: Ultimate borrowers, Ultimate lenders, and Financial intermediaries.

Investors attempt to accumulate wealth, to alter or smooth their pattern of consumption, or to change the risks attached to their consumption.

Borrowers transact to gain investable funds, to consume or to alter the risks attached to their liabilities. Financial intermediaries earn a return by packaging financial assets for borrowers or lenders-increasing the variety of securities directly available in the market. They can also act as brokers by arranging deals between borrowers and lenders.

Participants in International Financial Systems

- Individuals
- Corporations
- Governments
- Financial intermediaries
- Brokers

INTERNATIONAL MONETARY SYSTEM

It has complex set of rules, mechanisms and agreements that determines the behavior of the foreign exchange market.

Gold and Gold Bullion Standard

- The first modern international monetary system was the gold standard.
- Operating during the late 19th and early 20th centuries.
- The gold standard provided for the free circulation between nations of gold coins of standard specification.
- Gold was the only standard of value.
- During the 1920s, the Gold standard was replaced by the Gold Bullion Standard.

The Gold Exchange System

- In the decades following World War II, international trade was conducted according to the Gold Exchange Standard.

- Nations fix the value of their currencies not with respect to gold, but to some foreign currency, which is in turn fixed to and redeemable in gold.
- At the Bretton Woods International Conference in 1944, a system of fixed exchange rates was adopted and International Monetary Fund came into picture.

Two-tier System

- Modified version of Gold Standard adopted by US.
- The US treasury would buy and sell gold for foreign currency only to another government agency.
- Export and import of gold was prohibited.
- The gold price was fixed at $35 an ounce, and the US government guaranteed that it would control the price at this level.

Floating Exchange Rate

- After the collapse of the Bretton Woods Agreements, the world observed a period of high risk in financial markets. High government deficits, high inflation and the OPEC oil embargo increased financial price volatility.
- In this system the gold standard became obsolete and the values of various currencies were to be determined by the market.

BRETTON WOODS AGREEMENT

- During the 1930s, many of the world's major economies had unstable currency exchange rates.
- Many nations used restrictive trade policies.
- In the early 1940s, the United States and Great Britain developed proposals for the creation of new international financial institutions that would stabilize exchange rates and boost international trade.
- In the first three weeks of July 1944, delegates from 45 nations gathered at the United Nations Monetary and Financial Conference in Bretton Woods, New Hampshire.
- Delegates met to discuss the postwar recovery of Europe as well as a number of monetary issues, such as unstable exchange rates and protectionist trade policies.
- There was also a recognized need to organize a recovery of Europe in the hopes of avoiding the problems that arose after the First World War.
- The delegates at Bretton Woods reached an agreement known as the Bretton Woods Agreement to establish a postwar international monetary system of convertible currencies, fixed exchange rates and free trade and subsequently led to establishment of IMF.

INTERNATIONAL MONETARY FUND (IMF)

- Agreement came into force on December 27, 1945.
- The organization came into existence in May 1946 (29 countries signed the article of agreement).
- Established to promote the health of the world economy.
- Headquartered in Washington, D.C.
- 184 member countries

Primary purposes

- Promote International Monetary Cooperation.
- Facilitate the expansion and balanced growth of International Trade.
- Promote exchange stability and maintain orderly exchange arrangements among members.

International Monetary Fund (IMF) is an international organization that provides financial assistance and advice to its member countries and it helps to:

- Foster global monetary cooperation.
- Secure financial stability.
- Facilitate international trade.
- Promote high employment and sustainable economic growth.
- Reduce poverty.

The IMF works for global prosperity by promoting

- The balanced expansion of world trade.
- Stability of exchange rates.
- Avoidance of competitive devaluations, and orderly correction of balance of   payments problems.
- Providing loans to its member states to help alleviate balance of payments problems.

The IMF is responsible for the creation and maintenance of the international monetary system, the system by which international payments among countries take place. It thus strives to provide a systematic mechanism for foreign exchange transactions in order to foster investment and promote balanced global economic trade. To achieve these goals:

- The IMF focuses on and advises the macroeconomic policies of a country, which affect its exchange rate and its government's budget, money, and credit management
- The IMF will also appraise a country's financial sector, its regulatory policies, as well as structural policies within the macroeconomic that relate to the labor market and employment.
- In addition, as a fund, it may offer financial assistance to nations in need of correcting balance of payments discrepancies. The IMF is thus entrusted with nurturing economic growth and maintaining high levels of employment within countries.

How Does It Work?

The IMF gets its money from quota subscriptions paid by member states. The size of each quota is determined by how much each government can pay according to the size of its economy. The quota in turn determines the weight each country has within the IMF and hence it's voting rights as well as how much financing it can receive from the IMF.

Twenty-five percent of each country's quota is paid in the form of Special Drawing Rights (SDRs), which are a claim on the freely usable currencies of IMF members.

Special Drawing Right

The SDR, or Special Drawing Right, is an international reserve asset introduced by the IMF in 1969 (under the First Amendment to its Articles of Agreement) out of concern among IMF members that the current stock, and prospective growth, of international reserves might not be sufficient to support the expansion of world trade. The main reserve assets were gold and US dollars, and members did not want global reserves to depend on gold production, with its inherent uncertainties, and continuing US balance of payments deficits, which would be needed to provide for continuing growth in US dollar reserves. The SDR was introduced as a supplementary reserve asset, which the IMF could "allocate" periodically to members when the need arose, and cancel, as and when necessary.

INTERNATIONAL BANK FOR RECONSTRUCTION AND DEVELOPMENT (IBRD)

About IBRD

- The International Bank for Reconstruction and Development better known as the World Bank.
- Came into existence on December 27, 1945.
- It started its operations on June 25, 1946.
- The IBRD was established mainly for reconstruction of Europe and Japan after World War II, with an additional mandate to foster economic growth in developing countries in Africa, Asia and Latin America.
- The bank focused mainly on large scale infrastructure projects, building highways, airports, and power plants.

Goal of World Bank

- The World Bank provides long term loans, grants, and technical assistance.
- It provides advice and assistance to developing countries on almost every aspect of economic development.
- To help developing countries implement their poverty reduction strategies. It also help in different areas like health and education sector.
- To environmental and infrastructure projects, including dams, roads, and national parks.

The IBRD's Affiliated Agencies

- The International Finance Corporation (IFC), established in 1956.
- The International Development Association (IDA), established in 1960.
- The Multilateral Investment Guarantee Agency (MIGA), established in 1988, and
- The International Centre for Settlement of Investment Disputes (ICSID), established in 1966.

FOREIGN EXCHANGE TRANSACTIONS

The term 'foreign exchange' refers to the process of converting home currency into foreign currency and vice versa.

It consists of a number of dealers and brokers and also includes the central bank of each country.

A market for the purchase and sales of foreign currencies is called "foreign exchange market".

CONSTITUTIONS OF FOREIGN EXCHANGE MARKET

The foreign exchange made up of following:

1. *The Market*

2. *The market maker:* Foreign exchange market makers are the Central banks, major multinational commercial banks, non-banking establishment for the purpose of hedging and arbitragers and speculators.

    ### Inter bank market

    - It's a wholesale market through which most of the currency transactions are channeled.
    - It is used for trading among bankers.
    - It's a market through which around 95% of the foreign exchange transactions are carried out.

3. *Quotations:* Banks usually make two way quotations one for the purchase and the other for the sale of the currency.

4. *Operation of market maker:* Banks operates at two levels (1) Retail level-deal with individual and corporations, and (2) Wholesale in nature.

5. *Communication:* Foreign exchange dealers should have well established computer networks capable of handling several transactions at a time.

6. *SWIFT:* It is an international bank communications network that links electronically **all** brokers and traders in foreign exchange.

CHARACTERISTICS OF FOREIGN EXCHANGE MARKET

- Electronic market
- Geographical dispersal
- Transfer of purchasing power
- Intermediary
- Volume
- Provision of credit
- Minimizing risks

Participants in Foreign Exchange Markets

Foreign Exchange Dealers

Bank and non-bank agencies take part in activities of these dealers. Their role comprises in actual market making. They actively deal in foreign currency for their own account. They help in maintaining the foreign currency within the trading limit. Their profit comes from buying exchange at bid price and selling it at a higher offer/ask price.

Individuals and Firms

Exporters, importers, international portfolio investors, MNC's, tourists and others who use foreign exchange market to facilitate the execution of commercial or investment transaction.

Speculators and Arbitragers

Speculators buy and sell currencies solely to profit from anticipated changes in exchange rates, without engaging in the other sorts of business dealing for which foreign exchange is essential. Biggest speculator includes leading bank and investment bank.

Central Bank and Treasuries

- They use FEM for the purpose of buying and selling country's foreign exchange reserves.
- Government make deliberate attempt for altering the exchange rate between two countries by buying one and selling another is called interventions.

Foreign Exchange Brokers

- These are commission agents who bring together suppliers and buyers of foreign currency.
- Some of the service give by them are:-
  a) Provision of information on prevailing and future rates of exchange.
  b) Maintaining confidentiality of participants in foreign exchange market.
  c) Helping banks to keep at minimum the contacts with other traders.

FUNCTIONS OF FOREIGN EXCHANGE MARKETS

- To make necessary arrangements to transfer purchasing power from one country to another.
- To provide adequate credit facilities for the promotion of foreign trade.
- To cover foreign exchange risks by providing hedging facilities.

EXCHANGE RATE QUOTATION

Rate and Quotations

- Inter-bank Quotations
- Direct Quotations
- Indirect Quotations
- Bid Quotations
- Ask (offer) Quotations
- Cross rates

1. *Direct Quotations:* When the exchange rate for a unit of foreign currency is expressed in terms of units of home currency, it is referred to as "direct" or "home currency" quotations

   Here unit of foreign currency is kept constant. The change in exchange rate is denoted by changes in the value of the foreign currency in terms of the home currency.

   Example: US1$ = 46.6. If new price indicate:

   US 1$= 47. Then, we can say that US$ is costlier by 40 paisa.

   In India, exchange rate was expressed indirectly till August 1993.

2. *Indirect Quotations:* When the quotation is in terms of number of units of foreign currency equal to a home currency, it is referred to as "Indirect" foreign currency quotations.

Here the unit of home currency is kept constant. To record any change in values is adjusted.

Example: Rs. 100 = US$ 2.1549 (100/46.6)

If there is any shift like Rs. 100 = US$ 2.1276 (100/47)

Bid and Offers Rates

Banks usually give two way quotations.

Example: Quotation like 1US$ = 46.695/60 implies that the bank is willing to purchase dollars at the rate of 46.695 Rs, willing to sell at Rs. 46.60 per dollar.

The purchase price called bid price and the sale price is referred to as the offered rate.

The bid rate of one currency is the offered ate of the other currency. The difference between the bid and offered rate represents profits and is called the "Spread".

Cross Rate

Exchange rates are usually quoted and traded against a reference currency (a "vehicle" currency).

* The US dollar is most widely used as reference currency now,
* It used to be Pound, and
* It May soon change to Euro.

When exchange rate between two currencies is determined via third currency (usually US$ or Euro) then it is referred to as cross rate.

In such cases for a transaction first the home currency has to be converted to US$ or Euro dollars. Next the US$ or Euro dollars has to be converted in to foreign currency. Cross rate is obtained by dividing the spot rate between the home currency and dollars by the spot rate between the dollar and the foreign currency.

Spot Rate

When the delivery of foreign exchange is made two days after the date of the contract, it is referred to as "Spot" contract or transactions.

The spot market consists of foreign-exchange transactions that are to be consummated immediately (usually within two days of the trade date).

Forward Rates

The forward market consists of foreign-exchange transactions that are to occur some time in the future. Prices are often published for foreign exchange that will be delivered in 30 days, 90 days, and 180 days in the future.

When the delivery of a foreign currency takes place some days after the date on which the transaction takes place is referred to as a forward contract transaction. The rate of the forward transaction is called as a forward rate.

Forward rates are generally difference from spot rates because the spot rate is adjusted with a forward margin. The forward margin is said to be a discount, if the forward rate is lower than the spot rate. If the forward rate is higher than spot rate, the forward margin represent a premium.

US$1 = 45.60

1 month = 80/85

2 months = 85/90

Spot and Forward Rates

The spot rate is the quote for immediate delivery of foreign exchange,

- although there is usually a one or two-day settlement lag.

The forward exchange rate is for delivery at any later date,

- forward quotes are available easily at 30 days, 90 days, 180 days and 360 days horizons.

- and at any other date by bilateral negotiation.

Swap Transactions

Foreign exchange transaction where by simultaneously and sale of given amount of foreign exchange for different value takes place.

MARKET FOR CURRENCY FUTURES

This market came into being in 1972, when the Chicago Mercantile Exchange had set up its monetary market division for trading of currency futures. Other exchanges were established for this purpose in the subsequent period. Some of them are London International Financial Futures Exchange, Singapore International Monetary Exchange and Sydney Futures Exchange.

A currency future contact is a standardize agreement with an organized exchange to buy or sell some items, such as a currency or commodity, at a fixed price at a certain date in the future. Currency futures are similar to foreign exchange forwards in that they are contracts for delivery of a certain amount of a foreign currency at some future date and at known prices.

FEATURES OF CURRENCY FUTURES

- Transactions through clearing house
- Margin money
- Marking to the market

CURRENCY OPTION

The currency option allows, but does not require, a firm to buy or sell a specified amount of foreign currency at a specified price at any time up to a specified date. A call option grants the right to buy the foreign currency in question; a put option grants the right to sell the foreign currency.

- A Foreign Exchange Option is a contract for delivery of a specific currency.

- In exchange for another in which the holder of the option has the right to buy or sell the currency at an agreed price.

- The strike or exercise price, but is not required to do so.

- The right to buy is a call and the right to sell is a put. For such a right the buyer pays a price called the option premium.

Currency Call Option

1. A currency call option is a contract that gives the buyer the right to buy a foreign currency at a specified price during the prescribed period.

2.   People buy currency call options because they anticipate that the spot rate of the underlying currency will appreciate.

3.   Currency option can take place for hedging or speculation.

Currency Put Option

It is simply a contract that gives the holder the right to sell a foreign currency at a specified price during a prescribed period. People buy currency put option because they anticipate that the spot rate of the underlined currency will depreciate.

ARBITRAGE AND THE CURRENCY MARKET

Arbitrage is the riskless purchase of a product in one market for immediate resale in a second market in order to profit from a price discrepancy.

There are two types of arbitrage activities that affect the foreign-exchange market:

● Arbitrage of goods
● Arbitrage of money

Example:

In New York : $ 1.980 – 10/pound; and

In London: $1.9710 – 10/pound

We will buy the dollar in New York and sell it in London making a profit of $ 1.980 – 1.9710 = $0.009 per pound.

FORWARD MARKET

In forward market, contracts are made to buy and sell currencies for future delivery. The fixed price contract is made today for delivery of a certain amount of currency at a specified future date. The specified date is the settlement date. The agreed-upon price is termed the forward rate.

● No money actually changes hands today.

● Forward-exchange contracts may be used, to hedge a future import payment or export receipt.

● A forward contract can be used by the companies for speculation.

SPECULATION IN FORWARD MARKET

The purpose of speculator is to reap profits from the changes in the exchange rates. The source of profit to them being the difference between the forward rate and the future spot rate.

Example

A speculator sells US$ 1000 three months forward at the rate of Rs. 40.50/US$. On maturity US$ depreciates to Rs.40, the speculator will get Rs. 40,500 under the forward contract. He will exchange Rs. 40,500 at the then future spot rate of Rs. 40/US$ and will get US$ 1012.50. He will make profit of US$ 12.50.

FORWARD CONTRACT V/S CURRENCY FUTURES

CHARACTERISTIC	FORWARD CONTRACT	CURRENCY FUTURES
Nature	Any size is possible..	Only standardized amount is available for trading.
Maturity	The contracts may be for any period, usually up to one year.	Contracts last for a fixed maturity period usually up to a year.
Location	Trading takes place between individuals and banks with other banks through the mechanism of telecommunications linkages.	Trading takes place only on the floor of the organized exchanges.
Pricing	Prices are arrived at through the bid and offer quotes.	Pricing is done through the open outcry system.
Collateral	Only bank-standing is necessary and there is no explicit collateral needed.	Collateral in the form of margins are necessary for marking to market.
Settlements	Contract is normally delivered upon.	Contract delivery takes place through the purchase of an offsetting position.
Commission	Commissions gained through bid offers are spread through retail customers.	Single commission covers both purchase and sales.
Trading Hours	As the trading takes place through the telecommunications linkages, 24 hours trading is possible.	Fixed regulated hours of trading are applicable.
Liquidity	Liquid and relatively large in sales volume.	Although liquid, the volume is relatively small.'
Counter parties	Parties are in direct contact with each other for arriving in terms of forwards.	Parties are unknown to each other due to auction oriented style of functioning.

ARBITRAGE OF GOODS-PURCHASING POWER PARITY

The arbitrage of goods across national boundaries is represented by the theory of Purchasing Power Parity (PPP). This theory states that the prices of tradable goods, when expressed in a common currency, will tend to equalize across countries as a result of exchange-rate changes.

INTERNATIONAL FISHER EFFECT

Yale economist Irving Fisher demonstrated that a country's nominal interest rate reflects the real interest rate plus expected inflation in that country. National differences in expected inflation rates thus yield differences in nominal interest rates among countries, a phenomenon known as the International Fisher Effect.

FOREIGN EXCHANGE RISK

Where some of the assets of an enterprise are not denominated in the currency of its home country, foreign exchange risk or exposures arises. Owing to the exchange rate fluctuations, loss arises when domestic currency is exchanged for a foreign currency in relation to business proposed to be under taken. The occurrence of exchange risk can be explained as follows:

Illustration 1:

Indian entrepreneur enters into a contract for the purchase of machinery with American supplier, payment to be made after 3 months. Exchange rate at the time of contract 47.50/$1. Value of machinery $ 50,000. The value of Indian rupee declines to 49.00/$1 after 3 months.

Results

Amount paid to US exporter at the time of contract (US dollar) = $ 50,000

Amount to be paid to US exporter at spot rate (Indian rupees): $50000 x Rs.47.50 = Rs.23,75,000.

Amount paid to US exporter at future rate (Indian rupees)/amount required for purchasing US $ 50,000 on that date: $ 50,000 x Rs. 49.00 = Rs. 24,50,000.

Loss suffered: Rs.75,000

TYPES OF EXCHANGE RISKS

- Transaction Exposure
- Translation Exposure
- Economic Exposure
- Interest Rate Exposure
- Political Exposure

TECHNIQUES OF HEDGING FOREIGN EXCHANGE RISK

Forward Contract

Contract between banks which calls for delivery, at a future date, of a specified amount of one currency against dollar payments at the rate that is determined at the time of contract.

Future Contract

Firm legal commitment to buy or sell a stipulated quantity of a specified asset at a predetermined price on a predefined future, which is traded on a well-organized exchange.

Currency Arbitrage

Buying currency in one market and selling the same in another market simultaneously.

Covered Arbitrage

Movement of short-term funds between two currencies to take advantage of interest differentials with exchange risk eliminated by means of forward contracts.

SWAPS

Private arrangements where by cash flows in future are exchanged according to prearranged formulas are called swaps.

Currency Swap

Exchange of principal and fixed rate interest payments on a loan in one currency for principal and fixed rate interest payments on approx. equivalent loan in another currency.

Types of Currency SWAP

- Fixed currency SWAP
- Floating currency SWAP

FOREIGN EXCHANGE BONDS AND INSTRUMENTS

What are Bonds

Bonds are "fixed income" investments that have a fixed interest rate or coupon, payable on the principal amount, usually $100. There are many different types of fixed income investments: bonds, mid-term notes, debentures, mortgages, asset-backed securities, savings bonds, Guaranteed Investment Contracts (GICs), and Certificates of Deposits (CDs).

Types of Bonds

- *Fixed rate bonds:* fixed interest rate throughout the life of the bond.
- *Floating-rate bonds:* variable interest rate - money market index.
- *Zero-Coupon bonds:* no interest, as such, sold at a discount, full face value at maturity.
- "Spread" between the issue price and redemption price is the bond's yield. May be created from normal bonds by finance institutions "stripping" the coupons.
- Inflation Indexed bonds, principle is indexed to inflation.
- Ex TIPS (Treasury Inflation-Protected Securities) and I-bonds
- Securitized Bonds: interest and principal payments are backed by an underlying cash flow from another asset.

FOREIGN BONDS

A "foreign currency" bond is a bond that is issued by an issuer in a currency other than its national currency. Issuers make bond issues in foreign currencies to make them more attractive to buyers and to take advantage of international interest rate differentials. Foreign currency bonds can "swapped" or converted in the swap market into the home currency of the issuer. Bonds issued by foreign issuers in the United States market in US dollars are known as "Yankee" bonds. Bonds issued in British pounds in the British market are known as "Bulldogs". Yen denominated bonds by foreign issuers are known as "Samurai" bonds.

The development of the world bond markets allowed bond issuers to bring issues in other than their home markets. For example, since the 1970s, the Canadian provinces have used US bond market as a major source of funding. The Canadian province of Ontario is one of the world's largest and most sophisticated non-sovereign borrowers. It brings bond issues in many different currencies and markets, seeking to fund at the lowest possible absolute rate. In US bond market, Ontario and Ontario Hydro have many "Yankee" issues and is considered an alternative to domestic US corporate issuers.

Foreign currency bonds have a much different risk and return profile than domestic bonds. Not only is their price affected by movements in a foreign country's interest rate, they also change in value depending on the foreign exchange rates. In Canada, for example, the Canadian dollar has moved upwards to 4% in U.S. dollar terms in very short period of time. This exchange rate movement would result in price changes of 4% in Canadian dollars, which completely overwhelms the coupon income of a bond. Studies have shown that the longer term risk and return characteristics of foreign bonds in domestic currencies are closer to domestic equity returns than domestic fixed income returns.

Vocabulary in Bonds

Foreign currency bonds have a vocabulary of their own. Bonds issued in foreign currencies are given the names listed beside the currencies below:

- **"Yankee Bonds"** for U.S. dollars;
- **"Samurai Bonds"** for Japanese Yen;
- **"Bulldog Bonds"** for British pounds; and
- **"Kiwi Bonds"** for New Zealand dollars.

Types of Foreign Bonds

Yankee bonds: These foreign bonds pay coupons in dollars and mature in US dollars. They are like domestic bonds, except they might pay slightly higher interest rates, if foreign interest rates are higher. They do not carry currency exchange risk. The key questions here involve the credit worthiness of the foreign bonds and understanding why interest rates in a particular foreign country may be higher than in US. Yankee bonds are best for situations where US is bringing its own inflation under control, the dollar is likely to hold or gain in value relative to other currencies, and foreign bonds with higher interest rates are likely to avoid default. The "golden era" for Yankee bonds began at the peak of double digit interest rates in the early 1980's and followed the gradual decline in interest rates for the following two decades. One class of bonds, called Brady bonds, actually carried US Government guarantees.

Foreign bonds denominated in their home currency: These types of bonds have currency exchange risk. Under certain circumstances, this may be exactly what you want. The key question here is why the dollar is likely to decline relative to certain foreign currencies. Foreign bonds are best for a situation where it looks like the US is going to experience rising interest rates and inflation, therefore the investor wants to escape the domestic bond environment to avoid having the value of his bonds getting slammed by rising interest rates. Since 2000, bonds of countries such as Australia, New Zealand, and Canada have performed very well, benefiting from the eighteen month slide in the dollar beginning in late 2001, as well as a reduction in the Purchase Power Parity (PPP) valuation gaps between the currencies of those countries and the US dollar (PPP-related queries are discussed later in the chapter).

IDR

Basically, a depository receipt is a negotiable trustworthy security that is issued by a foreign public-listed company and listed on a local stock exchange of a country in which it is issued. By this, investors can hold securities of a foreign company through depository mode. This type of instrument has been in existence since 19th century and was common in American and New York Stock Exchanges. IDRs are just like shares but of a foreign company trading on a local stock exchange.

Norms

The Indian Depository Receipts (IDRs) will operate within the framework of rules framed by the Government in this regard, known as Companies (Issue of Indian Depository Receipts) Rules, 2004.

- The issuing company (a company incorporates outside India) has pre-issue paid-up capital and free reserves are at least US$100 millions.

- It has and had an average turnover of US$ 500 million during the three financial years preceding the issue.

- It has been making profits for at least five years preceding the issue and declaring dividend of not less than 10% each year during such period.

- Its pre-issue debt-equity is not more than 2:1.

- It also fulfills other criteria set by SEBI.

- The repatriation of the proceeds of issue of IDRs is subject to laws relating to export of foreign exchange.

- IDRs shall not be redeemable into equity shares for at least one year from the date of its issue.

- IDRs shall be listed in the recognized local stock exchange and they may be purchased, possessed and are freely transferable.

- IDRs shall be denominated in Indian Rupees.

Pricing Strategies and Privileges

- Basically, IDRs are arbitrage instruments and therefore, the pricing mechanism is based on the purchasing power of currencies and its exchange rate valuations and fluctuations in the local market. In order to trade at the best price for IDR's, one compares the price of IDR's at which it is issued with the equivalent value of that currency in the local market. If the domestic value of the currency is lower than the price at which it has been issued, then it may be worthwhile to buy shares in the domestic market. The continuous buy and sell action may lead to the parity, and the price differential in the process will be minimal or sometimes very close.

- The holders of IDRs are like equity shareholders who enjoys voting rights, title to dividends, participation in rights issue and share of bonus issue.

Benefits of IDR

1. A new instrument for the capital market to attract capital from domestic investors.

2. Better security through safe depository mode.

3. Scope for integration and convergence of global financial market.

4. Higher liquidity due to international exposures and risks.

5. Better portfolio management and diversification for investors.

Depositary Receipts (D R)

In the area of global investment, the term Depositary Receipts ("DRs") refers to a category of financial instrument representing shares in a corporation that is not resident and does not operate in the country or countries in which the DRs are intended to trade.

DRs are created by having shares in a particular company transferred to a "Depositary" (usually a bank) who acts as a custodian. The Depositary, in turn, issues DRs to the public which represent the underlying shares held by that Depositary. A DR certificate resembles a share certificate and trades in much the same manner as such.

In the last few years, DRs have been used with increasing frequency by corporations in a variety of countries who have recognized the benefits in making their shares available to non-resident investors without actually listing their shares directly on foreign stock exchanges.

GDR

A negotiable certificate held in the bank of one country representing a specific number of shares of a stock traded on an exchange of another country. GDR makes it easier for individuals to invest in foreign companies, due to the widespread availability of price information, lower transaction costs, and timely dividend distribution. It is also called European Depositary Receipt (EDR).

Nature of GDR

- EDRs are used by corporations (of whatever country) to enable their shares to be indirectly purchased by individuals in Europe but not in the US market or other markets.

- EDRs in Europe trade through various Euromarket clearing systems such as Euroclear and Cedel and many are listed on the major European stock exchanges.

- A share ownership interest in overseas companies may be easily purchased by non-resident investors even though the non-resident companies involved do not have their actual shares listed on the stock exchanges of the non-resident's jurisdiction.

- EDRs and GDRs have low commission costs compared with shares bought directly in the overseas markets. EDRs and GDRs also provide the following benefits to issuer companies:

  a) They serve to increase the liquidity of the shares of the issuer company globally.

  b) They provide a means of accessing international capital markets.

  c) EDRs and GDRs may be purchased through most major brokerage firms and international financial institutions.

Features of GDR

These are special instruments, which are created from ordinary shares to generate funds abroad

1. The shares of a company are deposited with a bank, which will issue GDRs and ADRs of equivalent value in a foreign currency (normally dollars).

2. The holder of a GDR does not have voting rights.

3. The proceeds are collected in foreign currency thus enabling the issuer to utilize the same for meeting the foreign exchange component of project cost, repayment of foreign currency loans, meeting overseas commitments and for similar other purposes.

4. Dividends are paid in Indian rupees due to which the foreign exchange risk or currency risk is placed totally on the investor.

5. It has less exchange risk as compared to foreign currency borrowings or foreign currency bonds.

6. The GDRs are usually listed at the Luxembourg Stock Exchange as also traded at two other places besides the place of listing e.g. on the OTC market in London and on the private placement market in USA.

7. An investor who wants to cancel his GDR may do so by advising the depositary to request the custodian to release his underlying shares and relinquishing his GDRs in lieu of shares held by the Custodian. The GDR can be cancelled only after a cooling-period of 45 days. The depositary will instruct the custodian about cancellation of the GDR and to release the corresponding shares, collect the sales proceeds and remit the same abroad.

8. Marketing of the GDR issue is done by the investment banks that manage the road show presentations made to potential investors. During the road shows, an indication of the

investor response is obtained. The issuer fixes the range of the issue price and finally decides on the issue price after assessing the investor response at the road shows.

9. Cost of floating an ADR or GDR issue is quite high and is only justifiable, if the amount of finance to be raised is quite large.

American Depository Receipts

With the opening up of the financial markets, Indian companies joined the 1990's worldwide rush to raise capital by issuing DRs. While Indian companies have issued American Depository Receipts (ADRs) since the early 90s, most of these earlier issues were privately placed.

What is ADR?

American Depository Receipts are instruments issued in the United States in lieu of non-US company's shares. They are tradable in USA (or in another country) though usually the term Global Depository Receipt (GDR) is used for Depository Receipts outside the USA) though the company itself is not listed in US exchange.

Advantages of ADR

DRs thus provide companies in emerging economies with a way of tapping industrialized markets, particularly United States market, for equity capital -arguably the least expensive way to make a company's equity available to foreign investors. The 1990s witnessed an explosion in the number of ADRs issued and the amount of capital raised by companies mostly from developing countries.

ADRs of Indian origin trading in major US Exchanges

1. Dr. Reddy's Laboratories Ltd.
2. HDFC Bank Ltd.
3. ICICI Bank Ltd.
4. ICICI Ltd. (now merged)
5. Infosys Technologies Ltd.
6. Mahanagar Telephone Nigam Ltd.
7. Rediff.Com India Ltd.
8. Satyam Computer Services
9. Satyam Infoway Ltd.
10. Silverline Technologies
11. Videsh Sanchar Nigam Ltd.
12. Wipro Ltd.

• Considering the ten ADRs of Indian origin that currently trade in the American stock exchanges and also have the underlying stocks trading in Indian bourses, the extent to which the usual predictions about ADR returns hold for this important type of cross-border securities.

• ADR returns appear to have unanticipated movers. The return on the underlying stock, the US-India exchange rate, the BSE national index movements as well as the movement on two important US indices – the S&P 500 and NASDAQ – together account for less than half of the total volatility of ADR returns in most cases.

• The ADRs enjoy considerable premium over their underlying stocks, indicating effective market segmentation between US and Indian markets.

- Infosys enjoys particularly high premiums but much of its premium is determined by the swings in the NASDAQ index. US market indices also affect the premium on other ADRs from India, though to a smaller extent.

- The ADR returns also have low correlation with the underlying stock returns and the exchange rate, but there is no evidence of any systematic bias in the ADR returns their excess return over their underlying stock is essentially zero in all cases.

- As with returns, volumes appear to have little cross-border connection as well. Only a small part of the variation in traded volume for ADR is explained by the variation in traded volume for the underlying stock.

- ADR issue appears to boost underlying stock prices temporarily. There is an increase in abnormal returns of the stocks just prior to the ADR listing. There is, however, considerable variation in this effect.

- ADR issues do not appear to have made the Indian stocks less connected to the Indian market. The impact of US market also does not increase in most cases.

Thus, the inclusion of foreign investors in a stock's pool of shareholders do not appear to have made a considerable impact in the pattern of returns for the Indian companies with exchange traded ADRs.

PRACTICE YOURSELF SOLVED QUESTIONS

Illustration 1: It is given here that USD/CHF - 1.5350/55
a)   What are two currencies involved?
b)   Is the rate being stated as USD per CHF or CHF per USD?
c)   At what rate will the bank giving the quote buy USD?
d)   At what rate will it sell USD?
e)   How much is the bid-offer spread in points?

Solution:

a)   The two currencies are US dollar and Swiss franc.
b)   The rate is being stated as CHF per USD or CHF price of 1 USD.
c)   The bank will buy 1 USD for 1.5350 CHF
d)   The bank will sell 1 USD for 1.5355 CHF
e)   The bid – offer spread is 5 points or 0.0005 CHF.

Illustration 2 : You see the following two quotes from two different banks.

Bank A-GBP/USD spot : 1.4540/45, Bank B-GBP/USD spot 1.5010/15

Is there an opportunity to make riskless profits without any investment? If so, how?

Solution:

Bank A is selling a pound for USD 1.4545 while Bank B is willing to buy pounds at the rate of USD 1.5010 per pound. Buy pounds from A and sell to B, netting a riskless gain of USD 0.0465 per pound with no investment.

Illustration 3: You see the following quotation on the screen.

EUR/USD spot 0.8710/15

Work out the reciprocal quote USD/EUR.

Solution

$(USD/EUR)_{bid} = 1/(EUR/USD)_{ask} = 1/0.8715 = 1.1474$

This is the rate for the bank buying 1 USD against EUR. The bank sells 1 EUR for USD 0.8715. Hence, in exchange for USD 1 it will give EUR (1/0.8715) which is $(USD/EUR)_{bid}$

$(USD/EUR)_{ask} = 1/(EUR/USD)_{bid} = 1/0.8710 = 1.1474$

The bank buys 1 EUR in exchange for USD 0.8710. Hence, to give you 1 USD it will charge EUR(1/0.8710) which is (USD/EUR).

Illustration 4: The following rates are the quoted in the market:

USD / JPY spot	121.2500/10
3- Months	119.5000/15
6- Months	117.8000/20

A customer wants an option forward contract to buy Yen with settlement anytime between three months and six months. What is the rate the bank will quote?

Solution

Yen is at premium at three and six months. The bank will take six months premium. For every dollar, the bank will give JPY 117.80

Illustration 5: The computer screen in a foreign exchange trading room shows the following :

Currency	Spot	1 – month	3 – month	6 - month
Mexican Peso	9.3850-80	70-80	210-215	410-440
South Africa Rand	61200-300	425-445	1100-1200	1825-1900
Pound Sterling	1.6320-35	40-34	105-95	190-170

The Peso and Rand are quoted against the US dollars as the base currency. The sterling is quoted with sterling as the base currency.

a)   Express all the above quotations as an outright basis.

b)   You want to buy Mexican Pesos three months forward with Pounds Sterling. What is your effective exchange rate?

c)   You want to buy Pound Sterling three months forward with delivery option between one and three months. What rate will you get?

Solution:

a)   The outsights:

USD/MEP :	1 Month : 9.3920 – 9.3960	
	3 Month : 9.4060 – 9.4095	
	6 Month : 9.4260 – 9.4320	
USD/SAR :	1 Month : 6.1625 – 6.1745	
	3 Month : 6.2300 – 6.2500	
	6 Month : 6.3025 – 6.3200	
GBP/USD :	1 Month : 1.6280 – 1.6301	
	3 Month : 1.6130 – 1.6165	
	6 Month : 1.6130 – 1.6165	

b) Three - month forward rates are

USD / MEP : 9.4060/ 9.4095 GBP /USD : 1.6215/1.6240

$(GBP/MEP)_{bid}$ = $(GBP/USD)_{bid}$ = $(USD/MEP)_{bid}$ = (1.6215)(9.4060)

= 15.2518.

c) The sterling is at a one month discount and a large three month discount. Since you are buying sterling with 1-3 months delivery option, the bank will give you only one month discount. You will have to pay $ 1.6301 per GBP.

Illustration 6: Your company has to make a US $1 million payment in three months time. The dollars are available now. You decide to invest them for three months and you are given the following information:

- The US deposit rate is 8% per annum.
- The Sterling deposit rate is 10% per annum.
- The spot exchange rate is $1.80/ Pound.
- The three month forward rate is $1.78/ Pound.

    a. Where should your company invest for better returns?

    b. Assuming that the interest rates and the spot exchange rate remains as above, what forward rate would yield an equilibrium situation?

    c. Assuming that the US interest rate and the spot and forward rates remain as in the original question, where would you invest if the sterling deposit rate were 14% per annum?

    d. With the original stated spot and forward rates and the same dollar deposit rate, what is the equilibrium sterling deposit rate?

Solution:

a. Alternative I

Invest in $ deposits @ 8 % p.a. for three months.

Income = 1,00,000*8/100*3/12 = $ 20,000

Alternative II

Convert dollars to pounds at spot rate. Cover forward position and invest @ 10 % p.a for three months.

Spot Exchange rate $1.80 = £ 1.00

∴.$1 Million = £ 555,555 {1m x 1/1.80 }

Interest earned on £ 555,555 @ 10 %

= 555,555 x 10/100 x 3/12 = £ 13, 888

∴amount after 3 month = 555,555

Add interest   13, 888
                569, 443

∴total, in dollars, at 1.78 forward rate = 569,443 x 1.78 = $ 1,013, 610.

So with alternative I, gain is $ 20000.

With alternative II, gain is $13,610 ...Hence, invest in US at 8%.

b. For an equilibrium situation, amount at the end of three months should be equal.

Hence,

Amount invested in sterling covered by forward rate = \$1,20,000

Let forward rate be \$x/£

∴ At equilibrium, £ 569, 443 equals \$ 569,443x = 1,02,000

$$\therefore \therefore x \times \frac{10,20,000}{56,9443} = 1.791$$

∴ Forward rate = \$ 1.791/£

c. Interest earned in pounds given same spot and forward rates

=555,555 x 14/ 100 x 3/12 = 19,444

∴ Total £   = 574,999

And total \$ = 574,999 x 1.78 = 1,023,498

∴ Gain   = \$ 23,498

Earlier gain = \$20,000

Hence at 14%, we should invest in sterling.

d. For equilibrium sterling deposit rate, amount invested in sterling equals \$1,020,000 after three months.

Now \$1,020,000 converted to £ at forward rate   = 1,020,000

                                                                          1.78

                                                                      = £ 5,73,033

Let sterling rate be X% p.a

∴ [555,555 x /100 x 3/12] + 555,555 = 573,033

∴ X = 17,478/555,555 x 12/3 x 100 = 12.58%

Ans: = 12.58% p.a

TEST YOUR KNOWLEDGE

1. What is International Financial System?
2. What is the role of an International Finance Manager?
3. Write the note on Economic frame work of International Financial Management.
4. What are the goals of the Global Financial System?
5. Write a Financial system architecture and Challenges.
6. Write unique elements of International Financial Systems.
7. What are global benefits from International Financial Systems?
8. Write a short note on International Monetary System.
    - Gold and gold bullion standard
    - The gold exchange system
    - Two-tier system
    - Floating exchange rate
    - Bretton woods agreement
    - International Monetary Fund
    - International bank for reconstruction and development (IBRD)

9.   Write a short note on foreign exchange transactions.

10. Benefits and participants of foreign exchange.

11. Constitutions of foreign exchange market.

12. Functions of foreign exchange markets.

13. Characteristics of foreign exchange market.

14. Participants in foreign exchange markets.

15. Factors/determinates of foreign exchange market.

16. Exchange rate quotation.

17. Write a short note on Cross rate, Spot rate, Forward rates, Spot and forward rates, Currency future, Features of currency futures, and Currency option.

18. Define Arbitrage and the currency market.

19. Write Forward contract v/s currency futures.

20. Arbitrage of goods-purchasing power parity.

21. Define International fisher effect.

22. What is Foreign exchange risk.

23. Write a note on Types of exchange risks.

24. Techniques of hedging foreign exchange risk.

25. Write a note Foreign exchange bonds and instruments.
     ● Types of bond
     ● Foreign bonds
     ● Vocabulary in bonds
     ● Indian Depository Receipts (IDRs)
     ● Depositary receipts (DRs)
     ● European depositary receipt or global depositary receipt (GDR)
     ● American depository receipts

26. Explain the following terms :
     a) Bid rate
     b) Offer rate
     c) Bid offer spread
     d) Value rate
     e) Swap transaction

27. Explain the terms European Quotes, American Quotes, Direct Quotes, and Indirect Quotes. On a particular day at 11:00 am the following DEM/$ spot quote is obtained from a bank 1.6225/35.
     a)   Explain this quotation.
     b)   Compute the implied inverse quote $/DEM.
     c)   Another bank quoted $/DEM 0.6154/59. Is there an arbitrage opportunity? If so, how would it work?

28. The following quotes are obtained from two banks :
     Ffr/$ Spot : 4.9570/80, 4.9578/90
     i.   Is there an arbitrage opportunity?
     ii.   What kind of a market will result?
     iii. What might be the reasons for this?

Securities Market

24

Know technical analysis

Understand fundamental analysis

company analysis

Know efficient capital markets

Understand the weak-form basis, semi strong-form analysis and strong-form analysis

Know implications of efficient capital markets

Objectives

After studying this chapter, you should be able to :

1 Know organization and functioning of securities markets

2 Understand characteristics of a well-functioning market

3 Understand primary capital markets

4 Understand secondary markets

5 Know call versus continuous markets.

6 Understand competitive bids, negotiation, private placement, call markets, continuous markets detailed analysis of exchange markets

7 Understand exchange membership

8 Understand commission broker

9 Understand floor brokers, registered traders, the specialist

10 Know the types of orders

11 Understand market orders, limit orders, a limit-buy order, a short sale special orders stop-loss orders, stop-buy orders

12 Understand margin transactions

13 Understand security-market indicator series

14 Know price-weighted series

15 Understand dow Jones industrial average (DJIA)

16 Understand nikkei Dow Jones average

17 Know stock split

18 Understand Standard and Poor's indexes

19 Understand structural features of major indexes

20 Understand global equity indexes

21 Know bond indexes

22   Know efficient capital markets

23   Understand the weak-form hypothesis, semi strong-form hypothesis, and strong-form hypothesis

24   Know implications of efficient capital markets

25   Know technical analysis

26   Understand fundamental analysis

27   Know market analysis

28   Understand industry and company analysis

ORGANIZATION AND FUNCTIONING OF SECURITIES MARKETS

Characteristics of a Well-functioning Market

A good market for goods and services has the following characteristics:

1. *Availability of information:* Timely and accurate information is available on the price and volume of past transactions and the prevailing bid-price and ask-price.

2. *Liquidity:* As an asset can be bought and sold quickly (that is, it has marketability, which means an asset's likelihood of being sold quickly) at a price close to the prices for previous transactions (price continuity), assuming no new information has been received. In turn, price continuity requires depth, which means the numerous potential buyers and sellers must be willing to trade at prices above and below the current market price.

3. *Transaction cost:* Low costs (as a percentage of the value of the trade) include the cost of reaching the market, the actual brokerage costs, and the cost of transferring the asset. This attribute is often referred to as internal efficiency.

4. *Informational (or external) efficiency:* Prices rapidly adjust to new information; thus the prevailing price is fair because it reflects all available information regarding the asset.

Primary Capital Markets

The primary markets are those in which new issues of bonds, preferred stock, or common stock are sold by government units, municipalities, or companies to acquire new capital.

♦ New issue
♦ *Key factor:* issuer receives the proceeds from the sale

SECONDARY MARKETS

The secondary markets permit trading in outstanding issues that is, stocks or bonds already sold to the public are traded between current and potential owners.

♦ Existing owner sells to another party.

♦ Issuing firm does not receive proceeds and is not directly involved. Secondary markets support primary markets.

♦ The secondary market provides liquidity to the individuals who acquired these securities, and the primary market benefits greatly from the liquidity provided by the secondary market because investors would hesitate to acquire securities in the primary market if they thought they could not subsequently sell them in the secondary market.

♦ Secondary markets are also important to issuers because the prevailing market price of the securities is determined by transactions in the secondary market. New issues of outstanding securities (seasoned securities) in the primary market are based on the prices in the secondary market. Forthcoming IPOs in the primary market are priced based on the prices of comparable stocks in the public secondary market.

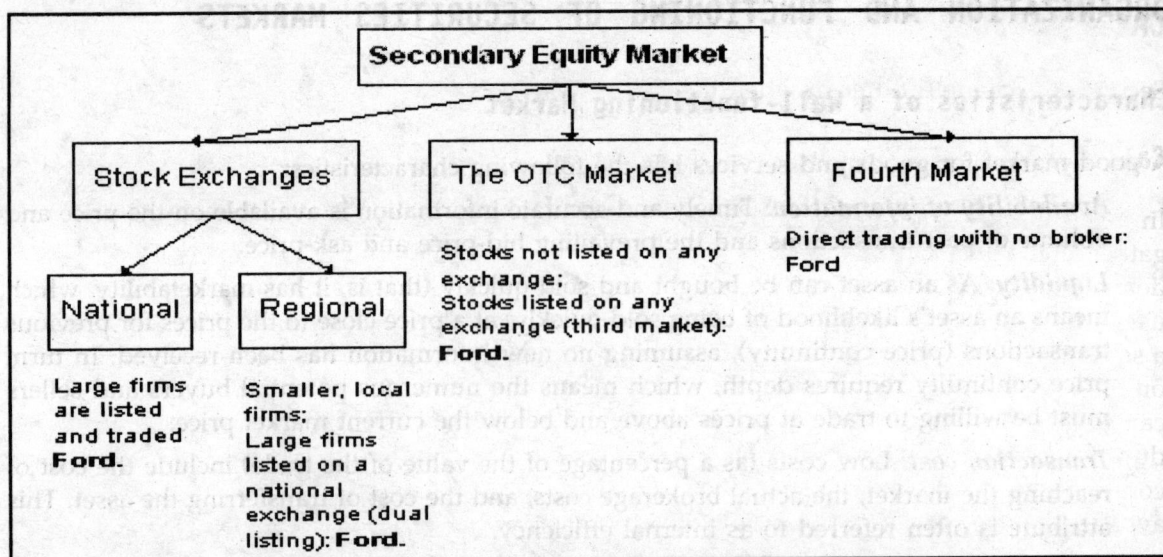

```
                    ┌─────────────────────────────┐
                    │   Secondary Equity Market   │
                    └─────────────────────────────┘
           ┌──────────────────┬──────────────────────┐
  ┌─────────────────┐  ┌─────────────────┐  ┌─────────────────┐
  │ Stock Exchanges │  │ The OTC Market  │  │  Fourth Market  │
  └─────────────────┘  └─────────────────┘  └─────────────────┘
```

Stock Exchanges → National / Regional

National: Large firms are listed and traded **Ford.**

Regional: Smaller, local firms; Large firms listed on a national exchange (dual listing): **Ford.**

The OTC Market: Stocks not listed on any exchange; Stocks listed on any exchange (third market): **Ford.**

Fourth Market: Direct trading with no broker: Ford

As an example, the shares of Ford Motor Company may be traded on:

♦ The national exchange,

♦ The OTC market (the third market), and

♦ The fourth market.

NEW MUNICIPAL BOND ISSUES ARE SOLD BY ONE OF THE THREE METHODS

1. *Competitive Bids:* It typically involves sealed bids. The bond issue is sold to the bidding syndicate of underwriters that submits the bid with the lowest interest cost in accordance with the stipulations set forth by the issuer. The underwriter is responsible for risk bearing and distribution, not for origination of the issue. However, the underwriter may help originate the issue for a separate fee.

2. *Negotiation:* It involves contractual arrangements between underwriters and issuers, wherein the underwriter helps the issuer prepare the bond issue and set the price and has the exclusive right to sell the issue.

3. *Private Placement:* It involves the sale of a bond issue by the issuer directly to an investor or a small group of investors (usually institutions). Note that two of the three methods require an underwriting function. Specifically, in a competitive bid or a negotiated transaction, the investment banker typically underwrites the issue, which means the firm participates in the design and initial planning of the issue (origination), purchases the entire issue at a specified price, relieving the issuer from the risk and responsibility of selling and distributing the bonds (risk bearings). Subsequently, the underwriter sells the issue to the investing public (distribution). Corporate bond issues are almost always sold through a negotiated arrangement with an investment bank. The investment bank is responsible for origination, risk bearing and distribution.

CALL VERSUS CONTINUOUS MARKETS

Securities exchanges differ in when the stocks are traded.

Call Markets

In a call market, trading for individual stocks takes place at specified times. The intent is to gather all the bids and ask for the stock and attempt to arrive at a single price where the quantity demanded is as close as possible to the quantity supplied. This trading arrangement is generally used during the early stages of development of an exchange when there are few stocks listed or a small number of active investors/traders. Call markets also are used at the opening for stocks on the BSE, if there is an overnight buildup of buy and sell orders, in which the opening price can differ from the prior day's closing price. The concept is also used if trading is suspended during the day because of some significant new information. The mechanism is considered to contribute to a more orderly market and less volatility in such instances because it attempts to avoid major up and down price swings.

Continuous Markets

In a continuous market, trades occur at any time the market is open. Stocks are priced either by auctions or by dealers. In an auction market, there are sufficient willing buyers and sellers to keep the market continuous. In a dealer market, enough dealers are willing to buy or sell the stock. Please note that dealers may exist in some auction markets. These dealers provide temporary liquidity and ensure market continuity if the market does not have enough activity. Although many exchanges are considered continuous, they (e.g. NYSE) also employ a call-market mechanism on specific occasions.

EXCHANGE MEMBERSHIP

Listed SEBI exchanges typically offer four major categories of membership:

1. *Commission Broker:* The investor places an order with a broker. The brokerage firm owning a seat on the exchange contacts its commission broker, who is on the floor of the exchange, to execute the order.

2. *Floor Brokers:* These are independent members of the exchange who own their own seats and handle work for commission brokers when those brokers have too many orders to handle. They act as brokers for other members.

3. *Registered Traders:* These are frequent traders who use their membership to execute trades for their own accounts. By trading directly, they avoid the commissions that would be incurred if they had to trade through a broker. They are believed to have an advantage because they are on the trading floor. They now have specific trading obligations set by the exchange, and thus are called registered competitive market makers.

4. The Specialist is central to the trading process. Specialists (market makers) maintain a market in one or more listed securities. A specialist has two major functions:

   - Serve as a broker to match buy and sell orders, and to handle special limit orders placed with member brokers.

   - Act as a dealer to maintain a fair and orderly market by dealing personally in the stock. The specialist provides liquidity to the market by standing ready to trade at quoted bid and asked prices. Specialists are not expected to prevent prices from rising or declining, but only to ensure that the prices change in an orderly fashion (that is, to maintain price continuity). For example, if there is an inadequate flow of orders, specialists buy and sell shares for their own accounts to narrow the bid and improve the price continuity.

● The specialist derives income from the broker (commissions) and the dealer (spread between the bid and asked prices at which they buy and sell securities) functions. It also appears that specialists' access to their book of limit order gives them unique knowledge about the probable direction of price movement over short period of time.

TYPES OF ORDERS

Investors may issue several types of orders to their brokers.

◆ Market orders are simply buy or sell orders that are to be executed immediately at current market prices. They provide immediate liquidity for someone willing to accept the prevailing market price.

◆ Investors can also issue limit orders, whereby they specify prices at which they are willing to buy or sell a security. For example, if the stock falls below the limit on a limit-buy order, then the trade is to be executed. Orders also can be limited by a time period (1 day, 1 week, 1 month, or good till cancelled, etc). Limit orders are sent to the specialist who controls the limit-order book.

◆ A short sale allows investors to profit from a decline in a security's price. It is the sale of stock that you do not own with the intent of purchasing it back later at a lower price.

◆ Special orders often accompany short sales, and they are used to limit potential losses from the short position. They include:

(a) Stop-loss orders, which are similar to limit orders in that the trade is not to be executed unless the stock hits a price limit. It specifies the price at which the stock must be sold if the price drops to a level. For example, you buy a stock at Rs. 5 and wants to limit your loss if prices drop. So you issue a stop loss order at Rs. 3. If the price drops to Rs. 3, the stock will be sold at the prevailing market price.

(b) Stop-buy orders specify that the stock should be bought when its price rises above a given limit.

Margin Transactions occur when investors who purchases stocks on margin borrow part of the purchase price of the stock from their brokers, and leave purchased stocks with the brokerage firm in street name because the securities are used as collateral for the loan.

SHORT SALES

A short sale allows investors to profit from a decline in a security's price if they believe the security is overpriced. In this procedure, an investor (the seller) borrows shares of stock from another investor (the lender) through a broker and sells the shares. The lender keeps the proceeds of the sale as collateral. Later, the investor (the short seller) must repurchase the shares in the market in order to return the shares that were borrowed (covering the short position) to the lender. If the stock price has fallen, the shares will be repurchased at a lower price than that at which they were initially sold, and the short seller reaps a profit equal to the drop in price into the number of shares sold short.

Three Technical Points Affect Short Sales

1. Exchange rules permit short sales only after an **uptick**, that is, only when the last recorded change in the stock price is positive. This rule is meant to prevent waves of speculation against the stock. Specifically, a short sale must be traded at a price:

● Higher than the last trade price (uptick trade), or

- Equal to the last trade price only if the last trade is higher than its previous trade (zero uptick). For example, if the transaction prices of the last two trades are 7.50 and 7.25, then you must trade higher than 7.25 because that prior trade was not an uptick.

2. The short seller must pay any dividend due to the investor who lent the stock, because the lender of the shares would have received the dividends directly from the firm had the shares not been lent.

3. Exchange rules require that proceeds from a short sale must be kept on account with the broker so the seller cannot invest those funds to generate income. In addition, short sellers must post the same margin as an investor who had acquired stock.

MARGIN TRANSACTIONS

Margin transactions occur when investors who purchase stocks on margin borrow part of the purchase price of the stock from their brokers, and leave purchased stocks with the brokerage firm in street name because the securities are used as collateral for the loan. The interest rate of the margin credit charged by the broker is typically 1.5% above the rate charged by the bank making the loan. The bank rate (called the call money rate) is normally about 1% below the prime rate.

- *Percentage margin:* The ratio of the net worth, or "equity value" of the account to the market value of the securities.

- *Maintenance margin:* The required proportion of your equity to the total value of the stock. It protects the broker if the stock price declines.

- *Margin call:* If the percentage margin falls below the maintenance margin, the broker issues a margin call requiring the investor to add new cash or securities to the margin account. If the investor fails to provide the required funds in time, the broker will sell the collateral stock to pay off the loan.

Example

Suppose an investor initially pays Rs. 6,000 towards the purchase of Rs. 10,000 worth of stock (Rs. 100 shares at Rs. 100 per share), borrowing the remaining from the broker. The maintenance margin is set to be 30%. The initial percentage margin is 60%. If the price of the stock falls to Rs. 57.14, the value of his stock will be Rs. 5,714. Since the loan is Rs. 4,000, the percentage margin now is (5,714 – 4,000) / 5714 = 29.9%. The investor will get a margin call.

When investors acquire stock or other investments on margin, they are increasing the financial risk of the investment beyond the risk inherent in the security itself. They should increase their required rate of return accordingly.

Return on margin transaction = (change in investor's equity – interest – commission)/initial investor's equity

Example

Suppose an investor is bullish (optimistic) on Microsoft stock, which is currently selling at Rs. 100 per share. The investor has Rs. 10,000 to invest and expects the stock to go up in price by 30% during the next year. Ignoring any dividends and commissions, the expected rate of return would thus be 30% if the investor spent only Rs. 10,000 to buy 100 shares. If the investor borrows Rs. 10,000 from his broker and invest it in the stock (along with his own Rs. 10,000). Assume that the interest rate is 9% per year.

- If the stock goes upto 30%, his 200 shares will be worth Rs. 26,000. After paying off Rs. 10,000 of principal and interest on the margin load leaves Rs. 15,100. The rate of return, therefore will be (Rs. 15,100 – Rs. 10,000) / Rs. 10,000 = 51%. Good investment, huh?

♦ Doing so, however, magnifies the downside risk. Suppose the stock actually goes down by 30%: his 200 shares of stock are worth Rs. 14,000 now. After paying off Rs. 10,900 he is left with only Rs. 3,100. The result is a disastrous rate of return of 69%.

♦ If there is no change in the stock price, he will lose 9% on the cost of the loan.

SECURITY-MARKET INDICATOR SERIES

Three Dominant Weighting Schemes for Stock Market Series

Security market indexes are used:

♦ To evaluate the portfolio performance on a risk-adjusted basis.

♦ To create index funds to track the performance of the specific market series over time.

♦ To examine factors that affect aggregate market movements.

♦ To help "technicians" predict future market movements.

♦ As a proxy for the market portfolio to calculate the systematic risk of an asset. To compute an index, the following factors are important:

   (a) The size of the sample: the larger, the better but eventually the costs of taking a larger sample will outweigh the benefits.

   (b) The breadth of the sample: the sample must represent the total population.

   (c) The source of the sample: samples must be taken from each different segment of the population.

   (d) The weight given to each member in the sample.

   (e) Computational procedure.

PRICE-WEIGHTED SERIES

It is an arithmetic average of current prices. Index movements are influenced by the differential prices of the components.

Dow Jones Industrial Average (DJIA)

It is the best-known price-weighted series and is also the oldest and the most popular stock market indicator series. The DJIA is computed by adding the prices of the 30 companies of NYSE and dividing by a "divisor". The weight of each firm in the index is proportional to the share price rather than the total outstanding market value of the shares. As stocks are added or dropped from the average, or stock split over time, the divisor is continually adjusted to leave the average unaffected by the change.

The Limitations Are

The sample used for the series is limited to 30 large, mature and blue-chip companies only: small sample size and narrow sample breadth. When a firm has a stock split, its price declines, and therefore its weight in the DJIA is reduced even though it may be large and important - the weighting scheme causes a downward bias in the DJIA: the stocks that have higher growth rates will have higher prices, and because such stocks tend to split, they will consistently lose weight within the index

♦ *Nikkei-Dow Jones Average:* It includes 225 stocks on the First Section of the Tokyo Stock Exchange. The price-weighted series has a downward bias.

- High-priced stocks have greater impact on the index than low-priced stocks, as the scheme assumes that an investor purchases an equal number of shares for each stock in the index.

- As illustrated for DJIA, large, successful firms consistently lose weight within the index since high-growth companies tend to split their stocks more often. Over time, low growth, small firms with high prices will dominate the index. A price-weighted series is computed by:
  - ❖ Adding up the market price of each stock in the index, then
  - ❖ Dividing this total price by the number of stocks in the index: price-weighted series = sum of stock prices/number of stocks in the series. The divisor must be adjusted when a stock splits.

Example

The shares of firm A sells for Rs. 100, and the shares of firm B sells for Rs. 25. The initial price index is $(100 + 25)/2 = 62.5$. The divisor is therefore 2.

Normal situation: suppose that A increases by 10% to Rs. 110, and B increases by 20% to Rs. 30, the price index would be $(110 + 30) /2 = 70$. The rate of return would be: $(70 - 62.5) / 62.5 = 12\%$.

Stock Split: If A were to split two for one, and its share price were, therefore to fall to Rs. 50, we would not want the average to fall since that would incorrectly indicate at all levels of market prices. Following a split, the divisor must be reduced to a value that leaves the average unaffected by the split. The new divisor is: $(50 + 25)/62.5 = 1.2$, which will make the initial value of the average unaffected.

Value-Weighted Series

It is generated by deriving the initial total market value of all stocks used in the series. The importance of individual stocks in the sample depends on the market value of the stocks. There is an automatic adjustment for stock splits and other capital changes in this series.

Standard and Poor's Index

It is based upon 500 firms from NYSE and OTC. The number of stocks in the index is different from that of DJIA, but more importantly, the source of the sample is also different. However, the index does not reflect cash dividends paid out by those firms.? NASDAQ Composite: Based on almost 5,000 OTC firms. Amex Market Value Firms with large market value have greater impact on the index than firms with small market value. Thus, over time the large market value stocks will dominate changes in a market-value-weighted series. A market-value-weighted series is generated by:

- Adding up the total market value of all stocks in the index: market value = number of shares outstanding x current market value.
- Dividing this total by the total market value for the base period.
- Multiplying this ratio by the beginning index value: new market value = (current market value / base value) x beginning index value.

The shares of firm A sells for Rs. 100 with 1 million shares, and the shares of firm B sells for Rs. 25 with 20 million shares. Their market value is therefore Rs. 100 million and Rs. 500 million, respectively. If A increases by 10% to Rs. 110, and B increases by 20% to Rs. 30, their market value will be Rs. 110 million and Rs. 600 million, respectively. The rate of return would be: $(710 - 600) / 600 = 18.3\%$.

STRUCTURAL FEATURES OF MAJOR INDEXES

Global Equity Indexes

Local indexes of individual countries lack consistency in sample selection, weighting, or computational procedures. Global equity indexes are created to solve this comparability problem.

◆ *FT/S&P Actuaries World Indexes:* about 2,461 equity securities in 30 countries are measured. Market-value weighted.

◆ *Morgan Stanley Capital International (MSCI) Indexes:* they consist of over 50 market-value weighted indexes worldwide.

◆ *Dow Jones World Stock Index:* 2,200 companies in 33 countries.

Bond Indexes

The creation and computation of bond-market index is more difficult than a stock market series:

1. The universe of bonds is much broader than that of stocks.

2. The universe of bonds is changing constantly because of new issues, bond maturities, calls and bond sinking funds.

3. The volatility of prices for individual bonds and bond portfolios changes because bond price volatility is affected by duration, which is changing constantly.

4. Pricing individual bonds is more difficult compared to the current and continuous transactions prices available for most stocks used in stock indexes.

EFFICIENT CAPITAL MARKETS

Why should Capital Markets be Efficient?

An **efficient capital market** is one in which security prices adjust rapidly to the arrival of new information and the current prices of securities reflect all the information about the security. Therefore, it is also called an **informationally efficient capital market**. Why should capital markets be efficient? Competition is the source of efficiency, and price changes should be independent and random.

◆ A large number of competing profit-maximizing participants analyze, and value securities, each independently of the others.

◆ New information regarding securities comes to the market in a random fashion, and the timing of the announcement is generally independent of others.

◆ The competing investors attempt to adjust security prices rapidly to reflect the effect of new information. The price adjustment is unbiased sometimes the market will over- adjust and other times it will under-adjust, but you cannot prefect its behavior.

In an efficient market, the expected returns implicit in the current price of the security should reflect its risk. Investors buying the security should receive a return that is consistent with the perceived risk of the security.

There are three versions of the 'Efficient Market Hypothesis' (EMH); they differ by their notions of what is meant by the term "all available information".

1. The **Weak-Form Hypothesis** asserts that stock prices already reflect all information that can be derived by examining market trading data such as the history of past prices, trading

volume, or short interest. This implies that trend analysis is fruitless, if such data ever conveyed reliable signals about future performance, all investors would have learnt already the exploit the signals.

2. The Semistrong Form Hypothesis states that all publicly available information regarding the prospects of a firm must be reflected already in the stock price. Such information includes, in addition to past prices, fundamental data on the firm's product line, quality of management, balance sheet composition, patents held, earning forecasts, and accounting practices. Obviously, this version encompasses the weak-form EMH. This hypothesis implies that an investor cannot achieve risk adjusted excess returns using important public information.

3. The Strong Form Hypothesis states that stock prices reflect all the information (from public and private sources) relevant to the firm, even include information available only to company insiders. This version of EMH encompasses both the weak-form and the semistrong-form EMH. It is quite an extreme. It implies that no investor has monopolistic access to information that influences prices. Thus, no investor can consistently derive risk-adjusted excess returns. In fact, the strong-form EMH assumes perfect markets, in which all the information is cost free and available to everyone at the same time. In contrast, in an efficient market prices adjust rapidly to new public information.

IMPLICATIONS OF EFFICIENT CAPITAL MARKETS

Technical Analysis

The assumptions of technical analysis directly oppose the notion of efficient markets:

♦   The process of disseminating new information takes time.

♦   Stock prices move to new equilibriums in a gradual manner.

♦   Hence, stock prices move in trends that persist.

Therefore, technical analysts believe that good traders can detect the significant stock price changes before others do. However, as confirmed by most studies, the capital market is weak-form efficient as prices fully reflect all market information as soon as the information becomes public. Though prices may not be adjusted perfectly in an efficient market, it is unpredictable whether the market will over-adjust or under-adjust at any time. Therefore, technical analysts should not generate abnormal returns and no technical trading system should have any value.

FUNDAMENTAL ANALYSIS

Fundamental analysts believe that:

1. At any time, there is a basic intrinsic value for the aggregate stock market, various industries, or individual securities.

2. These values depend on underlying economic factors such as cash flows and risk variables.

3. Though market price and the intrinsic value may differ across time, the discrepancy will get corrected as new information arrives.

Therefore, by accurately estimating the intrinsic value, a fundamental analyst can achieve abnormal returns by making superior market timing decisions or acquiring undervalued securities. Fundamental analysis involves aggregate market analysis, industry analysis, company analysis and portfolio management. However, using historical data to estimate the relevant variables is as much an art and a product of hard work as it is of a science. A fundamental analysis must do a superior job to predict earnings to beat the market.

1. *Market analysis:* Analysis relying solely on historical data will not yield superior, risk-adjusted returns as the EMH asserts that the market adjusts rapidly to public information. The analyst must be good at estimating the relevant variables that cause long-run trends of market movements.

2. *Industry and company analysis:* The EMH implies that to achieve abnormal returns, an analyst must correctly estimate future values for variables that influence rates of return and predict future earnings. The estimates must differ from the consensus. There will be no superior return if the analyst predicts the consensus and the consensus is correct. Therefore, the analyst should pay more attention to areas where the market is inefficient, such as stocks that are neglected by other analysts, stocks with high book value/market value ratios, and stocks with small market capitalization. Since the capital markets are primarily efficient, the majority of portfolio managers cannot beat a buy-and-hold policy on a risk-adjusted basis. However, in many occasions the market fails to adjust prices rapidly to public information, and it is likely to achieve superior investment performance through active security valuation and portfolio management. This relies on superior analysts who can time major market trends or identify undervalued securities. Hence, the decision of how one manages the portfolio (actively or passively) should depend on whether the manager has access to superior analysts or not.

If a portfolio manager has access to superior analysts, he or she can manage a portfolio actively, looking for undervalued securities based upon superior fundamental analysis (including predicting earnings surprise), and attempting to time the market wherein asset allocation is shifted between aggressive and defensive positions. The portfolio manager should ensure that the risk preferences of the client are maintained. If a portfolio manager does not have access to superior analysts, he or she should:

1. Determine and quantify his risk preferences.
2. Construct the appropriate risk-level portfolio by dividing the total portfolio between.
3. Lending or borrowing risk-free assets and a portfolio of risky assets.
4. Diversify completely on a global basis to eliminate all unsystematic risk.
5. Maintain the specific risk level by rebalancing when necessary.
6. Minimize taxes and total transaction costs (reduce trading turnover and trade relatively liquid stocks to minimize liquidity costs).

MACRO ECONOMIC ANALYSIS

The analysis of the following factors indicate the trends in macro economic that brings about change in the effect of the risk and return on investment:

1. Money supply
2. Industrial production
3. Capacity utilization
4. Unemployment
5. Inflation
6. Growth in GDP
7. Institutional lending
8. Stock prices
9. Monsoons
10. Productivity of factors of production
11. Fiscal deficit

12. Credit/Deposit ratio
13. Stock of food grains and essential commodities
14. Industrial wages
15. Foreign trade and balance of payments positions
16. Status of political and economic stability
17. Technological innovation
18. Infrastructural facilities
19. Economic and industrial policies of government
20. Debt recovery and loans outstanding
21. Interest rates
22. Cost of living Index
23. Foreign investment
24. Trends in Capital markets
25. Stages of business cycle
26. Foreign exchange reserves

ECONOMIC FORECASTING

Economic forecasting consists of making forecasts of economic activity at the national level. It considers movements of factors like national income, aggregate industrial production or employment and total imports and exports. Techniques used are:

Economic indicators

Diffusion index

Surveys

Economic Model Building

$$\text{Diffusion Index} = \frac{\text{No. of members set in the same direction}}{\text{Total No. of members set}}$$

In the example, Diffusion index = 4/10 = 0.4

Next month, if the index moved to 0.6, certainly it is strong confirmation of economic advances.

Component Evaluation Index

A narrow type of index is one which examines a particular series taking into consideration components of it. It measures the breadth of the movement within a particular series.

Opportunities and threats in Macro Economic Environment

S.No	Economic Indicator	Opportunity	Threat
1	Economic cycle stage	Boom	Recession
2	Gross National product	Growth	Decline
3	Employment	Increase	Decrease
4	Aggregate demand	Rise	Fall
5	Personal disposable income	Increase	Decrease
6	House constriction	Increase	Decrease
7	Personnel savings during inflation	Increase	Decrease
8	Rate of interest	Low	High
9	Corporate taxation	Low	High
10	Balance of trade	Positive	Negative
11	Rupee in foreign exchange market	Strong	Weak
12	Prices	Stable	unstable

INDUSTRY ANALYSIS

♦ Importance of industry analysis.

♦ Why should a security analyst do industry analysis?

(1) Firms in each different industry do typical experience similar level of risk and return. As such industry analysis can also be useful in knowing investment worthiness of a firm.

(2) To know industry prospectus.

CLASSIFICATION OF INDUSTRY

Classification of reporting agency:

1. According to RBI – 32 groups
2. According to SEBI – 10 Groups
3. Economics times – 10 Groups

Classification by business cycle:

1. Cyclical industry
2. Defensive industry
3. Cycle growth industry

Key Indicators in Industry Analysis

The security analyst will take into consideration the following factors in assessing the industry potential in making investments.

1. Past sales and earning performance
2. Government attitude towards industry
3. Labour conditions
4. Performance of the industry
5. Industry share price relative to industry earnings
6. Stage of industry life cycle
7. Industry trade cycle
8. Inventories build up in the industry
9. Investors performance over the industry
10. Technological innovation

With reference to key factors, evaluations shall be done to identify:

♦ Strengths and weakness

♦ Opportunities and threat

Some relevant questions which may be asked in this connection are given here:

1. Are the sales of industry growing in relation to the growth in gross national product (GNP)?
2. What is overall return on investment (ROI)?
3. What is the cost structure of the industry?
4. Is the industry in a stable position?
5. What is the impact of taxation on the industry?

6. What is the industrial scenario of the industry?
7. Is the industry highly competitive?
8. Is the industry highly technology-based?
9. How does stock market evaluate the industry?

COMPANY ANALYSIS

Frame Work of Company Analysis

The two major components of company analysis are:

1. Financial, and
2. Non-Financial

Internal analysis: Internal analysis consist of the data and events relating to the enterprise as published by it.

External analysis: Information comprises the reports and analysis made by sources outside the company viz., media and research agencies.

Factors influencing company analysis

A. Company analysis
   - Sales
   - Growth in Sales
   - Stability of Sales
B. Accounting Policies
   - Inventory Pricing
   - Depreciation Methods
   - Non Operating Income
   - Tax Carry over
C. Profitability
   - Gross Profit Margin
   - Net Profit Margin
   - Earning Power
   - Return on Equity
   - Earning Per Share
   - Cash Earning Per Share
D. Dividend Policy
   - Preference Shares
   - Debt:
     1. *Earning limit of Debt*
     2. *Assets Limit of Debt*
   1. Profitability Ratio
      ❖ Return on capital employed

        ❖ Earning per share
        ❖ Return on assets
        ❖ Cash profit ratio
        ❖ Gross profit margin

   2.   Activity Ratio/Turnover Ratio
        ❖ Inventory turnover ratio
        ❖ Inventory ratio
        ❖ Debtors turnover ratio
        ❖ Debtors collection period
        ❖ Creditors payment period
        ❖ Creditors turnover ratio
        ❖ Assets turnover ratio
        ❖ Working capital turnover ratio
        ❖ Sales to capital employed

   3.   Market Test Ratio
        ❖ Dividend payout ratio (DPS/EPS)
        ❖ Dividend yield (DPS/MP*100)
        ❖ Book value (Equity+ R&S/ No. of Equity Shares)
        ❖ Price earning ratio

E.   Internal Non-Financial Factors
    • History and business of the company
    • Top management team
    • Collaboration agreements
    • Product range
    • Future plans of expansion
    • R&D
    • Market standing-competition and market share
    • Corporate social responsibility
    • Industrial relations
    • Corporate image etc.,

F.   External Factors
    • Statutory control
    • Government policies
    • Industrial life cycle
    • Environmentalism
    • Consumerism

PRACTICE YOURSELF SOLVED QUESTIONS

1. You are considering purchasing the equity stock of B Company. The current price per share is Rs 10. You expect the dividend after a year to be Rs. 1.00. You expect the price per share of B stock after a year to have the following probability distribution.

Price a price hence	Rs. 10	11	12
Probability	0.4	0.4	0.2

(a) What is the expected price per share after a year?

(b) What is the probability distribution of the rate of return on B's equity stock?

Solution:

(a) Expected price per share a year hence will be:

= 0.4 x Rs.10 + 0.4 x Rs.11 + 0.2 x Rs.12 = Rs.10.80

(b) Probability distribution of the rate of return is:

Rate of return (R_i)	10%	20%	30%
Probability (p_i)	0.4	0.4	0.2

Note: The rate of return is defined as:

$$\frac{\text{Dividend} + \text{Terminal price}}{\text{Initial price}} - 1$$

(c) The standard deviation of rate of return is :

$$\sigma = \sum p_i (R_i - \overline{R})^2$$

The σ of the rate of return on B's stock is calculated below:

R_i	p_i	$p_i r_i$	$(R_i \overline{R})$	$(R_i \overline{R})^2$	$p_i (R_i \overline{R})^2$
10	0.4	4	-8	64	25.6
20	0.4	8	2	4	1.6
30	0.2	6	12	144	28.8

$$\overline{R} = \sum p_i R_i = 18 \qquad \sum p_i (R_i - \overline{R})^2 = 56$$

$$\sigma = \sqrt{56} = 7.48\%$$

2. The stock of X Company performs well relative to other stocks during recessionary periods. The stocks of Y Company, on the other hand, do well during growth periods. Both the stocks are currently selling for Rs 50 per share. The rupee returns (dividend plus price change) of these for the next year would be as follows:

	Economics Condition			
	High Growth	Low Growth	Stagnation	Recession
Probability	0.3	0.3	0.2	0.2
Return on X stock	55	50	60	70
Return on Y stock	75	65	50	40

Calculate the expected return and standards deviation of :

a) Rs 1,000 in the equity stock of X.

b) Rs 1,000 in the equity stocks of Y.

c) Rs 500 in the equity stock of X and Rs. 500 in the equity stock of Y.

d) Rs 700 in the equity stock of X and Rs. 300 in the equity of Y.

Which of the above four options would you choose? Why?

Solution:

3. (a) For Rs.1,000, 20 shares of X's stock can be acquired. The probability distribution of the return on 20 shares is

Economic Condition	Return (Rs)	Probability
High Growth	20 x 55 = 1,100	0.3
Low Growth	20 x 50 = 1,000	0.3
Stagnation	20 x 60 = 1,200	0.2
Recession	20 x 70 = 1,400	0.2

Expected return = (1,100 x 0.3) + (1,000 x 0.3) + (1,200 x 0.2) + (1,400 x 0.2)

= 330 + 300 + 240 + 280

= Rs.1,150

Standard deviation of the return = $[(1,100 - 1,150)^2 \times 0.3 + (1,000 - 1,150)^2 \times$

$0.3 + (1,200 - 1,150)^2 \times 0.2 + (1,400 - 1,150)^2 \times 0.2]^{1/2}$

= Rs.143.18

(b) For Rs.1,000, 20 shares of Y's stock can be acquired. The probability distribution of the return on 20 shares is:

Economic condition	Return (Rs)	Probability
High growth	20 x 75 = 1,500	0.3
Low growth	20 x 65 = 1,300	0.3
Stagnation	20 x 50 = 1,000	0.2
Recession	20 x 40 = 800	0.2

Expected return = (1,500 x 0.3) + (1,300 x 0.3) + (1,000 x 0.2) + (800 x 0.2)

= Rs.1,200

Standard deviation of the return = $[(1,500 - 1,200)^2 \times .3 + (1,300 - 1,200)^2 \times .3$

$+ (1,000 - 1,200)^2 \times .2 + (800 - 1,200)^2 \times .2]^{1/2}$ = Rs.264.58

(c) For Rs.500, 10 shares of X's stock can be acquired; likewise for Rs. 500, 10 shares of Y's stock can be acquired. The probability distribution of this option is:

Return (Rs)		Probability
(10 x 55) + (10 x 75)=	1,300	0.3
(10 x 50) + (10 x 65)=	1,150	0.3
10 x 60) + (10 x 50)=	1,100	0.2
(10 x 70) + (10 x 40) =	1,100	0.2

Expected return = (1,300 x 0.3) + (1,150 x 0.3) + (1,100 x 0.2) + (1,100 x 0.2)

= Rs.1,175

Standard deviation = $[(1,300 - 1,175)^2 \times 0.3 + (1,150 - 1,175)^2 \times 0.3 +$

$(1,100 - 1,175)^2 \times 0.2 + (1,100 - 1,175)^2 \times 0.2]^{1/2}$

= Rs.84.41

(d) For Rs.700, 14 shares of X's stock can be acquired; likewise for Rs.300, 6 shares of Y's stock can be acquired. The probability distribution of this option is:

Return (Rs)		Probability
(14 x 55) + (6 x 75)=	1,220	0.3
(14 x 50) + (6 x 65)=	1,090	0.3
(14 x 60) + (6 x 50)=	1,140	0.2
(14 x 70) + (6 x 40)=	1,220	0.2

Expected Return $\quad = \quad (1,220 \times 0.3) + (1,090 \times 0.3) + (1,140 \times 0.2) + (1,220 \times 0.2)$

$\quad\quad\quad\quad\quad\quad = \quad$ Rs.1,165

Standard deviation $\quad = \quad [(1,220 - 1,165)^2 \times 0.3 + (1,090 - 1,165)^2 \times 0.3 +$
$\quad\quad\quad\quad\quad\quad\quad\quad (1,140 - 1,165)^2 \times 0.2 + (1,220 - 1,165)^2 \times 0.2]^{1/2}$

$\quad\quad\quad\quad\quad\quad = \quad$ Rs.57.66

The expected return to standard deviation of various options are as follows:

Option	Expected return (Rs)	Standard deviation (Rs)	Expected / Standard Return deviation
a	1,150	143	8.04
b	1,200	265	4.53
c	1,175	84	13.99
d	1,165	58	20.09

Option 'd' is the most preferred option because it has the highest return to risk ratio.

4. The return on four stocks X,Y,Z and A over a period of 6 years have been as follows :

	1	2	3	4	5	6
X	10%	12%	-8%	15%	-2%	20%
Y	8%	4%	15%	12%	10%	6%
Z	7%	8%	12%	9%	6%	12%
A	9%	9%	11%	4%	8%	16%

Calculate the returns on :

a) A portfolio of one stocks at a time
b) Portfolios of two stocks at a time
c) Portfolios of three stocks at a time
d) A portfolio of all four stocks

Assume equiv. proportional investment.

Solution:

Expected rates of returns on equity stock X, Y, Z and A can be computed as follows:

$$X = \frac{0.10 + 0.12 + (-0.08) + 0.15 + (-0.02) + 0.20}{6} = 0.0783 = 7.83\%$$

$$Y = \frac{0.08 + 0.04 + 0.15 + 0.12 + 0.10 + 0.06}{6} = 0.0917 = 9.17\%$$

$$Z = \frac{0.07 + 0.08 + 0.12 + 0.09 + 0.06 + 0.12}{6} = 0.0900 = 9.00\%$$

$$A = \frac{0.09 + 0.09 + 0.11 + 0.04 + 0.08 + 0.16}{6} = 0.095 = 9.50\%$$

(a) Return on portfolio consisting of stock X = 7.83%
(b) Return on portfolio consisting of stock A and B in equal proportions

$\quad\quad\quad\quad = 0.5\ (0.0783) + 0.5\ (0.0917)$

$\quad\quad\quad\quad = 0.085 = 8.5\%$

(c) Return on portfolio consisting of stocks X, Y and Z in equal proportions

$$= \quad 1/3(0.0783) + 1/3(0.0917) + 1/3(0.090)$$

$$= \quad 0.0867 = 8.67\%$$

(d) Return on portfolio consisting of stocks X, Y, Z and A in equal proportions

$$= \quad 0.25(0.0783) + 0.25(0.0917) + 0.25(0.0900) + 0.25(0.095)$$

$$= \quad 0.08875 \quad = 8.88\%$$

5. The returns on the equity stocks of ACE limited and the market portfolios over a 12 year period are given below :

Year	Return on auto ACE Ltd. (%)	Return on market portfolio (%)
1	15	12
2	-6	1
3	18	14
4	30	24
5	12	16
6	25	30
7	2	-3
8	20	24
9	18	15
10	24	22
11	8	12

a) Calculate β for the stock of ACE limited

b) Establish the characteristics line for the stock of ACE limited.

Solution:

Define R_A and R_M as the returns on the equity stock of ACE Limited and Market portfolio, respectively. The calculations relevant for calculating the beta of the stock are shown below:

Year	R_A	R_M	R_A-$\overline{R}_A$	R_M-$\overline{R}_M$	$(R_A$-$\overline{R}_A)$	$(R_M$-$\overline{R}_M)$	R_A-$\overline{R}_A/R_M$-$\overline{R}_M$
1	15	12	-0.09	-3.18	0.01	10.11	0.29
2	-6	1	-21.09	-14.18	444.79	201.07	299.06
3	18	14	2.91	-1.18	8.47	1.39	-3.43
4	30	24	14.91	8.82	222.31	77.79	131.51
5	12	16	0-3.09	0.82	9.55	0.67	-2.53
6	25	30	9.91	14.82	98.21	219.63	146.87
7	2	-3	-13.09	-18.18	171.35	330.51	237.98
8	20	24	4.91	8.82	24.11	77.79	43.31
9	18	15	2.91	-0.18	8.47	0.03	-0.52
10	24	22	8.91	6.82	79.39	46.51	60.77
11	8.	12	-7.09	-3.18	50.27	10.11	22.55

$$\overline{R}_A = 15.09 \qquad \overline{R}_M = 15.18$$

$$\sum (R_A - \overline{R}_A)^2 = 1116.93 \quad \sum (R_M - \overline{R}_M)^2 = 975.61 \quad \sum (R_A - \overline{R}_A)(R_M - \overline{R}_M) = 935.86$$

Beta of equity stock of ACE Limited:

$$= \frac{\sum (R_A - \overline{R}_A)(R_M - \overline{R}_M)}{\sum (R_M - \overline{R}_M)^2}$$

$$= \frac{935.86}{975.61} = 0.96$$

$$\text{Alpha} = \overline{R}_A - \beta_A \overline{R}_M$$
$$= 15.09 - (0.96 \times 15.18) = 0.52$$
Equation of the characteristic line is
$$R_A = 0.52 + 0.96\, R_M$$

TEST YOUR KNOWLEDGE

1. Write a note on organization and functioning of securities markets.

2. What is the characteristics of a well-functioning market.

3. Write a short note on Primary capital markets and Secondary markets.

4. Write note on Call versus continuous markets, Competitive bids, Negotiation, Private placement, Call markets, Continuous markets detailed analysis of exchange markets, and exchange membership.

5. Write short note on Commission broker, Floor brokers, Registered traders, The specialist, Types of orders, Market orders, Limit orders, A limit-buy order, A short-sale special orders stop-loss orders, Stop-buy orders, Margin transactions.

6. What is Security-market indicator series?

7. Define Price-weighted series.

8. Define Dow Jones industrial average (DJIA).

9. Write a note on Stock split, Standard & poor's index.

10. Write Structural features of major index.

11. What is Global equity index, and Bond index.

12. Define Efficient capital markets.

13. Write Implications of efficient capital markets.

14. Define Technical analysis, and Fundamental analysis,

15. What is Market analysis.

16. What is the importance of industry and company analysis?

Mergers and Acquisitions

25

1 Meaning of M&A, Types of
M&A.

2 Differential efficiency and
financial synergy

3 Evaluation of a merger as a
capital budgeting.

4 Framework for evaluating M&A.

MERGERS & ACQUISITIONS

When two or more companies agree to combine their operations, where one company survives and the other loses its corporate existence, a merger is affected. The surviving company acquires all the assets and liabilities of the merged company. The company that survives is generally the buyer and it either retains its identity or the merged company is provided with a new name.

TYPES OF MERGERS

Horizontal Mergers

This type of merger involves two firms that operate and compete in a similar kind of business. The merger is based on the assumption that it will provide economies of scale from the larger combined unit.

Example: Glaxo Wellcome Plc. and SmithKline Beecham PLC. megamerger

The two British pharmaceutical heavyweights Glaxo Wellcome PLC and SmithKline Beecham PLC, early this year announced plans to merge resulting in the largest drug manufacturing company globally. The merger created a company valued at $182.4 billion and with a 7.3 per cent share of the global pharmaceutical market. The merged company expected $1.6 billion in pretax cost savings after three years. The two companies have complementary drug portfolios, and a merger would let them pool their research and development funds would give the merged company a bigger sales and marketing force.

Vertical Mergers

Vertical mergers take place between firms in different stages of production/operation, either as forward or backward integration. The basic reason is to eliminate costs of searching for prices, contracting, payment collection and advertising, and may also reduce the cost of communicating and coordinating production. Both production and inventory can be improved on account of efficient information flow within the organisation.

Unlike horizontal mergers, which have no specific timing, vertical mergers take place when both firms plan to integrate the production process and capitalise on the demand for the product. Forward integration takes place when a raw material supplier finds a regular procurer of its products while backward integration takes place when a manufacturer finds a cheap source of raw material supplier.

Example: Merger of Usha Martin and Usha Beltron

Usha Martin and Usha Beltron merged their businesses to enhance shareholder value, through business synergies. The merger will also enable both the companies to pool resources and streamline business and finance with operational efficiencies and cost reduction and also help in development of new products that require synergies.

Conglomerate Mergers

Conglomerate mergers are affected among firms that are in different or unrelated business activity. Firms that plan to increase their product lines carry out these types of mergers. Firms opting for conglomerate merger control a range of activities in various industries that require different skills in the specific managerial functions of research, applied engineering, production, marketing and so on. This type of diversification can be achieved mainly by external acquisition and mergers and is not generally possible through internal development. These types of mergers are also called concentric mergers. Firms operating in different geographic locations also proceed with these types of mergers. Conglomerate mergers have been sub-divided into:

◆   Financial Conglomerates

◆   Managerial Conglomerates

◆   Concentric Companies

Financial Conglomerates

These conglomerates provide a flow of funds to every segment of their operations, exercise control and are the ultimate financial risk takers. They not only assume financial responsibility and control but also play a chief role in operating decisions. They also:

◆   Improve risk-return ratio

◆   Reduce risk

◆   Improve the quality of general and functional managerial performance

◆   Provide effective competitive process

◆   Provide distinction between performance based on underlying potentials in the product market area and results related to managerial performance.

Managerial Conglomerates

Managerial conglomerates provide managerial counsel and interaction on decisions thereby, increasing potential for improving performance. When two firms of unequal managerial competence combine, the performance of the combined firm will be greater than the sum of equal parts that provide large economic benefits.

Concentric Companies

The primary difference between managerial conglomerate and concentric company is its distinction between respective general and specific management functions. The merger is termed as concentric, when there is a carry-over of specific management functions or any complementarities in relative strengths between management functions.

ACQUISITIONS

The term acquisition means an attempt by one firm, called the **acquiring** firm, to gain a majority interest in another firm, called **target** firm. The effort to control may be a prelude:

◆   To a subsequent merger, or

◆   To establish a parent-subsidiary relationship, or

◆   To break-up the target firm, and dispose off its assets, or

◆   To take the target firm private by a small group of investors.

There are broadly two kinds of strategies that can be employed in corporate acquisitions. These include:

FRIENDLY TAKEOVER

The acquiring firm makes a financial proposal to target firm's management and board. This proposal might involve the merger of the two firms, the consolidation of two firms, or the creation of parent/subsidiary relationship.

HOSTILE TAKEOVER

A hostile takeover may not follow a preliminary attempt at a friendly takeover. For example, it is not uncommon for an acquiring firm to embrace the target firm's management in what is colloquially called a bear hug.

DIFFERENTIAL EFFICIENCY & FINANCIAL SYNERGY: THEORY OF MERGERS

Differential Efficiency

According to the differential efficiency theory of mergers, if the management of firm A is more efficient than the management of firm B and if, after firm A acquires firm B, the efficiency of firm B is brought up to the level of firm A, then this increase in efficiency is attributed to the merger.

According to this theory, some firms operate below their potential and consequently have low efficiency. Such firms are likely to be acquired by other, more efficient firms in the same industry. This is because, firms with greater efficiency would be able to identify firms with good potential operating at lower efficiency. They would also have the managerial ability to improve the latter's performance.

However, a difficulty would arise when the acquiring firm overestimates its impact on improving the performance of the acquired firm. This may result in the acquirer paying too much for the acquired firm. Alternatively, the acquirer may not be able to improve the acquired firm's performance up to the level of the acquisition value given to it.

The managerial synergy hypothesis is an extension of the differential efficiency theory. It states that a firm, whose management team has greater competency than is required by the current tasks in the firm, may seek to employ the surplus resources by acquiring and improving the efficiency of a firm, which is less efficient due to lack of adequate managerial resources. Thus, the merger will create a synergy, since the surplus managerial resources of the acquirer combine with the non-managerial organizational capital of the firm.

When these surplus resources are indivisible and cannot be released, a merger enables them to be optimally utilized. Even if the firm has no opportunity to expand within its industry, it can diversify and enter into new areas. However, since it does not possess the relevant skills related to that business, it will attempt to gain a 'toehold entry' by acquiring a firm in that industry, which has organizational capital alongwith inadequate managerial capabilities.

FINANCIAL SYNERGY

The managerial synergy hypothesis is not relevant to the conglomerate type of mergers. This is because, a conglomerate merger implies several, often successive acquisitions in diversified areas. In such a case, the managerial capacity of the firm will not develop rapidly enough to be able to transfer its efficiency to several newly acquired firms in a short time. Further, managerial synergy is applicable only in cases where the firm acquires other firms in the same industry.

Financial synergy occurs as a result of the lower costs of internal financing versus external financing. A combination of firms with different cash flow positions and investment opportunities may produce a financial synergy effect and achieve lower cost of capital. Tax saving is another consideration. When the two firms merge, their combined debt capacity may be greater than the sum of their individual capacities before the merger.

The financial synergy theory also states that when the cash flow rate of the acquirer is greater than that of the acquired firm, capital is relocated to the acquired firm and its investment opportunities improve.

OPERATING SYNERGY & PURE DIVERSIFICATION: THEORY OF MERGERS

Operating Synergy

The operating synergy theory of mergers states that economies of scale exist in industry and that before a merger takes place, the levels of activity that the firms operate at are insufficient to exploit the economies of scale.

Operating economies of scale are achieved through horizontal, vertical and conglomerate mergers. Operating economies occur due to indivisibilities of resources like people, equipment and overhead. The productivity of such resources increase when they are spread over a large number of units of output. For instance, expensive equipment in manufacturing firms should be utilised at optimum levels so that cost per unit of output decreases.

Operating economies in specific management functions such as production, R&D, marketing or finance may be achieved through a merger between firms, which have competencies in different areas. For instance, when a firm, whose core competence is in R&D merges with another having a strong marketing strategy, the two businesses would complement each other.

Operating economies are also possible in generic management functions such as, planning and control. According to the theory, even medium-sized firms need a minimum number of corporate staff. The capabilities of corporate staff which are responsible for planning and control are underutilised. When such a firm acquires another firm, which has just reached the size at which it needs to increase its corporate staff, the acquirer's corporate staff would be fully utilised, thus achieving economies of scale.

Vertical integration, i.e. combining of firms at different stages of the industry value chain also helps achieve operating economies. This is because vertical integration reduces the costs of communication and bargaining.

PURE DIVERSIFICATION

Diversification provides several benefits to managers, other employees and owners of the firm as well as to the firm itself. Moreover, diversification through mergers is commonly preferred to diversification through internal growth, since the firm may lack internal resources or capabilities required. The timing of diversification is an important factor since there may be several firms seeking to diversify through mergers at the same time in a particular industry.

Employees: - The employees of a firm develop firm-specific skills over time, which makes them more efficient in their current jobs. These skills are valuable to that firm and job only and not to any other jobs. Employees thus have fewer opportunities to diversify their sources of earning income, unlike shareholders who can diversify their portfolio. Consequently, they seek job security and stability, better opportunities within the firm and higher compensation (promotions). These needs can be fulfilled through diversification, since the employees can be assigned greater responsibilities.

♦ *Owner-managers:* The owner-manager of a firm is able to retain corporate control over his firm through diversification and simultaneously reduce the risk involved.

♦ *Firm:* A firm builds up information on its employees over time, which helps it to match employees with jobs within the firm. Managerial teams are thus formed within the firm.

This information is not transferred outside and is specific to the firm. When the firm **shuts** down, these teams are destroyed and value is lost. If the firm diversifies, these teams can be shifted from unproductive activities to productive ones, leading to improved profitability, continuity and growth of the firm.

♦ *Goodwill:* A firm builds up a reputation over time through its relationships with suppliers, creditors, customers and others, resulting in goodwill. It does this through investments in advertising, employee training, R&D, organizational development and other strategies. Diversification helps in preserving its reputation and goodwill.

♦ *Financial and tax benefits:* Diversification through mergers also results in financial synergy and tax benefits. Since diversification reduces risk, it increases the corporate debt capacity and reduces the present value of future tax liability of the firm.

COSTS AND BENEFITS OF MERGER

When a company 'A' acquires another company say 'B', then it is a capital investment decision for company 'A' and it is a capital disinvestment decision for company 'B". Thus, both the companies need to calculate the Net Present Value (NPV) of their decisions.

To calculate the NPV of company 'A', there is a need to calculate the benefit and cost of the merger. The *benefit* of the merger is equal to the difference between the value of the combined identity (PV_{AB}) and the sum of the value of both firms as a separate entity. It can be expressed as Benefit = $(PV_{AB}) - (PV_A + PV_B)$

Assuming that compensation to firm B is paid in cash, the cost of the merger from the point of view of firm A can be calculated as

Cost= Cash - PV_B

Thus, NPV for A = Benefit –Cost = $(PV_{AB} - (PV_A + PV_B)) - (Cash - PV_B)$

The net present value of the merger from the point of view of firm B is the same as the cost of the merger for 'A'. Hence,

NPV to B = $(Cash - PV_B)$

NPV of A and B in case the compensation is in stock

In the above scenario, we assumed that compensation is paid in cash, however in real life compensation is paid in terms of stock. In that case, cost of the merger needs to be calculated, carefully. It is explained with the help of an illustration – firm A plans to acquire firm B. Following are the statistics of firms before the merger –

	A	B
Market price per share	Rs.50	Rs.20
Number of Shares	500,000	250,000
Market value of the firm	Rs.25 million	Rs.5 million

The merger is expected to bring gains, which have a PV of Rs.5 million. Firm A offers 1,25,000 shares in exchange for 2,50,000 shares to the shareholders of firm B.

The cost in this case is defined as –

Cost = $aPV_{AB} - PV_B$

Where, A represents the fraction of the combined entity received by shareholders of B. In the above example, the share of B in the combined entity is:

a = 125,000 / (500,000 + 125,000) = 0.2

Assuming that the market value of the combined entity will be equal to the sum of present value of the separate entities and the benefit of merger. Then,

$PV_{AB} = PV_A + PV_B + \text{Benefit} = 25 + 5 + 5 = \text{Rs.35 million}$

$\text{Cost} = aPV_{AB} - PV_B = 0.2 \times 35 - 5 = \text{Rs. 6 million}$

Thus,

NPV to A = Benefit − Cost

$= 5 - 2 = \text{Rs. 6 million}$

NPV to B = Cost to A = Rs 2 million.

EVALUATION OF A MERGER AS A CAPITAL BUDGETING DECISION

When a firm plans to acquire any firm then it should consider the acquisition as a capital budgeting decision. Hence, such a proposal must be evaluated as a capital budgeting decision.

Framework for evaluating acquisition

It consists of the following steps –

Step 1 – Determine CF (X), the equity related post-tax cash flows of the acquiring firm, *X*, without the merger, over the relevant planning horizon period.

Step 2 – Determine PV (X), the present value of CF (X) by applying a suitable discount rate.

Step 3 – Determine CF (X'), the equity-related post cash flows of the combined firm *X,'* which consists of the acquiring firm X and the acquired firm Y over the planning horizon. These cash flows must reflect the post merger benefits.

Step 4 – Determine PV (X'), the present value of CF (*X'*)

Step 5 – Determine the ownership position (OP) of the shareholders of firm X in the combined firm *X'*, with the help of the following formula –

$$OP = N_x / [N_x + ER (N_y)]$$

where:

N_x = number of outstanding equity shares of firm X (the acquiring firm) before the merger.

N_y = number of outstanding equity shares of firm Y (the acquired firm) before the merger.

ER = exchange ratio representing the number of shares of firm X exchanged for every share of firm Y.

Step 6: Calculate NPV of the merger proposal from the point of view of X as follows:

NPV (X) = OP [PV (X')] − PV (X)

where:

NPV (X) = NPV of the merger proposal from the point of view of shareholders of X.

OP = Ownership position of the shareholder of firm X.

PV (X') = PV of the cash flows of the combined firm X'.

PV (X) = PV of the cash flows of firm X, before the merger.

Illustration 1: Consider the firm X limited.

Step 1: Estimated equity related post tax cash flow CF (X)$_t$ of X limited are as follows-

Year	1	2	3	4	5
CF (X)$_t$	200	220	236	248	260

After five years, CF (X)$_t$ will grow at a compound rate of 5% per annum.

Step 2: Determination of PV of cash flows using the discount rate of 15%

$$PV(X) = 200/1.15 + 220/(1.15)^2 + 236/(1.15)^3 + 248/(1.15)^4 + 260/(1.15)^5$$
$$+ 260(1.05)/[(0.15-0.05)(1.15)^5] = 2123.79.$$

The last item in the above equation represents the PV of the perpetual stream of cash flows beyond the fifth year.

Step 3: Estimation of the equity – related cash flows of the combined firm X' is as follows –

Year	1	2	3	4	5
CF (X')$_t$	320	360	410	430	450

After 5 years cash flows of the combined firm is expected to grow at the compounded rate of 6% per year.

Step 4: Determination of PV of expected cash flows of the combined firm.

$$PV(X') = 320/1.15 + 360/(1.15)^2 + 410/(1.15)^3 + 430/(1.15)^4 +$$
$$450/(1.15)^5 + 450(1.06)/[(0.15-0.06)(1.15)^5] = 3660.6$$

Step 5: Determining the ownership position of the shareholders of X. The number of outstanding shares of firm X before merger are 100. The number of outstanding shares of firm Y are 100. The proposed exchange ratio (ER) is 0.6. The ownership position of the shareholders of firm X in the combined firm X' will be –

$$OP = 100/[100 + 0.6(100)] = 0.625$$

Step 6: Calculation of NPV of the merger proposal from the point of view of shareholders X -

$$NPV(X) = (0.625)\,3660.6 - 2123.79 = 164.085$$

Calculation Of Exchange Ratio From The Perspective Of The Acquired And The Acquiring Firm

Whenever a firm 'A' acquires another firm 'B', the compensation to the shareholders of the acquired firm is usually paid in the form of shares of the acquiring firm. In other words, shares of firm A will be given in exchange for shares of firm B. Thus, the exchange ratio is a very important factor in any kind of merger. Firm A will want to keep this ratio as low as possible, while firm B will want it to be as high as possible. In any case, both firms would ensure that post merger, their equivalent price per share will at least be equal to their pre-merger price per share.

Given below is the model developed by Conn and Nielson for determining the exchange ratio.

The symbols used in this model are: -

ER = Exchange ratio
P = Price per share
EPS = Earning per share
PE = Price earning multiple

E	=	Earnings
S	=	Number of outstanding equity shares
AER	=	Actual exchange ratio

In addition, the acquiring, acquired and combined firms will be referred to by subscripts A, B and AB, respectively.

Firm A would ensure that the wealth of its shareholders is preserved. This implies that the price per share of the combined firm is at least equal to the price per share of firm A before merger:

$P_{AB} >= P_A$

For the sake of simplicity consider that $P_{AB} = P_A$

Price earnings ratio of the combined firm X is equal to the earnings per share of the combined firm, which further gives the market price per share.

$$P_{AB} = PE_{AB} \times EPS_{AB} = P_A \qquad \text{...(1)}$$

Earnings per share of the combined firm can be expressed as:

$$EPS_{AB} = (E_A + E_B) / [S_A + S_B(ER_A)] \qquad \text{...(2)}$$

ER_A = number of shares of firm A given in lieu of one share of firm B.

Substituting formula of EPS_{AB} in equation 1, we get –

$$P_A = PE_{AB}(E_A + E_B)/[S_A + S_B(ER)]$$

From the above equation, we may solve for the value of ER_A as follows –

$$ER_A = -(S_A/S_B) + [(E_A + E_B) PE_{AB}] / P_A S_B$$

After discussing the maximum exchange ratio acceptable to the shareholders of firm A above, we will now calculate the minimum exchange ratio acceptable to the firm B (ER_B)

The basic condition is –

$$P_{AB}(ER_B) >= P_B \qquad \text{...(3)}$$

Using the equality form of above equation and substituting P_{AB} from equation 1 in equation 3, we get:

$$PE_{AB} \times EPS_{AB} \times ER_B = P_B$$

Substituting, the value of EPS_{AB} from the above mentioned equation 2, and solving the equation for ER_B, we get:

$$ER_B = P_B S_A / [(PE_{AB})(E_A + E_B) - P_B S_B]$$

POISON PILLS

Poison pills refers to securities that are created by a firm to safeguard itself from hostile takeover bids. These securities take time to provide exercisable rights to their holders, thereby, making it costly and difficult to gain control of a firm. If an acquirer still manages to takeover, then the securities will be akin to "economic poison" for them.

The Board of Directors generally adopt 'poison pills' without the approval of shareholders. The rights that are provided by a poison pill plan that can be changed by the Board or redeemed by the firm, as and when required. These provisions force the acquirer to negotiate directly with the Board, thus enhancing its bargaining power for a fair price.

TYPES OF POISON PILLS PLANS

The first poison pills plan was introduced in late 1982. There are five main types of poison pill plans:

(1) *Preferred Stock Plans:* Poison pill plans used prior to 1984 were also known as original plans. Under this plan, a firm issues a dividend of convertible preferred stock to its common shareholders. Here, the holders are entitled to one vote per share, and a higher dividend amount than that given to a common stock holder. The holders of the preferred stock can exercise special rights, when an outside party acquires a large block of the firm's voting stock.

First, preferred stock holders (apart from the large block holder) can redeem the preferred stock for cash at the highest price paid during the past year, by the large block holder for the firm's common or preferred stock.

Second, in case of a merger the preferred stock can be converted into voting securities of an acquirer, with a total market value no less than the redemption value in the first case.

Thus, this plan was designed to avoid dilution that could be effected by the majority shareholder.

(2) *Flip-over Rights Plans:* The most popular poison pill plan, it was introduced in late 1984 and was adopted by many firms. In this plan, shareholders receive a common stock dividend in the form of rights to acquire the firm's common stock or preferred stock, at an exercise price well above the current market price. In case of a merger, the rights would "flip over" to permit the holders to purchase the acquirer's shares, at a substantial discount. The flip-over plan does not prevent an acquirer from obtaining a controlling interest in the target, though it does make takeovers expensive, for an acquirer must obtain most of the rights. This is not easy, since most shareholders will prefer to hold on to their rights, which are more valuable than any premium that the acquirer may offer.

(3) *Ownership Flip-in Plans:* Under this plan, holders of rights are allowed to purchase the shares of the targeted firm (i.e. targeted for acquisition) at a large discount. If an acquirer accumulates target shares in excess of a threshold or "kick-in" point (i.e. 25 – 50%), his rights will become void. In most cases, the ownership flip-in plans deter acquisition of a substantial equity position. If the acquirer makes a cash tender offer for all outstanding shares, the flip-in provision is waived.

(4) *Back-end Rights Plans:* In this plan, shareholders receive a rights dividend. If an acquirer obtains shares of a firm in excess of a limit, holders (excluding the acquirer) can exchange a right and a share of the stock for senior securities or cash equal in value to a backend price set by the board of directors of the targeted firm. As the backend price is higher than the stock's market price, it acts as a minimum takeover price, which deters acquisition of a controlling interest.

(5) *Voting Plans:* Voting plan is an anti-takeover defence plan. These plans are implemented by issuing a dividend of preferred stock with voting rights. Here, if an investor acquires a substantial block of a firm's voting stock, preferred holders (other than the large block holder) become entitled to super voting privileges. Hence, it is difficult for the block holder to obtain voting control.

PROJECT RISK

Project risk can be defined as follows- '**A risk is a combination of constraint and uncertainty**'. The risk may be reduced to an acceptable level by reducing either uncertainty or constraint, or both. In practice, few people have the opportunity to reduce constraint, so most of them focus on the reduction of uncertainty.

Types of project risk

♦   *Stand-alone risk:* This is the risk of a project when viewed in isolation.

♦   *Firm risk:* This represents the contribution of the project to an overall risk of the company.

♦   *Systematic risk:* This represents the risk of the project in the context of the market portfolio.

Measures of risk

The following are the measures of risk:

♦   Range

♦   Mean absolute deviation

♦   Coefficient of variation

♦   Semi-variation

Project risk management: This is the systematic process of managing an organisation's risk exposures to achieve its objectives in a manner consistent with public interest, human safety, environmental factors, and the law. It consists of the planning, organising, leading, co-ordinating, and controlling activities undertaken with the intent of providing an efficient plan that incorporates an acceptable level of loss that minimises the adverse impact of risk on the organisation's resources, earnings and cash flows.

There are two stages in the process of Project Risk Management- Risk Assessment and Risk Control.

Risk assessment involves identifying uncertainties, analysing and prioritising risks.

Risk control involves mitigating risks, planning for emergencies, measuring and controlling.

In order to reduce the loss caused by uncertainties, the company undertakes the following measures, even before accepting a project:

♦   **Sensitivity analysis** also known as the 'What If' analysis.

♦   **Scenario analysis** looks at various scenarios and its effect on the finances.

♦   **Decision tree analysis** a technique for analysing situations where sequential decision making in risk is involved.

TURNAROUND STRATEGY

There are three stages of a turnaround strategy:

I.   Pre-turnaround

II.   Period of Crisis

III.   Period of Recovery

The first stage is the period just before the profitability begins to decline. The company is still considered profitable at this point, but losing ground. The second period is known as the period of crisis. At this point the company needs to turnaround. This stage is marked by a decline in profits (even negatives), a fall in market share and the company's poor cash situation.

The third stage is the period of recovery or the turning point. This is the stage where serious action is taken to turnaround the company. Important decisions like scaling back production or returning to an aggressive growth stage are taken. At this point, the company's strategy is clear.

The company can choose to rely on a centralized, low cost system to continue profitably. Alternatively, it might decide to combine these benefits with a growth strategy. This is the longest period and may last for years.

STEPS IN TURNAROUND STRATEGY

♦ *Changing the leadership:* A change in leadership ensures that those techniques, which resulted in the company's failure, are not used. The new leader has to motivate employees, listen to their views and delegate powers.

♦ *Redefining strategic focus:* This involves re-evaluating the company's business and deciding, which ones to change and which ones to retain. Diversified companies need to review their portfolio on the basis of long-term profitability and growth prospects.

♦ *Selling or divesting unnecessary assets:* Sometimes, although the assets are profitable, they must be liquidated to contribute to the strategic focus. The cash received from the sale of such assets should be used to repay debts. Self-sustaining businesses are ideal candidates to do so.

♦ *Improving Profitability:* To do this the company has to take drastic steps like:-

1. Assigning profit responsibility to individual divisions.

2. Tightening finance controls and reducing unnecessary overheads.

3. Laying off workers wherever necessary.

4. Investing in labour saving equipment.

5. Building a new inventory management system and manage debt efficiently through negotiating long-term loans.

♦ *Making careful acquisitions:* The company must be careful while making acquisitions. It should be in an area related to its core business enabling the company to quickly rebuild or replace its weak divisions.

CORPORATE VALUATION

In the wake of economic liberalisation, a critical issue to be addressed among issues concerning corporate restructuring, mergers and joint ventures is - how a company should be valued. There are several approaches to valuation. These are briefly described as below:

Discounted Cash Flow Technique

This is the most popularly used method for valuing a company. This method involves the following steps:

♦ *Forecasting the Free Cash Flow (FCF):*

FCF = Free cash flow from operations + non operating cash flow

Free cash flow from operations = Gross cash flow – Gross investment

Gross Cash Flow = EBIT– Taxes on EBIT– change in deferred taxes = Net Operating Profit less adjusted taxes (NOPLAT) + Depreciation.

Gross Investment= Increase in fixed assets + Current assets + Other assets.

Computing The Cost of Capital:

Cost of Capital = $K_e \times E/V + K_d(1-t) \times D/V + K_p \times P/V$

Where :

K_e is the cost of equity capital,

K_d is the cost of debt,

K_p is the cost of preference capital,

E is the market value of equity,

D is the market value of debt,

P is the market value of preference capital, and

V is the market value of the firm.

Estimating The Continuing Value: This can be calculated as follows: Continuing value (CV) = PV of free cash flow during the explicit period + PV of free cash flow after the explicit forecast period.

Cash flow as well as non-cash flow methods can be used to calculate continuing value.

The Cash Flow Methods Include

♦ *Growing Free Cash Flow Perpetuity Method:* This method assumes that the free cash flow grows at a constant rate after the explicit forecast period.

♦ *Value Driver Method:* This method uses the same logic as the above method but the connotations of the formula are different.

♦ *Non-Cash Flow* methods include:

1. Replacement cost method
2. Price-to-earnings ratio method
3. Market to book ratio method

Steps to calculate the value of the company include

♦ Discount the projected free cash flow and the continuing value, using the cost of capital.

♦ Deduct the market value of all debt claims.

Comparable Company Approach

This approach involves valuing a company on the basis of how similar companies are valued. This approach involves the following steps:

Analyse the economy: This provides a basis for evaluating the individual companies within an industry.

Analyse the industry: This involves studying various aspects like the relationship between the industry and the economy, profit potential of the industry, nature of regulations applicable etc.

Analyse the subject company: This involves studying the various functional aspects of the company life manufacturing, human resources, technological position, financial aspects etc.

♦ Select comparable companies: Companies, which are similar to the subject company in the various respects mentioned earlier, must be selected.

♦ Analyse the financial aspects of the subject and comparable companies.

Analyse the multiples: The multiples to be considered include price to cash flow, price to earnings, price to EBIT, price to EBDIT, price to sales, and price to book value.

Adjusted Book Value Approach

This approach involves determining the fair market value of the assets and liabilities of the company as a going concern.

VALUATION MODELS

There are four basic models available using free cash flow concept for valuations. They are:

♦   No growth
♦   Constant growth
♦   Super normal growth followed by no growth
♦   Super normal growth followed by constant growth

   The basic methodology to develop a general model will be helpful in explaining the above-mentioned four models because only some variables need to be added in special situations. The general model is:

$$V_0 = \frac{X_0(1-T)(1-b)(1+g)}{(1+k)}\left[1+\frac{(1+g)}{(1+k)}+\frac{(1+g)^2}{(1+k)^2}+........+\frac{(1+g)^{n-1}}{(1+k)^{n-1}}\right]$$

Where,

   X_t = Cash inflows

   k_t = Cost of capital

   T_t = Tax rate

   g = Growth rate in cash inflows

   b = Investment requirements (opportunities) per unit of after-tax cash flows

No Growth Model

The basic assumption in this model is that growth (g) = 0. As a result, the firm will not make investment, so b = 0. The formula in a no growth model implies that there is a constant level of inflows up to infinity. The formula is:

$$V_0 = \frac{X_0(1-T)}{k}\text{ for } k>0$$

Constant Growth Model

Here, the assumption is that growth rate (g) of cash inflows is constant instead of zero(0). Using the assumption under constant growth model for valuation of companies, the formula is:

$$V_0 = \frac{X_0(1-T)(1-b)(1+g)}{(k-g)}\text{ for } g<k.$$

   This formula is applied when cost of capital (k) is larger than growth rate (g) to perpetuity.

Super Normal Growth Followed By No Growth

The basic assumption for this model is that there is super normal growth in cash inflows temporally and no growth scenario will follow.

Following the assumptions, the formula will be:

$$V_0 = X_0(1-T)(1-b_s) = \sum_{t=1}^{n} \frac{(1+g_s)^t}{(1+k)^t} + \frac{X_0(1-T)(1+g_s)^{n+1}}{k(1+k)^n}$$

Super normal growth followed by constant growth

The basic assumption is that there is temporary super normal growth and constant growth to perpetuity will follow. The formula for this assumption is:

$$V_0 = X_0(1-T)(1-b_s) \sum_{t=1}^{n} \frac{(1+g_s)^t}{(1+k)^t} + \frac{X_0(1-T)(1+b_c)}{k-g_c} \times \frac{(1+g_s)^{n+1}}{(1+k)^n}$$

Application of the Valuation Model on XYZ Ltd.

The following example relates to the valuation of XYZ Ltd. under the assumption of temporal super normal growth followed by a period of no growth. The formula used is given below:

$$V_0 = X_0(1-T)(1-b_s) \sum_{t=1}^{n} \frac{(1+g_s)^t}{(1+k)^t} + \frac{X_0(1-T)(1+g_s)^{n+1}}{k(1+k)^n}$$

Where,

V_0	=	Total firm value [value of equity (S) plus Debt (B)]
X_0	=	EBIT or NOI
T	=	Tax rate
b	=	Investment rate
r	=	Profit rate
g	=	Growth rate
k	=	Cost of capital
N	=	Growth period

The various key parameters in terms of data and projections are given under two scenarios:

♦ *Optimistic Scenario:* Here, growth rate in EBIT is 15% per year, investment rate (b) is 50%, tax rate (T) is 34%, profit rate (r) is 30%, growth period (N) is 10 years, and cost of capital (k) is 10%.

The calculation of valuation is as follows:

$$V_0 = 946 \times (1-0.34)(1-0.5) \sum_{t=1}^{10} \frac{(1+0.15)}{(1+0.10)} + \frac{946(1-0.34)}{0.10}\left(\frac{1.15}{1.10}\right)(1.15)$$

$$V_0 = Rs.\ 4{,}019 + Rs.\ 11{,}199 = Rs.\ 250000$$

♦ *Pessimistic Scenario:* Under pessimistic scenario, the growth rate 'g' in earnings (EBIT) is reduced to 13% per year, profit rate 'r' = 26% , cost of capital 'k' = 11% and other assumptions are same.

The calculation of valuation is as follows:

$$V_0 = 946 \times (1-0.34)(1-0.5) \sum_{t=1}^{10} \frac{(1+0.13)}{(1+0.11)} + \frac{946(1-0.34)}{0.11}\left(\frac{1.13}{1.11}\right)(1.13)$$

$$V_0 = Rs.\ 3{,}449 + Rs.\ 7{,}668 = Rs.\ 250000$$

Valuation items	Optimistic method	Pessimistic method
First term EBIT	Rs. 4,020 Crores	Rs. 3,500 Crores
Second term EBIT	Rs. 11,200 Crores	Rs. 7,800 Crores
Value of firm	Rs. 15,220 Crores	Rs. 11,300 Crores
Less: Total debt	Rs. 630 Crores	Rs. 630 Crores
Value of equity	Rs. 14,590 Crores	Rs. 10,670 Crores
Number of shares	Rs. 150 Crores	Rs. 150 Crores
Value per share	Rs. 97.27	Rs. 71.13

CORPORATE GOVERNANCE

Corporate governance carries great depth of meaning. To most people, it means the way a company manages its business, in a manner that is accountable and responsible to someone—usually the shareholders. In a broad sense, responsibility and accountability are seen to be to broader audiences that also include the company's other stakeholders such as employees, suppliers, customers, and the local community. It suggests ethics and morals, as well as the best practices.

Corporate governance is usually expressed in the form of a code—such as the Cadbury code in the UK. The CII has established its committee on corporate governance. The challenge for corporate India will be to establish a set of principles or a code that is acceptable in international best practice terms. This set of codes will lead to change in the Companies Act, and auditing and reporting requirements eventually.

Corporate governance practices in India are likely to be changed for the better in the coming years. Promoters are becoming more answerable and responsive to shareholders. Financial institutions are appreciating the interventionist role they need to play in ensuring sound corporate governance.

Corporate governance refers to the relationship among the owners, directors and managers.

The Cadbury Committee Recommendations (Highlights)

In Britain, the Cadbury Committee was set up to go into the details of Corporate Governance prevailing there. After detailed studies, the committee made the following recommendations:

♦ Boards should have separate audit and remuneration committees made up entirely of independent directors.

♦ Audit committees should meet with the external auditors at least once a year and without executive directors.

♦ The full remuneration package of all directors—including performance-related elements-should be disclosed in annual reports.

♦ Director's terms of office should run for no more than three years without shareholders' approval.

♦ Companies must make funds available to non-executive directors who wish to get independent professional advice.

♦ The board must meet regularly.

♦ It ought to have a formal schedule of matters for decision.

♦ Independent directors should be appointed for specified terms.

♦ Independent directors should be appointed through a formal process.

- Independent directors should have a standing outside the company which ensures that their views carry weight.

- Independent directors should be fully independent and free from links with the company other than the fees and shareholdings.

- Fees for independent directors should reflect the time they spend on company business.

- There should be an accepted division at the head of the company, which will ensure a balance of power and authority such that no one individual has unfettered powers of decision. Where the chairman is also chief executive, there should be a strong independent element on the board with an independent leader.

What is Corporate Governance?

Although there is no single acceptable definition of corporate governance, it is a means to maximise the long-term shareholder value in a legal and ethical manner, ensuring fairness, courtesy and dignity in all transactions of the company.

The Securities and Exchange Board of India (SEBI) under the Chairmanship of Shri Kumaramangalam Birla set up a committee on corporate governance on 7th May 1999, to promote and raise the standards of corporate governance. The committee recently tabled its recommendations, and the highlights are given below:

- *Have an Appropriate Mix in the Board:* The Confederation of Indian Industry recommends that at least 30% of the board should consist of outsiders, if the chairman is one of them. If the chairman is an insider then 50% of the board should consist of non-executive directors. However, the major emphasis is to have directors who have a thorough understanding of the business, the market and the needs of the company.

- *Ensure that the Board is Aware of its Functions:* As per law, the board is responsible for decisions related to borrowing, lending, investing and maintenance, dividends and accounts, though good governance goes beyond that. The boards' contributions are needed to ensure customer satisfaction, employee satisfaction, succession, planning, financial prudence, a culture of performance and the protection of society and the environment.

- *Make Use of a Sub Committee :* Conformance to both the letter and the spirit of the law, transparency, honesty and fair play in financial practices and disclosures are essential. This can be done by setting up an audit committee with at least three members.

- *Provide Transparency:* Transparency is the basis for corporate governance. A good corporate governance model ensures fairness, courtesy and dignity in all transactions within and outside the company. Indian disclosure norms presently being inadequate, directors should benchmark international standards such as US Generally Accepted Accounting Practices.

Corporate governance also addresses issues of insider trading. It is very important that directors who have inside information of the company should not use it for unfair disadvantage of the uninformed stockholders. This calls for companies to devise an internal procedure for adequate and timely disclosures, reporting requirements, confidentiality norms and code of conduct for their directors and employees with regard to their dealings in securities.

CASE STUDY FOR CLASS DISCUSSION CASE I
ELECTROLUX: THE ACQUISITIONS AND INTEGRATION OF ZANUSSI (A)

While recounting the story of Electrolux's acquisition of Zanussi, Lefit Johansson, Head of Electrolux's major appliance division, had reasons to feel pleased. Through financial restructurings and operating improvements Zanussi had, in only three years since the acquisition, gone from a massive loss of £ 120 billion in 1983 to a tidy profit of £ 60 billion in 1987* - a turnaround that astounded outside analysts and was perhaps more impressive than the expectations of even the optimists within Electrolux. More important was the progress made in integrating Zanussi strategically, operationally, and organizationally within the Electrolux group, while protecting is a distinct identity and reviving the fighting spirit that had been the hallmark. Having been the first suggest to President Anders Scharp that Electrolux should buy financially troubled Zanussi, Johansson had a major personal stake in the operation's continued success.

By early 1988, however, the task was far from complete. Not every thing was going well at Zanussi : the company had recently lost some market share within Italey to Merloni, its arch-rival. Merloni had taken over domestic market leadership following its acquisition of Indesit.

* SI = £ 117 = Skr. 5.85 (International Financial Statistics, December, 1987)

© 1989, 1990 by INSEAD-CEDEP, Fontainebleau, France

This case was prepared by Dag Andersson, Nicola De Sancitis, Beniamino Finzi, and Jacopo Franzan. Research Assistants, under the supervision of Sumantra Ghoshal and Philippe Haspesalah, Associate Professors at INSEAD. It is intended to be used as the basis for class discussion rather than to illustrate either effective or ineffective handling of an administrative situation.

Reprinted with the permission of INSEAD-CEDEP

The case writers gratefully acknowledge the co-operation of the Electrolux company and its executives, and financial support from the INSEAD Alumni Fund European Case Programme.

(Another large Italian producer of household appliances). There had been some delays in Zanussi's ambitions programme for plant automation. Moreover, a recent attitude survey had shown that, while the top 60 managers of Zanussi fully supported the actions taken since the acquisition, the next rung of 150 managers felt less motivated and less secure. It was not clear whether these problems were short-term in nature and would soon be resolved, or whether they were the warning signals for more basic and fundamental maladies.

Though Leifit Johansson felt it was useful to review the integration process, his concerns focused on the next stage of the battle for global leadership. The industry was changing rapidly with competitors like Whirlpool and Matsushita moving outside their home regions (see Chapter 8 'Note on the Major Appliance Industry in 1988'). At the same time some local European competitors, for example, GEC-Hotpoint in UK and Merloni (Ariston) in Italy, were making aggressive moves to expand their shares in a relatively low-growth market. The Zanussi's takeover and the subsequent acquisition of White Consolidated in the United States, catapulted Electrolux to the top of the list of the world's largest producers of household appliances.

The challenge for Johansson now was to mould all the acquired entities into an integrated strategy ad organization that would protect this leadership role and leverage it into a profitable worldwide operation.

Electrolux

In 1962, Electrolux was on a downward curve. Profits were falling and the company had not developed any significant in-house research and development capability. Compared with other appliance manufacturers such as Philips, Siemens, GEC and Matsushita, it had a limited range of products : the core business was made up of vacuum cleaners and absorption-type refrigerators. These refrigerators were increasingly unable to compete with the new compressor-type refrigerators developed by the competitors and sales of the once highly successful lines of vacuum cleaners were rapidly declining.

That same year ASEA was launched. A company in the Wallenberg network (an informal grouping of major Swedish companies in which the Wallenbergs – the most influential business family in Sweden – has some equity shares) sold Electro-Helios to Electrolux for shares and thereby, became a major shareholder. Electro-Helios was a technological leader in compressor – type refrigerators, and a significant producer of freezers and cooking ranges. This led to a major expansion of Electrolux's role in the Swedish household appliance market, but the company found itself in financial difficulty again due to rapid expansion of production capacity during a period of severe economic downturn.

In 1967, Hans Werthen was appointed as CEO of Electrolux. In the next two decades, he and the other two members of what was known as the 'Electrolux Troika', Anders Scharp and Gosta Bystedt, managed to develop the company from a relatively small and marginal player in the business into the world's manufacturer of household appliance.

Growth Through Acquisitions

At the core of the dramatic transformation of Electrolux was an aggressive strategy of expansion through acquisition. At the beginning, Electrolux concentrated on acquiring firms in the Nordic countries, its traditional market, where the company already had a dominant market share. Subsequent acquisitions served not only to strengthen the company's positions in its household appliance activities, but also to broaden its European presence and open the way to entirely new product area. Exhibit I illustrates Electrolux's major acquisitions between 1988.

With more than 200 acquisitions in 40 countries, and 280 manufacturing facilities in 25 countries, the Electrolux group had few equal in managing the acquisition and integration processes. The company generally bought competitors in its core businesses, disposing of operations, which either failed to show long-term profit potential or appeared to have a better chance of prospering under the management of another company. In addition, Electrolux always tried to ensure that there were sufficient realizable assets available to help finance the necessary restructuring of the acquired company. Thus, from the beginning of the 1970s up to 1988, the groups made capital gains from selling off idle assets of more than Skr. 2.5 billion.

At the same time, flexibility had been maintained in order to pick up new product areas for further development. A typical example of this was the chain-saw product line that came with the acquisition of the Swedish appliance manufacturer, Husqvarna in 1978. By developing this product line through acquisitions and in-house-development. Electrolux emerged as one of the world's leading chain-saw manufacturers with about 30% of the global market. Another example, was provided by the new business area of outdoor products (mainly forestry ad garden products), which had grown from the small base of the Flymo lawnmower business through the acquisition of firms like Poulan/Weed Eater in the US and Staub/Bernard Moteur in France.

The two most notable departures from the strategy of buying familiar businesses had been the 1973 acquisition of Facit, A Swedish office equipment and electronics manufacturer, and the 1980 purchase of Granges, a metal and mining company. Both companies were in financial trouble. Electrolux had difficulty in fully mastering Facit, after bringing the profit up to a reasonable level, it was sold off to Ericsson in 1983. The borrowing because necessary to buy Granges, combined with the worldwide economic downturn and rising interest rates, pushed Electrolux into a sobering two-year period (1981-83) when profit margins declined. However, through the Granges takeover Electrolux also acquired new business for future growth. An example, was the manufacturing of seat belt, now concentrated in the subsidiary Electrolux Autoliv. Nevertheless, the acquisition of Granges would be the last diversifying acquisition.

Even though Electrolux had dealt with a large number of acquisitions, specific companies were seldom targeted. In the words of Anders Scharp, 'You never choose an acquisition, opportunities just come'. The company made it a practice to simulate what the merger combination with other companies would result in if they come up for sale. The financial aspects of an acquisition were considered to every important. The company usually ensured that it paid less for a company than the total asset value of the company, and not for what Electrolux would bring to the party.

Based on their experience, managers at Electrolux believed that there was no standard method for treating acquisitions : each case was unique and had to be dealt with differently. Typically, however, Electrolux moved quickly at the beginning of the integration process. It identified the key action areas and created task forces consisting of managers from both Electrolux and the acquired company in order to address each of the issues on a time-bound basis. Such joint task forces were believed to help foster management confidence and commitment and create avenues for reciprocal information flows. Objectives were clearly specified, milestones were identified, and the first phase of integration was generally completed within three to six months so as to create and maintain momentum. The top management of an acquired company was often replaced, but the middle management was kept intact. As explained by Anders Scharp, 'The risk of losing general management competence is small when it is a poorly performing company. Electrolux is prepared to take this risk. It is, however, important that we do not change the marketing and sales staff'.

Electrolux prior to the Acquisition of Zanussi

The activities of the Electrolux group in 1984 , prior to the acquisition of Zanussi, covered 26 products line within five business areas, namely household appliances, forestry and garden products, and industrial products. After acquiring commercial services, and metal and mining (Granges), The total sales revenue had increased from Skr.1.1 billion in 1967 to Skr 34.5 billion in 1984. The household appliance area (including white goods special refrigerators, floor-care products and sewing machines) accounted for approximately 52% of total group sales in 194. Granges was the second largest area with nearly 21.5% of total sales. The third area, industrial products provided heavy equipment for food services, semi-industrial laundries, and commercial cleaning.

By the 1980s, Electrolux had become one of the world's largest manufacturers of white goods with production facilities in Europe and North America, and a small presence in Lain America and the Far East. The Group's reliance upon the

Scahdinavian markets was still considerable. More than 30% of sales came from Sweden, Norway, and Denmark European sales, focusing mainly of Scahdinavia and Western Europe, constituted to 65% of total group sales. The US had emerged as the single most important market with 28.9% (1987) of total sales.

Electrolux's household appliances were manufactured in plants with specialized assembly lines. Regional manufacturing operations were focused on local brands and designs and established distribution networks. Sales forces for the various brands had been kept separate, though works. Sales forces for the various brands had been kept separate, though support functions such as physical distribution, stocking, order taking, and invoicing might be integrated with increasing plant automation and product differentiation, the number of models and the volume produced in any given plant had risen sharply. As described by Anders Scharp, 'We recognized that expansion means higher volumes, which create scope for rationalization. Rationalization, means better margins, which are essential to boost our competitive strength'.

One important characteristic of Electrolux was the astonishingly small corporate headquarters of Lilla Ewsingen, six kilometers outside the centre of Stockholm, and the relatively few people who worked in central staff department. The size of headquarters was a direct outcome of the company's commitment to decentralization. "I believe that we have at least two hierarchical. Levels fewer than other companies of the same size,' said Scharp, 'and all operational matters are decentralized to the subsidiaries'. 'However, most strategic issues such as investment programmes and product range decisions were dealt with at head quarters. The subsidiaries were considered to be profit centres and were evaluated primarily on their returns on net assets as compared with the targets set by the corporate office. Presidents of the diversified subsidiaries reported directly to Scharp, while others reported to the heads of the different products lines.

THE ACQUISITION OF ZANUSSI

In June 1983, Leifit Johansson, the 32-year-old head of Electrolux's major appliances division. Received a proposal from Mr. Candotti, head of Zanussi's major appliance division in France, from whom he had been 'sourcing' refrigerators for the

Exhibit 1: Consolidated financial statements for Zanussi Group				
Consolidated Income statements for Zanussi Group (in million Skr.)				
	1980	1981	1982	1983
Sales	3826	4327	4415	5240
Operating cost	-3301	-3735	-3957	-4654
Operating income before depreciation	525	552	458	586
Depreciation	-161	-98	-104	-130
Operating income after depreciation	364	454	354	456
Financial income	192	330	284	279
Financial expenses	-407	-489	-647	-627
Income after financial items	149	295	-9	108
Extraordanary items	-53	-228	-223	81
Income before appropriations	96	67	-232	189
Appropriations	-53	-42	-409	-382
Income before taxes	43	25	-641	-193
Taxes	-7	-7	-10	-10
Net income	36	18	-651	-203
Consolidated Balancesheet for Zanussi Group(in million Skr.)				
	1980	1981	1982	1983
Current assets exct. Inventory	1559	1987	1811	2108
Inventory	965	1054	998	956
Fixed assets	1622	1539	2366	2902
Total assets	4146	4580	5176	5966
Current liabilities	1590	1832	1875	2072
Long-term liabilities	1273	1441	1864	2349
Reserves	259	301	472	627
Shareholder's equity	1024	1006	965	918
Total liabilitiy sand shareholders' equity	4146	4580	5176	5966

French market. The proposal called for an investment of a small amount of money in Zanussi so as to secure future supplies from the financially troubled Italian producer. The next day Johansson called Anders Scharp to ask, 'Why don't we buy all of it', thereby triggering a process that led to the largest acquisition in the history of the household appliance industry and in the Swedish business world.

Zanussi

Having begun in 1916 as a small in Prodenone, a little town in northeast Itlay, where Antonio Zanussi produced a few wood-burning cookers, Zanussi had grown by the early 1980s to be the second largest privately owned company in Italy with more than 30,000 employees.

50 factories and 13 foreign sales companies. Most of the growth came in the 1950s and 1960s under the leadership of Lino Zanussi, who understood the necessity of having not only a complete range of products but also a well-functioning distribution and sales network. Lino Zanussi established several new factories within Italy and added cookers, refrigerators, and washing machines to the product range. In 1958, he launched a major drive to improve exports out of Italy and he established the first foreign branch office in Paris in 1962. Similar branches were soon opened in other European countries and the first foreign manufacturing subsidiary, IBELSA, was set up in Madrid in 1965. Though a series of Italian producers of appliances and components, Zanussi became one of the most vertically integrated manufacturer to Europe, achieving full control over all activities ranging from component manufacturing to final sales and service. It is rumored that, during this period of heady success, Zanussi had very seriously considered launching a takeover bid for Electrolux. Then a struggling Swedish company less than half Zanussi's size.

The company's misfortunes started in 1968, when Lino Zenussi and several other company executives died in an air crash. Over the next 15 years, the new management carved out a costly programme of unrelated diversification into field such as colour televisions, prefabricated housing real estate, and community centre. The core business of domestic appliances languished for want of capital, while the new businesses incurred heavy losses. By 1982, the company had huge amount of debts of over £ 1300 billion and was losing £ 100 billion a year on operations (see Exhibit 1 for the consolidated financial statements during this period).

The Acquisition Process

The process of Electrolux's acquisition of Zanussi formally commenced when Enrico Cuccia, the informal head of Mediobanca and the most powerful financier in Italy, approached Hans Werthen on 30th November 1983, about the possibility of Electrolux reducing Zanussi from impending financial collapse. It was not by chance that the grand old man of Mediobanca arrived in Sweden. Enrico Cuccia had close links to the Agenelli family – the owners of Fiat, the largest industrial group in Italy – and the proposal to approach Electrolux came from Mr. Agnelli, who wanted to save the second largest private manufacturing company in his country. As a board member of SKF, the Swedish bearing manufacturer, Agnelli had developed a healthy respect for Swedish management and believed that Electrolux alone had the resources and management skills necessary turn Zanussi around.

Mean while, Electrolux had been looking around for a good acquisition to expand its appliance business. Its efforts to take over AEF's appliance business in Germany had failed because the conditions stipulated for the takeover were found to be too tough. Later, Electrolux had to back away from acquiring the TI group in the UK because of too high a price-tag. Zanussi now represented the best chance for significant expansion in Europe. 'It was a very good fit', recalled Anders Scharp, 'There were not many overlaps : we were strong where Zanussi was weak, and vice-versa'. There were significant complementarities in products, markets, and opportunities for vertical integrations. For example, while Electrolux was well established in microwave ovens, cookers and fridge-freezers, Zanussi was Europe's largest producer of 'wet product' such as washing machines, traditionally a weak area for Electrolux. Similarly, while Electrolux had large market shares Scanhdinavia and Switzerland where Italy and Spain, two markets that Electrolux had failed to crack. Zanussi was also strong in France, the only market where Electrolux had failed to crack. Zanussi was also strong in France, the only market where Electrolux was losing money, and had a significant presence in Germany, where Electrolux had limited strength except in vacuum cleaners. Finally, while Electrolux had historically avoided vertical integration and sourced most of its components externally, Zanussi was a vertically integrated company with substantial spare capacity for component production the Electrolux could profitably use.

From 30th November 1983 until 14th December 1984, the date when the formal deal was finally signed, there ensured 12-months period of intense negotiation in which, alongside the top management of the two companies, Gianmario Rossignolo, the Chairman of SKF' Italian subsidiary, took an increasingly active role. The most difficult parts of the negotiations focused on the following three issues.

Union and Workforce Reduction: At the outset, the powerful unions at Zanussi were against selling the company to the 'Viking from the North'. They would have preferred to keep Zanussi independent, with a government subsidy, or to merge with Thomos from France. They also believed that under Electrolux management all important functions would be transferred to Sweden, thereby eroding the skills of the Italian company and also reducing local employment opportunities.

In response to these concerns, Electrolux guaranteed that all Zanussi's important functions would be retained within Italy. Twenty union leaders were sent from Sweden to Italy to reassure the Italians. The same number of Italian union leaders were invited to Sweden to observe Electrolux's production system and labour relations. Initially, Mr. Rossignolo signed a letter of assurance to the unions on behalf of Electrolux confirming that the level of employment prevailing at that time would be maintained. Soon, however, it became obvious that Zanussi could not be made profitable without workforce reductions. This resulted in difficult renegotiations. It was finally agreed that within three months of the acquisition Electrolux would present the unions a three-year plan for investment sand reduction in personnel. Actual retrenchments would have to follow the plan, subject to its approval by the unions.

Prior commitments of Zanussi: A number of problems were posed by certain commitments on the part of Zanussi. One major issue was SELECO, an Italian producer of television sets. A majority of shares in SELECO were held by REL, a government holding company, and the rest were owned by Zanussi and Indesit. Zanussi had made a commitment to buy REL's majority holdings of SELECO within a period of five years ending in 1989. Electrolux had no interest in entering the television business but finally accepted this commitment despite considerable apprehension.

Another major concern was the unprofitable Spanish appliance company IBELSA owned by Zanussi. Zanussi has received large subsidies form the Spanish government against a commitment to help restructure the industry in Spain, and heavy fines would have to be paid, if the company decided to pull out. Once again, Electrolux had to accept these terms despite concern about IBELSA's long-term competitiveness.

Nevertheless, there was one potential liability that Electrolux refused to accept. In the later stages of the negotiations, an audit team from Electrolux discovered that a previous managing director of Zanussi had sold a large amount of equipment and machinery to a German company and had then leased them back. This could potentially lead to severe penalties and large fines, as the actions violated Italian foreign exchange and tax laws. Electrolux refused to proceed with the negotiations until the Italian government had promised no to take any punitive actions in this case.

Financial structure and ownership: Electrolux was not willing to take over majority ownership of Zanussi immediately since it would then be required to consolidate Zanussi into group accounts, and the large debts would have major adverse effects on the Electrolux balance sheet and share prices. Electrolux wanted to take minority holdings without relinquishing its claim to majority holdings in the future. To resolve this issue, a consortium was organized that included prominent Italian financial institutions and industrial companies such a Mediobanca, IMI, Crediop, and a subsidiary of Fiat. The consortium took on a large part of the shares (40.6%), with another 10.4% bought by the Friuli region. This allowed Electrolux to remain at 49%. While the exact financial transactions were kept confidential, since some of the parties opposed any payment to the Zanussi family, it is believed that Electrolux injected slightly under $100 into Zanussi. One-third of that investment secured 49% shareholding, and the remainder went towards debentures that could be converted into shares at any time to give Electrolux a comfortable 75% ownership. An agreement with over 100 banks, which had some form of exposure to Zanussi assured a respite from creditors, freezing payments on the Italian debt until January 1987. At the same time, the creditors made considerable concessions on interest payments.

One of the most important meetings in the long negotiation process took place in Rome on 15th November, 1984, when, after stormy discussions between the top management of Electrolux and the leaders of the Zanussi union, a document confirming Electrolux 's intention to acquire Zanussi was jointly signed by both parties. During the most crucial hour of the meeting, Hens Werthen stood up in front of the 50 union leaders and declared: 'We are not buying companies in order to close them down, but to turn them into profitable ventures..... and, we are not the Vikings, who were Norwegians, anyway'.

The Turnarounds of Zanussi

It was standard Electrolux practice to have a broad but clear plan for immediate post-acquisition action well before the negotiation process for an acquisition was completed. Thus, by August 1984, well before the deal was signed in December, a specific plan for the turn around and the eventual integration of Zanussi was drawn up in Stockholm as started by Leifit Johnsson. 'When we make an acquisition, we adopt a centralized approach from the outset. We have definite plan worked out when we go in and there is virtually no need for extended discussions'. In the Zanussi case, the general approach had to be amended slightly since a feasible reduction in the employment levels was not automatic. However, clear decisions were taken to move the loss-making production of front-loaded washing machines for France of Zanussi's factory in Pordenone. On the other hand, the production of all top-loading washing machines was to be moved from Italy to France. In total, the internal plan anticipated shifting production of 600000-800000 product units from Electrolux and from subcontractor's plants to Zanussi, thereby increasing Zanussi's capacity utilization. Detailed financial calculations led to an expected cost savings of Skr. 400-500 millions through rationalization. Specific plans were also drawn up to achieve a 2-3% reduction in Zanussi's marketing and administrative costs by integrating an organization of the two companies in different countries.

Immediate post- acquisition actions

On 14th December, which year, within a matter of few hours after the signing of the final agreement, Electrolux announced a complete change in the top management of Zanussi. The old board, packed with nominees of the Zanussi family, was swept clan and Gianmario Rossignolo was appointed as Chairman of the company. An Italian, log-experienced in working with Swedish colleagues because of his position as chairman of SKF's Italian subsidiary, Rossignolo was seen as an ideal bridge between the two companies with their vastly different cultures and management styles. Carlo Verri, who was Managing Director of SKF's Italian subsidiary, was brought in as the new Managing Director of Zanussi. Rossignolo and Verri had turned around SKF's Itatlian operations and had a long history of working together as a team. Similarly, Hans Werthen, Anders Scharp, Gosta Bystedt and Lennart Fibohn joined the reconstituted Zanussi board. The industrial relations manager of Zanussi was the only senior manager below board level to be replaced. The purpose was to give a clear signal to the entire organization of the need to change work practices.

Consistent with the Electrolux style, a number of task forces were formatted immediately to address the scope of integration and rationalization of activities in different functional area. Each team was given a specific time period to come up with recommendations. Similarly, immediate actions were initiated in order to introduce Electrolux's financial reporting system within Zanussi, the clear target being to have the system fully in place and operative within six months from the date of the acquisition.

Direct steps taken at the business level to enhance capacity utilization, reduce costs of raw materials and components purchased, and revitalize local sales.

Capacity utilization : It was promised that Electrolux would source 5,00,000 units from Zanussi including 2,80,000 units of household appliances, 2,00,000 units of components, and 7,500 units of commercial appliances. This sourcing decision was given wide publicity both inside and outside the company, and a drive was launched to achieve the chosen levels as soon as possible. By 1985, 70% of the target had been reached.

Cost cutting in purchases : Given that 70% of production costs were represented by raw materials and purchased components, an immediate programme was launched to reduce vendor prices. The assumption was the vendors had adjusted their prices to compensate for the high risk of supplying to financially distressed Zanussi and should lower their prices now that risk was eliminated A net saving of 2% on purchase was achieved immediately. Over time approximately 17% gains in real terms would be achieved, not only for Zanussi, but also for Electrolux.

Revitalizing sales: Local competitors in Italy reacted vigorously to the announcement of Electrolux's acquisition of Zanussi. Anticipating a period of inaction while the new management took charge, they launched an aggressive marketing programme and Zanussi's ales slumped almost immediately. After consulting with Electrolux, the new management of Zanussi responded with a dramatic move of initially extending trade credit from 60 to 360 days under specified conditions. Sales surged immediately and the market was assured once and for all that 'Zanussi was back'.

Agreement with the Unions

In the next phase, starting from February 1985, the new management turned its attention to medium – and long-term needs. The most pressing of these was to fulfill a promise made to the unions before the acquisition : the presentation of a complete restructuring programme. This programme was finalized and discussed with the union leaders on 28th March 1985, at the Ministry of Industry in Rome. It consisted of a broad analysis of the industry and market trends, evaluation of Zanussi's competitive position and future prospects, and a detailed plan for investments and workforce reduction. The meeting was characterized by a high level of openness on the part of management. Such openness, unusual in Italian industrial relations, took the unions by surprise. In the end, after difficult negotiations, the plan was signed by all the parties in 25th May.

The final plan provided for a total reduction of the workforce by 4848 employees (the emergency phone number in Italy) to be implemented over a three-year period (2850 in 1985, 850·in 1986, and 1100 in 1987) through early retirement and other incentives for voluntary exit. In n1985, as planned, the workforce was reduced by 2800.

Paradoxically, from the beginning of 1986 a new problem arose. With business doing well and export demands for some of the products strong, a number of factories had to restore to overtime work and even hired new skilled workers, whilst at the same time the original reduction plans continued to be implemented. Management claimed that there was no inconsistency in these actions since the people being laid off lacked the skills that would be needed in the future. With the prospect of factory automation clearly on the horizon, a more educate and skilled workforce was necessary and the new hires conformed to these future needs. Some of the workers resisted, and a series of strikes followed at the Porcia plant.

Management decided to force the issue and brought out advertisements in the local press to highlight the situation publicly. In the new industrial climate in Italy, the strategy proved effective and the strikes ended. In 1987, the company made further progress in its relationship with the unions. In a new agreement, wage increases were linked to productivity and no limits were placed on workforce reductions. Further, it was agreed that the company could hire almost 1000 workers on a temporary basis, so as to take advantage of the subsidy provided by the government to stimulate worker training through temporary employment. It was clear that Zanussi management benefited significantly from the loss of union power that was a prominent feature of the recently changed industrial scene in Italy. However, its open and transparent approach also contributed to the success by gaining the respect of trade union leaders, both at company and national levels.

Strategic Transformation: Building Competitiveness

The new management recognized that in order to build durable competitive advantage, more basic changes were necessary. The poor financial performance of the company before the acquisition was only partly due to low productivity, and sustainable profits could not be assured through workforce reduction alone. After careful analysis, three areas were chosen as the focal points for a strategic transformation of Zanussi; improving production technology ; spurring innovations and new product development ; and enhancing product quality.

Improving production technology: Recalling his first visit to Zanussi, Halvar Johansson, then head of Electrolux's technical R & D, commented : 'What we found on entering Zanussi's factories was, in many respects, 1960s technology! The level of automation was far too low, especially in assembly operation. We did not find a single industrial robot or even a computer either in the product development unit or in the plant. However, we also discovered that Zanussi engineers and production personnel were of notably high standards. As part of a broad programme to improve production technology, Electrolux initiated an investment programme of £ 340 billion to restructure Zanussi's two major plants at Susegana and Porica.

The Susegana proposal foresaw an investment of L.100 billion to build up the facility into a highly automated, high-capacity unit able to produce 1.2 million refrigerators and freezers per year. The project was expected to come on stream by the end of 1988. The Porcia project anticipated a total investment of about £ 200 billion to build a highly automated, year flexible plant capable of producing 1.5 million washing machines per year. This project, scheduled for completion in 1990, was the largest individual investment project in the history of the Electrolux group. When on stream, it would be the largest washing-machine factory in the world. Both projects involved large investments to build flexibility through the use of CAD-CAM systems and just-in-time production methodology. As explained by Carlo Verri, 'The automation was primarily to achieve flexibility and to improve quality, and not to save on labour costs'.

Implementation of both projects was somewhat delayed. While the initial schedules may have been over-optimistic, some of the delays were caused by friction among Zanussi and Electrolux engineers. The Electrolux approach of building joint teams for implementation of projects was seen by some Zanussi managers as excessive involvement of the acquiring company in tasks for which the acquired company had ample and perhaps superior capabilities. Consequently, information flows were often blocked, resulting in, for example, a more than one-year delay in deciding the final layout of the Susegana factory. The delays were a matter of considerable concern to the top management of Electrolux. On the one hand, they felt extensive involvement of Electrolux's internal consultants to be necessary for effective implementation of the projects, since Zanussi lacked the requisite expertise. On the other hand, they acknowledged Zanussi's well-established engineering skills and the need to provide local engineers with the opportunity to learn and to prove themselves. They were also worried about whether the skill-levels of the local workforce could be upgraded in time for operating the new units, and looked for ways to expedite the training process.

Innovation and New Product Development: Zanussi had build it strong market presence o the reputation of being an innovator. This ability had, unfortunately, languished during the lean period. Both Rossignolo and Verri placed the greatest emphasis on reviving the innovative spirit of the company, and projects that had idled for years due to lack of funds revitalized and assigned high priority.

The results were quite dramatic and a virtual torrent of new product ideas emerged very quickly. The most striking example was a new washing-machine design – the 'Jet System' – that cut detergent and water consumption by a third. The product was developed within only nine months and the new machine was presented at the Cologne fair in February 1986. Through a direct television link with Cologne, Carlo Verri himself presented the assembly line at Pordenone where the Jet-System was to be mass produced. By July 1986, demand for the new machine had reached the level of 250000 per year and the company was facing delivery problems.

While the Jet System was the most visible outcome of the new emphasis on innovation, other equally important developments were in the pipeline. For example, the company developed a new rotary compressor to replace the reciprocating compressors that were being used in refrigerators. A major drive was also underway to improve product design and features through the introduction of integrated circuit (IC) chips. Interestingly, most of these proposal came not from the sophisticated and independent research centre of the company, but from development groups located within the line organizations which produced the products. How to maintain the momentum of innovation was a major concern for Verri, particularly as the company moved into the larger and more complex project necessary for significant technological breakthroughs.

Enhancing Product Quality : Quality enhancement was viewed as the third leg of the strategy for long-term revitalization of Zanussi. At Electrolux, high objectives of the company : satisfied customers, committed employees, and sound profitability. Zanussi had a good reputation for quality, but the standards had slackened during the turmoil faced by the company for almost a decade prior to the acquisition. Committed to the policy that quality levels must be the same within the group no matter where a product was produced, Electrolux initiated a major drive to enhance product quality at Zanussi and set extremely ambitious targets to reduce failure rates and post-sales service requirements. The targets were such that incremental improvements did not suffice for their attainment and a new approach towards quality was necessary. The technical staff of Electrolux provided requisite guidance and assistance and helped set up the parameters for a series of quality improvement programmes launched by Zanussi.

Carlo Verri was involved in these programmes on almost day-to-day basis. First, he headed the working group that set up the basic policy on quality for the entire Zanussi organization. In accordance with this policy, a total quality (TQ) project was started in May 1986 and a series of education and training programmes were introduced in order to diffuse the new philosophy and policy to all company employees. Supplier's involvement was an integral part of the TQ project. As described by Verri:

Supplier involvement was crucial. Zanussi's suppliers had to demonstrate their commitment to effective quality control. This meant that all the procedures for quality assurance, for tracking down failures etc., had to be approved by us. In other words, suppliers had to have the capability to provide self-certification for the quality of their products. They had to provide service within days rather than weeks, given that our plants were becoming automated. Our gains in flexibility and quality through new production techniques could be lost, if the suppliers did not become equally efficient.

Organizational revitalization :changing attitudes

One of the biggest challenges faced in the turnaround process lay in the area of revitalizing the Zanussi organization. During the troubled years, the management process at Zanussi had become a way of life, and information flow within the organization had become severely constrained. Most issues were escalated to the top for arbitration, and the middle management had practically no role in decision making. Front-line managers had become alienated because of direct dealings between had lost faith in the integrity of the system, in which seniority and loyalty to individuals were seen as more important than competence or commitment to the company.

In addition, the acquisition had also created a strong barrier of defensiveness within the Zanussi organization. In its own acquisitions, Zanussi typically eliminated the middle management in the acquired companies. As the acquired company expected similar actions from Electrolux. Moreover, some Zanussi managers were not convinced of any need for change. They believed that Zanussi's financial problems were caused not by any strategic, operational or organizational short-comings, but by the practices of the previous owners, including diversion of overseas profits through a foreign holding company in Luxembourg. Finally, most of the Managers were also concerned that both Rossignolo and Verri, with their backgrounds in the Italian subsidiary of a Swedish company, 'were closer to Stockholm than to Pordenone'.

In an attempt of overcome these barriers, Verri and the entire executive management group at Zanussi participated in a number of team-building sessions that were facilitated by an external consultant. These meetings gave rise to a number of developments that constituted the core of the organizational revitalization of Zanussi.

Statement of Mission, Values, and Guiding Principles : One of the direct outcomes of the team-building meetings was a statement of mission, values, and guiding principles, developed to serve as the charter for change (see Exhibit 2). The statement identified the four main values of the company—to be close to the clients and satisfy them through innovation and service; accept challenges and develop a leader mentality ; to pursue total quality not only in production but in all

Exhibit 2: Mission Values and Guiding Principles of Zanussi

Mission

To become the market leader in Europe, with a significant position in other world areas, in supplying homes, institutions, and industry with systems. Appliances components and after-sales services.

To be successful in this mission, the company and management legitimization must be based on the capability to be near the customer and satisfy his needs : to demonstrate strength, entrepreneurship, and creativity in accepting and winning external challenges. To offer total quality on all dimensions, more than the competition, and to be oriented to an internal vision and engagement.

Values

Our basic values, ranked, are:

1.   To be near the customer,

2.   To accept challenges,

3.   To deliver total quality, and

4.   With an international perspective.

Our central value, underlying all of the above, is transparence, which means that Zanussi will reward behaviour that is based on constantly transparent information and attitudes, safeguarding the interest of the company.

Guiding principles

1.   A management group is legitimized by knowing what we want, pursuing it coherently, and communicating our intent in order to be believable.

2.   Shared communication means shared responsibility, not power and status index.

3.   The manager's task is managing through information and motivation, not by building 'power islands'.

4.   Time is short: the world will not wait for our 'perfect solutions'.

5.   Strategic management implies:

    ● Professional skills.

    ● Risk-taking attitudes and the skill to spot opportunity.

    ● Integration with the environment and the organization, flexibility and attention to change.

    ● Identification with the mission of the firm, and helping in the evolution of a culture that supports it.

    ● Team work ability.

    ● Skill in identifying strengths and weaknesses.

Policies to be developed

Specific policies were being developed in the following areas to support the implementation of the above mission, values and guiding principles : personnel image and public relations, administration, purchasing, asset control, legal representation, R & D and innovation, and information systems. Members of senior management were assigned responsibility for developing policies in each of these areas, with completion expected by the end of 1986.

Areas of activity; and to become a global competitor by developing an international outlook. Apart from these specific points, the statement also confirmed the new management's commitment to create a context that would foster transparent and coherent behavior at both the individual and company levels under all circumstances. As described by Rossignolo: 'We adopted the Swedish work ethic – everybody keeps his word and all information is correct. We committed ourselves to being honest with the local authorities, the trade unions and our customers. It took some time for the message to get across, but I think everybody has got it now'.

Management Development Workshops: In order to improve the flow of information among senior managers and to co-opt them into the new management approach, a set of management development workshops was organized. The 60 most senior managers of Zanussi, including Verri, participated in each of three two-day workshops that were held between November 1985 and July 1986. The next tier of 150 middle managers of the company were subsequently exposed to the same programme.

Middle Management Problems : An organizational climate survey in 1987 revealed an interesting problem. The top 60 managers of the company confirmed strong support for the mission statement and the new management style. Conversely, the 150 middle managers, who seemed to feel threatened by the changes, appeared considerably less enthused. Their subordinates – approximately 1000 front-line managers and professional employees – like the top management, fully approved the change and demanded greater involvement. In response to this problem it was decided that the 60 top managers should establish direct communication with the 1000 front –line managers, bypassing the middle management, as and when necessary. The decision was made known within the organization and a clear signal was sent to the middle managers that they should 'get on board' or else they would risk 'missing the boat'. At the same time, a special training programme was launched for the front-line managers and professional employees in order to broaden their management skills and outlook.

Structural Reorganization: Before the acquisition, Zanussi was organized in five 'sectors', with the heads of each sector reporting to the managing director. The sectors, in turn, controlled the operating companies in their business areas. In practice, the sector managers were closely involved with the day-to-day operations of the companies under their charge. Both the managing director at the corporate level and the different sector managers had strong staff organizations to support their activities.

Verri abandoned the sector concept, even thought the operating companies continued to report to the former sector managers who were now called managing directors. However, staff at the sector level were virtually eliminated and the operating companies were given full responsibility and authority for taking all operating-level decisions. Similarly, staff at the corporate level were also reduced very substantially, and the heads of planning, finance and control, organization and human resources, general administration, and legal and public affairs all reported directly to Verri. The four managing directors, the five heads of major corporate staff departments, and Verri constituted to the executive management group of Zanussi. As Chariman, Rossignolo concentrated primarily on external relations.

Integration of the Companies

As described by Leifit Johansson, 'With the acquisition of Zanussi, the Electrolux group entered an new era. In several respects we were able to adopt a completely new way of thinking'. Much of the new thinking emerged from the discussions and recommendations of the task forces that had been appointed, involving managers from both companies, to look at specific opportunities for integrating the activities of the two organizations. In total, eight such task forces were formed : two each for components, product development, and commercial appliances; and one each for the marketing function and management development. Each of these task forces had met three to four times, typically for half a day each time. Their recommendations formed the basis for the actions that were taken to integrate the production and sales operations of the two companies, rationalize component production, and develop specialization in product and brand development within the entire Electrolux group. At the level of individuals, a bridge had been built between the top management of Electrolux and the senior management team of Zanussi, and further were underway for creating similar understanding and mutual respect among managers lower down in the two organizations.

Electrolux Components Group (ECG)

Following Electrolux's acquisition of White Consolidated in the US in March 1986, an international task force consisting of manager from Electrolux, White and Zanussi was created within the activities of the three companies. The task force concluded that integration opportunities were relatively limited at the level of finished products because of factors such as differences in customer preferences and technical standards, and the high transportation costs. However, at the component level there were many similarities in the needs of the companies, implying greater scope for standardization and production rationalization. As a result of this analysis, CEG was formed at the beginning of 1987 as part of the newly created industrial products division at Electrolux. The group was made responsible for the co-ordination and development of all strategic components used by Electrolux worldwide. Since over 50% of the group's component production came from Zanussi, Verri was appointed head of this group in addition to his responsibilities as Managing Director of Zanussi ; the group headquarters were located in Turin, Italy. In order to preserve and enhance the competitiveness of the component sector, it was decided that 50% of the component group's sales must be made to outside parties and at least 20% of the internal requirement for components must be sourced from outside the newly formed group.

Exhibit 3: Electrolux Group : Key Data.					
1. Group sales and employees worldwide					
Nordic countries			North America		
	Sales (Skr.m)	No. of employees		Sales (Skr.m)	No. of employees
Sweden	11128	29456	USA	19488	29750
Denmark	1735	3078	Canada	1580	2150
Norway	1505	1299		21068	31900
Finland	1445	1563			
	15813	35396			
Rest of Europe			Latin America		
Great Britain	6377	10589	Brazil	302	6215
France	5098	8753	Venezuela	208	1032
West Germany	4045	3317	Peru	181	750
Italy	3684	15282	Colombia	104	1865
Switzerland	1818	1814	Mexico	66	1735
Spain	1445	2851	Ecuador	34	232
Netherlands	1238	1016	Guatemala	24	31
Belgium and			Others	443	198
Luxemburg	913	1040		1362	12058
Austria	392	958			
Portugal	96	193			
Others	604	41			
	25710	45854			

Contd...

Asia			Africa		
Japan	707	1175		414	
Saudi Arabia	215	738			
Hong Kong	152	1340	Oceania		
Philippines	150	525			
Kuwait	147	2220			
Taiwan	119	2178	Australia	497	2216
Malaysia	72	1833	Newzealand	114	557
Thailand	56	15	Others	14	
Singapore	50	556		625	2773
Jordan	28	137			
Lebanon	22	35			
Others	720	1729			
	2438	12481	Total	67016	140462

2.   Sales by business area

	1987	1986	1985	% of total
	(Skr.m)	(Skr.m)	(Skr.m)	(1987 sales)
Household appliances	39487	31378	19200	58.6
Commercial appliances	5619	4250	3348	8.3
Commercial services	2893	2504	2266	4.3
Outdoor products	4475	2909	2990	6.6
Industrial product	11784	9087	9232	17.5
Building components	3172	2962	2652	4.7
Total	67430	53090	39688	100

3.   Operating income after depreciation by business area

Household appliances	2077	1947	1589	49.2
Commercial appliances	484	349	260	11.4
Commercial services	169	172	132	4
Outdoor products	421	241	373	10
Industrial product	910	474	657	21.5
Building components	164	138	126	3.9
Total	4225	3321	3137	100

Integration of Production

At Electrolux, production, sales and marketing had traditionally been integrated market-by-market. After the acquisition of Zanussi, all these activities were reorganized into international product divisions and national marketing/ sales companies.

The larger volumes from the combined operations made it feasible to switch to system in which large-scale specialized plants, equipped with flexible manufacturing technology, each would produce a single product for the entire European market. This new 'one-product-one factory' strategy was exemplified by the new plants in Susegana and Porica. Each of the product divisions carried full responsibility not only for manufacturing. But also for development and internal marketing of their products. In order to co-ordinate long-term development among these 43 divisions, three co-coordinators were appointed for 'wet', 'hot', and 'cold' products, respectively. Based in Stockholm without staff each of these co-coordinators would be on the road most of the time.

Integration of Sales/Marketing

Similarly, it was decided to create single umbrella companies over the separate sales/marketing organizations in all countries. Given the long-standing history of competition between the Electrolux and Zanussi organizations, this would turn out to be a difficult and complex process. It was planned that in each country the stronger organization would absorb the weaker one. This did not mean, however, that the head of the larger organization would absorb the weaker one. This did not mean, however, that the head of the larger organization. A number of complaints arose on both sides over this issue, which became a source of much irritation. For example, it was because of this that Candotti, who had been the first to approach Electrolux for investment in Zanussi, resigned. In what remained a source of considerable frustration, Zanussi continued to operate through directly controlled sales companies in Germany, France, Denmark and Norway.

Co-ordination among the marketing companies was achieved through an equally lean coordinating structure reporting to Leifit Johansson, with an Italian manager co-ordinating all European countries and a Swedish manager looking after the rest of the world.

To facilitate operational co-ordination between sales and production, a number of new system were develop. One, the Electrolux Forecasting and Supply System (EFS), involved the automatic co-ordination of sales forecasts and delivery orders. By 1998, computer links with EFS would be established in all European Sales subsidiaries and factories. The Zanussi evaluation system was changed to that Electrolux, in which both sales and factories were assessed on the basis of 'return on net assets' (RONA) rather than on a profit and cost basis. An overall RONA target of 20% was set for the group as a whole.

Appendix

Year	1%	2%	3%	4%	5%	6%	7%	8%	9%	10%
TABLE A-1 The Compound Sum of One Rupee										
0	1.000	1.000	1.000	1.000	1.000	1.000	1.000	1.000	1.000	1.000
1	1.010	1.020	1.030	1.040	1.050	1.060	1.070	1.080	1.090	1.110
2	1.020	1.040	1.061	1.082	1.102	1.124	1.145	1.166	1.188	1.210
3	1.030	1.061	1.093	1.125	1.158	1.191	1.225	1.260	1.295	1.331
4	1.041	1.082	1.126	1.170	1.216	1.262	1.311	1.360	1.412	1.464
5	1.051	1.104	1.159	1.217	1.276	1.338	1.403	1.469	1.539	1.611
6	1.062	1.126	1.194	1.265	1.340	1.419	1.501	1.587	1.677	1.772
7	1.072	1.149	1.230	1.316	1.407	1.504	1.606	1.714	1.828	1.949
8	1.083	1.172	1.267	1.369	1.477	1.594	1.718	1.851	1.993	2.144
9	1.094	1.195	1.305	1.423	1.551	1.689	1.838	1.999	2.172	2.358
10	1.105	1.219	1.344	1.480	1.629	1.791	1.967	2.159	2.367	2.594
11	1.116	1.243	1.384	1.539	1.710	1.898	2.105	2.332	2.580	2.853
12	1.127	1.268	1.426	1.601	1.796	2.012	2.252	2.518	2.813	3.138
13	1.138	1.294	1.469	1.665	1.886	2.133	2.410	2.720	3.066	3.452
14	1.149	1.319	1.513	1.732	1.980	2.261	2.579	2.937	3.342	3.797
15	1.161	1.346	1.553	1.801	2.079	2.397	2.759	3.172	3.642	4.177
16	1.173	1.373	1.605	1.873	2.183	2.540	2.952	3.426	3.970	4.595
17	1.184	1.400	1.653	1.948	2.292	2.693	3.159	3.700	4.328	5.054
18	1.196	1.428	1.702	2.026	2.407	2.854	3.380	3.996	4.717	5.560
19	1.208	1.457	1.753	2.107	2.527	3.026	3.616	4.316	5.142	6.116
20	1.220	1.486	1.806	2.191	2.653	3.207	3.870	4.661	5.604	6.727
25	1.282	1.641	2.094	2.666	3.386	4.292	5.427	6.848	8.623	10.834
30	1.348	1.811	2.427	3.243	4.322	5.743	7.612	10.062	13.267	17.449

TABLE A-1 The Compound Sum of One Rupee (Contd.)										
Year	11%	12%	13%	14%	15%	16%	17%	18%	19%	20%
0	1.000	1.000	1.000	1.000	1.000	1.000	1.000	1.000	1.000	1.000
1	1.110	1.120	1.130	1.140	1.150	1.160	1.170	1.180	1.190	1.200
2	1.231	1.254	1.277	1.300	1.322	1.346	1.369	1.392	1.416	1.440
3	1.368	1.405	1.443	1.482	1.521	1.561	1.602	1.643	1.685	1.728
4	1.518	1.574	1.630	1.689	1.749	1.811	1.874	1.939	2.005	2.074
5	1.685	1.762	1.842	1.925	2.011	2.100	2.192	2.288	2.386	2.488
6	1.870	1.974	2.082	2.195	2.313	2.436	2.565	2.700	2.840	2.986
7	2.076	2.211	2.353	2.502	2.660	2.826	3.001	3.185	3.379	3.583
8	2.305	2.476	2.658	2.856	3.059	3.278	3.511	3.759	4.021	4.300
9	2.558	2.773	3.004	3.252	3.518	3.803	4.108	4.435	4.785	5.160
10	2.839	3.106	3.395	3.707	4.046	4.411	4.807	5.234	5.695	6.192
11	3.152	3.479	3.836	4.226	4.652	5.117	5.624	6.176	6.777	7.430
12	3.498	3.896	4.334	4.818	5.350	5.936	6.580	7.288	8.064	8.916
13	3.883	4.363	4.898	5.492	6.153	6.886	7.699	8.599	9.596	10.699
14	4.310	4.887	5.535	6.621	7.076	7.987	9.007	10.147	11.420	12.839
15	4.785	5.474	6.254	7.138	8.137	9.265	10.539	11.974	13.589	15.407
16	5.311	6.130	7.067	8.137	9.358	10.748	12.330	14.129	16.171	18.488
17	5.895	6.866	7.986	9.276	10.761	12.468	14.426	16.672	19.244	22.186
18	6.543	7.690	9.024	10.575	12.375	14.462	16.879	19.673	22.900	26.623
19	7.263	8.613	10.197	12.055	14.232	16.776	19.748	23.214	27.251	31.948
20	8.062	9.646	11.523	13.743	16.366	19.461	23.105	27.393	32.429	38.337
25	13.585	17.000	21.230	26.461	32.918	40.874	50.656	62.667	77.387	95.395
30	22.892	29.960	39.115	50.949	66.210	85.849	111.061	143.367	184.672	237.373

TABLE A-1 The Compound Sum of One Rupee (Contd.)									
Year	21%	22%	23%	24%	25%	26%	27%	28%	29%	30%
0	1.000	1.000	1.000	1.000	1.000	1.000	1.000	1.000	1.000	1.000
1	1.210	1.220	1.230	1.240	1.250	1.260	1.270	1.280	1.290	1.300
2	1.46	1.488	1.513	1.538	1.562	1.588	1.613	1.638	1.664	1.960
3	1.772	1.816	1.861	1.907	1.953	2.000	2.048	2.097	2.147	2.197
4	2.144	2.215	2.289	2.364	2.441	2.520	2.601	2.684	2.769	2.856
5	2.594	2.703	2.815	2.932	3.052	3.176	3.304	3.436	3.572	3.713
6	3.138	3.297	3.463	6.635	3.815	4.001	4.196	4.398	4.6 3	4.827
7	3.797	4.023	4.259	4.508	4.768	5.042	5.329	5.629	5.945	6.275
8	4.595	4.908	5.239	5.589	5.960	6.353	6.767	7.206	7.669	8.157
9	5.560	5.987	6.444	6.931	7.451	8.004	8.595	9.223	9.893	10.604
10	6.727	7.305	7.926	8.594	9.313	10.086	10.915	11.806	12.761	13.786
11	8.140	8.912	9.749	10.657	11.642	12.708	13.862	15.112	16.462	17.921
12	9.850	10.872	11.991	13.251	14.552	16.012	17.605	19.343	21.236	23.298
13	11.918	13.264	14.749	16.386	18.190	20.175	22.359	24.759	27.395	30.287
14	14.421	16.182	18.141	20.319	22.737	25.420	28.395	31.691	35.339	39.373
15	17.449	19.742	22.314	25.195	28.422	30.030	36.062	40.565	45.587	51.185
16	21.113	24.085	27.446	31.242	35.527	40.357	45.799	51.923	58.808	66.541
17	25.547	29.384	33.758	38.740	44.409	50.850	58.165	66.461	75.862	86.503
18	30.912	35.848	41.523	48.038	55.511	64.071	73.869	85.070	97.862	112.454
19	37.404	43.735	51.073	59.567	69.389	80.730	93.813	108.890	126.242	146.190
20	45.258	53.357	62.820	73.863	86.736	101.720	119.143	139.379	162.852	190.047
25	117.388	144.207	176.857	261.539	264.698	323.040	393.628	478.901	581.756	705.627
30	304.417	389.748	497.904	634.810	807.793	1025.904	1300.477	1645.488	2078.208	2619.936

Year	1%	2%	3%	4%	5%	6%	7%	8%	9%	10%
1	1.000	1.000	1.000	1.000	1.000	1.000	1.000	1.000	1.000	1.000
2	2.010	2.020	2.030	2.040	2.050	2.060	2.070	2.080	2.090	2.100
3	3.030	3.060	3.091	3.122	3.152	3.184	3.215	3.246	3.278	3.310
4	4.060	4.122	4.184	4.246	4.310	4.375	4.440	4.506	4.573	4.641
5	5.101	5.204	5.309	5.416	5.526	5.637	5.751	5.867	5.985	6.105
6	6.152	6.308	6.468	6.633	6.802	6.975	7.153	7.336	7.523	7.716
7	7.214	7.434	7.662	7.898	8.142	8.394	8.654	8.923	9.200	9.487
8	8.286	8.583	8.892	9.214	9.549	9.897	10.260	10.637	11.028	11.436
9	9.368	9.755	10.159	10.583	11.027	11.491	11.978	12.488	13.021	13.578
10	10.462	10.950	11.464	12.006	12.578	13.181	13.816	14.487	15.193	15.937
11	11.567	12.169	12.808	13.486	14.207	14.972	15.784	16.65	17.560	18.531
12	12.682	13.412	14.192	15.026	15.917	16.870	17.888	18.977	20.141	21.384
13	13.809	14.680	15.618	16.627	17.713	18.882	20.141	21.495	22.953	24.523
14	14.947	15.974	17.086	18.292	19.598	21.015	22.550	24.215	26.019	27.975
15	16.097	17.293	18.599	20.023	21.578	23.276	25.129	27.152	29.361	31.772
16	17.258	18.639	20.157	21.824	23.657	25.672	27.888	30.324	33.003	35.949
17	18.430	20.012	21.761	23.697	25.840	28.213	30.840	33.750	36.973	40.544
18	19.614	21.412	23.414	25.645	28.132	30.905	33.999	37.540	41.301	45.599
19	20.811	21.840	25.117	27.671	30.539	33.760	37.379	41.446	46.018	51.158
20	22.019	24.297	26.870	29.778	33.066	36.785	40.995	45.762	51.169	57.274
25	28.243	32.030	36.459	41.645	47.726	54.864	63.248	73.105	84.699	98.346
30	34.784	40.567	47.575	56.084	66.438	79.057	95.459	113.282	136.305	164.491

TABLE A-2 The Compound Value of an Annuity of One Rupee

TABLE A-2 The Compound Value of an Annuity of One Rupee (Contd.)

Year	11%	12%	13%	14%	15%	16%	17%	18%	19%	20%
1	1.000	1.000	1.000	1.000	1.000	1.000	1.000	1.000	1.000	1.000
2	2.110	2.120	2.130	2.140	2.150	2.160	2.170	2.180	2.190	2.200
3	3.342	3.374	3.407	3.440	3.472	3.506	3.539	3.572	3.606	3.640
4	4.710	4.779	4.850	4.921	4.993	5.066	5.141	5.215	5.291	5.338
5	6.228	6.353	6.480	6.610	6.742	6.877	7.014	7.154	7.297	7.442
6	7.913	8.115	8.323	8.535	8.754	9.897	9.207	9.442	9.683	9.930
7	9.783	10.089	10.405	10.730	11.067	11.414	11.772	12.141	12.523	12.916
8	11.859	12.300	12.757	13.233	13.727	14.240	14.773	15.327	15.902	16.499
9	14.164	14.776	15.416	16.085	16.786	17.518	18.285	19.086	19.923	20.799
10	16.722	17.549	18.420	19.337	20.304	21.321	22.393	23.521	24.709	25.959
11	19.561	20.655	21.814	23.044	24.349	25.733	27.200	28.755	30.403	32.150
12	22.713	24.133	25.650	27.271	29.001	30.850	32.824	34.931	37.180	39.580
13	26.211	28.029	29.984	32.088	34.352	36.786	39.404	42.218	45.244	48.496
14	30.095	32.392	34.882	37.581	40.504	43.672	47.102	50.818	54.841	59.196
15	34.405	37.280	40.417	43.842	47.580	51.659	56.109	60.965	66.260	72.035
16	39.190	42.753	46.671	50.980	55.717	60.925	66.648	72.938	79.850	87.442
17	44.500	48.883	53.738	59.117	65.075	71.673	78.978	87.067	96.021	105.930
18	50.396	55.749	61.724	68.393	75.836	84.140	93.404	103.739	115.265	128.116
19	56.939	63.439	70.748	78.968	88.211	98.603	110.283	123.412	138.165	154.739
20	64.202	72.052	80.946	91.024	102.443	115.379	130.031	146.626	165.417	186.687
25	114.412	133.333	155.616	181.867	212.790	249.212	292.099	342.598	402.038	471.976
30	199.018	241.330	293.192	356.778	434.738	530.306	647.423	790.932	966.698	1181.865

	TABLE A-2 The Compound Value of an Annuity of One Rupee (Contd.)									
Year	21%	22%	23%	24%	25%	26%	27%	28%	29%	30%
1	1.000	1.000	1.000	1.000	1.000	1.000	1.000	1.000	1.000	1.000
2	2.210	2.220	2.230	2.240	2.250	2.260	2.270	2.280	2.290	2.300
3	3.674	3.708	3.743	3.778	3.813	3.848	3.883	3.918	3.954	3.990
4	5.446	5.524	5.604	5.684	5.766	5.848	5.931	6.016	6.101	6.187
5	7.589	7.740	7.893	8.048	8.207	8.368	8.533	8.700	8.870	9.043
6	10.183	10.442	10.708	10.980	11.259	11.544	11.837	12.136	12.442	12.756
7	13.321	13.740	14.171	14.615	15.073	15.546	16.032	16.534	17.051	17.583
8	17.119	17.762	18.430	19.123	19.842	20.588	21.361	22.361	22.995	23.858
9	21.714	22.670	23.669	24.712	25.802	26.940	28.129	29.369	30.664	32.015
10	27.274	28.657	30.113	31.643	33.253	34.945	36.723	38.592	40.556	42.619
11	34.001	35.962	38.039	40.238	42.566	45.030	47.639	50.398	53.318	56.405
12	42.141	44.873	47.787	50.895	54.208	57.738	61.501	65.510	69.510	74.326
13	51.991	55.745	59.778	64.109	68.760	73.750	79.106	84.853	91.016	97.624
14	63.909	69.009	74.528	80.496	86.949	93.925	101.465	109.611	118.411	127.912
15	78.330	85.191	92.669	100.815	109.687	119.346	129.860	141.302	153.750	167.285
16	95.779	104.933	114.983	126.010	138.109	151.375	165.922	181.867	199.337	218.470
17	116.892	129.019	142.428	157.252	173.636	191.733	211.721	233.790	258.145	285.011
18	142.439	158.403	176.187	195.993	218.045	242.583	269.855	300.250	334.006	371.514
19	173.351	194.251	217.710	244.031	273.556	306.654	343.754	385.321	431.868	483.968
20	210.755	237.986	268.783	303.598	342.945	387.384	437.568	494.210	558.110	630.157
25	554.230	650.944	764.596	898.082	1054.791	1238.617	1454.180	1706.790	2002.608	2348.765
30	1445.111	1767.044	2160.459	2640.881	3227.172	3941.953	4812.891	5873.172	7162.785	8729.805

Year	1%	2%	3%	4%	5%	6%	7%	8%	9%	10%
				TABLE A-3 The Present Value of One Rupee						
0	1.000	1.000	1.000	1.000	1.000	1.000	1.000	1.000	1.000	1.000
1	0.990	0.980	0.971	0.962	0.962	0.943	0.935	0.926	0.917	0.909
2	0.980	0.961	0.943	0.925	0.907	0.890	0.873	0.857	0.842	0.826
3	0.971	0.942	0.915	0.889	0.864	0.840	0.816	0.794	0.772	0.751
4	0.961	0.961	0.924	0.888	0.855	0.823	0.792	0.763	0.708	0.683
5	0.651	0.906	0.863	0.822	0.784	0.747	0.713	0.681	0.650	0.621
6	0.942	0.888	0.837	0.790	0.746	0.705	0.666	0.630	0.596	0.564
7	0.933	0.871	0.813	0.760	0.711	0.665	0.623	0.583	0.547	0.513
8	0.923	0.853	0.789	0.731	0.677	0.627	0.582	0.540	0.502	0.467
9	0.914	0.837	0.766	0.703	0.645	0.592	0.544	0.500	0.460	0.424
10	0.905	0.82	0.744	0.676	0.614	0.558	0.508	0.463	0.422	0.386
11	0.896	0.804	0.722	0.650	0.585	0.527	0.475	0.429	0.388	0.350
12	0.887	0.789	0.701	0.625	0.557	0.497	0.444	0.397	0.356	0.319
13	0.879	0.773	0.681	0.601	0.530	0.469	0.415	0.368	0.326	0.290
14	0.870	0.758	0.661	0.577	0.505	0.442	0.388	0.340	0.299	0.263
15	0.861	0.743	0.642	0.555	0.481	0.417	0.362	0.315	0.275	0.239
16	0.853	0.728	0.623	0.534	0.458	0.394	0.339	0.292	0.252	0.218
17	0.844	0.714	0.605	0.513	0.436	0.371	0.317	0.270	0.231	0.198
18	0.836	0.700	0.587	0.494	0.416	0.350	0.296	0.250	0.212	0.180
19	0.823	0.686	0.570	0.475	0.396	0.331	0.227	0.232	0.194	0.164
20	0.820	0.673	0.554	0.456	0.377	0.312	0.258	0.215	0.178	0.149
25	0.780	0.610	0.478	0.375	0.295	0.233	0.184	0.146	0.116	0.092
30	0.742	0.552	0.412	0.308	0.231	0.174	0.131	0.099	0.075	0.057

Year	11%	12%	13%	14%	15%	16%	17%	18%	19%	20%
\multicolumn{11}{l}{**TABLE A-3 The Present Value of One Rupee (Contd.)**}
0	1.000	1.000	1.000	1.000	1.000	1.000	1.000	1.000	1.000	1.000
1	0.901	0.893	0.885	0.877	0.870	0.862	0.855	0.847	0.840	0.833
2	0.812	0.797	0.783	0.769	0.756	0.743	0.731	0.718	0.706	0.694
3	0.731	0.712	0.693	0.675	0.658	0.641	0.624	0.609	0.593	0.579
4	0.656	0.636	0.613	0.592	0.572	0.552	0.534	0.516	0.499	0.482
5	0.593	0.567	0.543	0.519	0.497	0.476	0.456	0.437	0.419	0.402
6	0.535	0.507	0.480	0.456	0.432	0.410	0.390	0.370	0.352	0.335
7	0.482	0.452	0.425	0.400	0.376	0.354	0.333	0.314	0.296	0.279
8	0.434	0.404	0.376	0.351	0.327	0.305	0.285	0.266	0.249	0.233
9	0.391	0.361	0.333	0.308	0.284	0.263	0.243	0.225	0.209	0.194
10	0.352	0.322	0.295	0.270	0.247	0.227	0.208	0.191	0.176	0.162
11	0.317	0.287	0.261	0.237	0.215	0.195	0.178	0.162	0.148	0.135
12	0.286	0.257	0.231	0.208	0.187	0.168	0.152	0.137	0.124	0.112
13	0.258	0.229	0.204	0.182	0.163	0.145	0.130	0.116	0.104	0.093
14	0.232	0.205	0.181	0.160	0.141	0.125	0.111	0.099	0.088	0.078
15	0.209	0.183	0.160	0.140	0.123	0.108	0.095	0.084	0.074	0.065
16	0.188	0.163	0.141	0.123	0.107	0.093	0.081	0.071	0.062	0.054
17	0.170	0.146	0.125	0.108	0.093	0.080	0.069	0.060	0.052	0.045
18	0.153	0.130	0.111	0.095	0.081	0.069	0.059	0.051	0.044	0.038
19	0.138	0.116	0.098	0.083	0.070	0.060	0.051	0.043	0.037	0.031
20	0.124	0.104	0.087	0.073	0.061	0.051	0.043	0.037	0.031	0.026
25	0.074	0.059	0.047	0.038	0.030	0.024	0.020	0.016	0.013	0.010
30	0.044	0.033	0.026	0.020	0.015	0.012	0.009	0.007	0.005	0.004

Year	21%	22%	23%	24%	25%	26%	27%	28%	29%	30%
				TABLE A-3 The Present Value of One Rupee (Contd.)						
0	1.000	1.000	1.000	1.000	1.000	1.000	1.000	1.000	1.000	1.000
1	0.826	0.820	0.813	0.806	0.800	0.794	0.787	0.781	0.775	0.769
2	0.683	0.672	0.661	0.650	0.640	0.630	0.620	0.610	0.601	0.592
3	0.564	0.551	0.537	0.524	0.512	0.500	0.488	0.477	0.466	0.455
4	0.467	0.451	0.437	0.423	0.410	0.397	0.384	0.373	0.361	0.350
5	0.386	0.370	0.355	0.341	0.328	0.315	0.303	0.291	0.280	0.269
6	0.319	0.303	0.289	0.275	0.262	0.250	0.238	0.227	0.217	0.207
7	0.263	0.249	0.235	0.222	0.210	0.198	0.188	0.178	0.168	0.159
8	0.218	0.204	0.191	0.179	0.168	0.157	0.148	0.139	0.130	0.123
9	0.180	0.167	0.155	0.144	0.134	0.125	0.116	0.108	0.101	0.094
10	0.149	0.137	0.126	0.116	0.107	0.099	0.092	0.085	0.078	0.073
11	0.123	0.112	0.103	0.094	0.086	0.079	0.072	0.066	0.061	0.056
12	0.102	0.092	0.083	0.076	0.069	0.062	0.057	0.052	0.047	0.043
13	0.084	0.075	0.068	0.061	0.055	0.050	0.045	0.040	0.037	0.033
14	0.069	0.062	0.055	0.049	0.044	0.039	0.035	0.032	0.028	0.025
15	0.057	0.051	0.045	0.040	0.035	0.031	0.028	0.025	0.022	0.020
16	0.047	0.042	0.036	0.032	0.028	0.025	0.022	0.019	0.017	0.015
17	0.039	0.034	0.030	0.026	0.023	0.020	0.017	0.015	0.013	0.012
18	0.032	0.028	0.024	0.021	0.018	0.016	0.014	0.012	0.010	0.009
19	0.027	0.023	0.020	0.017	0.014	0.012	0.011	0.009	0.008	0.007
20	0.022	0.019	0.016	0.014	0.012	0.010	0.008	0.007	0.006	0.005
25	0.009	0.007	0.006	0.005	0.004	0.003	0.003	0.002	0.002	0.001
30	0.003	0.003	0.002	0.002	0.001	0.001	0.001	0.001	0.000	0.000

	**TABLE A-4 The Present Value of Annuity One Rupee**	

Year	1%	2%	3%	4%	5%	6%	7%	8%	9%	10%
0	1.000	1.000	1.000	1.000	1.000	1.000	1.000	1.000	1.000	1.000
1	0.990	0.980	0.971	0.962	0.952	0.943	0.935	0.926	0.917	0.909
2	1.970	1.942	1.913	1.886	1.859	1.833	1.808	1.783	1.759	1.736
3	2.941	2.884	2.829	2.775	2.723	2.673	2.624	2.577	2.531	2.487
4	3.902	3.808	3.717	3.630	3.546	3.465	3.387	3.312	3.240	3.170
5	4.853	4.713	4.580	4.452	4.329	4.212	4.100	3.993	3.890	3.791
6	5.795	5.601	5.417	5.242	5.076	4.917	7.767	4.623	4.486	4.355
7	6.728	6.472	6.230	6.002	5.786	5.582	5.389	5.206	5.033	4.868
8	7.652	7.326	7.020	6.733	6.463	6.210	5.971	5.747	5.535	5.355
9	8.566	8.162	7.786	7.435	7.108	6.802	6.515	6.247	5.995	5.759
10	9.471	8.983	8.530	8.111	7.722	7.360	7.024	6.710	6.418	6.145
11	10.368	9.787	9.253	8.760	8.306	7.887	7.499	7.139	6.805	6.495
12	11.255	10.575	9.954	9.358	8.863	8.384	7.943	7.536	7.161	6.814
13	12.134	11.348	10.635	9.986	9.394	8.853	8.358	7.904	7.487	7.103
14	13.004	12.106	11.296	10.563	9.899	9.295	8.746	8.244	7.786	7.367
15	13.865	12.849	11.938	11.118	10.380	9.712	9.108	8.560	8.061	7.606
16	14.718	13.578	12.561	11.652	10.838	10.106	9.447	8.851	8.313	7.824
17	15.562	14.292	13.166	12.166	11.274	10.477	9.763	9.122	8.544	8.022
18	16.398	14.992	13.754	13.134	11.690	10.828	10.059	9.372	8.756	8.022
19	17.226	15.679	14.324	13.590	12.085	11.158	10.336	9.604	8.950	8.365
20	18.046	16.352	14.878	14.029	12.462	11.470	10.594	9.818	9.129	8.514
25	22.023	19.524	17.413	15.622	14.094	12.783	11.654	10.675	9.823	9.007
30	25.808	22.397	19.601	17.292	15.373	13.765	12.409	11.258	10.274	9.427

TABLE A-4 The Present Value of Annuity One Rupee (Contd.)

Year	11%	12%	13%	14%	15%	16%	17%	18%	19%	20%
0	1.000	1.000	1.000	1.000	1.000	1.000	1.000	1.000	1.000	1.000
1	0.901	0.893	0.885	0.877	0.870	0.862	0.855	0.847	0.850	0.833
2	1.713	1.690	1.668	1.647	1.626	1.605	1.585	1.566	1.547	1.528
3	2.444	2.402	2.361	2.322	2.283	2.246	2.210	2.174	2.140	2.106
4	3.102	3.037	2.974	2.914	2.855	2.798	2.743	2.690	2.639	2.589
5	3.696	3.605	3.517	3.433	3.352	3.274	3.199	3.127	3.058	2.991
6	4.231	4.111	3.998	3.889	3.784	3.685	3.589	3.498	3.410	3.326
7	4.712	4.564	4.423	4.288	4.160	4.039	3.922	3.812	3.706	3.605
8	5.146	4.968	4.799	4.639	4.487	4.344	4.207	4.078	3.954	3.837
9	5.537	5.328	5.132	4.946	4.772	4.607	4.451	4.303	4.163	4.031
10	5.889	5.650	5.426	5.216	5.019	4.833	4.659	4.494	4.339	4.192
11	6.207	5.938	5.687	5.453	5.234	5.029	4.836	4.656	4.487	4.327
12	6.492	6.194	5.918	5.660	5.421	5.197	4.988	4.793	4.611	4.439
13	6.750	6.424	6.122	5.842	5.583	5.342	5.118	4.910	4.715	4.533
14	6.982	6.628	5.303	6.002	5.724	5.468	5.229	5.008	4.802	4.611
15	7.191	6.811	6.462	6.142	5.847	5.575	5.324	5.092	4.876	4.675
16	7.379	6.974	6.604	6.265	5.954	5.669	5.405	5.162	4.938	4.730
17	7.549	7.120	6.729	6.373	6.047	5.749	5.475	5.222	4.990	4.775
18	7.702	7.250	6.840	6.467	6.128	5.818	5.534	5.273	5.033	4.812
19	7.839	7.366	6.938	6.550	6.198	5.877	5.585	5.136	5.070	4.843
20	7.963	7.469	7.024	6.623	6.259	5.929	5.628	5.353	5.101	4.870
25	8.422	7.843	7.330	6.873	6.464	6.097	5.766	5.467	5.195	4.948
30	8.694	8.055	7.496	7.003	6.566	6.177	5.829	5.517	5.235	4.979

TABLE A-4 The Present Value of Annuity One Rupee (Contd.)

Year	21%	22%	23%	24%	25%	26%	27%	28%	29%	30%
0	1.000	1.000	1.000	1.000	1.000	1.000	1.000	1.000	1.000	1.000
1	0.826	0.820	0.813	0.806	0.800	0.794	0.787	0.781	0.775	0.769
2	1.509	1.492	1.474	1.457	1.440	1.424	1.407	1.392	1.376	1.361
3	2.074	2.042	2.011	1.981	1.952	1.923	1.896	1.868	1.842	1.816
4	2.540	2.494	2.448	2.404	2.362	2.320	2.280	2.241	2.203	2.166
5	2.926	2.864	2.803	2.745	2.689	2.635	2.583	2.532	2.483	2.436
6	3.245	3.167	3.092	3.020	2.951	2.885	2.821	2.759	2.700	2.643
7	3.508	3.416	3.327	3.242	3.161	3.083	3.009	2.937	2.868	2.802
8	3.726	3.619	3.518	3.421	3.329	3.241	3.156	3.076	2.999	2.925
9	3.905	3.786	3.673	3.566	3.463	3.366	3.273	3.184	3.100	3.019
10	4.054	3.923	3.799	3.682	3.570	3.465	3.364	3.269	3.178	3.092
11	4.177	4.035	3.902	3.776	3.656	3.544	3.437	3.335	3.239	3.147
12	4.278	4.127	3.985	3.851	3.752	3.606	3.493	3.387	3.286	3.190
13	4.362	4.203	4.053	3.912	3.780	3.656	3.583	3.427	3.322	3.233
14	4.432	4.265	4.108	3.962	3.824	3.695	3.573	3.459	3.351	3.249
15	4.489	4.315	4.153	4.001	3.859	3.726	3.601	3.483	3.373	3.268
16	4.536	4.357	4.189	4.033	3.887	3.751	3.623	3.503	3.390	3.283
17	4.576	4.391	4.219	4.059	3.910	3.771	3.640	3.518	3.403	3.295
18	4.608	4.419	4.243	4.080	3.928	3.786	3.654	3.529	3.413	3.304
19	4.635	4.442	4.263	4.097	3.942	3.799	3.664	3.539	3.421	3.311
20	4.657	4.460	4.279	4.110	3.954	3.808	3.673	3.546	3.427	3.316
25	4.721	4.514	4.323	4.147	3.985	3.834	3.694	3.564	3.442	3.329
30	4.746	4.534	4.339	4.160	3.995	3.842	3.701	3.569	3.447	3.332

Index